A general and true history of the lives and actions of the most famous highwaymen, murderers, street-robbers, &c. To which is added, a genuine account of the voyages and plunders of the most noted pirates.

Daniel Defoe

A general and true history of the lives and actions of the most famous highwaymen, murderers, street-robbers, &c. To which is added, a genuine account of the voyages and plunders of the most noted pirates. Interspersed with several remarkable tryals ... By Capt. Charles Johnson.

Defoe, Daniel
ESTCID: T120316
Reproduction from British Library
Titlepage in red and black.
Birmingham : printed by R. Walker, 1742.
[4],427,[1]p.,plates : ports. ; 2°

Eighteenth Century
Collections Online
Print Editions

Gale ECCO Print Editions

Relive history with *Eighteenth Century Collections Online*, now available in print for the independent historian and collector. This series includes the most significant English-language and foreign-language works printed in Great Britain during the eighteenth century, and is organized in seven different subject areas including literature and language; medicine, science, and technology; and religion and philosophy. The collection also includes thousands of important works from the Americas.

The eighteenth century has been called "The Age of Enlightenment." It was a period of rapid advance in print culture and publishing, in world exploration, and in the rapid growth of science and technology – all of which had a profound impact on the political and cultural landscape. At the end of the century the American Revolution, French Revolution and Industrial Revolution, perhaps three of the most significant events in modern history, set in motion developments that eventually dominated world political, economic, and social life.

In a groundbreaking effort, Gale initiated a revolution of its own: digitization of epic proportions to preserve these invaluable works in the largest online archive of its kind. Contributions from major world libraries constitute over 175,000 original printed works. Scanned images of the actual pages, rather than transcriptions, recreate the works *as they first appeared.*

Now for the first time, these high-quality digital scans of original works are available via print-on-demand, making them readily accessible to libraries, students, independent scholars, and readers of all ages.

For our initial release we have created seven robust collections to form one the world's most comprehensive catalogs of 18th century works.

Initial Gale ECCO Print Editions collections include:

History and Geography

Rich in titles on English life and social history, this collection spans the world as it was known to eighteenth-century historians and explorers. Titles include a wealth of travel accounts and diaries, histories of nations from throughout the world, and maps and charts of a world that was still being discovered. Students of the War of American Independence will find fascinating accounts from the British side of conflict.

Social Science

Delve into what it was like to live during the eighteenth century by reading the first-hand accounts of everyday people, including city dwellers and farmers, businessmen and bankers, artisans and merchants, artists and their patrons, politicians and their constituents. Original texts make the American, French, and Industrial revolutions vividly contemporary.

Medicine, Science and Technology

Medical theory and practice of the 1700s developed rapidly, as is evidenced by the extensive collection, which includes descriptions of diseases, their conditions, and treatments. Books on science and technology, agriculture, military technology, natural philosophy, even cookbooks, are all contained here.

Literature and Language

Western literary study flows out of eighteenth-century works by Alexander Pope, Daniel Defoe, Henry Fielding, Frances Burney, Denis Diderot, Johann Gottfried Herder, Johann Wolfgang von Goethe, and others. Experience the birth of the modern novel, or compare the development of language using dictionaries and grammar discourses.

Religion and Philosophy

The Age of Enlightenment profoundly enriched religious and philosophical understanding and continues to influence present-day thinking. Works collected here include masterpieces by David Hume, Immanuel Kant, and Jean-Jacques Rousseau, as well as religious sermons and moral debates on the issues of the day, such as the slave trade. The Age of Reason saw conflict between Protestantism and Catholicism transformed into one between faith and logic -- a debate that continues in the twenty-first century.

Law and Reference

This collection reveals the history of English common law and Empire law in a vastly changing world of British expansion. Dominating the legal field is the *Commentaries of the Law of England* by Sir William Blackstone, which first appeared in 1765. Reference works such as almanacs and catalogues continue to educate us by revealing the day-to-day workings of society.

Fine Arts

The eighteenth-century fascination with Greek and Roman antiquity followed the systematic excavation of the ruins at Pompeii and Herculaneum in southern Italy; and after 1750 a neoclassical style dominated all artistic fields. The titles here trace developments in mostly English-language works on painting, sculpture, architecture, music, theater, and other disciplines. Instructional works on musical instruments, catalogs of art objects, comic operas, and more are also included.

The BiblioLife Network

This project was made possible in part by the BiblioLife Network (BLN), a project aimed at addressing some of the huge challenges facing book preservationists around the world. The BLN includes libraries, library networks, archives, subject matter experts, online communities and library service providers. We believe every book ever published should be available as a high-quality print reproduction; printed on-demand anywhere in the world. This insures the ongoing accessibility of the content and helps generate sustainable revenue for the libraries and organizations that work to preserve these important materials.

The following book is in the "public domain" and represents an authentic reproduction of the text as printed by the original publisher. While we have attempted to accurately maintain the integrity of the original work, there are sometimes problems with the original work or the micro-film from which the books were digitized. This can result in minor errors in reproduction. Possible imperfections include missing and blurred pages, poor pictures, markings and other reproduction issues beyond our control. Because this work is culturally important, we have made it available as part of our commitment to protecting, preserving, and promoting the world's literature.

GUIDE TO FOLD-OUTS MAPS and OVERSIZED IMAGES

The book you are reading was digitized from microfilm captured over the past thirty to forty years. Years after the creation of the original microfilm, the book was converted to digital files and made available in an online database.

In an online database, page images do not need to conform to the size restrictions found in a printed book. When converting these images back into a printed bound book, the page sizes are standardized in ways that maintain the detail of the original. For large images, such as fold-out maps, the original page image is split into two or more pages

Guidelines used to determine how to split the page image follows:

• Some images are split vertically; large images require vertical and horizontal splits.
• For horizontal splits, the content is split left to right.
• For vertical splits, the content is split from top to bottom.
• For both vertical and horizontal splits, the image is processed from top left to bottom right.

A General and True

HISTORY

OF THE

LIVES and ACTIONS

Of the moſt FAMOUS

Highwaymen, Murderers, Street-Robbers, &c.

To which is added,

A Genuine Account of the *VOYAGES* and *PLUNDERS*
of the moſt Noted PIRATES.

Interſperſed with ſeveral Remarkable

TRYALS

Of the moſt

NOTORIOUS MALEFACTORS,

AT THE

Seſſions-Houſe in the *Old Baily, London.*

Adorn'd with the Effigies, and other material Tranſactions of the moſt
remarkable Offenders, engraved on Copper-Plates.

By Capt. *CHARLES JOHNSON.*

—— *Little Villains oft' ſubmit to Fate,*
That Great Ones may enjoy the World in State.
GARTH.

BIRMINGHAM:

Printed by R. WALKER, at the Sign of the PRINTING-PRESS, over-
againſt the *Swan-Tavern* in the *High-Street.*
MDCCXLII.

THE

INTRODUCTION.

WERE we to give our Readers an universal History of Robbers, of all Ranks and
Degrees, from the Beginning of the
World to this Time, our Scheme would be
almost as extensive, as if we proposed to
write the History of all Nations We should be oblig'd to
look back as far as the most antient Records would
guide us, and the greatest Names of Antiquity would
claim a Place in our Memoirs What was Nimrod
but a successful Free-booter? and what were all the
Founders of Monarchies, but Encroachers on the Properties of their Brethren and Neighbours? Alexander was a Plunderer of the first Magnitude, and
all his extraordinary Exploits, with which we have
been so long amused, and which we have been taught to
speak of with so much Admiration, were only Robberies
committed upon Men every Way better than himself
Cæsar, that other prodigious Name, was a Plunderer
of his native Country, or (as the great Cowley has
warmly and nobly express'd it) a Ravisher of his own
Mother What better can we call any of his Successors who have sacrific'd the Lives and Liberties of
thousands of their Fellow-Creatures to an extravagant
Passion? Whether we name it Tyranny, Ambition, or only Greatness of Soul, 'tis much the same,
while the Effects of it are so very terrible Happy is
it that we can produce, at least, no modern Instances
of Robbers of this Kind from our own Histories!
But even in Great-Britain, where Property is better
secur'd than any where else in the Universe, and where
the Hands of the Prince (were he inclin'd to make a
Prey of the People) are restrain'd, even here, I say,
'tis impossible to prevent Men of the lower Class from
plundering their Fellow-Subjects 'Twill be little to
the Purpose to enquire how far this rapacious Disposition
may spread itself, I mean, to name all the Degrees of
Men that have been, or may be infected with it 'Tis
sufficient to observe, that little Villains are oftenest
convicted, and obliged (as Garth says) to submit to
Fate, tho' a Story in this Collection will inform us,
that it is not unprecedented for a very great Knight to
be a very great Robber The poorer Sort of People,
to be sure, were disturb'd to see such a Man as Falstaff do what they might have some Excuse for But
what did Falstaff care, so long as he could laugh and
grow fat?
We would by no Means have our Readers expect an
Account of all the Plunderers that have been dignified,
unless they are willing to buy 500 Sheets, instead of
a hundred, the Number we propose If the Reason of
this vast Disproportion should be demanded, we answer,
a great Villain may commit more Depredations in a
short Time, than a hundred little ones can in a long
Course of Years, and consequently the Memoirs of such
a Man must swell to a very large Bulk Even Falstaff himself had been omitted, had not his Crimes been of

a publick Nature, but as Sir John condescended to be
an humble Highwayman, rather than a State Offender, he very well merits a Place among his Brother
Collectors
As we shall not, in this Collection, venture to meddle with those that are above us, so neither shall we
trouble our Heads with those that are without us Our
own Countrymen have taken great Care that Justice
should never be idle, and that Biographers of the inferior Sort should never want Materials We are daily
sensible of the Improvements they make, and Tyburn
once in six Weeks is obliged to groan under the Burden of their Iniquities
Lives of particular Persons have been commonly
esteem'd the most useful Pieces of History, they display
human Nature more familiarly than general Histories,
and the Impressions they leave are stronger General
History seems not so much the Concern of a private
Man, who has nothing to govern but his own Passions,
nor can he receive any extraordinary Advantage to
himself from the greatest Acquaintance with it, unless
he is Philosopher enough to apply the Convulsions and
Revolutions of State to his own Appetites and Inclinations, and even then 'tis like going to Bristol by the
Way of York, when he might otherwise accomplish his
Journey in a fourth part of the Time
We shall not pretend to determine whether Examples
of virtuous Men labouring with Difficulties, or of vicious Persons who are at last brought to Justice, may be
of most Use in this Age, (tho' we must confess, if the
Advantage be given to the latter, 'tis a great Sign of
our Degeneracy,) 'tis certain both may be of considerable Service, and 'tis as certain that Terror may have
some Effect upon a Mind that is past all Sense of Honour and Virtue The unhappy Wretches, indeed, whose
Lives we are to give the Publick, have generally spent
their Days in Rioting and Debauchery, which contain
all the Ideas that their abandon'd Minds could form of
Pleasure But alas! what are these, when compared
with the Pleasures of a good Conscience, which every
honest Man enjoys! Add to this, that whatever they
may pretend, and endeavour to appear, no reasonable
Man can think that a Person under perpetual Apprehensions of Justice, (as all who are conscious of the most
flagrant Crimes must be,) can enjoy a Moment's delight
even in the Way that they seek it, unless he may be said
to enjoy himself when all his Senses are entirely drown'd
in Liquor
But as it is not our Business to prescribe to our Readers,
or if it were, they would attend to us just as much as
they pleased We shall take Care that every one who
reads our Collection may be diverted, and that as many
as will may be instructed, which is all we can promise,
and, we believe, all that can be expected
The Reader may depend upon having the most authentic Accounts of every Highwayman, &c that can be

A 2   any

The INTRODUCTION.

any where procured, and of having those Accounts in a more agreeable Manner than they have ever yet appeared in Our Reflections, when we make any, shall be just, and naturally arising from the Story, whether they are calculated to raise a Smile or a serious Thought, for Occasion of both Kinds will frequently offer themselves in a Work of this Nature We have nothing more to say to our Male Readers in this Place, and therefore beg Leave to conclude with a Word or two to the Females; which is, that besides the Pleasure which they may find by perusing this Book in common with the Men, they may expect to feel the same Pity frequently reviv'd in their Breasts, which they, or some of their fair Predecessors, were formerly touched with, when several of our celebrated Heroes made their Exit

Having premis'd so much, we shall now lay before the Reader a few of the most material Persons, whose Lives and Dying Speeches will be inserted in this Work

THE Life of Sir Henry Morgan, a Pyrate, who took Panama from the Spaniards

The Life of Sir John Falstaff

The Life of Capt Avery, a Pirate, with a particular Account of his taking one of the Great Mogul's Ships

The Exploits of John Cottington alias Mull Sack; with the Particulars of his robbing the Oxford Waggon, wherein he found four thousand Pounds in ready Cash

The Adventures of Thomas Waters, with the pleasant Story of his robbing some Gipsies.

The Lives of Nan Holland and Tristram Savage, and the Manner of their robbing Dr Trotter

The Life of Jonathan Wilde, the noted Thief-taker.

The History of Jack Shephard

The Life of Capt George Lowther; with his Adventure at Mayo in the Gulph of Matique

The Lives of Capt Bartholomew Roberts, Capt Edward England, and Capt Edward Low, three famous Pirates

The Life of Whitney the Butcher, with the Particulars of his robbing an old Usurer, and tying his Hands behind him, with his Face to the Horse's Tail

The Life of the German Princess

The Life of Thomas Savage

The Life of Sawney Beane

Some Account of Sawney Cunningham, and his Adventure with the Astrologer

The Life of the Golden Farmer, and his merry Robbery of the Tinker

The History of Col Jack alias Jacque

The Life of Capt Hind, a Highwayman

The History of Capt Teach, a Pirate, commonly call'd Black Beard

The Life of the famous Claude Du Vall, a Highwayman

The Life of Sarah Malcolm, executed in Fleet Street for the Murder of Mrs Duncomb, and two others

The Lives of Edward Burnworth alias Frazier, William Blewit, Thomas Berry, Emanuel Dickenson, Peter Levee and John Higgs, who were executed for the Murder of Thomas Ball in the Mint.

The Life of Lewis Howsart, a French Barber, executed in Spittlefields, for the inhuman Murder of his Wife

The Life of Joseph Blake alias Blueskin, a Housebreaker

The History of the Waltham Blacks, and their Transactions, to the Death of Richard Parvin, Edward Elliot, Robert Kingshal, Henry Marshal, John and Edward Pine, and James Ansell alias Phillips, at Tyburn, whose Lives are also included

The Lives of Hawkins and Sympson, famous for robbing the Bristol Mail

The Lives of John Trippuck, the Golden Tinman, Robert Cane, Thomas Charnock and Richard Shephard

The Life of James Filewood

The Life of Gilder-Roy

An Account of the Murder of the Reverend Mr. John Talbot

The Lives of Capt. Uratz, and his Accomplices, Highwaymen, and Murderers, of Thomas Thynn, Esq, in Pall-Mall

The History of Moll Cutpurse, a Pick-pocket and Highway-woman.

The Tryals of upwards of sixty Pirates, taken by his Majesty's Ship the Swallow.

The Life of Capt John Phillips, a Pirate

The Life of Capt John Jaen, executed for the Murder of his Cabbin Boy.

T H I

Capt Hen. Morgan before Panama which he took from the Spaniards.

A General and True

HISTORY

OF THE

LIVES and ACTIONS

Of the most Famous

Highwaymen, Murderers, Street-Robbers, &c.

E begin this History with the Life of Sir Henry Morgan, who perhaps, distinguished himself in the Freebooting Way so much as no Man that ever engaged in it and had as large a Share of personal Courage and Bravery.

This Gentleman was born in Wales, and descended of a very good Family there, as indeed are almost all of that Name. His Father was a rich Yeoman or Farmer, but young Morgan had no Inclinations to follow that Employment, and therefore left his Country and went to seek his Fortune on the Seas, which he imagined would better suit his Temper. He was entertained at a certain Port where several Ships lay at Anchor, that were bound to the Isle of Barbadas. With these Ships he resolved to go unto the Service of one Man, according to what is commonly practised in those Parts of the English and other Nation, sold him as soon as he came on Shoar. He served his time at Barbadas, and when he had obtained his Liberty, thence transferred himself unto the Port of Jamaica, there to seek new Fortunes. Here he found two Vessels of Pyrates that were ready to go to Sea. Being destitute of Employ, he put himself in one of these Ships, with Intent to follow the Exercises of that Sort of People. He learned in a little while their manner of Living, and so exactly, that having performed three or four Voyages with some Prohibit and good Success, he agreed with some of his Comrades who had gotten by the same Voyages a certain Parcel of Money, to join Stocks and buy a Ship. The Vessel being bought, they unanimously chose him to be their Captain and Commander thereof.

With this Ship he set forth from Jamaica to cruise upon the Coast of Campeche, in which Voyage he had the Fortune to take several Ships, with which he returned triumphant to the same Island. Here he found an old Pyrate, named Mansfield, who was then busy in equipping a considerable Fleet of Ships, with Design to land upon the Continent, and pillage whatsoever he could.

In this Way, Mansfield seeing Captain Morgan return with so many Prizes, judged him, from his Actions, to be of undaunted Courage, and hereupon was moved to chuse him for his Vice-Admiral in that Expedition. Thus having fitted out fifteen Ships, between great and small, they set Sail from Jamaica with five hundred Men, both Walloons and French. With this Fleet they arriv'd not long after at the Isle of St. Catherine, situated nigh unto the Continent of Costa Rica, in twelve Degrees and a half, Northern Latitude, and distant thirty five Leagues from the River of Chagre, between North and South. Here they made their first Descent, landing most of their Men presently after.

Being now come to try their Arms and Fortune, they in a short Time forced the Garrison that kept the Island to surrender, and deliver into their Hands all the Forts and Castles belonging thereunto. All these they instantly demolished, reserving only one, wherein they placed an hundred Men of their own Party, and all the Slaves they had taken from the Spaniards. With the rest of their Men they march'd unto another small Island, adjoining to near unto that of St. Catherine, that with a Bridge they could get over. In a few Days they made a Bridge, and passed thither, conveying also over it all the Pieces of Ordnance which they had taken upon the great Island. Having ruined and destroyed, with Sword and Fire, both the Islands, leaving what Orders were necessary at the Castle above-mentioned, they put forth to Sea again with the Spaniards they had taken Prisoners. Yet these they set on shoe, not long after, upon the main Land, nigh unto a Place call'd Puerto Velo. After this they began to cruise upon the Coasts of Costa Rica, till finally they came to the River of Colla, designing to rob and pillage all the Towns they could find in those Parts, and afterwards to pass unto the Village of Natt, to do the same.

The President or Governor of Panama having had Advice of the Arrival of these Pyrates, and the Hostilities they committed every where, thought it his Duty to forth to send them to encounter with a Body of which this coming, called the Pyrates retired deeply, deal, with all Speed and Care. Pisces his seeing the whole Country alarm'd at his Arrival, and that their Designs were known, and consequently could be of no great Effect at that present. Hereupon they turned to the Isle of St. *Catharine*, to visit the hundred Men they left in Garrison there. The Governor of these Men was a certain *Frenchman*, named *Le Sieur Simon*, who behaved himself very well in that Charge, while *Mansvelt* was there. Insomuch that he had put the great Island in a very good Posture of Defence, and the little one he had caused to be cultivated with many fertile Plantations, which were sufficient to revictual the whole Fleet with Provisions and Fruits, not only for present Refreshment, but also in case of a new Voyage. *Mansvelt's* Inclinations were very much bent to keep these two Islands in perpetual Possession, as being very commodious, and profitably situated for the Use of the Pyrate; which, because they were so near the *Spanish* Dominions, and easily to be defended against them.

Hereupon *Mansvelt* determined to return to *Jamaica*, with Design to send some Recruits to the Isle of St. *Catharine*, that in case of any Invasion of the *Spaniards*, the Pyrates might be provided for a Defence. As soon as he arrived, he propounded his Martial Intentions unto the Governor of that Island, but he lik'd not the Propositions of *Mansvelt*, fearing lest, by granting such Things, he should displease his Master the King of *England*. Besides that, by giving him the Men he desired, and other Necessaries for that Purpose, he must of necessity diminish and weaken the Forces of that Island, whereof he was Governor. *Mansvelt* seeing the Unwillingness of the Governor of *Jamaica*, and that of his own Accord he could not compass what he desired, with the same Intent and Designs went unto the Island of *Tortuga*.

But there, before he could accomplish his Desires, or put in Execution what was intended, Death suddenly surpriz'd him, and put a Period to his wicked Life, all Things hereby remaining in Suspence, till the Occasion we shall hereafter relate, put them again into Motion.

Le Sieur Simon, who remained at the Isle of St. *Catharine*, in quality of Governor thereof, receiving no News from *Mansvelt* his Admiral, was greatly impatient and desirous to know what might be the Cause thereof. In the mean while, Don *John Perez de Guzman*, being newly come to the Government of *Costa Rica*, thought it no ways convenient for the Interest of the King of *Spain*, that that Island should remain in the Hands of the Pyrates. And hereupon he equipp'd a considerable Fleet, which he sent to the said Island to retake it. But before he came to use any great Violence, he writ a Letter to *le Sieur Simon*, wherein he gave him to understand that if he would surrender the Island unto his Catholick Majesty, he should be very well rewarded, but in case of Refusal, severely punish'd when he had forced him to do it. *Le Sieur Simon* seeing no Appearance or Probability of being able to defend it alone, nor any Emolument that by so doing could accrue either to him or his People, after some small Resistance, deliver'd up the Island into the Hands of its true Lord and Master, under the same Articles they had obtain'd it from the *Spaniards*. Few Days after the Surrender of the Island, there arriv'd from *Jamaica* an *English* Ship, which the Governor of the said Island had sent under-hand, wherein was a good Supply of People, both Men and Women. The *Spaniards* from the Castle having spy'd this Ship, put forth *English* Colours, and perswaded *le Sieur Simon* to go on board, and conduct the said Ship into a Port the assign'd him. This he perform'd immediately with Dissimulation, whereby they were all made Prisoners. A certain *Spanish* Engineer hath published an exact

Account of the retaking of the Fleet at *Cuba* by the *Spaniards*, which printed Paper, we have thought fit to insert in this Place.

A true and particular Relation of the Victory obtain'd by the Arms of his Catholick Majesty against the English Pyrates, by the Direction and Valour of Don John Perez de Guzman, Knight of the Order of St. James, Governor and Captain General of Terra Firma, and the Province of Veraguas.

THE Kingdom of *Terra Firma*, which of itself is sufficiently strong to repel and extirpate great Fleets, but more especially the Pyrates of *Jamaica*, had several Ways notice, under several Hands imported to the Governor thereof, that to certain *English* Vessels had Course upon the Coasts belonging to his Catholick Majesty. The News came to *Panama*, that the *English* Pyrates of the said Fleet were arrived at *Puerto de Naos*, and had forced the *Spanish* Garrison of the Isle of St. *Catharine*, whose Governor was Don *Estevan del Campo*, and that they had posted themselves of the said Island, taking Prisoners the Inhabitants and destroying all that ever they met. Moreover, about the same Time Don *John Perez de Guzman* received particular Information of these Robberies from the Relation of some *Spaniards* who escaped out of the Island, and whom he order'd to be conveyed unto *Puerto Velo*, who more distinctly told him, that the aforemention'd Pyrates came into the Island the 2d Day of *May*, by Night, without being perceived by any body. And that the next Day, after some Disputes by Arms, they had taken the Fortresses, and made Prisoners of all the Inhabitants, and Soldiers, not one excepted, unless those that by good Fortune had escaped their Hands. This being heard by Don *John*, he called a Council of War, wherein he declar'd the great Progress the said Pyrates had made in the Dominions of his Catholick Majesty.

Here likewise he propounded, *That it was absolutely necessary, to send some Forces to the Isle of St. Catharine, sufficient to retake it from the Pyrates, the Honour and Interest of his Majesty of Spain being very notoriously concerned herein. Otherwise the Pyrates, by such Conquests, might easily, in Course of Time, Possess themselves of all the Country's thereabouts.* Unto these Reasons some were found, who made Answer, *that the Pyrates, as not being able to subsist in the said Island would of necessity consume and waste themselves, and be forc'd to quit it, without any Necessity of retaking it, That consequently it was not worth while to engage in so many Expences and Troubles, as it might be foreseen this would cost.*

Notwithstanding these Reasons to the contrary, Don *John*, as one who was an expert and valiant Soldier, gave Orders that a Quantity of Provision should be conveyed to *Puerto Velo*, for the Use and Service of the Militia. And neither to be idle or negligent in his Master's Affairs, he transported himself thither, with no small Danger of his Life. Here he arriv'd the 7th Day of *July*, with no ill Things necessary to the Expedition in Hand, where he found in the Port a good Ship, called St. *Vincent*, that belonged to the *Company of Negroes*. This Ship being of itself a strong Vessel, and well mounted with Guns, he mann'd and victuall'd very well, and sent unto the Isle of St. *Catharine*, constituting Captain *Joseph Sanchez Ximenez*, Major of the City of *Puerto Velo*, Commander thereof. The People he carried with him were two hundred, threescore, and ten Soldiers, and thirty seven Prisoners of the same Island. Besides thirty four *apamaris* belonging to the Garrison of *Puerto Velo*, and twenty nine Mullitoes of *Panama*, twelve *Indians* very dextrous at shooting with Bows

ard

and Arms a Gunner and a Gunner's mate, a Pilot, one Surgeon, and one Knight ... of the Order of St. *Francis* for their Chaplain.

Don John soon after gives an Order unto every one of the Officers, instructing them how they ought to behave themselves, telling them that in case of the Governor of *Carrera*, he would fill them with more ... in a Boat, and it in any wise he thought it ...

... he proceeded thus far, *Don John* commanded the Ships to weigh Anchor, and sail out into the Port. The time ... when it took close, he called before him all the People design'd for that Expedition, and made them a Speech, exhorting them to fight against the Enemies of the Crown and Religion, but more especially against those inhuman Pirates, who had heretofore committed so many horrid and cruel Actions against the Subjects of his Catholick Majesty. With ... promising not to ... each of the most liberal Rewards, but especially unto such as should behave themselves as they ought in the Service of their King and Country. *Don John* ... and immediately the Ship weigh'd Anchor, and set sail under a favourable Gale of Wind. They soon arriv'd at *Carrera*, and presented a Letter to the Governor of the said City from the noble and valiant *Don John*, who received it with Testimonies of great Affection to the Person of *Don John*, and his Majesty's Service. And seeing their resolute Courage to ... to his Desire and Expectations, he ... *Militia*, which should be one hundred from *Carrera* in one Boat, and one hundred and ... Men, ... out of his own Garrison, and the other half Militia. Thus all of them being well provided with Necessaries, they set out from the Port of *Carrera*, and in eight Days they arriv'd within sight of the Isle of St. *Catharine*, towards the western Point thereof. And although the Wind was contrary, yet they reach'd the Port, and came to an Anchor within it, having lost one of their Boats by foul Weather, at the Rock call'd *Quai a Signos*.

The Pyrates seeing the *Spanish* Ships come to an Anchor, gave them presently three Guns with Bullets, the which were soon answer'd in the same manner. Hereupon the Major *Joseph Sanchez Ximenez*, sent on shore, unto the Pyrates, one of his Officers, to require them, in the Name of the Catholick King his Master, to surrender the Island, seeing they had taken it in the midst of the Peace between the two Crowns of *Spain* and *England*, and that in case they would be obstinate, he would certainly put them all to the Sword. The Pyrates made answer, *That Island had once before belong'd to the Government and Dominions of the King of England, and that instead of surrendring it, they preferr'd to lose their Lives.*

Some Days after this, three Negroes from the Pyrates, came swimming aboard the *Spanish* Admiral. These brought Intelligence, that all the Pyrates that were upon the Island were only threescore and twelve in Number, and that they were under a great Consternation, seeing such considerable Force come against them. With this Intelligence the *Spaniards* resolved to land, and advance towards the Fortresses which ceased not to fire so many great Guns against them, as they possibly could, and which were still answer'd in the same manner on the other side, till dark Night. Two Days after this, the Weather being very calm and clear, the *Spaniards* began to advance in the following manner. The Ship named St. *Vincent*, which the Admiral, discharg'd two whole Broadsides upon the Battery call'd the *Conception*. The Ship call'd St. *Peter*, that was Vice-Admiral, discharg'd likewise her Guns against the other Battery, call'd St. *James*.

... the main Guard ... Port ... ... in the Castle of St. *Jerome* ... Port ... remained ... ... towards the Castle called ... the Fortress ... Port ... which ... their Men was ... together unto ... both of them in certain ... which pass'd to turn it ... the Place were they ... Thus ... Pirates on a Piece of Land ... said Isles, and the Officers of the Church, or ... gave a ... short time soon ... the Town.

Notwithstanding ... the Heat of the ... Captain *Don Joseph Ramirez de Leyva*, who attacked the ..., made a strong Attack, wherein he fought on both Sides very desperately, till that at last he overcame, and forced the Pirates to surrender the Fort he had then in Hand.

On the other Side, Captain *John Galeno*, with fourscore and ten Men, pass'd over the Hills, to advance that Way towards the Castle of St. *Teresa*. In the mean while, the Major *Don Joseph* and Admiral, the Commander in chief, with the rest of his Men, set forth from the Battery of St. *James*, passing the Port with four Boats, and landing in Despite of the Enemy. About this time Captain *John Galeno* began to advance with the Men he had to the aforementioned Fortress. So that the *Spaniards* made three attacks on the Pirates on three several Sides, at one and the same time, with great Courage and Valour. The Pirates upon the ... seeing many of their Men already kill'd, and that they could in no manner subsist any longer, resolved to avoid *Contumacy*, where they surrender'd themselves, and likewise the whole Island, unto the *Spaniards* Hands, who possessed themselves of all, and set up the *Spanish* Colours, as soon as they had render'd Thanks to God Almighty for the signal Victory they had obtained. The Number of dead were six Men of the Pirates, with many wounded, and threescore and ten Prisoners. On the other Side was found only one Man kill'd, and four wounded.

There was found upon the Island eight hundred Pound of Powder, two hundred and fifty Pound of small Bullets, with many other military Provisions. Among the Prisoners were taken also two *Spaniards*, who had born Arms under the *English* against his Catholick Majesty. These were order'd to be shot to Death the next Day, by the Command of the Major. In less than a Month after this, there arriv'd at the Isle an *English* Vessel, which being seen at a great Distance by the Major, he gave Orders to le *Sieur Simon*, who was a *Frenchman*, to go and visit the said Ship, and tell them that were on board, that the Island belong'd still to the *English*. He perform'd the Commands, and found in the said Ship only fourteen Men, one Woman, and her Daughter, who were all instantly made Prisoners.

The *English* Pyrates were all transported to *Puerto Velo*; excepting only three, who by Order of the Governor were carried to *Panama*, there to work in the Castle of St. *Jerom*. This Fortification is an excellent Piece of Workmanship, and very strong, being raised in the Middle of the Port, of a quadrangular Form, and of very hard Stone. Its Elevation or Height is of eighty eight geometrical Feet, the Walls being of fourteen, and the Curtains of twenty five Feet diameter. It was built at the Expence of several private Persons, the Governor and the City furnishing the greatest Part of the Money; so that it did not cost his Catholick Majesty any Sum at all.

Captain *Morgan* seeing his Predecessor and Admiral, *Mansvelt*, was dead, endeavoured, by all the Means that were possible, to preserve and keep in

perpetual

perpetual Poſſeſſion, the Iſle of St *Catherin* ſeated nigh unto that of *Cuba* His principle Intent was to conſecrate it to a Refuge and Sanctuary to the Pyrates of thoſe Parts, partaking it in a ſufficient Condition of being a Receptacle or Store-houſe of their Preys and Robberies Unto this Effect he left no Store unmov'd whereby to compaſs his Deſigns, writing for the ſame Purpoſe to ſeveral Merchants that lived in *Virginia* and *New-England*, and perſwading them to ſend him Proviſions and other neceſſary Things to wards the putting the ſaid Iſland into ſuch a Poſture of Defence, as it might neither be ſeiſen by external Danger, nor be moved at any Suſpicion of Invaſion from any ſide, that might attempt to diſquiet it At Laſt, all his Thoughts and Cares proved ineffectual, by the *Spaniards* retaking the ſaid Iſland Yet notwithſtanding, Captain *Morgan* retain'd his ancient Courage, which inſtantly put him on new Deſigns Thus he equipp'd a that a Ship, with Intention to gather an entire Fleet, both as great and as ſtrong as he could compaſs By Degrees he put the whole Matter in Execution, and gave Orders to every Member of his Fleet, that they ſhould meet at a certain Port of *Cuba* Here he determin'd to call a Council, and deliberate concerning what was beſt to be done, and what Place firſt they ſhould fall upon Leaving theſe new Preparations in this Condition, we ſhall here give our Readers ſome ſmall Account of the aforementioned Iſle of *Cuba*, in whoſe Ports this Expedition was hatched

A Deſcription of the Iſland of CUBA

THE Iſland of *Cuba* lieth from Eaſt to Weſt, in the Situation of twenty to three and twenty Degrees, Northern Latitude, being in Length one hundred and fifty *German* Leagues, and about forty in Breadth Its Fertility is equal to that of the Iſland of *Hiſpaniola* Beſides which, it affordeth many Things proper for Trading and Commerce, ſuch as are Hides of ſeveral Beaſts, particularly thoſe that in *Europe* are call'd *Hides of Havana* On all Sides it is ſurrounded with a great Number of ſmall Iſlands, which go altogether under the Name of *Cayos* Of theſe little Iſlands the Pyrates make great Uſe, as of their own proper Ports of Refuge Here moſt commonly they make their Meetings, and hold their Councils, how to aſſault more eaſily the *Spaniards* It is thoroughly water'd on all Sides with the Streams of plentiful and pleaſant Rivers, whoſe Entries form both ſecure and ſpacious Ports Beſides many other Harbours for Ships, which along the calm Shores and Coaſts adorn many Parts of this rich and beautiful Iſland

All which contribute very much to its Happineſs, by facilitating the Exerciſe of Trade, whereinto they invite both Natives and Foreigners The chiefeſt of theſe Ports are St *Jago*, *Bayame*, *Santa Maria*, *Eſpiritu Santo*, *Trinidad*, *Xagua*, *Cabo de Corrientes*, and others, all which are ſeated on the South-ſide of the Iſland On the Northern-ſide hereof are found theſe following La *Havana*, *Puerto Mariano*, *Santa Cruz*, *Mata Ricos*, and *Barracoa*

This Iſland hath two principal Cities, by which the whole Country is govern'd, and to which all the Towns and Villages thereof are in Obedience The firſt of theſe is nam'd St *Jago*, or St *James*, being ſeated on the South-ſide, and having under its Juriſdiction one half of the Iſland The chief Magiſtrates hereof are a Biſhop and a Governour, who command over the Villages and Towns belonging to the half above mentioned The chiefeſt of theſe are, on the Southern-ſide, *Eſpiritu Santo*, *Puerto del Principe*, and *Bayame* On the North-ſides it hath *Barracoa*, and the Town call'd *de los Cayos*, The greateſt Part

of the Commerce driven at this former ſort and City of St *Jago* conſiſt from the *Cayos* Iſland, whither they tranſport great Quantities of Tobacco, Sugar, and Hides, which Sort or Merchandize neceſſary to the ſaid City from the ſuburbs and neighbouring Villages In former Times this City of St *Jago* was inceſſably ſack'd by the Pyrates of *Jamaica* and *Tortuga*, notwithſtanding that it is defended by a conſiderable Caſtle

The City and Port *de la Havana*, lieth between the North and Weſt Side of the Iſland This is one of the moſt renow'd and ſtrongeſt Places of all the *Weſt-Indies* Its Juriſdiction extendeth over the other Half of the Iſland, the chiefeſt Places under it being *Santa Cruz*, on the Northern Side, and *la Trinidad* on the South From hence is tranſported huge Quantities of Tobacco, which is ſent in great Plenty to *New-Spain* and *Coſta Rica*, even as far as the *South-Sea* Beſides many Ships, laden with this Commodity, that are conſign'd unto *Spain*, and other Parts of *Europe*, not only in the Leaf, but, alſo, in Rowls This City is defended by three Caſtles, very great and ſtrong, two of which ſtanding towards the Port, and the other is ſeated upon a Hill that commandeth the Town 'Tis eſtimated to contain ten thouſand Families, more or leſs, among which Number are of People, the Merchants of this Place trade in *New Spain*, *Campeche*, *Honduras*, and *Florida* All the Ships that come from the Parts aforementioned, as alſo from *Caracas*, *Cartagena*, and *Coſta Rica*, are neceſſitated to take their Proviſions in at *Havana*, wherewith to make their Voyage for *Spain*, this being the neceſſary and ſtreight Courſe they ought to ſteer for the South of *Europe*, and other Parts The Hote Fleet of *Spain*, which the *Spaniards* call *Flota*, being Homeward bound, toucheth here yearly, to take in the reſt of their full Cargo, as Hides, Tobacco, and *Campeche* Wood

Captain *Morgan* had been no longer than two Months in the abovementioned Ports of the South of *Cuba*, when he had got together a Fleet of twelve Sail, between Ships and great Boats, wherein he had ſeven hundred fighting Men, part of which were *Engliſh*, and part *French* They call'd a Council, and ſome were of Opinion 'twere convenient to aſſault the City of *Havana*, under the Covert of the Night, which Enterprize, they ſaid, might eaſily be perform'd, eſpecially if they could but take any few of the Eccleſiaſticks, and make them Priſoners Yea, that the City might be ſack'd, before the Caſtles could put themſelves in a Poſture of Defence Others propounded, according to their ſeveral Opinions, other Attempts Notwithſtanding, the former Propoſal was rejected, becauſe many of the Pyrates had been Priſoners at other Times in the ſaid City, and theſe affirm'd, nothing of Conſequence could be done, unleſs with fifteen hundred Men Moreover, that with all this Number of People they ought firſt to go to the Iſland *de los Pinos*, and land them in ſmall Boats about *Matamano*, fourteen Leagues diſtant from the aforeſaid City, whereby to accompliſh, by theſe Means, and order their Deſigns

Finally, they ſaw no Poſſibility of gathering ſo great a Fleet, and hereupon, with that they had, they concluded to attempt ſome other Place Among the reſt, was found, at laſt, one who propounded, that they ſhould go and aſſault the Town of *el Puerto del Principe* This Propoſition he endeavour'd to perſuade, by ſaying, he knew that Place very well, and that being at a Diſtance from the Sea, it never was ſack'd by any Pyrates Whereby the Inhabitants were rich, as exerciſing their Trade for ready Money, with thoſe of *Havana*, who kept here an eſtabliſh'd Commerce, which conſiſted chiefly in Hides This
Propoſal

Propofal was prefently admitted by Captain *Morgan*, and the chiefeft of his Companions, and, hereupon, they gave Orders to every Captain to weigh Anchor, and fet Sail, fteering their Courfe towards that Coaft that lieth neareft to *El Puerto del Principe*. Hereabouts is to be feen a Bay, nam'd, by the *Spaniards*, *El Puerto de Santa Maria*. Being arriv'd at this Bay, a certain *Spaniard*, who was Prifoner on board the Fleet, fwam a-fhore by Night, and came to the Town of *El Puerto del Principe*, giving Account to the Inhabitants of the Defign the Pyrates had againft them. This he affirm'd to have over-heard in their Difcourfe, they thinking, at the fame Time, he did not underftand the *Englifh* Tongue. The *Spaniards*, as foon as they received this fortunate Advice, began inftantly to hide their Riches, and carry away what Moveables they could. The Governor, alfo, immediately rais'd all the People of the Town, both Freemen and Slaves, and, with part of them, took a Poft, by which, of Neceffity, the Pyrates were to pafs. He commanded, likewife, many Trees to be cut down, and laid amidft the Ways, to hinder their Paffage. In like manner, he plac'd feveral Ambufcades, which were ftrengthen'd with fome Pieces of Cannon, to play upon them on their March. He gather'd, in all, about eight hundred Men, of which he diftributed feveral into the aforemention'd Ambufcades, and with the reft he begirt the Town, difplaying them upon the Plain of a fpacious Field, from whence they could fee the coming of the Pyrates at Length.

Captain *Morgan*, with his Men, being now upon the March, found the Avenues and Paffages to the Town impenetrable. Hereupon, they took their Way through the Wood, traverfing it with great Difficulty, whereby they efcap'd divers Ambufcades. Thus, at laft, they came into the Plain aforemention'd, which, from its Figure, is call'd by the *Spaniards*, la *Savana*, or The Sheet. The Governor feeing them come, made a Detachment of a Troop of Horfe, which he fent to charge them in the Front, thinking to difperfe them, and by putting them to Flight, purfue them with his main Body. But this Defign fucceeded not as it was intended, for the Pyrates march'd in very good Rank and File, at the found of their Drums, and with flying Colours. When they came nigh to the Horfe, they drew into the Form of a Semicircle, and thus advanc'd towards the *Spaniards*, who charg'd them like valiant and courageous Soldiers, for a while. But feeing that the Pyrates were very dexterous at their Arms, and their Governor, with many of their Companions, kill'd, they began to retreat towards the Wood. Here they defign'd to fave themfelves with more Advantage, but before they cou'd reach it, the greateft Part of them were unfortunately kill'd by the Hands of the Pyrates. Thus they left the Victory to thefe new-come Enemies, who had no confiderable Lofs of Men in this Battle, and but very few wounded. However, the Skirmifh continu'd for the Space of four Hours. They enter'd the Town, though not without great Refiftance of fuch as were within, who defended themfelves as long as poffible, thinking, by their Defence, to hinder the Pillage. Hereupon, many feeing the Enemy within the Town, fhut themfelves up in their own Houfes, and from thence made feveral Shot againft the Pyrates, who perceiving the Mifchief of this Difadvantage, prefently began to threaten them, faying, *If you don't furrender voluntarily, you fhall foon fee the Town in a Flame, and your Wives and Children torn in Pieces before your Faces.* With thefe Menaces, the *Spaniards* fubmitted entirely to the Difcretion of the Pyrates, believing they could not continue there long, and would foon be forc'd to diflodge.

As foon as the Pyrates had poffefs'd themfelves of the Town, they enclos'd all the *Spaniards*, both Men, Women, Children, and Slaves, in feveral Churches, and gather'd all the Goods they could find by way of pillage. Afterwards they fearch'd the whole Country round about the Town, bringing in, Day by Day, many Goods and Prifoners, with much Provifion. With this, they fell to banqueting among themfelves, and making great Chear after their cuftomary Way, without remembering the poor Prifoners, whom they permitted to ftarve in the Churches for Hunger. In the mean Time, they ceas'd not to torment them daily after an inhuman Manner, thereby to make them confefs where they had hid their Goods, Monies, and other Things, though little or nothing was left them. To this Effect they punifh'd alfo the Women and little Children, giving them nothing to eat, whereby the greateft part perifh'd.

When they could find no more to rob, and that Provifions began to grow fcarce, they thought it convenient to depart, and feek new Fortunes in other Places. Hence they intimated to the Prifoners, *That they fhould find Monies to ranfom themfelves, elfe they fhould be all tranfported to Jamaica.* Which being done, if they did not pay a fecond Ranfom for the Town, they would turn every Houfe into Afhes. The *Spaniards* hearing thefe fevere Menaces, nominated among themfelves four Fellow-prifoners to go and feek for the abovemention'd Contributions. But the Pyrates, to the Intent they fhould return fpeedily with the Ranfoms prefcrib'd, tormented feveral in their Prefence, before they departed, with all the Rigour imaginable. After a few Days, the *Spaniards* return'd from the Fatigue of their unfeafonable Commiffion, telling Captain *Morgan*, *That they had run up and down, and fearched all the neighbouring Woods and Places they moft fufpected, and yet had not been able to find any of their own Party, nor confequently any Fruit of their Embaffy. But if (faid they) you are pleafed to have a little longer Patience with us, we fhall certainly caufe all that you demand to be paid within the Space of fifteen Days.* Captain *Morgan* was contented, as it fhould feem, to grant them this Petition, but, not long after, there came into the Town feven or eight Pyrates, who had been ranging in the Woods and Fields, and got thereabouts fome confiderable Booty. Thefe brought, among other Prifoners, a certain Negroe, whom they had taken with Letters about him. Captain *Morgan* having perus'd them, found they were from the Governor of St *Jago*, being written to fome of the Prifoners. Wherein he told them, *They fhou'd not make too much Hafte to pay any Ranfom for their Town, or Perfons, or any other Pretext, but, on the contrary, they fhould put off the Pyrates as well as they could with Excufes and Delays, expecting to be reliev'd by him within a fhort Time, when he would certainly come to their Aid.* This Intelligence being heard by Captain *Morgan*, he immediately gave Orders that all they had robb'd fhould be carried on board the Ships, and, withal, he intimated to the *Spaniards*, that the very next Day they fhould pay their Ranfoms, forafmuch as he would not wait one Moment longer, but reduce the whole Town to Afhes, in cafe they fail'd to perform the Sum he demanded.

With this Intimation, Captain *Morgan* made no mention to the *Spaniards* of the Letters he had intercepted. Whereupon, they made him anfwer, *That it was totally impoffible for them to give fuch a Sum of Money in fo fhort a Space of Time, feeing their Fellow-townfmen were not to be found in all the Country thereabouts.* Captain *Morgan* knew full well their Intentions, and, withal, thought it not convenient to remain there any longer Time. Hence

3   C   he

he demanded of them only five hundred Oxen, or Cows, together with sufficient Salt wherewith to salt them

Hereunto he added only this Condition, that they should carry them on board his Ships, which they promised to do Thus he departed with all his Men, taking with him only six of the principal Prisoners, as Pledges of what he intended The next Day the *Spaniards* brought the Cattle and Salt unto the Ships, and required the Prisoners. But Captain *Morgan* refused to deliver them, till such Time as they had helped his Men to kill and salt the Beeves This was likewise performed in great Haste, he not caring to stay there any longer, lest he should be surprized by the Forces that were gathering against him Having received all on board his Vessels, he set at Liberty the Prisoners he had kept as Hostages of his Demands While these Things were in Agitation, there happen'd to arise some Dissentions between the *Englishmen* and *French* The Occasion of their Discord was, as followeth A certain *Frenchman* being employed in killing and salting one of the Beeves, an *English* Pyrate came to him, and took away the Marrow-bones he had taken out of the Ox, which sort of Meat these People esteem very much Hereupon they challenged one another Being come to the Place of Duel, the *Englishman* drew his Sword treacherously against the *Frenchman*, wounding him in the Back, before he had put himself in a just Posture of Defence, whereby he suddenly fell dead upon the Place The other *Frenchmen* desirous to revenge this base Action, made an Insurrection against the *English* But Captain *Morgan* soon extinguished this Flame, by commanding the Criminal to be bound in Chains, and thus carry'd to *Jamaica*, promising to them all, he would see Justice done upon him. For although it were permitted unto him to challenge his Adversary, yet was it not lawful to kill him treacherously, as he did

As soon as all Things were in a readiness, and on board the Ships, and likewise the Prisoners set at Liberty, they sailed from thence, directing their Course to a certain Island, where Captain *Morgan* intended to make a Dividend of what they had purchased in that Voyage Being arrived at the Place assigned, they found nigh the value of fifty Thousand Pieces of Eight, both in Money and Goods The Sum being known, it caused a general Resentment and Grief, to see such a small Purchase, which was not sufficient to pay their Debts at *Jamaica* Hereupon, Captain *Morgan* propounded to them, that they should think upon some other Enterprize and Pillage, before they returned Home But the *Frenchmen* not being able to agree with the *English*, separated from their Company, leaving Captain *Morgan* alone with those of his own Nation, notwithstanding all the Perswasions he used to reduce them to continue in his Company Thus they parted with all external signs of Friendship, Captain *Morgan* reiterating his Promises to them, that he would see Justice done upon the Criminal before mentioned This he performed, for being arrived at *Jamaica*, he caused him to be hanged, which was the Satisfaction the *French* Pyrates could expect

Some, perhaps, may think, that the *French* having deserted Captain *Morgan*, the *English* alone could not have been sufficient to perform such great Actions as before their Division But Captain *Morgan*, who always communicated Vigour with his Words, infused such Spirits into his Men, as were able to put every one of them instantly upon new Designs, They being all perswaded by his Reasons, that the sole Execution of his Orders would be a certain Means of obtaining great Riches This Perswasion had such Influence upon their Minds, that

with immutable Courage, they all resolved to follow him. The same likewise did a certain Pyrate of *Campeche*, who, on this Occasion joined with Captain *Morgan*, to seek new Fortunes under his Conduct, and greater Advantages than he had found before Thus Sir *Henry*, in a few Days, gather'd a Fleet of Nine Sail, between Ships and great Boats, wherein he had four hundred and threescore military Men

After that all Things were in a good Posture of Readiness, they put forth to Sea, Captain *Morgan* imparting the Design he had in his Mind, to no Body for that Present He only told them on several Occasions, that he held it as indubitable, that he should make a good Fortune by that Voyage, if strange Occurrences alter'd not the Course of his Designs They directed their Course towards the *Continent*, where they arrived in a few Days upon the Coast of *Costa Rica*, with all their Fleet entire No sooner had they discovered Land, but the Commodore declared his Intentions to the Captains, and presently after unto all the rest of the Company He told them, he intended in that Expedition to Plunder *Puerto Velo*, and that he would perform it by Night, being resolved to put the whole City to the Sack, not the least Corner escaping his Diligence Moreover, to encourage them, he added, that this Enterprize could not fail to succeed well, seeing he had kept it secret in his Mind, without revealing it to any Body, so that they could not have Notice of his coming Unto this Proposition some made Answer, by alledging, they had not a sufficient Number of Men wherewith to assault so strong and great a City But Captain *Morgan* replied, *If our Number is small, our Hearts are great, And the fewer Persons we are the more Union and better Shares we shall have in the Spoil* Hereupon, being stimulated with the Ambition of those vast Riches they promised themselves from their good Success, they unanimously concluded to venture upon that Design. But now, to the Intent our Reader may better comprehend the incomparable Boldness of this Exploit, it may be necessary to say something before-hand of the City of *Puerto Velo*

The City which beareth this Name in *America*, is seated in the Province of *Costa Rica*, under the Altitude of ten Degrees northern Latitude, at the distance of fourteen Leagues from the *Gulf of Darien*, and eight westwards, from the Port called *Nombre de Dios* It is judged to be the strongest Place that the King of *Spain* possesseth in all the *West-Indies*, excepting two, that is to say, *Havana* and *Cartagena*. Here are two Castles, almost inexpugnable, that defend the City, they being situated at the Entry of the Port, so that no Ship nor Boat can pass without permission The Garrison consisteth of three hundred Soldiers, and the Town is constantly inhabited by four hundred Families, more or less The Merchants dwell not here, but only reside for a while, when the *Galeons* come or go from *Spain*, by Reason of the Unhealthiness of the Air, occasioned by certain Vapours that exhale from the Mountains Notwithstanding this, their chief Warehouses are at *Puerto Velo*, tho' their Habitations are all the Year long at *Panama*. From whence they bring the Plate upon Mules, at such Times as the Fair beginneth, and when the Ships, belonging to the *Company of Negroes*, arrive here to sell Slaves

Captain *Morgan*, who knew very well all the Avenues of this City, as also all the neighbouring Coasts, arrived in the Dusk of the Evening, at the Place call'd *Puerto de Naos*, distant ten Leagues towards the West of *Puerto Velo* Being come to this Place, they mounted the River in their Ships, as far as another Harbour, call'd *Puerto Pontin*, where they came to an Anchor. Here they put themselves immediately into

Boats

Boats and Canoes, leaving in the Ships only a few Men to keep them, and conduct them the next Day unto the Port About Midnight they came to a certain Place call'd *Estera longa Lemos,* where they all went on Shore, and marched by Land to the first Watch of the City, They had in their Company a certain *Englishman,* who had been formerly a Prisoner in those Parts, and who now served them for a Guide Unto him and three or four more, they gave Commission to take the Centinel, if possible, or kill him upon the Place Accordingly, they laid Hands on him, and apprehended him with such Cunning, that he had no Time to give Warning with his Musket, or make any other Noise Thus they brought him, with his Hands bound, to Captain *Morgan,* who asked him, *How Things went in the City, and what Forces they had,* with many other Circumstances, which he was desirous to know After every Question, they made him a thousand Menaces to kill him, in Case he declared not the Truth Thus they began to advance towards the City, carrying always the same Centinel bound, before them Having marched about one Quarter of a League, they came to the Castle that is nigh to the City, which presently they closely surrounded, so that no person could get either in or out of the said Fortress

Being thus posted under the Walls of the Castle, Captain *Morgan* commanded the Centinel, whom they had taken prisoner, to speak to those that were within, and charge them to surrender, and deliver themselves up to his Discretion, threatning that otherwise they should be all cut in pieces, without giving Quarter to any one But they would hearken to none of these Threats, beginning instantly to fire, which gave Notice to the City, and suddenly alarmed the Garrison Yet notwithstanding the Governor and Soldiers of the said Castle made as great Resistance as could be performed, they were constrained to surrender to the Pyrates These no sooner had taken possession of the Castle, but they resolved to be as good as their Word, in putting the *Spaniards* to the Sword, thereby to strike a Terror to the rest of the City Hereupon, having shut up all the Soldiers and Officers, as prisoners, into one Room, they instantly set fire to the powder (whereof they found a great Quantity) and blew up the whole Castle into the Air, with all the *Spaniards* that were within This being done, they pursued the Course of their Victory, falling upon the City, which, as yet, was not in Order to receive them Many of the Inhabitants cast their Jewels and Monies, and other valuable Things, into Wells and Cisterns, or hid them in other places under Ground, to prevent, as much as were possible, their being totally robb'd One party of the Pyrates, being assigned to this purpose, ran immediately to the Cloysters, and took as many religious Men and Women as they could find The Governor of the City, not being able to rally the Citizens, through the huge Confusion of the Town, retir'd to one of the Castles remaining, and from thence began to fire incessantly at the Pyrates But these were not in the least negligent, either to assault him or defend themselves with all the Courage imaginable Thus it was observable, that amidst the Horror of the Assault, they made very few shot in vain For aiming, with great Dexterity at the Mouths of the Guns, the *Spaniards* were certain to lose one or two Men every time they charged each Gun a-new

The Assault of this Castle where the Governor was, continu'd very furious on both Sides, from Break of Day till Noon, and even then the Case was very dubious which party should conquer, or be conquer'd. At last, the Pyrates, perceiving they had lost many Men, and, as yet, advanc'd but little towards the gaining either this or the other Castles

remaining, thought to make use of Fire-balls, which they threw with their Hands, designing, if possible, to burn the Doors of the Castle But going about to put this in Execution, the *Spaniards,* from the Walls, let fall a great Quantity of Stones, and earthen Pots full of Powder, and other combustible Matter, which forc'd them to desist from that Attempt. Captain *Morgan,* seeing this generous Defence made by the *Spaniards,* began to despair of the whole Success of the Enterprize. Hereupon, many faint and calm Meditations came into his Mind, neither could he determine which Way to turn himself in that Distress of Affairs Being involv'd in these Thoughts, he was suddenly animated to continue the Assault, by seeing the *English* Colours put forth at one of the lesser Castles, which was just then enter'd by his Men A Troop of these immediately came to meet him, proclaiming Victory with loud Shouts of Joy This instantly put him upon new Resolutions, of making fresh Efforts to take the rest of the Castles that stood out against him Especially seeing the chiefest Citizens were fled to them, and had convey'd thither great part of their Riches, with all the Plate belonging to the Churches, and other Things dedicated to divine Service

To bring about this, therefore, he order'd ten or twelve Ladders to be made in all possible Haste, so broad, that three or four Men at once might ascend by them These being finished, he commanded all the religious Men and Women, whom he had taken Prisoners, to fix them against the Walls of the Castle. Thus much he had before-hand threaten'd the Governor to perform, in case he deliver'd not the Castle. But the Answer of that gallant Commander was, *That he wou'd never surrender himself alive* The Captain's Knowledge of the Superstition of these People, furnished him with this fine Stratagem, for he was persuaded himself that the Governor would not employ his utmost Forces, seeing religious Women, and Ecclesiastical Persons, exposed in the Front of the Soldiers to the greatest Dangers Thus the Ladders, as we have said, were put into the Hands of religious Persons of both Sexes; and these were forced, at the Head of the Companies, to raise and apply them to the Walls However, Captain *Morgan* was fully deceiv'd in his Judgment of this Design For the Governor, who acted like a brave and couragious Soldier, and who had little of the religious Temper of his Country, refused not, in Performance of his Duty, to use his utmost Endeavours to destroy whosoever came near the Walls The religious Men and Women ceas'd not to cry to him, and beg of him, by all the Saints of Heaven, that he would deliver the Castle, and thereby spare both his and their own Lives But nothing could prevail with the Resolution and Fierceness that had possess'd the Governor's Mind Thus many of the religious Men and Nuns were kill'd before they could fix the Ladders; which, at last, being done, though with great Loss of the said Brethren and Sisters, the Pyrates mounted them in great Numbers, and with no less Valour; having Fire-balls in their Hands, and earthen Pots full of Powder All which Things, being now at the Top of the Walls, they kindled, and cast in among the *Spaniards*

This Effort of the Pyrates was very bold and successful; insomuch, as the *Spaniards* could no longer resist nor defend the Castle, which was now enter'd Whereupon, they all threw down their Arms, and craved Quarter for their Lives; only the Governor of the City would neither admit nor crave Mercy, but continued to kill many of the Pyrates with his own Hands, and not a few of his own Soldiers, because they did not stand to their Arms And though the Pyrates asked him if he would have Quarter, yet he
constantly

conftantly anfwer'd, *By no Means I had rather die as a valiant Soldier, than be hang'd as a Coward* They endeavour'd, as much as they cou'd, to take him Prifoner But he defended himfelf fo obftinately, that they were forced to kill him, notwithftanding all the Cries and Tears of his own Wife and Daughter, who begg'd of him, upon their Knees, to demand Quarter, and fave his Life When the Pyrates had poffefs'd themfelves of the Caftle, which was about Night, they enclos'd therein all the Prifoners they had taken, placing the Women and Men by themfelves, with fome Guards upon them All the wounded were put into a certain Apartment by itfelf, to the Intent their own Complaints might be the Cure of their Difeafes; for no other was afforded them

This being done, they fell to eating and drinking, after their ufual Manner, that is to fay, committing in both thefe Things all manner of Debauchery and Excefs Thefe two Vices were immediately follow'd by many infolent Actions of Rape and Adultery, committed upon abundance of very honeft Women, as well married as Virgins, who being threaten'd with the Sword, were conftrain'd to fubmit their Bodies to the Violence of thofe lewd and wicked Men After fuch a Manner they deliver'd themfelves up to all Sorts of Debauchery of this Kind, that if there had been found only fifteen couragious Men, they might eafily have retaken the City, and kill'd all the Pyrates The next Day, having plunder'd all they could find, they began to examine fome of the Prifoners, who had been perfuaded by their Companions to fay they were the richeft of the Town, charging them feverely, to difcover where they had hidden their Riches and Goods But not being able to extort any Thing out of them, as they were not the right Perfons that poffefs'd any Wealth, they at laft refolv'd to torture them. This they perform'd with fuch Cruelty, that many of them died upon the Rack, or prefently afterwards Soon after this, the Prefident of *Panama* had News brought him of the Pillage and Ruin of *Puerto Velo* This Intelligence caus'd him to employ all his Care and Induftry to raife Forces, with Defign to purfue and caft out the Pyrates from thence But thefe car'd little for what extraordinary Means the Prefident us'd, as having their Ship nigh at Hand, and being determin'd to fet fire to the City, and retreat They had now been at *Puerto Velo* fifteen Days, in which Space of Time they had loft many of their Men, both by the Unhealthinefs of the Country, and the extravagant Debaucheries they had committed

Hereupon, they prepar'd for a Departure, carrying on board their Ships all the Pillage they had gotten But, above all, they provided the Fleet with fufficient Victuals for the Voyage While thefe Things were getting ready, Captain *Morgan* fent an Injunction to the Prifoners that they fhould pay him a Ranfom for the City, or elfe he would by Fire confume all to Afhes, and blow up all the Caftles into the Air Withal, he commanded them to fend fpeedily two Perfons, to feek and procure the Sum he demanded, which amounted to one hundred thoufand Pieces of Eight To this Effect, two Men were fent to the Prefident of *Panama*, who gave him an Account of all thefe Tragedies The Prefident, having now a Body of Men in Readinefs, fet forth immediately toward *Puerto Velo*, to encounter the Pyrates before their Retreat But thefe People, hearing of his coming, inftead of flying away, went to meet him at a narrow Paffage, through which, of Neceffity, he was to pafs Here they plac'd an hundred Men very well arm'd, who, at the firft Encounter, put to Flight a good Party of thofe of *Panama* This Accident oblig'd the Prefident to retire, for that Time, as not

being yet in a Pofture of Strength to proceed any further Prefently after this Rencounter, he fent a Meffage to Captain *Morgan*, to tell him, *That in cafe he departed not fuddenly with all his Forces from Puerto Velo, he ought to expect no Quarter for himfelf nor his Companions, when he fhould take them, as he hoped foon to do* Captain *Morgan*, who fear'd not his Threats, as knowing he had a fecure Retreat in his Ships, which were nigh at Hand, made him anfwer, *That he would not deliver up the Caftles, before he had received the Contribution money he had demanded, and that in cafe it were not paid down, he would certainly burn the whole City, and then leave it, demolifhing, before-hand, the Caftles, and killing the Prifoners*

The Governor of *Panama* perceiv'd by this Anfwer, that no Means would ferve to mollify the Hearts of the Pyrates, nor reduce them to Reafon Hereupon he determined to leave them, as alfo thofe of the City, whom he came to relieve, involved in the Difficulties of making the beft Agreement they could with their Enemies Thus in a few Days more, the miferable Citizens gathered the Contribution wherein they were fined, and brought the entire Sum of one hundred thoufand Pieces of Light to the Pyrates, for a Ranfom out of the cruel Captivity they were fallen into

The Prefident of *Panama*, confefs'd that thefe Tranfactions put him into an extreme Admiration, confidering that four hundred Men had been able to take fuch a great City, with fo many ftrong Caftles, efpecially feeing they had no Pieces of Cannon, nor other great Guns, wherewith to raife Batteries againft them And what was more, knowing that the Citizens of *Puerto Velo* had always been in great Repute for good Soldiers themfelves, and who had never wanted Courage in their own Defence This Aftonifhment was fo great, that it occafioned him, in order to be fatisfied herein, to fend a Meffenger to Captain *Morgan*, defiring him to fend him fome fmall Pattern of thofe Arms wherewith he had taken fo fuddenly fuch a great City Captain *Morgan* received this Meffenger very kindly, and treated him with great Civility Which being done, he gave him a Piftol and a few fmall Bullets of Lead, to carry back to the Prefident, his Mafter telling him, withal, *That he defired him to accept that flender Specimen of the Arms wherewith he had taken* Puerto Velo, *and keep them for a Twelvemonth, after which Time, he affured him he would come to Panama and fetch them away* The Governor of *Panama* return'd the Prefent very foon to Captain *Morgan*, giving him Thanks for the Favour of lending him fuch Weapons as he needed not, and withal fent him a Ring of Gold, with this Meffage, *That he defired him not to give himfelf the Trouble of coming to Panama, for he did certify unto him, that he fhould not fpeed fo well there as he had done at* Puerto Velo

After thefe Tranfactions, Captain *Morgan* (having provided his Fleet with all Neceffaries, and taken with him the beft Guns of the Caftles, nailing up the reft which he could not carry away) fet fail from *Puerto Velo* with all his Ships With thefe he arrived in a few Days, at the Ifland of *Cuba*, where he fought out a Place wherein with all Quiet and Repofe he might make the Dividend of the Spoil they had gotten They found in ready Money, two hundred and fifty thoufand Pieces of Eight, befides Variety of Merchandizes, fuch as Cloth, Linnen, Silks, and other Goods With this rich Purchafe they failed again from thence to their common Place of Rendezvouz, *Jamaica* Being arrived there, they paffed fome Time in all Sorts of Vices and Debauchery according to their common Practice, fpending with huge Prodigality, what others had gained with no

fmall

small Labour and Toil, tho' they, indeed, came to the Possession of it as easily as they parted with it

Not long after the Arrival of the Pirates at *Jamaica*, when they had stayed there precisely that short Time they needed to lavish away all the Riches abovemention'd, they concluded upon another Enterprize, wherein to seek new Fortunes To this Effect the Captain gave Orders to all the Commanders of his Ships, to meet together at the Island called *de la Vaca*, or *Cow-Isle*, seated on the South-side of the Isle of *Hispaniola*, as hath been mentioned above As soon as they came to this Place, there flocked to them great Numbers of other Pirates, both *French* and *English*, by Reason the Name of Captain *Morgan* was now rendered Famous in all the neighbouring Countries, for the great Enterprizes he had perform'd There was at that present Time, at *Jamaica*, an *English* Ship newly come from *New-England*, well mounted with thirty six Guns This Vessel, likewise, by Order of the Governor of *Jamaica*, came to join with *Morgan* to strengthen his Fleet, and give him greater Courage to attempt Things of great Consequence With this supply Captain *Morgan* judged himself sufficiently strong, as having the Addition of a Ship of such Port, for it was really the greatest of his Fleet Notwithstanding this, there being in the same Place another great Vessel, that carried twenty four iron Guns, and twelve of Brass, belonging to the *French*, Captain *Morgan* endeavoured as much as he could, to join this Ship in like Manner to his own But the *French* not daring to repose any Trust in the *English*, of whose Actions they were not a little jealous, denied absolutely to content to any such Thing

The *French* Pirates belonging to this great Ship, had accidentally met at Sea in an *English* Vessel, and being then under an extreme Necessity of Victuals, they had taken some Provisions out of the *English* Ship, without paying for them, as having, peradventure, no ready Money on Board Only they had given them Bills of Exchange, for *Jamaica* and *Tortuga*, to receive Money there for what they had taken Captain *Morgan* having Notice of this Accident, and perceiving he could not prevail with the *French* Captain to follow him in that Expedition, he resolved to lay hold on this Occasion, as a Pretext to ruin the *French*, and seek his own Revenge Hereupon, he invited, with a masterly Dissimulation, the *French* Commander, and several of his Men, to come with him, on board the great Ship that was come from *Jamaica*, as was said before Being come thither, he made them all Prisoners, pretending the Injury aforemention'd done to the *English* Vessel, in taking away some few Provisions without Pay

This unjust Action of Captain *Morgan* was soon followed by entire Punishment, as we may very rationally conceive The Manner we shall instantly relate Presently after he had taken the *French* Prisoners aforesaid, he called a Council, to deliberate what Place they should first pitch upon, in the Course of this new Expedition At this Council it was determin'd to go to the Isle of *Savona*, there to wait for the *Flota*, which was then expected from *Spain*, and to take any of the *Spanish* Vessels that might chance to straggle from the rest This Resolution being taken, they begin on board the great Ship to feast one another, for Joy of their new Voyage and happy Council, as they hoped it would prove In testimony hereof, they drank many Healths, and discharged many Guns, as the common Sign of Mirth among Seamen us'd to be Most of the Men being drunk, by what Accident is not known, the Ship suddenly was blown up into the Air, with three hundred and fifty *Englishmen*, besides the *French* Prisoners abovemention'd, that were in Hold Of all

which Number, there escap'd only thirty Men, who were in the great Cabin, at some Distance from the main Force of the Gunpowder Many more, 'tis thought, might have escap'd, had they not been so much overtaken with Wine

The Loss of such a great Ship was no inconsiderable Affliction, as well as Surprize, to the *English* They knew not whom to blame, but at last the Accusation was laid upon the *French* Prisoners, whom they suspected to have fir'd the Gunpowder of the Ship wherein they were, out of Design to revenge themselves, though with the Loss of their own Lives Hereupon, they sought to be reveng'd on the *French* a-new, and accumulate fresh Accusations to the former, whereby to seize the Ship, and all that was in it With this Design they forg'd another Pretext against the said Ship, by saying the *French* design'd to commit Piracy upon the *English* The Grounds of this Accusation were given them by a Commission from the Governor of *Barracoa*, found on board the *French* Vessel, wherein were these Words *That the said Governor did permit the* French *to trade in all* Spanish *Ports, &c ———As also to cruize upon the* English *Pirates in what Place soever they cou'd find them, because of the Multitude of Hostilities they had committed against the Subjects of his Catholick Majesty, in Time of Peace betwixt the two Crowns.* This Commission for Trade was interpreted by the *English* as an express Order to exercise Piracy and War against 'em, notwithstanding it was only a bare Licence for coming into the *Spanish* Ports, for the Cloak of which Permission, were those Words inserted, *That they should cruize upon the* English. And though the *French* sufficiently expounded the true Sense of the said Commission, yet they could not clear themselves to Capt *Morgan*, nor his prejudic'd Council, but in Revenge for the supposed Injury, the Ship and Men were seiz'd, and sent to *Jamaica* Here they also endeavour'd to obtain Justice, and the Restitution of their Ship, by all the Means possible But all in vain, for, instead of Justice, they were a long Time detain'd in Prison, and threatened with Hanging

Eight Days after the Loss of the said Ship, Capt *Morgan* commanded the Bodies of the miserable Wretches who were blown up, to be searched for, as they floated upon the Waters of the Sea, not to give them Christian Burial, but for the Sake of their Cloaths, &c If any had Gold Rings on their Fingers, they were cut off, and their Bodies left to the Monsters of the Sea At last they set Sail for the Isle of *Savona*, the place of Rendezvous, consisting in all of fifteen Vessels, carrying nine hundred and sixty Men, Capt *Morgan* commanding the biggest, having but fourteen Guns In a few Days after, they arriv'd at the Cape *Cabo de Lobos*, on the South-side of the Isle of *Hispaniola*, between the Capes of *Tiburon* and *Punta de Espada*, from hence they could not pass, (there being contrary Winds three Weeks) notwithstanding all the Endeavours Capt *Morgan* used. They doubled the Cape, and soon spoke with an *English* Vessel, buying for ready Money such Provisions they stood most in Need of

Captain *Morgan* proceeded in the Course of his Voyage, till he came to the Port of *Ocoa* Here he landed some of his Men, sending them into the Woods to seek Water, and what Provisions they could find, the better to spare such as he had already on board his Fleet They killed many Beasts, and among other Animals some Horses But the *Spaniards* being not well satisfy'd at their Hunting, attempted to lay a Stratagem for the Pirates To this Purpose they order'd three or four hundred Men to come from the City of *Santo Domingo*, not far distant from this Port, desiring them to hunt in all

4

the Parts thereabouts adjoining to the Sea, to the intent if any Pirates should return, they might find no subsistence. Within a few Days the same Pirates returned, with Design to hunt, but, finding nothing to kill, about fifty of them straggled farther into the Woods. The *Spaniards*, who watch'd all their Motions, gather'd a great Herd of Cows, and set two or three Men to keep 'em, which the Pirates espying, kill'd a sufficient Number, and tho' the *Spaniards* could see 'em at a Distance, yet they would not spoil their Sport for the present. But as soon as they attempted to carry them off, they set upon 'em with all imaginable Fury, crying, *Mata, mata;* that is, *Kill, Kill,* obliging the Pirates to quit the Prey, and retreat to their Ships as fast as they could. This was perform'd in good Order, retiring gradually, and when they had a favourable Opportunity, by discharging full Vollies of Shot upon the *Spaniards,* kill'd many, tho' not without some Loss on their own Side.

The rest of the *Spaniards*, seeing what Damage their Companions had sustained, endeavour'd to save themselves by Flight, and carry off the Dead and Wounded. The Pirates, perceiving the *Spaniards* to run, pursu'd them immediately to the Woods, killing the greatest Part of those that were remaining. The next Day Capt *Morgan*, enrag'd, went with two hundred Men into the Woods to seek for the rest of the *Spaniards*, but finding no-body, he revenged their Death, by burning the Houses of the poor and miserable Rusticks, inhabiting scatteringly about those Fields and Woods. Having done this, he return'd to his Ships, well-pleas'd he had done the Enemy such considerable Damage, which was always his most ardent Desire.

The huge Impatience wherewith Capt *Morgan* had waited so long for some of his Ships, which were not arriv'd, made him resolve to sail without them, and steer his Course for the Isle of *Savona*, the Place he had always design'd for. Being arriv'd there, and not finding any of his Ships as yet come, he was more impatient than before, fearing they might be lost, or that he must proceed without 'em. Nevertheless, he waited their Arrival some Days longer. In the Interim, having no great Plenty of Provisions, he sent a Crew of one hundred and fifty Men to the Isle of *Hispaniola*, to pillage some Towns nigh the City of *Santo Domingo*. But the *Spaniards* having had Intelligence of their coming, were now so vigilant, and in so good a Posture of Defence, that the Pirates thought it not convenient to assault them, chusing rather to return empty-handed into Capt *Morgan*'s Presence, than perish in that desperate Enterprize.

The Captain, at last, seeing the other Ships did not come, made a Review of his People, finding only five hundred Men, or thereabouts, and but eight Ships out of fifteen, and the greatest Part of those were very small. Thus, having hitherto resolved to cruize upon the Coasts of *Caraccas*, and plunder all the Towns and Villages he could meet, finding himself at present with such small Forces, he chang'd his Resolution, by the Advice of a *French* Captain belonging to his Fleet.

This *Frenchman* had serv'd *Lolonois*, his Countryman, in like Enterprizes, and was at the taking of *Maracaibo*, whereby he knew all the Entries, Passages, Forces, and Means, how to put in Execution the same again in the Company of Captain *Morgan*, to whom, having made a full Relation of all, the Captain concluded to sack it again a second Time, as being himself persuaded, with all his Men, of the Facility of what the *Frenchman* propounded. Hereupon, they weigh'd Anchor, and steer'd their Course towards *Curasao*. Being come within Sight of that Island, they landed at another, which is nigh to it,

and is call'd *Ruba*, seated about 12 Leagues from *Curasao*, towards the West. This Island is defended by a slender Garrison, and is inhabited by *Indians*, who are subject to the Crown of *Spain*, and speak *Spanish*, by reason of the *Roman Catholick* Religion, which is here cultivated by some few Priests, that are sent from Time to Time from the neighbouring Continent.

The Inhabitants of this Isle exercise certain Commerce, or Trade, with the Pirates that go and come this Way. These buy, of the Islanders, Sheep, Lambs, and Kids, which they exchange with them for Linnen, Thread, and other Things of this Kind. The Country is very dry, and barren, the whole Substance thereof consisting in those three Things abovemention'd, and in a small Quantity of Wheat, which is of no bad Quality. This Isle produceth a great Number of venomous Insects, such as Vipers, Spiders, and others, these last are so pernicious here that if any Man is bitten by them, he dies mad. And the Manner of recovering such Persons, is to tie them very fast, both Hands and Feet, and in this Condition to leave them for the Space of four and twenty Hours, without eating or drinking the least Thing imaginable. Captain *Morgan*, as was said, having cast Anchor before this Island, bought of the Inhabitants a great many Sheep, Lambs, and also Wood, which he needed for all his Fleet. Having been there two Days, he set sail again, in the Nighttime, to the Intent they might not see what Course he steer'd.

The next Day they arriv'd at the Sea of *Maracaibo*, taking always great Care of not being seen from *Vigilia*, for which Reason they anchor'd out of Sight of the Watch-Tower. Night being come, they set sail again towards the Land, and the next Morning, by Break of Day, found themselves directly over-against the Bar of the Lake abovemention'd. The *Spaniards* had here lately built a strong Fort, from whence they now fir'd continually against the Pirates, while they were putting their Men into Boats for them to land. The Dispute continu'd very hot on both Sides, being manag'd with a great deal of Courage and Valour from Morning till dark Night. Evening being come, Captain *Morgan*, in the Obscurity thereof, drew nigh to the Fort, which having examin'd, he found no Body in it, the *Spaniards* having deserted it not long before. They left behind them a Match kindled, nigh to a Train of Gunpowder, wherewith they design'd to blow up the Pirates, and the whole Fortress, as soon as they were out of it. This Design had taken Effect, had the Pirates fail'd to discover it the Space of one Quarter of an Hour. But Captain *Morgan* prevented the Mischief, by snatching away the Match with all Speed, whereby he sav'd both his own and his Companions Lives. They found here a great Quantity of Gunpowder, wherewith he furnish'd his Fleet, and afterwards demolish'd part of the Walls, nailing up fixteen Pieces of Ordnance, which carried from twelve to four and twenty Pounds of Bullet. Here they found, also, a great Number of Muskets, and other military Provisions.

The next Day they commanded the Ships to enter the Bar, among which they divided the Gunpowder, Muskets, and other Things they found in the Fort. These Things being done, they embark'd again, to continue their Course towards *Maracaibo*. But the Waters were very low, so that they could not pass a certain Bank that lies at the Entry of the Lake. Here upon, they were compell'd to put themselves into Canoes and small Boats, with which they arriv'd the next Day before *Maracaibo*, having no other Defence but some small Pieces, which they could carry in the said Boats. Being landed, they ran immediately to the

the Fort call'd *de la Barra*, which they found in like Manner as the preceding, without any Person in it. For all the Garrison and Inhabitants were fled before them into the Woods, leaving also the Town without any People, unless a few miserable poor Folk, who had nothing to lose.

As soon as they had entered the Town, the Pirates searched every Corner thereof, to see if they could find any People that were hidden, who might offend them at unawares. Not finding any Body, every Party, according as they came out of their several Ships, chose what Houses they pleased to themselves, in the best Manner they could find. The Church was deputed for the common *Corps de Garde*, where they lived after a military Manner, committing many insolent Actions. The next Day after their Arrival, they sent a Troop of one hundred Men to seek for the Inhabitants and their Goods. These returned the next Day following, bringing with them the Number of thirty Persons, Men, Women, and Children; and fifty Mules laden with several Sorts of Merchandize. All these miserable Prisoners were put to the Rack, to make them confess where the rest of the Inhabitants were, and their Goods. Amongst other Tortures then used, one was to stretch their Limbs with Cords, and at the same Time, beat them with Sticks and other Instruments. Others had burning Matches plac'd betwixt their Fingers, and were thus burnt alive, others had slender Cords, or Matches, twisted about their Heads, till their Eyes burst out of the Skull. Thus all Sorts of inhuman Cruelties were executed upon those innocent People. Those who would not confess, or who had nothing to declare, died under the Hands of these tyrannical Men, whose Tortures and Racks continu'd for the Space of three whole Weeks. In which Time they ceas'd not to send out, daily, Parties of Men, to seek for more People to torment and rob, they never returning Home without Booty and new Riches.

Captain *Morgan*, having now gotten, by Degrees, into his Hands about one hundred of the chiefest Families, with all their Goods, at last resolv'd to go to *Gibraltar*. With this Design, he equipp'd his Fleet, providing it very sufficiently with all necessary Things.

He put, likewise, on board, all the Prisoners, and thus weighing Anchor, set sail for the said Place, with Resolution to hazard the Battle. They had sent before them some Prisoners to *Gibraltar*, to denounce to the Inhabitants that they should surrender, otherwise Captain *Morgan* would certainly put them all to the Sword, without giving Quarter to any Person he should find alive. Not long after, he arriv'd with his Fleet before *Gibraltar*, whose Inhabitants receiv'd him with continual shooting of great Cannon-bullets. But the Pirates, instead of fainting here at, ceas'd not to encourage one another, saying, *We must make one Meal upon bitter Things, before we come to taste the Sweetness of the Sugar this Place affordeth.*

The next Day, very early in the Morning, they landed all their Men, and, being guided by the *French*-man abovemention'd, they march'd towards the Town, not by the common Way, but crossing through the Woods, by which Way the *Spaniards* scarce thought they wou'd have come. For, at the Beginning of their March, they made Appearance as if they intended to come by the next and open Way that led to the Town, hereby the better to deceive the *Spaniards*. But these remembering, as yet, full well what Hostilities had been committed upon them by Pirates before, thought it not safe to expect another Brunt, and hereupon they all fled out of the Town as fast as they could, carrying with them all their Goods and Riches, as also all the Gun-powder; having nailed up all the great Guns,

insomuch that the Pirates found not one Person in the whole City, excepting one only poor and innocent Man, who was born a Fool. This Man they asked whither the Inhabitants were fled, and where they had absconded their Goods. Unto all which Questions and the like, he constantly made Answer, *I know nothing, I know nothing.* But they presently put him to the Rack, and tortur'd him with Cords; which Torments forced him to cry out, *Do not torture me any more, but come with me, and I will shew you my Goods and my Riches.* They were perswaded, as it should seem, that he was some rich Person, who had disguised himself under those Cloaths so poor, as also that innocent Tongue. Hereupon, they went along with him; and he conducted them to a poor and miserable Cottage, wherein he had a few Earthen Dishes, and other Things of little or no Value, and amongst these, three Pieces of Eight, which he had concealed with some other Trumpery, under Ground. After this, they asked him his Name, and he readily made Answer, *My Name is Don Sebastian Sanchez, and I am Brother to the Governor of Maracaibo.* This foolish Answer, it must be conceived, these Men, tho' never so inhuman, took for a certain Truth. For no sooner had they heard it, but they put him again upon the Rack, lifting him up on high with Cords, and tying huge Weights to his Feet and Neck. Besides which cruel and stretching Torment, they burnt him alive, applying Palm-Leaves burning to his Face. Under these Miseries he died in half an Hour. After his Death, they cut the Cords wherewith they had stretch'd him, and dragg'd him forth into the adjoining Woods, where they left him without Burial.

The same Day they sent out a Party of Pirates to seek for the Inhabitants, upon whom they might employ their inhuman Cruelties. These brought back with them an honest Peasant, with two Daughters of his, whom they had taken Prisoners, and whom they intended to torture, as they used to do with others, in case they shewed not the Places where the Inhabitants had absconded themselves. The Peasant knew some of the said Places, and hereupon, seeing himself threatened with the Rack, went with the Pirates to shew them. But the *Spaniards*, perceiving their Enemies to range every where up and down the Woods, were already fled from thence much farther off, into the thickest parts of the said Woods, where they built themselves Huts, to preserve from the Violence of the Weather, those few Goods they had carried with them. The Pirates judged themselves to be deceived by the Peasant, and thereupon, to revenge their Wrath upon him, notwithstanding all the Excuses he could make, and his humble Supplications for his Life, they hang'd him upon a Tree.

After this, they divided into several Parties, and went to search the Plantations. For they knew the *Spaniards* that had hid themselves, could not live upon what they found in the Woods, without coming now and then to seek Provisions at their own Country-Houses. Here they found a certain Slave, to whom they promised Mountains of Gold, and that they would give him his Liberty by transporting him to *Jamaica*, in case he would shew them the Places where the Inhabitants of *Gibraltar* lay hidden. This Fellow conducted him to a Party of *Spaniards*, whom they instantly made all Prisoners, commanding the said Slave to kill some of them before the Eyes of the rest, to the Intent that by this perpetrated Crime, he might never be able to leave their wicked Company. The Negro, according to their Orders, committed many Murthers and base Actions upon the *Spaniards*, and followed the unfortunate Traces of the Pirates; who, after the Space of eight Days, returned to *Gibraltar* with many Prisoners,

Prisoners, and some Mules laden with Riches They examined every Prisoner by himself, (who were in all about two hundred and fifty Persons) where they had concealed the rest of their Goods, and if they knew of their fellow Townsmen Such as would not confess, were tormented after a most cruel and inhuman Manner Among the rest, there happened to be a certain *Portuguese*, who, by the Information of a Negro, was reported, though falsly, to be very rich This Man was commanded to produce his Riches But his Answer was, that he had no more than one hundred Pieces of Eight in the whole World, and that these had been stolen from him two Days before, by a Servant of his Which Words, tho' he sealed them with many Oaths and Protestations, would not satisfy these Wretches. Whereupon, they dragg'd him to the Rack, without any regard to his Age, as being threescore Years old, stretch'd him with Cords, and broke both his Arms behind his Shoulders

This Cruelty went not alone · For he not being able or willing to make any other Declaration than the abovesaid, they put him to another sort of Torment, that was worse, and more barbarous than the Preceding They tied him with small Cords, by his two Thumbs and great Toes, to four Stakes that were fix'd in the Ground at a convenient Distance, the whole Weight of his Body being pendent in the Air upon those Cords Then they thrash'd him upon the Cords with great Sticks, and all their Strength, so that the Body of this miserable Man was ready to perish at every Stroke, under the Severity of those horrible Pains Not satisfied, as yet, with this cruel Torture, they took a Stone which weighed about two hundred Pound, and laid it upon his Belly, as if they intended to press him to Death At which Time they also kindled Palm-Leaves, and applied the Flame to the Face of this unfortunate *Portuguese*, burning with them the whole Skin, Beard, and Hair At last, these cruel Tyrants, seeing that neither with these Tortures, nor others, they could get any Thing out of him, they untied the Cords, and carried him, being almost half dead, to the Church, where was their *Corps du Garde* Here they tied him anew, to one of the Pillars of the Place, leaving him in that Condition, without giving him any thing either to eat or drink for some Days, unless very sparingly, and so little as would scarce sustain Life

Four or five Days being past, he desired that one of the Prisoners might have the Liberty to come to him, by whose Means he promised he would endeavour to raise some Money to satisfy their Demands The Prisoner whom he required, was brought unto him ; and he ordered him to promise the Pirates five hundred Pieces of Eight for his Ransom But they were both deaf and obstinate at such a small Sum, and, instead of accepting it, beat him cruelly with Cudgels, saying to him, *Old Fellow, instead of five hundred, you must say, five hundred thousand Pieces of Eight, otherwise you shall here end your Life* Finally, after a thousand Protestations that he was but a miserable Man, and kept a poor Tavern for his Living, he agreed with them for the Sum of one thousand Pieces of Eight, These he raised in a few Days, and having paid them to the Pirates, got his Liberty ; altho' so horribly maimed in his Body, that 'tis scarce to be believed he could survive many Weeks after

Several other Tortures besides these, were exercised upon others, which this *Portuguese* endured not Some were hang'd up by the Testicles, or by their privy Members, and left in that Condition till they fell unto the Ground, those private Parts being torn from their Bodies If with this they were minded to shew themselves merciful to those Wretches, thus lacerated in the most tender Parts of their Bodies, their Mercy was to run them through and through

with their Swords , and by this Means rid them soon of their Pains and Lives Otherwise, if this were not done, they used to lay four or five Days under the Agonies of Death Others were crucified by these Tyrant, and with kindled Matches were burnt between the Joints of their Fingers and Toes Others had their Feet put into the Fire, and thus were left to be roasted alive, At last, having used both these and other Cruelties with the *Whitemen*, they begin to practise the same over again with the Negro's their Slaves, who were treated with no less Inhumanity than their Masters

Among these Slaves was found one, who promised Captain *Morgan*, to conduct him to a certain River belonging to the Lake, where he should find a Ship and four Boats richly laden with Goods, that belonged to the Inhabitants of *Maracaibo* The same Slave discovered, likewise, the Place where the Governor of *Gibraltar* lay hidden, together with the greatest Part of the Women of the Town But all this he revealed purely on account of the Menaces wherewith they threatned him, in case he told not what he knew Captain *Morgan* sent away presently two hundred Men in two *Sueties*, or great Boats, towards the River abovementioned, to seek for what the Slave had discovered But he himself, with two hundred and fifty more, undertook to go and take the Governor This Gentlemen was retired to a small Island, seated in the Middle of the River, where he had built a little Fort, after the best Manner he could, for his Defence But hearing that Captain *Morgan* came in Person with great Forces to seek him, he retired farther off, to the Top of a Mountain not much distant from that Place , to which there was no Ascent, but by a very narrow Passage This Place was even so streight, that whosoever pretended to gain the ascent, must of Necessity cause his Men to pass one by one Captain *Morgan* spent two Days, before he could arrive at the little Island abovementioned From thence he design'd to proceed to the Mountain where the Governor was posted, had he not been told of the Impossibility he should find in the Ascent, not only for the Narrowness of the Path that led to the Top, but also because the Governor was very well provided with all Sorts of Ammunition above Besides that, there was fallen an huge Rain, whereby all the Baggage belonging to the Pirates, and their Gunpowder, was wet By this Rain also they had lost many of their Men, at the Passage over a River that was overflown Here perished likewise, some Women and Children, and many Mules laden with Plate and other Goods , all which they had taken in the Fields from the fugitive Inhabitants So that all Things were in a very bad Condition with Captain *Morgan*, and the Bodies of his Men exceedingly harrass'd, as ought to be inferr'd from this Relation Whereby, if the *Spaniards* in that Juncture of Time had but had a Troop of fifty Men, well arm'd with Pikes or Spears, they might have entirely destroy'd the Pirates, without any possible Resistance on their Side But the Fears which the *Spaniards* had conceiv'd from the Beginning, were so great, that only hearing the Leaves on the Trees to stir, they often fancied them to be Pirates Finally, Captain *Morgan* and his People, having upon this March sometimes waded up to their Middles in Water, for the Space of half or whole Miles together, they at last escap'd, for the greatest part But of the Women and Children, that they brought home Prisoners, the major Part died

Thus, 12 Days after they set forth to seek the Governor, they return'd to *Gibraltar* with a great Number of Prisoners Two Days after arriv'd, also, the two *Sueties* that went to the River, bringing with them four Boats and some Prisoners. But as to the greatest

greatest part of the Merchandize that was in the said Boats, they found them not, the Spaniards having unladed and secur'd them, as having Intelligence before-hand of the coming of the Pirates Whereupon, they design'd also, when the Merchandize was all taken out, to burn the Boats Yet the Spaniards made not so much Haste as was requisite, to unlade the said Vessels, so that they left both in the Ship and Boats great Parcels of Goods, which, they being fled from thence, the Pirates seiz'd, and brought thereof a considerable Booty to Gibraltar Thus, after they had been in possession of the Place five entire Weeks, and committed there an infinite Number of Murders, Robberies, Rapes, and such like Insolencies, they concluded upon their Departure, but, before this could be perform'd, for the last Proof of their Tyranny, they gave Orders to some Prisoners to go forth into the Woods and Fields, and collect a Ransom for the Town, otherwise they would certainly burn every House down to the Ground. Those poor afflicted Men went forth as they were sent, and after they had search'd every Corner of the adjoining Fields and Woods, they return'd to Captain Morgan, telling him, that they had scarce been able to find any Body, but that unto such as they had found, they had propos'd his Demands, to which they had made Answer, that the Governor had prohibited them to give any Ransom for not burning the Town Yet, notwithstanding any Prohibition to the contrary, they beseech'd him to have a little Patience, and, among themselves, they would collect to the Sum of five thousand Pieces of Eight. And for the rest, they would give him some of their own Townsmen as Hostages, whom he might carry with him to Maracaibo, till such Time as he had receiv'd full Satisfaction

Captain Morgan, having now been a long Time absent from Maracaibo, and knowing the Spaniards had had sufficient Time wherein to fortify themselves, and hinder his Departure out of the Lake, granted them their Proposition abovemention'd, and, withal, made as much Haste as he could to set Things in Order for his Departure He gave Liberty to all the Prisoners, having before-hand put them every one to the Ransom, yet he detain'd all the Slaves with him They deliver'd to him four Persons, that were agreed upon for Hostages, till they could pay what Sums of Money more he was to receive from them And they desir'd to have the Slave of whom we made mention above, intending to punish him according to his Deserts But Captain Morgan would not deliver him, being persuaded they would burn him alive At last, they weigh'd Anchor, and set Sail with all the Haste they cou'd, directing their Course towards Maracaibo Here they arriv'd in four Days, and found all Things in the same Posture they had left them in when they departed Yet here they receiv'd News, from the Information of a poor distress'd old Man, who was sick, and whom alone they found in the Town, that three Spanish Men of War were arriv'd at the Entry of the Lake, and there waited for the Return of the Pirates out of those Parts Moreover, that the Castle at the Entry thereof was again put into a good Posture of Defence, being well provided with great Guns and Men, and all Sorts of Ammunition

This Relation of the old Man could not chuse but cause some Disturbance in the Mind of Captain Morgan, who now was careful how to get away through those narrow Passages of the Entry of the Lake Hereupon he sent one of his Boats, the swiftest he had, to view the Entry, and see if Things were as they had been related The next Day the Boat came back, confirming what was said, and assuring him, they had viewed the Ships so nigh, that they had been in great Danger of the Shot they had made at them Hereunto they added, that the biggest Ship was mounted with forty Guns, the Second with thirty, and the smallest with four and twenty These Forces were much beyond those of Captain Morgan; and consequently they caused a general Consternation among the Pirates, whose biggest Vessel had not above fourteen small Guns Every one judged that Captain Morgan desponded in his Mind, and was destitute of all manner of Hopes, considering the Difficulty of passing safely with his little Fleet amidst those great Ships and the Fort, and the Necessity he was otherwise under of perishing How to escape any other Way than this, either by Sea or by Land, they saw no Opportunity nor Convenience Only they could have wish'd that those three Ships had rather come over the Lake to seek them at Maracaibo, than to remain at the Mouth of the Streight where they were, for at that Passage they must of Necessity fear the Ruin of their Fleet, which consisted only, for the greatest part of Boats

Hereupon, being necessitated to act as well as he cou'd, Captain Morgan resum'd new Courage, and resolv'd to shew himself, as yet, undaunted with these Terrors To this Intent, he boldly sent a Spaniard to the Admiral of those three Ships, demanding of him a considerable Tribute or Ransom, for not putting the City of Maracaibo to the Flames This Man (who doubtless was receiv'd by the Spaniards with great Admiration of the Confidence and Boldness of our Pirates) return'd two Days after, bringing to Captain Morgan a Letter from the said Admiral, whose Contents were as followeth

A Letter of Don Alonso del Campo y Espinosa, Admiral of the Spanish Fleet, to Captain Morgan, Commander of the Pirates

HAving understood by all our Friends and Neighbours, the unexpected News, that you have dared to attempt and commit Hostilities in the Countries, Cities, Towns, and Villages, belonging to the Dominions of his Catholick Majesty, my sovereign Lord and Master, I let you understand by these Lines, that I am come to this Place, according to my Obligation, nigh to that Castle which you took out of the Hands of a Parcel of Cowards, where I have put Things into a very good Posture of Defence, and mounted again the Artillery which you had nailed and dismounted My Intent is, to dispute with you your Passage out of the Lake, and follow and pursue you every where, to the End you may see the Performance of my Duty Notwithstanding, if you will be contented to surrender with Humility all the Treasure you have taken, together with the Slaves and all other Prisoners, I will let you freely pass, without Trouble or Molestation, upon Condition that you retire home presently to your own Country But in case that you make any Resistance or Opposition against me, and refuse the Conditions that I proffer to you, I assure you I'll command Boats to come from Caracas, wherein I'll put my Troops, and, coming to Maracaibo, will cause you utterly to perish, by putting youand every Man to the Sword This is my last and absolute Resolution Be prudent, therefore, and do not abuse my Bounty with Ingratitude I have with me very good Soldiers, who desire nothing more ardently than to revenge themselves on you and your People, for all the cruel and base infamous Actions you have committed upon the Spanish Nation in America

From on board the Royal Ship named Magdalen, lying at Anchor at the Lake of Maracaibo

Don Alonso del Campo y Espinosa

As foon as Captain *Morgan* had received this Letter, he called all his Men together in the Market-place of *Maracaibo*, and after reading the Contents thereof, both in *French* and *Englifh*, he asked their Advice and Refolutions upon the whole Matter, and whether they had rather furrender all they had purchas'd, to obtain their Liberty, than fight like Men to keep what they were poffefs'd of.

They anfwered all unanimoufly, They had rather fight, and fpill the laft Drop of Blood they had in their Veins, than furrender fo eafily the Booty they had gotten with fo much Danger of their Lives. Among the Company, one was found who refolutely fpoke thus to Captain *Morgan*. *Take you Care for the reft, and I will undertake to deftroy the biggeft of thofe Ships with only twelve Men. The manner fhall be, by making a Brulot or Fire-fhip of that Veffel we took in the River of* Gibraltar. *And to the Intent fhe may not be known for a Fire-fhip, we will fill her Decks with Logs of Wood, ftanding with Hats and* Montera *Caps, to deceive their Sight with the Reprefentation of Men. The fame we will do at the Port-holes that ferve for the Guns, which fhall be filled with counterfeit Cannon. At the Stern we will hang out the* Englifh *Colours, and perfuade the Enemy fhe is one of our beft Men of War, and comes to fight them.* This Propofition being heard by the *Junta*, was admitted and approved by every one; neverthelefs their Fears were not quite difperfed.

For, notwithftanding what had been concluded there, they endeavoured the next Day to fee if they could come to accommodation with *Don Alonfo*. To this Effect Captain Morgan fent him two Perfons, with thefe following Propofitions. Firft, *That he would quit* Maracaibo, *without doing any Damage to the Town, or exacting any Ranfom for the firing thereof.* Secondly, *That he would fet at Liberty one half of the Slaves, and likewife all other Prifoners, without Ranfom.* Thirdly, *That he would fend home freely the four chief Inhabitants of* Gibraltar, *whom he had in his Cuftody, as Hoftages for the Contributions thofe People had promifed to pay him.* Thefe Propofitions from the Pirates being underftood by *Don Alonfo*, were inftantly rejected every one, as being difhonourable for him to grant. Neither would he hear a Word more of any Accommodation; but fent back this Meffage. *That in cafe they furrendered not themfelves voluntarily into his Hands, within the fpace of two Days, under the Conditions which he had offered them by his Letter, he would immediately come and force them to do it.*

No fooner had Captain *Morgan* received this Meffage from *Don Alonfo*, than he put all Things in order to fight, refolving to get out of the Lake by main Force, and without furrendring any Thing. In the firft Place, he commanded all the Slaves and Prifoners to be tied and guarded very well. After this, they gathered all the Pitch, Tar, and Brimftone, they could find in the whole Town, therewith to prepare the Fire-fhip abovementioned. Likewife, they made feveral Inventions of Powder and Brimftone, with great Quantities of Palm-Leaves, very well anointed with Tar. They cover'd, alfo, their counterfeit Cannon very dexteroufly, laying under every Piece thereof many Pounds of Gunpowder. Befides which, they cut down many Out-works belonging to the Ship, to the end the Gunpowder might exert its Strength the better. Thus they broke open, alfo, new Port-holes; where, inftead of Guns, they plac'd little Drums, of which the Negroes make Ufe. Finally, the Decks were handfomely befet with many Pieces of Wood, drefs'd up in the Shape of Men, with Hats, or Montera's, and likewife arm'd with Swords, Muskets, and Bandeleers.

The *Brulot*, or Fire-fhip, being thus fitted to their

Purpofe, they prepar'd themfelves to go to the Entry of the Port. All the Prifoners were put into one great Boat, and in another of the biggeft they plac'd all the Women, Plate, Jewels, and other rich Things which they had. Into others they put all the Bales of Goods and Merchandize, and other Things of greateft Bulk. Each of thefe Boats had twelve Men on board, very well arm'd. The *Brulot* had Orders to go before the reft of the Veffels, and prefently to fall foul with the great Ship. All Things being in a Readinefs, Captain *Morgan* exacted an Oath of all his Comrades, whereby they protefted to defend themfelves againft the *Spaniards*, even to the laft Drop of Blood, without demanding Quarter at any Rate, promifing them, withal, that whofoever thus behav'd himfelf, fhould be very well rewarded.

With this Difpofition of Mind, and couragious Refolution, they fet Sail to feek the *Spaniards*, and found their Fleet riding at Anchor in the Middle of the Entry of the Lake. Captain *Morgan*, it being now late, and almoft dark, commanded all his Veffels to come to an Anchor, with Defign to fight from thence even all Night, if they fhould provoke him thereto. He gave Orders that a careful and vigilant Watch fhould be kept on board every Veffel till the Morning, they being almoft within Shot, as well as within Sight of the Enemy. The Dawning of the Day being come, they weigh'd Anchors, and fet Sail again, fteering their Courfe directly towards the *Spaniards*, who obferving them to move, did inftantly the fame. The Fire-fhip, failing before the reft, fell prefently upon the great Ship, and grappled to her Sides in a fhort Time, which being perceiv'd by the *Spaniards* to be a Fire-fhip, they attempted to efcape the Danger by putting her off, but in vain, and too late. For the Flame fuddenly feiz'd her Timber and Tackling, and, in a fhort Space confum'd all the Stern, the Fore-part finking into the Sea, whereby fhe perifh'd. The fecond *Spanifh* Ship, perceiving the Admiral to burn, not by Accident, but by the Induftry of the Enemy, efcap'd towards the Caftle, where the *Spaniards* themfelves caus'd her to fink; chufing this Way of lofing their Ship, rather than to fall into the Hands of the Pirates, which they now held for inevitable. The third, as having no Opportunity nor Time to efcape, was taken by the Pirates. The Seamen that funk the fecond Ship nigh to the Caftle, perceiving that the Pirates came towards them, to take what Remains they could find of their Shipwreck (for fome part of the Hulk was extant above Water) fet fire in like Manner to this Veffel, to the End the Pirates might enjoy nothing of that Spoil. The firft Ship being fet on Fire, fome of the Perfons that were in her fwam towards the Shore. Thefe the Pirates would have taken up in their Boats, but they would neither ask nor admit of any Quarter; chufing rather to lofe their Lives, than receive them from the Hands of their Purfuers, for fuch Reafons as we fhall relate hereafter.

The Pirates were fo extreamly elevated, by this fignal Victory, obtain'd in fo fhort a Time, and with fo great Inequality of Forces, that they conceiv'd greater Pride in their Minds than they had before, and, thereupon, they all prefently ran afhore, intending to take the Caftle. This they found very well provided both with Men, great Cannon, and Ammunition, they having no other Arms than Muskets, and a few Fire-balls, in their Hands. Their own Artillery they thought incapable, for its Smalnefs, of making any confiderable Breach of the Walls. Thus they fpent the reft of that Day, firing at the Garrifon with their Muskets, till the Dusk of the Evening, at which Time they attempted to advance nigher to the Walls, with Intent to throw in the Fire-balls. But the *Spaniards*, refolving to fell their Lives

lives as dearly as they cou'd, continu'd firing so furiously at them, that they thought it not convenient to approach any nearer, nor persist any longer in the Dispute. Thus having experienc'd the Obstinacy of the Enemy, and seeing thirty of their own Men already dead, and as many more wounded, they retired to their Ships.

The *Spaniards*, believing the Pirates would return the next Day to renew the Attack, as also to make use of their own Cannon against the Castle, labour'd very hard all Night, to put all Things in Order for their coming; but, more particularly, they employ'd themselves that Night in digging down and making plain some little Hills and eminent Places, from whence, possibly, the Castle might be offended.

Captain *Morgan*, however, intended not to come ashore again, but busy'd himself the next Day in taking Prisoners some of the Men who still swam alive upon the Waters, hoping to get Part of the Riches that were lost in the two Ships that perish'd. Among the rest, he took a certain Pilot, who was a Stranger, and who belong'd to the lesser Ship of the two, with whom he held much Discourse, enquiring of him several Things; in particular, what Number of People had been in these three Ships; whether they expected any more Ships to come; from what Port they set forth the last Time, when they came to seek them out. His Answer to all these Questions, was as followeth; which he deliver'd in the *Spanish* Tongue ·

" Noble Sir, be pleas'd to pardon and spare me, and
" permit no Evil to be done to me, as being a Stran-
" ger to the Nation I have serv'd, and I shall sincere-
" ly inform you of all that pass'd till our Arrival at
" this Lake. We were sent by Orders from the
" Supreme Council of State in *Spain*, being six Men
" of War well equipp'd, into these Seas, with In-
" structions to cruize upon the *English* Pirates, and
" root them out from these Parts by destroying as
" many of them as we cou'd

" These Orders were given, by reason of the News
" brought to the Court of *Spain* of the Loss and
" Ruin of *Puerto Velo*, and other Places. Of all
" which Damages and Hostilities committed here
" by the *English*, very dismal Lamentations have of-
" tentimes penetrated the Ears of the Catholick
" King and Council, to whom belongs the Care
" and Preservation of this new World. And tho'
" the *Spanish* Court hath many Times, by their Am-
" bassadors, sent Complaints hereof to the King of
" *England*, yet it hath been the constant Answer of
" his Majesty of *Great Britain*, That he never gave
" any Letters Patents nor Commissions for the acting
" any Hostility whatsoever against the Subjects of the
" King of *Spain*. Hereupon, the Catholick King,
" being resolv'd to revenge his Subjects, and punish
" those Proceedings, commanded six Men of War
" to be equipp'd; which he sent into these Parts un-
" der the Command of *Don Augustin de Bustos*, who
" was constituted Admiral of the said Fleet. He
" commanded the biggest Ship thereof, nam'd *Nestra*
" *Senora de la Soledad*, mounted with eight and
" forty great Guns, and eight small ones. The Vice-
" Admiral was *Don Alonso del Campo y Espinosa*,
" who commanded the second Ship call'd *la Concep-*
" *tion*, which carried forty-four great Guns, and
" eight small ones. Besides which Vessels, there
" were also four more; whereof the first was nam'd
" *The Magdalen*, and was mounted with thirty-six
" great Guns, and twelve small ones, having on
" board two hundred and fifty Men. The second
" was call'd *St Lewis*, with twenty-six great Guns,
" twelve small ones, and two hundred Men. The
" third was call'd *la Marquesa*, which carried sixteen
" great Guns, eight small ones, and one hundred and

" fifty Men. The fourth and last, *Nestra Sennora*
" *del Carmen*, with eighteen great Guns, eight
" small ones, and likewise one hundred and fifty
" Men.

" We were now arriv'd at *Cartagena*, when the
" two greatest Ships receiv'd Orders to return to
" *Spain*, as being judg'd too big for cruizing upon
" these Coasts. With the four Ships remaining, *Don*
" *Alonso del Campo y Espinosa*, departed from thence
" towards *Campeche*; to seek out the *English*.
" We arrived at the Port of the said City, where
" being surpriz'd by a huge Storm that blew from
" the North, we lost one of our four Ships; it be-
" ing that which I named in the Place among the rest.
" From hence we set Sail for the Isle of *Hispaniola*;
" in sight of which we came within few Days, and
" directed our Course to the Port of *Santo Domingo*.
" Here we received Intelligence, that there had
" passed that Way a Fleet from *Jamaica*, and that
" some Men thereof having landed at a Place call'd
" *Alta Gracia*, the Inhabitants had taken one of
" them Prisoner, who confessed their whole Design
" was to go and pillage the City of *Caracas*. With
" this News *Don Alonso* instantly weighed Anchor,
" and set Sail from thence, crossing over to the *Con-*
" *tinent*, till we came in sight of *Caracas*. Here
" we found not the *English*; but happened to meet
" with a Boat, which informed us they were in the
" Lake of *Maracaibo*, and that the Fleet consisted of
" seven small Ships and one Boat

" Upon this Intelligence we arrived here; and
" coming nigh unto the Entry of the Lake, we shot
" off a Gun to demand a Pilot from the Shore. Those
" on Land perceiving that we were *Spaniards*, came
" willingly unto us with a Pilot, and told us that the
" *English* had taken the City of *Maracaibo*, and
" that they were at present at the Pillage of *Gibral-*
" *tar*. *Don Alonso*, having understood this News,
" made a handsome Speech to all his Soldiers and
" Mariners, encouraging them to perform their Duty
" and withal promising to divide among them all they
" should take from the *English*. After this, he gave
" Order that the Guns which he had taken out of
" the Ship that was lost, should be put into the Ca-
" stle, and there mounted for its Defence, with two
" Pieces more out of his own Ship, of eighteen
" Pounds each. The Pilot, conducted us into the
" Port, and *Don Alonso* commanded the People that
" were on Shore to come into his Presence, to whom
" he gave Orders to repossess the Castle, and re-en-
" force it with one hundred Men more than it had
" been before its being taken by the *English*. Not
" long after, we received News that you were re-
" turned from *Gibraltar* to *Maracaibo*, to which
" Place *Don Alonso* wrote you a Letter, giving you
" Account of his Arrival and Design, and withal ex-
" horting you to restore all that you had taken. This
" you refused to do, whereupon, he renewed his
" Promises and Intentions to his Soldiers and Seamen,
" and having given a very good Supper to all his
" People, he persuaded them neither to take nor
" give any Quarter to the *English* in the approach-
" ing Action. This was the Occasion of so many
" being drowned, who dared not to crave any
" Quarter for their Lives, as knowing their own In-
" tentions of giving none. Two Days before you
" came against us, a certain Negro came on board
" *Don Alonso*'s Ship, who spoke thus to him. *Sir,*
" *be pleased to have great Care of yourself, for the*
" *English have prepared a Fireship, with Design to*
" *burn your Fleet.* But *Don Alonso* would not believe
" this Intelligence, his Answer being, *How can that*
" *be? Can they have Wit enough to build a Fireship?*
" *Or what Instruments have they to do it withal?*"
The Pilot abovementioned, having related so distinctly

tinctly all the aforesaid Things to Captain *Morgan*, was very well used by him, and, after some kind Proffers made him, remained in his Service. He discovered moreover to the Captain, that in the Ship that was sunk, there was a great Quantity of Plate, even to the Value of forty thousand Pieces of Eight, and that it was certainly the Occasion they had oftentimes seen the *Spaniards* in Boats about the said Ship. Hereupon, Captain *Morgan* ordered that one of his Ships should remain there, to watch all Occasions of getting out of the said Vessel what Plate they could. In the mean While, he himself, with all his Fleet, returned to *Maracaibo*, where he refitted the great Ship he had taken of the three aforementioned. And now, being well accommodated, he chose it for himself, giving his own Bottom to one of his Captains.

After this, he sent again a Messenger to the Admiral, who was escaped on Shore and got into the Castle, demanding of him a Tribute or Ransom, for the Town of *Maracaibo*, to preserve it from Fire, which being denied, he threatened entirely to consume and destroy it. The *Spaniards*, considering how unfortunate they had been all along with those Pirates, and not knowing after what manner to get rid of them, concluded among themselves to pay the said Ransom, altnough *Don Alonso* would not consent to it.

Hereupon, they sent to Captain *Morgan* to ask what Sum he demanded. He answered them, that he would have thirty thousand Pieces of Eight, and five hundred Beeves, to the Intent his Fleet might be well victualled with Flesh. This Ransom being paid he promised them to give no farther Trouble to the Prisoners, nor to cause any Ruin or Damage to the Town. Finally, they agreed with him upon the Sum of twenty thousand Pieces of Eight, besides the five hundred Beeves. The Cattle the *Spaniards* brought in the next Day, together with one part of the Money. And while the Pirates were busied in salting the Flesh, they returned with the rest of the whole Sum of twenty thousand Pieces of Eight, for which they had agreed.

But Captain *Morgan* would not deliver, for that Present, the Prisoners, as he had promised to do, by Reason he feared the Shot of the Artillery of the Castle at his going forth of the Lake. Hereupon, he told them he intended not to deliver them, till such Time as he was out of that Danger, hoping by this Means to obtain a free Passage. Thus he set Sail with all his Fleet in quest of that Ship which he had left behind, to seek for the Plate of the Vessel that was burnt. He found her upon the Place, with the Sum of fifteen thousand Pieces of Eight, which they had purchased out of the Wreck, besides many other Pieces of Plate, as Hilts of Swords, and other Things of that kind. Also a great Quantity of Pieces of Eight, that were melted and run together by the Force of the Fire of the said Ship.

Captain *Morgan* scarce thought himself secure, neither could he contrive how to shun the Damages the said Castle might cause to his Fleet. Hereupon he told the Prisoners, that it was necessary they should agree with the Governor to open the Passage with Security for his Fleet; to which Point if he should not consent, he would certainly hang them all up in his Ships. After this Warning, the Prisoners met together to agree on the Persons they should depute to the said Governor *Don Alonso*, and they assigned some few among them for that Embassy. These went to him, beseeching and supplicating the Admiral that he would have Compassion and Pity on those afflicted Prisoners who were as yet, together with their Wives and Children, in the Hands of Captain *Morgan*. And that to this End he would be pleased

to give his Word to let the whole Fleet of Pirates freely pass, without any Molestation. Forasmuch as this would be the only Remedy of saving both the Lives of them that came with this Petition, as also of those who remained behind in Captivity, all being equally menaced with the Sword and Gallows, in case he granted not this humble Request. But *Don Alonso* gave them for Answer, a sharp Reprehension of their Cowardice, telling them, *If you had been as loyal to your King in hindring the Entry of these Pirates, as I shall be in opposing their going out, you had never caused these Troubles neither to yourselves nor to our whole Nation, which hath suffered so much through your Pusillanimity. In a Word, I shall never grant your Request, but shall endeavour to maintain that Respect which is due to my King, according to my Duty.*

Thus the *Spaniards* returned to their fellow Prisoners, with much Consternation of Mind, and no hopes of obtaining their Request, telling to Captain *Morgan* what Answer they had received. His Reply was, *If Don Alonso will not let me pass, I will find Means how to do it without him.* Hereupon, he began presently to make a Dividend of all the Booty they had taken in that Voyage, fearing lest he might not have an Opportunity of doing it in another Place, if any Tempest should arise, and seperate the Ships: As also being jealous that any of the Commanders might run away with the best Part of the Spoil, which then lay much more in one Vessel than another. Thus they all brought in, according to their Laws, and declared what they had, having before-hand made an Oath not to conceal the least Thing from the Publick. The Accounts being cast up, they found the Value of two hundred and fifty thousand Pieces of Eight, in Money and Jewels, besides the huge Quantity of Merchandizes and Slaves. The Dividend of which Purchase was made to every Ship or Boat, according to their proper Share.

The Division being made, the Question still remained on Foot, how they should pass the Castle, and get out of the Lake. At last, they agreed to make Use of a Stratagem, of no ill Invention, which was as followed. On the Day that preceded the Night wherein they determined to get forth, they embark'd many of their Men in Canoes, and rowed towards the Shore, as if they designed to land them. Here they concealed themselves, under the Branches of Trees that hung over the Coast, for a while, till they had laid themselves down along in the Boats. Then the Canoes returned to the Ships, with the only Appearance of two or three Men rowing them back, all the rest being concealed at the Bottom of the Canoes. Thus much only could be perceived from the Castle, and this Action of false Landing of Men, for so we may call it, was repeated that Day several Times. Hereby the *Spaniards* were brought into Persuasion, that the Pirates intended to force the Castle by scaling it, as soon as Night should come. This Fear caused them to place most of their great Guns on that Side which looks towards the Land, together with the main Force of their Arms, leaving the contrary Side, belonging to the Sea, almost destitute of Strength and Defence.

Night being come, they weighed Anchor, and by the Light of the Moon, without setting sail, committed themselves to the ebbing Tide, which gently brought them down the River, till they were nigh to the Castle. Being now almost against it, they spread their Sails with all the Haste they could possibly make. The *Spaniards* perceiving them to escape, transported with all Speed their Guns from the other Side of the Castle, and began to fire very furiously at the Pirates. But these, having a favourable Wind, were almost past the Danger, before those of
the

the Caftle could put Things into convenient order of Offence So that the Pirates loft not many of their Men, nor received any confiderable Damage in their Ships Being now out of the Reach of the Guns, Captain *Morgan* fent a Canoe to the Caftle with fome of the Prifoners and the Governor thereof gave them a Boat that every one might return to his own Houfe Notwithftanding this, he detained the Hoftages he had from *Gibraltar*, by reafon thofe of that Town were not as yet come to pay the reft of the Ranfom for not firing the Place Juft as he departed, Captain *Morgan* ordered feven great Guns with Bullets, to be fired againft the Caftle, as it were to take his Leave of them But they anfwered not fo much as with a Musket-fhot

The next Day after their Departure, they were furprized with a great Tempeft, which forced them to caft Anchor in the Depth of five or fix fathom Water But the Storm increafed fo much, that they were compelled to weigh again, and put out to Sea, where they were in great Danger of being loft For if on either fide they fhould have been caft on Shore, either to fall into the Hands of the *Spaniards*, or of the *Indians*, they would certainly have obtained no Mercy At laft, the Tempeft being fpent, the Wind ceafed, which caufed much Content and Joy in the whole Fleet

While Captain *Morgan* made his Fortune by pillaging the Towns abovementioned, the reft of his Companions who feparated from his Fleet at Cape *de Lobos*, to take the Ship of which were fpoken before, endured much Mifery, and was very unfortunate in all their Attempts For being arrived at the Ifle of *Savona*, they found not Captain *Morgan* there, nor any one of their Companions Neither had they the good Fortune to find a Letter, which the Captain, at his Departure, left behind him in a certain Place, where in all Probability they would meet with it Thus, not knowing what Courfe to fteer, they at laft concluded to pillage fome Town or other, whereby to repair their Fortune They were in all about four hundred Men, divided into four Ships and one Boat Being ready to fet forth, they conftituted an Admiral among themfelves, by whom they might be directed in the whole Affair To this Effect they chofe a certain Perfon, who had behaved himfelf very couragioufly at the taking of *Puerto Velo*, and whofe Name was Captain *Hanfel* This Commander refolved to attempt the taking of the Town of *Commana*, feated upon the Continent of *Caracas*, nigh threefcore Leagues from the Weft Side of the Ifle *de la Trinidad* Being arrived there, they landed their Men, and killed fome few *Indians* that were near to the Coaft But approaching to the Town, the *Spaniards*, having in their Company many *Indians*, difputed with them the Entry fo briskly, that, with great Lofs, and in great Confufion, they were forced to retire towards their Ships At laft, they arrived at *Jamaica*, where the reft of their Companions, who came with Captain *Morgan*, continu'd to mock and jear them for their ill Succefs at *Commana*, often faying to them, *Let us fee what Money you brought from* Commana, *and if it be as good Silver as that which we bring from* Maracaibo

But left we fhould weary our Readers with a too long Account of the Depredations of one Man, we fhall be more concife in the remaining Part of this Narrative, and reduce the great Number of Adventures that ftill remain to be related, into as little Room as poffible

Not long after Captain *Morgan's* Arrival at *Jamaica*, he found that Debauchery and Excefs had reduced the greateft Part of his Officers to the fame State of Indigency they were often in before This was a Motive fufficient to engage him in new Adventures, and tho' his Crew was pretty well difperfed about the Country, he found no Difficulty in getting them together again by Letters

The Place of Rendezvouz was Port *Coullton*, a *French* Town, over againft the Ifland *de la Vaca* Here he called a Council, who agreed to fend four Ships and one Boat, mann'd with four hundred Men, over to the *Continent*, to rifle fome of the neighbouring Villages for bread Provifions, while others of them hunted in the Woods, killed and falted a great Number of wild Beafts, and the reft were employed in refitting all their Veffels

The four Ships were becalmed near the Mouth of the River *de la Hacha*, for fome Days, in which Time they were perceiv'd by the *Spaniards*, who hid their Goods, and prepared to retire themfelves on Occafion Here they took a good Ship laden with and the next Morning landed in fpite of the Maiz, while the Men where endeavouring to efcape, Refiftance made by the *Spaniards*, whom they purfued a long Way, torturing thofe they took, in a grievous Manner, to make them difcover their Wealth, which fome of them did, fo that in fifteen Days they amafs'd a great Quantity of Plate and other moveable Goods This, however, did not content them, for they fent into the Woods for more of the Inhabitants, whom they oblig'd, with thofe they had already taken, to pay four thoufand Bufhels of Maiz for a Ranfom, and to prevent their burning the whole Town.

The Return of thefe Ships to the Fleet, after an Abfence of five Weeks, was the Occafion of great Joy Having equally divided the Maiz and Flefh, they fteered their Courfe for Cape *Tiburon*, being in all thirty feven Sail, with two thoufand fighting Men on board, befides Mariners and Boys *Morgan's* own Ship mounted twenty two great Guns, and fix fmall ones, all Brafs; the reft carried fome twenty, fome eighteen, fome fixteen, the fmalleft four; befides a great Quantity of Ammunition For the better Management of this Fleet, he divided it into two Squadrons, conftituting a Vice-Admiral to command one, with proper Officers under him, as in his own Divifion He then fummoned together all the Captains, gave them Letters-Patent, to commit all manner of Hoftilities againft the *Spaniards*, as Enemies of the *Englifh* Nation, and made them fign Articles, in which it was ftipulated, that he himfelf fhould have a hundredth Part of what was taken, every Captain the Share of eight Men, befides his own, the Surgeon two hundred Pieces of Eight, for his Cheft of Medicines, and every Carpenter one hundred Ditto, above common Salary The Rewards were as follows For the Lofs of both Legs, one thoufand five hundred Pieces of Eight, or fifteen Slaves, for the Lofs of both Hands, one thoufand eight hundred Pieces of Eight, or eighteen Slaves; for one Leg or one Hand, fix hundred Pieces, or fix Slaves, for an Eye, one hundred Pieces, or one Slave To him that fhould firft enter any Caftle, or otherwife fignalize himfelf, the Reward was fifty Pieces of Eight All thefe extraordinary Recompences were to be paid out of the firft Spoil.

From Cape *Tiburon* they failed for St *Catharine's*, at that Time in the Poffeffion of the *Spaniards*, where they anchored one Morning before Sun-rifing, and landed one thoufand Men, with which the Captain marched to the ufual Refidence of the Governor, but found the Garrifon retired to the leffer Ifland, which joins to the great one by a Bridge, and is almoft impregnable The *Spaniards* upon perceiving them, fired fo furioufly, that they hindred their advancing thither all that Day, fo that they were oblig-ed to lie on the Ground, where they fuffered a great Deal from the violent Rains that fell that Night, being almoft Naked, and withal very hungry In this Diftrefs

6 F

Diſtreſs the next Day, they even eat a diſtempered old Horſe that they found in the Fields, which was but a ſmall Relief among ſo many

In the Midſt of this Fatigue, Captain *Morgan* ordered a Canoe to be rigg'd, and a Flag of Truce to be hung out to the *Spaniards*, threatening withal, that if they did not ſurrender in a few Hours, he would put them all to the Sword To anſwer this Meſſage, the Governor deſired to call a Council, which being granted, after it was over, he ſent two Canoes with white Colours to treat Captain *Morgan*, ſending two Hoſtages in the mean Time to the Governor.

The Plenipotentiaries agreed that *Morgan* ſhould have the Iſland; but then, to ſave the Governor's Credit, he was to enter the Fort by Attack in the Night, ſo that he might ſeem to take it by Surprize, his Ships at the ſame Time making a formal Aſſault by Sea It was further concluded, that the Governor ſhould be taken Priſoner, and that no deviliſh miſchievous Bullets ſhould be us'd during the whole Engagement All this was punctually obſerv'd on both Sides.

The Pirates having taken the Iſland, their next War was with the Poultry, Cattle, and other Neceſſaries for the Belly Several Days were ſpent in feaſting, and a great many Houſes pull'd down to make Fuel of the Timber The Priſoners were about four hundred and fifty Perſons; one hundred and ninety of whom were Soldiers In the Iſland were nine Fortreſſes well mounted and provided the Store-houſe was furniſh'd with above thirty thouſand lb of Powder, beſides other Ammunition of all Sorts; which was all carry'd on board the Pirate-Ships, and the great Guns ſtopp'd and nail'd

Four Ships were now ſent with Guides to take the Caſtle of *Chagre*, under the Command of one *Brodele* This Caſtle is ſituated on a high Mountain, at the Entry of the River, ſurrounded with Palliſades, or wooden Walls fill'd with Earth On the Land-Side it has four Baſtions, and on the Sea-ſide is wholly inacceſſible Notwithſtanding all this Danger, theſe reſolute Fellows landed, hazarded an Aſſault, and were beaten back the firſt Time with ſome Loſs

In the Heat of the Action one of the Pirates was wounded with an Arrow, which he inſtantly pull'd out, wrapp'd ſome Cotton about it, and diſcharg'd it from his Muſquet This Arrow fell upon a Houſe thratch'd with Palm-Leaves, and the Cotton, being kindled by the Powder, ſet it on Fire, which the *Spaniards* did not perceive till it burnt to a great Quantity of Powder, blew it up, and caus'd a prodigious Conſternation

This Accident gave the Pirates an Opportunity to ſet the Palliſades on Fire alſo, while the *Spaniards* were labouring to extinguiſh the other It was not long now before a great many Breaches were made; which the *Spaniards* defended very bravely, till at laſt the Pirates got Poſſeſſion of one defended by the Governor himſelf, and from thence proceeded to the Caſtle, which they were alſo ſoon Maſters of The Governor was kill'd with a Muſquet-ſhot, and many of his Men jump'd into the Sea, to avoid being taken by theſe Fellows, of whom they entertain'd terrible Apprehenſions. So that at laſt the Priſoners amounted to no more than thirty (and of theſe twenty were wounded) out of three hundred and fourteen Soldiers, which were in Garriſon The Pirates themſelves loſt an hundred Men, and had ſeventy wounded.

As ſoon as *Morgan* receiv'd the News of this Action, he left St *Catherine*'s, and came to *Chagre*, loſing four Ships at the Entry of the River He was received with great Joy, and having order'd a Garri-

ſon for the Place, and ſeiz'd all the Veſſels that lay there, he departed towards *Panama*, at the Head of twelve hundred Men, with but a little Proviſions, becauſe he depended on his good Fortune

They were nine Days upon the March before they ſaw *Panama*, during which Time they ſuffer'd greatly, for want of Food, the *Spaniards* having deſerted all the Villages on a Rumour of their coming, and carry'd off with 'em all manner of Proviſions Some times a Pipe of Tobacco was all they liv'd on, one Day they eat Leather-Bags which they found, another Day Graſs and Herbs Cats, Dogs, Horſes or Aſſes, were delicate Food The ninth Day at Night they encamp'd near the City, expreſſing their Joy with the Sound of Drums and Trumpets, and feaſting plentifully on a great Number of Cattle which they took in the Neighbourhood

On the tenth Day, betimes, the Captain put his Men in Order, when one of his Guides advis'd him to ſhun the direct Road to the City, which Advice he follow'd, diſappointing by that Means the *Spaniards* who lay in Ambuſcade, and obliging them to draw together in a Body, and meet him openly The Forces with which the Governor of *Panama* advanc'd, were two Squadrons, four Regiments of Foot, and a huge Number of wild Bulls driven by *Indians*

The Pirates firſt ſpy'd the *Spaniards* from the Top of a little Hill, and were ſo terrify'd at their Number, that moſt of them dreaded the Event of a Battle however, they all reſolv'd to engage, and either conquer, or die on the Spot, as they could hope for no Quarter from People whom they had ſo much abus'd In this Confidence they march'd on, and were receiv'd by the *Spaniards* with a Shout, and an Attack from their Horſe, but the Field being quaggy, the Cavalry could not do the Service expected. A Party of two hundred Bucaniers, that march'd in the Front, gave them a Volley of Shot on their Knees, upon which the Battle kindled very warmly, with Advantage on the Side of the Pirates. This occaſion'd the *Indians* to drive the Bulls upon their Backs, which put them into ſome Diſorder, but the Beaſts were ſoon diſpers'd with the Noiſe of the Engagement

At the End of two Hours the greateſt part of the *Spaniſh* Horſe was kill'd, and the reſt fled The Foot diſcharg'd their Muſquets, threw them down, and follow'd the Example of the Horſe A great many hid themſelves, but were moſt of them taken and kill'd, among them ſeveral Monks and Prieſts A Captain of the *Spaniards*, who was brought before *Morgan*, inform'd him of the whole Strength of the Place, both with reſpect to the Men and Fortifications, which induc'd the March towards the Town by another Way

After numbring the dead Bodies, which amounted to ſix hundred *Spaniards*, and a pretty many Pirates, they advanc'd; but ſuffer'd much in the Attack from the great Guns planted at every Quarter yet they continu'd to gain Ground in Spite of all Difficulties, and in three Hours time carry'd the City Now they ſlew all that made the leaſt Oppoſition, and every Thing they found was their own, but the Inhabitants had conceal'd their moſt valuable Effects As ſoon as the Heat was over, *Morgan* aſſembled his Men, and order'd them to drink no Wine, telling them he was inform'd the *Spaniards* poiſon'd it all Tho' the true Reaſon, 'tis thought, of this Injunction, was to prevent their being drunk, and ſo encouraging the *Spaniards* to riſe, and put 'em all to the Sword

The Captain commanded the City to be privately ſet on Fire in ſeveral of the moſt magnificent Parts; ſo that before Night this fine Place was almoſt all burnt, tho' no-body ever knew his Motives. Some

of

of his own People murmuring at this Procedure, he endeavour'd to fling the Odium on the *Spaniards*, who, 'twas well known, with several of the Pirates, did all in their Power to extinguish the Flames; but, the Houses being all of Cedar, their Labour was to no Purpose The Monastries, Churches, Hospitals, &c in this Place were very nobly built, and richly adorn'd, the Number of Houses was about seven Thousand, of which two Thousand were grand Structures: Most of these were destroy'd, together with two hundred rich Ware-houses, and a great many Negroes, who hid themselves therein After doing all this Mischief, the Pirates retir'd, and encamp'd in the Field in Posture of Defence, apprehending they should be attack'd again by the *Spaniards*, who were still much their Superiors in Number

When they found themselves safe they return'd and plunder'd the Ruins, finding a great deal of Plate, and other Things that the Fire could not destroy They then pursu'd the Inhabitants who were fled and took above two hundred of them Prisoners

A Ship that had been sent to the *South-Sea*, now return'd, with three small Prizes, and informed the Captain that they had missed a Galeon richly laden, and but of small Strength Their Debaucheries had been the Occasion of this Neglect, which now sufficiently troubled them; and *Morgan* could not forbear sending a Boat well arm'd after the Booty, but in vain After this, four Boats more were sent out, with no other Success than the taking a few small Vessels; the Lading of some of which, indeed, was not inconsiderable *Alonvoy* that had been sent to *Chagre*, return'd also about this Time, and brought News of a *Spanish* Ship that had been taken there in the Captain's Absence

Thus while the Trade of Piracy went on at *Chagre*, *Morgan* continued at *Panama*, making daily Inroads in Parties, into all the adjacent Countries. The Riches hereof, were almost inestimable, as the Cruelties exercised were incredible One miserable Wretch they found in the House of a Man of Quality, with a Pair of Taffety Breeches on, and a silver Key hanging to them They ask'd him for the Cabinet which that Key belong'd to, and on his telling them he knew nothing of it, and had only put on the Breeches because he found them in his Masters House, they disjointed his Arms on the Rack, and twisted a Cord about his Forehead so hard, that his Eyes were ready to gush out, then they hung him up by the Testicles, and beat him violently in that Posture, afterwards they cut off his Nose and Ears, and sing'd his Face with burning Straw. When they found he could not speak, and consequently make no Confession, they ordered a Negro to run him thro' with a Lance

Priests and religious People were used the worst of all, and no Sex nor Condition was spared, except such Women as submitted to their Lust A Lady of good Quality was brought before the Captain, young and very beautiful: He ordered her to be lodg'd by herself, and attended with great Respect, notwithstanding she begged to be put with the other Prisoners, because she suspected he had a Design upon her Chastity. This civil Treatment continued several Days, so that she began to entertain a more favourable Opinion of the Captain, than she had been taught before But the Scene soon changed again, when, upon her obstinately refusing to comply with his lascivious Desires, she was ordered to be strip'd almost naked, put into a nasty Cellar, and almost starv'd to Death; so that the Pirates commiserated her Condition, and the Captain was oblig'd to charge her with holding Correspondence with the *Spaniards*, to defend himself from the Resentment of his own Company

We must not, however, omit one Act of Justice When the Prisoners were all put to the Ransom, this Lady informed the Captain, that she had sent two Monks for the Sum required, which they had receiv'd, and converted to their own Use This Fact was enquired into, and found true; whereupon the Lady was discharg'd, and the Monks taken and punish'd according to their Deserts Such an extraordinary Example of Constancy and Virtue, could not fail of having some Effect, even upon *Morgan* himself, in the midst of his Barbarities

A Plot among some of the Pirates was now discovered to *Morgan*, their Design was to have run away with a Ship, and set up for themselves in the *South-Sea* To prevent this, their Masts were cut down and burnt The Captain also ordered all the Artillery of the City to be spoil'd, and commanded all the Prisoners to procure a certain Sum for their Ransom, within three Days; threatning to transport such as fail'd to *Jamaica*. The Misery of these unhappy Wretches was very great, so that, what with the fear of Slavery, and want of Provisions, nothing was to be heard but Cries and Lamentations

When the Pirates left *Panama*, they had with them one hundred seventy five Beasts of Carriage, laden with Gold, Silver, and other valuable Goods Upon the Road they took more Prisoners, and such as could not pay their Ransoms, were actually transported At about half Way to *Chagre*, all the Company were searched, to see that they had concealed nothing contrary to their Articles; the Captain suffering the Enquiry to begin with himself. They found all Things in good Order at *Chagre*, till dividing the Booty put them into Confusion, several of the Company taxing *Morgan* to his Face with keeping the best Jewels to himself, for they thought it impossible that no more than two hundred Pieces of Eight per Head shou'd arise from so much as they had taken

Morgan, finding he began to grow obnoxious to the whole Company, stole away privately with two or three Ships from St *Catharine*'s, which he designed to have fortify'd and kept for himself. But he was soon stop'd in his Purpose, by the Arrival of a new Governor to *Jamaica*, who sent the old one Home to give an Account of his Actions Some of the Pirates were now taken and executed; and the Vigilance and Severity of this Gentleman put a final Period to the Depredations of Captain *Morgan*, and to all the Account that we have ever receiv'd concerning him.

We make no doubt but the surprizing Variety of Adventures contained in this Life, will sufficiently compleat the Whole, 'twou'd have been very easy to have made it as much longer, and yet have related nothing but authentic Facts.

The LIFE *of* **Capt. PHILLIP STAFFORD.**

CAPTAIN *Stafford* was born about the Year 1622 at a small Village in *Berkshire*, about seven Miles from *Newberry* His Father was a Sort of a Gentleman-Farmer, having about fifty Pounds a-Year of his own Estate ; upon which, by the Help of his Industry, he lived in a very comfortable Manner Our *Philip* was an only Child, which made the Farmer very careful to bring him up as handsomely as he was able He sent him to School first in the Country, afterwards to the Free-School at *Reading* , at both which Places his Improvements was as considerable as could be expected from one of his Age , and indeed might have been much greater, had his Application been equal to the Sprightliness of his Wit, and common Vivacity of his Temper. These Qualifications, however, shewed themselves more to Advantage in the other Parts of his Life, than they did in a sedentary Course of Study H s Conversation, even almost in his Childhood, was very agreeable, as his Resentment was generally fatal to those of his own Age and Stature Never a Lad in all the Parishes round, but would shudder at the Name of *Philip Stafford*, and if he was not always the best Scholar, he was indisputably the Head Boy in every School he went to

His Father design'd him for the Heir of his Industry, as well as of his Estate , and therefore put him out to no Trade , but when the Time generally allotted for the Education of young Men of a moderate Fortune, was expired, he took him Home to the Plow, and, as soon as he conceived him equal to the Burthen, gave him the whole Management of his Affairs *Phil* was a tolerable good Farmer, but a much better Ringer, Wrestler, and B ck-Sword-Player , in all which Exercises he was looked upon as the Hero of the whole Country The excellent Mr *Waller* tells us in one of his Poems, that if *Julius Cæsar* had been born in the Country, of obscure Parents,

> *He who subdu'd the World had been*
> *But the best Wrestler on the Green*

We may reverse these Lines, with respect to young *Stafford*, and venture to affirm, that a very little Assistance would have help'd such a promising Genius to have made a considerable Figure in some exalted Station.

He had imbib'd in his Infancy such Principles of Religion and Loyalty, as are common to Men in his Father's Circumstances ; these were strengthened by the Company he afterwards kept, and the manly Amusements he daily followed , so that when the Civil War broke out, between King *Charles* I and his Parliament, *Stafford* was one of the first of his County that voluntarily entered into the Service of his Sovereign He continued in the Army, through the whole Series of that unnatural Rebellion, and we have no Reason to doubt but he behaved with a great deal of Bravery, though his Actions are buried and lost in the universal Confusion of the Times. We have

not only all the other Particulars of his Life, which are recorded, to support such a Presumption, but the Military Honours he received, are an undeniable Proof, that he distinguished himself on some extraordinary Occasion ; for the Title of Captain, which he afterwards bore, was really conferred on him, while he was in the Service

Every one is acquainted with the dismal Catastrophe of those unhappy Troubles As soon as the King was dead, and the Rebels had got all into their Hands, the Royalists were obliged to shift from Place to Place all over the Nation ; and to use all the cautionary Means they could invent, to secure themselves. The small Patrimony of Mr. *Stafford* was sequestered, among the many larger Estates of Gentlemen, who had continued in their Duty to the last ; and he soon found himself in no Capacity of getting a moderate Subsistance What was to be done in such a Situation as this ? He looked every Way and could see no Prospect of an honest Livelihood This at last determined him in the Course which he immediately fell into, and which intitles him to a Place in this Collection The Resolution he set out with, was, to raise Contributions among the Enemies of his Master only, whom he vow'd never to spare in any Thing, wherein he had an Opportunity of doing any Damage either to their Persons or Estates

We shall now view our Captain in his new Character, and proceed to a Relation of the most remarkable and diverting Adventures, that are recorded of him, without proposing any particular Method, which it would be impossible to follow

An antient rich Republican, who was pretty deep in the Iniquity of the Times, had married a beautiful young Lady of large Fortune, the Daughter of a worthy Cavalier his Relation, by whose Death the Damsel fell into his tenacious Hands He had prophaned the sacred Ordinance of *Wedlock*, purely to keep the Substance of his deceased Kinsman to himself, and to gratify the leacherous Remains of his carnal Appetite Who could blame a Woman of Taste for being dissatisfy'd in such Circumstances ? *Stafford* had known her Father, and did not at all question getting the Lady's Favour, if he could but once get into her Company In order to this, he puts on the Habit of the Party, and gets himself recommended to the old Saint for a Servant He acted his part so well, that he was hired without much Difficulty, and in a very little while, had won the Heart of his Master , so that he was admitted to converse freely with both him and Madam The last was all he wanted, and it was not long before he found an Opportunity of disclosing his Mind to her, who was as sensible of the ill Usage she had met with, as *Stafford* could desire her In short, our Gentleman was now supplied with all the Money she could squeeze from her venerable Picture of Mortality, and enjoy'd besides, every other Favour, which a jolly personal Man could expect from a beautiful young Woman full of Desires They took every Opportunity of being in each other's

Company,

Company, and the good Grace this Affair was carried on with, made the old Gentleman imagine, if at any Time he found them together unexpectedly, that they only met to converse on spiritual Subjects, for the mutual Edification of each other. This Amour in Time brought the Lady heartily to despise her Husband, and to take a Pride in imposing upon his Credulity, and even upon his Senses, *Stafford* and she formed such a Plot of the latter kind, as, I believe, can hardly be parallelled, which they executed in the following Manner.

Our Cornuto lived in some Splendor, like the rest of the Saints, who at this Time had the Management of Affairs. He had a handsome well-built House, and a very decent Garden, enclosed with an high Wall, and planted, among other Things, with Variety of Fruit-Trees. At the furthest Recess of this Plot was a wide-spreading Pear-Tree, and it was now the Time of Year that the Pears were ripe. *Cornuto* and his dear Half were one Evening walking in the Garden, 'till they came to this Pear-Tree, when the Lady all of a sudden were seiz'd with a violent Longing for some of the Fruit. The compassionate old Gentleman would have help'd her, if he could, but there was not a Bough in his Reach, which Madam knew before. There was no other Way to get the Pears than by calling *Stafford*; accordingly, *Stafford* was called, and he immediately mounted up into the Tree. He was no sooner there, than he began to lift up his Eyes, and bless himself! *Dear Sir,* says he, *if you will do such Things, be so good as to go a little out of my Sight. One would think you should have a little more Regard to yourself, than to enjoy your Spouse before the Face of a Servant. Good God! are you in such a Hurry that you can't stay 'till you get back to the House? You have a good Bed and private Chambers there* —— *Besides, one would think the Nights are long enough to satisfy your Desires in* —— The poor Woman seemed to be in a strange Surprize to hear *Stafford* run on at this unaccountable Rate. *Is the Fellow in a Dream?* quoth she, *What is it you mean by enjoying one another, and satisfying our Desires? Are we not both sitting upon the Grass-Plot, and looking at you? Come down, pray now, and let us know what you are talking about.* Accordingly *Stafford* came down, and the old Gentleman began to be very merry with him! *Well* Stafford says he, *do you see me caress your Mistress now? Not just now,* reply'd *Stafford,* but *I'll be burn'd alive, if I did not see you do it about three Minutes ago, upon this very Place; or else the Pear-Tree is enchanted, and made it seem so* —— *Enchanted!* says the old Gentleman, *Fetch me a Ladder, and I'll examine this Enchantment.* Away goes *Stafford,* fetches a Ladder, sets it up against the Tree, and the old Man very orderly ascends. He was scarcely got up before our Wag had boarded Madam in earnest, and the poor Cuckold was struck with Admiration. *And are you really doing nothing now?* says he —— *Doing!* Madam replied in a seeming Passion, *what should we be doing of? I hope you don't think me such a Fool, as to let you see it, if I had a Mind to make you a Cuckold? Verily,* says he, *it appears to me, that* Stafford *has at this Time got thee in his Arms, but it must be the Tree then.* After this, he sat very contentedly, 'till the Pastime was over, and then came as contentedly down, wondering at what he had beheld. Madam proposed to have the Tree cut down immediately, that it might no more exhibit such wicked Sights, and *Stafford* was ordered to proceed to the Execution.

After this abominable Pear-Tree was reduced to Ashes, *Stafford* continued in the Family a considerable Time, without the least Suspicion on the Side of his Master, or the least Indifference on the Side of his Mistress. Favours were heaped upon him

by both Parties for his good Services, and Madam and he were every Day merry with the Story above related.

An Heir was born to the old Gentleman's Estate, whom he look'd upon as the Fruit of his own Labour, and our two Lovers were sufficiently pleased with the good Man's Credulity. But *Stafford,* after all, was no whining Inamorato, though Madam was heartily in love with his Person, 'twas her Wealth that kept him so long in her Arms. He began to look upon the whole Sex with an equal Eye, and waited only for an Opportunity to make a good Booty, and seek his Fortune upon other Ground. The Part of a Gallant no Man performed better, nor imitated that of a Lover more naturally than *Stafford.* He had besides all that was graceful and engaging in his Behaviour, as well as his Person. The Ascendant, which by these Means he had gained over the Soul of the young Gentlewoman, soon made him Master of all her Secrets. He learn'd that there was in the House a Casket of Jewels to the Value of fifteen hundred Pounds, and where it was deposited; nay, she had gone so far as to shew him this Treasure, one Day when her dear *Moiety* was gone out, and made him at the same Time a Present of a very pretty Diamond which she thought would not be missed. She had moreover given him the History of every Jewel, told which belonged to her Grandmother, which to her Aunt, and which the old Man had got by Sequestration, and made her a Present of. It is believed by the Country Wenches, that if they give a Gipsy any Piece of Money out of their Pocket, she will be sure to get the whole quickly after. *Stafford* in this Affair was a real Gipsy, and he accounted the whole Casket his own, from the very Moment she had dealt thus openly with him. He looked upon the Ring which she had given him, as a sort of Earnest, and waited only for a proper Opportunity to receive the whole Sum in Gross.

It was, however, necessary to take a pretty Deal of Precaution, in order to put such a Design as this in Execution. The whole Plot must be regularly laid in such a Manner, as that no Imputation of the Felony might light upon him. All this could not conveniently be done, without an Associate, and every one was not to be trusted in such an Affair. It was some Time therefore before he could bring every Thing to look favourably upon his Project. At last he met with a proper Tool, who had been an old School-Fellow of his, a Fellow abandoned to all Sense of Honour and Honesty, and who was always ready to execute the blackest Design, yet at the same Time so easily imposed upon, that it was no difficult Matter for such a Man as *Stafford* to reap all the Advantage of his Villainy. His Name was *Tom Pretty,* and being the Son of a *French* Refugee, he boasted, that he was descended from an Admiral of *France,* who was very famous in some War about a hundred Years before. This he would assert with a most consummate Assurance, and if any one ask'd him the Name of his Grandfather the Admiral, he would as confidently tell them a Name that was never seen in the *French* History; affirming with a thousand Imprecations, that he won Fights that were never heard of, in Years when all *Europe* were at Peace. *Tom* was a Hatter by Trade, and by his *Effrontery,* had got pretty good Business among a Company of young Gentlemen, who loved a Song better than they judged of it; for he pretended to be a great Master of Vocal Musick. He pretended, I say, to be so, for in Reality, though he had a Voice as strong as an Ass, he had no more Harmony in it, than the said unfortunate Animal, whom he also resembled in several other Respects, particularly in being a Beast of Burden. In the Theory of Musick he had so little Skill, that he

had

had never learn'd his Notes, and when the Scholaftic Word *Gammut* has been mention'd in his Company, he has been heard very gravely to afk, what *Gammer* they were talking of Befides this, he would frequently vapour with a very great Air, and fwear, that there was never a Man in *England* of his Inches, that could match him When he has been affronted by a Fellow much lefs than himfelf, in fuch Manner as no Man of Spirit would have born ; his ufual Method of coming off, was, by faying he was afham'd to fet his Wit to fuch an underfiz'd Braggadoccio If the Man happened to be full-fiz'd, he was certainly troubled either with the Gout, or the Gravel. In a Word, *Thomas Pretty* was a fecond *Falftaff* for Boafting and Cowardice, tho' for Wit and Contrivance he was many Degrees behind that antient corpulent Knight

This Digreffion on the Character of *Tom* will be pardoned, when the Reader fhall find by-and-by, that it was very-neceffary, in order to give his Actions their true Colour In writing the Life of any Man, 'tis one Half of the Work to draw a juft Picture To make *Tom's* Picture compleat, I fhould have added, That he was continually talking of Favours, which he had received from the Ladies, though in Reality, he was defpifed by the whole Sex

This Man, by neglecting his Bufinefs, and fpending his Money, on Purpofe to tell his Adventures, and let others hear him fing, being now reduced to Extremity, *Stafford* thought him the beft Inftrument he could make ufe of, provided he could employ him in the Work, when there was little Danger, otherwife he very much fufpected his Courage He had procured a Key to the Door where the Jewels were lodged, and he took an Opportunity to convey them out at a Window to *Pretty*, leaving the Cafement open, with all the vifible Marks of its having been forc'd without Side. He took Care alfo to have a Ladder left under the Window, and to have fo much Noife made as might confirm the Sufpicion of a *Scalado*, in the Morning when the Lofs was difcovered The Mafter and Miftrefs, while this was done, lodg'd in a Summer Houfe in the Garden, which they frequently did during the pleafant Time of the Year *Stafford* was the firft who gave the Alarm in the Morning, and all the reft of the Servants remembered the Noife, and faw the Ladder. There was not much Sufpicion of any of the Servants, and of *Stafford* there was the leaft of all, as he had always behaved in fuch an extraordinary Manner, fo that our good Couple quickly gave up their Jewels for loft

The Captain ftaid long enough in the Houfe after this, to prevent their thinking he went away with any other View, than that of getting a better Place, and he took Care, during this Time, to ferve his loving Miftrefs to the utmoft of his Strength and Ability The Jewels were all fold in a very private Manner, almoft to their full Value, and *Pretty* received a Gratuity fufficient to retain him in the Captain's Service, with whom he afterwards joined in feveral Adventures

Stafford was very careful to get a little Love, as well as Money in every Place he came to ; and therefore he always paid a particular Regard to the Ladies. He knew a proper Application to them was the beft Means of robbing their Hufbands in every Senfe of the Word ; for there are few Women who will not facrifice every Thing to a Man who has obtained what we commonly call the laft Favour, which is alfo commonly the firft Favour they grant. The Captain, however, met with one who was an Exception to this general Rule. She was young, and very handfome, but withal an unreafonable Coquet, though fhe had been married two Years. Our Hero found Means at

a Ball to declare his Paffion, which indeed, this once, was almoft real. But what a Surprize was it to one who had hitherto found his Perfon a fufficient Recommendation, when he heard a Woman talk of his making her a Prefent of an hundred Guineas, and continue deaf to all other Propofals, tho' he had feveral Times the Pleafure of her Company ! He got acquainted with the Hufband, went daily to fee him, eyed the Lady, fighed, writ Billets, and, as often as he could, fpoke his Mind ; but ftill an hundred Guineas were demanded *Stafford*, in fpite of his Readinefs upon all other Occafions, was very much to feek in this . An hundred Guineas was a great Deal of Money to give for a Miftrefs, Abundance too much for a Gentleman of his Trade, without a Profpect of doubling the Sum by the Bargain. At laft a lucky Thought came into his Head He had been now a pretty while intimate with her Hufband, and by his Appearance and Expences, given him Room to think he was a Gentleman of Fortune, he defired him, therefore, one Day to lend him an hundred Guineas upon his Word, in order to his making up a five hundred Pound Sum for a Purchafe, which he was about This he eafily obtain'd, by producing Bank Notes for the four hundred Pounds more, which he really had remaining from the Sale of the Jewels. The hundred Guineas being procured, he foon got the Lady's Good-Will, and a Day was appointed to make him happy, when the Hufband was to be out of the Way, and feveral to be invited to a fmall Collation, to prevent any Sufpicion

The Day being come, *Stafford* takes the hundred Guineas with him, and goes to the Houfe while they were all at Dinner He pulls out the Bag, *Madam,* fays he, *your Hufband lent me an hundred Guineas a few Weeks ago, and having the Money by me, I took this Opportunity to bring it you, which is the fame Thing, as though I gave it him provided, efe Gentlemen and Ladies will be Witneffes of the Payment* The Company all promifed to take Notice, and Madam, not knowing any Thing of her Hufband's Affair, and fuppofing it was the Money agreed on, which he prefented in this Manner only to impofe merrily upon the Company, received it with all the good Humour imaginable When the reft of the Guefts were gone, *Stafford*, who eafily enough found Excufe for ftaying laft, obtain'd all his Defires, and got the Favour repeated feveral Times into the Bargain.

In a little Time the good Man came Home, and the Captain took the firft Opportunity to pay him a Vifit, when he told him, that he had given the Money to his Wife fuch a Day, while he was abfent The Woman, to be fure, looked at him, but durft fay no more than juft to acknowledge the Receipt, with which her Hufband was very well contented *Stafford* had now all he wifhed for, and he took Care to get this Adventure whifpered all over the Neighbourhood

How odd foever it may feem for a profeffed Cheat as *Stafford* now certainly was, to part with an hundred Guineas, which he had once got Poffeffion of, every one who is acquainted with Intriguing will confefs, that fuch a mafterly Stroke as this, was worth two hundred of any Man's Money in *England*, efpecially, if he was fo full as *Stafford* was at the time when this was acted The Captain, through the whole Courfe of thefe Memoirs, will appear a perfect Gallant All the End he propofed to himfelf in getting Money, was the indulging his Appetites ; and is it any Wonder that a Libertine, with four or five hundred Guineas at Command, fhould fling away one hundred for the fake of enjoying a beautiful Woman, and outwitting an artful Coquete at the fame Time ? Befides, 'tis very probable he was unwilling

juft

it now to lose his Credit in the Country where he at present quartered, having perhaps some greater Advantage in View, than this would have been, had he thought good to embrace it

But we must not do by poor *Tom Pretty* as *P—s* did by his Bear and Fiddle, just excite the Reader's Curiosity, and then say no more about him We have already given you his Character, and we now proceed to one of his Adventures *Stafford* could never the Mistress, but *Tom.* would endeavour to do to the Maid; 'tis true he generally met with access, but then he always boasted of a great Deal While he talk'd of nothing above a Servant, the Captain took no Notice of the Matter but when the Adventure above recited was in Hand, our Bully pretended he had received the last Favour from a Lady whom *Stafford*, though not to his Man's Knowledge had before addressed to no Purpose The Captain had so good an Opinion of the Gentlewoman's Chastity and Sincerity, that he suspected the Truth of *Tom's* Assertion, and therefore communicated the Affair to *Iris* (for so we chuse to call her) She at first resented the Affront, as a Woman of Spirit ought to do, but when she was informed what the Fellow was, her Anger changed to Disdain, and she resolved to be revenged in the merriest Manner she could invent To this End it was proper to engage Persons who would promote her Design, and it was not long before she pitched upon a jolly Couple in the Neighbourhood. *Stafford* was to tell *Tom*, that such a Woman had consented to come and he with him all Night, provided she could get any Body to sleep in his Place *For*, says he, *to sleep is all you will have to do* Mrs — *has inform'd me, that her Husband has never turned to her, or so much as spoke to her in Bed, these seven Years past* He *comes Home about Eleven, half-drunk, falls asleep in two Minutes, and snores like a Hog till next Morning, when he gets up, and departs in the same peaceable Manner You have nothing to do, but to be quiet Leave the good Woman to introduce you* *Tom*, to be sure, was willing to oblige his Master, and accordingly promises to be ready The Hour is come, he is very decently dressed with a Night-Cap, and put into Mr ——'s Bed After he had been there about Half an Hour, comes his Bed-Fellow, without a Light, as he had been informed was his Custom, and slips into his Place *Tom*, from this Moment, was afraid to cough, spit, or even to breathe, much less to come near his Chum He lay upon the very extremity of his Bed, in such a Manner, that his Nose and his Knees met, he contracted himself that you might have put him into a Peck; all for fear his amorous Kit should seize his new Companion, and he should happen to put his Hand, or any Thing else, upon that unhappy Part which would discover all Now and then a Foot, now and then an Arm touches the unhappy *Tom*; he shrinks like a sensitive Plant Wh—n then was his Condition, when his Bed-Fellow embraced him closely, and lay a considerable Time in this Position? When Morning proceeded, the supposed Mr —— rings a Bell, *Tom* began to mutter over his Prayers to himself, and make a very solemn Vow for his Delivery, that if he came safe out of this Danger, he would never offend in the same Manner He thought over all the Sins of his Life, in particular the many Characters which he had aspersed of honest Women, at least for what he knew Suppose him now all in a cold Sweat a full Hour together, for so long it was from the Time of ringing the Bell, till any Person entered At last came in *Stafford*, the Gentleman of the House, who he thought was a-bed with him, and his Wife, all with Lights in their Hands Now was he more surpriz'd than ever, especially when he saw *Iris*, of whose Favours he had so often bragg'd, jump out of the Bed, and half discover her naked Breasts, to let him

see what a Heaven he had lost This once in his whole Life, *Tom* was asham'd 'Tis needless to say that all the rest of the Company were merry They were half an Hour contriving what further Punishment to inflict on him They concluded at last to toss him in a Blanket, and then make him, on his bare Knees, ask Pardon of *Iris*, and swear solemnly never more to boast of receiving Favours from Women, who had scarce ever spoke to him All this was punctually performed to the great Mortification of poor *Thomas*, and the entire satisfaction of all the rest present, more particularly of the injur'd and revengeful *Iris*

This Affront, one would have thought, was sufficient to have made *Tom* change his Master, but he was such an insensible Animal, that, except the few Minutes when he was immediately in Tribulation, he never resented the highest Indignity *Stafford* was as ready as any Man to take Advantage of his Temper, not only for his own Diversion, but for the Diversion of his Acquaintance; so that poor *Pretty* was the Fiddle of all Companies, nor was it a little that he contributed to his own Disquiet, by Relations which he would frequently make of his Adventures. One Thing he would boast of, was, his having been beset with two Foot-pads one Evening late, whom he disarm'd and stripped *And then*, said he, *as I do not delight in Blood, I very mercifully let the Rogues go about their Business* Then he would produce some of the Spoils, as he called them The Truth of this being enquired into, it was found, that at the very Time and Place which *Tom* specify'd two Gentlemen having left their Swords, Canes, and Cloaths under a Tree, while they washed themselves, before they came out of the Water, they were all carried off very dexterously, and they had never discovered the Thief

But we must leave the Servant a little, and return to the Master, in order to relate an Adventure, in which we have no Account that *Thomas* had any Hand It happen'd that *Stafford* was riding along very solitarily on the Western Road one miserable cold Day His Design was only to go and see his Relations, having at that Time Money enough; and it was not customary with him to rob any Body while the Stock was high But Fortune threw a very considerable Prize in his Way, in the following Manner

Just as he came to the Entrance of *Maidenhead-Thicket*, he espied an old formal Gentleman trotting before him As he looked upon him, by his plain Coat, and broad-brimmed Hat, to be one of the Godly, as they were then universally called, he immediately resolved, contrary to his Intention in travelling, to take hold of the Opportunity, and try the Depth of the old Man's Pocket He soon came up with Mr *Primitive*, and began such Conversation as is common to Travellers, more particularly the Severity of the Season occasioned a pretty many Reflections, as they both felt it to a high Degree. *I hope*, says *Stafford*, *after such a terrible Journey as this, I shall meet with a very good Lodging at Night, or else I shall think the Stars are against me indeed.* The old Man, upon this, assumes an Air of Piety, and begins to reprehend the Captain for his Prophaneness in mentioning the Stars, as if they had any Influence over a Man's Circumstances He told him, 'twas a heathenish Manner of expressing himself, and very unbecoming the Mouth of a Christian *For my Part*, says he, *I ascribe every Thing that befalls me to a wise Providence, and am always content with my Lot, as being assured in myself, that all Things are for the best, and work together for the Good of the Elect* — *And do you believe yourself to be one of those Elect?* says *Stafford* —— *It is the earnest Desire of my Soul,*

Soul, replied the old Man, *to find the Evidences of it in myself, it is what I pray for earneſtly Day and Night, and I truly hope, that my Prayers aſcend with a Saviour ſweet-ſmelling and acceptable, and that I ſhall receive an Anſwer of Joy and Peace* Of this I am the more confident, *as I have hitherto found, that the pious Ejaculations of my Heart have not been in vain upon particular Occaſions* Here the Captain endeavoured to reform his Phiz, and to look as demurely as his Companion *Verily Brother,* ſaid he, *whoever thou art, thy Reproof is juſt, but as I was upon a Journey, and uncertain what the Company was that I was thus providentially fallen into, I was willing to conform myſelf to it, for the Security of the outward Man If I had found thee ſpeaking in ſuch a Manner as bad diſcovered the Corruption of thy Heart, and proved thee to be one of the Unregenerate, I ſhould have endeavoured, as far as it would have appeared conſiſtent with my high Character as a Chriſtian, to have given thee thine own Way in Converſation But ſince, to my unſpeakable Joy and Conſolation in this deſart Place, I have found thee ſuch as my Heart would wiſh, I make no ſcruple to unboſom myſelf unto thee, begging that thou wouldſt extend thy Bowels of Chriſtian Compaſſion unto my Weakneſs, which occaſioned me to conceal the real Sentiments of my Soul, thro' Timidity of thy Perſon, to me unknown I would furthermore intreat, that thou wouldſt endeavour to make our Journeying together profitable unto our mutual Edification, by a Relation of ſome of thoſe Experiences, which thou haſt hinted to, as the Effect of thy being found in the Way of thy Duty*

The old Hypocrite was tranſported to hear ſuch a Speech as this, and made no Queſtion but he was luckily fallen into Compa y with a Stone of the ſpiritual Building, and a Brother Member of the ſacred Body of the Church " Foraſmuch, reply'd he, as it ſeemeth to be thy Deſire that I ſhould communicate unto thee ſomething of what I have done in the Courſe of my Duty, and inwardly experienced as the Return of my humble Petitions Know that I have always, ſince I have been made ſenſible what Heart-Work and the Divine Influence mean, conſtantly called for a Bleſſing upon what I have undertaken In an eſpecial Manner, when I have ſet out on a Journey, as at preſent, I have been more earneſt in intreating that I might paſs the Road in Safety, and that at Night in a good Inn I might take up my Quarters, and repoſe upon a Bed of Down Not ſo that I deſire to indulge my Tenement of Clay in the Courſe of this my Pilgrimage, i. that I look upon it to be Typical of that eternal Reſt in the which I hope to be received, when I ſhall put off this outward Man, this earthly Tabernacle of Fleſh It is, my Friend, a Help to my Meditation on theſe Things, when I lie extended at Eaſe in the Night; and I never yet found, but that every Particular has been anſwerable to my Deſires, and, indeed, proportioned to the Degree of Warmth with which I have expreſſed them It is for this Reaſon, that when I have been diligent in my Duty, and taken ſuch a Quantity of Money in my Pocket as will bear my expences in a comfortable Manner, I am under no Apprehenſions of any Danger that may attend me. I hope then quoth Stafford, thou wert not at all wanting this Morning in thy Exerciſes, both for thy ſake and my own; foraſmuch as with thy good liking I am determined to accompany thee this Evening" Hereupon the old Man aſſuring him, that he was never in all his Life more fervent than that Morning, the Captain ſeemed pretty contented, 'till they came to the Middle of the Thicket, when he thought it very proper to take the Advantage of the Place, and eaſe the old Hypocrite of his Money, which was of more Service

to him in his getting good Lodging, than all his boaſted Piety; the latter being only ſuperficial

To this End, he addreſſed him in the following Manner " Brother, I perceive by what you have related, that you are a Man favoured by Heaven in an extraordinary Degree; and that 'tis impoſſible to hinder you of any Thing that you have once pray'd for . To what Purpoſe then ſhould you carry Money with you? Now, for my Part, I cannot pretend to any ſuch particular Token of the Divine Regard; and therefore, I have no Room to expect any Thing out of the common Way; ſo that I think what Money you have about you will be much more ſerviceable to me than to you, who are certain of the beſt Uſage wherever you come ' The old Man began to ſtare upon his new Companion, and wondered what he was driving at; but he did not remain long in Suſpence, for Stafford told him very plainly, That it would be to no Purpoſe for him to make many Words, ſince he was now in Earneſt Therefore, ſays he, without Ceremony deliver your Money At theſe Words he clapped a Piſtol to his Breaſt, which terrify'd the venerable Saint to ſuch a Degree, that he pulled out a Purſe with forty Guineas in it, and gave it with a trembling Hand It was now plain, that how ſure ſoever our good Man was of Heaven, he was not willing to leave the World on a ſudden, which is no uncommon Caſe Stafford being willing to ſpoil the old Man's Lodging intirely, ſhot his Horſe, after he had rifled him of every Thing that he had which was valuable, and then forced him a conſiderable Way into the Thicket, where he bound him faſt, and left him on the cold Ground In this Condition he lay till next Morning, when he was taken up half dead.

The Captain, after this Robbery, was very ſenſible that how bad ſoever the Lodging of his Round-head Companion might be, his own would be as little to his Satisfaction if he were taken; he therefore, thought it moſt adviſeable to get out of the Main Road as faſt as he could This he did by croſſing the Country in to Buckinghamſhire, and riding till he thought he was out of all Danger for that Night He now began to look round him for a Light, the only Means he had of finding a Houſe at this Time, for it was Late At laſt he eſpied one at a conſiderable Diſtance, and with all the Speed his Horſe was Maſter of, rode ſtrait up to it When he was come to the Gate and had kcocked, a young Woman about twenty came with a Candle, and ſeemed not a little ſurprized as ſoon as ſhe ſaw him. The Captain told his Caſe in the beſt Manner he could, and after a little Converſation, he found that there was no Body in the Houſe but the Maid, who came to the Door, and her Miſtreſs, who was alſo up, and waiting for her Huſband to come Home from London

As the good Man had ſent her Word he would not fail that Evening, ſhe had prepared a very elegant Supper for his Refreſhment, which had now been ready a conſiderable Time; ſo long, that they almoſt deſpaired of his coming, and ſhe had, juſt as Stafford came, concluded to ſup by herſelf, and go to Bed When ſhe heard ſomebody at the Gate, ſhe concluded it muſt be her Huſband, and ſent the Maid to introduce him, while ſhe was preparing juſt within the Door to receive him with all the Formality of a Wife Wondring why the Maid ſtaid ſo long, ſhe alſo came out, and the Captain repeated how he had loſt his Way, and was grievouſly diſtreſſed for a Lodging It was impoſſible for a Woman of Breeding and Humanity to be inhoſpitable to a Stranger, who appeared ſo much like a Gentleman as Stafford did, eſpecially now ſhe had done expecting her Lord and Maſter. Betty was ordered to conduct him to the Stable,

Stable, and fee that his Horfe was well provided for, and then to bring the Gentleman in, who acknowledged her Civility in the moft obliging Manner; and made very large Proffeffions of Gratitude Madam, in Return, told him how fhe had been difappointed, affuring him, fhe was very glad, fince Things had fo fell out, that fhe could oblige fo deferving a Gentleman as he appeared to be, with what fhe had provided, adding, that the beft Bed in the Houfe was at his Service There is no Queftion but *Stafford* was fufficiently pleafed with his good Fortune · he reflected upon what had paft the Day before, and wondered how it came to pafs that the old Man's Prayer fhould be fulfilled to him, after he had fo much injured him He could hardly forbear thinking, that tne blind Goddefs had made a Miftake, and fhowered down her Favour upon the wrong Perfon In *a Word, they fat down to Table together, and *Stafford* could perceive that the Expectation of her Hufband had raifed fuch Sentiments in the Lady, as would fall in with his Wifhes After Supper they began to be more free, and the Captain offered to entertain his generous Hoftefs with a Song, which was as follows.

A SONG.

WHen firft Procreation began,
 Ere Forms interrupted the Blifs,
Each Woman might love any Man,
 Each Man any Woman might kifs.

The Youth who beheld a plump Lafs,
 Declar'd in few Words his Requeft;
Nor whin'd like an amorous Afs,
 Nor ever departed unbleft

The Girl who was ripe for the Game,
 Look'd out for a feeable Lad,
Then frankly difcover her Flame,
 And what fhe demanded fhe had

But while they thus revell'd at large,
 And Beatlings increas'd in their Kind,
The Mother fill bore all the Charge,
 The Father what Mortal could find?

So when great *Semiramis* reign'd,
 And Women repin'd at their Lot,
The Queen Matrimony ordain'd,
 That each might maintain what he got

While under this Petticoat Rule,
 The Men were oblig'd to fubmit;
The Wife went abroad; and the Fool
 Still own'd all that came to his Net.

The Men, when it came to their Turn,
 To keep their dear Spoufes at Home,
Decreed ev'ry Woman fhould burn,
 Who dar'd from her Hufband to roam.

'Twas all a Political Cheat,
 Tho' urg'd as a Sanction Divine,
It aw'd tne dull Croud, but the Great
 What Precept could ever confine?

The Jewifh Lawgiver of Yore,
 And all the old Sages of *Greece*,
Themfelves could difpenfe with a Score,
 Tho' all others had but one a Piece.

'Twas thought for the Good of Mankind,
 So by ev'ry Senate 'twas paft,
The Mob will for ever be blind;
 And therefore 'tis likely to laft.

8

Still may the Decrees of the State,
 Impofe on an ignorant Realm,
Let us our own Charter create,
 And do as they do at the Helm.

Since you have the Beauty to charm,
 And I have the Manhood to pleafe,
In Love can there be any Harm,
 That fprings from fuch Motives as thefe?

The Captain had an excellent Voice, and performed every Thing with fuch a Grace, that it was impoffible for any Woman living to hold it out long, when he began to lay clofe Siege The Maid was fent to warm his Bed and Madam, in the mean Time, artfully gave him to underftand how he might leave it, and come to hers, when every Thing was ftill. There is no Occafion to tell the Reader he did fo.

And now I wifh I could conceal the Sequel of this Story When fuch a gallant Man as our Captain robs only for Neceffity, and then makes Choice only of fuch Perfons to collect from, as he of whom we have been laft fpeaking, the Reader is not much difpleafed with him There appears fomething fo agreeable in the Manner and Circumftances of fuch a Story, as takes away a great Deal of the Refentment, which would otherwife arife againft the Felony But Gentlemen of this Profeffion can be engaged by no Favours to keep their Hands to themfelves, when fuch a fair Occafion as this is offered by Fortune If any Thing could prevail, certainly the Obligations of a beautiful Lady, who facrifices her Honour, would have this Effect But a vicious Habit will gain the Afcendant, even over a Man's own Refolutions For it has been hinted that *Stafford* did not ufually collect when he had Money, and at this Time in particulai he had determin'd only to vifit his Country, as a Gentleman, and return quietly to *London*, where he then refided It may be obferved further that almoft every Man, once in his Life, does fomething very unworthy of, and even contrary to his general Character If therefore this, which we are going to relate, be acknowledged as the Captain's one great Foible, the univerfal Weaknefs of human Nature will be ready to excufe him in fome Degree

But I prevent myfelf in my intended Story, by thus endeavouring to palliate it before-hand, and therefore I fhall be as brief as poffible in the Narration

When the Captain had been in Bed with the Gentlewoman will be thought the Time proper for his Purpofe He fuddenly bound her in her Bed, and threaten'd her with immediate Death, if fhe did not direct him to her Keys, and tell him where all the Treafure in the Houfe was depofited The Lady began at firft to exclaim againft his Ingratitude, but when fhe found there was no Remedy, fhe fubmitted, and directed him, where he found to the Value of three hundred Pounds in Money and Plate, which he fecured, and after he had bound the Maid, that fhe might not be able to come to her Miftrefs's Affiftance, and alarm the Neighbourhood before he was out of their Reach, he went to the Stable, took Horfe, and rode for *London*, by the moft By-Way in the whole Country, with which he was well acquainted

The Reader will perceive by the Song which we juft now recited, that Captain *Stafford* was fomething of a Poet He had indeed a very confiderable Knack of verfifying, and made frequent Ufe of it; not only, as in the Cafe above, to compliment his Miftrefs, but frequently to lafh the Hypocrify of the Times, for tho' he now and then condefcended to make Ufe of the fame Difguife, yet in his Soul he utterly abhorred it He very well knew there was no other Way, of infinuating himfelf into the Favour of the wealthieft Men in the Kingdom, than by making Religion his Pretence, and there was no Man who could counterfeit the affected Aufterity, that appeared on every Countenance, better than himfelf There was an abfolute Neceffity either of ftarving in his Profeffion, or of becoming frequently a Hypocrite, and of two great Evils he thought the Latter moft eligible As to his Poetry, it is confidently affirmed, by fome who pretend to authentick Informations, that many of the beft fatirical Pieces then publifhed, which have fince appear'd under other Names, where in reality all his Compofing In fhort his whole Life, with refpect to his Religion and Gallantry, was as confufed as the Account which we now give of it He was one Day a Saint, the next a Lover, the next a Satirift, and the next a Highwayman, or Impoftor, according as the Occafion offered But we proceed again to Particulars

Having, upon a certain Time, got together a confiderable Quantity of Money, and being under fome Apprehenfions of a Difcovery, he made off into the North of England, and took fhelter in a Country Village, fo obfcure that it was next to impoffible he fhould ever be detected He was afraid in this Place to make any great Figure, or to feem extravagant, becaufe he well knew the Country People are apt to be very inquifitive into the Circumftances of fuch Men, and, as he refolved to be as Godly as he was able, while he refided here, it was not expedient for him to put the Congregation to any Trouble, for he had now join'd himfelf to a People who affembled in the Neighbourhood, and it was cuftomary in thofe Days for a new Member, if he was in any refpect fufpicious, to give a very particular Account of himfelf By this prudent management, the Captain not only avoided their Inquifition, but made his ready Cafh laft a great Deal longer than it otherwife would have done

In this Place Stafford foon got the Reputation of a very good Man, he attended conftantly at publick Service, and not only to it, but alfo at all their private Meetings and Conferences, when he would frequently exercife his own Gift, and pour out a tedious Rhapfody of unintelligible Jargon, with a great Deal of feeming Warmth and Affection As it was no difficult Thing for a Man of the Captain's good Senfe to be the greateft Orator in fuch a Congregation as this, it was but a very little, while before his Tallents were every where talk'd of, he was fent for to all the Meetings round about, and publick Thanks were frequently return'd to Providence, who had fent fuch an eminent Chriftian among them It was not above a Year that he had been in this Place, before their venerable Paftor, who had formerly been an indifferent good Taylor, departed this Life The Sorrow on this melancholy Occafion was univerfal, and the Caufe of Religion was a Thoufand Times faid to be in Danger, by the Lofs of fuch a Subftantial Pillar of the Church (for fo they called themfelves) as their dear glorify'd Minifter When the general Lamentation was a little over, the Flock began to look round for one to feed them in the Room of the Deceafed All their Eyes were immediately fix'd on Stafford, who was efteemed the moft able Brother to the important Charge The Captain had by this time wafted his capital ftock pretty confiderably and he muft very foon have been under an abfolute Neceffity of recruiting by fome Means or other; he durft not as yet appear again upon the Road, for he had made himfelf fo notorious juft before his retirement, that a large Reward had been offered for taking him, and his Perfon had been fo particularly defcrib'd, that 'twas in vain to think of difguifing himfelf An offer of forty Pounds a Year, befides a Profpect of other

Acquifitions, was not, it may be imagin'd, at this Time very unacceptable, fo when the Elders of the Congregation waited upon him in a Body with their Refolution, he confented, after due Form, to accept of the Propofal

The Ceremony of his Ordination is foreign to our Purpofe, and therefore we omit it. Behold Captain Phillip Stafford, the Hero of thefe Sheets, in a ftiff Band, and a black Coat and Skull-Cap, mounted behind a velvet Cufhion, and holding forth with all the Eloquence he was Mafter of, againft all Sin, and even the very Appearance of Sin, advifing them to crufh the firft Motions of it in their Hearts, and never fuffer it to break forth into Practice Hear him defcribe the Pleafures of a good Confcience, void of Offence towards God and towards Man! What a Load of Accufations he lay upon his Friend Satan, the grand Enemy of Souls, enough to break the Back of any poor Devil in Chriftendom! Never was Preaching more effectual, never was more Weeping and Repentance, than among the old Women of Stafford's Congregation Every one excited herfelf to the uttermoft, that the Circumftances of their Minifter might be as eafy as poffible, and that fuch a faithful Labourer in the Vineyard of the Church, might not go without his Reward Prefents were fent him continually, he was invited to Dinner every Day by one or another of the Members, and he has frequently fince protefted, that, bateing the Hypocrify which he was obliged to ufe, the Time he was a Teacher was the pleafanteft Part of his Life

But the Captain had fomething farther to do for his Female Hearers, efpecially for the handfomeft of them, than juft to take care of their Souls. This he let fome of them underftand the firft Opportunity he had, after he had perceived himfelf abfolute Mafter of all their Hearts, and even their Fortunes He had all the Succefs he could wifh for, without being in the leaft fufpected of attempting any Thing that could poffibly caft the leaft Blemifh upon his Character Several married Women were delivered of Children, who very much refembled the Parfon, but the good Wives had an excellent Excufe for this, by urging the prodigious Attention with which they always heard Mr Stafford preach, and the deep Impreffion which he always made, both by his Voice and his Perfon, when he was in the Pulpit All this might have paffed very well as long as he had pleafed, had he carried the Jeft no further, but, alas, the Captain was fo voracious, that, though he had a continual Feaft, he could not be contented without fome Joints which no Body tafted but himfelf The Daughter of a leading Man began to grow thick about the Wafte, and her Parents were very inquifitive into the Meaning of it The Girl appeared very ignorant of the Matter, and ftood in it firmly, that fhe never in her Life knew the Difference between the Sexes The old People even began to credit what fhe faid, and to believe their Daughter, for her extraordinary Piety was favour'd by Heaven with a miraculous Conception Stafford, however, would have been the laft Man in the Univerfe that they could have any Sufpicion of, had not a Billet of his been intercepted by the old Man, through the Carelefnefs of a Maid Servant, who managed every Thing between them Who can exprefs the Grief and Surprize of the pious People upon this melancholy Difcovery? Mr Stafford to be fure was fent for, and the Damfel and he brought Face to Face, yet fo well had the young Lady been inftructed, that fhe continued firm in denying any Knowledge of the Affair Stafford had taken Care to fill the Mind of the Girl with Fears of eternal Damnation, if fhe ever difcovered a Secret that would turn to the Difgrace of the Priefthood, and being confident that his Lectures had made Impreffions, reſſions, too deep for any Arguments to eraze them, he did not ſtick to threaten every one that hinted his Suſpicions of his Guilt. The Father and Mother of the Damſel finding her inflexible, they concluded it would be much better to conceal their Daughter's Diſgrace, by providing for her Lying-in in a private Manner, than to expoſe her and themſelves to the Cenſures of an ill-natur'd World, by a too ſcrupulous Enquiry into an Affair of ſuch a tender Nature.

Our Eccleſiaſtical Captain now began to triumph, eſpecially when he underſtood that there was a Child born without any Father but Providence. He had no great Deſire to interfere with this common Parent of the Fatherleſs, in the Educating a Bantling which he had taken already ſo much Pains to throw entirely off his Hands. Abundance of the Members who had intimated Things to his Diſcredit, were now the Objects of Diſpleaſure in the higheſt Degree, and he took Care to employ Partizans, who abuſed almoſt all the honeſt Men, that were not ſatisfied with his Conduct on this Occaſion. The next *Sunday* after the young Gentlewoman was delivered, he had the Impudence to addreſs the following Harangue to the Congregation. *Friends, Brethren, and Siſters, you cannot any of you be ignorant, that a Baſtard Child is lately born in this Village, of the Body of Mrs* Anne B——, *the Daughter of Mr* Thomas B——, *a very worthy Chriſtian, and a Member of this Congregation. It cannot, moreover, be any ſtrange Thing to you, when I tell you, that ſundry cenſorious and evil-diſpoſed Perſons have not ſpared their ſcandalous Reflections and helliſh Machinations againſt me your Paſtor, whom you have never, in the whole Courſe of my Miniſtry, accuſed as guilty of any enormous Error, ſave only ſuch as it is impoſſible for frail human Nature to avoid, until this unhappy Time, when it ſeemeth as though the Prince of the Power of the Air had taken Poſſeſſion of the Hearts and Tongues of the Sons of Men, on Purpoſe to deceive them, and to do Deſpight unto that Holy Religion, which both I and you profeſs, and of which I am a weak and unworthy Teacher. But I return Thanks to Heaven, which has always ſtrengthened me in my Duty, and enabled me to curb the carnal Inclinations of my outward Man, and to keep the Fleſh weak and low, while the Spirit has been full of Conſolation. Tho' it might have been ſufficient to convince any among you of my Innocence in this Affair, that I have hitherto deſpiſed the Calumnies of the Wicked, and though no reaſonable Man or Woman can have any Doubts remaining, after this ſolemn Declaration in the Preſence of God and this Aſſembly, concerning this Thing, yet as the Cauſe of Religion ſeems to be wounded through my Sides, and as I would not for ten thouſand Worlds give the leaſt Offence to any tender Conſcience, I take this Opportunity to notify my Intentions of leaving this Place very ſhortly.*

This very inſolent Speech produced different Effects on the Minds of the different Perſons who heard it. All thoſe who had Penetration enough to ſee through the thin Artifice, which was only to make them engage him more ſtrongly to continue with them, from this Moment began to deſpiſe him, and not a few reſolved never to hear him any more; but moſt of the Women, and a few Men of the weakeſt Intellects, were almoſt driven to Deſpair by the Thought of loſing their Paſtor. They went to him immediately after Sermon, and requeſted him with Tears, as he tender'd the Good of their Souls, not to leave them; and our perfect Counterfeit pretended that it was with great Reluctance, and only as he preferred the Intereſt of Religion to all other Views, that he condeſcended to liſten to their Petition. The Effect of all theſe Diſputes was a dreadful Schiſm,

and *Stafford* continued ſome Time afterwards poſſeſſed of the Meeting-Houſe, which he made Uſe of as uſual, to the Edification of his faithful Adherents; but as the Revenue did not now anſwer his Purpoſe, he at laſt took an Opportunity to leave his little Flock without giving them any Warning, carrying off with him all the Sacramental Plate and Linnen to a pretty large Value.

We ſhall give our Readers a Sketch of Mr *Stafford*'s Opinion in Point of Religion, by preſenting them with a Copy of Verſes which are ſaid to have been written by him while he was in the miniſterial Function.

VERSES. *By Capt* Stafford.

Religion's a Thing very plain,
If Men would make uſe of their Eyes;
'Tis taught in a barbarous Strain,
And there all the Myſtery lies.

This Truth the old Catholicks knew,
So lock'd up its Rules from the Croud;
Amus'd them with Splendor and Shew,
And baul'd for the Church very loud.

At laſt a capricious old Monk,
Who elſe would have never been known,
The Name of his Holineſs ſunk,
And thereby exalted his own.

He us'd his vernacular Speech,
For reverend Hebrew and Greek;
Believe not, ſaid he, what I teach,
But take up your Bibles and ſeek.

The Seekers aroſe from this Hint,
(Each Man was the Head of a Sect)
Oppos'd one another in Print,
And won from their Hearers Reſpect.

New Parties 'twas eaſy to gain,
As eaſy to keep them when got,
By making obſcure what was plain,
And opening that which was not.

Since then 'tis a Trade to impoſe,
And Men will not judge for themſelves,
What Hurt can there be, by the Noſe
To lead a few ignorant Elves?

But 'tis Time to have done with the religious Part of the Captain's Life, and to return to that Part which more immediately gives him a Place in this Book. Indeed, as an Impoſtor and Cheat we might very juſtly mention him, if he had never been guilty of any Attempt upon the Subſtance of another Man in an open avow'd Manner. But this is not ſo directly keeping up to what we propoſe.

The laſt Adventure which we ſhall relate of the Captain, is, that for which he ſuffered. A Farmer of conſiderable Note in *Berkſhire*, had been at *Reading* to ſell his Corn, at a Time when that Commodity was very dear. The Farmer had the Reputation of being a very honeſt good Man, but as the Price of Corn was very advantageous to him, he could not help being a little elated by the Succeſs he had met with at Market. And he was now riding home in a very pleaſant Temper, meditating (as he himſelf confeſſed) on the Riches he was about to get for his Family. The Captain overtook him about four Miles from *Reading*, and accoſted him in a very friendly Manner, with *Pray, Farmer, what is it a Clock?* The Farmer being, as I ſaid before, pretty full of his good Fortune, immediately thought Mr. *Stafford*
had

known him; and ask'd him what Corn was a Load He therefore very readily answer'd, *Sixteen Pound ten the best Wheat* Stafford guessed the honest Countryman's Mistake? but thought at the same Time that their Conversation was likely to turn upon a Subject that would be to his Advantage: *And have you, Farmer*, said he, *sold any Wheat for that Price to Day? Yes*, says the Countryman, *I have sold two Loads, and I thank God I have got the Money for it in my Pocket* This was spoke very innocently, for the Farmer all the while thought himself with somebody that asked him these Questions out of Kindness, but he soon found to the contrary, for the Captain pulled a Pistol out of his Pocket in a very short Time; and clapping it to the Farmer's Breast, he made him refund the whole three and thirty Pounds, which he had just received

The Captain's Good-Fortune this Day began to leave him, for he was scarce got three hundred Yards from the Ground where he committed the Robbery, before two Gentlemen came up to the Farmer, who told them how he had been used The Gentlemen being well mounted rode after *Stafford* with all the Speed they could, and in less than a Quarter of an Hour, overtook and dismounted him The Money was all found upon him, and several of the Pieces were very remarkable; so that he was carried to the next Justice of the Peace, and by him committed to the County Jail, where he lay till the ensuing Assizes, which were not a great while afterwards.

At the Assizes the Farmer, who was a very conscientious Man, refused to appear against the Prisoner, because he was not certain whether or no it was the same Man that had robbed him The Evidence, nevertheless, of the two Gentlemen, and of the Money, which answered exactly to the Account which the Farmer had given of what he had lost, together with the bad Character of the Captain himself in his own Country, where he now was, were thought sufficient to condemn him; and the Sentence passed accordingly, and a Day was fixed for his Execution

While *Stafford* was in Prison, before his Condemnation, he lived in a very grand Manner He had a Wicket made before the Jail Porch to hide his Letters, where he used to sit frequently with one of the Keepers, and converse with Gentlemen of the best Fashion in the whole Town He had, moreover, settled a Correspondence with several of his own Profession, who came to see him in Prison These then undertook to rescue him from the Gallows, and afterwards to constitute him their Head The Report of this Compact, by some Means or other, took Wind, before the Time, and the Post-Boy was ordered what to say, if any Man should ask him any Questions on the Road This Charge to the Post-Boy was thought to be the only Reason why they did not come as they had promised, for two or three Men well mounted, one Day demanded of him when *Stafford* was to be executed, and the Boy told them the usual Day, which was now changed to another purely upon the Account of this Report.

The Captain had a new light-colour'd Suit of Cloaths made to go to the Gallows in (for he did not expect to be hang'd) in which he appeared as tho' he had been going to a Wedding He had a Nose-Gay in his Bosom, and his Countenance was without the least Appearance of Concern all the Way As he past by a Tavern, he order'd the Cart to stop, and called for a Pint of Wine, which he drank all off, and told the Vintner he would pay him when he came back At the Gallows he stood up, and look'd round him very wishfully some Minutes, still desiring more Time. At last when the Sheriff bid him prepare, and he saw no Remedy, his Colour was observed to change; and he trembled very much, but said nothing Just at the Instant that the Cart was ordered to be drawn away, he delivered a Paper to the Sheriff; and then was turned off in a great Deal of Confusion The Contents of the Paper were as follow

It is not merely in Compliance with the common Custom of Malefactors, that I Write any Thing to leave behind me in the World, if there had not seemed a more than Ordinary Necessity for this Declaration from me, upon the Account of my having been so universally talk'd of, I should have been contented to have suffer'd in Silence, what the Justice of the Law has required

I confess not only the Fact for which I Die, but also almost all those that are laid to my Charge by common Fame, besides innumerable others of the same Nature, yet I hope that what I am about to offer, will Plead a little in my Favour, and in some Measures abate the Horror which many sober People are apt to Conceive at the bare Recital of my Crimes

I was brought up in Principles of Honour and Virtue by my Parents, and I continued to Act agreeably to those Principles for many Years, as several worthy Gentlemen now Living can testify I can moreover call upon a greater Witness than any Mortal to attest, that I have always thought in my Soul nothing so mean and so Unworthy of human Nature as Fraud, of what kind soever it might be It has only the Iniquity of the Times, in which it has been my Unhappiness to have lived, that Occasion'd my abandoning in Practice with my Judgment always approved of, Notwithstanding the Pains I have taken to work myself into a Belief that Virtue is nothing but a vain Chimæra

The Cruelty with which all the loyal Party was Prosecuted during the late civil War, gave me a very dispiceable Opinion of those who Executed it This Opinion was afterwards strengthened when I beheld the same People dividing among themselves, and using an equal Severity towards each other, as any one Party got uppermost I soon found that their Religion was but a pretence, and their Appearance of Sanctity, nothing more than Hypocrisy; That Interest was the only Point they pursued, and their hyperbolical Cant concerning another World a mere Engine to draw to themselves larger Possessions in this, which they had the Confidence to affirm they had learn'd intirely to despise These things made me Determine, when my Estate was Quartered, and my Principles prevented my getting an honourable Subsistance, to take openly from some of those Hypocrites what they as unjustly, though more craftily, had taken from better People

What lies most heavily upon my Conscience, is, my having ever condescended to deal with these Men in their own Way, by imposing upon them under a Shew of Piety, May God forgive me in this Particular! I must, however, take the Freedom to say, That I was never able to match several that I have met with, to whom I have not thought myself inferior as to my Genius, in this their darling Vice, *Hypocrisy*, and that when I most succeeded in my Impostures, it was more owing to a Fluency of Words which I always had, than to my Art in counterfeiting their Formality in my common Behaviour

I shall not trouble the World with any more of these Things, which only relate to my Maker, and my own Conscience. Give me Leave to say, that as I have not been a common Offender, I would hope my Remains will be treated with a little more Decency, than the Bodies of the unhappy Wretches who suffer at this Place, commonly are

As I die justly, I have no Occasion to say any
Thing

The Golden FARMER and the TINKER

...hing concerning the Instruments of my Death, who ...ly excuse what the Law demands   If there are a-...other Persons, who are conscious that they have ...ven me just Cause of Offence, let them know that ...forgive them from my very Heart, and that I die ... Peace with all the World, to which I can very ...lmly bid *Farewel.*

In Compliance with Mr. *Stafford's* Request, con-cerning his Body, the Sheriff ordered him to be bu-ried under the Tower of *St Mary's* Church at *Rea-ding* Several Persons of Fashion honour'd his Fu-neral with their Attendance, and the Women in par-ticular were observed to shed Abundance of Tears.

We are inform'd that his Man *Pretty*, who had not Courage enough to engage singly in any Enterprize, took afterwards to Labour and got his Living in a handsome Manner

The LIFE of the GOLDEN FARMER.

THE Golden Farmer was so called from his Occupation, and paying People, if it was any considerable Sum, always in Gold, but his real Name was *William Davis*, born at *Wrexham* in *Denbighshire*, in *North-Wales*, from whence he re-moved, in his younger Years, to *Sudbury* in *Glouceſter-ſhire*, where he married the Daughter of a wealthy Inn-keeper, by whom he had eighteen Children, and followed the Farmer's Business to the Day of his Death, to shroud his robbing on the Highway, which irregular Practice he had followed for forty-two Years, without any Suspicion among his Neighbours

He generally robbed alone, and one Day meeting three or four Stage-Coaches going to *Salisbury*, he stopped one of them who was full of Gentlewomen, one of which was a Quaker All of them satisfied the Golden Farmer's Desire, excepting this *Perciscan*, with whom he had a long Argument to no Purpose; for upon her solemn Vow and Affirmation, she told him, she had no Money, nor any Thing valuable a-bout her, whereupon, fearing he should lose the Booty of the other Coaches, he told her, he would go and see what they had to afford him, and he would wait on her again; so having robbed the other three Coaches, he returned according to his Word, and the Quaker persisting still in her old Tone of having nothing for him, it put the Golden Farmer into a Rage, and taking hold of her Shoulder, shaking her as a Mastiff does a Bull, he cried, *You canting Bitch, if you dally with me at this Rate, you'll certainly provoke my Spirit to be damnable Rude with you You ſee theſe good Women here were ſo tender hearted, as to be charitable to me, and you, you whining Whore, are ſo covetous as to loſe your Life for the Sake of Mammon* —— *Come, come, you hollow-hearted Bitch, unpin your Purſe-Strings quickly, or elſe I ſhall ſend ſend you out of the Land of the Living* Now the poor Quaker being out of her her Wits at the bully-ing Expreſſions of the Wicked One, she gave him a Purse of Guineas, a Gold Watch, and a Diamond-Ring, and parted then as good Friends, as if they had never fallen out at all

Another Time this Desperado meeting with the Dutchess of *Albermarle* in her Coach, as riding over *Salisbury-Plain*, he was put to his Trumps before he could assault her Grace, by reason he had a long En-gagement with a Postillion, Coachman, and two Footmen, before he could proceed in his Robbery, but having wounded them all, by the discharging se-veral Pistoles, he then approached to his Prey, whom he found more Refractory than his Female Quaker had been, which made him very saucy, and more eager for Fear of any Passengers coming by the mean while, but still her Grace denied Parting with any Thing, whereupon by main Violence he pulled three Diamond Rings off her Fingers, and snatched a rich Gold Watch from her Side, crying to her, at the same Time, because he saw her Face painted, *You Bitch incarnate, you had rather read over your Face in the Glaſs every Moment, and blot out Pale to put in Red, than give an honeſt Men, as I am, a ſmall Matter to ſupport him on his lawful Occa-ſions on Road*, and then rode away as fast as he could without Searching her Grace for any Money, be-cause he perceived another Person of Quality's Coach, making towards them, with a good Retinue of Ser-vants belonging to it

Not long after this Exploit, the Golden Farmer meeting with Sir *Thomas Day*, a Justice of Peace liv-ing at *Briſtol*, on the Road betwixt *Gloucester* and *Worceſter*, they fell into Discourse together, and as riding along, he told Sir *Thomas*, whom he knew, though the other did not know him, how he had like to have been robbed but a little before by a Couple of Highwaymen, but as good Luck would have it, his Horse having better Heels than theirs, he got clear of them, or elſe, if they had robbed him of his Money, which was about forty Pounds, they had certainly undone him for ever Truly, quoth Sir *Thomas Day, that had been very hard, but neverthe-leſs, as you had been robbed between Sun and Sun, the County, upon ſuing it, muſt have been obliged to have made your Loſs good again*, But not long after this Chatting together, coming to a convenient Place, the Golden Farmer shooting Sir *Thomas's* Man's Horse under him, and obliging him to retire some Distance from it, that he might not make use of the Pistols that were in his Holsters, he presented a Pis-tol to Sir *Thomas's* Breast, and demanded his Money of him Quoth Sir *Thomas, I thought Sir, that you had been an honeſt Man* The Golden Farmer re-plied, *You ſee your Worſhip's miſtaken, and had you had any Guts in your Brains, you might have per-ceived by my Face, that my Countenance was the very Picture of mere Neceſſity, therefore deliver pre-ſently, for I am in Haſte* Then Sir *Thomas Day*, giving the Golden Farmer what Money he had, which was about Sixty Pounds in Gold and Silver, he humbly thanked his Worship, and told him, *that what he had parted with was not loſt, becauſe he was robbed betwixt Sun and Sun, therefore the Coun-ty*, as he told him, *muſt pay it again*

One Mr. *Hart*, a young Gentleman of *Enfield*, who had a good Estate, but not over-burden'd with Wit;

and.

and therefore, could sooner change a Piece of Gold, then a Piece of Sense, riding one Day over *Finchly-Common*, where the Golden Farmer had been hunting about four or five Hours for a Prey, he rides up to him, and giving the Gentleman a Slap with the Flat of his drawn Hanger o'er his Shoulders. Quoth he, *A Plague on you how slow you are to make a Man wait on you all this Morning Come deliver what you have, and be poxt to you, and go to Hell for Orders* The Gentleman who was wont to find a more agreeable Entertainment betwixt his Mistress and his Snuff-Box, being surprized at the Rustical Sort of Greeting, he began to make several Sort of Excuses, and say, he had no Money about him, but his Antagonist, not believing him, he made bold to search his Pockets himself, and finding in them above an Hundred Guineas, besides a Gold Watch, he give him two or three Slaps over the Shoulder again, with his Hanger, and at the same Time bid him not give his Mind to Lying any more, when an honest Gentleman desired a small Boon of him

Another Time this notorious Robber had paid his Landlord above forty Pounds for Rent, who going Home with it, the goodly Tenant disguising himself, met the old grave Gentleman, and bidding him stand Quoth he, *Come, Mr Gravity from Head to Foot, but from neither Head nor Foot to the Heart, deliver what you have in a Trice* The old Man, fetching a deep Sigh, to the Hazard of losing several Buttons of his Waistcoat, said, that he had not above two Shillings about him, therefore he thought he was more of a Gentleman, than to take a small Matter from a poor Man Quoth the Golden Farmer, *I have not the Faith to believe you, for you seem by your Mien and Habit to be a Man of better Circumstance than you pretend, therefore open your Budget, or else I shall fall foul about your House*——*Dea Sir*, replied his Landlord, *you can't be so barbarous to an old Man What! have you no Religion, Pity, or Compassion in you? Have you no Conscience? nor have you no Respect for your own Body and Soul, which must be certainly in a miserable Condition, if you follow unlawful Courses*——*Damn you* (said the Tenant to 'um) *don't talk of Age and Barbarity to me, for I shew neither Pity nor Compassion to any Damn you, what talk of Conscience to me! I have no more of that dull Commodity than you have, nor do I allow my Soul and Body to be governed by Religion, but Interest, therefore, deliver what you have, before this Pistol makes you repent your Obstinacy*, so delivering his Money to the Golden Farmer, he received it without giving the Landlord any Receipt for it, as his Landlord had him

Not long after committing this Robbery, overtaking an old Grasier at *Putney-Heath*, in a very ordinary Attire, but yet very rich, he takes Half a Score Guineas out of his Pocket, and giving them to the old Man, he said, *There was three or four Persons behind them, who looked very suspicious, therefore he desired the Favour of him to put that Gold into his Pocket, for in Case they were Highwaymen, his indifferent Apparel would make them believe he had no such Charge about him* The old Grasier looking upon his Intentions to be honest, quoth he, *I have fifty Guineas tied up in the fore Lappet of my Shirt, and I'll put it to that for Security*, so riding along both of them Cheek by Jole, for above Half a Mile, and the Coast being clear, the Golden Farmer said to the old Man, *I believe there's no Body will take the Pains of Robbing you or me to Day, therefore, I think I had as good take the Trouble of robbing you myself, so instead of delivering your Purse, pray give me the Lappet of your Shirt* The old Grasier was horridly startled at these Words, and began to beseech him not

to be so cruel in robbing a poor old Man ——*Pr'y, thee*, quoth the Golden Farmer, *don't tell me of Cruelty, for who can be more cruel than Men of your Age, whose Pride it is to teach their Servants their Duties, with as much Cruelty as some People teach their Dogs to fetch and carry?* So being obliged to cut off the Lappit of the old Man's Shirt himself, for he would not, he rode away to seek out another Booty

Another Time, this bold Robber lying at an Inn in *Uxbridge*, he happened into Company with one 'Squire *Broughton*, a Barrister of the *Middle-Temple*, which he understanding, pretended to him, that he was going up to *London*, to advise with a Lawyer about some Business, wherefore, he should be much obliged to him, if he could recommend him to a good one Counsellor *Broughton*, thinking he might be a good Client, he bespoke him for himself Then the Golden Farmer telling his Business was about several of his Neighbour's Cattle, breaking into his Grounds, and doing a great Deal of Mischief, the Barrister told him *That was very actionable, as being Damage Fesant Damage Fesant*, says the Golden Farmer, *what's that, pray Sir?* He told him, *That it was an Action brought against Persons when their Cattle broke through Hedges, or other Fences, into other People's Ground, and did them Damage* Next Morning, as they both were riding towards *London*, says the Golden Farmer to the Barrister, *If I may be so bold as to ask you, Sir, What is that you call Trover and Conversion?* He told him it signified in our Common Law, an Action which a Man has against another, that having found any of his Goods, refuses to deliver them upon Demand, and perhaps converts them to his own Use also The Golden Farmer being now at a Place convenient for his Purpose *Very well, Sir*, says he, *and so, if I should find any Money about you, and convert it to my Use, why then that is only actionable I find* ——*That's a Robbery*, said the Barrister, *which requires no less Satisfaction than a Man's Life* ——*A Robbery!* replied the Golden Farmer, *why then I must e'en commit one for once and not use it, therefore deliver your Money, or else behold this Pistol shall prevent you from ever Reading Cook upon Littleton any more* The Barrister, strangely surpriz'd at his Client's rough Behaviour, asked him, *If he thought there was neither Heaven nor Hell, that he could be guilty of such wicked Actions* Quoth the Golden Farmer, *Why, you Son of a Whore, thy Impudence is very great to talk of Heaven or Hell to me, when you think there's no Way to Heaven, but through Westminster-Hall Come, come, down with your Rino this Minute, for I have other guess Customers to mind, than to wait on your Arse all Day* The Barrister being very loath to part with his Money, he was still insisting on the Injustice of the Action, saying, *It was against Law and Conscience to rob any Man* However the Golden Farmer, heeding not his Pleading, he swore, *He was not to be guided by Law and Conscience any more than any of his Profession, whose Law is always furnished with a Commission to arraign their Consciences, but upon Judgment given, they usually had the Knack of setting it at large* So putting a Pistol to the Barrister's Breast, he quickly delivered his Money, amounting to about thirty Guineas, and eleven Broad Pieces of Gold, besides some Silver, and a Gold Watch

One Time overtaking a Tinker on *Black-Heath*, whom he knew to have seven or eight Pounds about him, quoth he, *Well overtaken, Brother Tinker, Methinks you seem very devout, for your Life is, a continual Pilgrimage, and in Humility you go almost barefoot, thereby making Necessity a Virtue* —— *Ay Master*, replied the Tinker, *needs must, when the Devil drives,*

and

Sawney Beane *at the Entrance of his* CAVE.

and had you no more than I, you might go without Boot and Shoes too ——That might be, quoth the Golden Farmer And I suppose you march all over England with your Bag and Baggage?——Yes; said the Tinker, I go a great Deal of Ground, but not so much as you ride ——Well, quoth the Golden Farmer, go where you will, it is my Opinion, your Conversation is unreproveable, because thou art ever mending ——I wish, replied the Tinker, That I could say as much by you ——Why you Dog of Egypt, quoth the other, you don't think that I am like you, in observing the Statutes; and therefore had rather steal than beg in Spite of Whips or Imprisonment Said the Tinker again, I'll have you to know to I take a great Deal of Pains for a Livelihood ——Yes, replied the Golden Farmer, I know thou art such a strong Enemy to Idleness, that mending one Hole, you make three, rather than want Work ——That s as you say, quoth the Tinker, however, Sir, I wish you and I were farther asunder, for i'faith I don't like your Company ——Nor I yours, said the other; for though thou art entertained in every Place, yet you enter no farther than the Door to avoid Suspicion ——Indeed replied the Tinker, I have a great Suspicion of you ——Have you so, replied the Golden Farmer, why then it shall not be without a Cause Come open your Wallet forthwith, and deliver that Parcel of Money that's in it Here their Dialogue being on a Con-

clusion, the Tinker pray'd heartily, that he would not rob him, for if he did, he must be forced to beg his Way Home, from whence he was above an hundred Miles Damn you, quoth the Golden Farmer, I don't care, if you beg your Way two hundred Miles; for if a Tinker escape Tyburn and Banbury, it is his Fate to die a Beggar So taking Money and Wallet too from the Tinker, he left him to his old Custom of conversing still in open Fields and low Cottages.

After this Encounter with the Tinker, our Adventurer had but a few Pranks to play upon the Stage of human Life, his Name being now spread all around the Country, so that Hue-and-Cries were pretty numerous after him In short, there was no Possibility to make his Escape, every one turning his Enemy now at the last Extremity, when, if Love of Man had in influenced them, they should have befriended him He was apprehended, and carried to Goal, where, during his Confinement, he behaved with the same Alacrity, as he had spent the merry Moment of his foregoing Life; neither the Thought of the Place, nor the Apprehensions of Death in the least terrifying him After three Weeks Imprisonment, he was tried and condemn'd, and the Gallows became the just Punishment of all the Miscarriages and Villanies he had been guilty of during his vicious Scene of Life

The LIFE of SAWNEY BEANE.

THE following Account, though as well attested as any historical Fact can be, is almost incredible, for the monstrous and unparallel'd Barbarities that it relates, there being nothing that we have ever heard of, with the same Degree of Certainty, that may be compar'd with it, or that shews how far a brutal Temper, untam'd by Education and Knowledge of the World, may carry a Man in such glaring and horrible Colours

Sawney Beane was born in the County of *East Lothian*, about eight or nine Miles eastward of the City of *Edinburgh*, some Time in the Reign of Queen *Elizabeth*, whilst King *James* I govern'd only in *Scotland* His Parents work'd at Hedging and Ditching for their Livelihood, and brought up their Son, to the same Occupation He got his daily Bread in his Youth by these Means, but being very much prone to Idleness, and not caring for being confined to any honest Employment, he left his Father and Mother, and run away into the desart Part of the Country, taking with him a Woman as viciously inclin'd as himself These two took up their Habitation in a Rock by the Sea-side, on the Shore of the County of *Galway*, where they lived upwards of 25 Years without going into any City, Town, or Village

In this Time they had a great Number of Children and Grand-Children, whom they brought up after their own Manner, without any Notions of Humanity or Civil Society. They never kept any Company, but among themselves, and supported themselves wholly by robbing; being, moreover, so very

cruel, that they never robb'd any one, whom they did not murder

By this bloody Method, and their living so retiredly from the World, they continued such a long Time undiscovered, there being no body able to guess how the People were lost that went by the Place where they lived As soon as they had robb'd and murder'd any Man, Woman, or Child, they used to carry off the Carcass to the Den, where cutting it into Quarters, they would pickle the mangled Limbs, and afterwards eat it, this being their only Sustenance And, notwithstanding, they were at last so numerous, they commonly had Superfluity of this their abominable Food, so that in the Night-time they frequently threw Legs, and Arms of the unhappy Wretches they had murdered, into the Sea, at a great Distance from their bloody Habitation The Limbs were often cast up by the Tide in several Parts of the Country, to the Astonishment and Terror of all the Beholders, and others who heard of it Persons who have gone about their lawful Occasions fell so often into their Hands, that it caused a general Out-cry in the Country round about, no Man knowing what was become of his Friend, or Relation, if they were once seen by these merciless Cannibals

All the People in the adjacent Parts were at last alarm'd, at such a common Loss of their Neighbours, and Acquaintance, for there was no travelling in Safety near the Den of these Wretches. This occasioned the sending frequent Spies into these Parts, many of whom never return'd again, and those who did, after the strictest Search and Enquiry could not
find

find how thefe melancholy Matters happen'd Several honeft Travellers were taken up on Sufpicion, and wrongfully hang'd upon bare Circumftances, feveral innocent Inn-keepers were executed for no other Reafon than that Perfons who had been thus loft, were known to have lain at their Houfes, which occafion'd a Sufpicion of their being murdered by them, and their Bodies privately buried in obfcure Places, to prevent a Difcovery. Thus an ill-plac'd Juftice was executed with the greateft Severity imaginable, in order to prevent thefe frequent atrocious Deeds, fo that not a few Inn-keepers, who lived on the Weftern Road of *Scotland*, left off their Bufinefs, for fear of being made Examples, and followed other Employments This on the other Hand occafion'd many great Inconveniencies to Travellers, who were now in great Diftrefs for Accommodation for themfelves and their Horfes, when they were difpofed to bait, or put up for Lodging at Night In a Word, the whole Country was almoft depopulated.

Still the King's Subjects were miffing as much as before, fo that it was the Admiration of the whole Kingdom how fuch Villanies could be carried on, and not the Villans to be found out A great many had been executed, and not one of them all made any Confeffion at the Gallows, but ftood to it at the laft, that they were perfectly innocent of the Crimes for which they fuffer'd When the Magiftrates found all was in vain, they left off thefe rigorous Proceedings, and trufted wholly to Providence, for the bringing to Light the Authors of thefe unparallel'd Barbarities, when it fhould feem proper to the Divine Wifdom

Sawney's Family was at laft grown very large, and every Branch of it, as foon as able, affifted in perpetrating their wicked Deeds, which they ftill follow'd with Impunity Sometimes they would attack four, five, or fix Footmen together, but never more than two if they were on Horfe-back They were, moreover fo careful, that not one whom they fet upon fhould efcape, that an Ambufcade was placed on every Side to fecure them, let them fly which Way they would, provided it fhould ever fo happen that one or more got away from the firft Affailants How was it poffible they fhould be detected, when not one that faw them ever faw any Body elfe afterwards ? The Place where they inhabited was quite folitary and lonefome, and when the Tide came up, the Water went for near two hundred Yards into their fubterraneous Habitation, which reached almoft a Mile under Ground, fo that when fome who had been fent arm'd to fearch all the By-Places about, have paft by the Mouth of their Cave; they have never taken any Notice of it, not fuppofing that any Thing human would refide in fuch a Place of perpetual Horror and Darknefs

The Number of the People thefe Savages deftroyed was never exactly known, but it was generally computed that in the twenty-five Years they continued their Butcheries, they had wafhed their Hands in the Blood of a thoufand at leaft, Men, Women, and Children The Manner how they were at laft difcover'd was as follows

A Man and his Wife behind him on the fame Horfe, coming one Evening Home from a Fair, and falling into the Ambufcade of thefe mercilefs Wretches, they fell upon them in a moft furious Manner The Man, to fave himfelf as well as he could, fought very bravely againft them with Sword and Piftol, riding fome of them down, by main Force of his Horfe In the Conflict the poor Woman fell from behind him, and was inftantly murdered before her Hufbands Face, for the Female *Cannibals* cut her Throat, and fell to fucking her Blood with as great a Guft, as if it had been Wine. This done, they ript up her Belly, and

pulled out all her Entrails Such a dreadful Spectacle made the Man make the more obftinate Refiftance, as expected the fame Fate, if he fell into their Hands. It pleafed Providence, while he was engaged, that twenty or thirty from the fame Fair came together in a Body, Upon which, *Sawney Beane* and his Blood-thirfty Clan withdrew, and made the beft of their Way through a thick Wood to their Den

This Man, who was the firft that had ever fell in their Way, and came off alive, told the whole Company what had happened, and fhewed them the horrid Spectacle of his Wife, whom the Murderers had dragg'd to fome Diftance, but had not Time to carry her entirely off They were all ftruck with Stupefaction and Amazement at what he related, took him with them to *Glafgow*, and told the Affair to the Provoft of that City, who immediately fent to the King concerning it

In about three or four Days after, his Majefty himfelf in Perfon, with a Body of about four hundred Men, fet out for the Place where this difmal Tragedy was acted, in order to fearch all the Rocks and Thickets, that, if poffible, they might apprehend this hellifh Cure, which had been fo long pernicious to all the Weftern Parts of the Kingdom

The Man who had been attacked was the Guide, and care was taken to have a large Number of Blood hounds with them, that no human Means might be wanting towards their putting an entire End to thefe Cruelties

No Sign of any Habitation was to be found for a long Time, and even when they came to the Wretches Cave, they took no Notice of it, but were going to purfue their Search along the Sea-Shore, the Tide being then out But fome of the Blood-hounds luckily enter'd this *Cimmerian* Den, and inftantly fet up a moft hideous Barking, Howling, and Yelping, fo that the King, with his Attendants, came back, and looked into it They could not yet tell how to conceive that any Thing human could be concealed in a Place where they faw nothing but Darknefs Neverthelefs, as the Blood-hounds encreafed their Noife, they went farther in, and refufed to come back again, they began to imagine there was fome Reafon more than ordinary, Torches were now immediately fent for, and a great many Men ventur'd in through the moft intricate Turnings and Windings, till at laft they arrived at that private Recefs from all the World, which was the Habitation of thefe Monfters

Now the whole Body, or as many of them as could, went in, and were all fo fhocked at what they beheld, that they were almoft ready to fink into the Earth Legs, Arms, Thighs, Hands, and Feet of Men, Women, and Children, were hung up in Rows, like dried Beef A great many Limbs lay in Pickle, and a great Mafs of Money, both Gold and Silver, with Watches, Rings, Swords, Piftols, and a large Quantity of Cloaths, both Linnen and Woollen, and an infinite Number of other Things, which they had taken from thofe whom they had murder'd, were thrown together in Heaps, or hung up againft the Sides of the Den

Sawney's Family at this Time, befides him, confifted of his Wife, eight Sons, fix Daughters, eighteen Grandfons, and fourteen Grand-Daughters, who were all begotten in Inceft

Thefe were all feiz'd and pinion'd, by his Majefty's Order in the firft Place, then they took what human Flefh they found, and buried it in the Sands, afterwards loading themfelves with the Spoils which they found, they return'd to *Edinburgh* with their Prifoners, all the Country, as they paffed along flocking to fee this curfed Tribe When they were come to their Journey's End, the Wretches were all
committed

committed to the Talbooth, from whence they were the next Day conducted under a ftrong Guard to *Leith*, where they were all executed without any Procefs, it being thought needlefs to try Creatures who were even profeffed Enemies to Mankind

The Men had firft their Privy-Members cut off, and thrown into the Fire before their Faces, then their Hands and Legs were fevered from their Bodies;

by which Amputations they bled to Death in fome Hours The Wife, Daughters, and Grand-Children, having been made Spectators of this juft Punifhment inflicted on the Men, were afterwards burnt to Death in three feveral Fires They all in general died without the leaft Signs of Repentance, but continued curfing and venting the moft dreadful Imprecations to the very laft Gafp of Life

---

The LIFE of Captain DUDLEY.

RICHARD *Dudley*, commonly called Capt *Dudley*, was born in *Leicefterfhire*, at a Place called *Swepfton* His Father was a Gentleman of a good Eftate, but had not the Fortune to keep it, he living in fuch a Manner, that his Expences by much exceeded his Income, fo that he was oblig'd to mortgage and fell the greateft Part to fatisfy his Creditors, and having about threefcore Pounds a Year left, came up to *London*, with his Family, hoping by the Obfcurity of his living, to contain himfelf within the Bounds of the fmall Remainder he had left, but we fhall leave the Father, and give an Account of the Son, who is the unhappy Occafion of our prefent Writing

Richard Dudley, the Son, had a good Education beftow'd upon him at St *Paul's School*, he feeming of a very promifing Genius, but when a vicious Inclination is rivetted in the Nature of any Perfon, no Care of his Education, no Rules of Religion or Morality are fufficient to controul him, as plainly appears by too fragrant an Inftance in the Life of this unfortunate Perfon; for when but nine Years old, he difcover'd his Tendency to Thieving, by robbing one of his Sifters Clofets of thirty Shillings, and marching off with it But being fome Days after found out, and brought Home again, he was fent back to School, but not liking that Sort of Confinement, he robb'd his Father's Houfe of a confiderable Sum of Money, and fo ran away again, yet his Father had the Luck to difcover him, and took him with a Couple of lewd Women, a little Way out of Town

After this, his Father defpairing of his doing any Good at Home, procured him the King's Letter to be a Reformade on Board a Man of War, in which Station, he went up the Streights, and behaved himfelf gallantly in feveral Actions Amongft the reft, this was one, being on Shore at *Cadiz*, in order to refrefh himfelf, and walking quietly along, he was abufed and attack'd by a *Spaniard*, but he not only defended himfelf, but run the Don quite through, left him dead on the Spot, and got fafe on Shipboard Upon his Arrival in *England*, he quitted the Ship, pretending he did fo on Account of a younger Reformade being preferr'd before him, on the Death of a Lieutenant, but whether that was his Motive, or not, this is certain, That he affociated himfelf with a notorious Gang of Thieves, ready for any Mifchief, and affifted them in breaking open and robbing the Houfe of Admiral *Carter* in the Country, and getting off undetected, came to *London*, and from that Time commenced a profeffed Thief The firft remarkable Robbery he was concerned in,

was, that of a Lady's Houfe at *Black-heath*, from whence he and his Accomplices ftole a very confiderable Quantity of Plate, which they brought to Town, and fold to a Refiner, but for this Robbery he was apprehended not long after, and when he was in *Newgate* he fent for the Refiner, and complain'd how hard a Thing it was to find an honeft Man, and a fair Dealer *For you curfed Rogue* (fays he) *among the Plate you bought, there was a Cup with a Cover, which you modeftly told us was but Silver gilt, and bought it at the fame Price with the reft, but it plainly appeared by the Advertifement in the Gazette, that it was a Gold Cup and Cover; but I fee you are a Rogue, and that there's no Trufting any Body* For this Robbery he was tried at *Maidftone*, convicted and condemn'd, but his Youth, and the Intereft of his Friends, firft procur'd him a Reprieve, and then a Pardon, which for about two Years, had fuch an Effect upon him, that he lived pretty foberly for that Time; fo that his Father bought him a Commiffion in the Army, in which Station he behaved very well, and had the good Fortune to marry a young Lady of a good Family, with whom he had an Eftate of feven fcore Pounds a Year, upon which and his Commiffion, they for fome Time lived comfortably, but the Captain loving Company too much, and having contracted a large Acquaintance, engaged himfelf for fome Money, which one of his Companions owed, who was afterwards arrefted for the Debt, in which Arreft a Bailiff was killed, and the Captain (being then prefent) was fufpected to have done it, he always declaring his Deteftation and Abhorrence of that Sort of Men, and often wifhing to kill fome of them, his Character and Opinion of them being as follows

A Serjeant is a Rogue that would undo one of twelve Companies for a Crown, the Counter Gate is his proper Kennel, and the Miferies of poor Men the Offal on which he feeds He does not carry his Captives directly to Hell (the Counter) but firft torments them in a Purgatory hard by, where you muft pay Two Shillings a Night for a lowfy Bed, and fpend as much in liquoring his Chops, as would pay Half the Debt. This he calls his Civility If you feem to fear other Actions coming againft you, he will pretend to pity you, and agrees for a Daub in the Fift to keep the Matter private, till you make an End of it, but goes directly to find out fome other Creditors, bids them ftrike whilft the Iron is hot, and thus when the poor Prifoner has fatisfied the firft Debt, and thinks to regain his Liberty, he is charged a-frefh Thus he picks your Pocket by Degrees, and when he finds that is empty,

10

K

he

he delivers you over to the Turnkey, where the Lord have Mercy on your Soul, for to be sure, they will have little enough on your Body.

A Common Bailiff exceeds a Serjeant as much as an *Irish* Maſtiff does a Spaniel in Fierceneſs. He is a Raven that pecks not out Mens Eyes, as others do, but all his Spite is at their Shoulders. Theſe Land Pirates cruiſe up and down *Holborn*, as thick as *Algier* and *Sallee* Men in the *Mediterranean*, and carry thoſe they take to a worſe Slavery. In the Country they are called Bums, being of the very Scum and Dregs of the People, Raſcalls who have generally eſcaped the Gallows once or twice, and yet muſt at laſt come to it; for a Rope is certainly their Deſtiny. 'Tis deplorable to think how they abuſe poor People, for there is hardly a Writ in five, againſt thoſe they arreſt, they are Setters by Day, Thieves in the Night, Bailiffs all the Week, and Informers on Sundays, and yet never Thrive. For as they live Rogues, they die Beggars.

A Marſhal's Man is yet a more inſufferable Grievance, a falſe Die of the ſame Bale, but not the ſame Cut, for it runs ſomewhat higher, and does more Miſchief. He is a perfect Blood-hound, that haunts upon the ſmalleſt Scent, and worries all to Death he lays hold on. The Circle this Devil is confin'd in, is twelve Miles over, and in that Circuit he commonly undoes above twelve hundred People a Year. He plies among poor People, and upon every petty Quarrel, Scoulding-bout, or Chandler's ſcore, he ſets them to Law; aſſoon as he has arreſted, one perſuades him to ſnap the other, and then they are both forced to be at his Mercy, till they pawn their Beds to raiſe what Money he pleaſes to demand; and that he may fleece them the more commodiouſly, he keeps a Tipling-houſe, where he impriſons them, by his own Authority, and his Wife over-reckons a Groat in a Shilling; and tho' you know it, you muſt not ſpeak, becauſe it is his Kindneſs to keep you there, and not carry you to the Lake of Perdition, on the other ſide the Water. There is nothing more frequent than to ſee here a Chimney-ſweeper proſecuting a Broom-Man for breaking his Head at Cudgels, and an Oyſter-Wench ſuing a Kitchen Stuff-Woman, for calling her Draggle-tail. What a deplorable Thing it is that a Family ſhall be ruin'd, and a poor Man buried alive, for ſuch an inconſiderable Matter!

As for the Yeomen, Followers, and ſetting Vermin, they are ſuch contemptible Raſcals, they are not worth thinking on. We may call them the Hooks that hang under Water, and their Maſter the Floats above, which pop down as ſoon as ever the Bait is ſwallowed. Neceſſity makes them Valiant, for they will greedily take a Cut with a Sword, and ſuck more Silver out of the Wound than a Surgeon, ſo that they commonly die with their Guts ripped up, or elſe the Devil by a ſudden Stale ſends a *Habeas cum anima* for them.

As to the Villains about *White-Chapel*, St *Katherine's*, the *Click*, and the reſt of the Devil's Houſes, I ſhan't trouble myſelf about, but I muſt have a Word or two with the Gaoler, for he is a Creature miſtaken in the making, for he ſhould be a Tyger, but the Shape being thought too terrible it is covered and he wears the Viſage of a Man, yet retains his Fierceneſs; his Conſcience, and his Shackles, he hangs up together, and they are made very near of the ſame Metal, ſaving that one is harder than the other, and hath one Property above Iron, that it never melts; he diſtills Money out of poor Mens Tears, and grows Fat by their Curſes, his Ears are ſtop'd to the Cries of others, and God's to his, by all Likelihood, for lay the Life of a Man in one Scale, and his Fees in the other, he would caſt away the Firſt to

get the Second, and in Brief is one that can look for no Mercy (if he deſires Juſtice to be done him) for he ſhews none.

But to return to the Captain, he abſented himſelf from his Houſe, lurking about in bye-Places; and by that idle way of living, he got acquainted with a Gang of Highwaymen, by whoſe Eaſineſs of living, and extravagant Expences, he was eaſily perſuaded to be one of their Gang, for few Perſuaſions were needful to one who had got the upper Hand of Virtue, who was more inclined to live upon the Ruins of his Countrymen, than by his own Induſtry, having been more uſed to Fight than Work. He was not long about earning his Trade, but in a little Time became Maſter of it; for there was ſcarce a notable Robbery committed, in which he had not a Hand, and finding it eaſy and profitable, he drew in his Brother (whoſe Name was *Will Dudley*) to be one of their Gang, he had not long gone on in his new Trade, before he was apprehended in the Country, for robbing a Gentleman of a Watch, a Sword, a Whip, and nine Shillings in Money; but the Evidence not being very clear, he eſcaped once more.

No ſooner had he obtained his Liberty, but he fell again to his old Trade, but did not confine himſelf to any particular Part, but robbed on the Highway, broke Houſes, or pick'd Pockets, or any Thing elſe that procured him any Money, in which ſeveral Ways he for a Time went on with Impunity, but was at length detected for breaking and robbing Sir *John Friend*'s Houſe, and for that Fact he received Sentence of Death, but his Friends again got him a Reprieve on Condition of Tranſportation, purſuant to which, he with ſeveral other Convicts, were put on board a Ship, in order for *Barbadoes*. But they were hardly got as far as the Iſle of Weight, before he had drawn in the reſt of the Rogues to a Conſpiracy, in order to eſcape, and having concerted their Meaſures, accordingly the Ships Company being under Hatches, they went off with the Long-Boat.

Being now on Shore, he left his Comrades, and travelled by himſelf through Woods and by-Ways, and being now in a very mean Habit, when he had no opportunity to ſteal, he begged, till he came to *Hounſlow-Heath*, where he attacked a Country Farmer, robbed and unhorſed him, and mounting himſelf, ſet forward to ſeek for more Prey, and before he got off the Heath, another Opportunity offered, for he met with a Man in a genteel Habit, and with a better Horſe than that which he took from the Farmer. He ſoon gave him the Word of Command to ſtand, and leading him into a Bye-Place, made him exchange Horſes and Cloaths with him, telling the Man that he ought never to accuſe him with robbing him, for ſays he, *you know the old Proverb, Exchange is no Robbery, ſo wiſhing him well, he made the beſt of his Way for* London, where he immediately reſorted to his old Haunts, to find out his Companions, which was very eaſy for him to do, and they all ſubmitted to his Conduct, and dubbed him with the Title of Captain. Thus got at the Head of a hardened Gang, no Part of the Country was ſecure from his Rapine, nor any Houſe ſtrong enough to keep him out, ſo that he became notorious every where.

To avoid the continual Searches made for him, and to divert Enquires, he paid a Viſit to the North, and being out one Day in ſearch of Booty, he met with a *Dutch* Colonel very well armed, but not couragious enough to fight for his Money, ſo that the Captain made bold with both Horſe and Arms, and took his laced Coat into the Bargain. Thus mounted and equipped, he committed Abundance of Robberies, but ſhifting the Colonels Accoutrements, he uſed only his Horſe upon which he robbed a great many People, particularly a Gentleman near *Epſom*, who

being

being a Man of Courage, would not deliver, but exchanged a Pistol with him. However, the Captain got the Better, and wounded the Gentleman in the Leg, upon which he rode up to him, lent him his Assistance, and conducted him to the next Village, to get some Help, and then left him; having first taken his Money As for the *Buckinghamshire* Lacemen, the Captain and his Gang robbed them for Pastime, and only called it an Airing for their Horses No Stage or other Coach, when they had Intelligence of any Passenger, could escape their Villany, that scarce a Day passed in which they did not commit some Robbery or other

Thus did he and his Confederates riot in the Spoils of others, and remained undiscovered for several Months, till at length robbing the *Southampton* Coach they were pursued, and several of them taken, yet he escaped not taken Warning. At this he joined himself with some House-breakers, and with them committed many Burglaries and Robberies, and in particular, he with three of his Accomplices, got into an old Woman's House, in *Spittle-fields*, they gag'd her, tied her in her Chair; rifled her House, and carried of a considerable Sum of Money, which the old Woman had been many Years hoarding up She hearing the Money chink, and going to be taken from her, struggled in the Chair, and fell down upon her Face, with the Gagg in her Mouth, and the Chair upon her, which means she was stifled; but they got safe off, and passed undiscovered, till the old Woman came to be Buried, when one of them (who was her Grand Child and privy to the Robbery) going to be fitted with Gloves, was observed to change his Countenance often, and Tremble very much, several Persons seeing the Disorder he was in, began to suspect him, and charged him with the Fact, he confessed the whole Affair, and two of them being found guilty on his Evidence, of the Murder and Robbery, were hang'd in Chains Yet the Captain all this while passed unapprehended, though his Name was publickly mentioned as an accessary to the Fact. But being at length taken up for divers Highway Robberies, (of which by his dextrous Management he was Acquitted) he was called to his Trial for that, also when the Evidence swore they saw him lurking about, go into and come out of the House of the murdered Woman; and several strong Circumstances appeared to prove him guilty; but he upon whole Evidence the two former were convicted, was not to be found; and this gave *Dudley* an Opportunity to make such a sham Defence, as would have deceived the most penetrating Judge and Jury on Earth He himself thought it so great a Master-piece, that he often boasted of it in Prison, and from his Account I shall acquaint the Reader with it

The first Witness that appeared in his behalf, was a young Gentleman, who deposed that he and another Gentleman, going through *Somerset-House* Yard on the Day set forth in the Indictment, to be that on which the Robbery and Murder was committed; he accidently met the Captain, who had been his Schoolfellow, and was surprized to see him, having heard that had been Transported for some Crime, which he was very sorry for That the Captain told him he was indeed ordered for Transportation, and expressed a very great Concern, that he should ever be guilty of a Crime to deserve such Punishment, but that his Relations being not so kind as he expected, he was put on board a Ship, with some more unfortunate Persons, as a common Convict, and made his Escape, and depended on his Friends good-Will, to put him in a Condition to Transport himself, resolving so to do the very first Opportunity The same Witness further deposed, that finding

him so very sorry for his Offence, he desired him to accompany him and his Friend to *Chelsea*, intending to make use of that Time, in exhorting him to lead his Life more regular for the Future That the Prisoner accepting the Offer, they took Boat at *Somerset* Stairs, and went to the Swan at *Chelsea*, where they staid till Seven at Night, and then walk'd to a publick House on the Bank-side, supped on a Dish of Fowls and Bacon, and stayed there till almost Eleven, when they took Boat again for *Somerset* Stairs, walked into the *Strand*, and there parted. The Witness being asked why he should take such particular Notice of the Day of the Month, answered, *That the next Day he heard a Paper cried about the Streets, concerning the Murder and Robbery of the old Woman, that buying it, he found the Captain's Name mentioned as an accessary in the Fact, and upon that made a Memorandum in his Pocket-Book, (which he produced in Court) and afterwards went to his Friend, who was with him at* Chelsea, *and to the Waterman who carried them, desiring them likewise to take Notice of the Day, for that* Dudley *being a Person of but an indifferent Character, some other Rogue might make use of his Name, and he be hanged for a Fact he was innocent of*

The next Witness, was the other Friend, who said, *that he saw him, and the Prisoner talk together in* Somerset-House *Yard, but did not know what they said; that they went to* Chelsea, *and there the former Witness was very earnest with the Captain (who then understood his Name to be, having never seen him before) to reform some ill Practices he had been too much addicted to, that the next Day the former Witness came and desired him to take particular Notice of the Day and Person who went with them to* Chelsea, *which he accordingly did, and was very positive that the Prisoner at the Bar, was the Man that they supped with at the Red-Lyon, at the Bank-side, that they afterwards came back to* Somerset-House *Stairs, and in the Strand parted with the Prisoner about eleven at Night*

The Waterman corroborated their Evidence, and affirmed, that he carried two Gentlemen aforesaid to *Chelsea*, and a third Person with them, and being asked if the Prisoner was that third Person, he said his Eyes were very bad, and went up close to the Bar to look him in the Face, and turning about said, *Yes, my Lord, this is the Gentleman* He also deposed that he waited on them at *Chelsea*, and carried them from thence to the Bank-side; where he received four Shillings and Sixpence for his Fare, upon Condition he would carry them back again, which he did, and landed them about eleven at Night. That the next Day his Master (the first Witness) came and bid him take Notice of the Day of the Month, which he did, and chalked it down at Home

The next who was called, was the pretended Landland, of the House, were they supped, *who swore that on such a Day of the Month, three Gentlemen came to his House about seven at Night, (of which the Prisoner was one) and ordered a couple of Fowls and Bacon to be got ready with all Speed, which was done; they supped, and between ten and eleven at Night, they took Boat, and ordered the Waterman to carry them to* Somerset *Stairs Being asked how he came to take such Notice of the Day, he readily answered, When these Gentlemen came on shore, I was starting of Beer, and they ordered me to give the Waterman four Shillings and Sixpence, I paid him, and told him he must stay till the Gentlemen went, and my Lord, I find by my Book now in my Hand, that it was on that Day my Beer was started*

The last Witness who appeared, was a Man who lived in *Burleigh street* in the *Strand, who said, the Captain was his Lodger, and came home at eleven of the*

the Clock on the Night before mentioned; that he knew it to be the same Night, because Dudley not being very well, did not stir out of Doors the next Day, and paid him his Rent for his Lodging, for which he gave him a Receipt, by the Date of which he knew the Time, and the Prisoner producing a Receipt, the Fellow swore it to be the same Such a set of profligate Witnesses as these, were enough to screen an Offender from Justice for a Time, and they had such an Influence over both Judge and Jury, so much, that the Captain was easily acquitted

His Liberty regain'd, he hastened to his old Companions, with whom he committed many notorious Robberies, especially one on a Nobleman, on *Hounslow-Heath*, from whom they took fifteen hundred Pounds. After a desperate skirmish with the Servants, three of whom they wounded, and killed two of their Horses; from thence they proceeded on the West Country Road, and near *Hartley-row* in *Hampshire*, robbed a Parson, whom they commanded to preach a Sermon in praise of Thieving, swearing his Destruction, if he refused to do it

The Parson was forced to comply However, to make him some amends, the Sermon being ended, they gave him his Money again that they took from him, and four Shillings to drink, for his Sermon

After they had this their Diversion, for we cannot call it a Robbery, they made the best of their Way for *London*, and for some Time left infesting the Highways During which Time the Captain's Brother, employ'd himself in shewing his Dexterity about Town, some of which we believe will prove Diverting to the Reader The first of his Tricks, was, he dressed himself like a Countryman, with a pair of dirty Boots, and a Whip in his Hand, and going into Bartholomew-Fair, met with no Prize worth speaking of But as he was going out, he met with a Countryman, and said to him, *honest Friend have a Care of your Pockets, you are going into a cursed Place, where are none but Whores, Rogues, and Pick-pockets, I am almost ruined by them, and I am glad they have not picked the Teeth out of my Head, let one take ever so much Care of one's Pockets, they'll be sure of your Money, I am sure the Devil helps them* I defie all the Devils in Hell, says the Countryman, to rob me of any Thing I Value, I have a Broad-piece that I'll secure, so clapping it into his Mouth, he went confidently into the Fair, *Will* desired no more than to know if he had any Money, and where it lay, he gives a Sign to a hopeful Boy of his, and telling him out some Six-pences and Groats, told him what he should do, the Boy immediately runs, and falls down just before the Countryman, and scattering the Money, starts up and roars like a Bedlamite, crying he was undone, he must run away from his Apprenticeship, his Master was a furious Fellow, he would certainly kill him The Countryman with other People gather'd about, helping the Boy to take up the Money, says one of them *have you found all?* Yes, all the Silver says the Boy, but what does that signifie, there is a Broad-piece of Gold, that I was carrying to my Master for a Token, sent from the Country, and I like a Fool must come thro' this unlucky Place to lose it, I shall be killed, what will become of me *Will* coming up, tells some of the by-standers who were pitying the Boy, he observed that Country Fellow there to stoop, and put something into his Mouth Whereupon, they flew upon him, and one of them wresting open his Chaps, made him spit out the Gold, and some Blood along with it, endeavouring to speak for himself, they kick'd him, punch'd him, and tossed him about, and some calling to Privy or Pump, he was glad to call for Mercy, and thought himself well off when he got out of their Clutches. The

Boy in the mean Time slipt into the Crowd, and went to *Will* with the Gold, to the appointed Place of Rendezvous

Will and his Boy changing Cloaths, and going into the Crowd heard some talking of the Country Fellow, how he had got into a House, and had sent for some responsible People that knew him, and his Master, a Knight of a vast Estate in the North, who was come to Town upon great Business with some Merchant *Will* knew the Gentleman and his Estate very well, and by what he heard expecting to see him at the Exchange, went immediately thither, and picked his Pocket of a great many Guineas, except one, which he left for the Gentleman's Dinner, or other Charges, till he should receive a Recruit The Knight going to the Tavern laugh'd heartily when his Tenant came and told him how he had been serv'd at the Fair But calling for the Reckoning, and telling the Company he was robbed too, 'twas comical to see how the Countryman laughed 'Sbud, Sir, says he, *let us make our Escape from this Roguish Place*, 'Slidking, Sir, they'll steal our small Guts to make Fiddle-Strings of them

The Gentleman lined his Pockets again, and went out the next Day to the Change, and notwithstanding all the Care he took, he was robbed again, but *Will* being not an ordinary Rogue and having something of a generous Principle, would not take all, but left him some The Knight admired how it was possible for the Wit of Man to rob one that had been so forwarned as he was, at last looking hastily about, he perceived *Will* standing by him, and recollecting he had seen him near him several Times before, he had a strong Suspicion he was the Man, and coming up to him, took hold of his Buttons, and told him, he had good Ground to think he was the Man that had robbed him several Times, but being a Gentleman of a great Estate, his Loss did not trouble him; and if he would be so generous, as to tell him by what means he had so serv'd him, he would not only forgive him, but treat him well at the Tavern, and help him to a better Way of living, if he pleased; *and this, says he, I promise upon my Honour.* Sir, says *Will*, your Word of Honour is sufficient I know the Greatness of your Estate I am the Man I'll wait on your Worship to the Tavern, and there shew you some of my Art, more freely than I would do to my Fellow Rogues As they went towards the Tavern, the Gentleman told him, he resolved to make a Frolick of it, and, to that End, he would send for some Gentlemen of his Acquaintance, and would take Care he should come to no Harm by any Discovery he should make to them I know you're a Gentleman, says *Will*, and Men of Honour scorn too keep base Company. Call as many as you please I'll take their Word, and I know I am safe

When the Gentry came, *Will* told them many Things to their Admiration and Satisfaction, and when he pulled out the Piece of Gold, and told them how he had served *Roger*, the Gentleman's Tenant, *Roger* was immediately sent for to make up the Frolick When he came, it 'twas good Sport to see how he scraped to the Ground His Master smiling asked of whom he learn'd to make such a handsome Leg But what would you say, says the Knight, if you saw your Gold again —— Oh! says he, *I would I could, but if my Mouth can't keep it, where should I put it?* 'Sbud I'd rather see the Rogue, I'd make a Jelly of his Bones —There he is, says the Knight, and there's your Broad-piece, — As *Roger* began to heave and bulk, his Master commanded him to take his Gold, and sit down by him *Roger* seeing which Way Things went, drank to *Will* One of the Gentlemen pulling out a curious Watch, another said, he wondered how it was possible for them to pick a Watch out of a Fob, and

and that it was certainly Carelesness. *No* says *Will*, *If the Gentleman will take a Turn or two in* Moorfields, *I'll wager a Guinea, I'll have the Watch before he returns, let him take what care he pleases, and I shan't stir out of his Room* ——*Done*, says the Gentleman However, every Gentleman in the Room laying down a Guinea, *Roger* laid down his Broad-piece, and went his Half The Gentleman went out with his Watch, and, as he walk'd was very careful not to suffer Man, Woman, or Child, to come within Arm's Length of him; thinking the Devil was in't, if any Body could rob him at a Distance, When it was almost Time he should return, a Boy came softly behind him; and when he came pretty near, he ran past him, yet not so near as to give the Gentleman Suspicion. As he pass'd him, he looks over his Shoulder, and tells the Gentleman his Back was cover'd with Lice, which he perceiving, loath'd the Sight, fretting, and wondering where he had been that Day *Good Boy*, says he, *take them off, and I'll give you a Shilling* The Boy does so, and picking the Lice off his Back, and the Watch out of his Fob, he received his Reward, and run. The Gentleman returns to the Tavern, wondering all the Way how he could have come by such Vermin, yet carefully avoiding any that came near him all the Way.

When he return'd, *Will* ask'd him what a-Clock it was by his Watch? Which thinking to pull out, he was amaz'd to find it gone *Will* pulls it out, and ask'd the Gentleman, if that was it? The Gentleman stood as dumb as a Fish, turning up the Whites of his Eyes. *Roger* laugh'd so loud and outragiously, that after the Gentleman had born him Company a good while, the Knight was forced to command him Silence, for he would have laughed all Night The Gentleman, full of Amazement, said, certainly he must have had the Assistance of the Devil *Of a Boy*, says *Will*. *Did not a Boy pick you clean?* ——*There's the Devil*, says the Gentleman, *and he threw them on too, I suppose? Ay, thro' a Quill*, says the other

The whole Company was mightily pleased with the Ingenuity of the Trick, especially *Roger*, who could not forget how the Gentleman looked, when he came in, and missed his Watch, and was now and then bursting out into a Laughter Says *Will*, *Pshaw, Gentlemen, this Trick is not worth the talking of, it is such a Thing as we send our Boys about There's a Nobleman goes now by the Window, with a very rich Coat on, I'll wager, as before, I'll steal it off his Back before all his Followers, and bring it hither on my own* The Gentlemen stak'd each their Guinea, and *Will* and *Roger* cover'd 'em Now, says *Will*, I'm to shew you a Master-Piece of my Art I must not send a Boy about it, but crave Leave to go myself; neither can I set a Time for my Return, but I hope to do it sooner than you imagine So out he runs, and dogging the Nobleman from Street to Street, at last follow'd him into a Tavern The Nobleman was conducted up Stairs. *Will* goes to the Bar-keeper, and desires her to lend him an Apron, *for the Nobleman, my Master, wherever he comes, will be served by none but myself He is a very good Customer, and expects the best of Wine I must go down into the Cellar, and taste it for him* Whereupon they let him have the Apron, and he went into the Cellar, and soon found out the best of every sort He ran so nimbly up and down Stairs, and was quick at his Work, none of the Servants kept Pace with him The Company looked upon him to be a Servant of the House, and were mightily pleased with his Quickness and Diligence, and the Goodness of the Wine, and every Thing he brought them. *Will* promised him that should have attended the Room, large Vails, and he was very well sa-

tisfy'd to receive Money for doing nothing. *Will* never came in the Room, but he passed some merry Jest, which pleased them wonderfully, and when they spoke to him, his Answers were so smart, that when he went for more Wine, they said one to another, *This is a merry witty Fellow, such a one as he is fit to make a House, he deserves double Wages* When *Will* had sufficiently amused the Company, and saw his Project ripe for Execution, he was resolved to trifle no longer Wherefore, when he returned into the Room with some Wine, and as he passed by my Lord, he laid Hold on the Opportunity, and with his Incision Knife, which he used in Pocket-Picking, he nicely, and with admirable Dexterity, made a Slit in the Seam of my Lord's Coat, and runs down Stairs for more Liquor When he returned with a Bottle in one Hand, and the other full of Glasses, before he came near my Lord, *Will* starts, saying, *What Cobling Fellows are they that made this Coat? Could they not sew a Coat to hold one Day? This Cabbagemonger deserved the Pillory before for filching, but now grudging to allow another Stitch, has committed a Scandalum Magnatum, and caused my Lord to go in a rent Coat the first Day of wearing perhaps* Some of the Company rising, and seeing the great Slash, told my Lord, the Taylor had affronted him Says my Lord, *I gave the Fellows sufficient Vails, and both they and their Master shall hear it* —— *My Lord*, says *Will*, *'tis only the End of a Thread has slipt Such Things will happen sometimes; the Coat may be faithfully sewed in other Places; it's not a Farthing the worse There's a Curious Fine-Drawer of my Acquaintance lives in the next Lane, be pleas'd to let me carry it to him, he will make it as good as at first I'll carry it secretly under my Master's Cloak, and return with it before you want more Wine* The Nobleman borrows a great Coat of one of the Company, and lets him have the Coat *Will* comes down to the Vintner, tells him what had happened to his Lord's Coat; and, to prevent its being seen in the Street, desires him to let him have a Cloak, and he would return immediately. The Vintner shewed him where the Cloak was, which *Will* put on, and claps the Vintner's Beaver on his Head, which hung on the next Pin Thus he troops off with them, and coming to the Tavern, where the Gentlemen were, he went into a Room, and having put on the Nobleman's Coat, the Cloak, and Beaver, he came into the Room where they sat, saluting them very civily. Says one of them, *What, instead of a Coat, you come with a Cloak, and great need for it, for*, says he, *there's a Deal of Knavery under it* So opening the Cloak, they were all amazed to see the rich embroider'd Coat, besides the Cloak and Beaver, which he told them how he had got into the Bargain, but when he told them how he had performed the Exploit, they all laugh'd heartily, and *Roger* with his Base made up the Consort

My Lord and his Company waited so long, that they were quite out of Patience, the People of the House likewise wondring they sat so long without calling, ordered the Fellow that should have waited on that Room, to go up Stairs and force a Trade. The Fellow comes in, and says, *Call here, call here, Gentlemen? Yes*, says one of them, *where is your Fellow-Servant that waited on us? My Fellow-Servant*, says the other, *He said, he was my Lord's Servant, and that my Lord would be attended by none but himself, and I should have good Vails notwithstanding* Says my Lord *how can that be, I have but one Gentleman here of my own Retinue, the Rest are with my Lady, he that served us, came in with an Apron, and is a Servant of the House, call up our Landlord* The Vintner coming up, a Gentleman of the Company asked him if he kept Sharpers in

the

II L

the House to affront Gentlemen, and rob them. *Nay*, says the Vintner, who was a very passionate Man, *Do you bring Sharpers along with you to affront me, and rob my House? I'm sure I have lost a fine new Cloak, and Beaver, and for ought I know, though you look like Gentlemen, you may be Sharpers yourselves, and of you I expect to be paid for my Losses and Reckoning to Boot* Immediately one of them drew upon him, but the Vintner ran down Stairs, and called all the House together, bidding them get what they could, and not to suffer one to come down Stairs, and snatching his Sword in a Fury, ran up Stairs, again, the Servants arming themselves with Spits, Fire-Forks, and such Weapons, as they could find, followed him The Uproar was very great and my Lord coming out first, to force his Way down, made a Pass at the Landland, but was put by with a Fire-Shovel, which was in one of the Drawer's Hands, narrowly escaping being thrust in the Guts with a long Spit, which *Margery*, the Cook Wench, pushed at him, so that my Lord seeing the Door so well guarded with stout Fellows and sturdy Wenches, retired into the Room, and told his Company, he had almost died by the Hands of a Wench with a Spit her Hand They seeing it neither safe nor honourable to sally out, shut the Door, and standing on the Defensive Part, began to consult what to do

Mean while, the Gentlemen foreseeing a Quarrel betwixt my Lord and the Vintner, immediately dispatched their own Landlord to tell them, they had caught the Rogue that had abused them, and had him in safe Custody, praying my Lord to know, if they should wait on him

The Landlord runs in Haste, and coming to the House, found it in an Uproar The Servants knowing him, let him go up Stairs, where he no sooner came, but he told his Brother Vintner, That they were all in Mistake, that the Rogue was catched, and in his House, whereupon, calling my Lord, informed him of the whole Business Immediately a Cessation of Arms was proclaim'd, the Swords sheath'd, the Spits, Fire-Forks, and Fire-Shovels disbanded, and an End happily made of a terrible War The Nobleman and his Company drinking Friends with the Vintner, promised to be a Friend to his House for the future, but resolved to go along with their Peace-maker to the Tavern where *Will* was to mend the Frolick The Vintner being well pleased with the Conceit, went along with them When they were come to the Place, after passing the usual Compliments, they sat down, and *Will* deliver'd the Coat, Cloak, and Beaver As for what he told them, and the other Tricks he then shewed them not having Room here to relate, we must now beg Leave to pass on to his Brother, the Captain

The Captain had committed so many and great Robberies, with his Companions and his Brother *Will*, (for the small Tricks he above committed were only his Pastime, when absent from the Road) that a Proclamation was issued out against them, with a Reward for the taking them, dead or alive, which made People more inquisitive after them, and not long after Captain *Dudley*, and some others were apprehended

The Manner of their being seiz'd was as follows The Captain, with five others, having committed a Robbery, and being closely pursued by the Country, were forced to ride hard for their Safety, and having got to *Westminster-Ferry*, they endeavour'd to pass, but the Wherrymen declared they would not go any more that Night, upon which two rid away, and the other four gave their Horses to a Waterman to lead to an Inn, which was not far off, being all of a Foam with their hard riding, which made the Waterman mistrust they were Highwaymen,

and had been pursued, that Day two of them, after their Horses were set up, took Oars to *Lambeth* The Waterman imparted his Suspicion to several People, the Constable got News of it, and he made it his Business to find them out Getting a good Guard, he went to the Inn, and enquired what Kind of Persons they were, secured the Horses, and made Search after the Men.

Being in the Yard, he observ'd a Person to walk up and down, as if he was sent for a Spy; he demanded what he wanted? The other ask'd him, if such a one lived there? He told him *No*, then he enquired for another Name, which was the Name of the Man of the House The Constable told him, he would go to the House with him, which he did; and knocking at the Door, inquired for a Person, whom the Maid denied, and suddenly shut the Door upon him, which gave the Constable a greater Mistrust, upon which he asked the Man, who he wanted? and told him, he suspected him to be one of those who had committed the Robbery that Day, or that he belong'd to some of them (the Constable being all this while at a Distance from his Guard, and without his Staff) and drawing the Fellow nearer to his Assistants, he boldly seiz'd him, and threatened to carry him before a Magistrate The Fellow being amazed at this unexpected Surprize, presently confessed he was sent by those who had made their Escapes, to see what became of their Horses, and whether any Enquiry or Pursuit was after them, and told the Constable two of them were in the House he knocked at, and the other two at an Inn in *Lambeth* Upon this the Constable takes his Guard with him, goes to the House, and knocks at the Door, which was not open'd, till he threaten'd to break it open He was no sooner enter'd, but he discovered *Dudley* going down a Pair of Stairs into the Cellar He followed him, but not so fast, but *Dudley* had Time to get into a further Cellar, and bolt himself in, but it was soon forced open, where they found *Dudley* with his Sword in one Hand, and a Pistol in the other, threatening the Death of the first Man that touch'd him, but seeing so many Men arm'd, and finding it in vain to resist, he surrender'd his Arms up, and was taken Prisoner. The Constable left a good Guard over him for his Security, and went to *Lambeth*, and took the other two, who in the Morning being carried before a Justice was by him committed to *Newgate*

At the next Sessions, Captain *Dudley* had his Trial, and was found Guilty on no less than five Indictments for the Highway, and received Sentence to be hang'd accordingly, with his Brother, and two of his Accomplices

After he had received Sentence, and was brought back to *Newgate*, he began to have a Sense of his near approaching End, and demean'd himself very well at Chapel He confessed he was a great Offender, that he justly deserved Death, but yet was very unfit to die, which troubled him much, for he desired longer Time to make his Peace with God An Acquaintance, who came to visit him, asked him if the Nearness of his Death (he being in perfect Health, and to die the next Day) did not startle him? He reply'd, *Yes, I have now but twenty four Hours to live*, and shaking his Head, desired of the Lord to forgive him, and to those who were with him, he said, *Pray for me* A Gentleman who came to see him, gave him some Tobacco, and would have given him more, which he refused, telling him, *He thanked him for what he had got already, that being sufficient for him, during the short Space he had to live*

He did not seem to be much cast down, but endeavour'd to appear as chearful as possible He confessed he had robbed many Men, but never committed any Murder, and when strongly charged with
killing

killing the Serjeant as above, he utterly denied it to the laſt, but own'd he promoted the doing of it. He was carried from *Newgate* with ſix Priſoners more. His Brother was very ſick, and lay all along in the Cart; but the Captain look'd pretty chearful all the Way. Being come to the Place of Execution he confeſſed he had been a notorious Offender, and that he juſtly deſerved Death, deſiring the Prayers of all good Chriſtians; and after the uſual Duties performed by the Ordinary, they were all turned off together. After hanging the uſual Time, they were cut down, and his Body, with his Brother's, put into ſeperate Coffins, to be carried to a diſconſolate Father, who at the Sight of them, was ſo much overwhelm'd with Grief, that he fell down upon the Dead Bodies, and never ſpoke more, but was buried at the ſame Time, and in the ſame Grave, with his two unfortunate Sons. It muſt needs be a ſad, ſhocking, and moſt affecting Spectacle to ſee ſo many Perſons going to an ignominious Death by the Impiety of their Lives; to behold ſuch a Sight, one would think, might awaken all who ſaw it, to fly from ſuch wicked Practices to leave off their vitious Company, and debauched Converſation, and ſeriouſly imploring Mercy and Forgiveneſs for paſt Iniquities, ſtrenuouſly endeavour to redeem their Time for the future.

The LIFE of OLD MOB.

THERE is a Beauty in all the Works of Nature, which we are unable to define, tho' all the World is convinced of its Exiſtence · So in every Action and Station of Life, there is a Grace to be attain'd which will make a Man pleaſing to all about him, and ſerene in his own Mind. This alſo as well as the former, every one will own, and at the ſame Time fancy he can reach, though almoſt all Mankind find themſelves miſtaken.

As every Virtue has its Foil, or a Sort of counterfeit Vice, which very nearly reſembles it, ſo near as often to impoſe upon the very Poſſeſſor, in like Manner the Beauty, Grace, or Decorum, which we have mentioned, often occaſions that we purſue a wrong Scent. We are convinced that there really is ſuch a Thing, and while we are inquiring what it is, our own favourite Paſſions preſent us with ſomething which we miſtake for it, and which we ever after make the Object of our Purſuit.

Thus a Man of a healthy, robuſt Conſtitution, who has at the ſame Time an impetuous and violent Temper, ſuch a one thinks of nothing ſo much as of being eſteem'd the braveſt Man of his Neighbourhood, and is never ſo well pleaſed as when he ſees others agree to his Opinion, for fear of incurring his Diſpleaſure. Manly Exerciſes are his whole Delight, and he can ſcarce bear to hear the Name of a Man given to one of leſs Strength and Fire than himſelf. Others on the contrary, delight only in the Exerciſes of Reaſon, and Amuſements of the Mind · Theſe frequently look upon the former, as a Sort of Creatures in human Shape, who differ from the irrational World in nothing but Figure and Speech. Theſe are the two Extremes of Mankind, and make, perhaps, the moſt diſcernable Difference, but there is a like Contraſt ſubſiſting throughout the whole Species.

Not to carry the Reader too far into this abſtracted Manner of Reaſoning, it will be obvious to every one who compares theſe Reflections with the Character of ſome Villains of the firſt Magnitude, that theſe unhappy Wretches, from a wrong Turn of thought, have even placed the Beauty we have been ſpeaking of, in Vice itſelf, and conceive a Sort of Excellence in being more vile and profligate than other Men, otherwiſe it is hardly probable, that they could commit ſo many Irregularities with a ſtrong Guſt, and an Appearance of Satisfaction.

What we are ſtill more to wonder at, is, that other People ſhould delight to hear the Actions of theſe Men rehearſed, and be even pleaſed with a Highwayman, who robs like a Gentleman. It ſeems as if it was, in Reality, ſomething great to excel upon any Account whatſoever. But let us conſider whether ſuch a Pleaſure as this be conſiſtent with a virtuous Inclination. Lives of wicked Men are doubtleſs both lawful and uſeful, for the ſame End as Sea-Marks, and no other; that we may avoid the Road in which they periſhed. Ought not therefore the greateſt Villain to raiſe in us the greateſt Abhorrence?

After theſe general Thoughts, we ſhall give the Reader a Sketch of the Life and Adventures of *Thomas Sympſon*, commonly called *Old-Mob*, who was perhaps, as notorious a Robber as almoſt any one of the laſt Age, for the Space of five and forty Years together, during which Time it was reported he never acted in any Company, except now and then a little with the *Golden Farmer*.

This Man was born at *Ramſey* in *Hampſhire* which continued to be the Place of his Habitation, when he reſided any where under his right Name, till the Day of his apprehending; and he had a Wife and five Children, beſides Grand-Children, living there at the Time of his Shameful Death.

We have no particular Account of his Education and private Life, from whence we may conclude, there was nothing remarkable in either. His Adventures on the Road we ſhall relate in the Order which we have received them, which is the only Method we can follow.

Riding one Time between *Honiton* and *Exeter*, he met with Sir *Bartholomew Shower*, whom he immediately called to an Account for the Money he had about him. Sir *Bartholomew* gave him all he had without any Words, which proved to be but a very little. *Old Mob* looked upon his Prize, and finding it infinitely ſhort of his Expectations, he readily told him, That there was not enough to anſwer his preſent Demands, which were very large, and very preſſing; *And therefore, Sir,* ſays he, *as you are my Banker, in general, you muſt inſtantly draw a Bill upon ſomebody at Exeter for one hundred and fifty Pounds, and remain in the next Field as Security for the Payment, till I have received*

received it The Knight would fain have made some Evasion, and protested that there was Body in *Exeter* who would Pay such a Sum at a Moment's Warning, but *Old Mobb* so terrified him with holding a Pistol to his Breast, that his Worship at last consented, and drew upon a rich Goldsmith.

As soon as *Old Mobb* had got the Note, he made Sir *Bartholomew* dismount, and walk far enough from the Road to be out of every Bodies hearing, then bound him Hand and Foot, and left him under a Hedge, while he rode to *Exeter*, and receiv'd the Money, which was paid without any Scruple, the Goldsmith knowing the Hand-Writing perfectly well. When he return'd, he found the poor Knight where he left him. *Sir*, says he, *I am come with a Habeas Corpus to remove you out of your present Captivity*, which he accordingly did by untying him, and sending him about his Business: But Sir *Bartholomew* was obliged to walk Home which was full three Miles, for our Adventurer had cut the Girths and Bridle of his Horse, and turn'd him astray, ever since he went to *Exeter* with the Note.

Old Mobb had one Time some high Words with a Woman in his Neighbourhood, when among other hard Names he called her a Whore. Every one knows what a tender Thing the Honour of a Woman is, and how ready poor *English* Husbands are to vindicate their Wives Virtue. Whether or no the Saddle fitted at this Time, or whatever else was the Occasion, we can't say, but a Prosecution in the Spiritual Court was set a Foot against *Old Mobb*, and the good Man was so zealous in Defence of his beloved Rib, that he put our Highwayman to a pretty Deal of Expence, for a spiritual Process generally hurts the temporal Estate, as much at least as a Suit at Common Law. To the Honour of our spiritual Courts be it spoken.

Soon after this Trouble was over, *Old Mobb* met the Proctor, who had managed against him, and drawn not a little Money out of his Pocket. He quickly knew his dear ghostly Friend, but being very much disguis'd, was not at all apprehensive of being known, which pleased him extremely. *Sir*, quoth he, *stand and deliver this Moment, or I shall have no more Mercy on you than the Devil, or, if you please, you yourself would have on an excommunicated Person.* The Proctor made some Resistance, but was soon obliged to surrender, and pull out a fine embroider'd Purse, with fifteen Guineas in it. He was a-going to take out the Guineas, and deliver them, but *Old Mobb* liking the Purse, assured him, he must have that also. The Proctor told him, it was given him by a particular Friend, and that he had promised to keep it as long as he lived, for which Reason he begged of him to leave that, *Suppose now*, says *Old Mobb*, *that you had a Process against me, and were come to me for your Fees, if I had no Money, nor any Thing of Value, but what was given me by a Friend, would you take it for Payment, if I told you that I had promised to keep it as long as I lived?* — *No, Sir*, stay there, *I love People should do as they would be done unto. What Business had you to promise a Thing that you were not sure of performing? Am I to be accountable for your Vows?* 'Twas in Vain for the poor Proctor to use any more Words, for he plainly saw that if he offer'd to separate the Purse and Money, his own Body and Soul would be in Danger of Separation; and notwithstanding his Spirituality, his inward Man did not much Care at this Time to leave its earthly Tabernacle, so e'en gave both together.

Mr. *John Gadbury*, the Astrologer, was another that fell into the Hands of *Old Mobb*, who notwithstanding his Familiarity with the Stars, was not wise enough to foresee his own Misfortune; which has been a common Case with Men of his Profession. This Rencounter was on the Road between *Winchester* and *London* Poor *Gadbury* trembled, and turned as white as a Clout, when *Old Mobb* told him what he wanted, professing that he had no more Money about him, than just enough to bear his Expences to *London*, but our Highwayman was not at all moved with Compassion at what he said. *Are not you a lying Son of a Whore*, quoth he, *to pretend you want Money, when you hold twelve large Houses of the Planets by Lease Parole, which you let out again to the Stationer's Company at so much per Ann. You must not sham Poverty upon me, Sir, who know as good Things as yourself and who have a Pistol that may prove as fatal as Sirius in the Dog Days, if you stand trifling with me.* Mr *Gadbury* was at this Time, indeed, more apprehensive of *Old Mobb*'s Pistol, than of any Star in the Firmament, for he was sensible the Influence of it, if discharged, would be much more violent and sudden; so that he looked like one out of his Senses. He was now even afraid to deliver his Money, least he should suffer for telling a Lye. However, as he saw there was no Remedy, he pulled out a Bag, in which was about nine Pounds in Gold and Silver, which he gave with a few grumbling Expressions. *Old Mobb* told him, he should take no Exceptions at what he said, for it was but just, that the Loser should have Leave to speak; so setting Spurs to his Horse, he left the Star-gazer to curse the disastrous Constellations.

One Day *Old Mobb* overtook the Stage-Coach going for *Bath*, with only one Gentlewoman in it. When he had commanded the Coachman to stop, and was come to the Door to raise Contribution after his usual Manner, the Passenger made a great many Excuses, and wept very plentifully, in order to move him to pity, she told him she was a poor Widow, who had lately lost her Husband, and therefore she hoped, he would have some Compassion on her. *And is your Losing your Husband then*, says he, *an Argument that I must lose my Booty? I know your Sex too well, Madam, to suffer myself to be prevail'd on by a Woman's Tears. Those Crocodile Drops are always at your Command, and no doubt but that dear Cuckold of yours, whom you have lately buried, has frequently been persuaded out of his Reason by their Interposition in your Domestick Debates. Weeping is so customary to you, that every Body would be disappointed, if a Woman was to bury her Husband, and not weep for him, but you would be more disappointed, if no Body was to take Notice of your Crying, for according to the old Proverb, the End of an Husband is a Widow's Tears, and the End of those Tears is another Husband.*

The poor Gentlewoman upon this ran out into an extravagant Detail of her deceased Husband's Virtues, solemnly protesting, that she would never be married again to the best Man that wore a Head, for she should not expect a Blessing to attend her afterwards, with a thousand other Things of the same Kind. *Old Mobb*, at last, interrupted her, and told her he would repeat a pleasant Story in Verse, which he had learn'd by Heart, so, first looking round him to see that the Coast was clear on every Side, he began as follows.

A Widow Prude had often swore
No Bracelet should approach her more ;
Had often prov'd that second Marriage
Was ten Times worse than Maid's Miscarriage,
And always told them of their Sin,
When Widows would be Wives agen:
Women who'd thus themselves abuse,
Should die, she thought, like honest Jews.
Let her alone to throw the Stones ,
If 'twere but Law, she'd make no Bones.

Thus

Thus long she led a Life demure ;
But not with Character secure.
For People said (what won't Folks say ?)
That she with Edward went astray
(This Edward was her Servant Man)
The Rumour thro' the Parish ran,
She heard, she wept, she called up Ned,
Wip'd her Eyes dry, sigh'd, sobb'd, and said:

Alas ! what sland'rous Times are these !
What shall we come to by Degrees !
This wicked World ! I quite abhor it !
The Lord give me a better for it !
On me this Scandal do they fix ?
On me ? who, God knows, hate such Tricks !
Have Mercy, Heav'n, upon Mankind !
And grant us all a better Mind !
My Husband——Ah that dearest Man !
Forget his Love I never can ;
He took such Care of my good Name,
And put all sland'rous Tongues to Shame.
But, ah ! he's dead —Here Grief amain,
Came bubbing up, and stop'd the Strain.

Ned was no Fool, he saw his Cue,
And how to use good Fortune knew
Old Opportunity at Hand,
He seiz'd the Lock, and bid him stand,
Urg'd of what Use a Husband was
To vindicate a Woman's Cause,
Exclaim'd against the sland'rous Age,
And swore he could his Soul engage,
That Madam was so free from Fault,
She ne'er so much as sinn'd in Thought,
Vowing he'd lose each Drop of Blood,
To make that just Assertion good

This Logic, which well pleas'd the Dame,
At the same Time eludes her Shame
A Husband, for a Husband's Sake,
Was what she'd ne'er consent to take.
Yet, as the Age was so censorious,
And Ned's Proposals were so glorious,
She thought 'twas best to take upon her,
A second Guardian of her Honour

This, says Old Mobb, is an exact Picture of Womankind, and as such I committed to Memory, you are very much obliged to me for the Recital, which has taken me up more Time than I usually spend in taking a Purse, let us now pass from the Dead to the Living, for it is these that I live by I am in a pretty good Humour, and so will not deal rudely by you. Be so kind therefore, as to search your self, and use me as honestly as you are able, you know I can examine afterwards, if I am not satisfied with what you give me The Gentlewoman found he was resolute, and so thought it the best Way to keep him in Temper, which she did by pulling forty Guineas in a silk Purse, and presented them to him 'Tis fifty to one but *Old Mobb* got more by repeating the Verses above, than the poor Poet that wrote them, ever made of his Copy Such is the Fate of the Sons of *Apollo*

Scarce was *Old Mobb* parted from this Gentlewoman before he saw the Appearance of another Prize at some Distance Who should it be, but the famous *Lincoln's-Inn Fields* Mountebank, *Cornelius a Tilburgh,* who was going to set up a Stage at *Wells* Our Adventurer knew him very well, as indeed, did almost every one at Time, which occasioned his demanding his Money in a little rougher Language than usual The poor *Quack-Salver* was willing to preserve what he had ; and to that End, used a great many fruitless Expostulations, pretending that he

had expended all the Money he had brought out with him, and was himself in Necessity. But *Old Mobb* soon gave him to understand, that he would not be put off with fine Words ; and that he had more Wit than to believe a Mountebank whose Profession is Lying *You get your Money,* says he, *as easily as I do, and 'tis only fulfilling an old Proverb, if you give me all you have Lightly come, Lightly go. Next Market-Day, Doctor, will make up all, if you have any Luck. 'Twill excite People to buy your Packets, if as an Instance of your great Desire to serve them, you tell them what you suffer'd upon your Journey, which nevertheless, could not hinder your coming to exercise your Bowels of Compassion among them, and restore such as are in a languishing Condition*

The Empirick could scarce forbear laughing to hear *Old Mobb* hold forth so excellently well, and lay open the Craft of his Occupation with so much Dexterity He was notwithstanding, very unwilling to part with his Money, and began to read a Lecture of Morality to our Desperado, upon the Unlawfulness of his Actions, telling him, that what he did might frequently be the Ruin of poor Families, and oblige them afterwards to follow irregular Courses, in order to make up what they had lost And then, says he, you are answerable for the Sins of such People This is the Devil correcting Sin with a Witness, quoth *Old Mobb,* Can I ruin more People than you, dear Mr. *Theophrastus Bombastus ?* You are a scrupulous, conscientious Son of a Whore, indeed, to tell me of ruining People I only take their Money away from them, but you frequently take away their Lives, and what makes it the worse, you do it safely, under a Pretence of restoring them to Health, whereas I should be hanged for killing a Man, or even Robbing him, if I were taken You have put out more Eyes than the Small-Pox, made more Deaf than the Cataracts of *Nile,* in a Word, destroy'd more than the Pestilence 'Tis in vain to trifle with me, Doctor, unless you have a Remedy against the Force of Gun powder and Lead If you have any such excellent Specifick, make Use of it instantly, or else deliver your Money

Our itinerant Quack still continuing his Delays, *Old Mobb* made bold to take a Portmanteau from his Horse, and put it upon his own, riding off with it, till he came to a convenient Place for opening it Upon examining the Inside, he found five and twenty Pounds in Money, and a large Golden Medal, which King *Charles* II had given him for Poysoning himself in his Majesty's Presence, besides all his Instruments, and Implements of Quackery.

Another Time *Old Mobb* met with the Dutchess of *Portsmouth,* on the Road between *New-Market* and *London,* attended with a small Retinue He made bold to stop the Coach, and ask her Grace for what she had about her, but Madam, who had been long used to command a Monarch, did not understand the Meaning of being spoken to in this Manner by a common Man Whereupon she briskly demanded, If he knew who she was ? Yes, Madam, *replied Old Mobb,* I known you to be the greatest Whore in the Kingdom, and that you are maintain'd at the Publick Charge.——I know that all the Courtiers depend on your Smiles, and that even the K—— himself is your Slave But what of all that ? A Gentleman Collector is a greater Man upon the Road, much more absolute than his Majesty is at Court You may now say, Madam, that a single Highwayman, has exercised his Authority, where *Charles* II. of *England* has often begged a Favour, and thought himself happy to obtain it, at the Expence of his Treasure, as well as his Breath

Her Grace continued to look upon him, with a superiour, lofty Air, and told him, he was a very insolent infolent Fellow ; that she would give him nothing, and that he should feverely fuffer for this Affront Adding, that he might touch her if he durft —— Madam, fays *Old Mobb*, that haughty *French* Spirit will do you no good here I am an *Englifh* Freebooter, and infift upon it as my Native Privilege to feize all Foreign Commodities Your Money indeed is *Englifh*, and the prodigious Sums that have been lavished on you will be a lafting Proof of *Englifh* Folly Neverthelefs, all you have is confifcated to me by being beftowed on fuch a worthlefs B——h I am King here, Madam, and I have a Whore to keep on the Publick Contributions, as well as King *Charles* 'Tis for this that I collect of all that pafs, and you fhall have no Favour from me —— As foon as he had fpoke, he fell on board her in a very boifterous Manner, fo that her Grace began to cry out for Quarters, telling him, fhe would deliver all fhe had She was as good as her Word, for fhe furrendered two hundred Pounds in Money, which was in the Seat of her Coach, befides a very rich Necklace, which her Royal Cully had lately given her, a Gold Watch, two Diamond Rings

Being once at *Abingdon*, on a Market-Day, when there is always a great Quantity of Corn bought and fold, *Old Mobb*, happened to fall into Company with a Perfon at the *Crown-Inn*, whom he knew to be a great Ingroffer of Corn, and that he had juft bought as much of that Commodity as came to fifty Pounds Having a pretty deal of Money in his Pocket at this Time, it came into his Head, how to cheat the Monopolizer out of his Bargain To this End, he put on the Appearance of a Man of Bufinefs, pretended that he was come from *London* to buy, and defired to fee this Purchafe of the Countryman's

As foon as he faw it, he feem'd to like it mightily; and demanded the Price of the Owner, who asked him but a fmall Advance above what he had juft given for it *Old Mobb* prefently paid down the Money, and fent the Goods away, where he was fure of having it difpofed of again at prime Coft

This was all that there was to be done that Day, for the Ingroffer did not go out of Town till the next Morning *Old Mobb* againft that Time, took Care to be well informed of the Way he was to take, and was at his Heels before he got two Miles out of Town He foon found an Opportunity to clap a Piftol to his Breaft; and tell him that he muft have the Money again, which he had lent him Yefterday, and whatfoever elfe he had about him The Countryman was fufficiently furpriz'd to fee himfelf addreffed to by his late Companion in fuch a Manner as this, and asked him, with Trembling, if it was Juftice, in him to take away both Goods and Money too Haft thou the Impudence to talk of Juftice, *fays Old Mobb?* Can any Man in the World act more unjuftly than an Ingroffer of Corn, who buys up the Produce of his Country, robs the Poor of their Bread, and pretends a Scarcity in Times of Plenty, only to increafe his own Subftance, and leave behind him Abundance of ill-gotten Wealth ? You are for inclofing all the Land in the Kingdom, and call our Fore-fathers Fools, becaufe they fold Corn for Twelve-pence a Bufhel. No Picture pleafes you fo well as that of *Pharoah*'s lean Kine, who eat up the fat ones ; this you hang up in your Parlours, recommend to your Neighbours, and pray fecretly to fee the Interpretation of it frequently fulfilled. Such Vermin as you are unfit to live upon the Earth, for you dread what *all the World befides* efteem a *Bleffing*, and dare not wifh well to your Country left her Profperity fhould difappoint your Hopes, and oblige you to bring out your hoarded Stock, and fell it for lefs than it coft you Talk no more of Juftice, Sir, but deliver your Money, or I fhall do the World

fo much Juftice as to fend you out of it Hereupon the Countryman delivered a Bag with all *Old Mobb*'s Money in it, and about as much more, which occafion'd our Adventurer to ride away with a great Deal of Satisfaction

Not long after the committing of this Robbery, *Old Mobb* met with Sir *George Jefferies*, at that Time Lord Chief Juftice of the *King's Bench*, as he was going to his Country Seat My Lord Chief Juftice upon the Road, was no more than another Man, for he firft difabled two Servants that attended him, by fhooting one through the Arm, and the other through the Thigh, and then ftopped the Coach, and demanded his Lordfhip's Money *Jefferies* had before this made himfelf fufficiently famous, by his Weftern Affizes, and other very fevere Proceeding, fo that he imagined his Name carried Terror enough in it, to intimidate any Man, but he was miftaken in *Old Mobb*, who had Courage to fpeak his Mind without any refpect to Perfons, and when his Lordfhip told him his Name, only faid, *He was glad he could be revenged on him in any Manner for putting him in Bodily Fear at* Hartford *Affizes a few Months before According to Law, my Lord*, fays he, *I might charge a Conftable with you, and bind you over to the Quarterly Seffions, for threatning to take away my Life However, if you pleafe, as I don't love to be fpiteful, I will make up the Matter with you for what Money you have in the Coach, which, I think, is as eafy as you can defire, and eafier than you can defire, and eafier than you deferve*

Jefferies expoftulated with him, upon the great Hazard he ran, both of Soul and Body, by following fuch wicked Courfes, telling him, that he muft expect Juftice to follow his Crimes, if he believed there was any fuch Thing as a Providence, that govern'd the World I don't doubt, *fays Old Mobb*, but that when Juftice has overtaken us both, I fhall ftand at leaft, as good a Chance as your Lordfhip, who have already writ your Name in indelible Characters of Blood, by putting to Death fo many hundred innocent Men, for only ftanding up in Defence of our Common Liberties, that you might fecure the Favour of your Prince 'Tis enough for you to preach Morality upon the Bench, where no Body dares to contradict you, but your Leffons can have no Effect upon me at this Time, for I know you too well not to fee that they are only calculated to preferve Money —— This Speech of *Old Mobb*, was followed with fifty Oaths and Imprecations against the poor Judge, which threaten'd him with nothing but immediate Death, if he did not deliver his Money. *Jefferies* faw his Authority would now ftand him in no Stead, fo he gave what Money he had, which amounted to about fiftyfix Guineas

We took notice at the beginning of this Life of *Old Mobb*, that he fometimes was engaged with the *Golden Farmer*, the Reader may therefore juftly expect an Account of fome of their Actions in Concert two Stories, the moft remarkable and diverting that we have feen concerning them, now follow

Having both of them a pretty deal of ready Cafh and being willing to retire a little while from the Highway, where they had lately made a great Noife and were now very much fought after, they came to *London*, in order to make ufe of their Wits, of which they had both as great fhares as they of ftrength and Courage. Here their firft Work was to obferve the Humours and Manners of the Citizens, whom neither of them was well acquainted with before, that they might know the better how to proceed, and impofe upon them in their own Way

Every one knows that *London* is all hurry and Noife, every Man there is a Man of Bufinefs, and thofe who make good Appearances never want Cre-
du

dit, all People there live by mutual Dependance upon one another, and he who has dealt for two or three hundred Pounds, and made good his Payments, may afterwards be trusted for five Our Adventurers soon perceived all this, and what Advantages many designing Men made of the general confidence, that People reposed in each other, they saw that no Body could teach them how to cheat a Citizen, so well as a Citizen himself, and thereupon he concluded, that the best Way they could take, was, to both turn Tradesmen.

Each of them now, takes a large handsome House, hires two or three Servants, and sets up for a great Dealer The *Golden Farmer's* Habitation was in *Thames-street*, where he passed for a Cornchandler, which Occupation he had the most Knowledge in of any. *Old Mobb* took up his residence somewhere near the *Tower*, and call'd himself a Holland Trader, he having been abroad when a Boy, and knowing pretty well what Commodities were exported to that Country, of the Language of which he had also a small Smattering They went for near Relations, of the Name of *Bryan*, and said they were North-Country Men.

They now employ all their Time in enquiring after Goods in their several Ways, buying whatever comes to their Hands, and either paying ready Money themselves, or drawing upon each other, for one, two, or three Days, at which Time Payment was always punctually made This constant Tide of Money was kept up by their continually selling privately what they bought (sometimes, perhaps, not a little to Loss) to such Persons as are glad to make use of their Cash in this Manner, and always wink at Things, which they can't comprehend, while they find their Interest in it As they deal in very different Ways, the Chapmen of the one, had no Knowledge of those of the other; so that though every one of them had been sent at one Time or another, by his respective Customer, to receive Money of his Kinsman, none of them had any Notion, that the Correspondence was mutual, and consequently no Suspicion of a Fraud at the Bottom

Thus they continued till they both found their Characters thoroughly established Perhaps in this Time, they might each of them lose a hundred or two of Pounds, but they very well knew that this Loss would get them as many Thousands When they saw that all who dealt with them were ready to send in what Goods they required, and not in the least Care about their Money, they thought their Project ripe for Execution, accordingly a Day was appointed for that Purpose.

They now order all their Customers to bring them in Goods on such a Day, as much, at least in Quantity, as they had ever before received at one Time of the respective Sorts, confining them all to particular Hours for the Delivery of what they brought, that they might not interfere with one another, and so suspect that some unfair Design was on Foot At the same Time they inform'd those who usually bought every Thing off their Hands, that they should have such and such Quantities of so many Sorts to dispose of, naming the next Day to that when they were to receive them, that they would sell them cheap, because they were obliged to make up a large Sum of Ready Money; that therefore they desired them to be punctual, and bring only Cash for what they design'd to buy The whole Scheme succeeded as well as they could wish; on one Side there was no Suspicion; and on the other, if there was any, it was not the Interest of the Parties to discover what they thought, because every one of them promised himself some Advantage

The Goods were all delivered according to Order,

at the Day and Hour appointed, and Notes were mutually drawn by the Kinsman in *Thames-Street* upon him by the *Tower*, and by the Kinsman by the *Tower*, upon him in *Thames-Street*, for the several Sums, to be paid at three Days after Date. Never were Men better satisfied than these poor Dupes, not one of them doubting but he should have all his Money the Moment he went for it, as usual. They went Home, and slept soundly that Night, and the two Nights succeeding

Next Day came the Buyers, and entirely cleared both Houses, paying down Ready Money for all they carried off These too were as well pleased as the rest, and with much better Reason. They imagined indeed, that their Chapmen were going to break, but what was that to them? No Matter how the poor Men were to live for the future, so long as they could have good Bargains at present

There was now Time enough before the Day of Payment, for our two Merchants to take Care of themselves, and the Money they had raised, which they did very effectually

When they came to Computation they found, that by this one bold Stroke, they had got clear into their Pockets, about sixteen Hundred and thirty Pounds: A pretty considerable Sum for three Months, which was the longest Time they were in Trade.

When the Creditors came to receive their Money, they were surpriz'd at both Places to see the Doors fast, and the Windows shut, till they were informed by the Neighbours, that the Birds were flown the Day before, and that all their Furniture was either carried off in the Night, or seiz'd for Rent How the Men now looked upon one another! Every one began to suspect that the rest who were attending came about the same Business as himself; and indeed when they came to examine the Matter, they found themselves not mistaken. Those who were earliest in *Thames-Street*, and had heard the melancholy News, went forthwith to the *Tower* to complain that Mr. *Cousin* was gone; and those at the *Tower* set out for *Thames-Street* Now was the whole Plot unravell'd, when they saw both were departed quietly, and had learned of each other how they had been mutually imposed upon by the pretended Relations, when they told their several Cases,

One such Trick as this, is enough for a Man's whole Life, and as much as he can safely play in the same Kingdom. Our two *Bryans* now, therefore, resum'd their old Names and Habits, taking to the Highway again for some Time, till fresh Danger of being apprehended, put them once more to their Shifts There was not less Art in what they now did, than in what we have just related; only they acted in a lower Sphere, not daring to aspire so high as to be Merchants, after they had brought so much Scandal upon the Name.

Men whose Thoughts are all turn'd upon Money, have no Regard to the Manner in which they get what they desire, nor need they, provided they come off with Impunity, for all People honour the Rich, without enquiring how they came to be so.

There were two wealthy Brothers of the Name of *Seals*, *Philip* and *Charles*, both Jewellers: *Philip* lived in *London*, and *Charles* resided at *Bristol*; where they were both born, in a House which his Father left him The *Golden Farmer* and *Old Mobb* knew every Circumstance of the Family, from which these Men were descended, and were moreover particularly instructed in the private History of our Brothers. This made our Desperado's fix on them for their next Prize, now they were again reduced to Extremity. The Brothers were sickly consumptive Men, which inclined these arch Villains to undertake and perform what will

will be as diverting in the Relation, as it was unparallel'd in itself, and worthy of the Men who acted in it.

Having contriv'd and order'd the whole Affair, the first Step they took towards executing it, was writing, and copying the following Letter, making only the Alteration of the Place and Name, as they saw necessary.

March 26 1686.

Dear Brother,

THIS *comes to bring you the sorrowful News, that you have lost the best of Brothers, and I the kindest of Husbands, at a Time when we were in Hopes of his growing better, as the Spring advanced, and continuing with us at least one Summer longer: He died this Morning, about Eleven of the Clock, after he had kept his Bed only three Days*

I send so hastily to you, that you may be here before we prepare for the Funeral, which was the Desire of my dear Husband, who informed me, that he had made you joint Executor with me. The Will is in my Hands, and I shall defer opening it till you arrive here I am too full of Grief to add any more, the Messenger, who is a very honest Man, and a Neighbour of mine, shall inform you of such Particulars as are needful from

Your Sorrowful Sister

——SEALS

P. S *I employ'd a Friend to write for me, which I desire you to excuse, for I was not able to do it myself, nor indeed to dictate any more*

These Letters being sealed, and properly directed, our two Adventures dressed themselves according to the Characters they were to bear, and parted from each other, one of them riding towards *London*, and the other towards *Bristol*, having so ordered it before-hand, that they might both come to the End of their Journey at the same Time

They arrived, they delivered their Credentials, and were kindly received 'Tis not to our Purpose to declare how many Tears were shed upon opening the Letters, and how many *Eulogias* each of the living Brothers bestow'd upon him whom he supposed to be dead. Much less shall we pretend to describe the Secret Joy which they both concealed under a sorrowful Countenance, but which naturally arose in their Breasts, when they understood that an Addition would now accrue to their Fortunes by the Death of a Brother 'Tis true, they both loved one another, but of all Love, Self-Love is the strongest

The Evening at each Place was spent in talking over several Particulars of the Family. Subjects that at such a Time as this always come in the Way Our Messengers were both very expert, and each Brother was convinced, that the Man whom his Sister had sent, had been long conversant in the Family, by the exact Account which he gave of Things They moreover, added of their own Heads a great Deal of Stuff concerning the Manner of the respective Mr *Seal*'s Death, and what he said in his last Moments, which at this Time, was doubtless very moving In a Word, the best Bed in both Houses was made ready for our two Sharpers, who were to depart the next Morning, and tell the Sisters-in-Law that their Brothers would come two Days after, which was as soon as their Mourning could be made, and other Things prepared for the Journey.

It may be proper to observe, that *Old Mobb* went to *Bristol*, and tho *Golden Farmer* to *London* The first of these found Means in the Evening to secure Jewels, to the Value of two hundred Pounds, which was all the Booty he had any Opportunity to make But the *Golden Farmer* having well observed the Position of Mr. *Philip Seal*'s Shop, arose in the Night, came silently down Stairs, and took to a much greater Value, among other Things a Diamond Necklace, which was just made for a Lady of the first Quality, but not to be delivered 'till some Days after, three very large Diamond Rings, and five small ones.

In the Morning both our Adventurers set out, one from *Bristol*, and the other from *London*, They met at a Place before appointed, and congratulated one another upon their Success.

But we must leave them together, and return to the Brothers, who were both getting ready for their Journey

Such was the Hurry and Confusion which our Messengers had put the two Families in, that no Body in either of them took any Notice of the Shops, so that nothing of the Robberies was discovered Time enough to prevent the Masters setting out, and let them see that they were imposed on The Shops were well furnished out, and what was carried off, took up but little Room, wherefore 'twas not surprizing, that such a Thing should be overlooked, at a Time when no Business was thought of, but the Preparations for Travelling, and appearing decently at the Funeral.

The merriest Part of the whole Story was our two Brothers setting out the same Morning, and coming the same Evening to *Newberry*, where they took up their Lodging also at the same Inn He from *London* came in first, and being fatigued went to Bed before the other arrived The *Bristol* Man about two Hours after, passed through his Brother's Room, and a Companion with him, whom he had engaged to attend him, and reposed themselves where but a thin Partition was between the two Chambers *Philip*, the *Londoner*, was asleep when his Brother went by him, but the Discourse between *Charles*, and his Friend, surpriz'd him, he could not tell what they talk'd off, but was certain one of the Tongues was his Brothers, whom he was going to see buried.

By and by *Charles* had Occasion to go to the necessary House, upon which he rises, and attempts to go through *Philip*'s Chamber again, who by the Moon-light was still more convinced that he had not been deceived in the Voice Upon this he screamed out, and *Charles* was now as much surpriz'd as his Brother, so that he ran back to Bed half dead with Fear

In a Word, they both continued sweating, and frightning themselves till Morning, when they arose and dressed themselves in their Mourning Apparel Below Stairs for some Time they shunn'd one another till they were taken Notice off by the People of the House, who with some Difficulty brought them together, after they had heard both their Stories They now saw themselves imposed on, but could not imagine the Reason of it, till after spending two Days together at the Inn, they both returned, and found themselves robbed. Now was the Plot unravell'd

Old Mobb, was at last apprehended in *Tuthill-street, Westminster*, committed to *Newgate*, and tried at the *Old-Bailey* on thirty-six Indictments; of thirty-two of which he was found Guilty

On *Friday* the 30th of *May*, 1690, he was executed at *Tyburn*, without making any Speech or Confession a

...tion; but continuing to act with his usual Intrepi-
ty.

Thus does the divine Vengeance pursue the Workers
f Iniquity, and very seldom suffers them to depart out
f this Life, without exposing them to Shame and Ini-
uty This, one would think, would be sufficient to
convince the greatest Libertine of the Government of a
just Providence, and make him tremble at his own
Thoughts and Actions, 'Tis also very shocking to reflect
upon the Departure of such a Man out of the World, in
such an insensible Manner as Old Mobb made his Exit,
since at best Death is a Launching forth into a State of
Uncertainty.

The LIFE of Major STEDE BONNET.

MAJOR *Bonnet* was a Gentleman of good
Reputation in the Island of *Barbadoes*, where
he was Master of a plentiful Fortune, hav-
g, besides, the Advantage of a liberal Education.
e had the least Temptation of any Man to follow
ch a Course of Life, from the Condition of his Cir-
mstances, and therefore it was very surprizing to
very one, in the Island where he liv'd, when they
eard of his Enterprizes As he was generally esteem'd
d honour'd, before he broke out into open Acts of
iracy, so he was afterwards rather pitied than con-
emned, by those that were acquainted with him; who
liev'd that this Humour of going a pirating pro-
eded from a Disorder in his Mind, which had been
t too visible in him, some Time before this wicked
ndertaking, and which is said to have been occasi-
n'd by some Discomforts he met with in a married
ate But be that as it will, the Major was but ill
ualify'd for the Business, for he did not understand
aritime Affairs

When he was resolv'd in his wicked Purpose, he
tted out a Sloop, with 10 Guns, and 70 Men, en-
rely at his own Expence, and in the Night-time
il'd from *Barbadoes* He call'd his Sloop *The Re-
enge*, and his first Cruize in her was off the Capes
f *Virginia*, where he took several Ships, and plun-
er'd them of their Provisions, Cloaths, Money, Am-
unition, &c in particular the *Anne*, Captain
Montgomery, from *Glasgow*, the *Turbet*, from *Barbadoes*, which latter, for the Country's Sake, after
hey had taken out the principal Part of the Lading,
he Pirate Crew set on Fire They took, also, the
Endeavour, Captain *Scot*, from *Bristol*, and the *Young*
Tom Leith From hence they went to *New-York*,
nd off the East End of *Long-Island* they took a Sloop
ound for the *West-Indies*, after which they stood in
nd landed some Men at *Gardners-Island*, but in a
eaceable Manner, for they bought Provisions for
he Company's Use, which they paid justly for, and
o went off again without Molestation

Some Time after, in the Month of *August* 1717,
Bonnet came off the Bar of *South-Carolina*, and took
Sloop and a Brigantine inwards-bound; the Sloop
elong'd to *Barbadoes*, *Joseph Palmer* Master and
as laden with Rum, Sugar, and Negroes, the Bri-
antine came from *New-England*, *Thomas Porter* was
Master, her they plunder'd, and then dismiss'd
ut they sail'd away with the Sloop, and at an Inlet
n *North-Carolina* were careen'd by her, and then
hey set her on Fire

After the Sloop had clean'd, they put to Sea, but
ame to no Resolution what Course to take, for the
rew were divided in their Opinions, some being for

one Thing, and some for another, so that nothing
but Confusion seem'd to attend all their Schemes.

The Major was no Sailor, as was said before, and
therefore was often oblig'd to yield to many Things
that were impos'd on him, during their Undertaking, for want of a competent Knowledge in maritime
Affairs, till at length he happen'd to fall in Company
with *Edward Teach*, commonly call'd *Black-Beard*,
as we shall observ'd in his Life This Fellow was a good
Sailor, but a most cruel harden'd Villain, bold and
daring to the last Degree and would not stick at perpetrating the most abominable Wickedness imaginable;
for which, he was made chief of that execrable Gang
It might be said, that his Post was not unduly fill'd,
Black-Beard being truly the Superior in Roguery of
all the Company, as shall be related in his Life, hereafter

To him *Bonnet*'s Crew join'd in Consortship, and
Bonnet himself was laid aside, notwithstanding the
Sloop was his own The Major went a-board *Black-
Beard*'s Ship, not concerning himself with any of
their Affairs, and continu'd there till she was lost in
Topsail Inlet, and one *Richards* was appointed Captain in his Room. The Major now saw his Folly, but
could not help himself, which made him melancholy:
He reflected upon his past Course of Life, and was
confounded with Shame when he thought upon what
he had done His Behaviour was taken Notice of by
the other Pirates, who lik'd him never the better for
it and he often declar'd to some of them, that he
would gladly leave off that Way of Living, being perfectly tir'd of it, but he should be asham'd to see the
Face of any honest *English* Man again Therefore he
said if he could get to *Spain* or *Portugal*, where he
might live undiscover'd, he would spend the Remainder of his Days in either of those Countries, otherwise he must continue with them as long as he
liv'd

When *Black-Beard* lost his Ship at *Topsail* Inlet,
and surrender'd to the King's Proclamation, *Bonnet*
re-assum'd the Command of his own Sloop, *The Revenge*, went directly away to *Bath Town* in *North-
Carolina*, surrender'd likewise to the King's Pardon,
and receiv'd a Certificate The War was now broke
out between the *Triple Allies* and *Spain*; so Major
Bonnet gets a Clearance for his Sloop at *North-Carolina*,
and goes to the Island of St *Thomas*, with a Design,
at least as he pretended, to get the Emperor's Commission to go a privateering upon the *Spaniards*.
When *Bonnet* came back to *Topsail* Inlet, he found
that *Teach* and his Gang were gone, and that they
had taken all the Money, small Arms, and Effects of
Value, out of the great Ship, and set ashore seventeen
Men

Men on a small sandy Island above a League from the Main, no Doubt with a Design they should perish, for there was no Inhabitant, or Provisions to subsist withal, nor any Boat; nor Materials to build or make any kind of Launch or Vessel, to escape from that desolate Place; They had remain'd there two Nights and a Day, without Subsistance, or the least Prospect of any, expecting nothing else but a lingering Death, when, to their inexpressible Comfort, they saw Redemption at Hand Major *Bonnet* happening to get Intelligence of their being there, by two of the Pirates who had escap'd from *Teach's* Cruelty, and had got to a poor little Village at the upper End of the Harbour, sent his Boat to make Discovery of the Truth of the Matter, which the poor Wretches seeing, they made a Signal to them, and were all brought on board *Bonnet's* Sloop

Major *Bonnet* told all his Company, that he would take a Commission to go against the *Spaniards*, and to that End, would sail to St *Thomas's*; therefore he said if they would go with him, they should be welcome. To this they all consented, but as the Sloop was preparing to sail, a Bom Boat which brought Apples and Cyder to sell to the Sloop's Men, informed them, that Captain *Teach* lay at *Ocracock* Inlet, with only 18 or 20 Hands. *Bonnet*, who bore him a mortal Hatred for some Insults offered him, went in pursuit of *Black-beard*, but it happened too late, for he missed of him there They cruized after him four Days; when hearing no farther News of him, they steered their Course towards *Virginia*

In the Month of *July*, these Adventurers came off the Capes, and meeting a Pink, with a Stock of Provisions on board, which they happened to be in Want of, they took out of her ten or twelve Barrels of Pork, and about 400 Weight of Bread They would not, however, have this set down to the Account of Piracy, and therefore they gave them eight or ten Casks of Rice, and an old Cable, in lieu thereof

Two Days afterwards they chased a Sloop of sixty Ton, and about two Leagues off of Cape *Henry* they took her. They were so happy here as to get a Supply of Liquor to their Victuals, for they brought from her two Hogsheads of Rum, and as many of Molosses, which, it seems, they had need of; tho' they had no ready Money to purchase them What Security they intended to give, I can't tell; but *Bonnet*, sent eight Men to take Care of the Prize Sloop, who, perhaps, not caring to make Use of those accustom'd Freedoms, took the first Opportunity to go off with her, and *Bonnet* (who was now pleased to have himself call'd Captain *Thomas*) saw them no more

After this, the Major threw off all Restraint; and, tho' he had just before received his Majesty's Mercy, in the Name of *Stede Bonnet*, he relaps'd in good Earnest into his old Vocation, by the Name of Captain *Thomas*, and recommended a down-right Pirate, by taking and plundering all the Vessels he met with He took off Cape *Henry*, two Ships from *Virginia*, bound to *Glascow*, which furnished them with but very little besides an hundred Weight of Tobacco The next Day they took a small Sloop bound from *Virginia* to *Bermudas*, which supply'd them with twenty Barrels of Pork, and some Bacon They gave her in return, two Barrels of Rice, and a Hogshead of Molosses, out of this Sloop two Men enter'd voluntarily into their Service The next they took was another *Virginia* Man, bound to *Glascow*, out of which they had nothing of Value, save only a few Combs, Pins and Needles, instead of which they gave her a Barrel of Pork, and two Barrels of Bread. From *Virginia* they sailed to *Philadelphia*, and in the Latitude 38 North, they took a Scooner, com-

ing from *North-Carolina*, and bound to *Boston* They deprived her only of two Dozen of Calf-Skins to make Covers for Guns, and two of her Hands, but they detained her some Days All this was but small Gain, and seem'd as if they design'd only to make Provision for their Sloop against they arrived at St *Thomas's*, for they hitherto had dealt favourably with all that fell into their Hands, but those that were so unhappy as to come after, fared not so well, for in the Latitude of 32; off of *Delaware* River, near *Philadelphia*, they took two Snows bound to *Bristol*, out of which they got some Money, beside Goods to the Value of about 150 *l* At the same time they took a Sloop of sixty Tons, bound from *Philadelphia* to *Barbadoes*, *Thomas Read* Master She was loaded with Provisions, which they kept, and put four or five of their Hands on Board her. The last Day of *July*, they took another Sloop of 60 Tons, commanded by *Peter Manwaring*, bound from *Antigoa* to *Philadelphia*, her they likewise kept with all the Cargo, consisting chiefly of Rum, Molosses, Sugar, Cotton, Indigo, and about 25 *l* in Money, valued in all at 500 *l*

The last Day of *July*, our Rovers, with the Vessels last taken, left *Delaware* Bay, and sailed to Cape *Fear* River, where they staid too long for their Safety; for the Pirate Sloop, which they now new named the *Royal James*, proved very leaky, so that they was obliged to remain here almost two Months, in order to refit and repair their Vessel · They took in this River a small Shallop, which they ripped up to mend their Sloop By these Means the Prosecution of their Voyage, as before mention'd, was deferred till the News came to *Carolina*, of a Pirate Sloop's being there to carreen with her Prizes

Upon this Information, the Council of *South-Carolina* was alarmed, apprehending they should receive another Visit from them speedily, to prevent which, Colonel *William Rhet*, of the same Province, waited on the Governor, and generously offered himself to go with two Sloops and attack this Pirate T.. Governor readily accepted his offer, and accordingly gave the Colonel a Commission, and full Power, to fit out such Vessels as he thought proper for the Design

In a few Days two Sloops were equipped and manned · The *Henry* with 8 Guns and 70 Men, commanded by Captain *John Masters*, and the *Sea Nymph*, with 8 Guns and 60 Men, commanded by Captain *Fayrer Hall*, both under the entire Direction of the aforesaid Colonel *Rhet*, who, on the 14th of *September*, went on Board the *Henry*, and, with the other Sloop, sailed from *Charles-Town* to *Swillivants* Island, to put themselves in order for the Cruize Just then arrived a small Snip from *Antigoa*, one *Cock* Master, with an Account, that, in Sight of the Bar, he was taken and plundered by one *Charles Vane*, a Pirate, in a Brigantine of 12 Guns, and 90 Men, who, they said, had also taken two other Vessels bound in there, one a small Sloop, Captain *Dill* Master, from *Barbadoes*, the other a Brigantine, Captain *Thompson* Master from *Guiney*, with ninety odd Negroes, which they took out of the Vessel, and put on Board another Sloop, then under the Command of one *Yeats*, his Consort, with 21 Men This prov'd fortunate to the Owners of the *Guiney* Man, for *Yeats*, having often before attempted to quit this Course of Life, took an Opportunity in the Night, to leave *Vane* and run into *North-Edisto* River, to the Southward of *Charles-Town*, where he surrendered to his Majesty's Pardon Thus the Owners got their Negroes, and *Yeats* and his Men had Certificates given them from the Government

Vane cruized some Time off the Bar, in hopes to catch *Yeats*, and, unfortunately for them, took two Ships

Ship, coming out, bound to *London* While the Crews of these were Prisoners a-board, some of the Pirates give out, that they designed to go into one of the Rivers to the Southward All this they told Colonel *Rhet*, who, upon hearing it, failed over the Bar the 15th of *September*, with the two Sloops before mentioned, and, having the Wind Northerly, went after *Vane*, scouring all the Rivers and Inlets to the Southward, however, meeting with him, he tacked about, and stood for Cape *Fear* River, in Prosecution of his first Design On the 26th following, in the Evening, the Colonel, with his small Squadron entered the River, and saw, over a Point of Land, three Sloops at an Anchor, which were Major *Bonnet* and his Prizes It happened, that, in going up the River, the Pilot run the Colonels Sloop aground, and it was dark before they were on Float, which hindered their getting up that Night The Pirates soon discovered the Sloops, but not knowing who they were, or upon what Design they came into that River, they mann'd three Canoes, and sent them down to make Prizes of them; but they quickly found their Mistake, and returned to the Sloop, with the unwelcome News Major *Bonnet* made Preparations that Night for engaging, and took all the Men out of the Prizes He shewed Captain *Manwaring*, one of his Prisoners, a Letter he had just wrote, which he declared he would send to the Governor of *Carolina*, the contents were to this Effect, *viz That if the Sloops, which then appeared, were sent out against him by the said Governor, and he should happen to get clear off, he would afterwards burn and destroy all Ships or Vessels going in or coming out of* South-Carolina The next Morning they got under Sail, and came down the River, designing only a running Fight Colonel *Rhet*'s Sloops got likewise under Sail, and stood for him, getting upon each Quarter of the Pirate, with Intent to board him, which *Bonnet* perceiving, he edged in towards the Shore, and, being warmly engag'd, ran his Sloop aground The *Carolina* Sloops, being in the same shoal Water, were in the same Circumstances, the *Henry*, in which Colonel *Rhet* was, grounded within Pistol shot of the Pirate, and on his Bow, the other Sloop grounded right a-head of him, and almost out of Gun-Shot, which made her of little Service to the Colonel, while they lay a ground

At this Time the Pirates had a considerable Advantage, for their Sloop, after she was a-ground, listed from Colonel *Rhet*'s, by which Means they were all covered, and the Colonel's Sloop listing the same Way, his Men were as much exposed, notwithstanding which, they kept a brisk Fire the whole Time they lay thus a-ground, which was near five Hours. The Pirates made a Wiff in their bloody Flag, and beckoned several Times with their Hats, in Derision to the Colonel's Men, to come on Board, which they answered with chearful Huzza's, and said, *that they would speak with them by and by* This accordingly happened, for the Colonel's Sloop being first afloat, he got into deeper Water, and after mending the Rigging, which was much shattered in the Engagement, they stood for the Pirate, to give the finishing Stroke, designing to go directly on Board him *Bonnet*, however, prevented this, by sending a Flag of Truce, and, after some Time capitulating, his whole Crew surrendered themselves Prisoners The Colonel took Possession of the Sloop, and was extremely pleased to find that Captain *Thomas*, who commanded her, was the individual Person of Major *Steede Bonnet*, who had done them the Honour several Times to visit their Coast of *Carolina*.

There were killed in this Action, on Board the *Henry*, ten Men, and fourteen wounded; on Board the *Sea Nymph* two were killed, and four wounded

the Officers and Sailors in both Sloops behaved themselves with the greatest Bravery, and, had they not so unluckily run a-ground, they had taken the Pirate with much less Loss of Men, but as he endeavoured to sail by them, and so make a running Fight, the *Carolina* Sloops were obliged to keep near him, to prevent his getting away Of the Pirates there were seven killed and five wounded, two of which latter died soon after, of their Wounds Colonel *Rhet* weighed the 30th of *September*, from Cape *Fear* River, and arrived at *Charles-Town* the 3d of *October* to the great Joy of the whole Province of *Carolina*

Bonnet and his Crew, two Days after, were put a-shore, and there not being a publick Prison, the Crew were kept at the Watch-House, under a Guard of Militia, but Major *Bonnet* himself was committed into to Custody of the Marshal, at his own House In a few Days after, *David Harriot* the Master, and *Ignatius Pell* the Boatswain, who were designed for Evidences against the other Pirates, were removed from the rest of the Company, to the said Marshal's House, and every Night two Centinels were set about the said House Whether it was thro' any Corruption, or want of Care in Guarding the Prisoners, we can't say; but so it was, that, on the 24th of *October*, the Major and *Harriot* made their Escape, the Boatswain refusing to go along with them This made a great Noise in the Province, and People were open in their Resentments, often reflecting publickly on the Governor, and others in the Magistracy, as tho' they had been brib'd, for conniving at their getting off These Invectives arose from their Fears, that *Bonnet* would be capable of raising another Company, and of prosecuting his Revenge against their Country, for what he had lately, tho' justly, suffered: But they were in a short Time made easy in those Respects, for as soon as the Governor had the Account of *Bonnet*'s Escape, he immediately issued out a Proclamation, and promised a Reward of 700 *l* to any that would take him, sending, besides, several Boats with armed Men, both to the Northward and Southward, in pursuit of him

Bonnet stood to the Northward, in a small Vessel, but wanting Necessaries, and the Weather being bad, he was forced back, and so returned with his Canoe to *Swillivants* Island, near *Charles-Town*, to fetch Supplies, there being now some Information given to the Governor, he sent for Colonel *Rhet*, and desired him to go in pursuit of *Bonnet*, and accordingly gave him a Commission for that Purpose Hereupon the Colonel, with a great Deal of Craft, and some Men, went away that Night for *Swillivant*'s Island, where, after a diligent Search, he discovered *Bonnet* and *Harriot* together The Colonel's Men fired upon them, killed *Harriot* upon the Spot and wounded one Negroe and an *Indian Bonnet* submitted, and surrender'd himself, and the next Morning, being *November* the 6th, was brought back by Colonel *Rhet* to *Charles-Town*, and, by the Governor's Warrant, committed there into safe Custody, in order for his being brought to his Trial

On the 28th of *October*, 1718, a Court of Vice-Admiralty was held at *Charles-Town*, in *South-Carolina*, and, by several Adjournments, continued to *Wednesday*, the 12th of *November* following for the Tryal of the Pirates taken in a Sloop formerly call'd *the Revenge*, but afterwards *the Royal James*, before *Nicholas Trot* Esq; Judge of the Vice-Admiralty, and Chief Justice of the said Province of *South-Carolina*, and other assistant Judges

The King's Commission to Judge *Trot* being read; and a Grand Jury sworn for the finding of the several Bills, a learned Charge was given them by the said Judge, wherein he first shewed *That the Sea was given by God, for the Use of Men, and therefore is subject*

subject to Dominion and Property, as well as the Land

2*dly,* He particularly remark'd to them, *the supreme Sovereignty of the King of England over the British Seas*

3*dly,* He observed, *that as Commerce and Navigation could not be carried on without Laws, so there have been always particular Laws, for the better ordering and regulating marine Affairs, to this he added,* an historical Account of those Laws, and their Origin

4*thly,* He proceeded to shew, *that there have been particular Courts and Judges appointed, to whose Jurisdiction maritime Causes properly belong; and that in Matters both Civil and Criminal*

And then 5*thly.* He particularly shewed them, *the Constitution and Jurisdiction of the present Court of Admiralty Sessions,*

And lastly, *the Crimes that were cognizable therein,* here he particularly enlarged *upon the Crime of Pyracy,* which was now to be brought before them.

The Indictments being found, a petit Jury was sworn, and the following Persons arraigned and tried

Stede Bonnet, alias *Edwards,* alias *Thomas,* late of *Barbadoes,* Mariner

Robert Tucker, late of the Island of *Jamaica,* Mariner

Edward Robinson, late of *New Castle* upon *Tine,* Mariner

Neal Paterson, late of *Aberdeen,* Mariner.

William Scot, late of *Aberdeen,* Mariner.

William Eddy, alias *Neddy,* late of *Aberdeen,* Mariner

Alexander Annand, late of *Jamaica,* Mariner

George Rose, late of *Glasgow,* Mariner

* *Thomas Nicholas,* late of *London,* Mariner.

John Ridge, late of *London,* Mariner

Matthew King, late of *Jamaica,* Mariner

Daniel Perry, late of *Guernsey,* Mariner

Henry Virgin, late of *Bristol,* Mariner

James Robbins, alias *Rattle,* late of *London,* Mariner

James Mullet, alias *Millet,* late of *London,* Mariner

Thomas Price, late of *Bristol,* Mariner

James Wilson, late of *Dublin,* Mariner

John Lopez, late of *Oporto,* Mariner

Zachariah Long, late of the Province of *Holland,* Mariner.

Job Bayly, late of *London,* Mariner

John-William Smith, late of *Charles-Town, South-Carolina,* Mariner.

Thomas Carman, late of *Maidstone* in *Kent,* Mariner.

John Thomas, late of *Jamaica,* Mariner

William Morrison, late of *Jamaica,* Mariner

Samuel Booth, late of *Charles-Town,* Mariner

William Hewet, late of *Jamaica,* Mariner

John Levit, late of *North-Carolina,* Mariner

William Livers, alias *Evis,* (without any particular Appellation)

John Brierly, alias *Timberhead,* late of *Bath-Town* in *North-Carolina,* Mariner

Robert Boyd, late of *Bath-Town* aforesaid, Mariner

* *Rowland Sharp,* late of *Bath-Town,* Mariner

* *Jonathan Clarke,* late of *Charles-Town,* Mariner.

* *Thomas Gerrard,* late of *Antegoa,* Mariner

All these, except the three last, and *Thomas Nicholas,* were found guilty of the Indictments exhibited against them, and received Sentence of Death accordingly

There were most of them try'd upon the two Indictments following.

' T H E Jurors for our Sovereign Lord the King, do upon their Oath present, that *Stede Bonnet,* late of *Barbadoes,* Mariner, *Robert Tucker, &c. &c.* The 2d Day of *August,* in the fifth Year of the

' Reign of our Sovereign Lord *GEORGE, &c* By ' Force of Arms, did piratically, and feloniously set ' upon, break, board, and enter, a certain Merchant ' Sloop, called the *Frances, Peter Manwaring* Commander, upon the High-Sea, in a certain Place called ' *Cape James,* alias Cape *Inlopen,* about two Miles ' distant from the Shore, in the Latitude of 39, or ' thereabouts, and within the Jurisdiction of the Court ' of Vice-Admiralty of *South-Carolina,* being the Property of certain Persons, to the Jurors unknown, ' and then, and there, piratically, and feloniously did ' make an Assault, in, and upon the said *Peter Manwaring,* and others his Mariners, whose Names to ' the Jurors aforesaid are unknown, in the same Sloop, ' against the Peace of God, and of our said now Sovereign Lord the King, then, and there being, and ' that the said *Stede Bonnet, &c* piratically and feloniously, did put the aforesaid *Peter Manwaring,* ' and others his Mariners, of the same Sloop aforesaid, in corporal Fear of their Lives, then and ' there, in the Sloop aforesaid, upon the *High-Seas,* ' in the Place aforesaid, called Cape *James,* alias ' Cape *Inlopen,* about two Miles from the Shore, in ' the Latitude of 39, or thereabouts, as aforesaid, ' and within the Jurisdiction aforesaid; and that the ' said *Stede Bonnet, &c* piratically and feloniously, ' did steal, take, and carry away the said Merchant ' Sloop, called the *Frances,* and also twenty six Hogsheads, *&c &c &c* being found in the aforesaid ' Sloop, in the Custody and Possession of the said ' *Peter Manwaring,* and others his Mariners of the ' said Sloop, and from their Custody and Possession, ' then and there, upon the High-Sea aforesaid, called Cape *James,* alias Cape *Inlopen,* as aforesaid, ' and within the Jurisdiction aforesaid, did remove, ' against the Peace of our now Sovereign Lord the ' King, his Crown and Dignity '

This was the Form of the Indictments they were arraigned upon, and tho' they might have proved several more Facts upon the major Part of the Crew, the Court thought fit to prosecute but two The Charge in the other was for seizing in a piratical and felonious Manner, the Sloop *Fortune, Thomas Read* Commander, which Indictment running in the same Words with the above-mention'd, *mutatis mutandis.*

All the Prisoners that were arraigned pleaded Not Guilty, and put themselves upon their Tryals, except *James Wilson,* and *John Levit,* who pleaded Guilty to both Indictments, and *Daniel Perry* to one only The Major would have gone through both the Indictments at once, which the Court not admitting, he pleaded Not Guilty to them both However, being convicted of one, he retracted his former Plea to the second Indictment, and pleaded Guilty to it, to prevent any farther Trouble

The Prisoners made little or no Defence, every one pretending only that they were taken off a Maroon Shore, and shipped with Major *Bonnet* to go to St *Thomas's,* but being out at Sea, and wanting Provisions, they were obliged to do what they did by the Vessels they met with Major *Bonnet* also himself, pretended that 'twas Force, not Inclination, that occasioned what had happened However, the Facts being plainly prov'd against them, and that they had all shared ten or eleven Pounds a Man, excepting the three last, and *Thomas Nicholas,* they were all but they found Guilty The Judge made a very grave moving Speech to them, setting forth the *Enormity of their Crimes, the Condition they were now in, and the Nature and Necessity of an unfeigned Repentance* He then recommended them to the Ministers of the Province, for more ample Direction to fit them for Eternity, *for* (concluded he) *the Priest's Lips shall keep Knowledge, and you shall seek* ek the Law at their Mouths, for they are the Meſſengers of the Lord, and the Ambaſſadors of Chriſt, and unto them is committed the Word of Reconciliation, after this he pronounced Sentence of Death upon them

On *Saturday Nov* the 8th, 1718. *Robert Tucker, Edward Robinſon, Neal Paterſon, William Scot, Job Bayley, John-William Smith, John Thomas, William Morriſon, Samuel Booth, William Hewit, William Eddy,* alias *Neddy, Alexander Annand, George Roſs, George Dunkin, Matthew King, Daniel Perry, Henry Virgin, James Robbins, James Mullet,* alias *Millet, Thomas Price, John Lopez,* and *Zachariah Long,* were executed at the *White-Point* near *Charles-Town,* purſuant to their Sentence.

As for the Captain, his Eſcape protracted his Fate, and ſpun out his Life a few Days longer, for he was not try'd till the 10th of *November,* when, being found Guilty, he received Sentence in like Manner as the former Judge *Trot* then made another excellent Speech particularly to him, which is rather ſomewhat too long to be inſerted in our Hiſtory; yet we could not tell how to paſs by ſo good and uſeful a Piece of Inſtruction, not knowing whoſe Hand. this Book may happen to fall into, and what Uſe ſuch ſound Inſtructions may be of.

The Lord Chief Juſtice's Speech, on his pronouncing Sentence of Death on Major Stede Bonnet.

MAJOR *Stede Bonnet,* you ſtand here convicted upon two Indictments of Piracy; one by the Verdict of the Jury, and the other by your own Confeſſion

Atho' you were indicted but for two Facts, yet you know that, at your Tryal, it was fully proved, even by an unwilling Witneſs, that you *piratically* took and rifled no leſs than *thirteen* Veſſels, ſince you ſailed from *North-Carolina*

So that you might have been indicted, and convicted of *eleven* more Acts of Piracy, committed ſince you took the Benefit of the King's *Act of Grace,* and pretended to leave that wicked Courſe of Life, if the Court had thought fit

Not to mention the many *Acts of Piracy* you committed before; for which, if your Pardon from Man was never ſo authentick, yet you muſt expect to give an Account before God, the great Judge

You know that the Crimes you have committed, are evil in themſelves, and contrary to the *Light* and *Law* of Nature, as well as to the *Law* of God. By which you are commanded, that *you ſhall not ſteal* Exod 20 15 And the Apoſtle St *Paul* expreſly affirms, that *Thieves ſhall not inherit the Kingdom of God,* 1 Cor 6 10

But to *Theft* you have added a greater Sin, which is *Murder* How many you may have *killed* of thoſe that reſiſted you in the committing your former *Pyracies,* I know not But this we all know, That, beſides the Wounded, you killed no leſs than eighteen Perſons out of thoſe that were ſent by lawful Authority to ſuppreſs you, and put a Stop to thoſe Rapines that you daily acted

And, however you may fancy that That was killing Men fairly in open *Fight,* yet this know, that the Power of the *Sword* not being committed into your Hands by any lawful Authority, you were not impowered to uſe any *Force,* or *fight* any one, and therefore thoſe Perſons that fell in that Action, in doing their Duty to their King and Country were *murdered,* and their *Blood* now cries out for *Vengeance* and *Juſtice* againſt you : For it is the *Voice of*

Nature, confirmed by the *Law* of God, That *whoſoever ſheddeth Man's Blood, by Man his Blood ſhall be ſhed.* Gen. 9. 6

And conſider that Death is not the only Puniſhment due to *Murderers*; for they are threatned to have *their Part in the Lake that burneth with Fire and Brimſtone, which is the ſecond Death,* Rev 21. 8 See alſo *Chap.* 22. 15. Words which carry that Terror with them, that, conſidering your Circumſtances and your Guilt, ſurely the Sound of them muſt make you tremble, *For who can dwell with everlaſting Burning?* Chap 33 14:

As the *Teſtimony* of your *Conſcience* muſt convince you of the great and many Evils you have committed, by which you have highly offended God, and provoked moſt juſtly his Wrath and Indignation againſt you, ſo I ſuppoſe I need not tell you, that the only Way of obtaining Pardon and Remiſſion of your Sins from God, is by a true and unfeigned *Repentance* and *Faith* in Chriſt, by whoſe meritorious Death and Paſſion, you can only hope for Salvation

You being a Gentleman that have had the Advantage of a *liberal Education,* and being generally eſteemed a Man of *Letters,* I believe it will be needleſs for me to explain to you the Nature of *Repentance* and *Faith* in Chriſt, they being ſo fully and ſo often mentioned in the Scriptures, that you cannot but know them For the ſame Reaſon, perhaps, it might be thought by ſome improper for me to have ſaid ſo much to you, as I have already, upon this Occaſion; neither ſhould I have done it, but that, conſidering the Courſe of your Life and Actions, I have juſt Reaſon to fear, that the Principles of Religion that had been inſtilled into you by your *Education,* have been at leaſt corrupted, if not entirely defaced, by the *Scepticiſm* and *Infidelity* of this wicked Age, and that what Time you allowed for Study, was rather applied to the *Polite Literature,* and the vain *Philoſophy* of the Times, than to a ſerious Search after the *Law* and *Will* of God, as revealed unto us in the holy *Scriptures* For had *your Delight been in the Law of the Lord, and had you meditated therein Day and Night,* you would then have found that God's *Word was a Lamp unto your Feet, and a Light to your Path,* Pſal 119 105 and that you would account all other Knowledge but *Loſt,* in Compariſon of *the Excellency of the Knowledge of Chriſt Jeſus,* Phil 3 8, *who to them that are called is the Power of God, and the Wiſdom of God,* 1 Cor 1 24 *even the hidden Wiſdom which God ordained before the World,* Chap 2 7.

You would then have eſteemed the *Scriptures* as the *Great Charter* of Heaven, and which delivered to us not only the moſt perfect *Laws* and *Rules* of Life, but alſo diſcovered to us the Acts of *Pardon* from God, wherein we have offended thoſe righteous Laws. For in them only is to be found the great *Myſtery* of fallen Man's *Redemption, which the Angels deſire to look into,* 1 Pet 1. 12

And they would have taught you that *Sin* is the debaſing of *Human Nature,* as being a *Deviation* from that *Purity, Rectitude,* and *Holineſs,* in which God created us, and that *Virtue* and *Religion,* and walking by the Laws of God, were altogether preferable to the Ways of *Sin* and *Satan*; for that the *Ways* of Virtue are *Ways of Pleaſantneſs, and all her Paths are Peace,* Prov. 3 17.

But what you could not learn from God's Word, by reaſon of your *careleſly,* or but *ſuperficially* conſidering the ſame, I hope the Courſe of his *Providence,* and the preſent *Affliction* that he hath laid upon you, have now convinced you of. For, however in your ſeeming Proſperity you might make a *Mock at your Sins,* Prov. 3. 17 yet now that you ſee that

God's Hand hath reached you, and brought you to publick Justice, I hope your present unhappy Circumstances have made you seriously reflect upon your past Actions and Course of Life; and that you are now sensible of the Greatness of your Sins, and that you find the Burthen of them is intolerable.

And that therefore, being thus *labouring, and heavy laden with Sin,* Mat. 11. 28. you will esteem that the most valuable *Knowledge,* that can shew you how you can be reconciled to that Supreme God whom you have so highly offended, and that can reveal to you Him who is not only the powerful *Advocate with the Father for you,* 1 John 2 1 but also who hath paid the Debt that is due for your Sins, by his own Death upon the Cross for you; and thereby made full Satisfaction for the Justice of God. And this is to be found no where but in God's Word, which discovers to us that *Lamb of God which takes away the Sins of the World,* John 1 29. which is *Christ* the Son of God: For this know, and be assured of, *that there is none other Name under Heaven given among Men, whereby we must be saved,* Acts 4 12 but only by the Name of the Lord *Jesus*

But then consider how he invites all Sinners to come unto him, and declares, *that he will give them rest,* Mat 11 28 for he assures us, *that he came to seek and to save that which was lost,* Luke 19 10 Mat 18 11 and hath promised, *that he that cometh unto him, he will in no wise cast out,* John 6. 37

So that if now you will sincerely turn to him, tho' late, even at the *eleventh Hour,* Mat 20 6, 9 he will receive you

But surely I need not tell you, that the *Terms* of his *Mercy,* are *Faith* and *Repentance*

And do not mistake the *Nature* of Repentance to be only a bare Sorrow for your Sins, arising from the Consideration of the *Evil* and *Punishment* they have now brought upon you; but your Sorrow must arise from the Consideration of your having offended a gracious and merciful God.

But I shall not pretend to give you any particular Directions as to the Nature of Repentance: I consider that I speak to a Person, whose Offences have proceeded not so much from his not *knowing,* as his *slighting* and *neglecting* his *Duty* Neither is it proper for me to give Advice out of the Way of my own Profession

You may have that better delivered to you by those who have made Divinity their particular Study, and who, by their Knowledge, as well as their Office, as being the *Ambassadors of Christ,* 2 Cor. 20. are best qualified to give you Instructions therein.

I only heartily wish, that what, in Compassion to your Soul, I have now said to you upon this sad and solemn Occasion, by exhorting you in general to *Faith* and *Repentance,* may have that due Effect upon you, as that thereby you may become a true *Penitent*

And therefore, having now discharged my Duty to you as a Christian, by giving you the best Counsel I can, with respect to the Salvation of your Soul, I must now do my Office as a *Judge*

The Sentence that the Law hath appointed to pass upon you for your Offences, and which this Court doth therefore award, is,

That you the said Stede Bonnet, *shall go from hence to the Place from whence you came, and from thence to the Place of Execution, where you shall be hanged by the Neck till you are dead*

And the God of infinite Mercy be merciful to your Soul.

The LIFE *of Sir* JOHN FALSTAFF.

SIR *John Falstaff* then was born at a Place called *Potten* in *Bedfordshire,* which is all we know concerning his Birth, and indeed if History had been as silent in this Article of Place as it is in that of the Time, when it had signified little, there being no remarkable Action, as we know of, to be settled by this Piece of Chronology. By the Courses he took, we may suppose his Estate was not very large; for the first Time he is mentioned, it is in Company with Thieves; tho' you may be sure it was none of your poor Pick-Pocket Gangs, forasmuch as *Henry* Prince of *Wales* (afterward King *Henry* V) appears among them *Poins, Bardolph, Gads-Hill,* and *Peto,* were the Names of the rest As we shall transcribe a great many of *Shakespear*'s inimitable Speeches, it would be a Folly to say any Thing in general of Sir *John*'s Person and Temper, besides what is contained in them. *When I was about thy Years,* Hal, (says Sir *John* to the Prince) *I was not an Eagle's Talon in the Waste; I could have crept into an Alderman's Thumb-Ring A Plague of Sighing and Grief, it blows a Man up like a Bladder!* For Sir *John,* you must know, when he said this, was not such a Skeleton as he describes. No,

he was a *Tun of Man, a Trunk of Humours a Bolting-hutch of Beastliness, a swoln Parcel of Dropsies, a huge Bombard of Sack, a stuff'd Clock-Bag of Guts, a roasted* Manning *Tree Ox, with a Pudding in his Belly,* &c as Prince *Henry* humorously draws his Picture

The first Scene between these two pleasant Companions gives us such a Sketch of our Hero, that I can't forbear transcribing some of it He addresses himself to the Prince in this merry Manner. Hal, *What Time of Day is it, Lad?* [Prince Henry.] *Thou art so fat-witted with drinking old Sack, and unbuttoning thee after Supper, and sleeping upon Benches in the Afternoon, that thou hast forgotten to demand that which thou wouldst truly know, What a Devil hast thou to do with the Time of the Day? unless Hours were Cups of Sack, and Minutes Capons, and Clocks the Tongues of Bawds, and Dials the Signs of Leaping-Houses, and the blessed Sun himself a fair hot Wench in Flame-colour'd Taffata, I see no Reason why thou shouldst be so superfluous to demand the Time of the Day.* [Falstaff] *Indeed you come near me now, Hal, for we that take Purses, go by the Moon and seven Stars,*

S.^R JOHN FALSTAFF & his Companions at GAD'S HILL.

by Phæbus, that wandering Knight so fair, but I pr'y thee, sweet Wag, when thou art King, — as God save thy Grace, (Majesty I should say, for Grace thou wilt never have so much as will serve as a Prologue to an Egg and Butter) Marry, I say, sweet Wag, when thou art King, let not us that are 'Squires of the Night's Body, be called Thieves of the Day's Beauty. Let us be Diana's Foresters, Gentlemen of the Shade, Minions of the Moon; and let Men say, we be Men of good Government, being govern'd as the Sea is, by our noble and chast Mistress the Moon, under whose Countenance we—steal. — But I pr'y thee, sweet Wag, shall there be Gallows standing in England when thou art King? and shall Resolution be thus fobb'd as it is, with the rusty Curb of old Father Antick, the Law? Do not thou when thou art King hang a Thief.

Immediately after this Sr John falls into a Strain of Repentance, and cries out, Thou art indeed, able to corrupt a Saint. Thou hast done much Harm to me, Hal, God forgive thee for it: Before I knew thee, Hal, I knew nothing, and now I am, if a Man should speak truly, little better than one of the Wicked. I must give over this Life, and I will give it over by the Lord, an I do not I am a Villain. I'll be damn'd for never a King's Son in Christendom. Hereupon the Prince asking him where he should take a Purse the next Day, Sir John answered, Where thou wilt, Lad, I'll make one; an I do not, call me Villain, and baffle me. And when the Prince told him, he saw a good Amendment in him, from Praying to Purse-taking, Why Hal, says Sir John, 'tis my Vocation, Hal: 'Tis no Sin for a Man to labour in his Vocation.

Poins, the bravest of all the Gang next to the Prince, understanding that there were Pilgrims going to St. Thomas Becket's Tomb at Canterbury, with rich Presents, and that at the same Time there were several wealthy Traders riding to London, he entered into an Agreement with his Highness, that Falstaff, Harvey, Rossil, and Gads-Hill (so called from the Place where they used to rob) should take the Booty from them; and that afterwards they (Poins and the Prince) should rob the Robbers in Disguise. This Design was accordingly executed; for the four that were appointed having got Possession of the shining Metal, which was the Piety of the Pilgrims, and the Life of the Tradesmen, our two Heroes fell upon them as they were dividing the Prey, put them all to Flight, and went off undiscovered, and sufficiently pleas'd. Some time after this, Falstaff and his stout-hearted Companions in the Exploit, meeting the Prince and Poins at a Tavern in Eastcheap, which they all frequented, the Knight began, after his usual Manner, to extol his own Valour, exclaiming bitterly against all Cowards, and professing that good Manhood was forgot upon the Face of the Earth. " There live not, quoth he, " three good Men unhang'd in England, and one of " them (meaning himself) is fat, and grows old. " God help the while a bad World, I say." His High-" ness asking the Occasion of this Bravado, Why, " says Sir John, here are four of us have taken a " thousand Pounds this Morning, but a hundred a " full hundred! fell upon us, and took it away again. " I am a Rogue, if I was not at Half-Sword with a " Dozen of them two Hours together. I have es-" cap'd by a Miracle, I am eight Times thrust " through the Doublet, four thro' the Hose, my " Buckler cut through and through, my Sword hack'd " like a Hand-Saw; here, look at it! I never dealt " better since I was a Man, all would not do. A " Plague of all Cowards, I say still." The Prince and Poins upon this, burst out a laughing, and told the whole Story, Harvey, Rossil, and Gads-Hill, Fal-staff's Companions, confess'd that he had hack'd his

Sword with his Dagger, and said, he would swear Truth out of England, but he would make Harry believe it was done in Fight, and that he had perswaded them to tickle their Noses with Spear-Grass to make them bleed, and then beslabber their Garments with it, and swear it was the Blood of true Men. This Instance of his Worship's Cowardice exposed him to the Ridicule of the whole Gang; but Sir John was not to be laugh'd out of Countenance; he had a Salve for every Sore. " By the Lord, says he, I " knew ye as well as he that made ye; but hark ye, " my Masters, was it for me to kill the Heir appa-" rent? should I turn upon the true Prince? Why, " thou knowest, I am as valiant as Hercules; but " beware Instinct — The Lion will not touch the " true Prince — Instinct is a great Matter, I was a " Coward on Instinct. I shall think the better of my-" self and thee during my Life; I for a valiant Lion, " and thou for a true Prince." An excellent Way of coming off!

Sir John however, seems contrary to his usual Custom, to have taken this Disgrace a little to Heart; for the next Time he meets Bardolph, he accosts him in this Manner: " Bardolph, am I not fallen " away vilely since this last Action? do I not bate? " do not I dwindle? why, my Skin hangs about me " like an old Lady's loose Gown: I am wither'd " like an old Apple-John. Well, I'll repent, and " that suddenly, while I am in some liking: I shall " be out of Heart shortly, and then I shall have no " Strength to repent. And I have not forgot what " the Inside of a Church is made of, I am a Pep-" per-Corn, a Brewer's Horse. The Inside of a " Church Company, villainous Company has been " the Ruin of me." Upon this Bardolph telling him he was fretful, and could not live long, " Why " there it is (quoth the Knight) come sing me a " bawdy Song to make me merry. I was a virtu-" ously given as a Gentleman need be, I swore " little, diced not above seven Times a Week; " went to a Bawdy-House not above once in a " Quarter of an Hour; paid Money that I borrow-" ed — three or four Times, liv'd well, and in good " Compass, but now I live out of all Order, out of " all Compass." This may serve for another Sketch of Sir John's Manner of repenting.

Some Time after this, the Civil Wars breaking out between the Houses of York and Lancaster, Prince Henry was sent for to Court to defend the Throne of his Father. Being unwilling to desert his humorous old squab Companion, he made him Captain of a Company of Soldiers, with Orders to march down to Shrewsbury, to meet the Enemy. But before we give an Account of our Knight's Behaviour in the Field of Battle, hear him describe his Company. " If " I be not asham'd of my Soldiers, I am a sous'd " Gurnet. I have misus'd the King's Press dam-" nably, I have got, in exchange of a hundred " and fifty Soldiers, three hundred and odd Pounds. " I press me none but good House-holders, Yeo-" mens Sons; enquire me out contracted Batchel-" lors, such as have been ask'd twice upon the " Banns; such a Commodity of warm Slaves, as " had as lieve hear the Devil as a Drum; such as " fear the Report of a Culverin worse than a struck " Fowl, or a hurt wild Duck. I press me none " but such Toasts and Butter, with Hearts in their " Bellies no bigger than Pins Heads, and they have " bought out their Services; and now my whole " Charge consists of Antients, Corporals, Lieutenants, " Gentlemen of Companies, Slaves as ragged as La-" zarus in the painted Cloth, when the Glutton's " Dogs lick'd his Sores, and such as indeed were " never Soldiers, but discarded unjust Servingmen, " younger Sons of younger Brothers, revolted Tap-sters,

" sters, and Hostlers Trade-fall'n, the Cankers of
" calm World and long Peace, ten Times more dif-
" honourably ragged than an old-fac'd Antient, and
" such have I to fill up the Rooms of those that
" have bought out their Services, that you would
" think I had an hundred and fifty tatter'd Pro-
" digals, lately come from Swine-keeping, from eat-
" ing Draff and Husks A mad Fellow met me
" on the Way, and told me I had unloaded all the
" Gibbets, and press'd the dead Bodies No Eye hath
" seen such Scare-Crows. I'll not march thro' *Co-*
" *ventry* with them, that flat. Nay, and the Vil-
" lains march wide between the Legs, as if they
" had Shackles on l for indeed, I had the most of
" them out of Prison There's but a Shirt and a
" half in all my Company, and the half is two
" Napkins tack'd together, and thrown over the
" Shoulders like a Herald's Coat without Sleeves;
" and the Shirt, to say the Truth, stollen from my
" Host of St *Alban's,* or the red-nos'd Inn-keeper of
" of *Daintry*; But that's all one, they'll find Linnen
" enough on every Hedge

The Forces of *Henry* IV. and Hot-spur *Piercy* being met at *Shewsbury,* the Place of Action, the
Morning before the Battle, *Falstaff* desires the Prince
to get astride him, and defend him, if he should happen to fall, telling him, that it would be a Point
of Friendship to do so To which the Prince pleasantly replying, that nothing but a *Collossus* could do him
that Service, and that he ow'd Heaven a Death, bidding him withal say his Prayers, and take his Leave,
we have the following humourous Speech of the
Knight's upon Record, which he made in Answer
to his Highness *The Debt to Heaven which you
speak of is not due yet, and I should be loth to pay him
before his Day What need I be so forward with
him that calls not on me? Well, 'tis no Matter, Honour
pricks me on But how if Honour pricks me off, when
I come on? How then? Can Honour set a Leg? No
Or an Arm? No Or take away the Grief of a
Wound? No Honour hath no Skill in Surgery then?
No What is Honour? a Word What is that word
Honour? Air, a trim Reckoning Who hath it? He
that died on Wednesday Doth he feel it? No Doth
he hear it? No It is insensible then? Yes, to the
Dead But will it not live with the Living? No
Why? Detraction will not suffer it Therefore I'll ha'
none of it Honour is a mere Scutcheon, and so ends
my Catechism* During the Battle, we find the valour-
ous Sir *John* getting as far as he can out of the Way,
and making this Soliloquy . *Tho' I could 'scape shot-
free at* London, *I fear the Shot here; here's no scoring, but upon the Pate Well, I am as hot as melted Lead, and as heavy too , Heaven keep Lead out of
me I need no more weight than mine own Bowels*
The Prince coming up, and chiding him for being
idle at such an important Time O Hal! pr'ythee
give me leave to breathe, says he, *Turk Gregory never did such Deeds in Arms as I have done this Day
I have paid* Piercy, *I have made him sure* The
Prince telling him *Piercy* was alive, and so leaving
him, Sir *John* goes on with the Soliloquy thus *If
Piercy be alive, I'll pierce him, if he comes in my
Way. If he do not, if I come in his, willingly, let
him make a Carbonado of me . I like not such grinning
Honour as Sir* Walter *hath,* (seeing the dead Body of
Sir *Walter Blunt,* a brave old Commander) *Give
me Life, which if I can save, I will, if not, Hon-
our comes unsought, and there's an End on't* Im-
mediately after this the Prince and *Hot-Spur* meet,
and a terrible Encounter ensues ; *Douglas,* a *Scots*
Nobleman, and Friend to *Hotspur,* falls at the same
Time on Sir *John,* and Sir *John* falls on the Ground,
to prevent any farther Mischief The Prince kills
Hotspur, and laments his old Friend *Jack,* whom he

fancies to be dead ; talks of having him imbowelled,
and so departs Sir *John,* who all this while had received no Hurt, rises at the Word imbowel, and
speaks as follows : " Imbowell'd l if you imbowel
" me To Day, I'll give you leave to powder me,
" and eat me To-Morrow 'Sblood' 'twas Time to
" counterfeit, or that hot Termagant *Scot* had paid
" me *Scot* and *Lot* too Counterfeit? I lie, I am
" no Counterfeit , to die is to be a Counterfeit,
" for he is but a Counterfeit of a Man who hath
" not the Life of a Man; but to counterfeit dying,
" when a Man thereby liveth, is to be no Counter-
" feit, but the true and perfect Image of Life in
" deed The better Part of Valour is Discretion, in
" the which better Part I have saved my Life But
" I am afraid yet of this Gunpowder *Piercy,* tho'
" he be dead How if he should counterfeit too,
" and rise? I am afraid he would prove the better
" Counterfeit? therefore I'll make him sure, yea,
" and I'll swear I kill'd him. Why may not he rise
" as well as I? Nothing confutes me but Eyes, and
" no body see me, therefore Sirrah, with a new
" Wound in your Thigh, come along with me."
Upon this, he very manfully ran the dead General
through the Thigh, and taking him upon his Back,
went to find out the King, that he might claim the
Honour of killing him He was met by the Prince,
who almost fancied he saw the Ghost of his old Cro-
ny . but Sir *John* soon convinc'd him that he was
the same individual *John Falstaff,* safe and sound,
and throwing down the Body, *There* says he, *is*
Piercy ; *if your Father will do me any Honour, to
him, if not, he may kill the next* Piercy *himself I
look to be either Earl or Duke, I assure you* The
Prince told him he kill'd *Piercy* himself, and saw him
lie, as he thought, dead. *Didst thou,* quoth *Falstaff?* Lord, Lord, *see how the World is given to lying I grant I was down, and so was he ; but we
rose both at an Instant, and fought a long Hour by*
Shrewsbury *Clock I'll take't on my Death, I gave
him that Wound in the Thigh, if the Man were alive,
and would deny it, I would make him eat a Piece of
my Sword*

One would have thought the Prince, after this,
should have had no more Employment for Sir *John* in
a martial Capacity , and by what has been said, there
is good Reason to think that Sir *John* would have
been very well satisfied at home in Quiet , but whether his Highness was willing to cross the capricious
old Fellow, or whatsoever else was the Cause, it is certain, that a fresh Insurrection was no sooner heard of,
but Captain *Falstaff* was again ordered to appear in
Arms When the Lord Chief Justice told him of it,
Well, says the Knight, " all you that kiss my Lady
" Peace at home, pray that our Armies join not in a
" hot Day , for I take but two Shirts out with me,
" and I mean not to sweat extraordinarily If it be
" a hot Day, if I brandish any thing but a Bottle,
" would I may never spit white again, There is not
" a dangerous Action can peep out his Head, but I
" am thrust upon it Well, I cannot last ever—
" But it was always the Trick of our Nation, if they
" have a good Thing, to make it too common I
" would to God my Name were not so terrible to
" the Enemy as it is ! I were better to be eaten to
" Death with a Rust, than to be scour'd to nothing
" with perpetual Motion " Sir *John* took as much
Care this Time in the Choice of his Men as had done
before, and was particularly cautious that he did not
get into the Field of Battle too soon , so that the Action was pretty well over when he made his Appearance However, he had the good Fortune to meet
a Knight of the Enemy's Party, called Sir *John Col-
ville of the Dale,* who was endeavouring to make his
Escape from the victorious *Henry Falstaff* bid him
surrender,

furrender, and Sir *John Coleville*, tho' otherwife a brave Man, did not think proper to difpute at this Time. By this Accident our Bully Knight got into his Poffeffion one of the nobleft Prifoners that were taken in the whole Engagement. He foon met the Prince, who began to call him to Account for his Delays, " I fhould be forry, my Lord, *fays* Falftaff, if ' it were not thus; I never knew yet but Rebuke ' and Check were the Reward of Valour Do you ' think me a Swallow, an Arrow or a Bullet? Have ' I in my poor old Motion the Expedition of ' Thought? I fpeeded hither with the very ex- ' tremeft Inch of Poffibility · I have founder'd nine ' Score and odd Pofts, and here, Travel-tainted as ' I am, in my pure and immaculate Valour, taken ' Sir *John Coleville of the Dale*, a moft furious ' Knight, and valorous Enemy But what of that? ' he faw me, and yielded. that I may juftly fay with ' the hook nos'd Fellow of *Rome*, I came, I faw, I ' *overcame* Here the Prince telling him it was more ' out of Sir John Coleville's *Courtefy* than his de- ' *ferving*, I know not that, *quoth* Sir John, but here ' he is, and here I yield him; and I befeech your ' Grace, let it be book'd with the reft of this Day's ' Deeds, or, by the Lord, I will have it in a par- ' ticular Ballad elfe, with mine own Picture at the ' Top of it, and *Coleville* kiffing my Foot, to the ' which Courfe if I be enforced, if you do not all ' fhew like gilt Two-pences to me, and I, in the ' clear Sky of Fame o'erfhine you as much as the ' Full Moon doth the Cinders of the Elements, which ' fhew like Pins Heads to her, believe not the Word ' of the noble, therefore let me have my Right, and ' let Defert mount " We have no Account what reward Sir *John* met with for this exemplary Piece of valour

The Reader, by this Time, may have heard enough of Sir *John Falftaff's* Courage, it may be proper, therefore, to relieve him a little with fome of our Knight's Gallantry, which was altogether as fingular as the Former; at leaft, in the inftance we are going to produce Two wealthy inhabitants of *Windfor*, call'd Mr *Ford* and Mr *Page*, liv'd in very good friendship, The Wives were as great Cronies as the Hufbands, and were befides, the witteft, merrieft Women in the whole Town. The gay eafy Tem- per of the Dames made Sir *John* fancy they were both in love with him, and in this Opinion, he writes to each of them a very amorous Epiftle, and fends 'em the fame Time The Confequence of this, was a Plot between the two Women, when they laid their Heads together, how to be reveng'd upon the leach- erous old Load of iniquity It was agreed, that Mrs *Ford* fhould give him Encouragement, and appoint a Time for him to come and fee her A Servant of Sir *John's* in the mean Time, goes and informs Mr. *Ford* who was before inclin'd to Jealoufy, of the whole affair? *Ford* goes to Sir *John* in Difguife, tells him his Name is *Broom*, and that he is in love with Mrs. *Ford*, offering him a huge Reward, if he could help him to the enjoying of her *Falftaff* hereupon dif- covers the Hour of Affignation, and promifes to in- troduce Mr *Broom*, who went away fully fatisfied of a terrible Plot againft his Head, which feemed already arm'd with Horns

At the Time appointed, *Falftaff* goes to *Ford's* Houfe, and the good natur'd Gentlewoman received him in the beft Manner imaginable, but they had not enjoy'd their Tranfport, before they were a- larm'd by Mrs *Page*, who was conceal'd in the next Room for that Purpofe She feemed to come from the Street, and told Sir *John* that Mr *Ford* was coming with a great many Neighbours, vowing Revenge A Basket of foul Linnen ftood by, and Sir *John* without Ceremony defired to be put into it, and fent to the

Wafherwoman's, or any whether, to efcape the Fury of the injur'd good Man The Bafket was placed there for this very Purpofe, and the Servants had their Leffons beforehand So the Knight was ftuff'd in and covered, and the two Men went away with the Burden, who carried all together, threw it into a fhallow Place in the *Thames*, and went their Way Sir *John* made a fhift to fcrabble out, and get home Hear him give a Defcription of this Misfortune to one of his Servants, " Go fetch me a Quart of Sack, " put a Toaft in it. Have I lived to be carried in a " Bafket, like a Barrow of Butcher's Offal, and to " be thrown into the *Thames*? Well, if I be ferved " fuch another Trick, I'll have my Brains taken out " and butter'd, and give them to a Dog for a New- " Year's-Gift The Rogues flighted me into the " River with as little Remorfe as they would have " drowned a blind Bitch's Puppies, fifteen in the Lit- " ter; and you may know by the Size, that I have a " kind of Alacrity in finking. If the Bottom were as " deep as Hell, I fhould down I had been drown- " ed, but that the fhore was fhelvy and fhallow, a " Death that I abhor for the Water fwells a Man: " And what a Thing fhould I have been when I had " been fwelled? I fhould have been a Mountain of " Mummy Come, let me pour in fome fack to the " *Thames* Water, for my Belly is as cold as if I had " fwallow'd Snowballs, for Pills to cool the " Reins."

The two Goffips, who knew nothing of the Infor- mation Mr *Ford* had received, were amaz'd to fee him come home in a real Fury They could not fo much as guefs at the Caufe, however, they were re- folved to have another Bout with Sir *John*, come what wou'd of it To this End, their former Go-between was again employ'd The Knight was at firft refrac- tory, becaufe of his late ill Ufage, but fo well did the Hag tell her Story, that at laft he yielded to come to Mrs *Ford's* again the next Morning between Eight and Nine No fooner was the Emiffary gone, but in comes the Sham Mr *Broom* *Falftaff* tells him how he had fucceeded with Mrs *Ford*, how the peaking Cornuto her Hufband had came Home at the Prologue of their Comedy, with a Rabble of his Companions; how he was cram'd into a Buck-Bafket, with foul Shirts, Smocks, Stockings, and greafy Napkins, and carried out; how he was met by *Ford*, and frighten'd terribly; in fhort, how he was thrown hiffing hot into the Thames " And think, Mafter *Broom*, fays " he, how all this muft be to a Man of my Kidney! " but I am to meet her again this Morning, her Huf- " band is gone a Birding, and then, Mr *Broom*, " for you!" *Ford*, who having fearched all the Houfe over before, and found no Body, was almoft reconcil'd to his rib, now went away more uneafy than ever, all the Circumftances agreed, and 'twas plain he was a Dupe —— Well, the Hour came, and *Falftaff* went, but was no fooner there, than he was again furpriz'd with *Ford's* coming The Women were very officious to drefs him in the Cloaths of a fat Woman, who pafs'd for a Witch, and whom *Ford* had forbid his Houfe Sir *John*, by this Means efcaped unknown, but was heartily bang'd in his Quality of an old Woman for prefuming to come there, and *Ford* and his Friends fearch'd the Houfe over again to no Purpofe

Mrs *Ford* thought it was now high Time to fet her Hufband at Eafe, fo fhe and Mrs *Page* produce their Letters, and tell the whole Story to all the Company The Man was fatisfied, the Women applauded, and a frefh Revenge was refolved on Mrs *Quickly*, the former Meffenger, was fent again, who informed Sir *John* fhe was come from the Par- ties " The Devil take one Party, and his Dam the " other, *fays he*, and fo they fhall be both beftow'd,

" I have suffer'd more for their fakes than the villai-
" nous inconstancy of Man's Disposition is able to
" bear I was beaten into all the Colours of the
" Rain-Bow, and like to be apprehended for the
" Witch of *Branford*: But that my admirable Dex-
" terity of Wit deliver'd me, I had been set in the
" Stocks, in the common Stocks, for a Witch! ——
" Well, *says the cunning old Hag*, but to prevent all
" Danger, sh'll meet you to Night in the Forest,
" where you may pass for *Herne* the Hunter, who,
" they say, walks with a great Pair of Horns on his
" Head Put on the Horns, and fear nothing!" *Fal-
staff* consented, the Woman went her Way, and Mr
Broom came again, not now to entrap his Wife, but
only to catch the Knight, who tells another lamen-
table Story of his being beaten grievously in the Shape
of a Woman *For in the Shape of a Man, Master*
Broom, says he, *I fear not* Goliath, *with a Weaver's
Beam* But meet me at Night, *and all shall be well*
So he recited the whole Story of his new Assignation
This was the worst Punishment of all, for *Ford*, *Page*,
their Wives, Children, and Friends, were ready a-
gainst the appointed Hour, all dress'd like Fairies.
Sir *John*, as before, went to the Place in Time, big
with the Hopes of enjoying what he had sought so
long, and suffer'd so much for. A huge Pair of
Stags Horns were upon his Head, which he esteem'd
as emblematical of those he was to fix upon the Head
of poor *Ford* In a Word, the Fairies came, and
pinched him almost to Death; which done, they all
discovered themselves And from this Time poor
Falstaff became a Laughing-Stock to all the good
People in *Windsor* He has humourously described
this Disposition of Mankind towards him in these
Words " Men of all Sorts take a Pride to gird at
" me The Brain of this foolish compounded Clay,
" Man, is not able to invent any thing that tends to
" Laughter more than I invent, or is invented on
" me I am not only witty in myself, but the Cause
" that Wit is in other Men ".

How much of the foregoing Stories we owe to
the fruitful Invention of *Shakespear*, we shall not pretend to determine 'Tis certain the whole Character of Sir *John Falstaff*, as he has drawn it, whether
it be entirely founded upon Truth or no, is one of
the most beautiful Pieces in our Language, which
may be a sufficient Excuse for our inserting so much
of it Those who are acquainted with the Plays from
which the foregoing is extracted, will see we have
bestowed a pretty deal of Labour, and, we hope,
some Judgment in what we have done, which is all
we shall say concerning ourselves Give us Leave,
however, to add, that the late celebrated Duke of
Buckingham, after he has discoursed very finely upon the humour of our Plays, uses these Words

But Falstaff *seems inimitable yet*

We now proceed to give a less poetical Account
of some of the merry Pranks which are recorded of
our Hero, and indeed a very different Account from
the foregoing. Instead of making him a Coward, a
Glutton, and a Drunkard, all other Authors that
mention him say, he was a very brave Commander;
and that, on the Account of his Valour against the
York Faction, King *Henry* IV knighted him, and
gave him a Pension of four hundred Marks *per Ann*
which was a great Income in those Days Be this as
it will, his Revenue was not sufficient to support his
Extravagancies, for all agree, he took up the Occupation of a Gentleman Highwayman

He first set out upon this unlawful Design by himself, but a Man need never want a Companion in
Wickedness, several other dissolute and disorderly
Gentlemen quickly enter'd themselves into his Service Their Names were the same as before recited
and the Robberies they committed were almost innumerable They were completely mounted and armed, and having been lately in the Service of the Hou[se]
of *Lancaster*, they wanted not for Skill to make u[se]
of those Advantages Scarce could a Traveller b[e]
safe for them upon any Road for a hundred Mile[s]
round *London*, tho' the Place which Sir *John* himself commonly collected at was *Gads-Hill* in *Kent*

It was here that he one Day met a Country Farmer, and demanding what Money he had about him
the Farmer replied, None, adding, that he did no[t]
use to carry Money about him for Fear of Robbing. Sir *John* hereupon, commanded him to knee[l]
down, and fall to Prayers, and at the same Time h[e]
pulled a little Manual out of his Pocket, and kneeled down by him The Countryman did not know
what to make of this unseasonable Piece of Devotion, and would willingly have taken another Time
and Place to make his Orisons. But there was no
resisting Necessity Sir *John* was inclined to be pious,
and the Farmer must be so too, at least must appea[r]
so, for very probably his Fear might abate the Fervour which he might else have shewn. The Knight
mumbled over some Words between his Teeth with
a great deal of seeming Devotion, and then enquir'd
of his Fellow Christian how it fared with him, *Fo[r]
Heaven*, he said, *would not be deaf to the pious Addresses of those that were sincerely devout, wherefore,
pr'ythee feel in thy Pockets, that we may see wha[t]
God hath sent thee* The Countryman did so, but
pretended he could find nothing Upon which Si[r]
John feeling in his own Pockets, pulls out a Ninepenny Piece, telling him withal, *That for certain he*
pray'd not heartily, therefore 'twas necessary for
him to pray again If you look, *says he*, directly
towards Heaven, it cannot be but you must get somewhat as well as I With that, putting his Hand
into his Pocket again, he pulls out a Thirteen-Pence
Half-penny Piece Still the other poor Man had no
Success He could not find a single Farthing, and
doubtless he pray'd, that no Body else might find
any Thing upon him He produces now no less
than a Noble, Six Shillings and Eight-Pence! The
Countryman continued firmly in the Negative Upon
which Sir *John* told him plainly, *That either he di[d]
not pray with Devotion, or else he would not let his*
him see how liberal Heaven had been to him? For says
he, *how comes it to pass, that my Prayers should b[e]
heard, and not yours? If you pray with as much sp[i]-
ritual Zeal, as you outwardly make Shew of, it mu[st]
needs be, that by this Time you have gained very considerably Therefore I am resolved to examine into th[e]
Truth of this Matter* He did so, and found in the
Countryman's Pockets twenty Broad-Pieces of Gol[d]
at which they were both amaz'd, Sir *John* seemin[g]-
ly at the Liberality of Heaven, and the other real[ly]
at the Loss of his Money *Falstaff*, however, deal[t]
better with the Farmer, than he expected For h[e]
gave him the Money, which he had at several Time[s]
taken out of his own Pocket, adding this severe Reprimand *What a hypocritical Rogue are you to endeavour to cheat me, your Companion, at this Rate! I[s]
this the Agreement we made before we went to Prayer[s]
Good Lord! how few People are just upon Earth! i[s it]
to punish you for your Wickedness, I shall keep wha[t]
Heaven has sent into your Pocket, but that you ma[y]
not want upon the Road, take what I have got b[y]
praying, and when you are got home; acquaint you[r]
Neighbours with what an honest Gentleman you me[t]
who gave you Eight Shillings and Six-Pence, who[m]
you endeavoured to cheat him of twenty Broad Piece[s]*

A little after this religious Enterprize Sir *John*, an[d]
some of his Comrades, met the common Hangman coming from an Execution at *Kingston* upon *Thame[s]*
They

[they] robb'd him of what little Money he had, and [th]en dragged him out of the Road, into an adjacent [W]ood, and hang'd him upon a Tree, as a dangerous [fe]llow to their Profession, which, in their Opinion, [w]as a very honourable one

On the same Day that the Executioner was exe[cu]ted Sir *John* received Notice of the Return of a [ce]rtain rich Merchant, who had been at a Fair at [Gu]ilford Upon this he dressed himself in Woman's [Ap]parel, and rode along 'till he came in Sight of his [in]tended Prey He then alighted; and lying down, [af]ter he had tied his Horse in a Wood, he filled the [Ro]ad with loud Cries and Lamentations, accusing [H]eaven and Earth as conspiring in his Misfortunes [T]he Merchant, being a Man of a brisk and airy [T]emper, and one who well understood the Delights [o]f a Female Conversation, was not a little mov'd [w]ith Joy at this happy Surprizal, imagining himself [i]n the easy Possession of a jolly young Woman; for [in]deed Sir *John*, though something of the thickest, [di]d not make a disagreeable Figure in his Female [Ha]bit There appeared so much Delicacy and Soft[ne]ss in his Skin, (at least what was seen of it, for he [w]as mask'd,) that not a few Women would have [be]en proud to have possest the like The honest [M]an, therefore, very generously a-lights from his [Ho]rse, and enquires of the fair Charmer (for so he [ca]lled Sir *John*) what was the Cause of her Com[pl]aints? She, poor Soul, for her Part tells him a long [St]ory of her piteous Adventures; as that she had [be]en to visit some Relations along with a barbar[ou]s inhuman Brother, who had left her in this unknown [P]lace, upon a very small Difference that had arisen. 'Twas impossible for the tender-hearted Merchant to [he]lp pitying her Misfortunes, which he looked upon [t]o be real, and joining with her in lamenting her [Co]ndition, and cursing the Cruelty of her Brother Pity, it has been observ'd, frequently tunes the Soul [t]o Love; and thus it was with our Merchant He [sa]te himself down, and spoke a great many soft Things, and, in short almost brought Matters to [th]e last Extremity Sir *John*, who was still covered [w]ith his Mask, made but a feeble Resistance, only [cr]ying, *I am undone, lost, ruin'd forever! Alas, dear Sir, what do you mean? What would you do with me? Is this your Compassion? This your Kindness to a poor, distressed, miserable Creature? What! rob me of my Honour, dearer to me than my Life? For Heaven's sake, Sir, forbear!* The Merchant was not to be repulsed with such a weak Opposition as this, he thought it was only Virgin Modesty that would presently be overcome, and therefore, comforted his dear Soul with all the kind Words, and fair Promises he could invent, taking her by the Hand, and leading her to the Entrance of the Wood, Sir *John*, seeing it now Time to draw towards a Conclusion, told him, *That since her Misfortunes had so ordered it, that she was fallen into his Hands, she entreated he would do her the Favour to advance further into the Wood, that she might not be openly prostituted* Still our excellent Droll sobbed, and cried, and called upon Death a thousand Times to come and succour her, before she was eternally disgrac'd. The Merchant complied with this last reasonable Request, and went with her into the most solitary Part of the Wood, where being just about to work his wicked Will upon the poor unhappy yielding Creature, to his great Surprize, as well as Pain, she drew a Poiniard out of her Bosom, and thrust him through one of his Arms. The amorous Gallant being hereby disabled, his supposed Female Beauty rifled his Pockets, took out three or four Purses of Gold, and immediately rode off with the Booty

Another Time, Sir *John*, in Company with but one of his Companions, met a couple of Friers, belong-

ing to a Monastery, which, in those Times of Popery, was at *Dartford in Kent* Our thieving Knight stripped them of their religious Habits, which was much against the Will of his Companion, 'till he gave him the following Reason for his so doing *You know*, says he, *that we are not far from* Lewisham, *where there is a noble large golden Chalice, belonging to the Church, and you ought to know as well, that there is no Habit which a Man can rob in so safely as a religious one My Advice then is, That we assume the Sheeps Cloathing, and make the best of our Way to the Curate's House Never doubt of Success, and leave the Conduct of the Affair to me* Falstaff's Comrade was now very well pleased with the Contrivance, and consented to assist in the putting it forthwith in Practice Away march our two Friars, and the generous Curate, believing them to be what they appeared, received them, in a Manner so very kindly as gave them fresh Hopes of succeeding in their Design At Night, as they lay together, they were a considerable Time consulting how they should carry on the Affair: But they at last concluded to both their Satisfactions, and went to Sleep The Morning being come, they got up very early, and went to the Curate's Chamber, telling him, *It was their Custom to say Mass always at that Time, and therefore they desired he would join with them.* The good Man, without mistrusting any Thing, arose and opened the Door; which he had no sooner done, but our two Ruffians rushed in upon him, knock'd him down, gagged him, and tied him Neck and Heels; after which, they broke open his Trunks, and took away all his Money, and not contented with this, they took the Keys of the Church, and carried away not only the Chalice, but all the other Ornaments that were portable, and so they marched off

One Day as Sir *John* was riding along the Road by himself, he met with two of his own Profession, who, not knowing him, and seeing he made a good Appearance, thought they had found a Prize. With this Confidence they rode up to him, who did not endeavour to avoid 'em, and bid him stand; swearing, damn 'em, and sink 'em, he was a dead Man, if he did not immediately deliver his Money. Sir *John* being accustomed not to give, but to take, could not heartily relish this Demand, and therefore, very boldly told them, he had none, at the same Instant laying his Hand suddenly upon one of their Swords, he wrenched it out of his Hand, and gave him such a Blow with it on his Arm, that the Pain took away all Sense Having done this, he set upon the other very furiously, who, being less valiant than his Companion, betook himself to the Swiftness of his Horse's Heels But Sir *John* pursued him so closely, that he made him yield himself to his Mercy Upon which he generously gave him his Life, after reprimanding him severely for attempting to meddle with one who was his Master at his own Trade Returning after this to the other, whom he had first struck, he threaten'd him with Death, if he deliver'd not his Money The poor Thief would willingly have excus'd himself by pretending he had none But *Falstaff* was not to be put off in that Manner, being well satisfied there was no Credit to be given to Persons of that Vocation He very orderly therefore applied to his Pockets, where he found a large Quantity of Gold and Silver, the Spoils of a great many honest People To be more completely revenged of his Antagonist, Sir *John* bound him strongly Neck and Heels, wrote his Crime upon a Paper, and pinned it to his Breast; then placed him where he might be exposed to the View of all Passengers

The unfortunate Highway-man had not lain long in this Position, before some whom he had lately robbed came by, who looking at the Paper, and at the same

same Time examining his Face, knew him to be the Man Upon this they carried him before a Magistrate, who committed him to Prison, where he remained 'till the next Assizes, when he was convicted, sentenc'd, and shortly after executed Thus was Sir *John* the Means of bringing one of his Brethren to Justice, while in the Height of his own Crimes, but the Action was honourable, and in his own Defence, for the Soul of our Knight was above submitting to the detested Office of a mercenary Thief-Catcher

Sir *John* followed this disorderly Course of Life a great many Years, and what made him the more daring in his unlawful Enterprizes, was the having a no less Man than the eldest Son of King *Henry* IV in his wicked Fraternity, with whom he was very familiar, as we have before observed This Prince being prompted on by his own vicious Inclinations, and the Fire of Youth, and encouraged by a Set of debauched and abandoned Courtiers, committed such Extravagancies as are almost incredible For he not only frequently robbed upon the Highway, in Company with *Falstaff* and others, whom we have mention'd, but went so far as to set upon his Father, and several Times put in Fear of some Design against his Person For Kings went not guarded in those Days as they do at present He attempted also to rescue a Prisoner from the Face of Justice, in the Court of *King's-Bench, Westminster*, for which he was himself committed a Prisoner by the Lord Chief Justice, whom he struck on the Seat of Judgment The Justice was admir'd and applauded for this Action, and the Prince, notwithstanding his ungovernable Temper, submitted to the Sentence, seemingly without Reluctance And indeed it appears this Prince, who had a prodigious natural Genius, often disapprov'd his own Extravances when he came to reflect seriously *Shakespear* has given us a Speech, or rather Soliloquy of his, suppos'd to be spoken at the Place of Haunt in *Eastcheap*, immediately upon parting with his scandalous Company 'Tis in these Words *I know you all, and will uphold your Humour a little, yet in this will I imitate the Sun, who permits the base contagious Clouds to hide his Beauty sometimes from the World, that when he pleases to be himself again, at a Time when he is over, much wanted, he may be the more wonder'd at, by breaking thro' the foul and ugly Mists and Vapours that seemed almost to smother and straggle him If all the Year were Holidays, it would be as tedious to sport as to work, but when Play-days come seldom, they come wish'd for, and nothing pleases but what is rare So when I throw off this base Behaviour, and pay the Debt I never promis'd, by how much I am better than my Word, by so much shall I falsify Men's Hopes and my Reformation glittering over my Fault, like bright Metal upon a sullen Ground, shall shew more goodly, and attract more Eyes than that which has no foil to set it off* And we find this illustrious Person was not at all worse than his Word, especially in the the Case of the Lord Chief Justice

This good Man, upon the Death of *Henry* IV. was under terrible Apprehensions of Severity from the Hands of his new Master The young King put on a sullen Countenance, and reprehended with a great Deal of seeming Warmth, and the Judge defended himself as nobly as he had acted before, by telling him, that upon the Bench he represented his Father, who was insulted in his Person, and desiring him to make the Case his own, and consider whether, now he was King, he would suffer his Dignity to be profan'd in a Chief Magistrate, by a disobedient Son But how agreeably was this venerable Person surpriz'd, when his Majesty returned him this Answer " You are right, Justice, and you weigh the Matter " well, therefore still bear the Ballance and the Sword,

" and I wish you Honours may increase till you " live to see a Son of mine offend you, and obey " you as I did So shall I live to speak the Words of " my Father, Happy am I, that I have a Magistra" so bold as to dare to do Justice upon my own " Son, and no less happy in having a Son that " would deliver up his Greatness into the Hand of " Justice You committed me, for which I com" mit into your Hand the unstain'd Sword that you " used to bear, remembring you still to use the same " with the like bold, just, and impartial Spirit as " you have done against me There is my Hand, " you shall be a Father to my Youth, and I will " humble myself to your wise Directions I will " mock the Expectations of the World, and frustrate " the Prophesies of the Vulgar My Tide of Blood, " that has proudly flow'd in Vanity till now, shall " turn back to the Sea, from whence it shall hence" forth flow in State and formal Majesty The wisest " of our Nation shall form our Council, of which " you, Father, shall be the Chief, and I will min" gle in your solemn Debates 'till Peace and War be " come familiar to me, and *England* is own'd the " best-govern'd Nation in the World " It is farther reported of this Prince, that he was wont every Day after Dinner to set apart two Hours to receive Petitions, and redress Grievances, which he would do with wonderful Equity, and that he sent to *Rome* to be absolved from the Death of King *Richard* II (of which 'tis thought his Father was guilty) tho' 'tis certain he had no Hand in it

This Account of the Reformation of King *Henry* V is doing Justice to the Memory of one of the greatest and best Monarchs that ever sate upon the *English* Throne Besides, it is not altogether foreign to our Design, as it makes Way for another Story of our Hero, Sir *John Falstaff* The Knight was in the Country, at the House of one Justice *Shallow*, an old Acquaintance of his, when the News was brought by *Pistol* of his Friend *Hal*'s Advancement He was unable to contain his Joy, and summoning all his own Gang and the Justice's Family about him, he made this Harangue Away *Bardolph*, saddle my Horses —— Master *Robert Shallow*, chuse what Office thou wilt in the Land, 'tis thine —— *Pistol*, I will double charge thee with Dignities —— Carry Master *Silence* to Bed —— Master *Shallow*, my Lord *Shallow*, be what thou wilt, I am Fortune's Steward Get on thy Boots, we'll ride all Night —— Oh! sweet *Pistol*, utter more to me, and withal advise something to do thyself good —— Boot, Boot, Master *Shallow*, I know the young King is sick for me —— Let us take any Man's Horses, the Laws of *England* are at my Commandment —— Happy are they who have been my Friends, and Wo to my Lord Justice Accordingly they all got ready, and Mr *Shallow* lent Sir John a thousand Pounds to maintain in his Dignity, 'till the King loaded him with Riches They rode post to *London*, and came just Time enough to see the Coronation The whole Company got among the Mob, and Sir John addressed himself to the Justice in this Manner Stand here by me, Master *Robert Shallow*, I will make the King do you Grace I will lear upon him as he comes by, and do but mark the Countenance that he will give me O if I had Time to have made new Liveries, I would have bestow'd the thousand Pounds I borrow'd of you But it is no Matter, this poor Show doth better, it infers the Zeal I had to see him, it shews my Earnestness of Affection, my Devotion, as it were, to ride Day and Night, and not to deliberate, not to remember, not to have Patience to shift me, but to stand stained with Travel, and sweating with Desire to see him, thinking ng of nothing elfe, putting all Affair in Oblivion, as if there were nothing elfe to be done but to fee him.

Thus did Sir *John* run on in a lofty Strain, indulging h s own Vanity, and the Hopes of all that were with him, till the Royal Perfon appear'd in all the Splendour and Magnificence that was futable to the Occafion *God fave thy Grace, King* Hal, *my fweet Boy, my Jove, my Heart!* faid Sir *John* with his wonted Air: But how was he difappointed, when, inftead of the Warmth he expected to be receiv'd with, his Majefty, with a forbidding Countenance, deliver'd thefe Words! *I know thee not, old Man, what is thy Meaning? Do thefe white Hairs become a Buffoon and a Jefter? I have long dream'd indeed of fuch a Man as thou art, fo furfeit-fwell'd, fo old, and fo prophane But being awake, I defpife my Dream—Make thy Body lefs, and thy Grace more; for Grave gapes for thee three Times wider than for other Men —Do not reply to me with a foolifh Jeft, nor be fo prefumptuous as to think me the Thing that I was Heaven knows, and the World fhall perceive, that I have turned away my former felf, fo will I thofe that have kept me Company When thou fhalt hear that I am what I have been, approach me, and be what thou waft, the Tutor and Feeder of my Riots; 'till then, I banifh thee from my*

Prefence, as I have done the reft of my Mifleaders; —dare not henceforth, on Pain of Death to come within ten Miles of our Perfon: I will allow you a Competence for Life, that Want may not induce you to Evil, and as we hear of your Amendment, we will advance you according to your Strength and Qualities The King did according to his Word in every Particular, and conquer'd himfelf in a manner that won the Hearts of all his People

Habits of Vice are very difficult to be worn off, even tho' the Occafions that firft produc'd them ceafe, *Henry's* Extravagancies were only the Sallies of a great and violent Soul, not yet fubjected to the Government of Reafon; but Sir *John* was grown grey in Iniquity, he acted his Crimes with Coolnefs and Deliberation; neither the Example, the Severity, nor the Promifes of his Sovereign, could have any Effect upon him He continued his diffolute Courfes 'till he was apprehended, and committed to *Maidftone* Goal for a Robbery at *Gad's-Hill* At the next Affizes he was capitally convicted, but the King unwilling he fhould fuffer Death, order'd him only to transport himfelf in a Month's Time out of the *English* Dominions It was thought this Sentence, tho' very mild, broke the Knight's Heart, for he died before the Time allow'd him was expir'd

The LIFE of ARTHUR CHAMBERS.

HAVING gone through the Life of *Falftaff*, or rather a Series of comic Adventures performed by him, and his Gang of merry Fellows, which we have exacted from authentick Memoirs, and fome Touches of our great *Shakefpear*, we fhall pafs over to latter Days, and prefent our Readers with Transactions of Modern Date, and which Thoufands now living may, probably, be no Strangers to We fhould, indeed, have premifed before, that our Countrymen were not to expect a fucceffive Order of the Perfons, whofe Exploits (if they may be termed fo) we have determined to write, but on the other Hand, fuch a mix'd Account as might have two Effects on the Minds of our candid Readers, by which Expreffion we beg leave to be underftood, that our Aim, throughout the Courfe of thefe Sheets, is, fometimes by fetting before them the oddeft Occurrences that ever happened in Life, fo to amufe them that they may receive a vaft deal of Pleafure while they read; and at other Times, by drawing horrid and melancholy Scenes of Death and Murder, fo to awaken them that they may deteft the like Vices, and in purfuing this Courfe, we have reafon think we fhall do no fmall Service to our Countrymen

The Perfon we are going to treat of, was named *Arthur Chambers*, one of bafe Extraction, and confequently void of Education, good Manners, or any other Qualification that was amiable, from his Infancy he had a natural Propenfity to Pilfering, and, becaufe the poor Circumftances of his Parents deprived him of acquiring what might fet him off in the World, the loofe Way of Living he had contracted from a vagabond and lazy Life, quite turned his

Thoughts to difhoneft Ways of fupporting himfelf 'Tis even afferted that he more than once play'd the Thief in Hanging-fleeve Coats, and if this be true, we need not wonder he became fo expert in his Employment, as he called it.

The firft Step, in his Opinion, to compleat him a thorough Mafter in the thieving Art, was to have at his Fingers Ends, all the canting Language (which comprehends a Parcel of invented Words, fuch as Thieves very well know, and by which they can diftinguifh one another from the other Claffes of Mankind) in order to the Attainment whereof, he put himfelf under the Direction of an experienced Teacher that Way, and what was foon obfervable, attended fo clofely to the Dictates of his Preceptor, that he not only out-rivalled him, but became fuperior to any of his cotemporary Thieves

Chambers quickly difcover'd how pleafing his new Language was to him, for he could not enter an Alehoufe, but he would be punning with the Landlord Indeed his gay Apparel (for *Arthur* could not endure the Thought of being called a Sloven) gained very often on the Mafters of the Houfes he frequented, to fit down by him, and liften to his jocular Way of talking Sometimes, from the Ignorance of fome of them, he would impudently affert that what he now and then mixed with his ordinary *English*, was the pureft *Greek* in the World, and, to convince them he was fincere in what he advanced, would frequently pull out of his Pocket a *Greek Teftament*, and fay, *Sir, this Book was made by one of the old Philofophers; believe me, I have ftudied it this dozen Years, and every Moment I look'd into it, I gain'd a Twelve-month's Knowledge.* The Landlord would be gazing all the while open-mouth'd at *Chambers*, and to be sure, he, on his Part, was very intent upon something besides his *Greek Testament*, for, soon after, a general Complaint was made of Abundance of Money being lost, but, which Way, was the Question.

A while after this, our Practitioner was sent to *Bridewell*, there to answer, with hard Labour, some petty Abuses he had committed, but, obtaining his Liberty he began to reflect, that some Way or other was of Necessity to be found out to make his Life more agreeable and less burthensome to him, than it had been of late; he found that the Town began to suspect him, and having very clear Eyes to see into those Things that concerned himself, he left it with a hearty Curse, and went down to *Launceston* in *Cornwall*

It seems the Inhabitants here received him with open Arms for a considerable Time, and his merry Disposition soon procured him the Acquaintance of Men of Note in that County: He had taken Care too before his leaving *London*, to supply himself with a great Number of false Crown and Half-Crown Pieces, which, on his Arrival, he uttered at all the Places he frequented, but Abundance of Persons having been deceived with these Pieces, and a general Complaint made round about, Search was made every where for the apprehending of the Cheat, and poor *Chambers* was taken up; the Consequence of which was sending him to Goal, where he remained a Year and a Half before he could get his Enlargement

Cornwall now became too hot for him to stay any longer there; he had forfeited his Reputation with his Acquaintance, he found no Relief, nor no Signs of any, and what could he do in these Circumstances? Why, he made the best Way he was able to *London*, where on the very first Day of his Arrival, he performed the most cunning, artful, and yet barefac'd Piece of Felony that ever was heard of The Fact stands thus recorded

Having alighted from the Waggon, he went directly to an Alehouse in *West-Smithfield*, where, seating himself in a Box, and calling for a Pint of Beer, and a Slice of Bread and Cheese, he comfortably refresh'd himself, then falling into Discourse with some Tradesmen in the next Box to him, about the Country and quiet Enjoyment of a rural Life, the Talk was insensibly turned upon Diving or picking of Pockets (a Circumstance of all others the most surprizing, as it was observed the Company had been reasoning very gravely a long Time on the Advantages of a Country before a City Life) *Chambers* improved the Hint, and said, *It was a thousand Pities no better Provision could be made for the Suppression of little Villains*; for added he, *Death was too ample a Punishment for a Person if he robbed the whole World, but why should I talk thus*, continued he, *if great Offenders are suffered, well may the poor and Necessitous say—We must live, and where's the Harm of taking a few Guineas from those who can spare them, or ten thousand to one who robbed others of them?—For my own Part, I look on a dextrous Pickpocket as a very necessary Man in any Government whatever; as such a Person draws so much from the Purses of his Countrymen, which otherwise would be spent in Gaming or Whoring. Look ye, Gentlemen, I can pick a Pocket as well as any Man in Great-Britain, and yet, tho' I say it, am as honest as the best Englishman breathing*, for an Instance of *what I say, observe the Country Gentleman just now passing by the Window I'll step out and take his Watch, tho' it is now scarce five o'Clock.*—A Wager of 10 s. was immediately laid that he did not perform it; *Chambers* answer'd the Bett, and presently pushing out of the

Door, made a quick Round, till he came to the End of *Long-Lane*, where he met with the Gentleman, and courteously pulling of his Hat to him, ask'd if he could inform him which was the nighest Way to *Knave's-Acre*,—to which the Gentleman replied,—*Lack-a-day Friend, you ask a very ignorant Person, for I am a Stranger here, and want to know the nearest Way to Moor-fields* ——*Oh! oh! Sir, I live there, and can acquaint you which Way to take, excuse me, Sir, I would willingly bear you Company thither, but extraordinary Affairs calling me to find out a Place called Knaves-Acre, I must necessarily be jogging on, but be pleased to take my best Direction* So saying he pointed with his Hand, *Look you, Sir, you have no other Way to go than directly along this Lane, which will bring you into a Street call'd Barbican, that into a dirty Lane over against it, and that into Chiswell-Street, the End whereof will lead you into Moorfields* All this while the Country Gentleman was staring the Way *Chambers* pointed, who in the Interim, made sure of his Watch, and after the Gentleman and he had left one another, returned back to the Company, laid down the Spoil on the Table, and claimed the Wager, which was accordingly paid ——*But*, said *Chambers, the Gentleman shall have his Watch again, and I myself will acquaint him with the whole Affair.* So said, he trudged after him, and coming up with him before he had got quite through *Barbican*, after having ask'd Pardon for his Rudeness, desired him to tell him if he had lost any Thing ——*Nothing I hope Friend, but I'll search my Pockets, to be sure of it, and see, my good Man*, in short, the Gentleman coming to his Fob, found his Watch gone; upon which *Chambers* civilly return'd it, but not without giving him a succinct Detail how he came by it, and the Reason why ——The Gentleman return'd him a thousand Thanks, admir'd his Dexterity, gave him half a Crown, and bad him put it to the 10 s and remember him among his Friends, and so they parted again

This Action performed in Broad-Day Light, and in a Lane where Abundance of People resort, and consequently where some must be passing and repassing at that Time, argued in *Chambers* not only a consummate Boldness, but the greatest Dexterity of Hand, with respect to the obtaining the Watch, that can be imagined But if this is looked upon as surprizing, the Sequel will discover Adventures of his, not any wise inferior, but I may venture to say, much superior to it

But before we enter into giving an Account of those which we deem vastly astonishing, we must beg Leave to fill the next Paragraph with a sharping Trick *Chambers* put on a raw Country Fellow that was just come to Town It seems that this Rustic was got among a Company of Sharpers, and gaping with the rest at a Marble-board, *Chambers* chanced to come by, drest in a very handsome Suit of Cloaths, and seeing *Robin* (for so was the Fellow named) intent on seeing the Diversion, gave him a Tap on the Shoulders, which made him turn about, upon this *Chambers* took him aside, and asking him what Countryman he was, and how long he had been in Town, which *Robin* acquainted him with, demanded if he wanted a Place, or had any Inclinations to serve a Gentleman To which *Robin* answer'd, *Indeed, Master, that be the very Errand I came to Town about* O then, replied *Chambers*, I can fit you to a Hair *I believe I can afford you myself; for the present, four Pounds a Year standing Wages, and six Shillings a Week Board-Wages, and all my cast-off Cloaths, which, let me tell you, are none of the worst* This was enough to make *Robin* ready to jump out of his Skin; he had never had such a fine Proffer made him, and he began to think that good Fortune me was going to smile upon him. *Chambers* observing the Gladness *Robin* was in, bid him take his Cloak and follow him, which he throwing over his Arm, away they went together to the *May-pole* in the *Strand*, where *Chambers* ordering his new Man to call him a Coach, he stept in and *Robin* after him. *Hold, hold,* (said *Chambers*,) *you must know, Robin, that Servants ride behind,* which he obeying, away drove the Coach to the *Bell-Tavern*, in *King-street, Westminster*, where *Chambers* alights, and goes into the Tavern, orders a Fowl to be roasted for his Dinner, and when it was ready, sets his Man down by him, who eat the best Part of it. During Dinner, *Chambers* acquaints *Robin* with the Ways of the Town, tells him he must be very circumspect in his Behaviour, and a thousand Tricks would be put upon him by the *Londoners*, who were ever sporting with Persons just come out of the Country, concluding his Discourse thus ' *Robin*, I am obliged wait on a Person Quality this Afternoon, and as I have a tolerable good Liking to you, I thought I could not do you a greater Piece of Justice than to acquaint you, that it is customary for Gentlemens Servants to get to gaming when they meet together, now you being a Youngster, may easily be drawn in and imposed on, but to prevent it, if you have any Money about you, put it into my Hands, and as you want it, 'tis but ask and have. *Robin* concluding from his Master's Words, that he had found out one of the honestest Men in the World, readily lugged out his Leathern Purse, wherein were nine and forty Shillings, and gave it to *Chambers*, who while he sent him to call a Coach, paid the Reckoning with his Man's Money, and then riding to the *Temple-gate* in *Fleet-Street*, *Robin* was ordered to pay the Coachman, who having a stout Oaken Stick in his Hand, began to lay about his Sides in a terrible Manner, upon which a fierce Encounter between him and the Coachman ensuing, and a numerous Mob immediately gathering about to see the Scuffle, *Chambers* found his Opportunity to move off, and leave his Man to provide for himself, and bemoan the Loss of so good a Master

If the following Story was not related by Captain *Smith* in his Collection, I would not have inserted the same here, considering the Circumstances, when put together, discover something of Improbability, tho' I confess, that Author assigns a Reason for the most unaccountable Fact of all, that makes the rest credit But without using any more Words, we shall give it our candid Readers

A Gentleman advanced in Years, who had a considerable Estate of his own, married a young Lady whom the Captain makes to be none of the wisest, with a Fortune agreeable to the large Possessions he held His Temper being sedentary, and devoted to the Quiet of a Country Life, he carried his new Spouse to a Seat of his about a Mile from *Huntington*, which stood by itself, and seemed to enjoy a very peaceful Recess But it seems our *Chambers* had frequently view'd it, to put in Force a Design he had long Time entertained to rob it, but still was disappointed For the good old Gentleman was too careful to let any of his Goods or Effects be taken from him without using proper Means to retain what he had about him Now, whether he was previously acquainted with *Chambers*'s Design, is not certain, but it seems probable he was, for Fire-Arms were Things he constantly kept in his Chamber, and he was several Times observed to be sitting behind the Curtain in his Window, especially in Moonlight Nights, to watch the Motions of such as should offer to molest his House.

Chambers perfectly understood this, yet was so far from declining from his Design, that he was the ra-

ther influenced now to put it directly in Execution. According he procured as many Cloaths as would just dress a Man, and with them made up the fictitious Appearance of one, which taking along with him to the House, he sets a Ladder to the Gentleman's Chamber Window, mounts it with the Scarecrow before him, and nods it full against the Sash The Gentleman hearing a Kind of Noise, and presently, to his Surprize, seeing the Scarecrow, discharges his Piece, upon which *Chambers* lets it drop, and instantly betakes himself to his Companions, who were behind the House. Old *Rusticus* thanks his Stars a thousand Times, that he has been so fortunate as to kill his mortal Enemy, and one whom he had been obliged to watch against so many Months. He goes to his Wife who was in Bed, and bids her congratulate with him for his Success, for that now he hoped they had no farther to fear *I will put on a few Things,* said he to her, *go out, and drag the Corps to a secret Place in my Grounds, where I will bury it, by which I shall avoid the burthensome Fees of the Parish* And having thus said, he drest himself, took a Pick Ax, Spade, and a Cord, which having tied about the Neck of the imaginary Dead, he haul'd it a considerable Way over his Grounds, dug a Pit, and tumbled it in. *Chambers*, all the while was not ignorant of the egregious Folly the old Gentleman was committing but to make amends for the Loss of Time, he had frequently had about the House before, mounted up the Ladder, and whipt open the Sash, and went to Bed to the Lady, with whom expressing his Gladness for what had happened, but withal giving Signs of some Diffidence, that still made his Mind uneasy, *What,* says he to her, *must we do, supposing this Rogue's Ghost should haunt us in Spite, and come and rob us still? This is what I have Reasons to fear, and I pray my Dear, let me take Care of your Diamond Ring and the Gold Watch by you.* No sooner said, than the Things were delivered up; and, as the Captain says, *Chambers* repaid her extraordinary Complacency, with gratifying her in the most sensible Manner; after which, acquainting her, he had only hauled the Body into a Field behind the House, he would get up again and bury him, to avoid coming into any Trouble for having killed him Accordingly he got up, drest himself, took a Cabinet of Jewels, thro' a Pretence of concealing it in the next Room, went privately down Stairs, and made off triumphantly to his Comrades, who waited in a convenient Place for him

All this while old *Rusticus* was busied in removing out of the World, as he thought, the greatest Torment he ever had. The Night being something cold, and his Apprehensions on one Side, of incurring Trouble about shooting the Deceased; and his Gladness, on the other, for having got out of the Way the much-dreaded Villain, made him dispatch the Business he was about in the quickest Manner. After he had finished every Thing to his Satisfaction, he returned Home extreamly cold, and getting into Bed to his Lady in the chilly Condition he was in, *Lord,* says she, *my Dear, how cold you are! You an't the same Man you was lately, how frigid! Lack-a-Day, what made you get up again* To which he made answer, *My Love, my Dear, certainly you must be in a Dream; for I assure you, I have not been in a Bed since the first Time I rose, which, let me tell you, is above an Hour ago. Nay, my Dear,* replied she, *it cannot be more than a Quarter of an Hour since you left me, when I gave you my Diamond Rings and Gold Watch, for fear the Rogue's Ghost should haunt us in Spite, and rob us still; and to convince you, that what I tell you is no other than the real Truth, you gave me that due Benevolence which we married Women require, better than ever I had it of you.* These were Hints the old Gentleman was confounded at He
swelled

swelled immediately into a violent Paffion, and faid, *By Heavens, Madnefs poffeffes the Woman! She dreams! What Diamond Rings? What Gold Watch? What Benevolence is this you fpeak of? For my Part, I have not touched your Rings, nor your Watch, it muft unavoidably be, that you are befides your felf But upon my Word, my dear Hufband, you did, and like-wife carried the fmall Cabinet there of Gold and Jew-els, for better Security, into the next Room* What an aftonifhing Piece of News is here? *Rufticus* begins to think there have been deplorable Things committed, during his Abfence; and that, while bufied in bury-ing one Rogue, he had been robbed by another But of all the Evils that perplexed his Mind, the Word Benevolence gauled him in the moft fenfible Manner. This was a Circumftance that gave him a thoufand Mortifications He fretted, foam'd at the Mouth, and ftar'd He calls to his Servants to bring him a lighted Candle to fee if there was Truth in what his injur'd Wife had told him. The Candle comes, but to his Coft, he finds his Effects funk fif-teen hundred Pounds in Value, but he is refolved to find the Bottom of the whole Affair; and, as foon as it was Break of Day, goes to the Place where he had interred the fictitious Corps, digs it up, and finds he had been fpending his Time in making a Hole for, and covering a Bundle of Rags, which unexpected Sight, raifed by Turns his Indignation and Laughter to think he had been fo abominably impofed on, fo cunningly robb'd, and fo unaccountably made a Cuckold.

Leave we the Reflections that may be made on this Story to thofe who perufe thefe Sheets. Let it fuf-fice to fay, that the Facts are very uncommon, and therefore liable to be varioufly conftrued. But proceed we to fome other Tranfactions of the dexterous Man we are treating of.

Chambers having had a pretty long Merry-Making, as he called it, about *Huntington*, and the adjacent Country, thought he could not do better, than to remove into fome other Place. Accordingly, *St Al-bans* was the Town he had a Longing for, the Ma-fter's Wife of the *Grayhound-Inn* there, had infpired him fome few Month's before, with a great Deal of Love, and in fpite of himfelf, he found he was not able to conquer his Paffion, 'till he had enjoy'd her 'Tis true indeed this Dame had an extraordinary Beauty in her Face, nor were the Charms of her Con-verfation lefs engaging, which made Abundance of Gentlemen call or lodge there, purely to have a Sight of her, or, what was more agreeable, to converfe with her The Hufband was a meer *Bacchanalian*, devoted to his Glafs and Bottle, and in every Com-pany muft unavoidably make a Party with them, du-ring which, Madam found Opportunities to difplay herfelf to Advantage, which the Guefts admiring, fhe conftantly improved Now it happened that *Cham-bers* alighted one Night at this Inn, in a very wretch-ed Condition, having been encounter'd on the Road by a Perfon of his own Vocation, and unhappily be-ing unfaddled, and thrown in the Road, had received all the Dirt and Mud about him by that Means At his firft Appearance the other Gentlemen that lodged there that Night, feemed to be forry for him, and every one through an Act of Humanity, frankly lent him fome of their own Apparel to wear 'till he went to Bed, and his own were cleaned and dry To requite thefe extraordinary Favours, *Chambers* defires the Gentlemen, who were about fix in Num-ber, to bear him Company at Supper, and partake of fuch Things as he had ordered to be provided for him, faying, *Half a Dozen Bottles of Wine were at their Service; and you, Landlord and Landlady, I beg may make two of the Company* In fhort, all ad-mired the Gentleman's Generofity; but the Land-

lady, though *Chambers* had frequently been at her Houfe before, thought him an entire Stranger, and handfomely accepted the Proffer Supper being ready, our Guefts with the handfome Dame at the Top of the Table, and *Chambers* next to her, fat down Every Thing was conducted with great Re-gularity, and every one were fatisfy'd extremely with each other's Company, but *Chambers* carried the Prize in the Eyes of the Landlady, who, after Supper, diverted the Company with feveral humorous Songs and merry Catches, admirably adapted to the Occa-fion The Glaffes moved brifkly about, and to be fure, *Chambers* made Madam drink very plentifully 'Twas now about one in the Morning, and all, ex cept *Chambers* and the Landlord, were laid faft, (not even excluding the Miftrefs of the Houfe) which made *Chambers* think he had a fine Opportunity to put in Schemes in Practice, fo, Defiring our Landlord to call his Servants to help the reft to Bed, (for he told him, it was much better to carry them there, than let them where they were) two or three lufty Fellows were called in, who taking them up, one after ano-ther, *Chambers* pretended to affift them, but was fo dexterous in the *Interim*, to fecure their Watches and Money, after which, telling the Landlord he would fmoke one Pipe more, and drink a ferious Bot-tle with him They fat down together again! be neither one, nor two Bottles excufed them, though *Chambers* all the while drank but little, letting the *Bacchanalian* Landlord take his juft Dofe, which he had the Satisfaction to fee compleated *Silenus* is now laid along two Chairs, and *Chambers* improves the Opportunity to fee the Linings of his Pockets, wherein he found great Spoil, but took only a third Share to himfelf, to avoid being fufpected of having robbed him, if any of his Servants fhould have fearched for his Money, to have kept it for him till the Morn ing In fine, every Thing concurred to compleat *Chambers*'s Wifhes He went himfelf civilly to Bed, and earneftly defired the Servants of the Houfe to have a ftrict Care of their Mafter, nay, he came down Stairs again, and would not go back, 'till he had feen the true Son of *Bacchus* laid by his handfome Wife, whereby he had Means of obferving the Situation of the Room, and every Thing be fides

All the Houfe being now in profound Reft, except *Chambers*, who could not fleep for the Succefs that had attended him, after having been about Half an Hour, or fomething more in Bed, rifes up in his Shirt, and opening his Chamber-Door very foftly, which was againft that of his Landlord's Room, which was open, he fteps in, and gets at the farther Side of the Bed where Madam lay Scarce was he enter'd, but roll-ing over to him, (not knowing but it was her beloved *Silenus*,) fhe grafped her Arms about his Wafte, and begin to carefs him in a very obliging Manner This was what *Chambers* came about He fatisfied his own Inclinations, and probably that of the Dame for that Time; for he rofe up immediately after, and went to his own Bed, leaving her calmly repofed, juft like a Child fet to Sleep by giving it the Bubby The Clock now ftrikes four, and the Sun invites our Ad venturer to be ftirring He rifes, puts on a Suit of Cloaths, all embroider'd, of a Gentleman's that lay in the next Room, and being ready to mount, calls the Hoftler for his Horfe, who ignorantly brings the right Owner's, and delivers it to *Chambers* He mounts, leaves a Couple of Guineas to anfwer his Expences, and Half a Crown for himfelf, telling him at his Departure, *That if any Thing fhould be wanting, he would fatisfy his Mafter, who was his intimate Acquaintance, the next Time he came that Way; and* having fo faid, rode off directly: But *Chambers*, hav ing rode not above three or four Miles out of Town, was

was agreeably furpriz'd at feeing fome Guineas tumble out of the Lining of the Saddle, by the violent Agitation of his Gallopping He difmounts, opens the Linings farther with his Knife, and finds to his Satisfaction two hundred Guineas; for which he pours a thoufand Bleffings on his fuccefsful Exchange, prays heartily that his Landlord may have his Houfe dignified with an Heir of his getting, and then rides directly to *London*.

Chambers being now in Town again, refolves not to let his Time be mifpent. To which End, he haunts all the Publick Places of Refort, in order to find out his Prey One Day, being very well dreft, he goes to the *Exchange*, and mixes with fome *Italian* Merchants, and after fome little Converfation, which ran on Trade and Shipping, calls one of them afide, who was a very comely and grave Perfon With him he feems to be in a clofe and eager Dialogue, the Merchant all the while nodding and biting his Thumb Mean Time one of *Chambers's* Confederates comes up and begins to difcourfe the Merchant much after the fame Way as he himfelf had done Upon which *Chambers* fays, Sir, I perceive you have no liking to my Propofition, but poffibly you may'nt meet with fuch another Bargain as mine, I mean as to Profit —— No liking, anfwer'd the Merchant, Yes, Yes, Sir, I'd as live chap with you as the beft Man alive, fo I find but my Advantage in it Upon this the Merchant fpoke a few Words to *Chambers's* Confederate, and then calling *Arthur* to him, faid, Here's another Gentleman has a Bargain much like your's to difpofe of, if you can join together, we'll throw the Commodities together, and make but one Lot of them —— Agreed, replied *Chambers*, who without any farther Ceremony, as the Merchant ftood clofe to his Confederate, div'd nimbly into his Pockets, and drew thereout a Purfe of Gold, and his Gold Watch, and imperceivably convey'd them to his Confederate But this Spoil not fatisfying the avaricious Temper of our Adventurer, who, feeing a very good Handkerchief hanging out of the Merchant's Coat-Pocket, fnaps at it, but unluckily for his firft Prize The Merchant, it feems, caught him in the Act, and, feiz'd him by the Collar, called out, Thief, Thief, which Words raifing Abundance of Perfons then on the Walks, about them, every one were defirous to know the Bottom of the Matter The Merchant was for having our Adventurer before a Magiftrate, and he, on his Part ftrenuoufly denied the Fact (for by this Time the Purfe and Watch were found gone) and even threaten'd the injur'd Tradefman to punifh him for defaming his Character among the only Perfons in the World he got his Living by During this Contention, the Confederate, who had received the Purfe and Watch from *Chambers*, was marched to the Porter at the Gate, to get Proclamation to be made on the *Exchange*, That if any Perfon had loft a Purfe with Gold in't, and a Gold Watch, on giving the true Marks, he might have it again Thefe Words reaching the Merchant's Ears, he, glad of the Opportunity of regaining his loft Things, lets go *Chambers*, with a thoufand Excufes for his Rudenefs and rafh Accufations, and goes directly to the Crier, but both *Chambers* and his Confederate procured Means of flipping away in the mean Time

This Difappointment but the more fharpened the Wit and Cunning of our Adventurer, who was refolved to ufe his Talents (as he called them) to a much better Purpofe than his laft Endeavour had produced To this End he takes a firft Floor of a Houfe in *Soho-Square*, and contracts with the Landlord to pay fourteen Shillings a Week for the fame For a while a good Harmony and Underftanding was between *Chambers* and the Gentleman of the Houfe,

who took him for a Man of Fortune, as his Drefs and Expences might have very well argued him One Evening as they were at Supper, I mean the Family of the Houfe, our Adventurer came in feemingly in a vaft Uneafinefs, which made the good Folks importune him to let them know what it was that difturbed him I have fo much Friendfhip for you, Mr. Woodville, faid the Landlord, (for you muft know this was the Name he had given himfelf,) that if I can be of any real Service to you, 'tis but opening your Mind to me, and you may depend to find me both your Counfellor and Benefactor —— Chambers, pleafed with the Landlord's frank Kindnefs, made no further Doubt to unravel the great Myftery he had at his Heart, and thus began 'Tis with a thoufand Struggles of Soul, that I find myfelf obliged to fpeak, Landlord, I am very fenfible of the Obligations I already owe you, and that Thought makes me decline being any further burthenfome to you, you muft know then, that having been at Hampftead this Afternoon, where I frequently ufed to go to divert myfelf with an affectionate Brother of mine, I was there a mournful Spectator of his Death 'Tis too much for me (here he pretended to weep) to acquaint you with every fad Particular about the Struggles he had before his Soul departed out of his Body; let it fuffice to fay, that he has left me Heir to his Poffeffions, (but his Life would have been of greater Value to me) and in his Will appointed me to inter him in the Cloifters in Weftminfter-Abby Now, Landlord, the Favour I have to defire of you is, for Conveniency of his Funeral, to have his Body brought here, and carried hence to the Grave Thefe laft Words *Chambers* pronounced with a deep Groan, which made the Landlord, and all the Family compaffionate him, they told him any thing they had was at his Service, and the Landlord left him at his own Liberty to bring the Corps, and chufe what Room ever he pleafed to place it in He thanked him for his Civility, and told him he would certainly repay it very fhortly, in a Way he fhould be very fenfible of Which indeed, he was as good as his Word to perform *Chambers* accordingly went out the next Morning, leaving Orders that the Herfe with the Corps would be with them about Six in the Evening And true he was to his Word For juft upon Six o'Clock a ftately Herfe with Six Horfes arrived at the Door, and Men fuborn'd to this End took thereout a beautiful Coffin with fine Hinges and Nails, wherein our Adventurer had put himfelf, there being private Holes in the Sides for Refpiration The Counterfeit Load was ftraightway born up one Pair of Stairs, and placed on a Table in the Dining-Room, where the Landlord, to grace the deceafed Brother of his Lodger, had fet out a very fine and rich Side-Board of Plate, befides other Valuables You muft know *Chambers* was laid in the Coffin in his Cloaths, and a Winding-Sheet wrapt round him, and one of his Confederates had taken Care to draw the Screws All this Time our Adventurer was miffing, which made the Landlord afk the Fellows where he was, who faid, he had bid them acquaint him, that having a Multitude of Things to difpatch about the Funeral, 'twas probable he might not come Home that Night, but fhould be obliged to ftay with a Friend of his in the *Strand*. The Landlord took the Excufe for granted, the Herfe and Men departed, and the Family of the Houfe, excepting the Maid, at their ufual Hour, went to Bed, leaving *Chambers* to rife out of his filent Manfion of Death, and perpetrate his villainous Defign Accordingly, he gets out with his Winding-Sheet about him, and going down Stairs, places himfelf in a Chair over-againft where the Maid

17 R was

was fitting, who, hereby frighted at the Apparition, as she thought, screamed out, *a Ghost, a Ghost,* and, without speaking another Word, ran as fast as could np into her Master's Chamber, and told him and his Wife the Story   *A Ghost,* says the Master, phoh? *you Fool, there's no such Thing in Nature , you have been asleep, Woman, and waking suadenly, have fancied you saw a Thing there never was*   Scarce were these Words out of the Mouth of the Landlord, but in steps, with a solemn Tread, our Adventurer *Chambers* in his Winding-Sheet, and presenting himself and his Face, which was covered over with Flour, full to the Maid, the Landlord, and his Wife, sets himself down in a Chair in the Room, where he continued full Half an Hour, putting the three Persons above into the greatest Pannic in the World all the Time   After which the imaginary Ghost stalks down Stairs, opens the Door to six of his Accomplices, who, while their Director *Chambers* raps the Doors too and fro to drown the Noise of more Persons being in the House than himself, strip the Dining-Room of all the Plate and other rich Furniture therein, and then making a general Search throughout the other Chambers and the Kitchen below, rifle and carry off every Thing of Value to the Amount of six Hundred Pounds   All this while the Family, believing a Spirit was actually in their House, and making the horrid Noise they heard, kept close hid under the Bed-Cloaths, but the Dawn of Day soon appearing, their Fears began to abate , whereupon the Maid gets up, and has the Courage to go down and see the Consequences of the late Bustle   She finds all her Pots, and her Pans removed effectually off out of the Way, and a dreadful Havock made among the Pewter, which, to the very last Plate was all vanished   She hastens to her Master, who was still in Bed, acquaints him with the Spirit's having robb'd the House, and tells him, that she can't in Conscience live with him any longer, since a bad and thieving Ghost visited his Family, which proved that his House was neither a good one, nor the Persons that composed his Family fit to be lived with.   Hereat the Landlord could not forbear bursting out into an extream Laughter, *Why, thou silly Jade, can it be supposed, that Ghosts, or Spirits, who have neither Flesh, Blood, or Bones, can rob, phoh!* banish thy foolish Conceits, and let me come and see what has been a working all this Night   The Maid displeas'd with her Master's Words, goes down Stairs, and finding some of her Fellow-Servants and Neighbours about the Door, tells them what she had seen, whereat all seem'd astonish'd, and say, They should not dare to stir an Inch out of their Houses in the Night, if the Case was so as she related it.   Mean Time the Landlord had roused his indolent Body from his Bed, and made a strict Search in those Places where he thought the most valuable Part of his Moveables lay, which he found entirely convey'd away, but coming into the Dining-Room, and seeing the Plate gone, and an empty Shell of a Coffin, he, too late is made sensible of the Imposition, which we'll leave him to mourn, or banish the Thoughts of, just as he pleases, and proceed to something else

Chambers being an extream Lover of a Woman, had made Choice of a singular Beauty, to whom he was in every Thing devoted except in the Case of his Secrets, and the Robberies he committed, which (if it may make to his Reputation) he would never entrust to any Female, which he justly knew to be too capricious and changeable to hold always in one Mind   Once as this Beloved and he were in Bed together, entirely resigned up to mutual Endearments, and the Pleasures of Love, she, with a Languishing Air, as she twined about his Neck, address him thus:

Dear Chambers (says she) *if I have proved sincere to you, or you have had any Affection for me, why may not I partake of your Secrets, since all I know in the World, is revealed to you? It must certainly argue extraordinary Diffidence of me in you, to be thus deprived of a Privilege which every Woman ought to enjoy who can say she has cohabited with a Man for some Years*   *Had you put me to the Trial once, and found me transgessing the Secret you had thought fit to impose on me, then you had had Plea suffi cient to have thought me an empty Person, unfit to hold any thing committed to me. But since nothing of the Nature has been put to my Experiment, nor you have any Ground to say I am a Betrayer of Secrets, indulge me, my dear Chambers, so far as to put me to the Trial, which if I happen to fail in, then my Veracity for ever shall be renounced, and you be at Liberty to make your Breast the sole Closet for your Actions*   This was a grave Harangue, indeed, to *Chambers*, who was so far from him having the least Notion of hearing such a Discourse that he had fully resolved within himself to devote that Night to Love , but he found his Humour cross, and the Woman he loved best in the World in his Way, unalterable in her Request till, wearied with her continual Intreaties, he told her he would some Time or other that Month, comply with her Desires and put her to the Test   After this Nocturnal Conference, several Days past without a Word made by Madam of being tried to keep a Secret   *Chambers* put divers Constructions on her Silence, sometimes he imputed it to her Want of hearing him speak any first about it, sometimes to a Sullenness in her for being refused so long to partake of his Mind, but, as he was too much acquainted with her condescending Temper, to think Moroseness had any Ascendant over her Mind, he could not find her guilty in this Respect   In short supposing the whole Affair entirely blotted out of her Mind (for he had strove to divert her with other Amusements) early one Morning as he was in Bed he feigns himself prodigious ill, which put Madam into much Concern, who asks him what he ail'd —*Ail'd*—say he, *Why, Peggy, out of the most wonderful and yet terrible Things has befallen me in the World? if you betray me now I am an undone Man for ever, for it is a Circumstance I cannot keep from you* —Oh !—What—*Another Good Lord! Good Lord help me* —*What is the Matter, Love? can I be of Service to you? Where is it you are pained! Let me see, Oh Laud! What a Couple of Eggs! surely they cannot be Eggs* —Eggs as sure as you are a Woman, and I have just now laid them.— *Oh! for Heaven's sake do not say a Syllable about them —— Not a Word for all the World, my Dear —— But pray, can I trust you? Ah! I cannot but trust you, now you have seen them* —— *Trust us, Chambers!* say you, *Oh! my Dear, I would not falsify myself in this Point for ten thousand Crowns* —— Here the Discourse ended   *Chambers* pretends to keep his Bed two or three Days, and Madam, that very Day in the Afternoon, being invited to drink a Dish of Tea with a Neighbour's Wife, amidst their Cups, tells the whole secret, and makes the Number of the Eggs four, the Neighbour some Time afterwards augments them to Eight, and a third Person to twenty   In short the Moment *Chambers* appeared out of Doors he heard it whisper'd, as he went along the Streets, *There goes the Man that laid an hundred Eggs*   He curses Womankind for their Folly, and determined never more to reveal a Secret to them, because he has found no Trial, that they are a Vessel with a leaky Bottom, that lets all the Water out.

Chamb.

Chambers having tried this Experiment upon his pretended Wife, took a small Journey into the Country, and coming into an open Road, met with a Couple of Men driving a Pair of fat Oxen He had an immediate Longing for the Cattle, and so to improve a Scheme he had in his Head as to obtain them, he put the following conceit in Practice Having a Cord in his Pocket, he put over the Foot-Path in the Fields, and by that means got about half a Mile before the Countrymen There was a tall Ash-Tree, into which *Chambers* having climbe'd, he put the Cord about his Neck, and so entangled himself among the Boughs, that to the Eye below he seemed as if he had been really hanging 'Twas not long before the Drivers came up, who seeing our Adventurer in this Condition, put various Constructions upon the Dismal Act as they thought it. One alledged, that it could be nothing else but Love that had induced him to so desperate an Action, while the other imputed this Piece of rash Conduct in *Chambers*, to Losses and Misfortunes in the World, conceiving that he had been some Tradesman In short, the first who spoke about it, had the truest Notions of the Matter, for *Chambers* did it purely for Love; but it was for Love of the Oxen, which the Countrymen were driving By this Time the Fellows were got at some Distance from *Chambers*, who descending immediately from the Tree, made the best Way he could over another Foot-Road, leading over the Meadows, and came again into the Highway He mounts another Tree, and puts himself into the very same Posture as before the Countrymen came up, see, and admire this strange Sight, and begin to have fears within themselves about it At first they look narrowly, in order to know whether it is the same Man or no, they had left behind them, they perceive the same Cloaths, and one of them concludes, it must be the same Man Hereupon a kind of Argument began between them, one asserting it was a different Man, the other insisting it was the same *How can that be,* answer'd the first, *that a Man can be hanging in two different Places at one Time? I cannot dive into the Reason of that, or indeed it is above my Understanding* At this the other tells him, *'Tis to no Purpose to make more Words for 'twas the same Man he was sure,* and, to confirm his Belief, *would lay him a Wager of a Shilling, and they two should go back to the first Place and see.* Hereupon both, to decide this important Wager, hasten back to satisfy themselves, but, coming to the Place where they thought to have found *Chambers* hanging, found nothing at all but the Tree Mean while our Adventurer was got down from his second Hanging Place, to the Countrymen's Oxen, which he drove to a Town in his Way to *Exeter*, where a fair happened to be at that Time, and sold them, and with the Money came up triumphantly to *London*

Chambers, during a few Years, committed Actions the most daring and artful that were ever known, we shall bring him to a Period, after two more of his Adventures, which shall conclude our Account of him —— The first proceeds thus Happening to be amongst some of his Companions, and very Hungry, but having little or no Money amongst them, they went together, with what they had, to an Alehouse by *Clare-Market*, and our Adventurer immediately borrowed of the Landlord a blue Apron, which tying about him, he went into the Market, and cheapen'd a Pig of a Woman, some little difference as to the Price, making the Bargain longer than ordinary, *Chambers*, whose Stomach was pretty sharp, at last took the Pig, and left the Price of it in the Woman's Hands, with a Power of bringing it back, if the Company, as he pretended, did not like it Away he returns to his Companions, who, in Concert with him, took the Pig out of the Cloath, and put a dead Dog into its Room, which *Chambers* pins up in the Cloath, and carries it back to the Woman, telling her his Company did not like it Whereupon he received his Money back again. Some little Time after, another Chapman comes to the Woman's Stall, and cheapens the supposed Pig, who tells him, *'Tis one of the whitest in the World, and one that she can very well put into his Hands* Hereupon she begins to unpin the Cloath, but coming to open it, finds, both to her Astonishment and Loss, a Dog The Artifice is soon blown over the Market, and the People put into an extraordinary Laughter, so that between Jeers and Jokes, and what between Loss and Disappointment, the Market-Woman is forced to pack up her All for that Evening, go home, and comfort herself in the best Manner she is able

The last Story of him is this Being at *Bristol* just before the Fair there, he hired himself as a Clicker to a Shoemaker, though no Ways skilled in the Business; but contracted with his Master not to enter upon actual Imployment 'till that Day Se'ennight However, he continued at the Door of the Shop, in order to let the rest of the Trade know he belonged to them *Chambers*, who was perpetually forming some Stratagem or other, to procure him either Goods, or Ready-Money, bethought him of an Expedient that would turn the Shoe-maker's Boots to his Advantage. Accordingly, he goes to a Neighbour of the Trade, and tells him, *That a Gentleman was at his Master's Shop, who wanted a Pair of Boots of the Eighth Size, and that he should be obliged to him to let him have one Boot for the Person to try on* The Shoemaker, not distrusting the Honesty of our Adventurer, gives him a Boot of that Size, hoping to have it soon returned, if the Gentleman did not like it, or it did not fit him *Chambers* immediately improves his Scheme, goes to all the rest of the Shoemakers, with the same Tale in his Mouth, and procures from each a single Boot of the Size with the first, when, on Computation, he had made himself Master of forty single Boots, which he pack'd off to a Customer for a Sum of Money something less than the real Worth of them. By this Time the several Masters wondered why their Boots were not returned, and consequently sent their Men to know the Reason; but *Chambers's* Master having lost his Man, in the *Interim*, and telling them, *He knew nothing of the Affair, nor any Boots borrowed,* every one became sensible of their Mistake, and found it too late to rectify the Cheat; for our Adventurer had moved his Quarters, and left his Master and the rest to admire his Dexterity and Contrivance.

Here we conclude the Scene of this Man's Life, who, after a Series of unaccountable and very surprizing Robberies and Actions, received a just Recompence for his ill-spent Life at *Tyburn*.

The

The L I F E *of Sir* GOSSELIN DENVILLE.

WE have ranked *Chambers* between two Knights, not to give him any Preference by such a Position, but only to pursue a mixt Account, as we have apologiz'd for in the Beginning of his Memoirs The Gentleman we are going to give an Account of, was descended of very honourable Parents at *Northallerton*, a Market Town in the *North-Riding* of *Yorkshire* The Family was very ancient, and came into *England* with *William the Conqueror*, who assign'd 'em Lands for the Services done him in the North of *England*, where they lived in great Esteem, and the Successors after them, for several Ages, till the Time of Sir *Gosselin*

The Father of this Gentleman being a pious and devout Man, sent his Son to *Peter-Colledge* in *Cambredge*, where, for some Time, he prosecuted his Studies with great Warmth, and, to outward Appearance, gave Signs of making a fine Man This gave the antient Father extreme Joy, who began to think of placing his Son in the Priesthood, but it seems *Gosselin* sat at his Books purely to amuse his Father, and to gain some Advantage he had in View by it It was found out afterwards that a religious Life, as his Father had design'd for him, was not the Thing he relished, but that the Prosecution of Amours and Love Intriegues, had the greatest Ascendant over his Mind nay, he began now to display his natural Propensity to a luxurious and profligate Life

These Steps creating great Discontent in the Breast of the Father, he took the violent Courses of his Son so much to Heart, that 'twas not long before he died leaving our Gentleman in full Possession both of the Dignity of the Family, and his Estate, valued at twelve hundred Pounds *per Annum*, a considerable Fortune in those Days Thus our Gentleman becomes a Knight, rolls in a plentiful Fortune, and gives a Loose, more extravagant than ever, to his ill Courses He associates a Brother of his, named *Robert*, with him, and they two together, by their Profuseness, soon made an End of the Estate

Being now out of the Reach of maintaining themselves as usual, and finding the Poverty of their Circumstances still encreasing upon them, they perceived there was no no other Way of supporting themselves, than by raising Contributions on the Highway To this End, being Men of extraordinary Valour and Courage, they equipt themselves out for a daring Enterprize, which was to rob two Cardinals, sent into this Kingdom by the Pope, to mediate a Peace between *England* and *Scotland*, and terminate the Differences then on Foot, between *Edward* II and the Earl of *Lancaster*

One *Middleton* and *Selby*, two Robbers of these Times, having heard of *Denville*'s Design, came and join'd him with all the Forces under their Command, which were no inconsiderable Number In short, the Cardinals were robbed, and a very large Booty taken from them, which put our Bravo into a tolerable Way of Subsistence for some Time, but there happening some Difference between *Middleton* and him, with regard to the sharing of this Booty, the former left the Association, and went some Time on the Road by himself, but being soon apprehended, was brought up to *London*, and there executed

All this while, Sir *Gosselin* pursued his illegal Practices, the Valour of his Arm, and the continual Prey, he and his Men made on all Travellers, put the whole Country into a terrible Pannic, for there was no such Thing as travelling with any Safety, and the great Number of Persons, of whom his Gang was composed, plainly shewed, that they defied the Laws, and every Thing else What they could not obtain on the Highway, they sought for in Houses, Monasteries, Churches, and Nunneries, which were rifled without any Distinction, and the most valuable and sacred Things carried off The Men under Sir *Gosselin*'s Conduct led a most licencious Life; and, like their Master, committed the worst of Villainies and Barbarities Persons were murdered in their Houses, when their Goods might have been taken without using Bloodshed So that killing and doing Havock, rather looked like Sport or Pastime with these Desperadoes Our Countryman *Tom. Shadwell* seems to point at our Knight, in his Play, called the *Libertine*, nay, to have founded the main Plot of that Piece upon his barbarous and licencious Conduct They who have a Mind to be further informed in this Particular, may, by perusing that Dramatic Performance, see how near the whole Conduct of the *Libertine* Squares with that of the Person we are speaking of

A while after our Knight and his Associates marching on the Road between *Marlow* in *Buckinghamshire*, and *Henley* upon *Thames*, met with a *Dominican* Monk, named *Andrew Symson*, who not only was obliged to deliver what little Gold he had, to them but also to climb into a Tree, and preach them a Sermon, which he did with a great Deal of Judgment and good Sense, though pronounced *Extempore*

This Sermon being at this very Time recorded in the *Bodleian* Library, as a Piece containing sound Divinity, and a great Deal of Wit, we shall make no Apology to our Readers for inserting it, but give it an immediate Place here Mr *Symson* having got into the Tree, chose for his Text the following Words

L U K E, Chap x Ver 30
A certain Man went down from Jerusalem *to* Jericho, *and fell among Thieves, which stript him of his Rayment, and wounded him, and departed, leaving him half dead*

" OUR Blessed Saviour himself pronounced
" these Words to a Lawyer by Way of Parable,
" who came with a View to tempt him, by putting
" this Question to him, *Master, What shall I do to*
" *inherit eternal Life?* Luke 10 30 The Law yet
" is taught by our Lord in the Context both before
" and

and after these Words, on which I lay the Foundation of my ensuing Discourse, That, in order to obtain Life Eternal, he was to esteem every Man his Neighbour, that stood in need of his Assistance; after which, the good *Samaritan* is introduced to shew the Love to one's Neighbour, for this Person, though a Priest and Levite, had before past by this poor Man spoken of in my Text, who was fallen among Thieves, had Compassion on him, went and bound up his Wounds, placed him on his own Breast, carried him to an Inn, and giving Orders to the Host to let him have any Thing he wanted, promised to defray all Expences, so the poor Man but recovered

" Having thus explained the Meaning of my Text, I shall now go on to a farther Illustration of it, by Discoursing on the three following Heads

I. The Hazard or Danger of taking a Journey
II Who it is that may bring this Danger
III What the Danger is, which is two fold, either the Loss of Goods, or Loss of Life, and sometimes Loss of both

" First then, I shall discourse on the first of these Heads, namely, the Hazard or Danger of taking a Journey. Now, this is when a Man leaves the City to go into the Country; in the former of which a Person need not be much apprehensive of himself, because the Numbers of Inhabitants are a sufficient Guard to protect him, but it is quite otherwise in the Country, I mean on the Road, where an honest Man, thro' the few People passing and repassing, and perhaps through the Obscurity of the Place, is exposed to the Insults of such abandon'd Wretches, whose Actions we should by no Means imitate or agree with For the Royal Psalmist seems to allude to this Doctrine *When thou sawest a Thief, then thou consentedst with him,* Psal 1 18 And I observe again, that if a Man but goes a few Miles from his Habitation, he cannot assure himself that he shall return unrobbed, for it seems that the Person here spoken of in the Evangelical Parable, went but to *Jericho,* which was only six Miles South Eastward from *Jerusalem* And what added to the Opportunity of the Thieves robbing him, was the Desart that lay between the two Places, which the Inhabitants call *Quarentem,* where great Thieving and egregious Robberies are committed to this Day

' Secondly, Who it is that may bring this Danger They who wilfully give themselves over to an insolent and lazy Life, and to covetous Pursuits, or they who abandon themselves to Drunkenness, to Gaming, or following lewd Women, for such as these turning Thieves, through their profligate Life, put honest Men into great Disorder, and commit great Damage upon them *Judas* thus for Example, coloured over his Actions, with a specious Pretence of loving the Poor, and with pretending to extraordinary Charity; when, on the contrary, he was neither a charitable Man, nor a Lover of the Poor, but a Thief, and a very covetous Wretch. This was his Hypocrisy, and one of the Evangelists witnesses thus much *Why was not this Ointment sold for Three Hundred Pence, and given to the Poor?* John xii 5, 6 I cannot but say, that depriving even a Man of an Advantage is a great Injustice, tho' robbing us of Things we hold the most considerable is much superior to this. But where both Life and Goods too are in the Case, then 'tis a most dismal Consideration; for not only the Laws of Man, but those of God likewise have made it a Capital Crime to take away any Thing unjustly from a

18

" Man, or to detain what of Right belongs to another; now this taking away which I am speaking of, is branched out into the three following Denominations, First, simple Theft, which means a private taking away of that which is another Man's Secondly, Rapine, by which Word is implied a forcible or compulsive Way of taking away of that which appertains to another Body's Right, And Thirdly, Sacriledge, which imports the taking away of Things deciucated to holy Uses, or in sacred Places Now the First and Last of these Kinds, are, for the Generality put in Execution in the Night-time, that being the most convenient Season to accomplish the Ends design'd by them If (says the Prophet) *Thieves comes to thee, if Robbers by Night, now art thou cut off; would not they have stollen till they had enough* Obad v 5 And our Saviour himself compares his coming on Earth to a Thief in the Night *The Day of the Lord so cometh as a Thief in the Night,* 1 Thes v 2, Says St *Paul* —— Agreeable to which is the following Passage of St *John* the Divine *Behold I come as a Thief,* Revel xvi 15 Which Words, if they were paraphrased, import thus much *Behold I come when you know nothing of it* But the other Kind of *taking away* is generally put in force (as you have now done) in the Day-time, putting Men and Women into terrible Frights, and vast bodily Fears

" But I must beg Leave to acquaint you, Gentlemen, by the way, that you are not the only Thieves in the World, for a great many others come under the Denomination, such as Kings and Princes, when they lay unnecessary Taxes and Excises upon their Subjects, Subjects when they do not pay the customary Tribute to their Princes, Tradesmen, when they use deceitful Weights and Measures, and unjustly enhance the Price of Commodities, Masters, when they defraud Servants of their Wages, and Servants when they embezzle the Goods of their Masters Nay, Apothecaries, and Taylors, when they make unconscionable Bills, Butchers, when they blow their Veil, Millers, for taking double Toll, Shoemakers, for stretching their Leather larger than their Consciences, Surgeons, for prolonging a Cure, Physicians, for taking away the Lives of their Patients, and Lawyers, for taking Bribes on both Sides, I say, that all these are no better than Thieves, and such as they, nor Covetous, nor Drunkards, nor Revilers, nor Extortioners, shall inherit the Kingdom of God, 1 *Cor* vi 10 Now what I have already observed brings me to the following Inferences *Thou shalt not steal* This is a positive Precept delivered to us by the Hand of God himself, who has also declared his avenging Hand on those that infringe it, yet this is so far from deterring Mankind from the Commission of it, that rather than not indulge your Headstrong Inclinations this Way, you will cut, hack, maim, wound, tie Hand and Foot, Neck and Heels together, you will rob, pilfer, and plunder any one, so this vicious Desire is but served What a melancholy Thing is this, and astonishing Considerations does it present to an honest and virtuous Mind! But, lack-a-day, why should I talk at this Rate, will not Courtiers rob People that solicit them for Favours? will not Judges pervert the Laws and administer Justice partially? These are shocking Reflections, and yet they are no more shocking than true I confess they are hard, but true, Instances of Injustice and Thieving But considering the Age we live in, 'tis not to be wondered at, for if Arts and Sciences are suffer'd to augment, much less is it to be admired why Vices and Immorality in all Shapes

S " increase;

" increase, *Satan* being industrious to plant his
" Schools of Wickedness, as much as our best In-
" structors there's, of good Learning and Mo-
" rality

" Now they who relinquish the Paths of Virtue,
" and will voluntarily pursue the Road of Iniquity
" and Thieving, Robbing, and Plundering, every
" one they meet, without any Distinction either of
" Sex or Person, expose themselves to an untimely
" Fate, which not only proves a miserable Exit to
" themselves, but also involves their Families, Friends,
" and Relations, in a great Deal of Scandal. And
" supposing they who pursue this profligate Course
" of Life, do not meet with the Gallows for their
" Reward, yet ten to one, they die no natural
" Death, for, 'tis possible, that one Time or other,
" meeting with a Prey, as they imagine, they may
" find some obstinate Resistance from the Person
" they attack, as may at last over-power them, and
" in the End take away one or other of their Lives,
" then pray what's the Consequence? Why, being
" thus cut off in their Sin, they tumble Head-long
" into Perdition, where endless Torments wait for
" them Probably you are dispatched and sent out
" of the World some Years before your appointed
" Time, whilst he that sent you packing out of this
" World, enjoys his Quiet, without being accoun-
" table to the Laws of his Country for what he did,
" and besides, we have the Levitical Law justifying
" the killing of a Thief *If a Thief be found break-*
" *ing up, and be smitten that he die, there shall no*
" *Blood be shed for him,* Exod xxii 2. And indeed
" all honest Men look upon Theft with such Detesta-
" tion, that on a Thief's being apprehended, they
" are ready to massacre him, before he is carried to
" Goal And under the Denomination of Theft we
" may justly place Usury, Bribery, and Cheating in
" Gaming Let us now suppose that the Thief may
" run on in his Villainous Course of Life several
" Years, without either being taken from his Ro-
" guery, or paying his Recompence to the Laws,
" yet what's this to the Purpose? All this Time he
" has something within him called Conscience, which
" incessantly tells him of his Ways, his Mind pre-
" sents to itself terrifying Ideas, nor can he purchase
" one Night's sound Sleep, he's haunted in every
" Corner, nor will Conscience suffer him to be at
" rest; possibly his pleasing Sins may delude his
" Thoughts with Gaiety and Mirth for a while, but
" this Scene lasteth not long, before a Vulture gnaw-
" eth his Heart, and eternally racks him For ill
" Actions are constantly attended with Perturbations;
" and the Punishment that follows is a thousand
" Times worse than all the Delight such Actions
" produced Ill acquired Gains are far more detri-
" mental than all the Losses of an adverse Fortune
" These latter but disturb us once, the first are per-
" petually teazing us And indeed that Man can
" never think of adding to his Contentment, who
" pursues Ways diametrically against it, still fixing
" his Eyes on the Beginning of Things, but has ne-
" ver once the Sense to consider where the End will
" reach

" Now, Gentlemen, if you are ignorant in this
" Particular, I will make bold to tell you, that the
" Beginning of Theft is an Entrance into Prison,
" where your chiefest Companions are Hunger,
" Thirst, Shackles, Bolts, Irons, and Vermin; and
" the End Hanging, unless you have the good For-
" tune to meet with an Adversary as favourable as
" King *Edward* the Confessor. I will produce the
" Instance for your Informations · It seems this
" Prince one Morning lying in Bed with his Curtains
" drawn, saw a poor Courtier come into his Cham-

" ber, and, going up directly to his Coffer, take as
" much Money away as he was able to carry, and
" came again, and was suffered to convey his second
" Booty off without being spoke to, but King *Ed-*
" *ward* finding him advance thither the third Time,
" reproved him for his Covetousness, and command-
" ed him to be gone, for if *Hugoline* his Treasurer
" came and caught him in the Fact, he would cer-
" tainly have a Rope for his Deserts Now it seems
" he was scarce got out of the Chamber, but the
" Treasurer, who had left open the Coffer, came
" and seemed in a vast Surprize at the Loss, but the
" King bid him not concern himself, for he had
" most Occasion for the Money, that had taken the
" Opportunity to convey it away

" Now I shall infer once more from this Discourse,
" Persons of your Profession, let your Lives be never
" so flagitious and enormous, may probably be of Opi-
" nion, that the same Mercy is laid up in Store for
" you, which the penitent Thief on the Cross found
" and enjoyed But let me tell you, and be you
" assured, that you are far from it, unless you can
" bring yourselves to repent as he did But pray
" what Man in his Senses would run the Risque of
" Damnation by suffering a reproachful Death,
" *When cursed is every one that hangeth on a Tree,*
" Gal xiii 21 Nay, he that is hanged is accursed
" of God Alas! no Man always sins unpunished,
" *Deut* xxi 23. Is it not a common Thing for us
" to see the Son punish'd for the Vices and profligate
" Life of the Father? I am very well assured that
" there are but few Vices of any Magnitude, which
" are not punished in this World God, let me tell
" you, Gentlemen, doth not bless or punish all at
" once, but by Degrees and Warnings. So much
" Knavery possesses the World at this Time of Day,
" that to be an honest Man is reputed Vice, and so
" many Mutations are hourly observed, that 'tis
" very rare to see the completed Race of another
" Our Lives are too short to take exact Notice how
" the most just God dispenses his Judgments, and
" how he strikes pernicious Mortals Some of his
" Corrections are performed in the Dark, nor does
" every notorious Act meet with its just Punishment,
" notwithstanding (as I have observed in the Forego-
" ing) private Punishments sometimes give a Man vast
" Uneasiness within, while Mankind observing only
" the Superficies of Things, see not how he smarts
" in secret

" Having proceeded thus far, I shall now come to
" some few Exhortations, and then close my Dis-
" course I must take the Freedom to acquaint you,
" Gentlemen, that the Sin of Theft is obligatory,
" that is, that you are obliged if you are able,
" to restore back the Things you steal, or forci-
" bly take from another, otherwise, let me tell
" you, your Sins are not forgiven I speak not
" this for the Sake of myself, but for the Benefit
" of your precious Souls, entertaining so favourable
" an Opinion of you, that I believe you to be good
" humour'd, generous, tender-hearted Gentlemen
" and such who, without being spurred on, have
" the Sense to shew a compassionate Honesty *All*
" *Things whatsoever you would that Men should do*
" *unto you, do ye even so to them For this is the*
" *Law and the Prophets* Some of you probably
" may object, and say, that it is impossible to keep
" the Commandments I answer to this, that it is
" because you have no Inclination to oblige your
" selves to the Observance of them, but are more
" willing that God should be thought the Author
" of Sin, which is exceedingly blasphemous and
" wicked Possibly too you may endeavour to justi

" fy your iniquitous and scandalous Lives, by al-
" ledging you cannot restrain yourselves, liking
" this Evasion much better than acknowledging your
" Iniquities, and confessing your Sins in order to
" amend, by engraving the Law of God upon your
" Hearts.

" It is my sincere Hope that the Words and Doc-
" trine I have already delivered, will have the same
" Influence on you, as the Advice once had on the
" Thief which the Apostle St. *John* gave him,
" which reclaimed him from his wicked Courses
" The Narrative is not very long, and for your
" Information, I will acquaint you with it St
" *John*, as soon as the Tyrant was dead, who had
" banish'd him to the Isle of *Pathmos*, returning to
" *Ephefus*, and being importuned to visit the Coun-
" tries adjacent, to put the Churches in Order,
" when he was come into a certain City, and see-
" ing a young Man of goodly Body, handsome Face,
" and fervent Mind, among the Brethren, he turned
" his Face to him, who was appointed chief over
" all the Bishops, and said, *I commend this young*
" *Man unto thy Custody, with an earnest Desire*
" *to take Care of him, as Christ and the Church*
" *bear me Witness* The Bishop having received his
" Charge, carried the young Man home, and took
" extraordinary Care of him But it seems that
" this young Convert, in spite of the Bishop's Pre-
" cepts and Admonitions, soon abandon'd himself
" to lewd and dissolute Courses, and associated with
" young Men of his Years, who were idle, debauch-
" ed, and acquainted with all Manner of Vice
" and Immorality The first Step these evil Coun-
" sellors take with their Pupil, is to bring him to
" costly Entertainments, afterwards to steal and pil-
" fer in the Night, and commit a great many o-
" ther Offences Thus our Convert soon became
" acquainted with all Manner of Wickedness, he
" plunges himself into a bottomless Pit of all Dis-
" order and Outrages, and in the End, despairs of
" the Saving Grace that cometh of God He is
" past all Hopes of Mercy, and therefore being
" quite regardless of the Consequences of his irre-
" gular Life, he proceedeth onward in his Impie-
" ties, and takes his Lot in common with the rest
" of his Companions It seems that a Gang of
" Thieves being gather'd together, he puts himself
" at their Head, and conducts them in the Execu-
" tion of their Enterprizes His Mind is now entirely
" bent to Robbing, extream Cruelty and Murder
" A while after this Bishop, being under some Ne-
" cessity, sent for St *John*, who having declared
" the Cause of his sending for him, the Apostle
" addressed him in the following Manner O *Bishop !*
" *I require the young Man, and the Soul of our Bro-*
" *ther whom I committed to thy Custody* The Bi-
" shop hearing this, with a dejected Countenance,
" and sobbing and sighing, told him that he was
" dead *Dead*, said St *John*, *how ? by what kind*
" *of Death ?* The Bishop replied, *he is dead to God,*
" *for he is become a very wicked and pernicious*
" *Wretch*, nay, a *Thief, keeping this Mountain over-*
" *against the Church, in Company with his Associates*
St *John* immediately rent his Garments, and beat
his Head, saying to the Bishop, *I have left a*
wise Keeper of our Brother's Soul, prepare me a
Horse, and let me have a Guide He hasten'd out
of the Church, and rode Post to the Place he intended, but was immediately apprehended by the
thievish Watch, yet he makes no Resistance, but
exclaims aloud, and says, *Bring me hither your*
Captain, who, in the mean time, as he was arm'd,
saw him coming As soon as the Captain saw the
Apostle's Face, knowing it to be St *John*'s, he
he was stricken with Shame, and ran away The

" old Man, unmindful of his great Age, pursues
" him flying, and cries, *My Son, why runnest thou*
" *away from me thy Father, unarm'd, and old ? Be*
" *not any away daunted, as there are Hopes of Sal-*
" *vation remaining*, *I will plead for thee with*
" *Christ*, nay, *I will expose my Life to Death for*
" *thee, if there be Occasion, as Christ exposed his*
" *for our Redemption, believe me, that I too will*
" *even hazard my Soul for thee and thine, for Christ*
" *sent me* Our Thief hearing this warm Expostu-
" lation, stood some Time stock still, with his Coun-
" tenance fix'd on the Ground, trembling like an A-
" spin Leaf, and all the while shed a Flood of Tears.
" He took St *John* in his Arms, and, with great E-
" motion, embraced him, making him as pertinent
" Answers as he could for his weeping, so that to
" outward Appearance he look'd as tho' he had been
" baptiz'd again with Tears After St *John* had
" promis'd and assured to obtain his Pardon with
" our Saviour, and pray'd, and fell on his Knees,
" and kissed his Right Hand, which Repentance had
" now purified, he conducted him to the Church a-
" gain, where rectifying his late fallen Soul with a-
" bundance of Prayers and Fastings, and confirm-
" ing his Mind with several excellent Sermons, he
" left him fully restored to the Church, a great Ex-
" ample of true Repentance, a brave Trial of a new
" Birth unto Righteousness, and a singular Pledge of
" a visible Resurrection from mortal Sin

" Wherefore, Gentlemen, if your Inclinations are
" to imitate the Example of this great Convert, and
" to put on the new Man, by being good Christians,
" associate yourselves with honest and good Compa-
" ny, for there is nothing more prejudicial than to
" keep that which is bad Our Fame and our Souls
" are utterly ruin'd by it, we receive Wounds by it
" which are incurable and past Remedy, besides,
" consider the Disgrace Was a Man a King, he
" would lose his Majesty and Dignity by it, for pray
" tell me, who would pay Obedience to his Com-
" mands or Government, when, in Imitation of *Nero*,
" he should waste his Time at Taverns with the
" Lewd and Debauched, play with Minstrels in his
" Chariot, and frolick with common Players on the
" Stage ? Bad Company may be compared very just-
" ly to the new Trimming of a Ship, whereso
" ever you but touch it, you are all bedaub'd, and
" supposing you are clean when you go aboard, yet
" the smallest Motion in the World will soon disco-
" ver the Blotches you have receiv'd How many
" hundreds could I enumerate, who, going to per-
" form the last Scene of an ignominious Death, have
" blamed ill Company as the Original of all the
" Failings they have made, as though some Witch
" had enchanted them into their Follies ? Bad Com-
" pany is an Engine which the Devil always is put-
" ting in Play to remove Man from the Pursuit of
" virtuous Ways· Bad Company is the spiritual
" Whore, that by fond Dalliances and Arts betrays
" a Man into his Destruction Bad Company is
" certainly a *Dailah*, if there be one under Heaven.
" But not to tire you with more of this Nature,
" I shall conclude my Discourse with this Admoni-
" tion in Scripture, *Let him that stole, steal no more*

This Sermon was vastly well received by Sir *Gos-*
selin and his Associates, who returned the Monk
their extraordinary Thanks for the excellent Sermon
he had made, in short, they gave back not only
the Gold they had taken from him, but making a
Collection among themselves, presented him with a
Purse (above his Money) by Sir *Gosselin* their Spokesman, who, after a few Ceremonies on both Side,
left the Monk to descend out of the Tree quietly ;
and go Home in Peace

One

One would have thought that the Doctor's impartial Handling of his Subject, and the open Manner in which he exposed Thieving, and the direful Consequences that waited upon it after this Life, would have awaked our Adventurers to a better Sense of themselves But, it seems they were too far plunged in their iniquitous Course of Life, to retreat back and reform Which will be proved in the Sequel Nay, if Accounts be true that are transmitted down to us concerning this Knight and his Confederates, whole Parties of Horse and Foot sent out to suppress their Career, were several Times defeated, at which the whole Kingdom was put into so much Terror and Amazement, that none durst take a Journey, or appear on the Roads The King then reigning having acquainted his Nobles of his Intention to make a Progress through the North of *England*, Sir *Gosselin* came timely to hear of it, and accordingly put himself and his whole Gang in Priests Habits Now the King being on his Progress and near *Norwich*, our Adventurers, being a considerable Number, drew up to him in their venerable Habits, which making the King halt to observe them a little more closely, Sir *Gosselin* closed up with him The King upon this seemed desirous to hear what he had to say, which Sir *Gosselin* observing, after a low Obeisance made to his Majesty, he told him that he was not come to discourse about Religious Matters, but Secular Affairs, which was to lend him and his needy Brothers what Money he had about him, otherwise not all the Indulgences he could obtain from the Pope should save him from being exposed to a very hard and rigid Penance. The King having but about Forty to attend him, found it impossible to get clear of his Adversary, to save his Money, but was obliged to surrender all, nay, look on while his Noblemens Pockets were search'd, after which Sir *Gosselin* and his Associates left them to perform the remaining Part of their Progress

This Attempt upon the King was highly resented, and several Proclamations with considerable Rewards inserted, issued to apprehend any of the Persons concerned in this Robbery alive or dead In less than Six Months above Sixty were treacherously taken by People, in order to obtain the Premium Notwithstanding, this Change of Fortune was so far from working any Reformation in our Knight, that he and his Brother robbed with greater Boldness, so that those Noblemen and Gentlemen, who had Seats in the Country, were afraid to reside at them, and were obliged to secure themselves and their Effects in the fortified Cities and Towns of the Kingdom

The last Adventure which we have on Record of this Knight was this Sir *Gosselin* and the remaining Part of his Associates being in the North of *England*, were determined to see what the rich Bishop of *Durham* could afford them, accordingly they got into his Palace, which they rifled from Top to Bottom of all the valuable Things in it; and, not content with the Spoil they found, bound the Reverend Prelate and his Servants Hand and Foot, while they went down into the Cellar, drank as much Wine as they could well digest, and then let the rest run out of the Barrels, after which they departed, leaving the Ecclesiastick to call upon God to deliver him in his Necessities

But Fortune now weighs down the Scale of our Knight's Iniquities It seems a Man kept a publick House in a By place in *Yorkshire*, where Sir *Gosselin* frequently went, not so much for the Liquor there, as for the Beauty of the Woman of the House A freer Acquaintance than consisted with Decency had been kept up very openly some Time between the Knight and the Landlady, which the Husband at first connived at, through a Notion his dignified Customer, and the Company he brought to his House, would be of considerable Advantage to his Trade But Sir *Gosselin* and his Wife pursuing their Love Intrigues in broad Day light, to the no small Scandal of his Family, and he beginning too late to think himself injured, found no other Resource to repair the ill Name thrown upon him by the People in the Neighbourhood, than by removing the Knight out of the Way To which End he goes to the Sheriff of the County, and acquaints him how Sir *Gosselin* might be apprehended with little Difficulty at his House, provided he came that Night. The Sheriff rejoiced at the Opportunity, but consider'd that the Knight and his Associates were Men of desperate Fortunes, vast Courage, and resolved to hazard the last, rather than surrender or be taken, upon which he muster'd up between five and six hundred Men in Arms, came privately in the Night with them to the House, which they vigorously attack'd as our Knight and his Company were revelling over their Cups Now or never was an important Battle, or rather Siege, to be determined The Persons within resolutely defended themselves for some Time, and the Men in Arms without were not less valiant Good Fortune seemed to incline to our Knight's Side, who, in Conjunction with his Men, laid two hundred of his Adversaries dead on the Spot, but being tired with the Slaughter, and fresh Enemies pouring in upon him, he was presently hemmed in on every Side, and obliged to surrender, tho' not without fighting to the last The Sheriff, exasperated to think at losing so many Men, took care to put the captive Knight, and three and twenty of his Comrades, who were made Prisoners at the same Time, under a very strong Guard, who safely conducted them to *York*, where, without any Trial or other Proceedings had upon them, they were executed, to the Joy of Thousands, the Satisfaction of the Great, and the Desire of the common People, who waited upon them to the Gallows, triumphing at their ignominious *Exit*

Th

The LIFE *of* ROBIN HOOD.

THE Accounts of this Man's Genealogy are exceeding various, and the Stories of him as fictitious among the Country People, as the Theft of Mercury among the Heathens, the one being accounted a God for his Dexterity of Pilfering, and the other being generally reputed a Nobleman I shall only confine myself to two, out of the several Accounts we have of this Man In the first he is said to be the Earl of *Huntington,* that his Father was Head-Ranger in the North of *England,* that his Mother was a Daughter of the Earl of *Warwick,* that he had an Uncle named *Gamwell* of *Gamwell-Hall* there, that his Father and Mother lived at a small Village called *Loxly,* near the Forest of *Sherwood,* and that he himself was born in *Henry* the Second's Time But in the second he is said to derive his Family *ab origine,* from no higher Persons than Shepherds, who for some time had inhabited in *Nottinghamshire,* in which County, at a small Village adjacent to the Forest of *Sherwood,* he was born, in the Reign of King *Henry* the Second, and bred up a Butcher , but being of a licentious and wicked inclination, left his Trade, and associating himself with several Robbers and Outlaws, put himself at their Head, because he was a Man of extraordinary Courage, and wou'd never entertain any in his fraternity, but such as had been sufficiently tried both as to their stoutness and dexterity in handling their Arms

But we are acquainted from the former of these two accounts, that *Robin* was put to School, where he made a surprizing Progress in his Books, and could answer to any Question put to him by his Master with wonderful facility and wit, which gave his Parents no small joy And that one *Christmas* he went to see his Uncle *Gamwell,* at whose House, in Company with *Little John* (who was a Servant there) he performed very unusual Tricks with Cups and Balls, which won the Heart of the aged Gentleman so much, that, dying not long after, he left *Robin* his sole Heir, who now began to be very beneficent and hospitable to all that came to see him , relieved the Poor, and did a thousand other meritorious Actions, which gained him the good-will and esteem of all about him, but that this open and free way of living did not last long, for, by his Profusion and too great Liberality having run thro' the Estate, he was obliged to support himself as well as he could That he had abundance of deep Reflection within himself how to maintain his usual Grandeur and Hospitality, which at length turned upon robbing the Rich, and always shewing kind to the Poor, who were always sending up their Prayers to Heaven for his Prosperity and long Life, because, if he met any of them, he would not only restrain from injuring or robbing them, but give them Money , nay, wheresoever he heard that any were sick or in want, he was sure to send his Succour and Assistance to relieve them in their necessitous Circumstances

By this time he and *Little John* (so called, tho' otherwise of lofty Stature) were become sworn Brothers They were together in all Parties of Pleasure,

of robbing, or otherwise And the first Adventure of theirs which we have on Record was performed by them, and fifteen more, on the Bishop of *Carlisle,* who had fifty in his Retinue The account of this Matter stands thus *Robin* having intelligence that the Prelate was in his way to *London,* met him on the South-side of Ferry-bridge in *Yorkshire,* and, notwithstanding his Retinue was so numerous, attacked him with his much inferior Number, took from him eight hundred Marks, and then tying him to a Tree, made him sing Mass , after which he unty'd him, set him on his Horse again with his Face to the Tail, and in that Condition obliged him to ride to *London,* where he made heavy complaint to the King of the indignity that had been offered him, who issued out a Proclamation for his being apprehended , but all endeavours were ineffectual

Some time after this the King having proposed a shooting-match in *Finsbury-fields, Robin* and his Gang, notwithstanding their late insulting the Bishop, had a mind to be Spectators of this Diversion, nay, to make Parties in it, and accordingly having disguised themselves, they came up to *London,* and mixed incognito among the company assembled on this Occasion Great Commendation were given to the King's Archers, who, to say the worst of them, shot exceeding well, and large Butts moving about, *Robin* steps up, and offers to lay an hundred Marks, that he singled out three Men who should shoot better than any three others that could be produced to oppose them , the King takes up our Adventurer, and the Queen, admiring the resolution of the Strangers, as she thought them, was incited to lay a thousand Pound on their Heads against their King, which example was followed by several of the Nobility *Robin* now bent his Bow and shot almost into the middle of the Clout, beating his Adversary about a Span , *Little John* hit the black Mark in it, and overcame his Antagonist, but *Midge* the Miller punn'd up the Basket, by cleaving with his Arrow the Pin in two which was in the middle of the Black , so that the Queen, and all those who laid on her side won the Bets But when the King came to know afterwards that it was *Robin Hood* and part of his Gang, that had beaten his Archers, he swore that he should be hanged whenever he was caught, and, in order thereto, sent out several Detachments of Soldiers into the Forest of *Sherwood* after him, which *Robin* having private notice of, made him withdraw into *Yorkshire,* thence to *Newcastle, Cumberland, Lancashire* and *Cheshire,* and last of all to *London,* till the Heat of the Hue and Cry was over, and then he returned to his old Place of Rendezvous, to the no small joy of his Companions, who had been from him full eight Months

Robin having a mind to make a Progress by himself, put into a by sort of a House, a little out of the Road, in which he found a very poor but a poor old Woman, who was weeping very bitterly, and in a flood of Tears *Robin,* moved the extraordinary crying, desired her to acquaint him with the cause of her Sorrow, to which she answered that she was a poor

poor Woman and a Widow, and being somewhat in debted to her Landlord for Rent, she expected him every moment to come and seize what few Goods she had, which would be her utter Ruin This news filling *Robin*'s Breast with Compassion, he bad her rest herself contented, and he would make things easy, so pulling off his rich laced Cloaths, and putting on an old Coat, which the old Woman lent him, and having likewise secured his Horse in an old Barn, in a little time came the old miserly Landlord, and demanded his Rent Upon this *Robin* rises out of the Chimney-corner with a short stick in his Hand, and says, *I understand, Sir, that my Sister here (poor Woman) is behind hand for Rent, and that you design to seize her Goods, but, she being a desolate Widow, and having nothing wherewithal to satisfy you at present, I hope you will take so much pity and compassion on her mean Circumstances, as not to be too severe upon her*. Pray, Sir, let me perswade you to have a little forbearance, to which the Landlord replied, *Don't tell me of forbearance, I'll have my Money, I want my Rent, and if I am not paid now, I'll seize her Goods forthwith, and turn her out of my House* When *Robin* found that no intreaties nor perswasions would prevail with the old miserly Cuff to have patience with the poor Woman, he pulled a Leathern Bag out of his Pocket, and said, *Come let's see a Receipt in full, and I'll pay it*, so accordingly a Receipt was given, and the Rent paid Then the Landlord being upon going away, says *Robin*, *'tis drawing towards Night Sir, and there's great robbing abroad, therefore I would advise you to stay here till to-morrow Morning, and take the Day before you* No, no, replied the Landlord, *I'll go Home now, I shall reach seven Miles before 'tis dark*. Pray Sir, says *Robin* to him again, *Let me perswade you to 'tarry here, for indeed there's great robbing abroad* I don't care, answered the Landlord, *what robbing there is abroad, I'll go home now, besides, I don't fear being robb'd by any one Man, let him be what he will* So taking his Horse, away he rode, and *Robin* after him, drest then in his fine Cloaths, and meeting him at a Pond where he knew he must pass by, bid him stand and fight, or deliver his Money Which words so terrified him, that he delivered all the Money he had received for Rent, and and as much more to it. Then *Robin* riding back to the old Woman again, and disguising himself as before, it was not long before the Landlord came back to the House again, and knock'd at the Door, upon which *Robin* asks who was there? The Landlord answers, *'tis I* what I? says *Robin*, why *'tis I*, answered the Landlord again At these words, the old Woman cried, *O dear! 'tis my Landlord*. So letting him in, he told his Grievance with a great deal of Sorrow, as how he was robbed by a Rogue in a lac'd Coat, who swore a thousand Oaths at him, and had certainly knock'd his Brains out had he not given him all his Money *Ay*, says *Robin*, *I told you there was great robbing abroad, but you would not take my Advice, now I hope you'll stay here till Morning* However he did not, for, having given an Account of his Misfortune, he made the best of his way homeward

The King having determined to make a Progress into the North of *England*, *Robin* came to hear of it, and was resolved to rob him Accordingly taking sixty of his Followers, put himself and his Associates in very rich Cloaths, with each Man his white Horse, well harnassed and accoutred They met the King at a small Village, with about thirty in his Retinue (for the Kings of *England* in those Days were not wont to be attended with Horse-guards as now) whereupon *Robin*, the foremost of his Com-

rades, stept up to the King, and addrest him in a very handsome manner, *My Liege, say he, by our extraordinary Garb and Dress we should seem to be Persons of Dignity and Fortune, but I must crave leave to be so sincere with you, as to inform you we are of a quite different Stamp and Condition to that which probably you and your Retinue may take us to be* For my part, having being descended of honourable Parents, and left, when very young, in Possession of a considerable Estate, which for several Years supported me in a generous and gay manner, I reckon my self among the Number of those your Countrymen (for Subject is too harsh a word for a Gentleman to pronounce) who think themselves the happiest Persons living, by having lost all through generous and polite Living What mean you Sir, by this mysterious way of Discourse, answered the King? Explain your self, for really I am at a loss to understand you To which *Robin* replies, *My Liege, my Action are already so much divulged throughout this Land, that there's no need of making enquiry about me, I am only to inform you, that, having run thro' all that I was born to, and double the Quantity, I made my self Captain over these brave Fellows whom you see before you Our Employment is to collect Tribute (not as, you do, to satiate the hungry Appetites of Ministers of State and Pensioners) of every one that travels thro' these Counties, which I have some time ago annexed to my Dominions I constantly take from the Rich to give to the Poor, for those share my Benevolence hourly, and I cannot think but your Generosity will look upon me as a Person deserving What I want Sir, is your Money, which will give you a free Passport to the Place you are going to* The King finding by the Number of *Robin*'s Attendance, that there was no such thing as resisting his Demand, voluntarily pulled out a Purse and gave it him, which found it, by the weight, sufficient to answer his present Occasions, without having recourse to the Noblemens Pockets who waited upon the King to increase the Booty

Our Readers are to be acquainted, that it was no Difficulty to rob our Kings at that Time of Day, Several of our Nobility of the present Age appear more splendid and numerous in their Attendance than they did Kings formerly used to make frequent Progresses to different Parts of the Kingdom, to diffuse among their Country Subjects their Riches, and see how Matters went among them, but now the Custom is quite varied, and nothing but large Bodies of Life-Guards are seen waiting upon our Kings, though it be but for three or four Miles, which makes it seem rather a Clog upon Majesty than an Augmentation of it

Robin, happening to be out one Morning by himself, observed a young Man, of a genteel Aspect, and well drest, sitting under the Shade of a Tree in a very melancholy and dejected Mood The Sight presently made our Adventurer step up to him, and ask the Reason of his sitting so disconsolately there The young Man, after many Sobs and Tears, broke out frequently into an Exclamation against Womenkind, who, he said, were the most perfidious Women es in the World *I this Morning, said he, had got Things ready in order to be married to the Gentleman's Daughter of that House, but Money being a stronger Perswasive than the truest Love, another Person in this Neighbourhood has supplanted me by the young Woman's own Appointment, though she's mine by all the sacred Oaths under Heaven* Ay, ay, says *Robin*, is your Case so? never be afraid Man, but put on a more chearful Look, I'll warrant you Success you shall not only have the Woman, but her Fortune too Having thus said, he took the young Man along with him

him to his Comrades, who went back to the Church together, and meeting the Bishop, *Robin* began to discourse him on some Points in Religion, till a wealthy Knight, and the young Man's Mistress came in to be married Upon which *Robin* said, 'Tis a great Shame that such a young beautiful Woman should be married to such a fumbling old Man as this, to lie grunting by her Side, and to make a Nurse of her all the Days of her Life No, no, she shall have her own Bridegroom, and he his right Mistress With that he blew a Blast, and straightway appeared the young Man, and twenty Yeomen Now, said *Robin*, you shall enjoy the Woman you love this very Day No, hold, *said the Bishop*, that's against the Laws of our Church, to marry any Person that has not been ask'd three Times *Robin* hearing this, immediately pulled off the Bishop's Robes, and put them on *Little John*, who went up directly into the Choir, and ask'd them seven Times before all the People, but the young Gentlewoman absolutely refused to make any Response, till Menaces and high Words forced her into a Compliance, when away they carried her to *Sherwood*, where they kept the Wedding

Another Time *Robin* being at *Coventry*, and having a Mind to play a Prank, which he mightily delighted in doing, and understanding that a certain Lord was to set out for *London* the next Day on horseback, with a great Retinue, he put himself in Woman's Apparel, and overtaking his Lordship on the Road, having a tolerable good Face, and young, the noble Peer was pleased to scrape Acquaintance with this young Damsel, as he suppos'd her, so after a great deal of Chat together, his Lordship, being amorously inclin'd, was for fulfilling the primary Command, *Encrease and multiply*, and putting the Question to her, this Masculine, Feminine Creature pretending great Modesty, said, *It became her Sex never to permit Dishonesty to come nearer than their Ears, and then, to save Virtue the Labour, Wonder and Defeftation ought to stop it.* However, his Lordship pursuing his Inclination very close, it made her hug the Conceit of it, and at last giving way to her Inamarato's Courtship, she told his Lordship, that if they had been in any Place of Privacy, she should have been very ready to gratify his Desire, but to expose herself before all his Men, she would not for the World His Lordship being very joyful at her Condescension to his Embraces, they had not rid above half a Mile further, before a Wood presented itself to their sight, where he ordered his Servants to halt till he came to them So he and his dear masculine Mistress rid into the Wood, and there alighting with an Intention of having a full Enjoyment of his proposed Lady, when his Lordship taking up her Petticoats, found under them a Pair of Breeches, and said, what's the meaning of your wearing Breeches, Madam? *Nothing*, replied our Adventurer, *but to put my Money in, and now you must pay for your peeping*, with that he beat his Lordship, and took above an hundred Marks from him, and then tied him to a Tree, to cool his Courage, and so bid my Lord farewell till the next meeting The Servants mean time waiting the Return of their Master, wondred, having staid an Hour, at his long Absence, but at last they determined to seek him out, and so entring the Wood, they heard a Voice crying out for Help, they followed the Sound as fast as they could, till at length they found his Lordship fast, he bad them untye him, and said, that the Villain whom he had taken for a Woman, proved to be neither better nor worse than an Highwayman and a Robber, and had taken all he had from him, that was valuable, but that for the future he would be hang'd, if ever he trusted himself alone with any thing in the shape of a Woman

Another time *Robin* disguised himself in a *Friar's* Habit, and traveling from his Companions, had not gone far before he met a Couple of Priests, and he making a pitiful moan to them, begg'd their Charity, and that they would relieve one of their Function, for the *Virgin Mary's* sake That we would willingly do, said they, was it in our Power, but we have lately met with a Gang of Villains, who have robbed us of all our Money, and left us nothing to relieve ourselves I am afraid, said *Robin*, you are all so addicted to Lying, that an honest Man cannot take your words Therefore let us all down on our Knees, and pray to the *Virgin Mary* to send us some Money to defray our Charges Upon which they offered to run away, but *Robin* soon put a stop to their Career, and made them go to Prayers They had not been long at their Supplications, before *Robin* bad one of the Priests feel in his Pockets, for what the *Virgin Mary* had sent, upon which both, to obey the word of Command, put their Hands in their Pockets, and pulled out nothing. *Robin* upon this fell into a great Passion, and told them, that he believed they were nothing but a parcel of lying deceitful Knaves, to make him believe that the *Virgin* had sent them nothing, when they had all prayed so heartily, therefore, don't deceive one another, but each of you stand a search So *Robin* began, and search'd their Pockets, and soon found five hundred pieces of Gold When he saw this glorious sight, he could not forbear calling them lying and deceitful Knaves Soon after this they rose up to go, but *Robin* stopt them and made them take an Oath never to tell lies to a *Friar* again, nor to tempt young Virgins, nor to lie with other Men's Wives After which he mounted his Horse, and returned to *Sherwood*

Another time a Gentleman as he was riding from *Coventry* to *London*, happened to meet with *Robin Hood*, and thinking him to be an honest Gentleman, desired him to turn back, and go some other way, or else he would certainly meet with Highwaymen, and be robb'd, for he had narrowly escaped them himself, and so advised him, if he had any Charge about him, not to venture that way I have no great Charge about me, Sir, said *Robin*, however, I'll take your Advice for fear of the worst So as they were riding along, said *Robin*, perhaps we may meet with some Rogues of the Gang, by the way, for this is an ugly robbing Road, therefore I'll secure that little I have, which is but ten Guineas, by putting it into my Mouth Now the Gentleman, not in the least suspecting him to be of that Profession, told him, that in case he should be set upon, he had secured his Gold in the feet of his Stockings, which he said was no small Quantity, and that he had receiv'd it that Day of his Tenants for Rent Discoursing thus together, they had not gone above half a Mile further, before they came into a very By-place, where *Robin* bad the Gentleman stand and deliver his Money The Gentleman was in a great Surprize, and told him, he took him for a very honest and worthy Person However there was no Remedy for the Loss of his Money, which was about fourscore and ten Marks So *Robin* left the Gentleman cursing his Folly for telling him where he had hid his Money

Some time after this *Robin*, meeting with a Butcher going to Market to sell his Meat, bought his whole Cargo, and his Mare with it, which came together to about twenty Pounds With these *Robin* immediately goes to the Market, and sells his Bargain presently, making such good Penny worths, that all the People thought he had stole the Meat, which now being converted into Money, he puts into an Inn at *Nottingham*, and treats all his Customers to the Value of Five Pounds, which coming to the Sheriff of the County's Ears, who was at the same time in the Inn.

Inn, and taking him to be some prodigal Spark, of whom he might make a Penny, intrudes into his Company, and after some short Discourse, ask'd him if he had any more Meat to sell. *Not ready dress'd*, said Robin, *but I have two or three hundred Head of Cattle at Home, and a hundred Acres of Land to keep them on, which, if you'll buy, I'll sell you them a Pennyworth* The Sheriff snapt at the Proffer, and took four hundred Pounds in Gold along with him. Away they rid together, but he was very much surpriz'd at the melancholy Place that Robin had brought him to. He told him, he wish'd they did not meet with a Man call'd Robin Hood, and began to wish himself back again, but 'twas then too late, for Robin winding his Horn, presently came Little John, with fifty of his Companions, who were commanded by their Captain Robin to take the Sheriff to Dinner with them, assuring them he had Money enough to pay his Share. Accordingly, they got a Collation ready for the Sheriff, and after Dinner was over, they led him into the Forest, and there took all his Gold from him, good Part of which he had borrow'd of the Inn-keeper, where he met with Robin Hood.

Our Adventurer being another time at Wigton in Yorkshire, and hearing how barbarously the Hostlers would cheat the Horses of their Provender, privately went into the Stable, and hid himself under the Manger. A little time after came the Hostler into the Stable, under Pretence of feeding Robin's Horse, no sooner had he put the Oats and Beans into the Manger, and laid down his Sieve, but he sweeps them all into a Canvas Bag fix'd under one Corner of the Manger, and so away he went. Robin all this while kept himself secretly hid under the Manger, and saw now the Hostler manag'd his Matters, upon which he got up from his private Recess, and went into the Kitchen again. After Dinner he seem'd to be for going, and calling for the Reckoning, ask'd the Hostler what Corn he had given his Horse? He said he had given him what Corn he had order'd him, and that the Gentleman who din'd with him, saw him bring it through the Kitchen. To which Robin answer'd, *Don't tell me a Lye, for I shall ask my Horse presently* This Saying put all the strange Gentlemen that were with him into Admiration, but above all, the Inn-keeper ask'd him if his Horse could speak. *Yes*, said Robin. *That's impossible*, reply'd the Landlord. *Not at all*, said Robin, *for my Horse is taught by Art Magic, So fetch him hither, and you'll soon see whether the Hostler has done him Justice or not* Accordingly, the Horse was fetch'd, and Robin striking him on the Belly, he laid his Mouth to his Master's Ear (by Custom) just as the Pidgeon did to Mahomet. *Look you there now*, said Robin, *did not I tell you that the Hostler had cheated him of his Corn* Why, said the Landlord, What does he say? *Say*, quoth Robin, *why he says your Hostler has flung all the Corn into a Bag plac'd at one Corner of the Manger*, upon which the Landlord and his Guest went into the Stable, and searching narrowly about the Manger, found the Bag of Corn at one Corner of it, for which cruel Villany he immediately turn'd away his Hostl.

It was customary for our Adventurer to go frequently in Disguise, so one Time he pull'd off his fine Cloaths, and dress'd himself like an old Shoemaker, and put an old Leather Apron about him, the better to colour his being one of the Gentle Craft. In this Disguise he set out to travel, and coming to alone Inn in the Road to Newcastle, it being near Night, he put in there, and being pretty liberal in his Expence, the Landlord lik'd him, and provided him a good Lodging, and Robin went went to bed betimes. The House, it seems, was full of Guests, so that all the Lodgings were taken up, and a Friar coming in very late, they had no Lodging for him. The Friar, rather than go farther, chose to accept of a Bed so low, but there was none that cared to be disturbed at that time of Night, but Robin (whom they took for a Shoemaker) was well enough pleas'd to have such a Bedfellow. Well, Matters being thus accommodated, and the Friar in Bed, he soon fell asleep, and slept very heartily, being tired with the Fatigue of his Day's Journey, but Robin having got a pretty good Nap before, had no mind to sleep any more that Night, but to lie awake and meditate Mischief, for he never lov'd any of that Function, so he studied how he should contrive to change Breeches with the Friar, and after having resolved upon what he would do, he gets up at Dawn of Day, and put on not only the Friar's Breeches, but also his sacerdotal or canonical Garment. Now Robin finding these sacred Habiliments fitted him very well, and being thus rigg'd down stairs he goes and calls the Hostler, bidding him bring his Boots, and make ready his Horse. The Hostler not in the least mistrusting, but that it was really the Friar, brought him his Boots and ask'd him what Corn his Horse must have. Half a Peck of Oats, says Robin, which was accordingly given him, Robin all the while being extremely uneasy till the Horse had eat them, but that he might be the sooner ready to go, he call'd for the Reckoning, and was answer'd that he had pa'd all last Night, but for his Horse. The Horse having eat up his Corn, he mounted him with all the Expedition imaginable, having paid for his Corn, and given the Hostler something to drink his Health. Away he rid as fast as the Friar's Horse could carry him, resolving to make himself merry at the first convenient Place he came to. The Friar mean time not dreaming what had happen'd, kept close within his Bed, but about seven in the Morning (it being in the Month of June) he rose out of his Sleep, and going to bid his Bedfellow good Morrow, soon found not only that the Bird was flown, but also that he was flown away with his Feathers, for he saw nothing but a Parcel of old Cloaths, which he suppos'd belong'd to his Bedfellow. Upon this the Friar in a great Surprize knocks and calls for some body to come up, but the Servants, who suppos'd it to be only the old Shoemaker, ask'd him, what a Pox ail'd him to make such a Noise, and bid him be quiet, or else they'd make him so. This vex'd the Friar, and made him knock the harder, upon which the Chamberlain went up, and threaten'd to thrash him if he made any more Noise. The Friar not understanding the Meaning of this rude Treatment, was amaz'd, and ask'd where his Cloaths were? The Chamberlain taking him for Sir Hugh, replied, *Where a Plague should they be, but upon the Chair where you left them? Who the Devil do you think would meddle with your nasty Cloaths, they ain't so much worth, that no need be afraid of any body's stealing them* The Man's mad, reply'd the Friar, do you know who you speak to, *Yes*, I do, says the Chamberlain. *If you did*, answer'd the Friar, you'd use better Language. *Better Language*, replied the Chamberlain, my Language is good enough for a pitiful drunken Shoemaker. What do you mean by drunken Shoemaker? Why, I am the Friar, said he, who came in here late last Night. The Devil you are, replied the Chamberlain, *I am sure the Friar went away as soon after three o'Clock this Morning* With that the Friar jumpt out of Bed in his shirt, and taking fast hold of the Chamberlain, Sirrah, says he, produce my Cloaths and Money, or I'll break your Neck down the Stairs. With this Noise and Scuffle up comes the Landlord of the Inn, and some of the Servants, who presently discover'd that this was the Person they had taken for the Shoemaker, and upon a little Enquiry into

into the Matter, found that Sir *Hugh* had made an Exchange with the Friar; upon which the Master of the Inn furnish'd him with a Suit of his own Cloaths, and Money to bear his Charges through his Journey

Robin Hood another Time was riding towards *London*, and being on *Dunsmore-Heath*, met with *William Longchamp*, then Bishop of *Ely*, with a small Retinue of about four or five in Number Immediately he rides up to one of the Bishop's Servants, whom he pretended to know; *Ah! Tom*, says he, *I'm glad with all my Heart that I am come up with you, for there's whipping Doings abroad, there's nothing but Robbing go where one will, I have got a great Charge of Money about me myself, but since I have the good Luck to get up with these honest Gentlemen, I'm not in fear of losing it; 'Egad let the Rogues come now if they dare, I'm resolved to have a Slap at them myself* This Discourse which *Robin* had with the Man, made his Lordship and his Retinue think him to be a very honest Man, and they held a great deal of Chat with him on the Road, till at last an Opportunity favouring his Intention, says he to the Bishop's Attendants, *I'm very dry, and since you are pleased to give me Protection from Danger as far as I shall go your Way, I'll ride before, and see if I can get any good Liquor, to treat you for your Civility, and shall be glad to find any worth your Acceptance* Accordingly *Robin* set Spurs to his Horse, and rid away as fast as if it had been for some Wager, when being out of Sight, he quickly tied his Horse to a Tree in a thick Wood, which was on one Side of the Road through which the Bishop was to pass, and *Robin* making what haste he could back again to the Company, says he, *O Gentlemen! I am run'd and undone, for in yonder's Lane, meeting with two Rogues, they have robb'd me of all I had, they have taken above forty Marks from me, but the Villains being but indifferently mounted, I don't doubt but that if you were to pursue them, you'd soon take them* This News put them into a Consternation, and the Bishop pitying *Robin*'s Loss, as he pretended, said to his Servants, *Let the poor Fellow shew you which Way the Rogues took, and go all of you after them as fast as you can, and take them if possible* They obeyed the Bishop's Command, taking *Robin* along with them, and when they came into a narrow Lane, he gave them the necessary Directions for pursuing the Highwaymen, and away they rid as fast their Horses could carry them, to catch the Rogues But *Robin*'s Business was with the Bishop, and back he goes immediately, and says to him, *Sir, my Time is but very short, and very precious too, therefore you must deliver what Money you have, or expect the worst of Usage* The Bishop was very much surpriz'd at his Impudence, but not knowing how to help himself, was forced to give him two hundred and fifty Marks, and then *Robin* making all the Expedition he could to the Wood, there mounted his Horse, and rid off with his Prize Soon after the Bishop being met by his Servants, they told him they could not hear of the Rogues high nor low *Ah! an* answer'd the Bishop, *the greatest Rogue has been with me, for he that pretended to be robb'd of forty Marks, hath just now made up the Loss by robbing me of six times the Money, but for his sake I shall never put Confidence in a Man who pretends to too much Honesty*

Robin, after coming into an Inn near *Buckingham*, heard a great Singing and Dancing, he enquired the Reason thereof, and found it was a Country Wake, at which were present most of the young Men and Maids for several Miles round about *Robin*, pleased at the Adventure, set up his Horse in the same Inn, and as he was drinking in the Kitchen, an old rich Farmer came in with a hundred Marks ty'd up in a

Bag under his Arm, which he had just received The Farmer, it seems, must needs step into this Inn, to see their Mirth and Pastime, instead of going directly home with his Money, which was not above a Quarter of a Mile from the Town. *Robin* seeing him admitted in the Room where the Wake was kept, ask'd the Landlord whether he might be permitted to see this Country Diversion without any Offence to the Company The Landlord told him he might and welcome; so he enter'd the Room likewise, but *Robin*'s Eyes were more fix'd upon the Farmer's Bag of Money than the young Folks dancing; and observing in the Room where they were, that there was a Chimney with a large Funnel, he went out and communicated his Design to the Hostler, who, for a Reward, drest up a great Mastiff Dog in a Cow's Hide that he had in the Stable, placing the Horns just on the Forehead, when, in the Height of their Jollity, by the Help of a Ladder and a Rope, he let him hastily down the Chimney into the Room where they were all assembled *Robin* was returned before the acting of this Scene, the Dog howled hideously as he descended, and rushing among them in that frightful Form, turn'd all into a Hurry and Confusion The Musick was immediately silenced, the Tables overthrown, the Drink spilt, the People screaming and crowding to get down Stairs as fast as they could, every one striving to be foremost, lest the Devil (as they supposed this to be) should take the hindmost Their Heels flew up, the Womens Coats over their Heads and Tails, whilst their Back-strings loosing, gave full Flushes, and made them in a very unsavoury Condition All the musical Instruments were trod under Foot, and broken to Pieces, and the supposed Devil making his Way over all, got into the Stable, whither the Hostler hasten'd to uncase him Sometime after, coming a little to their Senses, looking about them, and seeing no more of this supposed Devil, they all concluded he was vanished into the Air: But during this Hurly-burly, the old Farmer being in as dreadful a Fright as any one of them, and his Breeches as well befoul'd, dropt his hundred Marks, and fled for Safety The mean time *Robin* securing the Money under his Cloak, immediately took Horse, and made the best of his Way, but as soon as all Things were in a little Order again, there was a sad Outcry for the hundred Marks, which being not to be found, the Company supposed the late Devil had taken them away, and imputed the Loss as a Judgment inflicted on the Farmer, who was a covetous Wretch; one whose Study was how to cozen his Tenants, beggar the Widow, or undo the Orphan, or any body else, so he could but obtain their Money

Another Time *Robin* having been riding for his Pleasure, as he was returning home in the Evening, very well mounted, and drest like a Gentleman, coming near *Turnton-Bridge* in *Yorkshire*, he perceived from a rising Ground a Gentleman walking in his Gardens, which were indeed very fine, and of a large Extant Then *Robin* rode up to the Gardiner, who was standing at the Back-Door, and enquired of him whether a Gentleman, whose Curiosity had led him to see those famous Gardens, might not have the Liberty of taking a Walk in them The Gardiner, knowing his Master was willing that any Person appearing in good Fashion, might walk therein, gave him Admittance Then *Robin* alighting, he gave the Gardiner his Horse to hold, and seeing the Gentleman in the Walks, *Robin* paid his Respects to him in a very submissive Manner, at the same Time desiring he would pardon his Presumption of coming into his Gardens when his Worship was there recreating himself The Gentleman told him he very welcome, and invited him to see his Wilderness, where sitting down in a Arbour, they began to talk very merrily together, and at the latter End of their Discourse, Robin told him, That he heard he was a very charitable Gentleman, and that he must now make bold with him to borrow that little Money he had about him, for he had but little himself, and that he had a long Way to travel. At these Words the Gentleman began to startle, and was very much surpriz'd at his Impudence. But Robin told him he was a dead Man if he made any Resistance. Then he tied him to a Tree, and went away with a large Booty, but he bid the Gentleman be of good Cheer, for he would send one presently to relieve him. And accordingly going to the Gardiner, who held his Horse all this while, giving him a Ninepenny Piece, says Robin, Honest Friend, your Master wants to speak with you, then mounting, he rode off the Ground, whilst the Gardiner made haste to his Master, and very much surpriz'd to find him bound in that Manner, but he immediately loosed him and the Gentleman returned his Servant many Thanks for sending a Rogue to rob him in his own Gardens.

Our Adventurer was a Man of great Courage, and a noble daring and resolute Temper, and would often seek out for some new Adventures by himself. He had not gone far before he met the Lord Long-shamp, near Nottingham, with three Servants. His first Words were these, *Sir, I have a great Occasion for a little Money at this Time, so deliver what you have, or expect a Knock on the Pate.* Says his Lordship, *how dare you Sirrah, have the Impudence to stop a Nobleman? let me get off my Horse, and I'll fight you at Quarter Staff.* Why truly, replied Robin, *my Lord, that's a fair Challenge, and I should be very willing to accept of it, but I doubt when you are off your Horse, instead of fighting, you'll run away, as you did when you betray'd the poor Duke of ——— I won't put it into your Power to run away; so pray, Sir, don't stand prating, but deliver what you have presently.* Says his Lordship, *what the Devil are my Servants doing there? what! three great cowardly Dogs of you, and all stand still to see me robb'd by one poor Thief? Thief!* replied Robin, I am a Gentleman bred and born, and you see I live by my Sword and Staff, therefore don't rely on your Servants Assistance, for the first of them that offer to lay his Hand to his Sword, is a dead Man, as you are, if you make any more Words, offering as if he would strike him. His Lordship cried out for Quarter, and gave him a Brace of hundred Pounds, which he had in his Portmanteau, and then Robin returned to Sherwood, to make merry with his Companions.

Our Adventurer being endued with a great deal of Love and Charity for the Poor, insomuch that he would relieve any poor Family in Distress, was, on the contrary, a mortal Enemy to Misers and Engrossers of Corn, for he would often take from these to relieve the Necessitous. One Time being at Wantage, a great Market for Corn, he happened to fall into a Person's Company at an Inn there, whom he knew to be a great Engrosser of Corn, and who had bought as much Corn in the Market as cost him fourscore Marks, which Robin bought of him again, and paid him an hundred Marks ready Money for it, liking it, as he pretended, far beyond any he had seen that Day. The Corn he immediately sent to be distributed amongst the Poor of the Country. Robin understanding which Way his Corn-Merchant went, was soon at his Heels, and demanded his Money again, and what he had besides. The Countryman was in a great Surprize, shaking and trembling very much, asking him, *Whether he thought it Justice to take from him his Goods and Money too?* Says Robin, *why, han't I, you Villain, paid you for your Corn honestly, and can't you assume the Impudence to talk of*

Justice, *when there's none in the World acts more Injustice than an Engrosser of Corn? Sirrah, there's no Vermin in the Land like you, who slanders both Heaven and Earth with pretended Dearths, when there is no Scarcity at all. So talk no more of your Justice and Honesty, but immediately deliver your Money, or I shall crack your Crown for you.* Upon this he delivered him a Bag, in which Robin found his own Money, and as much more to it, so away he went with a great deal of Satisfaction.

As Robin was going one Morning to Nottingham, he met with a Tinker, and civilly ask'd him where he lived, for he heard there was nothing but bad News abroad. What bad News is it, answer'd the Tinker? for I live at Banbury, and am a Tinker by Trade, and as I came along I heard no bad News. Yes, says Robin, the News that I heard was bad, but true, for it was only two Tinkers in the Stocks for Drinking. Your News, says the Tinker, is not worth a Fart, and had they look'd you in the Face, they would have put you in to bear them Company, for I dare say you love Beer as well as any Tinker in Town. So I do, answer'd Robin, but pray tell me what News abroad; for you that go from Town to Town must needs hear some News. Why, replied the Tinker, I hear no other News than of a King Robin Hood, and I have a Warrant in my Pocket for apprehending him, wheresoever I find him, and if you can tell me where he is, I'll make a Man of you for your Pains. Let me see the Warrant, says Robin, whether it be made strong and good, and I'll go with you and take him this Night, for I know a House he uses at Nottingham. No, answer'd the Tinker, I'll let no Man see my Warrant, and if you won't help me to take him, I'll go and apprehend him my self.

So Robin perceiving how the Game went, ask'd him to go with him to Nottingham, for he said he was sure to meet with Robin Hood there, they where not long before they arriv'd at Nottingham, where they went into an Inn, and drank so plentifully, that the Tinker got drunk, and fell asleep; then Robin took away the Tinker's Money, and the King's Warrant, and left him ten Shillings to pay, but when he awak'd it would have made any one laugh to have beheld the poor Tinker's Fright at the Loss of his Money and Warrant, he call'd up his Landlord, and told him what a Mischance had befallen him; that the Stranger who was drinking with him was run away, and had robb'd him of all his Money, and had took a Warrant out of his Pocket, which he had from the King to apprehend Robin Hood. The Landlord told him, that was Robin Hood who had been drinking with him all that Day, then the Tinker rav'd and fretted like a Madman, and swore what he would have done, had he but known it had been him. In fine, the Tinker was oblig'd to leave his Budget to answer his Reckoning.

The above recited Stories are some of the great Number told of this Adventurer, and were we to give an Account of all, 'twould swell his History to an immoderate a Length, let it suffice to say, that Robin Hood was a very bold Man, of a charitable Disposition, generous and open to the last Degree. The long Distance of Time he liv'd in from these our Days make the Generality of People look upon his Actions as fabulous. It may be so, for we are at no Certainty about them, because, in several Books I have been obliged to peruse, I find the very Stories attributed to him, which are reported to be done by Falstaff and Glenville. These I have purposely omitted, not to give my Readers the same Things in two different Places. But I might have inserted the Story about our Adventurer and the Pinner of Wakefield, this having as much Veracity in as any thing that Captain *Alexander Smith* (who is too concise) says about him; but I have thought fit to omit it, as I am come to a Length large enough already, and shall only add, that *Robin Hood* having pursued his licentious Course of Living above twenty Years, when falling sick, was struck with Remorse of Conscience for his past misspent Life, and unlawful Practices, which made him privately withdraw to a Monastery in *Yorkshire*, where being led blood by a Monk, he bled to Death, aged forty three Years,

and was interr'd in *Kingsley*, with this Epitaph on his Grave-stone

Here underneath this Marble Stone,
Through Death's Assault, now lieth one,
Known by the Name of Robin Hood,
Who was a Thief, and Archer good,
Full twenty Years, or somewhat more,
He robb'd the Rich to feed the Poor,
Therefore his Grave bedew with Tears,
And offer for his Soul your Pray'rs

The LIFE *of* THOMAS DUN.

THIS Person was of very mean Extraction, and born in a little Village between *Kempston* and *Elstow* in *Bedfordshire* 'Tis said he had contracted Thieving so much from his Childhood, that every thing he touch'd stuck to his Fingers like Birdlime and that the better to carry on his Villanies, he chang'd himself into as many shapes as *Proteus*, being a Man who understood the World so well, I mean the Tricks and Fallacies of it, that there was nothing which he could not humour, nor any Part of Villainy that came amiss to him To Day he was a Merchant, to Morrow a Soldier, the next Day a Gentleman, and the Day following a Beggar In short he was every Day what he pleased himself

When he had committed any remarkable Roguery, his usual Custom was to cover his Body all over with nauseous and stinking Sear-Cloths and Ointments, and his Face with Plaisters, so that his own Mother could not know him. He would be a blind Harper to commit one Villany, and a Cripple with Crutches to bring about another, nay, he would hang artificial Arms to his Body Besides, his natural barbarity and cruel Temper was such, that two or three Men together durst scarcely meet him, for one Day being upon the Road, he saw a Waggoner driving his Waggon full of Corn to *Bedford*, which was drawn by five good Horses, the sight of which inflamed him to put the Driver to death, accordingly, without making any Reflection on the event, he falls on the Waggoner, and with two stabs killing him on the spot, boldly took so much time as to bury him, not out of any Compassion for the Deceased, for he never had any, but the better to Conceal his Design And then mounting the Waggon, drives it to *Bedford* where he sells it, Horses and all, and march'd off with the Mony

Dun at first thought it the best way to commit his Robberies by himself, but finding, upon trial, the method not so safe, as where there were a Company together, he betook himself to the Woods, where he was soon joined by Gangs of Thieves as wicked as himself These Woods served them as a Retreat on all Occasions, and the Caverns and hollow Rocks for hiding Places, from whence Night and Day they committed a thousand Villanies The report of their barbarity diffusing it self round about, caus'd all the Country to keep off from them, and more especially to avoid the Road leading from St *Alban's* to *Tocester*, betwixt which they every Day acted insupportable mischiefs, murdering and robbing all Travellers they met, insomuch that King *Henry* the First built the

Town of *Dunstable* in *Bedfordshire*, to bridle the outragiousness of this *Dun*, who gave Name to the aforesaid Place

However, this Precaution of the King was no impediment to *Dun's* Designs, who still pursued his old Courses, and tho' the Age he liv'd in was not so ripe for all manner of Villainy as it is now, yet the Gang under his Command consisted of several sorts of Artists who were made to serve different Purposes and Uses, just as he observed which Way every Man's particular Genius directed him Some of these being very expert in making false Keys and Betties, he never suffer'd them to remain idle or without Business Others were ingenious at wrenching off Locks, and making deaf Files, which wasted the Iron without Noise making the strongest Bolts give way for their Passage his Fraternity being thus compos'd of Lifters, Pickpockets and Filers, he refines, corrects augments and establishes their Laws, and one Day having read to them some few Comments on the Art and Mystery of robbing on the Highway, he for a while leaves them, but in a short time returns, and begins a pleasant Adventure, for being informed that a Company of Lawyers were to dine at a certain Inn at *Bedford*, he hastens directly to the Place appointed, where entring puffing and blowing, as a Man in extraordinary haste, he gives Orders, as if deputed by the Company to make ready a Dinner for ten or twelve Persons; which he had no sooner done, but the Company comes to the House, and *Dun* bustles about as if a principal Servant of the Inn, and was indeed believed so to be by the Lawyers, so notably did he bestir himself in the Business, when being about the Middle of their Dinner, he packs up the best of their Cloaks, and so marches off Scarcely had they made an End, but they began to miss them, demanding where they where, but they might look long enough before they found them, for *Dun* having done this Work, was got too far for the Lawyers to over-take him, or their Cloaks either.

After this Adventure, *Dun*, with some of this Associates, marches some Miles from whence they were known, and puts in at the first Inn he came at, where asking for a Chamber, the Mistress of the House, supposing them honest Men, shews them up Stairs, and perceiving her alone, they intended to force her, and in effect were ready to put their Intention into Practice, when the Master of the House just enter'd, upon which they were forced to wait a more favourable Opportunity Accordingly about Midnight one of *Dun's* Comrades feigns himself to be be extraordinary ill, and raises the Master and Mistress of the House, but it happening as he stept out of Bed, that he espied a Neighbour of his in the Chamber, upon which the Host, being transported with Jealousy, runs after the Man, while in the mean time these Rascals laid Hands on his Wife, who had gotten up Stairs in the Dark into *Dun's* Chamber, where they began to truss her up like a Woman of her Profession, but presently after the Husband coming to his Chamber, and missing his Wife, goes up to them, and finding her with them, would have put her to Death, but by a strange kind of Perfidiousness, she caused him to be murder'd by one of these Villains, thinking to come off well enough herself, but *Dun* would not be contented, for having understood of a long Time that there was Money in the House, he comes up to her, claps a Dagger to her Breast, (for there was no Pistols nor Use of Gunpowder in those Days,) and tells her, *That if she shew'd him not where the Money lay, there was an End of her Life*, but she making Resistance when there was a Demand for the Money, was immediately dispatch'd, and her House rifled of all the Money and Plate which *Dun* and his Confederates could find

Some time after this, *Dun*, being very well drest, went to an eminent Lawyer's House near *Bedford*, and demanded of the Lawyer a hundred Pounds, which, as he pretended, he had lent him on Bond The Barrister was surpriz'd at his Demand, as not knowing him, and looking on the Bond, his Hand was so exactly counterfeited, that he could not in a Manner deny it to be his own Hand Writing, but that he knew his Circumstances were such that he was never in any Necessity of borrowing so much Money in all his Life of any Man, therefore as he could not be indebted in any such Sum upon the Account of borrowing, he acquainted *Dun* that he would not pay a hundred Pounds in his Wrong Upon this *Dun* taking leave of him, told him, he must expect speedy Trouble, and in the mean time the Lawyer, expecting the same, sent for another, to whom opening the Matter, they concluded it was a forged Bond, upon which the Lawyer having got a general Release forged for the Payment of this hundred Pounds, and when Issue was joined, and the Cause came to be tried, the Witnesses to *Dun's* Bond swore so heartily to his lending the Money to the Defendant, that he was in a very fair Way of being cast, till the Lawyer's Council moving the Court in Behalf of his Client, acquainted the Judge that they did not deny the borrowing the hundred Pounds of the Plaintiff, but it had been paid for above three Months *Three Months*, said the Judge, *and why did not the Defendant then take up his Bond, or see it cancelled?* To this his Council replied, *That when they paid the Money, the Bond could not be found, whereupon the Defendant took a general Release for the Payment of it*, which being produced in Court, and two Knights of the Post swearing to it, the Plaintiff was cast, which putting *Dun* into a great Passion, he cried to his Companions, as he was coming from the Court, *Was ever such Rogues seen in this World before, to swear they paid that which was never borrowed?*

This very Story is related by Captain *Smith*, in the Life of one *Tom Sharp*, who lived some hundred of Years after our Adventurer We shall make no Remarks on it, but proceed to somewhat else

Dun having Intelligence that the Sheriff of *Bedford* with his Men were in search of him, and that they had determined to beset the Wood, where he then was, obliged him to put upon his Defence, which however did not make him lose his usual Courage, wherefore,

to prevent any Danger that might happen, he musters up his Company of grand Rogues, and retires into the thickest Part of the Wood, to a Place, in his Opinion, the most advantageous, where having left necessary Orders, he sent out Scouts; but judging it not safe to put his Confidence in Spies in Case of such Importance, he puts on a Canvas Doublet, and Breeches, old Boots without Spurs, and a Steeple-crown'd Hat on his Head, and so draws near them, where taking notice that they were unequal to him both in Number and Strength, he comes back to his Companions, makes them stand to their Arms, and so encourages them by Words and Example, that in setting upon them, as they did immediately, they were presently routed, and pursuing them closely, they took eleven Prisoners, whom they stript of their Liveries, and hanged them on several Trees in the Wood, after which they made their Coats serve them to commit several Robberies in For *Dun* going one Night to a Castle near this Wood, order'd, in the King's Name, the Gates to be open'd, pretending that *Dun* and his Companions had hid themselves there Accordingly the Gates were open'd, without the least Suspicion of what afterwards fell out *Dun* made a Pretence of searching into every Corner for Thieves, bustling every where throughout the Castle with the greatest Eagerness imaginable, but happening to find none, he would needs perswade the Waiters that they had concealed themselves in the Trunks Upon this he gave Orders for the Keys to be immediately brought him, when opening the Trunks, and having loaded himself and Companions with every thing that was any way valuable, he returns back to the Wood Mean time the Lord of the Castle was extremely enraged at this Proceeding, and could not brook to think that he should be thus robb'd, concluding that the Sheriff's Men, under Colour of searching for Thieves, had thus pillag'd him Upon this he addresses the King and Parliament, giving an Account by whom he thought he was thus robb'd, who immediately issued an Order for examining the Sheriff's Men, one of whom was hang'd to see what Influence it would have on the other, but they persisting (as well they might) on their Innocency, and discovering how eleven of their Companions had been used by *Dun* and his Associates, were set at Liberty

A very rich Knight living in the Neighbourhood, *Dun* was determined to ask his Benevolence, and accordingly went and knock'd at the House Door The Maid coming and opening it, *Dun* ask'd her if her Master was within, who told him he was Upon this he acquainted her he had earnest Business, and must needs speak with him The Maid taking *Dun* for a Gentleman by his Men and Dress, admits him within the House, and conducts him up Stairs to her Master's Chamber, into which *Dun* enters without any Concern, and after having complimented the Gentleman, sits down in a Chair, and begins a hotch potch Discourse, which the Knight admiring at, *Dun* steps up and demands a Word or two in his Ear *Sir*, says he, *my Necessities come pretty thick upon me at present, and I am obliged to keep even with my Creditors for fear of cracking my Fame, and Fortune too. Now having been directed to you, by some of the Heads of this Parish, as a very considerate and liberal Person, I am come to petition you in a modest Manner for the lending me a thousand Marks (which are thirteen Shillings and four Pence a Piece) which will just answer all the Demands upon me at present* A thousand *Marks!* answer'd the Knight, *why Man that's a capital Sum; and where's the Reason to lend you so much Money, who are a perfect Stranger to me, far to my Eyes and Knowledge, I never saw you before all this*

Dun

Days of my Life Lord, Sir, you must be mistaken, I am the honest Grocer at Bedford, who has spared so often your Favours, Really, Friend, I do not know you, nor shall I part with my Money but on a good Bottom Pray what Security have you? Why this Dagger (says Dun, pulling it out of his Breast) *is my constant Security, and unless yor let me have a thousand Marks instantly, I shall drive it into your Heart* This terrible Menace so frighted the Knight, that rather than expose his Life to any Danger, he thought it safer to deliver his Money, and get rid of his audacious Visiter

Another Time *Dun*, having a Mind to make a Journey some Miles off to see an old Aunt of his who was still alive, took Horse and set forward, but unluckily mistaking his Way, and the Night coming upon him, he was obliged to put in at the first House he came to Accordingly seeing a Light at a considerable Distance from him (for it was quite dark now) he made the best of his Way thither over Hedge and Ditch When he came to the House, he observed a great Bustle in the Stables and Court before the House, and enquiring of some of the Servants, who he saw were busied in rubbing down several Horses, *as* though lately come off a Journey, *if he could lodge there that Night, having lost his Way, and being benighted; so that he could not pursue his Journey any farther till the Morning,* he was answered, *That they believed their Master would not turn away at that Time of Night a Person of his Condition, but they would go and ask* In Consequence hereof, the Gentleman of the House was acquainted with our Adventurer's being in his Court, who immediately came to the Door, and after mutual Respects paid on both Side, told Dun, *That he was sorry to think he had not a Bed to spare to entertain a Gentleman, but that really his House was taken up from Top to Bottom by some Acquaintance and Relations who were come to honour him with their Presence at his Daughter's Marriage, which was design'd to be solemniz'd the next Day* However, he said, *there was one Room in his House which his Family from Time to Time told him was haunted, but he looked upon such a Thing as ridiculous, and could not for his Part be ever brought to come into such a Notion That if he pleased, the Room was at his Service, and if he required it, Persons should be appointed to sit up with him* No, replied *Dun, I have so little Faith, Sir, as to Stories of haunting Horses, or walks of Spirits, that I chuse to be entertain'd in such Places before any others* Upon this *Dun* dismounts, and is conducted by the Gentleman of the House into the Apartment where his Guests were, who receive him with extraordinary Civility, and all strive to banish out of his Mind the Thoughts of Fear But *Dun* is above vain Apprehensions, and looks on Tales of this Nature as the Produce of a romantick Brain He, on his Part, strives to divert the Company with several humourous Relations, which gain wonderful Approbation He sat over-against the Gentleman's Daughter, who was designed for Marriage, and eyed her with eager Looks, nor could all the Reason he was Master of restrain him from wishing that she was his The Clock strikes Twelve, and all are immediately desirous of going to rest They rise up, and with hearty Zeal wish our Adventurer all the Quiet in the World, nor would they leave him till they had seen him in Bed The House is now in a profound Rest, and *Dun* by himself to reflect on his Adventure Two large Tapers and a good Fire burn by him, he waits, every Moment for something to appear, which he could not well tell how to devise An Hour or more is past, but his Curiosity is disappointed, wherefore he is resolved to compose himself to Rest, and leave

the Consequence to Fate; but soon he is charm'd by the Appearance of the finest Woman his Eyes ever saw. The Gentleman's Daughter come into the Room, (for he had not lock'd the Door,) and stalks slowly to the Bedside Dun was in Amaze, and could not tell what to think Sometimes he thought 'twas a Ghost he saw, sometimes he consider'd the young Gentlewoman might be addicted to dreaming, and walk in her Sleep, (as Thousands have been known to do) and a thousand to one but that might be the real Cause of the House being thought to be haunted: but he was resolved to find the Truth of the Matter, and accordingly reaching his Hand softly to her, he gently touch'd her Shift, and then found how Matters went She seem'd earnestly to look upon him, but after some Time turn'd about, went to the farther Side of the Bed, and got in Here's an Adventure worth Notice If ever Man hugg'd himself on his good Fortune, certainly *Dun* did now He was in a thousand Doubts what to do, but his Surprize was at length prodigiously highten'd, by seeing the young Lady go to the farther Side of the Bed, gently turn up the Cloaths, and lay herself down by him. She had not lain above six or seven Minutes, before she pulled off her Finger a Diamond Ring, which *Dun* no sooner cast his Eyes on, but transporting Wishes prevailed within his Breast to seize it However, being determined within himself to see the Issue of the Adventure, he lay quietly, without offering either to take the Ring or incommode the Lady But this Surprize now vanishes, the Lady rises up, leaves the Ring on the Pillow, and goes out of the Room with the same silent Steps as she came in Now our Adventurer is convinced of the Reality of the Gentleman's House being haunted; he forms pleasing Ideas in his Mind about it, and cannot compose himself to Rest for a long Time, without having a thousand Thoughts about his good Fortune However, at last he falls asleep, and dreams that the same Gentlewoman comes to him again, and, enquiring for her Ring, seems solicitous about it She acquaints him *that she is going to be married to a Person that she can never love, and if he does not assist her in the critical Conjuncture she was in, she was lost to the Sense of all Pleasure and Satisfaction for ever, and then with a Sigh departs* The Morning now appears, and *Dun* awakes, his Dream fits fresh on his Mind, and he is at a Loss what to determine, whether to stay and see the Conclusion of the intended Nuptials, or get himself ready, and ride off with the extraordinary Prize he had made After some Deliberation, the latter Expedient seems best and safest *What have I to do,* says he, *with Matrimony, or the Copulation of Fools; I have got sufficient in my Hands to defray my Expences homewards, and that's the sole Affair I came about My Aunt now may go to the Devil if she will, for what I care* And so saying, he rises up, dresses himself, and, without once taking leave of the Gentleman his Benefactor, or so much as staying to gratify the Company with an Account of his Night's Transactions, leaves them to animadvert on his sudden Departure, and the Lady to look after her Ring

I believe this same Story has been fixed on ten other Persons of modern Date, but as I find a very grave Author seriously attribute it to *Dun*, I shall make use of his Authority, and let our Adventurer go with it

By this Time the Person we are speaking of was become formidable to all, for not only the Peers and other great Personages of the Kingdom stood in Awe of him, but also those of the lower Rank durst not frequent the Roads as usual What a melancholy Circumstance in his Conduct was, his general-

21

X

ly

ly committing Murder; and we find but one Instance, among the several Particulars of his Life, in which he refrained from this Barbarity, and that was in the Case above recited

We shall draw now to his last Period, and only endeavour to shew the extraordinary Struggles he made to obtain his usual Liberty, and preserve his Life, without being called to give an Account of his Actions, or answer the Laws of his Country what he was indebted to them for the many Villanies and Barbarities he had committed He had continued in this wild and infamous Course of Life for above twenty Years, and about the River *Ouse* in *Yorkshire*, was the general Scene where he play'd his pernicious and destructive Pranks, where Men, Women and Children fell a Prey to his Attempts, for he went constantly attended with fifty Horse, and the Men of the Country round about were so much terrified at his inhuman Cruelties, and the Number of his Partizans, that very few had the Courage, or even durst venture to attack him, in order to apprehend and bring him to Justice

We may venture to affirm, that if his Life contained many unaccountable and Strange Exploits, yet that his Death was as remarkable For having transacted Things beyond Imagination, his Fame, or rather Infamy, encreased every Day, so that the Country were determined to put up with his Insolencies no longer. It seems Threatnings against him came from all Parts, but these, instead of working a Reformation, or making him reflect on his past Conduct, only the more enflamed his audacious and villanous Temper. A stout Fellow, we are told, about *Dunstable*, had made five or six of the Sheriff's Officers to come to his House, with a Design to apprehend *Dun*, who sometimes would venture to walk out by himself But *Dun* having got previous Information of this Design against him, came in the Night Time with his Partizans to the Man's House, and filled it with a thousand Oaths and Curses, which presently got Wind throughout the Town, and among the Sheriff's Men, who came and pursued him with all their Force. The Fellows, his Partizans, finding they were closely pursued, divided themselves into separate Companies, and fled away to what Places they could come to, but *Dun* got into a certain Village, where he took up his Quarters for that Time However, the Pursuit still continued very warm, and his Adversaries arriving at the House where he had concealed himself, asked where he was hid, and at last found that he was concealed there Immediately, on this Report, the People, in Crowds, gathered together about the House, and two especially posted themselves in the Threshold of the Door to apprehend him, but *Dun* with an insurmountable Courage, started up, with his Dagger in his Hand, from the Table, and laid one dead that instant, and then dispatched his Companion, who ventur'd to oppose him. But what was the most surprizing, he had the Boldness to bridle his Horse in the very midst of this confused Uproar, mount, and force his Way out of the Inn The People no sooner saw this, but they fell upon him to the Number of one hundred and fifty, armed with Clubs, Forks, Rakes, and what else they could next come at With these Weapons, they forced him from his Horse, but this was so far from dismaying our Adventurer, that he mounted again in spite of all Opposition, and made his Way clear thro' the Crowd that opposed him, with his Sword The Countrymen, upon this found there was more Difficulty than they at first apprehended in taking him, but fresh Supplies coming in to their Assistance, they gave him chase still

Our Adventurer, now finding the last Period of his Life drawing on, made all the Haste he was able,

and got among the standing Corn, and then taking to his Heels (for by this Time he was forced to quit his Horse) outstript his Pursuers a Matter of two Miles, a Circumstance that seems almost incredible *Dun* having procured this Advantage, as he thought, would have lain him down to rest, and composed himself a while, but was presently, to his exceeding Suprize, hemmed in with no less a Number than 300 Men Thus was he brought into as great a Dilemma as before, but resuming his worsted Courage, he push'd valiantly through them, and got to some Vallies, where, considering there was but one Expedient left to save himself, he presently undrest himself, and taking his Sword between his Teeth, plunged into the River below, and fell to Swimming Instantly were all the Banks covered with Multitudes of People, some of whom were drawn together merely out of Curiosity to be Eye Witnesses of the Event, while others got ready Boats with a Design to give him chase, and try if they could take him 'Twas an astonishing Sight to behold him with the Sword all the Time between his Teeth, and swimming so many cross and various Ways, as still to elude his Pursuers At length he get upon a little Island which was in the River, where he sat down to get Breath a while, but his Adversaries having determined not to let him have any Rest, follow'd him in their Boats, but were forced to return back wounded in the Attempt After this he jumps in again, falls to swimming, and tries to gain the Shore at another Place, but ill Fortune attends him, and the People crouding thither, made at him with all their Oars, when they found it no way possible without Blows Several Times they struck him on the Head, and the Blows stunning him, it was no hard Matter then to apprehend him, which they did, and conveyed him to a Surgeon, in order to have his Wounds cured, and Care taken of him

When his Wounds were drest, he was conducted before a Magistrate, who, with very little Examination, sent him to *Bedford* Goal, under a strong Guard, to hinder his being rescued by his Companions Within a Fortnight after this, being tolerable well cured, he was brought into the Market Place at *Bedford*, without being put to the Trouble of undergoing a formal Trial, where a Stage was erected for his Execution, and two Executioners appointed to finish his last Scene of Life *Dun*, on beholding these dreadful Men, was so far from giving into the least Concern or Dismay, that he warned them, with an unconcerned Air, not to approach him for fear of the Consequences, telling them he would never suffer himself to undergo the Punishment determined him from their Hands Accordingly, to convince the Spectators round him, that his usual Intrepidity and Greatness of Mind had not left him, he grasped both the Executioners, and strugled so long with them, that he was seen nine Times successively upon the Scaffold, and the Men upon him However, he had still Strength to rise up from them, and taking his solemn Walks from one End of the Stage to the other, all which Time he cursed the Day of his Birth, and vented a thousand Imprecations on those who had been the Cause of his being apprehended, but chiefly on him who had been the first to beset him But his cruel Destiny is determined not to leave him, he finds his Strength diminish, and that he cannot, in spite of himself, defend himself any longer He yields, and the Executioners chopping off his Hands at the Wrists, then cut off his Arms at the Elbows, and all above next, within an Inch or two of his Soldiers, next his Feet were cut off beneath the Ankles, his Legs chopt off at the Knees, and his Thighs cut off about five Inches from his Trunk, which, after severing his Head from it, was burnt to Ashes

S. Cunningham's adventure with his Old Nurse and Astrologer

ſſies.   So after a long Struggle with Death, as dying by Piece-meal, he put a Period to his wicked and
abominable Life, And the ſeveral Members cut off
from his Body, being twelve in all, beſides his Head,
were fix'd up in thoſe of the principal Places in *Bed-
fordſhire*, to be a Terror to ſuch Villains as ſurvived
him

Here ends the Life of *Thomas Dun*, one of the moſt
profligate Wretches that ever lived, and had not ſo

many Murders ſtained his Actions, our Cenſures of
him might ſomewhat be abated, but where Blood
was ſo plentifully ſpilled, and his Robberies attended
with ſuch miſerable Cataſtrophes of the Perſons he
committed his Depredations on, we have no Room
left for Pity, notwithſtanding the infamous and extraordinary cruel Death he was put to   But waving
more about this Point, we ſhall proceed to another e-
qually as flagitious.

The LIFE *of* SAWNEY CUNNINGHAM.

THIS Perſon had no Reaſon to ſay he was
come of mean Parents, or that good Education or Tuition was denied him, whereby
he might have avoided the ſeveral pernicious Actions
and Villanies he committed, as will preſently be
ſhewn in the Sequel   His Family lived in tolerable
good Repute at *Glaſgow* in *Scotland*, where he was
born, but, in ſpite of all the Learning his Parents
had given him, or good Examples they had ſet before him, to regulate his Paſſions and direct his Conduct right, he abandoned himſelf, from his earlieſt
Acquaintance with the World, to little ſhuffling and
pilfering Tricks; which growing habitual to him, as
he advanced in Age, he increaſed in his wicked Practices, till at laſt he became a Monſter of Prophaneneſs and wicked Living   However, theſe (which
one would take to be) great Diſadvantages, hindred
him not from making a very honourable Match in
Wedlock as his Parents could not be blamed with
any Miſconduct, but ſtill kept up an honeſt and genteel Character in the Neighbourhood where they lived, and as it would have been infamous to have reproach'd them for thoſe Miſcarriages in the Son which
they had ſtrove all they could to root of his Mind,
and could not Help, ſo an old Gentleman, who had
preſerved for a long Time an inviolable Friendſhip
for the Family, entered into an Alliance with Mr
Cunningham the Elder, which at laſt terminated in
giving his Daughter to *Sawney*, and an Eſtate in
Portion with her of above one hundred and forty
Pounds *per Annum*, thinking that Marriage might be
a Means to reclaim our Adventurer from his ill Courſe
of Life, and at laſt ſettle his Mind, to the mutual
Satisfaction of both Families, for which he thought
his Daughter's Portion would be a good Purchaſe,
and well laid out   But how are Mankind deceived,
and, in ſhot, all our Foreſight and Conſultation
Sawney no ſooner found himſelf in Poſſeſſion of an
Eſtate able to ſupport his Extravagancies, but he immediately gave a more violent Looſe to his Paſſions,
than he had hitherto done   He made Taverns and
Alehouſes the frequent Places of his Reſort, and, not
content idly to waſte the Day in Debauches and
Drunkenneſs, the Night too muſt come in to make
up the Reckoning   Theſe deſtructive Steps could
not be attended but with hurtful Conſequences, and
he was too ſoon an Eye-Witneſs of ſome of them
For not having always wherewithal to indulge his
uſual Expences and Method of living, he was forced
to have Recourſe to indirect Meaſures, which ended
in pawning every thing he had, not only of his Wife's

but of his own   Melancholy Things were unavoidably to follow, if ſome Redreſs or Care was not taken to put a Reſtraint on this deſtructive Courſe.
Sawney laughed at his Follies, and could not bring
himſelf to believe he ſhould ever want, while he had
either Hands or Heart to ſupport him   He was determined to enter upon Buſineſs as ſoon as poſſible, I
mean ſuch Buſineſs as generally brings ſo many unhappy Men to the Gallows   His Wife, who was
vaſtly beautiful and handſome, ſaw this, but, with a
Prudence that became her Sex, ſtifled her Uneaſineſs
ſo long, till no longer able to bear the Torment upon
her Mind, ſhe firſt began with kind Entreaties, ſince
all they had in the World was gone, to fall into ſome
honeſt Way of Livelihood, to ſupport themſelves, for
'twas much and more commendable to do ſo, than
for him to give his Countrymen every Day ſo many
Inſtances of his riotous and profuſe Living   Had
Sawney been ſo good to himſelf as to have given Ear
to this Remonſtrance, without doubt Things had
ſucceeded well, and we ſhould never have read the
miſerable End he ſuffered   But all Admonition was
loſt on a Man abandoned to Wickedneſs, and determined to ſupport his uſual Extravagancies at any Rate.
The poor young Gentlewoman, inſtead of being anſwer'd civilly for her Love and Affection to him, met
with nothing but harſh and terrifying Words, attended with a thouſand Oaths and Imprecations.   The
Parents on both Sides obſerving this, were in extreme
Grief and Concern, and determined, after a ſerious
Conſultation, to diſſolve the Couple, but the young
and handſome Wife would never conſent to part from
her Huſband, tho' ſo baſe to her

Before we enter upon the firſt remarkable Tranſ-
action of *Sawney*'s Life, we think ourſelves under an
Obligation to lay before our Readers ſome Account of
this young Bride's rare Qualifications   In the firſt
place, as I have taken notice above, ſhe was extreamly
beautiful, not only in a perfect Symmetry of Features,
but likewiſe to theſe were joined an exquiſite Perſon.
She was tall, finely ſhap'd, full-breaſted, and had all
the other exterior Ornaments of her Sex   For her
Temper and the Qualifications of her interior Part of
Soul, ſhe was ſincere in her Love to the laſt, ever patient under the greateſt Difficulties, and ready at all
times to extricate her Huſband out of the Misfortunes
he involved himſelf in, by lawful and juſtifiable Methods, ſhe had a nice Conduct, and an extraordinary
Reſtraint upon every Paſſion that might betray her
into unforeſeen Miſcarriages   In *Glaſgow*, where
an Univerſity was, and conſequently young Gentlemen

men of Fortune and Addrefs, it was impoffible for Mrs *Cunningham* to hide the Charms of her Face and Perfon, fo as not to be taken notice of Several immediately offer'd their Refpects, and Money was not wanting to promote their Suits, but all were below the prudent Sentiments of her Mind She could not endure to think of difhonouring the Bed of her Hufband, by a bafe Compliance with the richeft Man in the Kingdom, and always fhe put off her Suitor with a Frown, and a feemingly difdainful Air But this only ferved to animate her Lovers the more, who now feemed to attack her with a Refolution not to quit the Siege till fhe had either capitulated or furrender'd herfelf Amongft the reft was a certain Lawyer, who was fo frequent in his Importunities, that fhe was quit tir'd out However, fhe was fo difcreet all the while, as to conceal from her Hufband *Sawney* the Importunities of her feveral Lovers, but their Sollicitations increafing, and being determin'd to be deliver'd of them as foon as poffible, fhe, one Night, as fhe lay in Bed with her Hufband, began to difcourfe him in Words to the following Effect *You are fenfible, my Dear, of the inviolable Love I have, from the firft Day of my Marriage to you, preferved for you, which fhall ftill, let whatever will happen, be as chaftely maintained, for the infernal Regions fhall fooner open and receive me alive, than I will dare to break the Laws of your Bed, or bring Difhonour to my Perfon, by a fhamelefs Proftitution of my Perfon in the Embraces of any Man alive As a Proof of what I tell you, you need only be acquainted, that for thefe feveral Months I have been ftrongly importuned by Mr* Hamilton *the Lawyer to confent to his Embraces, but ftill I have warded off from his Addreffes, yet cannot be free from him, which makes me now difcourfe this, in order to hear your Opinion in the Matter, and fee which will the fafeft and beft Expedient to be delivered of his Company* Here fhe ended, and *Sawney* being thoroughly convinced of his Wife's Loyalty and Fidelity, firft anfwered her with a *Defire fhe fhould forget all his Irregularities, confeffing their prefent Poverty had been the immediate Confequences of his too liberal and profufe Living, but that for the future fhe fhould fee a good Alteration in his Conduct, and he would make one of the beft of Hufbands* As for Mr *Hamilton*, faid he, *it is my Advice that you do not give him an abfolute Refufal, but pretending a kind of Love at a diftance, make him think that a confiderable Sum of Money will finifh his Expectations, and gain him what he fo much longs for; you have Youth and Beauty on your Side, and you may, confequently, command him as you pleafe, for I am not fo much a Stranger to Mr* Hamilton's *Temper, and Inclination, but that I know Love will influence him to perform generous Things My Dear, I have no Occafion to acquaint you with our Poverty at this time, which, to my extreme Grief, has been the Confequence of my irregular and profane Living, but our Wants and Neceffities may be amply made up by dexteroufly managing this Adventure, the Profecution of which I leave to your own Prudence and Conduct, and for my Part I fhall take effectual Care to extricate you and myfelf out of any Confequences that may happen upon it*

Mrs *Cunningham*, after this Conference with her Hufband, had a thoufand Thoughts in her Head, how to manage this Scheme, fo as to make the moft Advantage of it She faw that the Want of Money in her Family muft oblige her to it, tho' never fo much againft the Bent of her Inclination to the contrary, and therefore determining to put it in Execution as foon as poffible, fhe compofed herfelf to Reft for that Night The next Day *Sawney* got purpofely out of the Way, but not without a longing Expectation of receiving extraordinary Matters from his Wife's Con-

duct *Hamilton* appeared as ufual; and, protefting his Love for her was the fincereft in the World, faid, That it was impoffible for him to enjoy a Moment Reft without tafting thofe Joys fhe could fo eafily afford him Mrs *Cunningham*, at firft, reproved him for fuch a bare Declaration of his Defires, and faid, *That fo long as her Hufband liv'd, fhe could not without the moft manifeft Breach of conjugal Fidelity, and an eternal Infamy to herfelf, give way to comply with his Demands Your Perfon Mr* Hamilton, faid fhe, *is none of the worft, neither is your Senfe to be defpis'd, but alas! Heaven has decreed it, that I am already another Man's Wife and therefore deprived from gratifying you as I would were the Cafe otherwife And I have Apprehenfions of my Hufband, who is a choleric Perfon, and prefently urged into a Paffion upon the moft trifling Affair, which either he doth not like, or fquares not with his Happinefs or Intereft Intereft,* reply'd *Hamilton, Why, if that be the Cafe, neither your Hufband nor you fhall have any Reafon to complain for, let me tell you for once and all, I do not require a Gratification from any one, without making a fuitable Return, your Circumftances, Madam, are not unknown to me, and I am forry to think that after having brought Mr Cunningham fo plentiful a Fortune, I fhould have a juft Occafion to fay that you are poor, but miftake me not, I fcorn to make a Handle of your Circumftances, neither do I believe Mrs Cunningham would ever confent to my Defires on fuch fervile Terms* Upon this Madam anfwer'd him with a great deal of Prudence and Art, fhe told him, *That he pleaded handfomely for himfelf, and if fhe was not a married Woman, there fhould be nothing to obftruct their Defires* Mr *Hamilton* finding this, gave her a long Harangue, in which he endeavour'd to fhew how weak her Objection was, with refpect to her Hufband, concluding that what they did might be fo artfully contrived, that neither Mr *Cunningham* nor the World fhould know any thing of it In fine, the Lawyer pleaded as if it were for Life, for her Confent, which Madam obferving, and not caring to prolong the Time too far, but difpatch a great deal of Bufinefs in a little Time, fhe artfully told him, That fince her Stars had fo directed the Actions of her Life, that fhe had no Power of herfelf to contradict them, fhe refign'd herfelf to him, and faid, that it was to no purpofe to ftifle her Inclinations for him any longer, for to be plain with him, fhe had lov'd him from their firft Acquaintance together, before all the Men fhe had ever feen, and that fhe hop'd there was no Tranfgreffion in an Affair which her Deftiny over-ruled, and if the World proved cenforious, fhe did not care, and left her Caufe to be determined by the Stars, who, together with Mr *Hamilton's* fine Perfon, had influenced her to it To be fhort, an Affignation was made, and a Porch of one of the Churches in *Glafgow* defigned to be the Place where thefe two Lovers were to meet Nothing in the World gave the Lawyer fo much Satisfaction as the Thoughts of having obtained the Content of his fair Miftrefs, who had declared her Love to him, and refigned herfelf up to his Arms *Hamilton* promifed to make her a Prefent of a Purfe of a hundred Pounds Sterling before any thing was done, and fhe on her Side affured him fhe would pleafe him to the utmoft, and acquainted him, that he might expect all the Kindnefs fhe was able to afford him Here they parted, and the Lawyer thought the Time contained a thoufand Days till the Hour appointed was come, and he in the Arms of his Miftrefs It arrives, and both appear in the Porch, they carefs and toy, but no farther than the Laws of Modefty permitted. *Hamilton* wants to know where Mr *Cunningham* her Hufband is, and is acquainted that he was gone a fhort Journey into the Country, which however would take him up eight

Days,

Days, where as Madam had posted him, or he had done it himself, in a private Place in his Chamber at Home Hamilton seems extraordinarily pleased at his Success, and the Repose he should find in humouring his Appetite, now his Antagonist was out of the Way as he thought In a little time both these Lovers came to Sawney's House, and having entered his Bed-chamber, where he was concealed, and a good Fire burning, Mr Hamilton pulls out two Purses of Gold and gives them to her, and then going to unbreis himself, Swaney springs out from his secret Place, and with one Stroke lays Mr Hamilton flat on the Floor with a Club he had in his Hand , for, not contented with his Wife's having received the two Purses of Gold, he must have the Lawyer's Cloaths too , and therefore to make sure of them, he redoubles his Blows, till the poor Gentleman gave up the Ghost it Mrs Cunningham's Feet This was a Sacrifice to Love with a witness The Lawyer had contributed handsomely before for a Night's Lodging, and must ne give his Life into the Bargain? I know not how Mankind may think on't, but the Affair was carried to a desperate Length Now Mr Cunningham not dreaming her Husband would have carried Matters to such an Issue, seemed frighted to the last Extreme at what had been done, but Sawney endeavour'd to give her Ease, by telling her, that he would work himself out of the Scrape immediately, and so saying, hoisted the Body on his Shoulders, and went out at a Back-door which led directly to Hamilton's House, which easily opening, as a profound Sleep in the Family, and the Darkness of the Night favoured him, he carried the Lawyer to the Vault, and placed him upright on the Seat, to the end that the first who found him there might conclude he died in that Place and Posture

Now it seems Mr Hamilton the Day before had acquainted a particular Friend who lived in his House, with his Success, and how he was to have a Meeting with Mrs Cunningham that Night, This Friend had had the Gripes upon him for three or four Days, which made him have a violent Looseness, and being obliged to untruss a Point about Mid-night, rises in his Night Gown, and steps down to the Vault, where opening the Door, he spies Mr Hamilton sitting, as he supposed, and taking it that he was come there on the very same Errand as himself, stays without a while to let him have quiet Play , but finding he made no Motion to stir, after having waited a considerable Time, to his own Uneasiness, he opens the Door again, and taking him by the Sleeve of his Coat, was surprized to find him fall down He stoops to take him up, but finds him dead , at which being in a thousand Perplexities, and fearing to be thought the Murderer, he brings to mind his acquainting him with the Assignation between him and Mrs Cunningham, upon which he concludes his Friend had found no fair Play there, knowing the Husband to be none of the easiest of Men What should this Lodger do in this Case? Why he takes up the Body, throws it upon his Shoulders, and carries it to Sawney's House Door, where he sets it down Madam, a little after Midnight, having Occasion to discharge, gets out of Bed, and opening the Door, lets the Body of her late Lover tumble into the House, which putting her into a Fright, she runs up Stairs into the Chamber, and tells Sawney how that the Lawyer was come back Ay, ay says he, (just waking out of his Sleep) I'll warrant he shall come back no more, I'll secure him presently , and so saying, gets immediately out of Bed, puts on his Cloaths, and hoists the dead Lawyer once more on his Shoulders, with a Design to carry him to the River and throw him him in, but seeing some Persons at a Distance coming

22

ing towards him, he steps up to the Side of the Street, till they were got by, fearing his Design might be discovered, and Consequences were dangerous But what should these Persons be but Half a Dozen a Thieves, who were returning from a Plunder they had made, of two large Flitches of Bacon, out of a Cheesemonger's Shop And as they came along were talking of a Vintner hard by, who sold a Bottle of extraordinary Wine? Sawney was some what reliev'd from his Fears (for Fears he could not miss from having) at hearing this Conversation He had not been in his Post long, before he had the Satisfaction of seeing this Company put their Bacon, which was in a Sack, into an empty Cellar, and knock the Master of the Tavern up to let them in The Coast being now clear, Sawney conveys the dead Lawyer into the Cellar, and taking out the purloined Goods, put his uneasy Cargo in the Room, and then march'd home Mean while the Thieves were carousing, little dreaming what a Change they should presently find in their Sack Little or no Money was found amongst them, and the Flitches were to answer the full Reckoning, so that they continued drinking till they thought the Bacon was become an equivalent for the Wine they had drank

One of them, who pretended to be Spokesman, addressing the Landlord, told him, *That he must excuse him and his Comrades for bringing no Money in their Pockets to defray what they had expended, especially at such an unseasonable Time of Night, when he had been called out of his Bed to let them in , but Landlord, in saying this, we have no Design of doing you any Wrong, or drinking your Wine for nothing For if we cannot answer the Shot with the ready Cole, we will make it up by an Exchange of Goods Now we have got two Flitches of Bacon in a Cellar hard by, which will more than answer our Expences, and if you care to have them, they are at your Service, otherwise we must be obliged to leave Word with you where we live, or you lay under a Necessity of trusting us till the Morning, when, on sending any Body along with us, you may depend on receiving the Money, Gentlemen, says the Vintner, you are all meer Strangers to me, for to my Eyes and Knowledge, I cannot say I ever saw one of you before , but we will avoid making any Uneasiness about my Reckoning I do not care to purchase a Commodity I never saw, or , as the saying is, to buy a Pig in a Poke If the Flitches of Bacon, you say you have, are good, I'll take them off your Hands, and quit Scores with you, so they but answer my Demands* Immediately one of them, who had drunk plentifuller than the rest, said he would go and fetch them, and accordingly coming into the Cellar, strove to hoist the Sack up , *Zounds,* says he, *why I think the Bacon's multiplied, or I am damnably deceived What a Pox of a Loaf is here to gaul a Man's Shoulder's? Tom might well complain they were heavy, and by Gad, heavy and large ones they are, and the Vintner will have a rare Bargain of them,* much good go along with them, and so saying, he lugs the Corpse on his Shoulders to the Tavern On coming to open the Mouth of the Sack, Lord, what a Surprize were all in to see a Man's Head peep out Mr Dash presently knew the Lineaments of the deceased's Face, and cried out, *You eternal Dogs, did you think to impose a dead Corpse on me for two Flitches of Bacon? Why, you Rascals, this is the Body of Mr Hamilton the Lawyer, and you have murther'd him, have you, you Miscreants , but your Merits shall soon be soundly rewarded, I'll warrant you* At this all the six were in the saddest Plight that could be imagined, nothing but Horror and Dismay sat on their Looks, and they really appear-

Y ed

ed as the guilty Persons. But the Vintner, observing them bustling to get away, made such a thundering Noise of Mutherers, Murtherers, Murtherers, that immediately all the Family were out of
their Beds, and the Watch at the House Door to
know the Reason of such an Alarm The Thieves
were instantly convey'd to a Place of Durance for
that Night, and in the Morning were sent to the main
Prison, when after a little Time, they took their
Trials, were found guilty (though innocent) of Mr
Hamilton's Death, and executed accordingly

Sawney came off very wonderfully from this Matter, though neither his Wife's Admonitions, nor
his own frequent Asseverations to her to leave off
his irregular Course of Life, were of any Force to
make him abandon it, the Bent of doing ill, and
living extravagantly, was too deeply rooted within
him, ever to suppose now that any Amendment would
come ; nay, he began to shew himself a Monster
in Iniquity, and committed every Wickedness that
could exaggerate the Character of a most prophane
Wretch For 'tis impossible to enumerate, much
more to describe, the Quantity and Qualities of his
Villanies, they being a Series of such horrid and incredible Actions, that the very inserting them here
would only make the Reader think an Imposition
were put upon him, in transmitting Accounts so
shocking and glaring The Money he had obtained
of Mr *Hamilton* was a dear Purchase , it was soon
play'd away with and consumed, which made him
throw himself on other Shifts to support his Pockets ,
to which End he visited the Highway, and put
those to Death who offered to oppose him His
Character was too well known in the *West of Scotland*, to want any further Information about him,
which obliged him to retract towards *Edinburgh*,
where meeting with a Gang of his Profession, who
knew him to be most accomplish'd in their Way, he
was constituted Generalissimo of their Body, and each
Man had his particular Lodging in the City But
Sawney, who ever chose to act the principal Part in
all Encounters, industriously took Lodgings at a
House noted for entertaining Strangers, where he was
not long in insinuating himself into their Acquaintance *Sawney*, indeed had a most artful Method
to conceal the real Sentiments of his Mind, and hide
his Actions, which in a little Time so gained upon
the Belief of these Strangers, that they could not
help taking him for one of the sincerest Men breathing For it was his Custom sometimes to take them
along with him two or three Miles out of the City
to partake of some handsome Dinner or Supper, when
he was sure never to let them be at a Farthing Expence, but generously discharge the Reckoning himself The Design of all this was to make his Advantage of them, and force them to pay an extravagant Interest for the Money he had been out of
Pocket in treating them For constantly were Persons
planted in one Place or other of the Road by his immediate Direction, who fell uppn them as they returned to the City, and robbed them of what they
had But the Cream of all was, that to avoid Suspicion they always made *Sawney* their first Prize, and
rifled him, who was sure in the Morning to obtain
his own Loss back again, and a considerable Share of
the other Booty into the Bargain

Some time after this, our Adventurer, with two
of his Companions, meeting on the Road with three
Citizens of *Edinburgh*, affronted them in a very audacious Manner, and threw such Language at them
as plainly discovered that either Death or Bloodshed was near at Hand He had the Impudence to
tell the Person who seemed the genteelest and best
drest of the three, that the Horse he rode on was

his, and had been lately stolen from him, and that
he must return it him , or else the Sword he wore
should do him right *Sawney's* Companions began
with the others after the same Manner, and would
needs force them to believe that the Horses they
rid upon were theirs , The Citizens, astonish'd at such
gross Piece of Impudence, endeavour'd to convince
them the Horses rode on were their own, and they
had paid for them, and wondered how they durst
pretend to dispute an Affair which was so essential-
ly wrong, but these Words were far from having
any Effect on *Cunningham*, and the Citizens, in the
Conclusion were forced to dismount and give them
their Horses and Money into the Bargain, being
somewhat satisfied they had suffered no worse Consequences, for *Sawney*, by this Time was drenched
in all Manner of Villany, and Bloodshed was now
accounted a Trifle, so little Value did he set on
the Lives of any Persons

Sawney having run a merry Course of Roguery and
Villany in and about *Edinburgh* for some Time, when
he made a considerable Advantage to himself, so that
Fortune seem'd to have requited him for all the Poverty and Want he had before endured, determined
now to go home to his Wife, and spend the Remainder of his Days agreeably with her, on the Acquisi-
tions and Plunder he had made on his Countrymen.
Accordingly he came to *Glasgow*, where, among a
few Acquaintance he conversed with, for he did not
care to make himself too publick, he gave Signs of
Amendment, which struck those that knew him with
such Astonishment, that at first they could hardly be
brought to believe it One Night being in Bed with
his Wife, they had a close Discourse together on all
their foregoing Life, and the good Woman expressed
an extraordinary Emotion of Joy at the seeming Alteration and Change in her Husband, she could not imagine what Reason to impute it to ; for she had been
so much terrified from Time to Time with his Barbarities, that she had no Room to think his Conversion
was real , neither, on reflecting on the many Robberies and Murthers he had committed, could she perswade herself, that he could so soon abandon his licentious and wicked Courses , for she supposed, if his alter'd Conduct (as she thought) was real, it was mira-
lous, and an original Piece of Goodness hardly to be
met with The Sequel will prove that this Woman
had better Notions of her Husband, than the rest of
his Acquaintance, and those that knew him, and that
she built all her Fears on a solid and good Foundation.
The Proverb says, *What is bred in the Bone will never
be out of the Flesh* , and this will be remarkably verified in *Cunningham*, as we shall endeavour to shew in
its proper Place For all the Signs he gave of an alter'd Conduct, and all the plausible Hints to rectify
his former mistaken Steps, were no other than only to
amuse the World into a good Opinion of him, that so
he might make his Advantage, through this pretended
Conversion, with the greater Freedom and Impunity
And he w s not out in his Aim , for it seems, whenever he commit ed any thing sinister, or to the Disadvantage of any of his Countrymen, and he was pitch'd
on as the Transgressor, the Town would say, *It will
not be, for Mr* Cunningham *was too much reclaimed
from his former Course ever to give into them again*
I shall insert a very notable Adventure *Sawney* had
with a Conjurer, or Fortune-teller ; To which End I
shall trace it up from the Fountain-Head, and give my
Readers the first Cause that induced him to it When
Sawney was an Infant, he was put out to Nurse to a
poor Countrywoman in a little Village a Mile or two
out of *Glasgow* , the Woman, as the Boy grew up
could not help increasing in her Love for him, and he
being an exceeding snotty Child, would often say to
her

her Neighbours, *Oh! I shall see this Lad a rich Man out Day* This Saying coming to the Ears of his Parents, they would frequently make themselve, merry with it, and thought no more of it, than as a pure Result of the Nurse's-fondling Sawney having enrich'd himself with the Spoils about *Edinburgh*, actually thought his old Nurse's Words were verified, and sent for her to give her a Gratification for her Prediction. She came, but Sawney had chang'd his Cloaths, so that the poor Woman did not know him at first He told her that he was an Acquaintance of Mr *Cunningham*'s, who, on her coming, had order'd him to carry her to Mr *Peterson* the Astrologer's, where she would be sure to see and speak to him, for he was gone there to get some Information about an Affair that nearly concerned him The Nurse and her pretended Conductor goes to the Fortune-teller's, where desiring Admittance, *Peterson* thought they were Persons that wanted his Assistance, and bad them sit down, when Sawney taking a Freedom with the Reverend old Gentleman, as he was known to use with all Mankind, began to give an Harangue about Astrology, and the Laudable Practice of it " I and this old Woman, *said he*, a.e two of the most accomplish'd Astrologers or Fortune-Tellers in *Scotland*; but I would " not, Reverend Sir, by so saying, seem to depreciate " from your Knowledge and Understanding in so ve " nerable a Science I came to communicate a small " Affair to you, to the End, that not relying on my " Judgment and this Woman's, I might partake of " yours You are to know, Sir, that from six Years " of Age I have led a very untoward Life, and been " guilty of many egregious Sins, too numerous to " tell you at present, and what your Ears would not " care to hear, for my Employment has been to lay " with other Men Wives, make a Sharer of other " People's Money, balk my Lodging, and ruin the " Vintners, for a Whore and a Bottle I have told the " twelve Signs in the *Zodiack*, and all the Houses in " a *Horoscope*, neither Sextile, Quartile, or Trine " ever had Power over me to keep my Hands out of " my Neighbours Pockets, and if I had not a profound Respect for the Persons of my venerable " Order and Profession, I should call *Mercury* the Ascendant in the fourth House at this Minute, to lug " half a score Pieces of yours By my exceeding " deep Knowledge in Astrology, I can perfectly acquaint all manner of Persons, except myself, with " every Occurrence of their Lives, and were it not to " frighten yourself, I would conclude from the Appearance and Conjunction of *Saturn* and *Vulcan*, " that your Worship would be hanged for your Profession But, Sir, tho' Destiny hangs this unfortunate Death over your Head, it is at some Distance " from it, and may be some Years before it strikes " you

" Is it not surprizing that a Man shall be able to " to read the Fates of Mankind, and not have any " Pre-knowledge of his own? And is it not extremely ' afflicting to think, that one who has done so much " Good in his Generation, and assisted so many Thousands to the Recovery of Things, that would have " been inevitably lost, without his Advice, should " come at last to meet with an ignominious Halter, as " a fit Recompence for his Services? Good Heavens! " where is the Equity of all this? Certainly, Sir, if " we are to measure the Justice of Things, by the " Laws of Reason, we must naturally conclude that " laudable and good Actions deserve a laudable and " good Recompence, but can hanging be said to be " this good Recompence? No, but the Stars will " have it so, and how can Mankind say to the contrary?" *Cunningham* paused here a while, and the Astrologer and old Nurse wonder'd who in the Devil's Name they had got in Company with. Mr *Peterson*

could not help staring, and well he might, at the Physiognomy of our Adventurer, and, in spite of himself, began to be in a Pannick at his Words, which so terribly frighten'd him The Nurse was in Expectation of seeing Sawney come in every Minute, little dreaming the Person she was so near was the Man she wanted *Cunningham*'s Harangue was a Medley of Inconsistencies and downright Banter 'Tis true the Man had received tolerable Education in his Youth, and consequently might obtain a Jingle in several Sciences, as is evinced from the foregoing " Well, venerable " Sir, *says he*, do not be terrified at my Words, for " what cannot be avoided must be submitted to To " put you out of your Pain, I'll tell you a Story A " Gentleman had a Son who was his Darling, and " consequently trained up in all the virtuous Ways " that either Money could purchase, or good Examples teach The Youth it seems, took to a kind " and laudable Course of Life, and gave promising " Signs of making a fine Man, nor indeed were their " Expectations deceived; for he led a very exemplary " Life of Prudence, excellent Conduct, and good " Manners, which pleased the Parents so much, that " they thought every thing they could do for him " too little But the Mother, out of an inexpressible " Fondness for him, must needs go to an Astrologer, " and enquire how the remaining Part of his Life must " succeed Accordingly the Horoscope is drawn, but " a dismal Appearance results from it, it acquaints " the Mother that her Son shall remain virtuous for " two and thirty Years, and then be hanged Monstrous and incredible, *says he*, but I'll take care to " secure him in the right Way, or all my Care will " be to no Purpose Well, the Family are all soon " acquainted with this threatning Warning The " Person determined to be the Sacrifice, is already " nine and twenty Years old, and surely they suppose " they can easily get the other three Years, when all " shall go well with their Kinsman But what avails " all the Precaution of Mankind, this same Son obtains a Commission of a Ship, goes to Sea, and, " acting quite contrary to his Orders, turns Pyrate, " and, in an Encounter happens to kill a Man, for " which, on his Return to his native Country, he is " try'd, condemn'd and hang'd What think you " of this, venerable Brother? Is not he a sad Instance " of an over-ruling Influence of the Stars? But not " to prolong too much Time on a Discourse of this " Nature, let us come to the Purpose You are now " as I cannot do it myself, to tell me my Fortune, and " this old Woman is to confront you if you tell me a " Lie There is no Excuse to be made in the Matter; " for by Heavens, on your Refusal, I'll ease this Room " of your damnable Trumpery, and send you packing to the Devil after them *These Words were enough to frighten any Man out of his Senses, nor could* Peterson *well discover the Intention or Drift of his talkative and uneasy Visitant* What would you be at, *says the Astrologer?* Why, do not you see, " what a Terror you have put that good Woman " into, who trembles like an Aspen Leaf? I am not " used, Friend, to have Persons come into my House, " and tell me to my Face, that I am to be hanged, " and then to confirm it, as you pretend, tell me an " old Woman's Story of a Cock and a Bull, of a " young Man that went to Sea, and was hanged for " robbing, for which he certainly deserved the Punishment he met with As for telling your Fortune, " I'll be so plainly with you, that you'll swing in a " Halter as sure as your Name is *Sawney Cunningham*, " Sawney Cunningham, *quoth the Mauke, who straightway throwing her Arms about his Neck, began to kiss him very eagerly, and then looking earnestly in his Face, cry'd aloud, O Laird! And art thou* " *Sawney Cunningham!* Why, I thought thou come

" to

" to be a great Man, thou was such a Snotty Lad?
" Do you see now, *says* Sawney, what a damnable
" Lie you have told me, in impudently acquainting
" me that I shall be hanged, when my good Pro-
" phetess here tells me, I am a great Man, for
" great Men never can be hanged I do not care
" for what she says nor you neither, for hanged
" you'll be, and that in a Month's Time, or else
" there never was a Dog hanged in *Scotland* Pray,
" Brother, how came you to know this without
" consulting my Horoscope? — Know it, why
" your very Condition tells me you have deserved
" hanging this dozen Years, but the Laws have been
" too favourable to you, else Mr *Hamilton*'s Death
" had been revenged before this Time of Day Now
" to convince you of my superior Knowledge in
" Astrology, I mean, in telling how far their In-
" fluence extends over any Man's Actions, I will
" point to you the very Action and Persons that
" will bring you to the Gallows This very Day
" Month you shall go (in spite of all your Foresight
" and Endeavours to the contrary) to pay a Visit
" to Mr *William Bean*, your Uncle by the Mo-
" ther's Side, who is a Man of an unblameable
" Character and Conversation Him shall you kill,
" and assuredly be hang'd " Was there ever such a
prophetick or divining Tongue, especially in these
modern Days, heard of? For the Sequel will presently discover how every Circumstance of this prediction fell out accordingly Sawney, having observed
the Air of Gravity wherewith Mr *Peterson* delivered his Words, could not help falling into a serious
Reflection about them, and thinking the Place he was
in not convenient enough to indulge the Thoughts
he found rising within him, abruptly left the Fortune-teller, and giving his old Nurse five Shillings,
returned home

But what does he determine on now? After having seriously weighed on the several Particulars of
Peterson's Words, he could not for his Heart but
think, that the old Man, in order to be even with
him for telling him of being hanged, had only served
him in his own Coin, so that after a few Hours
every Syllable was vanished out of his Mind, and
he resolved to keep up to his usual Course of Life

King *James* I sitting on the Throne of *Scotland*
at this Time, and keeping his Court at *Edinburgh*,
the greatest Part of the *Scotish* Nobility resided there,
when our Adventurer used frequently to go to make
the best Hand he could of what Spoil he found there
The Earl of *Inchequin*, having a considerable Post
under the King, and several valuable Matters being under his Care, had a Centinel assigned, who
constantly kept Guard at this Lord's Lodgings
Door Guards were not much in Fashion at this
Time, and about two or three hundred in the same
Livery were kept only on the Establishment

Cunningham having a Desire of breaking into
this Minister's Lodgings, and having no Way so
likely to succeed by, as to put on a Soldier's Livery, went in that Dress to the Centinel, and after
some little Talk together, they dropt accidentally
into some military Duty and Exercise, which *Cunningham* so well display'd, that the Centinel, seeming to like his Brother's Notions, and smile extraordinarily, it made *Cunningham* stay a considerable
Time, till in the End he ask'd the Centinel to partake of two Mugs of Ale, and put Six-pence into
Hand to fetch them from an Alehouse, at some Distance from his Post, giving some Reason for it, that
it was the best Drink in the City, and none else
could please his Palate half so well as that Hereupon the Centinel acquainted him, that he could
not but know the Consequences that attended leaving his Post, and that he had rather enjoy his Com-

pany without the Ale, than run any Risque by fetching it Oh! says our Adventurer, I am not a Stranger to the Penalties we incur on such an Action,
but there can no harm come of it, if I stand in your
Place while you are gone And with that the Centinel gives *Cunningham* his Musket, and goes to the
Place directed for the Drink, but, on returning, he
must needs fetch a Pennyworth of Tobacco from
the same Place, during which, our Adventurer's Companions were broke into the Lord's
Apartments, and had rifled the same of Three Hundred Pounds Value *Cunningham* was, however, so
generous as to leave the Centinel his Musket The
poor Soldier returns in expectation of drinking with
his Friend, and enjoying his Company some Time
longer, but alas! the Bird is fled, and he is taken
up to answer for his forth coming, and committed
Talbooth Prison, where he was kept nine Months
in very heavy Irons, and had only Bread and Water allowed him to subsist on At length he is tried, condemned and hanged Thus did several innocent Persons suffer Death for that which ought
to have been the Portion of our Adventurer We
draw on to his last Scene now, which shall be dispatch'd with all the Brevity we are Masters of
Sawney having thus escaped so many Dangers,
and run through so many Villanies with Impunity,
must needs go to his Uncle *Bean*'s House, who
was a very good Christian, and a reputable Man,
as we have before observed, to pay him a Visit,
with no other Design than to boast to him of his
late Successes, and how Fortune had repaired the Injuries his former Misconduct and Remissness he had
done him

He went, and his Uncle with his moral Frankness,
bade him sit down, and call for any Thing his House
could afford him " Nephew, *says he*, I have desi-
" red a long Time to see an Alteration in your Con-
" duct, that I might say I had a Nephew worthy of
" my Acquaintance, and one to whom I might leave
" my Estate, as deserving of it, but I am acquainted
" from all Hands, that you go on worse and worse,
" and rather than produce an Amendment, abandon
" yourself to the worst of Crimes I am always wil-
" ling to put the best Interpretation I can upon Peo-
" ple's Conduct, but when so many fresh Reports
" come every Day to alarm my Ears of your Extra-
" vagances and profuse Living, I cannot help con-
" cluding but that the greatest Part of them are true.
" I will not go about to enumerate what I have
" heard, the Discovery of Mistakes only serving to
" increase one's Uneasiness and Concern But me-
" thinks if a good Education, and handsome Fortune,
" and a beautiful and loving Wife could have done
" any Service with respect to the reclaiming you, I
" should have seen it before now Your Wife has
" been an indulgent and faithful Friend to you in all
" your Misfortunes, and the lowest Employment in
" Life, could you but have confin'd yourself, would
" have proved more beneficial, and secured your Cha-
" racter, and the Esteem of your Family and Friend,
" better than the Ways you now tread in I am
" sensible my Advice is insignificant, and Men of my
" declining Years are little valued or thought of by
" the younger Sort, who, in this degenerate Age
" think none wiser than themselves, and are above
" Correction or Reproof Come, Nephew, Provi-
" dence may allot you a great many Years more to
" run, but let them not be such as those already past,
" if Heaven should grant you the Indulgence If I
" could build any Hopes on a good Foundation, that
" you would yet repent, methinks I could wish to
" have Vigour and Strength to live to see it, for what
" my Satisfaction would be then, none are able to de-
" clare, but such only as are in the like Case with
" myself

' myfelf Our Family has maintain'd an unfpotted
" Character in this City for fome hundred of Years,
" and fhould you be the firft to caft a ftain upon it,
" what will Mankind or the World fay You may
" depend that the Load of Infamy will be thrown on
' your Back, for all who know, or have heard the
' leaft of us, will clear us of the Difhonour, as know-
" ing how well you were educated, how handfomely
" fited out for the World, and how well you might
" have done If Fame fays true, you are to be
" charged with Mr *Hamilton*'s Death , but I cannot
" bring myfelf to think, you would ever be guilty of
" fo monftrous and Impiety It feems he had been
" your Benefactor, and feveral confiderable Sums of
" Money he had given you, in order to retrive your
" loft Circumftances , but was to give him his Death
" the Way to recompence him for his Kindnefs ? Fie
" on't Not Pagans or the worft of Infidels would
" repay their Benefactors with fuch Ufage , and fhall
" we Chriftians, who boaft fo much above them,
" dare to do that which they abhor from their Souls ?
" It cannot be, Nephew, but all Thoughts of Huma-
" nity and Goodnefs are banifh'd from your Mind,
" otherwife fome Tincture would ftill have remained
" of Chriftian Principles, that would have told you,
" you were highly indebted to that good and eminent
" Lawyer's Bounty I am more diffufive on this
" Head, becaufe it requires a particular Difquifition ,
" neither miftake me in this Matter, for I am not de-
" termin'd to reap up Things to the World, in order
" to blacken your Character more tnan 'tis already,
" nor to bring you under Condemnation , only repent
' and lead a foberer Life for the time to come, and
" all the Wifhes and Expectations of your Friends and
" Family are then fully anfwered Firft endeavour to
" reconcile your Paffions to the Standard of Reafon,
" and let that divine Emanation conduct you in every
" Action of your future Life, fo will you retrieve the
" Time you have loft, patch up your broken Repu-
" tation, be a Comfort to your Family, and a Joy
" to all who know you Ill Actions feem pleafing
" in their Commiffion, becaufe the Perfons that purfue
" them have fome Aim of Advantage in doing them ,
" but let me tell you there is nothing in the World
" like a virtuous Purfuit, tho' the Road is befet with
" Thorns and Briars, but there are inexpreffible De-
" lights and Pleafures in that Wildernefs, which not
" all the Vices in the World can balance This Ex-
" hortation probably may be the laft that may come
" from my Lips , but indeed you have need of Ad-
" vice every Moment, and want the Leading-ftrings
" of a Child, yet neither want you Senfe or Uuder-
" ftanding How comes it then you make fuch bad
" Ufe of them ? Are not all the miferable Catastro-
" pies of profufe and wicked Livers, fufficient to de-
" ter you from your licentious Courfe of Life ? If
" Gibbets and Gallows could have any Influence on a
" Mind, unlefs loft to all Senfe of Goodnefs, certainly
" the melancholy Ends fo many monthly make here,
' fhould be a means of opening your Eyes and re-
" claiming you But, alas ! the Wound I fear is too
' deep, and no Medicines can now prevail , your
" Enormities are of fuch an egregious Dye, that no
" Water can wafh t out Well, if neither the cruel
" Confequences of an iniquitous and mifpent Life,
" nor all the Advice which either your Friends and
" Relations can give you , if good Examples, Terrors
" or Death cannot awaken you from your profound
" Lethargy and Inactivity of Mind, I may well fay
" your Cafe is exceedingly deplorable, and what for

" my Part I would not be involved in for ten thoufand
" Worlds You cannot furely but know what you
" have to depend on now your Friends and Relations
" abandon you, for you are ftiled a Murderer ; and a
" Man that has once dipt his Hands in Blood, can ne-
" ver expect Enjoyment of any Felicity either in this
" or the next World , for there is an internal Senfa-
" tion called Confcience, which brings an everlafting
" Sting along with it, when the Deeds of the Body
" are heinous and black Indeed fome may pretend to
" ftifle their Iniquities for a confiderable Time, but
" the Paufe is but fhort, Confcience breaks thro' all
" the Barriers, and prefents before the Eyes of the
" guilty Perfon his Wickednefs in frightful Colours
" What would not fome give to be relieved of their
" racking Nights and painful Moments ; when freed
" from the Amufements of the Day, they lie down to
" Reft, but cannot 'Tis then that Providence thinks
" fit to give them a Foretafte of thofe Severities even
" in this Life, which will be Millions of times in-
" creafed in the next " Here the good old Man iffued
a Flood of Tears, which Pity and Compaffion had
forced from his Eyes, nor could *Sawney* forbear fhed
ding a Tear or two at hearing, but it was all Pre
tence, and an Imitation of the Crocodile , for he was
determin'd to take this reverend old Gentleman out
of the World to get Poffeffion of his Eftate, which, for
want of Male Iffue, was unavoidably to devolve upon
him after his Death With this View; after he had
made an End of his Exhortation, he fteps up, and
without once fpeaking, thrufts a Dagger to his
Heart, and fo ended his Life Thus fell a venerable
old Uncle for pronouncing a little feafonable Advice
to a Monfter of a Nephew, who finding the Servant
Maid come into the Room at the Noife of her Mafter's falling on the Floor, cut her Throat from Ear to
Ear, and then to avoid a Difcovery being made, fets
fire to the Houfe, after he had rifled it of all the valuable Things in it, but the Divine Vengeance was refolved not to let this barbarous Act go unpunifh'd
for the Neighbourhood obferving a more than ordinary
Smoke iffuing out of the Houfe, concluded it was on
fire, and accordingly unanimoufly joined to extinguifh
it , which they effectually did, and then going into the
Houfe, found Mr *Bean* and his Maid inhumanly murther'd. Our Adventurer was got out of the way, and
no one could be found to fix thefe Cruelties upon , but
it was not long before Juftice overtook *Cunningham*,
who, being impeach'd by a Gang of Thieves that had
been apprehended, and were privy to feveral of his
Villainies, he was taken up and committed a clofe
Prifoner to the Talbooth, where fo many Witneffes
appeared againft him, that he was condemn'd and
hang'd for his Tricks at *Leigh*, in Company with the
fame Robbers that had fworn againft him

This was the Cataftrophe of this Man, who deferved the Fate he fuffered long before it happened We
have not given our Readers a great many Adventures
of his, becaufe they were commonly attended with
Bloodfhed, an Account of which only prefents feveral
melancholy Ideas to the Reader But we have this to
fay, that we have far exceeded Capt *Smith*'s Narrative of him When he went to the Place of Execution, he betray'd no Signs of Fear, nor feemed any
way daunted at his approaching Fate As he lived, fo
he died, valiantly and obftinately to the laft, unwilling to have it faid, that he, whofe Hand had been the
Inftrument of fo many Murthers, proved pufillani-
mous at the laft

The LIFE *of* WALTER TRACEY.

THIS Perfon was the younger Son of a Gentleman, worth Nine Hundred Pounds *per Annum*, in the County of *Norfolk* He was fent to the Univerfity to qualify him for Divinity, and had a Hundred and Twenty Pounds left him by his Father when he died But his Studies not having a Relifh pleafing enough to his Mind, and his Eftate being too fittle to fupport his Extravagancies, he, to uphold himfelf in his profufe Expences, would now and then appear well accoutred on the Highway, and make his Collections But happening once to rob fome Perfons who knew him, he was obliged leave the College, and directly went down into *Chefhire*, where he put himfelf into the Service of a wealthy Grafier in the Country *Tracey*, having an excellently well-fhaped Body, and a Face that had Power to draw a thoufand Admirers after it, foon found the Country a pleafanter Scene of Life, than the wrangling and dull College. He had a genteel Air and Mien, and a hundred Liberties were given him by his Mafter, which the other Servants in the Family were not allowed to take The old Famer and his Wife, with their Daughters (for Sons they had none) would divert themfelves, after the Labour of the Day, with hearing our ruftick Gentleman play on the Violin, which he did with admirible Skill and Sweetnefs His fine Perfon and Face foon gain'd him Followers, and *Tracey* was not infenfible to Love, for if ever Man had Opportunity of indulging his Paffion that way, certainly he had, for whenever he took his mufical Inftrument into the Meadows or Paftures, he was fure to be furrounded with a Crowd of buxom Laffes, among whom fome had Beauty enough to make his Wifhes rife There was a fprightly brown Girl, who was his conftant Hearer, that feem'd to touch his Heart more than the reft, fhe would walk by his Side from Field to to Field, nay, accompany him into Caves and Solitudes, where fhe would liften with Admiration of his Mufick, *Tracey* employ'd thefe Moments to promote his Suit, for the Lafs was none of the faireft, yet had a charming Body, and a Delicacy in the plain Delivery of her Words that was irrefiftible *Tracey* durft not make an open Discovery of the real Intention of his Mind, for fear of fpoiling all the Adventure, he was convinced fhe admired his Mufick, and nothing but the Notion of Mufick, he thought, would gain upon her So he tells her he has another Inftrument that would afford the fweeteft Melody upon Earth, and that his Violin was no more to ftand in Competition with it, than a *Jew's* Harp with the Organ of their Church The Girl is ravifh'd till fhe hears it, and begs him a thoufand Times to bring it to-morrow to the Cave they were in, which *Tracey* complies with, and fo they part for that Night The Female Lover, you may befure, had little Reft till the Time appointed came, nothing but Harmony, and Melody, and Enchantment fill'd her Thoughts fhe longs to fee *Tracey* and his new Inftrument, which fhall not be long before

fhe has her Satisfaction accomplifh'd Both meet a the Cave, and both have different Views, the one is at Lofs ftill how to behave in fo critical a Minute, and the other importunes him to produce the Inftrument and play upon it I've brought the Inftrument, my Dear, along with me, which for its filent Melody exceeds every thing you ever faw or heard of But I muft acquaint you, before I fhew it, that it is no Compofition either of Wood or Horn, but that its Harmony proceeds from the Members of my Body The unpractifed Girl was fo fimple as to imagine, that from Geftures and Movements of the Bones of his Body, fome agreeable Harmony would proceed, or that his Hand by ftriking on the other Parts of his Body will raife a tranfporting Sound Come, my dear Girl, fays he, the Harmony that proceeds from my new Inftrument, cannot be raifed without your Affiftance, and therefore if you have a Defire of receiving Pleafure, you muft neceffarily be at fome Pains yourfelf, for 'tis a Tafk beyond my fingle Reach to perform, and I beg you'll give me Aid in it—If it is fo, reply'd fhe, let us fee what it is, and inftruct me in the Manner I am to act Upon this, *Tracey* clafped her in his Arm, and with great Eagernefs embraced her, and then offered to accomplifh the reft Oh fie, fays fhe, you are going to wrong me, let me alone, I cannot fuffer fuch Ufage, you prefs my Breaft too clofe, fie upon it, then, what's this you mean?—Do not be fearful, my Girl, there's no harm, I'll affure you in the Cafe,—For the Harmony and Melody is fo conceiv'd, and the ending will be much more pleafing than the beginning—She feels the tingling Pleafure, and fwoons away, but foon recovering her raptur'd Senfes, and feeing *Tracey* rifing up, fhe afk'd him, what! have you done already? you have but juft this Minute begun, fie, you baulk a Body of the Pleafure I expected—Indeed, fays *Tracey*, I imagined the Thing would do you no Damage, but that you would have fuch a longing Appetite, once you had found the Melody out, as to wifh for it again—Ay, truly, faid fhe, 'tis the beft Mufick in World, and I'll come hither any Night to enjoy it from you, but 'tis fo fhort, though I could not hear it, yet I felt an unaccountable Sweetnefs that warm'd all my Blood, prythee, wilt not you begin it again——I can do that, anfwered he, but I had a Mind to give you a Tafte before-hand, to fee how you liked it, fuch extraordinary Things as this are rare, very rare, my Dear, and too much Repetition but cloys us And, befides, fweet Meat is not always fo laid on the Stomach; you are fenfible, my Dear, that the Mufick and Harmony of our own two Bodies moving together, are inexpreffible, and that during the Raptures which they afforded, all our Senfes were loft—That's very true, fays fhe, but methinks I've a longing Defire to tafte once more of this divine Pleafure— and faying, then, fill to it again, which *Tracey* performed with more Vigour than at firft

Th.

The young Woman having had a Foretaste of this new Instrument of our Adventurer's, returned home exceedingly well pleased, and could not help the next Night she got among some of her Female Acquaintance, to take one of them aside, and acquaint her with the Satisfaction Mr *Blundel* the Grafier's Man had given her, by his pleasing Words, but more pleasing Harmony, which flowed from a new Instrument different to his Violin Upon this, both seem'd to meet together, and the Acquaintance ask'd her, if she might not be allowed to enjoy the same Liberty as herself, which the other said she might do, and accordingly both determined to meet our Adventurer at the Cave, who was previously acquainted with their Design Tracey was pleased to think his Humour should be so variously gratified, and rather than not keep touch with his Inamorates, would have sacrific'd all he had in the World Every one met at the Cave at the appointed Time, but, Heavens! What a Difference appeared between the two Country Girls The new Acquaintance had nothing to set her off, which might stand in Competition with the Brown Maid, and *Tracey* was so far from admiring, that he entertained at first View, an utter Aversion not only to her Person, but the Enjoyment of her Body But how to be rid of this Inconvenience was the Question, and absolutely to reject one or the other might endanger his Happiness with the Brown Maid Betwixt these he was in some Perplexity, but to extricate himself out of the Snare, he acquainted them he was sorry he could not gratify them according to their Expectations, but really he was indispos'd, and the Parts of his Body to compose the Harmony wish'd for, were so much out of Order with the Fatigues of the Day, that he was obliged to desire them they would forbear making any more Importunities about it then, and he would certainly crown their Satisfaction the next Night, the Girls could not forbear murmuring, and seem'd extraordinary uneasy, but at last, striving to combat their Disorder at his seeming Refusal, returned home, and left *Tracey* to go another Way As the Girls returned, the Acquaintance began to importune her, what, in the Name of the Stars, this Harmony was she had brought her to hear, that *Tracey* was so fond of, not to let her hear it Upon this the Brown Girl, out of her native Simplicity, acquainted her as well as she could, with the Manner of our Adventurer's playing, concluding, that in all her Life, she had never experienced such a pleasing and enchanting Piece of Diversion The Acquaintance, from the Language and Discovery of her Companion, drawing a right Judgment how Matters had gone, told her, that she was sorry to think she had betrayed so much ignorance and folly, for what *Tracey* had done was no more than any other Man could, and it was too much to extol him for it, because she herself, about four Years before, had received as much, or more Pleasure in the same Way, from her Father's Man *Arthur*, and therefore she need not think she had obliged her in bringing her to *Tracey*'s Cave, since he had no better Capacity that way than their Man *Arthur*, for had she known the Errand had been only about that, she would have got *Arthur* to perform his Musick with her, in order to see the Difference, who, she assured her, would have gratified her without making Scruples, or pretending indisposition And the next Time you see him, let me advise you to tell him, that he has wronged your Virginity, and, unless he will make some Reparation for it, convince him by Threats and Menaces, that your Father shall know his villainous Designs, and that you can tell how to revenge an Injury. For if you do not follow my Di-

rection herein, I myself will do his Business, and shew him that a neglected Woman, when rouz'd up to Resentment, can execute uncommon Things. What, added she, my Person was not lovely as yours, nor had my Face an Equality of Charms, but I'll make him quit Scores with me, or I'll know why. You, my Dear, may please yourself with as extraordinary Notions as you please, but for my part, I cannot help entertaining such an Aversion to his Baseness and ingratitude, that, of all Men living, he least sets in my Thoughts He's handsome, you'll probably say, and has a delicate Face, what's this to the Purpose? There are more such in the World, and, observe, he's a great deal inferior to you But why should *I* name inferiority, whan *I* myself have been guilty of the same indulgence, at a far younger Age than you. Such was the Discourse as these two went home together, and a thorough Resentment seemed to be working up for what *Tracey* had done, who was out of the Way of hearing, or else he had reconciled the uneasy Parties by proffering to them the utmost Submission

Lord, says the Brown Girl, what a Work you make? If *Tracey* had no Desire of making his pleasing Harmony with you, and that I obtained the Preference, can you blame the Man, let every Person exercise his Faculties as he thinks proper, for I take it, where the humour or inclination is obstructed, there can be no Enjoyment of Happiness, and it would be a Pity to make a Man of *Tracey*'s good Nature do a Thing which is against his Appetite You may defend him as you please, but observe by the Way, that e're ten Months are past, you may probably have an Harmonist of your own to play with, and then say how will it stand with you —— Why, answer'd the other, exceeding well, for were it to be done over again, I'd rather be thus pleasingly deceived again by *Tracey*, than all other Men in the World For it can be no Scandal to bear a Child by an handsome Fellow, and all the Country Lasses about us will agree with me in this, and supposing People should censure, I'll never disturb myself, or break my Repose about it, but rather impute it to Envy, because the same good Fortune has not happened to them As to your objecting to me an Harmonist before ten Months are past, I hope I shall see myself another long before that Time, which will not only be extreme Satisfaction to myself, but to my Parents also, and rather than be deprived of *Tracey*'s pleasing Company, I'll promote a better Understanding between him and me, with my antient Father, whom I'll bring over to a Consent of giving me in Marriage to him, when all the Expectations I have a long Time entertained in my Breast will be amply rewarded, and then the Brown Lass will be accounted the happiest Woman and Wife in the whole Parish

For *Tracey*, I am told for certain, is a Gentleman, though at present only in the Capacity of a menial Servant to my Father The Discourse ending here, they both went home, and on the Brown Girl's returning to her Father's, she found *Tracey* sitting under an Arbour with her Father and Mother, and diverting them with several comick Tales and Stories This made her make one of the Company, but soon she discovered an extraordinary Pleasure in her Countenance, which the Parents attributed to the Influence of *Tracey*'s Discourse, in which they were no bad Prophets. All that Night the Girl could take no Sleep, but her Head ran on the great Pleasure *Tracey* had given her As soon as it was Morning she took him aside, and blamed him heavily for refusing to yield the same Harmony to her Acquaintance as he had done to her, which he endeavoured to excuse, by telling her how impossible it was to give to another the same Satisfaction

aa

as he had done her, confidering the vaft Inequality of Perfons betwixt them, that the Charms of her Face were as fuperior to thofe of her Acquaintance, as the Radiance of a Star excelled the Flame of a Candle, that he had too long been in Love with her Perfon, to let another Share his Affection, and how could the other expect, who was fo much uglier than her, to be gratified in the fame Manner? Let me advife you, fays he, for the future, to confine yourfelf to me, who will conftantly ufe you in the fame extraordinary Manner as I have already done And though the fecret Place of our meeting has been difcovered by your Means, yet, never fear, I'll find another more fuitable for our Turn, where we may heighten this Harmony a great deal more Thefe Words revived the Brown Girl extremely, who could not but admire the winning Words of our Adventurer, and fix her Love upon him

It was neceffary to think now that the Acquaintance muft be difcarded, who faw it, and confequently was violently enraged At firft fhe began to fpread Reports no way to our Adventurer's Advantage, and got it divulged in his Mafter's Family that his Defigns were difhonourable, and only calculated to ruin the Reputation and Chaftity of her Daughter But this was the worft Way in the World to proceed with *Rufticus*, who was too much a Lover of our Adventurer, to form in his Breaft a fudden Averfion to him, neither had he any Reafon to raife a Mifunderftanding between them, for *Tracey* had managed his Cards with great Dexterity, and always took care fo to contrive his Matters, that no bad Confequences might be gather'd from them The old Man was entirely devoted to him on account of his gay and humourous Difpofition, which ferved to eafe his Mind and Body after the Fatigues of the Day were over, nor was the Grafier's Wife (who was a confiderable Number of Years younger than her Hufband, being his fecond Wife) lefs taken with the handfome Mien and winning Converfation of our Adventurer We fhall have occafion to mention a very comical Adventure between *Tracey* and this Woman prefently

Tracey finding the Inclination of the Grafier his Mafter fo much attach'd to his Advantage, that all the Reports fpread to ruin his Credit with him, were not able to prevail, and that his Miftrefs join'd in the fame Friendfhip for him, was extremely pleafed, and thought one Opportunity or other would foon be thrown into his Hands, to make a further Benefit of his Journey to *Chefhire*, than the obtaining the Goodwill of a Score of Country Girls But he foon found himfelf involved in a very troublefome Affair, which fenfibly touch'd him, and out of which he had a great deal of Work to extricate himfelf

The fecond Wife of the Grafier, on weighin in her Mind the Difference there was between the old fumbling Hufband and our Adventurer, who was young and fprightly, could not, after fhe had receiv'd a Foretafte of Pleafure from him, be reconciled to leave him, but fondly betrayed an exceffive Defire for him Her conjugal Affection began by degrees to turn off from the old Grafier, who was too good natur'd a Man to impute any Difhonefty to his Wife, for fear of creating Jealoufies and Alarms in his Family, which he naturally abhorr'd, being a Man who loved Peace, and had liv'd quietly till then *Tracey* had ftill Generofity enough left not to violate the Bed of his Mafter any longer, for what he had already done, was at the earneft Importunities of the Wife, who was always teazing him to a Compliance But the Miftrefs had too little Beauty to infpire a Man of our Adventurer's Gaiety and Temper with Love, and, befides, her frequent Intreaties and fulfome Dalliancies with him, when her Hufband was out of the Way, made him

quite averfe and naufeate her However, though was plain by his Conduct, that he had not that Affection for her which fhe wanted, yet fhe would not defift, but feemed rather the more inclined to win him over

One *Saturday* her Hufband being gone to Market, fhe finding all the Family at their Imployments, except *Tracey*, fhe took him to tafk, and afk'd the Reafon of his feeming Coldnefs *What, fays fhe, do you defpife my Perfon, who can be of fo much Advantage to you? What think you? Suppofing the old Man fhould die, of which there is fome Probability, would not the Farm and the Stock upon it, and my Perfon into the Bargain, be an equal Recompence for your Love I am forry, Tracey, to think I fhould humble myfelf thus far to make Declarations of Love to one fo much beneath me, but 'tis the Misfortune of fome Women, and they cannot help it You have given me a Foretafte of Enjoyment, and now decline gratify me any farther, which makes me long the more Had I never feen your Perfon, or been fo much acquainted with your Converfation, I had never been the Fool I now make myfelf, but the Remedy is paft Cure unlefs you apply the Medicine, for 'tis you alone that can heal me, and recover all my Hopes*

Tracey was confounded at this Speech, and knew not what to anfwer Here were Circumftances that both pointed at his Advancement, and yet threatned him with Confequences prejudical to his Repofe The Farm and the Stock upon it were worth a confiderable Sum of Money, which laid out prudently, might anfwer all the Purpofes of his Life, but then his Miftrefs cool'd his Purfuit, he could fee nothing in her that was either amiable or pleafing, for befides her Temper, which was none of the beft, fhe had feveral Defects in her Body, which together made him utterly hate her Yet that the Correfpondence between them might not be broke, he endeavoured to infinuate a feeming Kindnefs, though in Reality, he had much ado to comply with himfelf to perform it He told her, "That he fhould from that Time, owe her infinite Thanks, for making a Declaration of Love to him, which his Ambition could never have flattered him with That he had nothing to object againft fatisfying their mutual Defires, but her Hufband, who while alive, would be an eternal Impediment to their Wifhes That he look'd on violating his Bed as the groffeft Abufe in the World, and could not, confidering the Refpect he bore him, be brought to confent to fo notorious an Injury, tho he hoped fhe would think on his Conduct in this Refpect as Praife-worthy, and not to be blamed, fince, after his Deceafe, he was ready to join Hands with her, and be her Partner in her Pleafures and Pains That, to confefs his Mind, her Daughter in-law would make a more fuitable Match, not that he, by fo faying, endeavoured to depritiate from her, but then Years were more conformable, and it was more natural, that like and like fhould be link'd together However, rather than difoblige her by an abfolute Refufal, he would confent to embrace her once more, and would be ready to receive her that Night in his Chamber"

If any Thing in the World ever gave Woman Pleafure, thefe Words certainly did the Grafier's Wife, who was fo much tranfported with *Tracey's* pleafing Offer, that fhe had great Difficulty to contain herfelf till the Time of Affignation came, till when every Moment feem'd an Hour But Madam will dearly pay for this Appointment, for *Tracey*, acquainting in the mean Time, the Goatherd and Swineherd, how that every Night a Spirit tormented him, defired them to watch that Night in his Room to bear him Company The Fellows were terrified at the Relation, and

by

no Means could be brought to consent, till *Tracey* telling them they should come to no harm, and ordering each to bring a Bundle of Rods to whip the —— hout, they gave t—ir Consent, and said they would —re, the Fellows concluded from *Tracey*'s Words —ut the Rods, that there was ome Sport on Foot —at would give them Entertainment enough, which —ade them re—dy to embrace going *Tracey* told —em, that as soon as the Spirit appeared, they were —all to exercising their Rods, which would make —— retire, and probably never haunt his Chamber more —ll Things were now in a right Preparation, *Tracey* — Bed, and the other two Servants posted behind it — was not long before the Mistress came in, in her — mock, having double lock'd the Door of her Husband's Chamber, who was fast asleep, to prevent —s sudden surprizing them together, provided he —— d and found her missing As soon as she was —ntred, the two Men ru—ht out with the Rods in their —ads from their Post, and scourged the poor Wo— —n unmercifully, who durst not make any Noise —t her Husband should over-hear, and a—m t—e —o se, but when she found them so far from desisting —on their Stripes, that they laid on the heavier, she —uld not restr—in her Tongue any longer, but call— —g out Murder, so alarmed the Family, that the old —n immediately wak—ng out of his Sleep, wondered —hat was the Matter He put on his Cloaths to go —d see what it was that made such a Noise, but For—me at first directed him into Yard, still he listned, —l till he heard the Noise, and at left found that it —ame from *Tracey*'s Chamber Up-Stairs —e goes di—ctly but his Wife, in the inte—o, got to Bed On —oming into the Chamber the Fellows hid themselves —before, and asking our Adventurer what was the —eaning of all that Noise, was answer'd, that he —ght take his House to himself, for he would not — e hamper'd and beat about by Spirits as he had been, —r the best Place in *Fngland* Spirits, says the old —an! Ah, dear Master, Spirits, and so saying, the —ellows came suddenly upon him, and pulling down —s Breeches, gave him the same Lecture as they had —one his Wife But the Grafier was not contented —th this Usage, but lifting up his Hands, he poured —ch heavy Blows about the Shoulders of the Fellows, —t they no more imagin'd them the Cuffs of a mor— —l Man, but of an Hobgoblin, and so, being terri— —ed, ran again underneath the Bed At this the old —an in a violent Rage call'd out to *Tracey*, and ask'd —m where he was, who told him in Bed *Ah, my* —ar *Master,* says he, *these are the Spirits that con—* —nually *teaze me, I've suffered such Usage as this a* —g *Time, but being unwilling to put your House into* —y *Fears on my Account, have submitted to it with* —eat *Deal of Patience For God's Sake go to Bed,* —r *I'd rather endure their Blows, than you should* —dure *any Harm.* The Wife, all this Time, not— —withstanding the severe Smart she felt, was e tremely —pleased to think that her Husband had shar'd with —er in the same Punishm—ent and when he came to —d seem'd to con—de him in a very piteous Manner —th a Pox, says he, are you in Bed, where was — —u t—now? What are you a Ghost too? —gad — once a hand—sme House on't, indeed, and with —s he got to Bed, and rested pretty well the Re— —nder of the Night

— In the Morning the Grasier could not help bring— —g to his Thoughts what had happened to *Tracey,* —e was very fond of the Man, and w—nted to know —e Particulars that had befallen him *Tracey,* ha— —ng a ready and copious Invention, made a tho—sand —Things more of the Story than it really contain'd , —nd, by exaggerating it with Abundance of Falsities, —o terrified the old Man, that he could not forbear —ompassionating him, and shewing a great Deal of

Concern But, all the while, the Wife took the Notion of Spirits for a meer Whim, and concluded within herself that it had been all *Tracey*'s doing, for she observed a more than ordinary Coolness in his Behaviour, and, if at any Time she but spoke to him at Dinn—r or otherwise, was answered with a plain Negligence and Disrespect, which so exasperated her, that she was resolved to be even with him for his Inconcern and Indolence She had a thousand Thoughts what Expedient to make use of, in order to accomplish her Design in the surest Manner, and, on long Deliberation, found the only Way to ruin him, was to charge him before her Husband, with a Design upon her Honour, which she was not long before she put in Execution

Tracey was not a Stranger to her ill Temper, but was determined to see the Upshot of the whole Affair , so one Evening seeing the old Man walking in his Orchard alone, he goes to him, and after some Chat on indifferent Matters, begins to lay open his his Birth, Parentage and Education, by acquainting him, that he had been Master of a small Estate of Sixscore Pounds *per Annum,* but, living too profusely, had run it thro', which he was sorry for, because, had he known the same Frugality then as now, he had still been Master of it, or more , that his Father had sent him to the University to qualify him for the Ministry, but he had frustrated the Expectations of his Parents, who reposed all their Hopes in him That his former Extravagancies had oblig'd him to commit Actions he was now sorry for, and, to keep up his usual Way of Life, he was forced to support himself by indirect Means , but, that his coming to his House had entirely wiped out of his Mind the Desire of committing the like Follies, and thought that Heaven had favour'd him, in giving him the Grace, after having been brought up so well, and lived so liberally, to take to such an honest, painful, and laborious Life That he esteemed the Happiness of the Country much above that of the City, the Extravagancies of which he had seen, and the Ways the Men there pursued to support themselves , that the hard Bed he laid upon, was more soft to him than all the Down ones at his Father's House, and that to rise by Peep of Day, and go to his daily Employment, was more healthful and satisfactory, than to sleep snoring till Noon, and have no other Business than poring over a Parcel of wrangling Books , —— I beg, continued he, that you would mind my Discourse, because I have something to say that may be to your Advantage—— Now, Sir, you are to know, that after I had spent my Estate, I came into this Country with no other Mind than to do Penance for my former Miscarriages, by hiring myself to be a menial Servant to any Gentleman that wanted one Fortune has favour'd me in throwing me into your Family, among whom I take it, I have behaved with some Degree of Modesty, Honesty, and Diligence, my Conversation, Sir, has already drawn several Persons to covet my Acquaintance, and, if I may be indulged the Expression, the Lasses round about are ready to run mad for me, and I am sorry to have the Obligation to say, that your Wife, is not the least among them that sollicits my Favour——Hold that, not a Word more——My Wife run mad after thee ! Blood and Wounds——I'll cure her of her itching, *Wat*—— Why, Sir, that wou'd do exceeding well, but give me leave to make a Conclusion of my Discourse, and then say, and object what you please Your Wife, indeed, Sir, has more than once desired the Favour of my Bed, and to convince you that what I speak is true, she w—s the Person who raised the Spirit the Night you came into my Room, 'twas she her own self who walk'd, which may be verified by your Goatherd and Swineherd, who saw her in her Smock For my part, I have hitherto refrained violating your Bed, for Reasons which all Mankind ought to allow the justest in the World But if you don't restrain her, Flesh may be frail, though I had rather quit your Service a thousand Times over than commit so much Ingratitude against my Master and Benefactor But what is the real Occasion of all these Words of mine, is, that my Mistress is determined at Supper-time to charge me with several high Crimes against her Chastity, which are entirely groundless, and which I hope you'll give no Credit to And there is but one Thing more, which is, that as I was born a Gentleman to an Estate, and trained up at the University, and through my own Default, am now descended to the low Condition you see me in, you would bless me with an Alliance with your Daughter, who is a deserving young Woman, and one whom I have tenderly loved, ever since my first coming here

There will be no Scandal in this Match, for, was I not convinced of her sincere Affection for me, I would never presume on what I have said, and with her, to be a Servant, to be a Slave, nay, to be the worst of Mankind, I mean, in the lowest Degree, will be the greatest Joy, Happiness, and Contentment What could be more surprizing than these Words to the old Grasier, who was so far from imputing any kind of impudence to our Adventurer, that he seem'd vastly rejoic'd at the Tidings he had given him, and told him, that he thank'd him a thousand times for the Discovery he had made both of his Wife's Villainy and himself, adding thus, Wat, " I have a long " Time consider'd you in a very promising Light, " and been determin'd to put the Question to you se- " veral Times, to know if you entertain'd any " Thoughts of Marriage, judging that a Wife with " a little Money would be no unacceptable Thing in " your present Condition, which I have frequently " wish'd for the better, but now, Wat, for the " timely Service you have done me, perhaps it may " be in my Power shortly to recompence you hand- " somely, and repay your extraordinary Care and " Industry, suitably for your consulting my Repose, " and for your surprizing Modesty and Self denial, " in resisting such Temptations as might have ensna- " red others, but my Wife's Conduct is no more " than usual long before you came into my Service, " and whenever I am told of it, the Consideration " gauls me in the most sensible manner, as a Man in " the like Case would, you know, fret and fume " But, lack-a-day, Wat, my Wife is not the only " Thing that disturbs my Quiet, and molests my " Slumbers, I have other Causes of Disturbance, " which Time an another Opportunity, if you and " I hit in joining Horses together, may make you ac- " quainted with Never mind all she can either say " or invent against you, I am Master of my Family, " I believe, and who, tell me, dare pretend a Supe- " riority in it, besides myself ? Zounds, Wat, I " heartily love you, and had you been so free with " me a Quarter of a Year ago, you had been a bet- " ter Man behalf than you are now But, however, " I'll endeavour to requite you as you deserve, and " my Daughter, with three hundred Pounds, shall be " yours, Man, in spite of all the second Wives in " Christendom —— If I say it, who's the other to " controul me ? Here's my Hand, that she's yours " before eleven o'Clock to-morrow Morning But, " methinks, good Wat, I have a Mind to restore " you in some Degree to what you have lost I do " not question but your former Extravagancies have " set all your Relations and Friends you have entirely " against you ; to reconcile whom, and make up the " Breach between them and you, I take the best Ex-

" pedient to be, to send to the most considerable a- " mongst them a very submissive Letter, worded dex- " trously, but above all, containing your hearty Re " pentance for the Omissions you have formerly been " guilty of, and acquainting them, that having from " a Gentleman's Life descended to the low Condition " of a Peasant, you have forced yourself to a very " hard and laborious Penance for your Misdeeds, " which you now suppose you have justly perform'd, " and that Fortune smiling upon your Endeavours, " has, to reward your extraordinary Humility, made " your Master to think well of you, nay, to offer " you his Daughter in Marriage, provided they will " answer three hundred Pounds he designs to give in " Portion with her This, Wat, I take for a tolera- " ble good Beginning to succeed, and if you hear of " no Answer soon, you and I will then take Ho se, " go and negociate the whole Affair with them our " selves Let me tell you, six hundred Pounds will " purchase a pretty Farm for you two, and answer all " Necessaries so long as your Wife remains without " Children, but when those come on, and I find you " diligent, 'tis very likely I may add to your Estate, " and gratify you with a Present of thirty or forty " Acres more, which will effectually do your Business " Oh ! methinks, I congratulate you now on the fe- " licity you'll enjoy, so you mind yourself, prove an " endearing Husband, and a laborious Father " Here the old Grasier ended greatly to the Satisfaction of our Adventurer, who began to entertain a great many different Thoughts in his Head, now he should contrive to make the most Advantage to himself, and still keep a steddy Harmony in the Family He had frequent Thoughts how to accomplish his Ends, sometimes he was determin'd to throw for ever away his Desire of making Plunder on his Countrymen, and to embrace the generous Offer which his Master the Grasier had made him, thinking if he did so, his Life would be made easy, provided he could but conform himself to the Rules of Wedlock, and preserve the same good Thoughts he had all along entertain'd during his Abode in *Cheshire* Vast was his Desire to be reconcil'd to his Mistress, whom he look'd on now as his implacable Enemy, but he had so much Faith in his Master, that he could not, without doing him an Injustice, think he would act against his Interest Supper-time now comes, and no thing but Anger and Resentment glare in the Countenance of the Grasier's Wife, who seem'd resolv'd to do as she had determin'd, tho to her own Disadvantage, and even Ruin *Tracey* endeavour'd by all the external Signs he was Master of, to convince her that he had still left a dutiful Respect for her, and that she might expect to win him, provided the old Man was out of the Way

But Resentment rooted in the Breast of a Woman whose Love has been rejected, admits of no Bounds, nor had our Adventurer any room to hope for Success He drank to her, but she return'd the Compliment with a Disregard that plainly discover'd he was distasteful to her No, said she, *if my Husband is the Fool to humour you, it shall never be it that I will, you are an ungrateful Man, nay a Villain,* I say, *(now I am forc'd to open my Mind) after all the Civilities you have receiv'd in this Family, to use me, who ought to have some Sway in my own House, in the manner you have done Was not the receiving you poor, mean, and admitting you to such Privileges as few Servants can boast of, a Kindness deserving of some Acknowledgement ? Was not the preferring you to be the first of our Servants, when another, who had serv'd under us several Years, and better deserv'd it, a Favour which any one but you would have requited ? But it seems our Kindness and Generosity turn'd your Brain, and made you giddy-headed,*

headed, so that forgetting the Obligations you were under to us, you have had the Presumption not only of keeping up a close Communication with our Daughter, but also to address me with your fulsome Speeches, which my Virtue hath constantly guarded against, thinking that the Fame you so much boast of, could find no Refusal, and that I, as I fear my Daughter-in-law has already, should fall a Sacrifice to your inordinate Desires. Had not my Husband's Peace and Tranquility been struck, had not my Honour and Chastity been openly attack'd by you, and an Infamy endeavour'd to be laid on our Family, I would have scorn'd to have made this Discovery, but as I am tied by the solemn Rites of Religion to obey another Man, I was forc'd, even tho' against myself, to publish the Injustice that has a long time been design'd him. For 'tis not once or twice that is enough to exaggerate your Crime so as to deprive you of the Favours you enjoy at present, but, Tracey, you know how often have been the Times of this insulting and dishonourable Way of yours, had a thousand other Miscarriages proclaim'd your Conduct disrespectful to me, I should have put up with every of them, but an open Attack against my Honour, my Modesty and Fame, had no Excuses, nor ever shall with me.

Tracey, who heard this all the while with an attentive Ear, was surpriz'd at the Woman's Presumption and Boldness, he could not help staring upon her with an Eye full of Resentment, equal to that which she had in her own Breast. He could have crush'd all she had advanc'd in a Minute or two, had he been so minded, but he was in Expectation to hear his Master speak first, who, he depended on, was to vindicate him. Nor, indeed, was he long before he did, for putting the Tankard he was drinking out, out of his Hands, he began to question his Wife about her Insincerity and Baseness in taxing Tracey, whom he look'd upon as one of the best Friends he had, with a Crime he was no way guilty of, and which properly was her own Fault, but he need not be any way surpriz'd about it, since he had for some Years past receiv'd so many Complaints, which he had been unwilling to give Ear to, purely because he loved his Ease and Quiet. But now there was no longer room to distrust her Perfidy, since Tracey, who was so bashful a Man, had brought all Things to light. That for the future he would make himself very contented, and only desir'd her to return back to her Friends, for stay with him she should not, and all the Money she brought him was at her Service, to carry and dispose of just as she pleas'd ——Here the old Grasier stopp'd, and then Tracey took his Turn to speak, saying, The calling Goatherd and Swineherd would soon put an End to the Dispute, who would swear they saw her come into my Bed-chamber in her Shift, with a Design of procuring me to do that which you ought to perform, but far be it from me to create any Misunderstanding in a Family unjustly, to which I lay under so many Obligations——Misunderstanding, reply'd the old Grasier, none at all, for you shall be my Son, and I your Father, and having so said the Dispute broke up, and in a little time the Family retired to Bed.

All this Time the Grasier's Daughter, who was was the brown Lass above-mention'd, was full of Joy and Gladness at the good Fortune of Tracey, whom she look'd upon now as her real Husband. She found herself with Child by him, and was glad her Father was so considerate to join them together, in order to wipe off her Disgrace, but the old Man little thought of the Intercourse that had been betwixt his Daughter and his Man, else 'tis very probably all his intended Kindness had vanish'd

to Air. In short, the Morning came, and the old Man, to make sure of a Son-in-law, rode to the next Rural Dean, and got a Marriage-Licence; when about 11 o'Clock they were join'd together. The remaining Part of the Day was dedicated to Mirth and Jollity, the Neighbourhood being invited to partake of the Mirth.

Tracey was now in the Possession of a Bride already with Child by him, and what made more to his Happiness, was, the old Father's putting him immediately into part of his own Estate, out of which he reserv'd, a small annual Rent as an Acknowledgment: A Stock sufficient to live upon it was bought, and every Thing manag'd according to Tracey's Wish, who finding himself at Liberty to do and act just as he thought fit, had several serious Reflections within himself, how to make the best Advantage of all under his Care, and make the Father believe him a laborious and pains-taking Man. After he and his Wife had liv'd about two Months together, he often intimated to her, that 'twas true, the Country was a very pleasant Place, and a Life spent there vastly agreeable; but nevertheless, Society, to which he had always been used, was wanting, which made it not so recreating, that a Walk into the Meadows, or by the Side of some River, was a delightful Way to wipe off the Mind its gloomy and melancholy Ideas; and that murmuring Streams, rising Hills, and shady Woods, were the Recreation of Philosophic and contemplative Minds, but that they two, who were very young, had brisker Notions, and lov'd Gaity and an humourous Way of living, and that the Plough, Rake, and Sickle were too vulgar Things for such as they, and that the Means of obtaining what both earnestly desired, was to see London, where all the Pleasure which the World afforded, was to be found. That in Order to this, they were to get their Father to a Consent of selling their Farm, and with the Purchase-Money buy some Place or other of Profit, able to maintain them in a genteeler Way than at present, which he knew he would soon comply with, as he himself advised him to write to his Friends to obtain an Equivalent for the three hundred Pounds he had given him with her. That his Relations liv'd in Norfolk, and would comply with any reasonable Request, and would be so glad to see him, after so many Years Absence, that they would not know how to do too much for him. That he mention'd this with no manner of View, to leave his Father-in-law desolate, after he had, on his Account, sent his second Wife back to her Relations, but that he might see his Desire was no other than to honour his Family, by being preferr'd to a Post of Life more agreeable and profitable than the maintaining of a Farm ——The Wife having all her Lifetime been used to a rural Life, had little Thoughts of the Pleasures of a City so numerous and populous as London was, so that she was at a Loss how to answer her Husband. However, Tracey's Importunities, and the thousand Charms he told her was in a City Life, soon won her over, insomuch that nothing but London ran in her Mind, nothing now but Gaity and Pleasure, nothing but Dress and Acquaintance, nothing but Tea tables and Plays, nothing but Gallantry and Appointments, and nothing but Madam and Madam would now please her. Hence arose an Aversion to the Country, no more the Pastures and Meadows, no more the Woods and Hills, no more the Rivers and Fountains, no more the Shades and Haycocks, no more Wakes and rural Dances, and no more the Inhabitants in Cheshire delighted her. She is determin'd, the first Opportunity, to lay open her and her Husband's Mind with regard to their seeing London and sollicit him to take a Journey

ney into *Norfolk* to see his Relations Tracey approves well of his Wife's Conduct, and strives to Leighten it , and it was not long e're she found a feasonable Conjuncture one *Saturday* Evening, when the old Man retired from Market somewhat fuller with Liquor than ordinary She laid open the whole Affair with a great deal of Perswasion and Address, the Father readily granted all, and a Day was appointed for their Journey Mean time, *Tracey* made all the Advantage secretly he could of his Effects, and the old Grafier in about a Fortnight's Time got a Purchaser for *Tracey's* Farm, who gave Bills in the Room of Money

Every thing was now got ready, and our Adventurer, Wife, and Father in-law on the Road When they came to *Trentum* in *Staffordshire*, they put up at an Inn there, in order to stay two or three Days to refresh the old Man, who was already weary with his Journey During their Abode they happened to have a good deal of Company, among whom *Tracey* always found Admittance, for having a smooth Tongue, and a tolerable Voice for singing, every one were glad to get into his Company 'Twas here that *Tracey* was determin'd to put a finishing Stroke to his long Adventure with the Grasier, he was resolved not only to leave him his Daughter with Child by him to keep, but also to make himself Master of the Bills e're the Morning, and to that End, getting his Father to carouze that Night a little freer than ordinary (his Wife being already gone to Bed) he dextrously conveyed the old Man's Pocket-Book, wherein the Bills were, out of his Pocket, and then to colour over his Villany with some Pretence, wrote the following Letter, and left it in the room of the Pocket-Book

Dear Sir,

I Make no Wonder of your being surpriz'd at finding the Inclos'd, but I have innumerable Reasons for my doing thus, which I shall wave at this Time, and acquaint you with at my Return When my Wife and you read this in the Morning, be sure to think that I have done both of you the best Action in the World, which I could prove, were it not that I was in too much Haste when I wrote this For finding you fatigued with your Journey before we had got half Way, I thought I could not do a better Deed than leave you where you were, with your Money in your Pocket, and in the midst of Plenty and good Company As for the Bills, I take them to be properly mine, as they stand in the room of the Purchase-Money for the Estate which came to me by right of Marriage, and I humbly conceive I can make as right a Use of them as any Man living As for going into Norfolk, I apprehend the Journey is useless, till I have made myself certain of a Place in London, when probably they may do something for me, till which Time adieu

W TRACEY

Mean time the old Man and his Daughter were fast asleep in seperate Beds, and our Adventurer, to make sure of what he had, got up early in the Morning, and, under a Pretence of riding out half a dozen Miles till Breakfast-time got his Horse saddled, mounted, and rode off About Seven o'Clock the Father and Daughter rise, and missing *Tracey*, enquire of the People in the Inn if they had seen him, who are told by the Hostler that he went on Horseback at Three, and would return by Breakfast-time But no *Tracey* appears at that Time nor all that Day This astonishes the old Man , but more the Daughter, who began to lament his Absence They have different Thoughts about him, but all are in vain Sometimes they are afraid that some Mischance

has befallen him ; at other times, that having a Mind to view the Country, he had rode out for that Day , but at length, the old Man finding no Signs of his returning, goes and sees how Things stand about him The first that presents itself is the Letter, which being perused, put the old Man into a violent Fit of Trembling, which ended in a kind of convulsive Pang Drops are applied, which soon recovering the old Gentleman every one are desirous to know the Cause of his Uneasiness They are acquainted from the Beginning to the End, and all seemed concerned at his Sorrow What should the old Man do in this Case ? Why, he is determin'd this Minute to travel after him, the next to return home, but before he does that, he gets it proclaimed round about, that such a Man and such a Horse was missing, and if any one could inform him where they were, he she or they making such Information, should receive from him the Sum of five Pounds This was a tolerable good Way of Proceeding, for the Money induced several to make Enquiry, but in short all was to no Purpose, for our Adventurer was by this Time got to *Coventry*, and the old Man and his Daughter, after a two Week's Stay at *Trentum*, thought best to return home to *Cheshire*, to save more Expences, and wait there the Return of their hopeful Son-in law

Tracey, in the mean time, was got to *Coventry*, where he put up at the *Rose and Crown*, one of the best Inns in that City On his going into the Inn, he observed a more than usual Stillness, which he could not tell well what to attribute to He placed his Horse in the Stable, and then going up to the House, he heard a Dispute carrying on in the Room over his Head, which raising his Curiosity to know what it meant, he went directly up Stairs into the Chamber On his entring, the People within were somewhat astonish'd He look'd about him, and saw in the Bed a Man with only a Sheet over him, and near the Fire-side a Woman, the Mistress of the Inn, and a young Man *Tracey* ask'd them what made them take so little Care about the House, for had he been an ill-disposed Person, he might have run away with half the Things in the Kitchen Upon this the Man in the Bed, whom he took for dead, (being laid out as dead Men are) started up on his Backside, and address'd him in the following Manner " Sir, I'm
" heartily glad you are come in, since, you being
" an impartial Man, I may venture to lay open my
" Case without Offence You are to know then that
" the Woman sitting there is my Wife, which Word
" I wish I had never known , for from the Time the
" matrimonial Knot was tied between us, I may
" safely say I have not had a Day's Rest, put all
" together, and now we have lived together seven
" Years wanting but a single Month I believe I
" may alledge, without any Injustice, that during
" that Time I have been one of the most affectionate
" Husbands to her, for I have never debarr'd her
" from any thing, nor has she had the least Pretence
" for Complaint, occasion'd by me, wherever she
" wanted I readily gave her more than she asked
" for Whenever she was willing to go abroad, a
" Servant and a Chaise was at her Command, and
" whenever any new costly Fashion came up, I was
" the first to promote it, I never in shewing it upon
" her , and yet all these Favours and Confide ations
" would not do My Life upon this became a easy,
" and I had a thousand restless Moments about it I
" communicated my Uneasiness to a particular Friend
" who told me that she did not love me, and the only
" Way to discover it was to feign myself dead According
" cordingly I pretended myself dead, and presently
" this Wretch brought that old Woman, who together
" ther with her laid me out, as you saw me at your
" hard

" first coming in During my dead Penance, I had
" an Opportunity of hearing how the Cafe went, and
" foon found that Love, or rather Luft, was the real
" Caufe of all my late Miferies The young Raf-
" cal there is her Gallant, who I am fure has handled
" above five hundred Pounds of my Subftance, which
" from Time to Time I have found miffing This
" is a miferable Cafe, Sir, and deferves Compaffion
" But this is not all, fhe has already given Orders for
" my Funeral, for making of mourning Cloaths and
" Rings " — *Tracey* all this while ftood gazing with
due Attention, and could not but reflect on the Incon-
ftancy, Profufion, and Artifice of fome Women He
told the Perfon in Bed he was extremely forry for his
Misfortune in being wedded to fuch a She-Devil, who
was a thoufand Times worfe to him than a I his Money, but he would give him a feafonable Relief by-
and by

The Hufband hereupon thank'd him, and exprefs'd
his Gladnefs for his coming into his Chamber fo opportunely But Sir, fays he this Wretch had a
pretty long Confultation with the other to how fhe
fhould behave in fo nice a Circumftance, for, faid fhe,
I cannot weep, and the Town will admire at my not
fhedding a Tear over his Grave, who, they know
was fo tender and loving a Hufband Oh I added
fhe, I'll put Onions into my Handkerchief, and by
that Means I fhall deceive the World with a forc'd
Lamentation Ay, ay, replied *Tracey*, this is worfe
than all, but I'll fpoil her of her Artifices prefently,
and fo faying, he pulls a loaded Piftol out of his Breaft,
and commanded, on pain of Death, every one of
them, not excepting the Man in Bed, to deliver what
Money they had, for, faid he, 'tis Money that has
made this Confufion, and I'm refolv'd to eafe you of
it, in order to make you live together more quiet for
the future Upon thi going up to the Wife, he
received from her fifty Guineas, from the Gallant
thirty, and from the old Woman five an handfome fpoil i'faith, fays he, and pray, Landlord,
what can you afford me? Nothing in the World, reply'd he, for I humbly conceive I have given you
already five Guineas already, which is a tolerable good
Fee for your Advice, Sir Say you fo, Mr
Bufler — Well, I fhall call this Day Se'nnight a-
gain to fee how Affairs go, and if I do not find your
Wife reconciled by the Lofs of this Money, I'll then
remove double the Sum, and fo every Week in Proportion, till I have made a thorough Cure, and with
that he bad them farewel

Tracey, after this Adventure, made his Way to
Ware, where taking up his Lodgings for that Night,
he got into the Company of a young *Oxonian*, who
had brought a large Portmanteau behind him The
Student feemed very well pleafed at his Friend's Converfation, as he thought, and, to encreafe a better
Underftanding betwixt them, they fupped together,
and drank a Couple of Botles of Wine afterwards
They lay together in the fame Bed, and, an Hour or
two before they went to fleep, had a great Deal of
Converfation about the Ways of Mankind, which
terminated at laft about the Univerfity, which *Tracey*
pretended to be an entire Stranger to In the Morning both drank Sack Poffet, mounted and purfued their
Journey together *Tracey* endeavour'd to amufe his
Fellow Traveller with a Series of foreign Adventures,
which he had never perform'd, the Scholar, on his
Part, laid open the wicked Practices of the Colleges,
fo that both feem'd to be fit and choice Companions
for each other

Tracey would now and then take hold of the Student's Portmanteau, and tell him 'twas very heavy,
and wonder'd he did not bring a Servant along with
him, fo much undervaluing his Profeffion, by being
Mafter and Man himfelf? The Student conftantly an-

fwered, that the Times were exceeding hard, and he
travelled by himfelf to fave Charges How, replies
the other, Charges? Why, the Charges of a Servant
are vaftly infignificant in Comparifon of the Lofs you
may probably fuftain on the road for Want of one.
I hope, Sir, you have not got any great Charge of
Money within your Portmanteau, for I think you act
a very unwife Part, if you carry much about you,
without having fome one or other in Company with
you The Student told him, he had no lefs than
Threefcore Pounds within it, which he was carrying
to the Univerfity to defray the cuftomary Fees for taking up his Degree of Mafter of Arts Ah, fays Tracey, that's a round Sum, o' my Word, and 'tis a
thoufand Pitie fo much fhould be given away to Perfons that no way deferve a Farthing of it

If I had known of your having Threefcore Pounds
about you, when we were at the Inn, I could have
procured you a Crap that would have fold you a
Place for it much more beneficial than any Thing
you hope for, by being a Mafter of Arts, but as we
are too far a Diftance off from Ware to return in
Time, you fhall be eas'd of your Money and Portmanteau prefently, for I have an Occafion at this
very Conjuncture for fuch a Quantity of Money, and
there's no better Perfon than myfelf you can lend it
to; after which Words *Tracey* unloofes the Straps,
takes the Portmanteau, and puts it on his own Horfe.
The Student obferving this, immediately cried aloud,
Oh dear Sir, I hope Defign is not to rob me, I
fhall lofe a pretty good Perfonage that is offered me
in Eflex, *if you take away my Money from me Pray,*
Sir, confider the Crime you are going to act, for the
Lofs of my Threefcore Pounds will not only deprive me
of a competent Means of Livelihood, but alfo the Al-
mighty will lofe a Minifter of his Word And for the
Sake of Heaven, I befeech you to be compaffionate, and
not fo fevere on a poor Man that was obliged to borrow
this Money of feveral Perfons, who would not have
lent it, but through a View of being foon repaid Sir,
you commit a Thing againft the Laws of your Country,
and the Precepts of Humanity, to wreft thus by Force
what belongs to another Man, and I dare fay you are
not fo much a Stranger to the Injuftice of it, but you
know 'tis an Error, and a great one The Sin too is
vaftly enlarged, when a fpecious Pretence of Friendfhip
is made ufe of for fuch a difhonourable Deed, for how
will any Man know he is fafe in travelling, if every
one he meets with on the Road, converfes with him in
the fincere Manner (I mean outwardly) as you have
pretended to me But, Sir, not to enlarge further, let
me intreat you over and over again, not to take my All
from me, for if fo, I am inevitably ruin'd, and am an
undone Man for ever

Tracey feemed to mind the Student's Defire of having his Portmanteau again with a grave Attention,
but the Thought of having obtain'd fuch a confiderable Booty, made him banifh every compaffionate Sen-
timent out of his Breaft, till no longer able to bear
with the tedious Importunities of the Scholar, he pulled out of his Breeches Pockets a Leathern Purfe with
Four Pounds odd Money in it, and gave it the Collegian, faying, Friend, I am not yet fo much loft to
the Senfe of Compaffion, but I can extend my Charity
and Generofity, 'tis not cuftomary for a Gentleman of
my Fortune to give Money, but your Interceffion has
won me over to it Here are Four Pounds odd Money to bear your Expence to the Univerfity, fo that
you will not be all the Lofer, and when you come to the
College, acquaint all thofe whom t may concern, that
you have paid your Mafter of Arts Fees already to a
Collector on the Road, who had a thoufand Times more
Occafion for the Money than a Parcel of old Mollies,
that live by whoring, and ftealing out of other Authors
Works And fo faying he bad the poor Collegian
farewel,

25
B b

farewel, leaving him to pursue his Journey, and obtain his Degree as well as he could, while himself made the nearest Way to the next Village, where opening the Portmanteau, he found nothing but two old Shirts, half a Dozen dirty Bands, a thread bare Student's torn Gown, a Pair of Stockings without Feet, a Pair of Shoes, but with one Heel to them, some other old Trumpery, and a great Ham of Bacon, but not one Farthing of Money, which set him a swearing and cursing like a Devil, to think he should be such a preposterous Ass, to give Four Pounds and more for that which was not worth Forty Shillings.

We have but two Adventures more of *Tracey* which we find on Record, the first relating to a Robbery he committed on the famous Poet *Ben Johnson*, the other to another on the Duke of *Buckingham*, who was slain by *Felton*, as he was going to embark at *Portsmouth*, for which he was hanged, both which we shall be very brief in.

Ben Johnson had been down in *Buckinghamshire* to transact some Business, but in returning to *London* happened to meet with *Tracey*, who knowing the Poet, bad him stand and deliver his Money. But *Ben* putting on a courageous Look, spoke to him thus.

Fly Villain hence, or by thy Coat of Steel,
I'll make thy Heart my leaden Bullet feel,
And send that thrice as thievish Soul of thine
To Hell, to wean the Devil's Valentine.

Upon which *Tracey* made this Answer:

Art thou, great Ben? or the revived Ghost
Of famous Shakespear *? or some drunken Host?*
Who being tipsy with thy muddy Beer,
Dost think thy Rhimes will daunt my Soul with
   Fear,
Nay, know, base Slave, that I am one of those,
Can take a Purse, as well in Verse, as Prose,
And when thou art dead, write this upon thy
   Herse,
Here lies a Poet who was robb'd in Verse.

These Words alarmed *Johnson*, who found he had met with a resolute Fellow; he endeavoured to save his Money, but to no Purpose, and was obliged to give our Adventurer ten Jacobus's. But the Loss of these was not the only Misfortune he met with in this Journey, for coming within two or three Miles of *London*, it was his ill Chance to fall into the Hands of worse Rogues, who knock'd him off his Horse, stript him, and tied him Neck and Heels in a Field, wherein some other Passengers were enduring the same hard Fate, having been also robbed. One of them crying out, that he, his Wife and Children were all un-

done, while another, who was bound, over-hearing said, pray, if you are all of you undone, come and undo me. This made *Ben*, though under his Misfortunes, burst out into a loud Laugh, who being delivered in the Morning from his Bands by some Reapers, made the following Verses

Both robb'd and bound, as I one Night did ride,
With two Men more, their Arms behind them ty'd,
The one lamenting what did them befal,
Cry'd, I'm undone, my Wife and Children all,
The other hearing it, aloud did cry,
Undo me then, let me no longer lie;
But to be plain, those Men laid on the Ground,
Were both undone, indeed, but both fast bound.

Tracey might have made a good Man, had he turned those Talents Providence had given him to better Uses than he made of them. For he had a fine Way of Delivery, a Volubility of Speech, extensive Memory, and was well versed in the Books of the Antients. We may very well say, that his irregular Life was owing to the first immoderate Courses he learnt at the College, where so many young Gentlemen, by running beyond their Salary, are forc'd on dishonourable Artifices to support themselves. And *Tracey* happened to be one of these. While he remain'd in *Cheshire*, he gave Signs of being a frugal and provident young Man, and to descend so low as to hire himself, who had been born a Gentleman, to drudge into the Fields and Meadows, was what ten thousand, except himself, would have scorn'd to have done, but this heightens his Character, as it argues a real Sign of Humility, which, had our Adventurer continued in the Country with his Father, had made him one of the happiest of Men.

Tracey had amassed together in Money and Goods sufficient to support him handsomely during Life, and determining with himself to take up betimes, and live peaceably on what he had got, he placed his Money in a Friend's Hand, who made off with it, and left our Adventurer to pursue his old Trade towards obtaining more. He was heard to speak the following Words on this Occasion, 'Tis true that at this Time we are almost grown a Nation of Cheats, but that which is worst of all is, that Men will not cheat upon the Square, one engrosses more Knavery than the other, for if it went round equally there would be nothing lost.

The last Robbery he committed was on the Duke of *Buckingham* above-mention'd, but some say, he only endeavoured to commit one. Now as we have neither the Place, nor in what Manner this Attempt was made, nor how much he took from his Grace, nor any other Circumstances to help us to a Discovery of this Adventure, we are obliged to be silent, and only say that he suffered for it at *Winchester*

Van. Holland & Tristram Savage Robbing D:^r Trotter in Moorfields

The LIFE of ANN HOLLAND.

THIS was her right Name, tho' she went by the Names of *Andrews, Charlton, Edwards, Goddard* and *Jackson* This Practice, is very usual with Thieves, because falling oftentimes into the Hands of Justice, and being often convicted of Crimes, yet thereby it appears sometimes, that when they are arraign'd at the Bar again, that is the first Time that they have been taken, and the first Crime whereof they have ever been accus'd Moreover, if they should happen to be cast, People, by not knowing their right Names, cannot say the Son or Daughter of such a Man or Woman is to be whipp'd, burnt, or hang'd, on such a Day of the Month, in such a Year, from whence would proceed more Sorrow to them that suffer'd, as well as Disgrace to their Parents For this Reason an *alias* is prefix'd to several Names, when such Persons are indicted, as we have observed before, whose Delight is to be Gentlemen and Gentlewomen without Rents, to have other Folks Goods for their own, and dispose of them at their own Will and Pleasure, without costing them any more than the Pains of stealing them

As to *Anne Holland*, her usual Way of thieving was what they call the *Service-Lay*, which was hiring herself for a Servant in any good Family, and then, as Opportunity serv'd, she robb'd them

Thus living once with a Master Taylor, in *York-Buildings* in the *Strand*, her Mistress was but just gone to a Christening, when her Master came home booted and spurr'd out of the Country, and going up into his Chamber, where she was making his Bed, he had a great Mind to try his Manhood with her, and accordingly threw her on her Back *Nan* made a Resistance, and would not grant him his Desire without he pull'd off his Boots He consented, and at his Command she pluck'd one off, but whilst she was pulling off the other, somebody knocking opportunely at the Door, she ran down Stairs, taking a Silver Tankard off the Window, which would hold two Quarts, saying, she must draw some Beer, for she was very dry She not returning presently, poor *Stitch* was swearing, and staring, and bawling, for his Maid *Nan* to pull off his t'other Boot, which was half on and half off, but being extraordinary strait, he could neither get his Leg farther in nor out And there he might remain 'till Doomsday for *Nan*, for she was gone far enough off with the *Wedge*, that' to say, the Plate, which she had converted into another Shape and Fashion in a short Time

Another Time *Nan* having been at a Fair in the Country, as she was coming up to *London*, she lay at *Uxbridge*, where being a good Pair of Holland Sheets to the Bed, she was so industrious as set up most Part of the Night, and make her a Couple of good Smocks out of one of them, so in the Morning, putting the other Sheet double towards the Head of the Bed, she came down Stairs to Breakfast In the Interim, the Mistress sent up her Maid to see if the Sheets were there, who turning the single Sheet a little down as it lay folded, she came and whisper'd

in her Mistress's Ear, that the Sheets were both there; so *Nan* discharging her Reckoning, she brought more *Shifts* to Town than she carried out with her; and truly she had a pretty many before; or else she could not have liv'd as she did for some Years

This unfortunate Creature, at her first launching out into the Region of Vice, was a very personable young Woman, being clear-skinn'd, well shap'd, having a sharp piercing Eye, a proportionable Face, and an exceeding small Hand; which natural Gifts serv'd rather to make her miserable than happy; for several lewd Fellows flocking about her, like so many Ravens about a Piece of Carrion, to enter her under *Cupid's* Banner, and obtaining their Ends, she soon commenc'd, and took Degrees, in all manner of Debauchery, for if once a Woman passes the Bounds of Modesty, she seldom stops till she hath arriv'd to the very Height of Impudence

However, it was her Fortune to light on a good Husband; for one Mr. *French*, a Comb-maker, living formerly on *Snow-Hill*, taking a Fancy to her in a Coffee-house, where she was a Servant till she had an Opportunity to rob her Master, such was his Affection, without in the least knowing she had been debauch'd, that he married her, and was better satisfy'd with his matching with her who had nothing, than many are with Wives of great Portions But the Comb maker's Joys were soon vanish'd, for his Spouse being brought to Bed of a Girl within six Months after *Hymen* had join'd them together, it bred such a great Confusion betwixt them, that there was scarce any Thing in the Kitchen, or other Part of the House, which they did not continually fling at one another's Heads Whereupon her Husband confessing a Judgment to a Friend in whom he could confide, all his Goods were presently seiz'd, and she turn'd out of House and Home, to the great Satisfaction of Mr *French*, who shortly after went to *Ireland*, and there died

Nan Holland being thus metamorphos'd from a House keeper to a Vagabond, she was oblig'd to shift among the Wicked for a Livelihood, and to give her what was her due, tho' she was but young, yet she could cant tolerably well, wheedle most cunningly, lie confoundedly, swear desparately, pick a Pocket dexterously, dissemble undiscernably, drink and smoke everlastingly, whore insatiably, and brazen out all her Actions impudently

A little after this Disaster, she was married to one *James Wilson* an eminent Highwayman, very expert in his Occupation, for he never was without false Beards, Vizards, Patches, Wens, or Mufflers, to disguise the natural Physiognomy of his Face He knew how to give the Watch-word for his Comrades to fall on their Prey, how to direct them to make their Boots dirty, as if they had rid many Miles, when they were not far from their private Place of Rendezvous, and now to cut the Girts and Bridles of them whom they rob, and bind 'em

fast

fast in a Wood, or some other obscure Place. But these pernicious Actions justly bringing him to be hang'd in a little Time, at *Maidstone* in *Kent*, *Nan* was left a hempen Widow, and forc'd to shift for herself again.

After this Loss of a good Husband, *Nan Holland* being well apparell'd, she, in Company with one *Tristram Savage*, who had laid under a Fine for crying the scurrilous Pamphlet, entitled, *The Black List*, about the Streets, a long Time in *Newgate*, where they became first acquainted, went to Dr *Trotter* in *Moorfields*, to have her Nativity calculated. When they were admitted into the Conjurer's Presence, who took them to be both of the Female Sex, because *Savage* was also dress'd in Women's Clothes, and being inform'd by *Nan* what she came about, he presently drew a Scheme of the twelve Houses, and filling them with the insignificant Characters of the Signs, Planets, and Aspects, display'd about the Time and Place of her Birth in the Middle of them, the following Jargon.

That the Sun being upon the Cusp of the tenth House, and *Saturn* within it, but five Degrees from the Cusp, it denoted a Fit of Sickness, which would shortly afflict her, but then *Mercury* being in the eleventh House, just in the Beginning of *Sagittarius*, near *Aldebaran*, and but six Degrees from the Body of *Saturn*, in a Mundane Square to the Moon and *Mars*, it signified her speedy Recovery from it. Again, *Cancer* being in a Zodiacal Trine to the Sun, *Saturn*, and *Mercury*, she might depend upon having a good Husband in a short Time, and moreover, it was a sure Sign, that he who married her should be a very rich and thriving Man.

Thus having gone through this Astrological Cant, quoth *Tristram Savage* to Doctor *Trotter*, *Can you tell me, Sir, what I think?* The Conjuror replied, with a surly Countenance, *It is none of my Profession to tell Peoples Thoughts. Why then* (said Savage) *I'll shew 'em you.* Whereupon pulling a Pistol out

of his Pocket, and clapping it to the Doctor's Breast he swore he was a dead Man, if he made but the least Outcry, which so surpriz'd him, that, trembling like an Aspen Leaf, he submitted to whatever they desir'd. So while *Nan* was busy in tying him Neck and Heels, *Savage* stood over him with a Penknife in one Hand, and his Pop, (that's what they call any Thing of a Gun) in t'other, still swearing, that if he did but whimper, his present Punishment should be either the Blade of his Penknife thrust into his Wind-pipe, or else a Brace of Balls convey'd thro' his Guts. To be still more sure of the Conjurer's not cackling, they gagg'd him, and then rifling his Pockets, they found a Gold Watch, twenty Guineas, and a Silver Tobacco-Box, which they carry'd away, besides taking two good Rings off his Finger.

After these good Customers were gone, the Conjurer began to make what Noise he could for Relief, by rowling about the Floor like a Porpoise in a great Storm, and kicking on the Boards with such Violence, that the Servants verily thought there was a Combat indeed betwixt their Master and the Devil. But when they went up Stairs, and found him ty'd and gagg'd, they were in no small Astonishment, and quickly loosing him, he told them how he was robb'd, whereupon they made quick Pursuit after *Nan Holland*, and the other Offender, but to no Purpose, for they were got out of their Reach, and the Knowledge of all the Stars.

Altho' she had receiv'd Mercy once before, yet she took no Warning thereby, but when at Liberty still pursued her old Courses, which in 1705 brought her to *Tyburn*, where, instead of imploring for Mercy from above, she cry'd out upon the hard Heart of her Judge, and the Rigor of the Laws, also cursing the Hangman, but forgetting to repent of the Fact which brought her into the Executioner's Hands, and would, unrepented of, deliver her Soul into the far less merciful Hands of another hereafter.

The LIFE *of* DICK MORRIS.

WE have no Account of this Malefactor's Birth and Education, which we may therefore conclude were obscure enough. But be that as it will, his Actions were as extraordinary, and indeed as extravagant, in their Kinds, as any we have related. Some of them follow.

One Time *Dick Morris* drinking at an Inn in *Winchester*, and over-hearing a couple of Gentlemen declaring their Misfortunes in loving two Gentlewomen, by whom they were utterly slighted, he putting on a bold Face, which he always had, forc'd himself into their Company, which was not unacceptable to them, by reason, he pretended, that they should obtain their Sweethearts thro' his Means, for having liv'd with an Astrologer, who was also a great Magician, he had learnt of him many Secrets in matters of Love, which were so infallible, that if the Ladies Hearts, whom they lov'd, were harder than an *Adamant*, yet would he make them softer than Wax. But then they must help him to some of the Hairs of the Parties beloved, with which, and some Ceremonies that he would perform, he

would engage that both the Gentlewomen's Heart should be put in such a Flame, that they should never rest, Day nor Night, till they granted them their Desire.

This News pleas'd the Gentlemen to that Degree, that, between them, they kept *Dick Morris* very splendidly, both at Bed and Board, and also with Money in his Pocket, till he performed his Promise, which was to be within a Week, when the Moon was just encreasing, as the most proper Time for his Undertaking.

Next, according to *Dick's* Orders, the two Gentlemen bought a new Sack, a small Cord, another hempen one bigger, and four Ells long, a new Knife, a Chain, and a Brush, which were delivered into his Custody, and they thought every Minute an Age, till the Time of Conjuration came.

Long look'd for being come at last, and the Night approaching wherein the Gentlemen were to be made forever happy, they were drest, according to *Dick's* Directions, in their richest Apparel, giving each of them a Lock of their scornful Lover's Hair into his Hands, *With which,* (quoth our Conjurer,) *I will subdue your Mistresses; so that were their Hearts more frozen than the* Alps, *I will turn them into Mountains of Fire, hotter than those of* Vesuvius, *or ever-burning* Ætna Then all three taking Horse, they rid about two Miles out of *Winchester,* and alighting at the Place where this magical Trial was to be put in Execution, and tying their Horses to a Tree, *Dick* making strange four Faces, which looked as crabbed as the Letters of the *Arabick* Alphabet, he drew a Circle on the Ground, in which muttering many cramp Words, and turning himself in strange Postures, sometimes towards the *East,* and sometimes towards the *West,* withal using most surprizing Ceremonies with his Hands and Feet, he made the Gentlemen no less astonish'd than fearful.

After this, *Dick* began with the first Spark, making him to strip himself, and at the same Time teaching him to say certain insignificant Words in pulling off each Parcel of his Cloaths, which he pronounced so exactly, that he lost not one Syllable, as believing that if he had fail'd in one Jot, he should have spoilt all the Business. With this Ceremony *Dick* stript him to his Shirt, and tho' it was in the Depth of Winter, yet he order'd him to pull off that also, then giving him a Knife in his Hand, he commanded him to make some Stabs towards the four Quarters of the World, and to go into the Sack, which he did, as quiet as a Lamb

Thus having done with the first, after he had ty'd the Mouth of the Sack fast, and bid him not to stir Hand nor Foot for half an Hour, for then the Enchantment would be at an End, nor to speak a Word, for if he did, he would be in *Barbary* in the twinkling of an Eye · He then address'd himself to the other Gentleman, who, in a great Chafe, said to *Dick,* I'll be hang'd if thou hast not forgot something of my Business, for here I see neither Sack nor Knife for me, as for my Friend Whereupon, *Dick* told him there was no need of a Sack for his Matters, because his magical Operations were made stronger or weaker, according to the greater or lesser Cruelty that Gentlewomen have, and understanding his Friend's Mistress was the most disdainful of their two Sweet-hearts, he made the Inchantment of the Sack for her, as being the strongest of all *O! dear, Sir,* (reply'd the Gentleman) *what is this that thou hast done? My Mistress is more disdainful and hard hearted than any Tyger or Lioness Peace, be quiet,* (quoth *Dick*) *with these Hairs of her Head, and these Cords, I will twist such a Knot, that they shall have as much Force as your Friend's Sack, and though your Mistress is so cruel as you say, yet will I add thereto, that Charm which will make her never be able to take any rest till she sees you in her Arms* Said the Gentleman again, *'tis that which I want, therefore let us martyr her in such a Manner, that my Love may torment her Thoughts as much as she hath mine*

Then *Dick* bringing him to a Tree, where his Enchantment was to be made, he in an Instant drew a Circle, and making the Gentlemen go into it stark naked, because he thought two Shirts better than one, he took the Hairs of his Mistress, and twisting them with the Cord, he ty'd his Hands to the Tree, at the same Time telling him the Mystery that was hid in every Ceremony which he us'd, and *Dick* would also have ty'd his Feet, but that he fear'd the Gentleman would have suspected this Ceremony to be rather the Fact of a Robber than a Magician, however, as securing his Hands was enough for his Purpose, he took all their Cloaths and three Horses, and was in *London* before break of Day In the mean Time the Flames of *Cupid,*

26

which raged in these Gentlemen's Breasts, were pretty allay'd by the next Morning, for when they were releas'd from their Enchantments by some Passengers that happen'd to pass that Way, they were almost perish'd with Cold When they got home, they swore the Poets had a very good Reason to feign Love blind, because if they had not been so, they should have perceived all the pretended Magician's Promises to be nothing but Wind, and that the Means which he propounded to them for obtaining their Sweethearts Favours, was only to obtaining for himself their Cloaths and Equipage

Another Time *Dick Morris* being at *Northampton,* within half a Mile of which Place was a Meeting-House, and not above a quarter of a Mile farther dwelt a rich *Presbyterian Parson,* who was a single Man, he had once or twice attempted to rob him, but prov'd unsuccessful in his Design. However *Dick* thinking he could not go to *London* with a safe Conscience, unless he could outwit this dissenting Preacher He procures a Waggoner's old Linnen Frock, and dawbing it thick with Paste, he goes, on a *Saturday,* to the Meeting-house, and had the Opportunity of getting *incognito* into the Pulpit, whilst an old Woman was cleaning it against *Sunday* Then putting on the Frock, stuck full of Card Matches, he set them all on Fire, by the help of a Tinder Box which he had in his Pocket, then standing upright, quoth *Dick, Woman, Woman, hearken to my Voice!*

The old Woman seeing this blazing Spectacle, was running out in a great Fright, but upon *Dick*'s calling after her and saying, *Woman, unless thou comest back and hearken to my Voice, thou shalt presently perish,* she return'd, and, in a trembling Condition, gave great Attention to *Dick*'s Words, who bid her not to be fearful, for he was an Angel come to order her to go forthwith to the Minister of that Meeting-House, and tell him, that he was come to require his Soul of him that very Day, and that he must bring all his Money and Plate along with him, but to be sure must not come with a Lie in his Mouth; for if he did, it would be the worser for him

The poor old Woman dropping a low Church Courtsie to this dark Angel, she went with all Speed to the *Presbyterian Parson's* House, and told him all that had happened in the Meeting-House, but to be certain that the old Woman delivered her Message, *Dick,* having laid aside his flaming Garment, follow'd at a Distance, and softly stepping into the House after her, he heard the Parson, fetching a Sigh, say to his Maid, who was with Child by him, *Well, my Dear, my appointed Time is come, I find, so taking what Money and Plate, I have along with me, I must bid you farewel for ever in this World* Quoth the Maid, *I hope, Sir, you will not leave me in this Condition, you know my Reckoning is almost out, and I have nothing to keep me in my Lying-in That's true,* (reply'd the Parson) *and I pity you with all my Heart*——*There is ten Pounds in that silver Tankard, go take it, for perhaps, as it is an Act of Charity, it may be forgiven*

Then the Parson tying his Riches up in a Napkin, and putting it under his Cloak, he made the best of his Way to the Meeting House, where he was got before the Parson, in his former fiery Posture, which the Parson beholding with great Astonishment, he made his Obeisance to him, and the supposed Angel telling him he was come to fetch him into another World that Night, he ask'd, Whether he had brought all his Money and Plate along with him? The Parson, in a very faint Voice, answered, *Yes* quoth *Dick* then, *Where's the ten Pounds that was in the silver Tankard?* Ah! (reply'd the Parson trembling,) *I see now*

thou

thou art an Angel, for thou knoweſt the Secret of Mans Heart So telling *Dick* he would go and fetch it, he ran ſtraight home to his Maid, ſaying to her, *Oh! Hannah, Hannah, you muſt let me have the ten Pounds agan, for the Angel knew I had not brought all my Money* The Maid reſtor'd it him, for fear it ſhould be a hindrance to his Salvation, and he bringing it to *Dick*, put it with the reſt of the Money and Plate into a Bag, and then opening a great Sack, quoth he, *Come into this, and if you meet with any Difficulties in your ſpiritual Journey, you muſt not complain, becauſe* Narrow is the Way which leads to Life, and few there be that find it

Then tying him cloſe up, he throws him over his Shoulders, but many a hard knock had the poor Perſon, as he carry'd him over Gates and Stiles, and about a quarter of a Mile from the Meeting-Houſe, he threw this Lump of Iniquity into a Hogſty, and there left him

Not long after, ſome of the Servants going it, and ſeeing ſomewhat ſtir in the Sack, they were affrighted, and ran to tell their Maſter what they had ſeen in the Hog-ſty, who alſo coming thither, and finding the Report true, quoth he to one of his Servants, *Take the Pitchfork and run through it* This Command made the poor Parſon cry out for Quarters, whereupon, finding it was a Man, they open'd the Sack, and out he came, quaking like one with a Tertian Ague The Farmer aſking him how he was brought thither in that Manner, he told him an Angel had brought him thither *An Angel! (*reply'd the Farmer*) a D——l you mean? God knows what 'tis, but I'm ſure 'twas no Man,* ſays the Parſon, and ſo he went home to his Maid *Hannah* again, above one hundred and twenty Pounds worſer in his Pocket than when he left her.

In fine, *Richard Morris* one Day going to *Canterbury*, within a Mile of the City, he accidently lit into an old Woman's Houſe, to refreſh himſelf with a Piece of Bread and Cheeſe, and a Pint of Ale, and looking very dejected, the old Woman took Notice thereof, and aſked him the Cauſe of his ſad Countenance, ſo ſhaking his Head, he told her that Mouey was very ſhort with him, and that he ſhould be very glad if ſhe could help him to any Work, he being a Stocking-Weaver by Trade

The old Woman taking Compaſſion on him, helped him to a Maſter at *Canterbury*, where he had about five Months Work, at eleven Shillings *per* Week, leaving all that while, his Wages in his Maſters Hands, becauſe he would receive it all at a Lump, and then would pay the old Woman together, who all that Time found him in Victuals, Drink, Waſhing, and Lodging

At length, when the heat of Buſineſs was over, *Richard Morris* was paid off, and going ſtraight Home to his Landlady, he told her, with a great deal of Joy, that he had received all his Money, and the firſt Thing he did in the Morning, ſhould be to pay her what he owed her, to a Farthing Ay, Ay,

(quoth the old Woman) *I don't queſtion thy Honeſt, Richard!* So bidding the old Woman good Night, he went to Bed Early in the Morning, he comes down Stairs, in a *Diſabil*, as his Coat and Waſte-coat unbutton'd, and having no Garters, Wig, nor Neckcloth on, for he had them in his Pockets *Come Landlady,* ſays he *let's do nothing raſhly, we'll ha e a full Pot of humming Ale before we reckon, and a Toaſt* The old Woman, no doubt, was well pleas'd at this, and going into the Cellar to draw the Drink, *Dick* ſtept ſoftly to the Door, on the outſide of which was a Bolt, and bolted her in, where ſhe was ſquawling and bawling for ſome Hour, befo e any Body came by to let her out of her Confinement

But *Dick* was got quite off of the Ground, but betwixt *Settingborn* and *Rocheſter*, overtaking a Cart of Hay, which was going to be ſold in *Rocheſter* Market, he follows the Tail of it, ſwaying on the right and left thereof whenever it yielded more to one Side than the other, as going thro' a Rut, Slough, or hollow Place, and being in a great Country like Coat, and having a large oaken Plant in his Hand, an Inn-keeper, as paſſing thro' *Chatham,* call'd to *Dick,* (as ſuppoſing him to be the Owner of the Hay) to know the Price of it The Man that was driving on before, not hearing the Inn-keeper, keeps driving on, whilſt *Dick* ſtept up to his Chapman with a handful of Hay for him to ſmell to, telling him it was as good a Load of Hay as any was in *Kent* The Inn-keeper lik'd it very well, and after ſome *Pro*'s and *Con*'s about the Price, he paid him one Pound eight Shillings, for the Hay, out of which he ſpent Six-pence, and then ſaying to the Inn-keeper, *I ſuppoſe you will know my Cart again from the reſt in the Market, go and bid my Man bring the Load of Hay to your Houſe, and make haſte home with the Team,* he went about his Buſineſs

The Inn-keeper goes to Market ſtraight, and finding out the Cart, order'd the Man to bring that Load of Hay to his Houſe, for he had paid his Maſter for it. *S'blood* (quoth the Fellow) *I'de na Maſter come with me to Day* In ſhort, the Inn-keeper reſolving not to loſe his Money, nor the Bumpkin his Hay, from Words they came to Blows, till having blooded one another pretty well, they went to decide the Matter before a Juſtice of the Peace, where the Inn-keeper proved, by two or three Witneſſes, that he paid a Man eight and twenty Shillings for the Load of Hay which his Antagoniſt had now at Market, but the Servant proving his Maſter to be very ſick at Home, and that none came to Market along with him to ſell the Hay, but himſelf, the Inn-keeper, by the Magiſtrate's Order, was obliged to loſe his Money

But *Richard Morris* not making good uſe of the Mercy he had received once before, he ſtill purſu'd his villanous Practices till he was again condemn'd for his Life, and hang'd with *Arthur Chambers* and *Jack Goodwin,* alias *Plump,* at *Tyburn,* in 1706

The LIFE of JACK GOODWIN.

WHEN silver Tankards were more in vogue in the Alehouses than they at present, this Fellow going into one to drink, he call'd for a Tankard of Ale, which being brought, he drank it off, and having cut out the Bottom of it, paid the Victualler for his Liquor, who seeing the Tankard on the Table, had no Suspicion that any Damage had been done it. But shortly after some other Company came in, and the Tapster running into the Cellar to fill them that Tankard, which Mr Goodwin had been fingering, the Fellow wonder'd to see the Cock run and the Tankard never the fuller, whereupon, turning it up, he could find no more Bottom in it, than Mariners can in the Ocean.

Another Time *Jack Goodwin* being in the Country, as far as *Durham*, and destitute of Money, he happen'd to meet with another idle Companion, with whom he made a Bargain to beg their Way up to *London*, and in order to excite People's Pity the more, his new Companion was to act the Part of a Blind Man, and he was to be his Guide, instead of a Dog and a Bell. So getting a Penny-worth of searing Wax, with which Taylors sear the Edges of Silks and slight Stuffs, *Jack Goodwin* mollifying it over a Candle, he dawb'd his Comrade's Eyelids therewith, insomuch that he could not open them.

Our Couple thus proceeding on their Journey, they had by their cruizing or begging thro' the Countries pick'd up about the Sum of four Pounds sixteen Shillings, by that Time they had got up to *Ware*. Next making the best of their Way up to *London*, within ten or eleven Miles of the same, being to cross a small brook over a narrow wooden Bridge, with a Rail but on one Side of it, for the Conveniency of Foot Passengers, when they were upon it, Goodwin threw his blind Comrade into the Water, where he stood up to the Neck, but moving neither one Way nor t'other, for fear of being drowned. In the mean Time his Guide made straight to London. Soon afterwards some Passengers coming by, who took Pity on the Fellow, as supposing him to be really Blind, they help'd him out of the Brook, and setting him on *Terra firma*, he presently, by their Directions, arrived at a House, where getting some warm Water, he wash'd his Eye lids, which being then open'd, he march'd after his Fellow Traveller to *London*, where he might hunt about long enough before he found

him out, for *Jack* was got into some ill House or another, where he was as safe as a Thief in a Mill.

The Duke of *Bedford* being visiting a Person of Quality one Night very late, whilst the Footmen were gone to drink at some adjacent Boozing-Ken, or Alehouse, the Coachman was taking a Nap on his Box, and *Jack Goodwin* coming by at the same Time with some of his thieving Cronies, they took the two hind Wheels off the Coach, and supported it up with two Pieces of Wood, which they got out of a House which was building hard by. So having carried them away, His Grace not long after going into his Coach, and the Footmen getting up behind in a hurry, no sooner did the Horses begin to draw, but down fell His Grace, Footmen and all; who looking to see how the Accident came, they found the hind Wheels were stollen, whereupon the Duke was oblig'd to go home in a hackney Coach.

This *John Goodwin*, alias *Plump*, was condemned when he was but eleven Years of Age, for picking a Merchant's Pocket of one hundred and fifty Guineas, and was afterwards several Times in great danger of his Life, before Justice took hold of him in Earnest.

At last, committing a Burglary in company with another, when he was but eighteen Years of Age, he was apprehended and carried before Sir *Thomas Stamp*, Knight and Alderman of *London*, where, after he was examin'd, being searched, several Cords were found in his Pocket, upon which, his Worship asking Goodwin what Trade he was, he reply'd, *A Taylor*. Then Sir *Thomas* taking up the Cords, and looking very wistly on them, quoth he, *You use, methinks, very big Thread*. *Yes, Sir*, (said Goodwin) *for it is generally coarse Work which I'm employ'd about*.

Next searching his Comrade, *Henry Williams*, a Pistol was found loaded in his Bosom, upon which Sir *Thomas* asking what Trade he was, he reply'd, a Taylor too. *What {both Taylors* (said his Worship) *and pray what Implement is this belonging to your Trade?* Quoth *Williams, That Pistol, Sir, is my Needle-Case*.

To conclude, Sir *Thomas* was so astonish'd at their Impudence, that he immediately made their *Mittimus* for Newgate, and being try'd at *Justice-Hall* in the *Old-Bailey*, they were both condemned to die, and soon after executed at *Tyburn*.

The

The LIFE *of* WILL. ELBY.

THIS noted Malefactor was born at *Deptford*, in the County of *Kent*, of very honest Parents, who bound him Apprentice to a Block-maker at *Rotherhithe*, but he was no sooner out of his Time, than instead of setting up, or working for himself, he went rambling abroad, and delighting in bad Company, he soon grew in love with their Vices He went first of all upon the Waterpad, which is, going on Night with a Boat on board any Ship, or other Vessel lying down the River of *Thames*, or catching in no Persons to watch the same, or else catching the Watch asleep, break open the Padlocks of the Cabbins or Hatches, and rob 'em

William Elby, alias *Dun*, having been like to suffer twice or thrice for this sort of Robbery, he kept Company with several notorious House-breakers, particularly with one *Peter Bennet*, alias *Peter Flower*, but commonly called French *Peter*, from the Place of his Birth, as being born at *Niort*, in the Province of *Poictou* in *France* This Fellow, in the 25th Year of his Age, was hang'd at *Tyburn*, on *Wednesday* the 25th of *October*, 1704

Elby had also broke open several Houses with one *Samuel Scotland*, a Gardiner, who was condemned for 23 Fellonies and Burglaries, and hang'd for them on *Wednesday* the 30th of *December*, 1702, at *Tyburn*, where pulling off his Shoes, and flinging 'em among the Spectators, he said, *My Father and Mother often told me that I should die with my Shoes on, but you may all see that now I have made them both Liars* This impudent Speech has been used by more than one

At the same Time with *Scotland*, was one *John Goffe* executed there, with whom, and some others, *Will Elby* having taken a House in *Boswel* Court, in *Cary-street*, near *Lincolns-Inn-fields*, in the Name of a Lady whose Steward *Goffe* pretended to be, he had the Key thereof delivered to him, then he went to several Goldsmiths about Town, and telling them a plausible Story, that his Lady wanted several Pieces of Plate, as silver Tasters, Spoons, Forks, and Cups, they, by his Appointment, brought what he bespoke, to this empty House, where they expected to be paid for their Goods

But when these Tradesmen came thither, and were one after another let in by a genteel sort of a Fellow, with a green Apron ty'd before him like a Butler, and introduc'd into a back Parlour, they found no other Furniture but about half a dozen Rogues, who clapt Pistols to their Breasts, and told them, they were certainly dead Men, unless they quietly parted with their Plate Whereupon, Life being sweet, they surrender'd, as they came one after another, what they had, and suffer'd themselves to be ty'd Hand and Foot into the Bargain, and thrown into a Cellar, where they were found by a Porter's Wife, to whom *Goffe* (who lost his Life for this Fact) had given the Key of the Street Door, with Orders to make a Fire in the House, tho' when she went into the Cellar for Coals, she perceived nothing there to burn but three

Goldsmiths, who, by this Means, escap'd perishing by Hunger and Cold

Again, *William Elby* had committed many Burglaries with one *James Hacket*, a Taylor's Son, living in *Exeter-street*, behind *Exeter-Change*, in the *Strand*, who was hang'd when 24 Years of Age, at *Tyburn*, on *Friday* the 6th of *June*, 1707, for breaking and robbing the Houses of Mr *Churchill*, Mr *Battersby*, Mr *Hays*, and Mrs *Yalden* Moreover, he had done a few Felonies and Burglaries, with one Tooth less *Tom*, so call'd, from having most of his Teeth knock'd out, by a Person whose Pocket he was once attempting to pick, in St *Margaret*'s Church, at *Westminster*, and who was hang'd in the 23d Year of his Age, at *Tyburn*, on *Wednesday* the 22 d of *March*, 1703 4,

Will Elby was once concerned with one *John Estrick*, in robbing his Master *Thomas Glover*, Esq, at *Hackney*, of as much Plate as came to eighty Pounds, for which, one *Susannah Barnwell* an honest Servant, was wrongfully accus'd, and turn'd out of her Service, but when *Estrick* shortly after came to be hang'd for other Crimes, at *Tyburn*, on *Wednesday* the 10th of *March*, 1702-3, he there confess'd his coming to that untimely End, was occasioned by *John Prosser*, his Brother-in-law, and the Day before he suffer'd Death, sent the following Letter, to his former Master *Thomas Glover*, Esq.

March the 9th, 1702

SIR,

I heartily beg God's Pardon for all my Sins, and ask you forgiveness for the Damage I have done you But as I am a dying Man, Susan knows nothing of your Plate, tho' I falsely accused her of it, God forgive me!

JOHN ESTRICK

Afterwards he went upon the Foot-pad, with one *William Standley*, a Shoemaker, who having robb'd two Men in *Stepney fields*, from one of whom he 'd taken a Watch, the Person who lost it, put next Day an Advertisement thereof, in the *London Gazette*, and not long after, *Will Standley*, going to pawn it to Mr *Chambers*, a Pawnbroker, living at the Corner of *Blackmore street*, in *Drury-Lane*, he, knowing it to be that described in the News Papers, went to stop him, but then running out of his Shop as fast as he could along *Drury-Lane*, and being pursu'd by some who cry'd *Stop Thief* one *John Elliot*, a Watchman, going then on his Duty, and endeavouring to seize *Standley*, he ran him thro' the Body with his Sword, so that he dy'd on the Spot, and the Murderer was hang'd for it in the 28th Year of his Age, at *Tyburn*, on *Wednesday* the 26th of *January*, 1703-4

But tho' *Elby* had seen so many terrible Examples of his wicked Companions being cut off before, yet taking no Warning thereby, he rather grew more harden'd in his Sins, and never thought Justice would

over

overtake him He and his Associates one Evening, meeting with young *Pontack*, the famous Mutton Chop Seller, by *Chrift* Church Hospital, as coming from *Newington*, they leaped unawares upon him, out of a Ditch, and having first taken fourteen or fifteen Shillings in Money from him, they then ftripped him ftark naked; then tying his Hands behind him, they hung 5 or 6 Mutton Chops, which they had bought for Supper, about his Neck, and left him him, faying, at the fame Time, *Sir if your Impudence affumes a* French *Name, to put off boil'd Mutton and Broth, our Juftice directs us to fend you home in a* French *Fafhion, that is to fay, without Shoes or any Thing elfe*

Will *Elby* never pretended to be an Artift at picking Pockets, nevertheless, when Mr *Thomas* a Shoemaker, being drinking at the *Dog* Tavern in *Newgate ftreet*, laid a Wager that he would defie the beft Pick pocket in the World to get his Money from him, he was felected to manage *Crifpin*, who, to fecure a mark'd Guinea which he was to lofe, had put it in his Mouth So following him from Place to Place, till he came into the *Piazza's* in *Covent Garden*, *Will Elby* pull'd a Hankerchief out of his Pocket in which was fome old Shillings, and dropping the Money, a Mob came prefently round him, among whom was Mr *Thomas*, to help him to pick up his Money Afterwards the Rabble afking *Will* whether he had it? he faid, *I have all my Money, thank you, except a Guinea mark'd So and So, which I fancy the Gentleman there* [pointing to the Shoemaker] *has in his Mouth, by what I perceive of him* Whereupon, the vindictive Mob fearching the Shoemakers Mouth by force, and finding fuch a Guinea there as *Elby* defcribed, they did not only give it him, but had like to have knock'd Mr *Thomas* on the Head, who return'd back ftrait to the *Dog* Tavern, where the Guinea was got before him, and he was well laugh'd at befides, fo loling a Wager of two Guineas more

But once this Fellow meeting with one Lieutenant *Job Lord*, as he was coming from *Chelfea*, he attempted to rob him, at firft the Lieutenant was at a Lofs whether he fhould ftand on his own Defence, or no, as imputing the Refiftance would turn to no better Account than of one Pirate fighting another, when nothing is got betwixt them but blows and empty Barrels, but rather than lofe what he had, he engag'd the Foot-pad, and obtaining the Victory, gave him feveral Cuts over the Head, and then tying him Neck and Heels, did not only take about eighteen Guineas from him, but left him there bound to affault the next Paffenger which came that Way

After this great Malefactor received this Mifchance, being very poor a long Time, he was fo prophane as to fay to fome of his Comrades, that he would fell himfelf to the Devil for Money, who (as wicked as they were) exhorted him to the Contrary, telling him that Wizards and Witches were never rich, when they had any familiarity with infernal Powers,

but he faid, *I am refolved to do it, to better Advantage*

Being in a little Time after in *Newgate* again, and one *Sunday* up at Chapel, when feveral Strangers were there, to hear a Sermon preached to fome condemned Perfons, among whom was a Country Farmer, as the Bumpkin was leaning againft the wooden Grates, thro' which the Felons peep, like the Lions in the Tower, and taking a Nap with the high ftiff Collar of his Waftecoat unbuttoned, *Elby* was fo dextrous as to take off a Cheat which he wore in the Room of a Shirt, from under all his Cloaths, which was not miffed at all by the Country Hick, till he came home, and then he fwore and raved like a mad Man, to think which Way he fhould lofe that, without lofing his Coat and Waftecoat

Another Time *Elby*, and fome as good as himfelf at Roguery, being at *Bartholomew* Fa'r, where, among the Crowd, a Country Fellow on Horfeback was ftaring at a merry Andrew playing his Tricks, two of them fupporting the Saddle on their Shoulders, *Elby* privately cut the Girts and Bridle, and led away the Horfe unperceived, fo that the Mob difperfing, after the Fool had diverted them a little from the Gallery of the Booth, the Country Fellow tumbled down in the Dirt, in a great Surprize at the Lofs of his Fellow Creature, and was obliged to go home to *Enfield* a-foot

Mr *Abel*, that had once the Honour to fing before the King of *Poland's* Bear, keeping a Confort of vocal and inftrumental Mufick in *York* Buildings, *Will Elby*, who had been a Thief a long Time, and was refolved to be one till he dy'd, being well dreffed in an embroidered Coat, and a long Wig, and getting admittance *gratis*, among the Quality there, (for now a-days a mere Mountebank, or a Player, the two worft Profeffions upon Earth, in his laced Suit, fhall be more refpected than a Gentleman of Merit, in one that is out of Fafhion) whilft the People were in the heighth of their Jollity and Paftime, he privately ftole above half a Score gold Watches, which he carried clean off, without feeing the Conclufion of the mufical Entertainment.

But, at laft, this bafe Villain, tho' he had receiv'd both the Sentence of the Law, and the Mercy of his Prince before, breaking open the dwelling Houfe of Mr *James Berry*, at *Fulham*, and killing therein his Servant, *Nicholas Hatfield*, he was committed to *Newgate* Whilft Sentence of Death was paffing on him at the *Seffions-Houfe*, in the *Old Bailey*, his Impudence was fo great, as to curfe the whole Bench; nor was his ill Behaviour lefs remarkable under Condemnation, when, being perfwaded to difcover his Accomplice or Accomplices in the faid Murder, he faid, *That if any one fhould afk him again, any fuch Queftion, he would prefently knock him down* In this Refolution he continued till he was executed, and hang'd in Chains at *Fulham*, in the County of *Middlefex*, on *Saturday* the 13th of *September*, 1707, aged 32 Years

The LIFE *of* THOMAS WITHERINGTON.

THIS Perfon was the Son of a very wor-thy Gentleman of *Carlifle* in the County of *Cumberland*, who poffeffed a plentiful Eftate, and brought up his Children handfomely, and fuita-bly to his Condition. *Thomas*, of whom we are go-ing to fpeak had extraordinary Education given him and was defigned for a Gentleman, to live at his Eafe, free from the Toil and Hazard of Bufinefs The good old Gentleman dying, *Thomas* came into Poffeffion of a confiderable Eftate, which foon procured him a rich Wife, but fhe proving loofe, and violating his Bed, puſh'd him on, in Revenge, to Extravagancies, which otherwife he had no Inclination to, her Faf-hood to his Bed was a Mortification to his Thoughts he could never reconcile to his Mind, and being re-folved to reſent her Perfidy and Treachery, he aban-doned himfelf to the Company of all Manner of Wo-men Thefe by Degrees perverted all the good Qua-lities he poffeffed, nor was his Eftate lefs fubject to Ruin and Decay, for the Mortgages he made of it, in order to fupport his Profufion and Luxury, foon reduced his Circumftances to a low Ebb, and made him miferably poor What fhould a Gentleman of Mr *Witherington's* late affluent Fortune, do in this wretched Cafe ? He was above the mean Submiffion of ftooping to either Relations or Friends for a De-pendance ; and to afk Charity or crave the Benevo-lence of his Brother-Men, was a Circumftance his Soul abhorr'd One way he muft do to live, to ftarve prefented nothing but frightful and melancholy Ideas to the Mind The collecting Money on the Road was judged the beft, though not the fureft Expedient, of raifing his Fortune And with this View he com-mitted Robberies in moft Parts of *England* for fix or feven Years with admirable Succefs As none, or but very few Books of Robberies have given any Account of *Whitherington's* Tranfaction, we fhall infert a few here, with a View to humour our Readers, that they may not fay they have the Life of a Man without any Adventure in it

Witherington, having left his Wife, on Account of her Falfhood to his Bed, and being refolved to maintain himfelf by the Work of his own Hands, borrowed the Sum of forty Pounds of a Neighbour-ing Gentleman of his Acquaintance, pretending fuch a Sum of Money would do him an infinite piece of Service, as it would fet him up in fome little honeft Way to fupport him at prefent The Gentle-man, glad to find his Friend's Temper fomewhat alte ed from its vaft Prodigality, and being willing to ſecure him a vicious Inclination at fo fmall a Purchafe, readily lent him the Money, and pronounced feveral Bleffings along with it But *Witherington* fruftrat-ed the Expectations of his Friend, and with the Mo-ney bought him a Horfe, and other Neceffaries fit for his future Enterprizes ! He happened to lie one Night at the *Queen's Head* Inn in *Kefwick* in *Cum-berland*, where Dr *Flemming*, Dean of *Carlifle*, was alfo Our Adventurer, being no Way inferior to

the Doctor, either in Learning, or Point of Conver-fation or good Manners, fcraped Acquaintance pre-fently with the Clergyman, who was glad to have any one to converfe with, as he was alone Sup-per being fet before them, *Witherington*, to amufe the Doctor, told him he was but arrived a Fort night in *England*, having been abfent a matter of feven Years in the *Eaft-Indies*, where, thank God, he had got, by his Induftry and good Fortune to-gether, a competent Eftate, able to maintain him like a Gentleman all his Life, and that now he was go ing to fee his Friends at *Carlifle*, from whom he had been abfent fo long ——— The Doctor hearing him mention *Carlifle*, was defirous to know who thofe Friends were, acquainting him that he himfelf be-longed to that City, and he fhould be glad of his good Company thither in the Morning Upon this our Adventurer mention'd the Family of the *Wither-ingtons*, and told the Doctor, that having heard he Uncle was dead, and had left a confiderable Eftate behind him, he had haften'd his Return to *England*, and was come to fee what he had left him He had a Son, faid he, named Thomas, *a very hopeful young Man, when laft I left him, but the Letter which informed me of my Uncle's Death, told me likewife that his only Son was at the Point of Death and I know the Eftate can devolve (if every ont has his Right) on no other but me, who am next Heir at Law* The Doctor being perfectly acquaint-ed with Mr *Witherington's* Circumftances, as ha-ving made his Will, was furprized to think he had got into the Company of fo near a Relation of that Gentleman, and began to open his Mind to him with greater Freedom Sir, fays he, *I have been acquainted feveral times with a Relation of Mr Witherington's, being in the Eaft-Indies, but the Fa-mily, I can affure you, had frequent Letters (from whom I cannot tell) of his dying at Fort St George, and what Prejudice this may have done your Affairs at* Carlifle, *to Morrow will be the beft Witnefs As for* Thomas, *the only Son of Mr* Witherington, *I can affure you, that he is alive, and has run through the Eftate his Father left him very profufely, In-deed, at his coming into Poffeffion, he gave the World great Hopes of making an excellent Husband, which foon procured him a Wife with a confiderable Fortune but the Lady, I am told, not proving fo virtuous as fhe ought, forced him into a quite contrary courfe of Life, for inftead of living frugally and tempe-rately, as ufual, he abandon'd himfelf to the Embraces of lewd Women, kept high Company, profecuted Gam-ing, and a thoufand other wicked Courfes, which foon ruin'd his Eftate, and brought him to Want And if I am not mifinform'd, to fupport his open Extravagancies, he frequents the Road, and takes Purfes* Our Adventurer pretended all the while to liften with a world of Attention, and when the Doc-tor acquainted him with his Coufin's Extravagancies he feem'd in the deepeft Melancholy imaginable He

quirin

verend Sir, says Witherington, *I infinite Obligations to you for the Discovery you have made about my Uncle* Witherington *and his Son; and possibly you made be of extreme Service to my Affairs. I cannot impute our meeting together to any other thing than an Act of Providence, which is willing to incauze me, and, I pray, Sir, let me beg to be a Bottle of Wine for more Acquaintance.* The Doctor, who was a true *Bacchanalian*, readily accepted the Proffer, and *Witherington* and he made it up four Flasks before they went to Bed, where they repos'd very found till eight the next Morning. They got up together, eat their Breakfast, mounted, and took their Journey, when the Doctor, to make their Travelling as pleasing as possible, ran over a great many diverting Stories; and *Witherington*, to make his Part good, was not backward in producing Tales to anfwer his. All seem'd in good Harmony, the Doctor pleas'd with his Friend, as he suppos'd, and our Adventurer with his Traveller. But we shall soon see the Clergyman's Tone chang'd, for *Witherington* being arriv'd, with his Companion, at the Corner of a Wood, rode up to the Doctor, and whisper'd in his Ear, *Sir, tho' the Place we are at is very private, yet willing what I do should be more private, I take the Liberty to acquaint you, that you have something about you that will do me an infinite Piece of Service*—What's that, *reply'd the Doctor? You shall have it withal my Heart, if 'twill do you so much Service as you say I thank you, Sir, for your Civility, says Witherington*, well then, to be plain with you,—'tis the Money in your Breeches-pocket that will be infinitely ferviceable to me—Money, *reply'd the Doctor*, Way, Sir, you cannot want Money, your Garb and Perfon both tell me you are in no Want—Ay, but I am, for the Ship I came over in happen'd to be wreck'd, fo that I have loft all I brought, and I would not enter *Carlifle* for the whole World without Money in my Pocket—Friend, I may urge the fame Plea, and fay, I would not go into that City for the World without Money in my Pocket, but, what then? If you are Mr *Witherington's* Nephew, as you pretend to be, you would not thus peremptorily demand Money of me, for *Carlifle* being fo fmall a Diftance from us, it cannot be much that is wanting to defray your Expences thither, where, on reprefenting your Cafe, you'll find Friends enough to fupport you; and I declare, if you have nothing, I'll difburfe for you fo far. *Witherington* made Anfwer, Sir, the Queftion is not, whether I have any or no Money, but what you carry in your Pockets, for you fay my Coufin is oblig'd to take Purfes on the Road to fupport himfelf, and fo am I, fo that if I take your's, you may ride to *Carlifle*, and tell the Inhabitants, that Mr *Witherington* met you, and demanded your Charity—The Doctor plainly underftanding by this the Drift of his Companion's Intentions, told him, He was amaz'd to think, that a Perfon who had pretended fo much Honefty fhould deceive him in that manner, by requiring his Money, to which he had no Right—Right, reply'd the other, why, I tell you, Sir, that whether I have Right or no Right to it, 'tis my Cuftom to lay hold of it, if fo be that I can but get it. As he was fpeaking thefe Words, a Country Higgler, fitting between two Panniers full of Poultry, rode up to them, upon which, fays *Witherington*, You honeft Fellow, I have a Caufe of Confcience to put to you, whom I take to be fitteft Perfon to decide it. Here is a Clergyman, and a fat one let me tell you, who has four Livings, which bring him in an annual Rent of a thoufand Pounds, yet for all this, he has not the Sincerity or Heart to give a Par-

thing of his Money to the Poor, tho' he has now above fifty Guineas in his Pockets. What fay you, Countryman? Doth not Chriftianity the Rich that they are to give to the Poor, or elfe their Way to Heaven is as difficult, as for a Camel to go through the Eye of a Needle—The Countryman feeming confounded at the Sight of *Witherington's* Piftols, which he now began to fhew, was in a Dilemma what Anfwer to make, till our Adventurer forcing him to fpeak, he fpoke thus, Why, Sir, Ife tell you my Mind 'as faid, indeed, that the Rich fhould give to the Needy, but who knows what Occafions the rich Man may have for his Money. If there be an Object of Pity that really has nothing, there I take it, that the rich Man ought to give to the Poor—Than, my friend, I tell thee, I am that Object of Charity, for the Devil a farthing have I about me, and it coft me ten Shillings laft Night to treat this fire-nofe Son of a Whore of a Parfon—Come, my Lad, determine quickly, for I muft proceed on in my Bufinefs——Then I pronounce, reply'd the Countryman, That the Rich ought to give to the Poor,——Whereupon, *Witherington* drawing up to the Doctor, the Reverend Clergyman deliver'd him his Green Purfe, with fifty Guineas in it. *Witherington* was rejoiced at the Sight, and taking thence a Guinea, gave it the Countryman for the Equity of his Award, and then rode off, leaving the Doctor to purfue his Journey to *Carlifle*, and there tell his Misfortune.

Witherington another time being at *Newcaftle*, took up his Quarters at the Sign of the *George Inn*, which was then in a Street call'd the *Broad-Chair*. It happen'd, that abundance of young Clergymen, and other Scholars were come to follicit for a Schoolmafter's Place in the adjoining Country, worth about a hundred and fifty Pounds *per Ann*. It feems, the Gift went by Election, and he that could give the beft Proofs of his Capacity and Learning, was to have it. Several Gentlemen were prefent to gain Votes for their refpective Candidates, and no more than five and twenty Freeholders had Votes to difpofe of this Benefice. Our Adventurer finding how Matters were like'y to go, procured the Landlord to lend him a coarfer Suit of Cloathes than what he had on, faying, he was fure to obtain the School, provided Merit was to take Place. The Cloathes were inftantly procur'd, and *Witherington* appear'd in the Kitchen, where he fat down with his Mug of Ale by him, and fmok'd his Pipe. One or the Freeholders, who was alfo a Truftee for this School, obferving fomething in our Adventurer's Countenance that infenfibly pleas'd him, plac'd himfelf down in the next Chair to him, and began to tell him every Circumftance about chufing a new School-mafter. Ay! *fays Witherington*, I hope that Merit will take Place, but I am afraid fome one or other of thefe fine Sparks will carry the Day, by the mere Intereft of the Friends they have brought. Nay, nay, *replies the Freeholder*, as long as I have a Vote, Juftice fhall be done. What, did thou come hither to put up? Ay, *fays the other*, but I'll return Home, for I believe my Journy's loft—Not at all yet, Man, never fear, for egad, I fay, Merit fhall take Place, and if thou be found the beft Scholar, thou fhall certainly have it. And to convince thee, that I have fome Refpect for thy Perfon, tho' thou art a Stranger to me, I here promife thee my Vote before my Landlord, and will not only do that for thee, but gain thee fome others to thy Intereft. *Witherington* thank'd him heartily for his Civility, and the old Man was as good as his Word, for, till the Time of the Election's coming on, the good and frank Freeholder

took

took several of his Neighbours aside, and procured their Votes, in Opposition to the rest. The Election now is begun, and each by turns are examin'd. A fierce Contest arose between two of the last, (for our Adventurer was conceived all the while) who seem'd to have equal Abilities for the Imployment, and the Examiners and Freeholders were going to determine in favour of one of them, when our above mention'd Trustee, speaking to the Gentlemen assembled on the Occasion, told them he begged they would defer giving Judgment for a quarter of an Hour, till they had heard a Friend of his, a poor Man, examin'd him, and who was so modest, that he had declin'd appearing among a such guady Company.

All upon this were importunate to see him. He was brought, and several abstruse Questions was put to him, in order to puzzle his Understanding, but he answer'd all with a surprizing Facility and Judgment, so that the Company could not help staring upon one another. Come, said he, *you are my Antagonist, let us decide this Controversy by Dint and Force of Argument for 'tis not a Parcel of Greek and Latin Sentences cull'd out of ancient Authors, that ought to purchase a hundred and fifty Pounds a Year, let's see if you thoroughly understand what you read, or if you are Artist enough to distinguish betwixt good and bad Writing.*

The Books which he desired were immediately produced, but within half an Hour he made both the Examiners, Freeholders and other Gentlemen assembled on this Occasion, see clearly, that all the Candidates, who had been some Years at the University, except himself, were so far from having any real Knowledge in the Books, out of which they had made their Citations, that they had only gone thither to spend their respective Parents sixty or seventy Pounds a Year. This unexpected Success of our Adventurer made the rest of the Company stare on one another, the several Gentlemen who came to sollicit for their Friends were confounded, and obliged to return *re infecta*, and what was most surprizing, *Witherington*, who appear'd at this Election purely to gratify a roving Inclination he had, obtain'd the School with little or no Difficulty, while the others, who had been at considerable Expences in tampering with the Freeholders for their Votes, found themselves and their Hopes intirely frustrated. In short, *Witherington* was invested in the Jurisdiction of the School with the usual formalities, and happening to behave in his Place with a great deal of Moderation and Humility, the Churchwardens of the Parish taking a greater fancy for him, put their Books of Account in his Hands, and made him Overseer and Tax gatherer of their Parish, nay, so fond were all, and so believing in his Justice, that the Rector committed to his Care the collecting his Rents and Tythes. *Witherington* finding himself in a tolerable Way of Subsistence, was very well pleas'd with his Condition, which afforded him Opportunities enough to make his Advantage. The Trustees of the Parish, and the Parson himself were, if we may use the Expression, over credulous, and *Witherington*'s Words and Advice were sure to pass current when all the rest failed. So that never Man had better Opportunities (I mean one who had advantageous Views in prospect) of enriching himself. *Witherington* saw how the good Humour towards him diffused itself through the Body of the Parishoners, and was resolved to make a fine Handle of it. To this End he insinuated what Honour it would be to the Memory of the present Heads of the Parish to have a new School erected in the room of the old, which was in a very ruinous Condition, telling them at the same time, that, to promote so laudable an Undertaking he would sink a Year's Salary himself. This generous Proposition was received with Chearfulness, and it was unanimously agreed to have a new School erected. *Witherington* seeing his Proposal lik'd, got the Affair to be carry'd on with a great deal of Briskness. Contributions came in pretty thick from the neighbouring Gentlemen, and a Sum of above seven hundred Pounds was immediately rais'd. This enliven'd *Witherington*'s Hopes, who, finding he was desir'd by two Gentlemen who happened to come from *Carlisle* to see a Friend of theirs in this Place, he made off the following Night with the Money that had been given for rebuilding the School, and went directly into *Buckinghamshire*, where he committed several Robberies, the principal of which we shall set down in the Sequel.

Being one time at the Town of *Buckingham*, he fell into the Company of some Country Farmers, who who were come to pay their Rents, having all one Landlord. The Rustics were in a hot Debate about the Price of Corn, and unanimously said, that if their Goods brought them no more Money, 'twas impossible to maintain their Farms any longer, much less to pay their Landlord his Rent. *Witherington*, willing to have some Discourse with them, sat down in an Elbow-chair by the fire-side, and call'd for a Pint of Wine. The Rustics imagining by the Dress of our Adventurer, that he was some Gentleman who was travelling farther, ask'd him how forward the Corn was in those Countries he had travel'd through. This was what our Adventurer desir'd. God be thank'd, said he, there has not been three Weeks finer Weather than the last these six Years, as I know of, and if it continues much longer, 'tis to be hop'd the Fields will be quite clear'd —— Ay, *said the Countrymen*, but the same fair Weather has not bless'd *Buckinghamshire*, for we have had large intermissive Rains round about us for these six Weeks past, which has done our Corn considerable Damage, and I fear will do more, if the same uncertain Weather continue, yet our Landlord expects his Rent a fortnight after Quarter-day, not withstanding all the Misfortunes that attend us at present —— Pray what Rent may you pay, *replied Witherington?* For having all the same Landlord, *as you say*, the Sum must be pretty considerable —— Considerable indeed, *answer'd they*, for to tell you a Word of a Lye, we commonly bring him hither once every Quarter a matter of three hundred Pounds ——That is a round Sum upon my faith, *replied Witherington*, and, pray, does he make no Allowances in Cases of bad Weather or otherwise? — Not a Souce, Sir, for he's one of the most miserly Fellows this Day in the whole Land; he has upward of twelve hundred a Year, and yet grudges to allow himself Necessaries —Ay, he's a covetous Wretch, indeed, and 'tis a thousand Pities he should be Master of so much Money. Is there no Way to reclaim him d'ye think?—What do you mean Sir? —I mean, is there no Way to make him a better Man than he is?—We apprehend there is vast Difficulty in that —Well, Friends, if you'll leave the Affair to me, I'll manage the Payment of your Rents so well for you, that shall only pay half of the three hundred Pounds for this Quarter, 'tis true I'm a Stranger to you, but you may depend on my Sincerity in serving you —The Countrymen hearing this unexpected Speech from their new Acquaintance, seem'd extraordinarily glad at the News, but wonder'd, as they knew their Landlord's avaricious Temper, how he would pretend to serve them so beneficially. Pray, Sir, said they, *acquaint us how you into do us this particular Piece of Se-*

one, for we shall be ready to embrace it ——Why, I tell you, as soon as your Landlord comes, if he makes any Hesitation at seeing me in your Company you shall tell him, that being a Relation to one of you, and bred up in the Laws, I had a Mind to come and solicit a Favour from him in your Behalf This was immediately agreed to, and the Landlord appear'd in a Quarter of an Hour, who sat down among his Tenants, without seeming to take Notice of our Adventurer Witherington observing this spoke to the Farmers ——Gentlemen, I presume this is your Landlord, and now he's come, your Business may be dispatch'd presently Accordingly the Master of the inn was call'd to shew them to a private Room, because they had Business of the last Importance to transact to gether Mr Buffet ('o was the Person's Name) ordered one of his Men to conduct them into the Stir chamber, which was over the Brewhouse, and at some Distance from the overhearing of the rest of the House Hither they were convey'd, and all sat down round a large Table The Landlord was order'd to produce his last Receipts for Rents, which Witherington, as a pretended Lawyer, seem'd to read over with a world of Care ——Well, Mr Landlord, says he, I find by the Receipts which these Gentlemen, my Acquaintances have from time to time had from you, that they have been extraordinarily exact in paying their Rent every Fortnight after the Quarters became due, and I think you may bless your Fortune that you have so many honest and good Tenants, who, were they other Men than they are, would have left their Farms a considerable time ago I shall be very short in what I have to say, for abundance of Words are but unnecessary You must know, Sir, then, that these six good Men about you, have, as I am inform'd, been Tenants to you a considerable number of Years, which, I take it, makes for them It seems that none of them owe one Money they have acquired, to the Produce they have made of your Land, but to other Contingencies, which Fortune has thought fit to throw in their Way Whence comes it, then, that they preserve such an inviolable Esteem for you and your Farms, in paying your Rent so punctually, that no others will please them? They tell me, they are come this Day to pay you three hundred Pounds for a single Quarter's Rent Pray, what would it be, Sir, to throw them back this Money, as a small Gratuity for the Losses they are likely to sustain this Year, through the Rains that continue to fall in this Country Tenants, of other People, ought to have peculiar Indulgencies, who by their Labour and Industry so many miserable Wretches like yourself are supported And if Providence thinks fit to visit one particular County or Kingdom with an almost continued Tempest, and the Possessors of the Ground become Losers by it, 'tis my humble Opinion, that the Head should ought to abate of his Rent in Proportion to the Losses of his Tenants ——The avaricious Landlord look'd on his Tenants with a grim Aspect, shewing thereby the ill Opinion he had of the Stranger, and after some Pause broke out into the following Exclamation, Friend, you are an entire Stranger to me, and I cannot see what Business you have to intermeddle in the Affairs between me and my Tenants, who are all of them honest Men, and pay me my Rent without grumbling Have you a mind to create a Variance betwixt us, and break that good Understanding that has subsisted among us for so many Years, if so, declare your Mind, that I may know what I have to do As for Losses they are likely to sustain, is it in my Power to correct the Weather, or lay Commands on Providence, to make the Season wet or dry just as I or

28

they please? When a Compact is made between Landlord and Tenant for a Farm, the latter covenants to pay a stated annual Rent, without any Diminution for occasional or accidental Rains, for by the same Way of arguing, you may as well say, that provided a Farmer's entire Crop happens to be blighted with Lightning, the Landlord, in such Case, ought to abate of his Tenant's Rent in Proportion to the Loss he sustain'd Was ever such a Thing heard of? Supposing now, that the Houses my Tenants dwell in should be blown down by the high Winds that whistle about them at this present, pray who is to erect them again? Why, myself; might not I have just Reason to say, that my Loss and Damage was considerable, and therefore according to Equity, my Tenants ought to augment their Rents in Proportion to my Sufferings This, Sir, is fair Reasoning, and how you can controvert it, I cannot see, produce all the Laws of *England* on your Side, if you will ——I have nothing farther to say on this Point, but insist, in behalf of my Friends here, that you remit them a hundred and fifty Pounds of this Quarter's Rent, for I am told you have more than enough to support yourself and Family —— Not one Souce, reply'd the Landlord ——We'll try that presently ——But pray Sir, take your Pen, Ink and Paper in the mean time, and write them their Receipts, and the Money shall be forth coming immediately ——Not a Letter tell the Money is within my Hands ——It must be so then, answer'd Witherington, you will force a good-natur'd Man to use Extremes with you. and so saying, he laid a Brace of loaded Pistols on the Table Immediately the Landlord was on his Knees before Witherington O dear Sir, sweet Sir, kind Sir, loving Sir, for God of Heaven Sake, Sir, be merciful, Sir, and don't take away the Life of an innocent Man, Sir, who never intended you or any Person else any Harm in the whole Course of his Life ——Why, what Harm do I intend you, Friend? Cannot I lay the Pistols I travel with on the Table, but you must throw yourself into this unnecessary Fear? Pray proceed to the Receipts, and write them in full of all Accounts and Demands from the Beginning of the World to this Time, or else—or else—Dear God, Sir, you have an Intention ——Pray dear Sir, have no Intention against my Life ——To the Receipts then—or by Ju—pi—ter Am—mon, I'"—With this the old Landlord wrote full Receipts, and deliver'd them to the respective Farmers

Come, says Witherington, this is honest, and to see that you have met with Persons as honest as yourself, you shall have a hundred and fifty Pounds, which is a hundred and fifty Times more than you deserve, and, I promise you, if Things succeed well with these six good Men, you shall have the other Half made up by next Quarter And having thus said, he ordered the Countrymen to give him their Money, and he would pay him, which was accordingly done, and he paid him a hundred and fifty Pounds Whereupon the old Landlord seeming extremely cloudy at his Disappointment, but not daring to utter a Word about his Loss, nor the Countrymen venturing to speak a Syllable about what had befallen him, lest worse Consequences might attend this odd Proceeding The other People in the House plainly discovered an unusual Sadness diffused over the Countenance of the rich Landlord, but could not tell what to impute it to

Our Adventurer having made an End of this singular Transaction, ordered his Horse to be saddled immediately, and, walking into the Stable to see how the Hostler perform'd his Duty, ask'd him several Questions about the rich Landlord, as how much

E e

Land

Land he poffeffed, and where he lived, and having got a fuccinct Account from him, he mounted and rode off, with an Expectation of feeing his Twelve hundred Pounds a Year Landlord in a little Time He had not rode above a Mile out of Town, when when wanting to eafe Nature a little, he efpied the old Gentleman coming towards him on a gentle Trot, being followed by a Servant with a Portmanteau behind him. On their feeing one another, the old Gentleman feemed very willing to turn back, but *Witherington* taking hold of his Horfe's Bridle, defired him not to refufe him his Company, fince he had an Affair of great Importance to communicate to him. The old Gentleman, without making any Anfwer, fet Spurs to his Horfe, and feemed determin'd to wreft himfelf by main Force out of the Hands of one he had Reafon to hate the worft in the World. Our Adventurer feeing him a little refolute, told him, that fince it was fo, he was obliged to ufe fome Violence, which he was forry for, upon his Perfon, and therefore, as he tendred the Safety of his own Life, bid him give him the hundred and fifty Pounds, which remained of the Rent he had lately receiv'd, for, faid he, I have infinitely more preffing Occafions for fuch a Sum of Money than you, who, out of Twelve hundred Pounds *per Annum*, cannot find in your Confcience to allow yourfelf Neceffaries. What, d'ye think that Money was defigned for no other Ufe than to hoard up for a whoring Son, or fome diftant debauch'd Relation, who, after your Death, will curfe your Memory a thoufand Times a Day, and triumph over your Grave. No, Money is a Bleffing fent us by Heaven, in order that by its Circulation it may afford Nourifhment to the Body politick, for if fuch Rafcals as you, by laying up your Thoufands in your Coffers to no Advantage, caufe a Stagnation, there are Thoufands in the World that feel the Confequences, and I am to acquaint you of them, fo that a better Deed cannot be done, than to beftow what you have about to me, for to be plain with you, I am not to be refufed, and fo faying, he rode up with his Piftol in his Hand to the Footman, whofe Portmanteau he having unty'd, and put on his own Horfe, he then went up to the old Gentleman, who, extremely afraid of his Life, delivered him his green Purfe with the hundred and fifty Guineas, and fome old Medals *Witherington* having receiv'd the Spoil, told him, that Charity extorted in that Manner was of no Signification, for if the Heart was not inclined naturally of itfelf to give, all the Money he had in the World was but a Plague to him, and then turning his Horfe about, he march'd off, leaving this Admonition behind him, to be affable and generous to his Tenants, for they were the Perfons that fupported him, for had he Eyes to obferve with what Difficulty they obtain'd their Money, he would open his Heart little more, and faid, if he heard them fpeaking againft him any more, as he had done in *Buckingham*, he might depend on feeing him at his Houfe, and partake there of fuch Liberahty as his Apartments would afford him, and then he left him

But *Witherington* after this Adventure found the Country too hot for him to ftay any longer in it For the old Gentleman fent a Hue and Cry after him, and the Defcription of his Horfe, Drefs and Perfon was fo truly given, that he was obliged to ride round about the Country for a matter of two Days and a Night The firft Houfe he put up at was at *Nantwich* in *Chefhire*, at the *George* and *Vulture* there, where coming in all of a muck Sweat, and his Horfe in a weary Condition, the Gentlewoman of the

Houfe, who was a Widow Woman, thinking he was come off a large Journey (as indeed he was) took more than ordinary Care about him, for fear he fhould catch Cold, and order'd him fomething warm to drink. The Landlady was remark'd all round the Country for her extraordinary Civilities to Strangers, which drew Abundance of Travellers to her Houfe. She was not quite paft the fix'd Time of her Mourning, having loft a very good Hufband about eight Months before, fhe had Youth on her Side, and a tolerable good Face to fet her off, but what was the principal of all the reft, was, that her Hufband having had a rolling Trade while he liv'd, fhe was left in very good Circumftances. *Witherington*, though very much fatigu'd with his Journey, could not but turn his Eyes upon her, and think her a thoufand Times for the Care fhe fhew'd of him. She anfwer'd him always with a lively Brifknefs, that he was not Mafter of himfelf to go to Bed, but, in fpite of all the Fatigue of his long Journey, would make a Party among fome Gentlemen that came to fup there that Night. Thefe (who were four) it feems, made Pretenfions to the Dame, though in a private Way. *Witherington* had too good Eyes not to obferve it; and he would now and then fmartly point in his Difcourfe to the Landlady, that fhe might think herfelf vaftly happy and great, in making a Conqueft over fo many hearts. All was carried on with a wonderful deal of Mirth, but ftill the Widow, as fhe fpoke, drew the Attention of the whole Company. After Supper was over, the Widow addreffing herfelf to our Adventurer, begged him to give the Company a Song, for fhe was fure he could fing, having fo clear and fweet a Voice. *Witherington* wanting no further Importunity from a Perfon he had already fix'd his Affections on, began thus

While rofy Charms, and gay Delight
  Sit in thy blooming Looks confeft,
I tremble, yet admire the Sight,
  And feel the Rapture in my Breaft,
    Oh! footh my Flame
    Thou killing Dame,
And lull my Soul to balmy Reft

Can gazing, am'rous Man, behold
  Thofe beauteous Eyes, divinely gay,
Or view thy Treffes all of Gold,
  And not Love's mighty Hand obey?
    Come, and infpire,
    Or quench my Fire,
For foon my Soul will melt away

Come fair Venus, *Queen of Pleafure,*
And fair Widow, endlefs Treafure,
  Fold within my Arms,
For in Love there is no Meafure,
  When encircl'd with thy Charms

Thefe Verfes, and the Air our Adventurer delivered them with, were enough to warm an Imagination like that of the Widow's, fhe was too penetrating not to underftand who the Perfon was they were addreft to, fhe was at Lofs how to admire the Singer of them too much, and was even going to perhaps herfelf fome good Fortune was drawing near her, by having fo charming a Gallant under her Roof She confidered the reft of the Company fingly for a while within her Breaft, but found, on a clofe Examination, that our Adventurer had the Afcendant over them a great deal. But to make Trial of the Abilities of the Reft, fhe defired them to favour her with each a Song which was complied with, but how diftafteful and Furl how diſtant from the fine and genteel Manner, where-with *Witherington* pronounced his Words *I cannot but think,* ſays ſhe, *that as you have favour'd me with a friendly Song, you can alſo gratify me with ſome Adventure of your's, for your Perſon and Mein plainly diſcover there is ſomething extraordinary in you, more than a thouſand other Men can pretend to* Witherington thank'd her for the Honour ſhe did him, but deſired no further Commendation, as he very well knew there was nothing in him but what almoſt every Man might claim as well as he To pleaſe you, Madam, and if it be no Offence to the Gentlemen in Company here, I ſhall beg Leave to give a Recital of my coming hither, which may afford ſome Circumſtances of an Adventure not unworthy to be related The Company hearing this, were by ſo much the more ſollicitous to make him proceed, as they conjectured they ſhould hear ſome Hints which had been a Myſtery to them *Witherington* finding this, began thus I was born, Gentlemen and Lady, on the Confines of *Scotland,* of Parents not to be deſpiſed, for in my Family have been Perſons of Dignity and Repute, ſome of whom have ſacrificed their Lives in the Bed of Honour, in Defence of their Country and Religion, while others, trained up in the different Branches of a liberal and fine Education, have been advanced to conſider ble Poſts in the Kingdom, which they conſtantly maintained with Integrity and Uprightneſs of Mind At five years of Age I was put under the Tuition of an Uncle of mine, who, having a large Eſtate and no Children, took a particular liking to me, inſomuch that I became his Favourite, and whereſoever he went, I was ſure of being carried with him As my Age advanced, I was put under the Care of School-maſters, convenient for their Learning, and before I was full eleven Years old, I could make a Theme, or a Dozen *Latin* Hexameter and Pentameter Verſes tolerably well But coming into my Fourteenth Year, my Notions of Things began to extend themſelves farther, and I thought the School a meer Confinement Love then began to actuate within me, and, in ſpite of myſelf and School, found the Power of *Cupid* too much ſuperior to all my Endeavours to ſuppreſs it It happened that a neighbouring young Lady frequently made Viſits at my Uncle's Houſe, in Company with her Mother, who, as the Neighbourhood reported it, was deſigned for him They had a thouſand Interviews together, but to what End no Body could ever yet diſcover Various were the Diſcourſes about them And amidſt the different Sentiments of the Pariſhioners, the old Gentlewoman died, upon which the fair and young Daughter was removed to my Uncle's Houſe I had now an Opportunity of diſtinguiſhing more Charms than I had ever done before I had an intimate Acquaintance with her, and though a School-boy, had the Art to gain her Affections We loved one another with a Paſſion that is too difficult to deſcribe For neither of us could ever endure to be a Moment abſent from each other's Converſation We kiſs'd one another, and toy'd out thoſe half Days, when we had Play, in little but ſincere Dalliances I made her Verſes, and ſung her Songs We uſed to walk together in the Fields, and ſit two or three Hours at a Time under the Shade of ſome Tree, while I diverted her with reading Tales of Love, or Romances But alas! when we thought our Happineſs the moſt ſecure, we were unhappily ſeparated, for being at an Age capable of proſecuting nobler and genteeler Studies, my Uncle ſent me to the Univerſity, to the greateſt Regret I ever found in the World My Uncle was not ignorant of the Love that was between us; he gave us rather Liberty to indulge it, than any Way hindred us in the carrying on of our Amour The Lady had a conſiderable Fortune left her by her

Mother, who before ſhe died, made her Will, and declared therein my own Uncle her ſole Executor, with a Power of diſpoſing of her Daughter to whom he pleaſed I had behaved myſelf hitherto with great Circumſpection, ſo far as my tender Age would permit me, and nothing I thought in the World could hinder me from coming into the Arms of a beautiful Bride with an extenſive Portion, and enjoying my Uncle's Eſtate after his Deceaſe, but Experience tells Mankind, there is no Certainty to be found For during my being at the College, where I had already ſtudied ſix Years, my Uncle, though ſeventy Years of Age, takes her, who was mine by all the ſacred Ties of Truth and Love, and no more than ſeventeen Years old yet, to be his Wife The firſt News of this Revolution came incloſed in a Letter, a Correſpondent of mine in the Country ſent me I was confounded and bewildered, wholly unable to reconcile myſelf to a Belief of it for ſeveral Days But when I found the Thing too true, what Tongue can expreſs the Anguiſh of my Soul I wrote to my Uncle, and ſignified to him the Injuſtice he had done me in depriving me of the only Bleſſing I had in the World, and ſuggeſted the monſtrous Inequality there was between his and her Age, but my Letter was peruſed indeed, and afterwards torn to pieces This I was told of I was now determined to leave the College, and leaving all the Satisfaction I had received in Books, vindicate myſelf before my Uncle, and try, ſince he had done me ſo much Diſhonour, if he had any Inclinations to ſerve me otherwiſe Accordingly, I provided myſelf with a Horſe, and went down into the Country, where he received me with all the outward Marks of extreme Civility but I could not get a Sight of his Wife for a Fortnight or more, and what were the Reaſons of this Conduct I could not find out One Day I took my Uncle aſide into his Closet, and warmly expoſtulated the Matter with him How could you, Sir, offer to deprive me of the greateſt Jewel in the Univerſe? had not Love of a long ſtanding cemented our tender Hearts together, you might then pretend ſome Plea for what you have done Your great Age ought at leaſt to have convinced you, that the Match between you and her was prepoſterous, and what all the World would eſteem a downright Compulſion on the Lady's Thoughts For how could it be otherwiſe? Is it to be ſuppos'd that a Virgin in the Bloom of her Youth, can receive any Satisfaction from the Embraces of a Body wither'd like yours? If Perſons are but left to chuſe for themſelves, they'll match together a thouſand Times more equally than either Parents or Guardians will do for them Your marrying her has depriv'd her of all the Happineſs her Thoughts ſuggeſted to her, and to take the Advantage of my Abſence, was doing me and her the greateſt Injury that can be imagined, but what can Women guard againſt, when the Temptations of Money and Riches are conſtantly ſet before them? And ſo ſaying, I left him to ruminate on my Words

After this, I ſtrove to divert myſelf in the moſt agreeable manner I could, ſometimes by peruſing the choiceſt Books in my Uncle's Library, and ſometimes by walking in his Gardens, which were ſtiffly fine and beautiful One Evening, as the Sun was going to ſet, I happen'd to take a ſolitary Turn in his Wilderneſs, and a Thruſh ſinging very melodiouſly, I ſat down in an Arbour to enjoy the Muſick the Bird made I had not been there long before I heard ſomething tread ſoftly among the Trees, which at firſt putting me into ſome Confuſion I ſtarted from my Solitude, and caſting my Eyes around, what ſhould I eſpy but my once dear Love I ran to her with an Emotion of Mind not to be expreſs'd, and throwing my Arms about her Waſte, conducted her to a more ſecret Place in the Wilderneſs, where ſitting down, we at firſt gaz'd on one another with all the Joy imaginable, and then burſting out into Tears, our Tongues by degrees found Vent I began to expreſs my Concern that I had been depriv'd from ſeeing her ever ſince my Arrival, and could not well tell what to impute it to At this ſhe pauz'd a while, and then began thus *Oh ! ſays ſhe, were I to begin at the Original of my Troubles and anxious Hours ſince your firſt going to Cambridge, I ſhould ſwell the Narration to a Day s Length, which the Shortneſs of the Time will not permit me to relate, but take a Part You are ſenſible, my dear Witherington, how pleaſingly we liv'd and lov'd together for ſome Years, till your Abſence broke the Alliance between us, and reduc'd me to the miſerable Condition I am now in No ſooner was your Back turn'd, but I became too ſenſible under what a Maſter I was got, for I wanting to write to you, I was deny'd the Uſe of Pen, Ink, and Paper, and confin'd to the Limits of your Uncle's Houſe and Gardens, with a Woman Servant, one of his own procuring, to attend me If I ſpoke at any time of the Reſpect I had for you, I was anſwer'd, that my Reſpect was unſeaſonable, and I was now under the Care of one who had the abſolute Diſpoſal of my Perſon At this I would pour out a thouſand Tears, and ſeem'd drown'd with my crying, till ſooth'd with ſome flattering Promiſes he made me, I was made eaſy for a ſhort Time But, alas ! my dear Witherington, the Remembrance of you ſtill was uppermoſt in my Thoughts, and while that poſſeſt me, all the Pleaſures he allow'd me were taſteleſs and inſipid Finding this, he bought me rich Cloaths, as if he deſign'd to win me over by this, but his Aim was fruitleſs At length, after a thouſand Applications to no purpoſe, in order to wear your Idea out of my Mind, he propoſed Marriage, but without naming the Man. I told him I had entertain'd Thoughts of that honourable State a long Time, but none except his Nephew could make me happy ——— My Nephew, reply'd he, why, my Dear, he has nothing but what I ſupport him with, and that's but very little; 'tis true, I have a large Eſtate, and ſome tell me he is Heir at Law to it, nay, I have promiſed to leave him it, but 'tis all on a Proviſion that he acts in Obedience to my Commands, which in courting you he does not*

I found now how Things were likely to go, and therefore to make my unhappy Condition as pleaſing to me as I could, I fancy'd a thouſand romantick Dreams in my Head, purely to divert my Melancholy Sometimes I flatter'd myſelf I ſhould ſtill ſee you, and compleat my Happineſs, but I found I was only amuſing myſelf with Impoſſibilities One Evening your Uncle taking me in his Chaiſe, put the Queſtion about Marriage to me, I ſeem'd aſtoniſh'd at the Relation, and told him, I wondered at his making ſuch an Offer to me, when he knew the Engagements between you and me He ſeem'd offended at my Preſumption in acquainting him ſo, and told me, he had a Right to my Perſon and Fortune above all other Men in the World I generouſly reply'd to this, that if it was ſo, he muſt never expect to have either my Love or Duty This home Speech ſeemingly made no impreſſion upon me, we return'd Home, and ſupp'd together In the Morning the Parſon of the Pariſh came to Breakfaſt with us, and during the Time, he attack'd me with all the Force of Reaſon in order to induce me to comply with my Guardian's Commands, he repreſented to me the Advantages of ſuch a Match, and the Superiority ſuch an Alliance would give me over the low Circumſtances of a poor Collegian, who was forc'd to acknowledge all he had to the Benevolence of his Uncle I return'd ſuch an Anſwer as I was capable of giving; for what could I do, who was only myſelf, and unaſſiſted by

any body In ſhort, I found I muſt be marry'd to the Perſon I hated the worſt in the World, and marry'd I was within a Week after this Interview between the Parſon, my Uncle, and me

Here ſhe wept abundantly, and both of us, for ſome Time, were loſt in Pity in one another's Arms I ſtrove to divert her with all the Power of Language I was Maſter of, but was not able to recover her from her Uneaſineſs for a conſiderable Time, ſhe hung upon me, and kiſs'd me, I return'd the Salures with the ſame Warmth, till fired with uncommon Deſire we acted that together which nothing but the greateſt Diſhonour in the World could have prompted me to, had I been in my Senſes But alas ! 'twas too late to repent, and the dear Creature began to love me the more We continued in the Bower together till 'twas almoſt dark, tho' the riſing Moon gave us ſtill an Opportunity of ſeeing and gazing upon one another Ill Fortune attended this amorous interview, for her Maid having miſs'd her, had been ſearching all over the Garden for a long Time for her, but to no Purpoſe At laſt, Curioſity leading her into the Wilderneſs, ſhe came near the Place where we were ſitting together, and overhearing two Perſons talk, ſhe ſilently drew nigher, and diſcover'd us together What were the Conſequences d'ye think ? Why, the old Man was acquainted with the whole Affair, and to make the Accuſation heavier againſt me, the Maid confronted us in every Particular My Uncle rav'd and ſtorm'd, and appear'd like a mad Man, he reprimanded me very ſeverely, I ſtrove to vindicate the Lady's Honour, and juſtify myſelf; but he was above Conviction, and plainly told me, that I muſt never expect one Farthing from him, and for his Wife, he would take Care to ſecure her Conduct for the future, adding, that the World was wide enough for me, and and I was at Liberty to ſee what my Learning could gain me And having thus ſaid, he flung out of the Room and left me

Here was a ſad Mortification to grieve a Man's Spirits, I found I was inevitably rejected by my Uncle, and that there was no Recourſe left me in the World but to put myſelf into the Arms of it Accordingly I made ready in the Morning to depart, when taking Leave of my dear Creature, ſhe convey'd into my Boſom a Purſe of fifty Guineas, and bad me think of her Thus I left the Family, with a Reſolve to ſeek my Fortune ſome where or other, and Chance has thrown me into this hoſpitable Houſe, where I cannot but own, I have found as much Beauty as I have been ſadly depriv'd of

Our Adventurer here put an End to his fictitious and artful Tale, which ſo wrought on the Minds of the Company, eſpecially the fair Widow, that he plainly ſaw he was no unwelcome Gueſt He drew his Chair cloſe to her, and c reſt her in a very moving manner, which put one of the other Gentlemen into ſome Confuſion Witherington found he had a Rival to deal with, and ſhould he ſtay and proſecute his Suit with Warmth, he would ſee clearer into the Affair This Conſideration determin'd him to remain a Month at *Nantwich* All now withdrew, the Gentlemen to their Homes, and the Widow and her Family to Bed

Next Morning our Adventurer being with the Widow, they had a cloſe Diſcourſe together about the the Loſſes and Profits of Inn keeping *Witherington* ſeem'd to hint, as if the Care that attended ſo large a Family, was too much for a Woman to bear, and judged that a Man was the fitteſt Perſon to bear ſo large a Burthen on his Back The Widow return'd him Anſwer, that what he ſaid was very true, and ſhe ſhould think herſelf happy in finding a Man proper for it Why, ſays *Witherington*, I cannot think but there are Men enough to be found. ——— Methinks I obſerv'

obſerv'd one in the Company laſt Night diſcover how well he loved you   To this ſhe reply'd, That ſhe was too ſenſible of it, but could not return his Affection ſuitably ; that ſhe had had ſince her Huſband's Deceaſe abundance of Suitors, but that not one amongſt them all could pleaſe, that ſhe had a delicate Palate with reſpect to Man, for which the World ought not to cenſure her, ſince ſhe ſufficient to make the Perſon ſhe took for her Huſband exceeding happy, provided he was frugal and temperate

This Diſcourſe mightily pleaſed our Adventurer, who finding he had room enough to ſpeak for himſelf, ask'd if there was any thing in his Perſon that could with her   The Widow, confounded at the Advances ſhe had made, knew not how to retreat, but putting on a ſmiling Countenance, told him, That as he was ſo generous in ſpeaking for himſelf, he might go on, and doubtleſs Proſperity and Succeſs would attend him, that to be frank, ſhe could ſet her Affection on him as ſoon or ſooner than any Man in *England,* but Decency and the Cenſure of the World made her hop her Deſires, which otherwiſe ſhe ſhould think no Injury in gratifying   *Witherington* praiſed the Choice and Preference ſhe ſeem'd to make, but told her, " That he could not impute the Declaration ſhe had " made to any thing elſe but a Motive of Female " Gallantry — You may impute it to what you " will, Sir, *reply'd ſhe,* but I can aſſure you, if ever " Man had an Aſcendant over my Heart, you may " pretend to ſome Part of the Conqueſt, your Nar- " ration laſt Night too warmly engroſs'd my " Thought, to let it or the Idea of your Perſon die " ſo ſoon in my Memory   What I now ſpeak is " from the Reality of my Heart, and tho' you may " pretend to an eaſy Conqueſt over me, yet, let me " warn you to improve it moderately and with Diſ- " cretion, for, tho' a Woman, I can tell how to re- " venge an Injury, or requite a Kindneſs

What an *Ecclairciſſement* was here ? Sure *Withe- ington* wiſh'd a thouſand Bleſſings on his propitious Stars, who had thus befriended him in the Opinion and Sentiments of the Widow   All now was Rapture and Emotion, if the Widow lov'd the Perſon of *Witherington,* no leſs was he taken with her Money   Since this Licentious Courſe of Life, he had abandon'd a great many of his good Qualities, for Money was the only Thing he had any View to

We ſhall find in the Sequel a very barbarous Murder cloſe the End of this Courtſhip, which was attended with ſo promiſing a Beginning   By this Time a Gentleman, who, the Night before ſeem'd concern'd at the ſudden Familiarity between our Adventurer and the Widow, was acquainted how Things were going, he was confounded at the News, but knew that it was no more than he expected, he vow'd Revenge not on the Perſon of *Witherington,* but the beautiful Widow, his Intentions ſquar'd in every Article with thoſe of our Adventurer, for 'twas her alone, that made him offer Love   He had been inform'd by ſeveral of his Acquaintance, who knew her Deſigns better than himſelf, than to wed her, was the ſure and ready Way to his Deſtruction   That ſhe had been tax'd with ſending her late Huſband out of the World by Poiſon, and it might be his or any other Perſon's ill Fortune, who ſhould chance to marry her, to meet with the ſame inhuman Fate   As the Gentleman had courted her for ſome Time, and her bewitching Carriage had influenc'd him to a great Degree, it was not eaſy for him to wipe away ſo ſoon the Impreſſion he had receiv'd, he began to think within himſelf what he was going to do, and ſeriouſly conſider'd all the Conſequences that might attend him, was ſhe really as repreſented   He had but too flagrant an inſtance of her fluctuating Temper and

Inclination from what he had ſeen paſs the Night before between him and our Adventurer, therefore he was determined to reward her inconſtancy by a juſt Puniſhment, and do a Piece of Service to the Stranger-Gentleman, (as he term'd our Adventurer) by opening his Eyes againſt her

With this View he ſent a written Note by his Servant, directed to the Perſon that came in the Night before to the Inn   *Witherington* received it, and at firſt, ſeem'd confuſed, not knowing what the Deſign was   He peruſed it over three times before he gave any Anſwer, and then told the Man that he would wait on his Maſter preſently   They met together at the Gentleman's own Houſe, and the Widow was amuſed with this Tale, that Mr —— having took a Fancy to the Travellers Company and Converſation, muſt needs have him to dine with him that Day   This was a fine Artifice to make her eaſy   When they were ſat down together, the Gentleman excuſed himſelf for ſending for him in that manner, by acquainting him that he had an Affair of the laſt Importance to communicate with him, and that it was purely to do him a Piece of ſignal Service, that made him ſend for him

" You muſt know, Sir, that the Widow of the Inn " where you lodge now has bury'd her Huſband a- " bout eight Months ago   The Man was an excellent " Perſon in his Way, and a great Oeconomiſt, ſo " that by his Frugality and candid Behaviour to his " Cuſtomers at all Times, he acquir'd a competent " Eſtate, and leaving no Children behind him, he " bequeath'd every Penny of it by his Will to his " Wife   I am ſorry to think I have juſt Occaſion to " ſpeak what I am going to acquaint you with con- " cerning this Woman   I am told by a Abundance " of Perſons, whoſe Veracity may be depended on, " that ſhe poiſoned the poor Man to make way to " his Effects, tho' he had before ſecured them to her " by his Teſtament   'Tis true, I courted the Wo- " man, and have done ſo almoſt ſince her Huſband's " Deceaſe, thinking her Money ſufficient to make " me happy in my Circumſtances, which, without " hiding them from you, are a little involved at pre- " ſent, but having a Mind to prefer my Eaſe before " any other Conſideration, I have thought fit, at my " Friends importunities and Sollicitations, to wipe " her Memory out of my Mind, and be no longer a " Slave either to the Love of her Perſon or her Mo- " ney   Now the End of my ſending for you is this : " I had frequent Opportunities of diſcovering her " wavering inclination laſt Night, while you was re- " citing your Adventure, not, Sir, that I harbour'd " the leaſt Jealouſy in the World about it, for I " ſcorn ſo gnomious a Paſſion , but I am ſorry to " think I have made my Addreſſes to a Woman ſo " abominable, if Report be true   Beſides, I am ac- " quainted ſhe is making all the Haſte ſhe can to draw " you into Marriage, which, how conſequential, the " Lord above can only tell , but I am afraid of the " worſt, and would warn you as a Friend, to avoid " her inſinuations and artful Ways   I cannot help " thinking, but that both our Deſires are alike ? I " mean, that we want Money, and I think, I could " put us into a Way how to ſqueeze every Farthing " from this Woman, who values herſelf upon her " Effects "

Witherington for ſome Time could not tell what to reply , however, he return'd the Gentleman a great many Thanks for his timely forwarning him in ſuch an important Caſe , and told him, if he would leave the Affair to him for two or three Days longer, and not come to Extremes ſo ſoon, he'd warrant to find out all the Baſeneſs that lurk'd within her Breaſt, and then, if they had a Mind, they might make what Uſe of her they thought proper.   The Gentle-

29   F f

man feem'd fatisfy'd with this, and fo they parted for this Time.

Our Adventurer returning to the Inn, called the Widow afide, and then acquainted her with the whole Proceeding between him and the Gentleman She feemed in a Rage, and protefted the World was very cenforious, and declared fhe would have her Revenge on him, coft what it would Witherington forefeeing a Rupture was going to break out, thought it high Time to make his Advantage of the credulous Woman, who was ready to believe any thing he faid So that Night taking her afide, he told her, that the beft Way to revenge herfelf on him, would be, if fhe had any inclinations of marrying him, to give him fome Mark of her Favour that might diftinguifh him above his Rival Glad of this Opportunity, fhe conveys him into a Clofet, where fhewing him all her Money and Plate, fhe acquainted him, that all thofe were at his Service, provided he did her fo much Service as to deliver her from the Importunities of the Gentleman Witherington faid fhe might depend upon him, and fo they withdrew for that Night, which was indeed the laft of their feeing one another —— He retired into his Chamber, and there taking Pen, Ink and Paper, he wrote the following Letter

My Dear,

EVER mindful of what a Woman fays, efpecially one who has been pleas'd to fit her Affections on me, I have wrote this Letter purely to acquaint you, that being obliged to go to London, and the Journey being pretty long, I could not do better than make Ufe of the Money in the Clofet, which you was fo good as to fay, was at my Service I was in exceeding Hafte when I began to write this, fo that I cannot fpare more Time, than to tell you to be fure of thinking upon me till my Return,

                      Witherington.

After he had wrote this he went privately into the Clofet, and fecured all the Widow's real Money, which amounted to above Three Hundred Pounds, and returning into his Chamber, got all his Things ready, and going down Stairs into the Yard, got into the Stable, faddled his Horfe, mounted and rode out at a back Door, leaving the Family faft afleep, and the Widow and her Gentleman Lover to profecute their Amours as they thought fit

Witherington having obtained this large Booty of Money, purfued his Journey within twenty Miles of London, when between Acton and Uxbridge, not being fatisfied with his late Acqufitions, he committed a Robbery on the Highway, for which he was fent to Newgate, where he lived a very profligate Life to the very Day of his Execution

At the fame Time flourifh'd one Jonathan Wood-ward and James Philpot, two moft notorious Houfebreakers, who, in the Cities of London and Weftminfter, the Suburbs thereof, Southwark, and moft Towns and Villages in the Counties of Middlefex and Surrey, had committed daily Robberies for fome Years, for which they were fent to the Marfhalfea, and condemned to be hang'd upon St Margaret's-Hill, in the Borough of Southwark, but King James I happening this Year to come to the Throne of England, they were both pardoned upon an Act then put for all Criminals, excepting for High-Treafon and wilful Murther However, thefe Villains not making good Ufe of this Mercy, ftill purfued their old wicked Courfes, committing frequent Burglaries and Robberies, till at laft being apprehended again, and fent to Newgate, they were try'd with the abovementioned Thomas Witherington, at the Seffions Houfe

in the Old Bailey, and with eight other Malefactors were condemned, but thefe three being moft notorious Offenders, were only appointed for Death And while they continued in the Condemned-Hold, they led abominable Lives, abandoning themfelves to all Manner of curfing and fwearing, notwithftanding the extraordinary Pains and Care of the Ordinary to reclaim them

At the fame Time there was living one Mrs Elizabeth Elliot, who having a Son, that about two or three Years before, was condemned to be hanged for the like Practices, but received Mercy, and became a good Man, in Compaffion for other Criminals, and in Acknowledgment of the King's Royal Favour, on her Death Bed willed Two Hundred and Fifty Pounds to the Parifh of St Sepulchre's in London, to find a Man who fhould for ever, betwixt the Hours of Eleven and Twelve of the Clock of the Night before any Prifoners were to die, go under Newgate, and giving them Notice of his being come by a folemn Ringing of a Hand-Bell, fhould then put them in Mind of their approaching End, by repeating feveral goody Expreffions, tending to inftruct them for a true Preparation for Death After which he fays to the Prifoners appointed for Death — Gentlemen, are you Awake? Who from the Condemned-Hold, anfwering —— Yes —— he then proceeds thus

Gentlemen, I am the unwelcome Meffenger who brings you the fatal News that you muft to-morrow die Your Time is but fhort, the Hours flide away apace, the Glafs runs faft, and the laft Sand being upon dropping, when you muft launch out into boundlefs Eternity, give not yourfelves to fleep, but watch and pray to gain eternal Life Repent fooner than St Peter, and weep before the Cock crows, for now Repentance is the only Road to Salvation, be fervent in this great Duty, and without doubt to-morrow you may be with the penitent Thief on the Crofs in Paradife. Pray without ceafing Quench not the Spirit Abftain from all Appearance of Evil As your own Wickednefs has caufed all this Evil to fall upon you, and brought the Day of Tribulation near at Hand, fo let Goodnefs be your fole Comfort, that your Souls may find perpetual Reft with your bleffed Saviour, who died for the Sins of the World, he will wipe all Tears from your Eyes, remove your Sorrows, and affuage your Grief, fo that your Sin-fick Souls fhall be healed for evermore I exhort you earneftly not to be negligent of the Work of your Salvation, which depends upon your fincere Devotion betwixt this and to-morrow, before the Sword of Juftice fhall fend you out of the Land of the Living Fight the good Fight of Faith, and lay hold of eternal Life whilft you may, for there is no Repentance in the Grave, ye have pierced your felves through with many Sorrows, but a few Hours will bring you to a Place where you can't mufe, i might it Joy and Gladnefs. Love Righteoufnefs, and raife in quiry, then God, even your God, will anoint you with the Oil of Gladnefs, above your fellows Go we boldly to the Throne of Grace, that ye may obtain Mercy, and find Grace to help in Time of Need The God of Peace fanctify you wholly, and I pray God your whole Spirit, and Souls, and Bones, may be preferved blamelefs unto the coming of your bleffed Redeemer The Lord have Mercy upon you, Chrift have Mercy upon you Sweet Jefus receive your Souls, and to-morrow may you fup with him in Paradife To all which the Spectators cry, Amen.

Next Day on which they are to die, the Bell in the Steeple is to toll for them, and under St Sepulchre's Church yard Wall, the Cart or Carts ftopping,

ping, the aforesaid Man, after ringing his Hand-Bell again from over the Wall, repeats again some religious Exhortations to the Prisoners, which are as follow

Said by the Bell-man over St *Sepulchre*'s Church-Wall

Gentlemen, confider now you are going out of this World into another, where you will live in Happiness or Woe for evermore Make your Peace with God Almighty, and let your whole Thought be entirely bent upon your latter End Curfed is he that hangeth on a Tree, but 'tis hop'd the fatal Tree will bring your pre-

cious Souls to an Union with the great Creator of Heaven and Earth, to whom I recommend your Souls, in this your final Hour of Diftress Lord have Mercy upon you , Chrift look down upon you, and comfort you Sweet Jefus receive your Souls this Day into eternal Laft Amen.

I thought inferting thefe Particulars would not be unacceptable to the candid Reader, fince the three Perfons above-mention'd were the firft to whom thefe Exhortations and Warnings were given And thus ended the Life of our Adventurer *Thomas Witherington*

The LIFE *of* THOMAS RUMBOLD.

THIS *Thomas Rumbold* was defcended from honeft and creditable Parents at *Ipfwich* in *Suffolk* In his Youth he was put Apprentice to a Bricklayer, but evil Inclinations having an Afcendant over his Mind, he went from his Mafter before he had well ferved two Thirds of his Time This Elopement obliged him to purfue fome Irregularities to fupport himfelf He abfconded from his Father's Houfe, and having a Defire of feeing *London*, he came up to Town, where getting into the Company of a notorious Gang of Robbers, he went on the Highway, and frequently took a Purfe This Courfe he continued fome Time, in Conjunction with Confederates , but having a Mind to make Prizes by himfelf, he ventured by himfelf, committing feveral Depredations on his Countrymen , the following whereof have come to our Hands

The Archbifhop of *Canterbury* being to go from *Lambeth* to *Canterbury*, *Rumbold* was determin'd to Wy-lay him , and accordingly getting fight of him between *Rochefter* and *Sittingborn* in *Kent*, he gets into a field, and fpreading a large Tablecloth on the Grafs, on which he had placed feveral Handfuls of Gold, he then takes a Box and Dice out of his Pocket, and falls a playing at Hazard by himfelf His Grace riding by that Place, and efpying a Man fhaking his Elbows by himfelf, fent one of his Footmen to know the meaning of it The Man was no fooner come up to *Rumbold*, who was ftill playing very eagerly, fwearing and ftaring like a Fury at his Lofles, but he returns to the Reverend Prelate, and telling him what he had feen, his Grace ftept out of his Coach to him, and feeing none but him, afk'd him who he was at play with ? Damn it, faid *Rumbold*, there's five hundred Pounds gone Pray, Sir, be filent His Grace going to fpeak again, Ay, faid *Rumbold*, there's a hundred Pounds more loft Prithee, faid the Archbifhop, who art thou at play with ? *Rumbold* reply'd with —, And how will you fend the Money to him ? —— By, faid *Rumbold*, his Ambaffador, and therefore looking upon your Grace to be one of them extroydinary, I fhall beg the Favour of you to carry it him According, giving his Grace about fix hundred Pounds in Gold and Silver, he put it into the Seat of his Coach, and away he rid to *Sittingborn* to bait *Rumbold* rid thither alfo to bait in another

Inn , and riding fome fhort while before his Grace, as foon as he had Sight of him again, he had planted himfelf in another Field in the fame playing Pofture as he had before , which his Grace feeing as riding by, went again to fee this ftrange Gamefter, whom he then took to be really a Madman No fooner was his Grace approaching *Rumbold*, who then had little or no Money upon his Cloth, but he cry'd out —— Six hundred Pounds. —— What, faid the Archbifhop, loft again No, reply'd *Rumbold*, won, by Gad , I'll play this Hand out, and then leave off So Eight hundred Pounds more, Sir, won, I'll leave off while I'm well And who have you won of, faid his Grace ? Of the fame Perfon, reply'd *Rumbold* that I left the Six hundred Pounds with you for before you went to Dinner And how, faid his Grace, will you get your Winnings ? Says *Rumbold*, of his Ambaffador too So riding up with Sword and Piftol in Hand to his Grace's Coach, he took Fourteen hundred Pounds out of the Seat thereof over and above his own Money, which he had entrufted in his Hands to give to —— and rid off

When *Rumbold* had got this large Booty by playing, whofe Happinefs it was never to fee, without becoming a very great Convert indeed, he bought him a Place, but did not leave off robbing on the Road , and in order for his better Advantages, he kept in Fee with moft of the Hoftlers and Chamberlains of the chiefeft Inns in the Country for forty Miles about *London* So that having one Day a Blow fet him at *Colebrook*, that is to fay, being inform'd that a Couple of Travellers lay at a certain Inn in the abovefaid Town, he rofe early the next Morning, and way-laid them in their Journey to *Reading*, fo went before them to furprize them at *Maidenhead-Thicket*, but the Travellers being cunning, they had given out in Publick the wrong Road they were to go , for inftead of riding to *Reading*, they went to *Windfor*, fo that *Rumbold* miffing of his Pray, rode back again very melancholy, when meeting with the Earl of *Oxford*, who was attended only with one Groom and a Footman, he clapt his Hair into his Mouth to difguife himfelf for his intended Defign, and attack'd his Lordfhip with the terrifying Words, *Stand and Deliver*, withal fwearing, that if he made any Refiftance he was a dead Man The Expoftulations

tions the Earl used to save what he had, were as much in vain, as to pretend to wash a Blackamore white, however he swore too that since he must lose what he had, *Rumbold* should search his Pockets himself, for he would not be at that Trouble. Upon this our Adventurer commanding his Lordship's Servants to keep at above a hundred Foot Distance upon pain of Death, he took the Pains of searching the Earl, when finding nothing but Boxes and Dice in the Pockets of his Coat and Waistcoat, he began to rend the Skies with many First Rate Oaths, swearing also, that he believ'd he was the Groom Porter, else some gaming Sharper going to bite the poor Country People at their Fairs and Markets, till searching his Breeches he found within a good gold Watch and six Guineas, he changed his angry Countenance into smiling Features, and giving his Lordship eighteen Pence, bad him be of good Cheer, go up to his Regiment then at *London*, as fast as he could, and do his Duty as he ought, and when he next met with him, he would give him better Encouragement

Rumbold had an Acquaintance of his being one Day at *Canterbury*, in the Dress of a Country Fellow, they went to a Tavern to drink a Quart of Wine. It seems the Master of a House was a complete Sharper, who, taking his two Guests for ignorant Fellows, was determined to put the Chouse upon them, as he call'd it, accordingly he brought them a Wine Quart Pot, but it was little more than half full. He intended they should have it raw, but it being a cold Morning, they bid him roast it. The Vintner was at a Loss in filling out the first Glass, but not knowing how to help it, he set it down before the Fire, and, as was suppos'd, intended to fill it up afterwards, but he forgetting that, and our Adventurer and his Acquaintance being busy in Discourse, forgot to look after the Pot, when on a sudden they look'd, and the Pot was melted above have way down, which was as far as there was no Wine in it. The Maid observing the Pot melted, call'd out to them, What? honest Men do you melt your Pot? Not we, said they, it was the Wench. But are like to pay for it, reply'd the Wench That is when we do, said they. Upon this, the Master of the Tavern appears, to whom the Maid tells how the two Fools had been telling their *Canterbury* Tales together till the Pot was melted —— Then they must pay for it, answers the Vintner, for it was given into their Charge and Custody, and that therefore they ought to look after it, and since it was damag'd to pay for it They reply'd, they took no Charge of it, neither did they touch it, but only order'd him to burn the Wine well The Vintner insisted to be paid for his Pot They told him, they would not Upon this he threaten'd them with a Justice of Peace's Warrant This Menace somewhat troubling them, and unwilling to have any Dispute in the Affair, they told the Vintner they were content to pay for the Wine, and allow Sixpence more for mending the Pot The Vintner told them that would not do, for it could not be mended, and he must have a new one Our Adventurer and his Companion seeing the Vintner so unreasonable, were content to have the Justice determine the Controversy, wherefore before his Worship they went, and the Vintner made his Complaint, how that those two Men had melted his Quart-pot, and refused to pay for it The Justice perceiving how the Matter lay, and that he told his Tale wrong, desired the Men to speak, who, in plain Terms, told him they took no Charge of the Pot, but only desir'd the Drawer to cause the Wine to be burnt, that he had accordingly set it down by the Fire, and that without their handling or

touching it, the Pot was melted. So, said the Justice, and did neither of you drink of the Wine? No, not one Drop, reply'd our Adventurer, and yet we offer'd to pay for the Wine, and give Six pence towards mending the Pot This is more than you shall need to do, answer'd the Justice, and then he thus proceeded with the Vintner

Friend, with what Confidence can you demand any Money of these Men, who had nothing of you? Since you will not do them Justice, I will I do hereby acquit them from paying any thing for Wine, because they never had any, and for the melting the Pot, how did they do it? It was not they, but your Servant who drew the Wine, who, had he fill'd the Pot full of Wine, the Fire could not have melted no farther than it was empty, and farther, continu'd the Justice, this shall not serve your Turn, for I shall fine you for not filling your Pot Your Crime is very apparent and evident, and so shall your Punishment be, and I order you, as a Fine, to pay down twenty Shillings for your Misdemeanour, or else I shall make your Mittimus, and send you to Prison This was the Case alter'd, and the Tale now was of another Hog, for the Vintner, who expected Satisfaction, was forc'd to give it, and that immediately, or else go to Prison This went against the Hair, but Necessity had no Law, and therefore down he paid the Money, and came Home heartily vexed, not so much for the Money he had paid, as for the Disgrace he receiv'd, for he was now become the Town-talk

As *Rumbold* was riding along the Road he met a young Girl with a Milk-pail on her Head, but was amaz'd to see so much Perfection in her Face, he rode up pretty close to her, purposely to entertain some Discourse with her, introductory to a new Acquaintance. The first Questions he put to her were frivolous and indifferent, which she seem'd to answer with abundance of Modesty *Rumbold* seeing her open a Gate to milk a Cow, followed her, and tying his Horse to a Hedge, desir'd her Pardon for his Rudeness, and begg'd her to entertain a favourable Opinion of his Actions, for he would not offer the least Injury or Prejudice to her Chastity Being over persuaded with his Protestations and Vows to that Purpose, she admitted him to sit down and discourse with her, whilst she perform'd the Office of a Milk-maid *Rumbold* had much a do to contain his Hands within Bounds when he viewed her stroking the Cow's Dugs, which so heighten'd his amorous Passion that the Vows and Protestations he had so lately made soon vanish'd out of his Memory In short, after some Dalliances, Intreaties and Love persuasions, and using corporal Strength, he obtain'd his Desires After this they grew more familiar together, but the Burthen of the Song was, that *Rumbold* had undone her, but let the Reader judge the Truth of this It was concluded that she should go home to her Father's House, and that towards Night our Adventurer would come thither himself according to the Time appointed, as if he had never seen her before, and that he accidentally rode that Way in order to be inform'd what Course he was to take to pursue his Journey right

The Maid went cunningly in, and acquainted her Father and Mother, that there was a Gentleman without, who appear'd such by his Countenance, Garb and Dress, that fearing to travel farther, being Night, and not knowing the Way, he desir'd to rest himself until the Morning The Parents of the young Woman had more Respect for our Adventurer than to let him travel farther, whereby he might be expos'd to Difficulties, civilly admitted him into their House

Rumbold

Rumbold being handsomely entertain'd, was resolv'd to dedicate that Night to the Charms of his fair and young Mistress, but Heaven cross'd his amorous Design, and all the Stars were against him

Next Morning our Adventurer feign'd himself very ill, purely to have a Pretence of staying, which he acquainted the Daughter with. The old People were vastly loving and courteous, so that as soon as they heard of it, they came to see *Rumbold* in his Chamber, and express'd extraordinary Compassion and Pity for him. They provided every Thing they tho't necessary for him. Our Adventurer offer'd them Money for their Services, but they absolutely refused it, and to make them entertain the better Opinion of him, he shew'd a great Quantity of Gold

Rumbold lay at the Farmer's House at least a Fortnight in this pretended ill State of Health, several Doctors had been with him, but not one of them all had Knowledge enough to dive into his Distemper. During this Time he had the charming Daughter every Night, who, contrary to the Custom of most Women, did not seem coy and nice in gratifying his Passion which was the Centre of her Hopes. *Rumbold* fearing too long an Illness might give the old People some Uneasiness, or cause 'em to suspect him, left off counterfeiting any longer Indispositions, and shew'd them some Recovery of his Strength. When the old People at any time came into his Chamber, the main Subject of our Adventurer's Discourse commonly turn'd on the many signal Favours he had receiv'd, and that if he liv'd he would gratefully repay them. Being restor'd to his usual Strength, he told them that he could never well enough recompence the Care and Love they had over him, unless it were by marrying their Daughter, who had already won his Heart. The Parents made many Excuses upon this Article. The first Objection was, that she was but a poor Country Girl, and the like. However, *Rumbold* was not so backward to himself but he made several Enquiries in a neighbouring Town about the Circumstances of the Farmer, whom he found by the Report of every Body to be a very wealthy Person, and that Time had not been more careful in furnishing his Head with Silver Hairs, than he industrious to maintain them by the Procuration of a plentiful Estate. The Girl he pretended to love was the only Darling of the good old People, for the Father furrow'd the Surface of the Earth, and chose rather to sell than to eat his better Sort of Provision, in order to augment and increase her Portion. The old Farmer thought he had bestow'd his Labour to a good Purpose, since he had met with a blest Opportunity, wherein he should add Gentility to his Daughter's Riches. Of the Slaughter of Pigs, Geese and Capon, which, as to some idol, were sacrificed duly to procure our Adventurer's Favour. As he was not sparing of his Food, so was he liberal enough in sending for Wine, which he did to the Quantity of six Bottles at a time, so that the old Man was brought to this Pass, that he car'd not whether he spent his Estate on *Rumbold* or gave it him, and the Daughter was so pleas'd with the Person and Embraces of our Adventurer, that above all other Satisfactions in the World she lov'd his Company the best. The Endearments *Rumbold* and the Daughter had together are inexpressible, and the old Parents were never more pleas'd than when they saw them together, which gave our Adventurer more Opportunities of being with his Mistress than he could reason by hope for or expect. *Rumbold*'s main Design was to sift the young Woman in relation to the Quantity of Money her Father had, and where it lay. She told him that he had not above five Pounds in the House, having two or

three Days past laid out all his ready Money in a Purchase. This was no small Mortification to our Gentleman, who thought it Labour lost to stay any longer, when he could not glean the Father's Harvest, tho' he had cropt the Mother's Labour, and so resolv'd to be going, but not without one solemn Night's taking Leave of her. The Night being come, she purposely sat up till all the rest were gone to Bed. But Fortune now had a Mind to play our Adventurer an ill Turn, for he and his Mistress being too imprudently hasty in the Kitchen, both of them stumbled against two Barrels piled one on the other, and fell, and both were so entangled that they could not disengage themselves so soon, but that her Father came out crying —— In the Name of Goodness what is the Matter? And groping about, caught *Rumbold* by the naked Breech. Seeing there was no Remedy, he desir'd him to be silent, and not spread his Daughter's Disgrace, if so, he would shortly make her a Reconpence. The old Man was very much perplex'd, and could not forbear telling his Wife of what had past. They both cry'd out, that their Daughter was undone, and the Daughter was in the same Tone unless *Rumbold* would marry her

Rumbold, to colour the Matter, stay'd about three or four Days longer, and at last march'd off incognito, sending her twenty Pieces of Gold, and a Copy of Verses, which, as too plain and pertinent to the sweet Treatment that had pass'd between them, we shall at present here omit

Rumbold taking his Leave thus abruptly of the Farmer and his loving Daughter, rode a long Time, but met with no Body worthy of his Notice. Being weary, he struck into an Inn, and by the Time he had thoroughly refresh'd himself, the Evening began to approach. Upon this he mounted, and so put on. Passing by a small Coppice in a Bottom between two Hills, a Gentleman (as our Adventurer suppos'd him) well armed, and handsomely accoutred, started out upon him, and bid him deliver instantly. *Rumbold* hearing him say so, told him, if he would but have Patience he would, and with that drew out a Pocket-pistol, and fir'd at him without doing any Execution. If you are for a little Sport, reply'd the Gentleman, I'll shew you some instantly, whereupon drawing a Pistol he shot our Adventurer into the Leg, having so done, with his Sword, that hung ready at his Wrist, he neatly cut at one Blow the Reins of *Rumbold*'s Bridle, so that he was not able to manage his Horse, but he being good at Command, and used to the Charge, he gave him to understand with the winding of his Body what he was to do —— Come, Sir, said the Adversary, have you enough yet? In Faith, Sir, answer'd our Adventurer, I'll exchange but one Pistol more, and if that proves unsuccessful, I'll then submit to your Mercy. Upon this he shot but miss'd his Mark, however he kill'd his Horse, which instantly fell. The Gentleman, notwithstanding this Loss, was so nimble, that, before *Rumbold* could think what to do, he had sheathed his Sword in his Horse's Belly, which made our Adventurer come tumbling down too. Once more, said my Antagonist, we are upon equal Terms, and since the Obscurity of the Place gives us Freedom, let us try our Courage, one must fall. And upon that with his Sword, which was made for Cut and Thrust, he made a full Pass at his Body, but he put ing it by, closed in with him, and upon the Hug threw him with much Facility. Our Adventurer was surpriz'd at first, which he needed not have done, since his Nature (as he understood afterwards) was so prone to it. Having him down, Sir, said he, I shall take care of you for the future to be careful of whom you et, wherefore now yield, Sir, or I shall compel you. With

30   G g   much

much Reluctance he did, and ty'd his Hands and Feet with Cords he had for that Purpose, and so fell to rifling him. Unbuttoning his Coat to find if there was no Gold quilted therein, he wonder'd to see a Pair of Breasts so unexpectedly greater and whiter than any Man's; but being intent upon his Business, his Amazement soon vanish'd out of his Thoughts. Coming, after this, to his Breeches when he laid open, his curious Search omitted not any Place, in which he might suspect the Concealment of Money, at last, offering to remove his Shirt from between his Legs, he suddenly cry'd out, and strove to lay his Hand there, but could not ———— I beseech you, Sir, to be civil, said he. *Rumbold* imagined that some notable Treasure lay conceal'd there, and therefore he pull'd away her Shirt, (*alias* Smock) and found himself not much mistaken.

This unexpected Sight so surpriz'd him, that he look'd as if he had been converted into a Statue by the Head of some *Gorgon*, but after a little Pause he hastily unbound her, and taking her into his Arms, said, *Pardon me most courageous Amazon, for thus rudely dealing with you, it was nothing but Ignorance that caused this Error, for could my dimsighted Soul have distinguish'd what you were, the great Love and Respect I bear your Sex would have deterr'd me from contending with you, but I esteem this Ignorance of mine as the greatest Happiness, since Knowledge in this Case would have depriv'd me of the Benefit of knowing there could be so much Valour in a Woman.* For your Sake I shall for ever retain a very good Esteem for the worst of Females. Here our Adventurer paused, upon which she begg'd him not to be too tedious in his Expressions, nor pump for eloquent Phrases, alledging where they were, was no proper Place to make Orations in. But if you will declare yourself, *said she*, let us go into a Place not far distant from this, better known but to few besides myself. *Rumbold* approv'd well of her Advice, and returning what he had taken from her, follow'd her through several obscure Passages, till they came to a Wood, where in a Place the Sun had not seen since the Deluge, stood an House. At our first Approach the Servants were all in a Hurry who should obey Mrs *Virago*'s Commands, for they all knew her, being no Strangers to her Disguise, but wonder'd to see St *George* and his trusty Esquire on Foot, neither durst they shew themselves inquisitive presently.

After some short Time they were conducted into a very fine Apartment, where embracing one another, they tied an indissolvable Tie of Friendship. Having refresh'd themselves with what the House afforded, they began to discourse together with the same Familiarity as if they had been born together. *Rumbold* observing her Frankness, press'd her to tell him what she was, and what manner of Life she led. Sir, *said she*, I cannot deny your Request, wherefore to satisfy you, know I was the Daughter of a Swordcutler in my younger Days my Mother would have taught me to handle a Needle, but my martial Spirit gainsaid all Persuasions to that Purpose, I could never endure to be among Utensils of the Kitchen, but spent most of my Time in my Father's Shop, taking wonderful Delight in handling the Warlike Instruments he made. To take a Sword in my Hand well mounted and brandish it, was reckon'd by me among the chief of my Recreations. Being about a dozen Years of Age, I studied by all Ways imaginable how I might make myself acquainted with a Fencing-Master. Time brought my Desires to their Compliment, for such a one as I wish'd for accidentally came into my Father's Shop to have his Blade furbished, and Fortune so order'd it, there was none

to answer but myself. Having given him that Satisfaction he desired, tho' not expecting it from me, among other Questions, I ask'd him, whether he was not a Professor of that noble Science? (for I guess so much by his Postures, Looks, and Expressions.) *He told me, he was a Well-wisher to it.* Being glad of this Opportunity, desiring him to conceal my Intentions, I begg'd the Favour of him to give me some Instructions how I should manage a Sword. At first he seem'd amaz'd at my Proposal, but perceiving I was in Earnest, he granted my Petition, allotting me such a Time to come so aim as was most convenient. I became so expert at Backsword and Single Rapier in a little Time, that I needed not his Assistance any longer, my Parents not in the least mistrusting any such Thing.

I shall wave what Exploits I did by the Help of my Disguise, and only tell you, that when I arriv'd to the Age of fifteen Years, an Inn-keeper marred me, and carried me into the Country. For two Years we liv'd very peaceably and comfortably together, but at length the violent and imperious Temper of my Husband made me shew my natural Humour. Once a Week we seldom miss'd of a Combat betwixt us, which frequently prov'd so sharp, that it was a wonder if my Husband came off with a single broken Pate, by which the gaping Wounds of our Discontents and Differences being not presently salved up, they became in a manner incurable. I was not much inclin'd to love him, because he was of mean dastardly Spirit, and ever grieved that a Dunghill Cock should tread a Hen of the Game. Being tainted likewise of Money, my Life grew altogether comfortless, and I look'd on my Condition as insupportable, wherefore as the only Remedy or Expedient to mitigate my vexatious Troubles, I contriv'd a way now I might sometimes take a Purse. I judged this Resolve on safe enough, if I were not taken in the very Fact, for who could suspect me to be a Robber, wearing Abroad Men's Apparel upon such Designs, but at Home that which was more agreeable and suitable to my Sex, besides no one could have better Encouragement and Conveniency than myself, for, keeping an Inn, who is more proper to have in Custody what Charge my Guests brought into my House than myself? or is committed to my Husband's Tutelage, I could not fail to inform myself of the Richness of the Booty. Besides, the Landlady is the Person whose Company is most desired, before whom they are no ways scrupulous to relate which way they are going, and frequently what the Affair was that led them that Way.

Courage, I knew, I wanted not (be you my impartial Judge, Sir) what then could hinder me from being successful in such an Enterprize? Being thus resolv'd, I soon provided my necessary Habiliments for these my Contrivances, and never miscarried in any of them till now. Instead of riding to Market, or travelling five or six Miles about such a Business, (the usual Pretences with which I blinded my Husband) I would, when out of Sight, take a contrary Road to this House (in which we now are) and me tamorphose myself, and being fitted at all Points, pad incontroulably, coming off always victoriously. Not long since my Husband had about one hundred Pounds due to him about some twenty Miles from his Habitation, and design'd such a Day for receiving it. Glad I was to hear of this, resolving now to be reveng'd on him for all those Injuries and churlish Outrages he had committed against me. I knew very well which Way he went, and understood the Time of his coming Home. Upon which I Way-laid him at his Return, and fortunately,

nately, as I would have it, he did not make me wait above three Hours for him

I let him pass by me, knowing that by the Swiftness of my Horſe I cou'd eaſily overtake him, and ſo I did, riding with him a Mile or two before I cou'd do my intended Buſineſs At laſt looking about me, I ſaw the Coaſt clear on every Side, wherefore riding up cloſe to him, and taking hold on his Bridle, I clapt a Piſtol to his Breaſt, commanding him to deliver, or he was a dead Man This imperious Don ſeeing Death before his Face, had like to have ſav'd me the Labour, by dying voluntarily without Complaiſion, and ſo amaz'd was he at his being ſo ſuddenly ſurpriz'd, that he look'd like an Apparition, or one lately riſen from the Dead Sirrah, ſaid I, be expeditious, but a dead Palſy had ſo ſeiz'd every Part of him, that his Eyes were incapable of directing his Hands to his Pockets, but I ſoon recall'd his Spirits by two or three Blows with the Flat of my Sword, which ſo awaken'd him out of the deep Lethargy he was in, that, with much Submiſſion, he deliver'd all his Money After I had diſmounted him, and cut the Reins of his Bridle and Girts, I banſked him ſo ſoundly, till I had made almoſt Jelly of his Bones, and Egyptian Mummy of his Fleſh *Now you Rogue, ſaid I, I am even with you, have a Care the next time how you ſtrike a Woman, (your Wife I mean) for another ſuch as dare not fight a Man will lift up his Hand againſt the weaker Veſſel Now you ſee what it is to provoke them, for if irritated too much, they are reſtleſs till they accompliſh their Revenge to Satisfaction, I have a good Mind to end your wicked Croſſes with your Life, inhuman Varlet, but that I am loto to be hang'd for nothing, I mean for ſuch a worthleſs Man Farewel, this Money ſhall ſerve me to purchaſe Wine to drink Health to the Confuſion of ſuch raſcally and mean-ſpirited Things* And ſo I left him

She was about to proceed on farther with her Rencounters and Exploits, when Word was brought her up, that two Gentlemen below deſired to ſpeak with her, and ſo begging our Adventurer's Excuſe, ſhe went down, and in a little Time return'd with them She made an Apology to me for doing ſo, adding, that if ſhe had committed a Crime herein, my future Knowledge of thoſe Perſons wou'd extenuate it by their effeminate Countenances I cou'd not miſ-obliging who they were, I mean Females

What the female Warrior had advanc'd was too much, to having diſcourſed to her ſome time, Rumbold grew ſo well pleaſed with his new Acquaintance, that he reſolv'd to ſpend ſome Time in their Converſation and Company At the Time of going to Bed they were all conducted into one Chamber, where two Beds were, but what Satisfaction they enjoy'd there, we leave to the Thoughts of our candid Readers, who, we hope, can conſtrue as well as we The ſo, our Adventurer riſing betimes in the Morning, and finding his three Ions in faſt ſleep, examin'd the Pockets of the two laſt, out of which ſhe got a dozen Guineas, the very Sum he had returned to the firſt, ſo got his Horſe, and rode off

Rumbold having a long time obſerv'd a Goldſmith in Lombard-Street to be very intent in counting ſeveral Bags of Money, was reſolved to have a Share out of ſome of them, but, having tried ſeveral Eſſays, ſtill came off diſappointed He had ſeveral Rings about him which he had got by robbing, one of which had a very fine Diamond ſet in it Money being wanting, and ſo many Diſappointments croſſing his Deſires, he went to the Goldſmith's to ſell him the Ring, in Company with a Servant he kept On entring the Shop, he pull'd the Ring off his Finger, and aſk'd him what it was worth? The Goldſmith looking on him, and then on the Ring,

hoping to make the Ring his own for a ſmall Matter, and ſeeing our Adventurer (who had diſguis'd himſelf in a plain Country Dreſs) believ'd that he had little Skill in Diamonds, and that this came accidentally into his Poſſeſſion, and that he might purchaſe it very eaſily, wherefore being doubtful what to anſwer as to the Price, told the Countryman that the Worth of it was uncertain, for he could not directly tell whether it was a right or a counterfeit One As for that, ſaid our pretended Countryman, I believe it is a right One, and dare warrant it, and indeed I intend to ſell it, and therefore would know what you intend to give me for it Truly, reply'd the Goldſmith, it may be worth ten Pounds, yes, and more Money, ſaid the Countryman, not much more, anſwered the Goldſmith, for look you here, ſaid he, here is a Ring, which I will warrant is much better than yours, and I will alſo warrant it to be a good Diamond, and I will ſell it you for twenty Pounds This the Goldſmith ſaid ſuppoſing that the Countryman, who came to ſell, had no Skill, Inclination, or Money to buy, but our pretended Countryman believing that the Goldſmith only ſaid this, thinking to draw him on to part with his own Ring the more eaſily, and by that Means cheat him, reſolved if he could to be too wiſe for the Goldſmith, wherefore taking both the Rings into his Hands through a Pretence of comparing them together, he thus ſaid, I am ſure mine is a right Diamond, and ſo is mine replied the Goldſmith, and ſaid the Countryman ſhall I have it for twenty Pound? yes, replied the Goldſmith But ſaid he, I ſuppoſe you came to ſell and not to buy; and ſince you ſhall ſee I will be a good Cuſtomer, I will give you fifteen Pounds for yours Nay, replied the Countryman, ſince I have free Choice to buy or ſell, I will never refuſe a good Pennyworth, as I think this is, therefore maſter Goldſmith I will keep my own, and give you Money for your's, where is it, ſaid the Goldſmith haſtily? and endeavouring then to ſeize on his Ring, hold a Blow there ſaid Rumbold, here's your Money, but the Ring I will keep The Goldſmith ſeeing himſelf thus cheated, fretted and flounced like a Madman, and Rumbold pulling out a little Purſe, told down twenty Pieces of Gold, and ſaid, here Shopkeeper, here's your Money, but I hope you will allow me eighteen Pence a Piece in Exchange for my Gold Tell not me of Exchange, but give me my Ring, ſaid the Goldſmith It is mine, ſaid the Countryman, I have bought it, and paid for it, and have Witneſs of my Bargain All this would not ſerve the Goldſmith's Turn, but he curs'd and ſwore that Rumbold, the pretended Countryman, came to cheat him, and his Ring he would have, and at the Noiſe ſeveral People came about the Shop, but he was ſo perplex'd that he could not tell his Tale, and at length a Conſtable came, and altho' the Goldſmith knew not to what Purpoſe, yet before a Juſtice he would go Rumbold ſeem'd content, and therefore before a Juſtice they went together, when they came there, the Goldſmith, who was the Plaintiff, began his Tale, and ſaid, that the Countryman had taken a Diamond Ring from him worth one hundred Pounds, and would give him but twenty Pounds for it Have a Care, replied Rumbold, for if you charge me with taking a Ring from you I ſuppoſe that is ſtealing, and if you ſay ſo, I ſhall vex you more than I have yet done, and then he told the Juſtice the whole Story as here related, which was then a very plain Caſe, and for Proof of the Matter, our pretended Country Gentleman's Man was a Witneſs The Goldſmith hearing this, alledged, that he believed the Country Gentleman and his Man were both Impoſtors and Cheats To this our Adventurer reply'd as before, that he had beſt have a Care he did not make his Caſe worſe, and bring an old Houſe over

his

his Head by flandering him thus; for it was well known that he was a Gentleman of Three Hundred Pounds *per Annum*, and lived at a Place not above twenty Miles from *London*, and that he being defirous to fell a Ring, came to his Shop for that Purpofe, but he would have cheated him, but it prov'd that he only made a Rod for his own Breech, and what he intended to him was fallen upon himfelf Thus did our Adventurer make good his Cafe and the Juftice feeing there was no Injuftice done, difmifs'd him, but order'd that his Neighbour the Goldfmith fhould have the twenty Pieces of Gold for twenty Pound, though they were worth more in Exchange, and this was all the Satisfaction he had

Rumbold had a mighty itching after the Goldfmith's Money in *Lombard-Street*, he would not pafs thro' that Street, and hear thofe Tradefmen telling their Sums, but his Hands longed to be feeling of them He had a Boy that conftantly attended him, who, every Time his Mafter had a Mind to make fome Advantage to himfelf, went into a Goldfmith's Shop, took up an handful of Money, and then letting it all fall down on the Counter, ran out Once on a Time this Boy performed this Trick, the Servants in the Shop ran after him, and taxed him with ftealing fome of the Money. *Rumbold*, who always vindicated his Youngfter, bid them take Care what they faid, and pofitively affirm'd that his Boy had not taken a Farthing, and muft be fo plain with them, as to tell them, that the Goldfmith fhould pay for it Hereupon they fell to hot Words, and the Goldfmith calling our Adventurer a fhirking Fellow, faid, he would have both him and the Boy fent to *Newgate* for robbing him, and that in Conclufion, he muft, and fhould pay for it At firft our Adventurer defired to know with what Sum they pretended to charge the Boy, they faid they knew not, but that he had taken Money from a Heap they were telling, and which was a hundred Pounds.

Rumbold hearing them fay thus, told them, that he would ftay the telling of it, and then they might judge who had the Abufe. They were content with it, and accordingly went to telling Half an Hour had difpatch'd that Matter, and then they found all their Money was right to a Farthing; the Goldfmith feeing this, afk'd our Adventurer's Pardon for the Affront they had done him, faying it was a Miftake. *Rumbold* anfwered to this, that he muft pay for his prating, and that being a Perfon of Quality, he would not put up with the Affront, and that he muft expect to hear further from him. The Goldfmith feeing our Adventurer hot, was as cholerick as he, and fo they parted for that Time. *Rumbold*, the next Day got the Goldfmith to be arrefted in an Action of Defamation, and the Serjeant who arrefted him being well feed by our Adventurer, told the Goldfmith, that he had better by far compound the Matter, for the Gentleman he had injured was a Perfon of Quality, and would not put it up, but make him pay foundly for it, if he proceeded any farther The Goldfmith being defirous of Quiet, hearkened to his Counfel, and agreed to give ten Pounds, but that would not be taken, but twenty Pounds was given to our Adventurer, and fo the Bufinefs was made up for the prefent.

Rumbold having got fome of the Goldfmith's Money, was determined to have more, or venture hard for it, wherefore having again given inftructions to his Boy what to do, he made feveral Journeys to the Goldfmith's, walking by his Door to watch an Opportunity, at length he found one; for feeing the Servants telling a confiderable Quantity of Gold, he gave the Sign to the Boy, who prefently went in, and clapping his Hand on the Heap, took up, and brought

away a full Handful, and coming to his Mafter, gave it him. neither did the Boy make fo much Hafte out the Shop, but that he could hear a Stranger who was in the Shop receiving of Money, fay to the Apprentice, *Why do not you ftop the Boy? No*, faid the Apprentice, *I do not mean it, I know him well enough, my Mafter paid Sauce lately for ftopping of him*, and fo they continued telling of their Money

Rumbold being intimately acquainted with a Jeweller in *Fofter-Lane*, whom he often helped to the Sale of Rings and Jewels, which made his Credit good with him, went one Time into his Work-Room, and chancing to fpy a very rich Jewel, he told him, that he could help him to the Sale thereof My Lady fuch a one having fpoke to me, faid he, about fuch a Thing The Jeweller, glad of the Opportunity, delivered it to our Adventurer at fuch a Price to fell for him But *Rumbold* only carried it to another Workman, to have another made like it with counterfeit Stones Before he went, he afk'd if the Lady diflik'd it, whether he might leave it with his Wife or Servant Ay, ay, fays he, either will be fufficient *Rumbold* was forced to watch a whole Day to fee when he went out, and being gone, prefently went to the Shop, and enquired of the Wife for her Hufband, fhe anfwered him that he was but juft gone Well, Madam, faid he, you can do my Bufinefs as well as he, 'tis only to deliver thefe Stones into your Cuftody, and fo he went his way

Not long after, *Rumbold* met the Jeweller in the Street with difpleafing Looks, Sir, faid he, I thought a Friend would not have ferved me fo, but our Adventurer deny'd it ftifly, whereupon he was very angry, and told him he would profecute him *Rumbold* feem'd not to value his Threats, and fo left him *Rumbold* was not gone many Paces before he met with a Friend, who complain'd to him, that he had loft a very valuable Locket of his Wife's, it being ftolen from her *Rumbold* was glad to hear of fuch a Circumftance that had fallen out fo favourably to his prefent Purpofe, he afk'd him to give him a Defcription of it, which he did punctually. Now, faid *Rumbold*, what will you give me, if I tell you where it is Any thing in Reafon Then go to fuch a Shop in *Fofter Lane*, (the fame Shop where he had cheated the Man of his Ring) and there afk'd peremptorily for it, for I was there at fuch a Time, and faw it, nay he would have had me help'd him to a Cuftomer for it Mean Time, I'll ftay at the *Star* Tavern for you Away he went and demanded his Locket The Jeweller deny'd he had any fuch Thing (as well he might) Upon this, *Rumbold* advifed him to have a Warrant for him, and to fetch him before a Juftice of the Peace, and that he, and the Perfon who was with him, would fwear it The Goldfmith was inftantly feized on by a Conftable, and as foon as he faw who they were that would fwear againft him, defired the Gentleman to drink a Glafs of Wine, and then ordered him Satisfaction But *Rumbold* had fo ordered the Bufinefs that it would not be taken, unlefs he would give all three general Releafe. The Goldfmith knowing the Danger that might enfue to Life and Eftate if he perfifted, confented to the Propofal

Rumbold walking one time in the Fields with an Attendant or two, who fhould be conftantly bare before him, if in Company with any Perfon of Quality, but otherwife, *kind Fellow well met* He was got as far as *Hackney* before he knew he was, for his Thoughts were bufied in forming Defigns, and his Wit was contriving how to put them into Execution Cafting his Eye on one Side of him, he faw the prettieft built and well fituated Houfe that ever his Eyes beheld He had immediately a covetous Defire to be Mafter thereof. he was then, as Fortune would

have

have it in very handsome Dress He walk'd but a little Way farther before he found out a Plot to accomplish his Desires, and thus it was He return'd and knock'd at the Gate, and demanded of the Servant whether his Master was within? He understood he was, and thereupon desir'd to speak with him The Gentleman came out to him himself, and desir'd him to walk in After *Rumbold* had made a general Apology, he told him his Business, which was only to request the Favour of him, that he might have the Privilege to bring a Workman to survey his House, and to take his Dimensions thereof, because he was so well pleas'd with the Building, that he earnestly desir'd to have another built exactly after the same Pattern The Gentleman could do no less than grant him so much Civility Coming home, he went to a Carpenter, telling him he was about buying a House at *Hackney*, and that he would have him go along with him, to give him (in private) the Estimate Accordingly they went and found the Gentleman at Home, who entertain'd our Adventurer kindly as a Stranger In the mean Time the Carpenter took an exact Account of the Buts and Bounds of the House on Paper, which was as much as he desired at that Time

Paying the Carpenter well, he dismiss'd him, and by that Paper had a Lease drawn with a very great Fine (mentioned to have been paid) at a small Rent Witnesses he could not want to his Deed, and shortly after he demanded Possession The Gentleman thinking our Adventurer out of his Wits, only laugh'd at him *Rumbold* commenced a Suit of Law against him, and produc'd his Creatures to swear to his sealing and Delivery of the Lease, and the Carpenter's Evidence, with many other probable Circumstances to corroborate his Cause, whereupon he had a Verdict The Gentleman by this Time understanding who our Adventurer was, thought it safer to compound with him, and lose something rather than all

Another Time putting on one of the best Suits of Cloaths he had, he went to a Scrivener in *Bow-lane*, and acquainted him how he had a present Occasion for an hundred Pounds He demanded the Names of his Securities *Rumbold* told him where they liv'd, being Persons of eminent Worth, (but our Adventurer knew they were out of Town at that Juncture) and desir'd to make Enquiry, but to be private in the gaing of it The Scrivener accordingly went as he had desired him, and found them by Report to be what they were, really able and sufficient Men Two or three Days after *Rumbold* call'd upon him to know whether he might have the Money upon the Security propounded? He told him that he might on bringing the Persons, and nam'd a Day for meeting According to the Day he came with two of his Accomplices, dress'd like rich Citizens, who personated such Persons to the Life, that the Scrivener could not entertain the least Suspicion The Money being ready, he told it over, and put it into a Bag, upon which our Adventurer and his insignificant Bonds-men sealed the Writing, leaving the Scrivener to another Enquiry after them, whom, if he did not mean, 'twas very sufficiently to be believ'd that he could never find them, by reason of the several Names they went by It chanced that *Rumbold's* forged Name was the same with that of a Gentleman's in *Surrey*, who was a great Purchaser, which our Adventurer came to know by being accidentally in his Company the next Night after he had cheated the credulous Scrivener, understanding likewise the exact Place of his Abode, and as the D——l would have it his Christian Name was the same as well as his Sirname with that of our Adventurer's, which he had borrowed Upon this he went to the Scrivener again, and told him that now he had a fair Opportunity of benefiting himself very much by a Purchase, provided he wou'd assist him with two hundred Pounds more But, Sir, *said he,* take Notice (in a careless and generous Frankness) that it is out of a particular Regard and Respect to you that you might have profit by me, that I come again, neither will I give you any other Security than my own Bond, tho' I did otherwise before, but if you will be satisfy'd as to my Estate, pray let your Servant go to such a Place in *Surrey*, there is a Piece of Gold to bear his Charges, and I will satisfy you farther for the the Loss of Time occasion'd by sending him He being very greedy of Gain, very officiously promised to do what I requir'd, and would speedily give me an Answer Imagining what Time his Servant would return, *Rumbold* repaired to him again, and understood from him by the Sequel, that he had receiv'd as much Satisfaction as in Reason any Man wou'd desire Upon this he procured the two hundred Pounds upon his own Bond; which was accordingly paid him

Rumbold supported himself by these Cheats a considerable Time, tho' unlike his Companions, he was never known to be very extravagant He had amassed together a matter of eight hundred Pounds clear, and resolving to leave off in Time, put the Money into the Hand of a Banker a Friend of his, in order to live the Remainder of his Days comfortably on the Interest thereof, he had the Mortification, within a Month or two, to hear that his Trustee was march'd off not only with his Money, but a great many thousand Pounds more of other Peoples, so that being reduc'd to an impoverish'd State, he was forc'd, tho' somewhat against his Inclination, to betake himself again to his former irregular Courses, several merry Pranks of whom the Sequel will soon discover

Rumbold having a Design of robbing a Gentleman's House near *Uxbridge*, put up at an Inn in that Town, in order, on the first Opportunity, to put his Scheme in practice Several Companies were in the House, and lodg'd there, and it being the time of long Nights, much of that tedious Time was spent in Gaming and merry Conversation with one another. All Companies join'd with Pastime, but it growing late, they that were weary and sleepy dropp'd away to Bed, among the rest, a Man who had a very handsome Wife went to Bed, and his Lodging was in a Chamber where there was another Bed The Man being in Bed laid his Wearing-Cloaths upon him, and putting out the Candle went to sleep A little Time after our Adventurer, who was to lie in the Bed in the same Chamber, came up, and walking about, a Conceit came into his Head, that it was probable he might have a She-bedfellow, and in order thereto he thus carry'd on his Device, he put off his own Cloaths, and laid them very orderly on the Bed where the Man was asleep, first taking off those of his Chamber-fellows, and when he had done, he very fairly spread them on the Bed he was to lie in, and having done thus, he went to Bed and put out his Candle, and expecting the Event, which fell out according to his Hopes, for not long after up came the Woman intending to go to Bed to her Husband, undress'd herself, and feeling, and very well knowing her Husband's Cloaths, believing that to be a sufficient Sign of her Husband's being there, not looking on the Face, which was purposely hid, she put out the Candle and went to Bed to our Adventurer, who altho' he pretended to be then asleep, yet he did her Right before Morning, for she still supposing it was her Husband, gave him free Liberty to do what he would Her Bedfellow,

fellow, tho' he had taken much Pains, and was weary, yet towards Morning, confidering that if this Matter was discover'd, he might have fower Sauce to his Sweet Meat, studied and contrived how to come off as well as he had come on, and therefore turning to his Bedfellow and kissing her, &c. as a Farewel, he, pretending to rise and make Water, went out of the Bed, he soon found his Way to his Chamber-fellow's Bed side, and there took off his Cloaths, dress'd himself and departed. The Woman missing her Bedfellow, whom all the while she had took for her Husband, wonder'd much what was become him, and coy and studied in great Confusion without knowing either what to do or say, at length she began to mistrust she had wrong'd her Bedfellow, especially when she began to consider with herself that her Husband was not wont to be so kind. When she was partly sensible of the Mistake, she could not tell how to think of a Remedy, if she should arise and go into the other Bed, she might chance to be mistaken again, and therefore in this Confusion she knew not what to do. While she was in these Thoughts, a Maid with a Candle appear'd, who passing through the Room, gave her a clear View that her Husband was in the other Bed, accordingly she resolv'd to take her Cloaths and go to Bed to her Husband, but he who had slept hard all Night, was now awaken'd with the Noise of the Maid's passing through the Chamber, and therefore he crept out of Bed, and felt for a Chamber-pot, at length having found one, and us'd it, and going to return to Bed where had lain, his Wife then took the Opportunity to call to him, saying, *My Dear, whither are you going? You mistake your Bed. No, sure,* said the Man, *Where are you? Here,* reply'd she. He hearing her Voice, soon found out where she was, but could not presently be persuaded that he had lain there all Night. *You shall see that by and by,* said she, *when you can see your Cloaths on this Bed. If it be so, then you are in the right,* answer'd he. In fine, getting him to sleep again, she, in the Interim, got his Cloaths laid on the Bed, and Day-light coming on, and he seeing them there, was satisfy'd. Thus was this *Christmas* Adventure ended. She, towards one in the Morning, made great Enquiry after her Bedfellow, but no Tidings could be given of him.

Another time *Rumbold* coming early one Morning to an Inn in the Country, called for a Flaggon of Beer, and desir'd a private Room, for, *said he,* I have Company coming to me, and we have Business together. The Tapster accordingly shews him a Room, and brings him a Flaggon of Beer, and with it a Silver Cup worth three Pounds. *Rumbold* drank off his Beer, and call'd for another Flaggon, and at the same time desir'd the Landlord to bear him Company. The Landlord seeing him alone, sat and talk'd with him about State Affairs till they were both weary, and the Landlord was ready to leave him. *Well,* said our Adventurer, *I see my Company will not come, and therefore I will not stay any longer.* Neither did he, but having drunk up his Beer, he call'd to pay *Fourpence,* said the Tapster, *There it is,* answer'd our Adventurer, laying it down, and so he went out of the Room. The Tapster staid behind to bring away the Flaggon and Silver Cup, yet tho' he found the Flaggon, the Cup was not to be found, wherefore running hastily out of the Room, he cry'd, *Stop the Man. Rumbold* was not in such haste but that he quietly stopt of himself, he was not quite gone out of the Doors, and therefore soon return'd to the Bar, where when he was come. *Well,* said he, *what is the Matter? What would you have?* The Cup, answer'd the Tapster,

that I brought you. *I left it in the Room,* reply'd *Rumbold, I cannot find it,* answer'd the Tapster, and at this Noise the Landlord appear'd, who hearing what was the Matter, said, *I am sure the Cup was there but just now, for I drank out of it by, and it is there for me,* reply'd our Adventurer. *Look then further,* said the Landlord. The Tapster did so, but neither high nor low could he find the Cup. *Well then* said the Landlord, *if it be gone you must pay for it, Countryman, for you must either have it or know of its going, and therefore you must pay for it. Not I indeed,* reply'd our Adventurer, *you see I have none of it, I have not been out of your House, nor no Body has been with me, how then can I have it? You may search me.* The Landlord immediately caus'd him to be search'd, but there was no Cup to be found. However the Landlord was resolved not to lose his Cup so, and therefore he sent for a Constable, and charged him with our Adventurer, and threaten'd him with the Justice. All this would not do, and *Rumbold* told him, *That threaten'd Folk live long,* and if he would go before a Justice, he was ready to bear him Company to him. The Landlord was more and more perplex'd at this, and seeing he could not have his Cup, nor nothing confess'd, before the Justice they went. When they came, the Landlord told the Story as truly as it was, and our pretended Countryman made the same Answer there as he had done before to the Landlord. The Justice was perplex'd, not knowing how to do Justice. Here was a Cup lost, and *Rumbold* did not deny but he had it, but gone it was, and altho' *Rumbold* was pursued yet he did not fly, he had no Body with him, and therefore it could not be convey'd away by Confederacy, and for his own Part he had been, and was again searched, but no such Thing found about him, and he in all respects pleaded Innocency. —Tho' confider'd and weighed in the Balance of Justice, he could not think that our Adventurer had it, and therefore to commit him would be Injustice. He confider'd all he cou'd, and was inclin'd to favour the Countryman, who was altogether a Stranger, and he believed innocent, especially when he confider'd what a kind of Person the Landlord was of whose Life and Conversation he had both heard and known enough, and cause him to believe that it might be possible that all this might be a Trick of the Landlord's to cheat our Adventurer, and therefore he gave his Judgement, that he did not believe by the Evidence that was given that the Countryman had the Cup, and that he would not commit him, unless the Landlord would lay and swear point blank Felony to his Charge, and of that he order'd the Landlord to beware. The Landlord seeing how the Affair was like to go, said no more, but the he left to Mr. Justice, who being of the Opinion above-mention'd, then jg'd I could, and advised the Landlord to ... no more of such Matter, and if he could not account Plate, and know what Company he had deliver'd it to, then to keep it in. The Landlord thank'd the Justice for his Advice, and so departed, or pretended Countryman going about his Business, and he returning home being himself reviv'd at his Loss, and the ... of the whole Affair, which was neither to his Profit nor Credit, but he was forced to ... with the Loss, being extremely uneasy at it, resolving which way he should lose the Cup. He turn away some Money upon a Cunning-Man to know what was become of it, but all he could tell him was, that he would hear of it again, and so he did shortly after, tho' it was to his further Cost, and to little Purpose.

He had some Occasion to go to the Market Town

Town during the Time of the Assizes, and there seeing the Prisoners brought to their Tryals, among others he espied *Rumbold*, whom he had charged with the Silver Cup. He enquired what was his Crime, and was told it was for picking of a Pocket. Na, then, said the Landlord, *probably I may hear of my Cup again*, and therefore, when the Tryal was over, and the Prisoners carried back to the Goal, he went and enquired for our Adventurer, to whose Presence he was soon brought. O Lord, Master! how do you do? Who thought to have seen you here? I believe you have not met with so good Friends in this Country as you did in our Town of our *Squire*, but I't that pass. Come, let us drink together he upon a Jug of Ale was call'd for and some Tobacco, which they very lovingly drank off, and smoak'd together, which done, said the Landlord to our Adventurer, *I would gladly be resolv'd in one Point, and I question not but you can do. I suppose you may,* said Rambold, *about the old Business of the Silver Cup you lost.*——*Yes,* said the Landlord, *and the loss of it does not so much vex me, as the Manner how it was lost, and therefore,* continued he, *if you would do me the Kindness to give me Satisfaction what become of it, I do protest I will acquit you altho' you are directly guilty.* No, that will not do, reply'd Rumbold, there is somewhat else in the Case. Well then, said the Landlord, *if you will tell me, I will give you ten Shillings to drink. Ready Money does very well in a Prison,* said our Adventurer, *and will prevail much, but how shall I be assur'd that you will not prosecute me, if I should declare to be concern'd. For that,* reply'd the Landlord, *I assure you no other Warrant than my Oath, which I will inviolably keep. Well then,* said Rumbold, *do a with the merry Gigs, let me handle the None, and I'll be very true to you,* and as for your charging me with it I fear you not.

The Landlord being big with Expectation to know how this clean Conveyance was wrought, soon laid down the ten Shillings, when our Countryman thus proceeded "I must confess that I know which Way "your Cup went, but when you charg'd me with it "I did it not, neither was it out of the Room, "and I must tell you that, that if you had sought more "closely you might then have found it, but it was not there "long but. We who live by our Wits must all by "Policy more than Courage; Strength and raise our "not be done without Confederates, and I had such "in the Management of this Affair, for I left the Cup "I am with soft Wax under the Middle of the "Board of the Table where I am with, which Piece of "the Table, by reason it was cover'd with a Cloth, "as well I remember it was, it could be or would be "seen, and therefore you and your Servants miss'd "it. You know that very willingly I went with you "to the Justice, and whilst we were gone those "Friends and Confederates of mine, whom I had p——"ll said, and who first saw the Room and every thing "he, went to the House, and into the same Room, "where they found the Silver Cup, and without the "least Suspicion went fairly off with it, and at a "Place appointed we met, and there acquainted one "another with our Adventures, and what Purchases "we had made, we equally shared them between us. "The Landlord at the hearing this Discourse was extreamly surpriz'd, altho' full satisfy'd, but yet, "said he, I would be resolv'd one Question, which "is this, How is't we ne'er found it where you had "put it whilst you were there? Why, truly, said "Rumbold, then you could have charg'd me with "nothing and I would have put it off with a Jest, "and that would not have done, the most you could "have done would have been only to have kick'd and

"beaten me, as I those Things we of our Quality "must venture. You know the old Proverb, Nothing "venture, nothing have, and a stout heart never "won't fail I dy. And we have this other Proverb "to help us, *Fortune favours the Bold*, as it commonly does those of our Quality, and she did me, I "thank her in that Attempt." Rumbold thus descanted upon his Actions, and the Landlord finding no likelihood of getting his Cup or any Thing else of our Adventurer, return'd Home.

We shall give our Readers now the last Adventure of *Rumbold* which he perform'd upon this mortal Stage. It is this.

Our Adventurer in Company with two or three more Clerks going together, saw a Countryman who had a Purse of Money in his Hand, they had observ'd him to draw it out to pay for some Gingerbread he had bought on the Road, wherefore they clos'd with him, and once would to nip his Bung, pick his Pocket, but could not, for he knowing he was in a dangerous Place, and among as dangerous Company, put his Purse of Money into his Breeches, which being close to the Knees, secur'd it from falling out, and besides he was very sly in having any Body come too near him. Our Practitioners in the Art of Thieving seeing this would not do, set their Wits to working further, and having all their Tools ready about them, taking a convenient Time and Place, one of them goes before and drop a Letter, another of our Adventurers who had joined himself to the Countryman, seeing he lie fairly for the Purpose, says to him, *Look you what is here?* But altho' the Countryman did stoop to take it up, yet our Adventurer was too nimble for him in that, and, having it in Hand, said, *Here is somewhat else befals a Letter Crier, Half,* said the Countryman. *Well,* said Rumbold, *you stoop indeed as well as I, but I have it, however I will be fair with you, let us see what it is,* and whether it is worth the dividing, and thereupon he breaks open the Letter, and therein sees a fair Chain or Necklace of Gold. *Good Fortune,* says Rumbold *if this be right Gold. How shall we know that,* reply'd the Countryman, *let us see what the Letter says,* which being short, and to the Purpose, spoke thus.

Brother John,

I Have here sent you back this Necklace of Gold you have sent me, not for any Dislike I have to it, but my Wife is covetous, and would have a bigger, this comes not to above seven Pounds, and she would have one of ten Pounds, therefore pray get it chang'd for one of that Price, and send it by the Bearer to your loving Brother,

Jacob Thornton.

Nay then, we have good Luck, said the creating Dog our Adventurer, but I hope, continued he to the Countryman, you will not expect a full Share, for you know I found it, and besides, if we could divide it, I now not how to break it in Piece, but I doubt it would spoil it, therefore I had rather have my Share in Money. Well, said the Countryman, I'll give you your Share in Money, provided I may have a full Share. That you shall, said Rumbold, and therefore I must have of you three Pounds ten Shillings, the Price will be nine, you see seven Pounds. Ay, but said the Countryman, (though thinking to be too cunning for our Adventurer) it may be worth ten Pound in Money Fashion and all, but we must not value that, but only the Gold, therefore I think three Pounds in Money is better than half the Chain, and so much I'll give you it you'll let me have it. Well, I'm contented, said Rumbold, but then you shall give me a Pint of Wine over and above. To this the Countryman also agreed, and to a Tavern they went,

where

where *Rumbold* receiv'd the three Pounds, and the Countryman the Chain, who believ'd he had risen that Day with his Arse upwards, because he had met with so good Fortune　They drank off their Wine, and were going away, but *Rumbold* having not yet done with him, intended to get the rest of the Money from him, offered him his Pint of Wine, which the Countryman accepted of, but before they had drank it off, in comes another of the same Tribe, who asked whether such a Man, naming one, were there? *No*, said the Bar keeper, *Rumbold* and the Countryman sitting near the other Cheat all the while, asked of the Enquirer, Did not you enquire for such a Man? Yes, *said the Enquirer*　Why, said *Rumbold*, I can tell you this News of him, that it will not be long before he comes hither, for I met him as I came in, and he appointed me to come in here and stay for him　Well, then 'tis best for me to stay, said the Enquirer, but, continued he, it would be more proper for us to take a larger Room, for we cannot stir ourselves in this　Agreed, said *Rumbold*, so the Reckoning was paid, and they agreed to take a larger Room, leaving Word at the Bar, that if any Enquiry should be made for them, there they should find them, accordingly they went into another Room, and the Countryman having done his Business, gave Signs of going away　No, said *Rumbold*, I beg you would stay and keep us Company, it shall not cost you any thing　Well then, said the Countryman, I am content to stay a little　They being now entred into their Room, called for a Quart of Wine, and drank it off　What shall we do to spend our Time, said the last Cheat? For I am weary of staying for this Man, are you sure you are not mistaken? No, said the other　One of them upon this pretended to walk a Turn round the Room, and coming to the Window, behind a Cushion, finds a Pack of Cards, which indeed he himself had laid there · Look you here, said he to the Countryman, and the others, I have found some Fools, now we may go to work and spend our Time, if you will play Not I, said the Countryman, I'll not play, then I will, said *Rumbold*, but not for Money　Why then, said the other, for Sixpence to be spent, and the Game shall be Putt　They having agreed, and the Countryman being made Overseer of the Game, fell to playing, and the Countryman's first Acquaintance had the better of it, winning twelve Games to the other's four　Come, said he, what shall we do with all this Drink? We will play Two-pence wet, and Four-pence dry　To this the other agreed, and so they play'd, and at this low Gaming *Rumbold* had, in short, won of his Confederate ten Shillings in Money　The Looser seem'd to be angry, and therefore proposed to play for all Money, hoping to make himself whole again　Nay, said the other, I shall not refuse your Proposition, because I have won your Money; and therefore to it they went, and *Rumbold* had still the same Luck, and won ten Shillings more　Then the other would play for Twelve-pence a Game　No, said *Rumbold*, I am not willing to exceed Six-pence a Game, I will not alter what I have began, lest I change my Fortune, unless this honest Countryman will go my Halves　I have no Mind to Gaming, reply'd the Countryman　You need not play, said the other, I'll do that, and you see my Fortune is good, venture a Crown with me, *you know we both had Fortune, which I hope will continue propitious to us still*　Well, content, said the Countryman, and so they proceeded, still *Rumbold* had good Fortune, and he and the Countryman won ten Shillings apiece more of the other, which made them merry, and the other was extremely enraged, he therefore told them, he would either win the Horse or lose the Saddle, and venture all now, and drawing out about thirty Shil-

lings, Come, take it all, win it and wear it, and so they play'd, but they had now drawn the Countryman insufficiently, and he was flush, but it lasted not long thus, before he was taken down a Button hole lower, for the Fortune chang'd, and that what he had won was lost, and forty Shillings more　He was now angry, but to no Purpose, for he did not discover their foul Play and he, in Hopes of his good Fortune, ventur'd, and lost the other forty Shillings, and then he said he would go Halves no longer, for he thought he would be merry and wise, and if he could not make a Winning, he would be sure to make a secure Bargain, which he reckon'd he should do, because altho' he had lost four Pounds in Money, and giving *Rumbold* three Pounds for his Share of the Chain, that yet he should make seven Pounds of the Chain, and so be no Loser

They seeing he would not play, left off, and he that had won the Money, was content to give a Collation, which was called for, but *Rumbold* pretending much Anger at his Loss, was resolv'd to venture more, and to playing again he went, and in a short time he recover'd a great deal of his Losses　This vexed the Countryman, that he had not join'd with him, and in the End, seeing his good Fortune continue, and that he won, he again went Halves, but it was not long that they thrived　The Countryman was obliged to draw his Purse, and in the End lost all his Money, which was near twenty Pounds. He did not think his Condition to be so bad as it was, because he believed he had a Chain worth seven Pounds in his Pocket, and therefore he reckoned he had not lost all

By this time several other Confederates (having been Abroad, employ'd on the same Account, couzening and cheating of others) came into the Tavern, which was the Place appointed for their Rendezvous, then they acquainted one another of their several Gains and Prizes, afterwards fell to drinking, which they did very plentifully, and the Countryman for Anger did led up the Landlord to make one of the Company He soon understood what kind of Guests he had in his House, and how they had cheated the poor Countryman, and therefore he was resolved to serve them in the same Sort　Accordingly he put forward the Affair of Drinking, and some being h ngred, called for Victuals　he told them he would get them what they pleas'd, and they being determin'd to take up their Quarters there for that Night, a Supper was bespoke for all the Company, such as the Master of the House in his Discretion should think fit　He told them they should have it, and accordingly went down to provide Supper　He soon return'd, and helped them off with their Liquor till Supper-time, by this Time they were all perfectly drunk, he then commands up Supper, and they fall too with a Shoulder of Mutton and two Capons, *they Eat and Drink hard, and calls for more*, he tells them; *it's coming*　But they now having got still asleep, were all fallen asleep, he makes Use of this Opportunity, and brings up half a Dozen empty foul Dishes, or at least full of Bones of several Fowls, as Pigeons, Partridge, Pheasants, and all the Remains of Victuals that had been left in the House that Day, which he strewed and placed on their Plates, and so left them　Some of them sleeping, and sitting uneasily, fell from their Chairs, and so waked themselves, and their Companions, being thoroughly awak'd, they again fell to eating and drinking, some turning over the Bones that were brought, said, *How came these here? I do not remember that I eat any such Victuals*, *Nor I*, said another, upon which the Master of the House was call'd, and the Question was ask'd him　*It by surely, Gentlemen, you have forgot yourselves*, said he; *you*

Capt Hind Robbing Col Harrison in Maidenhead - Thicke

you have slept sound and fair indeed, I believe you will forget the Collar of Brawn you had too, that cost me six Shillings out of my Pocket How, Brawn, said one A, Brawn, answer'd the Lordlord, you had it, and are like to pay for it, you'll remember nothing presently, this is a fine drunken Bout indeed So it is, reply'd one of the Company, sure we have been in a Dream, but it signifies nothing, my Landlord, you must and shall be paid, give us another Dozen Bottles, and bring us a Bill, that we may pay the Reckoning we have run up

This Order was presently obeyed, and a Bill brought, which in all came to seven Pounds, in which 'tis taken for granted, that he misreckon'd them above one Hill, tho' he acquainted them, that he had used them very kindly, they were bound to believe him, and therefore every Man was call'd for to pay his share The Countryman shrunk behind, intending to escape, which one of the Company seeing, call'd him forwards, and said, *Come, let us tell Noses, and every Man pay alike* The Countryman desired to be excused, and said he had no Money, which they knowing well enough, at length they agreed to acquit him This done, they went to their several Lodgings to Bed, and it was time, for it was past Midnight, they all slept better than the Countryman, who could hardly sleep a Wink for thinking on his Misfortunes, and having such good Fortune in the Morning, it should prove to bad before Night

But Morning being come, he and they all arose, and the Countryman's Money being all spent, he knew it was to no Purpose for him to stay there, wherefore he resolv'd to go to a Goldsmith in the City, and sell, or pawn his Chain, that he might have some Money to carry him Home Being come to the Goldsmith's, he produced the Chain, which tho' at first Sight he took to be Gold, yet upon Trial he found it otherwise, and that it was but Brass gilt, he told the Countryman the same, who, at this heavy News was like to break his Heart The Goldsmith seeing the Countryman in such a melancholy Taking, he enquired of him how he came by it He soon acquainted him with the Manner, and every Circumstance, the Goldsmith, as soon as he understood the Cheat, advised him to go to a Justice, and get a Warrant for him that had thus cheated him, and the Countryman telling him that he had no Money, nor Friend, being a Stranger, he himself went with him to the Justice, who, soon understanding the Matter, granted his Warrant, and the Goldsmith procured a Constable to go with him to the Tavern or Night-House, where *Rumbold* was apprehended, but he found Means some Way or other to make his Escape out of the House, as did the rest by main Force

After *Rumbold* had lost the Money he had put in his Friend the Banker's Hands, he was forc'd to shift after this manner, cheating and cozening any one whom he took for a Prey He narrowly escap'd being apprehended at his Lodging in *Golden lane* near *Barbican*, but at length, still pursuing his Courses of Iniquity, he was taken, and sent to *Newgate*, when after five or six Days Imprisonment, he receiv'd his Trial at the *Old Bailey*, was condemned, and executed at *Tyburn*

The LIFE *of* Capt. JAMES HIND.

THE Father of Capt *Hind* was a Sadler, an Inhabitant of *Chipping-Norton in Oxfordshire*, where the Captain was born The old Man lived there many Years in very good Reputation among his Neighbours, was an honest Companion, and a constant Churchman As *James* was his only Son, he was willing to give him the best Education he was able, to that Purpose sent him to School till he was fifteen Years of Age, in which Time he learned to read and write very well, and knew Arithmetick enough to make him capable of any common Business

After this he was put Apprentice to a Butcher in his Native Town, where he served about two Years of his Time, and then ran away from his Master, who was a very morose Man, and continually finding something or another to quarrel with him about When he made this Elopement, he applied immediately to his Mother for Money to carry him up to *London*, telling her a lamentable Story of the Hardships he suffer'd from his Master's Severity Mothers are generally easily wrought upon with Stories of that Kind, she therefore very tenderly supplied him with three Pounds for his Expences, and sent him away with Tears in her Eyes

He had not been long in *London* before he got a Relish of the Pleasures of the Place (Pleasures I call them in Compliance with the Opinion of Gentlemen of the Captain's Taste) I mean, the Enjoyment of his Bottle and his Mistress, both which, as far as his Circumstances would allow, he pursued very earnestly One Night he was taken in Company with a Woman of the Town, who had just before picked a Gentleman's Pocket of five Guineas, and sent with her to the *Poultry Compter* till Morning, when he was released for want of any Evidence against him, he having, in Reality, no Hand in the Affair The Woman was committed to *Newgate*, but what became of her afterwards we are not certain, nor does it at all concern us The Captain by this Accident fell into Company with one *Thomas Allen*, a noted Highwayman, who had been put into the Compter upon Suspicion of some Robbery, and was released at the same Time with *Hind*, and for the same Reason These two Men going to drink together, after their Confinement, they contracted a Friendship which was the Ruin of them both, as the Reader will observe in the Perusal of these Pages

Their first Adventure was at *Shooters-Hill*, where they met with a Gentleman and his Servant *Hind* being perfectly raw and unexperienced, his Companion was willing to have a Proof of his Courage, and therefore stud at some Distance while the Captain rode up, and fingly took from them 15 Pounds, but returned the Gentleman twenty Shillings to bear his Expences on the Road, with such a pleasant Air, that the Gentleman protested he would never hurt a Hair of his Head, if it should at any Time be in his Power. *Allen* was prodigiously pleased both with the Bravery and Generosity of his new Comrade, and they mutually swore to stand by one another to the utmost of their Power.

It was much about the Time that the inhuman and unnatural Murder of King *Charles* I was perpetrated at his own Palace Gate, by the Fanaticks of that Time, when our two Adventurers began their Progress on the Road. One Part of their Engagement together was like Capt *Stafford's* Resolution, never to spare any of the Regicides that came in their Way. It was not before they met the grand Usurper *Cromwell,* as he was coming from *Huntingdon,* the Place of his Nativity, to *London.* *Oliver* had no less than seven Men in his Train, who all came immediately upon their stopping the Coach, and over-power'd our two Heroes, so that poor *Tom Allen* was taken on the Spot, and soon after executed, and it was with a great deal of Difficulty that *Hind* made his Escape, who resolved from this Time, to act with a little more Caution. He could not, however, think of quitting a Course of Life which he had just begun to taste, and which he found so profitable.

The Captain rode so hard to get out of Danger, after this Adventure with *Cromwell,* that he killed his Horse, and he had not at that Time Money enough to buy another. He resolved, therefore, to procure one as soon as possible, and to this Purpose tramped it along the Road on Foot. It was not long before he saw a Horse hung to a Hedge with a Brace of Pistols before him, and looking round him, he observed, on the other Side of the Hedge, a Gentleman untrussing a Point. *This is my Horse,* says the Captain, and immediately vaults into the Saddle. The Gentleman calling to him, and telling him, that the Horse was his. *Sir,* says Hind, *you may think yourself well off, that I have left you all the Money in your Pockets to buy another, which you had best lay out before I meet you again, lest you should be worse used;* so he rode away in Search of new Adventures.

There is another Story of the Captain's getting himself remounted, which I have seen in a printed Account of his Life. Whether it be only the same Action otherwise related, or another of our Adventurers Pranks, I shall leave the Reader to determine, and proceed.

Being reduced to the humble Capacity of a Foot-Pad, he hired a common Hack of a Man who made it his Business to let out Horses, and took the Road on his Back. He was overtaken (for he was not able to overtake any Body) by a Gentleman well mounted, with a Portmanteau behind him. They fell into Discourse upon such Topicks as are common to Travellers, and *Hind* was very particular in praising the Gentleman's Horse, 'till the Gentleman repeated every Thing his Horse could do. There was upon the Side of the Road a Wall, over which was another Way, and the Gentleman told *Hind,* that his Horse could leap that Wall. *Hind* offer'd to lay a Bottle of it, upon which the Gentleman attempted and accomplished what he proposed. The Captain confessed he had lost his Wager, but desired the Gentleman to let him try if he would do the same with him upon his Back, which the Gentleman consenting, the Captain rode away with his Portmanteau, and left him to return his Horse to the Owner.

Another Time Captain *Hind* met the celebrated Regicide, *Hugh Peters* in *Enfield-Chase,* and commanded him to deliver his Money. *Hugh,* who had his Share of Confidence, began to lay about him with Texts of Scripture, and to cue I our bold Robber with the eighth Commandment. *It is written in the Law,* says he, *That thou shalt not steal. And furthermore Solomon, who was surely a very wise Man, speaking in this Manner, Rob not the Poor, because he is poor.* Hind was willing to answer the finished old Cant in his own Strain, and for that End, began to rub up his Memory with some of the Scraps of the Bible, which he had learned by Heart in his Minority. *Verily,* says Hind, *if thou hadst regarded the Divine Precepts, as thou oughtest to have done, thou wouldst not have wrested them to such an abominable and wicked Sense as thou didst the Words of the Prophet, when he saith, Bind their Kings with Chains, and their Nobles with Fetters of Iron. Didst thou not, thou detestable Hypocrite, endeavour from these Words to aggravate the Misfortunes of thy Royal Master, whom thy cursed Republican Party, unjustly murdered before the Door of his own Palace?* Here Hugh Peters began to extenuate that horrid Crime, and to allege other Parts of Scripture in his Defence, and in Order to preserve his Money. *Pray Sir,* replied Hind, *make no Reflections on my Profession, for Solomon plainly says, Do not despise a Thief, but it is to little Purpose for us to dispute. The Substance of what I have to say, is this, Deliver thy Money presently, or else I shall send thee out of the World to thy Master in an Instant.*

These terrible Words of the Captain frighted the old Presbyterian in such a Manner, that he gave him thirty Broad Pieces of Gold, and then they parted. But *Hind* was not thoroughly satisfied with letting such a notorious Enemy to the Royal Cause depart in so easy a Manner. He, therefore, rode after him, full Speed, and overtaking him, spoke as follows. *Sir, now I think of it, I am convinced that this Misfortune has happened to you, because you did not obey the Words of the Scripture, which say, expressly, Provide neither Gold, nor Silver, nor Brass in your Purses for your Journey. Whereas it is evident that you had provided a pretty Deal of Gold. However, as it is now in my Power to make you fulfil another Command, I would by no Means slip the Opportunity. Therefore, Pray give me your Cloak.* Peters was so surpriz'd, that he neither stood to dispute, nor to examine what was the Drift of Hind's Demand, but *Hind* soon let him understand his Meaning, when he added, *You know, Sir, our Saviour has commanded, That if any Man take away thy Cloak, thou must not refuse thy Coat also, therefore, I cannot suppose you will act in direct Contradiction to such an express Direction, especially now you can't pretend you have forgot it, because I have reminded you of your Duty.* The old Puritan shrugged his Shoulders for some Time, before he proceeded to untie them, but *Hind* told him his Delay would do him no Service, for he would be punctually obey'd, because he was sure what he required was consonant to the Scripture. Accordingly *Hugh Peters* delivered his Coat, and Hind carried all off.

Next *Sunday* when *Hugh* came to preach, he chose an Invective against Theft for the Subject of his Sermon, and took his Text in the *Canticles,* Chap. v Ver. 3 *I have put off my Coat, how shall I put it on?* An honest Cavalier who was present, and knew the Occasion of his chusing those Words, cry'd out aloud. *Upon my Word, Sir, I believe there is no Body here can tell you, unless Capt Hind*

Hind *was here!* Which ready Answer to *Hugh Peters* Scriptural Question, put the Congregation into such an excessive Fit of Laughter, that the batiring Parson was ashamed of himself, and descended from his Prating Box, without proceeding any further in his Harangue

It has been observed before, that *Hind* was a professed Enemy to all the Regicides, and, indeed, Fortune was so favourable to his Desires, as to put one or other of those celebrated Villains often into his Power

····· one Day with that Arch-Traytor, Serjeant *Bradshaw*, who had some Time before the ····· to sit as Judge of his lawful Sovereign, and to pass Sentence of Death upon his Majesty The ····· where this Rencounter happened, was, upon the Road between *Sherbourn* and *Shaftsbury*, in Dorsetshire *Hind* rode up to the Coach Side, and demanded the Serjeant's Money, who, supposing his Name would carry Terror with it, told him who he was Quoth *Hind*, *I fear neither you, nor any King-killing Son of a Whore alive I have now as much Power over you, as you lately had over the King, and I should do God and my Country good Service, if I made the same Use of it, but live, I'll leave, to suffer the Pangs of thine own Conscience, till Justice shall lay her Iron Hand upon thee, and require an Answer for thy Crimes, in a Way more proper for such a Monster, who art unworthy to die by any Hands, but those of the common Hangman, and at any other Place than Tyburn Nevertheless, though I spare thy Life as a Regicide, be assured, that unless thou deliverest thy Money immediately, thou shalt die for thy Obstinacy*

Bradshaw began to be sensible that the Case was not now with him, as it had been when he sate at *Westminster-Hall*, attended with the whole Strength of the Rebellion A Horror naturally arising from a Mind conscious of the blackest Villanies, took Possession of his Soul, upon the Apprehensions of Death, which the Pistol gave him, and discovered itself in his Countenance He put his trembling Hand into his Pocket, and pulled out about forty Shillings in Silver, which he presented to the Captain, who swore he would that Minute shoot him through the Heart, if he did not find Coin of another Species The Serjeant at last, to save a miserable Life, pulled out that which he valued next to it, as of two Evils all Men chuse the least, and gave the Captain a Purse full of *Freeuses*

Hind, having thus got Possession of the Cash, he made *Bradshaw* yet wait a considerable Time longer, while he made the following *Eulogium* on *Money*, which, though in the Nature of it, it be something different from the Harangues, which the Serjeant generally heard on a *Sunday*, contains, nevertheless, much Truth, and might have been altogether as pleasing, had it come from another Mouth

This, Sir, is the Metal that wins my Heart for ever! O precious Gold, I admire and adore thee as well as either Bradshaw, Pryn, or any other Villain of the same Stamp, who, for the sake of thee, would sell their Redeemer again, were he now upon Earth Tis it that incomparable Medicament which the Republican Physicans call The Wonder-working Plaister It is truly Catholick in Operation, and somewhat of a Kin to the Jesuits Powder, but more effectual The Virtues of it are strange and various, it makes Justice deaf as well as blind, and takes out Spots of the deepest Treasons as easily as Castle Soap does common Stains, it alters a Man's Constitution in two or three Days, more than the Virtuoso's Transfusion of Blood can do in seven Years. 'Tis a great Alexipharmick, and helps

poisonous Principles of Rebellion, and those that Use them It miraculously exalts and purifies the Eye-sight, and makes Traytors behold nothing but Innocence in the blackest Malefactors 'Tis a mighty Cordial for a declining Cause, it stifles Faction and Schism as certainly as the Priests desire, d by Bitter and Brimstone In a Word, it makes Fools wise Men, and wise Men Fools, and both of them Knaves The very Colour of this precious Balm is bright and dazling If it be properly applied to the Fist, that is, in a decent Manner, and a competent Dose, it infallibly performs all the abovesaid Cures, and many others too numerous to be here mentioned

The Captain having finished his Panegyrick, he pulled out his Pistol, and said further

You and your infernal Crew have a long while run on, like Jehu in a Career of Blood and Impiety, pretending that Zeal for the Lord of Hosts has been your only Motive How long you may be suffered to continue in the same Course, God only knows I will, however, for this Time, stop your Race in a literal Sense of the Word. With that he shot all the Six Horses which were in the Serjeant's Coach, and then rode off in Pursuit of another Booty

Sometime after, *Hind* met a Coach on the Road between *Petersfield* and *Portsmouth*, filled with Gentlewomen He set it up to them in a genteel Manner, told them, that he was a Patron of the Fair-Sex, and that it was purely to win the Favour of a hard hearted Mistress, that he travelled the Country But Ladies, added he, *I am at this Time reduced to the Necessity of asking Relief, having nothing to carry me on in my intended Prosecution of Adventures* The young Ladies, who had read a pretty many Romances, could not help conceiting they had met with some *Quixot* or *Amadis de Gaul*, who was saluting them in the Stile of Knight Errentry Sir Knight, said one of the pleasantest among them, We heartily commiserate your Condition, and are very much troubled that we cannot contribute towards your Support, but we have nothing about us, but a sacred *Depositum*, which the Laws of your Order will not suffer you to violate

Hind was pleased to think he had met with such agreeable Gentlewomen, and, for the Sake of the Jest, could freely have let them pass unmolested, if his Necessities at this Time had not been very pressing "May I, bright Ladies, be favour'd with the Knowledge of what this sacred *Depositum*, which you "speak of, is, that so I may employ my utmost Abilities in its Defence, as the Laws of Knight-Errantry require?" The Lady who spoke before and who suspected the least of any one in Company told him, that the *Depositum* she had spoken of, was 3000l the Portion of one of the Company, who was going to bestow it upon the Knight who had won her Good-Will by his many past Services. "My humble Duty "be presented to the Knight, said he, and be pleased "to tell him, that my Name is Capt *Hind*, that "out of mere Necessity I have made bold to borrow "Part of what, for his Sake, I wish were twice as "much, that I promise to expend the Sum in Defence of injured Lovers, and the Support of Gen-"tlemen who profess Knight-Errantry" At the Name of Capt *Hind*, they were sufficiently startled, there being No body then stirring in *England* who had not heard of him *Hind* however bid them not be affrighted, for he would not do them the least Hurt, and desired no more than one thousand Pound, out of the Three These two Ladies very thankfully gave in an Instant (for the Money was ty'd up in seperate Bags)

Bag-) and the Captain wish'd them all a good Journey, and much Joy to the Bride

We must leave the Captain a little, to display the Corruption of human Nature, in an Instance, which the Captain has often protested was a great Trouble to him The Young Lady, when she met her intended Husband told him all that had past upon the Road, and the mercenary Wretch, as soon as he heard of the Money that was lost adjourned the Marriage, till he had sent to her Father to ask whether or no he would make up the Original Sum agreed upon, which he refusing (partly because he had sufficiently exhausted his Substance before, and partly, because he resented the sordid Proposal) our fervent Lover entirely broke through all his Vows, and the unfortunate young Lady died of Grief and Indignation This Account sufficiently demonstrates the Truth of what is advanced in the two Lines of Mr *Cowley's* Translation of one of the Odes of *Anacreon.*

Gold alone does Paffion move,
Gold monopolizes Love.

'nother Time *Hind* was obliged to abscond for a considerable Time in the Country, there being great inquiries made after him, during this interval, his Money begin to run short, and he was a great while before he could think of a Way to replenish his Purse He would have taken another Turn or two on the High way, but he had lived so long here that he had spent his very Horse While he was in this Extremity, a noted Doctor in his Neighbourhood went to receive a large Sum of Money, for a Cure which he had performed, and our Captain had got information of the Time It was in the Doctor's Way Home to ride directly by *Hind*'s Door, who had hired a little House on the Side of a Common Our Adventurer took Care to be ready at the Hour the Doctor was to return, and when he was riding by the House, he addressed himself to him in the most submissive Stile he was Master of, telling him, " That " he had a Wife within who was violent bad with a " Flux, so that she could not live without present " Help, intreating him to come in but two or three " Minutes, and he would shew his Gratitude as soon " is he was able "

The Doctor was moved with Compassion at the poor Man's Request, and immediately alighted, and accompanied him in, assuring him that he should be very glad if it was in his Power to do him any Service *Hind* conducted him up Stairs, and as soon as they were got into the Chamber, shut the Door, and pulled out a loaded Pistol, and an empty Purse, while the Doctor was looking round for his Patient *This,* quoth *Hind,* holding up the Purse, " is my Wife, " she has had a Flux so long, that there is now no- " thing at all within her I know, Sir, you have a " sovereign Remedy in your Pocket for her Distem- " per, and if you do not apply it without a Word, " this Pistol shall make the Day shine into your Body The Doctor would have been glad to have lost a considerable Fee, provided he might have had nothing to do with the Patient, but when he saw there was no getting off, he took forty Guineas out of his Pocket, and emptied them out of his own Purse into the Captain's, which now seemed to be in pretty good Health *Hind* then told the Doctor, That he would leave him in full Possession of his House, to make a-mends for the Money he had taken from him Upon which he went out and locked the Door on poor *Galen,* mounting his Horse, and riding away as fast as he was able, to find another Country to live in, well knowing that this would now be too hot to hold him

Hind has been often celebrated for his Generosity to all Sorts of People, more especially for his Kindness to the Poor, which it is reported was so extr. ordinary, that he never injured the Property of any Person, who had not a competent Share of Riches. We shall give one Instance, instead of a great many, which we could produce, which will sufficiently confirm this general Opinion of his Tenderness for those that were needy.

At a Time when he was out of Cash (as he frequently was, by reason of his Extravagancy) and had been upon the Watch a pretty while, without seeing any worth his Notice, he at last espied an old Man jogging along the Road upon an Ass He rides up to meet him, and asked him very courteously where he was going " To the Market, *said the old Man, at Wantage,* " to buy me a Cow that I may have some Milk for my " Children How many Children, *quoth* Hind, may you " have ? *The old Man answered* Ten And how much " do you think to give for a Cow, *said* Hind ? —— " I have but forty Shillings, Master, and that I have " been saving together these two Years, says the poor Wretch ——*Hind*'s Heart aked for the poor Man's Condition, at the same Time that he could not help admiring his Simplicity, but being in so great a Strait as I have intimated, he thought of an Expedient, which would both serve him, and the old Man too Father, " *said he,* the Money you have " got about you, I must have at this Time, but I " will not wrong your Children of their Milk My " Name is Hind, and if you will give me your forty " Shillings quietly, and meet me again this Day " Se'ennight at this Place, I promise to make the " Sum double Only be cautious that you never " mention a Word of the Matter to any Body be- " tween this and then." At the Day appointed the old Man came, and *Hind* was as good as his Word, bidding him buy two Cows, instead of one, and adding twenty Shillings to the Sum promised, that he might purchase the best in the Market

Never was Highwayman more careful than *Hind* to avoid Blood-shed, yet we have one Instance in his Life, that proves how hard it is for a Man to engage in such an Occupation, without being exposed to a Sort of wretched Necessity some Time or other, to take away the Life of another Man, in order to preserve his own, and in such a Case, the Argument of Self-Defence can be of no Service to extenuate the Crime, because he is only pursued by Justice, so that a Highwayman, who kills another Man, whatever Pretence, is as actually guilty of Murder, as a Man who destroys another in cold Blood without being able to give a Reason for his so doing

Hind had one Morning committed several Robberies in and about *Maidenhead-Thicket,* and, among others, had stopped Col *Harrison,* a celebrated Regicide, in his Coach and Six, and taken from him seventy odd Pounds The Colonel immediately procured a Hue-and-Cry for taking him, which was come into that Country before the Captain was aware of it However he heard at a House of Intelligence, which he always had upon every Road he used, of the Danger he was in, and thereupon, he instantly thought of making his Escape, by riding as fast as he could to find some safer Way of concealing himself

In this Condition, any one would imagine, the Captain was apprehensive of every Man he saw He had got no further than a Place called *Knowl Hill,* which is but a little Way of the Thicket, before he heard a Man riding behind him full Speed It was a Gentleman's Servant, endeavouring to overtake his Master who was gone before, with something that he had forgot *Hind,* just now thought of nothing but his own Preservation, and therefore resolved either to ride off, or fire at the Man, who he concluded was pursuing him As the other Horse was fresh, and
                                                                    Hind

Hat had pretty well tir'd his, he soon perceived the Vanguard of him, upon which he pulls out a Piſtol, and juſt as the unfortunate Countryman was at his Horſe's Heels, he turns about and ſhoots him through the Head, ſo that he fell down dead on the Spot. The Captain, after the Fact, got entirely off, but it was for this that he was afterwards condemn'd at *Reading*.

There have been a great many more Stories related of this celebrated Highwayman, which were either the Actions of other Men, or ſo improbable in themſelves, that we did not think them worth repeating. A Man who has excelled in his Way is always loaded with ſo much Praiſe as to make his whole Hiſtory ſeem a Fable. Whether this be occaſion'd by the Partiality of Writers, or by a Fate common to ſuch Men, I ſhall not determine. The *Hercules* of *Greece* was the moſt famous of all that bore that Name, therefore the Actions of all the reſt are attributed to him, almoſt the ſame may be ſaid of Captain *Hind*. One Relation more, which is univerſally known to be authentick, and redounds to the Honour of our Hero, ſhall cloſe our Account of his Life.

After King *Charles* I was beheaded, the *Scots* received and acknowledged his Son King *Charles* II and reſolved to maintain his Right againſt the reigning Uſurpation. To this End they raiſed an Army, and marched towards *England*, which they entered with great Precipitation. Abundance of Gentry, and others who were loyal to their Principles, flocked to the Standard of their Sovereign, and reſolved to loſe their Lives in his Service, or reſtore him to his Dignity. Among theſe *Hind*, who had as much natural Bravery as almoſt any Man that ever lived, reſolved to try his Fortune. *Cromwell* was ſent by the Parliament into the North to intercept the Royal Army, but in ſpite of that vigilent Traytor's Expedition the King advanced as far as *Worceſter*, where he waited the Enemies Coming.

Oliver came to *Worceſter* ſoon after, and the Conſequence of the two Armies meeting was a very fierce and bloody Battle, in which the Royaliſts were defeated. *Hind* had the Good-Fortune to eſcape at that Time, and came to *London*, where he lodged with one Mr *Denzie*, a Barber, over-againſt St *Dunſtan*'s Church in *Fleet-ſtreet*, and went by the Name of *Brown*. But Providence had now ordered, that he ſhould no longer purſue his Extravagancies, for he was diſcover'd by a very intimate Acquaintance. It muſt be granted, that he had ſufficiently deſerved the Stroke of Juſtice, but there yet appears ſomething ſo ſhocking in a Breach of Friendſhip, that we cannot help wiſhing ſomebody elſe had been the Inſtrument.

As ſoon as he was apprehended, he was carried before the Speaker of the Houſe of Commons, who then lived in *Chancery-Lane*, and, after a long Examination was committed to *Newgate*, and loaded with Irons. He was convey'd to Priſon by one Capt *Compton*, under a ſtrong Guard; and the Warrant for his Commitment commanded that he ſhould be kept in cloſe Confinement, and that no Body ſhould be admitted to ſee him without Orders.

On *Friday* the 12th of *December*, 1651 Captain *James Hind* was brought to the Bar of the Seſſions-houſe in the *Old Bailey*, and indicted for ſeveral Crimes, but nothing being proved againſt him that could reach his Life, he was convey'd in a Coach from *Newgate* to *Reading* in *Berkſhire*, where on the 1ſt of *March*, 1651 he was arraigned before Judge *Warberton* for killing one *George Sympſon* at *Knole*, a ſmall Village in that County. The Evidence here was very plain againſt him, and he was

found Guilty of *Wilful Murder*; but an Act of Oblivion being iſſued out the next Day, to forgive all former Offences but thoſe againſt the State, he was in great Hopes of ſaving his Life; 'till by an Order of Council he was removed by *Habeas Corpus* to *Worceſter Goal*.

At the beginning of *September*, 1652. he was condemn'd for High-Treaſon, and on the 24th of the ſame Month, he was drawn, hang'd and quartered, in Purſuance of the ſame Sentence, being thirty-four Years of Age. At the Place of Execution, he declared that moſt of the Robberies which he had ever committed, were upon the republican Party, of whoſe Principles he profeſſed he always had an utter Abhorrence. He added, That nothing troubled him ſo much as to die before he ſaw his Royal Maſter eſtabliſhed on his Throne, from which he was moſt unjuſtly and illegally excluded by a rebellious and diſloyal Crew, who deſerved Hanging more than him.

After he was executed, his Head was ſet upon the Bridge Gate, over the River *Severn*, from whence it was privately taken down, and buried within a Week afterwards. His Quarters were put upon the other Gates of the City, where they remained 'till they were deſtroy'd by Wind and Weather.

To the Memory of Captain H I N D.

By a Poet of his own Time.

WHenever Death attacks a Throne,
Nature thro' all her Parts muſt groan,
The mighty Monarch to bemoan.

He muſt be wiſe, and juſt, and good,
Tho' nor the State he underſtood,
Nor ever ſpar'd a Subject's Blood.

And ſhall no friendly Poet find,
A monumental Verſe for *Hind*?
In Fortune leſs, as great in Mind.

Hind made our Wealth one common Store;
He robb'd the Rich to feed the Poor.
What did immortal *Cæſar* more?

Nay, 'twere not difficult to prove,
That meaner Views did *Cæſar* move:
His was Ambition, *Hind*'s was Love.

Our *Engliſh* Hero ſought no Crown,
Nor that more pleaſing Bait, Renown:
But juſt to keep off Fortune's Frown.

Yet when his Country's Cauſe invites,
See him aſſert a Nation's Rights!
A Robber for a Monarch fights!

If in due Light his Deeds we ſcan,
As Nature points us out the Plan,
Hind was an honourable Man.

Honour, the Virtue of the Brave,
To *Hind* that Turn of Genius gave,
Which made him ſcorn to be a Slave.

This, had his Stars conſpir'd to raiſe,
His natal Hour, This Virtue's Praiſe
Had ſhone with an uncommon Blaze.

Some new Epocha had begun,
From ev'ry Action he had done;
A City built, a Battle won.

If one's a Subject, one at Helm,   Be henceforth then forever join'd,
'Tis the fame Violence, fays *Anfelm*,   The Names of *Cæfar*, and of *Hind*,
To rob a Houfe, or wafte a Realm   In Fortune different, one in Mind.

The LIFE *of* CLAUDE DU VALL.

SOME have affirmed that this very celebrated Highwayman was born in *Smock-Alley*, without *Bifhopfgate* ; but this is without Ground, for he really received his firft Breath at a Place called *Damfort* in *Normandy* His Father was a Miller, and his Mother the Daughter of a Taylor: By thefe Parents he was brought up ftrictly in the *Roman Catholick* Religion, and his promifing Genius was cultivated with as much Learning as qualified him for a Footman

But though the Father was fo careful, as to fee that his Son had fome Religion, we have good Reafon to think, that he had none himfelf He ufed to talk much more of good Chear, than of the Church, and of great Feafts, than great Faith, good Wine was to him better than good Works, and a found Courtezan was far more agreeable than a found Chriftian Being once fo very fick, there was great Hopes of his dying a natural Death, a ghoftly Father came to him with his *Corpus Domini*, and told him, that hearing of the Extremity he was in, he had brought him his Saviour to comfort him before his Departure Old *Du Vall*, upon this, drew afide the Curtain, and beheld a goodly fat Friar with the Hoft in his Hand *I know*, faid he, *that it is our Saviour, becaufe he came to me in the fame Manner as he went to* Jerufalem, C'eft un Afne que le porte *It is an Afs that carries him.*

Whether the old Man departed at this Time, or lived to difhonour his Family by fome more ignominious Death is ftill very uncertain, nor fhall we trouble ourfelves about it This we are credibly informed, neither Father nor Mother took any Notice of young *Claude*, after he was about thirteen Years of Age Perhaps their Circumftances might then oblige them to fend him abroad to feek his Fortune His firft Stage was at *Rouen*, the Capital City of *Normandy*, where he fortunately met with Poft Horfes to be returned to *Paris*, upon one of which he got leave to ride, by promifing to help to drefs them at Night. At the fame Time falling in with fome *Englifh* Gentlemen, who were going to the fame Place, he got his Expences difcharged by thofe generous Travellers

They arriv'd at *Paris* in the ufual Time, and the Gentlemen took Lodgings in the *Fanx-bourg St Germain*, where the *Englifh* generally quarter *Du Vall* was willing to be as near as poffible to his Benefactors, and by their Interceffion he was admitted to run on Errands, and do the meaneft Offices at the *St Efprit* in the *Rue de Bourchiere*, a Houfe of general Entertainment, fomething between a Tavern and an Alehoufe, a Cook's Shop and a Bawdy-Houfe In this Condition he continued till the Reftauration of King *Charles* II in 1660 at which Time Multitudes of all Nations flocking into *England*, among them came *Du Vall*, in the Capacity of a Footman to a Perfon of Quality.

The univerfal Joy upon the Return of the Royal Family, made the whole Nation almoft mad Every one ran into Extravagancies, and *Du Vall*, whofe Inclinations were as vicious as any Man's, foon became an extraordinary Proficient in Gaming, Whoring, Drunkennefs, and all Manner of Debauchery The natural Effect of thefe Courfes is the want of Money ; this our Adventurer experienced in a very little Time, and as he could not think of labouring he took to the Highway to fupport his Irregularities In this Profeffion he was within a little while fo famous, as to have the Honour of being named firft in the Proclamation for apprehending feveral notorious Highwaymen And here we have Reafon to complain that our Informations are too fhort for our Affiftance, in writing the Life of fuch a celebrated Offender However, fuch Stories as have been delivered down to us, we fhall give our Readers faithfully, and in the beft Manner we are able

He had one Day received Intelligence of a Knt. and his Lady that were travelling with four hundred Pounds in their Coach Upon this he takes four or five more along with him, and overtakes them on the Road The Gentry foon perceived they were like to be befet, when they beheld feveral Horfemen riding backwards and forwards, and whifpering one to another, whereupon the Lady, who was a young fprightly Creature, pulls out a Flagelet, and begins to play very brifkly *Du Vall* takes the Hint, and plays excellently well upon a Flagelet of his own, in anfwer to the Lady, and in this Pofture rides up to the Coach Door Sir, fays he to the Knight, *your Lady plays excellently, and I make no doubt but fhe dances well . Will you pleafe to ftep out of the Coach, and let me have the Honour to dance one Courant with her on the Heath?* I dare not deny any Thing, Sir, the Knight readily replied, *to a Gentleman of your Quality, and good Behaviour You feem a Man of Generofity, and your Requeft is perfectly reafonable* Immediately the Footman opens the Door, and the Knight comes out, *Du Vall* leaps lightly off his Horfe, and hands the Lady down It was furprizing to fee how gracefully he moved upon the Grafs, fcarce a dancing Mafter in *London*, but would have been proud to have fhewn fuch Agility in a Pair of Pumps, as *Du Vall* fhewed in a great Pair of *French* riding Boots As foon as the Dance was over, he waits on the Lady back to the Coach, without offering her the leaft Affront, but juft as the Knight was ftepping in, Sir, fays he, *you have forgot to pay the Mufick* His Worfhip replied, that he never forgot fuch Things, and inftantly put his Hand under the Seat of the Coach, and pulled out a hundred Pound in a Bag, which he delivered to *Du Vall*, who received it with a very good Grace, and courteoufly anfwered . Sir, you are liberal, and fhall have no Caufe to repent your being

f.

Du Vall *Robbing 'Squire* Roper, *Mast.ʳ of y̆ Buck Hounds to King* Charles II. *in* Windfor Foreſt.

fo *This hundred Pound given fo generoufly, is bet-*
better than ten Times the Sum taken by Force Your
noble Behaviour has excufed you the other three hun-
dred Pound, which you have in the Coach with you
After this he gave him the Word that he might
pafs undifturbed, if he met any more of their Crew,
and then very civilly wifhed them a good Journey

Another Time, as *Du Vall* with fome of his Companions were patrolling upon *Blackheath*, they met
with a Coach full of Ladies One of them had a
young Child in her Arms, with a Silver Sucking-
Bottle The Perfon appointed to act in this Adventure, robbed them very rudely, taking away their
Money, Watches, Rings, and even the poor B by's
Sucking-Bottle The Infant cried, as was natural on
fuch an Occafion, and the Ladies intreated him only
to return the Bottle, but the furly Thief refufed
to give any Ear to their Requeft, 'till *Du Vall*, obferving he ftaid longer than ordinary, rode up, and
demanded what was the Matter The Ladies, hereupon, renewed their Petition in Behalf of the Child,
and *Du Vall* threaten'd to fhoot his Companion,
unlefs he reftored what they required, adding thefe
Words *Sirrah, can't you behave like a Gentleman,*
and raife a Contribution, without ftripping People,
but, perhaps, you had fome Occafion for the Sucking-
Bottle, for by your Actions one would imagine, you
were hardly weaned This fharp reproof had the
defired Effect, and *Du Vall* took his Leave of the
Ladies in a courteous Manner

Capt *Smith* has been guilty of an unpardonable
Blunder in his Account of this Robbery, for he
tells us, that it was *Du Vall* himfelf, who behaved
in this ruftick Manner, and who was compelled
by one of his Comrades to reftore the Sucking-Bottle, but the Reader need only reflect on *Du Vall*'s
general Character, to convince him of the Captain's
Error

One Time *Du Vall* met with Efquire *Roper*, Mafter of the Buck-Hounds to King *Charles* II as he
was hunting in *Windfor-Foreft* As their Recoun-
ter happened in a Thicket, *Du Vall* took the Advantage of the Place, and commanded him to ftand
and deliver his Money, or elfe he would fhoot him
Mr *Roper*, to fave his Life, gave our Adventurer a
Purfe full of Guineas, containing at leaft fifty, and
Du Vall afterwards bound him Neck and Heels faftened his Horfe by him, and rode away a crofs the
Country

The Hunting, to be fure, was over for that Time,
but it was a pretty while before the Huntfman
could find his Mafter When the 'Squire was unbound, he made all the Hafte he could to *Windfor*,
and as he entered the Town, was met by Sir *Stephen*
Fox, who afking him whether or no he had had any
Sport, Mr *Roper* replied in a great Paffion, *Yes, Sir,*
I have had Sport enough from a Son of a Whore,
who made me pay damn'd dear for it He bound
me Neck and Heels, contrary to my Defire, and then
took fifty Guineas from me, to pay him for his La-
bour, which I had much rather he had omitted

But the Proclamation, which we fpoke of at the
Beginning of this Life, and the large Reward that
was promifed for taking him, made *Du Vall* think
it unfafe to ftay any longer in *England*, whereupon
he retired into *France* At *Paris* he lived very highly, boafting prodigioufly of the Succefs of his Arms
and Amours, and affirming proudly, that he never
encountered with any one Perfon of either Sex, whom
he did not overcome He had not been long here,
before he relapfed into his old Difeafe, Want of
Money, which obliged him to have Recourfe to his
Wits again He had an uncommon Talent at Contrivance, particularly at fuiting his Stratagems to the

Temper of the Perfon they were defigned to enfnare,
as the following Inftance will prove

A learned Jefuit, who was Confeffor to the *French*
King, was as much noted for his Avarice, as he was
for his Politicks; by which latter he had rendered
himfelf very eminent. His Thirft of Money was in-
fatiable, and though he was exceeding rich his Defires feemed to increafe with his Wealth It came
immediately into *Du Vall*'s Head, that the only
Way to fqueeze a little Money out of him, was to
amufe him with Hopes of getting a great Deal,
which he did in the following Manner

He put himfelf into a Scholar's Garb, to facilitate
his Admittance into the Mifer's Company, and then
waited very diligently for a proper Time to make
his Addrefs, which he met with in a few Days Seeing him alone in the Piazza of the *Fauxbourg*, he
went up to him very confidently, and faid *May*
it pleafe your Reverence, I am a poor Scholar, who
have been feveral Years travelling over ftrange
Countries, to learn Experience in the Sciences, purely
to ferve my native Country, to whofe Advantage I
am determined to apply my Knowledge, if I may be fa-
voured with the Patronage of a Man fo eminent as
yourfelf —— *And what may this Knowledge of*
yours be? replied the Father very much pleafed .
If you will communicate any Thing to me that may
be beneficial to France, *I affure you no proper En-*
couragement fhall be wanting on my Side ——
Du Vall, upon this growing bolder, proceeded
Sir, I have fpent moft of my Time in the Study of
Alchimy, or the Tranfmutation of Metals, and have
profited fo much at Rome *and* Venice, *from great*
Men learned in that Science, that I can change fe-
veral bafe Metals into Gold, by the Help of a Phi-
lofophical Powder, which I can prepare very fpee-
dily

The Father Confeffor appeared to be brightened
with the Joy of this Relation *Friend*, fays he, *fuch*
a Thing as this will be ferviceable indeed to the
whole State, and peculiarly grateful to the King,
who, as his Affairs go at prefent, ftands in fome need
of fuch a curious Invention But you muft let me
fee fome Experiment of your Skill, before I credit
what you fay fo far as to communicate it to his Ma-
jefty, who will fufficiently reward you, if what you
promife be demonftrated Upon this, he conducted
Du Vall home to his Houfe, and furnifhed him
with Money to build a Laboratory, and purchafe
fuch other Materials as he told him were requifite,
in order to proceed in this invaluable Operation,
charging him to keep the Secret from every living
Soul, 'till he thought proper, when *Du Vall* promifed to perform

The Utenfils being fixed, and every Thing in a
Readinefs, the Jefuit came to behold the wonderful
Operation *Du Vall* took feveral Metals and Mine-
rals of the bafeft Sort, and put them into a Cruci-
ble, his Reverence viewing every one as he put
them in Our learned Alchymift had prepared a
hollow Stick, into which he had convey'd feveral
Sprigs of pure Gold, as Black Lead is in a Pencil .
With this Stick he ftirred the Preparation as it melted, which with its Heat melted the Gold in the Stick
at the fame Time, fo that it funk imperceptibly into the Veffel When the exceffive Fire had con-
fumed in a great Meafure all the Lead, Tin, Brafs,
and Powder, which he had put in for a Shew, the
Gold remained pure to the Quantity of an Ounce and
an Half This the Jefuit caufed to be effayed, and
finding it what it really was, all fine Gold, he was
immediately devoted to *Du Vall*, and blinded with
the Profpect of future Advantage, that he believed
every Thing our Impoftor could fay, ftill furnifh-

ing

ing him with whatever he demanded in Hopes to be at laſt made Maſter of this extraordinary Secret, the who'e Fame, as well as Profit of which, he did not queſtion would redound to him, as *Du Vall* was but an obſcure Perſon

Thus were our Alchymiſt and Jeſuit, according to the old Saying, *as great as two Pickpockets*; which Proverbial Sentence, if we examine it a little cloſely, hits both their Characters *Du Vall* was a profeſſed Robber, and what is any Court-Favourite, but a Picker of the common People's Pockets? So that it was only two Sharpers endeavouring to out-ſharp one another. The Confeſſor was as open as *Du Vall* could wiſh He ſhewed him all his Treaſure, and among it, ſeveral rich Jewels, which he had received as Preſents from the King, hoping, by theſe Obligations to make him diſcover his Art the ſooner In a Word, he grew by Degrees, ſo importunate and urgent, that *Du Vall* began to apprehend a too cloſe Enquiry, if he denied the Requeſt any longer, and therefore he appointed a Day when every Thing was to be communicated In the mean time he took an Opportunity to ſteal into the Chamber, where all the Riches were depoſited, and where his Reverence generally ſlept after Dinner, and finding him at that Time very faſt, with his Mouth wide open, he gagged and bound him, then took his Keys, and unhoarded as much of his Wealth, as he could conveniently carry out unſuſpected; and ſo bid Farewel to both him and *France*

Du Vall had ſeveral other Ways of getting Money, beſides theſe which I have mentioned, particularly by Gaming, at which he was ſo expert, that few Men in his Age were able to play with him, No Man living could ſlip a Card more dexterouſly than he, nor better underſtood all the Advantages that could be taken of an Adverſary, yet, to Appearance, no Man play'd fairer He would frequently carry off ten, twenty, thirty, or ſometimes an hundred Pounds at a ſitting, and had the Pleaſure commonly to hear it all attributed to his good Fortune, ſo that few were diſcourag'd by their Loſſes with him from playing with him a ſecond, third, or fourth Time

He was moreover a mighty Man for laying Wagers, and no leſs ſucceſsful in this Particular than any of the former He made it a great Part of his Study to learn all the Intricate Queſtions, deceitful Propoſitions, and paradoxical Aſſertions, that are made uſe of in Converſation Add to this, the ſmattering he had attained in all the Sciences, particularly the Mathematicks, by means of which, he frequently won conſiderable Sums on the Situation of a Place, the Length of a Stick, and a hundred ſuch little Things, which a Man may Practice without being liable to any Suſpicion, or caſting any Blemiſh upon his Character, as an honeſt Man, or even a Gentleman, which *Du Vall* affected to appear

But what he was moſt of all celebrated for, was his Conqueſts among the Ladies, which were almoſt incredible to thoſe who had not been acquainted with Intriegue He was a handſome Man, and had Abundance of that ſort of Wit, which is moſt apt to take with the Fair Sex Every agreeable Woman he ſaw, he certainly died for, ſo that he was ten thouſand Times a Martyr to Love *Thoſe Eyes of yours, Madam, have undone me——I am captivated with that pretty good natur'd Smile——O that I could by any Means in the World recommend myſelf to your Ladyſhip's Notice——What a poor ſilly loving Fool am I!——*Theſe, and a Million of ſuch Expreſſions, full of Flames, Darts, Racks, Tortures, Death, Eyes, Bubbies, Waſte, Cheeks, &c were much more familiar to him than his Prayers, and he had the ſame Fortune in the Field

of Love, as *Marlborough* had in that of War, *viz* *Never to lay Siege, but he took the Place*

Our Hero had once a Mind to try the utmoſt of his Influence over the Fair-Sex; and to that End, he bought a good ſizeable Pocket-Book, and ſet out upon a Progreſs It were in vain to pretend to give the Reader a Catalogue of thoſe that fell Victims to his Addreſs Maids, Widows, and Wives, the Rich, the Poor, the Noble, the Vulgar, all, all ſubmitted to the powerful *Du Vall* In a Word his Pocket-Book was filled, and his Strength almoſt ſpent in leſs than ſix Months.

While he was on his Journey, he met with a young Gentleman of Wit and Humour, to whom he communicated the Occaſion of his traveling The Gentleman being alſo a very agreeable Perſon, and having been lately croſſed in Love, he ſoon conſented to try his Fortune with him They came together to an Inn, where was a beautiful demure Girl, an only Daughter, of about thirteen Years of Age It was ſoon agreed to ſee what they could do with the Damſel, of whoſe Virginity had no Room to doubt They ſoon found an Opportunity of ſpeaking to her alone, when they promiſed her a Ring which they then ſhewed her, if ſhe would come and lie with them every Night, while they tarried at her Father's Houſe The Wench made no Scruple of the Matter, after a few Words of Form But now the great Point to be debated was who ſhould have her Maidenhead The Gentleman claimed it a Thing due to his Dignity, and *Du Vall* as poſitively inſiſted upon it, that in ſuch Caſes there was no Reſpect of Perſons to be obſerved At laſt they both conſented to draw Cuts for the imaginary Treaſure, and the longeſt Share fell to *Du Vall*

At Night our young Innocent came and ſlippd in between them, when *Du Vall*, immediately, as he thought, took Poſſeſſion of what was his Right, and he was entirely ſatisfied with what he diſcover'd There is no Reaſon to ſay what further paſs'd that Night; it was ſufficient that *Du Vall* was very merry with his Companion in the Morning, who repined as much at his ill Fortune

There was a young Lad, Apprentice to her Father, who had ſome Months before been bleſſed in Reality (if there be any Reality in ſuch Bleſſings) with what *Du Vall* had now gotten in Imagination, and had every Night ſince came to the Girl's Bed He was ſurpriz'd when he found his Mate had left him, and as ſoon as he had Opportunity, he demanded the Reaſon of her Slight The poor Wench freely confeſs'd the whole Affair, promiſing, that if he would ſtay till the Gentlemen were gone, he ſhould have part of what they gave her, and the entire Poſſeſſion of her Perſon for the future *I ſtay,* ſaid the young Man, *I'll aſſure you Madam, no indeed, I will have a merry Touch this Night, or, by Heaven, I will never ſpeak to you again Don't the Gentlemen ſleep ſound?* Yes, *when they are aſleep,* ſaid ſhe, *but that is not often, for they teize me between them almoſt all the Night long However, I will give a gentle Tap on the Bed's Teſter when they are both faſt, and then do you come, without ſaying a Word* At proper Time the Sign was given, the Boy enter'd, and crept up between the two Gentlemen directly, in the right Place The Bed ſhook, the Travellers wak'd, and each thought his Companion was in the Saddle, till they both fell aſleep again, being weary with waiting And the young Man went away without being detected

In the Morning the Companions were ready to quarrel, each being angry at the other's unreaſonable Greedineſs. *Sure, ſays the Gentleman, you re-*

eat.

eaten *something more than ordinary yesterday* I *wish,* quoth Du Vall, *you have no Occasion of something to strengthen your Back to Day, for I am sure you laboured hard enough* At last it was agreed that the Girl should decide between them, who confess'd all They laugh'd at one another, gave the Ring, and departed Shortly afterwards, the young Virgin was married, and lost her Maidenhead for good and all, with many an artful Struggle

At another Place on the Road our two Adventurers perform'd another Prank of almost the same Nature They were benighted, and called at a House not an usual Place of Entertainment The good Man told them he was willing to serve them as much as he could, but he had no more than one Chamber, with two large Beds, and a Truckle Bed, in it *If you please,* says he, *to accept of one of the Beds, as you look like honest Gentlemen, you shall be very welcome I and my Wife will lay in the other, and my Daughter in the Truckle Bed* Any Proposal, at such a Time, without Doubt, was acceptable

The Daughter was about fixteen Years of Age, young, plump, and handsome, enough to make any Man's Mouth water Du Vall took Care to ogle her pretty sufficiently in the Evening without the old People's Notice, so that she understood his meaning, and let him perceive as much About eleven they went to Bed, and the good Landlord and Landlady as soon as our Assignators could wish When we heard them snore, Du Vall slipp'd out of his own Bed into the Wench's, where we leave them for the present

There was an Infant in a Cradle by the good People's Bed side, and the young Gentleman who was left alone, having some Occasion to go down, ran against the wooden Machine As he could not otherwise pass, he took and lifted it into the Middle of the Room, did what he wanted, and went to Bed again It was not long afterwards before the Landlad had a Motion of the same Nature, and it came into her Head at the same Time to feel for the Cradle She groped about so long in the Dark, that she lost the Bed side, and walked round about till she happened to fall on the other Bed, where the Gentleman was alone She felt of his head, and finding there was but one Man, concluded it must be her Husband, in which confidence she went to Bed

Our Gallant quickly discovered her mistake, and, by his Vigour, she soon perceived the same, however, she was not so ill-natur'd as to leave him immediately We must go no farther in our Relation, because we know not how many Ladies may read it In a Word, the old Man being still fast asleep, every one in the Room was entirely satisfied, and, getting all into their proper Places before Morning, their Satisfaction continued.

These two Stories may serve for Specimens of our Adventurer's Gallantry, all we shall add on that Head, is, that Du Vall has often protested, that, after he was deceived by the Inn-keeper's Daughter, he could never fancy he met with a Maid above fourteen

There's no certain Account how long Du Vall followed his vicious Courses in *England* before he was detected, after his coming from *France,* before he fell into the hand of Justice All we know, is, that he was taken drunk at the *Hole in the Wall* in *Chandois Street,* committed to *Newgate,* arraign'd, convicted, condemn'd, and (on *Friday* the 21st Day of *January* 1669-70) executed at *Tyburn,* in the 27th Year of his age

Abundance of Ladies, and those not of the meanest Degree, visited him in Prison, and interceded for his Pardon Not a few accompanied him to the Gallows, ... swoln Eyes and blubber'd

Cheeks After he had hanged a convenient Time, he was cut down, and, by persons well dress'd, convey'd into a Mourning Coach In this he was carried to the *Tangier* Tavern at *St Giles's,* where he lay in State all Night The Room was hung with black Cloth, the Herse cover'd with Scutcheons, eight Wax Tapers were burning, and as many tall Gentlemen attended With long Cloaks All was in profound Silence, and the Ceremony had lasted much longer, had not one of the Judges sent to interrupt the Pageantry

As they were undressing him, in order to his lying in State, one of his Friends put his Hand into his Pocket, and found therein the following Paper, which as appears by the Contents, he intended as a Legacy to the Ladies It was written in a very fair Hand

" I should be very ungrateful to you, fair *English*
" Ladies, should I not acknowledge the Obligations
" you have laid me under I could not have hoped
" that a Person of my Birth, Nation, Education,
" and Condition, could have had Charms enough to
" captivate you all, though the contrary has appeared, by your firm Attachment to my Interest, which
" you have not abandoned even in my last Distress
" You have visited me in Prison, and even accompanied me to an ignominious Death
" From the Experience of your former Loves, I
" am confident that many among you would be
" glad to receive me to your Arms, even from the
" Gallows
" How mightily, and how generously have you
" rewarded my former Services? Shall I ever forget
" the universal Consternation that appeared upon
" your Faces when I was taken, your chargable Visits to me in *Newgate,* your Shrieks and Swoonings when I was condemned, and your zealous Intercession and Importunity for my Pardon? You
" could not have erected fairer Pillars of Honour and
" Respect to me, had I been a *Hercules,* able to get
" fifty of you with Child in one Night
" It has been the Misfortune of several *English*
" Gentlemen to die at this Place, in the Time of the
" late Usurpation, upon the most honourable Occasion that ever presented itself, yet none of these,
" as I could ever learn, received so many Marks of
" your Esteem as myself How much the greater,
" therefore is my Obligation?
" It does not, however, grieve me, that your Intercession for me proved ineffectual, for now I
" shall die with a healthful Body, and, I hope, a
" prepared Mind, my Confessor has shewn me the
" Evil of my Ways, and wrought in me a true Repentance Whereas, had you prevailed for my
" Life, I must in Gratitude have devoted it to your
" Service, which would certainly have made it very
" short, for had you been found, I should have
" died of a Consumption, if otherwise, of a
" Pox "

He was buried with many Flambeaux, amidst a numerous Train of Mourners (most of them, Ladies) *Covent Garden* A white Marble Stone was laid over him with his Arms, and the following Epitaph engraven on it

Here lies Du Vall, Reader, if Male thou art,
Look to thy Purse, if Female, to thy Heart
Much Havock hath he made of both, for all
Men he made stand, and Women he made fall

The second Conqueror of the Norman *Race,*
Knights to his Arms did yield, and Ladies to his Face
Old Tyburn's Glory, England's bravest Thief,
Du Vall the Ladies' Joy! Du Vall the Ladies' Grief

L l   A PIN.

A PINDARICK ODE.
To the Happy Memory of the most Renown'd
DU VALL.

By the Author of HUDIBRAS.

I

'TIS true, to complement the Dead,
   Is as impertinent and vain,
As 'twas of old to call 'em back again
Or, like the *Tartars*, give 'em Wives,
With Settlements for After-Lives
For all that can be done or said,
Tho' ne'er so noble, great, and good,
By them is neither heard nor understood.
   All our fine Sights, and Tricks of Art,
First to create, and then adore Desert,
   And those Romances which we frame,
   To raise ourselves not them a Name
In vain are stuft with ranting Flatteries,
And such as, if they knew, they would despise
For as those Times, the golden Age they call,
   In which there was no Gold at all,
So we plant Glory and Renown,
   Where it was ne'er deserv'd, nor known.
But to worse Purpose many Times,
   To varnish o'er nefarious Crimes,
And cheat the World that never seems to mind,
How good or bad Men dye, but what they leave be-
                                        [hind.

II.

And yet the brave *Du Vall*, whose Name,
   Can never be worn out by Fame;
That liv'd and dy'd to leave behind
A great *Example* to Mankind.
   That fell a publick Sacrifice,
   From Ruin to prevent those few
Who, tho' born false, may be made true;
And teach the World to be more just and wise,
   Ought not, like vulgar Ashes, rest.
   Unmention'd in the silent Chest,
Not for his own, but publick interest.
He, like a pious Man, some Years before
   Th' Arrival of this fatal Hour,
   Made ev'ry Day he had to live
To his last Minute a Preparative
   Taught the wild *Arabs* on the Road
   To act in a more genteel Mode,
Take Prizes more obligingly than those
Who never had been bred *Filous*,
And how to hang in a more graceful Fashion,
Than e'er was known before to the dull *English* Na-
                                        [tion.

III.

In France, the Staple of new Modes,
Where Garbs and Courts are current Goods,
That serves the ruder Northern Nations
With Methods of Address and Treat,
Prescribes new Garnitures and Fashions,
And how to drink, and how to eat,
No out-of-Fashion Wine or Meat.

To understand Cravats and Plumes,
And the most modish from the old Perfumes
   To know the Age and Pedigrees,
   Of Points of *Flanders* and *Venice*,
Cast their Nativity, and to Day
Foretell how long they'll hold, and when decay,
   T'affect the purest Neghgences,
   In Gestures, Gaits, and Miens,
   And speak by Repartee *Routines*,
Out of the most authentick of Romances:
And to demonstrate with substantial Reason,
What Ribbands all the Year are in or out of Season

IV

To this great Academy of Mankind,
   He ow'd his Birth and Education,
Where all are so ingeniously inclin'd,
   They understand by Imitation,
Are taught, improve before they are aware,
As if they suck'd their Breeding from the Air,
   That naturally does dispense
To all a deep and solid Confidence
   A Virtue of that precious Use,
   That he whom bounteous Heav'n endues,
   But with a mod'rate Shew of it.
Can want no Worth, Abilities, nor Wit
   In all the deep *Hermetick* Arts,
   (For so of late the Learned call
   All Tricks, if strange and mystical)
   He had improv'd his nat'ral Parts,
   And with his magick Rod could found,
   Where hidden Treasure might be found
He, like a Lord o'th' Manor, seiz'd upon
   Whatever happen'd in his Way
   As lawful Waif and Stray
And after, by the Custom, kept it as his own

V.

From these first Rudiments he grew
   To nobler Feats, and try'd his Force
Upon whole Troops of Foot and Horse,
   Whom he as bravely did subdue.
   Declar'd all Caravans that go
Upon the King's High-Way, his Foe,
   Made many desperate Attacks,
   Upon itinerant Brigades
Of all Professions, Ranks, and Trades;
   On Carriers Loads, and Pedlars Packs,
   Made them lay down their Arms and yield,
   And, to the smallest Piece, restore
All that by cheating they had got before
And after plunder'd all the Baggage of the Field;
   In ev'ry bold Affair of War
He had the chief Command, and led them on
For no Man is judged fit to have the Care
Of other's Lives, until he as made it known,
How much he does despise, and scorn his own

VI

Whole Provinces 'twixt Sun and Sun,
Have by his conqu'ring Sword been won,
   And mighty Sums of Money laid
For Ransom upon ev'ry Man,
And Hostages deliver'd 'till 'twas paid
   Th' Excise, and Chimny-Publican,
   The Jew-forestaller and Inhanser,
   To him for their Crimes did answer
   He vanquish'd the most Fierce, and Fell,
   Of all his Foes, the Constable,
   That oft had beat his Quarters up,
   And routed him, and all his Troop.

f

He took the dreadful Lawyers Fees,
That in his own allow'd High-way,
Does Feats of Arms as great as his,
And when th' encounter in it, wins the Day,
Safe in his Garrison, the Court,
Where meaner Criminals are sentenc'd for't,
To the stern Foe he oft gave Quarter,
But as the *Scotchman* did to *Tartar*,
That he in Time to come
Might in Return from him receive his Doom

VII

He would have starv'd this mighty Town,
And brought his haughty Spirit down,
Have cut it off from all Relief,
And, like a wise and valiant Chief,
  Made many a fierce Assault,
Upon all Amunition-Carts,
And those that bring up Cheese and Malt,
Or Bacon from remoter Parts
No Convoy, e'er so strong, with Food
Durst venture on the desp'rate Road,
He made th' undaunted Waggoner obey,
And the fierce Higler Contribution pay,
  The savage Butcher, and stout Drover
Durst not to him their feeble Troops discover
And if he had but kept the Field,
In Time he'd made the City yield
For great Towns, like the Crocodiles, are found
I'th' Belly aptest to receive a mortal Wound.

VIII

But when the fatal Hour arriv'd,
In which his Stars began to frown,
And had in close Cabal contriv'd
To pull him from his Height of Glory down,
When he by num'rous Foes oppress'd,
Was in th' enchanted Dungeon cast,
  Secur'd with mighty Guards,
Lest he by Force or Stratagem,
Might prove too cunning for their Chains and them,
And break thro' all their Locks and Bolts, and Wards,
He'd both his Legs by Charms committed
To one another's Charge,
That neither might be set at large,
And all their Fury and Revenge out-witted.
  As Jewels of high Value are
Kept under Locks with greater Charge

Than those of meaner Rates;
So he was in Stone Walls, and pond'rous Chains, and
Iron Grates

IX.

Thither came Ladies from all Parts,
To offer up close Pris'ners, Hearts,
  Which he receiv'd as Tribute due,
And made 'em yield up Love and Honour too,
  But in more brave Heroicks,
Than e'er were practis'd yet in Plays.
For those two spiteful Foes who never meet,
  But full of hot Contest and Piques,
  About Punctilio's and meer Tricks,
Did all their Quarrels to his Doom submit,
  And far more generous and free,
With only looking on him did agree,
  Both fully satisfy'd, the one
  With the fresh Lawrels he had won,
And all the brave renowned Feats
  He had perform'd in Arms;
The other with his Person and his Charms:
  For just as Larks are catch'd in Nets,
  By gazing on a Piece of Glass:
So while the Ladies view his brighter Eyes,
  And smoother polish'd Face,
Their gentle Hearts, alas! were taken by Surprize.

X

Never did bold Knight to relieve
Distressed Dames such dreadful Feats atchieve,
  As feeble Damsels for his Sake
  Would have been proud to undertake,
And bravely ambitious to redeem
  The World's Loss and their own,
Strove who should have the Honour to lay down
  And change a Life with him:
But finding all their Hopes in vain,
To move his fix'd determin'd Fate,
  They Life itself began to hate,
And all the World beside disdain:
  Made loud Appeals and Moans
To less hard-hearted Grates and Stones,
Came swell'd with Sighs, and drown'd in Tears,
To yield themselves his Fellow-Sufferers:
And follow him like Prisoners of War,
Chain'd to the lofty Wheels of his triumphant Car.

The

The LIFE of JAMES BATSON.

THE following is the Life and Adventures of an Arch Villain, born in the first Year of the Reign of King *James* I which we hope will prove diverting, and afford an agreeable Amusement to our Readers

I suppose, according to Custom, the Reader will expect some Account of my Geneology, and as I was always a mighty Admirer of Fashions, I will follow the Mode, and give some Account of my Parents and Relations, beginning with my Grandfather, who had the great Fortune to marry a Woman excellently Skilled in Vaulting, and Rope-Dancing, and would play her Part with any Man She, tho' above fifty Years of Age, and troubled with the Phthisick, died in the Air. Her Husband would not marry again, to avoid seeing other Women fly as she had done, but kept a Puppet-Shew in *Morefields*, and it was reckon'd the curiousest that ever had been seen in the City Besides, my Grandfather was so little, that the only Difference between him and his Puppets, was, that they spoke through a Trunk, and he without one He made such Speeches before his Shews, that the Audience could wish he had never done, for he had a Tongue like a Parrot All the Apple-Women, Hawkers, and Fish-Women were so charmed with his Wit among his Puppets, that they would run to hear him without Leaving any Guard upon their Goods, but their Straw-Hats Unfortunate Man! being so like a Cock-Sparrow, he took to so many Hens, that when they had devoured his Money, Cloaths, and Puppets, they consumed his Health, and left him like a naked Baby in an Hospital

When he thought to have died soberly, he fell into a Frenzy to such a Degree, that one Day he fancied he was a *Bull* in a Puppet-Shew, and was to encounter a Stone Cross that stood near the Hospital-Gate, and, after several Essays, he made at the same Cross, crying, *Now I have you* This said, he run his Head so furiously against the Cross, that he dropt down, and said no more. A good Hospital-Nurse, who was one of the Family of the *Innocents*, seeing him die in that Manner, cried, *O the precious Soul, he died at the Foot of the Cross, and directing his Discourse to it*

My Father had two Trades, or two Strings to his Bow, for he was a Painter, and a Gamester, and a Master much alike at both, for his Paintings would hardly rise so high as a Sign-Post, and his Slight of Hand at Play was of such an ancient Date, that it would hardly pass upon the Mob He had one Misfortune, which he intail'd on all his Children, like Original Sin, and that was, his being born a Gentleman, which is as bad as a Poet, few of whom escape Eternal Poverty, or are above Perpetual Want

My Mother died unluckily of a Longing for Mushrooms, when they were not to be had, being then with Child by my *Father*, as she said, and departed

as quiet as a Bird She left two Daughters, great Devotees of *Venus*, tho' they were Christians, just at the Age the Doctors prescribe they are fit to e', both very handsome and very young, and I was left very little, but much better Skilled in Sharping than my Age seemed to promise When the Funeral Ceremonies were over, and the Tears dried up, which were not very many, my Father fell again to his *Daubing*, my Sisters to *Stitching*, and I returned to my little-frequented School, where my Posterior paid for the Slowness of my Feet, and the Lightness of my Hands

I had such an excellent Memory, that though my wicked idle Temper was the same it has ever since continued, yet I soon learned to read, write, and cast Accounts, well enough to have taken a better Course than I have done I put so many unlucky Tricks upon my Master, and so often set the Boys together by the Ears, that every Body called me the little *Judas* It was hard for any Book to escape me, and if once I cast my Eyes on a Picture, it was surely my own, which cost me many a Box ng Bout every Day, or else the Complaints were carried Home to my Father and Sisters The Eldest of them had it in Charge to reprove and convert me, she would sometimes give me a soft Cuff with her delicate white Hand, at other Times she would tell me I should be a Disgrace to the Family

All this Nonsense, and her Reproof, signified no more to me than the Barking of a Dog, it went in at ore Ear, and out at the other, so that, in short, I play'd so many unlucky Pranks, and was so full of Roguery, that I was expelled the School in as solemn a Manner, as if it had been by Beat of Drum My Father, after currying my Hide very well, carried me to a Friend of his, who was Barber to Count *Gondomar*, the *Spanish* Ambassador, then residing here, with whom he left me on Trial, in order to be bound Apprentice Having delivered his hopeful Son, and he returned Home, my Master ordered me into the Kitchen to my Mistress, who presently found me Employment, giving me a Basket full of Childrens Blankets, Clouts, Slabbering-Bibs, Barrows, &c and opening the Yard Door, furnished me with about an Ounce of Soap, then shewing me the Cistern with a great Trough under it, *Jemmy*, says she, *mind your Hits, there's a good Boy, for this Work belongs to the Apprentices* I hung down my Head, and tumbled all the filthy Clouts form the Basket into the Trough, and washed them as well as I could, and hung the Linnen to dry I mang'd it very well for myself, since I was soon discarded from my Office, which, had it continued longer, there had been an End of *Jemmy* in less than a Fortnight

The next Day I went over my Task again, and what I wanted in Washing of Clouts, was made up in Running on Errands

The third Day my Master having just given me a small Note to receive, there came into the Shop a
Bully

Bully Ruffian with a Pair of Whiskers that covered his Face, and would have been worth Money to have made Brushes on; he told my Master *he would have his Whiskers turned up* It being then so early that the Journeyman he kept was not come, he was going to turn them up himself, and bid me light a Fire, and heat the Irons. I did as I was ordered, and just as my Master had turned up one Whisker, there happened to be a Quarrel in the Street, and my Master being always a busy Man, must needs step out to see what was the Matter, leaving the stern Bravo, with one Whisker hanging quite down, and the other turned up The Scuffle lasting long, and my Master staying to see the End of it, the furious Kill crow never ceased swearing and cursing He asked me in a harsh Tone, *Whether I understood my Trade* , and I thinking it an undervaluing to myself to say I did not, boldly answered, *I did Why then you Son of a Whore,* says he, *turn up this Whisker for me, or I shall go into the Street as I am, and kick your Master* I was unwilling to be found in a Lye, and thinking it no hard Matter to turn up a Whisker, ne'er shew'd the least Concern, but took up one of the Irons that was at the Fire, and had been heating ever since the first Alarm of the Fray, and having nothing to try it on, but desiring to be thought Expeditious, I took a Comb, stuck it into his bristly Bush, and clapped the Iron to it No sooner did they meet, but there arose a Smoke, as if it had been out of a Chimney, with a whizzing Noise, and all the Hair vanished He cried out furiously, *Thou Son of a thousand Dogs, and ten thousand Whores, dost thou take me for Saint Laurence, that thou burnest me alive?* With that he let fly such a Bang at me, that the Comb dropping out of my Hand, I could not avoid in the Fright laying the hot Iron close along his Cheek, and cauterizing him on one Side of his Face This made him give such a Shriek, as shook the very House, and at the same Time drew his Sword to send me to the other World, but I remembring the Proverb, *That one Pair of Heels is worth two Pair of Hands,* got so nimbly into the Street, and so swiftly scoured out of that Part of the Town, that though I was a good Runner, I was amazed when I found myself above a Mile from Home, with the Iron in my Hand and the Spark's Whisker sticking to it As good Luck would have it, I was near the Person who was to pay the Note my Master gave me to receive for him, I carried it, and received the Money, but thought fit to apply it to my own Use, not daring to return Home again.

My Money lasted me for about a Month, when I began to think of returning to my Father, but I understood he was gone into the Country to receive some Money owing to him I rejoiced at the News, and went very boldly into the House as sole Lord and Master of it. My Sisters received me very coldly giving me many a sour Look, and upbraiding me with the Money my Father was forced to pay for my Pranks We had a thousand Squabbles every Day, particularly about their giving me small instead of strong Beer

These Animosities ran so high, that perceiving they did not mend, I resolved to make them know me Accordingly, one Day they having brought me four Beer, and the Meat being on the Table, I threw the Dish at my elder Sister, and the Pot with the Beer at the Younger, overthrew the Table, and marched out of Doors on a Ramble, but accidentally met a Messenger from the Country, who informed me of my Father's Death by a Fever At this News, I quickly went back to my Sisters, who were more compliable, finding by my Father's Will, I was left

Executor without Restraint of Age: I sold the Goods, got in what Debts I could, and led a merry Life, whilst the Money lasted, keeping all the Rakes about the Town Company, who at last drain'd me of every Farthing

They obliged me one Night to go Abroad with them, though much against my Will, and one of them having the Keys, like St *Peter,* opened the Door of a House, whence they took several Trunks to ease the owner of Lumber. A Cur Dog, who was upon Guard, gave the Alarm, and the People of the House came running into the Street, which compelled my Companions to lay down their Burdens, and act upon the Defensive with their Swords; for my Part I stood quaking for fear before the Robbery, at the Time of the Robbery, and after the Robbery, and always kept, at a Distance, repenting that I had not been acquainted with their Way of Living before I came out of my Lodging, that I might have avoided that Danger So that seeing my Companions fly, the wounded Men return to their Houses, I kept my Post all in a cold Sweat, least I should be taken up as a party concerned, and when I should have gone away, I had not the Power to stir one Foot At the Noise the Watch came in, who finding three Trunks in the Street, besides two Men dangerously wounded, and me not far off, they came up to see who I was By the Disorder they found me in, they concluded I was one of those who had done the Mischief. They took Care of me that Night, and the next Day I was ordered to a Place where I had Occasion to try all my Friends and Acquaintance, who all proved as I deserved In about ten Days, I was called to my Tryal, and my Excuses being very frivolous, and my Answers contradictory, I was condemn'd to be hoisted up by the Neck, and go to Heaven in a String However, just as I was singing the last Stave, a Reprieve came, and in about two Months after, I got a full Pardon

Frighten'd at this last Disaster, I was resolved to associate myself no more with any one, but went about the Streets, selling Wash-Balls, Tooth-Pickers, and Tooth-Powder I play'd the Merry-Andrew myself, cried up my Rubbish, extolled the Virtues of it, and sold it very dear. For whoever has a Mind to put off his Trumpery, and make a good Hand of it, must pretend his Trash comes from *Japan,* *Peru,* or *Tartary,* because all Nations undervalue their own Product and Workmanship, though never so excellent, and set a great Rate on foreign Trifles

All my Ware tending to make fine Teeth, and white Hands, the Ladies were my best Customers, but especially the Actresses There was at that Time one of the best Companies of Players that ever diverted *England,* and a Man at the Head of them famed for his Excellency that Way. By Virtue of my scurvy Ware, I became acquainted with his imaginary Queens, and pretended Princesses; one of whom, about eighteen Years of Age, and married to one of the Actors, told me one Day, *That she had taken a liking to me, because I was a confident sharp forward Youth, and therefore, if I would serve her, she would entertain me with all her Heart; and that when the Company went strolling, I might beat the Drum, and stick up the Bills* I fancied that was an easier Sort of a Life, so consented at first Word, desiring only two Days to sell my Ware off, which she courteously granted, and to encourage me, gave me a Crown

Having sold off my Trumpery, I waited on my Mistress, who appointed me four several Employments, the first was tiresome, the second uneasy,

         the

the third fluggifh, and the fourth dangerous At Home I was her *Valet de Chambre*, folding and laying up all her Cloaths. Abroad I was her Porter, fetching and carrying her Cloaths to the Play-houfe I was her Gentleman-Ufher in her Attiring Room, and her trufty Secretary and Ambaffador in all Places My Mafter quarrelled with her every Night about me, becaufe he fuppofed I was no *Eunuch*, faw I had a tolerable good Face, and thought me not fo young, but that I knew *What was What*, for which Reafon he was looking out for another Servant, that he might turn me off Such a Multitude of young Beauxs reforted daily to my Miftrefs's Houfe, that it looked like a Fair They all told me their Secrets, and acquainted me with their Sufferings Some made me Prefents, others promis'd Mountains, and others delivered me Copies of Verfes, which being gather'd in the Morning on *Parnaffus*, were buried at Night in the Neceffary Houfe I play'd the Part of a Prime Minifter, and Secretary of State and War, receiving thofe Memorials, and the Fees, promifing every one my Favour and Intereft Some of them I difpatch'd with my Miftrefs, and many more confidering fhe was fo dilatory, I anfwered of my own Head, after this Manner If the Petitioner was poor or niggardly, *Rejected* If he was a young Spark near coming to his Eftate, *He fhall be heard another Time* If rich and generous, *Granted* Thus I kept them all in Hand, abfolutely difmiffing none, but rather feeding them with Hopes

When I happen'd to lofe at Play, for 'tis impoffible a Scoundrel fhould ever be wife, as I took out or laid up her Cloath, I filled my Pocket with Ribbands and Garters, and giving them in her Name, as favours to the Gallants, they requited me fo plentifully, that I could make what I had filched, and enough left to game all the Week after

The Devil, who they fay never fleeps, fo ordered it, that my Mafter and Miftrefs being gone a vifiting, and I left at Home, two of the Servants belonging to the Play-houfe, and the Wardrobe-Keeper came to call me out to take a Walk, it being a leifure Day I went away with them We dropped into a Tavern, drank fix Bottles of the beft, play'd at Cards for the Reckoning, and that falling upon me, I was fo nettled, that I challenged the Wardrobe-Keeper, to play with me at *Putt*, and he being no Fool at that Sport, foon ftripped me of all I had This provoked me fo highly, that I told him, if he would but Stay, I would go fetch more Money. He confented, I ran Home with all Speed, took out a rich laced Petticoat my Miftrefs had, and carried it to a Paftry-Cook I was acquainted with, defiring to lend me three *Jacobus*'s upon it, pretending they were for my Miftrefs, who wanted fo much to make up a Sum to pay for a Ring fhe had bought, affuring him of his Money when my Mafter returned Home, with fomething for the Favour. The Paftry-Cook finding the Pawn fufficient, delivered me the Money, with which I hurried back to play, and loft as I had done before I got one *Jacobus* back again of the Winner, by way of Wrangling with him, as if he had not plaid fair, with which I turn'd out into the Street, full of Vexation, that I had loft fo beneficial a Place I went to an Inn, where I fupped and lay that Night, but with little Reft or Satisfaction

As foon as ever I difcovered the firft Dawn of Day, I got up full of Sorrow to think what a bafe Return I had made my Miftrefs for all her Kindnefs, and confidering the Danger I fhould be in, when fhe miffed her Petticoat, I left *London*, directing my Courfe towards *Colchefter*

Travelling fomewhat Haftily for fear of being followed, I overtook two of thofe Sort of Soldiers called *Decoy Ducks*, who ferve to draw in others, when they are Levies After fome Difcourfe, they told me they were going my Way, being informed that *at Colchefter there was a Captain raifing Men, and that none that lifted under him would ever want* I travelled on with them very fairly, every one paying his Club by the Way The next Day we got to that Town, and being kindly received by the Captain, and lifted, we lived in Clover for a fortnight, making our Landlords furnifh us with Dainties, and demanding Impoffibilies At laft, we received Orders to march, and having left the Town, our Captain moved like a Snail, ftill leaving the Quarters appointed us on one Side, and taking the contrary Way, becaufe the Towns paid him to be exempted He continued this Cheat three Days, but on the fourth, as we were paffing by a Wood, all his Men, about thirty in Number, left him with only the Colours, Drum, Serjeant, and Enfign, and five Wenches, who went with the Baggage, for being not likely to keep up a Company, who contrived how to make his Advantage of them without confidering, that it is very eafy to find a Captain, and no lefs difficult to get thirty Soldiers

However, I lik'd my Captain well enough, for he was civil to me, I ftuck by him, and came to London with him, where he was fo laugh'd at, that he refolved to quit the Kingdom, and having a good Eftate, intended to go abroad a Voluntier, and we fired my Company He embarked for *Barcelona*, and in a little Time got a Company, which was ordered with feveral others, to fail for *Alicant*, and being a good Accomptant, and writing a fair Hand, ftuck clofe all the while we were at Sea, to be Steward of the Ship to help him deliver out the Allowances to the Sailors, and Landmen He to keep up a good old Cuftom, and avoid being blamed by others of his Trade, gave the Soldiers all the broken Bifket, and kept that which was whole, and if for the Fifh, they had what was rotten As for the Bacon, he ftuck a Knife into it, and if it ftunk, the Soldiers had it, if otherwife, he put it up carefully, However he took Care to make much of the Officers, which made them all keep Council, and fee nothing and whilft the poor Soldiers fared hard, we lived well At length we arrived at *Alicant*, where we were quartered, and had a Mixture of good and bad, in as foon as they had fhewn us any Favour, they went over us with a *Cap de Deu*, which is that County Oath, and out came two or three Cafes of Piftols My Captain and I were at Variance, becaufe he had cheated me of my Pay, and I had made my Complaint to recover it For this Reafon he bore me ill Will there being nothing fo certain as that if a Soldier does not put up any Wrong in Point of Intereft, but intends to complain, or to ftand upon Terms with his Officers, all that he fays, though never fo true, will pafs for a Lie He will never be advanced, but their flighted and hated My Quarters were in a Tavern, where I was one Day a drinking with a Soldier and happened to fall out about a Lie given, when my Sword unluckily running into his Throat kick'd up his Heels, thro' his own Fault, for he fell upon my Point, fo that he may thank his own Bufinefs

To prevent my Captain's taking Revenge, or giving him an Opportunity of fruftrating his Malice, by taking upon himfelf to make an Example of me I went away to *Barcelona*, and took Refuge in a Monaftery My Captain, as if I had murdered his Father, ftolen his Goods, or taken away his Miftrefs, fent after me to have me fecured, and a little Whipper-Snapper of his, who was the Tale-Carrier of

Comp

company, followed his Business so Close, that in Despight of the Fathers, and in Contempt of the Church, he had me taken out of the Sanctuary, and it into the Prison of the *Arsenal* They put me into Irons bolted my Hands and Feet, and so left me. I was prosecuted as a Murderer, Deserter, and Raiser of Mutinies, and without any Regard to the Pain my Mother endured when she brought me into the World, they put me into a Fright with these terrible Words *You shall return to the Place from whence you came, and from thence to the Place of Execution, &c.*

In short, as if it had been a Thing of nothing, or a mere Matter of Pastime, they gave Sentence, *That I should be led in State along the Streets, then mount up a Ladder, kick up my Heels before all the People, and take a Swing in the open Air, as if I had another Life in my Snap Sack* I was made acquainted with this Publick Notary, who was so nice a *Christian*, that he never asked me any Gratuity for the good News, nor any Fees for the Trial It was impossible to avoid making some wry Faces, when I heard it, the Sighs broke loose in Spite of my Manhood, and the salt Tears trickled down my Cheeks The Jaylor bid me make Peace with God, without the least Supply from *Bacchus* to raise my Spirits, and I considering what I had to go through, gently squeez'd my Throat with my Hand, and tho' it was done very tenderly, I did not like the Test, but said to myself, *if the Hand, which is soft Flesh, hurts so much, what will it be when a hard hempen Rope is there* I kneeled down, and cried to Heaven for Mercy, solemnly protesting, if I regained my Liberty, that I would do Pennance for my Sins, and begin a new Life, but these were like Vows made in Storms The News was quickly spread, and several Friends came to see me, others to condemn me, some said it was pity I should lose my Life in the Prime of my Age, others that I looked like a rank Knave, and some, that I was not come to that for my Goodness At last, in came a *Franciscan Friar*, all in a Sweat, and full of Zeal, asking, *Where is the condemn'd Person?* I answer'd, *Father I am the Man, though you don't know me* He said, *Dear Child, it is now Time for you to think of another World, since Sentence is past, and therefore, you must imploy this short Time allow'd you, in confessing your Sins, and asking Forgiveness for your Offences* I answered, *Reverend Father, in Obedience to the Commands of the Church, I confess but once a Year, and that is in Lent But if, according to human Laws, I must attone with my Life for the Crime I've committed, your Reverence being so learned, must be truly sensible, that there is no Divine Precept, which says, Thou shalt not eat or drink, and therefore, since it is not contrary to the Law of God, I desire that you will give Order that I have Meat and Drink, and then we will discourse of what is best for us both, for I am in a Christian Country, and plead the Priviledge of Sanctuary*

The good Father, much disturbed to hear me talk so wildly at a Time when I should be serious, took a small Crucifix out of his Bosom, and began to make a Sermon to me on the Text of the lost Sheep, and the Repentance of the good Thief, and this with such an audible Voice, that he might he heard all over the *Arsenal* I turned pale, my Heart failed me, and my Tongue was numbed, when I heard the Charity Bells, which ring when Criminals are executed I cleared my Apartment, and kneeling down before my Ghostly Father, disgorged a wonderful Budget of Sins, and cleared my Store-house of Iniquity, and having received his Blessing and Absolution, found myself so changed, that it only troubled me to die, because I thought myself so truly contrite, that all

the Bells would ring out of themselves, the whole City would be in an Uproar, and the poor People would lose their Day's Work to come and see me

In the Height of this Fright, which I would freely bestow on any one that could be fond of it, the Marquis *D'Este*, then Commanding Officer, ordered me to be brought before him, I having got a Petition presented to him He like a merciful Man, being informed, that I pleaded the Priviledge of Sanctuary, ordered the Execution to be respited, the Sentence of Death reversed, and me sent to the Galleys for ten Years My Master was so much my Friend, that he opposed it, *alledging my Constitution was too Dainty to make a Water Thresher, and therefore it were better to send me out of this wicked World, that I might serve as an Example to all the Army, and that it would have been never the worse had it been done three or four Years sooner* Notwithstanding all this, I took a little Courage, finding myself backed by some Friends, and told the Marquis, it was Malice, Spight, and Hatred, made my Master so much my Enemy, that he had detain'd my Pay, upon which I threatened to complain, and he vow'd Revenge, and now would have it by my Death The General said, *It was strange, That two Countrymen could not agree, that he would not trouble himself with my Complaints, but ordered me to be immediately discharged without paying any Fees* I threw myself at his Feet for the Kindness he had done me, to the Disappointment of the Mob, and the Loss of the Executioner I presently departed the Palace, and went to be blooded to prevent any ill Consequence of the Fright I had been in

When the Bodily Fear I had been put into, was over, the Danger I had escaped forgotten, and the Blood I let out recruited in a Tavern, I went out one Day to take a Walk upon the Mole, and understanding there was a new Regiment to be raised, I enquired after the Officers, and by Accident met one of them, who asked me to list, I easily consented for the sake of a little Ready-Money My new Master seemed to take a Fancy to me, and ordered me to his own Quarters, where it was not long before I got a new Place, for the Cook going away, I was asked, if I understood any Thing that Way, and I always resolved to answer in the Affirmative, declared I did understand Cookery to the greatest Perfection, so that I was both Soldier and Cook

After several Voyages by Sea to *Rosas*, and other Places, we were ordered to succour *Alsace*, and for our Winter Residence had the Word of *Bavaria* My Master took up his Residence in the House of one of the richest Men in those Parts, though he pretended to be very poor, because he had drove away all his Cattle, and removed the best of his Goods This Contrivance did not serve his Turn, I got Information from the Servants With this, in a very stately Manner, I acquainted him, *That I was my Master's Steward, and Cook, and as such must inform him, that he had a Captain of Horse in his House, who was a Person of considerable Quality, and therefore must take Care to make very much of him and his Servants, that my Master was very much fatigued, and it was Dinner Time, and he must order all Things that were necessary* He answered, *I need only tell him what Provision I wanted for the Kitchen, and he would order his Servants to fetch it immediately* I told him we always kept three Tables, the first for the Gentlemen and Pages, the second for the Butler and under Officers, and the third for the Footmen, Grooms, and other Liveries, for all which Tables, he must furnish one Ox, two Calves, four Sheep, twelve Pullets, six Capons, two Dozen of Pidgeons,

Pidgeons, fix Pound of Bacon for Larding, four Pounds of Sugar, two of all Sorts of Spice, an hundred of Eggs, half a Dozen Dishes of Fish, a Pot of Wine to every Plate, and fix Hogsheads to stand by He blessed himself, as if he had seen all the Devils in Hell, and answered, *If all that your Worship speaks of be only for the Servants Tables, the whole Village will not be able to furnish the Masters* I reply'd, *My Master is such a worthy Person, that he had rather see the Servants made much of, than please himself, and therefore he and his Friends never put their Landlords to any more Charge, than a Dish of* imperial stuffed Meat, *with an Egg in it* He asked me, *what that stuffed Meat was made of?* And I bid him order me a new-laid Egg, a Squab Pidgeon, and two Loads of Coals, and to send for a Cobler with his Nawl and Ends, and a Grave-Digger with his Spade, and then he should know what else was wanting, that he might provide it whilst we were at Work. The Landlord went and fetched what I demanded, except the two Loads of Coals I took the Egg and the Pidgeon, which I gutted, and cutting it open enough with my Knife (for I had all my Tools about me) I clapped the Egg into the Belly of it, then said I to him, " Sir, take Notice, this Egg is
" in the Pidgeon, the Pidgeon is to be put into a
" Partridge, the Partridge into a Pheasant, the
" Pheasant into a Pullet, the Pullet into a Turkey,
" the Turkey into a Kid, the Kid into a Sheep, the
" Sheep into a Calf, the Calf into a Cow, all these
" Creatures are to be pulled, flead, and larded, ex-
" cept the Cow, which is to have her Hide on, and
" as they are thrust one into another, like a Nest of
" Boxes, the Cobler is to few every one of them
" with an End, that they may not flip out, and
" when they are all fast fewed into the Cow's Belly,
" *the Grave-Digger is to throw up a deep Trench,*
" into which one Load of Coals is to be cast, and
" the Cow laid a Top of it ; the other Load upon
" her, the Fuel set on Fire to burn about four
" Hours, more or less, when the Meat being ta-
" ken out, is incorporated, and becomes such a de-
" licious Dish, that formerly the Emperors used to
" dine upon it on their Coronation Day , for which
" Reason, and because an Egg is the Foundation of
" all that curious Mess, it was called, *the Imperial*
" *Egg Stuffed Meat* "
The Landlord, who stood listening to me with his Mouth open, and no more Motion than a Statue, gave such intire Credit to all I said, because I spoke fo feriously, and was very earnest to have the Ingredients, that squeezing me by the Hand, he said, *Sir, I am very poor,* and I understanding what he would be at, answer'd, *fear nothing.* Then leading him into the Kitchen, we agreed the Matter very well between us, and I told my Master he was very poor indeed, and ruined by our Troops, having had all his Cattle stolen My Master ordered he should not be oppressed, and left the Management of him to me
The other Servants observing that I had plenty of Wine in the Kitchen, and was supplied with choice Bits, suspected the Fraud, and informed my Master, who upon Enquiry found just the contrary to what I had told him He sent for my Landlord, and discovered all my Roguery My Master upon this paid me a Visit in the Kitchen, and taking up one of the neatest Cudgels he found about it, dusted my Jacket fo curiously, that he wanted a Cook for a Fortnight
During our Stay here we were attacked by a Parcel of *French* Scoundrels ; my Master ordered me out with the rest ; but I kept back, fearing a chance Bullet might mistake me for some Body else ; but

when I heard the *French* were beaten, I ventured into the Field with my drawn Sword, hacking and hewing the dead Carcases in a furious Manner It happen'd as a special instance of my Valour, that as I came up to one of the Enemies to give him half a Dozen good Gashes, thinking he was as dead as he rest, at the first Stroke I let fall, he gave such a dreadful Groan, that I was quite terrified, and thinking he made a Motion to get up to be revenged on me, I had not the Courage to stay fo long to draw my Sword out again , but faced about, and run as fast as I cou'd to the Place our Baggage was, looking back a thousand Times for fear he should overtake me I bought a good Sword of one who had been in the Pursuit, and some other Booty, boafling all about the Army, that I had gained it in the Fight I met my Master, who being brought along desperately wounded, and past all Hopes, said to me *You Scoundrel, why did you not do as I ordered you?* I answered, *because, Sir, I was afraid to be your Condition* He was carried into the Town, where he soon ended his Days for want of being fo discreet as I. He left me rather out of his own innate Goodness and Generosity, than for any good Service I had done him, a Horse, and fifty Ducats God grant him fifty thousand Ages of Blis for his Kindness, and double that Term to any one who shall hereafter fo far oblige me as to do the like
By this Time you may suppose I was pretty reasonable ; for I had got the Name of the merry *Englishman*, and being out of Place, spent my Money like a Lord My Purse being exhausted, I got into the Service of Count *Picolomeni* , and a little afterwards, we were ordered to march towards *Hainault*, and in a few Days encamped under the Walls of *Mons*
A comical Adventure befel me one Day in this Place I happen'd to go abroad, after dining in the Town, with my Head fo full, that I took Children for Men, and Blue for Black Staggering along in this Condition, I came up to a Chandler's Shop, which was all hung about with Rows of Tallow Candles, and I taking them for Bunches of Radishes, asked the Owner, why he pulled the Leaves off? He not understanding what I meant, and perceiving the Pickle I was in, made me no answer, but fell a laughing very heartily , but I who had doubtless a drunken Longing for Radishes, put out my Hand to one of the Rows that hung upon a long Stick, and laying hold of two Candles, pulled fo hard, that all the Range came down The Shopkeeper seeing his Goods broken, took up a Cudgel, and exercised it fo, you would have thought he had been beating of Stock fish Tho' drunk, I was fo fenfible of the Pain, that drawing my Sword, I charged him as my mortal Enemy He seeing me void of Fear and Reason, fled into a Room behind the Shop, and shut the Door after him Finding that though I made hundred Pushes at the Door, the Smart of my Bones did nothing abate, I vented my Spleen against the Candles, and laying about me, left the whole Shop strewed with Greafe
It happened a Gang of Soldiers were passing by, and they at the Request of the Neighbours, carried me out into the Street by Force, I still crying, *What cudgel me for a Radish or two which are not worth a Farthing* A Complaint was carried to my Master, who ordered me to be sent to Goal, and the next Day, when I awaked, I found myself in Irons
There I suffered for the Radish Fray, there I fasted though it was not Lent, and there was I dieted without any Liberty of getting drunk. At length my Mistress took Pity on me, and begged my Master to forgive me, who seeing me protected by such

an Angel, ordered me to be set free, on my paying for the Damage done to the Candles. I left the Goal with a full Resolution never more to disoblige my Master

I lived so sedate and modest for a little Time after this, that it surpriz'd my Master, who continually heaped new Favours upon me, and I leaving off drinking for the present, grew amorous To this Purpose I made Choice of a Waiting-Maid, a Country Lass in Dress, but a Courtier in keeping her Word She was young in Years, but old in Cunning, carried all her Fortune about her, and being Fatherless, for the more Decency and Security of her Person, served an Aunt of hers, who kept a Tavern, where I was acquainted I set my Heart on this Virgin-Pullet, and one Day putting my Hand upon her soft Bubbies she gave me such a Kick, that I defy the best *Flanders* Mare to have out-done her. She withdrew into her Chamber, and from that Time fled from me, as if I had been the Devil. I was up to the Ears in Love, and knew not what to do. However, at last, I wrote a *Billet-Doux*, and accompanied it with a Present The poor harmless Creature, who had been several Times upon Trial before, and still pleaded, *Lord, I know not what you mean*, bit at the Bait, received the Present, heard the Message, and gave me Leave, under the Pretence of quenching my Thirst, to pay her a Visit, which I did, and from that Moment she begin to fleece me, and her Aunt to pluck my Feathers Our Love grew so hot, that the Customers who used the Tavern, took Notice of it, therefore, to save her Reputation, for she passed for a Maid, I took Lodgings for her, and by that Means got her from her Aunt My Lady was so nice, that she could not eat Snails, because they had Horns; nor Fish, because of the Bones, nor Rabbits, because they had Tails She swooned away at the Sight of a Mouse; but rejoiced to see a Company of Grenadiers Before me she fed by Ounces, and in my Absence by Pounds She hated to be confined, and loved Liberty, and, under Colour of Melancholy, was never from the Window or Door At first, she used to receive Abundance of Visitors, pretending that all the Men were her Cousins; but I being informed they were carnal Kindred, put her into an Inclosure, taking a Room that had no Window to the Street, and when I went abroad, left a Spy upon her Actions.

Every now and then she would be lost, and rise again the third Day, as drowned Bodies do; though she shed Abundance of Tears, and swore a thousand Oaths to perswade me, that my ill Nature made her withdraw herself to her Aunt's; and that she had never been out of her Doors, nor seen by any Body, yet I did not forbear thrashing of her so severely, that she did not for a good while shew any more of her Tricks.

I was confoundedly Jealous of this Creature, and not without a Reason; for I had her not in keeping above four Months, before she very civilly tipped me a Distemper very common in *Naples*. Enraged at this, I beat her unmercifully, took away all her Cloaths, but a few Rags, and kicked her out of Doors I advised with a Surgeon and a Physician about my Case, who both condemned me to be anointed like a *Witch*, and to slabber like a *Natural* But I hoping to find some Way to avoid enduring the Pains of Hell in this World, went to every Doctor of Note: I told them my Distemper, and they all unanimously told me, *That if I designed to live, I must forbear Drinking* (and they had as good have bid me cut my own Throat) *and that the Wine I had so plentifully swallowed, was to be distilled out of my Body in Water.* Perceiving

36

they all agreed in the same Story, I resolved to get into the Hospital, and take a gentle Salivation.

I was kindly received, those good People being willing to entertain one Mad-man more in their godly House, and treating me like a Soul in Purgatory, they scalded my Intrails, and stifled me for want of Breath, keeping me always, like *Dives*, with my Tongue hanging out of my Mouth a Quarter of a Yard, still begging a Drop of Wine of some poor *Lazarus*, and preaching up the Works of Mercy; but they told me, *That Patience was a Virtue, and would carry me to Heaven; and that I must suffer for my former Excesses.* At the End of two Months, I had been in the Hospital, I was dismissed perfectly cured, but my Legs look'd like Trap-sticks, my Body like a Shotten-Herring, and my Voice like an Eunuch

The first Enquiry I made, was, for the next Tavern, and there I eat every Thing I could come at, as if I had been a Man in perfect Health, making a Jest of the Doctor, and laughing at the Surgeon, bestowing a thousand Blessings on the good Man that first found out the Vine, and double the Number on those who plant and prune it. After I had got a good Refreshment, I enquired after my kind Mistreis and her Aunt, both of whom had left the Place just after I had enter'd the Hospital. I was not at all sorry for it; but went to find out some of my old Comrades, whom I found merrily carousing At last a Dispute arose among them, and Swords were drawn. I was Fool enough to concern myself, and one of the Party against me, gave me such a Blow with his Sword (but as it happen'd it was the flat Part) that he made me void a Flood of Claret at my Mouth All the Skipkennel Troop took to their Heels, thinking I was killed, and I believing myself not far from it, bawled out for a Surgeon, who was called, and he feeling my Pulse beat very unregular, and observing how I reached and sweated, never enquired into the Cause of my Distemper, but bid the Landlord get a Priest to prepare me for Death The good Man being unwilling, I should die like a *Heathen* in a *Christian Country*, run in all Haste, and brought one, who being curious to see the Wound, took off my Hat, and found my Head clear from Blood, and without any other Hurt but a Bump raised by the Stroke I had received He asked those who had seen the Fray, *Whether I had any other Wounds besides that?* And being informed I had not, says to the Master of the House, *If this Man was to make his Confession every Time he is troubled with this Distemper, he ought always to have a Chaplain along with him Sleep is the only Thing will cure this Disorder; therefore carry him to Bed, and I will answer for his Life* His Orders were obeyed, and the next Morning I found myself out of Danger, and went to wait on my Master, who received me with a frowning Brow, and bid me begone about my Business, that he discarded me his Service, and left me at Liberty to go where I pleased. This was a terrible Blow to me, but I was comforted the next Morning by my generous Master's sending me a handsome Present in Gold, with a Command from him to leave the Place, which I did the next Morning, resolving to go to *France*, and from thence to my native Country.

The Carrier with whom I set out, was a great Gamester, and the second Night invited me to his Room, which was next the Stable, and there by the Light of a scurvy Lamp, I won all his Money. Enraged at his ill-fortune, he threw the Cards in my Face, and I in return, wiped him a-cross the Face with my Hat. He ran to a Corner to lay hold of a rusty Sword, and I discharged the Lamp

N n

at

at him so furiously, that he was all over Oil, and I half dead with Fear, being in the dark, and the Door shut. However, I was so fortunate to find the Salley-Port, and fled to the Watch, whither my greasy Carrier followed me with his rusty Tilter. A Corporal met and disarmed him, after giving each of us half a Dozen Bangs, and then inquired into the Affair, and endeavoured to reconcile us, but in vain, the Carrier refusing to consent, till I paid the Damage done to his Coat: I gave him Half his Money again, and the other Part I spent on the Corporal, Watchmen, myself, and the Carrier, drowning the Quarrel, and forgetting all Wrongs.

After travelling many a tedious Mile, I at last got to *Calais*, and from thence to *London* Being come to the Metropolis, I went directly to my Father's House, that had been, which upon Enquiry, I found in the Hands of a Stranger. I asked for my Sisters, and was told, they were remov'd into another World I found they had both been married, and had left Children; so that my Hopes of getting any Thing by their Death's proved abortive. Destitute of Friends, I knew not what to do, especially finding the Gout come upon me At last, by the Advice of an Acquaintance, I took a Publick-House, and understanding several Languages, have now very good Custom from Foreigners I intend to leave off my foolish Pranks, and as I have spent my juvenile Years, and Money in keeping Company, hope to find some Fools, as bad as myself, who delight in throwing away their Estates, and impairing their Healths.

This is all the Account he gives of himself, and all the information we can get further of him, is that he kept an Inn in *Smithfield*, and got a considerable Fortune; but being eager to be rich at once, he join'd with his Hostler committed a most barbarous and cruel Murder; for a Gentleman who had purchased an Estate in the Country was obliged to pay the Money in *London*, and accordingly came to Town for that Purpose, putting up at *Batson's-Inn*. The Hostler, in taking the Gentleman's Baggs off, perceived they were very heavy, and acquainted his Master with it, and they two soon agreed to murder the Gentleman, and divide the Booty, the first of which was barbarously executed by the Hostler, who cut the Guest's Throat, and then they removed the Body into a Closet, but a Dispute arose in dividing the Money, which made the Hostler leave his Master with what he could get; and he getting drunk the same Night, discovered the inhuman Deed, producing several Pieces of Gold as a Confirmation The Neighbours at first thought it was all Fiction, 'til the Fellow often calling God to Witness of the Truth, and vowing Revenge on his Master (thinking by his Discovery to save himself) that a Stander by, more penetrating than the rest, sent for a Constable, and got him secured, who being carried before a Magistrate persisted in it, and desired the House of his Master might be searched, which was accordingly done, and the Body found In a small Time after, they were both arraigned and convicted The Hostler died just after, but *Batson* was deservedly executed, dying penitent, and in the Communion of the Church of *Rome*, whose Principles he had imbibed by going into foreign Parts. And thus ended the Life of this detestable Villain about a Year before the Restauration of King *Charles* the Second

The LIFE *of* WILLIAM NEVISON.

AS Arts and Sciences of Use and Morality admit of improvement, so likewise those of Villainy grow up with them, the Devil being as industrious to improve his Followers in the Schools of Vice, as our best Instructors are in those of Virtue, which will be illustrated in the following Memoirs of the Life of *William Nevison*, who was born at *Pomfret* in *Yorkshire*, about the Year 1639. of well-reputed, honest, and reasonably-estated Parents, who bred him up at School, where he made some Progress as to his Learning, and in the Spring of his Youth promised a better Harvest, than the Summer of his Life produced; for, to say Truth, he was very forward and hopeful, 'till he arrived at thirteen or fourteen Years of Age, when he began to be the Ringleader of all his young Companions, to Rudeness and Debauchery.

So early as this he also took to Thieving, and stole a Silver Spoon from his Father, for which being severally punished at School, the Punishment was the Subject of the next Night's Meditation, which issued into a Resolution of Revenge on his Master, whatever Fate he met with in the Execution thereof; to which End, having hit on a Project for his Purpose, and lying in his Father's Chamber, he gets softly up before such Time as the Day appeared, and hearing that his Father was asleep, he puts his Hand into his Pocket, where he found the Key of his Closet, which unperceived he drew thence, and down he creeps to the said Closet, where he supplies himself with what Cash he could readily find, which amounted to about ten Pounds, and with this, knowing that his said Master had a Horse he had particular Delight for, that then grazed behind his House, he gets a Bridle and Saddle from his Father's Stable, and an Hour before Morning, arrays and mounts the said Horse onward for *London*, where he arrived with in four Days; when the Evening coming upon him, he cut the Throat of the Horse, within a Mile or two of the Town, for Fear he should prove a Means of his Discovery, if he should have carried it to an Inn.

When he came to *London*, he changed his Garb and Name, and being a lusty well-looking Lad, had put himself into the Service of a Brewer, where for two or three Years he lived, not at all changed in Mind, though Opportunity was not, during that Time, ripe to put his ill intentions in Practice, tho' he watched all Seasons to advance himself, by having several Times attempted to rob his Master, which at last he thus effected Taking the Advantage one Night of the Clerk's Drunkenness, who was his Master

ter's Cashier, he got up by Stealth after him into the Compting-House, where the said Clerk falling asleep, he rifled the same of all such Cash as he could conveniently come at, which amounted to near two hundred Pounds, and fled to *Holland*, where runing away with a Burgher's Daughter, that had robbed her Father of a great Deal of Money and Jewels, he was apprehended, had the Booty taken from him, and clapt in Goal; and, had he not broke out, he had certainly made his Exit beyond Sea. Having thus made his Escape, he got, after divers Difficulties, into *Flanders*, and listed himself amongst the *English* Volunteers, who were under the Command of the Duke of *York*, who 'bout the same Time was made Lieutenant-General of the *Spanish* Forces, under Don *John* of *Austria*, that were then designed to raise the Siege of *Dunkirk*, which was besieged by the *English* and *French* Armies, and behaved himself very well, while he was in a Military Employment; but not greatly liking it, and having got some Money whilst he was in the Service, he came over to *England*, and bought himself a Horse and Arms, and resolving for the Road, and perhaps a pleasant Life, at the Hazard of his Neck, rather than toil out a long Remainder of unhappy Days in Want and Poverty, which he was always averse to. Being thus supplied every Day, one Booty or other enriched his Stores, which he would never admit a Sharer in, chusing to manage his Designs alone, rather than trust his Life into the Hand of others, who by Favour or Misfortune might be drawn in to accuse him.

One Day *Nevison*, who went otherwise by the Name of *Johnson*, travelling on the Road, and scouring about in Search of a Prize, he met two Countrymen, who, coming up towards him, informed him, that it was very dangerous travelling forward, for that the Way was set, and they had been robbed by three Highwaymen, about half a Mile off; and if he had any Charge of Money about him, it were his safest Course to turn back. *Nevison*, asking them what they had lost, they told him 40 Pounds; whereupon he replied, Turn back with me, and shew me the Way they took, and my Life to a Farthing, I'll make them return you your Money again, they rid along with him till they had Sight of the Highwaymen; when *Nevison* ordering the Countrymen to stay behind him at some Distance, he rid up and spoke to the Foremost of them, Saying, Sir, by your Garb and the Colour of your Horse, you should be one of those I looked after, and if so, my Business is to tell you, that you borrowed of two Friends of mine 40 Pounds, which they desired me to demand of you, and which before we part you must restore. How! quoth the Highwayman, 40 Pounds! Darini you, Sir, what is the Fellow mad? So mad, replied *Nevison*, as that your Life shall answer me, if you do not give me better Satisfaction. With this he draws his Pistol, and suddenly claps it to his Breast, who finding then, that *Nevison* had also his Reign, and that he could not get his Sword or Pistol, he yielded, telling him, his Life was at his Mercy. No, says *Nevison*, 'tis not that I seek for, but the Money you robbed these two Men of, who are riding up to me, which you must refund.

The Thief was forced to consent, and readily to deliver such Part thereof, as he had, saying his Companions had the rest, so that *Nevison* having made him dismount, and taking away his Pistols, which he gave to the Countrymen, ordered them to secure him, and hold his own, whilst he took the Thief's Horse, and pursued the other two, who he soon overtook; for they thinking him their Companion, stopt as soon as they saw him, so that he came up to them in the Midst of a Common. How now, *Jack*, says

one of them, what made you engage with yon Fellow? No Gentlemen, replies *Nevison*, you are mistaken in your Man; Thomas, by the Token of your Horse and Arms, he hath sent me to you for the Ransom of his Life, which comes to no less than the Prize of the Day, which, if you presently surrender, you may go about your Business, if not, I must have a little Dispute with you at Sword and Pistol. At which, one of them let fly at him, but missing his Aim, received *Nevison*'s Bullet into his Right Shoulder; and being thereby disabled, *Nevison*, about to discharge at the other, he call'd for Quarter, and came to a Parley, which, in short, was made up, with *Nevison*'s Promise to send their Friend, and their delivering him all the ready Money they had, which amounted to 150 Pounds. With this, *Nevison* rides back to the two Countrymen, and releases their Prisoner, giving them their whole forty Pounds, with a Caution, for the future to look better after it, and not like Cowards, as they were, to surrender the same on such easy Terms again.

In all his Pranks he was very favourable to the female Sex, who generally gave him the Character of a civil obliging Robber; he was charitable also to the Poor, as relieving them out of their Spoils, which he took from them that could better spare it; and being a true Royalist, he never attempted any thing against that Party. One Time *Nevison* meeting with an old Sequestrator on the Road, he stop'd the Coach, and demanded some of that Money which he had churlishly extorted from poor Widows and Orphans, and ought to be returned. At which Words the old Man in a Fit of Terror, and especially to, when a Pistol was clap'd to his Breast, begun to expostulate for his Life; offering whatsoever he had about him for his Ransom, which he readily delivered to the Value of 60 Broad-pieces of Gold. But this not serving the Turn, *Nevison* told him that he must come thence; and go with him about some other Affairs he had to concert with him, and beg'd Leave of three young Gentlewomen that were also Passengers in the Coach with him, that they would spare one of the Coach-Horses for one Hour or two, which should certainly be returned that Night for the next Days Journey. So *Nevison* left them, and took his Prize with him on the Postilion, which he loos'd from his Coach, and carried him from them in a great Fright, thinking he was now near his End, the Gentlewomen pursued their Journey; about two Hours after they were got to their Inn, in comes the old Sequestrator on the Postilion's Horse before mentioned; and gave a lamentable Relation how he had been used, and forced to sign a Bill under his Hand, of 900 Pounds for his Redemption, payable by a Scrivener in *London* on sight, which he doubted not but wou'd be received before he could prevent the same; and indeed he did not doubt amiss, for *Nevison* made the best of his Way, all Night, and the next Day by Noon received the Money, to the no small Vexation of him that owned it.

Having one Day met a considerable Prize, to the Value 450 Pounds, from a rich Country Grazier, with this he was resolved to set down quietly; and go back to *Pomfret*, where he was most joyfully received by his Father, who never hearing of him in his Absence of seven or eight Years, thought he had been really dead. He lived very honestly with his Father till he died, and then returned to his old Courses again, committing such Robberies, as rendered his Name the Terror of the Road; insomuch, that no Carrier or Drover that pass'd the same, but was either forced to compound for their Safety by a constant Rent, which he usually received from them at such and such Houses, where he appointed them

them to leave it, or they were sure to be rifled for the Failure thereof.

Committing some Robberies in *Leicestershire*, he was there taken, and committed to *Leicester* Goal, where he was so narrowly watch'd, and strongly ironed, that he could scarce stir; yet, by a cunning Stratagem, he procured his Enlargement before the Assizes came. For one Day, feigning himself extremely ill, he sent for two or three trusty Friends, one of which was a Physician, who gave out that he was sick of a pestilential Fever; and that, unless he had the Benefit of some open Air, in some Chamber, he would certainly infect the whole Goal, and die of the said Distemper. Hereupon, the Goaler takes off his Fetters, and removes him into another Room, to lie by himself; in the mean Time, a Nurse was provided him, and his Physician came twice or thrice a Day to visit him, who gave out there was no Hopes of his Life, and that his Distemper was extremely contagious. On which Report, the Goaler's Wife would not let her Husband, nor any of the Servants, go nearer than the Door; which gave *Nevison*'s Confederates a full Liberty to practise their Intent, which they did thus: A Painter was one Day brought in, who made all over his Breast blue Spots, resembling those that are the Forerunners of Death in the Disease commonly called the Plague, as likewise, several Marks on his Hands, Face, and Body, which are usually on such that so die. All which being done, the Physician prepared a Dose whereby his Spirits were confined for the Space of an Hour or two, and then immediately gave out that he was dead. Hereupon his Friends demanded his Body, bringing a Coffin to carry him away in. The Goaler, as customary, orders a Jury, the Nurse having formerly laid him out to examine the Cause of his Death, who fearing the Contagion he was said to die of, staid not long to consider thereon; but having view'd him, seeing the Spots and Marks of Death about him, his Eyes set, and his Jaws close muffled, they brought in their Verdict that he died of the Plague, and thereupon he was put in the Coffin, and carried off.

Being thus discharged, he falls to his Trade again, and meeting several of his old Tenants the Carriers, who had used to pay him his Rents, as aforesaid, told them they must advance the same, for that his last Imprisonment had cost him a great Sum of Money, which he expected to be reimburs'd among them. They being strangely surprized at the Sight of Mr. *Nevison*, after the Reports of his Death, bruited about that his Ghost walked, and took upon him the Employment it was wont when living, which was the more confirmed by the Goaler at *Leicester*, who had brought in his Verdict of the Jury on Oath, who had examined the Body, and had found it dead, as abovemention'd, whereby he had been discharged by the Court, as to the Warrant of his Commitment. But afterwards, when the same came to be known, and the Cheat detected, the said Goaler was ordered to fetch him in, at his Peril. Whereupon great Search was made for him in all Places, and a Reward of twenty Pounds set upon his Head for any Person that should apprehend him.

Nevison, after this, was determined to visit *London*; and the Company he happen'd to fall into upon the Road, was a Crew of Canting Beggars, Pilgrims of the Earth, the Offspring of *Cain*, Vagabonds and Wanderers over the whole World, fit Companions for such who made a Trade of Idleness and Roguery, and these were at this Time fit Companions for him, who, seeing the merry Life they led, resolved to make one of their Company; whereupon, after he had a little more ingratiated himself

amongst them, and taken two or three Cups more of Rum-booz, he imparted his Inventions to one of the chief of them, telling him, he was an Apprentice, who had a curst Master, whose Cruelties had caused him to run away from him, and that whatever Fortune might betide him, yet should not the most necessitous Condition he could be plunged into ever make him return to him again. And therefore if he might be admitted into their Society, he should faithfully observe and perform what Rules and Orders were imposed upon him. The chief Beggar very much applauded him for his Resolution, telling him, that to be a Beggar was to be a brave Man, since it was then in Fashion. *Do not we, said he, come into the World like arrant Beggars, without a Rag upon us? And do not we all go out of the World like Beggars, without a Rag upon us? And do not we all go out of the World like Beggars, without any Thing, saving only an old Sheet over us? Shall we then be ashamed to walk up and down in the World like Beggars, with old Blankets pinn'd about us? No, no, that would be a Shame to us, indeed: Have we not the whole Kingdom to walk in, at our Pleasure? Are we afraid of the Approach of Quarter-day? Do we walk in Fear of Bailiffs, Serjeants, and Catch-poles? Who ever knew an arrant Beggar arrested for Debt? Is not our Meat dress'd in every Man's Kitchen? Does not every Man's Cellar afford us Beer? And the best Men's Purses keep a Penny for us to spend.*

Having by these Words, as he thought, fully fixed him in Love with Begging, he then acquainted the Company with *Nevison*'s Desires, who were all of them very joyful thereat, being as glad to add one to their Society, as a *Turk* is to gain a proselite to *Mahomet*; the first Question they asked him was, If he had any Loure in his Bung. He stared on them, not knowing what they meant; till, at last, one told him it was Money in his Purse. He told them he had but eighteen Pence, which he freely gave them. This, by a general Vote, was condemned to be spent in Booze for his Initiation. Then they commanded him to kneel down, which being done, one of the chief of them took a Gage of Booze, which is a Quart of Drink, and poured the same on his Head, saying, *I do by Virtue of this Sovereign Liquor, install thee in the Rouge, and make thee a free Denizon of our Ragged Regiment. So that henceforth it shall be lawful for thee to cant, and to carry a Doxy or Mort along with thee, only observing these Rules: First, that thou art not to wander up and down all Countries, but to keep to that Quarter that is allotted to thee. And, secondly, thou art to give Way to any of us that have born all the Offices of the Wallet before, and upon holding up a Finger, to avoid any Town or Country Village, where thou seest we are foraging for Victuals for our Army that march along with us. Observing these two Rules, we take thee into our Protection, and adopt thee a Brother of our numerous Society.*

Having ended his Oration, *Nevison* rose up, and was congratulated by all the Company's hanging about him like so many Dogs about a Bear, and leaping and shouting like so many Madmen, making such a confused Noise with their Gabling, that the Melody of a Dozen of Oyster-Wives, the Scolding at ten Conduits, and the Gossiping of fifteen Bake-houses, were not comparable unto it. At length he that installed him, cried out for Silence, bidding the *French* and *English* Pox to light on their Throats for making such a Yelping. Then fixing their Eyes upon *Nevison*, he read a Lecture to him out of the Devil's Horn Book, as followeth.

Now, saith he, thou art entered into our Fraternity
the

thou must not scruple to act any Villainies, which thou shalt be able to perform, whether it be to nip a Bung, like the Peter Cloy, the Lurries Crash, either a Bleating Cheat, Cackling Cheat, Grunting Cheat, Quacking Cheat, Tib oth-buttery, Margery Prater, or to cloy a Mish from the Crackman's, that is, to cut a Purse, steal a Cloak-Bag, or Portmanteau, convey all Manner of Things, whether a Chicken, Sucking-Pig, Duck, Goose, Hen, or steal a Shirt from the Hedge; for he that will be a Quier Cove, a profest Rogue, must observe this Rule, set down by an antient Patrico in these Words

> Wi't thou a begging go
> O per se o, O per se-o
> Then must thou God forsake,
> And to the Devil thee betake
> O per se-o, &c

And because thou art yet but a Novice in begging, and understandest not the Mysteries of the Canting Language, to principle thee the better, thou shalt have a Doxy to be thy Companion, by whom thou mayst receive fit Instructions for thy Purpose. And thereupon he singled him out a Girl of about fourteen Years of Age, which tickled his Fancy very much, that he had gotten a young Wanton to dally withal, but this was not all, he must presently be married to her, after the Fashion of their Patrico, who amongst Beggars, is their Priest, which was done after this Manner

They got a Hen, and having cut off the Head of it, laid the dead Body on the Ground, placing him on the one Side, and his Doxy on the other, this being done, the Patrico standing by, with a loud Voice, bid us live together till Death did us part; then one of the Company went into the Yard, and fetched a dry Cow-Turd which was broken over his Doxy's Head in Imitation of a Bride-Cake, and so shaking Hands and kissing each other, the Ceremony of the Wedding was over, and for Joy of the Marriage, they where all as drunk as Beggars; but then to hear the Gabling Noise they made would have made any one burst himself with laughing Some were Jabbering in the Canting Language, others in their own; some did nothing but weep, and protest Love to their Morts, others swore Swords and Daggers to cut the Throats of their Doxies, if they found them tripping, one would drink a Health to the Bride till he slaver'd again, some were for singing Bawdy Songs, others were divising Oaths for Justice of Peace, Headboroughs and Constables At last Night approaching, and all their Money being spent, they betook to a Barn not far off, where they couched a Hogshead in the Darkman's, and went to Sleep

Nevison having met with this odd Piece of Diversion in his Journey, slipt out of the Barn, when all were asleep, took Horse and posted directly away But coming to London, and finding his Name too much noised about to induce him to stay there, he returned into the Country, and fell to his own Pranks again Several who had been robbed by him, happened to meet him, and could not help thinking but his Ghost walk'd, considering the Report of his Pestilential Death in Lincoln Goal In short, his Crimes became so notorious, that a Reward was offered for any that would apprehend him. This made many way-lay him, especially two Brothers, named Fletchers, one of whom Nevison shooting dead, he got off, from whence going into a little Village about thirteen Miles from York, he was taken by Capt Hardcastle, and sent to York Goal, where in a Week's Time he was tried, condemned, and executed, aged Forty-Five.

The LIFE of JACK BIRD.

THIS notorious Malefactor was born at Stainford in Lincolnshire, of very honest Parents, by whom, after he had been at School to learn Reading, Writing, and Accounts, he was put Apprentice to a Baker at Godmanchester, near Huntington He had not served three Years before he run away from his Master, came to London, and listed in the Foot-Guards While he was in the Army, he was at the Siege of Maestricht, under the Command of the Duke of Monmouth, who was General of the English Forces in the Low Countries.

Here he was reduced to such Necessities as are common to Men, who engage themselves to kill one another for a Groat or Five-Pence a Day, This occasion'd him to run away from his Colours, and fly to Amsterdam, where he stole a Piece of Silk off a Stall, for which Fact he was apprehended, and dragged before a Migistrate The Effect of this was a Commitment to the Rasp-House, where he was put to hard Labour, such as Rasping Log-wood and other Drudgeries, for a Twelve-Month

As Jack had never been used to Work, he fainted under the Sentence, though to little Purpose, for his Task-Masters imputing it to a stubborn Laziness, inflicted a severer Punishment upon him · The Manner of which was as follows He was chained down to the Bottom of a dry Cistern by one Foot, immediately upon which, several Cocks were set a running into it, and he was obliged to pump for his Life The Cistern was much deeper that he was high; so that if the Water had prevailed he, must inevitably have been drowned without Relief or Pity Jack was very sensible of his Danger, which occasioned him to labour with all his Might for an Hour, which was as long as the Sentence was to continue.

Having overcome this Difficulty, he ply'd his Business very well the remaining Part of the Year, when being released, he returned into England, with a Resolution to try his Fortune on the Highway. Near St Edmundsbury he stole a Horse, and he had before provided half a Dozen good Pistols, and a Sword Success attended him in his three or four first Robberies, but an unluckly Adventure soon brought about a Turn of his Affairs

In the Road between _Gravesend_ and _Chatham_, he met with one Mr _Joseph Pinnis_, a Pilot of _Dover_, who had lost both his Hands in an Engagement He had been at _London_ to receive ten or twelve Pounds for carrying a _Dutch_ Ship up the River When _Bird_ accosted him with the Salutation common to Gentlemen of his Profession, _You see, Sir_, quoth Pinnis, _that I have never a Hand, so that I am not able to take my Money out of my Pocket myself Be so kind, therefore, as to take the Trouble of Searching me_ _Jack_ soon consented to this very reasonable Request, but while he was very busy in examining the Contents of the Pilot's Purse, the boisterous old Tar suddenly clapp'd his Arms about his Neck, and spurring his own Horse, pulled our Adventurer from his; then falling directly upon him, and being a very strong Man, he kept him under, and maul'd him with his Stumps, which were plated In the Midst of the Scuffle some Passengers came by, and enquired the Occasion of it. Mr _Pinnis_ replied with telling them the Particulars, and desiring them to supply his Place, and give the Villain a little more of the same, adding, _That he was almost out of Breath with what he had done already_. When the Company understood what was the Reason of the Pilot's labouring so hard upon the Bones of our Ruffian, they apprehended him, and carried him before a Justice, who committed him to _Maidstone_ Goal, where he continued till the Assizes, and then was condemned to be hang'd

This Time _Jack_ had the good Fortune to receive Mercy, and afterwards to obtain his Liberty The Remembrance of his being so heartily thumped by a Man without Hands, stuck so much in his Stomach that he had almost a Mind to grow honest, and indeed he continued pretty orderly, till he was again reduced to necessitous Circumstances, for Want of Employment He had no Trade that he was Master of, nor Learning enough to secure him a Maintenance in a genteel Way, so that when he found himself in the utmost Streights, he could see no other Method of supporting himself, than what he had formerly followed

The first that he met with, after he had resolved to set out in Pursuit of new Enterprizes, was a _Welch Drover_, about a Mile beyond _Acton_ The Fellow being almost as stout as Mr _Pinnis_, would not obey the usual Precept, but was going to lay about him with a good Quarter-Staff, which he had in his Hands. _Jack_, when he saw _Taffy's_ Courage, leapt nimble out of the Way of his Staff, and told him, _That he had been taken once by a Son of a Whore without Hands, and for that Trick_, says he, _I shall not venture my Carcass within Reach of one that has Hands, for fear of something worse_. While he was speaking, he pulled out a Pistol, and instantly shot him through the Head Rifling his Pockets, and finding but Eighteen-Pence, said ironically, _This is a Prize worth killing a Man for at any Time_ He then rode away about his Business as little concern'd as if he had done no Mischief at all

Another Time _Jack Bird_ met with _Poor Robin_ the Almanack Writer, on the Road going to _Waltham-Abbey_ Poor and rich were all the same to him, when they came in his Way; so the honest Astrologer was greeted with the Salutation of _Stand and Deliver_ It was the first Time that _Robin_ had been attacked on the Highway; and as he received no Intimation of this from the Stars, he stood and star'd as if he had been Planet-struck _Bird_ told him he was in Earnest, and _Robin_ reply'd with a Complaint

of his Poverty. _That_, says _Jack_, _is a common Thread-bare Excuse, and will not save your Bacon_—For quoth the Star-Gazer, _my Name is Poor Robin I am the Author of those Almanacks that come out yearly in my Name, and I have canoniz'd a great many Gentlemen of your Profession_ Look in my Calendar for Guzman, Jonas Allen, Hind, Du Val, Du Cor bray-Beis, Moll Cutpurse, _and others_ Let this be my Protection All was in vain, our inexorable Free Booter ransack'd his Pockets of fifteen Shillings, took a new Hat from his Head, and then told him, _That now he had given him Cause to cannonize him too_ Which _Robin_ promised to do the first Year after he had suffered Martyrdom at _Tyburn_, and so they parted

Being again encouraged by a Series of successful Adventures, and having remounted himself on a very good Horse, he was resolved to venture on higher Exploits An Opportunity for putting this Resolution into Practice, soon fell in his Way, by meeting the mad Earl of P———, and his Chaplain, who was little better than himself, in a Coach, with no more Attendants than the Coachman, and one Footman _Stand and deliver_ was the Word His Lordship told him, that he did not trouble himself about losing the small Matter he had about him · But then, says he, _I hope you will fight for it_ _Jack_, upon this, pulled out a Brace of Pistols, and let off a Volley of Imprecations _Don't put yourself into a Passion, Friend_, says his Honour, _but lay down your Pistols, and I will box you fairly for all the Money I have, against nothing_ _That's an honourable Challenge, my Lord_, quoth _Jack_, _provided none of your Servants be near us_ The Earl immediately order'd them to keep at a Distance

The Chaplain, like _Withrington_ in the old Ballad of _Chevy-Chace_, could not bear to see an Earl fight on Foot, while he stood looking on, so he desired the Honour of espousing the Cause of his Lordship To which both Parties readily agreeing, off went the Divinity in a Minute, and to Blows and Bloody Noses they came

Tho' _Jack_ had once the ill-Fortune to be stumped out of his Liberty by a sturdy old Sailor, he was nevertheless too hard for his Reverence in less than a Quarter of an Hour He beat him in such a Manner that he could not see, and had but just Breath enough to cry, _I'll fight no more_ About two Minutes after this Victory (which he took for a breathing Time) _Jack_ told his Lordship, _That now, if he pleased, he would take a Turn with him_——_By all Means_, quoth the Earl, _for if you beat my Chaplain, you will beat me, he and I having tried our Manhood before_. So giving our Hero twenty Guineas, his Honour rode off in a whole Skin

While _Jack_ resided in Town, he married a young Woman, who had been Servant to a Dyer near Exeter Exchange in the _Strand_ This Girl, while she was in Place, us'd to set up a-Nights for her Master, and, in short, to use him so very civily, that it was the Occasion of her Destruction A particular Account of this Affair will not be disagreeable, nor entirely foreign to our Design

The Dyer's Wife, having entertain'd a Jealousy from some Observations she had made, as well as from her Husband's Backwardness in the Performance of Family Duty, she was resolved to examine into the Bottom of the Affair Accordingly, one Night commanded the Maid to go to Bed, and undertook to sit up for her Husband herself Betwixt twelve and one he came Home, and Madam open'd the Door in the Dark, without speaking a Word. The good Man was silent as his supposed Maid

CAP^{t.} AVERY & his Crew taking one of y^e GREAT MOGULS Ships

B Cole sculp.

aloud, and very orderly laid her on a Coanter, exerted his Manhood, and gave her Half-a-Crown, according to Custom   Madam immediately slipp'd away to Bed, and her dear Spouse follow'd her, as soon as he had fasten'd up the Street-Door, without the least Suspicion of what had passed

The next Morning Mr ——— was amaz'd to see his Servant packing up her Cloaths, as soon as he was out of Bed   The Surprize encreased when he observed the surly Behaviour of his Wife, saw her pay the Girl her Wages, and bid her be gone forthwith   The young Woman without Doubt, was as much confused as her Master, being altogether as ignorant of the Cause, she durst not speak one Word for herself, such a Hurry was her Mistress in   At last M. ——— took the Courage to speak *Pray, my Dear, what's the Meaning of all this?   What has the poor Wench done to be thus turn'd out of Doors at an Hour's Warning?   I never found her dishonest, if you have, let her know what you accuse her with. Perhaps she may do better another Time   Or, if you are bent upon discharging her, don't give People Room to say you have us'd her unhandsomely*   The Devil a Word could he get more than, *She was a saucy Baggage, and go she should*   Accordingly, when her Things were all ready, she came into the Parlour to bid her Master and Mistress Good-b'ye. Just as she was going out of Doors, *Hold! Hold!* Betty says the Mistress, *here's Half-a-Crown that I earn'd for you last Night upon the Counter, take that along with you*   The Dyer, upon this, apprehended how Matters went, and was willing afterwards to make his Submission, that he might come to Terms with his dear offended Wife, who continually teiz'd him with the *Half-Crown* and the *Counter*.

The *Athenian* Society, who made themselves sufficiently famous about this Time by their Monthly Productions, took a great Deal of Pains in the Case above, before they could resolve whether or no the Dyer had committed Adultery with his own Wife They concluded at last, that tho' the Act of Copulation was with his own Spouse, yet he was chargeble with the Crime of Adultery, as his Design was on another Person, whom he could not lawfully touch   This Enquiry gave considerable Diversion to the Town, and made the poor Dyer a general Subject of Ridicule

But though *Bird* was married, he did not confine himself to any one Woman; for we are told that he was continually in Company with Whores and Bawds One Night in Particular, having a Woman with him, he knock'd down a Man, between *Dutchy-Lane*, and the *Great Savoy-Gate* in the *Strand*, and having robb'd him, made off safely, but the Woman was apprehended, and sent to *Newgate*   *Jack* went to her, in Hopes to make up the Affair with the Prosecutor, and was thereupon taken, on Suspicion, and confin'd with her

At his Trial he confessed the Fact, and took it wholly upon himself, so that the Woman was acquitted, and he condemn'd to suffer Death, which Sentence was inflicted on him at *Tyburn*, on *Wednesday* the 12th of *March*, 1690. he being forty-two Years of Age   After Execution his Body was convey'd to Surgeons Hall, and there anatomiz'd.

He spoke but very little at the Gallows, what he did say consisted chiefly of Invectives against lewd Women, and Advice to young Men not to be seduc'd, by their Conversation, from the Rules of Virtue and Morality.

The LIFE of Captain AVERY.

NONE of the bold Adventurers on the Seas were ever so much talk'd of, for a While, as *Avery*   He was represented in *Europe* as one that had rais'd himself to the Dignity of a King, and was likely to be the Founder of a new Monarchy; having, as it was said, taken immense Riches, and married the *Great Mogul's* Daughter, who was taken in an *Indian* Ship which fell into his Hands, by whom he had many Children, living in great Royalty and State ·   That he had built Forts, erected Magazines, and was Master of a stout Squadron of Ships, mann'd with able and desperate Fellows of all Nations

That he gave Commissions out in his own Name to the Captains of his Ships, and to the Commanders of his Forts, and was acknowledg'd by them as their Prince A Play was writ upon him, call'd, *The Successful Pirate*, and these Accounts obtain'd such Belief, that several Schemes were offer'd to the Council, for fitting out a Squadron to take him; while others were for offering him and his Companions an Act of Grace, and inviting them to *England*, with all their Treasure, lest his growing-Greatness might hinder the Trade of *Europe* to the *East-Indies*.

Yet all these were no more than false Rumours, improv'd by the Credulity of some, and the Humour of others who love to tell strange Things, for, while it was said he was aspiring at a Crown, he wanted a Shilling, and, at the same Time it was given out he was in Possession of such prodigious Wealth in *Madagascar*, he was starving in *England*.

No doubt but the Reader will have a Curiosity of knowing what became of this Man, and what were the true Grounds of so many false Reports concerning him, therefore I shall, in as brief a Manner as I can, give his History

He was born in the West of *England*, near *Plymouth* in *Devonshire*   Being bred to the Sea, he served as a Mate of a Merchant-Man, in several trading Voyages   It happen'd, before the Peace of *Ryswick*, when there was an Alliance betwixt *Spain*, *England*, *Holland*, &c against *France*, that the *French* in *Martinico* carried on a Smuggling Trade with the *Spaniards* on the Continent of *Peru*, which by the Laws of *Spain* is not allow'd to Friends in Time of Peace, for none but native *Spaniards* are permitted to traffick in those Parts, or set their Feet on Shore, unless at any Time they are brought as Prisoners

Where-

Wherefore they cônstantly keep certain Ships cruizing along the Coaſt, whom they call *Guardas del Coſta*, who have Orders to make Prizes of all Ships they can light of within five Leagues of Land Now the *French* growing very bold in Trade, and the *Spaniards* being poorly provided with Ships, and thoſe they had being of no Force, it often fell out, that when they met the *French* Smugglers, they were not ſtrong enough to attack them; therefore it was reſolved in *Spain*, to hire two or three ſtout foreign Ships for their Service This being known at *Briſtol*, ſome Merchants of that City fitted out two Ships of thirty odd Guns, and 120 Hands each, well furniſh'd with Proviſion and Ammunition, and all other Stores; and the Hire being agreed on, by ſome Agents for *Spain*, they were commanded to ſail for *Corunna*, or the *Groine*, there to receive their Orders, and to take on Board ſome *Spaniſh* Gentlemen, who were to go Paſſengers to *New-Spain*

Of one of theſe Ships, which I take to be call'd the *Duke*, Captain *Gibſon* Commander, *Avery* was firſt Mate; and being a Fellow of more Cunning than Courage, he inſinuated himſelf into the good Will of ſeveral of the boldeſt Fellows on board the two Ships, having founded their Inclinations before he open'd himſelf Finding them ripe for his Deſign, he at length propos'd to them to run away with the Ship, telling them what great Wealth was to be had upon the Coaſts of *India* It was no ſooner ſaid then agreed to, and they reſolv'd to execute their Plot at Ten o'Clock the Night following

It muſt be obſerv'd, that the Captain was one of thoſe who are mightily addicted to Punch, ſo that he paſs'd moſt of his Time on Shore in ſome little drinking Ordinary; but this Day he did not go on Shore as uſual However, this did not ſpoil the Deſign, for he took his uſual Doſe on Board, and ſo got to Bed before the Hour appointed for the Buſineſs The Men, alſo who were not privy to the Deſign, turn'd into their Hammocks, leaving none upon Deck but the Conſpirators, who, indeed, were the greateſt Part of the Ship's Crew. At the Time agreed on, the Long-Boat of the other Ship, call'd the *Dutcheſs*, appear'd, which *Avery* hailing in the uſual Manner, he was anſwer'd by the Men in her, with, *Is your drunken Boatſwain on Board?* which was the Watch-Word agreed between them *Avery* replying in the Affirmative, the Boat came a-board with ſixteen ſtout Fellows, and join'd the Company.

When our Gentry ſaw that all was clear, they ſecur'd the Hatches, and ſo went to work They did not ſlip the Anchor, but weigh'd it leiſurely, and ſo put to Sea without any Diſorder or Confuſion, though there were ſeveral Ships then lying in the Bay. Among theſe was a *Dutch* Frigate of forty Guns, the Captain of which was offer'd a great Reward to go out after her, but *Mynheer*, who perhaps would not have been willing to have been ſerv'd ſo himſelt, could not be prevail'd upon to give ſuch Uſage to another, and ſo he let Mr *Avery* purſue his Voyage without Moleſtation.

The Captain, who by this Time was awak'd, either by the Motion of the Ship, or the Noiſe of working the Tackles, rung the Bell, whereupon *Avery* and two others went into the Cabbin The Captain, half aſleep, and in a kind of Fright, ask'd *What was the Matter?* *Avery* anſwer'd coolly, *Nothing* The Captain replied, *Something's the Matter with the Ship, Does ſhe drive? What Weather is it?* Thinking nothing leſs than that it had been a Storm, and that the Ship was driven from her Anchors *No, no*, anſwer'd *Avery*, *we're at Sea, with a fair Wind, and good Weather* At Sea! ſays the Captain, *How can that be?* *Come*, ſays *Avery*, *don't be in a Fright,*

but put on your Cloaths, and I'll let you into a Secret You muſt know, that I am Captain of this Ship now, and this is my Cabbin, therefore you muſt walk out I am bound to Madagaſcar, with a Deſign of making my own Fortune, and that of all the brave Fellows join'd with me

The Captain, having a little recover'd his Senſes, began to apprehend the Meaning However, his Fright was as great as before, which *Avery* perceiving, bad him fear nothing. For, *ſays he*, if you have a Mind to make one of us, we will receive you, and if you'll turn ſober, and mind your Buſineſs, perhaps in Time I may make you one of my Lieutenants, if not, here's a Boat a-long-ſide, and you ſhall be ſet aſhore.

The Captain was glad to hear this, and therefore accepted of his Offer, and the whole Crew being call'd up, to know who was willing to go on Shore with the Captain, and who to ſeek their Fortunes with the reſt, there were not above five or ſix who were willing to quit this Enterprize, wherefore they were put into the Boat with the Captain that Minute, and made their Way to the Shore as well as they could

They proceeded on their Voyage to *Madagaſcar*, but I do not find they took any Ships in their Way When they arriv'd at the N E Part of that Iſland, they found two Sloops at Anchor, who, upon ſeeing them, ſlipp'd their Cables, and run themſelves aſhore, the Men all landing, and running into the Woods Theſe were two Sloops which the Men had run away with from the *Weſt-Indies*, and ſeeing *Avery*, they ſuppos'd him to be ſome Frigate ſent to take them Wherefore, not being of Force to engage him, they did what they could to ſave themſelves

He gueſs'd what they were, and ſent ſome of his Men on Shore, to let them know they were Friends and to offer them a Union for their common Safety The Sloop's Men were well arm'd, and had poſted themſelves in a Wood, with Centinels juſt on the out-ſide, to obſerve whether the Ship landed her Men to purſue them Theſe Centinels, obſerving only two or three Men coming towards them without Arms, they did not oppoſe them, but having challeng'd them, and been anſwer'd that they were Friends, they led them to their Body, where they deliver'd their Meſſage At firſt, they apprehended it was a ſtratagem to decoy them on board, but when the Ambaſſadors told them that the Captain himſelf, and as many of the Crew as they ſhould name, would meet them on Shore without Arms, they believ'd them to be in earneſt Thus they ſoon enter'd into a Confidence with one another, thoſe on Board going on Shore, and ſome of thoſe on Shore going on Board

The Sloop's Men were rejoic'd at the new Ally, for their Veſſels were ſo ſmall that they could not attack a Ship of any Force, ſo that hitherto they had not taken any conſiderable Prize, but now they hop'd to fly at high Game *Avery* was as well pleas'd at this Reinforcement, to ſtrengthen them for any brave Enterprize, and though the Booty muſt be leſſen'd to each, by being divided into ſo many Shares, yet he found out an Expedient not to ſuffer by it himſelf, as ſhall be ſhewn in its Place

Having conſulted what was to be done, they reſolv'd to ſail out together upon a Cruize, the Galley and two Sloops, they therefore fell to work to get the Sloops off, which they ſoon effected, and ſteer'd towards the *Arabian* Coaſt Near the Rio *Indus*, the Man at the Maſt-Head ſpied a Sail, upon which they gave Chace As they came nearer to her, they perceiv'd her to be a tall Ship, and fancied ſhe might be a *Dutch Eaſt India* Man homeward bound, but

but she prov'd a better Prize For, when they fir'd at her to bring too, she hoisted *Mogul*'s Colours, and seem'd to stand upon her Defence *Avery* only cannonaded at a Distance, and some of his Men began to suspect that he was not the Hero they took him for However, the Sloops made use of their Time, and coming one on the Bow, and the other on the Quarter of the Ship, they clapp'd her on Board, and enter'd her, upon which, she immediately struck her Colours, and yielded She was one of the *Great Mogul*'s own Ships, and there were in her several of the greatest Persons of his Court, among whom it was said was one of his Daughters, who were going on a Pilgrimage to *Mecca*, (the *Mahometans* thinking themselves oblig'd once in their Lives to visit that Place) and they were carrying with them rich Offerings, to present at the Shrine of *Mahomet* It is known that the Eastern People travel with the utmost Magnificence, so that they had with them all their Slaves and attendants, their rich Habits and Jewels, with Vessels of Gold and and Silver, and great Sums of Money to defray the Charges of their journey by Land, wherefore, the Plunder got by the Prize, not easy computed

Having taken all the Treasure on board their own Ship, and plundered their Prize of every Thing else they either wanted or liked, they let her go, and she, not being able to continue her Voyage, returned back As soon as the News came to the *Mogul*, and he knew that they were *English* who had robbed them, he threatened loud, and talked of sending a mighty Army with Fire and Sword, to extirpate the *English* from all their Settlements on the *Indian* Coast The *East-India* Company in *England*, were very much alarmed at it, however, by Degrees, they found Means to pacify him, by promising to do their Endeavours to take the Robbers, and deliver them into his Hands The great Noise this Thing made in *Europe*, as well as *India*, was the Occasion of all those romantick Stories, which were formed of *Avery's* Greatness

In the mean Time, our successful Plunderers agreed to make the best of their Way back to *Madagascar*, intending to make that Place their Magazine, or Repository, for all their Treasure, to build a small Fortification there, and leave a few Hands always ashore to look after it, and defend it from any Attempts of the Natives, but *Avery* put an End to this Project, and made it altogether unnecessary

As they were Steering their Course, he sends a Boat on Board of each of the Sloops, desiring the Chiefs of them to come on Board of him, in order to hold a Council, they did so, and he told them he had something to propose to them for the common Good, which was to provide against Accidents He bid them consider, that the Treasure they were possess'd of, would be sufficient for them all, if they could secure it in some Place on Shore, therefore all they had to fear, was some Misfortune in the Voyage, he told them the Consequence of being separated by bad Weather, in which Case the Sloops, if either of them should fall in with any Ships of Force, must be either taken or sunk, and the Treasure on Board her lost to the rest, besides the common Accidents of the Sea As for his Part, he was so strong, that he was able to make his Party good with any Ship they were like to meet in those Seas, for if he met with any Ship of such Strength, that he could not take her, he was sure from being taken, because he was so well mann'd, besides, his Ship was a quick Sailer, and could carry Sail when the Sloops could not, wherefore, he proposed to them, to put the Treasure on Board his Ship, to seal up each Chest with three Seals, whereof each was

to keep one, and to appoint a Rendezvous in Case of Separation

Upon considering this Proposal, it appeared so reasonable to them, that they readily came into it, for they argued to themselves, that an accident might happen to one of the Sloops, and the other escape, wherefore it was for the common Good The Thing was done as agreed to, the Treasure put on Board of *Avery*, and the Chests sealed, they kept Company that Day and the next, the Weather being fair, in which Time *Avery* tampered with his Men, telling them they now had sufficient to make them all easy, And what, said he, *should hinder us from going to some Country, where we are not known, and living on Shore all the rest of our Days in Plenty?* They understood what he meant, and, in short, they all agreed to bilk their new Allies, the Sloop's Men, nor do I find, that any one of them felt any Qualms of Honour rising in his Stomach, to hinder him from consenting to this Piece of Treachery In fine, they took Advantage of the Darkness that Night, steer'd another Course, and, by Morning, lost Sight of them

I leave the Reader to judge, what Swearing and Confusion there was among the Sloop's Men in the Morning, when they saw that *Avery* had given them the Ship, for they knew, by the Fairness of the Weather, and the Course they had agreed to steer, that it must have been done on purpose But we leave them at present to follow Mr *Avery*

Avery, and his Men, having consulted what to do with themselves, came to a Resolution, to make the best of their Way towards *America*, and, none of them being known in those Parts, they intended to divide the Treasure, change their Names, and go ashore, some in one Place, some in another, to purchase Settlements, and live at Ease The first Land they made, was the Island of *Providence*, then newly settled, here they stay'd some Time, and having considered, that when they should go to *New-England*, the Greatness of their Ship would cause much Enquiry about them, and possibly some People from *England*, who had heard the Story of a Ship's being run away with from the *Groine*, might suspect them to be the People, they took a Resolution of disposing of their Ship at *Providence* Upon which, *Avery* pretending that the Ship being fitted out upon the privateering Account, and having had no Success, he had received Orders from the Owners, to dispose of her to the best Advantage, he soon met with a Purchaser, and immediately bought a Sloop

In this Sloop he and his Companions embarked, they touch'd at several Parts of *America*, where no Person suspected them, and some of them went on Shore, and dispersed themselves about the Country, having received such Dividends as *Avery* would give them, for he concealed the greatest Part of the Diamonds from them, which, in the first Hurry of plundering the Ship, they did not much regard, as not knowing their Value

At length he came to *Boston* in *New England*, and seem'd to have a Desire of settling in those Parts Some of his Companions went on Shore here also, but he changed his Resolution, and proposed, to the few of his Companions who were left, to sail for *Ireland*, which they consented to He found that *New England* was not a proper Place for him, because a great deal of his Wealth lay in Diamonds, and should he have produced them there, he would have certainly been seized on Suspicion of Pyracy

In their Voyage to *Ireland*, they avoided St *George's* Channel, and, sailing North about, they put into one of the Northern Ports of that Kingdom There they disposed of their Sloop, and com-

ing

ing on Shore they separated themselves, some going to *Cork*, and some to *Dublin* Some of them obtained their Pardons afterwards of King *William* When *Avery* had remained some Time in this Kingdom, he was afraid to offer his Diamonds to Sale, lest an Enquiry into his Manner of coming by them should occasion a Discovery Considering therefore with himself what was best to be done, he fancied there were some Persons at *Bristol*, whom he might venture to trust Upon this, he resolved to pass over into *England*, he did so, and, going into *Devonshire*, sent to one of these Friends to meet him, at a Town called *Biddiford* When he had communicated himself to his Friend, and consulted with him about the Means of his Effects, they agreed, that the safest Method would be, to put them into the Hands of some Merchants, who being Men of Wealth and Credit in the World, no Enquiry would be made how they came by them One of these Friends told him he was very intimate with some who were very fit for the Purpose, and who, if he would but allow them a good Commission, would do the Business very faithfully *Avery* liked the Proposal, for he found no other Way of managing his Affairs, since he could not appear in them himself, therefore his Friend going Back to *Bristol*, and opening the Matter to the Merchants, they made *Avery* a Visit at *Biddiford*, where, after several strong Protestations of Honour and Integrity, he delivered them his Effects, consisting of Diamonds and some Vessels of Gold They gave him a little Money for his present Subsistance, and so they parted

He changed his Name and lived at *Biddiford*, without making any Figure, and therefore there was no great Notice taken of him, yet he let one or two of his Relations know where he was, and they came to see him In some Time his little Money was spent, yet he heard nothing from his Merchants, he writ to them often, and, after much Importunity, they sent him a small Supply, but scarce sufficient to pay his Debts In fine, the Supplies they sent him from Time to Time, were so small, that they were not sufficient to give him Bread, nor could he get that little without a great deal of Trouble and Importunity This Usage made him weary of his Life, and obliged him to go privately to *Bristol*, to speak to the Merchants himself, where, instead of Money, he met a most shocking Repulse : For, when he desired them to come to an Account with him, they silenced him by threatning to discover him, so that our Merchants were as good Pirates at Land as he was at Sea

Whether he was frightened by these Menaces, or had seen some Body else he thought knew him, is not known, but he went immediately over to *Ireland*, and from thence sollicited his Merchants very hard for a Supply, but all to no Purpose, so that he was even reduced to Beggary In this Extremity, he was resolved to return and cast himself upon them, let the Consequence be what it would He put himself on board a trading Vessel, and work'd his Passage over to *Plymouth*, from whence he travelled on Foot to *Biddiford* Here he had been but a few Days before he fell sick and died, not being worth so much as would buy him a Coffin

Thus have I given all that could be collected of any Certainty concerning this Man, rejecting the idle Stories which were made of his fantastick Greatness, by which it appears that his Actions were inconsiderable, in comparison of those of other Pirates since him, though he made more Noise in the World

Now we shall turn back, and give our Readers some Account of what became of the two Sloops.

We took Notice of the Rage and Confusion, which must have seized them, upon their missing of *Avery*, however, they continued their Course, some of them still flattering themselves, that he had only out-sailed them in the Night, and that they should find him at the Place of Rendezvous But when they came there, and cou'd hear no Tidings of him, there was an End of Hope It was Time to consider what they should do with themselves, their Stock of Sea Provision was almost spent, and tho' there was Rice, and Fish, and Fowl to be had ashore, yet these would not keep for Sea, without being properly cured with Salt, which they had no Conveniency of Doing This determined them, since they could not go a Cruizing any more so think of establishing themselves at Land, to which Purpose they took all Things out of the Sloop, made Tents of the Sails, and encamp'd themselves, having a large Quantity of Ammunition, and Abundance of small Arms

Here they met with several of their Countrymen, the Crew of a Privateer Sloop, which was commanded by Captain *Thomas Tew*, and, since it will be but a short Digression, we will give an Account how they came here

Captain *George Dew* and Captain *Thomas Tew*, having received Commissions from the then Governor of *Bermudas*, to sail directly for the River *Gambia* in *Africa*, there, with the Advice and Assistance of the Agents of the Royal *African* Company, to attempt the taking the *French* Factory at *Goorie*, lying upon that Coast In a few Days after they sailed out, *Dew*, in a violent Storm, not only sprung his Mast, but lost Sight of his Consort Upon this he returned back to refit, and *Tew*, instead of proceeding on his Voyage, made for the *Cape of Good Hope*, doubled the said Cape, and shaped his Course for the Straits of *Babel-Mandel*, being the Entrance into the *Red Sea* Here he came up with a large Ship, richly laden, bound from the *Indies* to *Arabia*, with three hundred Soldiers on Board, besides Seamen, *Tew* had nevertheless the Hardiness to board her, and he soon carried her, he said, that, by this Prize, his Men shared near three thousand Pounds a Piece They had Intelligence from the Prisoners, of five other rich Ships to pass that Way, which *Tew* would have attacked, tho' they were very strong, if he had not been over-ruled by the Quarter Master and others ——— This dissenting in Opinion created some ill Blood amongst them, so that they resolved to leave off Pirating, and no Place they thought was so fit to receive them as *Madagascar* Hither therefore they steered, resolving to live on Shore and enjoy what they had got

As for *Tew* himself, he, with a few others, in a short Time went off to *Rhode-Island*, from whence he made his Peace

Thus have we accounted for the Company our Pirates met with here

It must be observed, that the Natives of *Madagascar* are a kind of Negroes, they differ from those of *Guiney* in the length of their Hair, and their Complexion is not so good a Jet, they have innumerable little Princes among them who are continually making War upon one another, their Prisoners are their Slaves, and they either sell them, or put them to death, as they please When our Pirates first settled amongst them, their Alliance was much courted by these Princes, so they sometimes joyned one, sometimes another, but wheresoever they sided, they were sure to be victorious, for the Negroes here had no Fire-Arms, nor did they understand their Use, so that at length these Pirates became

came so terrible to the Negroes, that if two or three of them were only seen on one Side, when they were going to engage, the opposite Side would fly without striking a Blow

By these Means they not only became feared, but powerful, all the Prisoners of War they took to be their Slaves, they married the most beautiful of the Negroe Women, not one or two only, but as many as they liked, so that almost every one of them had as great a Seraglio as the grand Seignior at *Constantinople* Their Slaves they employ'd in planting Rice, in Filing, Hunting, &c Besides which, they had a-bundance of others, who lived, as it were, under their Protection, and, to be secure from the Disturbances or Attacks of their powerful Neighbours, they seemed to pay them a willing Homage Now they began to divide from one another, each living with his own Wives, Slaves and Dependants, Like a separate Prince, and, as Power and Plenty naturally beget Contention, they sometimes quarrelled with one another, and attacked each other at the Head of their several Armies In these civil Wars, many of them were kill'd, but an Accident happened, which oblig'd them to unite again for their common Safety

It must be observed, that these sudden great Men had us'd their Power like Tyrants, for they grew wanton in Cruelty, and nothing was more common, than, upon the slightest Displeasure, to cause one of their Dependents to be tied to a Tree, and shot thro' the Heart Let the Crime be what it would, whether little or great, this was always the Punishment This occasioned the Negroes to conspire together, to rid themselves of these Destroyers, all in one Night; and, as they now lived separately, the Thing might easily have been done, had not a Woman, who had been Wife or Concubine to one of them, run near twenty Miles, in three Hours, to discover the Matter to them Immediately upon the Alarm, they ran together as fast as they could, so that when the Negroes approached them, they found them all up in Arms, and retired without making any Attempt

This Escape made them very cautious from that Time, and it will be worth while to describe the Policy of these brutish Fellows, and to shew what Measures they took to secure themselves

They found that the Fear of their Power could not secure them against a Surprize The bravest Man may be kill'd when he is asleep, by one much his Inferior in Courage and Strength; therefore, as their first Security, they did all they could to foment War betwixt the neighbouring Negroes, remaining Neuter themselves By these Means, those who were overcome constantly fled to them for Protection, otherwise they must be either killed or made Slaves Thus they strengthened their Party, and always tied some to them by Interest When there was no War, they contrived to spirit up private Quarrels among them, and, upon every little Dispute or Misunderstanding, persu'd on one Side to take revenge on the other, to this Purpose they instructed them how to attack or surprize their Adversaries, and lent them loaded Pistols or Firelocks to dispatch them with The Consequence of these Things was, that the Murderer was forc'd to fly to them for the safety of his Life, with his Wives, Children, and Kindred Such as these were best Friends, as their Lives depended upon the Safety of their Protectors, for, as we observed before, our Pirates were grown so terrible, that none of their Neighbours had Resolution enough to attack them in an open War

By such Arts as these, in the Space of a few Years, their Body was greatly encreased They then began

to separate themselves, and remove at a greater Distance from one another, for the Convenience of more Ground Thus they were divided, like the *Jews,* into Tribes, each carrying with him his Wives and Children, (of which by this Time they had a large Family) as also their Quota of Dependants and Followers If Power and Command are the Things which distinguish a Prince, these Ruffians had now all the Marks of Royalty about them, nay more, they had the very Fears which commonly disturb Tyrants, as may be seen by the extreme Caution they took, in fortifying the Places where they dwelt

In their Plan of Fortification they imitated one another, and their Dwellings were rather Citadels than Houses They made Choice of a Place overgrown with Wood, and situate near a Water, they raised a Rampart or high Ditch round it, so strait and steep, that it was impossible to climb it, and especially by those who had not the Use of scaling Ladders Over the Ditch there was one Passage into the Wood, the Dwelling, which was a Hut, was built in that Part of the Wood which the Prince, who inhabited it, thought fit, but so covered that it could not be seen till you came at it But the greatest Cunning lay in the Passage which led to the Hut, which was so narrow, that no more than one Person could go a Breast, and contrived in so intricate a Manner, that it was a perfect Maze or Labyrinth The Way going round and round, with several little cross Ways, a Person that was not well acquainted with it, might walk several Hours round without being able to find the Hut Moreover, all along the Sides of these narrow Paths, certain large Thorns, which grew upon a Tree in that Country, were stuck into the Ground with their Points uppermost, and the Path itself being made crooked and serpentine, if a Man should attempt to come near the Hut at Night, he would certainly have struck upon these Thorns

Thus Tyrant-like they lived, fearing and feared by all, and in this Situation they were found by Captain *Woods Rogers,* when he went to *Madagascar,* in the *Delicia,* a Ship of forty Guns, with a Design of buying Slaves in order to sell to the *Dutch* at *Batavia* or *New-Holland* He happened to touch upon a Part of the Island where no Ship had been seen for seven or eight Years before, here he met with some of the Pyrates, when they had been upon the Island above 25 Years, having a large motly Generation of Children and Grand-Children descended from them, there being, at that Time, eleven of them remaining alive

Upon their first seeing a Ship of this Force and Burthen, they supposed it to be a Man of War sent to take them, they therefore lurked within their Fastnesses But when some from the Ship came on Shore, without any Shew of Hostility, and offered to trade with the Negroes, they ventured to come out of their Holes, attended like Princes, and since they actually were Kings De Facto, which is a kind of a Right, we ought to speak of them as such

Having been so many Years upon this Island, it may be imagined, their Cloaths had long been worn out, so that their Majesties, according to the Phrase, were extremely out at the Elbows, I cannot say they were ragged, since they had nothing to cover them but the Skins of Beasts without any tanning, with all the Hair on, not even a Shoe nor Stocking, so that they looked like the Pictures of *Hercules,* in the Lion's Skin, and, being overgrown with Beard, and Hair upon their Bodies, they appeared the most savage Figures that a Man's Imagination can frame

However they soon got rigg'd, for they sold great Numbers of the poor People under them, for Cloaths, Knives, Saws, Powder and Ball, and many other

Things,

Things, they became moreover so familiar, that they went aboard the *Delicia*, and were observed to be very curious, examining the Inside of the Ship, and talking very familiarly with the Men, inviting them ashore Their Design in doing this, as they afterwards confessed, was to try if it was not practicable to surprize the Ship in the Night, which they jucged very easy, in case there was but a slender Watch kept on Board They had Boats and Men enough at command, but it seems the Captain was aware of them, and kept so strong a Watch upon Deck, that they found it was in vain to make any Attempt, wherefore when some of the Men went ashore, and they were for drawing them into a Plot, for seizing the Captain and securing the rest of the Men under Hatches, when they should have the Night-Watch, promising a Signal to come on Board to join them, and proposing if they succeeded, to go a Pyrating together, the Captain, observing an Intimacy growing betwixt them, thought it is could be for no Good, and therefore broke it off in Time, not suffering them so much as to talk together After this, whenever he sent a Boat on shore with an

Officer, to treat with them about the Sale of Slaves, the Crew remained on board the Boat, and no Man was suffered to talk with them, but the Person deputed by him for that Purpose

Before he sailed away, when they found that no thing was to be done, they confessed all the Designs they had formed against him Thus he left them as he found them, in a great Deal of dirty State and Royalty, but with fewer Subjects than they had, having, as we observed, bought many of them, and, if Ambition be the darling Passion of Men, no doubt, they were happy One of these great Princes had formerly been a Waterman upon the *Thames*, where having committed a Murder, he fled to the *West Indies*, and was of the Number of those who run away with the Sloops, the rest had been all fore-mast Men, nor was there a Man amongst them, who could either read or write, their Secretaries of State having just as much Learning as themselves This is all the Account we can give of these Kings of *Madagascar*, some of whom it is probable are reigning to this Day

---

The LIFE *of Captain* MARTEL.

WE come now to the Pirates that have rose since the Peace of *Utrecht*; in War Time there is no Room for any, because all those of a roving advent'rous Disposition find Employment in Privateers Thus our Mobs in *London*, when they come to an Height, our Superiors order out the Train Bands, and when once they are raised, the others are suppressed of Course; I take the Reason of it to be, that the Mob go into the tame Army, and immediately, from notorious Breakers of the Peace, become, by being put into order, solemn Preservers of it Should our Legislators, therefore, put some of the Pirates into Authority, it would not only lessen their Number, but, I imagine, set them upon the rest, and they would be the likeliest People to find them out, according to the Proverb, *set a Thief to catch a Thief*

To bring this about, there needs no other Encouragement, than to give all the Effects taken on Board a Pirate Vessel to the Captors, for, in Case of Plunder and Gain, they like it as well from Friends, as Enemies, but are not fond, as Things are carry'd, *of ruining poor Fellows, as the Creoleans express it, with no Advantage to themselves*

The Multitude of Men and Vessels employ'd this Way, in Time of War, in the *West-Indies*, is another Reason for the Number of Pirates in a Time of Peace This cannot be supposed to reflect on any of our *American* Governments, much less on the King himself, by whose Authority such Commissions are granted, because of the Reasonableness of the Thing, and absolute Necessity there is for doing of it. Yet the Observation is just, for so many People employing themselves in Privateers, for the sake of Plunder and Riches, which they always spend as fast as they get, when the War is over, and they can have no far-

ther Business in the Way of Life they have been used to, they too readily, and, indeed, too naturally engage in Acts of Piracy And this being but the same Practice without a Commission, they make very the Distinction betwixt the Lawfulness of the one, and the Unlawfulness of the other

In all our Enquiries back, we have not been able to find the Original of this Rover, of whom we are now to speak, but we believe he and his Gang were some Privateer's Men, belonging to the Island of *Jamaica*, in the preceeding War, his Story is but short, for his Reign was so, an End having been put to his Adventures in good Time, when he was growing strong and formidable

In the first Accounts we have of him, we find him Commander of a Pirate Sloop of eight Guns, and 80 Men, cruising off *Jamaica*, in the Month of September, 1716 about which Time he took the *Berkley* Galley, Captain *Saunders*, and plundered him of 1000 *l* in Money, and afterwards met with a Sloop call'd the *King Solomon*, from whom he took some Money and Provisions, besides Goods to a great Value

They proceeded after this to the Port of *Cavena*, at the Island of *Cuba*, and in their Way took two Sloops, which they plundered and let go Off the Port they fell in with a fine Galley, of 20 Guns, call'd the *John* and *Martha*, Captain *Wilson*, which they attacked under the pyratical black Flag, and made themselves Masters of her They put some of the Men ashore, and others they demand'd, as they had done at several other Times, to encrease their own Company Captain *Martel* then charged Captain *Wilson*, to advise his Owners, that their Ship would answer his Purpose exactly, by taking one Deck down, and as for the Cargo, which consisted chiefly of of Logwood and Sugar, he would take Care it should be carry'd to a good Market

Having fitted up the aforesaid Ship, as they design'd, they mounted her with 22 Guns, and 100 Men, left 25 Hands in the Sloop, and so proceeded to cruize off the Leeward Islands, where they met but with too much Success After the taking of a Sloop and a Brigantine, they gave Chase to a stout Ship, which came up with, and which, at Sight of the Pyrate's Flag, struck to the Robbers. This was a Vessel of 20 Guns, call'd the *Dolphin*, bound for New-foundland Captain *Martel* made the Men Prisoners, and carry'd the Ship with him

About the Middle of *December*, the Pirates took another Galley in her Voyage from *Jamaica*, call'd the *Kent*, Captain *Lawton*, shifted her Provisions aboard their own Ship, and let her go This obliged her to sail back to *Jamaica* for a Supply for her Voyage Some Time after they met with a small Ship and a Sloop, belonging to *Barbadoes*, out of both they took Provisions, and then parted with them, having first taken such of their Hands, as were willing to be forced to go along with them The *Greyhound* Galley of *London*, Captain *Evans*, from Gurney to *Jamaica*, was the next that had the Misfortune to fall into their Hands ; they did not detain her long, for, as soon as they could get out of her Gold-Dust, E'ephant's Teeth, and Slaves, which were about 40, they sent her onward upon her Voyage

They concluded now, that 'twas very necessary to get into Harbour and refit, hoping at the same Time to get Refreshments for themselves, and an Opportunity to dispose of their Cargo With this View, 'twas resolv'd to make the best of their Way to *Santa Cruz*, a small Island in the Latitude of 18, 30, N ten Miles long, and two broad, lying South-East of *Porto Rico*, and belonging to the French Settlements Here they thought they might lie privately enough for some Time, and fit themselves for further Mischief They met with a Sloop by the Way, which they took along with them, and, in the Beginning of the Year 1716-17, they arrived at their Port. They had now a Ship of 20 Guns, a Sloop of eight, and three Prizes, *viz* another Ship of 20 Guns, a Sloop of 4 Guns, and the Sloop last taken With this little Fleet, they got into a small Harbour, or Road, the N W Part of the Island, and wrap'd up two Creeks, which were made by a little Island lying within the Bay, (we are the more particular now, because we shall take Leave of the Gentlemen at this Place) They had here bare 16 Foot of Water, at the deepest, and but 13 or 14, at the shallowest ; and nothing but Rocks and Sands without, which secured them from Wind and Sea, and likewise hinder'd any considerable Force from entering, if any such should come against them

When they were all got in, the first Thing they had to do, was to guard themselves in the best Manner they could , this they did by making a Battery of four Guns upon the Island, and another of two Guns on the North Point of the Road They also wrap'd in one of the Sloops with eight Guns, at the Mouth of the Channel, to hinder any Vessel from coming in When this was done, they went to work on their Ship, unrigging and unloading, in order to clean ; but we shall leave them a while, till we bring other Company to 'em

In the Month of *November*, 1716, General *Hamilton*, Commander in chief of all the *Leeward Caribee Islands*, sent a Sloop Express to Capt *Hume*, at *Barbadoes*, Commander of his Majesty's Ship the *Scarborough*, of 30 Guns, and 140 Men, to acquaint him, that two Pirate Sloops, having plunder'd several Vessels The *Scarborough* had bury'd twenty Men, and, at this Time, had near forty sick, and therefore was but in ill State to go to Sea However, Captain *Hume* left his sick Men behind, and sail'd to the other Islands, for a Supply of Men He took 20 Soldiers from *Antegoa*, at *Nevis* 10, and 10 at St. *Christopher*'s, and then sail'd to the Island of *Anguilla* Here he learn'd, that, some Time before, two such Sloops had been at *Spanish-Town*, otherwise call'd one of the *Virgin* Islands From this Information, the next Day, the *Scarborough* came to *Spanish-Town*, but could hear no other News of the Sloops, than that they had been there about *Christmas*, it being now the 15th of *January*

Captain *Hume*, finding no certain Account could be had of the Pirates, design'd to go back, the next Day, to *Barbadoes* , but it happen'd that Night, that a Boat anchor'd there from *Santa Cruz*, and inform'd him, that he saw a Pirate Ship of 22 or 24 Guns, with other Vessels, going into the North-West Part of the Island aforesaid The *Scarborough* weigh'd immediately, and the next Morning came in Sight of the Rovers and their Prizes, and stood to them , but the Pilot refus'd to enter in with the Ship

All this while the Pirates fir'd red-hot Bullets from the Shore. At length, the Ship came to an Anchor, along Side the Reef, near the Channel, and canonaded, for several Hours, both the Vessels and Batteries About Four in the Afternoon, the Sloop that guarded the Channel was sunk, by the Shot of the Man of War, then she canonaded the great Pirate Ship of 22 Guns, that lay behind the Island The next Night, *viz.* the 18th, it falling calm, Captain *Hume* weigh'd, fearing he might fall on the Reef, and in this Apprehension he stood off and on for a Day or two, to block them up On the 20th, in the Evening the Pirates observ'd the Man of War to stand off to Sea, and took the Opportunity to warp out, in order to slip away from the Island, which entirely ruin'd them At 12 o'Clock they run aground, and then, seeing the *Scarborough* about standing in again, as their Case was desperate, they were put into the utmost Confusion , they quitted their Ship, and set her on Fire, with 20 Negroes in her, who were all burnt Nineteen of the Pirates made their Escape in a small Sloop, but the Captain and the rest, with 20 Negroes, betook themselves to the Woods, where, 'tis probable, they might starve , for we never heard what became of 'em afterwards. Captain *Hume* releas'd the Prisoners, with the Ship and Sloop that remain'd, and then went after the two Pirate Sloops first mention'd. ,

The LIFE of Captain TEACH, alias BLACK-BEARD.

EDward Teach was a *Bristol* Man born, but had sail'd several Times out of *Jamaica* in Privateers, in the late French War Though he had often distinguish'd himself by his uncommon Boldness, and personal Courage, he was never rais'd to any Command till he went a pyrating, about the latter End of the Year 1716 It was then, that Captain *Benjamin Hornigold* put him into a Sloop, that he had made Prize of, and these two continued in Consortship till a little while before *Hornigold* surrender'd

In the Spring of the Year 1717, *Teach* and *Hornigold* sail'd from *Providence*, for the Main of *America*, and took, in their Way, a Billop from the *Havanna*, with 120 Barrels of Flour, which they put on board their own Vessels They took, also, a Sloop from *Bermuda Thurbar* Master, whom they rifled only of some Gallons of Wine, and then let her go , and a Ship from *Madeira* to *South Carolina*, out of which they got Plunder, to a considerable Value.

After cleaning, on the Coast of *Virginia*, they return'd to the *West-Indies*, and, in the Latitude of 24 made Prize of a large French Guiney Man, bound to *Martinico*, which, by *Hornigold*'s Consent, *Teach* went aboard of as Captain, and took a Cruize in her *Hornigold* return'd with his Sloop to *Providence*, where, at the Arrival of Captain *Rogers*, the Governor, he surrender'd to Mercy, pursuant to the King's Proclamation

Teach mounted 40 Guns aboard of his Guinea Man, and nam'd her *The Queen Ann's Revenge* Cruising near the Island of St *Vincent*, he took a large Ship, call'd *The Great Allen*, *Christopher Taylor*, Commander ; and, having plunder'd her of what he thought fit, and put all the Men a-shore upon the Island abovemention'd, he gave Orders to set Fire to the Ship

A few Days after, *Teach* fell in with the *Scarborough* Man of War, who engag'd him for some Hours, but the *Scarborough*, finding the Pirate well mann'd, and having tried her Strength, gave over the Engagement, and return'd to *Barbadoes*, the Place of her Station , *Teach* immediately sailing towards the Spanish *America*

In his Way, he met with a Pirate Sloop, of 10 Guns, commanded by Major *Bonnet*, whose Life we mention'd before He was lately a Gentleman of good Reputation and Estate in the Island of *Barbadoes*, but now he readily join'd with *Teach* ; but in a few Days after, *Teach*, finding that *Bonnet* knew nothing of a maritime Life, with the Consent of his own Men, put in one *Richards* to be Captain of *Bonnet*'s Sloop, and took the Major on board his own Ship , telling him, *That, as he had not been us'd to the Fatigues and Care of such a Post, it would be better for him to decline it, and live easy, and at his Pleasure, in such a Ship as his, where he should not be obliged to perform Duty, but follow his own Inclinations*

At *Turniff*, 10 Leagues short of the Bay of *Hondu-*

ras, the Pirates took in fresh Water, and while they were at an Anchor there, they saw a Sloop coming in, whereupon *Richards*, in the Sloop call'd *The Revenge*, slipp'd his Cable, and ran out to meet her, who, upon seeing the black Flag hoisted, struck his Sail, and came to, under the Stern of *Teach* the Commodore She was call'd *The Adventure*, from *Jamaica*, *David Harriot* Master They took him and his Men aboard the great Ship, and sent a Number of their own People with *Israel Hands*, Master of *Teach*'s Ship, to man the Sloop for the piratical Service

On the 9th of *April* they weigh'd from *Turniff*, having lain there about a Week, and sail'd to the Bay, where they found a Ship and four Sloops Three of the latter belong'd to *Jonathan Barnard*, of *Jamaica*, and the other to Captain *James* The Ship was of *Boston*, call'd *The Protestant Cæsar*, Captain *Wyar* Commander *Teach* hoisted his black Colours, and fir'd a Gun, upon which, Captain *Wyar*, and all his Men, left their Ship, and got ashore in their Boat *Teach*'s Quarter-Master, and eight of his Crew, took Possession of *Wyar*'s Ship, and *Richards* secur'd all the Sloops, one of which they burnt out of Spite to the Owner The *Protestant Cæsar* they also burnt, after they had plunder'd her, because she belong'd to *Boston*, where some Men had been hang'd for Piracy But the three Sloops belonging to *Barnard* they let go

From hence, the Rovers sail'd to *Turkill*, and then to the *Grand Caimanes*, a small Island about 30 Leagues to the Westward of *Jamaica* Here they took a small Turtler, and so sail'd to the *Havana*, from thence to the *Bahama* Wrecks, and from the *Bahama* Wrecks to *Carolina*, taking a Brigantine and two Sloops in their Way They lay on the *Carolina* Coast, off the Bar of *Charles-Town*, for five or six Days They took here a Ship as she was coming out, bound for *London*, commanded by *Robert Clark*, with some Passengers on board for *England*, the next Day they took another Vessel coming out of *Charles-Town*, and also two Pinks coming into *Charles-Town*, likewise, a Brigantine with 14 Negroes aboard All this being done in the Face of the Town, it struck a great Terror into the whole Province of *Carolina*, which had just before been visited by *Vane*, another notorious Pirate The Inhabitants even abandon'd themselves to Despair, being in no Condition to resist their Force There were eight Sail in the Harbour, ready for Sea, but none dar'd to venture out, it being almost impossible to escape their Hands The inward bound Vessels were under the same unhappy Dilemma, so that the Trade of this Place was totally interrupted What made these Misfortunes yet heavier to them, was a long expensive War, which the Colony had had with the Natives, and which was but just ended when these Robbers infested them

Teach detain'd all the Ships and Prisoners, and
being

Captain Teach commonly call'd Black Beard.

being in want of Medicines, resolv'd to demand a Chest from the Government of the Province Accordingly, *Richards*, the Captain of the *Revenge* Sloop, with two or three more Pirates, were sent up along with Mr *Marks*, one of the Prisoners whom they had taken in *Clark*'s Ship, to make their Demands, which they did in a very insolent Manner, threatening, that if they did not send immediately the Chest of Medicines, and let the Pirate-Ambassadors return, without offering any Violence to their Persons, they wou'd murder all their Prisoners, send up their Heads to the Governor, and set the Ships they had taken, on Fire

Whilst Mr *Marks* was making Application to the Council, *Richards*, and the rest of the Pirates, walk'd the Streets publickly, in the Sight of all People, who were fir'd with the utmost Indignation, looking upon them as Robbers and Murderers, and particularly, as the Authors of their present Wrongs and Oppressions But they durst not so much as think of executing their Revenge, for Fear of bringing more Calamities upon themselves, and so they were forc'd to let the Villains pass with Impunity The Government were not long in deliberating upon the Message Though 'twas the greatest Affront that could have been put upon them, yet, for the saving so many Mens Lives, (among them Mr *Samuel Wragg*, one of the Council) they comply'd with the Necessity, and sent on board a Chest, valu'd at between 3 and 400 *l* and the Pirates went back safe to theirs Ships

Blackbeard, (for so *Teach* was generally call'd, as we shall hereafter shew) as soon as he had receiv'd the Medicines and his Brother Rogues, let go the Ship and the Prisoners, having first taken out of them, in Gold and Silver, about 1500 *l* Sterling, besides Provisions and other Matters

From the Bar of *Charles Town*, they sail'd to *North-Carolina*, Captain *Teach* in the Ship which they call'd the Man of War, Captain *Richards* and Captain *Hands* in the Sloops, which they term'd Privateers, and another Sloop serving them as a Tender Teach began now to think of breaking up the Company, and securing the Money and the best of the Effects for himself, and some of his Companions whom he most Friendship for, and to cheat the rest Accordingly, on Pretence of running into *Top-sail* Inlet to clean, he grounded his Ship, and then (as if it had been done undesignedly, and by Accident) he orders *Hands*'s sloop to come to his Assistance, and get him off again, which he endeavouring to do, ran the sloop a Shore near the other, and so they were both lost. This done, *Teach* goes into the Tender Sloop, with 40 Hands, and leaves the *Revenge* there After this, he took 17 others, and marroon'd them upon a small sandy Island, about a League from the Main, where there was neither Bird, Beast, or Herb, for their Subsistence, and where they must have perish'd if Major *Bonnet* had not, two Days after, taken them off

Teach now goes up to the Governor of *North-Carolina*, with about 20 of his Men, surrenders to his Majesty's Proclamation, and receives Certificates thereof from his Excellency, but it did not appear that their submitting to this Pardon was from any Reformation of Manners, but only to wait a more favourable Opportunity to play the same Game over again, which he soon after affected, with greater Security to himself, and with much better Prospect of Success, having in this Time cultivated a very good Understanding with *Charles Eden*, Esq the Governor above-mention'd.

The first Piece of Service this kind Governor did to *Black Beard*, was, to give him a Right to the Vessel which he had taken, when he was a pirating in the great Ship call'd *The Queen Anne's Revenge*, for which Purpose a Court of Vice-Admiralty was held at *Bath Town*, where, though *Teach* had never any Commission in his Life, and the Sloop belong'd to the *English* Merchants, and was taken in Time of Peace, yet was she condemn'd as a Prize taken by *Teach* from the *Spaniards* These Proceedings shew that Governors are but Men

Before he sail'd upon his Adventures, he married a young Creature of about sixteen Years of Age, the Governor performing the Ceremony For, as it is a Custom to marry here by a Priest, so it is there by a Magistrate, And this, I have been inform'd, made *Teach*'s fourteenth Wife, about a Dozen of whom might be still living His Behaviour in this State was something extraordinary, for whilst his Sloop lay in *Okerecock* Inlet, and he was a-shore at a Plantation, where his Wife liv'd, after he had lain with her all Night, it was his Custom to invite five or six of his brutal Companions a-shore, and he would force her to prostitute herself to them all, one after another, before his Face

In *June* 1718, he went to Sea, upon another Expedition, and steer'd his Course towards *Bermudas* He met with two or three *English* Vessels in his Way, but robb'd them only of Provisions, Stores, and other Necessaries, for his present Expence, but when he came near the Island aforemention'd, he fell in with two *French* Ships, one of which was loaded with Sugar and Cocoa, and the other light, both bound to *Martinico* The Ship that had no Lading, he let go, having first put all the Men of the loaded Ship aboard her; the other he brought Home, with her Cargo, to *North Carolina*, where the Governor and the Pirates shar'd the Plunder

When *Teach* and his Prize arriv'd, he and four of his Crew went to his Excellency, and made Affidavit that they found the *French* Ship at Sea, without a Soul on board her; whereupon, a Court was called, and the Ship condemn'd The Governor had 60 Hogsheads of Sugar for his Dividend, and ore Mr *Knight*, who was his Secretary, and Collector for the Province, 20, the rest was shar'd among the other Pirates, as we may properly enough express it

The Business was not yet done, the Ship remained, and it was possible one or other might come into the River, that might be acquainted with her, and so discover the Roguery But *Teach* thought of a Contrivance to prevent this, for, upon a Pretence that she was leaky, and that she might sink, and so stop up the Mouth of the Inlet or Cove where she lay, he obtain'd an Order from the Governor to bring her out into the River, and set her on Fire This was accordingly executed, and she was burnt down to the Water's Edge, then her Bottom was sunk, and, with it, their Fears of her ever rising in Judgment against them

Captain *Teach*, alias *Black Beard*, pass'd three or four Months in the River, sometimes lying at Anchor in the Coves, at other Times sailing from one Inlet to another, trading with such Sloops as he met for the Plunder he had taken, and often giving them Presents for the Stores and Provisions took from them, that is, when he happen'd to be in a giving Humour, for at other Times he made bold with 'em, and took what he lik'd, without saying *by your Leave*, knowing well that they dar'd not send him a Bill for the Payment He often diverted himself with going a-shore among the Planters, where he revell'd Night and Day By these he was well receiv'd, but, whether out of Love, or Fear, I cannot say Sometimes he us'd them courteously enough, and made them, also, Presents of Rum and Sugar, in return for what he took from them: but, as to the Liberties which,

'tis

'tis said, he and his Companions often took with the Wives and Daughters of these Planters, I cannot take upon me to say, whether he paid them *ad Valorem*, or no   At other Times he carried it in a lordly Manner towards 'em, and would lay some of them under Contribution, nay, he often proceeded to bully the Governor, not, as I can discover, that there was the least Cause of Quarrel betwixt them, but it seem'd only to be done to shew he dar'd do it

The Sloops trading up and down this River, being so frequently pillag'd by *Black-Beard*, consulted with the Traders, and some of the best of the Planters, what Course to take   They saw plainly, it would be in vain to make any Application to the Governor of *North-Carolina*, to whom it properly belong'd to find some Redress, so that if they could not be reliev'd from some other Quarter, *Black-Beard* would be like to reign with Impunity   This determin'd them, with as much Secrecy as possible, to send a Deputation to *Virginia*, to lay the Affair before the Governor of that Colony, and to sollicit an arm'd Force, from the Men of War lying there, to take or destroy this Pirate

This Governor consulted with the Captains of the two Men of War, viz the *Pearl* and *Lime*, who had lain in St *James's* River about ten Months   It was agreed, that the Governor should hire a Couple of small Sloops, and the Men of War should man them, this was accordingly done, and the Command of them given to Mr *Robert Maynard*, first Lieutenant of the *Pearl*, an experienc'd Officer, and a Gentleman of great Bravery and Resolution, as will appear by his gallant Behaviour in this Expedition   The Sloops were well mann'd, and furnish'd with Ammunition and small Arms, but had no Guns mounted

About the Time of their going out, the Governor call'd an Assembly, in which it was resolv'd to publish a Proclamation with an Offer of certain Rewards, to any Person or Persons, who, within a Year after that Time, should take or destroy any Pirate   The original Proclamation being in our Hands, we shall give it to our Readers, it runs as follows.

By his Majesty's Lieutenant-Governor, and Commander in Chief, of the Colony and Dominion of *Virginia*,

A PROCLAMATION,

Publishing the Rewards to be given for apprehending or killing Pirates.

WHereas, by an *Act of Assembly*, made at a Session *of Assembly*, begun at the *Capital in Williamsburgh*, *the eleventh Day of* November, *in the fifth Year of his Majesty's Reign*, entitled, An Act *to encourage the apprehending and destroying of Pirates*, *it is*, amongst other Things, enacted, *That all and every Person, or Persons*, who, from and after the fourteenth Day of November, *in the Year of our Lord One thousand seven Hundred and Eighteen, and before the* Fourteenth Day of November, *which shall be in the Year of our Lord One Thousand seven Hundred and Nineteen, shall take any* Pirate, *or* Pirates, *on the Sea or Land*, *or*, *in case of Resistance, shall kill any such* Pirate, *or* Pirates, *between the Degrees of thirty four and thirty nine of Northern Latitude, and within one hundred Leagues of the Continent of* Virginia, *or* North-Carolina, *upon the Conviction, or making due Proof of the killing of all, and every such* Pirate, *and* Pirates, *before the Governor and Council, shall be entitled to have, and receive out of the publick Money, in the Hands of the Treasurer of this Colony, the several Rewards following, that is to say, For* Edward Teach, *commonly call'd Captain* Teach, *or* Black-Beard, *one hundred Pounds, for every other Commander of a Pirate Ship, Sloop, or Vessel, forty Pounds, for every Lieutenant, Master, Quarter-Master, Boatswain, or Carpenter, twenty Pounds, for every other inferior Officer, fifteen Pounds, and for every private Man, taken on Board such Ship, Sloop, or Vessel, ten Pounds, and, that for every* Pirate, *which shall be taken by any Ship, Sloop, or Vessel, belonging to this Colony, or* Nortn-Carolina, *within the Time aforesaid, in any Place whatsoever, the like Rewards shall be paid, according to the Quality and Condition of such* Pirates   *Wherefore, for the Encouragement of all such Persons as shall be willing to serve his* Majesty, *and their Country, in so just and honourable an Undertaking, as the suppressing a Sort of People who may be truly call'd Enemies to Mankind, I have thought fit, with the Advice and Consent of his* Majesty's *Council, to issue this Proclamation, hereby declaring, that the said Rewards shall be punctually and justly paid, in current Money of* Virginia, *according to the Directions of the said Act   And I do order and appoint this Proclamation to be published by the Sheriffs, at their respective County Houses, and by all Ministers and Readers, in the several Churches and Chapels, throughout the Colony*

Given at our Council-Chamber at *Williamsburgh*, this 24th Day of *November*, 1718, in the fifth Year of his Majesty's Reign
GOD SAVE THE KING
A SPOTSWOOD

The 17th of *November*, 1718, the Lieutenant sailed from *Kicquetan*, in *James* River in *Virginia*, and the 21st in the Evening came to the Mouth of *Okerecock* Inlet, where he got Sight of the Pirate   This Expedition was made with all imaginable Secrecy, and the Officer managed with all the Prudence that was necessary, stopping all Boats and Vessels he met with in the River, from going up, and thereby preventing any Intelligence from reaching *Black-Beard*, and receiving at the same Time an Account from them all, of the Place where the Pirate was lurking   However, notwithstanding this Caution, *Black-Beard* had Information of the Design, from his Excellency of the Province; and his Secretary, Mr *Knight*, wrote him a Letter particularly concerning it, intimating, *That he had sent him four of his Men, which were all he could meet with in or about Town*, and so bidding him be upon his Guard   These Men who belonged to *Black-Beard*, were sent from *Bath-Town* to *Okerecock* Inlet, where the Sloop lay, which is about 20 Leagues.

Black-Beard had heard several Reports, which happened not to be true, and so gave the less Credit to this; nor was he convinced till he saw the Sloops   When they came in sight, he put his Vessel in a Posture of Defence, having no more than twenty five Men on Board, tho' he gave out to all the Vessels he spoke with, that he had 40.   When he had prepared for Battle, he fate down and spent the Night in Drinking, with the Mafter of a trading Sloop, who, 'twas thought, had more Bufinefs with *Teach* than he fhould have had

Leutenant *Maynard* came to an Anchor, for the Place being fhoal, and the Channel intricate, there was no getting in where *Teach* lay that Night The next Morning he weighed, and fent his Boat a head of the Sloop to found, which, coming within Gun-Shot of the Pirate, received his Fire *Maynard*, hereupon, hoifted the King's Colours, and ftood directly towards him, with the beft Way that his Sails and Oars could make *Black-beard* cut his Cable, and endevoured to make a running Fight, keeping a continual Fire at his Enemies, with his large Guns, Mr *Maynard*, not having any, as we before obferv'd, kept a conftant Fire with fmall Arms, while fome of his Men labour'd at their Oars In a little Time *Teach*'s Sloop ran a ground, and Mr *Maynard*'s, drawing more Water than that of the Pirate, could not come near him, fo that he anchor'd within half Gun Shot of the Enemy In order to lighten his Veffel, that he might run him aboard, the Lieutenant ordered all his Ballaft to be thrown overboard, and all the Water to be ftav'd, and then weighed and ftood for him *Black-beard*, upon this, hail'd him in this rude Manner *Damn you for Villain, who are you? and from whence came you?* The Lieutenant made him anfwer, *You may fee by our Colours we are no Pirates* *Black beard* bid him fend his Boat on Board, that he might fee who he was, but Mr *Maynard* reply'd thus *I cannot fpare my Boat, but I will come aboard of you as foon as I can, with my Sloop* Whereupon, *Black-beard* took a Glafs of Liquor, and drank to him with thefe Words *Damnation feize my Soul if I give you Quarter, or take any from you* In Anfwer to which, Mr *Maynard* told him, *That he expected no Quarters from him, nor fhould he give him any*

By this Time *Black-beard*'s Sloop floated, as Mr *Maynard*'s Sloops were rowing towards him Thefe Sloops being not above a Foot high in the Wafte, confequently the Men were all expofed, as they came near together, therefore (there being hitherto little or no Execution done on either Side,) the Pirate fired a Broadfide, charged with all manner of fmall Shot——A fatal Stroke to them! The Sloop the Lieutenant was in had twenty Men killed and wounded, and the other Sloop nine This could not be help'd, for, there being no Wind, they were obliged to keep to their Oars, otherwife the Pirate would have got away from them, which, it feems, the Lieutenant was refolute to prevent

After this unlucky Blow, *Black-beard*'s Sloop fell Broadfide to the Shore, Mr *Maynard*'s other Sloop, which was call'd the *Ranger*, fell a-ftern, being for the prefent difabled Now, the Lieutenant finding his own Sloop had Way, and would foon be on Board of *Teach*, ordered all his Men down, for fear of another Broadfide, which muft have been their Deftruction, and have entirely ruined their Expedition Mr *Maynard* was the only Perfon that kept the Deck, except the Man at the Helm, whom he directed to lye down fnug, and the Men in the Hold were ordered to get their Piftols, and their Swords ready, for clofe fighting, and to come up at his Command, in order to which, two Ladders were placed in the Hatch way for the more Expedition When the Lieutenant's Sloop boarded the other, Captain *Teach*'s Men threw in feveral new fafhioned fort of Grenadoes, *viz* Cafe-Bottles fill'd with Powder, fmall Shot, Slugs, and Pieces of Lead or Iron, with a quick Match in the Mouth of them This Match, being lighted without Side, prefently runs into the

Bottle to the Powder, and as that is inftantly thrown on board, it generally does great Execution, befides the Confufion it occafions. By good Providence, however, they had not that Effect here; for the Men being in the Hold, *Black beard*, feeing few or no Hands aboard, told his Men, *That they were all knock'd on the Head, except three or four, and therefore*, fays he, *let's jump on Board, and cut them to Pieces that are alive*

Upon this, under the Smoak of one of the Bottles juft mention'd, *Black beard* enters, with fourteen Men, over the Bows of *Maynard*'s Sloop, and were not feen by him till the Air cleared; however, as it happened, he juft then gave the Signal to his Men, who all rofe in an Inftant, and attack'd the Pirates with as much Bravery as ever was fhewn upon fuch an Occafion *Black-beard* and the Lieutenant fired the firft Piftol at each other, by which the Pirate received a Wound, then they engaged with Swords, till the Lieutenant's unluckily broke; who, thereupon, ftepping back to cock a Piftol, *Black-beard*, with his Cutlafh, was ftriking at that Inftant, when one of *Maynard*'s Men gave him a terrible Wound in the Neck and Throat, by which the Lieutenant came off with a fmall Cut over his Fingers

They were now clofely and warmly engag'd, the Lieutenant and twelve Men, againft *Black beard* and fourteen, till the Sea was tinctur'd with Blood round the Veffel Tho' *Black-beard* receiv'd a Shot into his Body from the firft Piftol that Lieutenant *Maynard* difcharg'd, yet he ftood his Ground, and fought with great Fury, till he received twenty Cuts, and five more Shot At length, as he was cocking a Piftol, having fired feveral before, he fell down dead By this Time eight more out of the fourteen dropp'd, and all the reft, much wounded, jump'd over-board, and call'd out for Quarters, which was granted, tho' it was only prolonging their Lives for a few Days The Sloop *Ranger* came up, and attack'd the Men that remained in *Black-beard*'s Sloop, with equal Bravery, till they likewife cry'd for Quarters

Here was an End of that courageous Brute, who might have pafs'd in the World for a Heroe, had he been employ'd in a good Caufe, his Deftruction, which was of fuch Confequence to the Plantations, was entirely owing to the Conduct and Bravery of Lieutenant *Maynard* and his Men, who might have deftroy'd him with much lefs Lofs, had they had a Veffel with great Guns But they were oblig'd to ufe fmall Veffels, becaufe the Holes and Places he lurk'd in, would not admit thofe of greater Draught, and it was no fmall Difficulty for this Gentleman to get to him, even with thefe, having grounded his Veffel, at leaft, a hundred Times, in getting up the River, befides other Difcouragements, enough to have turn'd back any Man without Difhonour, who had been lefs refolute and bold than this Lieutenant The Broadfide that did fo much Mifchief before they boarded, in all Probability faved the reft from Deftruction, for before that *Teach* had little or no Hopes of efcaping, and therefore had pofted a refolute Fellow, a Negroe, whom he bred up, with a lighted Match, in the Powder-Room, with Commands to blow it up, when he fhould give him Orders, which he defigned to have done, as foon as the Lieutenant and his Men could have enter'd, that fo he might have deftroy'd his Conquerors with himfelf. And when the Negroes found how it went with *Black-beard*, he could hardly be perfuaded from the rafh Action, by two Prifoners that were then in the Hold of the Sloop

What feems a little odd, is, that fome of thefe Men, who behaved fo bravely againft *Black-beard*, went afterwards a pirating themfelves, and one of

40 R r them

them was taken along with *Roberts*, but I do not find that any of them were provided for, except one that was hang'd However, this is a Digreſſion

The Lieutenant cauſed *Black-beard's* Head to be ſevered from his Body, and hung up at the Bolt-ſprit End, then he ſailed to *Bath-Town*, to get Relief for his wounded Men

It muſt be obſerv'd, that, in rummaging the Pirate's Sloop, they found ſeveral Letters and written Papers, which diſcovered the Correſpondence betwixt Governor *Eden*, the Secretary and Collector, and alſo ſome Traders at *New-York*, and *Black-beard* It is likely he had had Regard enough for his Friends, to have deſtroyed theſe Papers before the Action, in order to hinder them from falling into ſuch Hands, where the Diſcovery would be of no Uſe, either to the Intereſt or Reputation of theſe fine Gentlemen, had not his fix'd Reſolution to have blown up all together prevented him, when he found no poſſibility of eſcaping

When the Lieutenant came to *Bath-Town*, he made bold to ſeize, in the Governor's Store-Houſe, the ſixty Hogſheads of Sugar, and from honeſt Mr *Knight* the twenty, which, it ſeems were their Dividends of the Plunder taken in the *French* Ship, as we before noted; the latter did not long ſurvive this ſhameful Diſcovery, for, being apprehenſive that he might be called to an Account for theſe Trifles, he fell ſick with the Fright, and died in a few Days

After the wounded Men were pretty well recovered, the Lieutenant ſailed back to the Men of War in *James's River*, in *Virginia*, with *Black-beard's* Head ſtill hanging at the Bolt ſprit End, and fifteen Priſoners, thirteen of whom were afterwards hanged It appeared upon Trial, that one of them, *viz Samuel Odell*, was taken out of the trading Sloop but the Night before the Engagement This poor Fellow was a little unlucky at his firſt entering upon his new Trade, there appearing no leſs than 70 Wounds upon him after the Action, notwithſtanding which, he lived, and was cured of them all. The other Perſon that eſcaped the Gallows, was one *Iſrael Hands*, the Maſter of *Black-beard's* Sloop, and formerly Captain of the ſame, before the *Queen Anne's Revenge* was loſt in *Topſail* Inlet

The aforeſaid *Hands* happened not to be in the Fight, but was taken afterwards aſhore at *Bath-Town*, having been ſometime before diſabled by *Black-beard*, in one of his ſavage Humours, after the following Manner ———One Night drinking in his Cabin with *Hands*, the Pilot, and another Man, *Black-beard*, without any Provocation, privately draws out a ſmall Pair of Piſtols, and cocks them under the Table, which being perceived by the Man, he withdrew and went upon Deck, leaving *Hands*, the Pilot, and the Captain together When the Piſtols were ready, he blew out the Candle, and, croſſing his Hands, diſcharged them at his Company , *Hands*, the Maſter, was ſhot thro' the Knee, and lam'd for Life; the other Piſtol did no Execution ———Being ask'd the meaning of this, he only anſwered, by damning them, that *if he did not now and then kill one of them, they would forgot who he was*

Hands being taken, he was try'd and condemned; but juſt as he was about to be executed, a Ship arrived at *Virginia*, with a Proclamation for prolonging the Time of his Majeſty's Pardon, to ſuch of the Pirates as ſhould ſurrender by a limited Time therein expreſſed Notwithſtanding the Sentence, *Hands* pleaded the Pardon, and was allowed the Benefit of it He was alive a few Years ago in *London*, where he begged his Bread

Now that we have given ſome Account of *Teach's* Life and Actions, it will not be amiſs that we ſpeak of his Beard, ſince it did not little contribute towards making his Name ſo terrible in thoſe Parts

Plutarch, and other grave Hiſtorians, have taken Notice, that ſeveral great Men amongſt the *Romans* took their Sir-Names from certain odd Marks in their Countenances, as *Cicero*, from a Mark of a Vetch on his Noſe So our Heroe, Captain *Teach*, aſſumed the Cognomen of *Black-Beard*, from that large Quantity of Hair, which, like a frightful Meteor, covered his whole Face, and frightned *America* more than any Comet that has appeared there a long Time

This Beard was black, which he ſuffered to grow to an extravigant Length, as to the Breadth, it came up to his Eyes, he was accuſtomed to twiſt it with Ribbons, in ſmall Tails, after the Manner of our Ramilies Wigs, and turn them about his Ears In Time of Action, he wore a Sling over his Shoulders, with three brace of Piſtols, hanging in Holſters like Bandaliers He ſtuck lighted Matches under his Hat, which appearing on each Side of his Face, and his Eyes naturally looking fierce and wild, made him altogether ſuch a Figure, that Imagination cannot form an Idea of a Fury from Hell, to look more frightful.

If he had the Look of a Fury, his Humours and Paſſions were ſuitable to it , we ſhall relate two or three more of his Extravagancies, which we omitted in the Body of his Hiſtory, by which it will appear, to what a Pitch of Wickedneſs human Nature may arrive, if it's Paſſions are not checked.

In the Commonwealth of Pirates, he who goes the greateſt Length of Wickedneſs, is looked upon with a kind of Envy amongſt them, as a Perſon of a more extraordinary Gallantry , he is therefore entitled to be diſtinguiſhed by ſome Poſt, and, if ſuch a one has but Courage, he muſt certainly be a great Man. The Hero of whom we are writing was thoroughly accompliſhed this Way, and ſome of his Frolicks of Wickedneſs were as extravagant, as if he aim'd at making his Men believe he was a Devil incarnate Being one Day at Sea, and a little fluſhed with Drink ——— *Come*, ſays he, *let us make a Hell of our own, and try how long we can bear it* Accordingly he, with two or three others, went down into the Hold, and, cloſing up all the Hatches, fill'd ſeveral Pots full of Brimſtone, and other combuſtible Matter, then they ſet it on Fire, and ſo continu'd till they were almoſt ſuffocated, when ſome of the Men cried out for Air At length, he open'd the Hatches, not a little pleas'd that he held out the longeſt

The Night before he was kill'd, he ſat up and drank till the Morning, with ſome of his own Men, and the Maſter of a Merchant Man , notwithſtanding his having had Intelligence of the two Sloops coming to attack him, as has been before obſerv'd It was then that one of his Men aſk'd him, in caſe any Thing ſhould happen to him in the Engagement with the Sloops, whether his Wife knew where he had buried his Money? He anſwer'd, *That no Body but himſelf and the Devil knew where it was, and the longeſt Liver ſhould take all*

Thoſe of his Crew who were taken alive, told a Story which may appear a little incredible, however, we think it will not be fair to omit it, ſince it had it from their own Mouths That once, upon a Cruize, they found out that they had a Man on board more than their Crew , ſuch a one was ſeen ſeveral Days amongſt them, ſometimes below, and ſometimes upon Deck, yet no Man in the Ship could give any Account who he was, or from whence he came , but that he diſappear'd a little before they
were

Captain Edward England

were caft away in their great Ship, and, it feems, they verily believ'd it was the Devil.

One would think thele Things fhould have induc'd them to reform their Lives ; but being fo many Reprobates of them together, they encourag'd and fpirited one another up in their Wickednefs, to which a continual Courfe of Drinking did not a little contribute In *Black Beard*'s Journal, which was taken, there were feveral Memorandums of the following Nature, all writ with his own Hand. —— *Such a Day, Rum all out* —— *Our Company fomewhat fober* —— *A damn'd Confufion amongft us!* —— *Rogues a plotting*, —— *Great Talk of Separation* —— *So I look'd fharp for a Prize*, —— *Such a Day took one, with a great deal of Liquor on board, fo kept the Company hot, damn'd hot, then all Things went well again*

Thus it was thefe Wretches pafs'd their Lives, with very little Pleafure or Satisfaction, in the Poffeffion of what they violently took away from others, and fure to pay for it at laft, by an ignominious Death

The Names of the Pirates kill'd in the Engagement, are as follow :

Edward Teach, Commander.
Philip Morton, Gunner,
Garrat Gibbens, Boatfwain
Owen Roberts, Carpenter
Thomas Miller, Quarter-Mafter.

John Hufk,
Jofeph Curtice,
Jofeph Brooks (1)
Nath. Jackfon.

All the reft were ____ and, except the two laft, after ____ in *Virginia*

John Carnes,	*Jofeph Philips*,
Jofeph Brooks (2)	*James Robbins*,
James Blake,	*John Martin*,
John Gills,	*Edward Salter*,
Thomas Gates,	*Stephen Daniel*,
James White,	*Richard Greenfail*,
Richard Stiles,	*Ifrael Hands*, pardon'd,
Cæfar,	*Samuel Odell*, acquitted

There were in the Pirate Sloops, and a fhore in a Tent near where the Sloops lay, 25 Hogfheads of Sugar, 11 Tierces, and 145 Bags of Cocoa, a Barrel of Indigo, and a Bale of Cotton ; all which, with what was taken from the Governor and Secretary, and the Sale of the Sloop, came to 2500 *l* befides the Rewards paid by the Governor of *Virginia*, purfuant to his Proclamation The whole was divided among the Companies of the two Ships, the *Lime* and the *Pearl*, that lay in *James* River, the brave Fellows that took them coming in for no more than their Dividend amongft the reft, and it was a long Time before even that was paid.

The LIFE of Captain EDWARD ENGLAND.

Edward England went Mate of a Sloop, that failed out of *Jamaica*, and was taken by Captain *Winter*, a Pirate, juft before their Settlement at *Providence* ; from which Ifland *England* had afterwards the Command of a Sloop in the fame laudable Employment It is furprizing that Men of good Underftanding fhould engage in a Courfe of Life, that fo much debafes human Nature, and fets them upon a Level with the wild Beafts of the Foreft, who live and prey upon their weaker Fellow Creatures. A Crime fo enormous ! That it includes almoft all others, as Murder, Rapine, Theft, Ingratitude, &c. and tho' they make thefe Vices familiar to them by their daily Practice, yet thefe Men are fo inconfiftent with themfelves, that a Reflection made upon their Honour, their Juftice or their Courage, is looked upon as an Offence that ought to be punifhed with the Life of him that commits it *England* was one of thefe Men, who feemed to have fuch a Share of Reafon, as fhould have taught him much better Things. He had a great deal of good Nature, and did not want for Courage, he was not avaritious, and always averfe to the ill Ufage Prifoners received He would have been contented with moderate Plunder, and lefs mifchievous Pranks, could his Companions have been brought to the fame Temper, but he was generally over-rul'd, and, as he was engag'd in that abominable Society, he was oblig'd to be a Partner in all their vile Actions, in fpite of his natural Inclinations.

Captain *England* fail'd to the Coaft of *Africa*, after the Ifland of *Providence* was fettled by the *Englifh* Government, and the Pirates had furrendered to his Majefty's Proclamation Here he took feveral Ships and Veffels, particularly the *Cadogan* Snow belonging to *Briftol*, at *Sierraleone*, one *Skinner* Mafter, who was inhumanly murthered by fome of *England*'s Crew, that had lately been his own Men, and ferved in the faid Veffel It feems fome Quarrel had happened between them, fo that *Skinner* thought fit to remove thefe Fellows on Board of a Man of War, and at the fame Time refufed them their Wages ; not long after they found Means to defert that Service, and, fhipping themfelves aboard a Sloop in the *Weft-Indies*, were taken by a Pirate, and brought to *Providence*, whence they failed upon the fame Account along with Captain *England*

As foon as *Skinner* had ftruck to the Pirate, he was ordered to come on Board in his Boat, which he did, and the Perfon that he firft caft his Eye upon, proved to be his old Boatfwain, who ftar'd him in the Face like his evil Genius, and accofted him in this Manner —— *Ah, Captain Skinner! Is it you? The only Man I wifhed to fee; I am much in your Debt, and now I fhall pay you all in your own Coin.*

The poor Man trembled every Joint, when he found into what Company he had fallen, and dreaded the Event, as he had Reafon enough fo to do;

do · for the Boatſwain immediately called to his Conſorts, laid hold of the Captain, and made him faſt to the Windleſs, where they pelted him with Glaſs Bottles, till they cut him in a ſad Manner. After this, they whipp'd him about the Deck, till they were weary, being deaf to all his Prayers and Intreaties ; and, at laſt, becauſe he had been a good Maſter to his Men, they ſaid, he ſhould have an eaſy Death, and ſo they ſhot him thro' the Head. They took ſome few Things out of the Snow, but gave the Veſſel and all her Cargo to *Howel Davis* the Mate and the reſt of the Crew, as will be hereafter mentioned in the Life of Captain *Davis.*

Captain *England* took a Ship caled the *Pearl*, Capt. in *Tyzard* Commander, for which he exchanged his own Sloop, fitted her up for the pyratical Account, and new chriſtened her by the Name of the *Royal James.* With her he took ſeveral Ships and Veſſels of different Nations, at the *Azores* and *Cape de Verd Iſlands.*

In the Spring 1719, the Rovers returned to *Africa*, and beginning at the River *Gambia*, ſailed all down the Coaſt, between that River and *Cape Corſo*, they took the following Ships and Veſſels.

The *Eagle* Pink, Captain *Ricketts* Commander, belonging to *Cork*, taken the 25th of *March*, having 6 Guns and 17 Men on Board, ſeven of whom turned Pirates.

The *Charlotte*, Captain *Oldſon* of *London*, taken *May* the 26th, having 8 Guns and 18 Men on Board, 13 of whom turned Pirates.

The *Sarah*, Captain *Stunt*, of *London*, taken the 27th of *May*, having 4 Guns and 18 Men on Board, 3 of whom turned Pirates.

The *Bentworth*, Captain *Gardener*, of *Briſtol*, taken the 27th of *May*, having 12 Guns and 30 Men on Board, 12 of whom turned Pirates.

The *Buck* Sloop, Captain *Silveſter*, of *Gambia*, taken the 27th of *May*, having 2 Guns and only 2 Men on Board, who both turned Pirates.

The *Carteret*, Captain *Snow*, of *London*, taken the 28th of *May*, having 4 Guns and 18 Men on Board, 5 of whom turned Pirates.

The *Mercury*, Captain *Maggot*, of *London*, taken the 29th of *May*, having 4 Guns and 18 Men on Board, 5 of whom turned Pirates.

The *Coward* Galley, Captain *Creed*, of *London*, taken the 17th of *June*, having 2 Guns and 13 Men on Board, 4 of whom turned Pirates.

The *Elizabeth* and *Katharine*, Captain *Bridge* of *Barbadoes*, taken *June* the 27th, having 6 Guns and 14 Men on Board, 4 of whom turned Pirates.

The *Eagle* Pink being bound to *Jamaica*, the *Sarah* to *Virginia*, and the *Buck* to *Maryland*, they let them go, but the *Charlotte*, the *Bentworth*, the *Carteret*, and the *Coward* Galley, they burnt. The *Mercury*, and the *Elizabeth* and *Katharine*, were fitted up for Pirate Ships, the former was new nam'd *Queen Anne's Revenge*, and commanded by one *Lane*, and the other was called the *Flying King*, of which *Robert Sample* was appointed Captain. Theſe two left *England* upon the Coaſt, and ſailed to the *Weſt-Indies*, where they took ſome Prizes, cleaned, and ſailed to *Braſil* in *November*, they took ſeveral *Portugueſe* Ships there, and did a great Deal of Miſchief, but in the height of their Undertakings, a *Portugueſe* Man of War, which was an excellent Sailor, came a very unwelcome Gueſt to them, and gave them Chace. The *Queen Anne's Revenge* got off, but was loſt a little while after upon that Coaſt, and the *Flying King*, giving herſelf over for loſt, ran aſhore. There

were then 70 Men on Board, 12 of whom were killed, and the reſt taken Priſoners, the *Portugueſe* hanged 38 of theſe, of which 32 were *Engliſh*, three *Dutch*, two *French*, and one of their own Nation.

England, in going down the Coaſt, took the *Peterborough* Galley of *Briſtol*, Captain *Owen*, and the *Victory*, Captain *Ridout*, the former they detained, but plundered the latter, and let her go. In *Cape Corſo* Road, they ſaw two Sail at Anchor, but before they could reach them, they ſlipp'd their Cables, and got cloſe under *Cape Corſo Caſtle*, theſe were the *Whydah*, Captain *Prince*, and the *John*, Captain *Rider*. The Pirates, upon this, made a fire Ship of a Veſſel they had lately taken, and attempted to burn them, as tho' they had been a common Enemy, which if they had effected, they could not have been one Farthing the better for it, but the Caſtle firing warmly upon them, they withdrew, and ſailed down to *Whydab* Road, where they found another Pirate, one Captain *la Bouche*, who, having got thither before *England* arrived, had foreſtall'd the Market, and greatly diſappointed his Brethren.

Captain *England*, after this Baulk, went into a Harbour, clean'd his own Ship, and fitted up the *Peterborough*, which he called the *Victory.* They liv'd there very wantonly for ſeveral Weeks, making very free with the Negroe Women, and committing ſuch outragious Acts, that they came to an open Rupture with the Natives, ſeveral of whom they killed, and one of their Towns they ſet on Fire.

When the Pirates came out to Sea, they put it to a Vote what Voyage to take, and the Majority carrying it for the *Eaſt Indies*, they ſhap'd their Courſe accordingly, and arrived at *Madagaſcar*, at the Beginning of the Year 1720. They ſtaid not long there, but, after taking in Water and Proviſion, ſail'd for the Coaſt of *Malabar*, which is a fine fruitful Country in the *Eaſt-Indies*, in the Empire of the *Mogul*, but immediately ſubject to its own Princes · It reaches from the Coaſt of *Canara* to *Cape Camorin*, which is between 7 D 30, and 12 North Latitude, and in about 75 Eaſt Longitude, counting from the Meridian of *London.* The old Natives are Pagans, but there are a great Number of *Mahometans* inhabiting among them, who are Merchants, and generally rich. On the ſame Coaſt, but in a Province to the Northward, lies *Goa*, *Curat*, and *Bombay*, where the *Engliſh*, *Dutch*, and *Portugueſe* have Settlements.

Hither our Pirates came, having made a Tour of half the Globe, *going about like roaring Lions, ſeeking whom they might devour*, as the Pſalmiſt ſays of the Devils. They took ſeveral Country Ships, that is, *Indian* Veſſels, and one European, a *Dutch* Veſſel, which they exchanged for one of their own, and then came back to *Madagaſcar.*

They ſent ſeveral of their Hands on Shore, with Tents, Powder, and Shot, to kill Hogs, Venion, and ſuch other freſh Proviſions as the Iſland afforded, and a Whim came into their Heads to ſeek out for the Remains of *Avery's* Crew, whom they knew to be ſettled ſomewhere in the Iſland ——— Accordingly, ſome of them travelled ſeveral Days Journey, without getting any Intelligence of them, and ſo they were forced to return with the Loſs of their Labour, for theſe Men were ſettled quite on the other Side of the Iſland, as has been taken Notice of in the Life of *Avery.*

They ſtaid not long here, after they had clean'd their Ships, but ſailing to *Juanna*, they met two *Engliſh*, and one *Oſtend* Ship, all *India* Men, coming out of that Harbour ; one of which, after a deſperate

rate Refiftance, they took The Particulars of this Aftion are at length related in the following Letter, wrote by the Captain from *Bombay*

A LETTER from Captain *Mac-kra*, dated at *Bombay*, November 16, 1720.

'WE arrived the 25th of *July* laft, in Company with the *Greenwich*, at *Juanna*, an 'Ifland not far from *Madagafca*, Putting in there 'to refrefh our Men, we found fourteen Pirates, 'that came in their Canoes from the *Mayotta*, 'where the Pirate Ship to which they belonged, ' viz the *Indian Queen*, two hundred and fifty Tons, 'twenty eight Guns, and ninety Men, commanded 'by Captain *Oliver de la Bouche*, bound from the 'Guinea Coaft to the *Eaft-Indies*, had been bulged 'and loft They faid they left the Captain and 40 'of their Men, building a new Veffel to proceed 'on their wicked Defign Captain *Kirby* and I, 'concluded it might be of great Service to the 'Eaft-India Company to deftroy fuch a Neft of 'Rogues, were ready to fail for that Purpofe on 'the 17th of *Auguft*, about eight o'Clock in the 'Morning, when we difcovered two Pirate Ships 'ftanding into the Bay *Juanna*, one of the thirty 'four, and the other of thirty Guns I immediate-'ly went on Board the *Greenwich*, where they feem-'ed very diligent in Preparations for an Engagement, 'and I left Captain *Kirby* with mutual Promifes 'of ftanding by each other I then unmoored, got 'under Sail, and brought two Boats a-head to row 'me clofe to the *Greenwich*, but he, being open 'to a Valley and a Breeze, made the beft of his 'Way from me, which an *Oftender* in our Com-'pany, of 22 Guns, feeing, did the fame, tho' the 'Captain had promifed heartily to engage with us, 'and I believe would have been as good as his 'Word, if Captain *Kirby* had kept his About half 'an hour after Twelve, I called feveral Times to the '*Greenwich* to bear down to our Afiftance, and 'fir'd Shot at him, but to no Purpofe For tho' 'we did not doubt but he would join us, becaufe 'when he got about a League from us, he brought 'his Ship to, and looked on, yet both he and the '*Oftender* bafely deferted us, and left us engag'd 'with barbarous and inhuman Enemies, with their 'black and bloody Flags hanging over us, without 'the leaft Appearance of ever efcaping but to be 'cut to Pieces But God, in his good Providence, 'determined otherwife, for, notwithftanding their 'Superiority, we engag'd 'em both about three 'Hours, during which Time, the biggeft of them 'received fome Shot betwixt Wind and Water, which 'made her keep off a little to ftop her Leaks The 'other endeavoured all fhe could to board us, by 'rowing with her Oars, being within half a Ship's 'length of us above an Hour, but by good For-'tune we fhot all her Oars to Pieces, which pre-'vented them, and by confequence faved our Lives 'About four o'Clock, moft of the Officers and 'Men pofted on the Quarter-Deck being kill'd and 'wounded, the largeft Ship making up to us with 'Diligence, being ftill within a Cable's Length of us 'often giving us a Broadfide, there being now no 'hopes of Capt *Kirby*'s coming to our Afiftance, 'we endeavoured to run a fhoar, and tho' we drew 'four foot of Water more than the Pirate, it pleafed 'God that he ftuck faft on a higher Ground than 'we did 'till in with; fo was difappointed a

'fecond time from boarding us Here we had a 'more violent Engagement than before All my 'Officers, and moft of my Men, behaved with un-'expected Courage, and as we had a confiderable 'Advantage by having a Broadfide to his Bow, we 'did him great Damage, fo that had Captain *Kir-by* 'come in then, I believe we fhould have taken 'both the Veffels, for we had one of them fure ? 'but the other Pirate (who was ftill firing at us) 'feeing the *Greenwich* did not offer to affift us, he 'fupplied his Confort with three Boats full of frefh 'Men About Five in the Evening, the *Greenwich* 'ftood clear away to Sea, leaving us ftruggling hard 'for Life, in the very Jaws of Death, which the 'other Pirate, that was a-float, feeing, got a-warp 'out, and was hauling under our Stern By this 'time many of my Men being killed and wounded, 'and no Hopes left us of efcaping being all mur-'dered by enraged barbarous Conquerors, I order'd 'all that could, to get into the Long-Boat, under 'the Cover of the Smoak of our Guns, fo that 'with what fome did in Boats, and others by fwim-'ing, moft of us that were able got a-fhore by 'feven o'Clock When the Pirates came a-board, 'they cut three of our wounded Men to Pieces I, 'with a few of my People, made what hafte I could 'to the *King's-Town*, twenty five Miles from us, 'where I arrived next Day, almoft dead with the 'Fatigue and lofs of Blood, having been forely 'wounded in the Head by a Mufket Ball

' At this Town I heard, that the Pirates had of-'fered ten thoufand Dollars to the Country People 'to bring me in, which many of them would have 'accepted, only they knew the King and all his chief 'People were in my Intereft. Mean Time, I cau-'fed a Report to be fpread, that I was dead of my 'Wounds, which much abated their Fury About 'ten Days after, being pretty well recovered, and 'hoping the Malice of our Enemies was nigh over, 'I began to confider the difmal Condition we were 'reduced to, being in a Place where we had no 'Hopes of getting a Paffage home, all of us in a 'manner naked, not having had Time to get off 'another Shirt, or a Pair of Shoes, than what we 'had on

' Having obtained Leave to go on Board the 'Pirates, and gotten a Promife of Safety, feveral 'of the Chief of them knew me, and fome of them 'had failed with me, which I found to be of great 'Advantage, becaufe, notwithftanding their Pro-'mife, fome of them would have cut me, and all 'that would not enter with them, to Pieces, had 'it not been for the chief Captain, *Edward Eng-land*, and fome others whom I knew They talk-'ed of burning one of their Ships, which we had fo 'intirely difabled, as to be no farther ufeful to 'them, and to fit the *Caffandra* in her room, but 'in the End I managed the Affair fo well, that 'they made me a Prefent of the faid fhattered Ship, 'which was Dutch built, and called the *Fancy*, her 'Burden was about three hundred Tons I pro-'cured alfo a hundred and twenty nine Bales of the 'Company's Cloth, tho' they would not give me 'a Rag of my own Cloaths

' They failed the 3d of *September*, and I, with 'Jury-Mafts, and fuch old Sails as they left me, 'made a fhift to do the like on the 8th, together 'with 43 of my Ship's Crew, including two Paf-'fengers and 12 Soldiers, having no more than five 'Tons of Water aboard After a Paffage of forty 'eight Days, I arrived here on the 26th of *Oc-tober*, almoft naked and ftarved, having been redu-'ced to a pint of Water a Day and almoft in defpair 'of ever feeing Land, by Reafon of the Calms we

S f ' met

'met with between the Coaft of *Arabia* and *Ma-*
'labar——We had in all thirteen Men killed, and
'twenty four wounded, and we were told, that we
'had deftroyed about ninety or a hundred of the
'Pirates When they left us, they were about 300
'Whites, and 80 Blacks, in both Ships I am
'perfuaded, had our Confort the *Greenwich* done
'his Duty, we had deftroyed both of them, and
'got two hundred thoufand Pounds for our Owners
'and felves; whereas the Lofs of the *Caffandra* may
'juftly be imputed to his deferting us I have de-
'livered all the Bales that were given me into the
'Company's Warehoufe, for which the Governor
'and Council have ordered me a Reward Our
'Governor, Mr *Boon,* who is extreme kind and
'civil to me, had ordered me home with this
'Pacquet, but Captain *Harvey,* who had a prior
'Promife, being come in with the Fleet, goes in
'my room The Governor hath promis'd me a
'Country Voyage to help to make up my Loffes,
'and would have me ftay, and accompany him to
'*England* next Year

Captain *Mackra* certainly run a great Hazard, in
going aboard the Pirate, and began quickly to repent his Credulity; for though they had promifed,
that no Injury fhould be done to his Perfon, he found
their Words were not to be trufted, and it may be
fuppofed, that nothing but the defperate Circumftances he imagined himfelf to be in, could have
prevailed upon him to fling himfelf and Company
into their Hands Perhaps he did not know how
firmly the Natives of that Ifland were attach'd to
the *Englifh* Nation, for about 20 Years ago, Captain *Cornwall,* Commodore of an *Englifh* Squadron,
affifted them againft another Ifland called *Mohilla,*
for which they have ever fince communicated all
the grateful Offices in their Power, infomuch that
it became a Proverb, *That an* Englifhman, *and a*
Juanna Man *were all one*
England was inclined to favour Captain *Mackra,*
but he was fo free as to let him know, that his Intereft was declining amongft them, and that the
Pirates were fo provoked at the Refiftance he made
againft them, that he was afraid he fhould hardly
be able to protect him He therefore advifed him to
footh up and manage the Temper of Captain *Tay-*
lor, a Fellow of a moft barbarous Nature, who was
become a Favourite amongft them, for no other Reafon than becaufe he was a greater Brute than the reft
Mackra did what he could to foften this Beaft, and
ply'd him with warm Punch, notwithftanding which,
they were in a Tumult whether they fhould make
an End of him, or no, when an Accident happen'd
which turn'd to the Favour of the unfortunate Captain; a Fellow with a terrible pair of Whiskers, and
a wooden Leg, being ftuck round with Piftols, like
the Man in the Almanack with Darts, comes fwearing and vapouring upon the Quarter Deck, and afks,
in a damning Manner, which was Captain *Mackra*
The Captain expected no lefs than that this Fellow
would be his Executioner,——but when he came
near him, he took him by the Hand, fwearing, *Damn*
him he was glad to fee him, and fhew me the Man,
fays he, *that offers to hurt Captain* Mackra, *for*
I'll ftand by him, and fo with many Oaths he told
him, *he was an honeft Fellow, and that he had for-*
merly fail'd with him
This put an End to the Difpute, and Captain
Taylor was fo mellow'd with the Punch, that he
confented that the old Pirate Ship, and fo many
Bales of Cloth, fhould be given to Captain *Mac-*
kra, and fo he fell afleep *England* advifed Captain
Mackra, to get off with all Expedition, leaft when

the Beaft fhould awake, he might repent his Generofity Which Advice was followed by the Captain

Captain *England* he having fided fo much to Captain *Mackra's* Intereft, was a Means of making him
many Enemies among the Crew, they thinking fuch
good Ufage inconfiftent with their Polity, becaufe it
looked like procuring Favour at the Aggravation of
their Crimes, therefore, upon an Imagination or Report, foon after raifed that Captain *Mackra* was fitting out againft them, with the Company's Force,
England was pulled out of his Government, and ma-
rooned, with three more, on the Ifland of *Mauritius,*
An Ifland, indeed, not to be complained of, had
they accumulated any Wealth by their Villainies,
they wou'd have afforded fome future comfortable
Profpect, for it abounds with Fifh, Deer, Hogs, and
other Flefh Sir *Thomas Herbert* fays, the Shores are
ftocked with Coral and Ambergrife, but I believe
the *Dutch* had not deferted it, had there been much
of thefe Commodities to have been found It was in
1722, refettled by the *French,* who have a Fort at
another neighbouring Ifland, called *Don Mafcarene,*
which is touched at for Water, Wood, and Refrefh-
ments, by *French* Ships bound to, or from *India,* as
St Helena and *Cape Bon Efperance,* are by us and
the *Dutch* From this Place, Captain *England* and
his Companions, having made a little Boat of Staves
and old Pieces of Deal left there, went over to *Mada-*
gafcar, where they fubfift at prefent on the Charity
of fome of their Brethren, who had made better Provifion for themfelves, that they had done
The Pirates detained fome Officers and Men belonging to Captain *Mackra,* and having repaired the
Damages received in their Rigging, they failed for
India The Day before they made Land, they faw
two Ships to the Eaftward, who, at firft Sight, they
took to be *Englifh,* and the crew ordered one of
the Prifoners, who had been an Officer with Captain
Mackra, to tell them the private Signals between the
Company's Ships, the Captain fwearing he would
cut him in pound Pieces, if he did not do it immediately, but the poor Man being unable, was forced
to bear their Scurrility, till they came up with the
Veffels, and found they were two *Moor* Ships from
Mufcat, loaded with Horfes They brought the Captains of them, and the Merchants, on Board, torturing them, and riding the Ships, in order to difcover
their Riches, as believing they came from *Moha,*
but being baulked in their Expectation, and next
Morning feeing Land, and at the fame Time a Fleet
in Shore plying to Windward, they were puzzled how
to difpofe of them To let them go, was to difcover
and ruin the Voyage, and it was cruel to fink the
Men and Horfes with the Ships, tho' many of them
were inclined to do it, therefore, as a Medium, they
brought them to an Anchor, threw all their Sails
over-board, and cut one of the Ships Mafts half
through

While they lay at an Anchor, and were all the
next Day employ'd in taking out Water, one of the
afore-mentioned Fleet bore towards them with *Eng-*
lifh Colours, and was anfwered with a red Enfign
from the Pirates, but they did not fpeak with one another At Night they left the *Mufcat* Ships, weighed
with the Sea Wind, and ftood to the Northward after this Fleet About four next Morning, juft as
they were getting under fail with the Land Wind,
the Pirates came amongft them, made no ftop, but
fir'd their great and fmall Guns very brifkly, till
they got thro'. As Day-Light cleared, they were
in a great Confternation in their Minds, having all
along taken them for *Angria's* Fleet What to do
was now the Point, to difpute whether to run or Purfue,

fue?) They were sensible of their Inferiority of Strength, having no more than 300 Men in both their Ships, and 40 of these were Negroes, besides, the *Victory* had then four Pumps at Work, and must inevitably been lost before, had it not been for some Hand-Pumps, and several Pair of Standards brought out of the *Cassandra*, to relieve and strengthen her. At last, observing the Indifference of the Fleet, they chose rather to chase than run, and thought that the best Way to save themselves, was to play at Bull-beggar with the Enemy. So they came up with the Sea Wind, about Gun-Shot to Leeward, the great Ships of the Fleet were a-head, and some others a-stern, which latter they took for Fire-Vessels. Those a-head gaining from them by cutting away their Boats, they could do nothing more than continue their Course all Night. This they did, and found them next Morning out of Sight, excepting a Ketch and some few Gallivats, which are a small sort of Vessels something like the Feluccas of the *Mediterranean*, and masts like them, triangular Sails. They bore down, which the Ketch perceiving, transported her People on Board a Gallivat, and set fire to her, the other proved too nimble, and made off. The same Day they chased another Gallivat and took her, being come from *Gogo* with Cotton, and bound for *Callicut*. Of these Men they enquired concerning the Fleet, supposing they must have been in it, but they protested they had not seen a Ship or Boat since they left *Gogo*, and pleaded very earnestly for Favour; nevertheless, the Pirates threw all their Cargo over-board, and squeez'd their Joynts in a Vice, to extort Confession. The poor Wretches entirely ignorant of who or what this Fleet should be, were oblig'd to sustain this Torment, and the next Day a fresh easterly Wind having split the Gallivats Sails, the Pirates put her Company into the Boat to shift for themselves, with nothing but a Trysail, no Provisions, and only four Gallons of Water, (half of it Salt) and being then out of Sight of Land.

For the better elucidating of this Story, it may be convenient to inform the Reader, who *Angria* is, and what the Fleet were, that had so scurvily behaved themselves.

Angria, is a famous *Indian* Pirate, master of considerable Strength and large Territories, that gives continual Disturbance to the *European* Trade, and especially to the *English*. His chief Hold is *Callaba*, no many Leagues from *Bombay*, and he has one Island in Sight of that Port, whereby he gains frequent Opportunities of annoying the Company. It would not be so insuperable a Difficulty to suppress him, if the Shallowness of the Water did not prevent Ships of War coming nigh, and if he had not till a better Art of bribing the *Mogul*'s Ministers for Protection, when he finds an Enemy too powerful.

In the Year 1720, the *Bombay* Fleet, consisting of four Grabs, which are Ships built in *India* by the Company, with three Masts, a Prow like a Row-Galley, instead of a Bolsprit, and of about 150 Tons Burden, officered and armed like a Man of War, for Defence and Protection of the Trade, assisted by the *London*, the *Candois*, and two other Ships, with Gallivats, attempted to bombard and batter *Gayra*, a Fort belonging to *Angria*, on the *Malabar* Coast. Besides their proper Complement, they carried down a thousand Men for this Enterprize. This was the Fleet that our Pirates fell in with, who were now returning to *Bombay*, without any Success in what they had undertaken. Captain *Upton*, Commodore of that Fleet, upon Sight of the Rovers, prudently objected to Mr *Brown*, the General, That the Ships were not to be hazarded, since they sailed without

their Governor *Boon*'s Orders to engage, and besides, that they did not come out with such a Design. Their missing this favourable Opportunity of destroying the Pirates, angered the Governor so, that he transferred the Command of the Fleet to Captain *Maskra*, who had Orders immediately to pursue and engage, wherever he met them.

The Viceroy of *Goa*, assisted by the *English* Company's Fleet from *Bombay*, after this, engaged for the Reduction of *Caslaba*, *Angria*'s principal Place, and to that Purpose landed 8 or 10000 Men the next Year, the *English* Squadron of Men of War being then in those Seas, but having viewed the Fortification well, and expended some of their Army by Sickness, and the Fatigues of a Camp, he carefully withdrew again.

We return to the Pirates, who, after they had sent away the Gallivats People, were resolved to cruize to the Southward. The next Day, between *Goa* and *Carwar*, they heard several Guns, which brought them to an Anchor, and they sent their Boat on the Scent, who returned about two in the Morning, and brought Word of two Grabs lying at Ancroi in the Road. They weighed and ran towards the Bay, till Day-Light, gave the Grabs Sight of them, and there was but just Time enough to get under *India Diva* Castle, out of their Reach. This displeased the Pirates the more, in that they wanted Water. Some of them were for making a Descent that Night, and taking the Island, but it not being approved of by the Majority, they proceeded to the Southward, and took next in their Way a small Ship, out of *Onnore* Road, with only a *Dutch* Man and two *Portugueze* on Board. They sent one of these on Shore to the Captain, to acquaint him, that if he would supply them with some Water, and fresh Provisions, he should have his Ship again, and the Master returned for answer, by his Mate *Frank Harmless*, that if they would deliver him Possession over the Barr, he would comply with their Request. This Proposal the Mate thought was collusive, and the Pirates rather jump'd into *Harmless*'s Opinion, who very honestly entered with them, and resolved to seek Water at the *Laccadeva* Islands. So having sent the other Persons on Shore, with Threats that he should be the last Man they would give Quarter to, by reason of this uncivil Usage, they put directly for the Islands, and arrived there in three Days. Here, being informed by a *Munchew*, they took with the Governor of *Carwar*'s Pass, that there was no Anchor-Ground among them, and *Melinda* being the next convenient Island, they sent their Boats on Shore, to see if there was any Water, and whether it was inhabited or not. The Boats returned with an Answer to their Satisfaction, *viz*. that there was abundance of good Water, and many Houses, all deserted by the Men, who had fled to the neighbouring Islands on the Approach of Ships, and left only the Women and Children to guard one another. The Women they forced in a barbarous Manner to their Lusts, and, to requite them, destroyed their Cocoa-Trees, and fired several of their Houses and Churches, which we suppose were built by the *Portugueze*, who formerly used to put in there in their Voyages to *India*.

While they were at this Island, they lost three or four Anchors, by the Rockiness of the Ground, and Freshness of the Winds, and at last were forced thence by a harder Gale than ordinary, leaving 70 People, Blacks and Whites, and most of their Water-Casks. In ten Days they regained the Island again, filled their Water, and took the People on Board.

Provisions were grown very scarce, and they now resolved to visit their good Friends the *Dutch*, at *Cochin*, who, if you will believe these Rogues, never

fail

fail of supplying Gentlemen of their Profession After three Days fail, they arrived off *Tellechery*, and took a small Veffel belonging to Governor *Adams*, *John Tawke*, Mafter, whom they brought on Board very drunk This Man giving them an Account of Captain *Mackra's* fitting out, it put them into a Tempeft of Paffion *A Villain*, faid they, *that we have treated fo civilly, as to give him a Ship and other Prefents, and now to come armed againft us*, he ought to be hanged And fince we cannot fhew our Refentment on him, let us hang the Dogs his People, who wifh him well, and would do the fame, if they were clear If it be in my Power, fays the Quarter-Mafter, both Mafters and Officers of Ships fhall be carried with us, for the future, only to plague them Now — d—— n England, we may thank him for this

Thence they proceeded to *Calicut*, where they endeavoured to take a large *Moorifh* Ship out of the Road, but were prevented by fome Guns mounted on Shore, and difcharged at them, Mr *Lafinby*, who was one of Captain *Mackra's* Officers, and detained by them, was under the Deck at this Time, and commanded, both by the Captain and Quarter-Mafter of the Pirates, to tend the Braces on the Brooms, in Hopes, it was believed, that a Shot would take him before they got clear When he would have excufed himfelf, they threatened, on the leaft Neglect, to fhoot him, at which, the other beginning to expoftulate farther, and claim their Promife of putting him a-fhore, he got an unmerciful beating from the Quarter-Mafter, Captain *Taylor*, who was now Succeffor to *England*, and whofe Priviledge it was to ufe the Cudgel, being lame of his Hands, and unable

The next Day, in their Paffage down, they came up with a *Dutch* Galliot, bound for *Calicut*, with Lime-Stone, a-board of which they put Captain *Tawke*, and fent him away At this Time, feveral of the People interceded for *Lafinby*; but in vain For, fays *Taylor* and his Party, if we let this Dog go, who has heard our Defigns and Refolutions, we overfet all our well-advifed Projections, and particularly this Supply we are now feeking for, at the Hands of the Dutch

It was but one Day more before they arrived off *Cochin*, where, by a Fifhing-Canoe, they fent a Letter on Shore; and in the Afternoon, with the Sea-Breeze, ran into the Road and anchored, faluting the Fort with 11 Guns each Ship, and receiving the Return in an equal Number This they look'd upon as a good Omen of the welcome Reception they afterwards found, for at Night there came on Board a large Boat, deeply laden with frefh Provifions and Liquors, and with it a Servant of a favourite Inhabitant, called *John Trumpet* He told them then they muft immediately weigh, and run further to the Southward, where they fhould be fupplied with all Things they wanted, whether naval Stores, or Provifions

They had not been long at Anchor again, before they had feveral Canoes on Board, with both black and white Inhabitants, who continued, without Interruption, all good Offices, during their Stay *John Trumpet*, in particular, brought a large Boat of Arrack, than which, nothing could be more pleafing, as alfo 60 Bales of Sugar, an Offering, it is prefumed, from the Governor and his Daughter, who, in Return, had a fine Table-Clock fent himfelf, the Plunder of Captain *Mackra's* Ship, and a large Gold Watch for the Lady, Earnefts of the Pay they defigned to make

When they had all on Board, they paid Mr *Trumpet* to his Satisfaction; it was computed to the Sum of 6 or 7000 *l* gave him three Cheers, 11 Guns each

Ship, and throw'd Ducatoons into his Boat by Handfuls, for the Boat-Men to fcramble for

That Night there being little Wind, they did not weigh, and *Trumpet*, in the Morning, waked them to the Sight of more Arrack, Chefts of Piece-Goods, and ready-made Clothes, bringing the Fifcal of the Place alfo with him At Noon, while thofe were on Board, they faw a Sail to the Southward, which they weighed, and chaced after, but fhe, having a good Offing, got to the Northward of them, and anchor'd at a fmall Diftance from *Cochin* Fort The afore-mention'd Gentlemen affuring the Pirates that they would not be molefted in taking her from under the Caftle, follicited before-hand for the buying her, and advifed them to ftand in, which they did boldly, to board her, but when they came within a Cable's Length or two of the Chace, now near Shore, the Fort fired two fmall Guns, whofe Shot falling nigh their Muzzles, they inftantly bore out of the Road, made an eafy Sail to the Southward and anchored at Night in their former Birth where *John Trumpet*, to engage them Stay a little longer, informed them, that in a few Days, a very rich Ship was to pafs by, commanded by the General of *Bombay's* Brother

This Governor is an Emblem of foreign Power, What Inconvenience and Injury muft the Mafter's fubjects fuftain, under one who can truckle to fuch treacherous and bafe Means, as correfponding and trading with Pirates to enrich himfelf? Certainly fuch a Man will ftick at no Injuftice to repair or make a Fortune He has the *Argumentum bacillum* always in his own Hands, and can convince, when he pleafes, in half the Time of other Arguments, that Fraud and Oppreffion is Law That he imploys Inftruments in fuch dirty Work, expreffes the Guilt and Shame, but no way mitigates the Crime *John Trumpet* was the Tool, but, as the Dog faid in the Fable, on another Occafion, *What is done by the Mafter's Orders, is the Mafter's Action.*

I cannot but reflect, on this Occafion, what a vile Government *Sancho Pancho* had of it; he had not only fuch *Perquifites* refcinded, but was really almoft ftarved, the Victuals was taken from him almoft every Day, and only under a Pretence of preferving his Excellency's Health But Governments differ

From *Cochin* fome were for proceeding to *Madagafcar* directly, others thought it proper to cruize till they got a Store-Ship Thefe latter being the Majority, they ply'd to the Southward, and, after fome Days, faw a Ship in Shore, which being to Windward of them, they could not get nigh, till, the Sea, Wind and Night favouring, they feparated, one to the Northward, the other to the Southward, thinking to enclofe her between But, to their Aftonifhment, and contrary to Expectation, when Day broke, inftead of the Chace, they found themfelves very near five Sail of tall Ships, who immediately making a Signal for the Pirates to bear down, put them in the utmoft Confufion, particularly *Taylor's* Ship, becaufe their Confort was at fo great a Diftance from them, as at leaft thrice Leagues to the Southward However, they ftood to one another, and joined, and then together made the beft of their Way from the Fleet, which they judged to be commanded by Captain *Mackra*, of whofe Courage having had Experience, they were glad to fhun any farther Proofs of it

In three Hours Chace, none of the Fleet gaining upon them, excepting one Grab, their dejected Countenances cleared up again, the more, in that a Calm fucceeded for the Remainder of that Day In the Night, with the Land Wind, they ran directly off

off Share, and found next Day, to their great Confolation, that they had loft Sight of all the Fleet

This Danger efcaped, they propofed to fpend their *Chriftmas*, which was the *Chriftmas* of 1720, in Carouzing and Forgetfulnefs, and, accordingly, they kept for three Days in a wanton and riotous Way, not only eating, but wafting their frefh Provifions in fo wretched and inconfiderable a Manner, that, when they had agreed after this to proceed to *Mauritius*, they were in that Paffage at an Allowance of a Bottle of Water *per Diem*, and not above two Pounds of Beef, and a fmall Quantity of Rice, every Day, for ten Men. So that had it not been for the leaky Ship, they muft moft of them have perifhed, but fhe had a large Quantity of Arrack and Sugar on Board.

In this Condition they arrived at the Ifland of *Mauritius*, about the Middle of *February*, fheathed and re fitted the *Victory*, and, on the 5th of *April*, failed again, leaving this terrible Infcription on one of the Walls: *Left this Place the 5th of April, to go to Madagafcar for Limes* This they did left any any Vifits fhould be paid in their Abfence, as it often happens to Lawyers, and Men of Bufinefs: However, they did not fail directly for *Madagafcar*, but the Ifland *Mafcarine*, where, luckily as Rogues could wifh, they found at their Arrival, on the 8th, a *Portugueze* Ship at Anchor, of 70 Guns, but moft of them thrown over-board, her Mafts loft, and the whole Veffel fo much difabled by a violent Storm they had met with in the Latitude of 13° South, that fhe became a Prize to the Pirates, with very little or no Refiftance. A glorious Prize fhe was, indeed, having the *Conde de Ericeira*, Viceroy of *Goa*, who made that fruitlefs Expedition againft *Angria*, the *Indian*, and feveral other Paffengers on Board Thefe Perfons could not be ignorant of the Treafure fhe had in her; and they afferted, that, in the fingle Article of Diamonds, there was to the Value of between three or four Millions of Dollars

The Viceroy, who came on Board that Morning, in Expectation of the Ships being *Englifh*, was made a Prifoner, and oblig'd to pay a Ranfom, which in Confideration of his great Lofs (the Treafure being partly his own,) they agreed, after fome Demurrings, fhould be only 2000 Dollars for himfelf and the other Prifoners, whom they fet afhore, with Promifes to leave a Ship, that they might tranfport themfelves, becaufe the Ifland was not thought in a Condition to maintain fo great a Number However, tho' they had learned from them the Account of an Oftender being to Leeward of the Ifland, and taken her on that Information, fo that they could conveniently have comply'd with fo reafonable a Requeft, yet they fent the *Oftender* (which was formerly the Greyhound Galley of *London*), with fome of their People to *Madagafcar*, with News of their Succefs, and Orders to prepare Mafts for the Prize; and followed themfelves foon after, without Regard to the Sufferers, carrying 2000 *Mozambique* Negroes with them in the *Portugueze* Ship

Madagafcar is an Ifland larger than *Great-Britain*, moft of it within the Tropick of *Capricorn* It lies Eaft from the Eaftern Side of *Africa*, and abounds with Provifions of all Sorts, as Oxen, Goats, Sheep, Poultry, Fifh, Citrons, Oranges, Tamarinds, Dates, Cocoa-Nuts, Banana's, Wax, Honey, Rice, Cotton, Indigo, or, in fhort, with any other Thing they will take Pains to plant, and have Underftanding to manage They have likewife Ebony, a hard Wood like Brafil, of which they make their Lances, and Gum of feveral Sorts, Benzin, Dragon's Blood, Aloes, &c What is moft incommodious, are the nu-

merous Swarms of Locufts on the Land, and the Crocodiles, or Alligators, in their Rivers Hither, in St *Auguftine's* Bay, the Ships fometimes touch for Water, when they take the inner Paffage in *India*, and do not defign to ftop at *Johanna*, and we may obferve, from the fixth general Voyage fet forth by the *Eaft-India* Company in Confirmation of what is hereafter faid in Relation to Currents in general, that this inner Paffage or Channel, has its Northern and Southern Currents ftrongeft where the Channel is narroweft, and is lefs, and varies on different Points of the Compafs, as the Sea comes to fpread again in the Paffage crofs the Line

Since the Difcovery of this Ifland by the *Portugueze*, A D 1506, the *Europeans*, and particularly the Pirates, have encreafed a dark Mulatto Race there, tho' ftill few in Comparifon with the Natives Thefe latter are Negroes, with curl'd fhort Hair, Active, and formerly reprefented malicious and revengeful, now tractable and communicable, perhaps owing to the Favours in Cloathing and Liquors, that they from Time to Time have received from thefe Fellows, who live in all poffible Friendfhip with them; and, can any fingle Man of them, command a Guard of 2 or 300 at a Minute's warning: This friendfhip is farther the Native's Intereft to cultivate with them, becaufe the Ifland, being divided into petty Governments and Commands, the Pirates, fettled here, who are now a confiderable Number, and have little Caftles of their own, can carry the Day wherever they think fit to fide.

When *Taylor's* Crew came with the *Portuguefe* Prize hither, they found the *Oftender* had played their Men a Trick, for they took Advantage of their Drink, rofe upon them, and as (they heard afterwards) carried the Ship to *Mozambique*, whence the Governor ordered her for *Goa*.

Here the Pirates cleaned the *Caffandra*, and divided their Plunder, fharing 42 fmall Diamonds a Man, or in lefs Proportion according to their Magnitude An ignorant, or a merry Fellow, who had only one in this Divifion, as being judged equal in Value to 42 fmall ones, muttered very much at his Lot, went and broke it in a Morter, fwearing afterwards, he had a better fhare than any of them, for he had beat it, he faid, in 43 Sparks.

Thofe who were not for running the Hazard of their Necks, with 42 Diamonds, befides other Treafure, in their Pockets, knocked off, and ftayed with their old acquaintance at *Madagafcar*, on mutual Agreements, that the longer Livers fhould take all. The Refidue having therefore no Occafion for two Ships, and the *Victory* being Leaky, fhe was burnt, the Men (as many as would) coming into the *Caffandra*, under the Command of *Taylor*, whom we muft leave a Time, projecting either for *Cochin*, to difpofe of their Diamonds among their old Friends the *Dutch*, or elfe for the *Red* or *China* Seas, to avoid the Men of War, that continually clamoured in their Ears a Noife of Danger; and proceed to give the *little* Account we are able, of that Squadron who arrived in *India*, early in the Year 1721.

At the *Cape* of *Good Hope*, in *June*, the Commodore met with a Letter, which was left for him by the Governor of *Maderas*, to whom it was wrote by the Governor of *Pandicherry*, a *French* Factory, on the *Coromondel* Coaft, fignifying, that the Pirates, at the Writing of it, were then ftrong in the *Indian* Seas, having 11 Sail and 1500 Men; but that many of them went away about that Time, for the Coaft of *Brazil* and *Guinea*, that others fettled and fortified themfelves at *Madagafcar*, *Mauritius*, *Johanna* and *Mohilla* And that others, under *Condin*, in a Ship called the *Dragon*, took a large *Moor's* Veffels,

Veſſel, coming from *Judda* and *Mocho*, with thirteen Lackies of Rupees on Board, (i e 1300000 half Crowns,) which Plunder having divided, they burnt their Ship and Prize, and ſat down quietly with their other Friends at *Madagaſcar*

The Account contained ſeveral other Things which we have before related——Commodore *Mattheus*, upon receiving this Intelligence, and being fond of the Service he came out for, haſtened to thoſe Iſlands, as the moſt hopeful Places of Succeſs ; at St *Mary*'s he would have engaged *England* with Promiſes of Favour, to communicate what he knew, concerning the *Caſſandra*, and the reſt of the Pirates, and aſſiſt in the Pilotage, but *England* was wary, and thought this was to ſurrender at Diſcretion . So they took up the Guns of the *Judda* Ship that was burnt, and the Men of War diſperſed themſelves on ſeveral Voyages and Cruizes afterwards, as was thought likelieſt to ſucceed, tho' all to no Purpoſe . Then the Squadron went down to *Bombay*, were ſaluted by the Fort, and came home

The Pirates, I mean thoſe of the *Caſſandra*, now Captain *Taylor*, fitted up the *Portugueſe* Man of War, and reſolved upon another Voyage to the *Indies*, notwithſtanding the Riches they had heaped up ; but, as they were preparing to ſail, they heard of the four Men of War coming after them to thoſe Seas, therefore they altered their Minds, ſailed for the Main of *Africa*, and put in at a little place called *Delagoa*, near the River *de Spiritu Sancto*, on the Coaſt of *Monomotapa*, in 26° South Latitude They believed this to be a Place of Security, in regard that the Squadron could not poſſibly get Intelligence of them, there being no Correſpondence over Land, nor any Trade carried on by Sea, between that and the Cape, where the Men of War were then ſuppoſed to be The Pirates came to in the Evening, and were ſurprized with a few Shot from the Shore, not knowing of any Fortification or *European* Settlement in that Part of the World, ſo they anchored at a Diſtance that Night In the Morning, they perceived a ſmall Fort of ſix Guns, whereupon, they run up to it, and battered it down

This Fort was built and ſettled by the *Dutch Eaſt-India* Company, a few Months before, for what Purpoſe, I know not ; they had left 150 Men upon the Place, who were then dwindled to a third Part by Sickneſs and Caſualties, and never after received any Relief or Neceſſaries, ſo that Sixteen of thoſe that were left, upon their humble Petition, were admitted on Board the Pirates, and all the reſt would have had the ſame Favour (they ſaid) had they been any other than *Dutch* I mention this, as an Inſtance of the Pirates Ingratitude, who had been ſo much obliged to their Countrymen for Support But Rogues ſeldom love one another, tho' their Intereſt often unites them

Here they ſtaid above four Months, carreened both their Ships, and took their Diverſions with Security, till they had expended all their Proviſions ; then they put to Sea, leaving conſiderable Quantities of Mu-

ſlins, Chintzes, and ſuch like Goods behind, to the half ſtarv'd *Dutch* Men, which enabled them to make good Penny'worths to the next that came, with whom they bartered for Proviſions, at the Rate of three Farthings an *Engliſh* Yard

They left *Delagoa* about the latter End of *December*, in 1722, but not agreeing whither, or how to proceed, they concluded to part, ſo thoſe who were for continuing that ſort of Life, went on Board the *Portugueſe* Prize, and ſteered for *Madagaſcar* to their Friends, with whom I hear they are now ſettled, and the reſt took the *Caſſandra* and ſailed for the *Spaniſh Weſt-Indies* The *Mermaid* Man of War happening then to be down on the Main with a Convoy, about 30 Leagues from theſe Pirates, would have gone and attacked them, but, on a Conſultation of the Maſters, whoſe Safety he was particularly to regard, they agreed their own Protection was of more Service than deſtroying the Pirate, and ſo the Commander was unwillingly with-held He diſpatched a Sloop to *Jamaica*, with the News, which brought down the *Lanceſtun*, only a Day or two too late they having juſt before he came, ſurrendered, with all their Riches, to the Governor of *Porto-Bello*

Here they ſat down to ſpend the Fruits of their diſhoneſt Induſtry, dividing the Spoil and Plunder of Nations among themſelves, without the leaſt Remorſe or Compunction ; ſatisfying their Conſciences with this Salvo, that other People would have done as much had they the like Opportunity We can't ſay, but that if they had known what was doing in *England*, at the ſame Time, by the South-Sea Directors, and their Directors, they would certainly have had this Reflection for their Conſolation, *viz. That whatever Robberies they had committed, they might be pretty ſure they were not the greateſt Villains then living in the World*

It is a difficult Matter to make a Computation of the Miſchief that was done by his Crew, in about five Years Time, which amounted to much more than the Plunder they gained, for they often ſunk or burnt the Veſſel they took, as it ſuited their Humour or Circumſtances, ſometimes to prevent giving Intelligence, ſometimes becauſe they did not leave Men to navigate them, and at other Times out of Wantonneſs, or becauſe they were diſpleaſed at the Maſter's Behaviour, for any of theſe Reaſons, it was but to give the Word, and down went the Ships and Car goes to the Bottom of the Sea

Since their Surrender to the *Spaniards*, I am informed ſeveral of them have left the Place, and diſperſed themſelves elſewhere, one of them were ſhipped about *November* laſt, in one of the South Sea Company's Aſſiento Sloops, and paſſed for Shipwreck'd Men, with which Pretence they came to *Jamaica*, and there ſailed in other Veſſels, and we know one of them that came to *England* laſt Spring from that Iſland 'Tis ſaid, that Captain *Taylor* has taken a Commiſſion in the *Spaniſh* Service, and that he commanded the Man of War, that lately attacked the *Engliſh* Log-Wood Cutters in the Bay of *Honduras*.

The LIFE of Captain CHARLES VANE.

CHarles Vane was one of those who stole a-way the Silver, which the *Spaniards* had fished up from the Wrecks of the Galleons, in the Gulph of *Florida*, and was at *Providence* when Governor *Rogers* arrived there with two Men of War, as the Reader has been informed before.

All the Pirates who were then found at this Colony of Rogues, submitted, and received Certificates of their Pardon, except Captain *Vane* and his Crew, who, as soon as they saw the Men of War enter, slipp'd their Cable, set Fire to a Prize they had in the Harbour, sailed out with their pyratical Colours flying, and fired at one of the Men of War, as they went off from the Coast.

Two Days after they went out, they met with a Sloop belonging to *Barbadoes*, which they made Prize of, and kept the Vessel for their own Use, putting abroad five and twenty Hands, with one *Yeats* to command them. A Day or two afterwards they fell in with a small interloping Trader, with a Quantity of *Spanish* Pieces of Eight aboard, bound into *Providence*, called the *John* and *Elizabeth*, which they also took along with them. With these two Sloops *Vane* went to a small Island and cleaned, where they shared their Booty, and spent some Time in a riotous Manner of Living, as is the Custom of Pirates after such Success.

About the latter End of *May*, 1718, they sailed, and, being in Want of Provisions, they beat up for the Windward Islands, in the Way they met with a *Spanish* Sloop, bound from *Porto Rico* to the *Havanna*, which they burnt, stowed the *Spaniards* in a Boat, and left them to get to the Island, by the Light of their Vessel. Steering afterwards between St. *Christopher*'s and *Anguilla*, they fell in with a Brigantine and a Sloop, freighted with such Cargo as they wanted, from whom they got Provisions for Sea-Store.

Sometime after this, standing to the Northward, in the Track the *Old-England* Ships take in their Voyage to the *American* Colonies, they took several Ships and Vessels, which they plundered of what they thought fit, and let them pass on in their Course.

The latter End of *August*, *Vane*, with his Consort *Yeates*, came off *South-Carolina*, and took a Ship belonging to *Ipswich*, one *Coggershall* Commander, laden with Logwood. This was thought convenient enough for their own Business, and therefore they ordered their Prisoners to work, and throw all the Lading over-board, but when they had more than half cleared the Ship, the Whim changed, and then they would not have her, so *Coggersh. all* had his Ship again, and he was suffered to pursue his Voyage home. In this Cruize the Rovers took several Ships and Vessels, particularly a Sloop from *Barbadoes*, one *Dill* Master, a small Ship from *Antegoa*, one *Cock* Master, a Sloop belonging to *Curacco*, one *Richards* Master, and a large Brigantine, Captain *Thompson*, from *Guinea*, with ninety odd Negroes aboard. The Pirates plundered them all and let them go, putting the Negroes out of the Brigantine a-board of *Yeat*'s Vessel, by which Means they came back again to the right Owners.

For Captain *Vane* always treated his Consort with very little Respect, and assumed a Superiority over him and his Crew, regarding the Vessel but as a Tender to his own. This gave them a Disgust; for they thought themselves as good Pyrates, and as great Rogues as the best of them, so they caball'd together, and resolved the first Opportunity to leave the Company, and accept of his Majesty's Pardon, or set up for themselves, either of which they thought more honourable than to be Servants to *Vane*. The putting a-board so many Negroes, where they were so few Hands to take Care of them, still aggravated the Matter, tho' they thought fit to conceal or stifle their Resentments at that Time.

A Day or two afterwards, the Pyrates lying off at Anchor, *Yeats* in the Evening slipp'd his Cable, and put his Vessel under Sail, standing into the Shore, which when *Vane* saw, he was highly provoked, and got his Sloop under Sail to chace his Consort, who, he plainly perceiv'd, had a Mind to have no more to do with him. *Vane*'s Brigantine sailing best, he gain'd Ground of *Yeats*, and would certainly have come up with him, had he had a little longer Run for it, but just as he got over the Bar, when *Vane* came within Gun-shot of him, he fir'd a Broad-side at his old Friend (which did him no Damage) and so took his Leave.

Yeats came into *North Edisto*, River, about Ten Leagues to the Southward of *Charles-Town*, and sent an Express to the Governor, to know if he and his Comrades might have the Benefit of his Majesty's Pardon, promising that, if they might, they would surrender themselves to his Mercy, with the Sloops and Negroes. Their Request being granted, they all came up, and receiv'd Certificates, and Captain *Thompson*, from whom the Negroes were taken, had them all restor'd to him, for the Use of his Owners.

Vane cruiz'd some Time off the Bar, in Hopes to catch *Yeats* at his coming out again, but therein he was disappointed, however, he there, unfortunately for them, took two Ships from *Charles Town*, which were bound home to *England*. It happen'd, that just at this Time, that two Sloops, well mann'd and arm'd, were equipp'd to go after a Pirate, which the Governor of *South Carolina* was inform'd lay then in Cape *Fear* River, a cleaning. But Colonel *Rhet*, who commanded the Sloops, meeting with one of the Ships that *Vane* had plunder'd, going back over the Bar, for such Necessaries as had been taken from her, and she giving the Colonel an Account of her being taken by the Pirate *Vane*, and, also, that some of her Men, while they were Prisoners on board of him, had heard the Pirates say they should clean in one of the Rivers to the Southward, he alter'd his first Design, and, instead of standing to the Northward, in pursuit of the Pirate in Cape *Fear* River, he turn'd to the Southward after *Vane*, who had

had order'd such Reports to be given out, on purpose to send any Force that should come after him upon a wrong Scent, for, in Reality, he stood away to the Northward, so that the Pursuit proved to be of no Effect

Colonel *Rhet*'s speaking with this Ship, was the most unlucky Thing that could have happen'd, because it turn'd him out of the Road, which, in all Probability, would have brought him into the Company of *Vane*, as well as of the Pirate he went after, and so they might have been both destroy'd; whereas, by the Colonel's going a different Way, he not only lost the Opportunity of meeting with one, but, if the other had not been infatuated to lie six Weeks together at Cape *Fear*, he would have miss'd of him likewise. However, the Colonel having searched the Rivers and Inlets, as directed, for several Days, without Success, he at length sail'd in Prosecution of his first Design, and met with the Pirate accordingly, whom he fought, and took, as has been before related in the History of Major *Bonnet*, for which Reason we shall say no more of it here.

Captain *Vane* went into an Inlet to the Northward, where he met with Captain *Teach*, otherwise call'd *Black-beard*, whom he saluted (when he found who he was) with his great Guns, loaded with Shot, it being the Custom among Pirates when they meet to do so, tho' they are fired wide of one another, or up into the Air. *Black-beard* answered the Salute in the same Manner, and mutual Civilities passed between them some Days, when, about the Beginning of *October*, *Vane* took Leave, and sailed further to the Northward

On the 23d of *October*, off of *Long-Island*, he took a small Brigantine, bound from *Jamaica* to *Salem* in *New-England*, *John Shattock* Master, besides a little Sloop They rifled the Brigantine, and sent her away From hence, they resolv'd on a Cruize between Cape *Meise* and Cape *Nicholas*, where they spent some Time, without seeing or speaking with any Vessel, till the latter End of *November*, then they fell upon a Ship, which, 'twas expected, would have struck as soon as their black Colours were hoisted, but, instead of that, she discharg'd a Broadside upon the Pirate, and hoisted Colours, which shew'd her to be a *French* Man of War *Vane* desir'd to have nothing further to say to her, but tremmed his Sails, and stood away from the *French* Man, however, Monsieur, having a Mind to be better inform'd who he was, set all his Sails, and crowed after him During this Chace, the Pirates were divided in their Resolutions what to do. *Vane*, the Captain, was for making off as fast as he could, alledging, the Man of War was too strong for them to cope with, but one *John Rackam*, who was an Officer, and who had a kind of a Check upon the Captain, rose up in Defence of a contrary Opinion, saying, *That though she had more Guns, and a greater Weight of Metal, they might board her, and then the best Boys would carry the Day.* *Rackam* was well seconded, and the Majority was for boarding; but *Vane* urg'd, *That it was too rash and desperate an Enterprize, the Man of War appearing to be twice that Force, and that their Brigantine might be sunk by her before they could reach to board her* The Mate, one *Robert Deal*, was of *Vane*'s Opinion, as were about fifteen more, and all the rest joined with *Rackam*, the Quarter-Master. At length, the Captain made use of his Power to determine this Dispute, which, in these Cases, is absolute and uncontrolable, by their own Laws, viz in fighting, chasing, or being chased, in all other Matters whatsoever, he is govern'd by a Majority. So the Brigantine having the

Heels, as they term it, of the *French* Man, she came clear off

But, the next Day, the Captain's Behaviour was oblig'd to stand the Test of a Vote, and a Resolution pass'd against his Honour and Dignity, which branded him with the Name of Coward, depos'd him from the Command, and turn'd him out of the Company, with Marks of Infamy; and with him went all those who did not vote for boarding the *French* Man of War They had with them a small Sloop, that had been taken by them some Time before, which they gave to *Vane* and the discarded Members, and, that they might be in a Condition to provide for themselves by their own honest Endeavours, they let them have a sufficient Quantity of Provisions and Ammunition along with them.

John Rackam was voted Captain of the Brigantine in *Vane*'s Room, and he proceeded towards the *Caribbee Islands*, where we must leave him, till we have finish'd our Story of *Charles Vane*

The Sloop sail'd for the Bay of *Honduras*, and *Vane* and his Crew put her into as good a Condition as they could by the Way, that they might follow their old Trade They cruiz'd two or three Days off the North-West Part of *Jamaica*, and took a Sloop and two Pettiaga's, all the Men of which enter'd with them The Sloop they kept, and *Robert Deal* was appointed Captain of her

On the 16th of *December* the two Sloops came in to the Bay, where they found only one Vessel at an Anchor She was call'd *The Pearl*, of *Jamaica*, Captain *Charles Rowland* Master, who got under Sail at the Sight of them, but the Pirate Sloops coming near *Rowland*, and shewing no Colours, he gave them a Gun or two, whereupon, they hoisted the black Flag, and fir'd three Guns each at *the Pearl* She struck, and the Pirates took Possession, and carried her away to a small Island call'd *Barnacho*, where they clean'd By the Way they met with a Sloop from *Jamaica*, Captain *Wallden* Commander, as she was going down to tne Bay, which they also made Prize of

In *February*, *Vane* sailed from *Barnacho*, in order for a Cruize, but some Days after he was out, a violent Turnado overtook him, which separated him from his Consort, and, after two Days Distress, threw his Sloop upon a small uninhabited Island, near the Bay of *Honduras*, where she was staved to Pieces, and most of her Men drowned *Vane* himself was saved but reduced to great Streights for want of Necessaries, having no Opportunity to get any Thing from the Wreck He lived here some Weeks, and was supported chiefly by Fishermen, who frequented the Island with small Craft, from the Main, to catch Turtles, &c

While *Vane* was upon this Island, a Ship put in there from *Jamaica*, for Water, the Captain of which, one *Holford*, an old Buccaneer, happened to be *Vane*'s Acquaintance, he thought this a good Opportunity to get off, and accordingly he applied to his old Friend; but *Holford* absolutely refused him, saying to him, Charles, *I shan't trust you a board my Ship, unless I carry you as a Prisoner, for I shall have you caballing with my Men, knock me on the Head, and run away with my Ship a pyrating* *Vane* made all the Protestations of Honour in the World to him; but, it seems, Captain *Holford* was too intimately acquainted with him, to repose any Confidence at all in his Words or Oaths. He told him, *He might easily find a Way to get off, if he had a Mind to it. I am now going down the Bay,* says he, *and shall return hither in about a Month, and if I find you upon the Island when I come back, I'll carry you to* Jamaica, *and*

and there hang you Which Way can I get away? Answers *Vane* Are there not *Fishermen's* Dories up- on the Beach? Can't you take one of them? Re- plies *Hilford* What, says *Vane*, would you have me *steal* a *Dory* then? Do you make it a Matter of Con- *science?* Said *Holford*, to *steal* a *Dory*, when you *have* been a common Robber and Pirate, stealing Ships and Cargoes, and plundering all Mankind that fell in your *Way?* Stay there and be damn'd, if you are so squeamish And he left him to consider of the Matter

After Captain *Holford's* Departure, another Ship put into the same Island, in her Way home, for Water, none of the Company knowing *Vane*, he easi- ly passed upon them for another Man, and so was shipp'd for the Voyage One would be apt to think that *Vane* was now pretty safe, and likely to escape the Fate which his Crimes had merited, but here a cross Accident happen'd that ruined all *Holford*, returning from the Bay, was met with by this Ship, and the Captains being very well acquainted toge- ther, *Holford* was invited to dine aboard of him, which he did, as he passed along to the Cabin, he chanced to cast his Eye down into the Hold, and

there saw *Charles Vane* at work; he immediately spoke to the Captain, saying, *Do you know who you have got aboard there?* Why, says he, *I have shipp'd a Man at such an Island, who was there cast away in a trading Sloop, and he seems to be a brisk Hand I tell you,* says Captain *Holford*, it is *Vane*, the noto- rious Pirate If it be him, replies the other, *I won't keep him* Why then, says *Holford*, *I'll send*, and take him aboard, and surrender him at *Jamaica* This being agreed to, Captain *Holford*, as soon as he re- turned to his Ship, sent his Boat with his Mate, armed, who coming to *Vane*, shewed him a Pistol, and told him, *He was his Prisoner*, no Man oppos- ing, he was brought aboard, and put into Irons, and when Captain *Holford* arrived at *Jamaica*, he de- livered his old Acquaintance into the Hands of Jus- tice, at which Place he was try'd, convicted, and exe- cuted, as was, some Time before, *Vane's* Consort, *Robert Deal*, who was brought thither by one of the Men of War Thus we may see how little ancient Friendship will avail a great Villain, when he is de- prived of the Power that had before supported him, and made him formidable

The LIFE of Captain JOHN RACKAM.

THIS *John Rackam*, as has been reported in the foregoing Pages, was Quarter Master to *Vane's* Company, till the Crew were di- vided, and *Vane* turned out of it, for refusing to board and fight the French Man of War, in his room *Rackam* was voted Captain of that Division that remained in the Brigantine The 24th of No- *vember*, 1718, was the first Day of his Command, and his first Cruize was among the *Caribbee Islands*, where he took and plunder'd several Vessels

We have already taken Notice, that, when Cap- tain *Woods Rogers* went to the Island of *Providence*, with the King's Pardon to such as should surrender, this Brigantine, which *Rackam* now commanded, made its Escape thro' another Passage, bidding De- fiance to the Mercy that was offered

To the Windward of *Jamaica*, a *Madeira* Man fell into the Pirates Way, which they detained two or three Days, till they had made their Market out of her, and then they gave her back to the Master, and permitted one *Hosea Tisdel*, a Tavern-Keeper at *Jamaica*, who had been pick'd up in one of their Prizes, to depart in her, she being then bound for that Island

After this Cruize, they went into a small Island and cleaned, and spent their *Christmas* ashore, drink- ing and carousing as long as they had any Liquor left, and then they went to Sea again for more. They suc- ceeded but too well, tho' they took no extraordi- nary Prize for above two Months, except a Ship la- den with Convicts from *Newgate*, bound for the Plantations, which, in a few Days, was retaken, with all her Cargo, by an *English* Man of War that was stationed in those Seas

Rackam stood off towards the Island of *Bermudas*,

and took a Ship bound to *England* from *Carolina*, and a small Pink from *New-England*, both which he brought to the *Bahama* Islands, where, with the Pitch, Tar, and Stores, they clean'd again, and refitted their own Vessel; but staying too long in that Neighbour- hood, Captain *Rogers*, who was Governor of *Provi- dence*, hearing of these Ships being taken, sent out a Sloop well mann'd and arm'd, which retook both the the Prizes, tho' in the mean while the Pirate had the good Fortune to escape

From hence they sail'd to the Back of *Cuba*, where *Rackam* kept a little kind of a Family; at which Place they staid a considerable Time, living ashore with their *Dalilahs*, till their Money and Provisions were expended, and they concluded it Time to look out for more They repaired to their Vessel, and were making ready to put to Sea, when a *Guarda de Costa* came in with a small *English* Sloop, which she had taken as an Interloper on the Coast The *Spa- nish* Guardship attacked the Pirate, but *Rackam* be- ing close in behind a little Island, she could do but little Execution where she lay, therefore the Dons warp'd into the Channel that Evening, in order to make sure of her the next Morning *Rackam*, find- ing his Case desperate, and that there was hardly any possibility of escaping, resolved to attempt the following Enterprize The *Spanish* Prize lying for better Security close into the Land, between the little Island and the Main, our Desperado takes his Crew into the Boat, with their Pistols and Cutlashes, rounds the little Island, and falls aboard their Prize silently, in the dead of the Night, without being discovered, telling the *Spaniards* that were aboard her, that, if they spoke a Word, or made the least Noise, they all were dead Men, and so they became Masters of her

U u

her When this was done, he slipt her Cable, and drove out to Sea The *Spanish* Man of War was so intent upon their expected Prize, that they minded nothing else, and as soon as Day broke, they made a furious Fire upon the empty Sloop, but it was not long before they were rightly apprized of the Matter, when they cursed themselves sufficiently for a Company of Fools, to be bit out of a good rich Prize, as she proved to be, and to have nothing but an old crazy Hull in the room of her

Rackam and his Crew had no Occasion to be displeased at the Exchange, as it enabled them to continue some Time longer in a Way of Life that suited their depraved Tempers In *August,* 1720, we find him at Sea again, scouring the Harbours and Inlets of the North and West Parts of *Jamaica,* where he took several small Craft, which proved no great Booty to the Rovers, but they had but few Men, and therefore they were oblig'd to run at low Game, till they could encrease their Company and their Strength

In the Beginning of *September,* they took seven or eight Fishing-Boats in *Harbour-Island,* stole their Nets and other Tackle, and then went off to the *French* Part of *Hispaniola,* where they landed, and took Cattle away, with two or three *French* Men they found near the Water-Side, hunting of wild Hogs in the Evening· The *French* Men came on Board, whether by Consent or Compulsion I can't say They afterwards plundered two Sloops, and returned to *Jamaica,* on the North Coast of which Island, near *Porto Maria* Bay, they took a Scooner, *Thomas Spenlow* Master; it being then the 19th of *October* The next Day, *Rackam* seeing a Sloop in *Dry Harbour* Bay, he stood in and fired a Gun, the Men all run ashore, and he took the Sloop and Lading, but when those ashore found them to be Pirates, they hailed the Sloop, and let them know they were all willing to come aboard of them

Rackam's coasting the Island in this Manner proved fatal to him, for Intelligence came to the Governor of his Expedition, by a Canoe, which he had surprized ashore, in *Ocho* Bay Upon this, a Sloop was immediately fitted out, and sent round the Island in quest of him, commanded by Captain *Barnet;* and mann'd with a good Number of Hands *Rackam* rounding the Island, and drawing near the Wester-most Point, call'd *Point Negril,* he saw a small Pettiauger, which, at Sight of the Sloop, run ashore and landed her Men, when one of them hail'd her, Answer was made, *They were English* Men, and desired the Pettiauger's Men to come on Board, and drink a Bowl of Punch, which they prevailed upon them to do Accordingly the Company came all aboard of the Pirate, consisting of nine Persons, in an ill Hour; they were armed with Muskets and Cutlashes, but what was their real Design by so doing, we shall not take upon us to say, They had no sooner laid down their Arms, and taken up their Pipes, but *Barnet's* Sloop, which was in Pursuit of *Rackam's* came in Sight

The Pirates, finding she stood directly towards them, fear'd the Event, and weighed their Anchor, which they but lately let go, and stood off Captain *Barnet* gave them Chace, and, having the Advantage of little Breezes of Wind, which blew off the Land, came up with her, and brought her into *Port Royal,* in *Jamaica.*

About a Fortnight after the Prisoners were brought ashore, *viz November* 16, 1720 A Court of Admiralty was held at St. *Jago de la Vega,* before which the following Persons were convicted, and Sentence of Death passed upon them, by the President, Sir *Nicholas Laws, viz John Rackam,* Captain, *George Fetherston,* Master, *Richard Corner,* Quarter Master, *John Davis, John Howell, Patrick Carty, Thomas Earl, James Dobbin* and *Noah Harwood* The five first were executed the next Day at *Gallows-Point,* at the Town of *Port-Royal,* and the rest next Day after at *Kingston, Rackam, Fetherston* and *Corner,* were afterwards taken down, and hang'd up in Chains, one at *Plumb* Point, one at *Bush* Key, and the other at *Gun* Key

But what was very surprizing, was the Conviction of the nine Men that came aboard the Sloop on the same Day she was taken They were try'd at an Adjournment of the Court, on the 24th of *January,* the Magistracy waiting all that Time, it is suppos'd, for Evidence, to prove the pyratical Intention of going aboard the said Sloop, for it seems there was no Act of Piracy committed by them, as appeared by the Witnesses against them, who were two *Frenchmen* taken by *Rackam,* off from the Island of *Hispaniola,* and who deposed in the following Manner

' That the Prisoners at the Bar, *viz John Eaton,*
' *Edward Warner, Thomas Baker, Thomas Quick,*
' *John Cole, Benjamin Palmer, Walter Rouse, John*
' *Hanson,* and *John Howard,* came aboard the Pirates
' Sloop, at *Negril Point, Rackam* sending his Canoe
' ashore for that Purpose That they brought Guns
' and Cutlashes on Board with them That when
' Captain *Barnet* chased them, some were drinking,
' and others walking the Deck That there was a
' great Gun and a small Piece fired by the Pirates
' Sloop, at Captain *Barnet's* Sloop, when he chaced
' her, and, that when Captain *Barnet's* Sloop fired
' at *Rackam's* Sloop, the Prisoners at the Bar went
' down under Deck That during the Time Captain *Barnet* chased them, some of the Prisoners at
' the Bar (but which of them he could not tell) help
' ed to row the Sloop, in order to escape from *Barnet* That they all seemed to be consorted together '

This was the Substance of all that was alledg'd against them The Court considered the Prisoners Cases, and the Majority of the Commissioners being of Opinion, that they were all Guilty of the Piracy and Felony they were charged with, which was, the *going over with a piratical and felonious Intent to* John Rackam, &c *then notorious Pirates, and by them known to be so,* they all received Sentence of Death, and were executed on the 17th of *February,* at *Gallows Point* at *Port Royal*

The LIFE *of* MARY READ.

WE are now to begin a History full of furprizing Turns and Adventures, I mean, that of *Mary Read* and *Ann Bonny*, alias *Bonn*, which were the true Names of thefe two Women Pirates, the Incidents that befel them, are fuch, that fome may be tempted to think the whole Story no better than a Novel or Romance, but fince it is fupported by many thoufand Witneffes, I mean the People of *Jamaica*, who were prefent at their Trials, upon the firft Difcovery of their Sex, and heard the Story of their Lives; the Truth of it can be no more contefted, than that there were fuch Men in the World, as *Avery* and *Black beard*, Pirates of whom we have given an Account

Mary Read was born in *England*, her Mother was married young, to a Man who ufed the Sea, and going a Voyage foon after their Marriage, left her with Child, which Infant proved to be a Boy As to the Hufband, whether he was caft away, or died in the Voyage, *Mary Read* could not tell, but, however, he never returned more The Mother, who was young and airy, met with an Accident in his Abfence, which has often happened to Women who are young, and do not take a great deal of Care, which was, fhe foon proved with Child again, without a Hufband to father it; but how, or by whom, none but herfelf could tell, for fhe carried a pretty good Reputation among her Neighbours I inding her Burthen grow, in order to conceal her Shame, fhe takes a formal Leave of her Hufband's Relations, giving out, that fhe went to live with fome Friends of her own, in the Country Accordingly fhe went away, and carried with her, her young Son, at this Time not a Year old Soon after her Departure her Son died, but Providence, in Return, was pleafed to give her a Girl in his room, of whom fhe was fafely delivered, in her Retreat, and this was our *Mary Read*

Here the Mother liv'd three or four Years, till what Money fhe had was almoft gone, then fhe thought of returning to *London*, and confidering that her Hufband's Mother was in good Circumftances, fhe did not doubt but to prevail upon her to provide for the Child, if fhe could but pafs it upon her for the fame, but the changing a Girl into a Boy feem'd a difficult Piece of Work, and how to deceive an experienc'd old Woman, in fuch a Point, was altogether as impoffible, however, fhe ventured to drefs it up as a Boy, brought it to 'Town, and prefented it to her Mother-in-law, as her Hufband's Son, the old Woman would have taken it, to have bred it up, but the Mother pretended it would break her Heart to part with it, fo it was agreed betwixt them, that the Child fhould live with the Mother, and the fuppofed Grandmother fhould allow a Crown a Week for it's Maintenance

Thus the Mother gained her Point, fhe bred up her Daughter as a Boy, and when fhe grew up to fome Senfe, fhe thought proper to let her into the Secret of her Birth, to induce her to conceal her Sex. It

happen'd that the Grandmother died, by which Means the Subfiftance, that came from that Quarter, ceafed, and they were more and more reduced in their Circumftances, wherefore fhe was obliged to put her Daughter out, to wait on a *French* Lady, as a Foot-boy, being now thirteen Years of Age Here fhe did not live long, for growing bold and ftrong, and having alfo a roving Mind, fhe entered herfelf on Board a Man of War, where fhe ferved fome Time At length, fhe quitted the Sea Service, went over into *Flanders*, and carried Arms in a Regiment of Foot, as a *Cadet*, and tho' in all Actions, fhe behaved herfelf with a great deal of Bravery, yet fhe could not get a Commiffion, they being generally bought and fold, therefore fhe quitted the Service, and took on in a Regiment of Horfe Here fhe behaved fo well in feveral Engagements, that fhe got the Efteem of all her Officers, but her Comrade, who was a *Fleming*, happening to be a handfome young Fellow, fhe fell in Love with him, and, from that Time, grew a little more neglegent in her Duty, fo that, it feems, *Mars* and *Venu* could not be ferved at the fame Time, her Arms and Acoutrements, which were always kept in the beft Order, were quite neglected 'Tis true, when her Comrade was ordered out upon a Party, fhe ufed to go without being commanded, and frequently run herfelf into Danger, where fhe had no Bufinefs, only to be near him The reft of the Troopers, little fufpecting the fecret Caufe which moved her to this Behaviour, fancied her to be mad, and her Comrade himfelf could not account for this ftrange Alteration in her, but Love is ingenious, and, as they lay in the fame Tent, and were conftantly together, fhe found a Way of letting him difcover her Sex, without appearing that it was done with Defign

He was much furprized at what he found out, and not a little pleafed, taking it for granted, that he fhould have a Miftrefs folely to himfelf, which is an unufual Thing in a Camp, fince there is fcarce one of thofe Campaign Ladies, that is ever true even to a Troop or Company, fo that he thought of nothing but gratifying his Paffions with very little Ceremony But he found himfelf ftrangely miftaken, for fhe proved very referved and modeft, and refifted all his Temptations, yet, at the fame Time, was fo obliging and infinuating in her Carriage, that fhe quite changed his Purpofe, and made him fo far from thinking of making her his Miftrefs, that he now courted her for a Wife

This was the utmoft Wifh of her Heart, in fhort, they exchanged Promifes, and when the Campaign was over, and the Regiment marched into Winter-Quarters, they bought Woman's Apparel for her, with fuch Money as they could make up betwixt them, and were publickly married

The Story of two Troopers marrying each other made a great Noife, fo that feveral Officers were drawn by Curiofity to affift at the Ceremony, and they agreed among themfelves, that every one of them fhould make a fmall Prefent to the Bride towards Houfe-

House-keeping, in Confideration of her having been their fellow Soldier Thus being fet up, they feemed to have a Defire of quitting the Service, and fettling in the World , the Adventure of their Love and Marriage had gained them fo much Favour, that they eafily obtained their Difcharge, and they immediately fet up an Eating-Houfe or Ordinary, with the Sign of the *Three Horfe-Shoes*, near the Caftle of *Breda*, where they foon got into a good Trade, a great many Officers eating with them conftantly

But this Happinefs did not laft long , for the Hufband foon died, and the Peace being concluded, there was no Refort of Officers to *Breda*, as ufual , fo that the Widow, having little or no Trade, was forced to give up Houfe keeping, and her Subftance being by Degrees quite fpent, fhe again affumes her Man's Apparel, and, going into *Holland*, there takes on in a Regiment of Foot, quarter'd in one of the Frontier Towns Here fhe did not remain long, for there was no Likelihood of Preferment in Time of Peace , therefore fhe took a Refolution of feeking her Fortune another Way , and, withdrawing from the Regiment, fhip'd herfelf on Board of a Veffel bound for the *Weft-Indies*.

It happened that this Ship was taken by *Englifh* Pirates, and *Mary Read* was the only *Englifh* Perfon on Board , they kept her amongft them, and having plundered the Ship, let it go again , after following this Trade for fome Time, the King's Proclamation came out, and was publifh'd in all Parts of the *Weft-Indies*, for pardoning fuch Pirates, as fhould voluntarily furrender themfelves by a certain Day therein mention'd The Crew of *Mary Read* took the Benefit of this Proclamation, and, having furrender'd, liv'd afterwards quietly on Shore ; but Money beginning to grow fhort, and our Adventurefs hearing that Captain *Woods Rogers*, Governor of the Ifland of *Providence*, was fitting out fome Privateers to cruize againft the *Spaniards*, fhe, with feveral others, embark'd for that Ifland, in order to go upon the privateering Account, being refolved to make her Fortune one way or other

Thefe Privateers were no fooner fail'd out, but the Crews of fome of them, who had been pardoned, rofe againft their Commanders, and turned themfelves to their old Trade In this Number was *Mary Read*, 'Tis true, fhe often declared, that the Life of a Pyrate was what fhe heartily abhor'd, and went into it only upon Compulfion, both this Time and before, intending to quit it, whenever a fair Opportunity fhould offer itfelf, yet fome of the Evidences againft her, upon her 'Tryal, who were forced Men, and had failed with her, depofed upon Oath, that, in Times of Action, no Perfons amongft them were more refolute, or ready to board, or undertake any Thing that was hazardous, than fhe and *Anne Bonny* , and particularly at the Time they were attack'd and taken, when they came to clofe Quarters, none kept the Deck except *Mary Read* and *Anne Bonny*, and one more , upon which, fhe *(Mary Read)* called to thofe under Deck, to come up and fight like Men, and, finding they did not ftir fired her Arms down the Hold amongft them, killing one, and wounding others.

This was part of the Evidence againft her, which fhe denied , whether this was true or no, thus much is certain, that fhe did not want Bravery , nor indeed, was fhe lefs remarkable for her Modefty, according to her Notions of Virtue . Her Sex was not fo much as fufpected by any Perfon on Board, till *Anne Bonny* took her for a handfome young Fellow, and, for fome Reafons beft known to herfelf, firft difcovered her Sex to *Mary Read Mary Read*, knowing what fhe would be at, and being very fenfible of her own

Incapacity that Way, was forced to come to a right Underftanding with her, and fo, to the great Difappointment of *Anne Bonny*, fhe let her know fhe was a Woman alfo , but this Intimacy fo difturb'd Captain *Rackam*, who was the Lover and Gallant of *Anne Bonny*, that he grew furioufly Jealous, fo that he told *Anne Bonny*, he would cut her new Lover's Throat , whereupon, to quiet him, fhe let him into the Secret alfo

Captain *Rackam*, (as he was enjoin'd,) kept the Thing a Secret from all the Ship's Company, yet, notwithftanding all her Cunning and Referve, Love found her out in this Difguife, and hindered her from forgetting her Sex In their Cruize they took a great Number of Ships, belonging to *Jamaica*, and other Parts of the *Weft-Indies*, bound to and from *England*, and whenever they met any good Artift, or other Perfon that might be of any great Ufe to their Company, if he was not willing to enter, it was their Cuftom to keep him by Force Among thefe was a young Fellow of a moft engaging Behaviour, or, at leaft, he was fo in the Eyes of *Mary Read*, who became fo fmitten with his Perfon and Addrefs, that fhe could not reft, either Night or Day , but as there is nothing more artful than Love, it was no hard Matter for her, who had before been practis'd in thefe Wiles, to find a Way to let him difcover her Sex She firft infinuated herfelf into his Liking, by talking againft the Life of a Pirate, which he was altogether averfe to , fo that they became Mefs-Mates and ftrict Companions When fhe found he had a Friendfhip for her, as a Man, fhe fuffered the Difcovery to be made, by careflely fhewing her Breafts, which were very White and Swelling

The young Fellow, who, we may fuppofe, was made of Flefh and Blood, had his Curiofity and Defire fo rais'd by this Sight, that he never ceafed importuning her, till fhe confeffed what fhe was Now begins the Scene of Love , as he had a Liking and Efteem for her, under her fuppofed Character, it was now turned into Fondnefs and Defire , her Paffion was no lefs violent than his, and fhe expreffed it, by one of the moft generous Actions, perhaps, that ever Love infpir'd It happened that this young Fellow had a Quarrel with one of the Pirates, and their Ship then lying at an Anchor, near one of the Iflands, they had appointed to go a-fhore and fight, according to the Cuftom of thefe People *Mary Read* was to the laft Degree uneafy and anxious, for the Fate of her Lover , fhe would not have had him refufe the Challenge, becaufe fhe could not bear the Thoughts of his being branded with Cowardise , on the other Side, fhe dreaded the Event, and apprehended the Fellow might be too hard for him When Love once enters into the Breaft of a Perfon who has any Sparks of Generofity, it ftirs the Heart up to the moft noble Actions In this Dilemma, fhe fhew'd, that fhe feared more for his Life than fhe did for her own , for fhe took a Refolution of quarrelling with this Fellow herfelf, and, having challenged him a fhore, fhe appointed the Time two Hours fooner than that when he was to meet her Lover, where fhe fought him at Sword and Piftol, and killed him upon the Spot

It is true, fhe had fought before, when fhe had been infulted by fome of thofe Fellows, but now it was altogether in her Lover's Caufe, for fhe ftood as it were betwixt him and Death, as if fhe could not live without him If he had had no regard for her before, this Action would have been enough to have bound him to her for ever, but there was no Occafion for Ties or Obligations, his Inclination towards her was fufficient, in fine, they applied their Troth to each other, which *Mary Read* faid, fhe look'd upon

upon to be as good a Marriage, in Conscience, as if it had been done by a Minister in Church; and to this was owing her great Belly, which she pleaded at her Trial, to save her Life

She declared she had never committed Adultery or Fornication with any Man, she commended the Justice of the Court, before which she was tried, for distinguishing the Nature of their Crimes, her Husband, as she called him, with several others, being acquitted When she was ask'd, who he was? she would not tell, but said he was an honest Man, and had no Inclination to such Practices, and that they had both resolved to leave the Pirates the first Opportunity, and apply themselves to some honest Livelihood

There is no doubt, but many had Compassion for her, yet the Court could not avoid finding her Guilty, for, among other Things, one of the Evidences against her deposed, that, being taken by *Rackam*, and detained some Time on Board, he fell accidentally into Discourse with *Mary Read*, whom taking for a young Man, he ask'd her, what Pleasure she could have in being concern'd in such En-

terprizes, where her Life was continually in Danger, by Fire or Sword, and not only so, but she must be sure of dying an ignominious Death, if she should be taken alive?——She answer'd, that, as to the hanging, she thought it no great Hardship, for, were it not for that, every cowardly Fellow would turn Pirate, and so infest the Seas, that Men of Courage must starve ——That if it was put to the Choice of the Pirates, they would not have the Punishment less than Death, the Fear of which kept some dastardly Rogues honest, that many of those who are now cheating the Widows and Orphans, and oppressing their poor Neighbours, who have no Money to obtain Justice, would then rob at Sea, and the Ocean would be crowded with Rogues, like the Land, so that no Merchant would venture out, and the Trade, in a little Time, wou'd not be worth following

Being found quick with Child, as has been observed, her Execution was respited, and it is possible she would have found Favour, but that she was seiz'd with a violent Fever, soon after her Trial, of which she died in Prison

---

The LIFE of ANNE BONNY.

WE are so particular in the Lives of these two Women, purely on Account of their Sex Otherwise, as they did not rise to Command, we should no have mention'd them, except in the List of condemn'd Persons However, we hope our Attempt will not be displeasing, and so, without more Apology, we proceed to *Anne Bonny*, who was born at at a Town near *Cork*, in the Kingdom of *Ireland* Her Father was an Attorney at Law, but *Anne* was not one of his legitimate Issue, which seems to cross an old Proverb, which says, *That Bastards have the best Luck* Her Father was a married Man, and his Wife, having been brought to Bed, contracted an Illness in her Lying in, so that, in order to recover her Health, she was advis'd to remove for Change of Air The Place she chose, was at a few Miles Distance from her Dwelling, where her Husband's Mother liv'd Here she sojourn'd some Time, her Husband staving it Home, to follow his Affairs

The Servant Maid, whom she left to look after the House, and attend the Family being a handsome young Woman, she was courted by a young Man of the same Town, who was a Tanner This Tanner us'd to take all Opportunities, when the Family was out of the Way, of coming to pursue his Amour, and being with the Maid one Day, as she was employ'd in one Houshold Business, not having the Fear of God before his Eyes, he takes his Opportunity, when her Back was turn'd, of whipping three Silver Spoons into his Pocket The Maid soon miss'd the Spoons, and knowing that no Body had been in the Room, but herself and the young Man, since she saw them last, she charg'd him with taking them He very stifly denied it, upon which, she grew outragious, and threaten'd to go to a Constable, in order to carry him before a Justice of Peace These Menaces frighten'd him out of his Wits, well know-

ing he could not stand Search Wherefore he endeavour'd to pacify her, by desiring her to examine the Drawers and other Places, by doing which, perhaps, she might find them In this Time he slips into another Room, where the Maid usually lay, puts the Spoons betwixt the Sheets, and then makes his Escape by a Back-Door, concluding, she must find them when she went to Bed, and so, next Day, he might pretend he did it only to frighten her, and the Thing might be laugh'd off for a Jest

As soon as she miss'd him, she gave over her Search, concluding he had carried them off, and went directly to a Constable, in order to have him apprehended The young Man was inform'd that a Constable had been in Search of him, which he regarded but little, not doubting but all would be well next Day Three or four Days pass'd, and still he was told the Constable was upon the hunt for him. This, at last, made him he conceal'd, he could not comprehend the Meaning of it, he imagin'd no less, than that the Maid had a mind to convert the Spoons to her own Use, and put the Robbery upon him

It happen'd, at this Time, that the Mistress, being perfectly recover'd of her late Indisposition, was return'd Home, in Company with her Mother-in-Law, the first News she heard was of the Loss of the Spoons, with the Manner how, the Maid telling her, at the same Time, that the young Man was run away The Fellow had Intelligence of the Mistress's Arrival, when considering with himself that he could never appear again in his Business, unless this Matter was got over, and that Madam was a good natur'd Woman, he took a Resolution of going directly to her, and of telling her the whole Story, only with this Difference, that he did it for a Jest

The Mistress could scarce believe it, however, she went directly to the Maid's Room, and turning down nin downing the Bed-Clothes, there, to her great Surprize, she found the three Spoons Upon this, she desir'd the young Man to go Home and mind his Busness, for he should have no farther Trouble about it

The Mistress could not imagine the Meaning of this , she never had found the Maid guilty of any pilfering, and therefore it could not enter her Head, that she design'd to steal the Spoons herself Upon the whole, she concluded the Maid had not been in her Bed from the Time the Spoons were miss'd , so that she grew immediately jealous upon it, and suspected that the Maid supplied her Place with her Husband during her Absence, and that this was the Reason why the Spoons were no sooner found

She call'd to Mind several Actions of Kindness which her Husband had shew'd the Maid, Things that pass'd unheeded by when they happen'd, but now she had got that Tormenter, Jealousy, in her Head, they amounted to Proofs of their Intimacy Another Circumstance which strengthen'd the whole, was, that though her Husband knew she was to come Home that Day, and had had no Communication with her in four Months before, which was ever since her Lying-in , yet he took an Opportunity of going out of Town that Morning, upon some slight Pretence ——All these Things put together, confirm'd her in her Jealousy

As Women seldom forgive Injuries of this Kind, she thought of discharging her Revenge upon the Maid In order to this, she leaves the Spoons where she found them, and orders the Maid to put clean Sheets upon the Bed; telling her, she intended to lie there herself that Night, because her Mother-in-Law was to lie in her Bed, and that she (the Maid) must lie in another Part of the House The Maid, in making the Bed, was surpriz'd with the Sight of the Spoons, but there were very good Reasons why it was not proper for her to tell where she found them , therefore she takes them up, puts them in her Trunk, intending to leave them in some Place where they might be found by chance

The Mistress, that every Thing might look to be done without Design, lies that Night in the Maid's Bed, little dreaming of what an Adventure it would produce After she had been a Bed some Time, thinking on what had pass'd (for Jealousy kept her awake,) she heard some Body enter the Room At first she apprehended it to be Thieves, and was so frighten'd, that she had not Courage enough to call out But when she heard these Words, *Mary, are you awake ?* she knew it to be her Husband's Voice Then her Fright was over , yet she made no Answer, lest he should find her out, if she spoke, therefore she continu'd to counterfeit Sleep, and take what follow'd

The Husband came to Bed, and that Night play'd the vigorous Lover , but one Thing spoil'd the Diversion on the Wife's Side, which was the Reflection that it was not design'd for her, however, she was very passive, and bore it like a numble Christian Early before Day she stole out of Bed, leaving him asleep, and went to her Mother-in-Law, telling her what had pass'd, not forgetting how he had us'd her, as taking her for the Maid , the Husband also stole out, not thinking it convenient to be catch'd in that Room In the mean time, the Revenge of the Mistress wrought strongly against the Maid, and without considering that to her she ow'd the Diversion of the Night before, and that one good Turn deserv'd another, she sent for a Constable, and charged her with stealing the Spoons The Maid's Trunk was broke open, and the Spoons found , upon which,

she was carried before a Justice of Peace, and by him committed to Goal.

The Husband loiter'd about till Twelve a-Clock at Noon, then came Home, and pretended he was just come to Town As soon as he heard what had pass'd, in Relation to the Maid, he fell into a great Passion with his Wife This set the Thing into a greater Flame , the Mother takes the Wife's Part against her own Son, insomuch that the Quarrel increasing, the Mother and Wife took Horse immediately, and went back to the Mother's House, and the Husband and Wife never bedded together after

The Maid lay a long Time in the Prison, it being near half a Year to the Assizes, but before it happen'd, it was discover'd she was with Child When she was arraign'd at the Bar, she was discharg'd for want of Evidence The Wife's Conscience touch'd her, and as she did not believe the Maid guilty of any Theft, except that of Love, she did not appear against her Soon after her Acquittal, she was deliver'd of a Girl

But what alarm'd the Husband most, was, that it was discover'd the Wife was with Child also, he taking it for granted, that he had had no Intimacy with her since her last Lying in, grew jealous of her also, in his Turn, and made this a Handle to justify himself for his Usage of her , pretending, now, he had suspected her long, but that here was Proof Madam was deliver'd of Twins, a Son and a Daughter

The Mother fell ill, and sent to her Son to reconcile him to his Wife, but he would not hearken to it, therefore she made a Will, leaving all she had in the Hands of certain Trustees, for the Use of the Wife and the two Children lately born, and died a few Days after

This was an ugly Turn upon him, his greatest Dependance being upon his Mother However, his Wife was kinder to him than he deserv'd , for sh made him a yearly Allowance out of what was her, though they continu'd to live separate It lasted near five Years At this Time, having a great Affection for the Girl he had by his Maid, he had a mind to take it Home, to live with him , but as all the Town knew it to be a Girl, the better to disguise the Matter from them, as well as from his Wife, he had it put into Breeches, as if it had been a Boy, pretending it was a Relation's Child, whom he was to breed up to be his Clerk

The Wife heard he had a little Boy at Home that he was very fond of, but as she did not know any Relation of his that had such a Child, she employ'd a Friend to enquire further into it This Person, by talking with the Child, found it to be a Girl, discover'd that the Servant-Maid was its Mother, and that the Husband still kept up his Correspondence with her

Upon this Intelligence, the Wife, being unwilling that her Children's Money should go towards the Maintenance of Bastards, stopp'd the Allowance The Husband enrag'd, in a kind of Revenge takes the Maid home, and lives with her publickly, to the great Scandal of his Neighbours , but he soon found the bad Effect of it , for by Degrees he lost his Practice, so that he saw plainly he could not live there This made him think of removing, and turning what Effects he had into ready Money , whereupon he goes to *Cork*, and there, with his Maid and Daughter, embarks for *Carolina*

At first he follow'd the Practice of the Law in that Province but afterwards fell into Merchandize, which prov'd more successful to him , for he gain'd by it sufficient to purchase a considerable Plantation

His Maid, who pass'd for his Wife, happen'd to die, after which, his Daughter, our *Anne Bonny,* now grown up, kept his House

She was of a fierce and couragious Temper, wherefore, when she lay under Condemnation, several Stories were reported of her much to her Disadvantage, as that she had kill'd an *English* Servant Maid once in her Passion, with a Case-Knife, while she look'd after her Father's House; but upon further Enquiry, we found this Story to be groundless 'Tis certain, she was so robust, that once, when a young Fellow would have lain with her against her Will, she beat him so that he lay ill of it a considerable Time

While she liv'd with her Father, she was look'd upon as one that would have a considerable Fortune, wherefore it was thought her Father design'd a good Match for her; but she spoil'd all, for, without his Consent, she marries a young Fellow who belong'd to the Sea, and was not worth a Groat This provok'd her Father to such a Degree, that he turn'd her out of Doors, upon which, the young Fellow who married her finding himself disappointed in his Expectation, shipp'd himself and Wife for the Island of *Providence,* expecting Employment there

Here she became acquainted with *Rackam* the Pirate, who, making Courtship to her, soon found Means of withdrawing her Affections from her Husband, so that she consented to elope from him, and go to Sea with *Rackam* in Men's Cloaths She was as good as her Word, and after she had been at Sea some Time, she proved with Child When she began to grow big, *Rackam* landed her on the Island of

Cuba , and, recommending her there to some Friends of his, they took Care of her till she was brought to Bed When she was up, and well again, he sent for her to bear him Company in his future Expeditions

The King's Proclamation for pardoning of Pirates being out, he took the Benefit of it, and surrender'd, afterwards, being sent upon the privateering Account, he return'd to his old Trade, as has been already hinted in the Story of *Mary Read* In all these Expeditions *Anne Bonny* bore him Company, and when any Business was to be done in their Way, no Body was more forward or couragious than she, and particularly, when they were taken, when she and *Mary Read,* with one more, were all the Persons that durst keep the Deck, as has been before hinted

Her Father was known to a great many Gentlemen, Planters of *Jamaica,* who had dealt with him, and among whom ne had a good Reputation, and some of them, who had been in *Carolina,* remember'd to have seen her in his House This made them inclin'd to shew her Favour, but the Action of leaving her Husband was an ugly Circumstance against her The Day that *Rackam* was executed, by special Favour, he was admitted to see her, but all the Comfort she gave him, was, *that she was sorry to see him there, but if he had fought like a Man, he need not have been hang'd like a Dog*

She was continu'd in Prison till the Time of her Lying-in, and afterwards repriev'd from Time to Time, but what is become of her since, we cannot learn Only this we know, that she was never executed

The LIFE *of Captain* HOWEL DAVIS.

Captain *Howel Davis* was born at *Milford,* in *Monmouthshire,* and from a Boy brought up to the Sea Service The last Voyage he made from *England* was in the *Cadogan* Snow of *Bristol,* Captain *Skinner* Commander, bound for the Coast of *Guinea,* of which Snow *Davis* was chief Mate They were no sooner arriv'd at *Sierraleon,* on the aforesaid Coast, but they were taken by the Pirate *England,* who plunder'd them Captain *Skinner* was at this Time barbarously murder'd, as has been related before in the Story of Captain *England*

After the Death of Captain *Skinner, Davis* pretended that he was mightily sollicited by *England* to engage with him, but that he resolutely answer'd, he would sooner be shot to Death than sign the Pirates Articles Upon which, *England,* pleas'd with his Bravery, sent him and the rest of the Men on board the Snow again, appointing him Captain of her, in the Room of *Skinner,* and commanding him to pursue his Voyage He also gave him a written Paper seal'd up, with Orders to open it when he should come into a certain Latitude, and, at the Peril of his Life follow the Orders therein set down This was done with an Air of Grandeur, like what Princes

practise to their Admirals and Generals —— It was punctually complied with by *Davis,* who read it to the Ship's Company It contain'd no less than a generous Deed of Gift of the Ship and Cargo to *Davis* and the Crew, and an Order, that they should go to *Brasil* and dispose of the Lading to the best Advantage, making a fair and equal Divedend of the Profit,

Davis demanded of the Crew, whether they were willing to follow their Directions, when, to his great Surprize, he found the Majority of them altogether averse to it, whereupon, in a Rage, he bad them be damn'd, and go where they would They knew that Part of their Cargo was consigned to certain Merchants at *Barbadoes,* wherefore they steered for that Island When they arrived, they related to these Merchants, the unfortunate Death of *Skinner,* and the Proposal which had been made to them by *Davis,* upon which, *Davis* was seized and committed to Prison, where he was kept three Months; however, as he had been in no Act of Piracy, he was discharged without being brought to any Trial yet he could not, after this, expect any Employment there Knowing therefore, that the Island of *Providence* was a kind of Rendezvous of Pirates, he

was

was refolved to make one amongft them, if poffible, and, to that Purpofe, found Means of fhipping himfelf for that Ifland, but, he was again difappointed, for, when he arrived there, the Pirates had newly furrrendered to Captain *Woods Rogers*, and accepted of the Act of Grace, which he had juft brought from *England*

However *Davis* was not long out of Bufinefs, for Captain *Rogers* having fitted out two Sloops for Trade, one call'd *the Buck*, the other the *Mumvil Trader*, *Davis* found an Employment on board of one of them The Lading of thefe Sloops was of confiderable Value, confifting of *European* Goods, which were to be exchang'd with the *French* and *Spaniards*, and many of the Hands on board of 'em were the Pirates lately come in upon the Act of Grace The firft Place they touch'd at, was the Ifland of *Martinico*, belonging to the *French*, where *Davis* having confpir'd with fome others, they rofe in the Night, fecur'd the Mafter, and feized the Sloop As foon as this was done, they call'd to the other Sloop, which lay a little Way from 'em, among whom they knew there were a great many Hands ripe for Rebellion, whom they order'd to come on board of them They did fo, and the greateft Part of them agreed to join with *Davis*, thofe who were otherwife inclin'd, were fent back on board the *Mumvil* Sloop, to go where they pleas'd, *Davis* having firft taken out of her every Thing which he thought might be of Service

After this a Council of War was call'd, over a large Bowl of Punch, at which it was propos'd to choofe a Commander The Election was foon over, for it fell upon *Davis* by a great Majority of *legal Pollers*, fo that there was no Scrutiny demanded, for all acquiefced in the Choice As foon as he was poffefs'd of his Command, he drew up Articles, which were fign'd and fworn to by himfelf and the reft, then he made a fhort Speech, the Sum of which was, a Declaration of War againft the whole World

After this, they confulted about a proper Place where they might clean their Sloop, a light Pair of Heels being of great Ufe either to take, or efcape being taken For this Purpofe, they made Choice of *Coxon's Hole*, at the Eaft End of the Ifland of *Cuba*, a Place where they might fecure themfelves from Surprize, the Entrance being fo narrow that one Ship might keep out a hundred

Here they clean'd with much Difficulty, for they had no Carpenter in their Company, who is a Perfon of great Ufe upon fuch Exigencies From hence they put to Sea, making to the North fide of the Ifland of *Hifpaniola* The firft Sail which fell in their Way, was a *French* Ship of twelve Guns, it muft be obferv'd that *Davis* had but thirty-five Hands, notwithftanding which, Provifions began to grow fhort with him Upon this Account he attack'd this Ship, which foon ftruck, and he fent twelve of his Hands on board of her, in order to plunder This was no fooner done, but a Sail was fpied a great Way to the Windward of them, they enquir'd of the *Frenchman* what fhe might be; he anfwer'd, that he had fpoke with a Ship the Day before, of 24 Guns, and 60 Men, and he took this to be the fame

Davis then propofed to his Men to attack her, telling them fhe would be a rare Ship for their Ufe, but they look'd upon it to be an extravagant Attempt, and difcover'd no Fondnefs for it However, he affur'd them he had a Stratagem in his Head that would make all fafe, wherefore he gave Chace, and order'd his Prize to do the fame The Prize being a flow Sailor, *Davis* firft came up with the Enemy, and, ftanding a long Side of them, fhew'd his pira-

tical Colours · They, much furpriz'd, call'd to *Davis*, telling him, that they wonder'd at his Impudence in venturing to come fo near them, and ordering him to ftrike, but he anfwer'd, that he intended to keep them in Play, till his Confort came up, who was able to deal with them, and that if they did not ftrike to him, they fhould have but hard Quarters, whereupon he gave them a Broad-Side, which they returned

In the mean Time the Prize drew near, who obliged all the Prifoners to come upon Deck in white Shirts, to make a Shew of Force, as they had been directed by *Davis*, they alfo hoifted a dirty Tarpawlin, by Way of black Flag, they having nothing better, and fir'd a Gun The *French* Men were fo intimidated by this Appearance of Force, that they ftruck *Davis* called out to the Captain to come on Board of him, with twenty of his Hands, he did fo, and they were all, for the greater Security, clapt into Irons, the Captain excepted Then he fent four of his Men on Board the firft Prize, and, in order ftill to carry on the Cheat, fpoke aloud, that they fhould give his Service to the Captain, and defire him to fend fome Hands on Board the Prize, to fee what they had got, but, at the fame Time, gave them a written Paper, with Inftructions what they fhould really do Here he ordered them to ril up the Guns in the little Prize, to take out all the ruft Arms and Powder, and to go every Man of them on Board the fecond Prize, when this was done, he ordered that more of the Prifoners fhould be removed out of the great Prize, into the little one, by which he fecured himfelf from any Attempt which might be feared from their Numbers, for thofe on board of him were faft in Irons, and thofe in the little Prize had neither Arms nor Ammunition to defend themfelves

Thus the three Ships kept Company for 2 Days, when finding the great Prize to be a very dull Sailor, he thought fhe would not be fit for his Purpofe, wherefore he refolv'd to reftore her to the Captain, with all his Hands, but firft, he took Care to take out all her Ammunition, and every Thing elfe which he might poffibly want The *French* Captain was in fuch a Rage, at being fo outwitted, that, when he got on Board his own Ship, he was going to throw himfelf over-board, if he had not been prevented by his Men

Having let go both his Prizes, he fteered North-ward, in which Courfe he took a fmall *Spanifh* Sloop, after this he made towards the *Weftern* Iflands, but met with no Booty thereabouts, then he fteered for the *Cape de Verde* Iflands, where they caft Anchor at St *Nicholas*, hoifting *Englifh* Colours, the *Portuguefe* inhabiting there, took him for an *Englifh* Privateer, and *Davis* going a-fhore, they both treated him very civilly, and alfo traded with him Here he remained five Weeks, in which Time he and half a Crew, for their Pleafure, took a Journey to the chief Town of the Ifland, which was 19 Miles up the Country *Davis*, making a good Appearance was careffed by the Governor and the Inhabitants, and no Diverfion was wanting which the *Portuguefe* could fhew, or their Money could purchafe After about a Week's Stay, he came back to the Ship, and the reft of the Crew went to take their Pleafure up the Town, in their Turn, as the Captain had done

At their Return they clean'd their Ship, and put to Sea, but not with their whole Company, for five of them, like *Hannibal's* Men, were fo charm'd with the Luxuries of the Place, and the free Converfation of fome Women, that they ftaid behind, and one of them, whofe Name was *Charles Franklin*, a *Monmouthfhire* Man married and fettled himfelf, and

and lived there several Years, being, for ought we know, alive at this Day

From hence they failed to *Bonevifta*, and looked into that Harbour, but finding nothing, they steered for the Ifle of *May* When they arrived here, they met with a great many Ships and Veffels in the Road, all which they plundered, taking out of them whatever they wanted; they also ftrengthened themfelves with a great many frefh Hands, who moft of them enter'd voluntarily One of the Ships they took to their own Ufe, mounted her with twenty fix Guns, and call'd her the *King James* There being no frefh Water hereabouts, they made towards St *Jago*, which belonged to the *Portuguefe*, in order to lay in a Store. *Davis*, with a few Hands, going a-fhore, to find the moft commodious Place to water at, the Governor, with fome Attendants, came himfelf, and examined who they were, and whence they came Not liking *Davis*'s Account of himfelf, his Excellency was fo plain as to tell them, that he fufpected them to be Pirates. *Davis* feemed mightily affronted, ftanding much upon his Honour, and replying to the Governor, that he fcorn'd his Words, however, as foon as his Back was turn'd, for fear of Accidents, he got on Board again as faft as he could *Davis* related what had happened, and his Men feemed to refent the Affront which had been offered him *Davis*, upon this, told them, he was confident he could furprize the Fort in the Night, they agreed with him to attempt it, and accordingly, when it grew late, they went a-fhore well arm'd, and the Guard which was there kept, was fo negligent, that they got within the Fort before any Alarm was given When it was too late there was fome little Refiftance made, and three Men killed on *Davis*'s Side Thofe in the Fort, in their Hurry, run into the Governor's Houfe to fave themfelves, which they barricadoed fo ftrongly, that *Davis*'s Party could not enter it, however, they threw in Granadoe Snells, which not only ruin'd all the Furniture, but kill'd feveral Men within

When it was Day the whole Country was alarm'd, and came down to attack the Pirates, who, confidering it was not their Bufinefs to ftand a Siege, made the beft of their Way on Board their Ship again, after having difmounted the Guns of the Fort By this Enterprize they did a great deal of Mifchief to the *Portuguefe*, and got but very little Good to themfelves

Having put to Sea, they mufter'd their Hands, and found themfelves near feventy ftrong, then it was propofed what Courfe they fhould fteer, and, differing in their Opinions, they divided, tho' by a Majority it was carried for *Gambia* on the Coaft of *Guinea* Of this Opinion was *Davis*, who having been employ'd in that Trade, was acquainted with the Coaft He told them, that there was a great deal of Money always kept in *Gambia* Caftle, and that it would be worth their while to make an Attempt upon it They afk'd him how it was poffible, fince it was garrifoned? He defired they would leave the Management of it to him, and he wou'd undertake to make them Mafters of it They began now to conceive fo high an Opinion of his Conduct, as well as Courage, that they thought nothing impoffible to him that he had a mind to undertake, therefore they agreed to obey him, without enquiring further into his Defign

Having come within Sight of the Place, he order'd all his Men under Deck, except as many as were abfolutely neceffary for working the Ship, that thofe from the Fort, feeing a Ship with fo few Hands, might have no Sufpicion of her being any other than a trading Veffel, then he ran clofe under the Fort,

and there caft Anchor, and having order'd out the Boat, he commanded fix Men into her, with old ordinary Jackets, while he himfelf, with the Mafter and Doctor, drefs'd themfelves like Gentlemen, his Defign being, that the Men fhould look like common Sailors, and they like Merchants In rowing a-fhore, he gave his Men Inftructions what to fay, in cafe any Questions fhould be afk'd them by the Garrifon

Being come to the Landing-Place, he was receiv'd by a File of Mufquetteers, and conducted into the Fort, where the Governor, accofting them civilly, afk'd them who they were, and whence they came? They anfwer'd, they were of *Liverpool*, bound for the River of *Sinnegal*, to trade for Gum and Elephant's Teeth, but that they were chas'd on that Coaft by two *French* Men of War, and narrowly efcap'd being taken, having the Heels of them but a very little *We are now refolved*, fays he, *to make the beft of a bad Market, and would willingly trade here for Slaves* Then the Governor afk'd them, What was the chief of their Cargo? They anfwer'd, Iron and Plate, which were good Things there The Governor told them he would flave them to the full Value of their Cargo, and afk'd them if they had any *European* Liquor on board? They anfwer'd a little for their own Ufe, however, a Hamper of it fhould be at his Service The Governor then very civilly invited them all to ftay and dine with him, but *Davis* told him, that, being Commander of the Ship, he muft go on board to fee her well moor'd, and give fome other neceffary Orders, *But thefe two Gentlemen*, fays he, *may ftay, and I myfelf will alfo return before Dinner, and bring the Hamper of Liquor with me.*

While he was in the Fort, his Eyes were very bufy in obferving how Things lay, he took Notice that there was a Centry at the Entrance, and a Guard-Houfe juft by it, where the Soldiers upon Duty commonly waited, their Arms ftanding in a Corner, in a Heap, he faw alfo, a great many fmall Arms in the Governor's Hall Now, when he came on board, he affur'd his Men of Succefs, defiring them not to get drunk, and telling them, that as foon as they faw the Flag upon the Caftle ftruck, they might conclude he was Mafter, and fend twenty Hands immediately a-fhore; in the mean Time, there being a Sloop at Anchor near them, he fent fome Hands in a Boat, to fecure the Mafter and all the Men, and bring them on board of him, left they obferving any Buftle, or arming in his Ship, might fend a-fhore and give Intelligence

Thefe Precautions being taken, he order'd his Men, who were to go in the Boat with him, to put two Pair of Piftols each under their Cloaths, he doing the like himfelf, and gave them Directions to go into the Guard-Room, enter into Converfation with the Soldiers, and obferve, when he fhould fire a Piftol through the Governor's Window, to ftart up at once, and fecure the Arms in the Guard-Room

When *Davis* arriv'd, Dinner not being ready, the Governor propos'd that they fhould employ themfelves in making a Bowl of Punch till Dinner Time. It muft be obferv'd, that *Davis*'s Cockfwain waited upon them, who had an Opportunity of going about all Parts of the Houfe, to fee what Strength they had He whifper'd *Davis*, there being no Perfon then in the Room but themfelves, the Mafter, and the Doctor, when *Davis* on a fudden drew out a Piftol, and clapp'd it to the Governor's Breaft, telling him, he muft furrender the Fort, and all the Riches in it, or he was a dead Man The Governor, being no ways prepar'd for fuch an Attack, promis'd to be very paffive, and do all they defir'd, therefore they fhut

the

the Door, took down all the Arms that hung in the Hall, and loaded them Davis fires his Piftol through the Window, upon which, his Men without executed their Part of the Scheme, like Heroes, in an Inftant, getting betwixt the Soldiers and their Arms, all with their Piftols cock'd in their Hands, while one of them carried the Arms out. When this was done, they lock'd the Soldiers into the Guard Room, and kept Guard without

In the mean Time, one of them ftruck the Union Flag on the Top of the Caftle, at which Signal, thofe on Board fent on Shore a Reinforcement of Hands, and they got Poffeffion of the Fort without the leaft Hurry or Confufion, or fo much as a Man loft of either Side

Davis harangued the Soldiers; upon which, a great many of them took on with him, thofe who refufed, he fent on board the little Sloop, and becaufe he would not be at the Trouble of a Guard for them, he ordered all the Sails and Cables out of her, which might hinder them from attempting to get away

This Day was fpent in a kind of Rejoicing, the Caftle firing her Guns to falute the Ship, and the Ship paying the fame Compliment to the Caftle, but the next Day they minded their Bufinefs, that is, they fell to plundering They found Things fall vaftly fhort of their Expectation, for they difcovered, that a great deal of Money had been lately fent away, however, they met with the Value of about two thoufand Pounds Sterling in Bar Gold, and a great many other rich Effects: Every Thing they liked, which was portable, they brought a board their Ship, fome Things which they had no Ufe for, they were fo generous as to make a Prefent of to the Mafter and Crew of the little Sloop, to whom they alfo returned his Veffel again, and then they fell to work in difmounting the Guns, and demolifhing the Fortifications

After they had done as much Mifchief as they could, and were weighing Anchor to be gone, they fpy'd a Ship bearing down upon them in full Sail, they foon got their Anchors up, and were in a Readinefs to receive her This Ship proved to be a French Pirate, of fourteen Guns, and fixty-four Hands, half French, half Negroes. The Captain's Name was La Boufe, he expected no lefs than a rich Prize, which made him fo eager in the Chace, but when he came near enough to fee their Guns, and the Number of their Hands upon Deck, he began to think he fhould catch a Tarter, and fuppofed her to be a fmall Englifh Man of War, however, fince there was no efcaping, he refolv'd to do a bold and defperate Action, which was to board Davis As he was making towards her, for that Purpofe, he fired a Gun, and hoifted his black Colours, Davis returned the Salute, and hoifted his black Colours alfo The French Man was not a little pleafed at this happy Miftake, they both hoifted out their Boats, and the Captains went to meet and congratulate one another, with a Flag of Truce in their Sterns A great many Civilities paffed between them, and La Boufe defired Davis to fail down the Coaft with him, that he might get a better Ship Davis agreed to it, and very courteoufly promifed him, that the firft Ship he took, fit for his Ufe, he would give him being very willing to encourage an induftrious Brother

The firft Place they touched at, was Sierraleon, where, at firft going in, they fpied a tall Ship at Anchor; Davis, being the beft Sailor, firft came up with her, and wondering that fhe did not try to make off, fufpected her to be a Ship of Force As foon as he came along Side of her, fhe brought a Spring upon

her Cable, and fired a whole Broadfide upon Davis at the fame Time hoifting a black Flag Davis hoifted his black Flag in like Manner, and fired one Gun to Leeward

In fine, fhe proved to be a Pirate Ship of twenty four Guns, commanded by one Cocklyn, who expecting thefe two would prove Prizes, let them come in, left his getting under Sail might frighten them away, and fo he fhould mifs the Booty

The Satisfaction was great on all Sides, at this Junction of Confederates and Brethren in Iniquity, two Days they fpent in improving their Acquaintance and Friendfhip, the third Day Davis and Cocklyn agreed, to go in La Boufe's Brigantine, and attack the Fort, they contrived it fo, as to get up thither by high Water, thofe in the Fort fufpected then to be what they really were, and therefore ftood upon their Defence When the Brigantine came within Musket Shot, the Fort fired all their Guns upon her, the Brigantine did the like upon the Fort, and fo they held each other in Play for feveral Hours, when the two confederate Ships came up to the Affiftance of the Brigantine Thofe who defended the Fort, feeing fuch a Number of Hands on Board thefe Ships, had not the Courage to ftand it out any longer, but abandoning the Fort, left it to the Mercy of the Pirates

They took Poffeffion of it, and continued there near feven Weeks, in which Time they all cleaned their Ships We fhould have obferved, that a Galley came into the Road while they were there, which Davis infifted fhould be yielded to La Boufe, according to his Word of Honour before given, Cocklyn did not oppofe it, fo La Boufe went into her, with his Crew, and, cutting her half Deck, mounted her with twenty four Guns

Having called a Council of War, they agreed to fail down the Coaft together, and, for the greater Grandeur, appointed a Commodore, who was Capt Davis, but they had not kept Company long, when drinking together on Board of Davis, they had like to have fallen together by the Ears, the ftrong Liquor ftirring up a Spirit of Difcord among them Davis, however, put an End to the Quarrel, by this fhort Speech ——Heark ye, you Cocklyn and La Boufe, I find by ftrengthening you, I have put a Rod into your Hands to whip myfelf, but I'm ftill able to deal with you both, however, fince we met in Love, let us part in Love, for I find, that three of a Trade can never agree long together ——Upon this, the other two went on Board their refpective Ships, and immediately parted, each fteering a different Courfe.

Davis held on his Way down the Coaft, and making Cape Appollonia, he met with two Scotch and one Englifh Veffels, all which he plundered, and then let them go About five Days after, he fell in with a Dutch Interloper of thirty Guns and ninety Men, (half being Englifh,) off Cape Three Points Bay Davis coming up along Side of her, the Dutch Man gave the firft fire, and pouring in a broad-fide upon Davis, killed nine of his Men, Davis returned it, and a very hot Engagement followed, which lafted from one a Clock at Noon till nine next Morning, when the Dutch Man ftruck, and yielded her felf their Prize

Davis fitted up the Dutch Ship for his own Ufe, and called her the Rover, aboard of her he mounted thirty two Guns, and 27 Swivels, and then proceeded, with her and the K James to Anamaboe He entered this Bay betwixt the Hours of twelve and one at Noon, and found there three Ships lying at Anchor, who were trading for Negroes, Gold and Teeth The Names of thefe Ships were the Hink Pink, Capt Hall Commander; the Princefs, Capt Plumb, of which Roberts, who will make a confiderable

derable Figure in the sequel of this History, was second Mate, and the *Morice* Sloop, Capt. *Fin*, he takes these Ships without any Resistance, and having plundred them, he makes a Present of one of them, *viz.* the *Morice* Sloop, to the *Dutch* Prisoners.

On Board of this Sloop alone were found a hundred and forty Negroes, besides dry Goods, and a considerable Quantity of Gold-Dust

It happened that several Canoes were along Side of this last, when *Davis* came in, who saved themselves and got ashore; these gave Notice at the Fort, that these Ships were Pirates, upon which the Fort fired upon them, but without doing any Execution, for their Mettle was not of Weight enough to reach them, *Davis* therefore, by Way of Defiance, hoisted his black Flag, and returned their Compliment

The same Day he sail'd with his three Ships, making his Way down the Coast towards *Princes*, a *Portuguese* Colony. But before we proceed any farther in *Davis*'s Story, we shall give our Reader an Account of the *Portuguese* Settlements on this Coast, with other curious Remarks, as they were communicated to us by an Ingenious Gentleman, lately arrived from those Parts

A Description of the Islands of St. Thome, Del Principe, and Annobono.

AS the *Portuguese* were the great Improvers of Navigation, and the first *Europeans* who traded to, and settled on, the Coasts of *Africa*, even round to *India*, and made those Discoveries, which now turn so much to the Advantage of other Nations, it may not be amiss, previously to give a Description of those Islands, to hint on that wonderful Property of the Loadstone, that a little before had been found out, and enabled them to pursue such new and daring Navigations

The a tractive Power of the Loadstone was universally known to the Ancients, as may be believed by its being a native Fossil of the *Grecians*, for 'tis call'd *Magnes* from *Magnesia*, but its directive, or polar Virtue, has only been known to us within this 350 Years, and is said to be found out by *John Goia*, of *Malphi*, in the Kingdom of *Naples*, *Prima dedit nautis usum magnetis Amalphi*, tho' others think and assure us, it was transported by *Paulus Venetus* from *China* to *Italy*, like the two other famous Arts of modern Use with us, PRINTING and *the Use of* GUNS

The other Properties or Improvements of the Magnet, *viz.* its Variation, or Defluxion from an exact N or S Line, Variation of that Variation, and its Inclination, were the Inventions of *Sebastian Cabot*, Mr *Gellibrand*, and Mr *Norman*, the Inclination of the Needle, or that Property whereby it keeps in its elevation above the Horizon, in all Places but under the Equator, where 'tis Parellel, is as surprizing a Phænomenon as any, and was the Discovery of our Countrymen, and could it be found regular, I imagine it would very much help towards the Discovery of the Longitude, at least 'twould point out better Methods than are hitherto known, when Ships drew nigh Land, which would answer as useful an End almost as the other

Before the Verticity and Use of the Compass, the *Portuguese* Navigations had extended no farther than Cape *Non*, which was their *ne plus ultra*, and therefore so called Distress of Weather indeed, had

drove some Coasters to *Porto Santo*, and *Madera*, before any certain Method of steering was invented, but after the Needle was seen thus inspired Navigation every Year improv'd, under the great Encouragements of *Henry*, *Alphonsus*, and *John* II Kings of *Portugal*, in Part of the 14th and in the 15th Century

King *Alphonsus* was not so much at leisure as his Predecessor, to pursue these Discoveries, but, having seen the Advantages that accrued to *Portugal* by them, and that the Pope had confirmed the perpetual Donation of all they should discover between Cape *Bajadore* and *India*, inclusively, he resolv'd not to neglect the proper Assistance, and so farm'd the Profits that did or might ensue, to one *Bernard Gomez*, a Citizen of *Lisbon*, who was every Voyage obliged to discover 100 Leagues still farther on About the Year 1470, he made these Islands, the only Places of all the considerable and large Colonies they had in *Africa*, that do now remain to that Crown

St *Thome* is the principal of the three, whose Governor is stiled Captain-General of the Islands, and from whom the other at *Princes* receives his Commission, tho' nominated by the Court of *Portugal* It is a Bishoprick, with a great many secular Clergy, who appear to have neither Learning nor Devotion, as may be judged by several of them being Negroes. One of the Chief of them invited us to hear Mass, as a Diversion to pass Time away; where he, and his inferior Brethren, acted such affected Gestures and Strains of Voice, as shewed, to their Dishonour, that they had no other Aim, than that of pleasing us, and, what I think was still worse, it was not without a View of Interest, for as these Clergy are the chief Traders, they stoop to pitiful and scandalous Methods for ingratiating themselves They and the Government, on this trading Account, maintain no great Harmony, being ever jealous of each other, and practising little deceitful Arts, to monopolize what Strangers have to offer for sale, whether Toys or Cloaths, which of all sorts are ever profitable Commodities with the *Portuguese* in all Parts of the World An ordinary Suit of Black will sell for seven or eight Pound, a Middle-row Wig of four Shillings, for a Moidore, a Watch of forty Shillings, for six Pound, &c

The Town is of mean Building, but large and populous, 'tis the Residence of the greater Part of the Natives, who, thro' the whole Island, are computed at 10000, the Militia at 3000, and are, in general, a rascally thievish Generation, as an old grave Friend of mine can witness, for he, having carried a Bag of second-hand Cloaths on Shore, to truck for Provisions, seated himself on the Sand for that Purpose, and presently gathered a Crowd round him, to view them, one of these desired to know the Price of a Black Suit, that unluckily lay uppermost, and was the best of them, agreeing to the Demand, with little Hesitation, provided it would but fit him, he put them on immediately, in as much hurry as possible, without any *co licentia Seignor*, and when my Friend was about to commend the Goodness of the Suit, and Exactness they set with, not dreaming of the Impudence of his running away from a Crowd, the Rascal took to his Heels, my Friend followed and bawled very much, and, tho' there was 500 People about the Place, it served to no other End but making him a clear Stage, that the best Pair of Heels might carry it, so he lost the Suit of Cloaths, and, before he could return to his Bag, others of them had beat off his Servant, and shared the rest

Most of the Ships from *Guiney*, of their own Nation and frequently those of ours, call at one or other of these Islands, to recruit with fresh Provisions, and

take

take in Water; which on the Coast are not so good, nor so conveniently to come by. Their own Ships likewise, when they touch here, are obliged to leave the King his Custom for their Slaves, which is always in Gold, at so much a Head, without any Deduction at *Brasil*, for the Mortality that may happen afterwards, this, by being a constant Bank to pay off the civil and military Charges of the Government, prevents the Inconveniency of Remittances, and keeps both St *Thome* and *Princes* Isle rich enough, to pay ready Money for every Thing they want of the *Europeans*

The Beefs are small and lean, few of them exceeding two hundred Weight, none of them much more, but the Goats, Hogs and Fowls are very good, their Sugar is coarse and dirty, and their Rum very ordinary, as these Refreshments lay most with People who are in want of other Necessaries, they come to us in a Way of bartering very cheap A good Hog for an old Cutlash, a fat Fowl for a Span of *Brasil* Tobacco, (no other Sort being valued) and so in Proportion to the rest. But in Money you give eight Dollars *per* Head for Cattle, three Dollars for a Goat, six Dollars for a grown Hog, a Testune and a half for a Fowl, a Dollar *per* Gallon for Rum, two Dollars a Roove for Sugar, and half a Dollar for a Dozen of Paroquets Here is Plenty likewise of Corn and Farine, of Limes, Citrons and Yamms

The Island is reckoned to be almost Square, each Side being 18 Leagues long; 'tis hilly, and under the *Æquinoctial*, a wooden Bridge, just without the Town, being said not to deviate the least Part of a Minute, either to the Southward or Northward; and, notwithstanding this warm Situation, and the continual vertical Suns, the Islanders are very healthy, which is imputed by those who are disposed to be merry, in a great Measure, to the Want of even so much as one Surgeon or Physician amongst them

The Isle *Del Principe*, the next in Magnitude, is a pleasant and delightful Spot to the grave and thoughtful Disposition of the *Portuguese*, 'tis an Improvement of Country Retirement, in that this may be a happy and uninterrupted Retreat from the whole World

I shall divide what I have to say on this Island, into Observations made on our Approach to it, and on the Seas round it, the Harbour, the Produce of the Island and Seasons, the Way of Living among the Inhabitants, and some Customs of the Negroes, with such proper Deductions on each, as may illustrate the Description, and inform the Reader

We were bound hither from *Whydah*, at the latter Part of the Month *July*, when the Rains are over, and the Winds hang altogether S W as they do before the Rains, S. E yet with this Wind we found the Ship gained unexpectedly so far to the Southward, that is the Windward, that we could with ease have weathered any of the Islands, and it seems next to impossible how this should be, if the Currents, which were strong to Leeward, in the Road of *Whydah*, had extended in like Manner cross the Bite of *Benin* No, it must then have very difficult to have weathered even Cape *Formosa* On this Occasion, I shall farther expatiate upon the Currents on the whole Coast of *Guiney*

The Southern Coast of *Africa* runs in a Western Line of Latitude, the Northern on an Eastern Line, but both strait, with the fewest Inlets, Gulphs or Bays, of either of the four Continents, the only large and remarkable one, is that of *Benin* and *Calabar*, towards which the Currents of each Coast tend, and which is strongest from the Southward, because more open to a large Sea, whose rising it is (tho' little and scarce discernable at any Distance from the Land,)

that gives rise to these Currents close in Shore; which are nothing but Tides, altered and disturbed by the Make and Shape of Lands

For Proof of this, I shall lay down the following Observations as certain Facts That in the Rivers of *Gambia* and *Sierraleon*, in the Straits and Channels of *Benin*, and in general along the whole Coast, the Flowings are regular on the Shores, with this Difference, that, in the abovemention'd Rivers, and in the Channels of *Benin*, where the Shore contracts the Waters into a narrow Compass, the Tides are strong and high, as well as regular, but on the dead Coast, where it makes an equal Reverbation, flow and low, (not to above two or three Foot,) increasing as you advance towards *Benin*, and this is farther evident, in that at Cape *Corso*, *Succonda* and *Commenda*, and where the Land rounds and gives any Stop, the Tides flow regularly on four Foot and upwards, when on an evener Coast, (tho' next adjoining) they shall not exceed two or three Foot, and ten Leagues out at Sea, (where no such Interruption is,) they become scarcely, if at all, perceptible

What I would deduce from this, besides a Confirmation of that ingenious Theory of the Tides, by Captain *Halley*, is first, that the Ships bound to *Angola*, *Cabenda*, and other Places on the Southern Coast of *Africa*, should cross the *Æquinoctial* from Cape *Palmas*, and run into a Southern Latitude, without keeping too far to the Westward, and the Reason seems plain, for if you endeavour to cross it about the Islands, you meet Calms, southerly Winds, and opposite Currents, and if too far to the Westward, the Trade Winds are strong and unfavourable, for it obliges you to stand into 8 or 30° Southern Latitude, till they are variable

Secondly, On the Northern Side of *Guiney*, if Ships are bound from the *Gold-Coast* to *Sierraleon*, *Gambia*, or elsewhere to Windward, considering the Weakness of these Currents, and the Favourableness of Land Breezes, and Southerly the Rains, Turn does, and even the Trade Wind, when a breast of Cape *Palmas*, it is more expeditious to pursue the Passage this Way, than by a long perambulatory Course of 4 or 500 Leagues to the Westward, and as many more to the Northward, which must be before a Wind can be obtained, that could recover the Coast.

Lastly, It is, in a great Measure, owing to this want of Inlets, and the Rivers being small and unnavigable, that the Seas rebound with so dangerous a Surff thro' the whole Continent

Round the Shores of this Island, and in *July*, *August* and *September*, the Months we were there, there is a great Resort of Whale Fish, *time*, and sporting very high the Ships as they sail in, they are always in Pairs, the Female being much the smaller, and are often seen to turn on their Backs for Dalliance, the Prologue to engendring This Fish has an enemy, called the Thresher, a large Fish too, that has it Haunts here at this Season, and encounters the Whale, raising himself out of the Water a considerable Heighth, and falling again with great Weight and Force It is commonly said also, that there is a Sword Fish in these Battles, who pricks the Whale up to the Surface again, but without this, I believe, he would suffocate when put to quick Motions, unless frequently approaching the Air, to ventilate and remove the Impediments to a swifter Circulation Nor do I think he is battled for Prey, but to remove him from what is, perhaps, the Food of both The Number of Whales here has put me sometimes on thinking than an advantageous Fishery might be made of it; but I presume these no more than those of *Brasil* are the Sort which yield the profitable Part, called

called Whale Bone· All therefore that the Iſlanders 'do, is now and then to go out with two or three Canoes, and ſet on one for their Diverſion

The Rocks and outer Lines of the Iſland, are the Haunts of variety of Sea-Birds, eſpecially Boobies and Noddies, the former are of the Bigneſs of a Gull, and a dark Colour, named ſo from their Simplicity, becauſe they often ſit ſtill and let the Sailors take them up in their Hands, but I fancy this ſucceeds more frequently from their Wearineſs, and the Largeneſs of their Wings, which when they once have reſted, cannot have the Scope neceſſary to raiſe and float them on the Air again The Noddies are ſmaller and flat footed alſo

What I would remark more of them, is, the admirable Inſtinct in theſe Birds, with reſpect to the proper Seaſons, and the proper Places for Support In the aforemention'd Months, when the large Fiſh are here, numerous Flocks of Fowl attend for the Spawn and Superfluity of their Nouriſhment; and in January few of either For the ſame Reaſon, there are ſcarce any Sea Fowl ſeen on the African Coaſt, Rocks and Iſlands being generally their beſt Security and Subſiſtance

The Harbour of Princes is at the E S E Point of the Iſland, the North Side has gradual Soundings, but here is deep Water, having no Ground at a Mile off Shore, with 140 Fathom of Line. The Port when entered, is a ſmooth narrow Bay, ſafe from Winds, (unleſs a little Swell when Southerly) and draughted into other ſmaller and ſandy Ones, convenient for raiſing of Tents, Watering, and hawling the Seam; the whole protected by a Fort, or rather Battery, of a dozen Guns on the Larboard-Side At the Head of the Bay ſtands the Town, about a Mile from the anchoring Place, and conſiſts of two or three regular Streets of wooden built Houſes, where the Governor and chief Men of the Iſland reſide Here the Water grow ſhallow for a conſiderable Diſtance, and the Natives, at every Ebb, (having before encompaſſed every convenient Angle with a ſite of Stones, ſometimes like the Weirs in England) reſort for catching of Fiſh, which, with them, is a daily Diverſion, as well as Subſiſtance, 500 attending with Sticks and wicker Baſkets; and if they cannot dip them with one Hand, they knock them down with the other The Tides riſe regularly 6 Foot in the Harbour, and yet not half that Height without the Capes that make the Bay

Here are conſtantly two Miſſionaries, who are ſent for ſix Years, to inculcate the Chriſtian Principles, and more eſpecially attend the Converſion of the Negroes, the preſent are Venetians ingenious Men, who ſeem to deſpiſe the looſe Morals and Behaviour of the Seculars, and complain of them as of the Slaves, ut Colore More ſunt nigri They have a neat conventual Houſe and a Garden appropriated, which, by their own Induſtry and Labour, not only thrives with the ſeveral Natives of the Soil, but many Exoticks and Curioſities A Fruit in particular, larger than a Cheſnut, yellow, containing two Stones, with a Pulp, or clammy Subſtance about them, which, when ſuck'd, exceeds in ſweetneſs Sugar or Honey, and has this Property beyond them, of giving a ſweet Taſte to every Liquid you ſwallow for the whole Evening after The only Plague infeſting the Garden, is a Vermin called Land Crabs, which are in all Numbers, they are of a bright red Colour, but in other Reſpects like the Sea ones. They burrough in theſe ſandy Soils like Rabbets, and are altogether as ſhy The Iſland is a pleaſant Intermixture of Hill and Valley, the Hills are ſpread with Palms, Cocoa-Nuts, and Cotton-Trees, with Numbers of Monkeys and Parrots among them, the Valleys with fruitful

Plantations of Yamms, Kulalu, Papas, Variety of Sallating, Ananas, or Pine-Apples, Guavas, Plantanes, Bonanas, Manyocos, and Indian Corn, with Fowls, Guinea Hens, Muſcovy Ducks, Goats, Hogs, Turkies, and wild Beefs, with each a little Village of Negroes, who, under the Direction of their ſeveral Maſters, manage the Cultivation, and exchange or ſell their Product for Money, much after the ſame Rates with the People of St Thome

We ſhall run thro' a Deſcription of the Vegetables, with their Properties, not only becauſe they are the Produce of this Iſland, but moſt of them of Africa in general

The Palm-Trees are numerous on the Shores of Africa, and may be reckoned the firſt of their natural Curioſities, in that they afford them Meat, Drink, and Cloathing, they grow very ſtraight to 40 and 50 Foot high, and, at the Top only, have 3 or 4 Circles of Branches, that ſpread and make a capacious Umbrella The Trunk is very rough with Knobs, either Excreſcencies, or the Healings of thoſe Branches, that were loop'd off to forward the Growth of the Tree, and make it anſwer better in its Fruit The Branches are ſtrongly tied together with a Cortex, which may be unravelled to a conſiderable Length and Breadth, the inward Lamella of this Cortex, are woven like a Cloath at Benin, and afterwards died and worn Under the Branches, and cloſe to the Body of the Tree, hang the Nuts, thirty Bunches perhaps on a Tree, and each of thirty Pound Weight, with prickly Films from between them, not unlike Hedge-Hogs Of theſe Nuts comes a liquid and pleaſant ſcented Oyl, uſed as Food and Sauce all over the Coaſt, but chiefly in the Windward Parts of Africa, where they ſtamp, boil and ſkim it off in great Quantities, underneath, where the Branches fatten, they tap them for Wine, called Cockra, in this Manner, the Negroes, who are moſtly limber active Fellows, encompaſs themſelves and the Trees with a Hoop of ſtrong With, and run up with a great deal of Agility, at the Bottom of a Branch of Nuts, he that aſcends makes an Excavation of an Inch and a half over, and tying faſt his Calabaſh, leaves it to diſtil, which it does to two or three Quarts in a Night's Time, when done he plugs it up, and chooſes another, for if ſuffered to run too much, or in the Day Time, the Sap is unwarily exhauſted, and the Tree ſpoiled The Liquor thus drawn is of a wheyiſh Colour, very intoxicating It ſours in 24 Hours, but when new drawn, is pleaſant to thirſt and hunger both It is from theſe Wines they draw their Arrack in India On the very Top of the Palm grows a Cabbage, called ſo, we believe, from ſome Reſemblance its Taſte is thought to have with ours, being uſed like it, the Covering has a Down that makes the beſt of Tinder, and the Weavings of other Parts are drawn out into ſtrong Threads

Coca-Nut-Trees are branch'd like, but not ſo tall as Palm Trees, the Nut like them, growing under the Branches, and cloſe to the Trunk, the milky Liquor they contain, to the Quantity of half a Pint, or more, is often drank to quench Thirſt, but is apt to ſurfeit, and this may be obſerved in their Way of Nouriſhment, that when the Quantity of Milk is large, the Shell and Meat are very thin, and they harden and thicken in Proportions, as that loſes

Cotton Trees alſo are the Growth of all Parts of Africa, as well as the Iſlands, they are of vaſt Bigneſs, yet not ſo apt to increaſe as the Shrubs or Buſhes of five or ſix Foot high, theſe bear a Fruit (if it may be ſo called) about the Bigneſs of Pigeons Eggs, which, as the Sun ſwells and ripens it, burſts forth and diſcovers three Cells loaded with Cotton, and Seeds in the Middle of them: This in moſt

Parts the Negroes know how to fpin, and here, at *Nicongo*, and the Ifland St. *Jago*, how to weave into Cloths

Yamms are a common Root, fweeter but not un-like Potatoes *Kubalu* is a herb like Spinnage *Papa*, a Fruit lefs than the fmalleft Pumkins, they are all three for boiling, and to be eat with Meat, the lat-ter are improv'd by the *Englifh* into a Turnip or an Apple Tafte, with a due Mixture of Butter or Limes

Guava's are a Fruit as large as a Pipin, with Seeds and Stones in it, of an uncouth aftringing Tafte, tho' never fo much be faid in Commendation of it At the *Weft Indies*, it is common for the *Cerolians*, (who have tafted both,) to give it a Preference to Peach or Nectarine, no amazing Thing for Men, whofe Taf-tes are fo degenerated, as to prefer a Toad in a Shell, (as *Ward* calls Turtle,) to Venifon, and Negroes to fine *Englifh* Ladies

Plantanes and *Bonano's* are Fruit of oblong Fi-gure, that I think differ only *fecundum Majus & Mi-nus*, if any, the latter are preferable, and, by being lefs, are jucier, they are ufually, when ftripped of their Coat, eat at Meals inftead of Bread The Leaf of this *Plantane* is an admirable Detergent, and ex-ternally applied, has been known to cure the moft ob-ftinate fcorbutick Ulcers

Manyoco is a Root that fhoots its Branches about the heighth of a Currant Bufh, from this Root the Iflanders make a Farine of Flower, which they fell at three Ryals a Roove, and drive a confiderable Trade for it with the Ships that call in The man-ner of making it, is, firft to prefs the Juice from it, (which is poifonous) by the help of Engines, and then the Negroe Women, upon a rough Stone, rub it into a granulated Flower, which they referve in their Houfes, either to boil, as we do our Wheat, when it makes a hearty Food for the Slaves, or to make it into a Bread, fine, white, and well tafted, for them-felves One thing worth taking Notice about *Ma-nyoco* in this Ifland, is, that the Woods abound with a wild, poifonous, and more mortiferous Sort, which fometimes Men, unfkilled in the Preparation of it, feed on to their Deftruction This the Miffiona-ries affured me they often experimented in their Hogs, and believed we did in the Mortality of our Sailors

Indian Corn is likewife, as well as the *Farine de Manyoco* and Rice, the common Victualling of our Slave Ships, and is afforded here at 1000 Heads for two Dollars This Corn grows eight or nine Foot high, on a hard Reed or Stick, fhooting forth at every fix Inches Heighth, fome long Leaves; it has always an Ear, or rather Head, at the Top of it, perhps containing 400 Fold Increafe, and often two, three, or more, about Midway

Here are fome Tamarind Trees, another Tree called *Cola*, whofe Fruit, or Nut about twice the Bignefs of a Chefnut, and bitter) is chewed by the *Portuguefe*, to give a fweet Guft to their Water which they drink, but above all, the Bark of one is gratel affirmed by the Inhabitants, to have a peculiar Pro-perty of enlarging the Virile Member, thofe who are not fond of fuch Conceits, nor believe it in the Power of any Vegetables, have acknowledged they have feen Sights of this kind among the Negroes very ex-traordinary; yet, that there may be no Wifhes a mong the Ladies for the Importation of this Bark I muft acquaint them, that they are found to grow lefs merry, as they encreafe in Bulk I had like to have forgot their Cinnamon Trees, there is only one Walk of them, which is the Entrance of the Gover-nor's Villa; they thrive extreamly well, and the Bark is not inferior to our Cinnamon from *India*

The Reafon why they and other Spices, in a Soil fo proper, receive no farther Cultivation, is, probably their Sufpicion, that fo rich a Produce might make fome potent Neighbour take a Fancy to the Ifland

They have two Winters, or rather Springs, and two Summers Their Winters, which are the rainy Seafons, come in *September* and *February*, or *March*, and Lold two Months, returning that Fatnefs and ge nerative Power to the Earth, that makes it yield a double Crop every Year, with little Sweat or La bour

Hic Ver affiduum atque Alienis Menfibus Æfta
——Bis gravidæ Pecudes, bis Pomis utilis arbos

Their firft coming is with Travado's, i e fudden and hard Gufts of Wind, with Thunder, Lighning, and heavy Showers, but the Continuance of thele Tempefts is very fhort, and the next new or ful Moon at thofe Times of the Year infallibly intro duces the Rains, which once begun, fall with little Intermiffion, and are obferv'd to be coldeft in Febru ary Similar to thefe are rainy Seafons alfo over all the Coaft of *Africa* If there may be allowed a general Way of calculating their Time, they happen from the Courfe of the Sun, as it refpects the Æqui noctial only, for if thefe Æquinoxes prove rainy Sea fons all over the World (as we are apt to think they do) whatever fecret Caufe operates with that States of the Sun to produce them, will more effectually do it in thofe vicine Latitudes, and therefore, as the Sun advances, the Rains are brought on the *Whydah* and Gold Coaft by *April*, and on the Windwardmoft Part of *Guiney* by *May* The other Seafon of the Sun's returning to the Southward, makes them more uncertain and irregular in North *Africa*, but then to the Southward again, they proceed in like man-ner, and are at Cape *Lopez* in *October*, at *Angola* in *November*, and fo in proportion at the other Parts

The Manner of living among the *Portuguefe* here, is, with the utmoft Frugality and Temperance, even to Penury and Starving, a familiar Inftance of this appears in the Voracity of their Dogs, who, finding fuch clean Cupboards at home, are wild in a manne with Hunger, and tear up the Graves of the Dead for Food, as has been often feen They themfelves are lean with Covetoufnefs, and that Chriftian Ver tue, which is often the Refult of it, Selfdenial, they would even train up their Cattle in the fame Way, could they fetch as much Money, or had not they their Provifion more immediately of Providence The beft of them (excepting the Governor now and then) neither pay nor receive any Vifits of Efcapade or Re creation, they meet and fit down at each other Doors in the Street every Evening, and as few of them, in fo fmall an Ifland, can have their Planta tons at any greater Diftance, than that they may fee them every Day if they will, fo the Subject of their Talk is moftly how Affairs went there, with their Negroes, or their Ground, and then they part one with another innocently, but as empty as when they came together

The Negroes have yet no hard Duty with them, they are rather Happy in Slavery, for as their Food is chiefly Vegetables, that could no Way elfe be ex pended, there are no Murmurs bred on that Account and as their Bufinefs is Domeftick, either in the Ser vices of the Houfe, or in Gardening, Sowing or Planting, they have no more than what every Maf would prefer for his Health and Pleafure, the hard eft of their Work, is, the Carriage of their Mafters or their Wives, to and from the Plantations, which they do in Hammocks (called at *Whydah*, Serpentin fling crot a Pole with a Cloth overhead, to fcreen the

the Perfon, fo carried, from Sun and Weather, and the Slaves are at each End; and yet even this, me-thinks, is better than the fpecious Liberty a Man has for himfelf and his Heirs to work in a Coal Mine

The Negroes are moft of them, thro' the Care of their Patroons, Chriftians, at leaft nominal, but, excepting fome few, they adhere ftill to many filly Pagan Cuftoms, in their Mournings and Rejoicings, and in fome Meafure, a powerful Majority of thefe People has introduced their Manners among the Vul-gar of the *Mulatto* and *Portuguefe* Race

If a Perfon die in that Colour, the Relations and Friends of him meet at the Houfe, where the Corpfe is laid out decently on the Ground, and covered all except the Face, with a Sheet, they fit round it, crying and howling dreadfully, not unlike what the Natives are faid to do in *Ireland* This Mourning lafts for eight Days and Nights, but not equally in-tenfe, for as the Friends, who compofe the Chorus, go out and in, they grow weary, and unequally af-fected, fo that the Tone leffens daily, and the Inter-vals of Grief are longer

In Rejoicings and Feftivals they are equally ridi-culous, thefe are commonly made on fome Friend's Efcape from Shipwreck or other Danger. They meet in a large Room of the Houfe, with a Strum, Strum, to which one of the Company, perhaps, fings wofully, the reft, ftanding round the Room clofe to the Pai-tions, take it in their Turns, one or two at a Time to ftep round, in a manner which they call Dancing, the whole clapping their Hands continual-ly, and hooping out every Minute *Abeo*, which fignify no more, than, *How do you do?* And this foolifh Mirth will continue three or four Days to-gether at a Houfe, and, perhaps, twelve or fixteen Hours at a Time

The *Portuguefe*, tho' eminently abftemious and temperate in all other Things, are unbounded in their Lufts, and perhaps they fubftitute the former, in the room of a Surgeon, as a Counterpoifon to the Mif-chiefs of a promifcuous Salacity They have moft of them Venereal Taints, and with Age become mea-ger and hectick I faw two Inftances here of Ve-nereal Ulcers that had cancerated in the Bowels, Spectacles enough to have effectually perfwaded Men how Salutary the Reftriction of Laws are.

Annabono is the laft, and of the leaft Confequence of the three Iflands, there are Plenty of Fruits and Povifions, which they exchange for old Cloaths and Trifles of any Sort, they have a Governor nomi-nated from St *Thome*, and two or three Priefts, neither of which are minded, every one living at Difcretion, filled with Ignorance and Luft

The Pleafure which we conceive the Reader has found in our Account of thefe Iflands, will, we hope, attone for the length of the Digreffion

To return to *Davis*, the next Day after he left *Anamaboe*, early in the Morning, the Man at the Maft Head efpied a Sail It muft be obferved, they keep a good Look out; for, according to their Ar-ticles, he who firft efpies a Sail, if fhe proves a Prize, is entitled to the beft Pair of Piftols on board, over and above his Dividend, in which they take a fingu-lar Pride, for a Pair of thefe honorary Piftols has fometimes been fold for thirty Pounds, from one to another

Immediately they gave Chafe, and foon came up with her, the Ship proved to be a *Hollander*, and, being betwixt *Davis* and the Shore, fhe made all the Sail fhe could, intending to run aground *Davis* guef-fed her Defign, and putting out all his fmall Sails, came up with her before fhe could effect it, and fired a Broadfide, upon which fhe immediately ftruck

and called for Quarter. It was granted; for accord-ing to *Davis*'s Articles, it was agreed, that Quar-ter fhould be given whenever it was called for, up-on Pain of Death

This Ship proved a very rich Prize, having the Governor of *Acra* on Board, with all his Effects, going to *Holland*, there was in Money to the Value of 15000 *l* Sterling, befides other valuable Merchan-dizes, all which they brought on Board of themfelves

Upon this new Succefs, they reftored Captain *Hall* and Captain *Plumb*, before-mentioned, their Ships again, but ftrengthened their Company with thirty five Hands, all white Men, taken out of thefe two and the *Morrice* Sloop, they alfo reftored the *Dutch* their Ship, after having plunder'd her, as is men-tioned

Before they got to the Ifland of *Princes*, their Ship the *King James* fprung a Leak; *Davis* order'd all Hands out of her, on Board his own Ship, with every thing elfe of Ufe, and left at an Anchor at *High Cameroon* As foon as he came in Sight of the Ifland, he hoifted *Englifh* Colours The *Portuguefe*, obferving a large Ship failing towards them, fent out a Sloop to examine what fhe might be, this Sloop hailing of *Davis*, he told them he was an *Englifh* Man of War, in queft of Pirates, and that he had received Intelligence there were fome upon that Coaft, upon this they received him as a welcome Gueft, and piloted him into the Harbour He fa-luted the Fort, which they anfwered; and he came to an Anchor juft under their Guns, and hoifted out the Pinnace, Man of War fafhion, ordering nine Hands and a Coxen into it, to row him afhore

The *Portuguefe*, to do him the greater Honour, fent down a File of Mufqueteers to receive him, and conduct him to the Governor. The Governor, not in the leaft fufpecting what he was, received him very civilly, promifing to fupply him with whatever the Ifland afforded *Davis* thanked him, telling him the King of *England* would pay for whatever he fhould take, fo, after feveral Civilities pafs'd be-tween him and the Governor, he returned again on Board

It happened that a *French* Ship came in there, to fupply it felf with fome Neceffaries, which *Davis* took into his Head to plunder, but to give the thing a Colour of Right, he perfuaded the *Portuguefe*, that fhe had been trading with the Pirates, and that he found feveral Pirates Goods on Board, which he feized for the King's Ufe This Story paffed fo well upon the Governor, that he commended *Davis* for his Diligence

A few Days after, *Davis*, with about fourteen more, went privately afhore, and walk'd up the Country towards a Village, where the Governor, and the other chief Men of the Ifland, kept their Wives Their Intent, as we may fuppofe, was to fupply their Hufbands Places with them, but being difco-vered, the Women fled to a neighbouring Wood, and *Davis* and the reft retreated to their Ship, without effecting their Defign The Thing made fome Noife, but as no body knew them, it paffed over.

Having cleaned his Ship, and put all Things in Or-der, his Thoughts now were turned upon the main Bufinefs, viz the Plunder of the Ifland Not know-ing where the Treafure lay, the following Stratagem came into his Head, to get it with a little Trouble, he confulted his Men upon it, and they liked the Defign His Scheme was, to make a Prefent to the Governor of a Dozen Negroes, by Way of Return for the Civilities received from him, and afterwards to invite him, with the chief Men of the Ifland, and fome of the Friars, on board his Ship, to an Entertainment, the Minute they came on Board, they were

were to be fecured in Irons, and there kept till they fhould pay a Ranfom of 40000 *l.* Sterling

But this Stratagem proved fatal to him, for a *Portuguefe* Negroe fwam afhore in the Night, and difcovered the whole Plot to the Governor, and alfo let him know, that it was *Davis* who had made the Attempt upon their Wives However, the Governor diffembled, received the Pirates Invitation civilly, and promifed that he and the reft would come

The next Day *Davis* went on Shore himfelf, as if it were out of greater Refpect, to bring the Governor on Board He was received with the ufual Civility, as were feveral other principal Pirates Some of thefe, by the Way, had affumed the Title of Lords, and as fuch took upon them to advife or councel their Captain, upon any important Occafion, and likewife held certain Priviledges, which the common Pirates were debarr'd from, fuch as walking the Quarter-Deck, ufing the great Cabin, going

afhore at Pleafure, and treating with foreign Powers, that is, with the Captains of Ships they made Prize of *Davis* and fome of the Lords were defired to walk up to the Governor's Houfe, to take fome Refreshment before they went on Board again; they accepted it without the leaft Sufpicion, but never returned again An Ambufcade was laid, and, a Signal being given, a whole Volley was fired upon them, they every Man dropped, except one, this one fled back, efcaped into the Boat, and got on Board the Ship *Davis* was fhot thro' the Bowels, yet he rofe again, and made a weak Effort to get away, but his Strength foon forfook him, and he dropp'd down dead Juft as he fell, he perceived he was followed, and drawing out his Piftols, he fired them at his Purfuers Thus, like a game Cock, giving a dying Blow, that he might not fall unrevenged

---

The LIFE *of Captain* BARTHO. ROBERTS.

Bartholomew Roberts failed from *London* in an honeft Employ, aboard of the *Princefs*, Capt *Plumb* Commander, of which Ship he was fecond Mate He left *England* in *November*, 1719, and arrived at *Guiney* about *February* following, when being at *Anamaboe*, taking in Slaves for the *Weft-Indies*, he was taken in the faid Ship by Capt *Howel Davis*, as mention'd in his Life In the Beginning he was very averfe to this fort of Life, and would certainly have efcaped from them, had a fair Opportunity prefented itfelf, yet afterwards he changed his Principles, as many befides him have done upon another Element, and perhaps for the fame Reafon too, *viz* Preferment ———— What he did not like as a private Man, he could reconcile to his Confcience as a Commander

Davis being cut off in the manner beforementioned, the Company found themfelves under a Neceffity or filling up his Poft, for which there appeared two or three Candidates, among the felect Part of them, that were diftinguished by the Title of LORDS, fuch were *Sympfon, Afhplant, Anftis,* &c Upon canvafing this Matter, and confidering how fhatter'd and weak a Condition their Government muft be in without a Head, fince *Davis* had been remov'd, in the manner beforemention'd, my Lord *Dennis* propos'd, 'tis faid, over a Bowl, to this Purpofe

That it was not of any great Signification who was dignify'd with the Title, fince really and in Truth, all good Governments, and among them theirs, had the fupream Power lodg'd with the Community, who might doubtlefs depute and revoke as fuited Intereft or Humour. We are the Original of this Claim (fays he) and fhould a Captain be fo fawcy as to exceed Prefcription at any Time, why down with Him! It will be a Caution after he is dead to his Succeffors, of what fatal Confequence any fort of affuming may be However, it is my Advice, that, while we are fober, we pitch upon a Man of Courage, and fkill'd in Navigation, one who, by his Council and Bravery, feems beft

able to defend this Common-wealth, and ward us from the Dangers and Tempefts of an unftable Element, and the fatal Confequence of Anarchy, and fuch one I take Roberts to be A Fellow, I think, in all Refpects, worthy your Efteem and Favour

This Speech was loudly applauded by all but Lord *Sympfon*, who had fecret Expectations himfelf, and who, on this Difappointment, grew fullen, and left them, fwearing, *he did not care who they chofe Captain, fo it was not a Papift for againft them he had conceived an irreconcileable Hatred, becaufe his Father had been a Sufferer in* Monmouth*'s Rebellion*

Roberts was accordingly elected, tho' he had not been above fix Weeks among them, the Choice was confirm'd both by the Lords and Commoners, and he accepted of the Honour with faying, *That fince he had dipp'd his Hands in muddy Water, and muft be a Pirate, it was better being a Commender than a common Man*

As foon as the Government was fettled, by promoting other Officers in the room of thofe that were kill'd by the *Portuguefe*, the Company refolve to revenge Captain *Davis*'s Death, he being more than ordinarily refpected by the Crew, for his Affability and good Nature, as well as his Conduct and Bravery upon all Occafions, and purfuant to this Refolution, about 30 Men were landed, in order to make an Attack upon the Fort, which muft be afcended to by a fteep Hill againft the Mouth of the Cannon. Thefe Men were headed by one *Kennedy*, a bold daring Fellow, but very wicked and profligate; they march'd directly up under the Fire of their Ship Guns, and as foon as they were difcover'd, the *Portuguefe* quitted their Poft and fled to the Town, upon which the Pirates march'd in without Oppofition, fet Fire to the Fort, and threw all the Guns off the Hill into the Sea, which after they had done, they retired quietly to their Ship

But this was not look'd upon as a fufficient Satisfaction

Cap.ᵗ Bartholomew Roberts

faction for the Injury they received, therefore most of the Company were for burning the Town, which *Roberts* faid he would yield to, if any means could be propofed of doing it without their own Deftruction, for the Town had a fecurer Situtation than the Fort, a thick Wood coming almoft clofe to it, and affording Cover to the Defendants, who under fuch an Advantage, he told them, it was to be fear'd, would fire and ftand better to their Arms, befides, that bare Houfes would be but a flender Reward for their trouble and Lofs This prudent Advice prevailed, however, they mounted the *French* Ship which they had feiz'd at this Place, with 12 Guns, and lighten'd her, in order to come up to the Town, the Water being fhoal, and with her they battered down feveral Houfes After this, they all returned on Board, gave back the *French* Ship to thofe that had moft Right to her, and failed out of the Harbour by the Light of two *Portuguefe* Ships which they were pleafed to fet on Fire there

Roberts ftood away to the Southward, and met with a *Dutch Guiney* Man, which he made Prize of, but after having plundered her, the Skipper had his Ship again Two Days after, he took an *English* Ship, called the *Experiment*, Captain *Cornet*, at *Cape Lopez* The Men went all into the Pirate Service, and having no Occafion for the Ship, they burnt her, and then fteered for St *Thome*, but meeting with nothing in their Way, they failed for *Anamabona*, and there watered, took in Provifions, and put it to a Vote of the Company, whether their next Voyage fhould be to the *Eaft-Indies*, or to *Brafil*, the latter being refolv'd on, they failed accordingly, and in 28 Days arrived at *Ferdinando*, an uninhabited Ifland on that Coaft Here they water'd, boot-top'd their Ship, and made ready for the defigned Cruize

Now we are upon this Coaft, we think it will be very proper to prefent our Readers with a Defcription of the Country, and fome ingenious Remarks of a Friend, which fhew how beneficial a Trade might be carried on here by our *Weft-India* Merchants, at a little Hazard.

A
DESCRIPTION
OF
BRASIL, &c.

BRASIL (a Name fignifying the holy Crofs) was difcovered for the King of *Portugal*, by *Pedro Alvarez Cabral, Anno Dom* 1501, it extends almoft from the *Æquinoctial* to 28° South The Air is temperate and cool, in comparifon of the *Weft-Indies*, from ftronger Breezes and in opener Country, which gives lefs Interruption to the Winds

The northernmoft Part of it, ftretching about 180 Leagues, is a fine fertile Country, and was taken from the *Portuguefe* by the *Dutch Weft-India* Company, *Anno* 1637, or thereabouts, but the Conquerors, as in turn where there is little or no Religion fubfifting, made fuch heavy Exactions on the *Portuguefe*, and extended fuch Cruelty to the Natives, that prepared them both to rife in a voluntary Revolt, facilitated by the *Dutch* Mifmanagement For tre States, being at this Time very intent on their *India* Settlements, not only recalled Count *Maurice* their Governor, but neglected Supplies to their Garrifons,

however, tho' the others were countenanced with a Fleet from *Portugal*, and had the Affection of the Natives, yet they found Means to withftand and ftruggle with this fuperior Power, from 1643, to 1660, and then was wholly abandoned by them, on Articles difhonourable to the *Portuguefe*, viz

That the *Dutch*, on Relinquifhing, fhould keep all the Places they had conquered in *India* from *Portugal* That the *Portuguefe* fhould pay the States 800000 *l* and permit them ftill the Liberty of Trade to *Africa* and *Brafil*, on the fame Cuftoms and Duties with the King of *Portugal*'s Subjects But fince that Time, new Stipulations and Treaties have been made, wherein the *Dutch*, who have been totally excluded the *Brafil* Trade, have, in lieu thereof, a Compofition of 10 *per Cent* for the Liberty of trading to *Africa*, and this is always left by every *Portuguefe* Ship, before fhe begins her Slaving, with the *Dutch* General of the *Gold-Coaft*, at *Des Minas*

There are only three principal Towns of Trade on the *Brafil* Coaft, St *Salvadore*, St *Sebaftian*, and *Pernambuca*

St *Salvadore*, in the *Bahia los todos Santos*, is an Archbifhoprick and Seat of the Viceroy, the chief Port of Trade for Importation, where moft of the Gold from the Mines is lodged, and whence the Fleets for *Europe* generally depart The Seas about it abound with Whale-Fifh, which in the Seafon they catch in great Numbers, the Flefh is falted up generally to be the Victualling of their Slave Ships, and the Train referved for Exportation, at 30 and 35 Millrays a Pipe

Rio Janeiro, or the Town St *Sebaftian*, is the Southernmoft of the *Portuguefe* Ports, and the worft provided of Neceffaries, but commodious for a Settlement, becaufe nigh the Mine, and convenient to fupert the Slaves, who, as we have been told, do ufual, allow their Mafter a Dollar *per Diem*, and have the Overplus of their Work to themfelves

The Gold from hence is efteemed the beft, it being of a coppery Colour, and they have a Mint to run it into Coin, both here and at *Bahia*, the Moidores of either having the initial Letters of each Place upon them

Pernambuca, though mention'd laft, is the fecond in Dignity, a large and populous Town, and has its rife from the Ruins of *Olinda*, or *The Handfome*, a City of a far pleafanter Situation, fix Miles up the River, but not fo commodious for Traffick and Commerce Juft above the Town the River divides it felf into two Branches, not running directly into the Sea, but to the Southward, and in the Nook of the Ifland made by that Divifion, ftands the Governor's Houfe, a fquare plain Building of Count *Maurice*'s, with two Towers, on which are only this Date infcribed, *Anno* 1641 The Avenues to it are every pleafant, through Vifto's of tall Coco Nut Trees

Over each Branch of the River is a Bridge, that leading to the Country is all of Timber, but the other to the Town, confifting twenty fix or twenty eight Arches, is half of Stone, and made by the *Dutch*, who in their Time had little Shops and gaming Houfes on each Side for Recreation

The Pavements alfo of the Town are in fome Places of broad Tiles, the remaining Fragments of their Conqueft The Town has the outer Branch of the River behind it, and the Harbour before it, jetting into which latter are clofe Keys, for the weighing and receiving of Cuftomage on Merchandize, and for the meeting and conferring of Merchants and traders The Houfes are ftrong built, but hourely latticed, like thofe of *Lifbon*, for the Admiffion of Air, without Clofets, and, what is

worfe,

47   3

worse, without Hearths, which makes their Cookery confist all in frying and stewing upon Stoves, and that they do till the Flesh becomes tender enough to shake it to Pieces, when one Knife is thought sufficient to serve a Table of half a Score

The greatest Inconvenience of *Pernambuca*, is, that there is not one Publick-House in it, so that Strangers are obliged to hire any ordinary one they can get, at a Guinea a Month And others, who come to transact Affairs of Importance, must come recommended, if it were only for the sake of Privacy

The Market is stocked well enough, Beef being at five Farthings *per lb* a Sheep or a Goat at nine Shillings, a Turkey at four Shillings, and very large Fowls at two Shillings a-Piece These may be procured much cheaper, by hiring a Man to fetch them out of the Country The dearest in its kind is Water, which being fetched in Vessels from *Olinda*, will not be put on Board in the Road under two Crusado's a Pipe

The *Portuguese* here are darker than those of *Europe*, not only from a warmer Climate, but their many Intermarriages with the Negroes, who are numerous there, and some of them of good Credit and Circumstances The Women here, like the Mulatto Generation every where else, are fond of Strangers, not only the Courtezans, whose Interest may be supposed to wind up their Affections, but also the married Women, who think themselves obliged, when you favour them with the Secrecy of an Appointment, but the Unhappiness of pursuing Amours, is, that the generality of both Sexes are touched with venereal Taints, without so much as one Surgeon among them, or any Body skilled in Physick, to cure or palliate the progressive Mischief The only Person pretending that Way, a few Years ago, was an *Irish* Father, whose Knowledge was all comprehended in the Virtues of two or three Simples, and those, with the Salubrity of the Air and Temperance, is what they depend on, for subduing the worst of Malignity It may not be unworthy of Notice, that, tho' few are exempted from the Misfortune of a Running, Eruptions, or the like, yet few or none are precipitated into those deplorable Circumstances so common in unskilful mercurial Processes

There are three Monasteries, and about six Churches, none of them Rich or Magnificent, unless one dedicated to St *Antonio*, the Patron of their Kingdom, which shines all over with exquisite Pieces of Paint and Gold

The Export of *Brasil*, besides Gold, is chiefly Sugars and Tobacco, the latter are sent off in Rolls of a Quintal Weight, kept continually moistened with Molosses, which, with the Soil it springs from, imparts a strong and peculiar Scent, more sensible in the Snuff made from it, which, tho' under Prohibition of importing to *Lisbon*, sells here at 2 s *per lb* as the Tobacco does at about 6 Milreas a Roll The finest of their Sugars sells at 8 s *per* Roove, and a small ill tasted Rum, drawn from the Dregs, and Molosses, at two Testunes a Galon

Besides these, they send off great Quantities of Brasil Wood, and Whale Oyl, with some Gums and Parrots, the latter are different from the *African* in Colour and Bigness, for as they are blue and larger, these are green and smaller, and the Females of them ever retain the wild Note, and cannot be brought to Talk

In lieu of this Produce, the *Portuguese*, once every Year by their Fleet from *Lisbon*, import all manner of European Commodities, and whoever is unable to lay in Store, or neglect of supplying himself at that Season, buys at a very advanced Rate before the Return of another

To transport Passengers, Slaves, or Merchandize, from one Settlement to another, or in fishing, they make use of Bark-Logs, by the *Brasilians* called *Jingadahs* They are made of four Pieces of Timber, the two outermost being the longest, pinned and fastened together, and shrupened at the Ends Towards each Extremity a Stool is fix'd, to sit on for paddling, or to hold by, when the Agitation is more than Ordinary, with these odd sort of Engines, continually washed over by the Water, do these People, with a little triangular Sail spreeted about the Middle of it, venture out of sight of Land, and along the Coast for many Leagues, in any sort of Weather, and if they overset with a Squall, which is not uncommon, they swim and presently turn it upright again

The Natives are of the darkest Copper Colour, with thin Hair, of a square strong make, and muscular, but not so well looking as the Wooley Generation They acquiesce patiently to the *Portuguese* Government, who use them much more humanly and Christian-like than the *Dutch* did, and by that means have extended Quietness and Peace, as well as their Possessions, three or 400 Miles into the Country A Country abounding with fine Pastures and numerous Herds of Cattle, and which yields a vast Increase from every Thing that is sown Hence they bring down to us Parrots, small Monkeys, Armadillos and Sanguins, and we have been assured, they have, in the inland Parts, a Serpent of a vast Magnitude, called *Siboya*, able they say, to swallow a whole Sheep, several have seen the Skin of another Specie full six Yards long, and therefore we think the Story not improbable

The Harbour of *Pernambuca* is perhaps singular, it is made of a Ledge of Rocks, half a Cables Length from the Main, and but little above the Surface of the Water, running at that equal Distance and Height several Leagues, towards Cape *Augustine*, a Harbour running between them, capable of receiving Ships of the greatest Burthen The Northern End of this Wall of Rock, is higher than any Part of the contiguous Line, on this a little Fort is built commanding the Passage either of Boat or Ship, as they come over the Bar into the Harbour On the Starboard Side, or the Side towards the Main, after you have entered a little Way, stands another Fort, which is a Pentagon, that would prove of small account, I imagine, against a few disciplined Men, and yet in these consist all their Strength and Security, either in the Harbour or Town They have besides indeed a Wall, once their removing from Olinda, designed to surround the latter, but the slow and great difficulty in making it, leaves room to it respect it will be a long Time a finishing

The Road without is used by the *Portuguese* when they are nigh sailing for *Europe* and wait for the Convoy, or are bound to *Bonia* or *Rio*, and by Strangers only when Necessity compels them, for of it is in ten Fathom Water, from the Main to N W from the Town, nigher it is foul with the many Anchors lost there by the *Portuguese* Ships, and rides out in about 14 Fathom It is coming on Pocky *July* is the worst and Winter Season on this Coast, the Trade Winds being then very strong and dense, hanging in a prodigious and terrible Swell to the Road, intermixed every Day with Squalls, Rain, and a heavy Horizon, but at other times terrible Skies and Sunshine

In these Southern Latitudes is a Constellation, which, from some Resemblance it bears to a *Jerusalem* Cross has the name of *Crosiers*, the brightest of this Hemisphere m fphere, and Obfervations are taken by it, as by the North Star in Northern Latitudes. What we mention this for, is to introduce the admirable Phænomenon in thefe Seas of the Magellanick Clouds, whofe Rifings and Sittings are fo regular, that, we have been affured, the fame Nocturnal Obfervations are made by them as by the Stars They are two Clouds, fmall and whitifh, no larger in Appearance than a Man's Hat, and are feen here in *July* in the Latitude of 58 S about four of the Clock in the Morning, if their Appearance fhould be faid to be the Reflection of Light, from fome Stellary Bodies above them, yet the Difficulty is not eafily anfwered, how thefe, beyond others, become fo durable and regular in their Motions

From thefe cafual Obfervations on the Country, the Towns, Coaft, and Seas of *Brafil*, it would be an Omiffion to leave the Subject, without fome Effay or an interloping Slave Trade here, which none of our Countrymen are adventrous enough to purfue, though very probably, under a prudent Manager, it would be attended with Safety and very great Profit, and I admire the more it is not ftruck at, becaufe Ships from the Southern Coaft of *Africa*, lengthen the Voyage to the *Weft-Indies* but a very little, by taking a Part of *Brafil* in their Way

The Difadvantages the *Portuguefe* are under for purchafing Slaves, are thefe, that they have very few proper Commodities for *Guiney*, and the Gold, which was their chiefeft, by an Edict in *July* 1722, ftands now prohibited from being carried thither, fo that the Ships employed therein are few, and infufficient for the great Mortality and Call of their Mines befides, would they venture at breaking fo deftructive a Law as the abovementioned (as no doubt they do, or they could make little or no Purchafe) yet Gold does not raife its Value like Merchandize in travelling, efpecially to *Africa*, and when the Compofition with the *Dutch* is alfo paid, they may be faid to buy their Negroes at almoft double the Price that the *Englifh Dutch*, or *French* do, which neceffarily raifes their Value extravagantly at *Brafil*, thofe who can purchafe one, buying a certainer Annuity than *South-Sea* Stock.

Thus far of the Call for Slaves at *Brafil*, I fhall now confider and obviate fome Difficulties objected againft any Foreigners, *Englifh* or others, interpofing in fuch a Trade, and they are fome on theirs, and fome on our Side

On their Side it is prohibited under Pain of Death, a Law lefs effectual to the Prevention of it than pecuniary Mulcts would be, becaufe a Penalty fo inadequate and difproportioned is only *In terrorem*, and makes it merciful in the Governor, or his Inftruments, to take a Compofition of eight or ten Moidores, when any Subject is catched, and 'tis the common Cuftom fo to do as often as they are found out

On our Side it is Confifcation of what they can get, which, confidering they have no Men of War to guard the Coaft, need be very little, without fupine Neglect or Careleffnefs

Suppofe me a Man of War, or Privateer, and that, being in want or Provifions, or in Search of Pirates, I put into *Pernambuca* for Intelligence, to enable me to the Purfuit The Dread of Pirates keeps every one off, till you have firft fent an Officer with the proper Compliments to the Governor, who immediately gives Leave for your buying every Neceffary you ftand in want of, provided it be with Money, and not in Exchange of Merchandize, which is againft the Laws of the Country

On this firft time of going on Shore depends the Succefs of the whole Affair, and it requires a cau-

t ous and difcreet Management in the Perfon entrufted He will be immediately furrounded at landing with the great and the fmall Rabble, to enquire who he is, and whence he comes? and whither bound, &c And the Men are taught to anfwer, from *Guiney*, denying any thing of a Slave on Board, they being put under Hatches, that they may make no Snew, nor need they, for thofe who have Money to lay out will conclude on that themfelves

By that time the Compliment is paid to the Governor, the News has fpread all round the Town, and fome Merchant addreffes you as a Stranger, and offers you the Civility of his Houfe, but privately defires to know what Negroes he can have, and at what Price A Governor may poffibly ufe an Inftrument in fifting this, but the Appearance of the Gentleman, and the Circumftance of being fo foon engaged after leaving the other, will go a great way in forming a Man's Judgment, and leaves him no room for the Sufpicion of fuch a Snare, to have a due Guard, Infinuations will fuffice, and bring him Friends enough to carry off the beft Part of a Cargo in two Nights time, from 20 to 30 Moidors a Boy, and from 30 to 40 a Man Slave The Hazard is lefs at *Rio Janeiro*

There has been another Method attempted, of fettling a Correfpondence with a *Portuguefe* Merchant or two, who, as they may be certain with in a Fortnight of any Veffels arriving on their Coaft with Slaves, might fettle Signals for the debarquing them at an unfrequented Part of the Coaft, but whether any Exceptions were made to the Price, or that the *Portuguefe* dread Difcovery, and the fevere Profecution in fo notorious a Breach of the Law, we cannot tell, but it has hitherto proved abortive

However, Stratagems fo landable, and attended with fo much Profit, at no other Hazard than lofs of Time, are worth attempting, it is what is every Day practifed with the *Spaniards* from *Jamaica*

Upon this Coaft our Rovers cruiz'd for about nine Weeks, keeping generally out of Sight of Land, but without feeing a Sail, which difcouraged them fo, that they determined to leave the Station, and fteer for the *Weft-Indies*, and, in order thereto, they ftood in to make the Land for the taking of their Departure, by which means they fell in, unexpectedly, with a Fleet of the Sail of *Portuguefe* Ships, off the Bay of *de todos Santos*, with all their Lading in for *Lisbon*, feveral of them of good Force, who lay there waiting for two Men of War of 70 Guns each for their Convoy However, *Roberts* thought it fhould go hard with him but he would make up his Market among them, and thereupon he mix'd with the Fleet, and after his After had took proper Refolutions could be form'd, that done, they came clofe up to one of the deepeft, and ordered her to fend the Mafter on board quietly, thretning to give them no Quarters, if any Refiftance, or Signal of Diftrefs was made The *Portuguefe*, being furprized at thefe Threats, and the fudden flourifh of Cutlaffes from the Pirates, fubmitted without a Word, and the Captain came on Board Roberts faluted him after a friendly manner, telling him, that they were Gentlemen of Fortune, and that their Bufinefs with him, was only to be informed which was the richeft Ship in that Fleet, and if he directed them aright, he fhould be reftored to his Ship without any Diminution, otherwise, he muft expect immediate Death

whereupon this *Portuguefe* Mafter pointed to one of 40 Guns, and 150 Men, a Ship of greater force than the *Rover*, but this no Ways difmayed them, They were only Portuguefe, they faid, and fo immediately fteered away for him When they came within Hail,

Hail, the Mafter whom they had Prifoner was ordered to afk, *How Signior Captain did?* And to invite him on Board, *for that he had a Matter of Confequence to impart to him*, which being done, he returned for Anfwer, *That he would wait upon him prefently* But by the Buftle that immediately followed, the Pirates perceived, they were difcovered, and that this was only a deceitful Anfwer to gain Time, to put their Ship in a Pofture of Defence, fo, without further Delay, they poured in a Broad-Side, boarded and grapled her The Difpute was fhort and warm, wherein many of the *Portuguefe* fell, and two only of the Pirates By this Time the Fleet was alarmed, Signals of Top-gallant Sheets flying, and Guns fired, to give Notice to the Men of War, who rid ftill at an Anchor, and made but fcurvy haft out to their Affiftance, and, if what the Pirates themfelves related be true, the Commanders of thofe Ships we e blameable to the higheft Degree, utterly unworthy their Title, or fo much as the Name of Men For *Roberts*, finding the Prize to fail heavy, and yet refolving not to lofe her, lay by for the headmoft of them, which much out failed the other, and prepared for Battle, which was igromimoufly declined, tho' the *Portuguefe* was of fuch fuperior Force, for not daring to venture on the Pirate alone, he tarried fo long for his Confort, that he gave them both time to make off leifurely

They found this Ship exceeding rich, being laden chiefly with Sugar, Skins, and Tobacco, and 4000 Moidors in Gold; befides Chains and Trinckets, of confiderable Value, particularly a Crofs fet with Diamonds, defigned for the King of *Portugal*, which they afterwards prefented to the Governor of *Caiana*, by whom they were obliged

Elated with this Booty, they had nothing now to think of but fome fafe Retreat, where they might give themfelves up to all the Pleafures that Luxury and Wantonnefs could beftow, and for the prefent they pitch'd upon a Place called the *Devil's Iflands*, in the River of *Surinam*, on the Coaft of *Caiana*, where they arrived, and found the civileft Reception imaginable, not only from the Governor and Factory, but their Wives, who exchanged Wares, and drove a confiderable Trade with them

They feiz'd a Sloop in this River, and by her gained Intelligence, that a Brigantine had alfo failed in Company with her, from *Rhode-Ifland*, laden with Provifions for the Coaft A Welcome Cargo! They growing fhort in the Sea Store, and as *Sancho* fays, *No Adventures to be made without Belly-Timber* One Evening as they were rumaging their Mine of Treafure the *Portuguefe* Prize, this expected Veffel was defcry'd at Maft-Head, and *Roberts*, imagining no Body could do the Bufinefs as well as himfelf, takes 40 Men in the Sloop, and goes in purfuit of her, but a fatal Accident followed this rafh, tho' inconfiderable Adventure, for *Roberts*, thinking of nothing lefs than bringing in the Brigantine that Afternoon, never troubled his head about the Sloop's Provifion, nor inquired what there was on Board to fubfift fuch a Number of Men Out he fails after his expected Prize, which he not only loft further Sight of, but after eight Days contending with contrary Winds and Currents, found they were thirty Leagues to Leeward The Current ftill oppofing their Endeavours, and perceiving no Hopes of beating up to their Snip, they came to an Anchor, and inconfiderately fent away the Boat, to give the reft of the Company Notice of their Condition, and to order the Ship to them, but too foon, even the next Day, their Wants made them fenfible of their Infatuation, for their Water was all expended, and they had taken no thought how they fhould be fupply'd, till either the Ship came, or

the Boat returned, neither of which was likely to be under five or fix Days Here, like *Tantalus*, they almoft famifhed in Sight of the frefh Streams and Lakes, being drove to fuch Extremity at laft, that they were forc'd to tare up the Floor of the Cabin, and patch up a fort of Tub or Tray with Rope Yarn, to paddle afhore, and fetch off immediate Supplies of Water to preferve Life

After fome Days, the long-wifh'd-for Boat came back, but with the moft unwelcome News in the World, for *Kennedy*, who was Lieutenant, and left in Abfence of *Roberts*, to command the Privateer and Prize, was gone off with both This was Mortification with a Vengeance, and, you may imagine, they did not depart without fome laid Speeches from thofe that were left, and had fuffered by their Treachery That there may need no further mention of this *Kennedy*, I fhall leave Captain *Roberts*, for a Page or two, with the Remains of his Crew, to vent their Wrath in a few Oaths and Execrations, and follow the other, whom me in my reckon, from that Time, as fteering his Courfe towards *Execution Dock*

Kennedy was now chofen Captain of the remaining Crew, but could not bring his Company to any determined Refolution, fome of them were for purfuing the old Game, but the greater part of them feem'd to have Inclinations to turn from thofe evil Courfes, and get home privately, there being now no Act of Pardon in Force, therefore they agreed to break up, and every Man to fhift for himfelf, as he fhould fee Occafion The firft Thing they did, was to part with the great *Portuguefe* Prize, having the Mafter of the Sloop, whofe Name was *Cane*, aboard, who they faid was a very honeft Fellow, for he had humoured them upon every Occafion, and told them of the Brigantine that *Roberts* went after This *Cane*, when the Pirates firft took him, complimented them at an odd Rate, telling them they were welcome to his Sloop and Cargo, and wifh'd that the Veffel had been larger, and the Loading richer, for their Sakes To this good natured Man they gave the *Portuguefe* Ship, which was then above half loaded, three or four Negroes, and all his own Men, for which he returned Thanks to his kind Benefactors, and departed

Captain *Kennedy*, in the *Rover*, failed to *Barbadoes*, near which Ifland they took a very peaceable Ship belonging to *Virginia*, the Commander was a Quaker, whofe Name was *Knot*, he had neither Piftol, Sword, nor Cutlafh on Board Mr *Knot* appearing fo very paffive to all they faid to him, fome of them thought this a good Opportunity to go off, accordingly eight of the Pirates went aboard, and were carried fafe to *Virginia* They made the Quaker a Prefent of 10 Chefts of Sugar, 10 Rolls of Brafil Tobacco, 30 Moidores, and fome Gold Duft, all to the value of about 250 *l* They alfo made Prefents to the Sailors, fome more, fon e lefs, and lived a jovial Life all the while they were upon their Voyage, Captain *Knot* giving them their Way, nor in deed could he help himfelf, unlefs he had taken an Opportunity to furprize them, when they were either drunk or afleep, for awake they wore Arms aboard the Ship, and put him in a continual Terror it not being his Principle to fight, unlefs with Art and Colufion However, he managed thefe Weapons well till he arrived at the Capes, after which four of the Pirates went off in a Boat, which they had taken with them, for the more eafily making their Efcape, and made up the Bay towards *Maryland*, but were forced back by a Storm into an obfcure Place of the Country Here meeting with good Entertainment among the Planters, they continued feveral Days without being difcovered to be Pirates. In the mean Tim

Time Captain *Knot*, leaving four others on Board his Ship, who intended to go to *North-Carolina*, made while he could to discover to Mr *Spotswood* the Governor, what sort of Passengers he had been forced to bring with him. The Governor, by good Fortune, got them seized, and Search being made after the others, who were revelling about the Country, they were also taken, and all try'd, convicted and hang'd. Two *Portuguese* Jews, who were taken on the Coast of *Brasil*, and whom they brought with them to *Virginia*, were the principal Evidences. The latter had found Means to lodge Part of their Wealth with the Planters, who never brought it to Account. But Captain *Knot* surrendered up every Thing that belonged to them that were taken aboard, even what they presented to him, in Lieu of such Things as they had plundered him of in their Passage, and obliged his Men to do the like.

Some Days after the taking of the *Virginia* Man left mentioned, in cruising the Latitude of *Jamaica*, *Kennedy* took a Sloop bound thither from *Boston*, loaded with Bread and Flower, aboard of this Sloop went all the Hands who were for breaking the Gang, and left those behind that had a Mind to pursue further Adventures. Among the former were *Kennedy*, their Captain, of whose Honour they had such a despicable Notion, that they were about to throw him over-board, when they found him in the Sloop, as fearing he might betray them all, at their return to *England*, he having in his Childhood been bred a Pick-pocket, and before he became a Pirate, a House breaker, both which are Professions that these Gentlemen have a very mean Opinion of. However, Captain *Kennedy*, by taking solemn Oaths of Fidelity to his Companions, was suffered to proceed with them.

In this Company there was but one that pretended to any Skill in Navigation, for *Kennedy* could neither write nor read, he being preferred to the Command merely for his Courage, which indeed he had often signaliz'd, particularly in taking the *Portuguese* Ship. This Man proved to be a Pretender only for, shaping their Course to *Ireland*, where they agreed to land, they ran away to the North West Coast of *Scotland*, and there were tost about by hard Storms of Wind for several Days, without knowing where they were, and in great Danger of perishing. At length they pushed the Vessel into a little Creek, and went all ashore, leaving the Sloop at an Anchor for the next Comers.

The whole Company refreshed themselves at a little Village, about five Miles from the Place where they left the Sloop, and passed there for ship-wreck'd Sailors, nor is there any doubt but they might have travelled on without Suspicion, but the mad and riotous Manner of their Living on the Road occasioned their Journey to be cut short, as we shall observe presently.

Kennedy and another left them here, and, travelling to one of the Sea-Ports, ship'd themselves for *Ireland*, and arrived there in Safety, Six or seven wilfully withdrew from the rest, travelled at their leisure, and got to their much desired Port of *London*, without being disturbed or suspected, but the main Gang alarm'd the Country wherever they came, drinking and roaring at such a Rate, that the People shut themselves up in their Houses in some Places, not daring to venture out among so many mad Fellows. In other Villages they treated the whole Town, squandering their Money away, as if, like *Æsop*, they wanted to lighten their Burthens. This expensive manner of Living procured two of their drunken Stragglers to be knock'd on the Head, they being found murdered on the Road, and their Money

taken from them. All the rest, to the Number of seventeen, as they drew nigh to *Edinburgh*, were arrested and thrown into Goal, upon Suspicion of they knew not what. However, the Magistrates were not long at a loss for proper Accusations for two of the Gang offering themselves for Evidences, they were accepted of; and the others were brought to a speedy Tryal, at which nine were convicted and executed.

Kennedy having spent all his Money, came over from *Ireland*, and kept a common Bawdy-House on *Deptford* Road, and now and then, 'twas thought, made an Excursion abroad in the Way of his former Profession, till one of his Houshold Whores gave Information against him of a Robbery, for which he was committed to *Bridewell*. But because she would not do the Business by halves, she found out a Mate of a Ship that *Kennedy* had committed Piracy upon, as he foolishly confessed to her. This Mate, whose Name was *Grant*, paid *Kennedy* a Visit in *Bridewell*, and, knowing him to be the Man, procured a Warrant, and had him committed to the *Marshalsea* Prison.

The Game that *Kennedy* had now to play, was to turn Evidence himself, according'y he gave a List of eight or ten of his Comrade, but not being acquainted with their Habitations, one only was taken, who, tho' condemn'd, appeared to be a Man of a fair Character, was forced into their Service, and took the first Opportunity to get from them, and therefore receiv'd a Pardon, but *Walter Kennedy*, being a notorious Offender, was executed the 19th of *July*, 1721, at Execution Dock.

The rest of the Pirates who were left in the Ship *Rover*, staid not long behind, for they went ashore to one of the *West-India* Islands, what became of them afterwards, we can't tell, but the Ship was found at Sea by a Sloop belonging to St *Christophers*, and carried into that Island with only nine Negroes aboard.

Thus we see what a disastrous Fate ever attends the Wicked, and how rarely they escape the Punishment due to their Crimes, who, abandon'd to such a profligate Life, rob, spoil, and prey upon Mankind, contrary to the Light and Law of Nature, as well as the positive Command of God. It might have been hoped, that the Examples of these Deaths, would have been as Marks to the Remainder of this Gang, how to shun the Rocks their Companions had split on, and that they would have surrendered to Mercy, or diverted themselves for ever from such Pursuits, lest in the End they might be subjected to the same Law and Punishment, which they must be conscious they now equally deserved, *an impending Law*, which never can let them sleep soundly unless when they are drunk. But all the Use that was made of it here, was to commend the Justice of the Court that condemn'd *Kennedy*, *for he was a sad Dog* (they said) *and deserved the Fate he met with*.

But to go back to *Roberts*, whom we left on the Coast of *Guiana*, in a grievous Passion at what *Kennedy* and the Crew had done, and who was now projecting new Adventures with his small Company in the Sloop. Considering how that hitherto they had been but as a Rope of Sand, they formed a set of Articles, to be signed and sworn to, for the better Conservation of their Society, and doing Justice to one another, excluding all *Lopp Men* from the Benefit of it, to whom they had an implacable Aversion upon the Account of *Kennedy*. How indeed *Roberts* could think that an Oath would be obligatory where Defiance had been given to the Laws of God and Man, I can't tell, but he thought their greatest Security lay in this, *That it was every one's Interest* to obferve the Articles, if they were minded to keep up fo abominable a Combination.

The following is the Subftance of the Articles, as taken from the Pirates own Informations

I.

EVERY Man has a Vote in Affairs of Moment, and an equal Title to the frefh Provifions, or ftrong Liquors, at any Time feized, which he may ufe at Pleafure, unlefs a Scarcity make it neceffary, for the good of all, to vote a Retrenchment

II.

Arother Particular was, that every Man fhould be called fairly in turn, by Lift, on Board of Prizes, becaufe, over and above their proper Share, they were on thefe Occafions allowed a Shift of Cloaths But if they defrauded the Company to the Value of a Dollar, in Plate, Jewels, or Money, MAROONING was their Punifhment (This was a barbarous Cuftom of putting the Offender on Shore, on fome defolate or uninhabited Cape or Ifland, with a Gun, a few Shot, a Bottle of Water, and a Bottle of Powder, to fubfift with, or ftarve) If the Robbery was only between one another, they contented themfelves with flitting the Ears and Nofe of him that was Guilty, and fet him on Shore, not in an uninhabited Place, but fomewhere, where he was fure to encounter Hardfhips.

III.

No Perfon to game at Cards or Dice for Money

IV

The Lights and Candles to be put out at eight o'Clock at Night If any of the Crew, after that Hour, ftill remained inclined for Drinking, they were to do it on the open Deck This Roberts believed would give a Check to their Debauches, for he was a fober Man himfelf, but he found at length, that all his Endeavours to put an End to this Debauch, proved ineffectual.

V

To keep their Piece, Piftols, and Cutlafs clean, and fit for Service In this they were extravagantly nice, endeavouring to out do one another in the Beauty and Richnefs of their Arms, giving fometimes at an Auction made at the Maft, 30 or 40 l a Pair, for Piftols Thefe were flung in Time of Service, with different coloured Ribbands, over their Shoulders, in a Way peculiar to thefe Fellows, in which they took great Delight.

VI

No Boy or Woman to be allowed amongft them If any Man were found feducing any of the latter Sex, and carried her to Sea, difguifed, he was to fuffer Death So that when any fell into their Hands, as it chanced in the Onflow, they put a Centinal immediately over her, to prevent ill Confequences from fo dangerous an Inftrument of Divifion and Quarrel, but then here lies the Roguery, they contend who fhall be Centinel, which happens generally to one of the greateft Bullies, who, to fecure the Lady's Virtue, will let none lie with her but himfelf

VII.

To defert the Ship, or their Quarters in Battle, was punifhed with Death, or Marooning

VIII

No ftriking one another on Board, but every Man's Quarrels to be ended on Shore, at Sword and Piftol, Thus The Quarter-Mafter of the Ship, when the Parties will not come to any Reconciliation, accompanies them on Shore with what Affiftance he thinks proper, and turns the Difputants Back to Back, at fo many Paces Diftance At the Word of Command, they turn and fire immediately, or elfe the Piece is knocked out of their Hands If both mifs, they come to their Cutlafhes, and then he is declared Victor who draws the firft Blood

IX.

No Man to talk of breaking up their Way of Living, till each had fhared 1000 l If in order to this, any Man fhould lofe a Limb, or become a Cripple in their Service, he was to have 800 Dollars, out of the publick Stock, and for leffer Hurts proportionably

X

The Captain and Quarter-Mafter to receive two Shares of a Prize, the Mafter, Boatfwain, and Gunner, one Share and a half, and other Officers one and a Quarter

XI

The Muficians to have Reft on the Sabbath Day, but the other fix Days and Nights, none, without fpecial Favour

Thefe, we are affured, were fome of Roberts Articles, but as they had taken Care to throw over board the Original they had figned and fworn to, there is a great deal of Room to fufpect, that the Remainder contained fomething too horrid to be difclofed to any, except fuch as were willing to be Sharers in the Iniquity of them, let them be what they will, they were together the Teft of all new Comers, who were initiated by an Oath taken on a Bible, referv'd for that Purpofe only, and were fubfcrib'd to in Prefence of the Worfhipful Mr Roberts And in Cafe any Doubt fhould arife concerning the Conftruction of thefe Laws, and it fhould remain Difpute whether the Party had infring'd them or no, a Jury was appointed to explain them, and bring in a Verdict upon the Cafe in Doubt

Since we are now fpeaking of the Laws of this Company, I fhall go on, and, in as brief a Manner as I can, relate the princial Cuftoms, and Government, of this roguifh Common Wealth, which are pretty near the fame with all Pyrates

For the Punifhment of fmall Offences, which are not provided for by the Articles, and which are not of Confequence enough to be left to a Jury of the Mens own chufing, the Quarter-Mafter, who is a princial Officer among the Pyrates, claims all Authority this Way, excepting in Time of Battle If they difobey his Command, are quarrelfome and mutinous with one another, mifufe Prifoners plunder beyond his Order, and, in particular, if they be negligent of their Arms, which he mufters at Difcretion, he punifhes at his own Arbitrement, with a drubbing or whipping, which no one elfe dare do
w hout

without incurring the Lash from all the Ships Company In short, this Officer is Trustee for the whole, is the first on Board any Prize, separating for the Company's Use what he pleases, and returning what he thinks fit to the Owners, excepting Gold and Silver, which they have voted not returnable

After a Description of the Quarter-Master, and his Duty, who acts as a sort of a civil Magistrate on Board a Pirate Ship, we shall consider their military Officer, the Captain, and what Privileges and Powers he exerts in such anarchy and unruliness of the Members Why truly very little, they only permit him to be Captain, on Condition that they may be Captain over him, they seperate to his Use the great Cabin, and sometimes vote him small Parcels of Plate and China, (for it may be noted that *Roberts* drank his Tea constantly) but then every Man, as the Humour takes him, will use the Plate and China, intrude into his Apartment, swear at him, seize a Part of his Victuals and Drink, if they like it, without his offering to find Fault or contest it Yet *Roberts*, by a better Management than usual, became the chief Director in every Thing of Moment, and it happened thus ——— The Rank of Captain being obtained by the Suffrage of the Majority, it falls on one superior for Knowledge and Boldness, who is *Pistol Proof*, as they call it, and can make those fear, who do not love him, *Roberts* is said to have exceeded his Fellows in these Respects, and when he was advanced, he enlarged the Respect that followed it, by making a sort of Privy-Council of half a Dozen of the greatest Bullies, such as were his Competitors, and had Interest enough to make his Government easy, yet even these, in the latter Part of his Reign, he had run counter to in every Project that opposed his own Opinion, for which, and because he grew reserved, and would not drink and roar at their Rate, a Cabal was formed to take away his Captainship, which Death did more effectually

The Captain's Power is uncontrolle in Time of Chace, or in Battle, when he drubs, cuts, or even shoots any one who dares deny his Command The same Privilege he takes over Prisoners, who receive good or ill Usage, mostly as he approves of their Behaviour, for tho' the meanest would take upon them to misuse a Master of a Ship, yet *Roberts* would controul herein, when he saw it, and merrily, over a Bottle, give his Prisoners this double Reason for it First, That it preserved his Precedence, and secondly, That it took the Punishment out of the Hands of a much more rash and mad Set of Fellows than himself When he found that Rigour was not expected from his People, (for he often practised it to appease them,) then he would give Strangers to understand, that it was pure Inclination that induced him to a good Treatment of them, and not any Love or Partiality to their Persons, for, says he, *there is none of you but will hang me, I know, whenever you can clinch me within your Power*

And now, seeing the Disadvantages they were under for pursuing the Account, viz. a small Vessel ill repaired, and without Provisions or Stores, they resolved one and all, with the little Supplies they could get, to proceed for the *West-Indies*, not doubting to find a Remedy for all these Evils, and to retrieve their Loss

In the Latitude of *Deseada*, one of the Islands, they took two Sloops, which supply'd them with Provisions and other Necessaries, and a few Days afterwards, took a Brigantine belonging to *Rhode Island*, and then proceeded to *Barbadoes*; off of which Island, they fell in with a *Bristol* Ship of 10 Guns in

her Voyage out, from whom they took abundance of Cloaths, some Money, twenty five Bales of Goods, five Barrels of Powder, a Cable, Hawser, 10 Casks of Oatmeal, six Casks of Beef, and several other Goods, besides five of her Men; and after they had detained her three Days, let her go This Vessel being bound for the abovesaid Island, she acquainted the Governor with what had happened, as soon as she arrived

Upon this, a *Bristol* Galley that lay in the Harbour, was ordered to be fitted out with all imaginable Expedition, with 20 Guns, and 80 Men, there being then no Man of War upon that Station, and also a Sloop with 10 Guns, and 40 Men The Galley was commanded by one Captain *Rogers*, of *Bristol*, and the Sloop by Captain *Graves*, of that Island, and Captain *Rogers*, by a Commission from the Governor, was appointed Commodore

The second Day after *Rogers* sailed out of the Harbour, he was discovered by *Roberts*, who, knowing nothing of their Design, gave them Chace The *Barbadoes* Ships kept an an easy sail till the Pirates came up with them, and then *Roberts* gave them a Gun, expecting they would have immediately struck to his piratical Flag, but instead thereof, he was forced to receive the Fire of a Broadside, with three Huzzas at the same Time An Engagement ensued, in which *Roberts*, being hardly put to it, was obliged to crowd all the Sail the Sloop would bear, to get off The Galley sailing pretty well, kept Company for a long while, keeping a constant Fire, which galled the Pirate, however, at length, by throwing over their Guns, and other heavy Goods, and thereby lightening the Vessel, they, with much ado, got clear, but *Roberts* could never endure a *Barbadoes* Man afterwards, and when any Ships belonging to that Island fell in his Way, he was more particularly severe to them than others

Captain *Roberts* sailed in the Sloop to the Island of *Dominico*, where he watered, and got Provisions of the Inhabitants, to whom he gave Goods in Exchange At this Place he met with 13 *Englishmen*, who had been set a shore by a *French Guard de la Coste*, belonging to *Martinico*, taken out of two *New-England* Ships, that had been seized, as Prize, by the said *French* Sloop The Men willingly entered with the Pirates, and it proved a seasonable Recruit

They staid not long here, tho' they had immediate Occasion for cleaning their Sloop, because they did not think this a proper Place, and herein they judged right, for the touching at this Island, had like to have been their Destruction, because they having resolved to go away to the *Granada* Islands, for the aforesaid Purpose, by some Accident it came to be known to the *French* Colony, who sending Word to the Governor of *Martinico*, he equipped and manned two Sloops to go in Quest of them The Pirates sailed directly for the *Granadilloes*, and hall'd into a Lagoon, at *Corvocoo*, where they cleaned with unusual Dispatch, staying but a little above a Week, by which Expedition they missed of the *Martinico* Sloops only a few Hours, *Roberts* sailing over Night, and the *French* arriving the next Morning This was a fortunate Escape, especially considering, that it was not from any Fears of their being discovered, that they made so much hast from the Island, but, as they had the Impudence themselves to own, for the want of Wine and Women

Thus narrowly escaped, they sailed for *Newfoundland*, and arrived upon the Banks the latter End of *June*, 1720 They entered the Harbour of *Trepassi*, with their black Colours flying, Drums beating, and Trumpets sounding There was two and twenty

Vessels

Veſſels in the Harbour, which the Men all quitted upon the Sight of the Pirate, and fled aſhore It is impoſſible particularly to recount the Deſtruction and Havock they made here, burning and ſinking all the Shipping, except a *Briſtol* Galley, and deſtroying the Fiſheries, and Stages of the poor Planters, without Remorſe or Compunction, for nothing is ſo deplorable as Power in mean and ignorant Hands; it makes Men wanton and giddy, unconcerned at the Misfortunes they are impoſing on their Fellow Creatures, and keeps them ſmiling at the Miſchiefs, that bring themſelves no Advantage *They are like mad Men, that caſt Fire-Brands, Arrows, and Death, and ſay, are not we in Sport?*

Roberts mann'd the *Briſtol* Galley he took in the Harbour, and mounted 16 Guns on Board her, afterwards cruizing out upon the Banks, he met with nine or ten Sail of *French* Ships all which he deſtroyed except one of 26 Guns which they ſeized and carried off for their own Uſe This Ship they chriſtened the *Fortune* and leaving the *Briſtol* Galley to the *French* Men they ſail'd away in Company with the Sloop on another Cruize, and took ſeveral prizes *viz.* the *Richard* of *Biddeford Jonathan Whitfield* Maſter, the *Willing Mind* of *Poole*, the *Expectation* of *Topſham*; and the *Samuel*, Captain *Cary*, of *London*; out of theſe Ships they encreaſed their Company, by entring all the Men they could well ſpare, in their own Service The *Samuel* was a rich Ship, and had ſeveral Paſſengers on Board, who were uſed very roughly, in order to make them diſcover their Money, threatening them every Moment with Death, if they did not reſign every Thing up to them They tore up the Hatches and entered the Hold, like a parcel of Furies, and, with Axes and Cutlaſhes, cut and broke open all the Bales, Caſes and Boxes, they could lay their Hands on, and when any Goods came upon Deck, that they did not like to carry a-board, inſtead of toſſing them into the Hole again, they threw them over-board into the Sea, all this was done with inceſſant curſing and ſwearing, more like Fiends than Men They carried with them, Sails, Guns, Powder, Cordage, and 8 or 9000 *l* worth of the choiceſt Goods, and told Captain *Cary, That they ſhould accept of no Act of Grace, that the* K—— *and* P——*t might be damned with their Acts of* G—— *for them, neither would they go to* Hope-Point, *to be hanged up a Sun-drying, as* Kidd's *and* Bradiſh's *Company were, but that if they ſhould ever be over-power'd they would ſet Fire to the Powder, with a Piſtol, and go all merrily to Hell together*

After they had brought all the Booty a board, a Conſultation was held whether they ſhould ſink or burn the Ship, but whilſt they were debating the Matter, they ſpy'd a Sail, and ſo left the *Samuel*, to give her Chace At Midnight they came up with the ſame, which prov'd to be a Snow from *Briſtol*, bound for *Boſton*, Captain *Bowles* Maſter They us'd him barbarouſly, becauſe of his Country, Captain *Rogers*, who attack'd them off *Barbadoes*, being of the City of *Briſtol*

July 16. which was two Days afterwards, they took a *Virginia* Man call'd *The Little York, James Philips* Maſter, and *The Love*, of *Liverpool*, which they plunder'd, and let go The next Day, a Snow, from *Briſtol*, call'd *The Phœnix, John Richards* Maſter, met with the ſame Fate from them, as alſo a Brigantine, Captain *Thomas*, and a Sloop call'd *The Sadbury* They took all the Men out of the Brigantine, and ſunk the Veſſel.

When they left the Banks of *Newfoundland*, they ſail'd for the *Weſt-Indies*, and the Proviſions growing ſhort, they went for the Latitude of the Iſland *Diſea-*

da, to cruize, it being eſteem'd the likelieſt Place to meet with thoſe Ships that (as they us'd in their Mirth to ſay) were conſign'd to them with Supplies And it has been very much ſuſpected, that Ships have loaded with Proviſions at the *Engliſh* Colonies, on pretence of trading on the Coaſt of *Africa*, when they have, in Reality, been conſign'd to them And though a Shew of Violence is offer'd to them when they meet, yet they are pretty ſure of bringing their Cargo to a good Market.

However, at this Time they miſs'd of the uſual Luck, and Proviſions and Neceſſaries becoming more ſcarce every Day, they retir'd towards St *Chriſtopher*'s, where, being denied all Succour or Aſſiſtance from the Government, they fir'd, in Revenge, on the Town, and burnt two Ships in the Road, one of them commanded by Captain *Cox*, of *Briſtol* They then retreated farther, to the Iſland of St *Bartholomew*, where they met with much handſomer Treatment, the Governor not only ſupplying them with Refreſhments, but he and the Chiefs careſſing them in the moſt friendly Manner And the Women, from ſo good an Example, endeavour'd to out-vie each other in Dreſs, and Behaviour, to attract the good Graces of ſuch generous Lovers, that paid well for their Favours

Sated, at length, with theſe Pleaſures, and having taken on board a good Supply of freſh Proviſion, they voted unanimouſly for the Coaſt of *Guinea*, and, in the Latitude of 22 Degrees North in their Voyage thither, they met with a *French* Ship from *Martinico*, richly laden, and, which was unlucky for the Maſter, had a Property of being fitter for their Purpoſe than the Banker *Exchange was no Robbery*, they ſaid and ſo, after a little Mock-complaiſance to *Monſieur*, for the Favour he had done them, they ſhifted their Men, and took Leave This was their firſt *Royal Fortune*

In this Ship *Roberts* proceeded on his deſign'd Voyage, but, before they reach'd *Guinea*, he propos'd to touch at *Braza*, the ſouthermoſt of *Cape Verd* Iſlands, and clean But here, again, by an intollerable Stupidity, and Want of Judgment, they go ſo far Leeward of their Port, that, deſpairing to regain it, or any of the Windward Parts of *Africa*, they were oblig'd to go back again with the Trade-Wind, for the *Weſt-Indies*, which had very near been the Deſtruction of them all *Surinam* was the Place now deſign'd for, which was no leſs than 700 Leagues diſtant, and they had but one Hogſhead of Water left to ſupply 124 Souls for that Paſſage A ſad Circumſtance, that eminently expoſes the Folly and Madneſs common among Pirates, and he muſt be an inconſiderate Wretch, indeed, who, if he could ſeparate the Wickedneſs and Puniſhment from the Fact, would yet hazard his Life amidſt ſuch Dangers, as the Want of Skill and Forecaſt often makes them liable to

Their Sins, we may preſume, were never ſo troubleſome to their Memories, as now, when inevitable Deſtruction ſeem'd to threaten them, without a leaſt Glimpſe of Comfort or Alleviation to their Miſery, for, with what Face could Wretches, who had ravag'd and made ſo many neceſſitous, look up to Heaven for Relief? They had to that Moment liv'd in Defiance of the Power that now alone they muſt truſt to for their Preſervation, and, indeed, without the miraculous Intervention of Providence, there appear'd only this miſerable Choice, *viz.* a preſent Death by their own Hands, or a ling'ring one by Famine

They continu'd their Courſe, and came to an Allowance of one ſingle Mouthful of Water for — Hours Many of them drank their Urine, or Sea Water

Water, which, instead of allaying, gave them an inextinguishable Thirst, that kill'd 'em Others pined, and wasted a little more Time in Fluxes and Apyrexies, so that they dropp'd away daily. Those that sustain'd the Misery best, were such as almost starv'd themselves, forbearing all Sorts of Food, unless a mouthful or two of Bread, the whole Day So that those who surviv'd, were as weak as it was possible for Men to be, and alive

But if the dismal Prospect they set out with gave them Anxiety, Trouble, or Pain, what must their Fears and Apprehensions be, when they had not one Drop of Water left, or any other Liquor to moisten or animate? This was their Case when (by the working of Divine Providence, no doubt) they were brought into Soundings, and at Night anchor'd in seven Fathom Water This was an expressible Joy to them, and, as it were, fed the expiring Lamp of Life with fresh Spirits But this could not hold long When the Morning came, they saw Land from the Mast Head, but it was at so great a Distance, that it afforded but an indifferent Prospect to Men who had drank nothing for the two last Days However, they dispatch'd their Boat away, and late the same Night it return'd, to their no small Comfort, with a load of Water, informing them, that they had got off the Mouth of *Merewinga* River, on the Coast of *Surinam*

One would have thought so miraculous an Escape should have wrought some Reformation, but, alas! they had no sooner quench'd their Thirst, but they had forgot the Miracle, till Scarcity of Provisions awaken'd their Senses, and bid them guard against starving Their Allowance was very small, and yet they would profanely say, *That Providence which had gave them Drink, would, no doubt, bring them Meat also, if they would use but an honest Endeavour*

In pursuance of these honest Endeavours, they were steering for the Latitude of *Barbadoes,* with what little they had left, too look out for more, or starve, and in their Way, they met a Ship that answer'd their Necessities, and after that a Brigantine The former was call'd *The Greyhound,* belonging to St *Christopher's,* and bound to *Philadelphia,* the Mate of which sign'd the Pirate's Articles, and was afterwards Captain of *The Ranger,* Consort to *The Royal Fortune*

Out of the Ship and Brigantine the Pirates got a good Supply of Provisions and Liquor, so that they gave over the design'd Cruize, and water d at *Tobago,* where nearing of the two Sloops that had been fitted out and sent after them at *Corvecoo,* they sail'd to the Island of *Martinico,* to make the Governor some sort of an Equivalent for the Care and Expedition he had shewn in that Affair

It is the Custom at *Martinico* for the *Dutch* Interlopers, that have a Mind to trade with the People of the Island, to hoist their Jacks when they come before the Town *Roberts* knew the Signal, and, being an utter Enemy to them, he bent his Thoughts upon Mischief Accordingly, he came in with his Jack flying, which, as he expected, they mistook for a good Market, and thought themselves happiest that could soonest dispatch off their Sloops and Vessels for Trade When *Roberts* had got them within his Power (one after another) he told them, he would not have it said that they came off for nothing, and therefore order'd them to leave their Money behind, for that they were a Parcel of Rogues, and he hop'd they would always meet with such a *Dutch* Trade as this was He reserv'd one Vessel to set the Passengers on shore again, and fir'd the rest to the Number of 20

Roberts was so enrag'd at the Attempts that had been made for taking of him, by the Governors of *Barbadoes* and *Martinico,* that he order'd a new Jack to be made, which they ever after hoisted, with his own Figure pourtray'd, standing upon two Skulls, and under them the Letters *A B H* and *A M H,* signifying a *Barbadian's* and a *Martinican's* Head As shall be seen in the Plate of Captain *Roberts*

At *Dominico,* the next Island they touch'd at, they took a *Dutch* Interloper of 22 Guns, and 75 Men, and a Brigantine belonging to *Rhodes* Island, of which one *Norton* was Master The former made some Defence, till some of his Men being killed, the rest were discourag'd, and struck their Colours. With these two Prizes they went down to *Guadalupe,* and brought out a Sloop, and a *French* Fly-Boat laden with Sugar, the Sloop they burnt, and went on to *Moonay,* another Island, thinking to clean But finding the Sea ran too high there to undertake it with Safety, they bent their Course for the North Part of *Hispaniola,* where, at *Bennet's* Key, in the Gulf of *Samanah,* they clean'd both the Ship and the Brigantine For though *Hispaniola* be settled by the *Spaniards* and *French,* and is the Residence of a President from *Spain,* who receives, and finally determines Appeals from all the other *Spanish West-India* Islands; yet is its People by no Means proportion'd to its Magnitude So that there are many Harbours in it, to which Pirates may securely resort, without Fear of Discovery from the Inhabitants

Whilst they were here, two Sloops came in, as they pretended, to pay *Roberts* a Visit, the Masters, whose Names were *Porter* and *Tuckerman,* address'd the Pirate as the Queen of *Sheba* did *Solomon,* to wit, *That,* having heard of his Fame and Atchievements, they had put in their to learn his Art and Wisdom in the Business of pirating, being Vessels on the same honourable Design with himself, and they hop'd, with the Communication of his Knowledge, they should also receive his Charity, being in Want of Necessaries for such Adventures *Roberts* was won upon by the Peculiarity and Bluntness of these two Men, and gave them Powder, Arms, and whatever else they had Occasion for, spent two or three merry Nights with them, and at parting, said, *He hoped the L————would prosper their Handy Works*

They passed some Time here, after they had got their Vessel ready, in their usual Debaucheries, they had taken a considerable Quantity of Rum and Sugar, so that Liquor was as plenty as Water, and few there were who denied themselves the immoderate Use of it, nay, Sobriety brought a Man under a Suspicion of being in a Plot against the Commonwealth, and in their Sense, he was looked upon to be a Villain that would not be drunk This was evident in the Affair of *Harry Glasby,* chosen Master of the *Royal Fortune,* who, with two others, laid hold of the Opportunity at the last Island they were at, to move off without bidding Farewell to his Friends *Glasby* was a reserv'd sober Man, and therefore gave Occasion to be suspected, so that he was soon miss'd after he went away A Detachment being sent in quest of these Deserters, they were all three brought back again the next Day This was a capital Offence, for which they were order'd to be brought to an immediate Tryal

Here was the Form of Justice kept up, which is as much as can be said of several other Courts, that have more lawful Commissions for what they do —— Here was no seeing of Council, and bribing of Witnesses was a Custom not known among them, no packing of Juries, no torturing and wresting the Sense of the Law, for bye Ends and Purposes, no puzzling or perplexing the Cause with unintelligible canting Terms, and useless Distinctions; nor was their Sessions burthened with numberless Officers, the Ministers of Rapine and Extortion, with ill boding Aspects, enough to fright *Astræa* from the Court

The Place appointed for their Trials, was the Steerage of the Ship, in order to the Procedure, a large Bowl of Rum Punch was made, and placed upon the Table, the Pipes and Tobacco being ready, the judicial Proceedings began; the Prisoners were brought forth, and Articles of Indictment against them read, they were arraigned upon a Statute of their own making, and the Letter of the Law being strong against them, and the Fact plainly proved, they were about to pronounce Sentence, when one of the Judges moved, that they should first Smoak t'other Pipe, which was accordingly done

All the Prisoners pleaded for Arrest of Judgment very movingly, but the Court had such an Abhorrence of their Crime, that they could not be prevailed upon to shew Mercy, till one of the Judges whose Name was *Valentine Ashplant*, stood up, and, taking his Pipe out of his Mouth, said he had something to offer to the Court in behalf of one of the Prisoners, which he delivered to this Effect —— *By G——, Glasby shall not die, d——n me if he shall* After this learned Speech, he sat down in his Place, and resumed his Pipe This Motion was loudly opposed by all the rest of the Judges, in equivalent Terms, but *Ashplant*, who was resolute in his Opinion, made another pathetical Speech, in the following Manner *G—— d——n ye Gentlemen, I am as good a Man as the best of you, d——n my S——l if ever I turned my Back to any Man in my Life, or ever will, by G——, Glasby is an honest Fellow, notwithstanding this Misfortune, and I love him, the D——l d——n me if I don't I hope he'll live and repent of what he has done, but d——n me, if he must die, I will die along with him.* Having delivered this, he pulled out a Pair of Pistols, and presented them to some of the learned Judges upon the Bench, who, perceiving his Argument so well supported, thought it reasonable that *Glasby* should be acquitted, and so they all came over to his Opinion, and allowed it to be Law

But all the Mitigation that could be obtained for the other Prisoners, was, that they should have the Liberty of choosing any four of the whole Company to be their Executioners The poor Wretches were ty'd immediately to the Mast, and there shot dead, pursuant to their villainous Sentence

When they put to Sea again, the Prizes, which had been detained only for fear of spreading any Rumour concerning them, a Thing that had like to hade been so fatal at *Corvocoo*, were thus disposed of They burnt their own Sloop, and mann'd *Morton*'s Brigantine, sending the Master away in the *Dutch* Interloper, not dissatisfied

With the *Royal Fortune*, and the Brigantine, which they christened the *Good Fortune*, they pushed towards the Latitude of *Diseada*, to look out for Provisions, being very short again; and just to their Wish, Captain *Hingstone*'s ill Fortune brought him in their Way, being richly laden for *Jamaica*, him they carried to *Berbadas* and plundered, then stretching back again to the *West-Indies*, they continually met with some Consignment or other, (chiefly *French*) which stored them with Plenty of Provisions, and recruited their starving Condition, so that, stocked with this sort of Ammunition, they began to think of something worthier their Aim, for these Robberies that only supplied what was in constant Expenditure, by no Means answered their Intentions, and accordingly, they proceeded again for the Coast of *Guiney*,

where they thought to buy Gold Dust very cheap. In their Passage thither, they took Numbers of Ships of all Nations, some of which they burnt or sunk, as the Behaviour or Characters of the Masters displeased them.

Notwithstanding the successful Adventures of this Crew, yet it was with great Difficulty they could be kept together, under any kind of Regulation, for being almost always mad or drunk, their Behaviour produced infinite Disorders, every Man being in his own Imagination, a Captain, a Prince, or a King When *Roberts* saw there was no managing of such a Company of wild ungovernable Brutes, by gentle Means, nor any Method of keeping them from drinking to excess, which was the Cause of all their Disturbances, he put on a rougher Deportment, and a more magisterial Carriage towards them, correcting whom he thought fit If any seemed to resent his Usage, he told them, *They might go a-shore and take Satisfaction of him, if they thought fit, at Sword and Pistol, for he neither valu'd or fear'd any of them*

About 400 Leagues from the Coast of *Africa*, the Brigantine, who had hitherto lived with them in all amicable Correspondence, thought fit to take the Opportunity of a dark Night, and leave the Commodore, which leads me back to the Relation of an Accident, that happened at one of the Islands of the *West-Indies*, where they water'd before they undertook this Voyage, which had like to have thrown their Government (such as it was) off the Hinges, and was partly the Occasion of the Separation. The Story is as follows

Captain *Roberts*, having been insulted by one of the drunken Crew, whose Name we have not learnt, he, in the Heat of his Passion, killed the Fellow on the Spot, which was resented by a great many others, but particularly by one *Jones*, a brisk active young Man, who died lately in the *Marshalsea*, and was his Mess-Mate This *Jones* was at that Time a-shore, a watering the Ship, but as soon as he came on Board, he was told that Captain *Roberts* had killed his Comrade, upon which he boldly cursed *Roberts*, and said, he ought to be served so himself *Roberts* hearing *Jones*'s Invective, ran to him with a Sword, and ran him into the Body; and *Jones*, notwithstanding his Wound, seized the Captain, threw him over a Gun, and beat him handsomely This Adventure put the whole Company in an Uproar, and some taking Part with the Captain, and others against him, there had like to have ensued a general Battle with one another, like my Lord *Thomont*'s Cocks however, the Tumult was at length appeas'd, by the Mediation of the Quarter-Master and as the Majority of the Company were of Opinion, that the Lignity of the Captain ought to be supported on Board, that it was a Post of Honour, and therefore the Person whom they thought fit to confer it on, should not be violated by any single Member, therefore they sentenced *Jones* to undergo two Lashes from every one of the Company for his Misdemeanour, which was executed upon him as soon as he was well of his Wound

This severe Punishment did not at all convince *Jones* that he was in the wrong, but rather animated him to some sort of a Revenge However, not being able to do it upon *Roberts*'s Person, on board the Ship, he and several of his Comrades correspond with *Anstis*, Captain of the Brigantine, and conspire with him and some of the principal Pirates on board that Vessel, to go off from the Company What made *Anstis* a Malecontent, was, the Inferiority he stood in with respect to *Roberts*, who carried himself with a haughty and magisterial Air to him and his Crew,

he

he regarding the Brigantine only as a Tender, and as such, left them no more than the Refuse of their Plunder In short, *Jones* and his Consort got on board of Captain *Anstis*, on Pretence of a Visit, and there consulting with their Brethren, they find a Majority for leaving *Roberts*, and so came to a Resolution to bid a soft Farewel, as they call it, that Night, and to throw over-board whosoever should stick out But they prov'd to be unanimous, and effected their Design as abovemention'd

We shall have no more to say of Captain *Anstis*, till the Story of *Roberts* is concluded, therefore we return to him, in the pursuit of his Voyage to *Guinea* The Loss of the Brigantine was a sensible Shock to the Crew, she being an Excellent Sailor, and having 70 Hands a-board However, *Roberts*, who was the Occasion of it, put on a Face of Unconcern at this ill Conduct and Mismanagement, and resolv'd not to alter his Purposes upon that Account

Roberts fell in to Windward nigh the *Senegal*, a River of great Trade for Gum, on this Part of the Coast, monopoliz'd by the *French*, who constantly keep Cruizers, to hinder the interloping Trade At this Time they had two small Ships on that Service, one of 10 Guns and 65 Men, and the other of 10 Guns and 75 Men, who, having got a Sight of Mr *Roberts*, and supposing him to be one of these prohibited Traders, chac'd, with all the Sail they could make, to come up with him, but their Hopes, which had brought them very nigh, too late deceived them. For, on the hoisting of *Jolly Roger*, which was the Name they gave their black Flag, their *French* Hearts fail'd, and they both surrender'd without any, or, at least, with very little Resistance With these Prizes they went into *Sierraleon*, and made one of them their Consort, by the Name of *The Ranger*, and the other a Store-Ship, to clean by

Sierraleon River disgorges with a large Mouth, the Starboard-Side of which draughts into little Bays, safe and convenient for cleaning and watering What still made it preferable to the Pyrates, was, that the Traders settled here are naturally their Friends There are about 30 *Englishmen* in all, who, in some Part of their Lives, have been either privateering, buccaneering, or pyrating, and still retain and love the Riots and Humours common to that sort of Life They live very friendly with the Natives, and have many of them, of both Sexes, to be their *Gromettas*, or Servants The Men are faithful, and the Women so obedient, that they are very ready to prostitute themselves to whomsoever their Masters shall command them The *Royal African Company* has a Fort on a small Island, call'd *Bence Island*, but tis of little Use, besides keeping their Slaves, the Distance making it incapable of giving any Molestation to their Starboard Shore Here lives at this Place an old Fellow, who went by the Name of *Crackers*, who was formerly a noted Buccaneer and, while he follow'd the Calling, had robbed and plundered many a Man He kept the best House in the Place, had two or three Guns before his Door, with which he saluted his Friends the Pyrates, when they put in, and liv'd a jovial Life with them all the while they are there

Here follows a List of the rest of those lawless Merchants, and their Servants, who carry on a private Trade with the Interlopers, to the great Prejudice of the *Royal African Company*, who, with extraordinary Industry and Expence, have made and maintain Settlements, without any Consideration from those, who, without such Settlements and Forts, would soon be under an Incapacity of pursuing any such private Trade Wherefore, 'tis to be hop'd, proper Means will be taken, to root out the Remainder of such a pernicious Set of People, who

have all their Lives supported themselves by the Labours of other Men

Two of these Fellows enter'd with *Robert's* Crew, and continu'd with them, till the Destruction of the Company

A LIST of the White Men, who lived on the High Land of Sierraleon, when Roberts was there, and the Craft they occupy.

JOHN *Leadstone*, three Boats and Periagoe.
 His Man *Tom*
 His Man *John Brown*
Alexander Middleton, one Long Boat
 His Man *Charles Hawkins*
John Pierce,
William Mead, } Partners, one Long-Boat.
 Their Man *John Vernon*
David Chatmers, one Long Boat
John Chatmers, one Long-Boat
Richard Richardson, one Long-Boat
Norton,
Richard Warren, } Partners, two Long-Boats, and two small Boats.
Robert Glynn,
 His Man *John Franks*
William Waits, and one young Man.
John Bonnerman
John England, one Long-Boat
Robert Samples, one Long Boat.
William Presgrove,
Harry,
Davis, } One Sloop, two Long Boats, a small Boat, and Periagoe
Mitchel,
Richard Lamb,
With *Roquis Rodrigus,* a *Portuguese*
George Bishop
Peter Brown
John Jones, one Long Boat
 His *Irish* young Man
At *Rio Pungo,* *Benjamin Gun*
At *Kidham,* *George Yeats*
At *Gallyneas,* *Richard Lemmons*

The Harbour is so convenient for Wooding and Watering, that it occasions many of our trading Ships, especially those of *Bristol*, to call in there, with large Cargoes of Beer, Cyder, and strong Liquors, which they exchange with these private Traders, for Slaves and Teeth, purchased by them at the *Rio Nunes's*, and other Places to the Northward So that here was what they call good Living

Hitherto *Roberts* came about the End of *June*, 1721 and had Intelligence that *The Swallow*, and *Weymouth*, two Men of War, of 50 Guns each, had left that River about a Month before, and design'd to return about *Christmas*, so that the Pirates could indulge themselves with all the Satisfaction in the World, in that they knew they were not only secure whilst there, but that in going down the Coast, after the Men of War, they should always be able to get such Intelligence of their Rendezvous, as would serve to make their Expedition safe So after six Weeks stay, the Ships being clean'd and fitted, and the Men weary of whoring and drinking, they bethought themselves of Business, and went to Sea the Beginning of *August*, taking their Progress down the whole Coast, as low as *Jaquin*, plundering every Ship they met of what

what was valuable in her, and sometimes, to be more mischievously wicked, they would throw what they did not want over board, accumulating Cruelty to Theft

In this Range, they exchanged their old *French* Ship, for a fine Frigate built Ship, call'd the *Onslow*, belonging to the Royal *African* Company, Captain *Gee* Commander, which happened to lye at *Sestos*, to get Water and Necessaries for the Company A great many of Captain *Gee's* Men were a-shore when *Roberts* bore down, and so the Ship was consequently surpriz'd into his Hands, tho' had they been all on Board, it was not likely the Case would have been otherwise, the Sailors, most of them, voluntarily joining the Pirates, and encouraging the same Disposition in the Soldiers, who were going Passengers with them to *Cape Corso-Castle* Their Ears being constantly tickled with the Feats and Gallantry of those Fellows, made them fancy, that *to go*, was only being bound on a Voyage of Night Errantry, to relieve the Distress'd, and gather up Fame, and so they likewise offered themselves, but here the Pirates were at a Stand, they entertained so contemptible a Notion of Landmen, that they put 'em off with Refusals for some Time, till at length being weary'd with Solicitations, and pitying a Parcel of stout Fellows, who, they said, were going to starve upon a little Canky and Plantane, they accepted of them, and allowed them a-quarter Share, as it was then term'd, out of Charity

There was a Clergyman on Board the *Onslow*, sent from *England*, to be Chaplain of *Cape Corso-Castle*, some of the Pirates were for keeping him, alledging merrily, that their Ship wanted a Chaplain, accordingly they offered him a Share to take on with them, promising that he should do nothing for his Money, but make Punch, and say Prayers, yet, however brutish they might be in other Things, they bore so great a Respect to his Order, that they resolved not to force him against his Inclinations, and the Parson, having no Relish for this sort of Life, excuse himself from accepting the Honour they designed him, they were satisfied, and generous enough to deliver him back every Thing he owned to be his The Parson laid hold of this favourable Disposition of the Pirates, and laid Claim to several Things belonging to others, which were also given up, to his great Satisfaction, in fine, they kept nothing which belonged to the Church, except three Prayer-Books, and a Bottle Screw

The Pirates kept the *Onslow* for their own Use, and gave Captain *Gee* the *French* Ship, and then fell to making such Alterations as might fit her for a Sea Rover, pulling down her Bulk Heads, and making her flush, so that she became, in all Respects, as compleat a Ship for their Purpose, as any they could have found, they continued to her the Name of the *Royal Fortune*, and mounted her with 40 Guns

She and the *Ranger* proceeded (as we said before) to *Jaquin*, and from thence to *Old Calabar*, where they arrived about *October*, in order to clean their Ships This Place was the most suitable along the whole Coast, for there is a Bar with not above 15 Foot Water upon it, and the Channel intricate, so that had the Men of War been sure of their being harboured here, they might still have bid Defiance to their Strength, for the Depth of Water at the Bar, as well as the Want of a Pilot, was a sufficient Security to the Rovers, and invincible Impediments to them Here therefore they sat easy, and divided the Fruits of their dishonest Industry, *and drank and drove Care away* The Pilot, who brought them into this Harbour, was Captain *L——e*, who, for this, and other Services, was extreamly well paid

according to the Journal of their own Account, which does not run in the ordinary and common Way, of *Debtor contra Creditor*, but much more concise, lumping it to their Friends, and so carrying the Debt in their Heads, against the next honest Trader they meet

They took at *Calabar* Captain *Loane*, and two or three *Bristol* Ships, the Particulars of all which would be an unnecessary Prolixity We therefore come now to give an Account of the Usage they received from the Natives of this Place The *Calabar* Negroes did not prove so civil as they expected, they refused to have any Commerce or Trade with them, when they understood they were Pirates An Indication that these poor Creatures, in the narrow Circumstances they were in, and without the Light of the Gospel, or the Advantage of an Education, have, notwithstanding, such a moral innate Honesty, as would upbraid and shame the most knowing Christian But this did but exasperate these lawless Fellows, and so a Party of 40 Men were detach'd to force a Correspondence, or drive the Negroes to Extremities, and they accordingly landed under the Fire of their own Cannon The Negroes drew up in a Body of 2000 Men, as if they intended to dispute the Matter with them, and staid till the Pirates advanced within Pistol shot, but finding the Loss of two or three made no Impression on the rest, the Negroes thought fit to retreat, when they did with some Loss The Pirates set Fire to the Town, and then return'd to their Ships This terrified the Natives, and put an entire stop to all the Intercourse between them, so that they could get no Supplies, which obliged them, as soon as they had finished the cleaning and triming of their Ships, to lose no Time, but depart for *Cape Lopez*, where they watered, and at *Anna-Bona* took a-board a Stock of fresh Provisions, and then sailed for the Coast again

This was their last and fatal Expedition, which we shall be the more particular in, because it can not be imagined, that they could have had the Assurance to have undertaken it, but upon a Presumption, that the Men of War, (whom they knew were upon the Coast,) were unable to attack them, or else, pursuant to the Rumour that had indiscretionally obtained at *Sierraleon*, were gone thither again

It is impossible at this Time, to think they could know of the weak and sickly Condition they were in, and therefore, we may suppose, they founded the Success of this second Attempt upon the Coast, on the latter Presumption, and this seems to be confirmed by their falling in with the Coast as low as *Cape Labou*, (and even that was higher than they designed) in the Beginning of *January*, and taking the Ship called the *King Solomon*, with 20 Men in her Boat, and a trading Vessel, both belonging to the Company The Pirate Ship happened to fall about a League to Leeward of the *King Solomon*, at *Cape Appollonia*, and the Current and Wind opposing their working up with the Ship, they agreed to send the Long Boat, with a sufficient Number of Men, to take her The Pirates are all Volunteers on these Occasions, the Word being always given, *who will go?* And presently the staunch and firm Men offer themselves, because, by such Readiness, they recommend their Courage, and have an Allowance also of a Suit of Cloaths, from Head to Foot, out of the Prize

They rowed towards the *King Solomon* with a great deal of Alacrity, and being hail'd by the Commander of her, answer'd, *Defiance* Captain *Trahern*, before this, observing a great Number of Men in the Boat, began not to like his Visitors, and prepared to receive them firing a Musket as they came
under

under his Stern, which they return'd with a Volley; and made greater Speed to get on board. Upon this, he applied to his Men, and ask'd them whether they would stand by him, to defend the Ship, it being a Shame they should be taken by half their Number, without any Repulse? But his Boatswain, *Philips*, took upon him to be the Mouth of the People, and put an End to the Dispute, he said plainly, he would not fight, laid down his Arms in the King's Name, as he was pleased to term it, and called out to the Boat for Quarters, so that the rest, by his Example, were misled to the losing of the Ship.

When they came on Board, they brought her under Sail, by the expeditious Method of cutting her Cable, *Walden*, one of the Pirates, telling the Master, that the heaving up the Anchor would be a needless Trouble, when they designed to burn the Ship. They brought her under Commodore *Roberts*'s Stern, and not only rifled her of what Sails, Cordage, &c. they wanted for themselves, but wantonly thrown'd the Goods of the Company over-board, like Spendthrifts, that neither expected or designed any Account.

On the same Day also they took the *Flushing*, a *Dutch* ship, robb'd her of Masts, Yards, and Stores, and then cut down her Fore-Mast, but sat as heavily as any Thing with the *Skipper*, was, their taking some fine Saulages he had on Board, of his Wife's making, and stringing them in a ludicrous Manner round their Necks, till they had sufficiently shew'd their Contempt of them, and then they threw them into the Sea. Others chopp'd the Heads of his Fowls off, to be dressed for their Supper, and courteously invited the Landlord, provided he would find Liquor. It was a melancholly Request to the Man, but it must be comply'd with, and he was obliged as they grew drunk, to sit quietly, and hear them sing *French* and *Spanish* Songs out of his *Dutch* Prayer Book, with other Prophaneis, that he (tho' a *Dutch* Man) stood amazed at.

In cruising too near it, they alarmed the Coast, and Expresses were sent to the *English* and *Dutch* Factories, giving an Account of it. They were sensible of this Error immediately, and, because they would make the best of a bad Market, they resolved to keep out of Sight of Land, and lose the Prizes they might expect between that and *Whydah*, to make the more sure of that Port, where commonly is the best Booty, all Nations trading thither, especially *Portuguese*, who purchase chiefly with Gold, the Idol their Hearts were bent upon. Yet notwithstanding this unlikely Course, they met and took several Ships between *Axim* and that Place, the circumstantial Stories of which, and the particular Terrors they struck into his Majesty's Subjects, being tedious and unnecessary to relate, I shall pass by, and come to their Arrival in that Road.

They came to *Whydah* with a St. *George's* Ensign, black Flag flying at their Mizzen-Peek, and a Jack and Pendant of the same. The Flag had a Death on it, with an Hour Glass in one Hand, and cross Bones in the other, a Dart by it, and underneath a Heart dropping three Drops of Blood —— The Jack had a Man pourtray'd on it, with a flaming Sword in his Hand, and standing on two Skulls, subscribed, *A B H* and *A M H* i. e. a *Barbadian*'s and a *Martinican*'s Head, as has been before taken Notice of. Here they found eleven Sail in the Road, *English*, *French*, and *Portuguese*, the *French* were stout Ships, of thirty Guns, and upwards of 100 Men each, yet when *Roberts* came to Fire, they, with the other Ships, immediately struck their Colours and surrendered to his Mercy. One Reason it may be of his easy Victory, was, that the Commanders and a good Part of the Men were a-

shore, according to the Custom of the Place, to receive the Cargoes, and return the Slaves; they being oblig'd to watch the Seasons for it, which otherwise, in so dangerous a Sea as this, would be impracticable. These all, except the *Porcupine*, ransom'd with him for eight Pound of Gold-Dust a Ship, not without the trouble of passing or repassing from the Shore, before they could settle it, and, notwithstanding the Agreement and Payment, they took away one of the *French* Ships, tho' with a Promise to return her, if they found she did not sail well, taking with them several of her Men for that End.

Some of the Foreigners, who never had Dealing this Way before, desired, for Satisfaction to their Owners, that they might have Receipts for their Money; which were accordingly given, a Copy of one of them we have here subjoin'd, *viz.*

THIS is to certify whom it may or doth concern, that we Gentlemen of Fortune, have received eight Pounds of Gold-Dust, for the Ransom of the Hardey, *Captain* Ditt witt *Commander, so that we discharge the said Ship*

Witness our Hands, this 13th of Jan 1721-2	Batt Roberts
	Harry Glasby

Others were given to the *Portuguese* Captains, which were in the same Form, but being sign'd by two waggish Fellows, *viz.* *Sutton* and *Simpson*, they subscrib'd by the Names of,

Aaron Whiffingpin,
Sim Tugmutton.

But there was something so singularly cruel and barbarous done here to the *Porcupine*, Captain *Fletcher*, as must not be passed over without special Remark. This Ship lay in the Road, almost slaved, when the Pirates came in, and the Commander, being on Shore settling his Accounts, was sent to for the Ransom, but he excused it, as having no Orders from the Owners, tho' the true Reason might be, that he thought it dishonourable to treat with Robbers, and that the Ship, separate from the Slaves, towards whom he could mistrust no Cruelty, was not worth the Sum demanded. Hereupon, *Roberts* sends the Boat to transport the Negroes, in order to set her on Fire, but being in haste, and finding that unshackling them would cost much Time and Labour, they actually set her on Fire, with eighty of these poor Wretches on Board, chained two and two together, under the miserable Choice of perishing by Fire or Water. Those who jumped over-board from the Flames, were seized by Sharks, a voracious Fish, very common in this Road, and, in their Sight, tore Limb from Limb alive. A Cruelty unparallel'd! And for which had every Individual been hanged, few could have thought that Justice had been rigorously executed.

The Pirates, indeed, were oblig'd to dispatch their Business here in haste, because they had intercepted a Letter from General *Phipps* to Mr *Baldwin*, the Royal *African*'s Company's Agent at *Whydah*, giving an Account, that *Roberts* had been seen to Windward of Cape *Three Points*, that *Baldwin* might the better guard against the Damages to the Company's Ships, if he should arrive at that Road before the *Swallow* Man of War, which he assured him, at the Time of that Letter, was pursuing them at that Place. *Roberts* call'd up his Company, and defied they would hear *Phips*'s Speech, (for so he was pleas'd to call the Letter,) and, no withstanding their vapouring, persuaded them of the Necessity

'of moving ; ' for, fays he, fuch brave Fellows can-
' not be fuppofed to be frightened at this News, yet,
' we muft all own, that it were better to avoid dry
' Blows, which is the beft that can be expected, if
' we are over-taken.

This Advice weighed with them, and they got under Sail, having ftay'd only from *Thurfday* to *Saturday* Night, and at Sea they voted for the Ifland
of *Anna Bona* ; but the Winds, hanging out of the
Way, croffed their Purpofe, and brought them to Cape
Lopez, where we fhall leave them for their approaching Fate, and relate fome further Particulars of his
Majefty's Ship the *Swallow, viz.* where it was fhe
had fpent her Time, during the Mifchief that was
done, and by what Means fhe was unable to prevent
it ; what alfo was the Intelligence fhe receiv'd, and
the Meafure thereon formed, that at laft brought two
fuch Strangers as Mr. *Roberts* and Capt *Ogle*, to
meet in fo remote a Corner of the World.

The *Swallow* and *Weymouth* left *Sierraleon, May*
28, where, we have already taken Notice, *Roberts*
arrived about a Month after, and doubtlefs learn'd
the Intent of their Voyage, and cleaning on the
Coaft · This made him fet down with more Security to his Diverfion, and furnifhed him with fuch In-
timations, as made his firft Range down the Coaft,
in *Auguft* following, more profperous ; the *Swallow*
and *Weymouth* being then at the Port of *Princes* a
cleaning

Their Stay at *Princes* was from *July* 28, to *Sept*
20, 1721, where, by a Fatality, common to the Irregularities of Seamen, who cannot in fuch Cafes be
kept under due Reftraints, they buried 100 Men in
three Weeks Time, and reduced the Remainder of
the Ships Companies into fo fickly a State, that it
was with Difficulty they brought them to fail, and
this Misfortune was probably the Ruin of *Roberts*,
for it prevented the Men of War's going back to
Sierraleon, as it was intended, there being a Neceffity of leaving his Majefty's Ship *Weymouth* (in
much the worfe Condition of the two) under the
Guns of Cape *Corfo*, to imprefs Men, being unable
at this Time, either to hand the Sails, or weigh her
Anchor Now *Roberts*, being ignorant of the Occafion or Alteration of the firft Defign, fell into the
Mouth of Danger, when he thought himfelf the
fartheft from it , for the Men of War did not endeavour to attain further to Windward, when they came
from *Princes*, but to fecure Cape *Corfo* Road under
their Lee, they luckily hovered in the Track he had
took

The *Swallow* and *Weymouth* fell in with the Continent at Cape *Appollonia, October* 20th and there
received the ungrateful News from one Captain *Bird*,
a Notice that awakened and put them on their Guard,
but they were far from expecting any Temerity
fhould ever bring him a fecond Time on the Coaft,
while they were there , therefore the *Swallow* having feen the *Weymouth* into Cape *Corfo* Road *Nov*
10th, fhe ply'd to Windward as far as *Baffam*, rather as an Airing, to recover a fickly Ship's Company, and fhew herfelf to the Trade, which was found
every where difturb'd, than to chafe the Pirate. E-
very Thing being quiet, they were returning to
their Confort, when accidently meeting a *Portuguefe*
Ship, fhe told them, that the Day before, fhe faw
two Ships chace an Englifh Veffel into *Junk*, which
fhe believed muft have fallen into their Hands. On
this Story, the *Swallow* clung her Wind, and endeavoured to gain that Place, but receiving foon after, *viz October* the 14th, a contrary Report from
Captain *Plummer*, an intelligent Man, in the *Jafon*
of *Briftol*, who had come further to Windward, and
neither faw or heard any Thing of this ; fhe turned

her Head down the fecond Time, anchored at Cape
Appollonia the 23d, at Cape *Tres Puntas* the 2-6
and in *Corfo* Road *January* the 7th, 1721 2

They learned that their Confort the *Weymouth*
was, by the Affiftance of fome Soldiers from the
Caftle, gone to Windward, to demand Reftitution of
fome Goods or Men belonging to the *African* Com
pany, that were illegally detained by the *Dutch* at
Des Minas , and while they were regretting fo long
a Separation, an Exprefs came to General *Phip*,
from *Axim*, on the 9th, followed by another from
Dixcove, an Englifh Factory, with Information that
three Ships had chafed and taken a Galley right *Axim*
Caftle, and a trading Boat belonging to the Company
No doubt was made concerning what they were, it
being taken for granted they were Pirates, and fuppofed to be the fame that had the *Auguft* before in-
fefted the Coaft The natural Refult therefore, from
thefe two Advices, was, to haften for *Whydah*, for
it was concluded the Prizes they had taken, had informed them how nigh the *Swallow* was, and with
al, how much better in Health than fhe had been for
fome Months paft, fo that, unlefs they were very
mad indeed, they would, after being difcovered,
make the beft of their Way for *Whydah*, and fecure
the Booty there, without which, their Time and
Induftry had been entirely loft, moft of the Gold
lying in that Corner.

The *Swallow* weighed from Cape *Corfo, January* the 10th, but was retarded by waiting fome Hours
on the *Margeret*, a Company's Ship, at *Accra*, a-
gain on the *Portugal*, and a whole Day at *Apong*, on
a Perfon they ufed to ftile *Mifs Betty* A Conduct
that Mr *Phips* blamed, when he heard the Pirates
were miffed at *Whydah*, altho' he had given it as his
Opinion, that they could not be paffed by, and intimated, that to ftay a few Hours would prove no
Prejudice.

This, however, hinder'd the *Swallow*'s catching
them at *Whydah*, for the Pirates came into that
Road, with a frefh Gale of Wind, the fame Day
the *Swallow* was at *Apong*, and fail'd the 13th of
January from thence, fhe arriving the 17th She
gained Notice of them by a *French* Shallop from
Grand Papa, the 14th at Night, and from *Little
Papa* next Morning by a *Dutch* Ship, fo that the
Man of War was on all Sides, as fhe thought, fure
of her Purchafe, particularly when fhe made two
Ships, and difcovered three of them to get under
Sail immediately at Sight of her, making Signals to
one another, as tho' they defigned a Defence, but
thefe were found to be three *French* Ships, and thofe
at Anchor, *Portuguefe* and *Englifh*, all honeft Trades,
who had been ranfack'd and ranfomed

This Difappointment chagrin'd the Ship's Company, who were very intent upon their Market,
which was reported to be in Arms Cheft full of Gold,
and kept with three Keys, tho' in all likelihood, had
they met with them in that open Road, one or
both would have made their Efcapes , or if they had
thought fit to have fought, an Emulation in their
Defence would probably have made it defperate

While they were contemplating on the Matter, a
Letter was received from Mr *Baldwin*, Governor
here for the Company, fignifying, that the Pirates
were at *Jaquin*, feven Leagues lower The *Swallow* weighed at two next Morning, *January* the
16th, and got to *Jaquin* by Day Light, but to no
other End, than frightening the Crews of two *Portuguefe* Ships on Shore, who took her for the Pirate
that had ftruck fo much Terror at *Whydah* She
returned therefore that Night, and having been
ftrengthened with thirty Voluntiers, *Englifh* and
French, the difcarding Crews of the *Porcupine*, and
the

the French Ship they had carried from hence, she put to Sea again *January* the 19th, conjecturing, that either *Calabar*, *Princes*, the River *Gabone*, Cape *Lopez*, or *Annabona*, must be touched at for Water and Refreshment, tho' they should resolve to leave the Coast As to the former of those Places, we have before observed, it was hazardous to think of it, or rather impracticable, *Princes* had been a sour Grape to them, but being the first in the Way, she came before the Harbour the 29th, where learning no News, without losing Time, they steered for the River *Gabone*, and anchored at the Mouth of it *February* the 1st.

This River is navigable by two Channels, and has an Island about five Leagues up, call'd *Papagays* or *Parrots*, where the *Dutch* Cruizers for this Coast generally clean, and where sometimes Pirates come in to look for Prey, or to refit, it being very convenient, by Reason of a soft Mud about it, that admits a Ship's lying on Shore, with all her Guns and Stores in, without Damage. Hither Captain *Ogle* sent his Boat and a Lieutenant, who spoke with a *Dutch* Ship above the Island, from whom he had this Account, *viz* That he had been four Days from Cape *Lopez*, and had left no Ship there However, they beat up for the Cape, without regard to this Story, and on the 5th, at Dawning, were surprized with the Noise of a Gun, which, as the Day brightened, they found was from Cape *Lopez* Bay, where they discovered three Ships at Anchor, the largest with the King's Colours and Pendant flying, which was soon after concluded to be Mr *Roberts* and his Consorts The *Swallow* being to Windward, and unexpectedly deep in the Bay, was obliged to steer off, for avoiding a Sand, called the *Frenchman's Bank*, which the Pirates observed for some Time, and rashly interpreting it to be Fear in her, righted the *French Ranger*, which was then on the Heel, and ordered her to chase out in all haste, bending several of her Sails in the Pursuit The Man of War, finding they had foolishly mistaken her Design, humoured the Deceit, and kept off to Sea, as if she had been really afraid, and managed her Steerage so, under the Direction of Lieutenant *e n*, an experienced Officer, as to let the *Ranger* come up with her, when they thought they had got so far as not to have their Guns heard by her Consort at the Cape The Pirates had such an Opinion of their own Courage, that they never could dream any Body would use a Stratagem to speak with them, and so were the more easily drawn into the Snare

The Pirates now drew nigh enough to fire their Chase Guns, they hoisted the black Flag that was worn in *Whydah* Road, and got their Spritsail Yard along ships, with Intent to board, no one having ever asked all this while, what Country Ship they took the Chase to be, they would have her to be a *Portuguese*, Sugar being then a Commodity among them, and were swearing every Minute at the Wind or Sails to expedite so sweet a Chase; but, alas! all turned sour in an Instant It was with the utmost Consternation they saw her suddenly bring to, and haul up her lower Ports, now within Pistol shot, and they struck their black Flag upon it directly After the first Surprize was over, they kept firing at a Distance, hoisted it again, and vapoured with their Cutlashes on the Poop, tho' wisely endeavouring at the same Time to get away Being now at their Wits End, Boarding was proposed by the Heads of them, and so to make one desperate Push, the Motion not being well seconded, and their Main-Top Mast coming down by a Shot, after two Hours firing, it was declined They

grew sick, struck their Colours, and called out for Quarters, having 10 Men killed out right, and 20 wounded, without the loss or hurt of one the King's Men The *Ranger* had 32 Guns, was mann'd with 16 French Men, 10 Negroes, and 77 English The Colours were thrown over board, that they might not rise in Judgment, nor be display'd in Triumph over them

While the *Swallow* was sending their Boat to fetch the Prisoners, a Blast and Smoak was seen to pour out of the great Cabin, and they thought they were blowing up, but, upon Enquiry afterwards, they found that half a Dozen of the most desperate, when they saw all Hopes fled, had drawn themselves round what Powder they had left in the Steerage, and fired a Pistol into it, but it was too small a Quantity to effect any Thing, more than burning them in a frightful Manner

This Ship was commanded by one *Skyrme*, a *Welchman*, who, tho' he had lost his Leg in the Action, would not suffer himself to be dressed, or carried off the Deck; but, like *Widrington*, fought upon his Stump The rest appeared gay and brisk, most of them with white Shirts, Watches, and Silk Vests, but the Gold-Dust belonging to them was most of it left in the *Little-Ranger* in the Bay, this Company's proper Ship, with the *Royal Fortune*.

I cannot but take Notice of two, among the Crowd of those disfigured from the Blast of Powder just before-mentioned, *viz. William Main* and *Roger Ball* An Officer of the Ship seeing a Silver Call hang at the Waist of the former, said to him, *I presume you are Boatswain of this Ship Then you presume wrong,* answer'd he, *for I am Boatswain of the Royal Fortune, Captain Roberts Commander Then Mr Boatswain you will be hang'd I believe,* replies the Officer *That is as your Honour pleases,* answered he again, and was for turning away But the Officer desired to know of him, how the Powder which had made them in that Condition, came to take Fire —— *By G——, says he, they are all mad and bewitch'd, for I have lost a good Hat by it* (the Hat and he being both blown out of the Cabin Gallery into the Sea) *But what signifies a Hat Friend,* says the Officer ——*Not much,* answer'd he The Men being busy in stripping him of his Shoes and Stockings, the Officer enquired further of him, whether *Roberts*'s Company were all as likely Fellows as these ——*There are 120 of them,* (answer'd he) *as clever Fellows as ever trod in Shoe Leather Would I were with them No doubt on't* says the Officer ——*By G—— it is naked Truth* answered he, looking down and seeing himself by this time quite stripp'd

The Officer then approached *Roger Ball*, who was seated in a private Corner, with a Look as sullen as Winter, and asked him how he came blown up in that frightful Manner —— *Why, says he, John Morris fired a Pistol into the Powder, and if he had not done it I would* (bearing his Pain all the while without the least Complaint) The Officer gave him to understand he was a Surgeon, and that if he desired it he would dress him; but he swore it should not be done, and that if any thing was applied to him he would tear it off Nevertheless the Surgeon had good Nature enough to dress him, tho' with much Trouble At Night he was in a kind of *Delirium*, and raved on the Bravery of *Roberts*, saying, he should shortly be released, as soon as they should meet him This procured him a lashing down upon the Forecastle, which he resisting with all his Force, it caused him to be used with the more Violence, so that he was tied down with so much Severity, that his Flesh being sore and tender with the blowing up, he died next Day of a Mortification.

They

They secured the Prisoners with Pinions and Shackles, but the Ship was so much disabled in the Engagement, that they had once Thoughts to set her on Fire. This however would have given them the Trouble of taking the Pirate's wounded Men on board themselves, and as they were certain the *Royal Fortune* would wait for her Consort's Return, they lay by her two Days, repaired her Rigging, and other Damages, and sent her into *France* with the *French* Men, and four of their own Hands

On the 9th in the Evening, the *Swallow* gained the Cape again, and saw the *Royal Fortune* standing into the Bay, with the *Neptune*, Captain *Hill*, of *London* A good Presage of the next Day's Success, for they did not doubt but the Temptation of Liquor and Plunder, which they might find in this their new Prize, would make the Pyrates very confused, and so it happened

On the 10th in the Morning, the Man of War bore away to round the Cape *Roberts*'s Crew, discerning their Masts over the Land, went down into the Cabin to acquaint him of it, he being then at Breakfast with his new Guest, Captain *Hill*, on a favory Dish of Solomongundy and some of his own Beer. He took no Notice of it, and his Men almost as little, some saying she was a *Portuguese* Ship, others a *French* Slave Ship, but the major Part swore it was the *French Ranger* returning, and they were merrily debating for some Time, on the Manner of Reception, as whether they should salute her or not, but as the *Swallow* approached nigher, Things appeared plainer, and though they were stigmatized with the Name of *Cowards*, who shewed any Apprehension of Danger, yet some of them, now undeceived, declared it to *Roberts*, especially one *Armstrong*, who had deserted from that Ship, and knew her well Those *Roberts* swore at as Cowards, who meant to dishearten the Men asking them if it were so, whether they were afraid to fight or no? In short, he hardly refrained from Blows What his own Apprehensions were, till she hawled up her Ports, and hoisted her proper Colours, is uncertain, but then, being perfectly convinced he slipped his Cable, got under Sail, and ordered his Men to Arms, without any Shew of Timidity, dropping a first Rate Oath, *that it was a Bite*, but, at the same Time, resolved, like a gallant Rogue, to get clear or die

There was one *Armstrong*, as I just mentioned, a Deserter from the *Swallow*, whom they enquired of concerning the Trim and Sailing of that Ship, he told them she sail'd best upon a Wind, and therefore, if they designed to leave her, they should go before it

The Danger was imminent, and the Time very short, to consult of Means to extricate himself, his Resolution in this Streight, was as follows To pass close to the *Swallow*, with all their Sails, and receive her Broadside, before they returned a Shot, if disabled by this, or that they could not depend on sailing, then to run on Shore at the Point, and every one to shift for himself among the Negroes, or sailing in these, to board, and blow up together, for he saw that the greatest Part of his Men were drunk, passively couragious, and unfit for Service.

Roberts himself made a gallant Figure, at the Time of the Engagement, being dressed in a rich crimson Damask Waistcoat and Breeches, a red Feather in his Hat, a Gold Chain round his Neck, with a Diamond Cross hanging to it, a Sword in his Hand, and two Pair of Pistols hanging at the End of a Silk Sling, flung over his Shoulders, according to the Fashion of the Pirates He is said to have given his Orders with Boldness and Spirit, coming, according to what he

had purposed, close to the Man of War, he received her Fire, and then hoisted his black Flag, and returned it, shooting away from her, with all the Sail he could pack, and had he took *Armstrong*'s Advice, to have gone before the Wind, he had probably escaped, but keeping his Tacks down, either by the Wind's shifting, or ill Steerage, or both, he was taken a-back with his Sails, and the *Swallow* came a second Time very nigh to him He had now, perhaps, finished the Fight very desperately, if Death, who took a swift Passage in a Grape Shot, had not interposed, and struck him directly on the Throat He seated himself on the Tackles of a Gun, which one *Stephenson*, from the Helm, observing, ran to his Assistance, and not perceiving him wounded, swore at him, and bid him stand up, and fight like a Man, but when he found his Mistake, and that his Captain was certainly dead, he gushed into Tears, and wished the next Shot might be his Portion. They presently threw him over-board, with his Arms and Ornaments on, according to the repeated Request he made in his Life-time

Roberts was a tall black Man near forty Years of Age born at *Newey-Lagh*, nigh *Haverford West* in *Pembrokeshire*, of good natural Parts, and personal Bravery, tho' he applied them to such wicked purposes as made them of no Commendation, frequently drinking D———n to him who ever lived to wear a Halter He forc'd himself at first among this Company out of the *Prince*, Captain *Plumb*, at *Anamaboe*, about three Years before, where he served as second Mate, and shed, as he us'd to tell the sad Men, as many Crocodile Tears then, as they did now, but Time and good Company had wore it off He could not plead Want of Employment, nor Incapacity of getting his Bread in an honest Way, to favour so vile a Change, nor was he so much a Coward as to pretend it, he frankly own'd, it was to get rid of the disagreeable Superiority of some Masters he was acquainted with, and the love of Novelty and Change that maritime Peregrinations had accustom'd him to In an honest Service, said he there is thin Commons, low Wages and hard Labour, in this, Plenty and Satiety, Pleasure and Ease, Liberty and Power, and who would not ballance Creditor on this Side, when all the Hazard that is run for it, at worst, is only a sour Look or two at chocking, No, A merry Life and a short one, shall be my Motto Thus he preach'd himself into an Approbation of what he at first abhorred, and, being duly required with Mirth, Drinking, and the Gaiety and Diversions of his Companions, these depraved Propensities were quickly eng'd and strengthened, to the extinguishing of Fear and Conscience Yet among all the vile and ignominious Actions herein perpetrated, he is said to have had an Aversion towards forcing Men into that Service, and had procured some their Discharge, notwithstanding so many made it their Plea

When *Roberts* was gone, as tho' he had been the Life and Soul of the Gang, their Spirits sunk, many deserted their Quarters, and all stupidly neglected any Means for Defence or Escape, and their Main-mast soon after being shot by the Board, they had no Way left, but to surrender and call for Quarters The *Swallow* kept aloof, while her Boat passed and repassed for the Prisoners, because they understood they were under an Oath to blow up, and some of the Desperadoes shewed a Willingness that Way, Matches being lighted, and Scuffles happening between those who would, and those who opposed it But we cannot easily account for this Humour, which can be termed no more than a false Courage, since any of them had Power to do

from his own Life, either by Pistol, or Drowning, without involving others in the same Fate, who were in no Temper of Mind for it: And, at best, it had been only dying for fear of Death

She had 40 Guns, and 157 Men, 45 whereof were Negroes, three only were killed in the Action, without any Loss to the *Swallow* There was found upwards of 2000 l. in Gold-Dust in her The Flag could not be got easily from under the fallen Mast, and therefore was recovered by the *Swallow*, it had the Figure of a Skeleton in it, and a Man pourtray'd with a flaming Sword in his Hand, intimating a Defiance of Death, but this has been before described

The *Swallow* returned back into Cape *Lopez* Bay, and found the little *Ranger*, whom the Pirates had deserted in haste, for the better Defence of the Ship She had been plundered, according to what we have learn'd, of 2000 l in Gold-Dust, (the Shares of those Pirates who belonged to her) and Captain *Hill*, in the *Neptune*, was not unjustly suspected, for he would not wait the Man of War's returning into the Bay again, but sail'd away immediately, making no scruple afterwards to own the Seizure of other Goods out of her, and surrendering, as a Confirmation of all, 40 Ounces at *Barbadoes* To sum up the whole, if it be considered, first, that the sickly State of the Men of War, when they sail'd from *Princes* was the Misfortune that hindered their being as far as *Sierraleon*, and consequently out of the Track the Pirates then took That those Pirates, directly contrary to their Design in the second Expedition, should get above Cape *Corso*, and that nigh *Axim* a Chace should offer, that inevitably must discover them, and be soon communicated to the Men of War That the satiating their evil and malicious Tempers at *Whydah*, in burning the *Porcupine*, and running off with the *French* Ship, had strengthened the *Swallow* with 30 Men That the *Swallow* should miss them in that Road, where probably she had not, or at least had not so effectually, obtained her End That they should be so far infatuated at Cape *Lopez*, as to divide their Strength, which, when collected, might have been so formidable And lastly, that the Conquest should be without Bloodshed I say, considering all these Circumstances, it shews that the Hand of Providence was concerned in their Destruction

As to the Behaviour after they were taken, it was found that they had great Inclinations to rebel, if they could have laid hold of an Opportunity For they were very uneasy under Restraint, having been lately all Commanders themselves, nor could they brook their Diet or Quarters, without cursing and swearing and upbraiding each other, with the Folly that had brought them to it

So that to secure themselves against any mad desperate Undertaking of theirs, the Crew of the *Swallow* strongly barricado'd the Gun Room, and made another Prison before it, an Officer, with Pistols and Cutlashes, doing Duty, Night and Day, and the Prisoners within being manacled and shackled.

They would yet in these Circumstances be impudently merry, saying, when they viewed their Nakedness That they had not left them a Halfpenny, to give old *Charon*, to ferry them over *Styx* And at their thin Commons, they would observe, that they fell away so fast, that they should no have Weight left to hang them *Sutton* used to be very prophane, he happening to be in the same Irons with another Prisoner, who was more serious than ordinary, and read and pray'd often, as became his Condition, this Man *Sutton* used to swear at, and ask him, *what he proposed by such Noise and Devotion?* Heaven, says the other, *I hope* Heaven,

you Fool, says *Sutton, did you ever hear of any Pirates gothing thither? Give me* H——ll, *it's a merrier Place: I'll give* Roberts *a Salute of* 13 *Guns at my Entrance* And when he found such ludicrous Expressions had no Effect on him, he made a formal Complaint, and requested that the Officer would either remove this Man, or take his Prayer-Book away, as a common Disturber

A Combination and Conspiracy was formed betwixt *Moody, Ashplant, Magnes, Mare,* and others, to rise, and kill the Officers, and run away with the Ship This they had carried on by Means of a Mulatto Boy, who was allow'd to attend them, and proved very trusty in his Messages between the Principals, but the Evening of that Night they were to have made this Struggle, two of the Prisoners that sat next to *Ashplant*, heard the Boy whisper them upon the Project, and name to him the Hour they should be ready, upon which, they presently gave Notice of it to the Captain, which put the Ship in an Alarm for a little Time, and, on Examination, they found that several of them had made Shift to break off, or lose, their Shackles, but all this tended only to procure to themselves worse Usage and Confinement

In the same Passage to Cape *Corso*, the Prize, *Royal Fortune*, was in the same Danger She was left at the Island of St *Thomas's*, in the Possession of an Officer, and a few Men, to take in some fresh Provisions, (which were scarce at Cape *Corso*,) with Orders to follow the Ship There were only some of the Pirates Negroes, three or four wounded Prisoners, and *Scudamore* their Surgeon, from whom they seemed to be under no Apprehension, especially from the last, who might have hoped for Favour on Account of his Employ, and had stood so much indebted for his Liberty, eating and drinking constantly with the Officer, yet this Fellow, regardless of the Favour, and lost to all Sense of Reformation, endeavoured to bring over the Negroes to his Design of murdering the People, and running away with the Ship He easily prevailed with the Negroes to come into the Design, but when he came to communicate it to his Fellow Prisoners, and would have drawn them into the same Measures, by telling them, he understood Navigation, that the Negroes were stout Fellows, and, by a Smattering he had in the *Angolan* Language, he had found them willing to undertake such an Enterprize; and that it was better venturing to do this, run down the Coast and raise a new Company, than to proceed to Cape *Corso*, and be hanged like Dogs, and sundry'd One of them abhorring the Cruelty, or fearing the Success, discovered it to the Officer, who made him immediately a Prisoner, and brought the Ship safe.

When they came to be lodged in Cape *Corso-Castle*, their Hopes of this kind were all cut off, and they were assured they must there soon receive a final Sentence The Note was now changed among most of them, and, from vain insolent jesting, they became serious and devout, begging for good Books, and joining in publick Prayers, and singing of Psalms, twice at least every Day

As to their Tryals, if we should give them at length, it might appear tedious to the Reader, for which Reason, we have, for the avoiding Tautology and Repetition, put as many of them together as were try'd for the same Fact, reserving the Circumstances which are most material, with Observations on the dying Behaviour of such of them as came to our Knowledge

And first, it may be observed, that a great Part of these Pirate Ships Crews, were Men entered on the

the Coaft of *Africa*, not many Months before they were taken, from whence it may be concluded, that the pretended Conftraint of *Roberts* on them, was very often a Complotment between Parties equally willing. And this *Roberts* feveral Times openly declared, particularly to the *Onflow*'s People, whom he called aft, and afk'd them *who was willing to go, for he would force no Body?* This was depofed, by fome of his beft Hands, after Acquital, nor is it reafonable to think he fhould reject *Irifh* Voluntiers, only from a Pique againft *Kennedy*, and force others, that might hazard, and, in Time, deftroy his Government. But their Behaviour foon put him out of this Fear, and convinc'd him, that the Plea of Force was the only beft Artifice they had no fhelter themfelves under, in Cafe they fhould be taken, and that they were lefs Rogues than others only in Point of Time.

It may likewife be taken notice of, that the Country, wherein they happened to be tried, is, among other Happineffes, exempted from Lawyers, and Law-Books, fo that the Office of Regifter, of neceffity, fell on one not verfed in thofe Affairs, which might juftify the Court in want of Form, more effentially fupply'd with Integrity and Impartiality.

But, perhaps, if there was lefs Law, there might be more Juftice, than in fome other Courts, for, if the civil Law be a Law of univerfal Reafon, judging of the Rectitude or Obliquity of Mens Actions, every Man of common Senfe is endued with a Portion of it, at leaft fufficient to make him diftinguifh Right from Wrong, or what the Civilians call, *Malum in fe*.

Therefore, here, if two Perfons were equally guilty of the fame Fact, there was no convicting one, and bringing the other off by any Quirk, or Turn of Law, for they form'd their Judgments upon the Conftraint, or Willingnefs, the Aim, and Intention of the Parties, and all other Circumftances, which make a material Difference. Befides, in Crimes of this Nature, Men bred up to the Sea muft be more knowing, and much abler than others more learned in the Law, for, before a Man can have a right Idea of a Thing, he muft know the Terms ftanding for that Thing. The Sea Terms being a Language by it felf, which no Lawyer can be fuppofed to underftand, he muft therefore of Confequence want that difcriminating Faculty, which fhould direct him to judge right of the Facts meant by thofe Terms.

The Court well knew, it was not poffible to get the Evidence of every Sufferer by this Crew, and

therefore, firft of all, confidered how the Defciency fhould be fupplied, whether or no they could pardon one *John Dennis*, who had early offered himfelf as King's Evidence, and was the beft read in their Lives and Converfations. Here indeed, they were at a Lofs for Law, and concluded in the Negative, becaufe it looked like compounding with a Man to fwear falfly, lofing by it thofe great Helps he could have afforded.

Another great Difficulty in their Proceedings, was, how to underftand thofe Words in the Act of Parliament, of, *particularly fpecifying in the Charg, the Circumftances of Time, Place, &c.* i.e. to to underftand them, as to be able to hold a Court, &c if they had been indicted on particular Robberies, the Evidence had happened moftly from the Royal *African* Company's Ships, on which thefe Gentlemen of Cape *Corfo-Caftle* were not qualified to fit, their Oath running, *That they have no Intereft, directly or indirectly, in the Ship or Goods, for the Robbery of which the Party ftands accufed*. And this the, thought they had, Commiffions being paid them of fuch Goods. And on the other Side, if they were incapacitated, no Court could be formed, the Commiffion abfolutely requiring three of them by Name.

To reconcile all Things, therefore, the Court refolved, to bottom the whole of their Proceedings on the *Swallow*'s Depofitions, which were clear and plain, and had the Circumftance of Time when, Place where, Manner how, and the like, particularly fpecified, according to the Statute in that Cafe made and provided. But this admitted only a general Intimation of Robbery in the Indictment, therefore, *to approve their Clemency*, (it looking Arbitrary on the Lives of Men, to lump them to the Gallows, in fuch a fummary Way as muft have been done, had they folely adhered to the *Swallow*'s Charge) they refolved to come to particular Tryals.

Secondly, *That the Prifoners might not be ignorant whereon to anfwer*, and fo have all fair Advantages to excufe and defend themfelves, the Court farther agreed, with Juftice and Equanimity, to hear any Evidence that could be brought, to weaken or corroborate the three Circumftances that compleat a Pirate, firft, being a Voluntier amongft them at the Beginning, fecondly, being a Voluntier at the taking or robbing of any Ship, or laftly, voluntarily accepting a Share in the Booty of thofe that did, for, by a Parity of Reafon, where thefe Actions were of their own difpofing, and yet committed by them, it muft be believed their Hearts and Hands joined together, in what they acted againft his Majefty's Ship the *Swallow*.

The TRIALS of the PIRATES,

Taken by His Majesty's Ship the Swallow, *begun at* Cape Corso-Castle, *on the Coast of* Africa, *March the* 28th, 1722.

THE Commission impowered any Three named therein, to call to their Assistance such a Number of qualified Persons, as might make the Court always consist of Seven And accordingly, Summons were signed to Lieut *Jo Barnsley*, Lieut. *Ch Fanshaw*, Capt *Samuel Hartseafe*, and Capt. *William Menzies*, viz

'BY Virtue of a Power and Authority unto us
' given, by a Commission from the King, un-
' der the Seal of Admiralty, You are hereby requi-
' red to attend and make one of the Court, for the
' trying and adjudging of the Pirates, lately taken
' on this Coast, by his Majesty's Ship the *Swal-
' low*

Given under our Hands this 28th of *March*,
1722, at Cape *Corso-Castle*

Mungo Heardman,	*Francis Boye*,
James Phips,	*Edward Hyde*
Henry Dodson,	

The Commissioners being met in the Hall of the Castle, the Commission was first read, after which, the President, and then the other Members, took the Oath prescribed in the Act of Parliament, and having directed the Form of that for Witnesses, as follows, the Court was opened

I A B *do solemnly promise and swear on the Holy*
Evangelists, to bear true and faithful Witness, be-
tween the King and Prisoner, or Prisoners, in Rela-
tion to the Fact, or Facts, of Piracy and Robbery, he
or they do now stand accused of
So help me God

The Court consisted of
Captain *Mungo Heardman*, President

James Phips *Esq*, *General*   Mr Edward Hyde, *Secre*
of the Coast   *tary to the Company*
Mr H Dodson, } Mer   Lieut. John Barnsley,
Mr F Boye,   }   Lieut. Ch. Fanshaw

There were 78 Prisoners, out of the Pirate Ship *Ranger*, having been commanded before them, the Charge, or Indictment, was exhibited

You, *James Skyrm, Michael Lemmon, Robert Hart-
ley, &c*

'YE, and every one of you, are, in the Name,
' and by the Authority, of our dread Sovereign
' Lord *George*, King of *Great Britain*, indicted as
' follows.

' Forasmuch as, in open Contempt of the Laws of
' your Country, ye have all of you been wickedly
' united, and articled together, for the Annoyance
' and Disturbance of his Majesty's trading Subjects by
' Sea And have, in Conformity to the most evil
' and mischievous Intentions, been twice down the
' Coast of *Africa*, with two Ships, once in the Be-
' ginning of *August*, and a second Time, in *January*
' last, sinking, burning, or robbing such Ships, and
' Vessels, as then happened in your Way
' Particularly, ye stand charged at the Instance,
' and Information, of Captain *Chaloner Ogle*, as
' Traytors and Pirates, for the unlawful Opposition
' ye made to his Majesty's Ship, the *Swallow*, under
' his Command
' For that on the 5th of *February* last past, upon
' Sight of the aforesaid King's Ship, ye did imme-
' diately weigh Anchor from under Cape *Lopez*, on
' the Southern Coast of *Africa*, in a *French* built Ship,
' of 32 Guns, called the *Ranger*, and did pursue and
' chase the aforesaid King's Ship, with such Dispatch
' and Precipitancy, as declared ye common Robbers
' and Pirates
' That about Ten of the Clock the same Morning,
' drawing within Gun-shot of his Majesty's afore-
' said Ship the *Swallow*, ye hoisted a piratical black
' Flag, and fired several chase Guns, to deter, as
' much as ye were able, his Majesty's Servants from
' their Duty
' That an Hour after this, being very nigh to
' the aforesaid King's Ship, ye did audaciously con-
' tinue in a hostile Defence and Assault, for about
' two Hours more, in open Violation of the Laws,
' and in Defiance to the King's Colours and Com
' mission
' And lastly, that in the acting, and compassing of
' all this, ye were all, and every one of you, in a
' wicked Combination, voluntarily to exert, and ac-
' tually did, in your several Stations, use your ut
' most Endeavours to distress the said King's Ship,
' and murder his Majesty's good Subjects

To which they severally pleaded, *Not Guilt,*

Then the Court called for the Officers of the
Swallow, Mr *Isaac Sun*, Lieutenant, *Ralph Buld
rick*, Boatswain, *Daniel Macklaughlin*, Mate, desir
ing them to view the Prisoners, and say whether
they knew them? And requiring them to give in Account in what Manner they had attack'd and fough
the King's Ship, and they agreed as follows

That

That they had viewed all the Prisoners, as they stood now before the Court, and were assured they were the same taken out of one, or other, of the Pyrate Ships, *Royal Fortune* or *Ranger*, but verily believe them to be taken out of the *Ranger*.

That they did in the King's Ship, at break of Day, on *Monday*, the 5th of *February*, 1721-2 discover three Ships at Anchor, under Cape *Lopez*, on the Southern Coast of *Africa*; the Cape bearing then W S W about three Leagues, and perceiving one of them to have a Pendant flying, and having heard their Morning-Gun before, they immediately suspected them to be *Roberts* the Pyrate, his Consort, and a *French* Ship, which they knew had been lately carried out of *Whydah* Road.

The King's Ship was oblig'd to hawl off N W and W N W to avoid a Sand called the *French Man's Bank*, the Wind then at S S E and found, in half an Hour's time, one of the three had got under Sail from the Careen, and was bending her Sails, in a Chace towards them. To encourage this Rashness and Precipitancy, they kept away before the Wind, as tho' afraid, but with their Tacks on Board, their Main-Yard braced, and making at the same Time, very bad Steerage.

About half an Hour after Ten, in the Morning, the Pyrates Ship came within Gun-shot, and fired four Chace Guns, hoisted a black Flag at the Mizzen-Peek, and got their Sprit-sail Yard under their Bowsprit, for boarding. In half an Hour more, approaching still nigher, they starboarded their Helm, and gave her a broadside, the Pyrate bringing to, and returning the same.

After this, the Deponents say, their Fire grew slack for some Time, because the Pyrate was shot so far a Head on the Weather-Bow, that few of their Guns could point to her; yet in this Interval their black Flag was either shot away, or hawled down a little Space, and hoisted again.

At length, by their ill Steerage, and the Favour of the Wind, they came near a second Time, and about Two in the Afternoon shot away their Main-Topmast.

The Colours they fought under, besides a black-Flag, were a red *English* Ensign, a King's Jack, and a *Dutch* Pendant, which they struck, at, or about, Three in the Afternoon, and called for Quarters, it proving to be a *French* built Ship of 32 Guns, called the *Ranger*,

Isaac Sun,
Ralph Baldrick,
Daniel Macklauglin.

When the Evidence had been heard, the Prisoners were called upon to answer, how they came on Board this Pyrate Ship, and their Reason for so audacious a Resistance, as had been made against the King's Ship was also demanded.

To this, each, in his Reply, owned himself to be one of those taken out of the *Ranger*, that he had signed their pyratical Articles, and shared in their Plunder, some few only accepted, who had been there too short a Time. But that neither in this signing, or sharing, nor in the Resistance that had been made against his Majesty's Ship, had they been Voluntiers, but had acted in these several Parts, from a Terror of Death; which by a Law amongst them, was to be the Portion of these who refused. The Court then ask'd who made those Laws? How those Guns came to be fired? Or why they had not deserted their Stations, and mutiny'd, when so fair a Prospect of Redemption offered? They replied still, with the same Answers, and could extenuate their Crimes with no other Plea, than

being forced Men. Wherefore the Court were of Opinion, that the Indictment, as it charged them with an unlawful Attack and Resistance of the King's Ship, was sufficiently proved; but then, it being undeniably evident, that many of these Prisoners had been forced, and some of them of very short standing, they did, on mature Deliberation, come to this merciful Resolution.

That they would hear further Evidence for, or against, each Person singly, in Relation to those Parts of the Indictment, which declared them Voluntiers, or charged them with aiding and assisting, at the burning, sinking, or robbing of other Ships, for if they acted, or assisted, in any Robberies or Devastations, it would be a Conviction they were Voluntiers, here such Evidence, though it might want the Form, still carried the Reason of the Law with it.

The Charge was exhibited also against 86 Prisoners, taken out of the *Royal Fortune.*

You, *Harry Glasby*, *William Davison*, *William Champnis*, *Samuel Morwell*, &c.

‘ YE, and every one of you, are, in the Name,
‘ and by the Authority, of our dread Sovereign
‘ Lord *George*, King of *Great Britain*, indicted as
‘ follows
‘ Forasmuch as, in open Contempt and Violation
‘ of the Laws of your Country, to which ye ought to
‘ have been subject, ye have all of you been wickedly
‘ united, and articled together, for the Annoyance
‘ and Disturbance of his Majesty's trading Subjects by
‘ Sea. And in Conformity to so wicked an Agree-
‘ ment and Association, ye have been twice lately
‘ down this Coast of *Africa*, once in *August*, and a se-
‘ cond Time in *January* last, spoiling and destroying
‘ many Goods and Vessels of his Majesty's Subjects,
‘ and other trading Nations.
‘ Particularly, ye stand indicted at the Information
‘ and Instance of Captain *Chaloner Ogle*, as Tray-
‘ tors, Robbers, Pirates, and common Enemies to
‘ Mankind.
‘ For that on the 10th of *February* last, in a Ship
‘ ye were possess'd of called the *Royal Fortune*, of
‘ 40 Guns, ye did maintain a hostile Defence and
‘ Resistance for some Hours, against his Majesty's Ship
‘ the *Swallow*, nigh Cape *Lopez* Bay, on the South-
‘ ern Coast of *Africa*.
‘ That this Fight and insolent Resistance against
‘ the King's Ship, was made, not only without any
‘ Pretence of Authority, more than that of your own
‘ private depraved Wills, but was done also under a
‘ black Flag, flagrantly by that, denoting yourselves
‘ common Robbers and Traytors, Opposers and Vio-
‘ lators of the Laws.
‘ And lastly, that in this Resistance, ye were all of
‘ you Voluntiers, and did, as such, contribute your
‘ utmost Efforts, for disabling and distressing the a-
‘ foresaid King's Ship, and deterring his Majesty's
‘ Servants therein from their Duty.

To which they severally pleaded, *Not Guilty.*

Whereupon the Officers of his Majesty's Ship, the *Swallow* were called again, and testified as follows.

That they had seen all the Prisoners now before the Court, and knew them to be the same who were taken out of one or other of the Pirate Ships, *Royal Fortune* or *Ranger*, and verily believed them to be those taken out of the *Royal Fortune*.

That the Prisoners were possess'd of a Ship of 4 Guns,

Guns, called the *Royal Fortune*, and were at an Anchor under Cape *Lopez*, on the Coast of *Africa*, with two others, when his Majesty's Ship the *Swallow*, to which the Deponents belong'd, and were Officers) stood in for the Place, on *Saturday* the 10th of *February, 1721 2* The largest had a Jack, Ensign and Pendant flying, being this *Royal Fortune*, who, on Sight of them, and their Boats passing and repassing, from the other two, which they supposed to be with them The Wind not favouring the aforesaid King's Ship, she was oblig'd to make two Trips to gain high enough the Wind, to fetch in with the Pirates, and, and being at length little more than random Shot from them, they found she slipped her Cable, and got under Sail

At Eleven the Pirate was within Pistol-Shot, a Breast of them, with a black Flag, and Pendant hoisted at their Main-topmast Head The Deponents say, they then struck the *French* Ensign, that had continued hoisted at their Staff all the Morning t ll then, and display'd the King's Colours, giving her, at the same Time, their Broadside, which was immediately return'd

The Pirates Mizzen-topmast fell, and some of her Rigging was torn, yet she still out sailed the Man of War, and slid half Gun Shot from them, while they continued to fire without Intermission, and the other to return such Guns as could be brought to bear, till, by favour of the Winds, they were advanced very nigh again, and, after exchanging a few more Shot, about half an Hour past one, his Main-Mast came down, having received a Shot a little below the Parrel

At Two she struck her Colours, and called for Quarters, proving to be a Ship formerly called the *Onslow*, but by them, the *Royal Fortune* and the Prisoners from her assured them, that the smallest Ship of the two, then remaining in the Road, belong'd to them, by the Name of the *Little Ranger*, which they had deserted on this Occasion

> *Isaac Sun,*
> *Ralph Baldrick,*
> *Daniel Macklaughlin*

The Prisoners were ask'd several Questions by the Court, to the same purpose with those put to the others in the Morning, as, What Exception they had to make against what had been sworn? And what they had to say in their Defence? And their Replies were much the same with the other Prisoners? that they were forced Men, had not fired a Gun in this Resistance against the *Swallow*, and that what little Assistance they did give on this Occasion, was to the Sails and Rigging, to comply with the arbitrary Commands of *Roberts*, who had threatened, and they were perswaded would, have shot them on Refusal

The Court, to dispense equal Justice, mercifully resolve for these, as they had done for the other Pyrite Crew, that further Evidence should be heard against each Man singly, to the two Points, of being a Volunteer at first, and to their particular Acts of Pyracy and Robbery, since That so Men, who had been freely received amongst them, and as yet had not been at the taking, or plundering, of any Ship, might have the Opportunity and Benefit of clearing their Innocence, and not fall promiscuously with the Guilty

By Order of the Court,

John Atk , Regist

Wm Magnes, &c, Oughterlavie, Wm Main, Wm Mackintsh, Vic Adylang, John Walden, Israel Hind, Marcus Johnson, Wm Petty, Wm Fer-

nan, *Abraham Harper, Wm Wood, Tho How John Stephenson, Ch Bunce,* and *John Griffin.*

Against these it was deposed by Captain *Joseph Trahern,* and *George Fenn* his Mate that they were all of them, either at the attacking and taking of the Ship *King Solomon,* or afterwards at the robbing and plundering of her, and in this Manner,

That on the 6th of *January* last, their Ship riding at Anchor near Cape *Appollonia* in *Africa,* they discovered a Boat rowing towards them, against Wind and Stream, from a Ship that lay about three Miles to Leeward They judged from the Number of Men in her, as she nearer advanced, that she was a Pirate, and made some Preparations for receiving her, believing, on a nigher View, they would think fit to withdraw from an Attack, that must be on their Side with great Disadvantage in an open Boat, and against double the Number of Men, yet by the Rashness and the Pusillanimity of his own People (who laid down their Arms, and immediately called for Quarter) the Ship was taken, and afterwards robbed by them

President Can you charge your Memory with any Particulars in the Seizure and Robbery?

Evidence We know that *Magnes,* Quarter-Master of the Pyrate Ship, commanded the Men in this Boat that took us, and assumed the Authority of ordering her Provisions and Stores out, which being of different kinds, we soon found were seized and sent away under more particular Directions, for *Main,* as Boatswain of the Pyrate Ship, carried away two Cables, and several Coils of Rope, as what belonged to his Province, beating some of our own Men for not being brisk enough at working in the Robbery *Petty,* as Sail-maker, saw to the Sails and Canvas, *Harper,* as Cooper, to the Cask and Tools; *Griffin,* to the Carpenter's Stores, and *Oughterlarney,* as Pilot, having shifted himself with a Suit of my Cloathes, a new tie Wig, and called for a Bottle of Wine, ordered the Ship, very arrogantly, to be steer'd under Commodore *Roberts's* Stern, which I supposed was to know what Orders there were concerning her So far particularly In the general, Sir, they were very outragious and emulous in Mischief

President Mr *Castel,* acquaint the Court of what you know in Relation to this Robbery of the *King Solomon,* in particular, after what Manner the Pyrate-Boat was dispatch'd for this Attempt

Tho Castel I was a Prisoner, Sir, with the Pirates, when their Boat was ordered upon that Service, and found, upon a Resolution of going, Word was passed through the Company, Who would go? And I saw all that did, did it voluntarily, there being no Compulsion, but rather a pressing who should be foremost

The Prisoners yielded to what had been sworn about the Attack and Robbery, but denied the latter Evidence, saying, *Roberts* hector'd and upbraided them with Cowardice on this very Occasion, and told some, they were very ready to step on board of a Prize when within Command of the Ship, but now there seem d to be a Trial of their Valour, they were backward and fearful

President So that *Roberts* forced ye upon this Attack

Prisoners Roberts commanded us into the Boat, and the Quarter Master to rob the Ship, neither of whose Commands we dared to have refused

President And granting it so, those are still your own Acts, since done by Orders from Officers of your own Election Why would Men, honestly disposed, give their Votes for such a Captain and such a Quarter Mafter, as were every Day commanding them on diftaftful fervice?

Here fucceeded a Silence among the Prifoners, but at length *Fennon* very honeftly own'd, that he did not give his Vote to *Magnes*, but to *David Simpfon* (the old Quarter-Mafter,) for in Truth, fays he, *I took Magnes for too honeft a Man, and unfit for the Bifnefs.*

The Evidence was plain and home, and the Court, without any Hefitation, brought them in *Guilty.*

William Church, Phil Haak, James White, Nich Brattle, Hugh Riddle, William Thomas, Thomas Roberts, Jo Richards, Jo Cane, R Wood, R Scot, Wm Davifon, Sam Morwell, Edward Evans, Wm Guaneys, and 18 *French* Men

The four firft of thefe Prifoners, it was evident to the Court, ferved as Mufick on board the Pirate, were forced lately from the feveral Merchant Ships they belonged to, and that they had, during this Confinement, an uneafy Life of it, having fometimes their Fiddles, and often their Heads broke, only for excufing themfelves, or faying they were tired, when any Fellow took it in his Head to demand a Tune.

The other *Englifh* had been a very few Days on board the Pirate, only from *Whydah* to Cape *Lopez*, and no Capture or Robbery done by them in that Time. And the *French* Men were brought with a Defign to reconduct their own Ship, or the *Little Ranger* in exchange, to *Whydah* Road again, and were ufed like Prifoners, neither quarter'd, nor fuffered to carry Arms. So that the Court immediately acquiefced in *acquitting them.*

THO Sutton, David Simpfon, Chrifto Moody, Phil Bill, R Harsay, Hen Dennis, David Rice, Wm Williams, R Harris, Geo. Smith, Ed. Watts, Jo Mitchell, and James Barrow

The Evidence againft thefe Prifoners, were *Geret de Haen*, Mafter of the *Flufhingham*, taken nigh *Axim*, about the Beginning of *January* laft.

Beny Kreft Mafter, and *James Groet* Mate of the *Gertruycht*, taken nigh *Gabone* in *December* laft, and Mr *Caftel, Wingfield*, and others, that had been Prifoners with the Pirates

The former depofed, that all thefe Prifoners (excepting *Hardy*) were on board at the Robbery and Plunder of their Ships, behaving in a vile outragious Manner, putting them in bodily Fears, fometimes for the Ship, and fometimes for themfelves, and in particular, *Kreft* charged it on *Sutton*, that he had ordered all their Gunner's Stores out, on which the Prifoner prefently interrupted, and faid, he was perjured, *That he had not taken Half.* A Reply, I believe, not defign'd as any faucy Way of jefting, but to give their Behaviour an Appearance of more Humanity than the *Dutch* would allow

From Mr *Caftel, Wingfield*, and others, they were proved to be diftinguifh'd Men, Men, who were confulted as Chiefs in all Enterprizes, belonged to the Houfe of Lords (as they call'd it) and could carry an Authority over others. The former faid particularly of *Hardy*, Quarter-Mafter of the *Ranger*, that when the *Diligence* Sloop was taken (whereto he belonged) none was bufier in the Plunder, and he was the very Man who fcuttled and funk that Veffel

From fome of the Prifoners acquitted, it was farther demanded, Whether the Acceptance or Refufal of any Office was not in their own Option? And it was declared, that every Officer was chofen by a majority of Votes, and might refufe, if he pleafed,

fince others gladly embraced what brought with it an additional Share of Prize   *Guilty*

The Court on the 31ft of *March*, remanded the following Six before them for Sentence, *viz David Simpfon, Wm Magnes, R Hardy, Thomas Sutton, Chrifto Moody*, and *Valen Afhplant*

To whom the Prefident fpoke to the following Purpofe   'The Crime of Piracy, of which all of 'you have been juftly convicted, is of all other Rob 'beries the moft aggravating, and inhumane; in that 'being removed from the Fears of Surprize, in re 'mote and diftant Parts, ye do in Wantonnefs of 'Power often add Cruelty to Theft

'Pirates, unmoved at Diftrefs or Poverty, not on 'ly fpoil and rob, but do it from Men needy, and 'and who are purchafing their Livelihoods thro' 'Hazards and Difficulties, which ought rather to 'move Compaffion, and what is ftill worfe, do of 'ten, by Perfwafion or Force, engage the inconfi 'derate Part of them, to their own hard Families 'Ruin; removing them from their Wives and Chil 'dren, and, by that, from the Means that fhould 'fupport them from Mifery and Want

'To a trading Nation, nothing can be fo deftruc 'tive as Piracy, or call for more exemplary Punifh 'ment, befides, the national Reflection it infers 'It cuts off the Returns of Induftry, and thofe 'plentiful Importations that alone can make an I 'fland flourifhing; and it is your Aggravation, that 'ye have been the Chiefs and Rulers in thefe licen 'tious and lawlefs Practices

'However, contrary to the Meafures ye have 'dealt, ye have been heard with Patience, and tho' 'little has, or poffibly could, have been faid in Ex 'cufe or Extenuation of your Crimes, yet Charity 'makes us hope, that a true and fincere Repentance '(which we heartily recommend) may entitle ye to 'Mercy and Forgivenefs, after the Sentence of the 'Law has taken Place, which now remains upon me 'to pronounce

YOU Dav Simpfon, Wm Magnes, R Hard Tho Sutton, Chrifto Moody, and Val Afhplant Ye, and each you, are adjudged and fentenced, to be carried back to the Place from whence ye came, from thence to the Place of Execution, without the Gates of this Caftle, and there, within the Flood-Marks, to be hanged by the Neck till ye are dead

After this, ye, and each of you, fha'l be taken down, and your Bodies hanged in Chains

Warrant of Execution

PUrfuant to the Sentence given on *Saturday* by the Court of Admiralty, at *Cape-Corfo Caftle*, againft *Dav Simpfon, Wm Magnes, R Hard, Tho Sutton, Chrifto Moody*, and *Val Afhplant*

You are hereby directed to carry the aforefaid Malefactors to the Place of Execution, without the Gates of this Caftle, To-morrow Morning at Nine of the Clock, and there, within the Flood-Marks, caufe them to be hanged by the Neck till they are dead, for which, this fhall be your Warrant. Given under my Hand this 2d. Day of *April*, 1722.

To *Jofeph Gordyn*,   *Mungo Headman*
    Provoft-Marfhal

The Bodies remove in Chains, to the Gibbets already erected on the adjacent Hillocks

                        M. H

William Phillips

IT appeared by the Evidence of Captain *Jo Trahern*, and *George Fenn*, Mate of the *King Solomon*, that this Prifoner was Boatfwain of the fame Ship,

Snip, when she was attacked and taken off Cape *Appoll nia*, the 6th of *January* last, by the Pirates Boat.

When the Boat drew nigh, (they say,) it was judged from the Number of Men in her, that they were Pirates, and being hailed, they answered, *Defiance*, at which the Commander snatched a Musquet from one of his Men, and fired, asking them at the same Time, Whether they would stand by him, to defend the Ship? But the Pirates returning a Volley, and crying out, they would give no Quarters if any Resistance was made, this Prisoner took upon him to call out for Quarters, without the Master's Consent, and missed the rest to the laying down their Arms, and giving up the Ship, to half the Number of Men, in an open Boat. It was further evident, he became, after this, a Voluntier amongst them. First, because he was presently very forward and brisk, in robbing the Ship *King Solomon* of her Provisions and Stores. Secondly, because he endeavoured to have his Captain ill used, and lastly, because he had confessed to *Finn* that he had been obliged to sign their Articles that Night (a Pistol being laid on the Table, to signify he must do it, or be shot) when the whole appeared to be an Untruth from other Evidence, who also asserted his being armed in the Action against the *Swallow*.

In Answer to this, he first observed, The Unhappiness he was under, of being Friendless in this Part of the World, which, elsewhere, by witnessing to the Honesty of his former Life, would, he believed, in a great Measure, have invalidated the wrong Evidence that had been given of his being a Voluntier with the Pirates. He own'd, indeed, he made no Application to his Captain, to intercede for a Discharge, but excused it with saying, he had a Dislike to him, and therefore was sure that such Application would have availed him nothing.

The Court observed the Pretences of this, and others of the Pirates, of a Pistol and their Articles being served up in a Dish together, or of their being misused and forced from an honest Service, was often a Complotment of the Parties, to render them less suspected of those they came from, and was to answer the End of being put in a News Paper or Affidavit, and the Pirates were so generous as not to refuse a Compliment to a Brother that cost them nothing, and, at the same Time, secured the best Hands, the best I call them, because such a Dependance made them act more boldly. *Guilty.*

Harry Glasby, Master

THERE appearing several Persons in Court, who had been taken by *Roberts's* Ship, whereof the Prisoner was Master, their Evidence was accepted as follows

Jo Trahern, Commander of the *King Solomon*, deposed, that the Prisoner, indeed, attempted to act as Master of the Pirate Ship, while he was under Restraint there, but was observed like no Master, every one obeying at Discretion, of which he had taken Notice, and complained to him, how hard a Condition it was, to be a Chief among Brutes, and that he was weary of his Life, and such other Expressions, now out of his Memory, as shewed him in a great Measure not inclined to that Course of Living.

Jo Wingfield, a Prisoner with them at *Calabar*, told the same, as to the Quality he acted in, but that he was civil beyond any of them, and verily believed, that when the Brigantine he served on board of as a Factor for the *African* Company, was ordered to be burnt, this Man was the Instrument of saving it, by pressing himself with a great deal

of Sorrow, for this and the like malicious Rogueries of the Company he was in, that to him shewed, he had acted with Reluctancy, as one who could not avoid what he did. He adds further, that when one *Hamilton* a Surgeon was taken by them, and the Articles were about to be imposed on him, he opposed, and prevented it. And that *Hunter*, another Surgeon among them, was clear'd at the Prisoner's Instance and Persuasion; from which last, this Deponent had it assured to him, that *Glasby* had once been under Sentence of Death, on board of them, with two more, for endeavouring an Escape in the *West-Indies*, and that the other two were really shot for it.

Elizabeth Trengrove, who was taken a Passenger in the *African* Company's Ship *Onslow*, strengthened the Evidence of the last Witness; for having heard a good Character of this *Glasby*, she enquired of the Quarter-Master, who was then on board a robbing, Whether or no she could see him? And he told her *No*, they never ventured him from the Ship, for he had once endeavoured his Escape, and they had ever since continued jealous of him.

Edward Crisp, Captain *Trengrove*, and Captain *Sharp*, who had all been taken in their Turns, acknowledged for themselves and others, who had unluckily fallen into those Pirates Hands, that the good Usage they had met with, was chiefly thro' the Prisoner's Means, who had often interposed, and was for leaving sufficient Stores and Instruments on board the Ships they had robbed, alledging they were superfluous and unnecessary on board their own Vessel.

James White, whose Business was Musick, and who was on the Poop of the Pirate Ship in Time of Action with the *Swallow*, deposed, that during the Engagement, and the Defence she made, he never saw the Prisoner busied about the Guns, or giving Orders, either to the loading or firing of them, but that he wholly attended to the setting or trimming of the Sails, as *Roberts* commanded, and that in the Conclusion, he verily believed him to be the Man, who prevented the Ship's being blown up, by setting trusty Centinels below, and opposing himself against such hot-headed Fellows, as had procured lighted Matches, and were going down for that Purpose.

Isaac Sun, Lieutenant of the Man of War, deposed, that when he came to take Possession of the Prize, in the King's Boat, he found the Pirates in a very distracted and divided Condition, some being for blowing up, and others (who supposed themselves least culpable) opposing it. That in this Confusion he enquired for the Prisoner, of whom he had before heard a good Character; who then rendered all the Service in his Power, for preventing the Mischief, in particular, he understood by all Hands, that he had seized and taken from one *James Philips*, a lighted Match, at the Instant he was going down to the Magazine, swearing, that he would send them all to H——l together. He had heard also, that, after *Roberts* was killed, the Prisoner ordered the Colours to be struck, and had since shewn, how opposite his Practice and Principles had been, by discovering who were the greatest Rogues among them.

The Prisoner in his own Defence said, That when he had the Misfortune of falling into the Pirates Hands, he was chief Mate of the *Samuel* of *London*, Captain *Carey*, and when he had hid himself, to prevent the Design of carrying him away, they found him, and beat him, and threw him over-board Seven Days afterwards, upon his objecting against, and refusing to sign their Articles, he was cut and abus'd again.

again. That tho' after this, he ingratiated himself, by a more easy Carriage, it was only to make Life easy; the Shares they had given him, having been from Time to Time returned again to such Prisoners as fell in his Way; till of late, indeed, he had made a small Reservation, and had desired Captain *Loane* to take two or three Moidores from him, to carry to his Wife, He was once taken, he said, at making his Escape in the *West-Indies,* and, with two more, sentenc'd to be shot for it, by a drunken Jury, the latter actually suffered, and he was preserved only by one of the chief Pirates taking a sudden Liking to him, and bullying the others. A second time he ran away at *Hispaniola,* carrying a Pocket Compass, for conducting him through the Wood, but that it being a most desolate wild Part of the Island he fell upon, and he ignorant how to direct his Course, he was obliged, after two or three Days wandring, to return towards the Ship again, denying with egregious Oaths, the Design he was charged with, for Fear they should shoot him. From this Time he hoped it would be some Extenuation of his Fault, that most of the acquitted Prisoners can witness, they entertained Jealousies of him, and *Roberts* would not admit him into his Secrets, and withal, that Captain *Cary,* and four other Passengers with him, had made Affidavit of his having been forced from his Employ, which tho' he could not produce, yet he humbly hoped the Court would think highly probable from the Circumstances offered.

On the whole, the Court was of Opinion, that Artists had the best Pretension to the Plea of Force, from the Necessity Pyrates are sometimes under of engaging such, and that many Parts of his own Defence had been confirmed by the Evidence, who had asserted, he acted with Reluctance, and had expressed a Concern and Trouble for the little Hopes that remained to him, of ever extricating himself. That he had used all Prisoners well, at the hazard of ill Usage to himself. That he had not in any military Capacity assisted their Robberies. That he had twice endeavoured his Escape with the utmost Danger. *Acquitted him*

Captain *James Skyrm.*

IT appeared from the Evidence of several Prisoners acquitted, that this *Skyrm* commanded the *Ranger,* in that Defence she made against the King's Ship, that he ordered the Men to their Quarters, and the Guns to be loaded and fired, having a Sword in his Hand to enforce those Commands, and beating such to their Duty, whom he espied any way negligent or backward. That altho' he had lost a Leg in the Action, his Temper was so warm, as to refuse going off the Deck, till he found all was lost.

In his Defence, he says, he was forced from a Mate's Employ on board a Sloop call'd the *Greyhound,* of St *Christophers, Oct* 1720. The Pirate having drubbed him, and broke his Head, only for offering to go away when that Sloop was dismissed. Custom and Success had since indeed blunted, and, in some Measure, worn out the Sense of Shame, but that he had really for several Months past been sick, and disqualified for any Duty, and though *Roberts* had forced him on this Expedition, much against his Will, yet the Evidence must be sensible, that the Title of Captain gave him no Pre-eminence; for he could not be obeyed, though he had often called to them, to leave off their Fire, when he perceived it to be the King's Ship.

The Sickness he alledged, but more especially the Circumstance of losing his Leg, were Aggravations of his Fault, shewing him more alert on such Occasions, than he was willing to be thought. As to the Name of *Captain* if it were allowed to give him no Precedence out of Battle, yet here it was proved a Title of Authority, such in Authority as could direct an Engagement against the King's Colours, and therefore he was in the highest Degree, *Guilty*

John Walden

CAptain *John Trahern,* and *George Fenn,* deposed, That the Prisoner was one of the Number, who, in an open Boat pyratically assailed, and took their Ship, and was remarkably busy at Mischief, having a Pole-ax in his Hand, which served him instead of a Key, to all the lock'd Doors and Boxes he came nigh. Also in particular, he cut the Cable of our Ship, when the other Pirates were busied at heaving up the Anchor, saying, *Captain, what signifies this Trouble of* Yo Hope, *and straining in hot Weather, there are more Anchors at London, and besides, your Ship is to be burnt*

William Smith (a Prisoner acquitted) deposed, That *Walden* was known among the Pirates, mostly, by the Nick name of *Miss Nanney* (ironically so presumed from the Hardness of his Temper) that he was one of the twenty who voluntarily came on board the *Ranger,* in the Chace she made out after the *Swallow,* and by a Shot from that Ship, he lost his Leg, his Behaviour in the Fight, till then, being bold and daring.

The President called for *Harry Glasby,* and bid him relate a Character of the Prisoner, and what Custom was among them, in Relation to these voluntary Expeditions, out of their proper Ship, and this of going on board the *Ranger,* in particular

And he gave in for Evidence, that the Prisoner was looked on as a brisk Hand (i.e. as he farther explained it, a stanch Pirate, and a great Rogue) that when the *Swallow* first appeared in Sight, every one was willing to believe her a *Portuguese,* because Sugar was very much in Demand, and had made some Jarring and Distinction between the two Companies (the *Fortune's* People drinking Punch, when the *Ranger's* could not) that *Roberts,* on Sight of the *Swallow,* hailed the new *Ranger,* and bid them right their Ship, and get under Sail, there is, says he, Sugar in the Offing, bring it in, that we may have no more mumbling, ordering at the same Time the Word to be pass'd among the Crew, who would go to their Assistance, and immediately the Boat was full of Men, to transport themselves

President. Then every one that goes on board of any Prize, does it voluntarily? Or were there any other Reasons for it?

H. Glasby. Every Man is commonly called in a List, and inits, in his Turn, to go on board of Prize, because they then allowed a Shift of Cloths (the best they can find) over and above the Divided from the Robbery, and this they are so far from being compell'd to, that it often becomes the Contest and Quarrel amongst them. But in the present such like Cases, where there appears a Prospect of Trouble, the Lazy and Timerous are often willing to decline their Turn, and yield to their Betters, who thereby establish a greater Credit.

The Prisoner, and the rest of those Men who came from the *Fortune* on board the *Ranger,* to his this Expedition, were Volunteers, and the truest Men among us

President. Was there no Danger of the *Ranger* leaving you in this Chace, or at some other time in order to surrender?

H. Glasb. Most of the *Ranger's* Crew were stout Men, Men who had been enter'd only since the taking on the Coast of Guinea, and thereto chiefly

liberal a Share in fresh Provisions, or Wine, as the *Fortune*'s People, who thought they had born the Burthen and Heat of the Day, which had given Occasion, indeed, to some Grumblings and Whispers, as tho' they would take an Opportunity to leave us, but we never supposed, if they did, that it would be with any other Design than setting up for themselves, they having, many of them, behaved with greater Severity than the old Standers.

The Prisoner appeared undaunted, and rather solicitous about resting his Stump, than giving any Answer to the Court, or making any Defence for himself till called upon, and then he related in a careless, or rather hopeless Manner, the Circumstances of his first Entrance, being forced, he said, out of the *Blessing of Lemmington*, at *Newfoundland*, about 12 Months past, this he was sure, most of the old Pirates knew, and that he was for some Time as sick of the Change as any Man, but Custom and ill Company had altered him. He then own'd very frankly, that he was at the Attack, and Taking of the *King Solomon*, that he did cut her Cable, and that none was forced on those Occasions.

As to the last Expedition in the *Ranger*, he confessed he went on board of her, but that it was by *Roberts*'s Order, and in the Chace he loaded one Gun, to bring her to, but when he saw it was a Bite, he declared to his Comrades, that it was not worth while to resist, forbore firing, and assisted to reeve the Braces, in order, if they could, to get away, in which sort of Service he was busied, when a Shot from the Man of War took off his Leg. And being asked, What he would have done, supposing the Chace had proved a *Portuguese*? Why then, says he, I don't know what I might have done, intimating withal, that every Body then would have been ready enough at plundering. *Guilty*

Peter Scudamore

Harry Glass, Jo Wingfield, and Nicholas Brattle, deposed thus much, as to his being a Volunteer with the Pirates, from Capt *Roel*, at *Calabar* First, That he quarrell'd with *Moody*, one of the Heads of the Gang, and fought with him, because he opposed his going, asking *Rolls* in a leering Manner, Whether he would not be so kind as to put him into the *Gazette*, when he came Home. And, at another Time, when as he was going from the Pirate Ship, in his Boat, a Tornado arose, *I wish*, says he, *the Rascal may be drowned, for he is a great Rogue, and has endeavoured to do me all the ill Offices he could among these Gentlemen* (i e Pirates)

And secondly, That he had signed the Pirate's Articles with a great deal of Alacrity, and gloried in having been the first Surgeon that had done so (for before this it was their Custom to change their Surgeons when they desired it, after having served a Time, and never obliged them to sign, but he was resolved to break thro' this, for the Good of those who were to follow,) swearing immediately upon it, he was now, he hoped, as great a Rogue as any of them.

Captain *Jo Trahern*, and *George Fenn*, his Mate, deposed, That the Prisoner had taken out of the *K Solomon* their Surgeon's capital Instruments, some Medicines, and a Back-Gammon Table, which latter became the Means of a Quarrel between one *Wilson* and he, whose Property they should be, and they were yielded to the Prisoner.

Jo Sharp, Master of the *Elizabeth*, heard the Prisoner ask *Roberts* leave, to force *Comry*, his Surgeon, from him, which was accordingly done, and with him, he carried also some of the Ships Medicines. But what gave a fuller Proof of the Dishonesty of his Principles, was, the treacherous Design he had formed of running away with the Prize, in her Passage to Cape *Corso*, tho' he had been treated with all Humanity, and very unlike a Prisoner, on Account of his Employ and better Education, which had rendered him less to be suspected.

Mr *Child* deposed, That in their Passage from the Island of St *Thomas*, in the *Fortune* Prize, this Prisoner was several Times tempting him into Measures of rising with the Negroes, and killing the *Swallow*'s People, shewing him, how easily the white Men might be demolished, and a new Company raised at *Angola*, and that Part of the Coast, for, says he, I understand how to navigate a Ship, and can soon teach you to steer, and is it not better to do this, than to go back to Cape Corso, and be hang'd and Sun-dry'd? To which the Deponent replying, That he was not afraid of being hang'd, *Scudamore* bid him be still, and no Harm should come to him, but before the next Day evening, which was the designed Time of executing this Project, the Deponent discovered it to the Officer, and assured him, that *Scudamore* had been talking all the preceding Night to the Negroes, in the *Angolan* Language.

Isaac Burnet heard the Prisoner ask *James Harris*, a Pirate who had been left with the wounded in the Prize, whether he was willing to come into the Project of running away with the Ship, and endeavouring to raise a new Company, but he turned the Discourse to Horse racing, as the Deponent crept nigher, he acquainted the Officer with what he had heard, who kept the People under Arms all Night, their Apprehensions of the Negroes not being groundless, for many of them, having lived a long Time in this piratical Way, were by the thin Commons they were reduced to, as ript for Mischief is any.

The Prisoner in his Defence said, That he was a forced Man from Captain *Rolls*, in *October* last, and if he had not shewn such a Concern as became him, at the Alteration, he must remark the Occasion to be, the Disagreement and Enmity between them, but that both *Roberts* and *Val Ashplant*, threatned him into signing their Articles, and that he did it in Terror.

The *King Solomon*, and *Elizabeth* Medicine-Chest, he own'd, he plundered, by Order of *Hunter*, the then chief Surgeon, who, by the Pirates Laws, always directs in this Province, and Mr *Child*, tho' now acquitted, had by the same Orders taken out a whole *French* Medicine Chest, which he must be sensible for me, as well as himself, we neither of us daring to have denied, it was their being the proper Judges, that made so ungrateful an Office imposed. If after this he was elected chief Surgeon himself, both *Camry* and *Wilson* were set up also, and it might have been their Chance to have carried it, and as much out of their Power to have refused.

As to the Attempt of rising and running away with the Prize, he denied it altogether as untrue. He own'd, indeed, a few foolish Words, but only by Way of Supposition, that if the Negroes should take in their Heads (considering the Weakness and ill look-out that was kept) it would have been an easy Matter, in his Opinion, for them to have done it, but that he encouraged such a Thing was false. His talking to them in the *Angolan* Language, was only a Way of spending his Time, and trying his Skill to tell Twenty, he being incapable of further Talk. As to his understanding Navigation, he had frequently

quently acknowledged it to the Deponent *Child*, and wonder'd he should so circumstantiate this Skill against him　*Guilty*

Robert Johnson.

IT appeared to the Court, that the Prisoner was one of the twenty Men, in that Boat of the Pirates, which afterwards robb'd the *King Solomon*, at an Anchor near Cape *Appollonia*　That all Pirates on this, and the like Services, were Voluntiers, and he, in particular, had contested his going on board a second Time, tho' out of his Turn.

The Prisoner, in his Defence, called for *Harry Glasby*, who witnessed to his being so very drunk, when he first came among their Crew, that they were forced to hoist him out of one Ship into the other, with a Tackle, and therefore without his Consent, but he had since been a trusty Man, and was placed to the Helm, in that running Battle they made with the *Swallow*

He insisted for himself likewise, on Captain *Turner's* Affidavit of his being forc'd on which others, who were his Ship-mates had been clear'd

The Court considering the Partiality that might be objected in acquitting one, and condemning another of the same standing, thought fit to remark it as a clear Testimony of their Integrity, that their Care and Indulgence to each Man, in allowing his particular Defence, was to exempt from the Rigour of the Law, such, who, it must be allowed, would have stood too promiscuously condemned, if they had not been heard upon any other Fact than that of the *Swallow*, and herein what could better direct them, than a Character and Behaviour from their own Associates, for tho' a voluntary Entry with the Pirates may be doubtful, yet his consequent Actions are not, and it is not so material how a Man comes among Pirates, as how he acts when he is there.　*Guilty*

George Wilson

JOhn *Sharp*, Master of the *Elizabeth*, in which Ship the Prisoner was Passenger, and which fell a second Time into the Pirates Hands, deposed, That he took the said *Wilson* off from *Sestos*, on this Coast, paying to the Negroes for his Ransom, the Value of three Pounds five Shillings in Goods, for which he had taken a Note, that he thought he had done a charitable Act in this, till meeting with one Captain *Canning*, he ask'd, Why he would release such a Rogue as *Wilson* was? For that he had been a Voluntier with the Pirates, out of *John Tarlton*　And when the Deponent came to be a Prisoner himself, he found *Thomas*, the Brother of this *John Tarlton*, a Prisoner also, who was immediately, on *Wilson's* Instigation, in a sad Manner misused and beat, and had been shot, through the Fury and Rage of some of those Fellows, if the Town-side (i e *Liverpool* Men) had not hid him in a Stay-sail, under the Bowsprit, for *Moody* and *Harper*, with their Pistols cock'd, searched every Corner of the Ship to find him, and came to this Deponent's Hammock, whom they had like fatally to have mistaken for *Tarlton*, but on his calling out, they found their Error, and left him with this comfortable Anodyne, That he was the honest Fellow who bought the Doctor　At coming away, the Prisoner asked about his Note, whether the Pirates had it or no? Who not being able readily to tell, he reply'd, it's no Matter, Mr *Sharp*, I believe I shall hardly ever come to *England* to pay it

Adam Comry, Surgeon of the *Elizabeth*, said, altho' the Prisoner had, on Account of his Indisposition and Want, received many Civilities from him,

before meeting with the Pirates, he yet understood it was thro' his and *Scudamore's* Means, that he had been compelled among them　The Prisoner was very alert and chearful, he said, at meeting with *Roberts*, hailed him, told him he was glad to see him, and would come on board presently, borrowing of the Deponent a clean Shirt and Drawers, for his better Appearance and Reception, he signed their Articles willingly, and used Arguments with him to do the same, saying, they should make their Voyage in eight Months to *Brasil*, share 6 or 700*l* a Man, and then break up　Again, when the Crew came to an Election of a chief Surgeon, and this Deponent was set up with the others, *Wilson* told him, he hoped he should carry it from *Scudamore*, for that a quarter Share, which they had more than others, would be worth looking after, but the Deponent missed the Preferment, by the good Will of the *Ranger's* People, who, in general, voted for *Scudamore*, to get rid of him, the chief Surgeon being always to remain with the Commodore

It appeared likewise, by the Evidence of Captain *Jo Trahern*, *Thomas Castel*, and others, who had been taken by the Pirates, and thence had Opportunities of observing the Prisoner's Conduct, that he seem'd thoroughly satisfy'd with that Way of Life, and was particularly intimate with *Roberts*, they often scoffing at the Mention of a Man of War, and saying, if they should ever meet with any of the Turnp man's Ships, they would blow up, and go o H——ll together　Yet, setting aside these sly Freaks to recommend himself, his Laziness got him many Enemies, even *Roberts* told him (on the Complaint of a wounded Man whom he refused to dress) that he was a double Rogue to be there a second Time, and threatned to cut his Ears off

The Evidence further assured the Court, from Captain *Thomas Tarlton*, that the Prisoner was taken out of his Brother's Ship, some Month before, a first Time, and, being forward to oblige his new Company, he presently ask'd for the Pirate's Boat, to fetch the Medicine Chest away, when the Wind and Current proving too hard to contend with, they were drove on Shore at Cape *Montzerado*

The Prisoner called for *William Darling*, *Samuel Morvel*, and *Nicholas Butler*

William Darling deposed, That the first Time the Prisoner fell into their Hands, *Roberts* mistook him for *Jo Tarlton* the Master, and being informed it was the Surgeon who came to represent him, he presently swore he should be his Mess mate, to which *Wilson* reply'd, he hop'd not, for he had a Wife and Child, which the other laughed at　This Evidence added, that he had been two Days on board, before he went in that Boat, which was drove on Shore at Cape *Montzerado*　And at his second coming, in the *Elizabeth*, he heard *Roberts* order he should be brought on board in the first Boat.

Samuel Morvel said, That he had heard him bewail his Condition, while on board the Pirate, and desire one *Thomas* to use his Interest with *Roberts* for a Discharge, saying, his Employ, and the little he had left at Home, would, he hop'd, exempt him from the further Trouble of seeking his Bread at Sea

Nicholas Butler, who had remained with the Pirates about 48 Hours, when they took the French Ships at *Whydah*, deposed, That in this Space the Prisoner addressed him in the *French* Language several Times, deploring the Wretchedness and ill Fortune of being confin'd in such Company

The Prisoner desiring the Liberty of two or three Questions, ask'd, Whether or no he had not expostulated with *Roberts*, for a Reason of his obliging Surgeon.

geons to fign their Articles, when heretofore they did not? Whether he had not expreffed himfelf glad of having formerly efcaped from them? Whether he had not faid, at the taking the Ships in *Whydah* Road, that he could not like the Sport, were it lawful? And whether he had not told him, that fhould the Company difcharge any Surgeon, he would infift on it as his Turn? The Deponent anfwered Yes, to every Queftion feparately, and farther, that he believed *Scudamore* had not feen *Wilfon* when he firft came and found him out of the *Elizabeth*

He added, in his own Defence, that being Surgeon with one *John Tarlton* of *Liverpool*, he was met a firft Time on this Coaft of *Guiney*, by *Roberts* the Pirate, who, after a Day or two, told him to his Sorrow, that he was to ftay there, and ordered him to fetch his Cheft, (not Medicines, as was afferted) which Opportunity he took to make his Efcape, for the Boat's Crew happening to confift of five *French* and one *Englifh* Man, all as willing as himfelf, they agreed to pufh the Boat on Shore, and truft themfelves with the Negroes of Cape *Montzerado* Hazardous, not only in Refpect of the dangerous Seas that run there, but the Inhumanity of the Natives, who fometimes take a liking to human Carcaffes Here he remained five Months, till *Thomas Tarlton*, Brother to his Captain, chanced to put in the Road for Trade, to whom he reprefented his Hardfhips and ftarving Condition, but was, in an unchriftian Manner, both refufed a Releafe of this Captivity, or fo much as a fmall Supply of Bifcuit and falt Meat; becaufe, as he faid, he had been among the Pyrates A little Time after this, the Mafter of a *French* Ship paid a Ranfom for him, and took him off, but, by Reafon of a nafty leperous Indifpofition he had contracted by hard and bad Living, he was, to his great Misfortune, fet afhore at *Seftos* again, when Captain *Sharp* met him, and generoufly procured his Releafe in the Manner himfelf has releated, and for which he ftands infinitely obliged —— That ill Luck threw him a fecond Time into the Pirates Hands, in this Ship *Elizabeth*, where he met *Thomas Tarlton*, and thoughtlefly ufed fome Reproaches of him, for his fevere Treatment at *Montzerado*, but without Defign that his Words fhould have had fo bad a Confequence, for *Roberts* took upon him, as a Difpenfer of Juftice, to correct Mr *Tarlton*, beating him unmercifully, which Severity, he hopes it will be believed, was contrary to any Intention of his, becaufe as a Stranger, he might be fuppofed to have no Influence, and he believed, there were fome other Motives for it —— He could not remember that he expreffed himfelf glad to fee *Roberts* this fecond Time, or that he dropped thofe Expreffions about *Comry*, as were fworn, but if immaturity of Judgment had occafioned him to flip rafh and inadvertent Words, or that he had paid any undue Compliments to *Roberts*, it was to ingratiate himfelf, as every Prifoner did, for a more civil Treatment, and in particular, to procure his Difcharge, which he had been promifed, and was afraid would have been revoked, if fuch a Perfon as *Comry* did not remain there to fupply his Room, and of this, he faid, all the Gentlemen (meaning the Pirates) could witnefs for him

He urged alfo his Youth in Excufe for his Rafhnefs —— The firft Time he had been with them, which was only a Month in all, and that in no military Employ, but in particular, the Service he had done, in difcovering the Defign the Pirates had to rife in their Paffage on board the *Swallow* Guilty

But Execution to be refpited till the King's Pleafure be known, becaufe the Commander of the

Swallow had declared, that the firft Notice he received of this Defign of the Pirates to rife, was from him

Benjamin Jefferys

BY the Depofitions of *Glafby* and *Lilburn*, (both acquitted) againft this Prifoner, it appeared, that his Drunkennefs was what at firft detained him from going away in his proper Ship, the *Norman Galley*; and next Morning, for having been abufive in his Drink, and faying to the Pirates, there was not a Man amongft them, he received for a Welcome, fix Lafhes from every Perfon in the Ship, which difordered him for fome Weeks, but on Recovery, he was made Boatfwain's Mate, the ferving of which, or any Office on board a Pirate, is at their own Option (tho' elected) becaufe others are glad to accept what brings an additional Share in Prize

The Deponents further faid, that at *Sierraleon* every Man had more efpecially the Means of efcaping, and that this Prifoner in particular neglected it, and came off from that Place, after their Ship was under Sail, and going out of the River

The Prifoner in his Defence, protefted he was at firft forced, and that the Office of Boatfwain's Mate was impofed on him, and what he would have been glad to have relinquifh'd That the barbarous Whipping he had received from the Pirates at firft, was for telling them, that none who could get their Bread in an honeft Way, would be on fuch an Account And he had certainly taken the Opportunity which prefented at *Sierraleon*, of ridding himfelf from fo diftaftful a Life, if there had not been three or four of the old Pirates on fhore at the fame Time, who, he imagin'd, muft know of him, and would doubtlefs have ferved him the fame, if not worfe, than they once had done *William Williams*, who, for fuch a Defign, being delivered up by the treacherous Natives, had received two Lafhes thro' the whole Snip's Company

The Court obferved, that the Excufe of thefe Pirates, about want of Means to efcape, was oftentimes as poor and evafive, as their Pleas of being forced at firft, for here at *Serraleon*, every Man had his Liberty on fhore, and it was evident might have kept it, if he, or they, had fo pleafed And fuch are further culpable, who, having been introduced into the Society by fuch uncivil Methods as whipping or beating, neglect lefs likely Means of regaining Liberty, it fhews ftrong Inclinations to Difhonefty, and they ftand inexcufably *Guilty*

Jo Mansfield

IT was proved againft this Prifoner, by Captain *Trahern*, and *George Fenn*, that he was one of thofe Voluntiers who was at the Attack and Robbery of the Company's Ship, called the *King Solomon* That he bully'd well among them who dar'd not make any Reply, but was very eafy with his Friends, who knew him, for *Moody*, on this Occafion, took a large Glafs from him, and threatned to blow his Brains out (a favourite Phrafe with thefe Pirates) if he muttered at it

From others acquitted, it likewife appeared, that he was at firft a Voluntier among them, from an Ifland call'd *Dominico* in the *Weft-Indies*, and had, to recommend himfelf, told them, he was a Deferter from the *Rofe* Man of War, and before they had been on the High-way, he was always drunk, they faid, and fo bad at the Time they met the *Swallow*, that he knew nothing of the Action, but came up vapouring with his Cutlafh, after the *Fortune* had ftruck her Colours, to know who would go on board the Prize, and it was fome Time before they could perfwade him into the Truth of their Condition

He

He could fay little in Defence of himfelf, and acknowledg'd this latter Charge of Drunkenneſs, a Vice, he faid, that had too great a Share in enfnaring him into this Courſe of Life, and had been a greater Motive with him than Gold *Guilty*

William Davis

Illiam *Allen* depoſed, That he knew this Priſoner at *Sierraleon*, belonging to the *Anne* Galley, that he had a Quarrel with, and beat the Mate of that Ship, for which, as he faid, being afraid to return to his Duty, he conſorted to the idle Cuſtoms and Ways of living among the Negroes, from whom he received a Wife, and ungratefully ſold her one Evening for ſome Punch to quench his Thirſt After this, having put himfelf under the Protection of Mr. *Plunket*, Governor there for the Royal *African* Company, the Relations and Friends of the Woman apply'd to him for Redreſs, who immediately ſurrendered the Priſoner, and told them, he did not care if they took his Head off, but the Negroes, wifely judging it would not fetch ſo good a Price, they ſold him in his Turn again to Seignior *Joſſee*, a Chriſtian Black, and Native of that Place, who expected and agreed for two Years Service from him, on Conſideration of what he had diſburſed, for the Redemption of the Woman But long before the Expiration of this Time, *Roberts* came into *Sierraleon* River, where the Priſoner (as Seignior *Joſſee* affur'd the Deponent) entered a Volunteer with them

The Deponent further corroborates this Part of the Evidence, in that he being obliged to call at *Cape Mount*, in his Paſſage down hither, met there with two Deſerters from *Roberts's* Ship, who affured him of the ſame, and that the Pyrates did deſign to turn *Davis* away the next Opportunity, as an idle good for-nothing Fellow

From *Glasby* and *Lilburn* it was evident, that every Pyrate, while they ſtaid at *Sierraleon*, went on ſhore at Diſcretion That *Roberts* had often affur'd Mr *Glyn* and other Traders, at that Place, that he would force no Body, and, in ſhort, there was no Occaſion for it, in particular, the Priſoner's Rowmate went away, and conſequently he might have done the ſame, if he had pleaſed

The Priſoner alledged his having been detained againſt his Will, and ſaid, that returning with Elephants Teeth for *Sierraleon*, the Pyrate's Boat purſued and brought him on board, where he was kept on Account of his underſtanding the Pilotage and Navigation of that River

It was obvious to the Court, not only how frivolous the Excuſes of Conſtraint and Force were among theſe People, at their firſt commencing Pyrates, but alſo it was plain to them, from theſe two Deſerters met at Cape *Mount*, and the diſcretional Manner they lived in at *Sierraleon*, through how little Difficulty ſeveral of them did, and others might, have eſcaped afterwards, if they could but have obtained their own Conſents for it *Guilty*

This is the Subſtance of the Tryals of *Roberts's* Crew, which may ſuffice for others that occur in this Book

We are not ignorant how acceptable the Behaviour and dying Words of Malefactors are to the generality of our Countrymen, and therefore ſhall deliver what occurr'd, worthy of Notice, in the Behaviour of theſe Criminals

The firſt Six that were called to Execution, were *Magnes, Moody Sympſon, Sutton, Aſhplant,* and *Hardy*, all of them old Standers and notorious Offenders When they were brought out of the Hold, on the Parade, in order to break off their Fetters, and fit the Halters; none of them, it was obſerved, appeared the leaſt dejected, unleſs *Sutton*, who ſpoke faint, but it was rather imputed to a Flux that had ſeized him two or three Days before, than Fear A Gentleman, who was Surgeon of the Ship, was ſo charitable at this Time, as to offer himſelf in the Room of an Ordinary, and repreſented to them, as well as he was able, the Heinouſneſs of their Sin, and the Neceſſity which lay on them of Repentance, one particular Part of which, he obſerved ought to be, acknowledging the Juſtice they had met with They ſeemed heedleſs for the preſent, ſome calling for Water to drink, and others applying to the Soldiers for Caps, but when this Gentleman preſs'd them for an Anſwer, they all exclaim'd againſt the Severity of the Court, and were ſo hardened, as to curſe, and wiſh the ſame Juſtice might overtake all the Members of it, as had been dealt to them *They were poor Rogues*, they ſaid, *and ſo hang'd, while others, no leſs guilty in another Way, eſcoped*

When he endeavoured to compoſe their Minds, exhorting them to die in Charity with all the World, and would have diverted them from ſuch vain Diſcourſe, by aſking them their Country, Age, and the like, ſome of them anſwer'd, *What was that to him, they ſuffered the Law, and ſhould give no Account but to God* They walked to the Gallows without a Tear in Token of Sorrow for their paſt Offences, or ſhewing ſo much Concern as a Man would expreſs at travelling a bad Road, nay, *Sympſon*, at ſeeing a Woman that he knew, ſaid, *he had lain with that B——h three Times, and now ſhe was come to ſee him hang'd* And *Hard*, when his Hands were ty'd behind him (which happened from their not being acquainted with the Way of bringing Malefactors to Execution) obſerved, *That he had ſeen many a Man hang'd, but this Way of the Hands being ty'd behind them, he was a Stranger to, and never ſaw before in his Life* We mention theſe two little Inſtances, to ſhew how ſtupid and thoughtleſs they were of their End, and that the ſame abandon'd and reprobate Temper that had carried them thro' their Rogueries, abided with them to the laſt

Samuel Fletcher, another of the Pirates order'd for Execution, but reprieved, ſeemed to have a quicker Senſe of his Condition, for when he ſaw thoſe that were alloted, gone to Execution, he ſent a Meſſage by the Provoſt Marſhal to the Court, to be, *inform'd of the Meaning of it, and humbly deſired to know, whether the, deſign'd him Mercy, or not? If they did, he ſtood infinitely obliged to them, and thought the whole Service of his Life an incompetent Return for ſo great a Favour, but that if he was to ſuffer the ſooner the better, he ſaid, that he might be out of his Pain*

There were others of theſe Pirates the reverſe of this, and, tho' deſtitute of Miniſters, or fit Perſons to repreſent their Sins to them, and aſſiſt them with ſpiritual Advice, were yet always employing their Time to good Purpoſes, and behaving with a great deal of ſeeming Devotion and Penitence, among theſe may be reckon'd *Scudamore, Williams, Philips, Stephenſon, Jefferys, Leſſ, Harper, Armſtrong, Bunce*, and others

Scudamore too lately diſcerned the Folly and Wickedneſs of the Enterprize that had chiefly brought him under Sentence of Death, from which, ſeeing there was no Hopes of Eſcaping, he petitioned for two or three Days Reprieve, which was granted, and ſo that Time he applied himſelf inceſſantly to Prayer, and reading the Scriptures, ſeem'd to have a deep Senſe of his Sins, and of this in particular, and deſire fired at the Gallows, that they would have Patience with him, to fing the firft Part of the thirty firft Pſalm, which he did by himſelf throughout.

Armſtrong, having been a Deferter from his Majeſty's Service, was executed on board the *Weymouth* (and the only one that was) there was no Body to preſs him to an Acknowledgment of the Crime he dy'd for, nor of ſorrowing in particular for it, which would have been exemplary, and made ſuitable Impreſſions on Seamen, ſo that his laſt Hour was ſpent in lamenting and bewailing his Sins in general, exhorting the Spectators to an honeſt and good Life, in which alone they could find Satisfaction In the End, he defired they would join with him in ſinging the two or three latter Verſes of the 140th Pſalm, and that being concluded, he was, at the firing of a Gun, tric'd up at the Fore-Yard Arm

Bunce was a young Man, not above 26 Years old, but made the moſt pathetical Speech of any at the Gallows He firſt declaim'd againſt the gilded Baits of Power, Liberty, and Wealth, that had enſnar'd him among the Pyrates, his unexperienc'd Years not being able to withſtanding the Temptation, but that the Briſkneſs he had ſhewn, which ſo fatally had procured him favour amongſt them, was not ſo much a Fault in Principle, as the Livelineſs and Vivacity of his Nature He was now extreamly afflicted for the Injuries he had done to all Men, and begg'd theirs and Gods Forgiveneſs, very earneſtly exhorting the Spectators to remember their Creator in their Youth, and guard betimes, that their Minds took not a wrong Byaſs, concluding with this apt Similitude, *That he ſtood there as a Beacon upon a Rock* (the Gallows ſtanding on one) *to warn erring Mariners of Danger*

The LIFE of Madam CHURCHILL.

Deborah *Churchill*, alias *Miller*, was born within ſix Miles of the City of *Norwich*, in the County of *Norfolk*, of worthy honeſt Parents, who gave her very good Education, and brought her up in her younger Years in the Ways of Religion and good Manners, but ſhe had wickedly thrown off all thoſe good Things, which were endeavoured to be fixed in her, and abandoned herſelf to all manner of Filthineſs and Uncleanneſs, which afterwards proved her Shame and Ruin She was firſt married to one *John Churchill*, an Enſign in Major General *Faringdon*'s Regiment, by whoſe Name ſhe commonly went, but ſeldom by her ſecond Husband's, who, two or three Years before her Misfortunes, was married to her in the *Fleet* Priſon, upon Agreement firſt made between them both, that they ſhould not live together, nor have any Thing to do with each other Which Agreement was ſtrictly performed, and ſo ſhe continued freely to keep Company with one *Hunt* a Life-Guard Man, as ſhe had begun to do in her former Husband's Time

She had lived with the aforeſaid Bully *Hunt* for ſeven Years together, in a laſcivious and adulterous Manner, which broke her firſt Husband's Heart, by whom ſhe had two Children ſurviving at the Time of her unfortunate Death She had liv'd alſo in Incontinency about three Months, with one *Thomas Smith*, a Cooper, who was hanged at *Tyburn*, on *Friday* the 16th Day of *December*, 1709, for breaking open and robbing the Houſe of the Right Honourable the Earl of *Weſtmoreland*, at which Time were likewiſe hanged *Aaron Jones* and *Joſeph Wells*, for the Murder of one Mr *Lamas* near *Marybone*

This noted Jilt bore a great Sway in *Drury Lane*, as in taking Tribute of all new Whores who preſumed to walk there at Night, to venture their Souls, if Men would their Bodies, for the ſmall Price of Two-pence wet, and Two-pence dry She was here a common Strumpet, and proſtituted herſelf to all Comers and Goers, whoſe Pockets ſhe conſtantly pick'd. An Inſtance of her Manner, was what ſhe did with one Mr *Jeffery W——*, a Bookſeller, living in St *Paul*'s *Church-Yard*, from whom taking a Pocket-Book, in which were ſeveral Notes and Bills of Value, *Hunt* her Bully, went the next Day to his Shop, and returning the Pocket-Book to him, ſaid, *By this I underſtand you have been more familiar with my Wife than became you, but take Notice, I ſhall require Satisfaction for the Affront, or otherwiſe take what follows,* The Bookſeller being conſcious of what was laid to his Charge, rather than the Scandal ſhould come to his Wife's Ears, to whom he was newly marr'ed, he gave him ten Guineas, with a Promiſe of paying him thirty more the next Day But in the mean Time acquainting a Bookbinder, living in *Little-Britain*, with the Matter, he, knowing the World pretty well, met *Hunt* at the Place where Mr *W——* was to give him thirty Guineas, and threatning to ſecure him with a Conſtable, the Sharper was forced not only to ſurrender his Pretenſions to the thirty Guineas, but to return the former Ten, for fear of being carry'd before his Betters

As ſhe was once going thro' *Cheapſide*, upon the Buttock and File, ſhe pick'd up a Linnen Draper living in *Cornhill*, who being as ſharp as ſhe, he found he had loſt his Watch in the Tavern where they were drinking, which was at the Three Tuns in *Newgate-ſtreet*, and charged her with it She deny'd it ſtifly, neither could it be found upon her, tho' the Maids of the Houſe had ſtript her ſtark naked But the Linnen-Draper ſwearing point-blank that ſhe had it, and ſending for a Conſtable to ſecure her, ſhe diſcovered the Watch, which was hid in the Bottom of a Leather Chair, whereupon ſhe was committed to *Woodſtreet* Compter

But the aboveſaid Linnen-Draper never appeared againſt Madam *Churchill*, when under Confinement, ſhe was at laſt diſcharged, but had not long enjoy'd her Liberty before ſhe was committed to *New Priſon*, for picking a Gentleman's Pocket of a Purſe, wherein was an hundred and four Guineas.

neas Whilst she was there, she seemed to be really a pious Woman; but only her Religion was of five or six Colours; for this Day she would pray that God would turn the Heart of her Adversary, and To-morrow curse the Time that ever she saw him.

She at last got out of this Mansion of Sorrow also, but soon forgetting her Afflictions, she pursued her Wickedness continually, till she had been sent no less than twenty Times to *Clerkenwell Bridewell*, where receiving the Correction of the House every Time, by being whipt, and kept to beating Hemp from Morning till Night, for the small Allowance of so much Bread and Water, which will but just keep Life and Soul together, she commonly came out like a Skeleton, and walked as if her Limbs had been ty'd together with Packthread; yet let what Punishment would light on this common Strumpet, she was no Changling, for as soon as she was out of Goal, she was still running into greater Evils, by deluding, if possible, all Mankind

One Night picking up one *William Fowler*, a Barber, living in *Bull-Inn-Court*, in the *Strand*, and carrying him to her Lodging in *Castle-street*, behind the North Side of *Long-Acre*, they went to Bed, where the amorous Folly of these two Lovers consisted, no doubt, more of Action than Expression. But in the Height of these Enjoyments, Bully *Hunt* unexpectedly came Home, and knocking hard at the Door, startled our two Inamorato's, who were more strictly entangled in each others Arms, than *Mars* was by *Vulcan*'s crafty Net, when entwin'd in amorous Folds with the *Cyprian* Goddess In the mean Time *Deborah Churchill*, being otherwise employ'd than to come out of a warm Bed, and endanger the catching of Cold, was as mute as a Fish; neither could she in Reason make Answer to the Disturber of her Joys, till the Business she was about consummated.

But Bully *Rock*, impatient of Delay, repeating his Strokes on the harmless Door, Madam found herself constrained to demand *Who was there?* tho' in Words imperfect, as one waked out of a profound Sleep Knowing the Voice, upon Reply, she capitulated with *Hunt*, till she might hide her Cully, for whom there was no other Refuge but crawling under the Bed; where being secured, she jumped out, and in great Haste ran to the Door, speaking as she was wont, *Oh! my Soul! Oh thou most welcome Man to me alive:* When in herself she thought, *What envious Devil has brought thee hither at this Juncture to disturb my Pleasure?*

The Bully thus entered, began to salute her in his usual Language, *You Whore, you Bitch, what Rogue have you got in Bed with you now?* But find-

ing no Body there, he kicked her about the Room like a Foot-ball, saying again, *Where have you hid the Scoundrel, that durst presume to bestow a Citizen's Fate upon my Honour, in making me a Cuckold?* Then drawing his Sword, quoth he, *I've not killed a Man this great while, but by G——d I'll send one out of the World now.* So thrusting his Sword under the Bed, poor *Tonsor* began to cry out for Quarter, at the same Time creeping out of his Nest so extreamly powder'd with Dust and Feathers, that Bully *Hunt* taking him rather for a Devil than a Man, the Fright he was in gave the as much frighted Cut beard the favourable Opportunity of making his Escape out of the House, with only the Loss of his Breeches, in which was a good silver Watch, and about four Pound in Money But for this Trick he swore, *He would never go a Whoring again,* which was as dangerous as trusting his Arms in the Throat of a Lyon, or his Purse with a Highwayman

Now after Madam *Churchill* had reign'd a long Time in her Wickedness, as she was coming one Night along *Drury-Lane*, in Company with *Richard Hunt*, *William Lewis*, and *John Boy*, they took an Occasion to fall out with one *Martin Were*, and she aggravating the Quarrel, by bidding them sacrifice the Man, they killed him between *King's Head Court* and *Vinegar-Yard* The three Men who committed this Murder made their Escape, but she being apprehended as an Accessary therein, was sent to *Newgate*, and shortly after condemned for it on the 26th of *February*, 1707-8

After Sentence of Death was passed on her, her Execution was respited, by virtue of a Reprieve given her, upon the Account of her being thought to be with Child; which she pretended to be, in Hopes it might be a Means to save her Life, or at least put off her Death for a Time But when she had laid under Condemnation almost ten Months, and was found not to be with Child, she was called to her former Judgment Then being convey'd in a Coach to *Tyburn*, on *Friday* the 17th of *December*, 1708, she was there hang'd in the 31st Year of her Age But, before she was turn'd off, she desired all the Spectators to pray for her, and that God would be pleas'd to be merciful to her poor Soul Moreover, calling to one she call'd Nurse, an Apple-Woman's Daughter in *Drury-Lane*, she earnestly begg'd of her to take Care of her poor Children, for whom she seemed to be very much concerned. These were her last Words, which she spoke in the Cart, into which she was put as soon as she came to the Place of Execution

The

The LIFE of JACK OVET.

THIS notorious Malefactor, *John Ovet*, a Shoemaker by Trade, was born at *Nottingham*, where his Abode was for four or five Years, after he had serv'd his Apprenticeship But being always of a daring, audacious Disposition, his unruly Temper induced him to keep very lewd and quarrelsome Company, and depending on his Manhood, it inspir'd him with an Inclination of laying aside his mechanical Employment, to translate himself into a Gentlemen, by maintaining that Quality on the Highway

Immediately equipping himself, as a Highwayman ought, with a good Horse, Hanger, and Pistols, he rid towards *London*, and on the Road had the good Success of robbing a Gentleman of Twenty Pounds; who being one of great Courage, told *Ovet*, that if he had not come upon him unawares, and surpriz'd him at a Disadvantage, he should have given him some Trouble before he wou'd have parted with his Money. Quoth *Ovet*, Sir, I have ventur'd my Life once already in committing this Robbery, however, if you have the Vanity to think yourself a better Man than me, I'll venture once more, for here's your Money again, let it be betwixt us, and whoever of us is the best Man let him win it and wear it The Gentleman very willingly accepted the Proposal, and making use of their Swords on Foot, *Jack Ovet* had the Fortune to kill his Antagonist on the Spot

Not long after he kill'd another Man in a Quarrel at *Leicester*, but flying from Justice, he still cheated the Hangman of his due, and without any Dread pursued his unlawful Courses to the highest Pitch of Villany One Day in particular meeting the Pack-Horses of one Mr. *Rogers*, who goes from *Leominster* in *Herefordshire* to *London*, and being in great want of Money, he turn'd one of them out of the main Road into a narrow Lane, where cutting open the Pack, he found therein about 280 Guineas in Gold, besides three Dozen of Silver-hafted Knives and Forks, and Spoons, which he carry'd off The other Pack-horses were gone above two Miles before Mr *Rogers* miss'd this, and then making a strict Search after it, he found it ty'd to a Tree, and the Pack thrown off his Back, and rifled of what was most valuable, but not knowing who had done this great Injury, he was forc'd to make the Loss good to the Owner of the Plate and Money

Another Time *Jack Ovet* being drinking at the Star Inn in the *Strand*, he overheard a Soap boiler contriving with a Carrier how he should send an Hundred Pounds to a Friend in the Country At length it was concluded upon, to put the Money into a Barrel of Soap, which Project was mightily approved off by the Carrier, who answer'd, *If any Rogues should rob my Waggon (which they never did but once) the Devil must be in them if they look for any Money in the Soap Barrel* Accordingly the Money and Soap was brought to the Inn, and next Morning the Carrier going out of Town, *Jack Ovet*

overtook him in the Afternoon, and commanding him to stop, or otherwise he would shoot him and his Horses too, he was oblig'd to obey the Word of Command Then quoth the honest Highwayman, *I must make bold to borrow a little Money out of your Waggon, therefore if you have any direct me to it, that I may not lose any time, which you know is always precious* The Carrier told him he had nothing but cumbersome Goods in his Waggon, as he knew of, however, if he would not believe him, he might search every Box and Bundle there if he pleased.

Ovet soon got into the Waggon, and threw all the Boxes and Bundles about, till at last he came to the Soap Barrel, which feeling somewhat heavy, quoth he to the Carrier, *What a pox do you do with this nasty Commodity in your Waggon? I'll fling it away.* So throwing it on the Ground the Hoops bursted, out flew the Head, and the Soap spreading abroad, the Bag appear'd Then jumping out of the Waggon, and taking it up, says he again, *Is not he that sells this Soap a cheating Son of a Whore, to put this Bag of Lead into it, to make the Barrel weigh heavy If I knew where he lived I'd go and tell him his own; however, that he may not succeed in his Roguery, I'll take it, and sell it at the next House I come to, for it will wet ones Whistle to the Tune of two or three Shillings*

He was going to ride away, when the Carrier cry'd after him, Hold, Hold, Sir, that is not Lead that's in the Bag, it is an Hundred Pounds, for which (if you take it away) I must be accountable. No, no, (reply'd *Jack Ovet*) this can't be Money, but if it is tell the Owner that I'll be answerable for it if he'll come to me Where, Sir, (said the Carrier) may one find you? Why, truly, (reply'd *Jack*) that's a Question soon ask'd, but not so soon to be answered, the best Directions I can give is, 'tis like you may find me in a Jail before Night, and then, perhaps, you may have again what I have took from you, and Forty Pounds to boot

Another Time *Jack Ovet* meeting with the *Worcester* Stage Coach on the Road, in which were several young Gentlewomen, he robb'd them all, but one of them being a very handsome Person, he entertain'd such a Passion for her exquisite Charms, that when he took her Money from her, he said, Madam, Cast not your Eyes down, neither cover your Face with those modest Blushes, your Charms have softened my Temper, and I am no more the Man I was; what I have took from you (through meer Necessity at present) is only borrow'd, for as no Object on Earth ever had such an Effect on me as you, assure yourself that if you please to tell me where I may direct to you, I'll upon Honour make good your Loss to the very utmost. The young Gentlewoman told him where he might send to her, and then parting, it was not above a Week after that before *Jack* sent the following Letter to the aforesaid Gentlewoman, who had gain'd such an absolute Conquest over his Soul, that his Mind ran now as much upon Love as Robbing

MADAM,

MADAM,

' THESE few Lines are to acquaint you, that
' tho' I lately had the Cruelty to rob you of
' Twenty Guineas, yet you committed a greater Rob-
' bery at the same time, in robbing me of my Heart,
' on which you may behold yourself entnroned, and
' all my Faculties paying their Homage to your un-
' parakll'd Beauty Therefore be pleased to propose
' but the Method how I may win your Belief, and
' were the Way to it as deep as from hence to the
' Centre, I will search it out For, by all my Hopes
' by all those Rites that crown a happy Union, by the
' Rosy Tincture of your Cheeks, and by your all
' subduing Eyes, I prize you above all the World
' Oh! then my fair *Venus*, can you be afraid of Love?
' His Brow is smooth, and his Face beset with Banks
' full of Delight, about his Neck hangs a Chain of
' golden Smiles Let us taste the Pleasures which *Cu-*
' *pid* commands, and for that unmerited Favour I
' shall become another Man to make you happy So
' requesting the small Boon of a favourable Answer to
' be sent me to Mr *Walker's*, who keeps an Ale-
' house at the Sign of the Bell in *Thornbury* in *Glocef-*
' *terfhire*, give me leave to subscribe myself your most
' humble Servant to command for ever,

JOHN BURTON

The Gentlewoman's Answer.

SIR,

' YOURS I received with as great Diffatisfac-
' tion as when you robbed me, and admire
' at your Impudence of offering me yourself for a
' Husband, when I am sensible 'twould not be long

' 'ere you made me a hempen Widow Perhaps
' some foolish Girl or another may be so bewitch'd
' as to go in White to beg the Favour of marrying
' you under the Gallows, but indeed I should nei-
' ther venture there, nor in a Church, to marry one
' of your Profession, whose Vows are treacherou,
' and whose Smiles, Words, and Actions, like small
' Rivulets, thro' a thousand Turnings of loose Paf-
' sions, at last arrived to the dead Sea of Sin Should
' you therefore dissolve your Eyes into Tears, was
' every Accent a Sigh in your Speech, had you all
' the Spells, and Magick Charms of Love, I should
' seal up my Ears that I might not hear your Diffi-
' mulation You have already broke your Word,
' in not sending what you villainously took from me,
' but not valuing that, let me tell you, for fear you
' should have too great a Conceit of yourself, that
' you are the first, to my Remembrance, whom I
' ever hated and sealing my Hatred with the Hopes
' of quickly reading your dying Speech, in case you
' die in *London*, I presume to subscribe myself Yours
' never to command,

D. C

This was the End of *Jack Ovet*'s warm Amour,
and he was soon after as unsuccessful in his Villany,
as he was here in Love, for committing a Robbery
in *Leicestershire*, where his Comrade was killed in
the Attempt, he was closely pursued by the Country,
apprehended, and sent to Jail At last the Affizes
being held at *Leicester*, he was condemned Whilst
he was under Sentence of Death, he seem to have no
Remorse at all for his Wickedness, nor in the least to
repent of the Blood of two Persons, which he had
shed, so being brought to the Gallows, on *Wednef-*
day the Fifth of *May* 1708, he was justly hang'd in
the thirty second Year of his Age

The LIFE of WILLIAM CADY.

THIS unhappy Gentleman was born at *Thetford* in the County of *Norfolk* His Father was an eminent Surgeon in that Place, and very careful of his Son's Education After a Courſe of Grammar Learning, *Will* was ſent to the Univerſity of *Cambridge*, where he was Servitor to the Father of the preſent Right Honourable the Lord Viſcount *Townſhend*, at that Time a Student in *Trinity College* He profited ſo well as in Time to be made Batchellor of Arts, and continued at his Studies till the Death of his Father.

The Deceaſe of a Parent to a young Gentleman, as *Cady* was, is often the Criſis of Fortune, and the Time that fixes his future Fate When a Man becomes his own Maſter, we learn in what he places his Happineſs, and what has before given a prevailing Turn to his Thoughts, then influences his Actions. *Will*, immediately upon the News, withdrew from the Muſes, and went up to *London*, where he profeſs'd Phyſick ; for his Father made ſo good Uſe of what he had in his Life-Time, as to leave nothing behind him The firſt Patient he had was his own Uncle, who was dangerouſly ill of an Impoſthume, and the Manner how he cured him is very well worth relating in this Place

When he came into his Uncle's Chamber, the firſt Thing he did was to examine the State of the old Gentleman's Stomach To this Purpoſe he hunted the Room all over, moved every Diſh, Plate, and Baſon he could ſee, all under a Pretence of finding out what they gave him to eat, tho' in Reality to find a proper Occaſion for the Experiment he afterwards tried At laſt he ſpied an old Saddle under the Bed . Upon which he ſeemed to ſtart, crying out, *Uncle, your Caſe is very deſperate* ——*Not ſo bad, I hope*, ſays the Uncle, *as to make me paſt Recovery* ——*Heaven knows that*, cried *Cady* , *but a Surfeit is a terrible Thing, and I perceive you have got a violent one A Surfeit!* replied the old Gentleman, *you miſtake, Nephew, 'tis an Impoſthume that I am afflicted with* ——*The Devil it is !* quoth *Cady*, *why I could have ſworn it had been a Surfeit , for I perceive you have eat a whole Horſe, and left us only the Saddle* At this he held up the Saddle in his Hands, and the old Gentleman fell into ſuch a Fit of Laughing, as inſtantly broke his Impoſthume, ſo that he became a well Man again in leſs than a Fortnight

This is not the only Inſtance that has been related of an Impoſthume's being broke by a violent and ſudden Fit of Laughter, occaſion'd by ſome odd Action or ſmart Saying We ſhall relate two Stories of the like Nature

The firſt is of a certain Cardinal at *Padoua*, who lay at the Point of Death, and ſeemed ſo far gone, that the Servants had begun to rifle the Chamber, and to pull down the very Hangings of the Chamber where his Eminence lay An Ape, in the Midſt of the Hurry, pick'd up an old Cap that lay by the Bed's Side, and clapp'd it on his own Head, ſhew-

ing ſo many out of the Way Tricks, that the Cardinal laugh'd, broke his Impoſthume, and ſav'd both his Life and his Money.

The other is of a Lady at *Orleance*, who was in a very dangerous Condition, and began to deſpair of any Remedy The Maid, who lay in a Pallet-Bed by her, happen'd to thruſt out her Poſteriors a little beyond the Cloaths, and at the ſame Time to let a rouſing Fart Upon which a Monkey who was in the Room, went immediately to the Part from whence the Noiſe came, ſmell'd to it, chatter'd, and made ſo many wry Faces, that the Lady laugh'd herſelf into a Recovery

Cady's Uncle gave him fifty Guineas for performing ſo ſpeedy and unexpected a Cure ; all which he ſpent in leſs than a Month. It was not long after, that he bid adieu to *Galen* and *Hippocrates*, and betook himſelf to the Highway for a Livelihood The firſt Exploit which he perform'd was on *Hounſlow-Heath*, where meeting with Monſieur *Chevalier*, Captain of Grenadiers in the firſt Regiment of Foot-Guards, afterwards kill'd in the *Weſt*, in the Engagement againſt the Duke of *Monmouth*, and another Gentleman, he rid boldly up to them, and enquired the Way to *Stains*, telling them he was a Stranger in the Country They courteouſly told him they were going thither themſelves , and that they ſhould be very glad of his Company, if he pleaſed to keep Pace with them *Will* thanked them for their Civility, and accepted of their Proffer, riding and talking by the Side of them for about a Mile At laſt ſeeing the Coaſt clear, he without Ceremony ſhot one of the good-natur'd Guides thro' the Head , then turning upon *Chevalier*, he told him, *If he did not deliver his Money, he ſhould ſuffer the ſame Fate with his Companion Chevalier* ſaid, *He was a Captain of the Guards, and therefore he muſt fight, if he got any Thing from him.* ——*If you are a Soldier, Sir*, quoth *Cady*, *you ought to obey the Word of Command, otherwiſe you know the Sentence I have nothing to do but to tie you Neck and Heels* ——*You are an unconſcionable Son of a B——h*, ſays Monſieur, *to demand Money of me, who never ow'd you any* ——*Sir*, reply'd *Cady*, *there's not a Man that travels the Road, but owes me Money, if he has any about him Therefore, as you are one of my Debtors, if you do not pay me inſtantly, your Blood ſhall ſatisfy my Demands* The noble Captain exchanged a Shot or two with our Highwayman, but had the Misfortune at laſt to have his Horſe killed , upon which, ſeeing it was in vain to make any more Reſiſtance, he ſurrender'd his Gold-Watch, a Diamond Ring, and a Purſe of twenty-ſix Guineas *Will*, having collected all he could, tied the *Frenchman* Neck and Heels, nailed the Hind-Lappets of his Coat to a Tree, and then rode off with his Booty

The next Perſon he robb'd was on *Bagſhot Heath* It was Lord Viſcount *Dundee*, who was killed at the Fight of *Gilly cranky in Scotland*, after the Revolution His Honour was on Horfe-back, attended only by a Couple of Footmen Cady rode up to them full Speed, enquiring if they did not fee a fingle Man ride that Way harder than ordinary Being told *Yes*, he prefently added, *he has robb'd me of twenty Pounds, which I was going to pay my Landlord, and I am utterly ruin'd.* The Man who had rid by was a Confederate of Cady's who had parted from him for that very Purpofe. My Lord was touched with Compaffion at *Will*'s Complaint, and immediately order'd his Footmen to purfue the Villain The Servants rode away full Stretch, and Cady after them fome Diftance, till he thought they were far enough, then he turn'd back on his Lord and robb'd him of a Gold-Watch, a Gold Snuff-Box, and fixty Guineas in Money To make all fafe, he fhot the Vifcount's Horfe, and then rode after the Footmen, whom he found a Mile off, with his Comrade between them, Prifoner The Fellows were furpriz'd, when *Will* bid them let the Man go, and feem'd to laugh at them for what they had done, till at laft they abfolutely refufed to part with their Prize. Cady, upon that, fwore they fhould, and a warm Engagement enfu'd, continuing till one of the Footmen was killed, and the other was obliged to fly, who found his Lord difmounted and robb'd

Dundee complain'd at Court of this Abufe, and a Reward of one hundred Pounds was promifed in the *London-Gazette* to any one that fhould apprehend Cady or his Comrade, who were both very particularly defcrib'd. Our Adventurer now thought it fafeft to get out of the Reach of Juftice; and to that End, made the beft of his Way to *Douay* in *Flanders*, where was an *Englifh* Seminary As he was a Scholar, he was eafily admitted, upon the Superior's Examination, into the Fraternity of *Benedictine Friars*, among whom he behaved with a great Deal of feeming Devotion and Piety, fo that he fhortly attain'd a very extraordinary Character The natural Refult of this was his having a great Number of Penitents continually reforting to him, to make a Confeffion of their Sins Cady's Pity, however, at laft began to fit very uneafy upon him, and he was afraid his Hypocrify would in Time be found out for he look'd upon himfelf as incapable of keeping the Vows of Poverty and Chaftity which he had made, This made him refolve to return into *England* again at all Hazards, choofing to enjoy a merry though but a fhort Life, rather then to drag out many Years under the Strictnefs of Ecclefiaftical Difcipline But there was money wanting before this could be done, and now his Invention was rack'd for fome Method of raifing a fufficient Quantity

He feign'd himfelf indifpofed, and kept his Chamber feveral Days, during which Time he received Vifits from Abundance of People, and among others, from all of the Fair-Sex, who ufually made him their Confeffor He had fingled out in his Mind a Couple of young Gentlewomen who commonly came together, and were both very rich and very handfome A Brace of Piftols he had alfo found Means to procure At laft the Ladies came, and when they had made their Confeffion, he defir'd them to hear his In fhort, he told them, he was in great Want of Money, and if they did not inftantly fupply him, they fhould never depart alive At the fame Time he held the Piftols to their Breafts, and commanded them not to make the leaft Noife The poor Gentlewomen were almoft out of their Wits for fear, and trembled like Afpen Leaves, while Cady made Enquiry into their Pockets, and found them lin'd with about fifty Piftoles. To this he compelled them to make an Offering of two Diamonds-Rings, which were on their Fingers, and then laying them both

on the Bed, he gave them, after one another, a Tafte of his Manhood, and robb'd them of their Virginity into the Bargain Next he gagg'd and ty'd them Neck and Heels, and then went out, pretending to the Father of the Convent, that he would only take the Air in the Fields a little But he went much farther a Field then they expected, for he never return'd again, but chang'd his Cannonical Habit, and return'd back into *England*

Even before he arriv'd at *London*, he fell again in to his old Courfes, tho' he had been two Years out of his native Country; for as he rode over *Black Heath*, he met with one *Sandal*, a great Hop Merchant, and his Wife, whom he commanded to *Stand and Deliver* Sandal ftood up fmartly in his own Defence, and fir'd two Piftols without Succefs, after which he was obliged to lie at the Marcy of the Enemy, who prefently difmounted them both, and killed their Horfe (for they had but one) and then fell to rifling their Pockets. He found about twenty eight Pounds upon the Husband, but the Wife had no more then Half a-Crown *Is this your Way of travelling*, fays Cady? *What I carry but Half-a-Crown in your Pocket, when you are to meet a Gentleman Collector on the Highway! I'll affure you, Madam, I fhall be even with you; therefore off with that Ring on your Finger* Mrs *Sandal* begg'd him to fpare her Wedding-Ring, becaufe fhe would not lofe it for double the Value, as fhe had kept and worn it above twenty Years *You whining Bitch*, quoth *Will, Marriage may be d——n'd, and you too What! becaufe you are a Whore by Licenfe, I muft be more favourable to you then another Woman I'll warrant Give me the Ring in a Moment without any more Cant, or I fhall make bold to cut off your Finger with it for Difpatch, as I have ferved feveral of your Sex before*

The remaining Part of this Story is of fuch a fhocking Nature, that it can neither be related nor read without Horror I could even with intirely to omit it, were not that fuch an unparallel'd Inftance of Cruelty may deter others from entering into a Courfe of Life, in which they will certainly be led on from bad to worfe, till at laft they will be capable of committing what they before would have trembled at the Rehearfal of

The good Woman finding all Entreaties were in vain pulled of her Ring, but inftead of giving it to Cady, inftantly clapp'd it into her Mouth, and fwallow'd it, in Hopes, by that Means of preferving what fhe fo fuperftitioufly priz'd Cady fell to fwearing and ftamping like a Madman, telling her, *That all her Tricks were in vain, for he would that Moment fend her to the Devil without her Wedding-Ring* Accordingly he fhot her through the Head ript her open and took the Ring out of her Body in the prefence of her Husband, whom he had before bound, and who was incapable of uttering a Word at the Sight of fuch an unheard of Piece of Barbarity *Your Wife's a Bite, Sir*, faid the Butcherly Villain, *but I think I have hit the Bun* fo remounting his Horfe, he rode away with as little Concern as if he had done no Crime, leaving the Sorrowful Widower bound by his Wife's Body, till fome Paffengers came by and loos'd him, and then carried the mangled Corps to the next Inn

The fame Night Cady came ftrait to *London*, but was afraid that even that great City was not large enough to conceal him from the Enquiry, which fuch a horrid Action would naturally Occafion He would not ftay therefore above an Hour before he took Horfe for *Scotland*, where he arrived and ftay'd about a Month, without any Notice being taken of him After this, he came into *England* again, and a liwas making towards *London* between *Ferry-bridge* and *Doncaster* in *Yorkshire* he overtook Dr *Moreton*, a Prebendary of *Durham* It would not be more strange to see a Horse refuse Oats, than to hear that such a Gentleman as *Cady* would let a plump, sleek Clergyman pass unmolested, when he was in his Power *Stand and deliver*, was the Precept, with the Addition of *D———n you are a dead Man, if you hesitate* The Clergyman had never been used to such Language before, and began to give him good Advice, counselling him very gravely to refrain from such ill Courses, and telling him the Hazard he ran, both with Respect to his Soul and his Body But all his preaching was in vain, for *Cady* look'd upon him with all the Moreseness he could collect in his Countenance, and told him, *That his Doctrine had no Effect, and the Pretence of Religion was framed only to preserve what he had before got in the same Way* Adding *That if he did not speedily deliver, what he had, he should send him out of the World But that, quoth he with a Sneer, is nothing to a Man of your Cloth, for doubtless all the Clergymen are prepared for Death at any Time, and certain of eternal Happiness*

While *Cady* was uttering these Words, a Stone-Horse in an adjacent Field, smelling his Mare, leaped over the Hedge, and came snorting and neighing to her, like a mad Creature *Will* was so busy with Mr Doctor, that he took no Notice of the Stallion, till his Mare was covered, and he dismounted The poor Parson was glad of an Opportunity to save his Bacon, so as soon as he saw *Cady* on the Ground, he rode off as fast as he could. *The Devil take all Whoring*, cry'd *Will*, *if Horses must practise it too However, Mr Mettle, I shall go nigh to spoil your Sport before the Game be over* He was as good as his Word, for instantly pulling out a Pistol, he shot the Horse, and then remounted his Mare, and rode after Divinity

In three Quarters of a Mile he overtook poor *Moreton*, and accosted him with, *You unreasonable unmannerly Dog, what do you mean to leave a Man in the midst of his Journey, without giving him any Thing to pay his Charges?* The Doctor had taken Care, as he rode off, to hide his Money in a Hedge, so that when *Cady* search'd him, he found never a Farthing He could not however, think that a Man of his Figure would travel on Horse back without any Money in his Breeches, so that he swore the Reverend Priest should never go Home alive, if he did not inform him what he had done with his Mammon The Doctor standing to it, that he had none, our bloody Wretch instantly shot him through the Heart, which to him was no more than making a good Meal when he was a hungry

After this he took a Journey into *Norfolk* with an Intent to see his Friends and Relations at *Thetford*, but meeting a Coach within two or three Miles of that Town, with three Gentlemen and a Gentlewoman in it, could not forbear riding up to it, and making the usual Compliment The Gentlemen were resolved to dispute a Point with him, and stood bravely upon their Guard, one of them firing off a Blunderbuss without doing him any other Damage than just grazing a-cross his Left-Arm, and tearing his Coat, Waistcoat, and Shirt This put him into a violent Passion, so that after he had taken about one hundred and thirty Pounds from them all, he swore that the Loss of his Money should not entitle him that had shot him to any Quarters. He was

always as good as his Word in these Cases, the poor Gentleman was left dead in the Coach; and then cutting the Reins and Traces of the Horses, he rode off, without going to *Thetford* to see his Acquaintance

Now he steers his Course towards *London*, as fast as he can; and coming over *Finchly-Common* attacks a Lady, who was riding there for the Air, attended by a single Footman He fell upon her in a very rude Manner, pulling a Diamond-Ring from her Finger, and a Gold-Watch from her Side, taking a Purse with eighty Guineas in it, out of her Pocket, and giving her a great Deal of ill Language. The honest Footman, though the Lady had commanded him not to meddle, could not forbear shewing his Resentment at *Cady's* unmanly Behaviour He returned his foul Words with others of the same Kind calling him Villain, Rascal, Thief, and other Names of the same Import, which were suitable to his Character *Will. Cady*, without speaking a Word, answer'd the poor Fellow, by sending a Brace of Balls thro' his Head; then he cut the Girts of the Lady's Saddle, and was a going to make off

But the Time which Providence had fixed for a Period to his wicked Actions was now come Two Gentlemen, who had seen the Transaction at a Distance, intercepted him, just as he put Spurs to his Horse, with Pistols in their Hands. *Cady* was very desperate when he saw his own Danger He fired as fast as he was able, and they as nimbly returned the same Compliment, till a lucky Ball lodged in his Horse, and made him fall under him After this, he resolutely maintain'd his Ground on Foot for a considerable Time, even till he had discharged all his Pistols, and entirely weary'd himself He was then apprehended, and carried before a Justice of the Peace at *Highgate*, who committed him under a strong Guard to *Newgate*, where he continued till the next Sessions without any Signs of Remorse for the Blood he had so plentifully shed within four Years before

When his Tryal came on at the *Old-Bailey*, he behaved agreeably to his Character before that venerable Court The Lord Mayor and Recorder, he said, were a Couple of old Almswomen, and the Jurymen was treated in the same Manner The Matter of Fact which he was indicted for, was proved so plainly against him, that he received Sentence of Death, and was put into the Condemn'd-Hold, but even this Place of Horror and Darkness had no Effect upon his Mind, for he continued to swear, curse, sing, roar, and get drunk, as he had always done before. What hardened him the more, was, the Dependence he had on some Friends at Court who had given him Room to hope for a Reprieve from King *James* II who then reign'd, but the many Murders he had committed put a Stop to the Mercy which he might otherwise have obtain'd

His Day of Execution being come, and the Cart stopping as usual, under *St Sepulchre's* Church Wall, whilst the Bellman rang his Bell, and repeated his exhortatory Lines instead of being affected with the Admonition, he fell a swearing at the Sheriff's Officers, asking them, *Why they detain'd him there to hear an old Puppy chatter Nonsense?* At *Tyburn* he was just the same, being turn'd off without either conversing with the Ordinary, praying by himself, or making any Speech to the People His Exit was in 1687 when he was just twenty-five Years of Age

The

The LIFE *of* THOMAS WYNNE, *A* House-breaker *and* Murderer.

THIS notorious Criminal was born at *Ipswich* in *Suffolk*, where, for aught we find to the contrary, he continued till he was between fifteen and sixteen, at which Age he betook himself to the Sea, which he followed between eight and nine Years Happening then to come to *London*, and habituating himself with ill Company, especially lewd Women, he left no Villainy unperpetrated for the Support of himself and them, in their Extravagancies, till, at laft, he became fo expert in Housebreaking, and in fhort, all Sorts of Theft, that he was reckon'd the moft notable Artift in his Way, of thofe Times.

It was in the Reign of that glorious Monarch, Queen *Elizabeth*, that our artift flourished, accordingly, we find, that fcorning a meaner Prey he had once the Boldnefs, or rather Impudence, to rob the Royal Lodgings at *Whitehall* Palace, of as much Plate as amounted to above four hundred Pounds, for which he had the ill Luck to be taken, and committed to *Newgate* But, fortunately for him, her Majefty's Act of Grace coming out foon afterwards, granting a free Pardon for all Offences, except Treafon, Murder, and fome other notorious Crimes, he was allow'd the Benefit thereof, and obtained his Liberty, amongft many other Criminals, whom their Evil Courfes had brought into the fame Condition

But *Wynne* making a very ill ufe of the Royal Mercy, and taking no Warning, ftill purfued his vitious Ways, till at laft being in eminent Danger of being apprehended, he got into the Service of the Earl of *Salisbury*, into whofe Kitchen he was received in the Capacity of a Scullion.

Whilft he was in this Poft, he had the Impudence to pretend Love to the Countefs's Woman, who admiring at fuch Infolence in a Fellow of his Rank, return'd his Addreffes with the greateft Scorn and Contempt This exafperating *Wynne*, his pretended Love turn'd to Hatred, and he vow'd Revenge, which he effected foon after in this Manner

As fhe was coming down Stairs one Night after undreffing her Lady, and putting her to Bed, he met her full Butt, and throwing her on her Back, run his Hand fuddenly up her Coats, *caught her by a Place which Women don't Care to have ufed too roughly, and pinch'd her by it fo terribly, that fhe roar'd out as bad as any Bull that is baited* In the mean while *Wynne* kept pulling and tugging at his Game as fierce and as eager as any Maftiff, never offering to quit his Hold, till feveral of the Servants came to her Affiftance, and refcued her The poor Gentlewoman was immediately put to Bed very ill, and the Earl being next Day made acquainted with the whole Story, took upon himfelf to be his Judge, and ordered him to be forthwith ftript, and feverely lafhed by

his Coachman, which was executed to fome Tune, upon the Spot However his Lordfhip not thinking this a fufficient Punifhment, threaten'd to have it repeated once a Week for a Month together, but *Wynne*, not liking his Sentence, thought proper to feek out frefh Quarters, and accordingly pack'd up his Awls and went off But refolving to be revenged of his Profecutors, before he took his final Leave of the Family, he broke open the Trunk of the Coachman that had flead him, and robb'd him of nine Pounds. He borrow'd likewife fifteen Pounds of the Mafter-Cook, a Silver-Difh of his Lord's, and all the beft Cloaths of the poor Woman whofe *Non refifting Part* he had handled fo unmercifully, after which he fet out in Queft of new Adventures

It feems in *Wynne*'s Time, Inn-keepers were not fo fharp as they are at prefent, wherefore our Artift would frequently drefs himfelf in a Porter's Habit, with a knot and Cord, and going to one of the beft Inns, fix his Eye on any Bundle or Parcel which feem'd to be of Value, and throwing it upon his Shoulders, when he faw the Coaft clear, walk off with it directly, without the Servants having the leaft Sufpicion of him, although they met him, each of them thinking he was known by one of his Fellow-Servants

He followed this Courfe about two Years, in which Time he got above two hundred Pounds, which fell heavy on the Carriers, who were obliged to make good what was loft But dear-bought Experience making them look better after what they were entrufted with for the future, he had no Opportunity of fupporting himfelf any longer that Way, which obliged him to have Recourfe to other Methods

One Day then hearing a Man, as he was going out of his Houfe, tell his Wife he fhould not be back again in lefs then five or fix Hours, he dogged him to the Place whither he went and going to an Alehoufe hard by enquir'd the Name of the People of the Houfe This done, he went back into the Tradefman's Neighbourhood, and getting his Name after the fame Manner goes to his Wife, and tells her, that he was fent by Mr. *Such-a one*, where her Husband was taken on a fudden fo violently ill, that 'twas queftion'd whether he would live or die wherefore fhe was defired to make all the Hafte fhe could thither At this the poor Wife fell a Shrieking terribly, and after bidding the Maid take Care of the Houfe, hurried away with the Sham-Meffenger either to affift her Husband, or take her Leave of him before he departed this World

They had not gone very far together before *Wynne* pretending Bufinefs another Way, left the Woman to purfue her Journey by herfelf, and returning to the

H

House again, told the Maid, *Her Miſtreſs had ſent him to acquaint her, That if ſhe did not come back by ſuch an Hour, ſhe might go to Bed, for ſhe ſhould not come Home all Night* As *Wynne* pretended to be mightily tried with having made ſo much Haſte, the Maid asked him very civilly to walk into the Kitchin and reſt himſelf, which being what he wanted, he readily accepted In the mean while the poor Wench going to fetch him ſomething to eat, whilſt her Back was turn'd he knock'd her down ſuddenly, and binding her Hand and Foot, and gagging her, rifled all the Trunks, Boxes, Cheſts, of Drawers, and Cup-boards, carrying off to the Value of 200 l in Plate and Money

He had now reign'd about eight years in his Villany, when taking Notice of an Old Man, who had formerly been a Linnen-Draper, but being rich had left off Trade, and liv'd on what he had, together with his Wife in *Honey-Lane* near *Cheapſide*, he had for a long Time a ſtrong Deſire of robbing him Accordingly one Night he reſolved to put it in Execution, and broke into their Houſes, but not content with robbing them, he determin'd alſo to murder them, to prevent a Diſcovery, which he did by cutting their Throats in a moſt barbarous Manner, as they were ſleeping in their Bed together, This done he robb'd the Houſe to the Value of 2500 l and fled away with his Wife and four Children he had by her, to *Virginia*

Next Day, the old People being not ſeen by their Neighbours either to go out or in as uſual, and the Houſe being cloſe ſhut up from Morning to Night they began to be ſurpriz'd at the Meaning of it, and ſome among them ſuſpecting ſome foul Play, a Conſtable was ſent for, and the Door broke open, when upon entering their Chamber the old Couple were found in their Bed, to their great Aſtoniſhment and Horror, with their Throats cut from Ear to Ear, and weltering in their Blood

A great Enquiry and Search was then made after the Murderer, and a poor Man, who begg'd his Bread having been obſerv'd to walk to and fro about the Door, and ſometimes to ſit on a Bench belonging to the Houſe, the Day before the Murder was perpetrated, he was apprehended on Suſpicion, and being carried before a Juſtice of Peace, was by him committed to *Newgate* The poor Wretch was afterwards brought upon his Trial, and though there was no other Proof againſt him, than ſome ſuſpicious Circumſtances, he was caſt for his Life, and ſentenced to be hanged before the Door of the murder'd Perſons, which was accordingly executed,

though he denied the Fact to the laſt, as well he might, and he was afterwards hang'd in Chains at *Holloway*

In the mean while *Wynne* was ſafe enough with his Family beyond Sea, where it pleaſed God, that he thrived prodigiouſly with his ill-got Money, the Price of innocent Blood But having now been abſent from his native Country twenty Years, and being very deſirous of ſeeing it once before he died, deſigning afterwards to return back and lay his Bones in *Virginia*, he took his Leave of his Wife, Children, and Grand-Children (for his Family had multiplied as well as his Riches) and came over to *England* ———— But mark how Providence purſued him

Being one Day at a Goldſmith's Shop in *Cheapſide* to buy a Parcel of Plate, which he deſign'd to carry with him to *Virginia*, whilſt he was bargaining for it, and the Maſter of the Shop was weighing it, a great Uproar aroſe in the Street, for ſome Serjeants having arreſted a Gentleman, and he breaking from the *Catchpoles*, who were in Purſuit of him Hereupon *Wynne* ran out of the Shop the ſame Way as the Mob, and ſome that were behind him, crying out, *Stop him, Stop him*, his Conſcience flew in his Face, ſo that he ſtopt ſhort, and ſaid, *I am the Man* ——— *You the Man*, cry'd the People, *What Man ?* ——— *The Man*, reply'd *Wynne*, *that committed ſuch a Murder in* Honey-Lane, *twenty Years ago, for which a poor Man was hang'd wrongfully*

Upon this Confeſſion he was taken into Cuſtody, and carried to a Magiſtrate, before whom he again owns the ſame, and being committed to *Newgate*, was try'd, condemn'd, and executed alſo before the Houſe, where he had perpetrated the Murder, after which he was carried to *Holloway*, and hanged in Chains

Thus the juſt Judgment of God at laſt overtook him for ſhedding innocent Blood, when he thought himſelf ſecure from the Stroke of Juſtice, neither was it wanting to puniſh his Wife and Poſterity for being privy thereunto, and living upon the Fruits thereof For his Wife ran diſtracted, upon receiving the News of his ſhameful End, and died ſo Two of his Sons alſo were hang'd in *Virginia*, for a Robbery and Murder they committed there, and what Plantations he had purchaſed were ſeiz'd upon for the Queen's Uſe, as forfeited by his Conviction of Murder and Felony, ſo that his Poſterity were reduced to Beggary ever after, and died very miſerable.

The LIFE *of* THOMAS SAVAGE.

THIS unhappy Wretch was born of very honest Parents in the Parish of *St. Giles's* in the Fields, and between fourteen and fifteen Years of Age, bound Apprentice to one Mr *Collins* a Vintner, at *the Ship-Tavern* at *Ratcliff Cross*, with whom he led but a very loose and profligate Sort of Life for about two Years

Breaking the Sabbath (by his own Confession, he having never once heard a whole Sermon during that Time) was the first Inlet to all his other Vices, especially Whoredom, Drunkenness, and Theft For he used commonly to pass away the Sabbaths at a Bawdy-House in *Ratcliff-Highway*, with one *Hannah Blay*, a vile common Strumpet, who was the Cause of his Ruin, and brought him to his shameful End

He was carried at first to drink there by an Acquaintance, who afterwards went to Sea, but having once found the Way, he went after that alone, without his Companion, and would often carry a Bottle or two of Wine to junket with her This however, not satisfying her wicked Desires, she told him frequently, *That if he would enjoy her Company, he must bring good Store of Money with him* To this he always replied, *That he could bring none but his Master's, and that he had never wronged him of Two-pence in his Life* Nevertheless she still continued urging him to rob him privately, but he answer'd, *he could not because the Maid was always at Home with him. Hang her, a Jade,* (said this Limb of the Devil) *knock her Brains out, and I'll receive the Money, and go any where with you beyond Sea, to avoid the Stroke of Justice*

She was often giving him this bad Advice, and preaching this infernal Doctrine; and she repeated it in particular on the very Day when he unhappily took her Counsel, and perpetrated the Murder For being at her House in the Morning, she made him drunk with burnt Brandy, and he wanting a Groat to pay his Reckoning, she again persuaded him to knock the Maid's Brains out, and bring her what Money he could find

Hereupon he went Home between twelve and one o'Clock, and seeing his Master standing at the Street Door, did not dare to go in that Way, but climbed over a Wall, and getting in at the Back-Door, went into the Room, where his Fellow-Servants were at Dinner O *Sirrah*, said the Maid to him, *you have been now at the Bawdy-House, you will never leave it till you are utterly ruin'd thereby*

These Words provok'd him highly, and he was so much enraged at her, that from that Moment the Devil took firm Possession of him, and he fully resolved, even while he was at Dinner, to be her Butcher Accordingly, when his Master, with the rest of the Family were gone to Church, leaving only the Maid and *Tom Savage* at Home, he goes into the Bar, and fetches a Hammer, with which he began to make a great Noise, as he sat by the

Fire, by knocking on the Bellows. Hereupon, says the Maid to him, *Sure the Boy is mad! Sirrah, What do you make this Noise for?*

To this he made no Answer, but going to the Kitchen Window began to knock, and make the same Noise there, of which the Maid then taking no Notice, he, to provoke her, got on the clean Dresser, and walk'd up and down thereon several Times with his dirty Shoes This Piece of Malice exasperating the Maid, so that she scolded at him pretty heartily, he threw the Hammer at her suddenly with such Violence, that hitting her on the Head, she fell to the Ground and shriek'd out He then went and took up the Hammer, intending to repeat the Blow, but laid it down again thrice, not being yet harden'd enough in Cruelty, to strike her any more, but at last taking it up the fourth Time, the Devil had then gain'd such an absolute Mastery over him, that he gave her several Strokes with all the Force he could, and quickly dispatch'd her out of the World.

The inhuman Wretch having perpetrated this hellish Piece of Barbarity, immediately broke open a Cupboard in his Master's Chamber, and taking out a Bag, wherein was about Sixty Pounds, hid it under his Coat, and went out at a Back-Door directly away to *Hannah Blay* again. When he came there, and had informed her what he had done, the cunning Slut, who was harden'd in Wickedness, would fain have had the Money from him, but he would part with no more than Half a Crown, which having given her, he went away without the least Remorse for what he had done

But he had not gone very far, when meeting with a Stile, he sat him down thereon to rest himself, and than began to reflect on the horrid Deed he had perpetrated, and to cry out to himself, *Lord, what have I done!* wishing that he could have recalled the fatal Blows, even at the Price of ten thousand Worlds, if so many had been in his Power After this, he was in so much Horror and dread of Mind, that he stirred not a Step, but he thought every one he met, came to apprehend him

That Night he reach'd *Greenwich*, where he took up his Lodging, telling the People of the House he was going to *Gravesend*, but being got to Bed, he could not sleep through the Terror of a guilty Conscience, but got up again, and walked about the Room for several Hours Next Morning the Mistress of the House, perceiving he had a large Quantity of Money in a Bag not sealed up, began to examine him about it, doubting he came not by it honestly Hereupon, to avoid her just Suspicion, he told her, *He was carrying it down to Gravesend to his Master, who was a Wine-Cooper, and lived on* London-Bridge, *and that if she would not believe him, she might send to his Mistress, and in the mean Time he would leave the Money in her Hands*

Thus

H.Burgh Sculpsit

THO SAVAGE *Returning to* HANAH BLAY'S *Lodgings*

This was agreed upon, and accordingly he wrote a Note himself to his pretended Mistress, which was to be carried by some People, who were then going to *London*, whilst he went his Way, wandering towards *Woolwich*, where he was in the *Ship-Yard*, much about the Time the Hue-and-Cry came to *Greenwich* of a Murder committed at *Ratcliff-Cross* by a Youth, upon a Maid, who was his Fellow-Servant, and that he had also robb'd his Master of a Bag of Money

Upon this News the Mistress of the House, where he lay, presently concluded, that it was the same Youth who had lodg'd there, and that the Bag he had left with her was that whereof he had robb'd his Master Hereupon, she immediately dispatch'd several Men in Search of him, who found him a-sleep in an Alehouse, with his Head upon a Table, and a Pot of Beer by him. Upon this, one of the Men calling him by his Name, said, *Tom, Did not you live at Ratcliff?* He answer'd, *Yes, And did not you murder your Fellow-Servant* He answer'd likewise in the Affirmative *And you took so much Money from your Master?* He acknowledg'd all *Then*, continued he, *you must go along with us* To which he replied, *Yes, with all my Heart* Accordingly they went forthwith to *Greenwich*, to the House where he had lain the Night before.

By that Time he got thither, his Master and some Friends were arriv'd there likewise, who exaggerated to him the Barbarity of the Fact, wherewith he was not much affected at first, though a little after he burst out into Tears: From thence he was carried back to *Ratcliff*, and had before a Justice of Peace, who committed him to *Newgate*

Being now in safe Custody, he was visited by one Mr *Baker*, to whom, after some little Acquaintance, he gave the foregoing Account, and he found him at first but little sensible of the Heinousness of the Crime he had committed But the next Time, asking him whether he was sorry for the Fact, he answer'd with Tears in his Eyes, wringing his Hands, and striking his Breast, " Yes, Sir, for it cuts me to the Heart " to think that I should take away the Life of an in-" nocent Creature, and that is not all, but for any " Thing I know, I have sent her Soul to Hell " Oh! how can I think of appearing before God's " Tribunal, when she shall stand before me, and " say, Lord, this Wretch took away my Life, and " gave me not the least Time to consider of the State " of my Soul, that so I might have repented of my " Sins, and have turned to thee, he gave me no " Warning at all, Lord Oh! then, What will " become of me "

He was then visited by Mr *Robert Franklyn*, Mr *Thomas Vincent*, Mr *Thomas Doolittle*, and Mr *James Janeway*, who ask'd him, *If he was the Person that murder'd the Maid at Ratcliff?* To which he answer'd, *Yes* Hereupon they endeavoured to set the Sin home upon his Conscience, telling him the Danger he was in, not only of a Temporal, but of an eternal Death, without true Repentance, and a sincere and strong Faith

The Day that he went down to the Sessions, his Fellow Prisoners gave him something to drink, which very much disorder'd him; and *Hannah Blay*, whom he had accused, and who was taken into Custody

thereupon, was heard to say to him. " Others " have made you drunk To-day, but I will make " thee drunk To-morrow *He lamented this Back-* " *sliding grievously, but said*, 'That it was not the " Quantity he had drank, which was much less than " he was able to drink at other Times, without be-" ing in the least disorder'd; but it was something " they had infused into his Liquor to intoxicate his " Senses." Which made him ever afterwards very cautious and fearful of drinking in their Company

After he had received Sentence of Death, he was again visited by Mr *Baker*, and the *Saturday* before his Execution was again with him, when *Savage* said to him, taking him by the Hand, " Oh! my " dear Friend, come hither *Then opening his Coffin*, " look here, *continued he*, this is the Ship where I " must launch out into the Ocean of Eternity Is it " not a terrible Thing to see one's own Coffin and " Burial Cloaths, when at the same Time (as to " my Bodily Health) I am every Whit as well as " you?"

On the *Sunday*, expecting to be executed next Day, he desir'd to be alone, and spent it in Prayer, and other religious Duties Next Morning the Sheriff's Men and Cart came for him, but the Sheriff of *Middlesex* not having Notice, it was deferred till *Wednesday*, when looking upon his Cloaths that he had put on to die in, he said, *What, have I got on my dying Cloaths? Dying Cloaths, did I say? They are my living Cloaths, the Cloaths out of which I shall go into eternal Glory; They are the best Cloaths that ever I put on*

Being brought to the Place of Execution at *Ratcliff-Cross*, he made a short Speech, wherein he exhorted People, both old and young, *To take Warning by his untimely End, how they offended against the Laws of God and Man* After which, having said a very pathetick Prayer, and breath'd forth such pious Ejaculations, as drew Tears from the Eyes of the Beholders he was turn'd off the Cart, and struggl'd for a while, heaving up his Body Which a young Man, his Friend, perceiving, he struck him several Blows upon his Breast with all his Strength, to put him out of his Pain, till no Motion could be perceived in him, wherefore after he had hung a considerable Time, and was to all Appearance dead, the People moving a Way, the Sheriff ordered him to be cut down When being received into the Arms of some of his Friends, he was convey'd into a House not far from the Place of Execution There being laid upon a Table, he began, to the Astonishment of the Beholders, to breath, and rattle in the Throat, so that it was evident Life was whole in him Hereupon he was carry'd from thence to a Bed in the same House, where he breath'd more strongly, and opered his Eyes and Mouth, though his Teeth were set before, and he offer'd to speak but could not recover the Use of his Tongue

However, his Reviving being blaz'd abroad within an Hour, the Sheriff's Officers came to the House where he was, and carrying him back to the Place of Execution, hung him up again till he he was really dead After which his Body was carried by his mourning Friends to *Islington*, and buried *October* 28. 1668 being seventeen Years of Age

The

The LIFE *of* Colonel JACK.

IN this Account of the Life of Colonel *Jack*, as written by himself, there is Room for just and copious Observations on the Blessings and Advantages of a sober and a well-govern'd Education, and the Ruins of many thousands of Youths of all Kinds for want of it: Also how much Publick-Schools and Charities might be improv'd to prevent the Destruction of so many unhappy Children, as in this City are every Year bred up for the Gallows The miserable Condition of unfortunate Children, many of whose natural Tempers are docible, and would lead them to learn the best Things rather than the worst, are truly deplorable, and is abundantly seen in the History of this Man's Childhood, where though Circumstances form'd him by Necessity to be a Thief, a strange Rectitude of Principles remain'd with him, and made him early abhor the worst Part of his Trade, and at last wholly leave it off If he had come into the World with the Advantages of Education, and been well-instructed how to improve the generous Principles he had in him, what a Man might he not have been ?

The various Turns of his Fortune in the World, make a delightful Field for the Reader to wander in. Every wicked Reader will be here encouraged to a Change, and it will appear, that the best and only good End of a wicked misspent Life is Repentance While these Things and such as these are the End and Designs of the Undertakers of this present Book, I think no Apology need be made for any single Life, No, nor for the whole, if discouraging every Thing that is evil, and encouraging every Thing which is virtuous and good. I say, if these appear to be the Scope and Design of publishing such Stories, no Objection can be against it, neither is it of the least Moment to inquire whether the Colonel hath told his own Story true or not If he has made it a History, or a Parable, it will be equally useful and capable of doing good, and in that it recommends itself without any further Introduction

Seeing my Life has been such a Chequer-Work of Nature, and that I am able now to look back upon it, from a safer Distance, than is ordinary to the Fate of the Clan, to which I once belong'd, I think my History may find a Place in the World, as we'll as some, who I see are every Day read with Pleasure, though they have in them nothing so diverting or Instructing, as I believe mine will appear to be

My Original may be as high as any Bodies, for ought I know, for my Mother kept very good Company, but that Part belongs to her Story more than to mine All I know of it is by oral Tradition thus . My Nurse told me my Mother was a Gentlewoman, that my Father was a Man of Quality, and she (my Nurse) had a good Piece of Money given her to take me off his Hands, and deliver him and my Mother from the Importunities that usually attend the Misfortune of having a Child to keep that should not be seen or heard of

My Father, it seems, gave my Nurse something more than was agreed for, at my Mother's Request, upon her solemn Promise, that she would use me well, and let me be put to School, and charged her, that if I lived to come to any Bigness, capable to understand the Meaning of it, she should always take Care to bid me remember, that I was a Gentleman, and this, he said, was all the Education he would desire of her for me ; for he did not doubt, but that some Time or other, the very Hint would inspire me with Thoughts suitable to my Birth, and that I would certainly act like a Gentleman, if I believ'd myself to be so

But my Disasters were not directed to end as soon as they began, 'tis very seldom that the unfortunate are so but for a Day, as the Great rise by Degrees of Greatness to the Pitch of Glory in which they shine, so the miserable sink to the Depth of their Misery by a continued Series of Disasters, and are long in the Tortures and Agonies of their distressed Circumstances before a Turn of Fortune, if ever such a Thing happens to them, gives them a Prospect of Deliverance

My Nurse was as honest to the Engagement she had enter'd into, as could be expected from one of her Employment ; and particularly as honest as her Circumstances would give her Leave to be, for she bred me up very carefully with her own Son, and with another Son of Shame, like me, who she had taken upon the same Terms

My Name was *John*, as she told me, but neither she nor I knew any Thing of a Sirname that belonged to me, so that I was left to call myself Mr any Thing what I pleased, as Fortune and better Circumstances should give Occasion It happen'd, that her own Son, (for she had a little Boy about one Year older than I) was called *John* too, and about two Years after, she took another Son of Shame, as I call'd it above, to keep, as she did me, and his Name was *John* too But my Nurse, who may be allow'd to distinguish her own Son a little from the rest, would have him call'd Captain, because forsooth he was the Eldest

I was provok'd at having this Boy called Captain, and cried and told my Nurse I would be called Captain, for she told me I was a Gentleman, and I would be a Captain, that I wou'd The good Woman, to keep the Peace, told me *Ay, ay, I was a Gentleman, and therefore I should be above a Captain, for I should be a Colonel, and that was a great Deal better than a Captain For, my Dear*, says she, *every Tarpawlin, if he gets but to be Lieutenant of a Press-Smack, is called Captain, but Colonels are Soldiers, and none but Gentlemen are ever made Colonels Besides*, says she, *I have known Colonels come to be Lords, and Generals, though they were Bastards at first, and therefore you shall be called Colonel* Well I was hush'd indeed, with this for the present, but not thoroughly pleased, till a little while after, I heard her tell her own Boy, that I was a Gentleman,

and

Colonel Jack Robbing Mrs Smith going to Kentish Town.

and therefore he muſt call me Colonel; at which her Boy fell a Crying, and he would be called Colonel too, ſo then I was ſatisfy'd that it was above a Captain So univerſally is Ambition ſeated in the Minds of Men, that not a Beggar Boy, but has his Share of it Before I tell you much more of our Story, it would be very proper to give ſomething of our ſeveral Characters, as I have gather'd them up in my Memory, as far back as I can recover Things either of myſelf, or my Brother *Jacks*, and they ſhall be brief and Impartial

Capt. *Jack*, the Eldeſt of us all by a whole Year, was a ſquat, big, ſtrong made Boy, and promiſed to be ſtout when grown up to be a Man, but not tall He was an original Rogue, for he would do the fouleſt and moſt villainous Things even by his own Inclination; he had no Taſte or Senſe of being honeſt, no not even to his Brother Rogues, which is what other Thieves make a Point of Honour of; I mean that of being honeſt to one another.

Major *Jack* was a merry, facetious, pleaſant Boy, and had ſomething of a Gentleman in him He had a true manly Courage, fear'd nothing, and yet, if he had the Advantage, was the moſt compaſſionate Creature alive, and wanted nothing but Honeſty to have made him an excellent Man He had learnt to write and read very well, as you will find in the Proceſs of this Story

As to myſelf, I paſs'd among my Comrades for a bold reſolute Boy, but I had a different Opinion of myſelf, and therefore ſhun'd fighting as much as I could I was wary and dexterous at my Trade, and was not ſo often catched as my Fellow-Rogues I mean while I was a Boy, and never after I came to be a Man, no not once for twenty ſix Years, being ſo old in the Trade, and ſtill unhang'd

I was almoſt ten Years old, the Captain eleven, and the Major eight, when our good old Nurſe died, her Husband was drown'd a little before in the *Gloucester* Frigate, which was caſt away going to *Scotland* with the Duke of *York*, in the *Reign* of King *Charles* II and the honeſt Woman dying very poor the Pariſh was obliged to bury her The good Woman being dead, we were turned looſe to the World, rambling about all three together, and the People in *Rosemary Lane* and *Ratcliffe*, knowing us pretty well, we got Victuals eaſy enough, as for Lodging, we lay in the Summer-Time on Bulk-Heads and at Shop-doors, as for Bed, we knew nothing what belong'd to it for many Years after my Nurſe died, but in Winter got into the Aſh-Holes, and Nealing-Arches in the Glaſs-Houſes, where we were accompanied by ſeveral Youngſters like ourſelves, ſome of whom perſuaded the Captain to go a kidd napping with them, a Trade at that Time much followed the Gang uſed to catch Children in the Evening, ſtop their Mouths, and carry them to ſuch Houſes, where they had Rogues ready to receive them, who put them on Board Ships bound to *Virginia*, and when they arrived there, they were ſold This wicked Gang were at laſt taken, and ſent to *Newgate*, and Capt *Jack*, among the reſt, though he was not then much above thirteen Years old, and being but a Lad was ordered to be three Times whipped at *Bridewell*, the Recorder telling him, it was done in order to keep him from the Gallows We did what we could to comfort him, but he was ſcourged ſo ſeverely, that he lay ſick for a good while, but as ſoon as he regain'd his Liberty, he went to his old Gang, and kept among them as long as that Trade laſted for it ceaſed a few Years afterwards

The Major and I, though very young, had ſenſible Impreſſions made on us for ſome Time by the ſevere Uſage of the Captain; but it was within the Year, that the Major, a good-condition'd eaſy Body was wheedled away by a Couple of young Rogues to take a Walk with them The Gentlemen were very well matched for the oldeſt of them was not above fourteen, the Buſineſs was to go to *Bartholomew-Fair*, and the End of going there was to pick Pockets

The Major knew nothing of the Trade, and therefore was to do nothing, but they promiſed him a ſhare with them, for all that, as if he had been as expert as themſelves, ſo away they went The two dexterous Rogues managed it ſo well, that by about eight o'Clock at Night, they came back to our duſty Quarters at the Glaſs-Houſe, and ſitting them down in a Corner, they began to ſhare their Spoil by the Light of the Glaſs-Houſe Fire The Major lugg'd out the Goods, for as faſt as they made any Purchaſe, they unloaded themſelves, and gave all to him, that if they had been taken, nothing might be found about them. It was a Deviliſh lucky Day to them, the Devil certainly aſſiſting them to find their Prey, that he might draw in a young Gameſter, and encourage him to the Undertaking, who had been made backward before by the Misfortune of the Captain The Liſt of their Purchaſe the firſt Night was as follows

1 *A white Handerchief from a Country Wench, as ſhe was ſtaring up at a Jack-Pudding There was three Shillings and Six-Pence, and a Row of Pins tied up in one End of it*

2 *A coloured Handkerchief out of a young Country Fellow's Pocket, as he was buying a China Orange.*

3 *A Ribband-Purſe with eleven Shillings and three Pence, and a Silver Thimble in it, out of a young Woman's Picket, juſt as a Fellow offered to pick her up ——— N B She miſs'd her Purſe preſently, but not ſeeing the Thief, charged the Man with it that would have picked her up, and cried out, A Pick-pocket ! and he fell into the Hands of the Mob, but being known in the Street, he got off with great Difficulty*

4 *A Knife and Fork that a Couple of Boys had juſt bought, and were going Home with, the young Rogue that took it within a Minute after the Boy had put it into his Pocket*

5 *A little Silver-Box with Seven Shillings in it, all in ſmall Silver 1 d, 2 d, 3 d, 4 d Pieces*

6 *Two Silk Handkerchiefs*

7 *A Jointed Baby, and a little Looking-Glaſs, ſtol'n off a Toy Seller's Stall in the Fair*

All this Cargo to be brought Home clear in one Afternoon, or Evening rather, and by only two little Rogues, ſo young, was, it muſt be confeſſed extraordinary, and the Major was elevated the next Day to a ſtrange Degree, for he came to me very early, and called me out into a narrow Lane, and ſhewed me almoſt his little hand full of Money I was ſurpriz'd at the Sight, when he puts it up again, and bringing his Hand out, Here, ſays he, you ſhall have ſome of it, and gives me a Six Pence and a Shilling's worth of the ſmall Silver Pieces This was very welcome to me, who never had a Shilling of Money together before in all my Life, that I could call my own I was very earneſt to know how he came by this Wealth, he quickly told me the Story, and that he had for his Share Seven Shillings and Six-pence in Money, the Silver-Thimble, and a Silk-Handkerchief

We went to *Rag Fair*, and bought each of us, a pair of Shoes and Stockings, and afterwards went to a Boiling Cooks in *Rosemary Lane*, where we treated ourselves nobly, for we had boil'd Beef, Pudding, a Penny-Brick, and a Pint of Strong-Beer, which cost us Seven Pence in all. That Night the Major triumph'd in our new Enjoyment, and slept in the usual Place, with an undisturb'd Repose. The next Day the Major and his Comrades went abroad again, and were still successful, nor did any Disaster attend them for many Months; and by frequent Imitation and Direction, Major *Jack* became as dexterous a Pick-Pocket as any of them, and went through a long Variety of Fortune, too long to enter upon now, because I am hast'ning to my own Story, which at present is the main Thing I have to set down

Overcome by the Persuasions of the Major, I enter'd myself into his Society, and went down to *Billinsgate* with one of them, which was crouded with Masters of Coal-Ships, Fish-Mongers, and Oyster-Women It was the first of these People my Comrade had his Eye upon. So he gives me my Orders, which was thus *Go you, says he, into all the Ale-Houses as we go along, and observe where any People are telling of Money, and when you find any, come and tell me* So he stood at the Door, and I went into the Houses. As the Collier Masters generally sell their Coals at the Gate, as they call it, so they generally receive their Money in those Ale-Houses, and it was not long before I brought him Word of several Upon this, he went in and made his Observations, but found nothing to his Purpose At length I brought Word, that there was a Man in such a House, who had received a great Deal of Money of somebody, I believed, of several People, and that it lay all upon the Table in Heaps, and he was very busy writing down the Sums, and putting it up in several Bags: *Is he, says he, I'll warrant him, I will have some of it*, and in he goes, walks up and down the House, which had several open Tables and Boxes in it, and listen'd to hear, if he could learn what the Man's Name was, and he heard somebody call him *Cullum*, or some such Name, then he watches his Opportunity, and steps up to him, and tells him a long Story, *That there was two Gentlemen at the Gun-Tavern sent him to enquire for him, and to tell him, they desired to speak with him*

The Collier-Master had got his Money before him just as I had told him, and had two or three small Payments of Money, which he had put up in little black dirty Bags, and laid by themselves, and as it was hardly broad Day, he found Means in delivering his Message, to lay his Hand upon one of those Bags, and carry it off perfectly undiscover'd When he had got it, he came out to me, who stood but at the Door, and pulling me by the Sleeve, *Run, Jack, says he, for our Lives*, and away he scours, and I after him, never resting, or scarce looking about me, till we got quite into *Moorfields* But not thinking ourselves safe there, we run on till we got into the Fields, and finding a By-place, we sat down, and he pulls out the Bag, *Thou art a lucky Boy Jack, says he, thou deservest a good Share of this Job, truly, for 'tis all along of thy lucky News*, So he pours it all out into my Hat, for, as I told you I now wore a Hat

How he did to whip away such a Bag from any Man who was awake and in his Senses, I can't tell There was about seventeen or eighteen Pound in the Bag, and he parted the Money, giving me one Third, with which I was very well contented As we were now so rich, he would not let me lie any longer about the Glass-House, or go naked and ragged as I had done; but obliged me to buy two Shirts, a Waistcoat, and a Great-Coat; for a Great-Coat was more proper for our Business than any other So I cloathed

myself, as he directed, and we lodged together in a little Garret.

Soon after this, we walk'd out again, and then we tried our Fortune in the Places by the Exchange a second Time. Here we began to act separately, and I undertook to walk by myself, and the first thing I did accurately, was a Trick I play'd that argued some Skill for a new Beginner, for I had never seen any Business of that kind done before, I saw two Gentlemen mighty eager in Talk, and one pulled out a Pocket-Book two or three Times, and then shipt it into his Coat-Pocket again, and then out came again, and Papers were taken out, and others put in, and then in it went again, and so several Times, the Man being still warmly engaged with another Man, and two or three others standing hard by them the last Time he put his Pocket-Book in to his Pocket with his Hand, and the Book lay End-Way, resting upon some other Book, or something else in his Pocket, so that it did not go quit down, but one Corner of it was seen above his Pocket. When seeing the Book pass and repass, I brushed smoothly, but closely by the Man, and took it clean away, and went directly into *Moorfields*, where my Fellow Rogue was to meet me I was not long before he came I had no Occasion to tell him my Success, for he had heard of the Action among the Crowd We searched the Book, and found several Goldsmith's and other Notes, but the best of the Booty was in one of the Folds of the Cover of the Book. There was a Paper full of loose Diamonds The Man, as we understood afterwards, was a *Jew*, and dealt in those glittering Commodities

We agreed that *Will* (which was my Comrade's Name) should return to the Change to hear what News was stirring, and there he heard of a Reward of one hundred Pound for returning the Things The next Day he went to the Gentleman, and told him he had got some Scent of his Book, and the Person who took it, and who, he believed, would restore it, for the sake of the Reward, provided he was assured that he should not be punish'd for the Fact After many Preliminaries, it was concluded, that *Will* should bring the Book, and the Things lost in it, and receive the Reward, which on the third Day, he did, and faithfully paid me my Share of it

Not long after this, it fell out, we were strolling about in *Smithfield* on a *Friday* There happened to be an old Country Gentleman in the Market, selling some very large Bullocks, it seems they came out of *Sussex*, for we heard him say, there were no such Bullocks in the whole County of *Sussex* His Worship, for so they call'd him, had received the Money for these Bullocks at a Tavern, whose Sign I have forgot now, and having some of it in a Bag, and the Bag in his Hand, he was taken with a sudden Fit of Coughing, and stands to Cough, resting his Hand with the Bag of Money in it, upon a Bulk-Head of a Shop, just by the Cloister-Gate in Smithfield, that is to say, within three or four Doors of it We were both just behind him, says *Will* to me, *Stand ready* Upon this, he makes an artificial Stumble, and falls with his Head just against the old Gentleman in the very Moment when he was coughing ready to be strangl'd and quite spent for want of Breath

The Violence of the Blow, beat the old Gentleman quite down, the Bag of Money did not immediately fly out of his Hand, but I run to get hold of it, and gave it a quick Snatch, pulled it clean away, and run like the Wind down the *Cloister* with it, till I got to our old Rendezvous *Will* in the mean Time, fell down with the old Gentleman, but soon got up The old Knight, for such, it seem he was,

was frighted with the Fall and his Breath so stopp'd with his Cough, that he could not recover himself to speak 'till some Time, during which nimble *Will*, was got up again, and walk'd off, nor could he call out stop Thief, or tell any Body he had lost any Thing for a good while, but coughing vehemently till he was almost black in the Face, he at last brought it out, *The Rogues has got away my Bag of Money*

All this while the People understood nothing of the Matter, and as for the Rogues indeed, they had Time enough to get clear away, and in about an Hour, *Will* came to the Rendezvous, there we sat down on the Grass again, and turned out the Money, which proved to be eight Guineas, and five Pounds eight Shillings in Silver. This we shar'd upon the Spot, and went to work the same Day for more, but whether it was that being flush'd with our Success, we were not so vigilant, or that no other Opportunity offer'd, I know not, but we got nothing more that Night, nor so much as any Thing offer'd itself for an Attempt

The next Adventure was in the Dusk of the Evening, in a Court which goes out of *Grace-Church-Street* into *Lombard-Street*, where the *Quaker's Meeting-house* is, there was a young Fellow, who, as we learn'd afterwards, was a *Woollen-Draper's* Apprentice in *Grace-Church Street*, it seems he had been receiving a Sum of Money, which was very considerable, and he comes to a Goldsmiths in *Lombard Street* with it, paid in the most of it there, insomuch that it grew Dark, and the Goldsmith began to be shutting in the Shop, and Candles to be lighted, we watched him in there, and stood on the other side of the Way, to see what he did, when he paid in all the Money he intended, he stayed a little longer to take Notes for what he had paid At last he comes out of the Shop with still a pretty large Bag under his Arm, and walks over into the Court, which was then very dark, in the middle of the Court is a boarded Entry, and at the End of it a Threshold, and as soon as he had set his Foot over the Threshold, he was to turn on his Left Hand into *Grace Church Street*

Keep up, says *Will* to me, be *nimble*, and as soon as he had said so, he flies at the young Man, and gives him such a violent Thrust, that pushed him forward with too great a Force for him to stand, and as he strove to recover the Threshold, took hold of his Feet, and he fell forward I stood ready, and presently fell out the Bag of Money, which I heard fall, for it flew out of his Hand I went forward with the Money, and *Will* finding I had it, run backward. And as I made along *Fenchurch-street* overtook me, and we scoured Home together The poor young Man was hurt a little with the Fall, and reported to his Master as we heard afterwards, that he was knocked down His Master was glad the rest of the Money was paid in to the Banker, and made no great Noise at the Loss, only cautioned his Apprentice to avoid such dark Places for the Future

This Booty amounted to 14l 18s apiece, and added extremely to my Store, which began to grow too big for my management, but still I was at a Loss with whom to trust it A little after this, *Will* brought me into the Company of two more young fellows, we met at the Lower part of *Gray's-Inn Lane*, about an Hour before Sun-set, and went out into the Fields, towards a Place called the *Pindar of Wakefield*, where are abundance of Brick-Hills, here it was agreed to spread from the Field Path, to the Road-way, all the Way towards *Pancras* Church, to observe any Chance Game, which, as they called it, they might shoot Flying. Upon

the Path within the Bank on the side of the Road going towards *Kentish Town*, two of our Gang, *Will*, and one of the other met a single Gentleman, walking apace towards the Town, being almost Dark, *Will* Cryed, *Mark, ho*, which, it seems was the Word at which we were all to stand still at a Distance, come in if he wanted Help, and give a Signal if any thing appeared that was Dangerous

Will steps up to the Gentleman, stops him, and put the Question, that is, *Sir, your Money*; the Gentleman seeing he was alone, struck at him with his Cane, but *Will* a nimble strong Fellow, flew in upon him, and with Strugling got him down, then he begged for his Life *Will* having told him with an Oath, that he would cut his Throat in that Moment While this was doing, comes a Hackney Coach along the Road, and the fourth Man who was that Way cries. *Mark, ho*, he which was to intimate that it was a Prize, not a Surprize, and accordingly the next Man went up to assist him, where they stop'd the Coach, which had a Doctor of Physick, and a Surgeon in it, who had been to visit some considerable Patient, and I suppose had considerable Fees, for here they got two gold Purses, one with 11 or 12 Guineas, the other Six, with some pocket Money, two Watches, one Diamond Ring, and the Surgeon's Plaister Box, which was most of it full of silver Instruments

While they were at this Work, *Will* kept the Man down, who was under him, and tho' he promis'd not to kill him, unless he offered to make a Noise, yet he wou'd not let him stir, till he heard the Noise of the Coach going on again, by which he knew the Jobb was over on that side Then he carried him a little out of the Way, ty'd his Hands behind him, and bid him lie still and make no Noise, and he would come back in half an Hour, and untie him upon his Word, but if he cry'd out he would come back and kill him The poor Man promis'd to lie still and make no Noise, and did so, and had not above 11s. 6d in his Pocket, which *Will* took, and came back to the rest, but while they were together, I who was on the side of the *Pindar of Wakefield*, cry'd *Mark, ho*, too

What I saw was a couple of poor Women, one a kind of a Nurse, and the other a Maid-Servant, going for *Kentish Town* As *Will* knew I was but young at the Work, he came flying to me, and seeing how easy a Bargain it was, he said Go Col fall to work I went up to them, and speaking to the Elderly Woman, Nurse said I don't be in such haste, I want to speak with you, at which they both stopp'd, and looked a little frighted, don't be frighted Sweet-heart said I to the Maid, a little of that Money in the Bottom of your Pocket, will make all easy, and I'll do you no harm, by this Time *Will* came up to us, for they did not see him before, then they began to scream out, hold says I, make no Noise, unless you have a Mind to force us to Murther you whether we will or no, give me your Money presently, and make no Words, and we shan't hurt you Upon this the poor Maid pull'd out 5 s 6d and the old Woman a Guinea and a Shilling, crying heartily for her Money, and said it was all she had in the World, well we took it for all that, tho' it made my Heart Bleed to see what Agony the poor Woman was in at parting with it; and I ask'd her where she lived, she said her Name was *Smith*, and she lived at *Kentish Town*, I said nothing to her, but bid them go on about their Business, and I gave *Will*, the Money; so in a few Minutes we were all together again, says one of the other Rogues come this is well enough for one Road, it's time to be gone So we jog'd away, crossing the Field out of the Path toward *Tottenham Court*, but hold says

H il.

Will, I muſt go and untie the Man⸺im him, ſays one of them, let him lye, no ſays *Will* I wont be worſe then my Word I will untye him So he went to the Place, but the Man was gone, either he had untied himſelf, or ſome-Body had paſſed by, and he had called for Help, and ſo was untied, for he could not find him, nor make him Hear, tho' he ventured to call twice for him aloud.

This made us haſten away the faſter, and getting into *Tottenham Court* Road, they thought it was a little too near, ſo they made into the Town at St *Giles's* and croſſing to *Piccadilly* went to *Hyde-Park* Gate, here they ventured to rob another Coach that is to ſay, one of the two other Rogues and *Will*, did it between the *Park* Gate and *Knightsbridge*; there was in it only a Gentleman and a Whore that he had pick'd up it ſeems at the Spring-Garden a little farther, they took the Gentleman's Money, and his Watch, and his ſilver hilted Sword; but when they came to the Slut, ſhe damn'd them and curſed them for robbing the Gentleman of his Money, and leaving him none for her, as for herſelf ſhe had not one Sixpenny-piece about her, tho' ſhe was indeed well enough dreſſed too Having made this Adventure, we parted, and went each Man to his Lodging

Two Days after this, *Will* came to my Lodging, for I had now got a Room by Myſelf, and appointed me to meet him the next Evening at ſuch a Place I went, but to my great Satisfaction miſs'd him, but met with the Gang at another Place, who had committed a notorious Robbery near *Hounſlow*, where they wounded a Gentleman's Gardener, ſo that I think he died, and robbed the Houſe of a very conſiderable Sum of Money and Plate. This, however, was not ſo clean carried, but the Neighbours were alarm'd, the Rogues purſued, and being at *London* with the Booty, one of them was taken, but *Will* being a dextrous Fellow made his Eſcape with the Money and Plate He knew nothing that one of his Comrades were taken, and that they were all ſo cloſely purſued that every one was obliged to ſhift for himſelf He happened to come in the Evening, as good Luck then directed him Juſt after Search had been made for him by the Conſtables, his Companion who was taken, having upon promiſe of Favour, and to ſave himſelf from the Gallows, Diſcovered his Confederates, and *Will* among the reſt, as the Principal Party in the whole undertaking, he got Notice of it, and left all his Booty at my Lodging, hiding it in an old Coat that Lay under my Bed, leaving Word he had been there, and had left the Coat that he borrowed of me, under my Bed I knew not what to make of it, but went up Stairs, and finding the Parcel, was Surprized to ſee wrapped up in it, above a hundred Pounds in Plate and Money, and heard nothing of Brother *Will*, as he called himſelf, for three or four Days, when we ſold the Plate after the Rate of two Shillings *per* Ounce, to a Pawn-Broker near *Cloth-Fair*

About two Days afterwards, going upon the Strole, who ſhould I meet but my former Brother Captain *Jack*? When he ſaw me, he came cloſe to me in his blunt Way, and ſays, *Do you hear the News* I aſked him, *What News*? He told me, *My old Comrade and Teacher was taken, and that Morning carried to Newgate, that he was charged with a Robbery and Murder, committed ſomewhere beyond Brentford, and that the worſt was, he was impeached* I thanked him for his Information, and for that Time parted, but was the very next Morning ſurpriz'd, when going croſs *Rag-Fair*, I heard one call *Jack*? I look'd behind me, and immediately ſaw three Men,

and after them a Conſtable, coming towards me with great Fury, I was in a great Surprize, and ſtarted to run, but one of them clapped in upon me, got hold of me, and in a Moment the reſt ſurrounded me, and told me they were to apprehend a known Thief, who went by the Name of one of the *Three Jacks of Rag-Fair*, for that he was charged upon Oath, with having been a Party in a notorious Robbery, Burglary, and Murther, committed in ſuch a Place, and on ſuch a Day

Not to trouble the Reader with an Account of the Diſcourſe that paſt between the Juſtice, before whom I was carried, and myſelf I ſhall, in brief, inform him, that my Brother Capt *Jack*, who had the Forwardneſs to put it to me, whether I was among them or no, when in Truth he was there himſelf, had the only Reaſon to fly, at the ſame Time that he adviſed me to ſhift for myſelf, ſo that I was diſcharged, and in about three Weeks after, my Maſter and Tutor in Wickedneſs, poor *Will*, was executed for the Fact

I had nothing to do now but to find out the Captain, who, though not without ſome Trouble, I at laſt got News of, and told him the whole Story He preſently diſcover'd by his Surprize, that he was guilty, and after a few Words more, told me, *It was all true, that he was in the Robbery, and had the greateſt Part of the Booty in Keeping, but what to do with it, or himſelf he did not know; but thought of flying into Scotland,* asking me, *if I would go with him?* I conſented, and the next Day he ſhewed me twenty two Pound he had in Money I honeſtly produced all the Money I had left, which was upwards of ſixteen Pounds We ſet out from *London* on Foot, and travelled the firſt Day to *Ware*, for we had learn'd ſo much of the Road, that our Way lay thro' that Town, from *Ware* we travelled to *Cambridge*, though that was not our direct Road. The Occaſion was this, In our Way through *Puckridge*, we baited at an *Inn*, and while we were there, a Countryman came and hung his Horſe at the Gate, while he went in to drink, We ſat in the Gate-way, having called for a Mug of Beer, we drank it up, we had been talking to the Hoſtler about the way to *Scotland*, and he bid us ask the Road to *Royſton* But ſays he, *there is a turning juſt here a little farther, you muſt not go that Way, for that goes to* Cambridge

We had paid for our Beer, and ſat at the Door only to reſt us, when on a ſudden comes a Gentleman's Coach to the Door, and three or four Horſemen rode into the Yard, and the Hoſtler was obliged to go in with them, ſays he to the Captain, *Young Man, Pray take Hold of the Horſe,* meaning the Countryman's Horſe I mention'd above, *and take him out of the Way that the Coach may come up* He did ſo, and beckoned to me to folow him We walk'd together to the Turning, ſays he to me, *Do you ſtep before, and turn up the Lane, I'll overtake you,* ſo I went on up the Lane, and in a few Minutes, he was got upon the Horſe, and at my Heels, and bidding me get up, and take a Lift

I made no Difficulty of doing ſo, and away we went at a good round Rate, having a ſtrong Horſe under us We ſuſpected the Countryman would follow us to *Royſton*, becauſe of our Directions from the Hoſtler, ſo that we went towards *Cambridge*, and went eaſier after the firſt Hour's Riding, and coming thro' a Town or two, we alighted by Turns, and did not then ride double, but by the Way pick'd a Couple of good Shirts of a Hedge, and that Evening got ſafe to *Cambridge*, where the next Day I bought a Horſe for myſelf, and thus equipped, we jogged on through ſeveral Places, till we got to *Stamford*

ford in *Lincolnshire,* where it was impossible to restrain my Captain from playing his Pranks, even at
Church, where he went, and placed himself so near
an old Lady, that he got her Gold Watch from her
Side unperceived, and the same Night we went a-
way by Moon-light, after having the Satisfaction to
hear the Watch cried, and ten Guineas offered for it
again, he would have been glad of the ten Guineas
instead of the Watch, but durst not venture to carry
it Home We went through several other Places,
such as *Grantham, Newark,* and *Nottingham,* where
we play'd our Tricks, without any Accident but one, which was
crossing a Foid, the Captain was really in Danger of
drowning, his Horse being driven down by the Stream,
and fell under him, but the Rider had a Proverb on
his Side, and got out of the Water

At *Edinburgh* we remain'd about a Month, when
on a sudden my Captain was gone, Horse and all,
and I knew nothing what was become of him, nor
did I ever see or hear of him for eighteen Months
after, nor did he so much as leave the least Notice
for me, either where he was gone, or whether he
would return to *Edinburgh* again or no I took his
leaving me very heinously, not knowing what to do
with myself, being a Stranger in the Place, and on
the other Hand my Money abated a-pace too I
had for the most Part of this Time my Horse upon
my Hands to keep; and as Horses yield but a sorry Price in *Scotland,* I found no Opportunity to
sell him to any Advantage However, at last I was
forced to dispose of him

Being thus eased of my Horse, and having nothing
at all to do, I began to consider with myself what
would become of me, and what I could turn my
Hand to. I had not much diminished my Stock of
Money, for though I was all the Way so wary, that
I would not join with my Captain in his desperate
Attempts, yet I made no Scruple to live at his Expence In the next Place, I was not so anxious a-
bout my Money running low, because I had made
a Reserve, by leaving upwards of ninety Pounds in
a Friend's Hands at *London,* but still I was willing
to get into some Employment for a Livelihood I
was sick of the wandering Life I had led, and resolved to be a Thief no more, but stuck close to
Writing and Reading for about six Months, till I
got into the Service of an Officer of the Customs,
who imploy'd me for a Time, but as he set me to
do little but pass and repass between *Leith* and *Edinburgh,* leaving me to live at my own Expence till
my Wages should be due, I run out the little Money I had left in Cloaths and Subsistance, and a little
before the Year's End, when I was to have twelve
Pounds *English* Money, my Master was turned out
of his Place, and which was worse, having been
charged with some Misapplications, was obliged to
take Shelter in *England,* so we that were Servants,
for there were three of us, were left to shift for
ourself Thus was a hard Case for me in a strange
Place, and I was reduced by it to the last Extremity I might have gone for *England,* an *English*
Ship being there, the Master proffered to take my
Word for ten Shillings, till I got there But just
as I was upon going, Captain *Jack* appeared again

I have mentioned how he left me, and that I
saw him no more for eighteen Months His
Ramble and Adventures were many, in that
Time he went to *Glasscow,* playing some very
remarkable Pranks there, escaped, almost miraculously, the Gallows, got over to *Ireland,* wandered
about there, escaped from *Londonderry* over to the
Highlands, and about a Month before, I was left
destitute at *Leith,* by my Master, noble Captain

Jack came in there, on board the Ferry boat from
Fife, being, after all his Adventures and Successes,
advanc'd to the Dignity of a Foot-soldier in a Body
of Recruits rais'd in the North for the Regiment
of *Douglas*

After my Disaster, being reduc'd almost as low
as *Jack,* I found no better Shift before me, at least
not for the present, than to enter my self a Soldier
too, and thus we were rank'd together, with each
of us a Musket upon our Shoulders I was extremely delighted with the Life of a Soldier, for I took
the Exercises naturally, that the Serjeant, who
taught us to handle our Arms, seeing me so ready at
it, ask'd me if I had never carried Arms before
I told him no At which he swore, though jesting, *they call you Colonel,* says he, *and I believe
you will be a Colonel, or you must be some Colonel's
Bastard, or you would never handle your Arms as you
do at once or twice showing* Whatever was my Satisfaction in that Part, yet other Circumstances did
not equally concur to make this Life suit me, for
after we had been about six Months in this Figure,
we were inform'd that we were to march for *England,* and be shipp'd off at *Newcastle,* or *Hull,* to
join the Regiment in *Flanders* Poor Captain *Jack*'s
Case was particular, he durst not appear publickly
at *Newcastle,* as he must have done had he march'd
with the Recruits In the next Place, I remember'd my Money in *London,* which was almost 100 *l*
and if it had been ask'd all the Soldiers in the Regiment which of them would go to *Flanders* a private Centinel, if they had 100 *l* in their Pockets, I
believ'd none of them would have answer'd in the
affirmative

These two Circumstances concurring, I began to
be very uneasy and very unwilling in my Thoughts
to go over into *Flanders* a poor Musketeer, to be
knock'd on the Head for 3 *s* 6 *d* a Week While
I was daily musing on the Hardship of being sent
away, as above, Captain *Jack* comes to me one
Evening, and ask'd me to take a Walk with him into
the Fields, for he wanted to speak with me We
walk'd together here, and talk'd seriously of the
Matter, and at last concluded to desert that very
Night The Moon affording a good Light, and
Jack had got a Comrade with him thoroughly acquainted with the Way cross the *Tweed,* and when
he arrived there we were on *English* Ground, and
safe enough, from thence we propos'd to get to *Newcastle,* and get some Collier Ship to take us in, and
carry us to *London*

About half an Hour past Eight in the Morning we
reach'd the *Tweed,* and here we overtook two more
of the same Regiment, who had deserted from *Had-
dingtoun,* where another Part of the Recruits were
quarter'd Those were *Scotsmen,* and very poor,
having not one Penny in their Pockets, and when
they saw us, who they knew to be of the same Regiment, they took us to be Pursuers, upon which,
they stood upon their Defence, having the Regiment
Swords on, as we had also, but none of the Mounting or Cloathing, for we were not to receive the
Clothes till we came to the Regiment in *Flanders.*
It was not long before we made them understand that
we were in the same Condition with themselves, and
so we became one Company Our Money was ebb'd
very low, and we contriv'd to get into *Newcastle* in
the Dusk of the Evening, and even then we durst
no venture into the publick Parts of the Town, but
made down towards the River below the Town.
Here we knew not what to do with ourselves, but,
guided by our Fate, we put a good Face upon the
Matter, went into an Alehouse, sat down, and called
for a Pint of Beer

THE Woman of the House appear'd very frank, and entertain'd us chearfully; so we, at last, told her our Condition, and ask'd her if she could not help us to some kind Master of a Collier, who would give us a Passage to *London* by Sea. The *subtil Devil*, who immediately found us proper Fish for her Hook, gave us the kindest Words in the World, and told us she was heartily sorry she had not seen us one Day sooner; that there was a Collier-Master of her particular Acquaintance who went away but with the Morning Tide, that the Ship was fallen down to *Sheilds*, but she believ'd was hardly over the *Bar* yet, and she would send to his House and see if he was gone on board (for sometimes the Masters do not go away till a Tide after the Ship;) and she was sure, if he was not gone, she could prevail with him to take us all in, but then she was afraid we must go on board immediately, the same Night

We begg'd of her to send to his House, for we knew not what to do; for as we had no Money, we had no Lodging, and wanted nothing but to be on board. We look'd upon this as a mighty Favour, that she sent to the Master's House, and, to our greater Joy, she brought us Word, about an Hour after, that he was not gone, and was at a Tavern in the Town, whither his Boy had been to fetch him, and that he had sent Word he would call there in his Way Home. This was all in our Favour, and we were extremely pleas'd with it In about an Hour he comes into the Room to us. *Where are these honest Gentlemen Soldiers*, says he, *that are in such Distress?* We stood all up, and paid our Respects to him. *Well, Gentlemen*, said he, *and is all your Money spent?*

Indeed it is, said one of our Company, *and we will be infinitely obliged to you, Sir, if you will give us a Passage We will be very willing to do any Thing we can, in the Ship, though we are not Seamen*

Why, says he, *were none of you ever at Sea in your Lives?*

No, says we, *not one of us*

You will be able to do me no Service, then; for you will all be sick. However, for my good Landlady's Sake here, I'll do it But are you all ready to go on board, for I go on board, myself, this very Night.

Yes, Sir, says we, again, *we are ready to go, this very Minute.*

No, no, said he, very kindly, *We'll drink together. Come Landlady,* says he, *make these honest Gentlemen a Sneaker of Punch*

We look'd at one another, for we knew we had no Money, and he perceiv'd it. *Come, come,* said he, *don't be concern'd at your having no Money, my Landlady, here, and I, never parts with dry Lips, Come, good Wife,* make the Punch, as I bid you

We thanked him, and said, *God bless you, noble Captain,* a hundred Times over, being over-joy'd at our good Luck While we were drinking the Punch, he told the Landlady he would step Home, and order the Boat to come at High-water, bad her get something for Supper, which she did

In less than an Hour, our Captain came again, and came up to us, and blam'd us that we had not drank the Punch out *Come,* said he, *don't be bashful, when that's out, we can have another When I am obliging poor Men, I love to do it handsomely*

We drank on, and drank the Punch out, more was brought up, and he push'd it about a-pace; Then came up a Leg of Mutton. I need not say we fed heartily, being several Times told we should pay nothing After Supper was done, he bids my Landlady ask if the Boat was come, and she brought

Word no, it was not High-Water by a great deal Then more Punch was call'd for, and, as was afterwards confess'd, something more than ordinary was put into it, that, by the Time the Punch was drank out, we were all intoxicated, and, as for me, I fell a-sleep

At last, I was rouz'd, and told that the Boat was come So I, and my drunken Comrades, tumbled out, almost one over another, into the Boat, and away we went with our Captain Most of us, if not all, fell a-sleep till after some Time, though how much, or how far going, we knew not The Boat stopp'd and we were wak'd and told we were at the Ship's Side, which was true and with much Help, and holding us, for Fear we should fall over board, our Captain, as we call'd him, call'd us thus *Here Boatswain, take Care of those Gentlemen, give them good Cabins, and let them turn into Sleep, for they are very weary* And so indeed, we were, and very drunk too

Care was taken of us, according to Order, and we were put into very good Cabins, where we were sure to go immediately to sleep, in the mean Time, the Ship, which was indeed just ready to go, and only on Notice given, had come to Anchor for us at *Sheilds* weigh'd stood over the Bar, and went off to Sea, and when we wak'd, and began to peep Abroad, which was not till near Noon the next Day, we found our selves a great Way at Sea, the Land in Sight, indeed, but at a great Distance, and all going merrily on for *London*, as I thought We were very well us'd, and very well satisfy'd with our Condition, for about three Days, when we began to enquire whether we were not almost come, and how much longer it would be before we should come into the River *What River?* says one of the Men *Why* the Thames, says my Captain *Jack* The Thames, say the Sailor, what d'ye mean by it? *What ha'n't you had Time enough to be sober, yet?* So Captain *Jack* said no more, but look'd very full, when, a While after, some other of us ask'd the same Question, and the Seamen, who knew nothing of the Cheat, began *to smell a Rat,* and, turning to another *Englishman,* who came with us, *Pray,* says he, *where do you fancy you are going, that you ask so often about it?* Why to London, says he, *where should we be going?* We agreed with the Captain to carry us to London

Not with the Captain says he, I dare say, poor Men you are all cheated, and I thought so, when I saw you come aboard with that Kidnapping Rogue *Gilliman,* poor Men adds he, you are all betray'd, for the Ship is bound to *Virginia* Assoon as we heard this News, we were raving M r, drew our swords and swore revenge, but we were soon over powered and carried before the Captain, who told us, he was sorry for what had happened, but that he had no hard in it, and it was out of his power to help us, and let us know very plainly what our Condition was, namely, that we were put on board his Ship as Servants to *Maryland,* to be delivered to a Person there, but that however, if we would be quiet and orderly in his Ship, he would use as well in the Passage, but if we were unruly, we must be Handcuffed and kept between Deck, for it was his Business to take care no Disturbance happened in the Ship

No hand in it! Damn him says my Captain *Jack,* aloud, do you think he is not Confederate in the Villainy? would any honest Man receive innocent People on board his Ship, and not enquire of their Circumstances, but carry him away, and not speak to them? Why does he not set us on Shore again, I tell you he is a Villain, and none but him, why does

       he

he not compleat his Villainy, and Murder us, and then he'll be free from our Revenge ? But nothing else shall deliver him from my Hands, but sending us to the D——l, or going thither himself; and I am honester in telling him so fairly, than he had been to me.

All this Discourse availed nothing, we were forced to be Quiet, and had a very good Voyage, no Storms all the Way; but just before we arrived, one of the Scotsmen asked the Captain of the Ship, whether he would sell us, Yes said he; why then Sir, says the Scotsman, the Devil will have you at the hinder End of the Bargain Say you so, says the Captain, Smiling, well, well, let the Devil and I alone to agree about that, do you be Quiet, and behave Civily as you should do

When we come ashore, which was on the Banks of a River they call *Potomack*, *Jack* says, I have something to say to you Captain, that is, I have promised to cut your Throat, and depend upon it I will be as good as my Word. Our Captain or Kidnapper, call him as you will, made no Answer, but delivered us to the Merchant to whom we were consigned, who again disposed off us as he thought fit, and in a few Days we were separated

As for my Captain *Jack*, to make short of the Story, that desperate Rogue had the good Luck to have an easy good Master, whom he abused very much, for he took an Opportunity to run away with a Boat, which his Master entrusted him, and another with, to carry Provisions to a Plantation down the River This Boat and Provisions they run away with, and sailed North to the Bottom of the Bay, *as they call it*, and there quitting the Boat, they wandered through the Woods, till they got into *Pensylvania*, from whence they made Shift to get a Passage to *New-England*, and from thence Home, where falling in among his old Companions, and to his old Trade, he was at length taken and hanged about a Month before I came to *London*, which was near twenty Years afterwards.

My Part was harder at the Beginning, tho' better at the Latter End; I was sold to a rich Planter, whose Name was *Smith* During this Scene of Life I had Time to reflect on my past Hours, and tho' I had no great Capacity of making a clear Judgment and very little Reflections from Conscience, yet it made some Impressions upon me I behaved myself so well, that my Master took Notice of me, and made me one of his Overseers, and was so kind as to send my Note of my Friends Hand for the 93*l*, before-mentioned, to his Correspondent, who received and returned me the Money My good Master a little Time after, says to me, *Colonel* don't flatter me, I love plain Dealing, Liberty is precious to every Body, I give you yours, and will take Care you shall be well used by the Country, and will get you a good Plantation

I insisted I would not quit his Service, for the best Plantation in *Maryland*, that he had been so good to me, and I believed I was so useful to him, that I could not think of it, and at last I added I hoped he could not believe but I had as much Gratitude as a *Negro*

He smiled and said he would not be served upon these Terms, that he did not forget what he had promised, nor what I had done in his Plantation, and that he was resolved in the first Place to give me my Liberty, so he pulls out a piece of Paper, and throws it to me, there, says he, is a Certificate of your coming on Shore, and being sold to me for five Years, of which you have lived three with me, and now you are your own Master

I Bowed and told him, that I was sure if I was

my own Master, I would be his Servant, as long as he would accept of my Service He told me he would accept of my Service, on these two Conditions First, That he would give me 30*l*, *per Ann* and my board, for my managing the Plantation I was then imploy'd in And Secondly, That at the same Time he would procure me a new Plantation to begin with upon my own account; for *Jack*, says he, smiling, tho' you are but a young Man, 'tis Time you was doing something for yourself

Not long after, he purchased in my Name about 300 Acres of Land, near his own Plantation, as he said, that I might the better take Care of his My Master, for such I must still call him, generously gave it me, but *Colonel* says he, giving you this Plantation is nothing at all, if I do not assist you to support it, and to carry it on, and therefore I will give you Credit, for whatever is needful Such as Tools, Provisions, and some Servants to begin Materials for Out houses, and Hogs, Cows, Horses, for Stock, and the Like, and I'll take it out out of your returns from abroad, as you can Pay it

Thus got to be a Planter, and encouraged by a kind Benefactor, that I might not be wholly taken up with my new Plantation, he gave me freely without any Consideration, one of his Negro's named *Mouchat*, whom I always esteemed Besides this, he sent to me two Servants more, a Man and a Woman; but these he put to my Account as above *Mouchat* and these two fell immediately to Work for me, they began with about two Acres of Land, which had but little Timber on it at first, and most of that was cut down by the two Carpenters who built my House It was a great Advantage to me, that I had so Bountiful a Master who help'd me out in every Case, for in this very first Year, I received a terrible Blow, having sent a large Quantity of Tobacco, to a Merchant at *London*, by my Master's Direction, which arrived safe there The Merchant was ordered to make the Return in a sorted Cargo of Goods for me, such as would have made a Man of me all at once, but to my inexpressible Terror and Surprize, the Ship was lost, and that just at the Entrance to the Capes, that is to say, the Mouth of the *Bay*, some of the Goods were recovered, but spoiled In short, nothing but the Nails, Tools, and Iron work were good for any Thing, and tho' the Value of them was very Considerable in proportion to the Rest, yet my Loss was irreparably great, and indeed, the greatness of the Loss consisted in its being irreparable

I was perfectly astonished at the first News of the Loss, knowing that I was in Debt to my Patron or Master, so much, that it must be several Years before I should recover it, and as he brought me the bad News himself he perceived my Disorder, that is to say, he saw I was in the utmost Confusion, and a kind of Amazement and so indeed I was, because I was so much in Debt But he spoke chearfully to me, come says he, do not be so discouraged, you may make up this Loss, no Sir, says I, that never can be, for it is my All, and I shall never be out of Debt, well, says he, you have no Creditor, however, but me, and now remember I once told you, I would make a Man of you, and I will not disappoint you, for this Disaster I thank'd him, and did it with more Ceremony and Respect than ever, because I thought myself more under the Hatches than I was before But he was as good as his Word, for he did not Baulk me in the Least, of any Thing I wanted, and as I had more Iron work saved out of the Ship in Proportion, that I wanted, I supplied him with some Part of it, and took up some Linnen and Cloaths, and other Necessarie from him in Exchange, and now I began

to

to increase visibly, I had a large Quantity of Land cured, that is freed from Timber, and a very good Crop of Tobacco in view, and I got three Servants more, and one Negro, so that I had five white Servants, and two Negro's, and with this my Affairs went very well on; the first Year indeed I took my Wages or Sallary, of 30 *l* a Year, because I wanted it very much, but the Second and Third Year, I resolved not to take it, but to leave it in my Benefactor's Hands, to clear off the Debt I had Contracted.

At the same Time my Thoughts dictated to me, that tho' this was the Foundation of my new Life, yet that this was not the Superstructure, and that I might still be born for greater Things than these, that it is Honesty and Virtue alone, that made Men Rich and Great, and gave them Fame, as well as Figure in the World, and that therefore I was to lay my Foundation in these, and expect what might follow in Time. To help these Thoughts as I had learned to Read and Write when I was in *Scotland*; so I began now to love Books, and particularly, had an Opportunity of Reading some very Considerable ones, some of which I bought at a Planter's House, who was lately Dead, and his Goods sold, and others I borrowed. I considered my present State of Life to be my meer Youth, tho' I was now above 30 Years old, because in my Youth I had learned nothing and if my daily Business, which was now great, would have permitted, I would have been content to have gone to School, however, Fate which had something else in Store for me, threw an Opportunity into my Hand, namely, a clever Fellow that came over a transported Felon from *Bristol*, and fell into my Hands for a Servant. He had led a loose Life that he acknowledged, and being driven to Extremities, took to the High way, for which had he been taken, he would have been hanged, but falling into some low priz'd Rogueries afterwards, for want of Opportunity for worse, was Catched, Condemn'd, and Transported, and, as he said, was glad he came off so.

He was an excellent Scholar, and I perceiving it, asked him one Time, if he could give a Method how I might learn the Latin Tongue, he said, smiling, yes, he could teach it me in three Months, if I would let him have Books, or even without Books if he had Time. I told him a Book would become his Hand better then a Hoe, and if he could promise to make me but understand Latin though to read it, and understand other Languages by it, I would ease him of the Labour which I was now obliged to put him to, especially if I was assured that he was fit to receive that Favour of a kind Master. In short, I made him to me, what my kind Benefactor made me to him, and from him I gained a Fund of knowledge infinitely more valuable than the Rate of a Slave, which was what I paid for it, but of this hereafter.

In this Posture I went on for 12 Years, and was very successful in my Plantation, and had gotten by means of my Master's Favour, who now I called my Friend, a Correspondent in *London*, with whom I Traded, shipped over my Tobacco to him, and received *European* Goods in Returns, such as I wanted to carry on my Plantation, and sufficient to sell to others also. In this interval, my good Friend and Benefactor died, and I was left very Disconsolate on account of my Loss, for it was indeed a great Loss to me, he had been a Father to me, and I was like a forsaken Stranger without him, tho' I knew the Country and the Trade too well enough, and had for some Time chiefly carried on his whole Business for him, yet I seem'd now at a Loss, my Councellor and my chief Supporter was gone; and I had no Confident to communicate myself too, on all Occasions as formerly but there was no Remedy I was however, in a better Condition to stand alone then ever I had a very large Plantation, and had near 70 Negro's, and other Servants.

Now I looked upon myself as one Buried alive in a remote Part of the World, where I could see nothing at all, and hear but a little of what was seen, and that little not till at least half a Year after it was done, and sometimes a Year or more, and in a Word, the old Reproach often came in my Way, namely, that even this was not yet the Life of a Gentleman. However. I now began to frame my Thoughts for a Voyage to *England*, resolving then to Act as I should see Cause, but with a secret Resolution to see more of the World if possible, and Realize those Things to my Mind, which I had hitherto only entertained remote Ideas of, by the Help of Books.

It was three Years after this, before I could get Things in Order, fit for my leaving the Country. In this Time I delivered my Tutor from his Bondage and would have given him his Liberty, but to my great Disappointment I found that I could not on power him to go for *England* till his Time was expired, according to the Certificate of his Transportation, which was register'd, so I made him one of my Overseers, and thereby raised him gradually to a Prospect of Living in the same Manner, and by like Steps, that my good Benefactor raised me, only that I did not assist him to enter upon Planting for himself as I was assisted, neither was I upon the Spot to do it, but this Man by his Diligence and honest Application delivered himself, even unassisted, any farther than by making him an Overseer, which was only a present Ease and Deliverance from the hard Labour and Fare, which he endured as a Servant. However, in this Trust he behaved so faithfully, and so diligently, that it recommended him in the Country, and, when I came back, I found him in Circumstances very differing from what I left him in, besides, his being my principal Manager for near 20 Years, as you shall hear in its Place.

I was now making Provision for my going to *England*, after having settled my Plantation in such Hands as was fully to my Satisfaction. My first Work was, to furnish myself with such a Stock of Goods and Money as might be sufficient for my Occasions abroad, and particularly, might allow to make large Returns to *Maryland*, for the Use and Supply of all my Plantations, but when I came to look nearer into the Voyage, it occur'd to me that it would not be prudent to put my Cargo all on board the same Ship that went in. So I shipp'd, at several Times, five hundred Hogsheads of Tobacco, in several Ships, for *England*, giving Notice to my Correspondent, in *London*, that I would embark about such a Time to come over myself, and ordering him to insure for a considerable Sum proportion'd to the Value of my Cargo.

About two Months after this, I left the Place, and embark'd for *England* in a stout Ship, carrying 24 Guns, and about 600 Hogsheads of Tobacco, and we left the Capes of *Virginia* on the first of *August* ——— We had a very sour and rough Voyage for the first Fortnight, though it was in a Season so generally noted for good Weather. We met with a Storm, and our Ship was greatly damag'd, and some Leaks we had, but not so bad, but, by the Diligence of the Seamen, they were stopp'd, after which, we had tolerable Weather, and a good Sea, till we came into the Soundings, for so they call the Mouth of the *British* Channel. In the Grey of the Morning a *French* Privateer, of 26 Guns, appear'd, and cross after us with all the Sail they could make. Our Captain exchang'd a Broad-fide or two with them, which was terrible Work to me; for I had never feen fuch before; the *Frenchman's* Guns, having rak'd us, and kill'd and wounded fix of our Men. In fhort, after a Fight long enough to fhew us that if we would not be taken, we muft refolve to fink by her Side, for there was no Room to expect Deliverance, and a Fight long enough to fave the Mafter's Credit, we were taken, and the Ship carried away for St *Malo's*. I had, however, befides my being taken, the Mortification to be detain'd on board the Cruifer, and feeing the Ship I was in, mann'd by *Frenchmen*, fet fail from us. I afterwards heard that fhe was re-taken by an *English* Man of War, and carried into *Portfmouth*.

The Rover cruis'd abroad again, in the Mouth of the Channel, for fome Time, and took a Ship richly laden, bound homeward from *Jamaica*. This was a noble Prize for the Rogues, and they haftened away with her to St. *Malo's*, and from thence I went to *Bourdeaux*, where the Captain ask'd me if I would be deliver'd up a State Prifoner, get myfelf exchang'd, or pay 300 Crowns. I defir'd Time to write to my Correfpondent in *England*, who fent me a Letter of Credit, and in about fix Weeks I was exchang'd for a Merchant Prifoner in *Plymouth*. I got Paffage from hence to *Dunkirk*, on board a *French* Veffel, and having a Certificate of an exchang'd Prifoner from the Intendant of *Bourdeaux*, I had a Paffport given me to go into the *Spanifh Netherlands*, and fo whither I pleas'd. I went to *Ghent*, afterwards to *Newport*, where I took the Packet-Boat, and came over to *England*, landing at *Deal* inftead of *Dover*, the Weather forcing us into the *Downs*.——When I came to *London*, I was very well receiv'd by my Friend to whom I had confign'd my Effects, for all my Goods came fafe to hand, and my Overfeers I had left behind, had fhipp'd, at feveral Times, 400 Hogfheads of Tobacco, to my Correfpondent, in my Abfence. So that I had above 1000*l* in my Factor's Hands, and 200 Hogfheads befides, left in Hand, unfold.

I had nothing to do now but entirely to conceal myfelf from all that had any Knowledge of me before, and this was the eafieft Thing in the World to do, for I was grown out of every Body's Knowledge, and moft of thofe I had known, were grown out of mine, my Captain who went with me, or rather who carried me away, I found by enquiring at the proper Place, had been rambling about the World, came to *London*, fell into his old Trade, which he could not forbear, and growing an eminent Highwayman, had made his Exit at the Gallows, after a Life of 14 Years moft exquifite and fuccefsful Rogueries, the Particulars of which, would make, as I obferved, an admirable Hiftory. My other Brother *Jack*, who I called *Major*, followed the like wicked Trade, but was a Man of more Gallantry and Generofity, and having committed innumerable Depredations upon Mankind, yet had always fo much Dexterity, as to bring himfelf off, till at length he was laid faft in *Newgate*, and loaded with Irons, and would certainly have gone the fame Way as the Captain, but he was fo dextrous a Rogue, that no Goal, no Fetters would hold him, and he with two more, found means to knock off their Irons, work'd their way thro' the Wall of the Prifon, and let themfelves down on the Outfide, in the Night. So efcaping, they found means to get into *France*, where he followed the fame Trade, and that with fo much Succefs, that he grew famous by the Name of *Anthony*, and had the Honour with three of his Comrades, who he had taught the *Englifh* Way of

Robbing generoufly, as they called it, without murthering, or wounding, or ill-ufing thofe they robbed, to be broke upon the Wheel, at the *Greve* in *Paris*.

All thefe Things I found means to be fully informed of, and to have a long Account of the Particulars of their Conduct from fome of their Comrades, who had the good Fortune to efcape, and who I got the Knowledge of, without letting them fo much as guefs at who I was, or upon what Account I enquir'd.

I was now at the height of my good Fortune, and got the Name of a great Merchant. I lived fingle, and in Lodging, and kept a French Servant, being very defirous of improving myfelf in that Language, and received 5 or 600 Hogfheads a Year from own Plantations; and fpent my Time in that, and fupplying my People with Neceffaries at *Maryland*, as they wanted them.

In this private Condition I continu'd about two Years more, when the Devil owing me a Spleen ever fince I refus'd being a Thief, paid me home, with Intereft, by laying a Snare in my Way, which had almoft ruin'd me.

There dwelt a Lady in the Houfe oppofite to the Houfe I lodg'd in, who made an extraordinary Figure, and was a moft beautiful Perfon. She was well bred, fung admirably fine, and fometimes I could hear diftinctly, the Houfes being over-againft one another in a narrow Court. This Lady put herfelf fo often in my Way, that I could not in good Manners forbear taking Notice of her and giving the Ceremony of my Hat, when I faw her at her Window, or at the Door, or when I pafs'd her in the Court. So that we became almoft acquainted at a Diftance. Sometimes fhe alfo vifited at the Houfe I lodg'd at, and it was generally contriv'd that I fhou'd be introduc'd when fhe came. And thus, by Degrees, we became more intimately acquainted, and often convers'd together in the Family, but always in publick, at leaft for a great While. I was a meer Boy in the Affair of Love, and knew the leaft of what belong'd to a Woman, of any Man in *Europe* of my Age, the Thoughts of a Wife, much lefs a Miftrefs, had never fo much as taken the leaft Hold of my Head, and I had been, till now, as perfectly unacquainted with the Sex, and as unconcern'd about them, as I was when I was ten Years old, and lay in a Heap of Afhes at the Glafs-houfe.

She attack'd me without ceafing, with the Finenefs of her Conduct, and with Arts which were impoffible to be ineffectual. She was ever, as it were, in my View, often in my Company, and yet kept herfelf fo on the Referve, fo furrounded continually with Obftructions, that for feveral Months after fhe could perceive I fought an Opportunity to fpeak to her. She render'd it impoffible, nor could I ever break in upon her, fhe kept her Guard fo well.

This rigid Behaviour was the greateft Myftery that could be, confidering, at the fame Time, that fhe never declin'd my feeing her, or converfing with me in publick, but fhe held it on. She took Care never to fit next me, that I might flip no Paper into her Hand, or fpeak foftly to her. She kept fome Body or other always between, that I could never come up to her. And thus, as if fhe was refolv'd really to have nothing to do with me, fhe held me at the Bay feveral Months. In fhort, we came nearer and nearer every Time we met, and at laft gave the World the Slip, and were privately married, to avoid Ceremony, and the publick Inconveniency of a Wedding.

No fooner were we married, but fhe threw off the

the Mask of her Gravity and good Conduct, and carried it to such an Excess, that I could not but be dissatisfied at the Expence of it   In about a twelve-month she was brought to Bed of a fine Boy, and her Lying-in cost me as near as I can now remember, 136 _l_ which, she told me, she thought was a Trifle.   Such Jarring continually between us, produced a Separation; and she demanded 300 _l per Annum_ for her Maintenance.   In the Interim of this, by means of two trusty Agents, I got Proof of my Spouse's being caught several Times in Bed with another Person, and by whom she had a Daughter I sued her in the Ecclesiastical Court, in order to obtain a Divorce; and, as she found it impossible to avoid it, she declin'd a Defence, and I gain'd a legal Decree of Divorce.

Things being at this Pass, I resolv'd to go over to _France_, where I fell into Company with some _Irish_ Officers of the Regiment of _Dillon_, where I bought a Company, and so went into the Army directly   Our Regiment, after I had been some Time in it, was commanded into _Italy_, and one of the most considerable Actions I was in, was the famous Attack upon _Cremona_ in the _Milaneze_, where the _Germans_ being treacherously let into the Town by Night, through a kind of Common Shore, surpriz'd the Town, and took the Duke _de Villeroy_ Prisoner, beating the _French_ Troops into the Citadel, but were in the Middle of their Victory so boldly attack'd by two _Irish_ Regiments, that, after a most desperate Fight, and not being able to break through us to let in their Friends, were obliged to quit the Town, to the eternal Honour of those _Irish_ Regiments.   Having been in several Campaigns, I was permitted to sell my Company, and got the Chevalier's _Brevet_ for a Colonel, in case of raising Troops for him in _Great Britain_   I, accordingly, embark'd on board the _French_ Fleet, for the Firth of _Edinburgh_, but they over-shot their Landing-place: And this Delay gave Time to the _English_ Fleet, under Sir _George Byng_, to come to an Anchor just as we did.

Upon this Surprize, the _French_ Admiral set sail, and crouding away to the North, got the Start of the _English_ Fleet escap'd, with the Loss of one Ship only, to _Dunkirk_, and glad I was to set my Foot on Shore again, for all the While we were thus flying for our Lives, I was under the greatest Terror imaginable, and nothing but Halters and Gibbets run in my Head, concluding, that if I had been taken, I should certainly have been hang'd

I took my Leave of the Chevalier and the Army, and made Haste to _Paris_, a Place full of Gallantry, and where I again foolishly tried my Fate in Matrimony, for in less than three Months I caught my good-natur'd Wife in Bed with a _French_ Marquis,

whom I the next Day fought, and left for dead I took Post Horses for _Flanders_, and, at last, got safe once more to _London_, from which Place I embark'd for _Virginia_, and had a tolerable Voyage thither, only that we met with a Pyrate Ship, who plunder'd us of every Thing they could come at that was for their Turn   But, to give the Rogues their Due, though they were the most abandon'd Wretches that ever were seen, they did not use us ill; and, as to my Loss, it was not considerable

I found all my Affairs in very good Order at _Virginia_, my Plantations prodigiously increas'd, and my Manager, who first inspir'd me with travelling Thoughts, and made me Master of any Knowledge worth naming, receiv'd me with a Transport of Joy, after a Ramble of four and twenty Years   I was exceedingly satisfied with his Management, for he had improv'd a very large Plantation of his own, at the same Time; however, I had the Mortification to see two or three of the _Preston_ Gentlemen there, who being Prisoners of War, were spar'd from the publick Execution, and sent over to that Slavery, which, to Gentlemen, must be worse than Death

During my Stay here, I married a Maid I brought over from _England_, who behav'd her self, for some Time, extraordinary well, but at last turn'd Whore, like the rest, got the Foul Disease, and died, and I, not liking to stay long in a Place, I was so much talk'd of, sent to one of my Correspondents for a Copy of the general free Pardon then granted, and wherein it was manifest I was fully included

After I had settled my Affairs, and left the same faithful Steward, I again embark'd for _England_, and, after a Trading Voyage (for we touch'd at several Places in our Way,) I arriv'd safe, determining to spend the Remainder of my Life in my native Country, for here I enjoy the Moments which I had never before known how to employ, I mean that of looking back upon an ill-spent Life

Perhaps, when I wrote these Things down, I did not foresee that the Writings of our own Stories would be so much the Fashion in _England_, or so agreeable to others to read, as I find Custom, and the Humour of the Times, has caus'd it to be   If any one that reads my Story pleases to make the same just Reflections, which I acknowledge I ought to have made, he will reap the Benefit of my Misfortunes, perhaps, more than I have done myself, 'tis evident, by the long Series of Changes and Turns which have appear'd in the narrow Compass of one private mean Person's Life, that the History of Men's Lives may be many Ways made useful and instructing to those who read them, if moral and religious Improvement, and Reflections, are made by those that write them

The LIFE of WHITNEY.

THIS notorious Malefactor was born at *Stevenage* in *Hertfordshire*, where he was put Apprentice to a Butcher, as soon as he was fit for Servitude He serv'd his Time, as far as we have heard, very faithfully, but was not long in his own Master before he took to the irregular Courses that brought Destruction upon him, and branded his Name with Infamy.

He was pleasantly disappointed, as he would himself frequently confess afterwards, in the first Piece of Knavery that ever he contrived. Going with another Butcher to *Rumford* in *Essex*, in order to buy Calves, they met with one which they had a particular Fancy to: but the Owner demanded what they thought an extravagant Price for it, so that they could not strike a Bargain However, as the Man kept a Publick House, our Companions agreed to go in and drink with him They were very much vex'd in their Minds, to think that they could not have their Wish, and were contriving how to be revenged of their Lordlord, when *Whitney* suddenly whispered these Words to his Comrade, *What Business have we to give so much Money out of our Pockets, for what we may by and by get for nothing? We know where the Calf is, and what should hinder our taking him, when we have an Opportunity?* The other came directly into his Measure, and so they sat boozing till Night

In the Evening there came a Fellow into the Town with a great She Bear, which he carried about for a Show, and was his Fortune to put up at the House where our two Butchers were drinking in an inner Room , for it being just at the Town's End, there was no Place so convenient besides The Man of the House was some Time before he conclude where to put the Bear, at last he resolved to move the Calf into another Out-house, and tie Madam *Bruin* up in his Place, which was done accordingly, without the Knowledge of *Whitney*, and his Friend, who continued drinking till they were told, it was Time to go to Bed

Upon this Warning they paid their Reckoning, and went out, staying in the Fields near the Town, 'till they imagined the Time favour'd their Design The Night was very dark, and they came to the Stall without making any Noise or Disturbance *Whitney* was to go in and fetch out their Prey, while the other watched without When he was entered, he groped about for the Calf till he got hold of the Bear, which lying after the sluggish Manner peculiar to these Creatures, he began to tickle it to made it rise At last being awaked, the poor Beast, being muzzled and blind, rose up on her Hind Legs, not knowing but it was her Master going to show her *Whitney* still continued feeling about, wondering at the length of the Calf's Hair, and that he should stand in such a Posture, till the Bear caught hold of him, and hugg'd him fast between her fore Feet.

In this Posture he remain'd, unable to move, and afraid to cry out, till the other Butcher, wondering at his long Stay, put his Head in at the Door, and said, with a low Voice, *What a Pox, will you be all the Night stealing a Calf? A Calf*, quoth *Whitney, I believe it's the Devil, that I am going to steal, for he hugs me as closely as he does the Witch in the Statue Let it be the Devil*, says t'other *bring him out however, that we may see what he is like, which is something that I should be very glad to know* *Whitney* was too much surprized to be pleased with the Jesting of his Companion, so that he replied with some Choller *Come and fetch him yourself , for may I be pox'd, if I half like him.* Hereupon t'other enter'd, and after a little Examination, found, how they were bit By his Assistance *Whitney* got loose, and they both swore, they would never attempt to steal Calves any more for this Trick.

Whitney, after this, took the *George-Inn* at *Cheshunt* in *Hertfordshire*, where he entertain'd all Sorts of bad Company , but not thriving in this Way, he was in a little Time obliged to shut up his Doors, and entirely give over the Occupation. He now came up to *London*, the common Sanctuary of such Men, where he lived very irregularly, and at last, when Necessitous Circumstances came on him apace, wholly gave himself up to Villainy

It was still some Time before he took to the Highway, following only the common Tricks practised by the Sharpers of the Town, in which he was the more successful as he always went dressed like a Gentleman ; it being easier to impose upon Mankind with a good Suit of Cloaths, than any other Way whatsoever But the World is governed by Appearances, and always will be, unless Providence should ever see fit to make the Characters of Virtue and Vice more visible A poor Man, tho' endow'd with ever so honest, and generous a Soul, is avoided by every Body , so that he can hardly in his Life find an Opportunity to discover himself, and let a mistaken World see what he possesses While the greatest Villain that ever was born, may be caressed by all Companies, if he has but Credit enough to get good Apparel, and Impudence to thrust himself forwards

One Morning, *Whitney* stood on *Ludgate-Hill*, at a Mercer's Door, waiting for a Friend whom he expected to come by, when two Misses of the Town well habited came along These Ladies took our Gentleman for the Master of the Shop, and supposing him by his Looks to be an amorous young Batchelor, one of them, in order to begin a little Conversation, asked him, if he had any fine Silks of the newest Fashion, *Whitney* readily replied, *That he had none by him at present, but in a Day or two's Time, he should have Choice Several Weavers being to bring him in Pieces made from the last Patterns that were going Then Ladies*, says he, *I shall be glad to supply you with what you want , and there is no Man in England will use you better Only please to leave*
                                                        your

your Names, and where you live, that I may do my-self the Honour to wait on you. Here our Madams were put to it for an Answer; but looking a little on one another, she that spoke first told him, *That being newly come to Town, they did not remember the Name of the Street where they lodged, but it was not far off, and if he pleased to go with them, they would shew him their Habitation, such as it was.*

Whitney, to be sure consented, and to make the Affair appear with a better Face, he stepp'd into the Shop as if he went to give Orders to the Apprentice, to whom he only put some impertinent Questions, and came out again unsuspected. Away trudge the Ladies and their 'Squire, who when they told him they were come to the Door, very civilly offered to take his Leave of them. *Nay, Sir,* says one of them, *but you shall walk in, and take a Glass of Wine with us, since you have been so good as to give your-self all this Trouble?* *Whitney* thanked them, and with Abundance of Complisance, accepted the Favour.

Hitherto both Parties were deceived. *Whitney* really took them for Gentlewomen of Fortune, and came Home with them only to learn something that might forward him to make a Prey of them, and they as confidently believed him to be the Mercer, who own'd the Shop at which they picked him up. Their Designs were to get his Money out of his Pocket, and if they could, a Suit or two of Cloaths into the Bargain. What confirm'd them in this Opinion was, the Notice he took of several Gentlemen as he passed along the Street, by pulling off his Hat to them, and their returning the same Compliment. *Whitney* did it for this very Purpose, and it is natural and common for Men of Fashion to re-salute those who salute them, whether they know them or no, because a Man may be known by one whom he can't remember on a sudden to have ever seen before.

The Ladies introduced their supposed Cully into an Appartment splendidly furnished, where a Table was instantly spread with a fine cold Collation. This being over, the Maid and one of the Mistresses withdrew, leaving the other to manage *Whitney*. She immediately fell into amorous Discourse, and soon proceeded to greater Freedoms, telling him, he was bashful, and offering to teach him a soft Love-Lesson. *Whitney* now began to understand his Company, yet, as he hoped to get a little Love by the Bargain, he was willing to keep on the Mask, and professed himself her Slave, devoted to her Service, and willing to fulfil her Pleasure, promising withal after a great many mutual Endearments, to give her as much Silk as would make a Suit of Cloaths. This was all she required of him before she granted him the last Favour, and upon this single Promise, she suffer'd him to play over the *Jeu d'amour* as often as he pleased, entertaining him, after all, with two or three more Bottles free-cost.

Whitney was so well pleased with his Reception at this Place, that he was resolved, if possible, to have a little more of the same Sport, and to that End went to a Mercer, and told him, that such a Lady had sent him to desire that he would let one of his Men carry two or three Pieces of the richest Silk in his Shop, for her to choose a Gown and Petticoat. The Mercer knew the Person of Quality whom he named, she having been his Customer before, and without mistrusting any Thing, sent a Youth, who was but newly come Prentice, telling him the Prices in *Whitney*'s Hearing. Our Adventurer led the Lad through as many By-Streets as he could, in order to carry him out of his Knowledge, till observing a House in *Suffolk-Street*, which had a Thorough-fare into *Hedge-Lane*, he desired the

young Man to stay at the Door, while he carried in the Silks to shew them to the Lady, who lodged there. The Youth obey'd very readily, and *Whitney* went into the House, and asked the People for somebody whom they did not know; upon their telling him no such Person liv'd in that Neighbourhood, he desired Leave to go through, which was granted.

Now, Good Night Mr *Mercer*, you may wait till you are weary, and go back lighter by all your Load. In a Word, *Whitney* went to his Mistress, and distributed the Prize between them. After which he revelled on all Manner of Excess for several Days, till he was glad to retire of himself.

He was resolved, however, that no Body but himself should enjoy the Fruit of his Industry, since he could not have the Profit of his Cheat, it would be a Piece of Honesty in him, he thought, to restore the Mercer's Goods again. To this End he writes a Letter where the Women lived, and the Shop-keeper getting a Warrant, and a Constable, went and found the Silks in their Custody. To be sure they were enough frighten'd to see themselves apprehended for what they thought had been given them by the Right Owner, but all their Excuses were in vain, they were hurried before a Magistrate, who committed them to *Tuthil-Fields Bridewell*, where they were taught the Discipline of the Place, by that celebrated Lictor, Mr *Redding*, and their Backs were covered with Stripes of the Cat and Nine Tails, instead of the Eleemosynary Silks, which they thought themselves so sure of.

When *Whitney* was grown a confirmed Highwayman, he one Day met a Gentleman on *Bagshot-Heath*, whom he commanded to stand and deliver, To which the Gentleman replied, *Sir, 'tis well you spoke first, for I was just going to say the same Thing to you* —— *Why, are you a Gentleman Thief then,* quoth *Whitney?* —— *Yes,* said the Stranger, *but I have had very bad Success to Day, for I have been riding up and down all this Morning, without meeting with any Prize.* *Whitney*, upon this, wished him better Luck, and took his Leave, really supposing him to be what he pretended.

At Night it was the Fortune of *Whitney*, and this Impostor to put up at the same Inn, when our Gentleman told some other Travellers by what a Stratagem he had escaped being robb'd on the Road. *Whitney* had so alter'd his Habit and Speech, that the Gentleman did not know him again; so that he heard all the Story without being taken any Notice of. Among other Things he heard him tell one of the Company softly, that he had sav'd an hundred Pounds by his Contrivance. The Person to whom he whisper'd this, was going the same Way the next Morning, and said, he had also a considerable Sum about him, and if he pleased, should be glad to travel with him for Security. It was agreed between them, and *Whitney* at the same Time resolved to make one with them.

When Morning came, our Fellow-Travellers set out, and *Whitney* about a Quarter of an Hour after them. All the Discourse of the Gentlemen was about cheating the Highwaymen, if they should meet with any, and all *Whitney*'s Thoughts were upon being revenged for the Abuse which was put on him the Day before.

At a convenient Place he got before them, and bid them stand. The Gentleman whom he met before, not knowing him, he having disguised himself after another Manner, briskly cried out, *We were going to say the same to you, Sir,* —— *Were you so?* quoth *Whitney*, *And are you of my Profession then?* —— *Yes,* said they both *If you are,* reply'd *Whitney, I suppose you remember the old Proverb,* Two of a Trade can never agree, *so that you must not expect any Favour on that Score.* But to be plain, Gentlemen, the Trick will do no longer I know you very well, and must have your hundred Pounds, Sir, and your considerable Sum, Sir, turning to the other, *let it be what it will, or I shall make bold to send a Brace of Bullets through each of your Heads* You, Mr. Highwayman, should have kept your Secret a little longer, and not have boasted so soon of having out-witted a Thief. There is now nothing for you to do but deliver, or die —— These terrible Words put them both into a sad Consternation. They were loth to lose their Money, but more loth to lose their Lives; so of two Evils, they chose the least, the Tell-tale Coxcomb disbursing his hundred Pounds, and the other a somewhat larger Sum, professing that they would be careful for the future not to count without their Host.

Another Time *Whitney* met with one Mr. *Hull,* an old Usurer in the *Strand,* as he was riding across *Hounslow-Heath* He could hardly have chosen a Wretch more in Love with Money, and consequently who would have been more unwilling to have parted with it

When the dreadful Words were spoken, he trembled like a Paralitic, and fell to expostulating the Case in the most moving Expressions he was Master of, professing that he was a very poor Man, had a large Family of Children, and should be utterly ruined, if he was so hard hearted as to take his Money from him He added, moreover, a great Deal concerning the Illegality of such an Action, and how very dangerous it was to engage in such evil Courses. *Whitney,* who knew him, cried out in a great Passion *Sirrah, do you pretend to preach Morality to an honester Man than yourself? Is it not much more generous to take a Man's Money from him bravely, than to grind him to Death with eight or ten per Cent, under Colour of serving him? You make a Prey of all Mankind, and Necessity in an honest Man, often is the Means of his falling into your Clutches, who are certain quite to undo him I am a Man of more Honour than to shew any Regard to one whom I esteem an Enemy to the whole human Species This once, Sir, I shall oblige you to lend me what you have without Bond, and consequently without Interest, so make no Words —* Old *Hull,* hereupon, pulled out about eighteen Pound, which he gave with a pretty Deal of Grumbling, telling him withal, that he should see him one Time or another, ride up *Holborn-Hill* backwards

Whitney was going about his Business, till he heard these Words, when he returned, and pulled the the old Gentleman off his Horse, putting him on a again with his Face towards the Horse's Tail, and tying his Legs Now, says he, *you old Rogue, let me see what a Figure a Man makes when he rides backwards, and let me have the Pleasure, at least, of beholding you first in that Posture* So giving the Horse three or four good Licks with his Whip, he set him a running so fast, that he never stop'd till he came to *Hounslow* Town, where the People fooled our Gentleman after they had made themselves a little merry with the Sight

Whitney, like a great many others of the same Profession, affected always to appear generous and noble There is one Instance of this Temper in him, which it may not be amiss to relate Meeting one Day with a Gentleman on *New-Market Heath,* whose Name was *Long,* and having robb'd him of an hundred Pounds in Silver, which was in his Portmanteau, tied up in a great Bag The Gentleman told him

that he had a great Way to go, and as he was unknown upon the Road, should meet with many Difficulties, if he did not restore as much as would bear his Expences. *Whitney* upon this opened the Mouth of the Bag, and holding it to Mr *Long* Here, says he, *take what you have Occasion for,* Mr *Long* put in his Hand, and took out as much as he could hold To which *Whitney* made no Opposition, but only said with a Smile, *I thought you would have had more Conscience, Sir*

Doubtless it must make some of our Readers merry, when they observe how often the Heroes of these Sheets are introduced as talking of Conscience, Virtue, Honour, Generosity, &c And it must be confessed, that they have Reason for their Mirth. This may, however, prove the real Beauty of these Perfections of human Nature, *That even those who have least of them, discover a Sort of Secret Value for them, and would affect to possess what they are of all Men the farthest from*

Our dexterous Butcher came once to *Doncaster* in *Yorkshire,* where he put up at the *Red-Lyon-Inn,* and made a very great Figure, having a pretty round Sum in his Possession. While he resided here, he was informed that the Landlord of the House was reputed rich, but that he was withal so covetous, as that he would do nothing to help a poor Relation or Neighbour in Distress, and so very sharp in his Business, that it was next to impossible for any one living to impose on him in the least Particular Nothing could be so pleasing to such a Man as *Whitney,* as out-witting one who was esteemed able to out-wit all the World, wherefore he was resolved to attempt this Master-stroke of Invention, as he supposed it must be, if he succeeded,

He now gives it out, that he had a good Estate, that he travelled about the Country merely for his Pleasure, and had his Money remitted to him as the Rents came in, still continuing for some Time to pay for every Thing he had, till, supposing his Host sufficiently satisfy'd that he was really what he pretended, he one Day took an Opportunity to tell him that his Money ran short, and he should be obliged to him for Credit, till he could have Returns O dear, Sir, says my Landlord, *you need not give yourself the least Uneasiness about such an Affair as this Every Thing that I have is at your Service, and I shall think myself honoured, if you please to make use of me as a Friend* *Whitney* returned the Compliment with Abundance of Thanks and other Expressions of Esteem, eating and drinking from Day to Day at the good Man's Table, his Horse also, all the while, being fed plentifully with the best of Corn and Hay And the better to Colour the Matter, and to prove that he really came out of Curiosity to see the Country, there was seldom a Day passed, but he rode out to some of the Neighbouring Villages, sometimes getting Mr *Inn-keeper,* sometimes other Gentlemen in the Town, to bear him Company, they being all proud of the Honour

It happened, that while he remain'd there, there was a Fair, according to annual Custom Upon the Fair Day in the Morning a small Box, carefully sealed, and very weighty, came directed to him He open'd it, took out a Letter, and read, lock'd it up, and gave it to his Landlady, desiring her to keep it in her Custody for the present, because it would be safer then in his own Hands, and ordering the Landlord, at the same Time to write out his Bill, that he might pay him next Morning. As soon as he had done thus, he went out, as though to see the Fair

In the Afternoon he comes home again in a great Hurry, and desires his Horse may be dressed and saddled, he having a Mind to shew him in the Fair, and, if he could, to exchange him for one which he had seen, and which he thought was the finest that ever he fix'd his Eyes on *I will have him,* says he, *if possible, whether the Owner will buy mine or no, and though he cost me forty Guineas* He then asked for his Landlady to help him to his Box, but was told she was gone to the Fair, whereupon he fell a Swearing like a Madman, That he supposed she had locked up what he gave her, and taken the Keys with her, *If she has,* quoth he, *I had rather have given ten Guineas, for I have no Money at all, but what is in your Possession* Enquiry was made, and it was found to be as he said, which put him into a still greater Passion, though it was what he wished for, and even expected, the whole Comedy having been invented for the sake of this single Scene

The Landlord quickly had Notice of our Gentleman's Anger, and the Occasion of it; upon which he comes to him, and begs of him to be easy, offering to lend him the Sum he wanted, till his Wife came Home   *Whitney* seemed to resent it highly, That he must be obliged to borrow Money when he had so much of his own, however, as there was no other Way, he condescended, with Abundance of Reluctance, to accept the Proposal, adding, That he desired an Account of all he was indebted as soon as possible, for it was not his Custom to run Hand over Head

Having received forty Guineas, the Sum he pretended to want, he mounts his Horse, and rides towards the Fair; but instead of dealing there, for another Horse, he spurred his own thro' the Crowd, as fast as he could conveniently, and made the best of his Way towards *London*   At Night the People of the Inn sat up very late for his coming Home, nor did they suspect any Thing the first, or even the second Night, when they saw nothing of him, he having been out before a Day or two together in his Progress round the Country, which they concluded was now the Case   But at the End of two or three Days, the Landlord was a little uneasy, and after he had waited a Week to no Purpose, it came into his Head to break open the Box, in order to examine it. With this View he goes to the Magistrate of the Place, procures his Warrant for so doing, and a Constable, with other proper Witnesses to be present.   We need not tell the Reader he was cheated, for every one will naturally conclude so, nor need we say, he was ready

to hang himself, when he found only Sand and Stones covered over, his Character may give an Idea of his Temper at this Time   But *Whitney* did not Care for his Landlord's Passion, so long as he got off safe with the Money.

This was however, the last of his Adventures in the Country, for not long after his Arrival in Town, he was apprehended in *White Friars,* upon the Information of one Mother *Cosens,* who kept a Bawdy-house in *Milford Lane,* over-against *St Clement's Church*   The Magistrate who took the Information, committed him to *Newgate,* where he remained till the next Sessions at the *Old-Bailey*

After his Conviction, Sir S——l L——e, Knt Recorder of *London,* made an excellent Speech before he passed Sentence of Death, to him, and the other Malefactors, setting forth the Nature of their several Offences in very strong Expressions, and addressing himself to *Whitney* in particular, who he exhorted to a sincere Repentance, as it was impossible for him to hope for any Reprieve, after such a Course of Villainies   Vindicating the Justice of the Law, and urging the Certainty of a Providence, which pursues such as him, and at last takes Vengeance on them for their Crimes

On *Wednesday,* the 19th of *December,* 1694, *Whitney* was carried to the Place of Execution, which was at *Porter's Block,* near *Smithfield*   When he came there, and saw no Hopes of any Favour, he addressed these few Words to the People

I Have been a very great Offender, both against *God, and my Country, by transgressing all Laws both Human and Divine. I believe there is not one here present but has often heard my Name, before my Confinement, and seen a large Catalogue of my Crimes, which has been made publick since   Why should I then pretend to vindicate a Life stain'd with so many enormous Deeds?*

The Sentence past on me is just, and I can see the Footsteps of a Providence, which I had before profanely laugh'd at, in my Apprehending and Conviction   I hope the Sense which I have of these Things, has enabled me to make my Peace with Heaven, the only Thing that is now of any Concern to me   Join in your Prayers with me, my dear Countrymen, that God would not forsake me in my last Moments.

Having spoke thus, and afterwards spent a few Moments in private Devotion, he was turned off, being about 34 Years of Age.

An Account of the Murder of the Reverend Mr. John Talbot.

THIS Gentleman had been Chaplain to a Regiment in *Portugal*, in the Reign of King *Charles* II. where he continued in the Discharge of his Office, till the Recalling of the said Regiment When arriving in *London*, he preached three Months at *St. Alphage in the Wall* Afterwards he was Curate to a Town called *Laindon* in *Essex*, where a Law-Suit commenced between him and some Persons of the said Parish, upon the Account of which me came up to *London* at the unhappy Time when a Period was put to his Life in the following Manner.

Several profligate abandon'd Wretches, to the Number of six Men, and one Woman, took into their Heads one Day to way-lay, rob, and murder this poor Man Whether hearing his Business, they might think he had a pretty Deal of Money about him or whether they acted at the Instigations of some of Mr *Talbot's* Enemies, is not certain, however it was, they dogged him from four a-Clock in the Afternoon, whetherfoever he went. The Names of some of these Miscreants were, *Stephen Eaton*, a Confectioner; *George Roades*, a Broker, *Henry Prichard*, Taylor; and *Sarah Swift*.

Mr *Talbot* had received Information, that his Adversaries design'd to arrest him, which made him a little circumspect while he was abroad, for every one who took any Notice of him, he imagined to be an Officer This occasioned him the sooner to be alarm'd when he saw himself followed by five or six People, from Place to Place, so that turn which Way foever he would, he was certain of meeting one or more of them

After he had shifted about a long Time to no Purpose, in order to avoid, as he thought, their clapping a Writ on his Back, he betook himself to *Gray's-Inn*, whither being still pursued, he had there a good Opportunity to take particular and accurate Notice of some or all of these evil-disposed Persons Here he took Shelter a little while, and writ Letters to some of his Acquaintance and Friends, requesting them to come and lend him their Assistance in order to secure his Person

The Persons whom he sent to failing him, he got Admittance into the Chambers of one of the Gentlemen of the Place, where he stay'd till he supposed all the Danger was over, then taking a little Refreshment, he took the back Way, through *Old Street*, and so over the Fields to *Shoreditch*

Not long after he had got into the Field, he perceived the same Persons at his Heels, who had dogged him before He was now more surprized than ever, it being Eleven a Clock at Night The most probable Method of escaping that he could see, was by breaking through a Reed Hedge to a Garden House, but before he could reach the Place, one or more of the Villains seiz'd him, and began to pick

his Pockets They found about twenty Shillings, and his knife, with which they attempted to kill him by cutting his Throat

Whether it was by Chance, on these Wretches pretended to an extraordinary Skill in Butchering Man, is uncertain, but they first cut out a Piece of his Throat, about the Breadth of a Crown-Piece, without touching the Wind-pipe, and then, in the dependant Part of the Orifice, they stabbed him with the knife so deep, that the Point almost reached his Lungs However, Providence so far over-ruled their Cruelty, that they did not cut the Reccurent Nerves, which would have stopped his Speech, nor the Jugular Veins and Arteris, which if they had done, he had instantly bled to Death without Remedy, and then possibly no Discovery had been made

There was a Cut in the Collar of his Doublet, which seemed to shew that they attempted this Piece of Butchery before they stripped him, but then the Nature of the Wound intimated, on the Contrary, that they pulled off his Coat and Doublet before they accomplished their Design

This bloody Deed was perpetrated at *Anniseed-Clear*, on *Friday* the 2d of *July* 1669 While the Wretches were committing their Butchery, the Dogs bark'd, and the Beasts bellow'd in an uncommon Manner, so that several Gardeners rose out of their Beds to prepare for the Market, supposing it had been Day light, soon after it thunder'd and rain'd in a terrible Manner, which drew several Brickmakers out of their Lodgings to secure their Bricks from the Weather, and was also the Occasion that the Murderers did not get far from the Place where their Barbarity was acted before they were apprehended, so that Heaven and Earth seem'd to unite in crying out against the inhuman Deed, and detecting the wicked Authors of it

Some of the Brickmakers, who had been alarm'd by the Thunder and Rain, discover'd Mr *Talbot* lying in his Shirt and Drawers all bloody These gave Notice to their Companions, who also came up They then raised him, and cherished him with a Dram which one of them had at Hand, whereupon he immediately pointed which Way the Murderers went The Watch near *Shoreditch* were soon inform'd what had happen'd, and some of them came as well to take Care of the wounded Gentleman, as to apprehend the Authors of his Misfortune One of the Number quickly discover'd a Man lying among the Nettles, and called up his Companions, supposing he also had been murder'd, but when they came to a nearer Examination, they saw a bloody Knife on one Side of him, and the Murderer's Doublet on the other Upon these Circumstances, presuming he was guilty of the Murder, they apprehended him At first he feign'd himself a-sleep, and then suddenly starting up, he attempted to make his Escape,

but

but in vain. A Pewter Pot, with the Mark was newly scraped out, was found near him, and one of the Watchmen broke his Head with it, which made him a little more tractable. In the mean Time, Mr. *Talbot*, by the great Care of the Officers of the Night, was carried to the *Star Inn* at *Shoreditch Church*, where he was put to Bed, and whither a Surgeon was sent for to dress, and take Care of his Wounds.

This Man, who was apprehended, was *Eaton*, the Confectioner, he was carried before Mr *Talbot*, who instantly knew him, and by Writing, declared that he was the Man who cut his Throat; and that five more Men, and a Woman, were his Associates. A second Time, upon Mr. *Talbot*'s own Request, *Eaton* was brought before him, when he continued his former Accusation against him, whereupon he was carried before Justice *Pitfield*, and by him committed to *Newgate*. It was not long after *Eaton*, before the Woman was found, who also pretended to be a-sleep. Mr. *Talbot* swore as positively to her, as he had done to the other, and enquired of the Constable whether her Name was not *Sarah*? For he had heard one of her Comrades say to her, when in *Holborn*, *Shall we have a Coach Sarah*? The Constable demanded her Name, and she not suspecting the Reason, told him right, which confirmed the Evidence of the dying Gentleman. Shortly after a Third, and then a Fourth was taken, who were also committed to Newgate, Mr. *Talbot* knowing one of these also.

The Care of Mr *Talbot*'s Wounds was committed to one Mr *Litchfield*, an able Surgeon, who diligently attended him; and that nothing might be omitted which might conduce to his Recovery, Dr. *Hodges* one of the Physicians employ'd by the City, during the dreadful Visitation in 1665, was likewise called. To these, at the Request of the Minister of the *Charter-house*, Dr *Ridgely* was added. By their joint Direction, he was in a fair Way to be cured, no ill Symptoms appearing from *Monday* Morning to the *Sabbath-Day* following, either upon Account of Wounds, or otherwise; for though he lay some Time in the Wet, yet thro' the Experience of these Gentlemen, he was kept from a Fever. Several other Surgeons also freely offered their Assistance.

About Noon on *Sunday* he was dressed, the Wound look'd well, and he seem'd more chearful than ordinary, but within two or three Hours after, a violent Fit of Coughing seiz'd him, which broke the jugular Vein, and caused such an Effusion of Blood, that he fainted, and his extreme Parts were cold, before any one could come to his Assistance. The Flux was once stop'd, but upon coughing he bled again, so that his Case was almost past Hopes. About one or two next Morning, he sent for Dr *Atfield*, Minister of Shorditch Church, to pray by him, and within two Hours after, he expired, having been very devout and composed to the last Moment.

Several Attestations were made before the Justice, and at the Tryal of the Prisoners, concerning Mr *Talbot*'s having been dogg'd and murdered, by those who had either seen him the Day before, or came up to him first, when he was left in the lamentable Condition we have been describing. Mr *Went*, in particular, who was Constable of the Night, when this Murder was committed, gave a particular Relation of taking the Prisoners, and of what Mr *Talbot* said and wrote, when he saw any one of them. The Papers which the Deceased wrote were likewise produced in Court, and it was observable that he particularly exclaim'd against the Woman, whom he called bloody every Time he mentioned her, affirming, that she said to her Companions several Times, *Kill the Dog, kill him.*

The Facts and Circumstances were so plain, that the Jury found all the four that had been taken, guilty of the Murder, not one of them being able to give a satisfactory Account of themselves, or to prove where they were after six o'Clock, the Night the bloody Deed was done. The Names of these four was given at the Beginning of this Relation.

Mr *Cowper*, the Coroner, and Mr *Litchfield* the Surgeon, gave in their Informations, an exact Account of Mr. *Talbot*'s Wound, and both of them deposed, *That they verily thought it to be the Occasion of his Death*. Mr *Litchfield* said, *The Knife really penetrated his Lungs.*

The Night before Mr *Talbot* died, he wrote to Mr *Went* the Constable, desiring him to go to the Ordinary, and enquire with him of *Eaton*, whether any of *Laindon*'s People, employ'd or abetted him in the Fact he had committed, if they did, to get their Names of him. But *Eaton* persisted in denying, not only that, but even the Fact itself, telling them in the most solemn Manner, *That, to his Knowledge, he never in his Life saw Mr. Talbot, till he was brought before him, after he was taken.* *Sarah Swift* likewise being questioned concerning her Guilt, and urged to confess what she knew, she answered, *That she would burn in Hell before she would own any Thing of the Matter.* To such an uncommon Degree had these Wretches hardened themselves in their Crimes.

Mr *Talbot* wrote also several Letters to his Friends, with an exact Account of the Manner how he had been followed for seven Hours together, and how he was at last set upon, and used in the barbarous Manner herein related; but the Substance of these Letters being interspersed in the Story itself, it is needless to give them at large.

On *Wednesday* the 14th of *July*, 1669. *Stephen Eaton*, *George Roades*, and *Sarah Swift* were convey'd in a Cart to *Tyburn*, where the two Men confessed the Murder; but the Woman continued obstinate to the last. *Henry Prichard* was reprieved upon some favourable Circumstances that were produced.

'Tis wonderful what could excite these poor Creatures to pursue the Blood of an innocent Man at this unaccountable Rate, and indeed 'tis scarce to be imagin'd, that they should pitch upon one from whom they could have no very great Expectations, unless they had been hired to do it, or had some Personal Quarrel with him, which latter could not be true. However as none of them own'd who were their Abbettors, or whether they were employ'd at all or no, we must not take upon us to judge in this Case, but leave the Decision of this Point to that great and awful Day, when the Secrets of Men's Hearts shall be revealed, and every Thing that has been hid shall be made manifest.

The LIFE *of the* GERMAN PRINCESS.

THIS Woman was so called from her pretending to be born at *Collogn* in *Germany*, and that her Father was *Henry Van Wolway* a Doctor of the civil Law, and Lord of *Holmsteim* But this Story was a Piece with her Actions, for she was really the Daughter of one *Meders* a Chorister at the Cathedral of *Canterbury*, or, as some say, only an indifferent Trader of that City, in which she was born the 11th of *January* 1642 We can say little of her Education, only from her Inclinations afterwards we may suppose she had as much Learning as is commonly given to her Sex. She took great Delight in Reading, especially of Romances, and Books of Knight Errantry, *Parismus* and *Parismanus*, *Don Bellianis* of Greece, and *Amadis de Gaul*, were some of her favourite Authors, and she was so touched with the Character of *Oriana* in the Latter, that she frequently conceited herself to be a Princess, or a Lady of high Quality *Casandra* and *Cleopatra* were also read in their turns, and her Memory was so Tenacious, that she could repeat a great Part of their Amours and Adventures very readily

Her Marriage was not agreeable to the high Opinion she had entertained of her own Merit ; instead of a Knight, or a Squire at least, which she had promised herself, she took up with a Journeyman Shoemaker whose Name was *Stedman*, by whom she had two Children, who both died in their Infancy This Man being unable to maintain her Extravagances, and support her in the Splendour she always aim'd at, she was continually discontented, till at last she resolv'd to leave him, and seek her Fortune A Woman of her Spirit is never long in executing Things of this Nature, she made an Elopement, she went to *Dover*, she married another Husband who was a Surgeon of that Town

Information of this Affair was soon taken, and she was apprehended and indicted at *Maidstone*, for having two Husbands, but by some masterly Stroke, which she never wanted on a pressing Occasion, she was quickly acquitted This emboldened her to a third Marriage, with one *John Carleton*, a Londoner, which was the Occasion of her being first publickly known in Town, for some of her old Acquaintance giving *Carleton*'s brother an Account of her former Weddings, she was again taken, committed to *Newgate*, and try'd at the Old Bailey for Polygamy. Here again the Evidence against her was insufficient, so that she was a second Time acquitted

'Tis requisite, before we proceed any further in our Relation, to observe, that between the two last Marriages, she embark'd on board a Merchant Ship which carried her to *Holland*, from whence she travelled by Land to the Place she had so often talk'd of the City of *Cologn*, where being now Mistress of a considerable Sum of Money, she took a fine Lodging at a House of Entertainment, and lived in greater Splendour then she had ever before done As it is customary in *England*, to go to *Epsom* or Tun-

bridge Wells in the Summer Season, so in *Germany*, the Quality usually frequent the *Spaw* Here our Adventuress had the picking of a few Feathers from an old Gentleman who fell in Love with her, and who had a good Estate not many Miles distant from *Cologn*, at *Liege* or *Lugat*. By the Assistance of the Landlady she managed this Affair with so much Artifice, that he presented her with several fine and valuable Jewels, besides a gold Chain, with a very costly Medal, which had been formerly given him for some remarkable good Service, under Count *Tilley* against the valiant King of *Sweden*, *Gustavus Adolphus* The foolish old Dotard urged his Passion with all the Vehemence of a young vigorous Lover, pressing her to Matrimony, and making her very large Promises, till at last she gave her Consent to espouse him in three Days, and he left the Preparation of Things necessary to her Care, giving her large Sums of Money for that purpose Madam now perceived it was high Time to be gone, and, in order to her getting off with the greater Security, she acquainted her Landlady with the Design, who had before shared pretty largely in the Spoils of the old Captain The Hostess to be sure, was willing to hearken to any Proposal that would help her a little more to fleece the doting Inamorato

The Princess, however, was resolved this Time to have all the Booty to herself ; and to accomplish this, she perswaded her Landlady to go into the Town, and get a Place for her in some Carriage that did not go to *Collogn*, because, she said her Lover should not know whether to follow her The old Trot saw that this Precaution was very necessary, and therefore a way goes she, to provide for the safety of her Guest, who was now sufficiently to reward her out of her Dotard's Favours. This was all our Adventuress wanted, for as soon as she found herself left alone, she brok open a Chest, where she had observed her Landlady to put all her Treasure, and there she found not only what she had shared with her out of the old Man's Benevolence, but also an additional Sum of Money not inconsiderable. There is little Reason to tell the Reader that she took all that was worth taking, there being none of her Character apt to spare what it is in their Power to Seize, tho' it be from a Brother or Sister of their own Profession Madam soon pack'd up her Parcel, and having before privately made sure of a Passage to *Utrecht* She fled thither, from thence she went to *Amsterdam* where she sold her gold Chain, Medal, and some of the Jewels, then proceeded to *Rotterdam*, and then, to the *Brill*, where she took Shipping for *England*

She landed at *Billingsgate* one Morning very early, about the latter End of *March*, in the Year, 1663. but found no House open till she came to the Exchange Tavern, where she first obtained the Title of the *German Princess*, in the following Manner.

She was got into the aforesaid Tavern, in Company with some Gentlemen who she perceived, were pretty full of Money These Gentlemen addressing her in the Manner usual on such Occasions, she immediately feigned a Cry which she had always at Command. The Tears trickled down her Cheeks, she sigh'd she sobb'd, and the Cause being demanded told them, that she little thought once of being reduced to such a wretched Necessity as she was now in, of exposing her Body to the Pleasure of every Bidder   Here she repeated the History of her Extractions and Education, telling them a great Deal about her pretended Father, the Lord *Henry Van Wolway* ; who, she said, was a sovereign Prince of the Empire, independent of any Man but his sacred imperial Majesty *Certainly, continued she, any Gentleman may suppose what a Mortification it must be to a Woman born of such noble Parents, and bred up in all the Pomp of a Court, under the Care of an indulgent Father, to suffer as I now do, yet why did I say indulgent Father? Alas! was it not his Cruelty that banished me his only Daughter, from his Dominions, only for marrying a Nobleman of the Court, whom I loved to Excess, without his Knowledge? Was it not my Father that occasioned my dear Lord and Husband to be cut off in the Bloom of his Age, by falsly accusing him of a Design against his Person, a Deed which his virtuous Soul abhorred* Here she pretended her Sorrow would permit her to rehearse no more of her Misfortunes, and the whole Company was touched with Compassion at the melancholly Relation, which she so well humoured, that they all looked upon it as true, giving her out of mere Pity, all the Money they had about them, promising to meet her again with more This they also accomplished, and ever afterwards called her, the poor unfortunate *German Princess* ; which Name she laid Claim to in all Companies

The Exchange Tavern was kept by one Mr *King*, who was the same as kept it when our Princess received her Honourary Title As she was now come from foreign Parts, with a great Deal of Riches, he believed more than ever the Truth of what she had before affirmed Nor was Madam backwards in telling him that she had raised all her Wealth by private Contribution from some Princes of the Empire, who were acquainted with her Circumstances, and to whom she had made herself known : Adding, that not one of those who had given her any Thing, dared to acquaint her Father that they knew where she was, because they were all his Neighbours, and vastly Inferior to him in the Number and Strength of their Forces, *For, said she, my Father is so inexorable, that he would make War upon any Prince, who he knew extended his Pity to me.*

John Carleton, whom we mentioned before as her third Husband, was Brother-in-Law to Mr *King*, He made his Addresses to the Princess *Van Wolway*, in the most dutiful and submissive Manner that could be imagined, making Use of his Brother's Interest, to negotiate the Affair between them, till with a great Deal of seeming Reluctance at Marrying one of common Blood, her Highness consented to take him to her Embraces Now was Mr. *Carleton* as great as his Majesty, in the Arms of an imaginary Princess , he formed to himself a thousand Pleasures, which the vulgar Herd could have no Notion of, he threw himself at her Feet in Transport, and made Use of all the Rhetoric he could collect, to thank her for the prodigious Honour she had done him But Alas! how was he surprized, when Mr *King* presented him with the following Letter.

SIR,

I *Am an entire Stranger to your Person, yet common Justice and Humanity obliges me to give you Notice, that the pretended Princess, who has passed herself upon your Brother, Mr* John Carleton, *is a Cheat and an Impostor*

If I tell you, Sir, that she has already married several Men in our County of Kent, *and afterwards made off with all the Money she could get into her Hands, I say no more than could be proved, were she brought in the Face of Justice*

That you may be certain I am not mistaken in the Woman, please to observe that she has high Breast, a very graceful Appearance, and speaks several Languages fluently

Yours unknown,

T B

After Mrs *Carleton* (for so we may at present call her) had got rid of her Husband, and of the Prosecution for marrying him, she was entertained by the Players, who were in Hopes of gaining by a Woman, who had made such a considerable Figure on the real Theatre of the World The House was very much resorted to upon her Account, and she got a great deal of Applause in her Dramatical Capacity, by the several Characters she performed, which were generally either Jilt, Coquette, or Chamber Maid, either of which was agreeable to her artful intriguing Genius , but what contributed most to her Fame, was a Play, written purely upon her Account, called the *German Princess*, from her Name, and in which she performed a principal Part, besides speaking the following Epilogue

I've past one Trial, but it is my Fear
I shall receive a rigid Sentance here
You think me a bold Cheat, but Case 'twere so,
Which of you are not? Now you'd swear I know,
But do not, lest that you deserve to be
Censur'd worse than you can Censure me ·
The World's a Cheat, and we that move in it,
In our Degrees, do exercise our Wit ,
And better 'tis to get a glorious Name,
However got, than Live by common Fame

The Princess had too much Mercury in her Constitution to be long settled in any Way of Life whatsoever The whole City of *London* was too little for her to Act in, how was it possible then that she should be confined in the narrow Limits of a Theatre? She did not, however, leave the Stage so soon but she had procured a considerable Number of Adorers, who having either seen her Person, or heard of her Fame, were desirous of a nearer Acquaintance with her As she was naturally given to Company and Gallantry, she was not very difficult of Access, yet when you were in her Presence, you were certain to meet with an Air of Indifferency

There were two of her Bullies who doted on her beyond all the Rest, a couple of smart young Fellows, who had abundance more in their Pockets, than they had in their Heads These from a deficiency of Wit in themselves, were very fond in the large Quantity of that Commodity which they discovered in her Company There is no Doubt but they had other Designs than just to converse with her, for they several Times discovered an Inclination to come a little nearer to her Body And Madam was not so ignorant, but she knew their Meaning by their Whining , she therefore give them Encouragement, till she had drained about 300*l* a piece

piece out of them, and then, finding their Stock pretty well exhausted, she turn'd them both off, telling them she wondered how they could have the Impudence to pretend Love to a Princess

After this, an elderly Gentleman fell into the same Condition, at seeing her, as several had done before, tho' he was fifty Years of Age, and not ignorant of her former Tricks He was worth about 400 *l per Annum*, and immediately resolv'd to be at the Charge of a constant Maintenance, provided she would consent to live with him To bring about which he made her several valuable Presents of Rings, Jewels, &c At last, after a long Siege, he became Master of the Fort, yet in such a Manner, that it seemed rather to be surrender'd out of pure Love and Generosity, than from any mercenary Views, for she always protested against being Corrupted, so far as to part with her Honour, for the sake of filthy Lucre, which is a common Artifice of the Sex Our Gentleman, tho', as has been remark'd, he was sensible what she was, yet by Degrees he became so enamour'd, as to believe every Thing she said, and to look upon her as the most virtuous Woman alive

Living now as Man and Wife, she seem'd to redouble her Endearments, and to give them all a greater Air of Sincerity, so that he was continually gratifying her with some costly present or another, which she always took Care to receive with an Appearance of being ashamed he should bear so many Obligations on her, telling him continually that she was not worthy of so many Favours Thus did she vary in her Behaviour, according to the Circumstances and Temper of the Person she had to deal with At last, our old Lover came home one Night very much in Liquor, and gave her a Jewel of 5 *l* Value, and our Princess thought this as proper a Time as any she was like to meet with, for her to make the most of his Worship's Passion Accordingly having got him to Bed, and seen him fast asleep, which he soon was at this Time, she proceeded to rifle him, finding his Pocket Book, with a Bill for 100 *l* upon a Goldsmith in the City, and the Keys of his Trunks and Escrutoires

She now proceeded to secure all that was worth her while, among other Things, she made herself Mistress of 20 pieces of old Gold, a gold Watch, a gold Seal, an old Silver Watch, and several pieces of Plate, with other valuable Moveables, to the Value in all of 150 *l* Now she thought it best for her to make off as fast as she could with her Prize So as soon as it was Day she took Coach, and drove to the Goldsmith, who mistrusted nothing, having seen her before with the Gentleman, and instantly paid the 100 *l* upon which she delivered up the Bill

Having thus over reached her old Lover, Madam took a convenient Lodging, at which she past for a Virgin, with a Fortune of a 1000 *l* left her by an Uncle, to this she added, that her Father was very Rich, and able to give her as much more, but that disliking a Man whom he had provided for her Husband, she had left the Country, and retired to *London*, where she was in Hopes none of her Relations would find her That this Story might appear the more probable, she contrived Letters from a Friend which were brought her continually, and in which, she pretended, she received an Account of all that past, with respect to her Father and Lover These Letters being loosely laid about the Chamber, were pick'd up by her Landlady, who out of Curiosity perused the Content, and by that Means became more and more satisfied in her Tennant. This Landlady had a Nephew of considerable Substance, and it was now all her Endeavour to make a Match

between him and her young Gentlewoman, whom she soon brought to be pretty intimately acquainted together

The new Lover presents her with a Watch, as a Token of his Esteem for her Person, but the poor innocent Creature refused it with abundance of Modesty However, she was at last prevailed upon to accept this little Favour, and the young Man thought himself with one Foot in Paradise already, that she was so condescending Their Amour after this, went on to both their Satisfactions, Madam seeing a fair Prospect of making a Penny of her Mamorato, and he not in the least doubting but he should obtain his Wish, and one Day or another enjoy that Heaven of Bliss, which, as he frequently expressed it, was treasured in her Arms

One Day as they were conversing together, and entertaining each other with all the soft and tender Endearments of young Lovers, a Porter knocks at the Door, and upon being admitted, delivers a Letter to our Lady, being introduced by the Maid, who had received her Instructions before-hand Madam immediately opens and reads the Letter, but scarce had she made an End, before altering her Countenance, she Shrieked out, *Oh! I am undone, I am undone* All the Company could scarce prevent her falling in a Swoon, tho' the smelling Bottle was at Hand, and her young Lover sitting by her, who, to be sure, did not fail to use all the Rhetoric he was Master of, in order to comfort her, and learn the Cause of her Surprise *Sir*, quoth she at last, *since you are already acquainted with most of my Concerns, I shall not make a Secret of this Therefore if you please, read this Letter, and know the Occasion of my Affliction* The young Gentleman received it at her Hands, and read as follows

Dear Madam,

'I Have several Times taken my Pen in Hand, 'on purpose to write to you, and as often laid 'it aside again, for fear of giving you more Trou- 'ble than you already labour under However, as 'the Affair so immediately concerns you, I cannot 'in Justice hide what I tremble to disclose, but 'must in Duty tell you the worst of News, whatever may be the Consequence of my so doing

'Know then, that your affectionate and tender 'Brother is Dead I am sensible how dear he was 'to you, and you to him, yet let me intreat you for 'your own sake to acquiesce in the Will of Provi- 'dence as much as possible, since our Lives are all 'at his Disposal who gave us Being

'I could use another Argument to comfort you, 'that with a Sister less loving than you would be of 'more Weight than that I have urged, but I know 'you your Soul is above all mercenary Views I 'cannot, however, forbear just to inform you 'that he has left you all he had, and you know 'further, that your Father's Estate of 200 *l* per 'Annum, can now devolve upon No-Body after his 'Decease, but yourself, who are now his only Child.

'What I am next to acquaint you with, may per- 'haps be almost as bad as the former Particular 'Your hated Lover has been so importunate with 'your Father, especially since your Brother's De- 'cease, that the old Gentleman resolves, if ever he 'should hear of you any more, to marry you to him, 'and he makes this the Condition of your being re- 'ceived again into his Favour, and having your 'former Disobedience, as he calls it, forgiven. 'While your Brother lived, he was every Day en- 'deavouring to soften the Heart of your Father, 'and we were but last Week in Hopes he would 'have consented to let you follow your Inclinations,

'If

' if you would come Home to him again; but now
' there is never an Advocate in your Caufe, who can
' Work upon the Man's peevifh Temper; for he
' fays, as you are now his fole Heir, he ought to be
' more refolute in the Difpofal of you in Mar-
' riage.

' While I am Writing, I am furprifed with an Ac-
' count that your Father and Lover are both prepar-
' ing to come to *London*, where they fay they can
' find you out. Whether or no this be only a De-
' vice, I cannot tell, nor can I imagine where they
' could receive their Information if it be true. How-
' ever, to prevent the Worft, confider, whether or
' no you can caft off your old Averfion, and fubmit
' to your Father's Commands, for if you cannot,
' it will be moft advifeable, in my Opinion, to change
' your Habitation. I have no more to fay in the Af-
' fair, being unwilling to direct you in fuch a very
' nice Circumftance, the Temper of your own Mind
' will be the beft Inftructor you can apply to, for
' your future Happinefs or Mifery, during Life, de-
' pends on your Choice. God grant that every
' Thing may turn for the Better.''

From your Friend,

S. E.

Our young Lover having read the Letter, found
that fhe had real Caufe to be afflicted Pity for her,
and above all, a Concern for his own Intereft, and the
Fear of lofing his Miftrefs to the Country Lover,
thro' the Authority of her Father, put him upon per-
fwading her to remove from her Habitation, and
come to refide with him, having very handfome
Rooms, fit for the Reception of a Perfon of fuch high
Quality Thither fhe went the next Day, with her
Maid, who knew her Defign, and had engaged to
affift her therein to the utmoft of her Ability When
they were come into Madam's Bed-Chamber, they
refolved not to go to Reft, that they might be ready
to move off in the Morning at the firft Opportunity
By turns they flept in their Cloaths on the Bed, and
towards Morning when all were faft, but themfelves,
they went to Work, broke open a Trunk, took a
Bag with 100 *l.* in it, and feveral Suits of Apparel,
and then flipt out, leaving our poor Lover to look
for his Money and Miftrefs together when he was ftirring, who were both by that Time far enough out of
his Way

In a Word, it would be impoffible to relate half
the Tricks which fhe play'd, and mention half the
Lodgings in which fhe at Times refided. Seldom did
fhe mifs carrying off a confiderable Booty wherefoever
fhe came, at beft fhe never fail'd of fomething, for
all was Fifh that came to her Net, where there was
no Plate, a pair of Sheets, half a dozen Napkins, or
or a Pillobier, nay, even Things of a lefs Value than
thefe would ferve her Turn, rather than fhe would
fuffer her Hands to be out of Practice. Captain
Smith, for the Sake of fwelling her Life, has made
her the Actrefs of feveral Things which he has in o-
ther Places apply'd to other People. We can fee no
Caufe he had to do thus, fince there are many more
genuine Facts that have come to knowledge then we
fhall infert

One Time fhe went to a *Mercer*'s in *Cheapfide*,
with her pretended Maid, where fhe agreed for as
much Silk as came to 6l. and pulled out her Purfe
to pay for it, but there was nothing therein but feveral particular pieces of Gold, which fhe pretended
to have a great Value for. The *Mercer* to be fure,
would not be fo rude as to let a Gentlewoman
of Figure part with what fhe had fo much efteem

for, fo he ordered one of his Men to go along
with her to her Lodging, and receive the Money
there A Coach was ready which fhe had brought
along with her, and they all three went up into it
When they came to the *Royal-Exchange*, Madam
ordered the Coachman to fet her down, pretending
to the *Mercer* that fhe wanted to buy fome Ribbon
fuitable to the Silk; upon which he fuffered the
Maid, without any Scruple, to take the Goods along
with her, ftaying in the Coach for their return
But he might have ftayed long enough, if he had
attended till they came again, for they found Means
to get off into *Threadneadle-ftreet* and the young
Man having waited till he was quite Weary, made
the beft of his Way home to rehearfe his Misfortune
to his Mafter.

Something of a Piece with this, was a Cheat fhe
put upon a French Mafter *Weaver* in *Spittlefield*,
of whom fhe bought to the of Value 40 l taking him
Home with her to her Lodging, and bidding him
make a Bill of Parcels, for half the Silk was for a
kinfwoman of hers in the next Room The Frenchman
fate down very orderly to do as fhe bid him, while
fhe took the Silk into the next Room that the ther
to fee it · Half an Hour he waited pretty contentedly,
drinking fome Wine, which Madam had left him
At laft beginning to be a little uneafy, he made
bold to Knock, when the People of the Houfe
came up, and upon his afking for the Gentle
woman, told him fhe had been gone out fome
Time, and was to come there no more. The poor
Man feeming furprifed, they took him into the next
Room, and fhewed him a pair of back Stairs which
was the proper Way to her Apartment Monfieur
was at firft in a Paffion with the People, till they
convinced him that they knew nothing of his Gentlewoman, any more then that fhe had taken their
Room for a Month, which being expired, fhe was
removed they could not tell whether.

The next Landlord fhe had was a *Taylor*, whom
fhe employed to make up what fhe bilked the Mercer and *Weaver* of The *Taylor* imagines he has
got an excellent Job, as well as a topping Woman
for his Lodger, fo he fell to Work immediately,
and by the Affiftance of fome Journeymen which he
hired on this Occafion, he got the Cloths finifhed
againft a Day which fhe appointed, when fhe
pretended fhe was to receive a great Number of Vi-
fiters Againft the fame Time fhe gave her Land
lady 20 s to provide a Supper, defiring her to
fend for what was needful, and fhe would pay the
Overplus next Day Accordingly an elegant Enter
tainment was prepared, Abundance of Wine was
Drank, and the poor *Taylor* was as Drunk as a
Beaft. This was what our Princefs wanted, for the
Landlady going up to put her Hufband to Bed, fhe
and all her Guefts flip'd out, one with a filver Tank
ard, another with a Salt, her Maid with the
Cloths which was not on their Backs, and, in a Word,
not one of them all went off empty-handed. Being
got into the Street, they put the Maid and the Booty
into the Coach, getting themfelves into others, and
driving by different Ways to the Place of their next
Refidence, not one of them being difcovered

Another Time, fhe had a mighty Mind, feem-
to put herfelf into Mourning, to which Purpofe, fhe
fent her Woman to a Shop in the *New-Exchange* in
the *Strand*, where fhe had bought fome Things the
Day before, to defire that the People would bring
Choice of Hoods, knots Scarves, Aprons, Cuffs,
and other Mourning Accutrements to her Lodging
inftantly, for her Father was dead, and fhe muft be
ready in fo many Days to appear at his Funeral
The Woman of the Shop prefently look'd out the
                                                    beft

st she had of each of these Commodities, and made the best of her Way to Madam's Quarters When she came there, the poor Lady was sadly indispos'd, that she was not able to look over the Things till her Dinner, when, if Madam Milliner wou'd please come again, she did not doubt but they shou'd The good Woman was very well satisfy'd, and refus'd to take her Goods back again, but desir'd she might trouble her Ladyship so far as to leave them where till she came again, which was very readily granted At the Time appointed comes our Tradeswoman, and ask if the Gentlewoman above Stairs was at Home, but was told, to her great Mortification, that she was gone out they could not tell whether, and that they believ'd she would never return again, for she had found Means, before her Departure, to convey away several of the most valuable Parts of Furniture in the Room which she had hir'd The next Day confirm'd their Suspicion, and made both the landlord and Milliner give her up for an Impostor, and their Goods for lost

Being habited, à la Mode, all in Sable, she took Rooms in *Fuller's-Rents* in *Holborn*, and sent for a young Barrister of *Gray's-Inn* When Mr *Justinian* came, she told him she was Heir to her deceas'd Father, but that having an extravagant Husband, with whom she did not live, she was willing to secure her Estate in such a Manner as that he might not enjoy the Benefit of it, or have any Command over it, for, if he had, she was certain of coming to want Bread in a little Time Here she wept plentifully, to make her Case have the greater Effect, and engage the Lawyer to stay with her till the Plot she had laid could be executed While the grave young Man was putting his Face into a proper Position, and speaking to the Affair in Hand with all the Learning of *Coke*, a Woman came up Stairs on a sudden, crying out, *O Lord, Madam, we are all undone! for my Master is below He has been asking after you, and swears he will come up to your Chamber I am afraid the People of the House will not able to hinder him, he appears so resolute O Heavens! says our Counterfeit, what shall I do? Why? says the Lawyer, Why! quoth she, I mean for you, dear me, what Excuse shall I make for your being here? I dare not tell him your Quality and Business, for that would endanger all And, on the other Side, he is extremely jealous Therefore, good Sir, step into that Closet till I can send him away* The Lawyer being surpriz'd, and not knowing what to do so on a sudden, complied with her Request, and she lock'd him into the Closet, drawing the Curtains of the Bed and going to the Door to receive her counterfeit Husband, who, by this Time, had demanded Entrance

No sooner was our Gentleman enter'd, but he began to give his Spouse the most opprobrious Language he could invent *O Mrs Devil, says he, I understand you have a Man in the Room! A pretty Companion for a poor innocent Woman, truly, one who is always complaining how hardly I use her Where is the Son of a Whore? I shall sacrifice him this Moment Is this your Modesty, Madam? This your Virtue? Let me see your Gallant immediately, or, by the Light, you shall be the first Victim your self* Upon this, he made to the Closet-Door, and forc'd it open in a great Fury, as he had before been directed Here he discovers our young Lawyer, all pale, and trembling, ready to sink through the Floor at the Sight of one from whom he could expect no Mercy Out flies the Sword, and poor *Littleton* was upon his Marrow-bones in a Moment Just in his Instant Madam interpos'd, being resolv'd rather to die herself than see the Blood of an innocent Man spilt in her Apartment, and upon her Account A

Companion, also, of our Bully Husband, stepp'd up, and wrested the Sword out of his Hand by main Strength, endeavouring to pacify him with all the Reason and Art he was Master of But still, that there might be no Appearance of Imposture, the more they strove, the more enrag'd our injur'd poor Cornuto appear'd, for such he thought to make the Lawyer believe he imagin'd himself

They could not, however, so effectually impose on our Limb of the Law as than he discern'd nothing of the Artifice He began to see himself trapann'd, and ventur'd to speak in his own Behalf, and tell the whole Truth of the Story But he might as well have said nothing, for the other insisted upon it that this was only Pretence, and that he came there for other Purposes His Honour was injur'd, and nothing would serve but Blood, or other sufficient Reparation It was at last referr'd to the Arbitration of the other Man, who came with the sham Husband, and he propos'd the Sum of 500 l. to make up the Matter This was a large Sum, and indeed, more than the Lawyer could well raise However, he at last consented to pay down 100 l. rather than bring himself into fresh Inconveniences, which they oblig'd him immediately to send for, first looking over the Note, to see that he did not send for a Constable instead of the Money Upon the Payment, they discharg'd him from his Confinement

Not long after this, our Princess was apprehended for stealing a Silver Tankard in *Covent Garden*, and after Examination, committed to *Newgate* At the following Sessions she was found guilty, and condemn'd, but was afterwards repriev'd, and order'd for Transportation This Sentence was executed, and she was sent to *Jamaica*, where she had not been above two Years, before she return'd to *England* again, and set up for a rich Heiress By this Means, she got married to a very wealthy Apothecary in *Westminster*, whom she robb'd of above 300 l. and then left him

After this, she took a Lodging, in a House where no body liv'd but the Landlady, a Watchmaker, who was also a Lodger, and herself and Maid When she thought her Character here pretty well establish'd, she one Night invited the Watchmaker and her Landlady to go with her and see a Play, pretending she had a Present of some Tickets They contented, and only Madam's Maid, who was almost as good as herself, was left at Home She, according to Agreement, in their Absence broke open almost all the Locks in the House, stole 200 l. in Money, and about thirty Watches, so that the Prize, in all, amounted to about 600 l. which she carried to a Place before provided, in another Part of the Town After the Play was over, our Princess invited her Companions to drink with her as the *Green Dragon* Tavern in *Fleetstreet*, where she gave them the Slip, and went to her Maid

We now proceed to the Catastrophe of this prodigious Woman, who, had she been virtuously inclin'd was capable of being the Phœnix of her Age, for it was impossible for her not to be admir'd in every Thing she said and did The Manner of her last and fatal Apprehension, was as follows, we having taken the Account from the Papers of those Times

One Mr *Freeman*, a Brewer in *Southwark*, had been robb'd of about 200 l. whereupon he went to Mr *Lowman*, Keeper of the *Marshalsea*, and desired him to search all suspicious Places, in order to discover the Thieves One *Lancaster* was the Person most suspected, and while they were searching a House near *New Spring Gardens* for him, they spied a Gentlewoman, as she seemed to be, walking in the two pair of Stairs Room in a Night-Gown

Mr *Louman* immediately enters the Room, spies three Letters on the Table, and begins to examine them Madam seems offended with him, and their Dispute caused him to look on her so stedfastly that he knew her, call'd her by her Name, and carried away both her and her Letters

This was in *December* 1672, and she was kept close Prisoner till the 16th of *January* following, when she was brought by Writ of *Habeas Corpus* to the *Old Bailey*, and ask'd whether or no she was the Woman who usually went by the Name of *Mary Carleton*, to which she answered, that she was the same, the Court then demanded the Reason of her returning so soon from the Transportation she had been Sentenced to Here she made a great many trifling Evasions, to gain Time, by which Means she gave the Bench two or three Days Trouble At last, when she found nothing else would do, she pleaded her Belly, but a Jury of Matrons being called, they brought her in not quick with Child So that on the last Day of the Sessions she received Sentence of Death, in the usual Form, with a great deal of Intrepidity

After Condemnation she had abundance of Visitants, some out of Curiosity, others to converse with her, learn her Sentiments of Futurity, and give her such Instructions as were needful Among the Latter, was a Gentleman to whom she gave a great many regular Responses; in which she discovered herself to be a *Roman Catholick*, profest her Sorrow for her past Life, and wish'd she had her Days to live over again, she also blam'd the Women who were her Jury for their Verdict, saying, that she believed they could not be sure of what they testify'd, and that they might have given her a little more Time

On the 22d of *January*, which was the Day of her Execution, she appeared rather more Gay and Brisk than ever before. When her Irons were taken off, (for she was shackled) she pinn'd the Picture of her Husband *Carleton* on her Sleeve, and in that manner carried it with her to *Tyburn* Seeing the Gentleman who had conversed with her, she said to him in French, *Mon Ami, le bon Dieu vous beniffe, My Friend, God bless you.* At hearing St. *Sepulchre's*

Bell toll, she made use of several Ejaculations One Mr *Crouch*, a Friend of hers, rode with her in the Cart, to whom she gave at the Gallows two Popish Books, called, *The Key of Paradise*, and *The Manual of Daily Devotion* At the Place of Execution she told the People, *That she had been a very vain Woman, and expected to be made a Precedent for Sin, that tho' the World had condemn'd her, she had much to say for herself; that she pray'd God to forgive her, as she did her Enemies*, and a little more to the same Effect After which, she was turn'd off, in the 38th Year of her Age, and in the same Month she was born in

Her Body was put into a Coffin, and decently buried in St *Martin's*-Church Yard, on which Occasion a merry Wag wrote this Distich

The *German Princess* here, against her Will,
Lies *Underneath*, and yet, Oh strange! *lies still*

Verses on the GERMAN PRINCESS.

I

WHAT might our Princess be esteemed,
If Women all are Wonders deem'd,
Since, from the same unfounded Cause,
Of Wonders, she the Wonder was?

II

A Woman's Arts, the learn'd pretend,
No Man alive can comprehend
Carleton in wiles, whenever try'd,
Exceeded all the Sex beside

III.

No Woman's Craving can be still'd,
So Solomon the wise Man held,
By any single Man he meant,
Not fifty Carleton *could content.*

IV.

In Vain her Qualities we trace,
O'er all the Sex she claims a Place;
For all the wondrous Sex combin'd
To call her Wonder of their Kind.

The LIFE of THOMAS WATERS.

THOMAS WATERS was born of very reputable Parents at *Henley upon Thames* in *Oxfordshire* His Father and Mother both dy'd when he was very young, and left him to the Care of an Uncle, who put him Apprentice to a Notary Publick behind the *Royal Exchange* But Business was what his Mind was not turn'd for, and the Servitude of seven Years appear'd to him a grievous Thing, whereupon he gave himself a Discharge without the Leave of his Master, before he had serv'd half the Term What little Money he had was soon expended, and he was expos'd to the wide World, without any visible Way of getting a Living in it These Circumstances soon inclin'd him to apply himself to the Highway, as the only Method he could see of supporting himself, there being this peculiar Advantage in the Life of an Highwayman, that he need not want a Livelihood so long as he has Occasion for it, if he will but be industrious in this Vocation He may rob till he is taken, then the County must maintain him till the Sessions or Assizes, and if he has the Luck to be hang'd, there's an End at once of all his Wants This was *Tom*'s Way of thinking, and his whole Life afterwards was a Series of Actions agreeable thereto

'Tis true he enter'd himself at first into the Earl of *Dover*'s Troop of Guards, but the Pay of this Service was not at all proportionab'e to his Expences, so that he was a Soldier rather to conceal himself than for the Profit of his Place The Highway was much more advantageous, and he soon entirely neglected his Duty, and deserted, for the sake of living more at Freedom upon the Stock of his good Fortune

His first Exploit was on about twenty or thirty Gypsies, whom he saw near *Bromley* in *Kent*, as they were coming one Morning early out of a Barn, where they had lain all Night He rid up to them, and commanded them to Stand, with threatening to shoot half a Score of them through the Head, if they did not obey his Command instantly These Strollers were pretty patient thus far, but when he order'd them to draw their Purse Strings, they set up an Outcry as terrible, as the *Holo loo* of the *Wild Irish*, when they lose a Cock or a Hen The being robb'd on the Highway was something new to them, who had all their Lives long been us'd to defraud every one they met with Some of them intreated his Pity and Compassion in a miserable Tone Others began to tell his Fortune, promising him abundance of Riches, and every Thing else they could think of that was desirable, and bestowing on him more Blessings than the *Pope* would have sold for all the Wealth they had to lose, tho' perhaps his Benedictions have not a Halfpenny more intrinsick Value in them theirs *Tom* was not so superstitious at this Time as to take Notice either of their Predictions or their Blessings, he wanted the ready Rhino, for the old Proverb, *That one Bird in Hand is worth two in the Bush*, was one of his daring Maxims A

Plague take you, says he, *for a Company of canting Whores and Roguet, I know what my Fortune is well enough I shall be hang'd, if I don't mend my Manners, and so 'tis possible some of you may be too* However, neither this Similitude in our Fortunes, nor all the Jargon you can muster, will do you any Service, so deliver, or I'll send half of you to your old Friend the Devil

When our Tribe of Jugglers found he was resolutely bent upon taking what they had, they began to empty their Pockets of a large Quantity of Silver Spoons, Tasters, Gold Rings, &c which they either stole, or persuaded some of the silly Country People to give them, for having their Fortunes told These Moveables, together with what Money they produc'd, amounted in all to Sixty Pounds By that Time *Tom* had got his Booty, several Country Fellows in the Neighbourhood, who were alarmed at the first Outcry, came running to see what was the Matter, with Clubs, Flails, and Pitchforks in their Hands *Tom* saw them coming, and rode to meet them, crying out, *That whilst one of the Gypsies was telling his Fortune, she pick'd his Pocket to a considerable Value, and would not return him any Thing again, for which Reason he had been lashing some of them with his Whip* You did very well, Master, said the Boors, *for there are not such Thieves in Hell as these Gypsies are* This turn'd the Rage of the Countrymen upon the Tawny Tribe, so that they drove them all out of Sight with their Sticks, and throwing Stones at them, while *Tom* rode laughing off, to think how he had impos'd on them

One Time he met with an Hostler on the Road from *Yorkshire* to *London*, who had once liked to have betray'd him at an Inn in *Doncaster* This fellow had sav'd together Forty Pounds, and was coming to Town in order to improve it, either by jockying, or keeping an Alehouse, the two Ways his Countrymen commonly apply themselves to *Tom* knew him again, and the Remembrance of such a gross Affront was enough to make him a little rough, however, he promis'd to spare his Life, tho' he did not deserve such a Favour, if he deliver'd what he had without Words The Hostler was conscious of what he had done, and so he surrender'd, but at the same Time begg'd that *Waters* would return him Part of it, because otherwise he was utterly undone But instead of hearkening his Request, *Tom* shot his Horse, and advis'd him to tramp down into *Yorkshire* again on Foot, and take to his old Vocation, at which he would soon find Ways and Means to make up his Loss If Travellers say true, our Adventurer might not be much mistaken, for the Honesty of an Hostler is a Proverb on the Road

Another of *Waters*'s Adventures was with Sir *Ralph Delaval*, at that Time Vice Admiral of the *English* Fleet, whom he very well The Meeting was on the Road between *Portsmouth* and *Petersfield* Well overtaken, Brother Tar, quoth Tom, pray what Religion

Religion are you of? Sir _Ralph_ ſtared at him, and ſeem'd aſtoniſh'd at his Impudence _What Buſineſs have you,_ ſays he, _to enquire about my Religion?_ Nay, Sir Ralph, Waters reply'd, _I had only a Mind to aſk a civil Queſtion, becauſe I have been inform'd that you Sailors have no Religion at all_ But ſince you are ſo cruſty upon this Head, give me Leave to aſk you another Thing _Pray do you apprehend you ſhall be robb'd before you come to the End of your Journey?_ Not at all, quoth the Admiral, _I have my Footman behind me_ Now there you and I are of two Opinions, ſays _Tom,_ for I believe you will be robb'd very quickly While he was ſpeaking his Piſtols were out, and Maſter and Man were threaten'd with Death, if they offer'd to ſtir Hand or Foot In this Condition the Knight thought it his beſt Way to ſave his Life by delivering his Money; which he did, to the Tune of ninety Guineas, beſides a Gold Watch _Tom_ thank'd him very heartily, bid him not be ſo poſitive another Time of eſcaping a Robbery, and ſo took his Leave to go in queſt of other Adventures, and ſpend the Profit of this.

On the ſame Day, between _Guildford_ and _Godalming,_ he met with the famous _Hermaphrodite,_ who liv'd formerly in _Lamb's Conduit-Fields,_ and afterwards at _Goſport_ A mere Frolick excited him to rob this Perſon, that he might have ſuch an Adventure to talk of afterwards He ſtopp'd her (for ſhe was dreſs'd in Woman's Apparel) with a Volley of Oaths and hard Names, calling her _Maſculo-Feminine_ Monſter; half Dog, half Bitch; and abundance to the ſame Purpoſe, telling her, _That he did not at all fear Proſecution._ For, as thou art neither Man nor Woman, ſays he, _'twill be impoſſible for thee to lodge a Bill againſt me_ He got from this Perſon about Twenty Pounds, which pleas'd him more than any other Booty he ever got in his Life, as he frequently us'd to declare.

For the Space of five Years and upwards he continued his Robberies, during which Time he committed almoſt an incredible Number But as few of theſe Fellows eſcape the Demerit of their Crimes, though they may elude it for ſome Time, ſo _Tom_ fell at laſt into the Hands of the Law His laſt Robbery was on _Hounſlow-Heath,_ a Place where almoſt all of them at one Time or another try their Fortunes He took from one _John Hoſey,_ a _Briſtol_ Carrier, above Fourteen Hundred Pounds in Money and Plate; ſome of which latter was found on him when he was apprehended For this Fact he receiv'd Sentence of Death, and being convey'd to _Tyburn_ in a Coach, on _Friday_ the ſeventeenth Day of _July,_ in the Year 1691, he was there executed, in the Twenty fixth Year of his Age, going off the Stage in a very reſolute Manner.

Before he was carry'd from _Newgate,_ he deliver'd a Paper to ſome of his Friends, the Subſtance of which was as follows

IT muſt be confeſs'd, that at firſt Thought a Perſon in my Condition ſeems to have the leaſt Cauſe to be merry of any one in the World I am juſt going to leave all my Companions, all my Pleaſures, and, in a Word, all that at preſent ſeems moſt engaging, either in a literal Senſe, To be no more, or to take a Leap in the Dark the Lord knows whither

If the firſt of theſe were certain, I ſhould have nothing more to do than to bid all my Friends, Good b' w' ye, and take the finiſhing Saving with the ſame Pleaſure that I go to ſleep at Night, or if, on the other Hand, I were ſure of taking a Supper this Evening, either in Paradiſe or Tartarus, and of keeping my Habitation there to Eternity, provided I were inform'd in which of theſe Places it was to be, I ſhould have no Occaſion to remain in this fluctuating, doubtful, State of Mind, but give Way either to Deſpair or Tranſport, according as my Entertainment would be pleaſing or dreadful

But none of theſe Things can be determin'd, and this very Uncertainty of Affairs is enough to make a Man thoughtful We are apt always to fear the worſt where two Extremes are before us, one of which cannot be avoided; eſpecially if we are conſcious of not having perform'd the Terms on which the beſt is promiſed

Yet, after all, why ſhould we fear the worſt, where every Thing is equally doubtful? Does the Sailor always think of drowning when he is at Sea? No, he is as cheerful, as though the Element he was upon expoſed him to no Danger Why then in Death only are our Fears ſo powerful? I can ſee no Reaſon for it, and therefore I will endeavour to think no more of it, but turn all my Thoughts to the Enjoyment of the few Moments I am to be here, in that Manner which has uſually afforded me the moſt Pleaſure, and as to Futurity —— be as eaſy as an old Shoe.

You ſee, Gentlemen, I have reaſon'd my ſelf quite out of Breath, and neither I nor you are the wiſer for all I have ſaid Things ſtill remain as they were, and will do ſo in ſpite of all our Enquiries I am going the Way of all Fleſh, and yet I know not a ſtep of the Road beyond Tyburn, _nor am I like to know till I come thither, and then I muſt take it as it runs I am to be hang'd, that's all you'll ever know of me, and all I would ever have you deſire to know When the Job's over, go home and be merry, and let_ Tom Waters _never more give you an uneaſy Thought_

The

The LIFE of Captain EVAN EVANS.

THE Title of Captain, was only assumed by this noted Criminal, who was born in *South-Wales*, and his Father, who kept an Inn at *Brecknock*, the chief Town in *Brecknockshire*, having given him good Education, put him Apprentice to an Attorney at Law, but his vicious Inclinations, together with the Opportunity he had of corresponding with some Gentlemen of the Road, (as such Rogues affected call themselves) who frequented his Father's House, he soon came to act in the same wicked Courses they follow'd, and in a little Time became the most noted Highwayman in these Parts, having made prodigious Booties of the *Welsh* Graziers and others

The Captain once happening to be under a Guard, who were conducting him to *Shrewsbury* Goal, with his Legs ty'd under the Belly of the Horse, one of his Attendants had got an excellent Fowling-Piece, which was then loaded, and the Prisoner espying a Pheasant pearching upon a Tree, with a deep Sigh express'd the Dexterity he had used formerly in killing such Game, so humbly requesting the Gun, that he might shoot at so fine a Mark, the ignorant Fellow readily complied with his Request But no sooner had the Captain got the Piece into his Hands, but he charged upon his Guard, and swore a whole Volley of Oaths, that he would fire upon them if they stir'd one Step farther Then retreating from them upon his little Poney to a convenient Distance, he commanded one of them that was best mounted, to come near him and alight, which being done, and the Bridle of the Horse on a Hedge, the poor Fellow was obliged to throw him his Pistols, and then was admitted to approach nearer the Captain, who, presenting one of them at his Head, obliged him to lose his Legs, and retire to his Companions this being also done, he soon left his little Scrub, mounted the fine Gelding, and rode off

The Captain then coming to *London*, the Country being too hot to hold him, upon his handsome Behaviour and Carriage, which was somewhat Extraordinary, as likewise his Person, he got to be Clerk to Sir *Edmund Andrews*, then Governor of *Guernsey*, and continued there in that Capacity for three or four Years, but Money not coming in fast enough in that honest Employment, to support his wicked Inclinations, he soon left that Service, return'd to *London*, and took a Lodging at the three Pleats Tongues in *Nicholas-Lane*, where he passed for a *Guernsey* Merchant, or a Captain of a Ship, and took his younger Brother *William Evans*, as a Servant to wait on him, giving him a Livery, under the Colour of which he committed several notorious Robberies on the Highways about *London*

One of his boldest and most daring Robberies, was committed on 'Squire *Harvey* of *Essex*, between *Bow-End* and *Bow*, in the Day-time, from whom he took a diamond Ring, and Money, to a considerable Value, as he was riding home in his Coach from the Cathedral Church of St *Paul's*, the late

Queen *Anne* having that Day honoured the City with Royal Presence

Sometime after that, meeting not far from *Hampstead*, with one *Gambol* a Writing-Master, living in *Exeter-street*, behind *Exeter-Exchange*, in the *Strand*, walking with his Wife, he made bold to command them to deliver what Money they had, which they very obstinately refusing, the Captain took what Money he found in their Pockets, which was about thirty or forty Shillings, and for their Presumption of not being obedient to the Doctrine of Non-resistance, obliged them upon pain of Death, to strip themselves stark naked, and then tying them close Belly to Belly, with their Clothes by them, (for he did not take them away) bound them to a Tree, and rode off But before he left them, he had chalk'd in great Letters just over their Heads on the Body of the Tree, that *Gambol* and his Wife were *Adamites*, which is a sort of Sect which teaches their Proselytes both Men and Women, to pray in their Meetings, and perform other divine Services, stark naked, which Posture they call the state of Innocency, and the Places they assemble in, Paradise

Another Time, Captain *Evans* and his Brother, with two other Persons, attacked a Member of Parliament on *Bagshot Heath*, who was travelling in a Coach and six Horses, with three other Gentlemen in it, and no less than four Gentlemen on Horseback well arm'd, besides three Footmen, a Coachman and Postillion This honourable Person and the rest had a Jealousy they were Highwaymen coming to approach them, and with their Arms, as two Blunderbusses, a Carbine, and Pistols loaded, stood upon the defensive Part, which occasion'd a Field Fight for above the Space of a Quarter of an Hour, several Charges and Discharges being made between them, but to no other Hurt done but the Horse shot dead on which the Captain's Brother *William*, alias his Footman, rode on

The Captain and the rest of his Accomplices being still desperate, the Parliament Man drew his Sword, and *Evans* his, and ventur'd to engage in a single Combat to save farther Bloodshed, but in this fairly trying their Skill, *Evans* disarming the other, generously return'd him his Sword again, accepting only of a good Horse to carry his Brooff, and what Money they pleas'd to collect among them, for which genteel Piece of Behaviour, that honourable Person afterwards endeavoured to save his Life

Not long after this Exploit, Captain *Evans* meeting by *Kilburn Warren*, one *Wargent* a Bricklayer, who for his vast Bulk might be term'd a Colos, his vast Bigness at first, put our Highwaymen into a Surprize, till approaching him nearer, he commanded him to stand, when narrowly searching his Head, and viewing his back Part, he found by his having no Horns and Tail, that he was no Ox, as he first supposed him to be at some Distance, he ventured to fearch his Breeches next, in which he found a fi'ver Watch, and feventeen or eighteen Shillings in Money, which converting to his own Ufe, he rode off in queft of another Prey

One remarkable Robbery he committed with his Brother, was this. As he was travelling *Portfmouth* Road in *Surrey*, meeting a parcel of Headboroughs or Conftables conducting about 30 poor Fellows they had preft to *Portfmouth* Garrifon, Captain *Evans* afked the Reafon of their being led fo as Captives ty'd with Cords. The Officers told him they were for the Service, and that they had ten Shillings for each Man they had fo impreft. He highly commended them for performing their Duty, and rode off But coming up with them again in a more convenient Place, he and his Brother attacked them with fo much Fury, that fetting all the Prifoners at Liberty, they robbed all the Headboroughs of every Penny they had, and then binding them Hand and Foot in a Field, they made the beft of their Way off

Another Time Captain *Evans* meeting on Finchly Common, one *Cornifh* an Informer, and common Affidavitman, he faluted him with the unwelcome Words *Stand and Deliver*, or otherwife he would fhoot him thro' the Head Poor *Cornifh* ftood trembling like an Afpin Leaf, and heartily begged and prayed that he would fave his Life, tho' he took all he had from him; but if he did rob him, he was certainly ruined and undone. Quoth *Evans*, *What a Plague are you a Spaniard, that you carry all your Riches about you?* No, Sir, (reply'd *Cornifh*) *I am a poor honeft Man, as all my Neighbours in St. Sepulchre's Parifh know, belonging to the Chamberlain.* Said *Evans* then, *What Inn do you live at? Perhaps you may do me a Piece of Service, by informing me of wealthy Paffengers lying at your Houfe; and if fo, I fhall generoufly reward you* Quoth *Cornifh*, *Sir, I belong to no Chamberlains of Inns, but to the Chamberlain of* London, *to whom I give an Information of Perfons fetting up in the City, that are not Freemen, of Apprentices not taking up their Freedom when out of their Times, and other Matters* which come under the Cognizance of that Officer Said *Evans*, D——n you and the Chamberlain of London *too, I thought all this while you had belonged to fome Inn, and fo might have given me Intelligence in my Way of Bufinefs, but as I find the contrary, I have no more Time to lofe with you Deliver, or you are a dead Man!* So fearching *Cornifh's* Pockets, in which he found but five Pence in Brafs Money, he was fo confounded mad, that he flung them over the Heath, and then feverely caning him, in the midft of twenty G——d——me's and more, he mounts his Horfe again, and rode off to feek a better Booty

Amongft the many Robberies which he committed, we fhall now proceed to that which prov'd moft fatal to him He having Intelligence of the *Chefter* Coach's coming with Paffengers to *London*, fent his Brother *William* the Night before to be at *Barnet*, and to be in *Baldock Lane* at a certain Time next Morning But the poor Lad happening to light of a Scotch Cheefmonger, who was travelling to *Edinburgh*, and he pretending to be going fome Part of the Way on his Mafter's Occafions, they muft needs lie together, and proceed on their Journey next Day. When they were got into *Baldock-Lane*, a Piftol, to the great Surprize of the *Scotchman* was fired over *Will's* Head by the Captain, that being the Signal propofed, they then foon commannded the *Scotchman* to lie by, and in Sight robbed all the Coaches Then in Thunderclaps of Oaths, the Captain riding up to the *Scotchman*, he robb'd him of feven Guineas, and two Watches, but by *Will's* Interceffion, who had lain with him all Night, return'd him his beft Watch, and three Guineas to bear his Charges in to his own Country; for which generous Action the fame *Scotchman* hang'd them both at the Affizes held at *Hartford*, in 1708, the Captain aged 29 Years, and his Brother *Will* 23 Several Perfons of Quality, and others of no fmall Diftinction, whom they robbed, would not appear againft them, but rather endeavoured to fave their forfeited Lives.

The LIFE of STEPHEN BUNCE.

THIS unfortunate Malefactor took to all manner or Disorderliness and Theft, even in his very Childhood, for playing very often with one of his Neighbour's Children, whose Father was a Charcoal-Man, he would privately fill his Pocket with that Commodity, and vend it for Codlings, to an old Apple-Woman that kept a little Bulk, or Stall, in *Newtners-Lane*, but, at length, being weary of this petty Thieving, he wanted once to have so many Codlings before-hand, and allow for them in the next Bargain, tho' he design'd to merchandize no more with her. The old Woman mistrusting his Intent, would not give him Credit Stephen was very angry to himself that she should scruple his Honesty, and resolved to be even with her. To this Intent, one could frosty Morning, bringing her a good Parcel of Charcoal, whose Hollowness in the Middle he had fill'd with Gun-Powder, and sealed it up with black-Wax, he had for it what the old Woman thought fit to give him in her Ware She presently thrust an Heap of it under her Kettle which was boiling, and being hard bitter Weather, she sat hovering over it with her Coats almost up to her Navel At length the Gunpowder concealed in the Charcoal taking Fire, up bounced the Kettle, out flew the Codlings and Water about her Ears, whilst in the midst of Fire and Smoak, the old Woman cry'd out, Fire and Murder in a hideous Manner, which brought a great Mob about her presently, to assist her in her great Distress However, it was the Goodness of her kind Stars, to let her come off in this imminent Danger, with the Damage only of scalding her a little, and burning a large Hole thro' her Smock, and the Trouble of picking up her Codlings again

After *Stephen Bunce* was grown to Years of Discretion, he soon undertook great Exploits For Instance, being one Day very genteely dress'd, and going into a Coffee-House, where an old Gentleman had then a Silver Tobacco Box, which opened in two separate Parts, lying the Table where this Sharper sate, after turning the News Papers over and over, whilst he was drinking a Dish of Tea, he paid for the same, and went privately away with the Lid of the Box, and had his Cypher presently engraved thereon, then returning back to the Coffee-House, and very courteously pulling off his Hat, quoth he, *Gentleman, have not I left the Bottom of my Tobacco Box behind me?* So rumbling among the News Papers, he there found it, crying, as he clapp'd the Lid on, *Oh, here it is!* At this, the Owner thereof claim'd it for his, but *Stephen* impudently shewing his Cypher on it, he challeng'd it as his Property, and kept it, which put all the Company in the Coffee Room into a great Consternation, about what should become of the other Gentlemen's Box

Another Time, *Stephen Bunce* being benighted near *Bromyard* in *Herefordshire*, and much straiten'd for want of Money, a Thought came into his Head to make up to the Parson's House, where knocking at the Door, he desired the Maid to tell her Master a Stranger fain would have the Honour of speaking with him, the Parson coming out, and enquiring his Business, he being a good Tongue Pad, told him he was a poor Student lately come from *Oxford*, in order to go home to his Friends, and being belated, he most humbly begged the Favour that he would give him Entertainment under his Roof, but for one Night. The Parson being taken with his modest Carriage and Behaviour, withal believing what he said to be true, he kindly received him, and courteously entertained him at Supper with him and his Family; which being over, the Maid was ordered to shew him his Bed Chamber

When he was bidding them all good Night, *Stephen* most humbly requested of the Parson, that he might give him a Sermon in the Morning, which was *Sunday*, and the Parson very thankfully accepted of his Proffer. So the Morning being come, the Levite equipp'd his young Student in his Gown and Cassock, and, because it was about a Mile to the Church, lent him his Horse too, whilst he, his Wife, and Children, would go the foot Path over the Fields When Sir Reverend came to Church, one was bowing, another scraping, to the Parson of the Parish, wondering to see him without his canonical Habit, on a Day when he should perform his sacred Function But he soon alleviated their Admiration, by telling his Parishoners, that a young Gentleman of the University of *Oxford*, would be there presently, that would preach to them an excellent Sermon Now Prayers were said, and the last Psalm sung, but none of the Gentleman came, so staying till Dinner Time, the Congregation was forc'd to go Home without a Sermon, as well as their Parson without his Gown and Horse, which *Stephen* to be sure had ordained for another Use than to ride to Church to preach in

Another Time this pickled Blade being upon his Patrole in *Essex*, as he was on one side of the Hedge, he espy'd at some Distance, a Gentleman very well mounted on a good Gelding, so getting into the Road, he lay all along on the Ground with his Ear close to it, till the Gentleman came up, who asking him the Reason of that Posture, *Stephen* held up his Hand to him, which was as much as to bid the Gentleman be silent, but the Gentleman being of a hasty Temper, quote he, *What a Pox are you a listening to?* Hereupon, *Stephen* sitting on his Breech, he said, *Oh, dear! Sir, I have often heard great Talk of the Fairies, but I could never have the Faith to believe there were any such Things in Nature, till now, in this very Place, I hear such a ravishing and melodious Harmony of all sorts of Musick, that it is enough to charm me to sit here, if possible, to all Eternity*

This Story made the Gentleman presently alight to hear this ravishing Musick too, so giving *Stephen* his Gelding to hold, and laying his Ear to the Ground,

quoth

quoth he, *I can hear nothing* Mr *Bunce* bid him turn t'other Ear, which he did, and then his Face being from him, *Stephen* presently mounted his Gelding, and galloped away with all Speed, till he came within Sight of *Rumford* Then alighting he let the Gelding loose, supposing that if the Owner us'd any Inn in that Town, he would make to it, as accordingly he did, and *Stephen* at his Heels The Hostler who was at the Door, cry'd out, *Master, Master, here's Mr* Bartlet*'s Horse come without him* By this Stratagem, *Stephen* having got the Owner's Name, quoth he to the Inn-keeper, Mr Bartlet *being engaged with some Gentlemen in Play at* Ingerstone, *he pray'd him to send him* 15 Guineas, *and to keep his Gelding in Pledge thereof till he came himself, which would be in the Evening. Ay, Ay,* (reply'd the Inn-keeper) 100 Guineas *if he wanted them* So giving *Stephen* 15 Guineas, he made the best of his Way to *London,* when in about four or five Hours, the Gentleman came puffing and blowing in his great Jack Boots to the Inn, and the Inn-keeper stepping up to him, said, *Oh, dear! Sir, what need you have sent your Gelding, and so put yourself to the Trouble of coming this sultry Weather on Foot, for the small Matter of fifteen Guineas, when you might have commanded ten Times as much without a Pledge?* Quoth the Gentleman, *Hath the Fellow then brought my Gelding hither? A Son of a Whore!* He was *pretty Honest in that ,* but *I find the Rogue hath made me pay fifteen Guineas for hearing his d——n'd Fairies Musick*

Stephen Bunce was a great Visiter of Billiard-Tables, and Cock-Pits, as leaving no Place unsearched wherein there might be any Thing worthy of a Bait. Tho' he had ever so fair an Opportunity of reclaiming, yet was he so profligate in all roguish Transactions, that he abhorr'd any Thing which looked virtuously Once turning Foot-Pad, he set upon a Butcher betwixt *Paddington* and *London,* who being also a lusty stout Fellow, he would not part with what he had without some Blows To cudgelling one another therefore they went ; but tho' the Butcher play'd his Part very well, yet after a very hard Battle, wherein they were both sadly battered and bruised, he was forced to cry for *Peccavi* Then the Victor searching him all over, from Head to Foot, and finding but a Groat in his Pocket, quoth he, *Is this all you have?* The Butcher reply'd, *Yes, and too much to lose* Said *Bunce* then, *Oh! d——n you for a Son of a Whore; if you'd fight at this rate but for a Groat, what a Plague would you have done if you'd had more Money?* So they both parted

But this small Sum not sufficing for one Night's Extravagancy, as *Stephen* was coming home by one Mr *Sandford's* Shop, a Goldsmith, in *Russel-Street, Covent Garden,* he saw the old Man telling a great Parcel of Money on the Compter, and presently stept to an *Oil Shop* for a Farthingworth of Salt, then coming back to the Goldsmith's House, and flinging it all in his Eyes, it caused such a terrible Smarting, that he did nothing but stamp and rub his Peepers, whilst Mr *Bunce* swept about fifty Pounds into his Hat, and went off with it

It is a true saying, *That what is got over the Devil's Back, is always spent under his Belly* , for *Stephen* going the same Night to a Bawdy-House in *Colson's Court* in *Drury Lane,* he let into a Strumpet's Company, call'd for her great Bulk, which was like a *Colossus,* the *Royal Sovereign,* who pick'd his Pocket of twenty Pounds, and vanish'd away with it in the Twinkling of an Eye This Disaster made him fret, fume, and Storm, like a mad Man, and vent more Oaths and Curses, than any losing Gamester at the Groom-Porter's But all his Exclamations

being to no Purpose, he began to vent his Passion next with a general Raillery against all the Female Sex, swearing that there was not a Woman on Earth but what was a Crocodile at Ten, a Whore at Fifteen, a Devil at Forty, and a Witch at Three score

Spending the Remainder of his Money in a Day or two for Vexation, Necessity (which is always the best Whetstone to sharpen the Edge of a Man's Invention) compell'd him to contrive Ways and Means for a fresh Supply , then going to one of his Comrades, whom the Sight of Line, Rope, or Halter, could not daunt with the Fear of coming home short at last, they went one Night, when the Shop was just shut up, to one Mr *Knowles,* a Woollen Draper, in *King-street, Westminster,* where, whilst *Stephen* was bargaining for three Quarters of a Yard of Cloth, to make him, as he said, a Pair of Breeches, his Companion had the Opportunity of taking the *Feather,* as Thieves call it, or Key, out of a Pin in the Window Then going away, but without buying any Thing, and the Man not thinking any otherwise than that his Shop was fast shut, as having secured all before, they came in the dead of the Night, which was very dark by reason the *Moon* did not shine, and taking the Pin out which had no Key, they had an easy Access into the Shop, from whence they took away as much Cloth as came to above eighty Pounds

When *Stephen Bunce* was but a Lad about 14 or 15 Years of Age, he was a Tapster at the *Nag's Head* Alehouse, in *Tuttle-street, Westminster,* where he had not been above a Month before he convey'd a silver Tankard privately to one of his thieving Companions, which held two Quarts At Night, when his Master came to lock up his Plate, the Tankard was missing, which put all the House into Disorder, Mr *Nick* and *Froth* swore like an Emperor, the Mistress scolded as bad as any Fish-Woman at *Billingsgate,* and the Servants had all a Grumbling in the Gizzard, but whom to blame none could tell However, after some small Inquisition about it, it was generally concluded, that some of the Guests had taken it away , whereupon it was agreed by a general Consent, that the next Morning the Maid and *Stephen Bunce* should go to *John Partridge,* the Astrologer and Translator of Shoes, in *Salisbury-street* in the *Strand,* who was cry'd up for his Dexterity in that Art, and thought to be little inferior to Friar *Bacon* For tho' he could not make a brazen Head to speak, yet he had such a brazen Face of his own as could outface the D——l himself for lying

Accordingly going to this Astrologer's House, and popping a Shilling into his Hand, he very formally set himself down in a Chair, laid half a Sheet of white Paper before him, and then taking a Pen in his Hand, he made thereon several Triangles about a Square, which he call'd the 12 Houses, and said, *Jupiter* being Lord of the Ascendent, signifies good Luck for the gaining of your Tankard again, did not *Mars* interpose with an Evil Aspect towards *Mercury* Now, *Venus* being on the fiery Trigon, denotes the Party that had it, lives either East or West, and *Saturn* being retrogado, and in the Cusp of *Taurus* it must needs be, that is it hid under Ground either North or South

Then he asked if there was not a red hair'd Man at the House that Day? They told him, No Nor a black hair'd Man neither? said he They still answered, No Nor was there not a brown hair'd Man there, with grey Cloaths, not very tall, nor very low? They told him, Yes Then he asked whether they knew him or not? They answered, No The *Sun* (saith he) being ill posited in the 11th House,

House, and *Mercury* in Trine with *Virgo*, it was without all Doubt a brown hair'd Man that had the Tankard Then *Stephen* asked, whether it might not be a Woman, as well as a Man? This put the Conjurer something to his Trumps, but when the Maid said that could not be, for there was never a strange Woman in the House all that Day, he grew bold, and said No, too, for *Venus* being weak in Reception with *Gemini*, and the *Moon* in her Detriment, both termine Planets, it plainly tells that it was a Man, and one betwixt 40 and 50 Years of Age Upon my Life, said the Maid, I saw the Party then that had it, he was a curl'd pated Fellow, with a sad coloured Sute, and about that Age, he drank in the Rose, but if ever I see the Rogue again, I'll teach him to steal Tankards, with a Murrain to him *Stephen* could not but laugh in his Sleeve at the Maid's Confidence, so taking their Leave of the *Astrologer*, they went homewards, with a deal of News to tell their Master, but by the way *Stephen* dropt the Maid, to go and take Share of his Booty, and never went any more to his Place.

We should not have rehearsed so much of this Astrological Cant, but to expose both the Professors of that pretended Science, and those who consult them, neither of whom can ever be sufficiently ridicul'd But to proceed

This notorious Fellow being once, by an Order of Court at the Sessions-House in the *Old Bailey*, sent for a Soldier into *Spain*, while he was there, in an Enemy's Country, he was so much upon the Duty of fasting, that the civil War which the Wind made in his empty Stomach, oblig'd him very often to look out sharp for some Employment for his Teeth So one Day *Stephen*, and a Comrade he had got, being as Hungry as two Tarpaulins kept upon short Allowance, but altogether Moneyless, they went loitering up and down the Market in *Barcelona*, to see what Fortune might offer in Relief of their Bellies, which had been mere Strangers to any Sustenance for above forty eight Hours At length they espy'd a Country Man going out of Town on an Ass They follow'd him at some Distance, and about half a Mile from the Town, there being a very high Hill, the Country Man alighted, and led the Ass up leisurely by a loose Bridle Hereupon *Stephen Bunce* going with his Comrade softly after them, he dexterously slipt the Bridle off the Ass's Head, and puts it on his own, then the other going off with the Booty, *Stephen* crawls upon all Fours, 'till he ascended on the Top of the Hill, when the Country-Man turning about to mount again, he was almost frighten'd out of his Wits, to see a Man bridled instead of an Ass *Stephen* perceiving his great Consternation, quoth he, *Dear Master, don't be troubled at this strange Alteration which you see in your Beast, for indeed was no Ass, as you suppos'd it, but a Man, real Flesh and Blood, as you may be, but you must know, that it being my Misfortune to commit a Sin against the Virgin Mary once, she resented it so heinously, that she trans-*

form'd me into the Likeness of an Ass for seven Years; and now the Time being expired, I assume my proper Shape again, and am at my own Disposal However, Sir, I return you many Thanks for your Goodness towards me, for since I have been in your Custody, you put me to no more Labour than what I, you, or any other Ass, might be able to bear

The Country Man was astonish'd at the Story; but nevertheless was glad that his Ass which was could not charge him with any ill Usage So parting, *Stephen* went to his Comrade, who had already chang'd the Ass again into Money, to put their Teeth in use once more, for fear they should forget the Way of eating, whilst the poor Country Man was oblig'd to return to Town again to buy him another Ass to carry him home When he came into the Ass-Market he espied his old Ass again, whereupon stepping up hastily to him, and whispering in his Ear, he said, *Oh! Pox on you, you have committed another Sin against the Virgin Mary, I find, but I shall take Care how I buy you again*

He was lawfully married at *Plymouth* to a Victualler's Daughter, who had so much Education bestow'd upon her, as to read, sew, and mark on a Sampler, after which she was kept at Home to sit in the Bar, and keep the Scores, which Post pleas'd the young Woman very well, because there was great Variety of Guests us'd the House, especially merry drunken Sailors, who, when they had Liberty to come ashore, would lustily booze it, and sing and dance all Weathers But *Stephen*, within a very little while after he was entertain'd into the State of Matrimony, catching the Gunner of the *Swiftsure* Man of War boarding his Wife, he quickly shew'd his Spouse a light Pair of Heels, and came up to *London*, where growing debauch to the highest Degree, he was very seldom out of the Powdering Tub, Nevertheless, the impairing of his Health after this profligate Way did not alienate his Inclination from keeping Company with such Cattle, who ruin both Body and Soul, and for the Maintenance of lewd Woman, he cared not what Hazards he underwent, as he confess'd when under Sentence of Death At last, as common Whores were his Ruin, he would, but it was then too late, exclaim against 'em, and say, a Strumpet was the Highway to the Devil, and he that look upon her with Desire began his Voyage to inevitable Destruction, he that stay'd to talk with her mended his Pace, and he who enjoy'd her was at his Journey's End

He had been an old Offender, and was such a debauch'd Fellow in his Conversation, that he could invent no other Method of gracing his Discourse, and making it taking, but by a complaisant Rehearsal of his own, and other Mens Uncleannesses; in fine, he could not find an Hours Talk, without being beholden for it to a common Whore, but his Wickedness made its End at *Tyburn*, in 1707, with *Jack Hall* and *Dick Low*, whose Lives immediately follow.

The LIFE _of_ DICK LOW.

THIS Perfon took to thieving in his Minority, and was become very expert in it at the Age when others ufually begin. One time when he was about 11 or 12 Years old, creeping privately in an Evening behind a Goldfmith's Compter in _Cheapfide_, the Goldfmith comes from a back Room, and goes himfelf behind the Compter; infomuch that _Dick Low_ had no Opportunity of going out invifible, whereupon he cries, _Whoop, Whoop_ At this the Goldfmith cry'd, _Hey, hey, is this a Place to play at Whooper's Hide? Get you gone, you young Rogue, and play in the Streets_, But _Dick_ yet lying ftill, cry'd again, _Whoop, Whoop_, which made the Goldfmith in a great Paffion cry, _Get you gone, Sirrah, or I'll Whoop you with a good Cane, if you want to play here_ Whereupon _Dick_ went away with a Bag of fifty Pound, which the Goldfmith mifs'd next Day.

But as he grew up in Years, his Statue made him paft thofe Exercifes which they call the Morning, Noon, or Night _Sneak_, which is privately fneaking into Houfes at any of thofe Times, and carrying off what next comes to Hand; for all's Fifh that comes to Net with them, who are term'd Saint _Peter_'s Children, as having every Finger a Fifh-hook. He went alfo upon other Lays, fuch as taking _Lobs_ from behind _Ratlers_, that is to fay, Trunks or Boxes from behind Coaches; and upon the _Mill_, which is breaking open Houfes in the Night; for which Purpofe they have their Tinder-Boxes, Matches, Flints, Steels, Dark-Lanthorns, Bags, Cords, Betties, and Chiffels to wrench This was then the manner, but at prefent they have a new Way, of uiing a large turning a Gimblet or Augar, with which boring Holes thro' a wooden Window, they prefently with a Knife cut out a Hole big enough to put in their Hand to unbolt it, whereby an honeft Man is foon undone by thefe fly Rafcals, who call themfelves _Prigs_, which, in their canting Language, denotes a Thief As for the Religion of thefe People, they term themfelves but half Chriftians, becaufe of the two principal Commandments they keep but one, which is to love God, but in no Cafe their Neighbour, from whom it is their Livelihood to fteal Thefe Thieves have a quick Eye to take hold on all Advantages of obtaining an unlawful Prize, and Highwaymen have commonly their Spies in all Fairs, Markets, and Inns, who view all that go and come, and learn what Money they carry, how much, where they leave it, and in what Hands, whereby they for whom they fpy may be mafters of it

When _Richard Low_ was a Foot Soldier in _Flanders_, he and his Comrade being one Day very peckifh, and meeting with a Boor in _Ghent_, loaded with Capons, Partridges, and Hens, they ftruck up a Bargain with him for half of them, which _Dick_'s Comrade carried off, whilft he was fumbling and pulling out all his Things in his Pockets to find out his Money. His Coin amounting to nothing anfwerable to the Poultry he had bought, he order'd the Boor to follow him, 'till at length he brought him into a Cloyfter of _Capuchine Fryars_, when fome of them were confeffing Folks, then he told the Boor, that the Provifion he had bought of him was for this Houfe, and a certain Father, who was there confeffing, was the Superior, to whom he would go, and acquaint his Reverence that he muft pay him Accordingly going up the Confeffor, and privately putting Sixpence in his Hand, he whifper'd him in his Ear, faying, _Reverend Father, this honeft Country Man here is a particular Acquaintance of mine, who's come hither to be confefs'd, being fix Miles off, and Bufinefs requiring him Home this Evening, I befeech you to be fo kind as to confefs him as foon as you can_

The good Father, oblig'd by the Alms given aforehand, promis'd him, that when he had ended the Penitent's Confeffion whom he had at his feet, he fhould difpatch him prefently; and at the fame Time calling to the Boor, quoth, _Dick, Go in hence and the Father will perform what you want prefently_

So _Dick_ going after his Comrade, when the afore faid Penitent had made an End of his _Canterbury_ Story to the Prieft, the fpiritual Juggler called the Clown to him, who ftood bolt upright, looking very wifhfully on the Confeffor, to fee if he put his Hand in his Pocket to pay him The Father Confeffor look'd as wifhfully on the Boor, to fee him ftand with fo little Devotion to be confefs, but in puting the Caufe thereof to his Simplicity, he bid him kneel, which the Clown did with fome Reluctancy, as thinking it to be an infulting Ceremony for a Man to kneel to receive his own Money However, obeying the Order with grumbling, the Prieft bids him make the Sign of the Crofs, at which the Boor being out of Patience, believing the Confeffor to be out of his Wits, he chatter'd, and rav'd, and fwore like a mad Man, which made the Confeffor imagine the Boor was poffefs'd with the Devil Upon this he put his hempen Girdle about the poor Fellow's Neck, and making the Sign of the Crofs over his Head, began to conjure him by faying fome devout Prayers This made the Man fo mad indeed, that he tore off the Confeffor's Habiliments, and throwing him down on the Ground, demanded loudly his Money for the Poultry

This ruftical Ufage made the Father fuppofe he had the Devil himfelf to deal with, fo that with a weak and affrighted Voice, he began to commend himfelf to all the Saints in the Almanack for their Affiftance, and at the Clamour and Noife that was betwixt him and the Prieft, while the Convent of Friars came out in Proceffion with Croffes and allow'd Lights in their Hands, and cafting holy Water about on every Side, as believing there was a Legion of Devils in their Chapel But the Boor ftill crying out for his Money for the Poultry, the Prior made a ftrict Enquiry into the Matter, and found

...d some Knave had impos'd on the Fellow, who
... no other Satisfaction, than that of the Con-
...ts cursing him that had cheated the Boor, by
..., Book, and Candle

In a short Time *Dick* came home again, and
...re being one Mr *Pennell*, an Apothecary, liv-
...in *Drury Lane*, it was his Misfortune to have
...Wife who kept Company with one *Davis* a Gla-
...r, but bad Circumstances obliging him to fly
...Secretly to *Thornbury* in *Gloucestershire*, his
...Adore was in great Want of another Gallant How-
...er, for being naturally prone to Liberality, and al-
...ys constantly rewarding Kindnesses of this Na-
...re, it was not long 'ere a particular Acquaintance
...her's undertook to supply her with a new Lover,
...ich was *Dick*

As soon as he was introduced into Company of
...Apothecary's Wife, she took a huge Fancy to
...m, for he behaved himself so pleasantly, and his
...resses were so agreeable, that his Mistress esteem-
...herself the happiest Woman in the World, in the
...joyment of a Person so facetious, and accomplish-
...with all the Mysteries of Love Whenever he
...me to her House, which was always when her
...sband was from Home, she entertained him with
...h unreserved Freeness, that she concealed no-
...ing from her Spark, that might either please his
...ncy or Curiosity. But one Day opening a Chest
...Drawers to take out somewhat, *Dick* espy'd a
...ple of Bags of Money, at which his Mouth in-
...ntly water'd, for altho' his Mistress told him,
...at as long as one Penny was in them, his Pockets
...uld never be unfurnished, yet he wanted to be
...ster of them presently, and indeed it was not
...ng before he had them at his Command, for Bu-
...ness requiring the Apothecary in the Country for
...at a Week, *Dick* then lay in his House at Rack
...d Manger, and having two other Rogues like
...mself at a great Supper prepared for them there,
...ey began about 12 of the Clock at Night, to de-
...are their Intention with Sword and Pistol, saying,
...at whoever presumed to speak but one Word,
...ffered present Death

To Work they now went, gagging and tying
...rst the Procurer In the mean Time the Apothe-
...ry's Wife seeing how her Friend was served, she
...ell on her Knees, and heartily beseeched them not
...o use her so Quoth *Dick*, No, no, Madam, we'll
...nly tie your Hands, lest you should ungag that serious,
...nd now silent Bawd there

After she was secured, they went down into the
...itchen, and gagg'd and ty'd the Maid and Ap-
...rentice, then rifling the House, they carry'd away
...wo hundred and fifty Pounds and some Plate, to a
...considerable Value But *Dick* thinking it unman-
...nerly to go away without saying any Thing, he
...went to his late beloved Mistress, and giving her a
Judas Kiss, Quoth he, *Dear Madam, farewell,
and when I am gone, say, I've done more than ever
your Husband did, for I've bound you to be constant
now*

After this, *Dick Low* going one Morning into
...he *Rose* and *Crown* Alehouse, kept by one Mr
Nayland, in *Clare-Court*, in *Drury-Lane*, he desired
...a private Room, by Reason he had some Company

coming to him, about some Business A private
Room was shew'd him, and a double Pot of Drink
brought with a silver Cup to drink out of; and being alone, the Man of the House sate with him chatting, till they were both weary At last, *Nayland*
was wanted by other Company, and whilst he was
gone out, *Dick* having with some soft Wax, fasten'd
the Bottom of the Cup under the Board of the Table, which was covered with a Carpet hanging somewhat down all round it, he came to the Bar, saying, *I see my Company will not come, therefore I'll
stay no longer* Then paying his Reckoning, and the
Man of the House going into the Room to bring a-
way the Pot and the Cup (which first he could find,
but not the other high nor low) he charges *Dick*,
who had not yet received his Change, with downright Theft The one curs'd and swore he had it
not, and the other swore and curs'd he had it, so
that between them both, they were ready to swear
the House down about their Ears

Dick was then searched, and tho' nothing was
found about him, yet *Nayland* swore still he must
have the Cup, or else know of the going of it;
therefore he should pay for the Loss But *Dick*
standing as stifly upon his Reputation, which was
never worth any Thing, he insisted he had it not,
nor knew any Thing of its being gone, whereupon a Constable being fetch'd, he was carry'd before Justice *Negus*, where the Loser making his
Complaint as truly the Matter was, and *Dick Low*
alledging his Innocency, the Magistrate was in a
Quandary how to do Justice For, quoth he to the
Complainant, *here's a Cup lost, and the Prisoner doth
not deny but he had it, but then it was missed whilst
he was in the House, and he searched without finding any Thing about him, besides, he had no Body
with him, therefore it could not be convey'd away
by Confederacy; so unless you'll lay point blank Felony to his Charge, I can do no otherwise than discharge him.*

Then the Victualler, who was an *Irishman*, reply'd, *Tiss fery true, Shir, what you shay, but by
Shalvashnon, rader dan he should go without hanging, I will shwear twenty Felonies against him,
or any Ting elsh what your Worship pleash to command me, for I love to oblige any shivel Shentle-
man as you be. Indeed*, said the Justice, *you will
not oblige me in hanging a Man wrongfully* In a
Word, there being no plain Proof to justify that
Dick Low either had the Cup, or convey'd it a-
way to another, and it being plain that he was
charg'd in Custody before ever he went out of the
House, he came off with flying Colours, and soon
sent another of his Clan to fetch off the Cup, by
going to drink in the same Room and removing it
from under the Table into his Breeches without
any Suspicion, paying for his Liquor, and fairly
returning that Cup that was brought to him

This Fellow, tho' he was not above 25 Years of
Age, when he was hang'd at *Tyburn*, with *Jack
Hall* and *Stephen Bunce*, in 1707, had reigned long
in his Villany; and the fortunate Success which he
had had in his manifold Sins, made him only repent that he had practis'd them no sooner

The LIFE *of* JACK HALL.

THIS most notorious Villain, was bred a Thief from his Mother's Womb; and there is no sort of Theft, but what he was expert in, as breaking open Houses, going on the Foot Pad, Shop-lifting, or pilfering any small Matter that lies in the Way, nay, if it was but Mops and Pails, the *Drag*, which is, having a Hook fastened to the End of a Stick, with which they drag any Thing out of a Shop Window in a dark Evening, and *filing a Cly*, which is picking Pockets of Watches, Money, Books, or Handkerchiefs. To this End he used to haunt Churches, Fairs, Markets, publick Assemblies Shows, and be very busy about the Play-house. And he that performs this last Part of Thieving, commonly gives what he takes to another, that in Case he should be found with his Hand in any Man's Pocket, he might prove his Innocency, by having nothing about him, but what he can justify to be his own.

Jack Hall was as dextrous in picking a Pocket, as ever he was in sweeping a Chimney; for on a Market Day once in *Smithfield*, a Grasier having received some Money for his Cattle, and put it into his Coat Pocket in a Bag, this nimble Spark, to whose Fingers any Thing stuck like Birdlime, observing the same, he soon became Master of it, and brought it to his Comrades that were drinking at an Alehouse hard by, and to shew his farther Dexterity in *filing a Cly*, emptying the Bag, he untruss'd a Point in it, and finding out the Man, who was still in the Market selling off the rest of his Cattle, he put it into his Pocket again. A little after which, a Person coming to the Farmer for some Money, he went with him to his Inn, and pulling out his Bag, and putting therein his Hand for Money to pay the Creditor, he eagerly pluck'd it out in a sad stinking Pickle, swearing, That he had thirty Pounds in his Bag but just now, but, woundkins, it was now turned to a T——d.

Jack Hall having a Design once to rob a great Merchant in the City of *London*, he went oftentimes hankering about his House, but could never effect it, whereupon he bethought himself of this Stratagem. He was to be put into a Pack done up like a Bale, and by the Contrivance of his Comrade, who was very well apparell'd, he was to be laid into this Merchant's House in the Evening, as so much Silk, which he was to see next Morning, and to buy off his Hands, in Case they agreed.

Accordingly this Bale full of Iniquity, wedg'd inwardly on all Sides with coarse Cloth and Fustian, was laid up in the Warehouse. Night being come, and the Apprentices weary, two of them, whilst their Master was at Supper, went to rest themselves, and by Accident lay along on this Bale, which was plac'd by some others, insomuch that the extreme Anguish of their Weight being very heavy upon *Jack Hall*, he could scarce fetch his Breath. Upon this, he drew out a sharp Knife, and making a great Hole in

the Fillet of the Bale, he also made a deep Wound in the Buttocks of him that lay most upon it, which made him rise, and roar out, his Fellow Apprentice had killed him. Running out to his Master in the Agony, his Fellow-Apprentice followed him, and was innocently secur'd, till a farther Examination of the Matter. In the mean while *Jack Hall* made his Escape out of a Window, with only taking two Pieces of Velvet along with him.

At the same Time the Merchant seeing his Apprentice in a very bloody Condition, and fearing, if the Bale of Silk he lay on should be spoilt with the Blood, he must be forced to pay whatever Price was required, he ran presently into the Warehouse to prevent any Damage coming to it, where finding it mightily shrunk in its Bulk, it rais'd some Suspicion of Roguery in him, for opening it, he found therein nothing of Value, Then searching about his Warehouse and missing the two Pieces of Velvet, he plainly perceived some Rogue had been pack'd up in the Bale, with an Intent to rob his House when he and his Family were in Bed, whereupon, the accus'd Apprentice was set at Liberty, and a Surgeon fetched for the wounded one, who cost his Master above five Pounds before he was well.

He was also very good for the *Lob*, which is the Going with a Consort into any Shop to change a *Pistole* or *Guinea*, and having about half of his Change, cries the Consort, *What need you to change? I have Silver enough to defray our Charges where we are going.* Upon this the other throws the Money back again into the Money Box; but with such Dexterity, that he has one of the Pieces, whether Shilling or Half Crown, sticking in the Palm of his Hand, which he carries clean off, without any Suspicion of Fraud. Again, he was very expert at the *Whalebone-Lay* which is, having a thin Piece of Whalebone daubed at the End with Birdlime, with which, going into a Shop with a Pretence to buy something, they make the Shop-keeper, by wanting this and that Thing, to turn his Back often, and then take the Opportunity of putting the Whalebone, so daubed with Birdlime, into the Teil of the Counter, which brings up any single Piece of Money that sticks to it. After which, to give no Mistrust, they buy some small Matter, and pay the Man with a Pig of his own Sow.

The Year before *Jack Hall*, the Chimney-Sweeper, was hang'd, having committed Sacriledge at *Bristol*, in robbing *Ratcliff Church* in that City, he made the best of his Way for *London*, where after a little While, his Extravagancies reducing him to the want of Money again, in order to recruit his Pockets, he went with some of his wicked Associates, upon the *Running-Smobble*, which is this. One of them goes into a Shop, and pretending to be drunk, after some troublesome Behaviour, he puts the Candles out, and taking away whatever comes first to Hand, he runs off, whilst another flings Handfuls of Dirt and Nastiness

Feb

s into the Mouth and Face of the Perfon that es out ftop Thief, which putting him or her into udden Surprize, it gives them an Opportunity of ing off without apprehending

One Time *Jack Hall* being dreft like a Gentle n, (tho' you muft fuppofe, like *Æfop's* Crow, he s decked in other People's Plumes) and fitting on Bench in the *Mall* in St *James's Park*, a Life-uard Man, and one Mr *Knight* an Attorney, liv-g in *Shandois Street*, near *Covent Garden*, meeting e another juft by the Place where *Jack* fate, after ne Complements were paffed between them, the wyer invited the Life-Guard Man, whom he had t feen a long Time before, to dine with him at a Houfe the next Day, for he fhould be very wel-me, and any Friend that he fhould bring along with m The Life-Guard Man promis'd he would be re to wait upon him, but afking his Friend whe-er he liv'd in the fame Place ftill, Yes, yes, (quoth e Lawyer) *I ftill live within three Doors of the athers Alehoufe in Shandois-ftreet* They then rted, and now *Jack Hall's* Wits were on the Ten-rs for making fome Advantage by this Invitation hich he had heard gvien. So the next Day, above Hour before the Time, when hungry Mortals het their Knives on Thefholds, and the Soles of hoes, he was lurking thereabouts, and at laft, fet-ng his Eyes on the Life Guard Man, whom he hew again, he was no fooner entred into his Friend's oufe, but *Jack* was at his Heels, and entred alfo th him, with as much Confidence as if he had been Acquaintance of the Lawyer. There were above lf a Score Gentlemen and Gentlewomen, among hom he fate down, and foon after, Dinner being t on the Table, with great Variety of Dainties, e ftrange Gentleman, *Jack Hall*, did eat as hearti-y, and talk as boldly, as any there

All the while the Life-Guard Man took him to e one of the Inviter's Acquaintance, and the Invi-er fuppos'd him to be the Life-Guard Man's Friend, ut in the End, he prov'd to be neither of their riends, efpecially the Lawyer's, for waiting his Op-ortunity, he went to the Side Board, which ftood n a convenient Place, and putting a dozen of filver poons and as many filver Forks, into his Pockets, he walk'd off *incognito* The Life-Guard Man, foon after, mifs'd *Jack*, and the Lawyer mifs'd his Friend's riend, as he thought him, but it was not much onger 'ere the Spoons and Forks were miffing, and altho' ftrict Search was made for them, yet were they not found, none but the Friend, or he that was thought fo on both Sides, being miffing, the Law-yer afked the Life Guard Man for him, but the Life-Guard Man telling the Lawyer he was none of his Friend or Acquaintance, it was concluded, *nemine contradicente*, that the abfent Perfon was the Rogue that had converted the Lawyer's Plate to his own Ufe

Another Time, *Jack Hall* being very well drefs'd, and pretending to be a Country Gentleman, he took Lodgings at the Houfe of one *Dogget*, a Quaker, and Button-feller, living in *Burleigh-ftreet*, in the *Strand*, where he behaved himfelf very foberly till an Opportunity offered to out-wit the Quaker, who thought it no harm to out-wit every Body For the Key of his Chamber being left one Day in the Door, he took the Impreffion of it in Clay, and had another made by it, a little after which, old *Dog-get* and his Wife going to their Country-Houfe, for two or three Days, leaving none at Home, but a wanton Kinfwoman, an Apprentice, and Maid, *Jack* in the mean Time had the Conveniency of entring their Bed-Chamber, when all in the Houfe were in Bed, and opening a Trunk he took out above eighty

65

Pounds in Money and Plate, and opening the Street Door went off with it But when the old Folks came Home again, and found what had happen'd, the Houfe was all in an Uproar; there was power-ful *Holding forth* by the Man, who ftorm'd and rav'd, and fell a kicking the Trunk about like a Foot Ball, which he did with a great deal more Eafe than he could when it was full.

After this Exploit, *Jack Hall*, *Stephen Bunce*, and *Dick Low*, going upon an Enterprize at *Hack-ney*, about 12 of the Clock at Night, they, by the help of their Betties and fhort Crows, made a forci-ble Entry into the Houfe of one *Clare*, a Baker, whofe Journeyman being ty'd Neck and Heels they threw him into the Kneading-Trough, and the Ap-prentice with him. *Jack Hall* ftood Centry over them, and with a great old rufty Back Sword, which he found in the Kitchen, and fwearing with a great Grace, that their Heads both went off as round as a Hoop, if they offered to ftir or budge In the mean Time *Dick Low* and *Stephen Bunce*, went up to Mr *Clare's* Room, whom they found in Bed with his Wife, and ty'd and gagg'd the old Folks, without any Confideration of their Age, which had left them but few Teeth, to barricade their Gums from the Injury they might receive from thofe ugly Inftruments that ftretched their Mouths afunder

Finding not fo much as they expected, the old Man they ungagged again, to bring to a Confeffion where he hoarded his Money; but extorting nothing out of him, *Jack Hall* being then come up to them, for fear they fhould fink upon him, which is an ufual Thing among Thieves, to cheat one an-other, he took up in his Arms the old Man's Grand-Daughter, about fix Years old, lying in a Trundle-Bed by him, and faid, *Damn me, if I won't bake the Child prefently in a Pye, and eat it, if the old Rogue will not be civil* Thefe fearing Words made Mr *Clare* beg'd heartily that they fhould not hurt the Child, and he would difcover what he had, fo fetching, by his Order, a little Iron-bound Cheft from under the Bed, and unlocking it, they took what was in it, which was about eighty Pounds, then obfcuring their dark Lanthorns, they bid the Baker Good Night, and commanded him to re-turn them Thanks that they fpared his Ears, which is againft the Law for any of their Occupation to wear.

Another Time *Jack Hall* going to one Mr *Afpin*, a Robe-maker, living in *Portugal-ftreet*, by *Lincolns Inn* Back-Gate, he pretended that he had Occafion for a Gown for his Brother, who was a Parfon in the Country, but he would have a very good one, though it coft him more Money *I can furnifh you with all Sorts and Sizes*, faid Mr *Af-pin*, and thereupon fetch'd feveral, and fhew'd him *Jack* turn'd many of them over, but ftill defired to fee better At length one was brought which he feem'd to like, but faid he to the Robe-maker, *I doubt it is too fhort?* T'other faid he did not doubt *but it was long enough in all Confcience*, and there-upon he was for trying upon *Jack*, who faid, *Alas! there will be no certain Meafure by me, for no Bro-ther is taller than I am by the Head and Shoulders, but as he is a Man about your Pitch, I defire the Favour of you to put it upon yourfelf, and then I fhall guefs the better whether it is long enough or no*

Mr *Afpin*, to fatisfy his Cuftomer, did fo, but as he was putting it on, *Jack* took up a Barrifter's Gown, and fhew'd him a fair Pair of Heels Mr *Afpin*, without putting off the Gown, purfu'd him, in the mean Time two of his Companions, who lefd Perdue, acted their Parts, for *Stephen Bunce* went

3 T   into

into the Shop, and taking the next Parcel of Goods which came to Hand, he marched off And *Dick Low*, fearing that if the Shop-keeper kept his Pace he might overtake *Jack Hall*, having placed himself in the Way on Purpose, catches hold on Mr. *Aspin*, and says, *O! dear, Doctor Cross, who thought of seeing you? I am glad I have met with you with all my Heart But pray, Sir, what makes you run in this distracted Manner about the Streets? Pish*, quoth Mr *Aspin*, *let me go, I am no Parson, you are mistaken in the Man, for I am running after a Rogue that has robb'd me.* Then *Dick Low* reply'd, but still holding him, *I beg your Pardon, Sir, for my Mistake, for you are as like my Friend Doctor Cross, as ever I saw two Men in my Life like one another*

Letting him go at last, *Jack* before now was turn'd the Corner of a Street or two, and was quite out of Sight By this Time also several of the Neighbours being gathered together, they were in an Admiration to see old *Aspin* in a canonical Habit, some saying, *Surely he was not going to christen his own Child himself, which is Maid Betty lay in with!*

whilst others perswaded him to go home, and ... off the Gown, and then make an Enquiry after ... Thief, since he was at present got clear away ... *Aspin* took their Advice, but when he came to ... Shop, he found a second Loss, which made ... more angry than before, and swear, that the Fel... that met him, might well call him Doctor C... for d——n him if he had not all the Crosses in ... World come upon him at once

This most notorious Malefactor though it no ... justice to rob every Body; and all his Vices, w... ever Deformity the Eye of the World apprehe... to be in them, his unaccountable Wickedness look... upon as no less excellent than the most absolu... all Virtues But his Villainy being so unparelle... that Justice was obliged to unsheath her Swor... gainst him, a shameful Catastrope put an End to h... wicked Crimes in the Year 1707, when he deserv... ly suffered Death at *Tyburn*, with his Compan... *Low* and *Bunce*, as before-mentioned.

The LIFE *of* DICK HUGHES.

THIS great Villian, *Richard Hughes*, was the Son of a very good Yeoman, living at *Bettus* in *Denbighshire*, in *North-Wales*, where he was born, and followed Husbandry, but would now and then be pilfering in his very Minority, as he found Opportunity When he first came up to *London*, in his Way, Money being short, his Necessity compell'd him to steal a Pair of Tongs at *Pershore* in *Worcestershire*, for which he was sent to *Worcester* Goal; and at the Assizes held there, the Matter of Fact being plainly proved against him, and the Judge asking the poor *Welshman* what he had to say in his Defence, he said, *Why, coud hur Lord Shudge, hur has nothing to say for hurself, but that hur found dam. Found them!* quoth his Lordship again, *Where did you find them?* *Taffy* reply'd, *Why truly, hur found dem in the Chimney Corner* Whereupon the Judge telling him, that the Tongs could not be lost there, because that was the proper Place they should be in; and finding the Fellow to be Simple, he directed the Jury to bring him in guilty only of *petty Larceny*, and accordingly giving in their Verdict Guilty to the Value of ten Pence, he came off with crying Carrots and Turnips, a Term which Rogues use for whipping at the Cart's Arse

After this Introduction to farther Villany, *Dick Hughes* coming up to *London*, he soon became acquainted with the most celebrated Villains in this famous Metropolis, especially with one *Thomas Lawson*, alias *Browning*, a Tripe Man, who was hang'd at *Tyburn* on *Tuesday* the 27th of *May*, 1712, for Felony and Burglary, in robbing the House of one Mr *Hunt*, at *Hackney* In a very short 'Time he became noted for his several Robberies, but at last breaking open a Victualling House at *Lambeth*, and taking from thence only the Value of three

Shillings, because he could find no more, he was ... and condemn'd for that Fact, at the Assizes ne... *Kingston upon Thames*, but was then repriev'c, a... afterwards pleaded his Pardon at the same P... Now being again at Liberty, instead of becoming... new Man, he became rather worse than before, ... breaking open and robbing several Houses at *Tu...ham Cross*, *Harrow on the Hill*, a Gentlewoman... House at *Hackney*, a Gentleman's at *Hammersmi...* a Minister's near *Kingston upon Thames*, a Tob... conist's House in *Red Cross Street*, and a House ... *Hounslow-Heath*

This Fellow was very intimate with one *Jac... Waldron*, who being a young Man, but an ol... Rogue, 'twill be very material to take Notice, tha... he was condemned to be hang'd when he was scar... in the Teens, for picking a Gentleman's Pocket, bu... receiving Mercy, in respect to his tender Age, h... travelled to *Ireland*, where, at *Dublin*, he went ... on the Glaze, which is robbing Goldsmiths Sho... Glasses on their Stalls by cutting them, as an Op... portunity offers, with Glaziers Diamond, waiting fo... a Coach coming by, and breaking them or else wi... the Hand, which sometimes, is not heard, thro' th... Noise which is made by the Rattling of the said Coach

This Trade *Waldron* followed in that Countr... till he was pretty well noted and punish'd ther... then coming to *London* again, such was his unac... countable Impudence and Insolence, that he wou... in a manner rob People before their Faces, and ha... done more Damage to the Goldsmiths, than any... six Rogues that went upon the like Villany Bu... after having been about 18 Times in *Newgate*, be... sides *New Prison*, and all the *Bridewells* in Town... often whipt at the Cart's Arse, burnt in the Hand... and once in the Face, he became very well known... whenever he came to the Sessions-House in the Old Baile...

y, as an old Offender. Whereupon, the Right
hipful Sir *Peter King*, then Recorder of *Lon-*
was pleas'd to tell him, *That if ever he came*
but for an Egg, he would hang him for the
But this notorious Villain yet taking no
ning, and coming before Sir *Peter* again, his
hip was as good as his Word, for tho' the
which he laſt committed was but ſimple Felony,
he caſt him for his Life, which he juſtly ſer-
d at *Tyburn* in 1711, aged but nineteen Years
ow to *Dick Hughes* again. When he firſt came
ondon, he lit on a ſad Miſchance, for happening
Night into a Lumber Houſe, not far from
nſgate, he had not been long there, before
Joe Haynes, the Commedian, and a broken Of-
, came raking thither too, without a Farthing
ither of their Pockets. *Joe Haynes* having ſav'd
reat deal of Duſt, which he got off an old rotten
, and wrapt it up nicely in a clean Sheet of Pa-
as ſoon as he and his Comrade were ſat down
Table, with a Tnkard of Beer before them, he
'd out the Duſt of the rotten Poſt, and was ſeal-
it up in ſeveral Pieces of Paper ; which occaſion-
ſome Folks that were drinking there, to enquire
t it was that he was ſo choicely making up. *Joe*
nes told them it was an incomparble Powder,
ich was the only Thing in the univerſal World,
a burnt Hand, a ſcalded Leg, or any Accident
atever that ſhould befal a Man by Fire , nay,
thermore, it would prevent alſo any Hurt that
ght happen by that raging Element. For proof
ereof, ſays he *make a Kettle of Water preſently*
alding hot, and my Friend here, by rubbing a
le of my Powder on his Leg, ſhall put it into the
d Water, and receive no Damage.
The People were very eager to try the Experi-
nt, and a kettle of Water was immediately made
alding hot. Then *Joe Haynes* rubbing ſome of
s Powder but on the Stocking of his Friend's right
g, which was artificially made of Wood, for his
tural one he had loſt three Years before in *Flan-*
rs, he put it into the ſcalding Water, and bringing
out unhurt, it put the Spectators into ſuch an Ad-
ration of its Virtue, that they bought in all as faſt
they could, as twelve Pence a Paper, ſo that
oe Haynes and his Friend, who had no Money be-
re, had now above 30 Shillings to pay what they
ad call'd for, and ſomething in their Pockets be-
de.

Dick Hughes being one of the Fools that was ta-
en in thus, the next Day he was in ſome Company,
here bragging what an excellent Powder he had
r a Burn or a Scald, he would lay a Wager with
em of ten Shilings, that he would put his Leg
to a Kettle of ſcalding Water and not hurt it.
Thereupon, his Companions thinking it a 'Thing
npoſſible, they laid what he propos'd , and a Kettle
f Water was forthwith put on the Fire, whilſt

Dick went into another Room, (becauſe they ſhould
not ſee how he prepared his Leg for the fiery
Trial) to rub ſome of the Powder on the Ssocking,
as *Joe Haynes* had on his Friend's. Then coming out, and putting his Leg all at once into the
ſcalding Water, he roar'd out in a moſt prodigious
Manner, and could not pull it out again till he was
help'd. Thus he did not only loſe his ten Shillings,
but had like to have loſt his Leg too ; for he was
above nine Months in St. *Bartholomew's* Hoſpital,
before he went abroad again.

No ſooner was this Villain roving about once
more, but he got into Old Bridewell, by Fleet-
Ditch. But obtaining his Liberty after one Court-
Day, he ſtill continued in his Villany, and attempted once to go on the Foot-pad. In which Enterprize, the firſt Perſon whom he attacked in this land,
was that very honeſt Coney-Wool Comber, *William*
Fuller ; taking from him about fourteen Shillings, in
the Road betwixt *Camberwell* and *Southwark*, for
all he might have inſiſted on a ſort of Privilege from
being robb'd, by telling *Dick Hughes, That tho' he*
was no Thief, yet he was a great Cheat , and ſince
he firſt pretended to diſcover the Pedigree of that
Son of a Whore the Prince of Wales, he had ruin-
ed more People by Tongue-Padding, than ever all
the Thieves in London had done. Damage by any bad
Practices whatever.

Another Time, he met on the Road betwixt
Clapham and *Vaux-Hall*, with D——n the broken
Bookſeller , and taking from him three half Crowns,
and ſtripping him ſtark naked beſide, he ty'd his
Hands behind him, and his Head betwixt his Legs,
to contrive, in that muſing Poſture, what ſeditious
Libel might be moſt edifying to a Republican Party.

Whilſt he lay under Condemnation, his Wife, to
whom he had been married in the *Fleet-Priſon*, conſtantly viſited him at Chapel. She was a very honeſt
Woman, and had ſuch an extraordinary Kindneſs
for her Huſband, under his great Afflictions, that
when he went to be hang'd at *Tyburn*, on Friday
the 24th of *June*, 1709, ſhe met at St *Giles's* Pound,
where the Cart ſtopping, ſhe ſtept up to him, and
whiſpering in his Ear, ſhe ſaid, *My Dear, Who*
muſt find the Rope that's to hang you, we or the She-
riff ? Her Huſband reply'd, *The Sheriff, Honey ,*
for who's obliged to find him Tools to do his Work ? Ah!
reply'd his Wife, *I wiſh I had a known ſo much be-*
fore, it would have ſaved me Two-pence, for I have
been and bought one already. Well, well, ſaid *Dick*
again, *perhaps it mayn't be loſt, for it may ſerve a*
ſecond Huſband. Yes, quoth his Wife, *if I have any*
Luck in good Huſbands, ſo it may. Then the Cart
driving on to *Hyde-Park* Corner, this notorious Villain ended his Days there, in the 30th of his Age ,
and was after anatomiz'd at *Surgeons-Hall*, in *Lon-*
don.

The

The LIFE *of* HARVEY HUTCHINS.

THIS Malefactor, *Harvey Hutchins*, was born of honeſt Parents, his Father being a Sword-Blade-maker by Trade; who, when this unhappy Son came to be about fourteen Years of Age, put him Apprentice to a Silver-Smith in *Shrewſbury*; but pilfering very often from his Maſter, he had him ſent at laſt, to *Shrewſbury* Gaol.

In this Priſon the young Lad came acquainted with ſome *London* Thieves, who, occupying their Calling in the County of *Salop*, they were alſo committed to the ſame Jail, where *Hutchins* hearing them tell of the ſeveral notable and ingenious Robberies that were committed in and about *London*, by ſome of the chief Maſters of their Profeſſion, he was reſolved to make the beſt of his Way thither after he obtained his Liberty

About three or four Months after his Confinement, came the Aſſizes, when being try'd, and whipt at the Cart's Arſe, upon his Friends paying his Fees he got his Enlargement and came up to *Iſlington*, where he lurk'd about the Town, and took up his Lodging in a Barn But his Mind ſtill ran upon the Ingenuity of the topping Thieves in *London*, particularly one *Conſtantine*, who, for the fine Stories he had heard told of him, he admired above the reſt At laſt he moves into the great Metropolis, where getting acquainted with ſome young Pick-Pockets, he enquired among them for this *Conſtantine*, who told him he might be found at one *Snotty-Noſe Hill's*, who kept the *Dog Tavern* in *Newgate-ſtreet*

The young *Salopian* being overjoyed he had found out where Mr *Conſtantine* uſed, one Evening he goes to the *Dog-Tavern* to enquire, ſaying, after his Country Dialect or Tone, *He had vary enneſt Buſueſs wod him* The Drawer preſently went up Stairs to Mr *Conſtantine*, who was then drinking with a great many of his thrieving Fraternity, and acquaints him, *That there was a young Country Lad below wanted earneſtly to ſpeak with him* Quoth *Conſtantine*, With me? D——n me, *I don't know any Country Lad What is he? Perhaps he's ſent for ſome Trepan, prithee go down and aſk him his Buſineſs* The Drawer comes to the Country Lad, aſking, *What he would have with Mr* Conſtantine, *and he would go up and tell him* Young *Shropſhire* told him, *No harm, but his Buſineſs was ſuch, that mornt tol it to eny Buddy bot hemſelf*.

The Drawer returns again with this Meſſage, and *Conſtantine* wondring who this Lad ſhould be, ordered him to be brought up to the Stairs Head, where coming out to him, quoth he, *Do you want me, Lad?* He reply'd *Yes, Meſter, vor I am come abvve a Hundered Moiles to zee you.* Said *Conſtantine*, *What is your Buſineſs with me?* He anſwered, *Vy, Meſter, I have been in* Shrewſbury *Jail, vere haring a grot morny vine Stories of you, by zum Gentlemen that ware Proſners with me, I am come up to* London *on Porpus to be and myzelf Prontiſe to yew.* Hereupon,

Conſtantine could not forbear ſmiling at the Lad's Fancy, and taking him into the Room, where he repeated the Story to his Company, it cauſed a great deal of Laughter among them

He gives the Boy Sixpence, and a Glaſs or two of Wine, and bade him *be ſure to come to him at the ſame Place about Seven the next Night, and he would take him upon Liking, and according as he found him tractable, diligent, and acute in his Buſineſs, he would take him Apprentice.* The Boy overjoyed at this good Fortune (as he unhappily thought it) took his Leave, and, according to Order, was next Night at the *Dog-Tavern* punctually at the Hour appointed, where his Maſter *Conſtantine* was ready to go with him upon a Trial of Skill; which was this *Conſtantine* having ſtole a ſilver Tankard, about three Months before, out of an Alehouſe in *Cheapſide*, he had, neverthelefs, been there in Diſguiſe ſeveral Times after, and obſerving much Plate ſtill in Uſe about the Houſe, he told the Boy the Story going along the Street, and promiſed him, that if he could carry off another clean, and bring it to him at a certain Houſe in *White Chapel*, he would certainly take him Apprentice, and make a Man of him when he was out of his Apprenticeſhip, at the ſame Time intimating to him, that the Houſe was juſt before him where he was going to drink.

The Boy took his Story right, but juſt as his Maſter was come to the Houſe, pulling him by the Sleeve, quoth he, *Meſter, Meſter, can you ran well? Yes,* (reply'd his Maſter,) *as well as moſt Men in* England, *I have often out-ran Hundreds together before now. Weel then,* (ſaid the Boy) *if you can ran well, ne'er fear but we'll have a Tonkad*

Into the Houſe *Conſtantine* goes firſt, and calling for a Room, the Boy fo'lowed him to the Bar, as his Servant, and with a low Voice aſked the Man of the Houſe, *If he did not loſe a ſilver Tankard about three Months ago? Yes,* reply'd he, which *Conſtantine* over hearing, took as faſt as he could to his Heels, the Boy at the ſame Time crying out, *That was the Man that ſtole it* Upon which the Victualler, and the Servants, ran preſently out in purſuit of him, but to no Purpoſe, for he was got out of Sight in an Inſtant, and in the mean Time the Boy took another ſilver Tankard out of the Bar, and got ſafely to the Place appointed by his Maſter, who no ſooner ſaw him, but he fell a curſing, and damning, and ſtuking, at him, like a Madman, for putting him into ſuch bodily Fear, withal telling him, *That if he had been taken, he ſhould have been certainly hang'd by the beſt Neck he had, but,* quoth he, *Sirrah, have you got a Tankard? Yes,* reply'd the Boy, and taking it from under his Coat, gave it him, ſaying at the ſame Time, *Meſter, if yow hed not virſt afor'd me thet yow cud ran well, I wud a gut it ſum uddar way*

A little after this running Bout, young *Harvey* and his Maſter going through *Denmark Court* in the
Strand,

Strand, they espy'd a silver Tankard, Cup, Salver, and some Spoons and Forks, lying on a Side-board in the Parlour of one *William Bunworth*, a School-Master; at which *Constantine*'s Mouth watering, quoth he to his Apprentice, who was now bound to him for three Years, *Is there no possibility, Harvey, of getting that Plate, whilst that damn'd Maid is in the Parlour? Yes, Mester*, quoth he, *if you will carry me up to the Mester of the School, and pretending I am a noughty Boy, give him sumthing to whop me, and then var menaging the Maud, I'll leve that to you, Mester*,

Accordingly they both went up Stairs without asking any Questions, and coming into the School, *Constantine*, who was drest much like a Gentleman, with his long tail Wig, and Sword by his Side, address'd himself to the School-Master, saying, " Sir, I have " got an unlucky Rogue of a Boy here for a Servant, " who is the saddest Dog as ever was known for go-" ing of an Errand, for send him but to the next " Door and he will stay two or three Hours before " he returns with an Answer. I have try'd fair " Means, and foul Means with him, and yet all will " not do, wherefore, I humbly beg the Favour of " you to do so much as give him a good whipping, " and next Week I shall send him to School to you, " to be instructed in Writing and casting Accompts, " for I would fain have the Rascal come to good if I " could " At the same Time he slipt a Crown-Piece into *Bunworth*'s Hand, who being such a miserly covetous Fellow, that he would never marry for fear of bringing a charge of Children on him, he was overjoyed at so large a Gift for doing so small a Piece of Service.

Immediately the School-Master takes *Harvey* to Task, who began to set up his Pipes, and cry'd heartily, but all to no Purpose, one of the lustiest Boys in the School was call'd out to hoist him, who getting him on his Back, the Master handsomely flank'd him In the mean Time *Constantine* went down Stairs, desiring him before to send his Boy after him, as soon as he had given him Correction Then approaching the Maid with fair Words, he gave her a Shilling, to fetch a Pint of Sack for him and her Master, who was just upon coming down to him upon some Business that was betwixt them The poor Servant mistrusting no harm, takes the Shilling, and went for the Wine; in the mean Time he went off with all the Plate, and presently came down *Harvey* and went after him

In less than four or five Minutes, School being done, down comes *Bunworth* himself, and seeing the Maid coming in at the Street-Door with a Pint of Wine in her Hand, quoth he, *Who is that for, Mary?* She told him, the Gentleman that was just now with him, ordered her to fetch it. Quoth he, " A very " generous civil Gentleman, I vow; he gave me a " Crown but for whipping that unlucky Rogue of " his, who, according to the Character of him, is, " indeed, a very naughty Boy. *Said the Maid again*, " Ay, but Sir, where is all the Plate that was on the " Sideboard here just now? Plate? *quoth* Bunworth, " what Plate? I saw no Plate. *Away they both went* " *searching the Closet, and every Hole and Corner of* " *the House, but not finding it,* Bunworth *cries out*, " Ruin'd and undone for ever! I'm robb'd, I'm " robb'd! Oh! that damn'd Son of a Whore of a " Gentleman, whilst I was whipping his unlucky Son " of a Whore his Boy, he has whipt away all my " Plate Thieves! Thieves! " At this Uproar all the Neighbours came in to assist him, thinking they were then in the House; but, indeed, the Thieves were farther a Field, without Doubt making merry over their Booty, whilst poor *Bunworth* was damning and sinking himself to the Pit of Hell for his Loss, which he did not long survive, for within a little while after he died with mere Vexation and Grief.

In fine, *Harvey* very truly and honestly served out his Time with his Master, when setting up for himself, he had very pretty Business in House-breaking, and liv'd very creditably and handsomely among those of his Profession, for about nine Years, in and about the Cities of *London* and *Westminster*, and in that Time had often paid Scot and Lot to *Newgate*, and other Jails about Town, but at last being apprehended for breaking open a *Jew*'s House at *Dukes Place*, and robbing it of above four hundred Pounds in Money and Plate, he was hang'd at *Tyburn* in 1704, aged twenty six Years

The LIFE of JACK WITHERS.

THE Malefactor we are now to give an Account of, was the Son of a Butcher, born at _Litchfield_ in _Staffordshire_, where he served an Apprenticeship with his own Father. For want of Business when he was out of his Time, made him come up to _London_, and his evil Genius when he was there, soon threw him into the Way of Destruction, for engaging himself with a Society of Thieves, by their Conversation he got into, from whence he was sent into _Flanders_ for a Soldier, as was then the Custom of dealing with Offenders, who were not judg'd worthy of Death.

While he was abroad, he could very indifferently brook the being obliged to live on a Foot Soldier's Pay, which bore no Proportion to his late Expences. This put him on a great many Shifts, and made him take all Opportunities of making up the Deficiency of his Income. One or two of the Pranks that he play'd in this View, will be very well worth rehearsing, and we shall give them as briefly as possible.

Going into a Church in _Ghent_, where the People were all at High Mass, and seeing most of them cast Money into a Box that stood under an Image of the Virgin _Mary_, it made his Fingers itch for the Coin, so watching a fair Opportunity, with a crooked Nail he pick'd the Lock, and cram'd as much of the Treasure as he could into his Pockets. But doing it over-hastily, and dropping some of the Pieces, they made such a jingling on the Marble Pavement, that, as ill Luck would have it, he was discovered, seized, and dragg'd before a great Cardinal then in that Town.

This arch Priest examining the Witnesses as to the Fact, and finding it plain, he exclaimed prodigiously against _Withers_, by the Titles of _Rogue, Rascal_, and _sacrilegious Villain_, and was just going to condemn him to a severe Punishment, when _Jack_ falling on his Knees, with uplifted Hands, and Tears in his Eyes, begg'd his Eminency to hear him. This, after much Storming, was granted, and Silence being made, _Jack_, in a piteous Tone, told him, That he was a vile wicked Wretch, bred up a Protestant, and an Heretick, and being in great Distress, he had made his Prayers before the Image of the Blessed Virgin, to relieve him in his hard Necessity, promising, in consideration thereof, to turn _Roman Catholick_, and ever be her Votary, when all on a sudden, the Box under her Image flew open, and she pointed with her Finger to the Money, making also a dumb Shew with nodding her Head, for him to supply his Necessities out of it, which he had thankfully done, with a Resolution of keeping his Vow for ever.

This Relation being heard with much Patience and Attention, the Cardinal cry'd out, _A Miracle! A Miracle!_ which all the rest rehearsed out aloud, concluding that none had more right to dispose of that Money, than the Virgin to whom it was offer-

ed. Instead of being punished, _Jack Withers_ was now carried back to the Church in solemn Procession, on Mens Shoulders, and borne round it in Triumph, whilst _Ave Maria_ was sung by the Priests, and he placed before the High Altar, after which he was dismissed with great Applause.

Proving so fortunate in this Cheat, he was thereby embolden'd to commit another like it; for one Day going into a Church in _Antwerp_, he perceiv'd the Priest put a silver Crucifix, of great Value, into a Sepulchre, as their Ceremony is, in representing the Resurrection, upon _Ascension Day_, and whilst the spiritual Juggler and the People were going round the Church, in their superstitious Way of Devotion, _Jack Withers_ was so dextrous as to convey the Crucifix into his Breeches, and shuffle among the Crowd, so that when the Priest came back to it, saying these Words in the Gospel, _Non est hic, surrexit enim_ that is, _He is not here, for he is risen_, he found it so indeed, for, after much fumbling, he perceiv'd his graven God was gone, and _Withers_ then made what Haste he could away, for fear of a Search.

But a little after the playing of this Prank, _Jack_ running away from his Colours, came into _England_ again, where, preferring an idle course of Life before any lawful Employment, he took to the High-way. One Day meeting with an old Miser upon the Road, who was his Father's Neighbour, he commanded him to stand, and deliver what he had, or otherwise he was a dead Man. The old Man being surpriz'd, pleaded great Poverty, in Hopes of saving about an hundred Guineas and Broad Pieces of Gold, which he had in the Pockets of his wide knee Breeches, containing Cloth enough to make a Gentlewoman a hoop'd Petticoat, but all his whining prevailed nothing with _Jack_. He was then for coming to Composition with him, by giving him one half of his Money to save t'other, but _Withers_ swore a great Oath of the first Rate that he would not abate him a Farthing of _Cent per Cent_. The old Man fumbling a good While in his Pocket, at length he lugg'd out his Purse and Pair of Spectacles, which putting on his Nose, he gave his money to _Jack Withers_, who ask'd him whether his Sight was so bad that he could not give him his Purse without using his auxiliary Eyes? To which the other reply'd, " That he hoped he " might have the Liberty of seeing to whom he gave " his Money. Ay, ay, and welcome, _quoth_ Jack, " and pray take notice, that when you see me again, " you must supply me with just such another Sum." So they parted, _Jack_ riding one Way, and the old Wretch another.

One Time _Jack Withers_, and two of his hopeful Comrades, having been all Night a rakeing in the Country, as they were coming on Foot over the Field by _Marybone_, by 4 o'Clock in a Summer's Morning, they observed a Gentleman walking all alone, making all the Gestures imaginable of Passion, Discontent, and Fury, such as casting up his Eyes to the

the Sky, displaying his Arms abroad, and then ringing them together again, This happened to be one Mr *Vanbruggen*, a celebrated Player, who was getting his Part; but they not knowing who he was, suppos'd he might be in despair for Love, or some other Cause, and so in that Condition might lay violent Hands upon himself Hereupon they watch'd his Motions at a Distance, but Mr *Vanbruggen*, at length, espying them, he, for the more Privacy, went thro' a Hedge into another Field, where these three Sparks found him by the side of a Pond, expressing, in a very passionate Manner, these Words of *Varanes*, in the Tragedy of *Theodosius*, or, *The Force of Love*

I charge thee not!
But when I am dead take the attending Slaves,
And bear me, with my Blood distilling down,
Streight to the Temple; lay me, O! Aranthes,
Lay my cold Coarse at Athenais's Feet,
And say, ——O! why, why do my Eyes run o'er!
Say with my latest Gasp I groan'd for Pardon
Just here my Friend; hold fast, and fix the Sword
I feel the Artery, where the Life Blood lies;
It heaves against the Point —— Now, O! ye Gods,
If for the greatly wretched you have room,
Prepare my Place, for dauntless, lo I come!
The Force of Love thus makes the mortal Wound,
And Athenais sends me to the Ground

Jack Whithers being foremost, cry'd out to his Camrades, Hallo! Make haste, by G——d 'tis e'en as we thought, the poor Gentleman is just going to kill himself for Love So making all up to *Vanbruggen*, one taking him by one Arm, and another by the other, they said, Pray, Sir, consider what you are going to do! What a sad Thing will it be for you to drown yourself here! Be advis'd, and have better Thoughts with you, Mr *Vanbruggen* not knowing their Meaning, quoth he, as they were pulling and halling him about, " What a Plague " is all this for? I am not going to hang, stab, " nor drown myself, I am not in Love, I am only " a Player getting my Part A Player are you? " reply'd *Withers*, if we had thought that, you

" should e'en have drown'd yourself, and been " d——n'd too, before we'd have took all this Pains " to follow your Arse up and down: But to make " us amends for our Trouble, you can do no less " then give us what Money you have. " Being in a bye Place, they ty'd his Hands and Legs together, and took from him about ten Shilling, and a silver hilted Sword

After this *Jack Withers*, and one *William Edwards*, setting on a Person of Quality within a Mile or two of *Beaconsfield*, in *Buckinghamshire*, the Lord that was assaulted, who had only one Footman with him, had the Courage to oppose them, and held so hot a Dispute to save what he had, that *Withers*'s Horse being shot, *Edwards* was obliged to carry him off behind him, and a close Pursuit being made after them, they were forced to quit that Horse, and make their Escape on Foot, thro' bye Lanes, and over Fields, where none on Horseback could ride after them Now hiding themselves in a Wood all Night, the next Morning they made the best of their way for *London*, but about a Mile out of *Uxbridge*, meeting with a Penny-Post Man they assaulted him on the Queen's Highway, and having taken from him about eight Shillings, to prevent his Discovery of them, *Withers* (tho' much against the Will of his Comrade *Edwards*) took a Butcher's knife out of his Pocket, and with it not only cut the Throat of the unhappy Man, but ript out his Bowels, and filling the Body full of Stones threw it into a Pond, where it was found the next Day. None could tell the Author of this inhuman Murder, till *Withers* and his Companion were apprehended about two Months after for a Country Robbery, when being condemn'd at the Lent Assizes at *Norfolk*, on the 16th of *April*, 1703, the Day of their Execution, at *Thetford*, *Withers* confess'd the Fact Thus we may see how the Providence of God generally brings to light the Authors of such horrid Deeds, for tho' a Murderer may for some Time escape, yet the divine Judgment will overtake him at last

The LIFE of WILL MAW.

THIS noted Villain, aged 50 Years when he was hang'd, was born at *Northallerton* in *Yorkshire*, from whence he came to *London*, at about 20 Years of Age, and served his Apprenticeship with a Cabinet-maker, and for a great while followed that Occupation, in the Parish of St. *Giles's Cripplegate*, where he dwelt for above eighteen Years together; and for many Years before his Death having left off working at his Trade, he maintained himself by some illegal Ways of living, such as the buying of stollen Goods, and thereby encouraging Thieves and Robbers, he had also been addicted to coining, and for some of his irregular Actions, had a Fine of ten Pounds laid in upon him, in *September* 1705, was burnt in the Hand in *April* 1710, and in *September* following, and twice ordered to hard Labour in *Bridewell*

Having once committed a Robbery, for which he was afraid to be apprehended, when he lived in *Golden Lane*, he pretended to be very sick at Home, and ordered his Wife to give out that he was dead. His Wife being a cunning Baggage, so ordered the Matter, that she cleanly executed his Command, bought him a Coffin, invited about 40 or 50 Neighbours to the Funeral, and followed the Corps in such a mournful Condition, as if her poor Husband had been dead indeed. As they were coming by the *Red-cross* Alehouse, at the End of *Red-Cross-street*, to St *Giles's* Church-Yard, near *Cripplegate*, some Company being drinking at the Door, who were inquisitive to know who was dead, they were told it was old *Maw*, whom they knew very well.

About five Years afterwards, one of those Persons that were drinking, as aforesaid, being a Prisoner in *Wood-street* Compter, for Debt, and *Maw* coming in also a little after him, the Person was so surpriz'd at the latter, that at first he had not Power to speak to him; but, at length, recovering some Courage, as dreading he had seen a Ghost, quoth he, *Is not your Name Maw, Sir?* *Maw* reply'd, *Yes, Sir, as sure as your Name is* Watkins The other said again, *Why, I thought you had been dead and buried five Years ago!* *Yes,* reply'd *Maw, so I was in Trespasses and Sins* But *I mean,* said *Watkins, laid yourself corporally in the Grave* No, (reply'd *Maw*) *I was not dead; but being at that Time under some Troubles, I was at the Charge of a Coffin to save my Neck, and my Wife gave out I was really defunct, as supposing then my Adversaries would not look for me in my Grave.*

Shortly after this Imprisonment being hang'd, as he was going up *Holborn*, another Person, who, like Mr. *Watkins*, had thought him dead and buried, seeing him in the Cart, he was in a great Admiration, calling thus out to him in the Cart, *Oh! dear, Mr Maw, I really thought you had been dead and buried five Years ago and more. Why so I wa., re*ply'd *Maw, but don't you know that we must all rise again at the Day of Judgment? Yes,* reply'd h. *Acquaintance, but the Day of Judgment is not come yet* Ay, but it is, quoth *Maw,* and pass'd to s, I. *Day. ago, at the Sessions-House in the Old Baily, where I am sure 'twas the Judgment of the Court.* send me to be hanged now So his Friend wishing him a good Journey, and a safe Return, they both parted

Will Maw having once stole a Trunk from behind a Coach, in which were several Goods, and among them a Clergyman's new Gown and Cassock, great Enquiry was made at most of the Brokers for the canonical Robes, by a Friend of the Minister who lost them. *Maw* had sold them to one *Seabrook* in *Barbican,* with whom they were at length found. *Seabrook* offered to sell them a Pennyworth, and the Gentleman bid him bring them to the *Sun-Tavern,* in *Aldersgate-street,* where the Person was that wanted them The Clergyman was there, and having viewed and tried the Robes, found them to be the same; whereupon, he asked the Broker how he came by them; who could neither give much Account of the Manner he bought them in, nor find the Person he bought them of In a Word, but an Act of Grace having been lately past, he pleaded the Benefit of it, and so escaped the Punishment which he must otherwise have suffered, tho' not the Disgrace that attends such Practices

After a long Course of Iniquities, *Maw* was at last committed to Newgate himself, and at the ensuing Sessions convicted of five Indictments 1 For breaking open the House of Mrs *Anne Johnson,* and taking thence eight Pewter Plates, and other Goods. 2 For breaking open the House of Mr *John Avery,* and taking thence 24 Pair of Leather Clogs 3 For assaulting and robbing Mr *Charles Potts,* on the Highway, and taking from him a silver Watch, five gold Rings, Money, and other Things 4 For assaulting Mrs *Anne Grover,* on the Highway and taking from her 3 s 6d And 5 For assaulting on the Queen's Highway, and robbing, Mr *Coleman,* of some Money, an Handkerchief, and other Goods 'Twas impossible for him now to think of coming off; and if it had been possible for him to have expected any Grace, he had been deceived, for on *Wednesday* the 29th of *October,* 1711, this Offender met with the Punishment he so well deserved, at the usual Place of Execution

The LIFE of NICHOLAS WELLS.

THIS noted Criminal, *Nicholas Wells*, was born at *Pemsworth*, in the County of *Kent*, but afterwards lived at *East-Grimstead*, with his Grandmother; and keeping a Horse, travelled from thence to *London*, and bought and sold Goods, by which he helped to keep two of his Younger Sisters He was a Butcher by Trade, and married a Woman in *Barnaby-street*, with whom he had one hundred and twenty Pounds for a Portion. Whilst his Money lasted, which was not long, he lived content with his Wife, but having by extravagant Courses quickly consumed it, they then lived like married Quality, for they would see one another once a Week perhaps, lie together once a Month, and eat together once a Year

Being by his Folly reduced to great Necessities, and much in Debt, he, for a Livelihood, drove a Woodmonger's Cart in *Southwark*; and one day carrying three Loads of Faggots to a Gentleman's House at *Lambeth*, as he was making Water not far from the Door, where the Gentleman's Wife stood, her extraordinary Beauty had such an Influence on his carnal Mind, that he was over heard by the Gentlewoman to say to himself these Words *Was I to lie with that handsome Creature, I vow and swear I'd give my Cart and Horses.*

The Gentlewoman, who was none of the Chastest, calling him into her Parlour, she wanted to know what 'twas he said, as he was making Water, or otherwise, if he would not tell her, she would call her Footman to kick him well Our new Carman was somewhat bashful to declare what he had said; but fearing to be ill us'd in case he did not satisfy the Gentlewoman's Demands, he very bluntly told her the Words above-mentioned. The Lady now taking him at his Word, she carried him to her Bed Chamber, were obtaining the Pleasure, for which he had forfeited his Cart and Horses, and finding no Difference betwixt her and his Wife in that sort of Sport, he swore, *They were all alike.*

In this Tone he hankered about the Street Door a great while, for home to his Master he durst not go, without the Cart and Horses, but, at last, the Gentlewoman's Husband coming home to Dinner, and hearing the Fellow swear, *They were all alike,* by G——d, quoth he, *What are all alike ?* The Faggots, reply'd the Carman Quoth the Gentleman again, *And what of that ?* To which *Nick* thus answered *An't please you, Sir, I have brought home the three Loads of Faggots which you bought, and your Lady being not satisfied, that the last Faggots which are not so big as the first, she hath ordered her Servant to lock up my Cart and Horses in your Coachyard, and says, that she will keep them,* O ! fie, fie, *Madam,* said the Gentleman to his Wife, *you must not do so, the Cart and Horses are none of the poor Man's, they're his Master's, therefore you must deal to him if he has not us'd you well*

The Gentlewoman than presently delivered the Cart and Horses, and privately gave the Carman a Guinea besides, for his handsome come off But the next Day *Nick* bringing some Coals to the same House, he then left the Gentlewoman his Cart and Horses for good and all, for finding an Opportunity of slipping into a Back Parlour, where a Scrutore was open, he took out of it, a rich gold Watch, several diamond Rings, and two hundred and fifty Guineas, which he carried clear off, without going to his Master any more

Not long after this Exploit, meeting with *Handsome Fielding,* riding on Horseback by himself over *Putney-Heath,* as he came by *Nick,* he knock'd him off his Gelding, and seconding his Blow with another, which stunn'd him worse than the first, he ty'd his Hands and Feet, and searched his Pockets, wherein he found about twenty Guineas, which made him break forth into this Exclamation *O ! Gold almighty, thou art good for the Heart sick at Night, sore Eyes in the Morning, and for the Wind in the Stomach at Noon; indeed, thou art a never failing Remedy for any Distemper, at any Time, in all Cases, and for all Constitutions*

Whilst *Nick* was expostulating to himself on the excellent Qualities of Gold, *Handsome Fielding* recovering his Senses, quoth he, *Sirrah, Dost know on whom thou hast committed this Insolence ?* Not I, (reply'd *Nick*) nor I don't care, for 'tis better you cry than I starve Quoth the robb'd Person again, *I'm General Fielding, who'll make you dearly suffer for this, if ever you come into my Clutches Art thou* (reply'd *Nick* then) *Beau Fielding ?* Why truly I've heard thy Fame and Shame long enough ago , I think thou art one of those amorous Coxcombs who never go without Verses, in praise of a Mistress, and write Elegies on the great Misfortune of losing your Buttons Thou art one of the whining Puppies, that waste Day and Night with her that you admire for a Whore, taking up her Glove, and robbing her of a Hankerchief, which you'll pretend to keep for her Sake In fine, let me tell you, thou art translated out of a Man into a Whimsy So leaving Beau *Fielding* to shift for himself, he made the best of his Way to *Rosemary-Lane,* where his Landlord and Landlady were transported at the sight of his Booty, for he treated them, as in Duty bound, plentifully , and there was never a Servant in the House of Iniquity but fared the better for his Villany.

Altho' *Nick Wells* was a Fellow that ventured his Neck in these dangerous Enterprizes, yet he was not Master of any true Courage, for he was much of the nature of those who are always challenging People that will not fight, and cuffing such as all the Town has kick'd, upon many Occasions it has appeared that he was as cautious of dealing with a Man that is truly rough, as an honest Man would have been of dealing with him. He was very Bloody-minded, where he had the Advantage of a Man, as may be perceived by an Enterprize which he once undertook for one *Elizabeth Harman,* alias *Bess Toogood.*

This Woman being condemned for picking the Pocket of one *Samuel Winfield*, a Lock-Smith, living near St *George*'s Church in *Southwark*, such was her implacable Malice before she was hanged, that she said she could not die satisfied, unless she had the Blood of her Prosecutor. Proposing her wicked Inclinations to *Nick Wells*, quoth he, *Bess*, not that I matter a Murder or two committing, but I don't love to work without Hire; what am I to have, first? and who am I to dispatch? But I care not who it is, if you content me. Then this wicked Wretch acquainting him where her Adversary liv'd, and giving him three Guineas to murder him, he took his last Farewell of her in the Chapel of *Newgate*, and that same Day going to Mr *Winfield's* House, with pretence of bespeaking a Lock, that he might have a sight of the Man he was to kill, in the Evening he watch'd his going out, and coming home, which was about twelve at Night, and coming behind him as he was knocking at his own Door, he ran him thro' the Back with a Tuck, of which Wound he presently died on the Spot: But the Murderer was never known till he confess'd this barbarous Crime at the Gallows.

Whilst he followed these ill Courses he was much addicted to all manner of Lasciviousness, and seldom saw his Wife, whom he greatly slighted; for he was often want to say, *He was not cursed with the Plague of Constancy*. Nay, how little Regard he had for his Wife, may plainly be seen by the following Contract, drawn betwixt him and *William Maw*, whose Life immediately precedes this.

We the Subscribers, *William Maw* of *London*, Joyner, and *Nicholas Wells* of *Pemsworth*, in the County of *Kent*, Butcher, being each of us burdened with an useless Moveable, the former with a Jack-Daw, and the latter with a Wife, declare, That we have thought fit, for the Convenience of one another, out of our own pure and free Will, to make a Barter and Truck of the Jack-Daw for the Wife; yielding up the one to the other, all Right and Title that we have to the said Wife and Jack-Daw, and quitting for ever all Claim to them, without any Manner of Complaint or Demand hereafter to the Premisses so trucked. To which Bargain and Agreement, in token of hearty Consent and Satisfaction, we have hereunto set our Hands and Seals. Dated at *Deptford*, the 10th Day of *May*, 1710.

William Maw.

Nicholas Wells.

Accordingly the Wife went with the Buyer, and her Husband, without repenting his Bargain, pursu'd his vicious Practices still. But at length being apprehended for robbing one *James Wilmot*, a Butcher, near *Epsom*, of thirty Guineas, some Silver, and a silver Watch, he was committed to the *Marshalsea* Prison in *Southwark*. For this Fact he was hanged in the twenty eighth Year of his Age, at *Kingston upon Thames*, on *Saturday* the 28th of *March*, 1712. Mr *Noble* an Attorney being also executed there at the same Time for the barbarous Murder of one *John Sayer*, Esq;

The LIFE of WILLIAM HOLLOWAY.

WAS born at *Newcastle-under-Line*, in *Staffordshire*, and was bred up to Husbandry; but not liking his Occupation, he came up to *London*, where falling into such Company as had rather be the Devil's Soldiers, than fight under the Banners of Honesty, he soon became such an Enemy to Virtue, that no sort of Theft miss'd his Inclination, to support himself in the Extravagancies of a most licentious Course of Life.

First he went upon petty Matters of Thieving, in which he was very successful, for one Day going to Knight's House in *Bloomsbury-Square*, with an Apron before him just like a Scowrer, he had the Impudence to go up Stairs and take three or four Footmens Liveries, but just coming out with them on his Arms, the Coachman stopping at the Door with his Coach, he stopp'd *Holloway*, and ask'd him, *Whether he was going with those Coats, and Waste-coats?* Quoth *Holloway, The Parliament being to sit within this Week, and your Master being willing his Mens Liveries should look somewhat fresh and decent, the Steward has ordered me to scower them against then. Here, here, then,* said the Coachman, *take my Cloak too, and scower it well.* So stepping on his Coach-Box, he took his Cloak off the Seat, and gave it *Holloway*, who never took the Pains to bring it back again. But the poor Coachman was sadly jeer'd about it, for whereever the Boys met him, who knew of the Trick, they would cry to him, *Here, here, take my Cloak too.*

Another Time there being a great Stop of Coaches in *Fleet-street*, Mr *Holloway* stepping up to a Gentleman's Coach, and pretending to have some earnest Business with him, whilst *Holloway* was talking to the Gentleman as he lean'd over the Door of the Coach to him, one of his Comrades took out a rich Coach Seat, and got clear off with it in the Dark, and whilst the Gentleman turn'd his Head out of the other Door to look after it, *Holloway* snatch'd off the other Seat, and in the Crowd went away with that. The Gentleman being in a great Surprize to see how suddenly he had lost both his Seats, he call'd out to his Coachman, saying, *Tom, hast thou got the Horses there?* Quoth *Tom, Yes, Sir. Ay, but* (said the Gentleman) *are you sure you have them? Why yes, Sir,* reply'd the Coachman, *I'm sure I have them, for their Reins are now in my Hand. Well,* (quoth the Gentleman) *see and keep them there, for I have lost the Seats out of the Coach, and by Heavens, if you've not a special Care, you'll lose my Horses too.*

Not long after this Exploit, Mr *Emes*, who kept the Punch-House in *Hemlock-Court*, having been one Day recreating himself in his Calash, *Will* observing it to come a soft Pace in the Road betwixt *Turnham-Green* and *Hammersmith*, he perceived the Driver thereof, who had been drinking very hard where he had been, to be fast asleep. Hereupon *Will* stopp'd the Horse, which was but one, and softly stepping up, rifled Mr *Emes's* Pockets, unfelt of him, of a Watch

and two Guineas, and so sneaked off from him, supposing that was all the Booty he could get at that Time, unless he stripped him of his Cloaths too, which he could not well carry off without some Suspicion, in that Place. However, the Road being clear of Passengers, and finding Mr *Emes* still in a profound Sleep, he ty'd his Legs together, and, that he might have the Pleasure to see what would be the Issue of it, he pull'd the Pins out of the Axle-Tree of the Wheels, and set the Horse a-going, which he had not done above an hundred Paces, but the Wheels flew off, and down came the Booby-Hutch.

Mr *Emes* now waked in a great Consternation, whilst *Will* lay peeping behind a Hedge, and could perceive his Surprize. But the Horse's Rein being cut, and he not able to unloose his Legs, for want of a Knife to cut the Cord, the Horse never stopp'd nor stard, till in that manner, he had drawn the Calash through Thick and Thin into *Hammersmith*; from whence sending for the Wheel, and having them put on again, he slept no more till he got quite Home.

Now *Holloway* having cast all Honesty and Goodness quite out of Doors he was resolved to prosecute his Villany to the highest Degree, so from committing small Matters of Theft, he was resolved to turn Highwayman, and being accoutred for this Purpose, with a good Horse, Hanger, and Pistols, he set out for such Enterprizes.

The first Action he went upon, was upon the Road betwixt *Faringdon* and *Abingdon*, in *Berkshire*, where meeting with a Country Farmer, and asking him the Time of the Day, he told him it was about twelve o'Clock. *Why then* (quoth *Holloway*,) " it may be about high Time to ask one Favour of you. What's that? *(said the Farmer)* " Why truly, *(reply'd Holloway)* understanding that " you received ten Pounds at the Inn from whence " you now came, (for I was drinking in the next " Room when it was paid you) Necessity obliges me " to borrow it, and if you are not willing to lend it " me by fair Means, I shall take it by foul Means." The Farmer being a Man of some Courage, presently drew his Hanger in his own Defence, but that being no Security against Pistols, which could kill at a Distance, *Holloway* shot his Horse under him, so dismounting his Antagonist, and riding up to him with another Pistol ready cock'd, and presenting it to the Farmer's Breast, he lent him his Money without taking a Note of his Hand for it.

Another Time *Holloway* meeting with a Gentleman on the Road, who had like to have been robb'd but a little before, he told the said *Holloway*, that there were some Highwaymen before, wherefore he advis'd him, if he had any Charge about him, to turn back. Quoth *Holloway*, " I have no great " Charge about me, Sir, however, I'll take your " Advice for fear of the worst. So as they were ri- " ding along, said *Will* again, Perhaps we may

" meet

" meet with more Rogues of the Gang by the Way,
" for this is an ugly robbing Road, therefore I'll
" secure that little I have, which is but three Gui-
" neas, by putting it in my Mouth *Now the*
" *Gentleman thinking him not of that Profession, quoth*
" *he*, And in case we should be set upon, I have se-
" cur'd my Gold in the Rowls of my Stockings,
" which is no small Quantity, for I received Rent
" this Day of some of my Tenants." They had not
gone above half a Mile farther, before they came into
a very bye Place, where he bidding the Gentleman
Stand and Deliver, he was in a great Surprize, however, there was no Remedy for preventing the Loss
of his Gold, which was about eighty Guineas, and
for fear he should have more of the same Metal in his
Boots too, he ript them from Top to Bottom, but
finding none there, he left the Gentleman cursing and
swearing, for discovering where he had laid up his
Hoard.

Will for a long Time had been very successful in
many Robberies on the Highway, but at length his
Devil failing him, he was apprehended for one committed on *Hounslow-Heath*, sent to *Newgate*, and
condemned for the same, but had the good Fortune
to receive Mercy Now having a Reprieve, and
being impatient till he pleaded to Her Majesty's Pardon, he broke out of *Newgate*, after which having
the Impudence, when he was drunk, to go to the
Sessions-House in the *Old Bailey*, while the Judges
were sitting upon a Commission of *Oyer* and *Termi-
ner*, some of the Turnkeys of *Newgate* offered
to apprehend him for breaking out of Gaol, which
causing a Scuffle betwixt him and them, he mortally
shot *Richard Spurling*, a Turnkey, thro' the Body,
in the Face of the whole Court, of which Wound he
died within eleven Minutes For this he was secured, with one Mrs *Housden*, who was try'd with
him for the said Murder, and condemned as an

Accessary to it; and to make their Punishment more
exemplary, he and the Woman were not only
hanged at the End of *Gilt-Spur-street* in sight of
Newgate, in *September*, 1712, but afterwards *Halloway* was also hanged in Chains at a Place call'd
by his own Name, on one side *Islington*

At the Place of Execution, he own'd he never
had any Antipathy against the Person deceas'd, and
did not know what he did, as being in Drink. Thus
we may evidently see the fatal Consequences of
Drunkenness; which odious Vice is now become
so fashionable, that we may, too often, behold Sots
contending for Victory over a Pot, and taking the
measure of their Bravery by the Strength of their
Brains, or Capacity of their Bellies Taverns and
Alehouses are the common Academies of Sin; where
Drunkards make themselves expert in all those Ani-
whereby they gratify *Satan*, and, as it were, in so
many open Bravadoes, challenge the Almighty in
the Field, and dare him to do the worst he can.

Doubtless *Satan*, hath but too much Power over
these Men when they are most sober, they need not
give him the Advantage of finding them so often
drunk, except in a Bravado they desire to show the
World how boldly they dare defy Heaven, and how
much they scorn to owe their Ruin to any but themselves Nay, it seems very evident, that even those
Bachanalians make this sottish Pastime their
beloved Recreation, and only account him fit for
their Company, that can take off his Cups handsomely,
and is versed in all the Methods and Maxims of this
hellish Art. Indeed, they have made it a kind of
Science, and have given it so many Rules and Laws
of late, that he that will now be expert in it, had
need to serve out an Apprenticeship, to learn all
the Circumstances and Terms tho' he ever so perfect
in the Substance before

Th

The LIFE of AVERY.

THIS Malefactor, *Avery* by Name, was born in *Oxfordshire*, and by his Parents was put out an Apprentice to a Bricklayer, in *London*, where, after he was out of his Time, which he served very faithfully and honestly, he married; and then following his Trade for himself, he seemed to be so industrious at his Business, that his Neighbours had no Suspicion in the least of his robbing on the Highway, which unlawful Practice he had followed for some Years, to the great Comfort of himself and all his Family; who saw him work so hard till at last it killed him, much against his Will.

One Time *Avery* going out to look for a Prize on the Road, he got one by the bye, and to make sure of what he had (for you must know it is a Maxim in Politicks, that it is a harder Matter to keep a Kingdom then to conquer one) he rid all bye Roads till he came into a Field where several Country Fellows were standing at a Gate. Now was he in a quandary what to do. Thinks he *Should I ride back again in any Precipitation, it will give them some Mistrust, therefore I will put on a good Face, and ride up to the Men.* But the Gate being lock'd he could not get out. However one of the Men who had the key of it, wanting a young Colt which he had in the Field, he told *Avery* that if he would catch that Colt, he would open the Gate for him. *Avery* rid up and down the Field after the Colt, and had a long Chace before he could catch him, then bringing him up to the Owner, he let him out.

Now being in the Road together, quoth he to the Man that own'd the Colt, *What must I have for catching the Colt for you? Have?* (reply'd the Countryman) *O dear! Sir, what can you expect for such a Matter? Why, I think that was a Kindness to let you through the Gate, or else you must have rid a great Way about.* *Avery* swore most horribly he would be paid for his Trouble. The Countryman seeing him in a great Passion, he promised him a Pot or two of Ale, if he would accept it. But this would not satisfy *Avery*, for pulling out his Pistols he swore he would not take all that Pains for nothing about his damn'd Colt, therefore, if they did not all deliver presently, he would shoot them every Man. The poor Country Fellows being in a great Consternation, and almost frighted out of their Wits, at the sight of his murdering Implements, they all pull'd out their leather Purses, and gave him what they had, after which he rode away in great Triumph for robbing half a dozen Men by himself and without Doubt he had made his Brags thereof to some of his intimate Cronies, for when he was going to be hang'd, one of them meeting him in the Cart, as he was riding up *Holborn*, thus call'd out to him *So ho! Friend* Avery, *what, are you going to catch another Colt?* But Mr *Avery* had then so much Business on his Hands, that he could not make him any Answer.

Another Time Mr *Avery* roving up and down the Road, to seek whom he might devour, he met with a good honest Tradesman betwixt *Kingston upon Thames* and *Guilford* in *Surry*, with whom holding some Chat, as they rode together, *Avery* asked him what Trade he might follow when at home. Said he, *I'm a Fishmonger, pray what Occupation may you be of?* *Avery* reply'd, *Why I am a Limb of St Peter too. What* (quoth the Fishmonger) *are you a Fisherman? Ay,* (said *Avery*) *I'm something towards it for every Finger I have is a Fishook.* Quoth the Fishmonger, *Indeed, I don't apprehend your Meaning, Sir,* Then *Avery* pulling out his Pistols *Now, says he my Meaning may soon be apprehended, for there's not a Finger on either of my Hands, but what will catch Gold or Silver without any Bait at all.* So taking twenty Pounds from him, and cutting the Girts and Bridle of his Horse, he rode as fast as he could for *London.*

Money growing short again with Mr *Avery*, he was forced to seek his Fortune as usual, on the Road; and meeting with an Exciseman on *Finchly-Common*, whom he knew very well, though he was not known by him, by reason he was very much disguised, with a Mask on his Face, *Avery* followed him at some Distance, and a fair Opportunity favouring his Design, he rode up to the Exciseman, demanding his Money at once. The assaulted Person being somewhat sullen and obstinate, he would not deliver any Thing till *Avery* threatened to kill him if he made any farther Refusal. The Exciseman being daunted at his Words, and almost frighted out of his Wits, to hear what dreadful Vollies of Oaths came out of his Mouth, he stopp'd it as fast as he could with a dozen Pounds saying, *Here take what I have; for if there is a Devil, certainly thou art one. It may be so,* (reply'd *Avery*) *but yet as much a Devil as I am, I see an Exciseman is not such a good Bait, as People say, to catch him. No, he is not,* quoth the Exciseman, *the Hangman is the only Bait to catch such Devils as you.* But *Avery* giving the Loose leave to speak, he rode away for fear of being caught indeed.

And it was not long after that he was apprehended, and sent to *Newgate* with one *Waterman*, that was condemned likewise for assisting him in these Exploits on the Highway; but he was reprieved. *Avery* being to die without his Comrade, he made what Friends he could to save his Life also, which he had often forfeited for his Villany, besides sending several Petitions to the Queen, and Mr. Recorder, in Hopes of obtaining Mercy for his manifold Crimes, but all being rejected he was executed at *Tyburn*, on *Saturday* the 31st of *January*, 1712-13.

The LIFE of DICK ADAMS.

THIS unhappy Person, *Richard Adams*, was born of very good and reputable Parents in *Gloucestershire*, who bestow'd some small matter of Education upon him, as Reading, Writing, and Casting of Accompts Coming up to *London*, he got into the Service of a great Dutchess at *St James's*, in which he continued about two Years, when for some Misdemeanor quitting his Place, he contriv'd to live by his Wits.

Having a general Key which opened the Lodgings in St. *James's* Palace, he went one Day to a certain Mercer's on *Ludgate-Hill*, and desired him to send with all Speed, a Parcel of the richest Brocades and Sattins, and other Silks he had in his Shop, for his Dutchess to make Choice of some on an extraordinary Occasion. The Mercer knowing him to have come often upon such a like Errand before, he presently sent away several Pieces by his Man and a Porter, and being come to St. *James's*, *Dick Adams* brought them up to a Door of some of the Royal Lodgings where he ordered them to wait, while he, seemingly, went to acquaint his Dutchess of their being without. In some short Time after, coming out again, quoth he, *Let's see the Pieces presently, for my Dutchess is just now at leisure to look on them.* So the Mercer's Man giving him the whole Bundle he convey'd it away backwards, and went clear off thro' St *James's* Park. The Mercer's Man and the Porter having waited two or three Hours, and receiv'd no Answer about their Goods, they began to make a strict Enquiry after them; and finding they were trick'd, were forced to go home much lighter then they went out

About a Month after, *Dick Adams* having been drinking somewhat hard in the City, and forgetting the Prank he had play'd the Mercer, he came by his House one Afternoon, and he being accidentally standing at the Door, and espying his Chapman, he presently seiz'd him, saying *Oh! Sir, have I caught you? you are a fine Spark, indeed, to cheat me out of two hundred Pounds worth of Goods, but before I part with you, I believe I shall make you pay dearly for them* Mr. *Adams* was much surpriz'd at his being so suddenly apprehended, and without doubt, curs'd his Fate to himself, for being so forgetful as to come into the very Mouth of his Adversary, but seeing the late Bishop of *London* at some Distance riding along in his Coach, and having a good Presence of Mind at the same Time, quoth he to the Mercer, *I must acknowledge I have committed a Crime, to which I was forced by mere Necessity, but I see my Uncle, the Bishop of London, is coming this Way in his Coach, therefore hoping you'll be so civil as not to raise any Hubbub of the Mob about me, whereby I shall be expos'd and utterly undone, I'll go speak to His Lordship about the Matter, if you please to step with me, and I'll engage he shall make you Satisfaction for the Damage I've done you.*

The Mercer liking his Proposal, as thinking it far better than sending him to Gaol, he stepped along with Mr. *Adams*, who boldly calling out to the Coachman to stop, he approached the Side of the Coach, and desired the Favour of speaking a few Words with the Bishop His Lordship seeing him have the Mien and Habit of a Gentleman, he was pleas'd to hear what he had to say, so leaning over his Coach Door, quoth *Adams*, " Begging your Lord " ship's Pardon for my Presumption, I make bold to " acquaint your Honour, that the Gentleman stand " ing behind me is an eminent Mercer, keeping " House just by here, and is a very upright godly " Man, but being a great Reader in Books of Divi " nity, especially polemical Pieces, he hath met " therein with some intricate Cases, which very much " trouble him, and his Conscience cannot be at rest, " till his Doubts and Scruples are cleared about them, " therefore I humbly requested your Lordship would " vouchsafe him the Honour of giving him some " Ease before he runs farther to Despair "

The Bishop being ready to serve any Person in Religious Matters, ordered *Adams* to bring his Friend to him the next Day. But said *Adams* again, " It " will be more satisfactory to him, if your Lordship " would be pleas'd to speak yourself to the Gentle " man to wait upon you " Whereupon his Lordship beckoning to the Mercer, who stood some Distance off, whilst they discours'd together, when he came up to the Side of the Coach, quoth the Bishop, " The Gentleman has informed me of all the Matter " about you, and if you please to give yourself the " Trouble of coming to my House at *Fulham*, I will " satisfy you then in every Point " The Mercer making twenty Bows and Cringes, was very well pleas'd with his Security, and taking *Adams* to the Tavern, gave him a very good Treat

Next Morning *Adams* came again to the Mercer, who was drawing out his Bill to give to the Bishop, and pretending that his coming in haste to go along with him to his Uncle, had made him forget to put Money in his Breeches, he desired the Mercer to lend him a Guinea, and put it down in his Bill, which he did very willingly; and then taking Water, away they went to *Fulham*, where acquainting the Bishop's Gentleman, that according to his Lordship's Order over Night, they were come to wait upon him at the Time appointed, the Gentleman introduc'd them into the Hall, and having regal'd them there with a Bottle or two of Wine and a Neat's Tongue, the Mercer was admitted into his Lordship's Presence, and in the mean Time Mr *Adams* made the best of his Way by Water again The Mercer being before the Bishop, quoth his Lordship, I understand that you are, or at leastwise have been, much troubled, how do you find yourself now, Sir? The Mercer reply'd, My Trouble is much abated since your Lordship was pleas'd to order me to wait on you So pulling out a Pocket-Book, he gave His Lordship the following Bill Mr.

Mr *Adams*'s Bill, *April* the 20th, 1711.

	l	s	d
FOR a Piece of green flowered Brocade, containing 23 Yards, at 1l 9s per Yard	33	07	00
For a Piece of white strip'd Damask, containing 20 Yards, at 14s per Yard	18	04	00
For a Piece of Cloth of gold Tissue, containing 18 Yards, at 4l 15s per Yard	85	10	00
For a Piece of black watered Tabby, containing 29 Yards, at 4s 8d per Yard	06	15	04
For a Piece of blue Satin, containing 21 Yards, at 16s per Yard	16	16	00
For a Piece of crimson Velvet, containing 17 Yards, at 1l 18s per Yard	32	06	00
For a Piece of yellow Silk, containing 25 Yards, at 8s per Yard	10	00	00
May the 17th. Lent your Lordship's Nephew.	01	01	06

Sum total, 203 19 10

His Lordship ftaring upon this large Bill, quoth he, ' What is the Meaning of all this ? The Gen-' tleman laft Night might very well fay your Con-' fcience could not be at reft, and I wonder how it ' fhould when you bring a Bill to me which I know ' nothing off *Said the Mercer then bowing and* ' *fcraping,* Your Lordfhip laft Night was pleas'd to ' fay that you would fatisfy me to Day Yes, reply'd ' his Lordfhip, and fo I would as to what the Gen-' tleman told me; who faid, that you being much ' troubled about fome Points of Religion, you de-' fired to be refolved therein, and in order thereto, ' I appointed you to come to me to Day Truly, ' (faid the Mercer again) Your Lordfhip's Nephew ' told me otherwife, for he faid you would pay me ' this Bill off, which Goods, upon my Word he ' had of me, and in a very clandeftine Manner, if I ' was to tell Your Lordfhip all, but only in Ref-' pect to your Honour, I would not difgrace your ' Nephew Quoth His Lordfhip, My Nephew ! ' he is none of my Nephew, I never, to my Know-' ledge, faw the Gentleman in my Life before ' Thus when they came to unriddle the Matter on both Sides, they could not forbear Laughing, the Bifhop at his Nephew, and the Mercer for lending a Man that had once cheated him, a Guinea to cheat him again

After this *Dick Adams* got into the Life-Guards, but his Extravagancy not permitting him to live on his Pay, he went on the Highway One Day he and fome of his Accomplices meeting with a Gentle-man on the Road, they took from him a gold Watch, and a Purfe, in which was one Hundred and eight Guineas But *Adams* not contented with this Booty, and feeing the Gentleman whom they robbed had a very fine Coat on, he rode a little Way back again, and faying to him, Sir, *you have a very good Coat on, I muft make bold to change with you,* he ftripped him of it, and put on his As the Gentleman was riding along after he was robbed, and hearing fomewhat jingle in the Pocket of the Coat which *Adams* had put on him, he felt therein, and, to his great Joy, found his Watch and Guineas again, which *Adams* in a Hurry and Confufion had forgot to put unto the other Coat Pocket when he changed Coats with the Gen-tleman But he and his Comrades coming to an Inn to fnack their Booty, when they found what a Mi-ftake had been made, there was fwearing and ftaring, curfing and raving, damning and finking, with one another, as if they would have fworn the Houfe down, but above all, they were ready to knock *Adams* on the Head for his Forgetfulnefs. However, fince it could not then be help'd, and *Adams* promifing to be more careful in his Bufinefs for the Future, his Neg-ligence was pardon'd for that Time

Dick Adams going out the fame Day again with his Comrades, they ftopp'd the *Canterbury* Stage-Coach on the Road betwixt *Rochefter* and *Sitting-bor*, in which were feveral Gentlewomen, and for the Miftake they made laft, they were very fevere and boifterous upon thefe Paffengers, one of which fay-ing to *Dick,* as he was fearching her Pockets; *Have you no Pity nor Compaffion on our Sex? Certainly ye have neither Chriftianity, Confcience, nor Religion in you.* Right, Madam, (reply'd *Dick*) *we have not much Chriftianity nor Confcience in us, but for my Part you fhall prefently find a little Religion in me* So falling next on fome fine Jewels hanging to her gold Watch, and a fine Pair of Bobs in her Ears, quoth *Dick, Indeed, Madam, fuppofing you to be an Ægyp-tian, I muft beg the Favour of you, as being a Jew, to borrow your Jewels and Ear Rings, according as my Forefathers were commanded by* Mofes Thus having rifled all the Gentlewomen, to above the Va-lue of two hundred Pounds in Money and Goods, they left them to proceed on their Journey, with very forrowful Hearts for their fad Mifchance.

But at laft *Dick* robbing a Man by himfelf, between *London* and *Brainford,* the Perfon robbed met with a Neighbour on the Road, who clofely purfued this Highwayman. He made a running Fight of it, in fhooting *Tarter* like behind him, but they at laft apprehended him, and carrying him before a Magi-ftrate, he was committed to *Newgate.* Tho' he was very wicked before his Affliction fell upon him, yet whilft he lay under Condemnation, he was very devout He was executed at *Tyburn,* in *March,* 1713.

The

The *History* of the Waltham Blacks *and their Transactions, to the Death of* Richard Parvin, Edward Elliot, Robert Kingshel, Henry Marshal, John *and* Edward Pink, *and* James Ansell, *alias* Phillips, *at* Tyburn, *whose Lives are also included.*

SUCH is the unaccountable Folly which Reigns in too great a Part of the human Species, that by their own ill Deeds, they make such Laws neceffary for the Security of Mens Persons and Properties, as would otherwise appear cruel and inhuman, and doubtless, those Laws which we esteem barbarous in other Notions, and even some which appear so, tho' anciently practiced in our own, had their rise from the same Cause I am led to this Observation, from the Folly which certain Persons were guilty of, in making small Insurrections for the Sake only of getting a few Deer, and going on, because they found the Lenity of the Laws could not punish them at present, until they grew to that Height as to ride in arm Troops, Blacked and Disguised, in order the more to terrify those whom they assaulted, and where ever they were denied what they thought proper to demand, whether Venison, Wine, Money, or other Neceffaries for their debauched Feasts, they would by Letters threaten to plunder and destroy with Fire and Sword, whomsoever they thought proper These Villanies being carried on with a high Hand for some Time, in the Year 1722 and 1723, their Insolence grew at last so intollerable, as to oblige the Legiflature to make a new Law against all who thus went Armed and Disguised, and affociated themselves together by the Name of *Blacks,* or entered into any other Confederacies to support and affift one another in doing Injuries and Violences to the Persons and Properties of the King's Subjects

By this Law it was enacted, *That after the first Day of* June, *1723, whatever Persons armed with offensive Weapons, and having their Faces Black'd, or went otherwise Disguised, should appear to any Forest Park, or Grounds enclos'd with any Wall or Fence, wherein Deer were kept, or any Warren where Hares or Conies are kept, or in any Highway, Heath, or Down, or unlawfully Hunt, Kill, or Steal, any Red or Fallow Deer, or rob any Warren, or steal Fish out of any Pond, or malicioussy break down the Head of any Fish-pond, or kill or wound Cattle, or set Fire to any House or Out-House, Stack, &c or cut down, or any other ways destroy Trees planted for Shelter or Profit, or should maliciously shoot at any Person, or send a Letter, demanding Money or other valuable Things, or should rescue any Person in Custody of an Officer, for any such Offences, or b, Gift or Promise, procure any one to join with them, should be deemed Guilty of Felony without Benefit of Clergy, and suffer Pains of Death as Felons so convicted*

Nor was even this Thought fufficient to remedy those Evil, which the idle Follies of some rash Persons had brought about, but a Retrospect was also, by the same Acts, had to Offences heretofore committed, and all Persons who had committed any Crimes punishable by this Act, after the Second of *February* 1722, were commanded to render themselves before the 24th of *July,* 1723, to some Justice of his Majesty's Court of *King's Bench,* or to some Justice of the Peace for the County where they lived, and there make a full and exact Confeffion of the Crimes of such a Nature which they had committed, the Times when, the Places where, and Persons with whom; together with an Account of such Person's Places of abode, as had with them been Guilty as aforefaid, in order to their being thereupon apprehended and brought to Judgment according to Law, on Pain of being deemed *Felon,* without Benefit of the Clergy, and fuffering accordingly But they were entitled to a free Pardon and Forgiveness, in Case that before the 24th of *July* they surrendred and made such Difcovery. Justices of Peace by the said Act, were required on any Information being made before them, by one or more credible Persons, against any Person charged with any of the Offences aforefud, to tranfmit it under their Hands and Seals, to one of his Majesty's principle Secretary's of State, who by the fame Act was required to lay fuch Information and Return before His Majesty in Council, whereupon, an Order was to iffue for the Perfon so charged, to surrender within forty Days, and in case he refufed or neglected to surrender within that Time, then from the Day in which the forty Days were elaps'd, he was to be deemed as a Felon convict, and Execution might be awarded as attainted of Felony by a Verdict Every Perfon also who after the Time appointed for the Surrender of the Person, should conceal, aid, or fuccour him, knowing the Circumstances in which he then stood, should fuffer Death as a Felon, without Benefit of the Clergy And that People might the more readily hazard their Persons for the apprehending fuch Offenders, it was likewise enacted, that if any Person should be wounded, so as to lose an Eye, or the use of any Limb, in

endeavouring

endeavouring to take Persons charged with the Commission of Crimes within this Law, then on a Certificate from the Justices of the Peace, of his being so wounded, the Sheriff of the County was commanded within thirty Days after the sight of such Certificate, to pay the said wounded Person 50 l. under pain of forfeiting 100 l. on failure thereof; and in case any Person should be killed in seizing such Persons as aforesaid, then the said 50 l. was to be paid to the Executors of the Person so killed.

It cannot seem strange, that in Consequence of so extraordinary an Act of the Legislature, many of these Presumptuous and silly People should be apprehended, and a considerable Number of them, having upon their Apprehension been committed to *Winchester* Goal, seven of them were, by *Habeas Corpus*, removed to the greater Solemnity of their Trial to *Newgate*, and for their Offences brought up and arraign'd at the *King's Bench-Bar, Westminster*, and were convicted on full Evidence, all of them of Felony, and three of Murder. We shall inform you, one by one, of what has come to our Knowledge in Relation to their Crimes, and the Manner and Circumstances with which they were committed.

Richard Parvin was Master of a Publick-house at *Portsmouth*, a Man of a dull and flegmatick Disposition, who continually denied his having been in any Manner concerned with these People, though the Evidence against him at his Trial, was as full and as direct as possibly could have been expected, and he himself evidently proved to have been upon the Spot, when the Violences committed by the other Prisoners were transacted. In Answer to this, he said, *That he was not with them, tho' indeed he was upon the Forest*, for which he gave this Reason. He had, he said, a very handsome young Wench who lived with him, and for that Reason being admired by many of his Customers, she took it in her Head one Day to run away; he hearing that she had fled cross the Forest, pursued her, and in that Pursuit, calling at the House of Mr *Parford*, who keeps an Alehouse on the Forest, this Landlord, it seems, who was an Evidence against the other *Blacks*, took him into the Number, tho' as he said, he could fully have cleared himself, if he had had any Money to have sent for Witnesses out of *Berkshire*, but the Mayor of *Portsmouth*, seizing as soon as he was apprehended, on all his Goods, put his Family into great Distress, and whether he could have found them or no, hindred his being able to produce any Witnesses at his Trial. He persevered in these Professions of his Innocency to the very last, still hoping for a Reprieve, and not only feeding himself with such Expectations while in Prison, but also gaz'd earnestly when at the Tree, in hopes that a Pardon would be brought him, till the Cart drew away, and extinguished Life and the Desire of Life together.

Edward Elliot, a Boy of about Seventeen Years of Age, who Father was a Taylor, at a Village between *Petworth* and *Guilford*, was the next who received Sentence of Death with *Parvin*. The Account he gave of his coming into this Society, has something in it very odd, and which gives a fuller Idea of the strange Whims which possessed these People. The Boy said, that about a Year before his being apprehended, thirty or forty Men met him in the County of *Surrey*, and hurried him away; he who appeared to be the Chief of them, telling him that he enlisted him for the Service of the King of the Blacks, in Pursuance of which he was to disguise his Face, obey Orders of whatsoever kind they were, such as breaking down Fish Ponds, burning Woods, shooting Deer, taking also an Oath to be true to them, or they by their *Art Magick* would him into a Beast, and as such make him carry their Burthens, and live like a Horse upon Grass and Water. And he said also, that in the Space of Time he continued with them, he saw several of their Experiments of their Witchcraft; for that once when two Men had offended them, by refusing to comply in taking their Oath, and obeying their Orders, they caused them immediately to be blindfolded, and stopping them in Holes of the Earth up to their Chin, ran at them as if they had been Dogs, bellowing and barking as it were in their Ears, and when they had plagued them a while in this ridiculous Manner, took them out, and bid them remember how they offended any of the Black Nation again, for if they did, they should not escape so well as they had at present. He had seen them also, he said, oblige Carters to drive a good Way out of the Road, and carry whatsoever *Venison* or other Thing they had plundered, to the Places where they would have them. Moreover, that the Men were generally so frighted with their Usage, and so terrified with the Oaths they were obliged to swear, that they seldom complained, or even spoke of their Bondage.

As to the Fact for which they died, *Elliot* gave this Account. That in the Morning when that Fact, for which he died, was committed, *Marshal, Kingshel*, and four others came to him and persuaded him to go to *Farnham Holt*, and that he need not fear disobliging any Gentlemen in the Country, some of whom were very kind to this *Elliot*. They persuaded him that certain Persons of Fortune were concerned with them, and would bear him harmless if he would go. He owned that at last he consented to go with them, but trembled all the Way; insomuch, that he could hardly reach the *Holt*, while they were engaged in the Business for which they came, *viz.* killing the Deer. The Keepers, he said, came upon him, for he was wandered a considerable Way from his Companions after a Fawn, which he intended to send as a Present to a young Woman at *Guildford*, him therefore they quickly seized and bound, and leaving him in that Condition, went in search of the rest of his Associates. It was not long before they came up with them, the Keepers were Six, the Blacks were Seven in in Number, they fell warmly to it with Quarter-Staffs; the Keepers unwilling to have Lives taken away, advised them to retire, but upon their refusing, and *Marshal's* firing a Gun, by which one of the Keepers belonging to the Lady *How* was slain, they discharged a Blunderbuss and shattered the Thigh of one *Barber* amongst the Blacks, upon which three of his Associates ran away, and the two others, *Marshal* and *Kingshel*, were likewise taken, and so the Fray for the present ended. *Elliot* lay bound all the while within hearing, and in the greatest Agonies imaginable, at the Consideration that whatever Blood was spilt, he should be as much unsearable for it as those who shed it, in which he was not mistaken; for the Keepers returning after the Fight was over, carried him away bound, and he never had his Fetters off after, till the Morning of his Execution. He behaved himself very soberly, quietly, and with much seeming Penitence and Contrition; he owned the Justice of the Law in punishing him, and said, He more especially deserved to suffer, since at the Time of the committing this Fact, he was Servant to a Widow Lady, where he wanted nothing to make him happy or easy.

Robert Kingshel was 26 Years old, lived in the same House with his Parents, being Apprentice to his Brother a Shoemaker. His Parents were very watchful

watchful over his Behaviour, fought by every Method to prevent his taking ill Courses, or being guilty of any Debauchery whatever. The Night before this unhappy Accident fell out, as he and the rest of the Family were sleeping in their Beds, _Barber_ made a Signal at his Chamber Window, it being then about Eleven a Clock. _Kingshel_ upon this, arose and got softly out of the Window, _Barber_ took him upon his Horse, and away they went to the _Holt_, twelve Miles distant, calling in their Way upon _Henry Marshal_, _Elliot_, and the rest of their Accomplices. He said it was Eight a Clock in the Morning before the Keepers attacked them; he owned they bid them retire, and that he himself told them they would, provided the bound Man (_Elliot_) was released, and deliver'd into their Hands, but that Proposition being refus'd, the Fight presently grew warm _Barber_'s Thigh was broke, and _Marshal_ killed the Keeper with a Shot. Being thereupon very hard pressed, three of their Companions ran away, leaving him and _Marshal_ to fight out, _Elliot_ being already taken, and _Barber_ disabled. It was not long before they were in the same unhappy Condition with their Companions From the Time of their being apprehended, _Kingshel_ laid aside all Hopes of Life, and applyed himself with great Fervency and Devotion, to enable him in what alone remained for him to do, viz. _dying Decently._

Henry Marshal, about 36 Years of Age, the unfortunate Person by whose Hand the Murther was committed, seem'd to be the least sensible of the Evils he had done of any, such was the Pleasure of Almighty God, that till the Day before his Execution, he neither had his Senses, nor the use of his Speech When he recovered it, and a Clergyman represented to him the horrid Crime of which he had been Guilty, he was so far from shewing any deep Sense of the Crime of shedding innocent Blood, that he made light of it, and said, _Sure he might stand upon his own Defence, and was not bound to run away and leave his Companions in Danger._ This was the Language he talked for the Space of twenty four Hours before his Death, when he enjoyed the Use of Speech, and so far was he from thanking those who charitably offered him their Admonitions, that he said, he had not forgot himself, but had already taken Care of what he thought necessary for his Soul, however, he did not attempt in the least to prevaricate, but fairly acknowledged that he committed the Fact for which he died, tho' nothing could oblige him to speak of it in a manner as if he was sorry for, or repented of it, farther than for having occasioned his own Misfortunes So strong is the Prejudice which vulgar Minds may acquire, by often repeating to themselves certain Positions, however ridiculous or false, that a Man had a right to imbrue his Hands in the Blood of another, who was in the Execution of his Office, and endeavouring him in the Commission of an illegal Act.

These of whom we have last spoken, were altogether concerned in the aforemention'd Fact, which was attended with Murder. But we are now to speak of the rest, who were concerned in the Felony only, for which they with the abovemention'd _Parvin_ suffered Of these there were two Brothers, whose Names were _John_ and _Edward Pink_, Carters in _Portsmouth_, and always accounted honest and industrious Fellows, before this Accident happened They did not, however, deny their being Guilty, but on the contrary, ingenuously confessed the Truth of what was

sworn, and mentioned some other Circumstances that had been produced at the Trial, which attended their committing it They said that they met _Parvin_'s House-keeper upon the Road, that they forced her to cut the Throat of a Deer which they had just taken upon _Bear Forest_, gave her a Dagger, which they forced her to wear, and to ride cross legg'd with Pistols before her. In this Dress they brought her to _Parford_'s House upon the Forest, where they dined upon a Haunch of Venison, feasted merrily, and after Dinner sent out two of their Companions to kill more Deer; not in the _King_'s Forest, but in _Waltham-Chace_, belonging to the Bishop of _Winchester_. One of these two Persons they called their King, and the other they called Lyon Neither of these two Brothers objected any Thing, either to the Truth of the Evidence given against, or the Justice of that Sentence passed upon them, only one insinuated that the Evidence given against, or the strong against him and _Ansel_, if it had not been so running away with the Witness's Wife, which so provok'd him that they were sure they should not escape when he was admitted a Witness These, like the rest, were hard to be persuaded that the Things they had committed were any Crimes in the Eyes of God, and said, Deer were wild Beasts, and they did not see why the Poor had not as good a Right to them as the Rich However, as the Law condemned them to suffer, they were bound to submit, and in Consequence of that Notion, they behaved themselves very orderly, decently, and quietly, while under Sentence.

James Ansel, alias _Stephen Philips_, the Seventh and last of these unhappy Persons, was a Man addicted to a worse and more profligate Life than any of the rest had ever been; for he had held no settled Employment, but had been a loose disorderly Person, concerned in all Sorts of Wickedness for many Years, both at _Portsmouth_, _Guilford_, and other Country Towns, as well as at _London_ Deer were not the only Things that he had dealt in, stealing, robbing on the Highway, had been formerly his Employment, and in becoming a Black, he did not, as the others, ascend in Wickedness, but came down on the contrary a Step lower Yet this Criminal, as his Offences were greater, so his Sense of them was much stronger than in any of the rest, excepting _Kingshel_, for he gave over all manner of Hopes of Life, and all Concerns about it as soon as he was taken, yet even he had no Notion of making Discoveries, unless they might be beneficial to himself, and tho' he owned the Knowledge of twenty Persons who were notorious Offenders in the same Kind, he absolutely refused to name them, since such naming would not procure himself a Pardon. Talking to him of the Duty of doing Justice, was beating the Air: He said he thought there was no Justice in taking away other Peoples Lives, unless it was to save his own, yet no sooner was he taxed about his going on the Highway than he confessed it, and said, he knew very well Bills would have been preferred against him at _Guilford_ Assizes, in case he had got off at the _King_'s-_Bench_, but that he did not greatly value them, for tho' formerly he had been Guilty of some Facts in that Way, yet they could not all now be proved, and he should have found it no difficult matter to have demonstrated it of those then charged upon him, of which he was not really Guilty, but owed his being thought so to a profligate Course of Life he had for some Time led, and his Aversion to all honest Employments As bold as the whole Gang of these Fellows appeared, yet what with Sickness, what with the Apprehension of Death, they were so terrified, that not one of 'em but *Ansel*, was able to stand up, or speak, at the Place of Execution, many who saw 'em there, affirming, that some of them were dead even before they were turned off

As an Appendix to the melancholly History of these seven unhappy Persons, we will add Part of a Letter written at that Time by a Gentleman of *Essex*, to his Friend in *London*, containing a more particular Account of the Humour of these People than we have seen any where else

A Letter to Mr. C. D. *in* LONDON.

DEAR, SIR,

'YOU cannot but have heard of the *Waltham Blacks*, as they are called, a set of whimsical merry Fellows, that are so mad to run the greatest Hazards for the Sake of a haunch of Venison, and passing a jolly Evening together. For my Part, I took the Stories of them for Fables, till Experience taught me the contrary, by the Adventure I am going to relate to you

' To begin then, my Horse got some Way a Stone in his Foot, so that finding it impossible to get him along, I was glad to take up at a little blind Ale-House, which I perceived had a Yard and Stable behind it The Man of the House received me very civily, but when I ask'd him whether I could lodge there that Night, he told me No, he had no room I desired him then to put something to my Horse's Foot, and let me sit up all Night The Man made me no Answer, but when we came into the House together, the Wife dealt more roughly and more freely with me, that truly I neither could, nor should stay there, and was for hurrying her Husband to get my Horse out: However, on putting a Crown into her Hand, and promising her another for my Lodging, she at last told me that there was indeed a little Bed above Stairs, on which she would order a clean Pair of Sheets to be put, for she was persuaded I was more of a Gentleman than to take any Notice of what I saw passed there. This made me more uneasy than I was before I concluded now I was got among a den of Highwaymen, and expected nothing less than to be robbed and have my Throat cut, however, finding there was no Remedy, I even set myself down, and endeavoured to be as easy as I could

' By this Time it was very dark, and I heard three or four Horsemen alight, and lead their Horses into the Yard As the Men where coming into the Room where I was, I overheard my Landlord say, Indeed Brother you need not be uneasy, I am positive the Gentleman's a Man of Honour To which I heard another Voice reply, What good could our Death do to any Stranger? Faith I don't apprehend half the Danger you do: I dare say the Gentleman would be glad of our Companies, and we should be pleas'd with his, come, hang Fear, I'll lead the Way ' So said, so done, in they came, Five of them, all disguis'd so effectually, that unless it were in the same Disguise, I should not be able to distinguish any one of them Down they sat, and he who was constituted their *Captain pro hac Vice*, accosted me with great Civility, and asked me, *If I would honour them with my Company*

at Supper I did not yet guess the Profession of my new Acquaintance But supposing my Landlord would not suffer either a Robbery or a Murder in his own House, by Degrees my Mind grew perfectly easy

' About Ten o'Clock, I heard a very great Noise of Horses, and soon after of Mens Feet trampling in a Room over my Head Then my Landlord came down and informed us, Supper was just ready to go upon the Table Upon this, we were all desired to walk up, and he, whom I before called the *Captain*, presented me with a humorous kind of Ceremony to a Man more disguis'd than the rest, who sat at the upper End of the Table, telling me at the same Time, he hoped I would not refuse to pay my Respects to *Prince Oroonoko King of the Blacks*. It then immediately struck into my Head, who those worthy Persons were, and I called myself a thousand Blockheads in my Mind for not finding it out before; but the Hurry of Things, or to speak the Truth, the Fear I was in, prevented my judging, even from the most evident Signs

' As soon as our aukward Ceremonies was over, Supper was brought in It consisted of eighteen Dishes of Venison in every Shape, roasted, boiled with Broth, hashed Collups, Pasties, Umble Pies, and a large Haunch in the Middle larded. The Table we sat at was very large, and the Company in all twenty one Persons, at each of our Elbows there was set a Bottle of Claret; and the Man and Woman of the House sat down at the lower End. Two or three of the Fellows had good natural Voices, and so the Evening was spent as merrily, as the Rakes pass theirs at the *King's Arms*, or the City Apprentices at *Sadler's Wells* About Two the Company seemed inclined to break up, having first assured me that they should take my Company as a Favour any *Thursday* Evening, if I came that Way

' Before I conclude my Epistle, it is fit I should inform you, that they did me the Honour, of acquainting me with those Rules by which their Society was govern'd. Their *Black Prince* assured me that their Government was perfectly *Monarchial*, and that when upon Expeditions, he had an absolute Command, But in the Time of Peace (continued he) and at the Table, I condescend to eat and drink familiarly with my Subjects as Friends. We admit no Man into our Society, 'till he has been twice drunk with us, that we may be perfectly acquainted with his Temper, but if the Person who sues to be admitted, declares solemnly he was drunk in his Life, this Rule is dispensed with, and the Person is only bound to converse with us a Month. As soon as we have determined to admit him, He is to equip himself with a good Mare or Gelding, a Brace of Pistols, and a Gun to lye on the Saddle Bow, then he is sworn upon the Horns over the Chimney; and having a new Name conferred by the Society, is thereby entered upon the Roll, and from that Day forward, considered as a lawful Member.

' He went on with abundance more of their wise Institutions which are not of Consequence enough to tell you In the Morning having given my Landlady the other Crown Piece, I speeded directly home, as much in Amaze at the new People I had discovered, as the *Duke* of *Alva*'s Huntsmen when they found an undiscovered Nation in Spain, by following their Master's Hawk over the Mountains Pray, in Return let me see if all your London

' dos

" don Rambles can produce such another Adventure."

I am yours, &c.

Before we leave these People we think it proper to acquaint our Readers, that their Folly was not to be extinguished by a single Execution; there were a great many young Fellows of the same Stamp, who were Fools enough to forfeit their Lives upon the same Occasion. However, the Humour did not run very long; Tho' some of them were impudent enough to murther a Keeper or two afterwards, in the Space of a Twelvemonth, the whole Nation of the *Blacks* was extinguished, and these *Country Rakes* were contented to play the Fool upon easier Terms The last Blood that was shed on either Side, being that of

a Keeper's Son at *Old Windsor*, whom some of these wise People fired at as he look'd out of the Window

A special Assizes was held at *Reading*, before three of his Majesty's Judges, to try the Persons concern'd in this Murther, and several others Four Men were Capitally convicted and executed; several others were ordered for Transportation, and in short this was the decisive Stroke which put a Period to their whimsical Monarchy. The Men that were hang'd, like those abovementioned, were so weak with lying in Prison, that one of them was borne between two to the *Town Hall*, and carry'd upon the Hangman's Back into the Cart that convey'd him to the Tree The rest were not in a much better Condition.

The LIFE of JOSEPH BLAKE, *alias* BLUESKIN.

AS there is Impudence and Wickedness enough in the Lives of most publick Malefactors, to make Persons of a sober Education and Behaviour, wonder at the depravity of human Nature; so there are sometimes superlative Rogues, who as far exceed the ordinary Class of Rogues, as they do honest People, and whenever such a Monster as this appears in the World, there are enough Fools to make such a Noise about his Conduct, as to invite others to imitate the Obstinacy of his Deportment, thro' that false Love of Fame, which influences those Wretches. Amongst the Number of these, *Joseph Blake*, better known by his nick Name of *Blueskin*, always deserves to be remembered, as one who studiously took the Paths of Infamy, in order to become Famous.

By Birth he was a Native of this City of *London*; his Parents being Persons in tollerable Circumstances, kept him six Years at School, where he did not learn half so much from his Master, as he did Evil from his School-Fellow *William Blewit*, from whose Lessons he copied so well, that all his Education signified nothing. He absolutely refusing, when he came from School, to go to any Employment, but on the contrary set up for a Robber when he was scarce Seventeen, but from that Time to the Day of his Death, was unsuccessful in all his Undertakings, hardly ever committing the most trivial Fact, but he experienced for it, either the Humanity of the Mob, or of the Keepers of *Bridewel*, out of which, or some other Prison, he could hardly keep his Feet for a Month together.

He fell into the Gang of *Lock, Wilkinson, Carrick, Lincoln*, and *Daniel Carrol* And being one Night out with this Gang, they robb'd one Mr *Clark* of eight Shillings, and a silver hilted Sword, just as Candles were going to be lighted A Woman looking accidentally out of a Window, perceived it, and

cry'd out Thieves *Wilkinson* fired a Pistol at her, which (very luckily) upon her drawing in her Head, graz'd upon the Stone of the Window, and did no other Mischief *Blake* was also in the Company of the same Gang, when they attack'd Captain *Langley* at the Corner of *Hide-Park Road*, as he was going to the *Camp*, but the Captain behaved himself so well, that notwithstanding they shot several Times thro' and thro' his Coat, yet they were not able to rob him Not long after this, *Wilkinson* being apprehended, impeached a large Number of Persons, and with them, *Blake* and *Lock Lock* hereupon made a fuller Discovery than the other before Justice *Blakerby*, in which Information there was contained no less than seventy Robberies, upon which he also was admitted a Witness, and having nam'd *Wilkinson, Lincoln, Carrick* and *Carrol*, with himself, to have been the five Persons who murder'd *Peter Martin* the *Chelsea Pensioner*, by the *Park Wall Wilkinson* thereupon was apprehended, tried, and convicted notwithstanding the Information he had before given, which was thereby totally set aside.

Blake himself also became now an Evidence against the rest of his Companions, and discovered about a dozen Robberies which they had committed, amongst these there was a one very remarkable one Two Gentlemen in Hunting Caps were together in a Chariot on the *Hampstead-Road*, from whom they took two gold Watches, Rings Seals and other things to a considerable Value, and *Junks*, alias *Levee*, laid his Pistol down by the Gentlemen all the while he search'd them, yet they wanted either the Courage or the presence of Mind, to seize it and prevent their losing Things of so great Value Not long after this *Oakly*, *Junks*, and this *Blake*, stopp'd a single Man with a Link before him in *Fig-Lane*, and he not surrendering so easily as they expected, *Junks* and *Oakly* beat him over the Head with their Pistols, and then

then left him wounded in a terrible Condition, taking from him one Guinea and one Penny. A very short time after this, *Junks, Oakley,* and *Flood,* were apprehended and executed, for robbing Colonel *Cope* and Mr *Young* of that very Watch, for which *Carrick* and *Malony* had been before executed, *Joseph Blake* being the Evidence against them

After this hanging Work of his Companions, he thought himself not only entitled to Liberty but Reward therein however he was mightily mistaken, for not having surrendered willingly and quietly, but being taken after long Resistance and when he was much wounded, there did not seem to be the least Foundation for this confident Demand He remained still Prisoner in the *Wood-street* Compter, obstinately refusing to be transported for seven Years, 'till at last procuring two Men to be bound for his good Behaviour, he was carried before a worthy *Alderman* of the City and there discharged At which time, some-body there present asking how long time might be given him, before they should see him again at the *Old-Bailey?* A Gentleman made answer, in about three Sessions, in which time it seems he guessed very right, for the third Sessions from thence, *Blake* was indeed brought to the Bar. For no sooner was he at Liberty but he was employed in robbing, and having picked up *Jack Shepherd* for a Companion, they went out together to search for Prey in the Fields. Near the half Way House to *Hampstead,* they met with one *Pargstar,* pretty much in Liquor, whom immediately *Blake* knock'd down into a Ditch, where he must inevitably have perished, if *John Shepherd* had not kept his Head above the Mud with great Difficulty For this Fact the next Sessions after it happened, the two Brothers (*Brightwells*) in the Guards were tried, and if a Number of Men had not sworn them to have been upon Duty at the Time the Robbery was committed, they had certainly been convicted, the Evidence of the Prosecutor being direct and full. The elder *Brightwell* died in a Week after he was released from his confinement, and so did not live to see his Innocence fully clear'd by the Confession of *Blake.*

A very short Space after this, *Blake* and his Companion *Shepherd,* committed the Burglary together in the House of Mr. *Kneebone,* where *Shepherd* getting into the House, let in *Blake* at the back Door and carry'd off Goods to a considerable Value For this, both *Shepherd* and he were apprehended, and the Sessions before *Blake* was convicted, his Companion received Sentence of Death; but at the Time *Blake* was taken up, had made his Escape out out of the Condemned Hold.

He behaved with great Impudence at his Trial, and when he found nothing would save him, he took the Advantage of *Jonathan Wild's* coming to speak with him, to cut the said *Wild's* Throat, a large Gash from the Ear beyond the Wind-pipe; of which Wound *Wild* languished a long Time, and happy had it been for him if *Blake's* Wound had proved fatal, for then *Jonathan* had escaped Death by a more dishonourable Wound in the Throat, than that of a Penknife But the Number of his Crimes, and the Spleen of his Enemies procured him a worse Fate. Whatever *Wild* might deserve of others, he seems to have merited better Usage from this *Blake,* for while he continued a Prisoner in the Compter, *Jonathan* was at the Expence of curing a Wound he had received, allowed him three Shillings and Six-pence a Week, and after his last Misfortune promised a good Coffin, actually furnished him with Money to support him in *Newgate,* and several good Books, if he would have made any Use of them. But because he freely declared to *Blueskin,* there was no Hopes of getting him Transported, the bloody Villain determined to take away his Life, and was so far from shewing any Signs of Remorse, when he was brought up again to *Newgate,* that he declared if he had thought of it before, he would have provided such a Knife as should have cut off his Head

At the Time that he received Sentence, there was a Woman also condemned, and they being placed as usual, in what is called the *Bail Dock* at the *Old-Bailey, Blake* offered such Rudeness to the Woman, that she cried out and alarmed the whole Bench All the Time he lay under Condemnation, he appeared utterly thoughtless and insensible of his approaching Fate. Tho' from the cutting of *Wild's* Throat, and some other Barbarities of the same Nature, he acquired amongst the Mob the Character of a brave Fellow, yet he was in himself but a mean spirited timorous Man, and never exerted himself, but either thro' Fury or Dispair He wept much at the Chapel before he was to die; and tho' he drank deeply to drive away Fear, yet at the Place of Execution he wept again, trembled, and shewed all the Signs of a timorous Confusion, as well he might, who had lived wickedly, and trifled with his Repentance to the Grave. There was nothing in his Person extraordinary, a dapper, well set Fellow, of great Strength, and great Cruelty; equally detested by the sober Part of the World, for the audacious Wickedness of his Behaviour, and despised by his Companions for the Villanies he committed even against them He was executed in the 28th Year of his Age, on the 11th of *November,* 1724.

The

The LIFE of JACK SHEPHERD.

Amongst the Prodigies of ingenious Wicked-ness and artful Mischief, which have surpri-zed the World in our time perhaps none has made so great a Noise as *John Shepherd*, the Malefactor of whom we are now going to speak. His Father's Name was *Thomas Shepherd*, who was by Trade a Carpenter, and liv'd in *Spittle-Fields*; a Man of an extraordinary good Character, and who took all the Care his narrow Circumstances would allow, that his Family might be brought up in the Fear of God, and in just Notions of their Duty towards their Neighbour yet he was so un-happy in his Children, that both his Son *John* and another took to ill Courses, and both in their Turns were convicted at he Bar in the *Old-Bailey.*

After the Father's Death, his Widow did all she could to get this unfortunate Son of hers admitted into *Christ's Hospital*, but failing of that, she got him bred up at a School in *Bishopsgate-Street*, where he learned to read, and might in all pro-bability have got a good Education, if he had not been too soon removed, being put out to the Trade of a *Cane-Chair-Maker*. His Master us'd him very well, and probably he might have liv'd honestly with him, but he dying in a short time afterwards, *Shepherd* was put to another, a much younger Man, who used him so harshly, that in a little time he ran away from him He was then put to another Master, one Mr. *Wood* in *Witch-Street*, from whose Kindness and of Mr *Kneebone's*, whom he robbed, he was taught to write, and had many other Favours done him by that Gentleman, whom he so ungratefully treated. But good usage or bad was grown all alike to him now; he had gi-ven himself up to the sensual Pleasures of low Life, Drinking all Day, and getting to some impudent Strumpet at Night

Amongst the Chief of his Mistresses there was one. *Elizabeth Lion*, commonly call'd *Edgeworth Bess*: the Impudence of whose Behaviour was shocking even to the greatest Part of *Shepherd's* Companions; but it seems charm'd him so much, that he suffered her for a while to direct him in every Thing, and she was the first who engaged him in taking base Methods to obtain Money wherewith to purchase baser Pleasures. This *Lion* was a large masculine Woman, and *Shepherd* a very little slight-limb'd Lad, so that whenever he had been drinking and came to her quarrelsome, *Bess* often beat him into better Temper, though *Shepherd* upon other Occasions ma-nifested his wanting neither Courage nor Strength Repeated Quarrels however between *Shepherd* and his Mistress as it does with People of better Rank, created such a Coldness, and at last a Seperation The Creature he picked out to supply the Place of *Betty Lion*, was one Mrs *Maggott*, a Woman somewhat less boisterous in her Temper, but full as wicked She had a very great Contempt for *Shep-*

herd, and only made Use of him to go and steal Money, or what might yield Money, for her to spend in Company that she lik'd better One Night when *Shepherd* came to her, and told her he had pawn'd the last Thing he had for half a Crown, *Prithee*, says she, *don't tell me such melancholly Stories, but think how you may get more Money I have been in* White-Horse Yard *this Afternoon, there's a Piece-Broker there worth a great deal of Money, he keeps his Cash in a Drawer under the Compter; and there's Abundance of good Things in his Shop that would be fit for me to wear*, a Word you know to the Wife is enough, *let me see now how soon you'll put me in Possession of them* This had the Effect that she desired; *Shepherd* left her about One o'Clock in the Morning, went to the House she talked of, took up the Cellar Window Bars, and from thence entered the Shop, which he plun dered of Money and Goods to the amount of 22 l. and brought it to his Doxy the same Day before she was stirring, who appeared thereupon very well satisfied with his Diligence, and helped him a short Time to squander what he had so dearly earned

He still attained some Affection for his old Fa-vourite *Bess Lion*, who being taken up for some of her Tricks, was committed to St *Giles's* Round house, where *Shepherd* going to see her, broke the Doors open, beat the Keeper, and like a true Knight Errant, set his distressed *Paramour* at Liberty, which heroick Act got him so much Reputation a mongst the Ladies of *Drury-Lane*, that there was no Body of his Profession so much esteemed by them as *John Shepherd* His Brother *Thomas*, who was himself a tollerable Estimation with that de-bauch'd part of the Sex, now importun'd some of them to speak to his Brother *John* to lend him a little Money, and for the Future allow him to go out a robbing with him To both these Propo-sitions, *Jack*, being a kind Brother, consented at the first Word, and from thence forward the two Bro thers were always of one Party

In about three Weeks after their coming toge ther, they broke open a Linnen-Draper's Shop, near *Clare-Market*, where the Brothers made good use of their Time, for they were not in the House above a quarter of an Hour, before they made shift to strip it of 50 l But the younger Brother acting impudently in disposing of some of the Goods, he was detected and apprehended, upon which the first Thing he did was to impeach his Brother, and as many of his Confederates as he could *Jack* was very quickly apprehended upon his Brother's In-formation, and committed by Justice *Parry* to the Round-house, for farther Examination, but in stead of waiting for that, he began to examine, as well as he could, the Strength of the Place of his Confinement; which being much too weak for a Fel low of his Capacity, he marched off before Night, and committed a Robbery into the Bargain, vowing

ing to be revenged on *Tom* who had so basely behaved himself (as *Jack* phrased it) toward so good a Brother.

That Information going off, *Jack* went on in his old Way as usual. One Day he and *J. Benson* being in *Leicester Fields*, *Benson* attempted to get a Gentleman's Watch, but missing his pull, the Gentleman perceived it and rais'd a Mob, where *Shepherd* passing briskly to save his Companion, was apprehended in his stead, and being carried before Justice *Walters*, was committed to *New-Prison*, where the first Sight he saw, was his old Companion *Bess Lion*, who had found her Way thither upon a like Errand *Jack*, who now saw himself beset with Danger, began to exert all his little Cunning, which was indeed his Master piece He applied himself first to *Benson*'s Friends, who were in good Circumstances, hoping by their Meditation to make the Matter up, but in this he miscarried. Then he attempted a slight Information, but the Justice to whom he sent it, perceiving how trivial a Thing it was and guessing well at the Drift thereof refused it *Shepherd* was now driven to his last Shift, when *Bess Lion* and he laid their Heads together how to break out, which they effected by Force, and got safe off to one of *Bess Lions* old Lodgings, where she kept him secret for some Time, frightening him with Stories of great Searches being made after him, in order to detain him from conversing with any other Woman

But *Jack* being not naturally timorous, and having a strong Inclination to be out again in his old Way with his Companions, it was not long before he gave her the slip, and lodged himself with another of his Female Acquaintance, in a little bye Court near the *Strand* Here one *Charles Grace* desired to become an Associate with him *Jack* was very ready to take any young Fellow in as a Partner of his Villanies especially as *Grace* told him that his Reason for doing such Things, was to keep a beautiful Woman without the Knowledge of his Relations *Shepherd* and he getting the Acquaintance of one *Anthony Lamb*, an Apprentice to Mr *Carter*, near St *Clements* Church, they inveigled the young Man to consent to let them in to rob his Master's House He accordingly perform'd it, and they took from Mr *Barton*, who lodged there, to a very considerable Value But *Grace* and *Shepherd* quarrelling about the Division, *Shepherd* wounded *Grace* in a violent Manner, and on this Quarrel betraying one another, *Grace* and *Lamb* were taken. But the Misfortune of poor *Lamb*, who had been drawn in, so far prevailed upon several Gentlemen who knew him, that they not only prevailed to have his Sentence mitigated to Transportation, but also furnished him with Necessaries, and procured an Order that on his Arrival there he should not be sold, as the other *Felons* were, but that he should be left at Liberty to provide for himself as well as he could

It seems that *Shepherd*'s Gang, which consisted of himself, his Brother *Tom*, *Joseph Blake*, alias *Blueskin*, *Charles Grace*, and *James Sikes*, whom his Companions called *Hell* and *Fury* not knowing how to dispose of the Goods they had taken, made use of *William Field* for that purpose, whom *Shepherd* in his Ludicrous Stile, us'd to characterize thus. That he was a Fellow wicked enough to do any thing, but his want of Courage permitted him to do nothing but carry on the Trade he did; which was that of selling stolen Goods when put into his Hands But *Blake* and *Shepherd* finding *Field* sometimes delatory, not thinking it always safe to trust him, they resolved to hire a Warehouse and lodge their Goods there; which accordingly they did near the *Horse-Ferry* in

Westminster. There they plac'd what they took out of Mr. *Kneebone*'s House, and the Goods made a great show there, whence the People in the Neighbourhood really took them for very honest Persons, who had so great wholesale Business on their Hands as occasion'd their taking a place there which lay convenient for the Water *Field* however importun'd them, having got scent they had such a Warehouse, that he might go and see the Goods, pretending that he had it just now in his Power to sell them at a very great Price They accordingly carried him thither and shewed him the Things Two or three Days afterwards, *Field*, tho' he had not Courage to rob any Body else, ventured however, to break open the Warehouse, and took every Rag that had been lodged there

Not long after, *Shepherd* was apprehended for robbing Mr *Kneebone*, and tried at the next Sessions at the *Old-Bailey*. His Appearance there was very mean, and all the Defence he pretended to make, was, that *Jonathan Wild* had helped to dispose of part of the Goods, and he thought that it was very hard that he should not share in the Punishment The Court took little Notice of so insignificant a Plea, and Sentence being passed upon him, he hardly made a sensible Petition for the Favour of the Court in the Report, but behav'd throughout as a Person either stupid or Foolish, so far was he from appearing in any Degree likely to make the Noise he afterwards did

When put into the *Condemned Hold*, he prevailed upon one *Fowls*, who was also under Sentence, to lift him up to the Iron Spikes placed over the Door which looks into the Lodge, a Woman of a large Make attending without, and two others standing behind her in Riding Hoods *Jack* no sooner got his Head and Shoulders thro' between the Iron Spikes, than by a sudden Spring his Body followed with Ease, and the Women taking him down gently, he was, without Suspicion of the Keepers, (tho' some of them was drinking at the upper End of the *Lodge*) convey'd safely out of the *Lodge* Door, when soon getting a Hackney Coach, he went clear off before there was the least Notice of his Escape; which, when it was known, very much surprized the Keepers, who never dreamt of an Attempt of that Kind before

As soon as *John* breathed the fresh Air, he went again briskly to his old Employment, and the first thing he did was to find out one *Page*, a Butcher of his acquaintance in *Clare-Market*, who dress'd him up in one of his Frocks, and then went with him upon the Business of raising Money No sooner had they set out, but *Shepherd* remembring one Mr *Martin*'s a Watch-maker, near the *Castle Tavern* in *Fleet-street*, and the Situation of the Shop, he prevailed upon his Companion to go thither, and screwing a Gimlet fast into the Post at the Door, they tied the Knocker of the Door thereto with a String, and then boldly breaking the Glasses, snatched three Watches before a Boy that was in the Shop could open the Door, and marched clear off, *Shepherd* having the Impudence upon this Occasion, to pass underneath *Newgate*

However, he did not long enjoy his Liberty, for, strolling about *Finchly Common*, he was apprehended and committed to *Newgate*, and was put immediately in the *Stone Room*, where they loaded him with a heavy pair of Irons, and then stapled him fast down to the Floor He being left there alone in the Sessions Time, most of the People of the Gaol then attending at the *Old-Bailey*, he with a crooked Nail opened the Lock, and by that Means got rid of his Chain, and went directly to the Chimney in the Room,

Room; where, with inceſſant working, he got out a couple of Stones, and by that Means entered a Room called the *Red Room*, where no Body had been lodged for a conſiderable Time Here he threw down a Door, which one would have thought impoſſible to have been mov'd by the Strength of a Man though with ever ſo much Noiſe From hence with a great deal to do, he forced his Paſſage into the Chapel, there he broke a Spike off the Door, forcing open by its help four other Doors Getting at laſt upon the Leads, he from thence deſcended gently, by the Help of the Blanket on which he lay, (for which he went back thro' the whole Priſon) upon the Leads of Mr *Bird* a Turner, next Door to *Newgate*, and looking in at the Garret Window, ſaw the Maid going to Bed. As ſoon as he thought ſhe was aſleep, he ſtepp'd down Stairs, went thro' the Shop, opened the Door, then into the Street, leaving the Door open behind him.

In the Morning when the Keepers were in ſearch after him, hearing of this Circumſtance by the Watchman, they were then perfectly ſatisfied of the Method by which he went off. However, they were obliged to publiſh a Reward, and make the ſtricteſt Enquiry after him, ſome fooliſh People having propagated a Report, that he had not got out without Connivance In the mean while *Shepherd* found it a very difficult Thing to get rid of his Irons, having been obliged to lurk about and lye hid near a Village not far from Town, 'till with much ado he procured a Hammer and took them off He was no ſooner freed from the Incumbrance that remained upon him but he came privately into the Town and that Night robbed Mr *Rawlin's* Houſe a *Pawn-Broker* in *Drury-Lane* Here he got a very large Booty, and amongſt other things a very handſome black Suit of Cloaths and a Gold Watch Being dreſſed with theſe he carried the reſt of the Goods and valuable Effects to two Women, one of whom was a poor young Creature whom *Shepheard* had ſeduced, and who was impriſoned on this account

No ſooner had he taken care of the Booty, but he went amongſt his Companions, the Pick-pockets and Whores in *Drury-Lane* and *Clare Market*, where being accidentally eſpied ſudling at a little Brandy-Shop, by a Boy belonging to an Alehouſe who knew him very well, the Lad immediately gave Information, upon which he was apprehended, and re-conducted with a vaſt Mob to his old Manſion-Houſe of *Newgate*, being ſo much intoxicated with Liquor, that he hardly was ſenſible of his miſerable Fate They now took effectual Care to prevent a third Eſcape, never ſuffering him to be alone a Moment, which as it put the Keepers to great Expence, they took Care to pay themſelves with the Money they took of all who came to ſee him.

In this laſt Confinement it was that Mr *Shepherd* and his Adventures became the ſole Topick of Converſation about Town. Numbers flocked daily to behold him, and he, far from being diſpleaſed at being made a Spectacle of, entertained all who came with the greateſt Gaiety that could be. He acquainted them with all his Adventures; related each of his Robberies in the moſt ludicrous Manner, and endeavoured to ſet off every Circumſtance of his flagitious Life, as well as his Capacity would give him leave, which, to ſay Truth, was excellent at Cunning, and Buffoonery, and nothing elſe. Nor were the Crowds

of People on this Occaſion, that throng'd to *Newgate*, made up of the Dregs of the People only, for then there would have been no Wonder; but inſtead of that, Perſons of the firſt Diſtinction, and not a few even dignified with Titles 'Tis certain that the Noiſe made about him, and this Curioſity of Perſons of ſo high a Rank was a very great Misfortune to the poor Wretch himſelf, who from theſe Circumſtances began to conceive grand Ideas of himſelf, as well as ſtrong Hopes of Pardon, which encouraged him to play over all his Airs, and divert as many as thought it worth their While, by their Preſence, to prevent a dying Man from conſidering his latter End Yet when *Shepherd* came up to Chapel, it was obſerved that all his Gaiety was laid aſide, and he both heard and aſſiſted with great Attention at Divine Service, tho' upon other Occaſions he as much as he could avoided religious Diſcourſe; and depending upon the Petitions he had made to ſeveral Noblemen to interceed with the King for Mercy, he ſeemed rather to aim at diverting his Time till he receiv'd a Pardon, than to improve the few Days he had to prepare himſelf for his laſt

On the 10th of *November*, 1724, *Shepherd* was by *Certaorari* removed to the Bar of Court of King's Bench at *Weſtminſter*, an *Affidavit* being made, that he is the ſame *John Shepherd* mentioned in the Record of Conviction before read Mr Juſtice *Powis* awarded Judgment againſt him, and a Rule was made for his Execution on the 16th

Such was the unaccountable Fondneſs this Criminal had for Life, and ſo unwilling was he to loſe all hopes of preſerving it, that he fram'd in his Mind all Reſolutions of cutting the Rope when he ſhould be bound in the Cart, thinking thereby to get amongſt the Crowd, and ſo into *Lincoln's-Inn-Fields*, and from thence to the *Thames* For this Purpoſe he had provided a Knife, which was with great Difficulty taken from him, by Mr *Watſon* who was to attend him to Death. Nay, his Hopes were carried even beyond hanging, for when he ſpoke to a Perſon to whom he gave what Money he had remaining, out of the large Preſents he had received from thoſe who came to divert themſelves at *Shepherd's* Show, or *Newgate* Fair, he moſt earneſtly entreated him, that as ſoon as poſſible his Body might be taken out of the Hearſe which was provided ſo him, put into a warm Bed, and, if it were poſſible, ſome Blood taken from him, for he was in great Hopes he might be brought to Life again, but if he was not, he deſired him to defray the Expences of his Funeral, and return the Overplus to his poor Mother Then he reſumed his uſual Diſcourſe about his Robberies, and in the laſt Moments of his Life endeavoured to divert himſelf from the Thoughts of Death Yet ſo unce't in and various was he his Behaviour, that he told one whom he had a great Deſire to ſee the Morning he died, that he had then as much Satisfaction to his Heart, as if he was going to enjoy two hundred Pounds *per Annum*

At the Place of Execution, to which he was convey'd in a Cart, with Iron Handcuffs on, he behaved himſelf very gravely, confeſſing his robbing Mr *Philips* and Mrs *Cook*, but denying that *Joſeph Blake* and he had *William Field* in their Company when they broke open the Houſe of Mr *Kneebone*. After this he ſubmitted to his Fate on the 16th of *November*, 1724, much pitied by the Mob.

The

The LIFE *of* MOLL RABY.

WE have chosen this Offender's most usual Name to distinguish her by, tho' she had almost as many Names as the fabulous *Hydra* had Heads She was born in the Parish of St *Martin's* in the Fields, and took betimes to ill Courses, in which she continued till her Death Madam *Ogle* was not more dextrous at bilking Hackney Coaches, than *Moll Raby* at bilking her Lodging. in which Species of Fraud her Talent originally lay, and at which she had more Success than at any Thing else she undertook We will give an Account of her first Exploit this Way, as a Specimen of the rest

This Adventure was at a House in *Great Russel-Street,* by *Bloomsbury-Square,* where passing for a great Fortune, who was oblig'd to leave the Country by reason of the importunate troublesomness of a great many Suitors, she was entertain'd with all the Civility imaginable This seeming honest Creature, who was a Saint without, but a Devil within, continued there about a Fortnight, to encrease her Character, making a very good Appearance as to her Habit, for she had a Talley-Man in every Quarter of the Town. At last, understanding one Day that all the Family was to take their Pleasure as to Morrow, at *Richmond,* she resolved to take this Opportunity, and when they were all absent, excepting the Maid, she desired her to call a Porter, and gave him a sham Bill drawn on a Banker in *Lombardstreet,* for one hundred and fifty Pounds, which she desired might be in Gold, but fearing such a quantity of Money might be a Temptation to make the Porter dishonest, she privately requested the Maid to go along with him, and she, in the mean Time, would take Care of the House The poor Maid, thinking no harm, went with the Porter to *Lombardstreet,* where they were stopp'd for a couple of Cheats, but alledging their Innocency, and proving from whence they came, a Messenger was sent home with them, who found it to be a Trick and come upon the Servant to rob the House, for before she came back, *Moll Raby* was gone off with above eighty Pounds in Money, one hundred and sixty Pounds worth of Plate, and several other Things of a considerable Value

For Offences of this Nature, she was thrice burnt in the Hand, after which she marry'd one *Humphry Jackson,* a Butcher, who was taught by her to leave off his Trade, and go upon the Pad in the Day time, while she went upon the *Buttock and Twang* by Night, which is picking up a *Cull* or *Spark,* whom pretending she would not expose her Face in a Publick-House, she takes into some dark Alley, where, whilst the decoy'd Fool is fumbling with his Breeches down, she picks his Fob or Pocket, of his Watch or Money, and giving a sort of a Hem as a signal she hath succeeded in her Design, the Fellow with whom she keeps Company, blundering up in the Dark, knocks down the Gallant, and carries off the Prize

But after the Death of this Husband, *Moll* turn'd arrant Thief, and in the first Exploit she then went upon, she had like to come scurvily off; the Adventure was this Going upon the *Night Sneak,* (as the Phrase of these People is) she found a Door half open, in *Downing-street* at *Westminster,* where stealing softly up Stairs into a great Bed Chamber, and hiding herself under the Bed, she had not been there above an Hour, before a couple of Footmen brought Candles into the Room, whilst the Maid with great Diligence, was laying the Cloth for Supper The Table being furnish'd with two or three Dishes of Meat, five or six Persons sat down, besides the Children that were in the House; which so affrighted *Moll,* that she verily thought, that if their Voices and the Noise of the Children had not hinder'd them, they might have heard her very Joints smite one against another, and the Teeth chatter in her Head But what was worst of all, there being a little Spaniel running about to gnaw the Bones that fell from the Table, where *Moll* lay *incognito,* the Dog snarling and striving to take the Bone from her, the Cat so well us'd her Claws to defend her Prize, that having given the *Buffer,* (that is their canting Name for a Dog) two or three Scratches on the Nose, there began so great a Skirmish betwixt them, that, to allay the Hurly Burly, one of the Servant took a Fire Shovel out of the Chimney, and flung it so furiously under the Bed, that it gave *Moll* a Blow on the Nose and Forehead, that stunn'd her for near half an Hour The Cat rush'd out as quick as Lightning, but the Dog stay'd behind, barking and grinning with such Fury, that neither her fawning nor threatning could quiet him, till one of the Servants flung a Fire Fork at him, which chas'd him from under the Bed, but gave her another unlucky Blow cross the Jaws At length, Supper was ended, but the Dog still growling in the Room, the Fear of his betraying her, rais'd such a sudden Looseness in her, that she could by no Means avoid discharging herself, which made such a great Stink, that it offended the People, who, supposing it to be the Dog, they turn'd him out, and not long after they all withdrew themselves, when *Moll* coming from under the Bed, she wrapt the Sheets up in the Quilt, and sneaking down Stairs, she made off the Ground as fast as she could

Another Time *Moll Raby* being drinking at an Alehouse in *Wapping,* she observed the Woman of the House, who was sleeping by the Fire side, to have a good Pearl Necklace about her Neck, at which her Mouth immediately water'd, and which she thus secured Having drank a Pot of Drink with a Consort which she had in her Company, she sent the Maid down in the Cellar again to fill the Pot, and in the mean Time cut off the Necklace with a Pair of Scissars, and taking the Pearls off the String, swallowed them Before they had done end of that Pot of Drink, the Woman awaking, she miss'd her Necklace, for which she made a great Outcry, and charged *Moll* and her Comrade with it, but they stood upon their Innocency, and going into a private Room, stript themselves, when nothing being found upon them, the Woman thought her Accusation might be false, and so was forced to lose her Necklace without being able to suspect in what Manner.

Mary Raby, alias *Rogers*, alias *Jackson*, alias *Brown*, was, at last, condemned for a Burglary, committed in the House of the Lady *Cavendish*, in *Soho Square*, the 3d of *March*, 1702-3, upon the Information of two Villains, namely, *Arthur Chambers* and *Joseph Hatfield*, who made themselves Evidences against her. At the Place of Execution, at *Tyburn*, on *Wednesday* the 3d of *November* 1703, she said she was thirty Years of Age, that she was well brought up at first, and knew good Things, but did not practise them, having given up herself to all manner of Wickedness and Vice, such as Whoredom, Adultery, and unjust Doings. As for the Fact she stood condemn'd for, she only own'd so much, and no more of it, than this. That some part of the Goods stollen out of that Lady's House, was brought to hers, in the *Spring Garden*, where she then liv'd, she understood, the next Day after the Robbery was committed, and not before, whose Goods they were.

She farther said, That she had a Husband, she thought, in *Ireland*, if still alive, but she was not certain of it, because it was now six Years since he left her. However, she was very sorry she had defiled his Bed, and wish'd he was present, that she might desire him to forgive her that Injury. She begg'd also Pardon of all the World in general, for the scandalous, impious, and wicked Life she had lived. And she pray'd, That all wicked Persons, especially those she had been concerned with, would take Warning by her, and that they might have Grace so to reform and amend their Lives betimes, never to be overtaken in their Sins. Before she was turn'd off, she was again press'd to speak the whole, in relation to the Fact she was now to die for, she persisted in what she had said before about it.

But still own'd she had been a very great Sinner, as being one that was guilty of Sabbath-breaking, swearing, drinking, lewdness, buying, receiving, and disposing of stollen Goods, and harbouring of ill People.

As an Appendix to the Life of *Moll Raby*, we shall add some Account of *Moll Hawkins*, from her living with a Fellow of that Name, who was a most notorious Pick-Pocket, was condemn'd on the 3d of *March*, 1702-3, for privately stealing Goods out of the Shop of Mrs *Hobday*, in *Pater noster Row*. She having been repriev'd for nine Months, upon the Account of her being then found quick with Child, tho' she was not, she was now call'd down to her former Judgment. When she came to the Place of Execution at *Tyburn*, on *Wednesday* the 22d of *December*, 1703, she said she was about twenty six Years of Age, born in the Parish of St *Giles*'s in the Fields, that she served three Years Apprenticeship to a Button-Maker in *Maiden-Lane*, by *Covent-Garden*, and followed that Employment for some Years after, but withal gave Way at the same Time to those ill Practices which were now the Cause of her Death.

Before this *Moll Hawkins* projected Shoplifting, she went upon the *Question Lay*, which is putting herself into a good handsome Dress, like some Exchange Girl, and then taking an empty Bandbox in her Hand, and passing for a Milliner's or Sempstress's Apprentice, she goes early to a Person of Quality's House, and knocking at the Door, asks the Servant if the Lady is stirring yet; for if she was, she had brought home, according to order, the Sute of Knots, (or what else the Devil puts in her Head) which her Ladyship had bespoke over Night; while the Servant goes up Stairs to acquaint the Lady with this Message, the Custom is in the mean Time to rob the House, and go away without an Answer. Thus she one Day served the Lady *Arabella Howard*, living in *Soho-Square*, when the Maid went up Stairs to acquaint her Ladyship that a Gentlewoman waited below with some Gloves and Fans, *Moll Hawkins* took the Opportunity of carrying away above fifty Pounds worth of Plate, which stood on a Side Board in the Parlour, to be clean'd against Dinner time.

The LIFE of WILLIAM GETTINGS.

THIS Malefactor was born in the Parish of *Wolhope*, in *Herefordshire*, where he lived with his Father, a Grazier, till he was sixteen Years of Age, and then came up to *London* He spent, after this, about 5 Years in the Service of several Gentlemen, sometimes in the Capacity of a Butler, at other Times as a Footman Had he continued honest, as he was at first, he might have done very well, for he was esteemed, but after these 5 Years, he took to bad Company, who soon debauch'd him, both in Principles and Practice

When he first took to ill Courses, he went by the Name of *William Smith*, and sought his Fortune originally by other Ways of Thieving than that of robbing on the Highway, as House-breaking, Shoplifting, or the like

Thus one Evening going privately, dress'd like a Porter, into the House of a Doctor of Physick, living in or near *Well-Close*, by the *Danes* Church in *Ratcliff-High-Way*, he there took down a rich Bed, and pack'd it up Then bringing it out of the Chamber, in order to carry it off, he fell headlong down Stairs, insomuch that he had like to have broke his Neck. The Noise alarming the old Doctor and his Son, they came running out of the Kitchen to see what was the Matter, whereupon *Gettings*, who was puffing and blowing, as if he was quite tired and out of Breath, perceiving them nearer than they should be, said to the Doctor, *Is not your Name so and so ? Yes*, reply'd the Doctor, *and what then ? Why then, Sir*, quoth William Gettings, *there's one Mr Hugh Hen and Penhenribus, I as ordered me to bring these Goods hither which have almost broke my Back, and for which he'll call about half an Hour hence, and fetch them away to a new Lodging which he has took somewhere hereabouts* Mr Hugh Hen and Penhenribus, reply'd the Doctor again, pray who's he ? for to the best of my Knowledge, I don't know any such Gentleman I can't tell for that, said Gettings, but indeed the Gentleman knows you, and ordered me to leave the Goods here I don't care, quoth the Doctor, now well he knows me, I tell you, I'll not take in People's Goods, unless they were here themselves, therefore I say carry them away Nay, pray Sir, said Gettings, let me leave the Goods here, for I am quite weary already in bringing them hither I tell you, reply'd the Doctor, there shall none be left here, therefore take them away, or I'll throw them into the Street else Well, quoth Gettings, I'll take the Goods away then, but I'm sure the Gentleman will be very angry, because he ordered me to leave them here I don't care, reply'd the Doctor, for his Anger, nor ours neither, I tell you I'll take no Charge of other People's Goods, unless they were here themselves to put 'em into my Custody Very well, Sir, quoth Gettings, but since I must carry them away, I beg the Favour of you, and the Gentleman there, to lift them on my Back Ay, ay, with all my Heart, reply'd

the Doctor, *come Son, and lend's a Hand to lift them on the Fellow's Back*

In a Word, the Goods being lifted on *Getting's* Shoulders, it was not long 'ere the Doctor's Wife came from Market, and going into the Room where the Bed was taken down, she came running openmouth'd at her Husband, and said, ' Why truly this ' is a most strange Thing, that I can never stir out ' of Doors, but you must be making one whimsical ' alteration or other in the House What's the Matter, reply'd the Doctor, with the Woman ? Are you ' beside yourself ? No, *said the Wife*, but truly you ' are, in thus altering Things as you do almost every ' Moment Certainly, my Dear, *reply'd the Doctor*, you must have been spending your Market ' Penny, or else you would not talk at this Rate as ' you do of Alterations, when none in the least have ' been made since you have been gone out *Quoth ' the Wife*, I am not blind, I think, for I am sure ' the Bed is took out of the Room one Pair of Stairs ' backwards, and pray Husband, where do you de- ' sign to put it now " At these Words the Husband and Son going presently up Stairs, they found the Bed was stollen, which, to be sure fretted them, but nevertheless, they durst not tell the old Woman that they had a Hand in the losing it, by helping the Thief to carry it away and so they now made the best of a bad Market, since all the fretting in the World would not bring it back again

Tho' *Gettings* was so successful in robbing this House, yet his Genius not agreeing with this sort of Theft, he was resolved to try his Fortune on the Highway, and one Day meeting with a noted Evidence, they pretended to make a Discovery of the World in the Moon, by telling who was the *Pretender's* Father and Mother, trudging it on Foot along the Road betwixt *Lewisham* and *Bromley* in *Kent*, he commanded the Sharper to stand and deliver, then taking from him two Pence halfpenny, for which he stood as hard as a Shoemaker would for a Piece of Carrion, but to no purpose, he said, *The World was come indeed to a very sad Pass, that one Rogue must prey on another*

Shortly after the robbing this incorrigible Villain, Gettings robbed a Man on the Way to *Chelsea*, and took from him about twelve Shillings, and a Pair of silver Buckles Next he robbed a Stage Coach upon *Hounslow Heath*, taking from the Passengers a silver Watch and some Money Next he robbed another Stage Coach, not far from *Reading* in *Berkshire*, and took from the Passengers four Guineas and some Silver And next he robbed Esq; *Dashwood's* Coach a little beyond *Putney*, and took from him and his Lady a gold Watch, and three or four Pieces of Gold, with some Money in Silver

But the most notable Action he ever committed, was this which follows Having been riding one Day into the Country for his Pleasure, as he was returning

turning

turning home in the Evening very well mounted, and drefs'd much like a Gentleman, juft at *Tooting*, by *Richmond*, he perceived from a rifing Ground Sir *James* B———— walking in his Gardens, which were very fine indeed, and of a large Extent. Then riding up to a Gardener ftanding at a Back-Door, he enquired of him, whether a Gentleman whom Curiofity led to fee thefe Gardens, of which he had heard fo much Talk in their Praife, might not have the Liberty of taking a Walk in them. The Gardener knowing Sir *James* was free that any Perfon appearing in good Fafhion might walk there, he gave *Gettings* Admiffion into them.

Gettings alighting, he gave the Gardener his Horfe to hold; and in the Walks feeing Sir *James* B———— to whom he paid Refpects in a very fubmiffive Manner, withal hoping, that he would pardon his Prefumption of coming into his Gardens, when his Worfhip was therein recreating himfelf, the courteous Knight affured him he was very welcome, and invited him to fee his Wildernefs, where fitting down in an Arbour, *Gettings* in their Difcourfe was pleas'd to fay, *Your Worfhip has got a very fine diamond Ring on your Finger* Yes, reply'd Sir *James*, *it ought to be a fine one, for it coft me a very fine Price* *Why then*, faid *Gettings* again, *it is the fitter to beftow on a Friend; therefore if your Worfhip pleafes, I muft make bold to take it, and wear it for your fake*

At thefe Words Sir *James* began to ftartle at his Impudence, but *Gettings* clapping a Piftol to his Breaft, told him, he was a dead Man if he made but the leaft Noife or Refiftance. So taking it from him, quoth he again, *I am fenfible your Lordfhip does not go without a good Watch too.* Converting this alfo to his own Ufe, and fome Guineas out of his Pocket, he then tied his Hands and Feet, and then came away with a Booty worth ninety Pounds, but bid Sir *James* be of good Cheer, for he would fend one prefently to relieve him And accordingly going to the Gardener, who held his Horfe all this while, and giving him a Shilling, quoth he, *Honeft Friend*, Sir James *wants to fpeak with you.* Then mounting he rode prefently off the Ground, whilft the Gardener made hafte to his Mafter, and was in a great Surprize to fee Sir *James* bound in that Manner which *Gettings* had left him in, but immediately fetting him loofe, his Worfhip returned his Servant many Thanks, for fending a Rogue to rob him in his own Gardens

He once went purpofely from *London* into the Country, to rob the Houfe of a dear Friend, and near Relation of his, which he effectually and eafily did, as being well acquainted with all the Parts of that Houfe, and the Ways to go into it, taking away from thence a Horfe, fome Money, gold Rings, and other Things And laftly, he robbed Efq; *Harrifon* and his Lady, riding in their Calafh towards *Fulham*, and took from them a Purfe with four Guineas in it, and fome Money in Silver For this Fact being apprehended by the Right Honourable the Lord *Bolingbroke*, one of whofe Servants he fhot in taking him, he was committed to *Newgate*, and hanged in the twenty fecond Year of his Age, at *Tyburn*, on Friday the 25th Day of *September*, 1713.

The Murder of Thomas Thynn Esq. in Pall-Mall

The LIFE of Capt. URATZ, *Highwayman, and Murderer of* THOMAS THYNN, *Esq; in the* Pall-Mall.

CHristopher Uratz, the youngeft Son of a very good Gentleman, and born in *Pomerania*, a Country adjoyning to *Poland*, having but a very fmall Patrimony left him, he was incited, thro' the Slendernefs of his Fortune, to betake himfelf to the Highway, and being a Man of a great Courage, and undaunted Spirit, he ventured on fuch Attempts by himfelf, which would not be undertook by half a dozen Man, for once *John Sobieski*, King of *Poland*, who with the Duke of *Lorrain*, raifed the Siege of *Vienna*, going difguifed out of the *Charistian* Camp, in Company only with three Officers, to obferve the Motion of the *Turks*, he intercepted his coming back, and robbed him and his Attendants of as many Diamonds, which he fold to a *Jew* at *Vienna*, for about 8000 Ducatoons, befides taking from them a confiderable Quantity of Gold. He had alfo committed fome Robberies in *Hungary*, but having fomewhat of a more generous Soul, than always to get his Bread by that diminutive Way of living, he was contrary to all others of that Profeffion, not extravagant whilft he maintained himfelf by thofe fearing Words, *Stand and Deliver*, therefore having faved a good Purfe by him, he bought a Captain's Commiffion in a Regiment in the Emperor of *Germany*'s Service.

Whilft he was in this Poft, he became acquainted whith Count *Coningfmark*, and came over with him into *England*; where the faid Count being biulked in his Amours with a certain Lady by *Thomas Thynn*, Efq; his ill Succefs therein he fo highly refented, that nothing could pacify his Refentment, but the Death of his Rival. Captain *Uratz* being made privy to his Difguft, he procured two other Affaffins, namely, *John Stern*, a Lieutenant, and *George Borosky* alias *Boratzi*, who, about a quarrel after Eight at Night, on *Sunday* the 12th of *February*, 1681, meeting Efquire *Thynn* riding in his Coach up St *James's-Street*, from the Countefs of *Northumberland*'s *Boroski*, a *Polander*, fhot him with a Blunderbufs, which mortify'd him after fuch a barbarous Manner, that Mr *Hobbs* an eminent Chyrurgeon, found in his Body four Bulets which had torn his Guts, wounded his Liver, and Stomach, and Gall, broke one of his Ribs, and wounded the great Bone below, of which Wounds he died.

Thefe Murderers being taken the next Day and carry'd before Juftice *Bridgman*, he committed them to *Newgate*, from whence being brought to the *Old Bailey* on *Tuefday* the 28th of *Fedruary* following, they were try'd before the Lord Chief Juftice *Pemberton*, and being caft for their Lives, the Recorder pafs'd Sentence of Death on them.

Whilft Captain *Uratz* was under Condemnation, Dr *Anthony Horneck*, and Dr *Gilbert Burnet*, the late Bifhop of *Salisbury*; went to vifit him the firft of which Divines thus writes: " That putting " the Criminal in Mind of the All-feeing Eye above, " who knew his Crimes, tho' he did conceal them " from Man, he was pleas'd to tell me, That he " had far other Apprehenfions of God; then I had, " and was confident God would confider a Gentle- " man, and deal with him fuitably to the Condi- " tion and Profeffion he had plac'd him in, and " would not take it ill, if a Soldier, who liv'd by " his Sword, reveng'd the Affronts offer'd to him " by another " I reply'd, That there was but one Way to eternal Happinefs, and that God, in his Laws has made no Exception for any Sorts or Degrees of Men, and confequently Revenge in a Gentleman, was a Sin God would not pardon without true Repentance, any more then he would forgive it in a Peafant. He asking me hereupon, What Repentance was? I told him, it was fo to hate the Sin we had done, that for the future no Argument fhould prevail with us to commit it again. To which he faid, That if he were to live, he fhould not forbear to give any one as good as he brings; with fome other Expreffions, which I am loth to repeat; for they made me fo melancholick, that I was forced to leave him. Yet I bid him confider what he had faid, as he lov'd his own Soul. The laft Time I vifited him, was on the 8th of *March*, whom, when I had faluted, I told him I hop'd he had taken his dangerous Condition into Confideration, and wrought himfelf into a greater Senfe of his Sins, then I could obferve in him when I was laft with him. He faid, he knew not what I meant by this Addrefs. I then explained my felf, gave him to underftand, that I fpake it with Relation to the late great Sin he had been engag'd in, and that I hop'd his approaching Death had made him more penitent, than I had found him t'other Day, To which he reply'd, That he was fenfible he was a great Sinner, and had committed divers Enormities in his Life time, of which he truly repented, and was confident that God had pardon'd him, but he could not well underftand the Humour of our *English* Divines, who prefs'd him to make particular Declarations of Things they had a Mind he fhould fay, tho' never fo falfe, or contrary to Truth, and at this, he faid, he wondered the more, becaufe in our Church we were not for auricular Confeffion I let him run on, and then I told him, that he was much miftaken in the Divines of the *Church of England*, who neither us'd to reveal private Confeffion, nor oblige Offenders in fuch Cafes, to confefs Things

         contrary

contrary to Truth, that this was both against their Practice and their Principles. The Confession, I said, he was fo often exhorted to, was no private, but a publick Confession, for as his Crime had been publick Confession, for as his Crime had been publick, fo his Repentance and Confession ought to be publick too; and farthermore, I told him, that *Chriſt*'s Blood was actually applied to none but the true Penitent, and that true Repentance muſt diſcover it felf in Meekneſs, Humility, Tender-hearted-neſs, Compaſſion, Righteouſneſs, making ingenious Confeſſions, and, fo far as we are able, Satisfaction too, elſe, notwithſtanding the Treaſure of *Chriſt*'s Blood, Men might drop into Hell Upon this, he replied, that he fear'd no Hell I anſwer'd, poſſibly he might believe none, or, if he did, it might be a very eaſy one of his own making He ſaid he was not ſuch a Fool as to believe that Souls could fry in material Fire, or be roaſted as Meat on a great Hearth, or in a Kitchin, pointing to the Chimney. His Belief was, that the Puniſhment of the Damn'd conſiſted in a Deprivation of the gracious and beatifick Preſence of God, upon which Deprivation, there aroſe a Terror and Anguiſh in their Souls, becauſe they had miſs'd of fo great a Happineſs He added, that poſſibly I might think him an *Atheiſt*, but he was fo far from thoſe Thoughts, that he could ſcarce believe there was any Man fo ſottiſh in the World, as not to believe the Being of a God, gracious, and juſt, and generous to his Creatures, nor could any Man, that was not either mad or drunk, believe Things came fortuitouſly, or that this World was govern'd by Chance I ſaid that this Truth I approv'd of, and was glad to ſee him well ſettled in the Reaſonableneſs of that Principle, and as for material Fire in the other World, I would not quarrel with him for denying it, but rather hold with him, that the Fire and Brimſtone ſpoken of in Scripture, were but Emblems of thoſe inward Terrors which would gnaw and tear the Conſciences of impenitent Sinners, but ſtill this was a greater Puniſhment than material Fire And this Puniſhment he had Reaſon to fear, if he could not make it out to me, or other Men, that his Repentance was ſincere I was at firſt in ſome Doubt whether I would publiſh the Captains Anſwers to my Queries and Expoſtulations, becauſe ſome of them favour of Prophaneneſs, yet, conſidering that the *Evangeliſt* hath thought fit to acquaint the World with the penitent Expreſſions of the other Malefactor, I was willing to follow that great Example, hoping that thoſe looſe Diſcourſes of the Man may ſerve as Sea-marks to warn Paſſengers from running upon thoſe Sands That which I chiefly obſerv'd in him, was, that Honour and Bravery was the Idol he ador'd, a Piece of poſteſterous Devotion, which he maintain'd to the laſt, as if he thought it would merit Praiſe, not to decede from what he had once ſaid, though it was with the Loſs of God's Favour, and the Shipwreck of a good Conſcience He conſider'd God as ſome genetous, yet partial Prince, who would regard Men's Blood, Deſcent, and Quality, more than their Errors, and would give vaſt Grains of Allowance to their Breeding and Education, and poſſibly the ſtout Behaviour of ſome of the ancient *Roman* Bravo's, (for he had read Hiſtory) might roll in his Mind, and tempt him to write Copies after thoſe Originals, or, to think that it was great to do ill, and to defend it to the laſt Whether after my laſt Conference with him he relented, I know not Thoſe that ſaw him go to his Execution, obſerv'd that he look'd undaunted, and with a Countenance fo ſteady, that it ſeem'd to ſpeak his Scorn, not only of all the Spectators that look'd upon him, but

of Death it ſelf But I judge not of the Thoughts of dying Men, thoſe the Searcher of all Hearts knows beſt, to whom Men ſtand or fall

Dr *Gilbert Burnet* writes thus of Captain *Uratz* It is certain, that never Man died with more Reſolution, and leſs Signs of Fear, or the leaſt Diſorder His Carriage in the Cart, both as he was led along, and at the Place of Execution, was aſtoniſhing, he was not only undaunted, but look'd chearful, and ſmil'd often. When the Rope was put about his Neck, he did not change Colour, nor tremble, his Legs were firm under him He look'd often about on thoſe that ſtood in Balconies and Windows, and ſoom'd to fix his Eyes on ſome Perſons, Three or four Times he ſmil'd, He would not cover his Face as the reſt did, but continu'd in that State, often looking up to Heaven, with a Chearfulneſs in his Countenance, and a little Motion of his Hands I ſaw him ſeveral Times in the Priſon, he ſtill ſtood to the Confeſſion he made to the Council, till the laſt Day of his Life He often ſaid to me, he would never ſay any Thing but what he had ſaid at firſt When I was with him on *Sunday* before his Death, he ſtill denied all that the Lieutenant and *Polander* had ſaid, and ſpake ſeverely of them, chiefly of the Lieutenant, as if he had confeſs'd thoſe Things, which he then call'd Lies, in Hopes of ſaving his own Life by it, or in Spite to him, that he might not be pardon'd, and all I could ſay, could not change his Mind in that I told him, it was in vain for him to dream of a Pardon, for I aſſur'd him, if any kept him up with the Hopes of it, they deceiv'd him He had two Opinions that were as I thought, hurtful to him, the one was, That it was enough if he confeſs'd his Sins to God, and that he was not bound to make any other Confeſſion, and he thought that was a Piece of Popery to preſs him to confeſs He had another odd Opinion, alſo, of the next State He thought the Damn'd were only excluded from the Preſence of God, and endur'd no other Miſery but that of ſeeing others happier than themſelves, and was unwilling to let me enter into much Diſcourſe with him for undeceiving him He ſaid it was his own Affair, and he deſir'd to be left to himſelf But he ſpake with great Aſſurance of God's Mercy to him I left him, when I ſaw that nothing I could ſay had any good Effect on him, and reſolv'd to have gone no more to him; but when I underſtood by a *German* Miniſter that attended him, and by the Meſſage which I heard deliver'd in his Name to the Lieutenant and the *Polander*, the Night before his Execution, that he was in another Temper then when I ſaw him laſt, I went to him He receiv'd me more kindly than formerly, moſt of his Diſcourſe was concerning his going to the Place of Execution, deſiring it might be in a Coach, and not in a Cart, and when I pray'd him to think of that which concern'd him more, he ſpake with great Aſſurance, that it was already done, that he knew God had forgiven him And when I wiſh'd him to ſee that he might not deceive himſelf, and that his Hopes, might not be ill grounded, he ſaid it was not Hope, but Certainty, for he was ſure God was reconcil'd to him, through *Chriſt* When I ſpake to him of confeſſing his Sin, he ſaid he had written it, and it would be publiſh'd to all *Europe*, but he did not ſay a Word concerning it to me So I left him, and ſaw him no more till I met him at the Place of Execution When he ſaw me, he ſmil'd on me, and whereas I had ſometimes warn'd him of the Danger of affecting to be a *Counterfeit Bravo*, (*Foux* brave) he ſaid to me, before I ſpake to him, *That I ſhould ſee it was not a falſe Bravery, but that he was fearleſs to the laſt* I wiſh'd him to conſider well upon what he grounded his

his Confidence: He said he was sure he was now to be receiv'd into Heaven, and that his Sins were forgiven him. I ask'd him if he had any Thing to say to the people. He said No. After he had whisper'd a short Word to a Gentleman, he was willing the Rope should be ty'd to the Gibbet. He call'd for the *German* Minister; but the Crowd was such, that it was not possible for him to come near. So he desir'd me to pray with him in *French*, but I told him I could not venture to pray in that Language, but, since he understood *English*, I would pray in *English*. I observ'd he had some Touches in his Mind, when I offer'd up that Petition, that for the Sake of the Blood of *Christ*, the innocent Blood shed in that Place might be forgiven, and that the Cry of the one for Mercy, might prevail over the Cry of the other for Justice. At these Words, he look'd up to Heaven with the greatest Sense that I had at any Time observ'd in him. After I pray'd, he said no-

thing, but that he was now going to be happy with God; so I left him. He continu'd in his undaunted Manner, looking up often to Heaven, and sometimes round about him, to the Spectators. After he and his two Fellow-Sufferers had stood about a quarter of an Hour under the Gibbet, they were ask'd when they would give the Signal for their being turn'd off. He answer'd, that they were ready, and that the Cart might be driven away when it pleas'd the Sheriff to order it. So, a little While after, it was driven away. And thus they all ended their Lives.

As for Lieutenant *Stern*, the illegitimate Son of a Baron of *Sweden*, afterwards made a Count, and *Borosky* the *Polander*, they were very penitent from first to last, being with Captain *Uratz*, aged 38, executed in the *Pall-Mall* on *Friday* the 10th of *March* 1681-2, but *Borosky* was afterwards hung up in Chains, a little beyond *Mile-End*, by the Command of King *Charles* the Second.

The LIFE of LEWIS HOUSSART.

AS there is not any Crime more shocking to human Nature, or more contrary to all Laws human and divine, than Murder, so perhaps there have been few Murders, in these last Years committed, accompanied with more odd Circumstances than that for which this Criminal suffered.

Lewis Houssart was born at *Sedan*, a Town in *Champaigne*, in the Kingdom of *France*, his own Paper says, *That he was bred a Surgeon, and qualified for that Business*, however that were, he was here no better than a Penny Barber, only that he let Blood, and thereby got a little Money. As to the other Circumstances of his Life, all we shall say of him is, that while his Wife *Anne Rondeau* was living, he married another Woman, and the Night of the Marriage, before sitting down to Supper, he went out a little Space. During the Interval between that and his coming in, it was judged from the Circumstances, that he cut the poor Woman's Throat, who was his first Wife, with a Razor. For this being apprehended he was tried at the *Old Baily*, but for Want of Proof sufficient was acquitted. Not long after he was indicted for *Bigamy*, upon which Indictment, scarce making any Defence, he was found guilty. He said thereupon, *That he did not trouble himself to preserve so much as his Reputation in this Respect, for in the first Place he knew they were resolved to convict him, and in the next Place his first Wife was a Socinian, an irrational Creature, entitled to the Advantages of no Nation nor People, because she was no Christian, and according as the Scripture says, with such a One have no Conversation, no, not so much as to eat with them.* An Appeal was then lodg'd against him by *Solomon Rondeau*, Brother and Heir to *Anne* his Wife, yet that appearing to be defective, it was quash'd, and he charged upon another, whereunto joining Issue upon six Points, they came to be tried at the *Old Bailey*, where the following Circumstances appeared upon the Trial.

That at the Time he was at Supper at his new Wife's House, he started on a sudden, looked agast, and seemed to be very much frighted. A little Boy deposed, that the Prisoner gave him Money to go to his own House in a little Court, and fetch the Mother of the deceased *Anne Rondeau* to a Gentleman who would be at such a Place and stay for her. When the Mother returned from that Place, and found nobody wanting her, or that had wanted her, she was very much out of Humour at the Boy's calling her, but that quickly gave way to the Surprize of finding her Daughter murder'd assoon as she enter'd the Room. This Boy who called her was very young, yet out of a Number of Persons that were in *Newgate*, he singled out *Lewis Houssart*, and declared that he was the Man who gave him Money to go for old Mistress *Rondeau*. Upon this and several other corroborating Proofs the Jury found him guilty. Upon which he arraigned the Justice of the Court, declaring that he was innocent, and that they might punish him if they would, but they could not make him guilty, and much more to the like Effect. But the Court was not troubled at that, and he scarce endeavoured to make any other Defence.

While in the Condemn'd-Hole, amongst the rest of the Criminals, he behaved himself in a very odd Manner, insisted upon it that he was innocent of the Fact laid to his Charge, and threw out most opprobrious Language against the Court that condemn'd him, and when he was advised to lay aside such Heats of passionate Expressions, he said, *He was sorry he did not more full, expose the British Justice upon the spot at the Old-Baily, and that now, since they had tied up his Hands from acting, he would at least have Satisfaction in saying what he pleased.*

When this *Houssart* was first apprehended he appeared to be very much affected with his Condition, was continually reading good Books, praying and meditating, and shewing the utmost Signs of a Heart full

full of Concern, and under the greatest Emotions; but after he had been once acquitted, it made a thorough Change in his Temper He quite laid aside all his former Gravity, and gave way, on the contrary, to a very extraordinary Spirit of Obstinacy and Unbelief He puzzled himself continually, and if Mr. *Deval*, who was then under Sentence, would have given Leave, would have puzzled him too, as to the Doctrines of a future State, and an identical Resurrection of the Body, saying, he could not be persuaded of the truth thereof in a literal Sense. But Mr *Deval*, after he had answered as well as he could these Objections once, refused to hearken a second Time to any such Discourses, and was obliged to have Recourse to harsh Language, to oblige him to desist In the mean while his Brother came over from *Holland*, on the News of this dreadful Misfortune, and went to make him a Visit in the Place of his Confinement, where going to condole with him on the Weight of his Misfortunes, instead of receiving the Kindness of his Brother in the Manner it deserved, *Houssart* began to make light of the Affair, and treated the Death of his Wife and his own Confinement in such a Manner, that his Brother leaving him abruptly, went back to *Holland*, more shocked at the Brutality of his Behaviour, than grieved for the Misfortune which had befallen him

It being a considerable Space of Time that *Houssart* lay in Confinement in *Newgate*, and even in the Condemn'd-Hole, he had there of Course Abundance of Companions; but of them all he affected none so much as *John Shepherd*, with whom he had Abundance of merry, and even loose, Discourses, once particularly, when the Sparks flew very quick out of the Charcoal Fire, he said to *Shepherd, See fee' I wish there were so many Bullets that might beat the Prison down about our Ears, and then I might die like Sampson*

It was near a Month before he was called up to receive Sentence, after which he made no Scruple of saying, That since they had found him guilty of Throat-cutting, he would verify their Judgment by cutting his own Throat Upon which when some, who were in the same sad State with himself, objected to him how great a Crime Self-murder was, he immediatey made Answer, He was satisfied it was no Crime at all. And upon this he fell to arguing in Favour of the Mortality of the Soul, as if certain that it died with the Body, endeavouring to cover his Opinions with false Glosses on that Text in *Genesis*, wherein it is said *That God breathed into Man a living Soul*, from whence he would have inferr'd, *That when a Man ceases to live, he totally lost that Soul*, and when it was asked of him, Where then it went, he said, *He did not know, nor did it much concern him* The Standers by, who, notwithstanding their profligate Course of Life, had a natural Abhorrence of this Theoratical Impiety, reproved him in very sharp Terms, for making use of such Expressions, upon which he reply'd, *Ay! would you have me believe all the strange Notions that are taught by the Parsons? that the Devil is a real Thing? that our good God punishes Souls for ever and ever? that Hell is full of Flames from material Fire? and that this Body of mine shall feel it? Well, you may believe it if you please, but it is so with me that I cannot*

Sometimes, however, he would lay aside these Sceptical Opinions for a Time, talk in another Strain, and appear mightily concerned at the Misfortunes he had drawn upon his second Wife and Child He would then speak of Providence, and the Decrees of God, with much seeming Submission, would own that he had been guilty of many and grievous

Offences, and say, *That the Punishment of God was just, and desired the Prayers of the Minister of the Place, and those that were about him.*

When he reflected on the Grief it would give his Father, who was near 90 Years old, to hear of his Misfortunes, he was seen to shed Tears, but as soon as these Thoughts were a little out of his Head he resumed his former Temper, and was continually asking Questions in relation to the Truth of the Gospel Dispensation, and the Doctrines therein taught of Rewards and Punishments after this Life. Being a *Frenchman*, and not perfectly versed in our Language, a Minister, of the Reformed Church of that Nation, was prevailed upon to attend him *Houssart* received him with tolerable Civility, seemed pleased that he should pray by him, but industriously waved all Discourses of his Guilt, and even fell out into violent Passions, if a Confession was pressed upon him as a Duty In this strange Way he consumed the Time allotted him to prepare for another World

The Evening before his Execution, the Foreign Minister, and he whose Duty it was to attend him, both waited upon him at Night, in Order to discourse with him, on those strange Notions he had of the Mortality of the Soul, and a total Cessation of Being after this Life, but when they came to speak to him to this Purpose, he said, *They might spare themselves any Arguments upon that Head, for he believed a God and a Resurrection as firmly as they did* They then discoursed to him of the Nature of a sufficient Repentance, and of the Duty incumbent upon him to confess that great Crime for which he was condemned, and thereby give Glory unto God He fell at this into his old Temper, and said with some Passion, *If you will pray with me, I'll thank you, and pray with you as long as you please but if you come only to torture me of my Guilt, I desire you would let me alone altogether*

His Lawyers having pretty well instructed him in the Nature of an Appeal, and he coming thereby to know that he was now under Sentence of Death at the Suit of the Subject, and not of the King, he was very assiduous to learn where it was he was to apply for a Reprieve But finding it was the Relations of his deceased Wife from whom he was to expect it, he laid aside all those Hopes, rightly conceiving it a Thing impossible to prevail upon People to spare his Life, who had almost undone themselves in prosecuting him

In the Morning of the Day of Execution he was very much disturbed at being refused the Sacrament, which, as the Minister told him, could not be given him without his Confession Yet this did not prevail, he said, " He would die then without receiving it " A French Minister having before said to him, " Lewis Houssart, since you are condemned on full " Evidence, I must inform you, that if you persist " in this Denial, you can look for nothing but to be " d——, Houssart replied, You must look for " Damnation yourself, for judging me guilty, when " you know nothing of the Matter " This confused Frame of Mind he continued in, till he entered the Cart for his Execution, persisting all the Way he went in like Declarations of Innocence, tho' sometimes intermixed with short Prayers to God to forgive his manifold Sins and Offences

At the Place of Execution he turned very pale, and grew very sick The Ministers told him, they would not pray by him, unless he would confess the Murder for which he died, whereupon he said, *He was very sorry for that, but if they would not pray by him he could not help it, he would not confess what he was totally ignorant of* He persisted even at the Moment

Moment of being tied up ; and when such Exhortations were again repeated, he said, *Pray do not torment me ! Pray ceafe troubling of me ! I tell you I will not make myfelf worfe than I am* And fo faving, he gave up the Ghoft, without any private Prayer when left alone, or calling upon God or Chrift to receive his Spirit : He delivered however a Paper, a Copy of which follows ; from whence our Readers will receive a more exact Idea of the Man than from any Picture we can draw

' I *Loun Houffart* am 40 Years old, and was born in *Sedan*, a Town in *Campaigne* near *Boulloons* I have left *France* above 14 Years I was ' Apprentice to a Surgeon at *Amfterdam*, and after ' Examination was allowed by the College to be ' qualified for the Bufinefs ; fo that I intended to ' go on board a Ship as a Surgeon ; but I could ' never have my Health at Sea I dwelt fometime ' at *Maeftrickt* in the *Dutch Brabant*, where my ' aged Father and Mother now dwell I travelled ' thro' *Holland*, and in almoft every Town My ' two Sifters are in *France*, and alfo many of my ' Relations for the Earth has fcarce any Family ' more numerous than ours Seven or eight Years ' I have been in *London*, and here I met with *Anne* ' *Rondeau*, who was born at the fame Village with ' me, and therefore I loved her After I had left ' her, fhe wrote to me, and faid, *She would reveal* ' *a Secret* , and fhe told me, *She had not been chafte,* ' *and the Confequence of it was upon her* Upon ' which I gave her my beft Help and Affiftance. ' Since fhe is dead, I hope her Soul is happy

---

The LIFE of JONATHAN WILD.

*J*ONATHAN *Wild* was the Son of mean Parents, but honeft and induftrious , their Family confifted of three Sons and two Daughters, whom they maintained in the beft Manner they could from their joint Labours, he as a Carpenter, and fhe by felling Fruit in *Wolverhampton* Market in *Staffordfhire* *Jonathan* was the eldeft of the Sons, and having receiv'd as good an Education as his Father's Circumftances would allow him, he was put out an Apprentice in *Birmingham* He ferved his Time with much Fidelity, and came up to Town in the Service of a Gentleman of the long Robe, about the Year, 1704, or a little later But not liking his Service he quitted it, and retired again to his old Employment in the Country, where he continued to work diligently for fome Time

At laft growing fick of Labour, and ftill entertaining a Defire of rafting the Pleafures of *London*, thither he came a fecond Time and worked Journey-Work at the Trade he was bred But this not producing Money enough, to fupport thofe Expences his love of Pleafure threw him into, he got pretty deeply in Debt, was fuddenly arrefted, and thrown into *Woodftreet Compter* Having no Friends to do any Thing for him, he liv'd very hardly there, fcarce getting Bread enough to fupport him from the Charity allowed to Prifoners, and what little Services he could render to Prifoners of the better Sort in the Goal However, as no Man wanted Addrefs lefs than *Jonathan*, fo no Body could have employed it more properly than he did upon this Occafion, for he got fo much into the Favour of the Keepers, that they quickly permitted him the Liberty of the Gate, and he thereby got fome little Matter for going of Errands This fet him above the very Pinch of Want, and that was all , but his Fidelity and Induftry in thefe mean Employments procured him fuch Efteem amongft thofe in Power there, that they foon appointed him an Under Keeper to thofe diforderly Perfons who were brought in every Night

Jonathan now came into a comfortable Subfiftance, having learnt how to get Money of fuch People, by putting them into the Road of getting Liberty for themfelves Here he met with a Lady, who went by the Name of *Mary Milliner*, and who foon taught him how to gain yet much greater Sums then in his Way of Life, by Methods which he till then never heard of By the help of this Woman, he grew acquainted with all the notorious Gangs of loofe Perfons with in the Bills of Mortality, and was perfectly vers'd in the Manner by which they carried on their Schemes He knew where and how their Enterprizes were to be gone upon and what Manner they difpofed of their ill got Goods, and having always an intreguing Head, he fet up for a *Director* amongft them, and foon became fo ufeful, that tho' he never went out with any of them, yet he got more Money by their Crimes, than if he had been a Partner there in, which upon one Pretence or other, he always declined

It muft be obferv'd that anciently when a Thief had got his Booty, there were Multitudes of People ready to help him off, with his Effects without any more to do , but this Method being totally beftroyed by an Act paffed in the Reign of King *William*, by which it was made Felony for any Perfon to buy Goods ftolen, knowing them to be fo, there were few or no Receivers to be met with , thofe that ftill carried on the Trade, taking exorbitant Sums for their own Profit, and leaving thefe who had run the Hazards of their Necks in obtaining them, the leaft Share in the Plunder This had like to have brought the thieving Trade to nought , but *Jonathan* quickly put Things again in order, and gave new Life to the Practitioners in the feveral Branches of Stealing The Method he took was this

As foon as any confiderable Robbery was committed, and *Jonathan* received Intelligence by whom, he immediately went to the Thieves, and enquired how the Thing was done, where the Perfons lived who were injured, and what the Booty confifted in that was taken away Then pretending to chide them for their Wickednefs, and exhorting them to live honeftly for the Future, he gave it them as his Advice, to lodge what they had taken in a proper Place which he appointed, and promis'd to take some Measures for their Security, by getting the People to give them somewhat to have their Goods restored them again Having thus wheedled those who had committed a Robbery, into a Compliance with his Measures, his next Business was to divide the Goods into several Parcels, and cause them to be sent to different Places, always avoiding taking them into his own Hands Things being in this Position, *Jonathan* and Mrs. *Milliner* went to the Persons who were robbed, and after condoling the Misfortune, pretended that they had some Acquaintance with a Broker, to whom certain Goods were brought, some of which they suspected to be stolen; and hearing that the Person to whom they thus applied had been robb'd, they said, though it the Duty of one honest Body to another, to inform them thereof, and to enquire what Goods they were they lost, in order to discover whether those they spoke of were the same or no. People who had such Losses, are always ready to hearken to any Thing that has a Tendency towards recovering their Goods. *Jonathan* or his Mistress therefore, had no great Difficulty in making People listen to such Terms In a Day or two therefore they were sure to come again, with Intelligence that they had found Part of the Things, and provided no Body was brought into Trouble, and the Broker had something in Consideration of his Care, they might be had again

This Practice of *Jonathan's*, if well considered, carries in it a great deal of Policy For first it seemed a very honest Act to prevail on evil Persons to restore the Goods which they had stole, and then 'twas a great Benefit to those were who robb'd, to have their Goods again upon a reasonable Premium, *Jonathan* all the While taking apparently nothing, his Advantages arising out of the Gratuity left with the Broker and out of what he had bargained to give to the Thief; who also found his Advantage in it, the Rewards being very near as large as the Price given by Receivers, since receiving became so dangerous, and affording a certain Security into the Bargain With respect to *Jonathan*, the Contrivance placed him in Safety from all the Laws then in Being, so that in a short Time he began to give himself out for a Person who made it his Business to procure stolen Goods to their right Owners When he first did this, he acted with so much Art, that he not only acquired a very great Reputation, not only from those who dealt with him, but even from People of higher Station, who observing the Industry with which he prosecuted Malefactors, took him for a Friend of Justice, and as such afforded him Countenance Certain it is, that he brought more Villains to the Gallows, than perhaps any Man ever did, and so sensible was he of the Necessity there was for him to act in this Manner, that he constantly hung up two or three of his *Clients* in a Twelvemonth, that he might keep up that Character to which he had attained; and so indefatigable was he in the Pursuit of those he endeavoured to apprehend, that in all his Course of acting, never so much as one single Man escaped him

When this Practice of *Jonathan's* became noted, it produced not only much Discourse, but some Enquiries into his Behaviour. *Jonathan* foresaw this, and in order to invade any ill Consequence he put on upon such Occasions, as an Air of Gravity, and complained of the evil Disposition of the Times, which would not omit a Man to serve his Neighbours and his Country without Censure. *For do I not*, quoth he, *do the greatest Good, when I persuade People who have deprived others of their Properties, to restore them again for a reasonable Consideration* And the Villains whom I have brought to suffer Punishment? Do not their Deaths shew how much Use I am of to the Country? Why then should People disperse me? Besides these Professions of Honesty, two great Things there were which contributed to his Preservation; and they were these First, the great Readiness the Government always shews in detecting Persons guilty of capital Offences, in which Case 'tis common to offer not only Pardon, but Rewards, to Persons guilty, provided they make Discoveries, and this *Jonathan* was so sensible of, that he did not only screen himself behind the Lenity of the supreme Power, but made Use of it also as a Sort of Authority taking upon him the Character of a Sort of a Minister of Justice, which assumed Character of his, however ill founded, prov'd of great Advantage to him in the Course of his Life The other Point, which contributed to keep him from any Prosecutions, was the great Willingness of People, who had been robbed, to recover their Goods, so that provided for a small Matter, they could regain Things very considerable, they were so far from taking Pains to bring the Offenders to Justice, that they thought the Premium a cheap Price to get off Thus by the Rigour of the Magistrate and the Lenity of the Subject *Jonathan* claim'd constant Employment, and according as the Case required, the poor Thieves were either trus'd up to satisfy the just Vengeance of the one, or protected and encouraged, to satisfy the Demands of the other Perhaps in all Histories there is not an Instance of a Man who thus openly dallied with the Laws, and play'd even with capital Punishment If any Title can be devised suitable to *Jonathan's* Character, it must be that of *Director General* of the united *Forces of Highwaymen, House-breakers, Foot-pads, Pick-Pockets* and *private Thieves* Now the Maxims by which he supported himself in this dangerous Capacity, where these In the first Place he continually exhorted the Plunderers to let him know punctually what Goods they at any Time took, by which Means he had it in his Power to give a direct Answer to those who came to make Enquiries If they complied faithfully with his Instructions, he was a certain *Protector* on all Occasions, and sometimes had Interest enough to procure them Liberty when apprehended But if they pretended to become Independent and despise his Rules, or if they threw out any threatning Speeches against their Companions, or grumbled at the Compositions he made for them, in such Cases as these, *Wild* took the first Opportunity of putting them into the Information of some of his Creatures, or the first fresh Fact they committed, he immediately set out to apprehend them, and labour so indefatigable therein, that they never escaped him Thus he not only procured the Reward for himself, but also gain'd an Opportunity of pretending, that he not only restored Goods to the right Owners, but also apprehended the Thief as often as it was in his Power In those Steps of his Business which were most hazardous, *Wild* made the People themselves take the first Steps, by publishing Advertisements of Things lost and directing them to be brought to Mr *Wild* who was impowered to receive them, and pay such a Reward as the Person that lost them thought fit to offer *Wild* in this Capacity appeared no otherwise than as a Person on whose Honour the injured People could rely After he had gone on in this Trade for about ten Years with Success, he began to lay aside much of his former Caution, taking a larger House in the Great *Old-Bailey*, then that in which he formerly lived, giving the Woman whom he called his Wife, abundance of fine Things, and keeping an o

pen

pent Office for restoring stolen Goods. His Fame at last came to that Height, that Persons of the highest Qualities would condescend to make use of his Abilities when at any *Installation, publick Entry*, or some other great Solemnity, they had the Misfortune of losing their Watches, Jewels or other Things, of real or imaginary Value. But as his Method of treating those who applied to him for his Assistance has been much represented, we shall next give an exact and impartial Account thereof.

In the first Place, when a Person was introduced to Mr *Wild*'s Office, it was hinted to him, that a Crown must be deposited by Way of Fee for his Advice. When this was complied with, a large Book was brought out: Then the Looser was examin'd with much Formality, as to the Time, Place, and Manner, wherein the Goods became missing; and then was dismissed with a Promise of careful Enquiries being made, and of hearing more concerning them in a Day or two. *Wild* had not the least Occasion for these Queries, but to amuse the Person he asked; for he knew beforehand all the Circumstances of the Robbery much better than they did, nay, perhaps had the very Goods in his House when the Folks came first to enquire for them. When, according to his appointment, the Enquirer came the second Time *Jonathan* took Care by a new Scene to amuse him. He was told that Mr *Wild* had indeed made Enquiries, but was very sorry to communicate the Event of them, for the Thief, who was a bold impudent Fellow, rejected with Scorn the Offer which had been made him, pretending he could sell the Goods at a double Price; and, in short, would not hear a Word of Restitution unless upon better Terms. But says *Jonathan*, *if I can but come to the Speech of him, I don't doubt bringing him to Reason*. At length, after one or two more Attendances, Mr *Wild* gave the definitive Answer, *That provided no Questions were ask'd, and you gave so much Money to the Porter who brought them you might have your Things returned at such an Hour precisely*. This was transacted with an outward Appearance of Friendship on his Side, and with great seeming Frankness and Generosity, but when you come to the last Article, viz what Mr *Wild* expected for his Trouble, then an Air of coldness was put on, and he answered with equal Pride and Indifference, *That what he did was purely from a Principle of doing Good, as to a Gratuity for the Trouble he had taken, he left it totally to yourself, you might do in it what you thought fit*. And even when Money was presented to him, he received it with the same negligent Grace, always putting you in Mind that it was your own Act, and that he took it as a great Favour, and not as a Reward.

Thus by this Dexterity in his Management, he fenced himself against the Rigour of the Law, in the midst of these notorious Transgressions of it. For what could be imputed to Mr *Wild*? He neither saw the Thief, who took away your Goods, nor received them after they were taken. The Method he pursued was neither dishonest nor illegal, if you would believe his Account on it, and no other than his Account of it could be gotten. Had he continued satisfied with this Way of dealing, in all human Probability he might have gone to his Grave in Peace. But he was greedy, and instead of keeping constant to this safe Method, came at last to take the Goods into his own Custody, giving those that stole them what he thought proper, and then making such a Bargain with the Looser as he was able to bring him up to, sending the *Porter* himself, and taking without Ceremony whatever Money had been giving him. But as this happened only in the two last Years of his

Life; it it fit we should give some Instances of his Behaviour before.

A Gentleman who deals in Silks near *Covent Garden*, had a Piece of extraordinary rich Damask, bespoke of him on Purpose for the *Birth-Day* Suit of a certain *Duke*; and the *Lace-Man* having brought such Trimming as was proper for it, the *Mercer* had made the whole up in a Parcel, tied it at each End with blue Ribband, sealed with great Exactness, and placed on one End of the Compter, in Expectation of his *Grace's* Servant, who he knew was directed to call for it in the Afternoon. According to the Fellow came, but when the *Mercer* went to deliver him the Goods, the Piece was gone, and no Account could possibly be had of it. As the Master had been all Day in the Shop; so there was no Pretence of charging any thing, either upon the Carelesness or Dishonesty of Servants. After an Hour's fretting therefore, seeing no other Remedy, he e'en determined to go and communicate his Loss to Mr *Wild*, in Hopes of receiving some Benefit by his Assistance; the Loss consisting not so much in the Value of the Things, as in the Disappointment it would be to the *Birth-Day*. Upon this Consideration an *Hackney-Coach* was immediately called, and away he was ordered to drive directly to *Jonathan*'s House in the *Old-Baily*. As soon as he came into the Room, and had acquainted Mr *Wild* with his Business, the usual Deposite of a Crown being made, and the common Questions of *how, when and where*, having been ask'd, the *Mercer*, being very impatient, said with some kind of Heat, Mr *Wild*, *tell me in a few Words, if it be in your Power to serve me, if it is, I have thirty Guineas here ready to lay down, but if you expect that I should dance Attendance for a Week or two, I assure you I shall not be willing to part with above half the Money*. Good Sir, reply'd Mr *Wild*, *have a little more Consideration. I am no Thief Sir, nor Receiver of stolen Goods, so that if you don't think fit to give me Time to enquire, you must e'en take what Measures you please*.

When the *Mercer* found he was like to be left without any hopes, he began to talk in a milder Strain, and with abundance of Intreaties fell to persuading *Jonathan* to think of some Method to serve him, and that immediately. *Wild* stepped out a Minute or two and as soon as he came back, told the Gentleman, *It was not in his Power to serve him in such a Hurry, if at all. However, in a Day or two he might be able to give him some Answer?* The *Mercer* insisted, that a Day or two would lessen the Value of the Goods one half to him, and *Jonathan* insisted as peremptorily, that it was not in his Power to do any thing sooner. At last a Servant came in a Hurry, and told Mr *Wild*, there was a Gentleman below desired to speak with him. *Jonathan* bowed, begged the Gentleman's Pardon, and told him, *he would wait on him again in one Minute*. In about five Minutes he returned with a very smiling Countenance, and turning to the Gentleman, said, " I " protest Sir, you are the luckiest Man I ever knew. " I spoke to one of my People just now to go to a " House where I knew some Lifters resort, and di- " rected him to talk of your Robbery, and to say, " you had been with me and offered thirty Guineas " for the Things again. This Story has had its " Effect, and if you go directly home, I fancy you'll " hear more News of it than I am able to tell you. " But pray, Sir, remember that the thirty Guineas " was your own Offer, you are at free Liberty to " give them, or let them alone, 'tis nothing to me, " though I have done all for you in my Power of " Gratuity."

A way

Away went the Mercer, wondering where this Affair would end, but as he walked up *Southampton ſtreet*, a Fellow overtook him, patted him on the Shoulder, delivered him the Bundle unopened, and told him the Price was twenty Guineas. The Mercer paid it him directly, and returning to *Jonathan* in half an Hour's Time, begged him to accept of the ten Guineas he had ſaved him for his Pains *Jonathan* told him, *That he had ſaved him nothing, but ſuppoſed that the People thought twenty enough, conſidering that they were now pretty ſafe from Proſecution* The Mercer ſtill preſſed the ten Guineas upon *Jonathan*, who after taking them out of his Hand, returned him Five of them, and aſſured him, *There was more than enough* ; adding, *'Tis Satiſfaction enough Sir, to an honeſt Man, that he is able to procure People their Goods again*. This was a remarkable Inſtance of his Moderation he ſometimes practiſed, the better to conceal his Villanies. We will add another Story, no leſs extraordinary.

A Lady whoſe Huſband was out of the Kingdom, and who had ſent for her over-draughts for her Aſſiſtarce, to the amount of between fifteen hundred and two thouſand Pound, loſt the Pocket Book in which they were contained, between *Bucklers-bury* and the *Magpye-Ale-houſe* in *Leadenhall-ſtreet*, where the Merchant lived upon whom they were drawn. She, however, went to the Gentleman, and he adviſed her to go directly to Mr *Jonathan Wild* Accordingly to *Jonathan* ſhe came, depoſited the Crown, and anſwered the Queſtions ſhe aſk'd him *Jonathan* then told her that in an Hour or two's Time, poſſibly ſome of his People might hear who it was that had pick'd her Pocket The Lady was vehement in her Deſires to have it again, and for that Purpoſe went ſo far at laſt as to offer an hundred Guineas *Wild* upon that made Anſwer, " Though they are of " much greater Value to you, Madam, yet they " cannot be worth any Thing like it to them, there-' fore keep your own Council, ſay nothing in the " Hearing of my People, and I'll give the beſt Di-" rections I am able for the Recovery of your " Notes , in the mean While, if you will go to any " Tavern near, and endeavour to eat a bit of Dinner, " I will bring you an Anſwer before the Cloth is " taken away " She ſaid ſhe was unacquainted with any Houſe thereabouts , upon which Mr *Wild* named the *Baptiſt-Head* The Lady would not be ſatiſfied unleſs Mr *Wild* promiſed to eat with her He at laſt complied, and ſhe ordered a Fowl and Sauſages at the Houſe he had appointed She waited there about three quarters of an Hour, when Mr *Wild* came over and told her he had heard News of her Book, deſired her to tell out ten Guineas upon the Table in caſe ſhe ſhould have Occaſion for them, and as the Cook came up to acquaint her that the Fowl was ready, *Jonathan* begged ſhe would juſt ſtep down and ſee whether there was any Woman waiting at his Door The Lady without minding the Myſtery, did as he deſired her, and perceiving a Woman in a Scarlet Riding-Hood walk twice or thrice by Mr *Wild*'s Houſe, her Curioſity prompted her to go near her ; but recollecting ſhe had left the Gold upon the Table up Stairs, ſhe went and ſnatched it up without ſaying a Word to *Jonathan*, and then running down again, went towards the Woman in a red Hood, who was ſtill walking before his Door It ſeems ſhe had gueſs'd right , for no ſooner did ſhe approach towards her, but the Woman came directly up to her, and preſenting her her Pocket-Book, deſired ſhe would open it and ſee that all was ſafe The Lady did ſo, and anſwering, *It was all right*, the Woman in the red Riding-Hood ſaid, *Here's another*

little Note for you, Madam · Upon which ſhe gave her a little Biller, on the out-ſide of which was wrote ten Guineas The Lady delivered her the Money immediately, adding alſo a Piece for herſelf, then ſhe returned with a great deal of Joy to Mr *Wild* and told him, *She had got her Book, and would now eat her Dinner heartily*

When the Things were taken away, ſhe thought it was Time to go to the Merchants, who probably now was returned from Change , but firſt thought it neceſſary to make Mr *Wild* an handſome Preſent, for which Purpoſe, putting her Hand in her Pocket, ſhe with great Surpirze found her green Purſe gone, in which was the Remainder of fifty Guineas ſhe had borrowed of the Merchant in the Morning, upon this ſhe look'd very much confus'd, but did not ſpeak a Word *Jonathan* perceived it, and aſk'd her, " If ſhe was not well I am tolerable in " Health, Sir, *anſwered ſhe*, but amaz'd that the ', Woman took but ten Guineas for the Book, and " at the ſame Time picked my Pocket of thirty " nine Mr *Wild* hereupon appeared in at great " Confuſion as the Lady, and ſaid, He hoped ſhe was " not in earneſt , but if it were ſo, begged her not " to diſturb herſelf, for ſhe ſhould not loſe one Fa, " thing " Upon this, *Jonathan* begging her to ſit ſtill, ſtepped over to his own Houſe, and gave, as may be ſuppoſed, neceſſary Directions ; for in leſs than half an Hour, a little *Jew*, that *Wild* kept, bolted into the Room, and told him the Woman was taken, and on the Point of going to the Compter " You ſhall ſee, Madam, (replied *Jonathan*, " turning to the Lady) what exemplary Puniſhment " I'll make of this infamous Woman " Then turning himſelf to the *Jew*, " *Abraham*, (ſays he) was " the green Purſe of Money taken about her ? Yes, " Sir, (replied his Agent) O la! (then ſaid th " Lady) I'll take the Purſe with all my Heart, I " would not proſecute the poor Wretch for the " World Would not you ſo, Madam, (repued " *Wild*) well then, we'll ſee what's to be done ' Upon this he firſt whiſper'd his Emiſſary, and then diſpatched him He was no ſooner gone, than, upon *Jonathan*'s ſaying the Lady would be too late at the Merchant's, they took Coach, and ſtopped over againſt the *Compter* Gate by *Stocks-Market* The Lady wonder'd at all this, but by that Time they had been in a Tavern there a very little Space, back comes *Jonathan*'s Emiſſary, with the green Purſe and the gold in it " She ſays, Sir, (ſaid the Fel-" low to *Wild*) ſhe has only broke a Guinea of the " Money for Garniſh and Wine, and here's all the " reſt of it Very well (ſays *Jonathan*) give it to " the Lady Will you pleaſe to tell it, Madam' " The Lady according did, and found there were " forty-nine Guineas Bleſs me! (ſays ſhe) I think " the Woman's bewitch'd, ſhe has ſent me ten " Guineas more than I ſhould have had, No Ma " dam (replied *Wild*) ſhe has ſent you the ten Gu eas " back again, which ſhe receiv'd for the Book I " never ſuffer any ſuch Practices in my Way , I ob " liged her therefore to give up the Money ſhe had " taken as well as that ſhe had ſtoln The Lady was ſo much confounded at theſe unaccountable Inc dent, that ſhe ſcarce knew what ſhe did , at laſt recollecting herſelf, " Well, Mr *Wild*, (ſays ſhe) then I think " the leaſt I can do is to oblige you to accept of theſe " ten Guineas. " No, (replied he) nor of ten har " things , I ſcorn all Actions of ſuch a Sort as much " as any Man of Quality in the Kingdom All the " Reward I deſire, Madam, is, that you will ac " knowledge I have acted like an honeſt Man, and a " Man of Honour " He had ſcarce pronounced theſe

ese Words, before he rose up, made her a Bow, nd went immediately down Stairs. We shall add ut one more Relation of this Sort, and then go on ith the Series of our History.

There came a little Boy with Viols to sell in a asket, to a Surgeon's Shop; it was in the Winter, hen one Day after he had sold the Bottles that ere wanted, the Boy complained he was almost hill'd to Death with Cold, and almost starved for Want of Victuals. The Surgeon's Maid, in Compas-on to the Child, who was not above nine or ten ears old, took him into the Kitchen, and gave im a Porringer of Milk and Bread, with a Lump r two of Sugar in it. The Boy eat a little of it, hen said, He had enough, gave her a thousand Blef-ngs, and marched off with a Silver Spoon, and a air of Forceps of the same Metal, which lay in he Shop as he passed through. The Instrument was rst missed, and the Search after it occasioned their issing the Spoon, yet noBody suspected any thing of he Boy, though they had all seen him in the Kitchen. The Gentleman of the House, however, having me Knowledge of *Wild*, and not living far from he *Old-Bailey*, went immediately to him for his dvice. *Jonathan* called for a Bottle of White Vine, and ordered it to be mull'd. The Gentle-an knowing the Custom of his House, laid down he Crown, and was going on to tell him the Man-er in which the Things were missed, but Mr Wild soon cut him short, by saying, ' Sir, step into the next Room a Moment, here's a Lady coming hither. You may depend upon my doing any Thing that is in my Power, and presently we'll talk the Thing over at Leisure.' The Gentleman went into the Room where he was directed, and saw, with no little Wonder, his Forceps and Silver Spoon ying upon the Table. He had hardly took them p to look at them, before *Jonathan* entered, ' So Sir, said he, I suppose you have no farther Oc-cafion for my Assistance. Yes indeed I have, said the Surgeon, there are a great many Servants in our Family, and some of them will certainly be blam-ed for this Transaction, so that I am under a Ne-essity of begging, that you will let me know how they were stolen? I believe the Thief is not far off, quoth *Jonathan*, and if you'll give me your Word he shall come to no Harm, I'll produce him immediately.' The Gentleman readily con-descended to this Proposition, and Mr. *Wild* step-ing out for Minute or two, brought in the young Viol Merchant in his Hand. Here Sir, says Wild, do you know this hopeful Youth, Yes, answered the Surgeon, but I could never have dreamt that a Crea-ture so little as he, could have had so much Wick-edness in him. However, as I have given you my Word, and as I have had my Things again, I will not only pass by his robbing me, but if he will bring me Bottles again, I shall make use of him as I used o do. I believe you may, added *Jonathan*, when he ventures into your House again. But it seems he was herein mistaken, for in less than a Week fterwards the Boy had the Impudence to come and fter his Viols again, upon which the Gentleman ot only brought of him as usual, but ordered two Quarts of Milk to be set on the Fire, put into it wo Ounces of gither Sugar, crumm'd it with a ouple of penny Bricks, and obliged this nimble inger'd Youth to eat it every Drop up before he vent out of the Kitchen Door, and then, without arther Correction, hurried him about his Business

This was the Channel in which *Jonathan's* Busi-efs usually ran, till he became, at last so very no-rious, that an Act of Parliament passed, levelled directly against such Practices, whereby Persons who took Money for the Recovery of stolen Goods, and did actually recover such Goods without apprehend-ing the Felon, should be deemed guilty of Felony in the same Degree with those who committed the Rob-bery. After this became a Law, a certain honour-able Person sent to *Jonathan* to warn him of going on any longer at his old Rate, for that it was now become a capital Crime, and if he was apprehend-ed for it, he could expect no Mercy. *Jonathan* received the Reproof with Abundance of Thankful-ness and Submission, but never altered the Manner of his Behaviour in the least, but on the contrary, did it more openly and publickly than ever. Indeed, to compensate for this, he seemed to double his Diligence in apprehending Thieves, and brought the most notorious amongst them to the Gallows, even tho' he himself had bred them up in their Art.

Of these none was so open and apparent a Case as that of *Blake*, alias *Blueskin*. This Fellow had from a Child been under the Tuition of Mr *Wild*, who paid for the curing his Wounds whilst he was in the Compter, allowed him three Shillings and six Pence a Week for Subsistence, and afforded his Help to get him out at last; yet soon after this he aban-doned him to his own Conduct, and in a short Space caused him to be apprehended for breaking open the House of Mr. *Kneebone*, which brought him to the Gallows. When this Fellow came to be tried, Mr *Wild* assured him, That his Body should be hand-somely interred in a good Coffin at his own Expence. This was strange Comfort, and such as by no Means suited with *Blueskin*, who insisted peremptorily upon a Transportation Pardon, which he said he was sure *Jonathan* had Interest enough to procure for him. But upon *Wild's* assuring him that he had not, and that it was in vain for him to flatter himself with such Hopes, *Blueskin* was at last in such a Passion, that though this Discourse happened in the Presence of the Court then sitting, *Blake* could not forbear taking Revenge for what he took to be an Insult on him, and therefore clap'd one Hand under *Jo-nathan's* Chin, and with the other cut him a large Gash a cross the Throat, which every Body at the Time it was done judged mortal. *Jonathan* was carried off, all covered with Blood; and though at that Time he professed the greatest Resentment for such base Usage, affirming that he had never de-served to be so treated, yet when he afterwards came to be under Sentence of Death himself, he re-gretted prodigiously the Escape he then made, often wishing that *Blake* had put an End to his Life, ra-ther than left him to so ignominious a Fate. Indeed it was not *Blake* alone, who had entertained Notions of putting him to Death, he had disobliged almost the whole Group of Villains, and there were Num-bers of them who had taken it into their Heads to deprive him of Life. His Escapes in the appre-hending such Persons were sometimes very narrow, having received Wounds in almost every Part of his Body, had his Skull twice fractured, and his whole Constitution so broken by these Accidents, and the great Fatigue he went through, that when he fell under the Misfortunes which brought him to his Death, he was scarce able to stand upright, and never in a Condition to go to Chappel

But we have broke a little into the Thread of our History, and must therefore go back, in order to trace the Causes which brought on *Jonathan's* last Adventures, and finally his violent Death, which we shall now relate in the clearest and concisest Manner that the Thing will allow.

The Practices of this Criminal continued long af-ter

74   4 E

ter the Act of Parliament, and that in so notorious a Manner at last, that the Magistrates of *London* and *Middlesex* thought themselves obliged to take Notice of him This occasioned a Warrant to be granted against him, by a worshipful Alderman of the City; upon which Mr *Wild* being apprehended somewhere near *Woodstreet*, he was carried into the *Rose* Spunging-House While he waited the Leisure of the Magistrate who was to examine him, the Crowd was very great; whereupon with his wonted Hypocrisy he harangued them to this Purpose *I wonder, good People, what it is you would see? I am a poor honest Man, who have done all I could to serve People when they have had the Misfortune to lose their Goods by the Villainy of Thieves. I have contributed more than any Man living, in bringing the most daring and notorious Malefactors to Justice Yet now by the Malice of my Enemies, you see I am in Custody, and am going before a Magistrate, who I hope will do me Justice Why should you insult me therefore? I don't know that I ever injured any of you Let me intreat you, as you see me lame in Body, and inflicted in Mind, not to make me more uneasy than I can bear. If I have offended against the Law it will punish me, but it gives you no right to use me ill, unheard and unconvicted* The People of the House, and the Compter Officers, by this Time, had pretty well cleared the Place; upon which he began to compose himself, and desired them to get a Coach to the Door, for that he was unable to walk About an Hour after, he was carried before a Justice and examined, and thereupon immediately committed to *Newgate* He laid there a considerable Time before he was tried, at last he was convicted capitally, upon the following Fact

He was indicted on the afore mentioned Statute, for receiving Money for the restoring stolen Goods, without apprehending the Persons by whom they were stolen In order to support this Charge, the Prosecutrix, *Catherine Stephens*, deposed as follows On the 22d of *January*, I had two Persons, came into my Shop under Pretence of buying some Lace, they were so difficult that I had none below would please them; so leaving my Daughter in the Shop, I stepped up Stairs and brought down another Box; we could not agree about the Price, and so they went away together. In about half an Hour after, I missed a tin Box of Lace that I valued at fifty Pound The same Night I went to *Jonathan Wild's* House, but not meeting with him at Home, I advertised the Lace that I had lost, with a Reward of fifteen Guineas, and no Questions ask'd But hearing nothing of it, I went to *Jonathan's* House again, and then met with him at home He desired me to give him a Description of the Persons that I suspected, which I did, as near as I could, and then he told me, That he would make Enquiry, and bid me call again in two or three Days I did so, and then he said, That he had heard something of my Lace, and expected to know more of the Matter in a very little Time I came to him again on that Day he was apprehended, and told him, that tho' I had advertis'd but fifteen Guineas Reward, yet I would give twenty or twenty five Guineas, rather than not have my Goods Don't be in such a Hurry, (says *Jonathan*) I don't know but I may help you to it for less, and if I can I will. The Persons that have it are gone out of Town, I shall set them to quarrelling about it, and then I shall get it the cheaper On the 10th of *March* he sent me Word, That if I could come to him in *Newgate*, and bring ten Guineas in my Pocket, he would help me to the Lace I went, he desired me to call a Por-

ter, but I not knowing where to find one he [...] a Person who brought one that appeared to be [...] Ticket-Porter The Prisoner gave me a Lea[...] which he said was sent him as a Direction where [...] go for the Lace; but I could not read, and so [...] delivered it to the Porter. Then he desired me [...] give the Porter the ten Guineas, or else (he said) [...] Persons that had the Lace would not deliver [...] gave the Porter the Money, he went away and in [...] little Time returned, and brought me a Box [...] was sealed up, but not the Box that was lost [...] opened it, and found all my Lace but one Pa[...] Now Mr *Wild* (says I) what must you have [...] your Trouble? Not a Farthing, (says he) not a [...] thing for me. I don't do these Things for world[...]ly Interest, but only for the good of poor Peop[...] that have met with Misfortunes As for the P[...] of Lace that is Missing, I hope to get you [...] be long; and I don't know but that I may h[...] you not only to your Money again, but to the Thi[...] too, and if I can, as you are a good Woman, [...] a Widow and a Christian, I desire nothing of y[...] but your Prayers, and for them I shall be thank[...]ful I have a great many Enemies, and God know[...] what may be the Consequence of this Imprison[...]ment.

The Fact suggested in the Indictment was [...] doubtedly fully proved by this Deposition, and [...] it happened in *Newgate*, and after his Confinement yet it still continued as much a Crime as if it [...] been done before The Law therefore condemn[...] him upon it But if he had even escaped thi[...] there were other Facts of a like Nature, which [...] evitably would have destroyed him, for the last Years of his Life, instead of growing more prudent he became less so, and the Blunders he committed were very little like the Behaviour of *Jonathan*, [...] the first Years of his Practice When he was brought up to the Bar to receive Sentence, he appeared to [...] very much dejected, and when the usual Question was proposed to him, *What have you to say wh[...] Judgment of Death should not pass upon you?* [...] spoke with a very feeble Voice in the following Terms,

My Lord, I hope I may even in the sad Condit[...] in which I stand, pretend to some little Merit [...] respect to the Service I have done my Country, in de[...]livering it from some of the greatest Pests with which it was ever troubled, My Lord, I have brought many bold and daring Malefactors to just Punish[...]ment, even at the Hazard of my own Life, my Body being covered with Scars I received in these Under[...]taking I presume, my Lord, to say, I have some Merit, because at the Time the Things were done they were esteemed meritorious by the Government, and therefore I hope, my Lord, some Compassion may be shewn on the Score of those Services I submit myself wholly to His Majesty's Mercy, and humbly beg a favourable Report of my Case

When Sir *William Thompson* pronounced Sentence of Death, he spoke particularly to *Wild*, put him in Mind of those Cautions he had received of going on in Practices, rendered Capital by a Law, made on Purpose for preventing that infamous Trade of becoming Broker for Felony, and standing in the Middle between the Felon and the Person injured, in order to receive a *Premium* for Redress And when he had properly stated the Nature and Aggravation of his Crime, he exhorted him to make a better Use of that small Portion of Time, which the Tenderness of the Law of *England* allowed Sinners for Repentance, and desired he would remember this Admonition, though he had slighted others as to the Repor[...]

eport, he told him, him, he might depend on Justice, and ought not to hope for more.

Under Conviction, no Man who appeared upon other Occasions to have so much Courage, ever shewed so little When Clergymen took the Pains to visit him, and instruct him in those Duties which it became a dying Man to practice, though he heard them without Interruption, yet he heard them coldly, and was continually suggesting Scruples and Doubts about a future State, and putting frequent Cases of the Reasonableness and Lawfulness of *Suicide*, where an ignominious Death was inevitable, and the Thing was perpetrated only to avoid Shame He was more especially swayed to such Notions, he pretended, from the Examples of the famous Heroes of Antiquity, who, to avoid dishonourable Treatment, had given themselves a speedy Death As such Discourses were what took up most of the Time between his Sentence and Death, so they occasioned some very useful Lectures upon this Head, from the charitable Divines who visited him One Letter was written to him by a learned Person, of which a Copy has been preferred 'Tis an excellent Piece, but too long to be inserted.

Jonathan pretended to be overcome with these Reasons, but it plainly appeared that in this he was an Hypocrite, for the Day before his Execution, not withstanding the Keepers had the strictest Eye on him imaginable, some-body conveyed to him a Bottle of *Liquid Laudanum*, of which having taken a very large Quantity, he hoped it would prevent his dying at the Gallows But as he had not been sparing in the Dose, so the Largeness of it made a speedy Alteration in him, which being perceived by his Fellow Prisoners, seeing he could not keep open his Eyes at the time that Prayers were said, they walked him about; which first made him sweat exceedingly and then very sick At last he vomited, and they continuing still to lead him, he threw the greatest Part of the *Laudanum* off from his Stomach He continued notwithstanding that, very drowsy, stupid and unable to do any thing but gasp out his Breath. He went to Execution in a Cart, and the People, instead of expressing any Compassion, threw Stones and Dirt all the Way he went along, reviling and cursing him to the last, and plainly shewing by their Behaviour, how much his Crimes had made him abhorred. When he arrived at *Tyburn*, having gathered a little Strength, (Nature recovering from the Convulsions into which the *Laudanum* had thrown him) the Executioner told him, *He might take what Time he pleased to prepare for Death* He therefore sat down in the Cart for some small time, during which the People were so uneasy, that they called out incessantly to the Executioner to dispatch him, and at last threatned to tear him in Pieces, if he did not tie him up immediately Such a furious Spirit was hardly ever discovered in the Populace, who generally behold even the Stroke of Justice with Tears, but so far were they from it in this Case, that had a Reprieve really come, 'tis highly questionable whether the Prisoner could ever have been brought back with Safety

Before we part with Mr. *Wild*, 'tis requisite to say

something of his Wives His first was a poor honest Woman, who contented herself to live at *Woolverhampton*, with the Son she had by him, without ever putting him to any Trouble, or endeavouring to take upon her the Title of Madam *Wild*, which his last Wife did with the greatest Affectation The next was the aforementioned Mrs *Milliner*, with whom he continued in very great Intimacy after they liv'd separately, and by her means he first carried on the Trade of detecting stolen Goods. The Third was one *Betty Man*, a Woman of the Town in her younger Years, but so suddenly struck with the Horrour of her Offences, that on the Persuasion of a *Romish Priest* she turn'd *Papist*, and appearing exceedingly devout and thoroughly penitent for all her Sins *Wild* even retained such an Impression of the Sanctity of this Woman, that he ordered his Body to be buried next hers in *Pancras Church-Yard*, which his Friends saw accordingly performed, about two a-Clock in the Morning after his Execution. The next of Mr. *Wild's Sultana's* was *Sarah Perrin*, alias *Grayston*, who surviv'd him The fifth was *Judith Nunn*, by whom he had a Daughter, who at the time of his Decease might be about ten Years old, both Mother and Daughter being then living The sixth and last was the celebrated Madam *Wild* This remarkable Damsel before her first Marriage was known by the Name of *Mary Brown*, afterwards by that of Mrs. *Dean*, being Wife to *Skull Dean*, who was executed about the Year 1716 or 1717 for House breaking. Some People have reported that *Jonathan* was receisary to the Hanging him, merely for the Sake of the Reward, and the Opportunity of taking his Relict; who, whatever Regard she might have for her first Husband, is currently reported to have been so much affected with the Misfortunes of the latter, that she twice attempted to make away with herself after she had the News of his being under Sentence By this last Lady he left no Children, and but two by his three other Wives, who were living at the Time of his Decease

As to the Person of this Man, it was homely to the greatest Degree, there being something remarkably villainous in his Face, which Nature had imprinted in stronger Terms, than perhaps she ever did upon any other However, he was strong and active, a Fellow of prodigious Boldness and Resolution, which made the Pusillanimity shew at his Death more remarkable He was not at all shy in owning his Profession, but on the contrary bragged of it upon all Occasions, into which perhaps he was led by that ridiculous Respect which was paid him, and the Meanness of his Spirit some Persons of Distinction were guilty of in talking to him freely Common Report has swelled the Number of Malefactors executed thro' his Means, to no less than one hundred and twenty. Certain it is, that they were very numerous, as well in Reality as his own Reckoning It has been said that there was a considerable Sum of Money due to him for his Share in the Apprehension of several Felons at the very Time of his Death, which happened on *Monday* the 24th of *May*, 1725, he being then about 42 Years of Age.

The LIFE *of* TOM JONES.

TOM JONES was born at *Newcastle upon Tine*, in the County of *Northumberland*, where his Father, being a Clothier, brought him up to the same Trade He follow'd this Calling till he was two and twenty Years of Age, though not without discovering his vicious Inclinations many Years before, by running in Debt, and taking to all manner of irregular Courses. At last, being reduc'd to Extremity, he resolv'd at once to apply himself to the Highway, as the only Way left to retrieve his Fortune. A very odd Way indeed ! but what is too often embrac'd by reduc'd Extravagants.

To make a Beginning, he robb'd his Father of 80*l* and a good Horse, upon which he rode cross the Country with all Speed, for fear of being pursu'd The Devil, he knew, was sometimes apt to leave his Children in the Lurch, and therefore he thought it safer to trust to the Legs of his Horse, than to his good Fortune This, and the conscious Dread of Justice, which is always ready to terrify young Villains, occasion'd his galloping 40 Miles before he stopp'd, all which Way, he was afraid of every one he saw, and every Noise he heard

After this, riding into *Staffordshire*, and meeting a Stage-Coach, with several Passengers in it, he commanded the Coachman to stop, and the People within to deliver Some of the Gentlemen were resolute, and refus'd to comply with his Demand ; upon which he fir'd several Pistols, taking Care to do no Hurt, and still preserving three or four, well loaded, for his Defence, if he should have Occasion of them The Fright which the Gunpowder put a Couple of Ladies into, who were in the Coach, obliged the Gentlemen to surrender, before there was any Mischief done, and Tom rode off with a considerable Booty

There is a pleasant Story related, as the Consequence of this Adventure, which we believe it will not be amiss to rehearse A Monkey, belonging to one of the Passengers, being ty'd behind the Coach, was so frighten'd at *Jones*'s firing, that with skipping about, he broke his Chain, and ran about the Fields so that the Owner could not catch him again. At Night, a Country-Fellow coming over a Stile, Pug leap'd out of the Hedge upon his Back, and there hung very fast The poor Man, having never seen a Monkey before, imagin'd the Devil had laid hold of him, in which Opinion he ran Home, and thunder'd at the Door like a mad Man His Wife look'd out at Window, and ask'd him what he had got He told her, the Devil, begging she would go to the Parson, and require his Assistance Nay, quoth she, *you shall not bring the Devil in here If you belong to him, I don't* So pray be content to go without Company Poor Hob was oblig'd to wait at his Door, till a Man, a little wiser than his Neighbours, came by, and with a few Apples and Pears, dispossess'd the unfortunate Wretch, who was very willing to let our Exorcist keep the Devil for his own Use, as a Reward for this signal Piece of Service And he, upon

hearing the Monkey cry'd, carry'd him to the Owner, and receiv'd a Reward

An Attorney of *Clifford's-Inn*, whose Name was *Story*, having been drinking at a Friend's House in the Country till he was entirely drunk, as he was riding along the Road towards Town, he was necessitated to alight and tie his Horse to a Tree, while he went under a Hedge to untruss a Point, It was *Tom Jones*'s Fortune to come by in the Interim ; whereupon he also dismounted, with the same Pretence, As soon as *Story* had done, *Jones* commanded him to deliver his Money ; but he, being in the Condition just mention'd, took no Notice of what was said Whereupon our Highwayman caught him by the Collar, and began to shake him *Have a Care what you do*, says the Attorney, *for I am brim full, and shall run over if you move me ever so little Brim full of what ?* quoth Jones *Of Liquors*, reply'd the other But '*tis your Money I want, Sir ; are you brim full of that ? If you are, run over as fast as you please* Story was so sick he could speak no more, but, before *Jones* was aware, giving a great Belch, he discharg'd a large Quantity of his Friend's Punch into the Face of our Adventurer, which almost blind ed him, and set him to swearing like a mad Man. At last, having clear'd his Phyz with a Handkerchief, he put his Hand into the Attorney's Pockets, and oblig'd them to discharge six Pounds odd Money, which shining Vomit a little pacify'd him, and made him forgive the Affront, and suffer our drunken Man, who was by this Time a little soberer, to remount and ride off

Tom was by this Time so grounded in Vice, that nothing less powerful than the Gallows was able to convert him from his wicked Courses This is, indeed, commonly the last Teacher which such Wretches have, and he never fails to make them as honest as any of their Neighbours, and as quiet as any of the Descendants of *Adam*, who have been departed in Peace some Thousands of Years The sooner he does his Duty, 'tis generally the better

But this is another Digression from our History, to which we now return Not long after the committing of the above recited Robbery, *Tom Jones* met with one *Samuel P———s* upon the Road, a Quaker, who formerly kept a Button Shop, between the two Gates of the *Savoy* in the *Strand*, to whom he put the usual Demand Mr *Primitive*, having reduced himself to very low Circumstances, as 'tis said, by Whoring, Gaming, and Drinking, he was now riding down into the Country to his Friends, in order to avoid an Arrest As he was therefore in much greater Apprehension of a Bailiff than of a Highwayman, and as he did not understand what *Tom* said, till he had got fast hold of him by the Throat, he very formally cried out, *At whose Suit dost thou detain me ? Jones*, who was not acquainted with our Friend's Condition, smartly reply'd, *I detain thee on my own Suit, and my Demand is for all thy Substance* The

Quake

Quaker now perceived how the Cafe ftood. nevertheless, being a dry queer fort of a Man, he was refolved to carry on the Jeft, whereupon he added. *Indeed Friend, I don't know thee, nor can I tell how to imagine that ever thee and I have had any Dealings together,* ——— *You fhall find then,* fays *Jones, that we muft deal together now.* So clapping a Piftol to his Breaft, he was going to explain himfelf, when Friend *Samuel* cry'd out; *Pray Neighbour ufe no Violence ! for if thou carrieft me to Goal, I fhall be utterly undone I have at leaft* 14 *Guineas about me, and if that will fatisfy thee, thou art welcome to take them Here they are, and give me leave to affure thee, that I have frequently ftopp'd the Mouth of a Bailiff with a much lefs Sum, and made him affirm to my Creditors, that he could not find me* Jones was pleas'd to receive the Money, upon any Account whatfoever ; yet, being willing to convince the Quaker of his Miftake, (tho' indeed the Quaker, as we have obferv'd, was not miftaken, but only willing to carry on the Affair in the Strain it began with) he faid to to him, *Friend, I am not fuch a Rogue as thou takeft me to be: I am no Bailiff, but an honeft generous Highwayman. I fhall not trouble myfelf,* the Friend reply'd, *about the Diftinction of Names ; if a Man takes my Money from me by Force, it concerns me but little what he calls himfelf, or what his Pretence may be for fo doing.* After this they rode about their feveral Affairs, the Quaker homewards, and *Tom* in queft of more Prey

Not long after this, he met the late Lord *Wharton* and his Lady on the Road, ftopp'd their Coach, and demanded their Money, tho' they had three Men on Horfeback to attend them His Lordfhip at firft made fome Hefitation, and afk'd him if he underftood what he was about ? " Do you know me, " Sir, *fays he,* that you dare be fo bold as to ftop " me on the Road ? Not I, *reply'd* Jones *very rea-* " *dily,* I neither know nor care who you are, tho' " before you fpoke, I took you for a Brewer, be- " caufe you carry your Cooler by your Side . Now, " indeed, I am apt to imagine you are fome great " Man, becaufe you fpeak fo big, but be as great " as you will, Sir, I muft have you to know, that " there is no Man upon this Road fo great as my- " felf ; therefore pray be quick in anfwering my " Demands, for Delays may prove Dangerous " His Honour now faw our Gentleman was refolute, fo he and his Lady e'en delivered up what they had about them, without more Words.

The whole Prize confifted of two hundred Pounds in Money, three diamond Rings, and two gold Watches All this being fecured, *Jones* commanded his Lordfhip to bid his Servants ride on to fome Diftance before, threatning him with Death if he refufed, which being done, and the Servants obeying, he had a fair Opportunity of riding off, without being purfued

Tom received Intelligence one Day, that a certain Gentleman was on the Road, with two hundred Pounds in his Coach This, to be fure, was a fufficient Invitation for him He got upon a Hill to wait for his Cuftomers coming, who fpy'd him at a Diftance without apprehending any Thing But a Steward of the Gentleman's, obferving the Behaviour of our Chapman at a Diftance, he told his Mafter, that he believed the Man on the Hill was a Highwayman. *If you pleafe Sir,* quoth he, *to truft me with your Money, I'll ride by him, which I may do unfufpected, for he certainly waits for you* The Gentleman was pleas'd at his Servant's Care, and lik'd his Propofal very well So giving him the Bag, he rode on as faft as he could, and pafs'd by *Jones,* without being examin'd, getting out of Sight before the Coach came up

In fhort, the Coach was ftopp'd, and the Money demanded, when our Gentleman gave him about ten Guineas, affuring him that he had no more *Jones* boldly nam'd the Sum he wanted, and fwore 'twas in the Coach, the Traveller as often afferting that he was miftaken At laft, the real State of the Cafe came into our Adventurer's Head ; whereupon, without taking his leave of the Gentleman, he fet Spurs to his Horfe, and rode after the Steward full Speed, who was by this Time got at leaft a Mile and a half from the Place. *Jones* was well mounted, and it was five Miles from the next Town, fo that he came in fight of the Steward before he could get into any Inn, but the Steward faw him, mended his Pace, and fav'd the Money This difappointment vex'd poor *Tom* to the Heart, but there was no Remedy. As to the Gentleman, he gave his Servant a handfome Gratuity for what he had done, as he deferved.

After many Adventures, moft of them of a Piece with the foregoing, *Tom* was apprehended in *Cornwal,* for robbing a Farmer's Wife, and afterwards ravifhing her. For this Fact he was try'd, and condemn'd, the Affizes following, and about ten Days afterwards, executed at *Launcefton,* on *Saturday* the 25th of *April,* 1702 being thirty two Years of Age

At the Gallows he gave a pretty large Account of his Robberies, to fome Gentlemen who defired it, behaving with more Modefty and Decency than fuch Wretches commonly do Before he was turn'd off, he delivered a pretty Deal of good Advice to the young Men prefent, in very pathetic Words Exhorting them to be induftrious in their feveral Callings, and careful not to entangle themfelves with Debts, contracted by their own Extravagances. Defiring them to follow the Dictates of their Reafon, and have a due Regard for every Man's Property ; and enforcing all his Admonitions, with putting his Hearers in Mind of a Providence, which governs the World, and will certainly call every Man to an Account for his Actions.

The LIFE *of* TIM. BUCKLEY.

TIMOTHY BUCKLEY, was an unparallel'd a Villain as ever liv'd in this Kingdom; he was born of very honest Parents at *Stamford* in *Lincolnshire*, where he serv'd three Years to a Shoemaker; but then running away from his Master, he came up to *London*, and soon became acquainted with ill Company, whose Vices he followed to support him in a most scandalous and infamous Course of Life. Having spent a great deal of his ill-got Money at a blind Alehouse in *Wapping*, he once ask'd the Victualler to lend him ten Shillings; which Favour he denied him; and *Tim* so highly resented his Ingratitude, that he left frequenting his House. Not long after *Tim.* and some of his thieving Companions, breaking in by Night, they bound the Victualler, his Wife and Maid, both Hand and Foot. As they were going to gag 'em, Mr *Taplish* desiring *Tim* to be more favourable, *No, no,* quoth he, *you must expect no Favour from my Hands, you surly Son of a B——h, whose Prodigality makes you lord it over the People here, like a Boatswain over a Ship's Crew, and look as bluff upon your Tarpaulin Guests, as a Mate newly rais'd to a Commander. Now if you'll go but about* Charing-Cross, *and that Way, you shall have the Ale-drapers so very humble and obliging for the taking but Three-pence, that a Gentleman Foot-Soldier, or a Lord's-Valet, shall have as many Scrapes and Cringes from the Man of the House, as if he was a French Dancing-Master. Whether it be Poverty, as living among Courtiers, or having been bred Gentlemen's Servants, and so kick'd and cuff'd into good Manners by their Masters formerly, makes them so mannerly, that I can't tell. But let it be as it will, I shall use that End of the Town for the future, and for their extreme Civility, make bold to spend some of your Money among 'em.* And accordingly *Tim* and his Comrades, robb'd the House, taking from thence Forty Pounds laid by for the Brewer, three Silver Tankards, a Silver-Watch, and eight Gold Rings.

Another Time, *Tim Buckley* taking a Walk towards *Hyde-Park-Corner*, the Air of which Place is generally very unwholsome for a Thief to take, it was his Fortune to meet with that famous *Merry Andrew* and *Mountebank*, Doctor *Cately*. He commanded that illiterately learned Gentleman to *stand and deliver*; which Words sounding as terribly in his Ears, as *Cut, Slash, Saw,* and *Sear*, does to those poor Patients whose Legs are cutting off in St *Bartholomew's*, or St *Thomas's* Hospital, he begg'd heartily of him to be merciful, and not to rob a poor Man, who took a great deal of Pains for an honest Livelihood. *Tim* knowing his Occupation, fell a laughing, withal saying, " Quacks pretend to Honesty! There is not such a Pack of cheating Knaves " in the Nation again, in making People believe " they are Scholars, when they know no more of " *Greek,* or *Latin*, than a sucking Child. Besides, " their Impudence is intolerable, for deceiving of ig-

" norant Folks with hard Names, and cramp Words " as Jugglers do with the old Cant of *Hictius doctius,* " *hi presto*, be gone, while their Confederates pick " their Pockets. Moreover, making credulous Fools " believe, that there was not more Men slain and " wounded at the Fight of the *Boyne* in *Ireland*, than " they have recover'd from the Point of Death, or " Death's Door, by beckoning their Souls back a-" gain, after they have been many Leagues from their " Bodies. Therefore quickly deliver what you have " or else this Pistol shall prevent your going any " more into, *France, Spain, Italy, Portugal, Den-*" *mark, Sweden, Poland, Germany*, and *the Devil's* " *Arse i'the Peak*, as your usual Cant is, tho' you " was never out of *England* in your Life." Our Doctor preferring his own Welfare before what he had about him, he humbly presented *Tim.* with Six Guineas, and a very good Watch, that he might keep Time in spending the Gold.

An informing Constable, who was a Baker in St *Giles's* Parish in the Fields, once taking up *Tim* and sending him for a Soldier into *Flanders*, he had not been long there before he deserted, and came to *London* again, and one Day meeting this Baker's Wife coming alone from *Hampstead*, forcing her into a private Place, and presenting a Pistol to her Breast, he swore he would shoot her dead on the Spot if she refus'd laying with him; he being bent upon it, to be reveng'd on her Husband, who had impress'd him a little while ago. The Baker's Wife being no *Lucretia*, to value her Chastity at the Loss of her Life, she was forced to submit to the Ravisher's Pleasure, who having obtain'd what he desir'd, he then commanded her to deliver her Money, and what other Things of Worth she had about her. Hereupon the honest Woman crying out, *Is this Justice or Conscience, Sir?* Quoth *Tim. You B——h, don't tell me of Justice, for I hate her as much as your Husband can, because her Scales are even. And as for Conscience, I have as little of that as any Baker in England, who cheats other Bellies to fill his own. Nay, a Baker is a worse Rogue than a Taylor, for whereas the latter commonly pinches his Cabbage from the Rich, the former, by making his Bread too light, robs all without distinction, but chiefly the Poor, for which he deserves more hanging than me, or any of my honest Fraternity.* So taking from her a Couple of Gold Rings, and eleven Shillings, he sent her home to tell her Husband of this Adventure.

Afterwards *Tim Buckley* stealing a very good Horse in *Buckinghamshire*, he turn'd Highwayman, and riding up to *London*, he met on the Road a certain Pawn-broker, living in *Drury Lane*, by whom having been some Loser in pawning some Things to him, which were lost for want of redeeming, he was resolved to have his Pennyworth out of him now, so commanding him to stand and deliver, he began to plead earnestly for Favour, saying, It is a very hard Case that an honest Man can not

not go about his lawful Occasions but he must be robb'd. D——mn you (quoth Tim.) hast thou so much brazen'd Impudence as to reckon thyself an honest Man, when I know thou art an unconscionable Pawn-broker, who lives and grows fat on Fraud and Oppression, as a Toad on Filth and Venom? Your Practice outvies Usury, as much as robbing on the Highway does a Petit-Larceny, so if one calls you a Tradesman, it must be by the same Rhetorical Figure which stiles the Legerdemain of a Pick-pocket an Art and Mystery. Your Shop, like the Gates of Hell, is always open, in which you sit at the Receipt of Custom, and having got the Spoils of the Needy, you hang 'em up in Rank and File, like so many Trophies of Victory To your Shop all sorts of Garments resort on a Pilgrimage, whilst you playing the Pimp, lodge the Tabby Petticoat, and the Russet Breeches together, in the same Bed of Lavender Thou art the Treasurer of the Thieves Exchequer, and the common Tender of all Booth heavers and Shoplifters in Town, to which Purpose you keep a private Warehouse, whence you ship away all ill-gotten Goods by wholesale, you do so fleece the poor, that you scarce leave them so much as a primitive Fig-leaf to cover their Nakedness, and so often do they bring what they have into your Lumber-House, that at last they know the Way, and can almost go to pawn alone by themselves Thus they are forc'd to purchase the same Clothes half a score times over, and for want of a Chest to keep them in at home, it costs thrice as much as they are worth for a Lodging in your Custody Six Pence per Month must they pay for every twenty Shillings, which (after your rate of thirteen Months to the Year) is six shillings and six pence per Pound per Annum, or thirty two Pound ten shillings per Cent besides a Shilling for a Bill of Sale, if the Matter be considerable

Upon the whole, since you seldom or never lend above half the Value on any thing, Plate excepted, you get near forty Pounds in every Hundred Pounds, and considering how many Thieves and Pick-pockets (your chiefest Customers, that bring the lumping Bargains) never intend to redeem, and how many poor People are not able, or that if they are redeemed the very next Day, yet are you so extortioning as to be paid a Month's Interest, one may reasonably conclude, that you make at least Cent per Cent. of your Money in a Year And all this by a Course tending only to the Encouragement of Thieves, and the Ruin of those that are honest, but indigent Come, come, Mr Blood sucker, open your Purse strings, or otherwise this Pistol shall instantly send you to Hell before the Wind But the Pawn-broker being very loath to go to the Devil before his Time, he ransom'd himself for Twenty-eight Guineas, a Gold Watch, a Silver Tobacco box, and a Couple of Gold Rings

Another Time Tim, Buckley meeting a Stockjobber on the Road, who had formerly prosecuted him for Felony, upon Conviction whereof he was burnt in the Hand, he was now resolved to be revenged on him, by robbing him of Forty eight Guineas, The Stockjobber desiring some small Matter of Tim to carry him forward on his Journey, quoth he I have no Charity at all for any Rogues of Stock jobbers, who are Animals that rise and fall like the ebbing and

flowing of the Sea, and their Paths are as unsearchable Thou art as changeable as the Wind, and certain in nothing but Uncertainty. I believe the Grashopper on the Royal-Exchange is an Emblem of you; for as that leaps from one Place to another, so do you from one Number to another, sometimes thirty per Cent Advance is too little for you; at other times thirty per Cent. Discount is not enough. I'll hold you a Wager, that if I should ask what Religion you profess, you'll cry, You'll sell me as cheap as any Body; or ask you of what Value such an Article of Faith is you'll tell me, You'll give me as much for Navy Bills as any Chapman Thou art so full of Contradiction, that you lower the Price of Things on purpose to raise it, yet I must acknowledge, you can't be said to be a Hypocrite, because you commonly boast of over reaching those you deal with. As for Christianity, thou art far enough from that, for tho' perhaps you have been baptiz'd, yet will it be highly improper to say, you was ever confirm'd, unless in Impudence And I verily think you could never shew more Impudence than you do now, in asking me for somewhat to help you on your Journey, out of so small a Matter as forty eight Guineas, which is scarce worth taking from you Indeed I shan't give you one Farthing, therefore wishing you the best of a bad Market, and that you may be as well stock'd when I see you next on the Road, farewel till the next merry meeting

Not long after, this same Stock-jobber accidentally meeting Tim Buckley in London, he caused him to be apprehended and committed to Newgate, and convicting him of this Robbery, he receiv'd Sentence of Death But obtaining a Reprive, and afterwards pleading to a free Pardon, as soon as he was at Liberty, resolving to be farther reveng'd on this Adversary, who had twice sat very close on his Skirts, he went to Hackney, where this Stock-jobber having a Country-House within a Mile of that Village, he one Night set Fire to it but a timely Discovery thereof preventing it from doing much Damage, it was quickly quench'd However Tim made his Escape, and flying into Leicestershire, where he broke open a House at a Place called Ashby de la Zouch, and from thence took above eighty Pounds He then went to a Fair at Derby, where he bought a good Horse, and went on the Highway again. Being thus mounted again to rob on the Road, within two Miles of Nottingham he attempted to stop a Coach, in which were three Gentleman, besides a Couple of Footmen riding a little behind, but they being resolv'd not to be robb'd of what they had by one Villain, one of 'em fired a Blunderbuss out of the Coach, which kill'd Tim's Horse, and then all the Gentlemen alighting, and the Footmen being by this time also come up to their Assistance, a bloody and obstinate Engagement begun between them, wherein Tim kill'd one of the Gentlemen and a Footman, but nevertheless, being overpower'd, after he had discharged eight Pistols, and was also grown faint thro' the Loss of much Blood (for he had receiv'd eleven Wounds in his Arms, Thighs, and Legs) he was seized and committed to Jail in Nottingham, where he was executed in 1701, aged twenty nine Years, and afterwards hang'd in Chains at the Place where he perpetrated the two Murders aforesaid.

The LIFE of MOL CUTPURSE, a
Pickpocket and Highway-woman.

*M*ARY *Frith*, otherwise call'd *Mol Cutpurse*, from her original Profession of cutting Purses, was born in *Barbican* in *Aldersgate-street*, in the Year 1589 Her Father was a Shoemaker; and though no remarkable Thing happened at her Nativity, such as the flattering Soothsayers pretend in Eclipses, and other the like Motions above, or Tides, and Whales and great Fires, adjusted and tim'd to the Genitures of crown'd Heads, yet, for a She-Politician, she was not much inferior to Pope *Joan*, for in her Time, she was Superior in the Mystery of diving in Purses and Pockets, and was very well read and skill'd too in the Affairs of the Placket among the great Ones.

Both the Parents (as having no other Child living) were very tender of this Daughter, but especially the Mother; according to the Tenderness of that Sex, which is naturally more indulgent than the Male; most affectionate she was to her in her Infancy, most careful of her in her Youth, manifested especially in her Education, which was the more strictly and diligently attended, by Reason of her boisterous and masculine Spirit, which then shewed itself, and soon after became predominant, she was above all Breeding and Instruction She was a very *Tomrig* or *Hoyden*, and delighted only in Boys-play and Pastime, not minding or companying with the Girls; many a Bang or Blow this Hoyting procured her, but she was not so to be tam'd, or taken off from her rude Inclinations; she could not endure that sedentary Life of sewing or stitching; a Sampler was as grievous to her as a Winding-sheet; and on her Needle, Bodkin, and Thimble, she could not t'unk quietly, wishing them chang'd into Sword and Dagger for a Bout at Cudgels Her Head-geer and Handkerchief (or what the Fashion of those Times was for Girls to be dress'd in) were alike tedious to her, she wearing them, as handsomly as a Dog would a Doublet; and so cleanly, that the footy Pot-hooks were above the Comparison This perplex'd her, Friends, who had only this Proverb favourable to their Hope, *That an unlucky Girl may make a good Woman*, but they liv'd not to the length of that Expectation, dying in her Minority, and leaving her to the Swing and Sway of her own unruly Temper and Disposition

She would fight with Boys, and courageously beat them, run, jump, leap, or hop with any of her contrary Sex, or recreate herself with any other Play whatsoever. She had an Uncle, Brother to her Father, who was a Minister, and of him she stood in some Awe, but not so much, as to restrain her in these Courses, so that seeing he could not effectually remedy that inveterating Evil in her Manners, he trappanned her on board a Merchant-Ship lying at *Gravesend*, and bound for *New-England*, whither he designed to have sent her, but having learn-

ed to swim, she one Night jump'd over board, and swimm'd to Shore, and after that Escape, would never go near her Uncle again Farthermore, it is to be observed, that *Mercury* was in Conjunction with, or rather in the House of *Venus*, at the Time of her Nativity; the former of which Planets is of a thievish, cheating, deceitful Influence; and the other hath Dominion over all Whores, Bawds, and Pimps, and, joyn'd with *Mercury*, over all Trepanners and Hectors · She hath a more general Influence than all the other six Planets put together, for no Place nor Person is exempted from her, invading alike both sacred and prophane, Nunneries and Monastries, as well as the common Places of Prostitution, *Cheapside* and *Cornhill*, as well as *Bloomsbury* or *Covent-Garden* Under these benevolent and kind Stars, she grew up to some Maturity, she was now a lusty and sturdy Wench, and fit to put out to Service, having not a competency of her own, left her by her Friends to maintain her without working; but as she was a great Libertine, she liv'd too much in common, to be enclos'd in the Limits of a private Domestick Life A Quarter-staff was fitter for her than a Distaff; she would go to the Ale-house when she had made shift to get a little Stock, spend her Penny, come into any one's Company, and Club till she had none left, and then she was fit for any Enterprize. Moreover, she had a natural Abhorrence to tending of Children, to whom she ever had an Averseness in her Mind, equal to the Sterility and Barrenness in her Womb, never (to our best Information) being made a Mother

She generally went dress'd in Man's Apparel, which puts me in Mind how *Hercules*, *Nero*, and *Sardanapalus* are laugh'd at and exploded, for their effeminacy and degenerated Dissoluteness in their extravagant Debauchery, the first is pourtrated with a Distaff in his Hand, the other recorded to be marry'd as a Wife, and all the conjugal and matrimonial Rites perform'd at the Solemnity of the Marriage; and the other lacks the Luxury of a Pen, as loose as his Female Riots to describe them, These were all Monsters of Men, and have no Parellels either in old or Modern Histories, till such Time as *Mol Cutpurse* approach'd their Examples; for her heroick Impudence hath quite outdone every Romance, never Woman before being like her No Doubt but *Mol*'s Converse with herself, informed her of her Defects, and that she was not made for the Pleasure or Delight of Man, and therefore, since she could not be honoured with him, she would be honoured by him, in that Garb and Manner of Raiment which he wore This she took to from her first Entrance into a competency of Age, and to her dying Day she would not leave it off

Though she was so ugly in any Dress, as never
to

to be woo'd nor follicited by any Man, yet she never had the *Green-Sickness*, that epidemical Difease of Maidens, after they have once pafs'd their Puberty, she never eat Lime, Coals, Oatmeal, Tobaccopes, Cinders, or fuch like Trafh, no Sighs, dejected Looks, or Melancholly clouded her vigorous Spirits, or reprefs'd her Joviality, she was troubled with none of those Longings which poor Maidens are fubject to. She had the Power and Strength to command her own Pleafure of any Perfon who had reafonable Ability of Body, and therefore she needed not whine for it, as she was able to beat a Fellow to a Compliance, without the unneceffary Trouble of Entreaties

Now *Moll* thinking what Courfe of Life she should betake herfelf to, she got acquainted with fome Fortune-tellers of the Town, from whom learning fome Smatch and Relifh of that Cheat, by their infignificant Schemes, and calculating of Figures, she got a tolerably good Livelihood, but her Income being not equivalent to her Expences, she enter'd herfelf into the Society of *Divers*, otherwise call'd *File-clyers, Cut-purfes*, or *Pick-pockets*, which People are a kind of Land Pirates, trading altogether in other Men's *Bottoms*, for no other Merchandife than *Bullion* and ready Coin, and they keep moft of the great Fairs and Marts in the World. In this unlawful Way she got a vaft deal of Money, but having been very often in *Old Bridewell*, the *Compters*, and *Newgate*, for her irregular Practices, and burnt in the Hand four Times, she left off this petty Sort of Theft, and went on the Highway, committing many great Robberies, but all of 'em on the Round-heads, or Rebels, that fomented the Civil War againft King *Charles* the Firft, againft which Villains she had as great an Antipathy as an unhappy Man, that, for counterfeiting a Half-Crown in those rebellious Times, was executed at *Tyburn*, where she faid, *That he was adjudg'd to die but for counterfeiting a Half-Crown, but thofe that ufurp'd the whole Crown, and ftole away its Revenue, and had counterfeited its Seal, were above Juftice, and efcap'd unpunifh'd*

A long Time had *Moll Cutpurse* robb'd on the Road, but, at laft, robbing General *Fairfax* of 250 *Jacobus*'s on *Hounflow Heath*, shooting him thro' the Arm for oppofing her, and killing two Horfes on which a couple of his Servants rid, a clofe Purfuit was made after her by fome Parliamentarian Officers, quartering in the Town of *Hounflow*, to whom *Fairfax* had told his Misfortune. Her Horfe fail'd her at *Turnham-Green*, where they apprehended her, and carried her to *Newgate* After this, she was condemn'd, but procur'd her Pardon, by giving her Adverfary 2000*l* Now *Moll* being fighten'd by this Difafter, she left off going on the Highway any more, and took a House, within two Doors of the *Globe* Tavern in *Fleet-ftreet*, over againft the Conduit, almoft facing *Shoe-Lane* and *Salifbury Court*, where she difpens'd Juftice among the wrangling Tankard-Bearers, by often exchanging their Burden of Water for a Burden of Beer, as far the lighter Carriage, though not fo portable

In her Time Tobacco being grown a great Mode, she was mightily taken with the Paftime of Smoaking, becaufe of its Singularity, and that no Woman ever fmoak'd before her, though a great many of her Sex, fince, have follow'd her Example

Moll being quite fcar'd from thieving herfelf, she turn'd *Fence*, that is to fay, a Buyer of ftolen Goods, by which Occupation she got a great deal of Money. In her Houfe she fet up a kind of Brokery, or a diftinct Factory for Jewels, Rings, and Watches, which had been pinch'd or ftolen any manner of

Way, at never fo great a Diftance, from any Perfon It might properly enough be call'd the *Infurance-Office* for fuch Merchandife, for the Lofers were fure, upon Compofition, to recover their Goods again, and the Pirates were fure to have a good Ranfom, and she fo much in the Grofs for Brokage, without any more Danger, the *Hue-and-Cry* being always directed to her for the Difcovery of the Goods, and not the Takers

Once, a Gentleman that had loft his Watch by the bufy Fingers of a Pickpocket, came very anxioufly to *Moll*, enquiring if she could help him to it again She demanded of him the Marks and Signs thereof, with the Time when, and where he loft it, or by what Crowd, or other Accident He replied, *That coming through Shoe-Lane, there was a Quarrel betwixt two Men, one of which, as he afterwards heard, was a Grafier, whom they had fet in Smith field, having feen him receive the Sum of 200l or thereabouts, in Gold There was one Bat Rud, as he was fince inform'd, who, obferving the Man hold his Hand in his Pocket where his Gold was, juft in the middle of a Lane whitherto they dogg'd him, overthrew a Barrel trimming at an Alehoufe Door, while one behind the Grafier pufh'd him over, who, withal, threw down Bat, who was ready for the Fall Betwixt thefe two prefently arofe a Quarrel; the Pickpocket demanded Satisfaction, while his Comrades interpofing, after two or three Blows in Favour of the Countryman, who had drawn his Hands out of his Pocket to defend himself, foon drew out his Treafure, and while he was looking on the Scuffle, fome of them had lent him a Hand too, and finger'd out his Watch* *Moll* fmill'd at this Adventure and told him, *He should hear further of it within a Day or two, at the fartheft* When the Gentleman came again, she underftood by his Difcourfe that he would not lofe it for twice the Value, becaufe it was given him by a particular Friend; fo she fqueez'd 20 Guineas out of him before he could obtain his Watch

One Night late, *Moll* going Home almoft drunk from the *Devil* Tavern, she tumbled over a great black Sow, that was roufting in a Dunghill near the Kennel, but getting up again, in a fad dirty Pickle, she drove her to her Houfe, where finding her full of Pigs, she made her a Drench to haften her Farrowing, and the next Morning she brought her eleven curious Pigs, which *Moll* and her Companions made fat and eat, and then she turn'd the Sow out of Doors, who prefently repair'd to her old Mafter, a Bumpkin at *Iflington*, who with Wonder receiv'd her again Having given her fome Grains, he turn'd her out of his Gates, watching what Courfe she would take, and intending to have Satisfaction for his Pigs wherefoever he should find her to have laid them The Sow, naturally mindful of her fqueaking Brood, went directly to *Moll*'s Door, and there kept a lamentable Noife to be admitted This was Evidence enough for the Fellow, that there his Sow had laid her Belly, when knocking, and having Entrance, he tells, *Moll* a Tale of a Sow and her Litter She replied, he was mad He fwore, he knew his Sow's Meaning by her grunting, and that he would give her Sauce to her Pigs *Goodman Coxcomb*, quoth Moll, *come in, and fee if this Houfe looks like a Hogftye*: when, going into all the Rooms, and feeing how neat and clean they were kept, he was convinced that the Litter was not laid there, and went Home curfing his Sow for mifinforming him

To get Money, *Moll* would not ftick out to bawd for either Men or Women, infomuch, that her Houfe became a double Temple for *Priapus* and *Venus*, frequented by Votaries of both Sorts Thofe who were generous to her Labour, their Defires were favourably

vourably accommodated, with Expedition; whilst she linger'd with others, laying before them the difficult but certain Attainment of their Wishes, which serv'd as a Spur to the Dulness of their Purses For the Lady *Pecunia* and she kept the same Pace, but still in the End she did the Feat. *Moll* having a great Antipathy against the Rump Parliament, she hit on a Fellow very dextrous for imitating People's Hands; with him she communicated her Thoughts, and they concurr'd to forge and counterfeit their Commissioners and Treasurers Hands to the respective Receivers and Collectors Hands, without Delay, to such as he in his counterfeited Orders appointed So that wheresoever he had Intelligence of any great Sum in the Country, they were sure to forestal the Market This Cheat lasted for half a Year, till it was found out at *Guild-hall*, and such a politick Course taken, to avoid Cozenage, that no Warrants would pass among themselves. But when the Government was seiz'd and usurp'd by that Arch-Traytor *Oliver Cromwell*, they began this Trade afresh, it being very easy to imitate his single Sign Manual, as that ambitious Usurper would have it stil'd; by which Means, her Man also drew great Sums of Money out of the Customs and Excise, nay, out of the *Exchequer* itself, till *Oliver* was forc'd to use a private Mark, to make his Credit authentick among his own Villains

After 74 Years of Age, *Moll* being grown crazy in her Body, and discontented in Mind, she yielded to the next Distemper that approach'd her, which was the Dropsy, a Disease which had such strange and terrible Symptoms, that she thought she was possess'd, and that the Devil was got within her Doublet. Her Belly, from a wither'd, dry'd, wrinckled Piece of Skin, was grown to the tutest, roundest Globe of Flesh, that ever any beauteous young Lady strutted with However, there was no Blood that was generative in her Womb, but only that destructive of the Grape, which by her Excesses was now turn'd into Water; so that the tympanied Skin thereof sounded like a Conduit-Door. If we anatomize her any farther, we must say her Legs represented a Couple of Mill-posts, and her Head was so wrapp'd with Cloaths, that she look'd like Mother *Shipton*.

It may well be expected, that, considering what a deal of Money she got by her wicked Practices, she might make a Will; but yet, of 5000*l.* which she had once by her in Gold, she had not above 100*l.* left her latterly, which she thought too little to give to the Charitable Uses of building Hospitals and Alms-houses The Money that might have been design'd that Way, as it came from the Devil, so it return'd to the Devil again, in the *Rump's* Exchequer and Treasury at *Haberdashers* and *Goldsmiths-Hall.* Yet, to preserve something of her Memory, and not leave it to the Courtesy of an Executor, she anticipated her Funeral Expences; for it being the Fashion of those Times to give Rings, to the undoing of the *Confectioners*, who liv'd altogether by the Dead and the New-born, she distributed some

that she had by her, among her chief Companions and Friends.

These Rings (like Princes Jewels) were notable ones, and had their particular Names likewise, as the *Bartholomew*, the *Ludgate*, the *Exchange*, and so forth; deriving their Appellations from the Places whence they were stolen. They needed no Admunition of a Death's Head, nor the Motto *Memento mori*; for they were the Wages and Monuments of their thieving Masters and Mistresses, who were interr'd at *Tyburn*, and she hop'd her Friends would wear them, both for her Sake and theirs. In short, she made no Will at all, because she had had it so long before to no better Purpose, and that if she had had her Desert, she should have had an Executioner instead of an Executor.

Out of the 100 Pounds which she had by her, she dispos'd of 30 Pounds to her three Maids which she kept, and charg'd them to occupy it the best Way they could; for that, and some of her Arts in which they had had Time to be expert, would be beyond the Advantage of their Spinning and Reeling, and would be able to keep them in Repair, and promote them to *Weavers*, *Shoe-makers*, and *Taylors* The rest of her personal Estate, in Money, Moveable, and Houshold-Goods, she bequeath'd to her Kinsman *Frith*, a Master of a Ship, dwelling at *Redriff*, whom she advis'd not to make any Ventures therewith, but stay at Home and be drunk, rather than go to Sea, and be drown'd with 'em

And now, the Time of her Dissolution drawing near, she desir'd to be bury'd with her Breech upwards, that she might be as preposterous in her Death as she had been all along in her infamous Life When she was dead, she was interr'd in St *Bridget's* Church-yard, having a fair Marble-stone put over her Grave, on which was cut the following Epitaph, compos'd by the ingenious Mr *Milton*, but destroy'd in the great Conflagration of *London*.

Here lies, under this same Marble,
Dust, for Time's last Sieve to garble:
Dust, to perplex a Sadducee,
Whether it rise a He or She,
Or two in one, a single Pair,
Nature's Sport, and now her Care.
For how she'll cloath it at last Day,
Unless she fighs it all away,
Or where she'll place it, none can tell:
Some middle Place 'twixt Heav'n and Hell——
And well 'tis Purgatory's found,
Else she must hide her under Ground
These Reliques to deserve the Doom,
Of that Cheat Mahomet's fine Tomb,
For no Communion she had,
Nor sorted with the Good or Bad;
That when the World shall be calcin'd,
And the mix'd Mass of human Kind
Shall sep'rate by that melting Fire,
She'll stand alone, and none come nigh her.
Reader, here she lies till then,
When, truly, you'll see her again

The LIFE of JONATHAN SIMPSON.

WHEN a Man who has had an Opportunity of living not only in Reputation but even in Splendour, all his Days, brings himself to the Gallows, we are apt to look on his Case as more deplorable than that of another Person, though in Reality he is much less to be pitied, because their must be violent Inclinations to Dishonesty where it seems to be preferr'd of Choice, and where a Person will be a Rogue in Spite of all that Providence can do to prevent it

We can't indeed judge the Hearts of Men so far as to say this was positively the Case with *Jonathan Simpson*, because he certainly receiv'd high Provocations from his Wife while he was in Trade; but then we can find no other Reason for his turning Highwayman than the Bent of his Mind notwithstanding, forasmuch as he had still enough either to have lived moderately on all his Days, or to have gone into Trade again in another Place, after he had shut up his Shop on his Wife's Account

But not to run into a Train of Reflections before we have given the Story on which they are built, we are to tell the Reader, that *Jonathan Simpson* was the Son of a very wealthy Inhabitant of *Launceston* in *Cornwall*, and that his Father put him Apprentice to a Linnen-Draper in *Bristol* when he was about fourteen Years of Age. When he had served out his Time, which he did with Reputation, the same indulgent Father gave him Fifteen Hundred Pounds to set up with in the City where he was free, and where he soon fell into great Business, and got Money apace

In less than a Year after he had kept Shop, he marry'd a Merchant's Daughter of the same Place, who brought him a Fortune of Two Thousand Pounds This was a great Addition to his Wealth, but the Union proved unhappy, because the young Lady was before engaged in Affection to a Gentleman of less Fortune in the Neighbourhood, whom her Father hinder'd her from having, and with whom she continued a Familiarity that soon displeased her Husband.

Jealousy doubtless is the most tormenting Plague that can haunt either Man or Woman, and it frequently drives both to Extravagancies that before they could not have thought of Possibly in Fact this Passion might be more than any thing the Occasion of *Simpson*'s Ruin, but to Appearance it wrought on him in a merry Manner, for it was the Occasion of the following pleasant Adventure.

He formed a Pretence of going into *Cornwall* to see his Friends, and so took his Leave of his Wife for ten or twelve Days, who as soon as he was gone, gave her Gallant Notice, being unwilling to lye so long alone He was to come in the Evening, and a Couple of Fowls and a Bottle of Wine were got ready for his Reception *Simpson* staid abroad till he imagined the Woodcock was got into his Springe,

and then he comes to the Door before the Maid, who was privy to her Mistress's Affairs, was gone to Bed He ran immediately up into the Chamber, and Madam could not conceal her Lover in a great Chest, that stood in the Room, so suddenly but that her Cuckold heard the Lid of it move. However he took no Notice, but told her he was glad she had got something for Supper, and made an Excuse for his returning so soon.

Mrs *Simpson*'s Spark was also marry'd since he had left his Mistress, and he had made some Pretence of going abroad for some Days, to spend that Time in the Company of one he liked better than his Wife, designing when he was once enter'd to have continued in *Simpson*'s House till near the Time of his Return. *Jonathan* found an Errand also to some Relations at the further End of *Bristol*, that must be done that Night, on which he dispatch'd his dear Rib, and sent immediately for the Spouse of her Gallant to come and sup with him in his Chamber on the two Fowls

While they were at Supper he told his Guest that he had lost his Wife that Evening, and that she had been seen with her Husband This immediately inflamed her with Jealousy, because she knew of their former Intimacy, so that there was no Difficulty to perswade her to revenge the Affront, which *Simpson* took Care to have done on the very Chest wherein poor *Pill Garlick* was almost stifled. As soon as the Job was over, he lifted up the Lid of the Chest, and cry'd, *Come out Brother Cuckold*, which he did in Confusion enough. The poor Woman was ready to swoon for what she had done when she saw her Husband; but *Simpson* made him swear not only to forgive her, but never to mention the Thing, under Penalty of losing his Ears; and so he turn'd them both home together very well reconciled.

But though this was all he did to his Neighbour, his Revenge on his Wife went yet further, for when she came back from the Place he had sent to, he refused her Admittance; and the next Day sold off his Stock, shut up Shop, and went off with all the Money he could raise, resolved never more to live in *Bristol*

Such a Crisis as this must be a great Tryal for any Man, but there can be no Excuse sufficient to defend a Person that invades the Property of another Almost any Man in such a Case would have run into Extravagancies, but none but a Man that was viciously inclined would have turned Highwayman, as *Simpson* now did He had above Five Thousand Pounds of his own, but his Expences were of a Piece with the rest of his Actions, for at the End of eighteen Months he had not a Penny left of all this large Sum, and of all the Money he had during that Time taken on the Road

While his Money lasted he play'd with the Law,
for

for though he was once or twice diſcover'd, he made up the Matter, and prevented a Proſecution The Law is chiefly for poor Rogues, who can neither daub a Plantiff, hire an Evidence, or corrupt a —— or a —— G——g was hang'd in Queen *Anne*'s Time becauſe he was not Principal in the Fact he ſuffer'd for, and conſequently had leſs Money than they that eſcaped When a Miniſtry of State is corrupted, there are commonly a great many of your little Officers, who are forced to make a wry Face, before their Maſters can be touch'd Nay, 'tis hardly once in an Age that a *Mazarine*, a *Mortimer*, or a *Blue-String* goes to Pot, and when ſuch a One does come to Juſtice, 'tis commonly after he has ſpent all his Money in his own Defence, unleſs a *Felton* undertakes to be the Executioner, and ſo the Job is finiſhed without the Help of the Law If *Charteris* had been piſtol'd for a private Affront, he might have met with his Deſert, but it was not for a Man to be hang'd with ſo much Money

No ſooner had *Simpſon* waſted all his Subſtance but he was apprehended and condemn'd at the *Old Baily* for a Robbery on the Highway, and he muſt certainly have ſwung for it, if ſome of his rich Relations had not procured him a Reprieve from Above. It came when he was at *Tyburn*, with the Halter about his Neck, and juſt ready to be turn'd off in Company with ſeveral others As he was riding back to *Newgate* behind one of the Sheriff's Officers, the Officer aſk'd him, if he thought any thing of a Reprieve, when he came to the Gallows *No more,* ſaid *Simpſon, than I thought of my Dying-Day* A very pretty Expreſſion at that Time

When he was brought to the Priſon-Door, the Turnkey refuſed to receive him, telling the Officer, that as he was ſent to be executed, they were diſcharged of him, and would not have any thing to do with him again, unleſs there was a freſh Warrant for his Commitment; whereupon *Simpſon* made this Reflection *What an unhappy caſt-off Dog am I! that both Tyburn and Newgate ſhould in one Day refuſe to entertain me* Well, I'll mend my Manners for the future, and try whether I can't merit a Reception at them both the next time I am brought hither He was as good as his Word; for 'twas believed he committed above forty Robberies in the County of *Middleſex* within ſix Weeks after his Diſcharge

He was a very good Skater, and made a Practice of robbing People on the Ice between *Fulham* and *Kingſton-Bridge*, in the great Froſt, 1689, which held thirteen Weeks He uſed to kick up their Heels, and then ſearch their Pockets

One Time a Gentleman whom he ſtopp'd gave

him a fine Silk Purſe full of Counters, which he took for Gold, and ſo did not examine them till he came to his Inn at Night When he found himſelf outwitted, he made no Words of it, but kept the Braſs Booty in his Pocket, looking out frequently for his Benefactor, whom he knew to be often on the Road At the End of about four Months, he met his Worſhip again on *Bagſhot-Heath*, when riding up to the Coach, *Sir*, ſays he, *I believe you made a Miſtake the laſt Time I had the Happineſs to ſee you, in giving me theſe Pieces; I have been troubled ever ſince for fear you ſhould have wanted them at Cards, and am glad of this Opportunity to return them Only for my Care I require you to come this Moment out of your Coach and give me your Breeches, that I may ſearch them at Leiſure, and not truſt any more to your Generoſity, leſt you ſhould miſtake again* The Gentleman was obliged to comply by a Piſtol, and *Simpſon* found at Night that the Freight of his Breeches, was a Gold Watch, a Gold Snuff-Box, and a Purſe, containing ninety eight Guineas and five *Jacobus*'s

Another Time he robb'd the Lord *Delamere* on *Dunmoor-Heath* of three hundred and fifty Guineas, perſwading his Lordſhip firſt to ſend away all his Attendants on a ſham Pretence of two Highwaymen that were juſt before, and had robb'd him of forty Pounds This Action made his Lordſhip ſwear never to do a good-natured Deed again to a Stranger

The Robberies he committed on Drovers, Pedlars Market-People, &c were almoſt innumerable He ſtopp'd in one Day nineteen of thoſe People between *London* and *Barnet*, and took from them above two hundred Pounds He even ventured to attack the Duke of *Berwick*, natural Son to King *James* the Second, and take from him his Watch, Rings, and Money, amounting in all to a great Value

This great Malefactor was at laſt apprehended near *Acton*, by Means of two Captains of the Foot-Guards, whom he attempted to rob both together. There was an obſtinate Fight between them, and *Simpſon* behaved himſelf with ſo much Bravery, that, in all Probability, he had not been taken, if one of the Officers had not ſhot his Horſe under him, though he was before that wounded in both his Arms and one of his Legs Nay even when he was diſmounted he defended himſelf till other Paſſengers came up and ſecured him, which his Adverſaries were ſcarce able to do, they being alſo both very much hurt When he was ſent to *Newgate* he now found the Keeper ſo much his Friend as to receive him, neither did *Tyburn* this Time refuſe to bear his Burden He was hang'd on *Wedneſday* the eighth of *September*, 1686, aged thirty two Years,

The LIFE of MOLL JONES.

MARY JONES was born in *Chancery-Lane*, where her Parents lived in a great deal of Credit. She was brought up to the making Hoods and Scarves at the *New-Exchange* in the *Strand*. She married an Apprentice, whom she loved extremely, and whose Extravagancies were thought to be the first Occasion of her taking to a dishonest Course of Life, for as he was not in a Capacity to get any Money himself, she was willing to do any Thing in order to furnish him with whatever he wanted, being fond of having him always appear like a Gentleman. The first Species of thieving she took to, was picking of Pockets.

One Day meeting, near *Rosamond's-Pond*, in St *James's* Park, with one Mr. *Price*, a Milliner, keeping Shop in the same Exchange in which she was bred, *Moll* pretended to ask him some Questions about Mrs *Zouch*, a Servant of his, who had murder'd her Bastard Child, whereupon he pull'd out a Tin Trumpet, which he usually carry'd in his Pocket to hold to his Ear, being so very deaf that he could not hear otherwise. Whilst he was earnestly hearkening to what *Moll* said to him thro' this Vehicle, she pick'd a Purse out of his Breeches, in which were fifteen Guineas and a Broad Piece. Mr *Price* never miss'd it, till he came home, and then where to find her he could not tell.

Shortly after this, she was apprehended for picking the Pocket of one Mr *Jacob Delafay*, a *Jew*, who was Chocolate-maker to King *James* II and King *William* III and lived over-against *York-Buildings* in the *Strand*. For this Fact she was committed to *Newgate*, and burnt in the Hand, which Punishment making her out of conceit with the Trade of Diving or *Filing*, she turn'd Shop-lifter, in which she was very successful for three or four Years, at the End of which, privately stealing half a dozen Pair of Silk Stockings from Mr *Wansel*, a Hosier in *Exeter-Change*, she was detected in her very committing the Theft, by one *Smith* a Victualler, at the *Rose and Crown* Ale house over-against the little *Savoy-Gate* in the *Strand*, who was buying a Pair of Stockings there at the same Time. This *Smith* being a Constable, seized her, and carrying her before Justice *Bridal*, he committed her to *Newgate*, after which she was burnt in the Hand again.

Once more *Moll* obtaining her Liberty, she was resolv'd to be reveng'd on *Smith* the Constable, at whose House she had spent a pretty deal of Money, for discovering her in thieving, therefore knowing this Victualler to be very vain-glorious, as well as covetous, usually boasting of his Friends in the Country, and his Wealth at home, she found thereby that he had some Relations about *Ludlow*, in the Confines of *Shropshire* and *Herefordshire*, which gave her Opportunity to put this Trick upon him.

In a Summer Evening, something late, a Rogue of her Acquaintance, booted and spurr'd, with a Horse in his Hand, and cover'd with Dust, came a-

long the *Strand*, and very solicitously and hastily enquired out for Mr *Smith*, and by his Neighbours was informed which was his House. The Fellow follow'd their Direction, yet like an ignorant Countryman that dared not to go one Step without new Directions in the Wood of this great Town, he kept the same gaping Enquiry in his Country Tone, where Mr *Smith* dwelt. The People thought the Fellow Mad, but it prepared Mr *Smith*, with very great Solemnity, to receive this importunate Visitant. Being come to his Door, he with some earnestness and elevation of Voice, demands which is his House? *Smith* gravely answer'd beyond the Question, *I am the Master, for want of a better. What would you please to have with me?*

Our Impostor, upon this, tells him, That if he be the Gentleman, he hath some News out of the Country, which most nearly concerns him, having come on purpose to be the first Messenger of such glad Tidings. Pray, Sir, come in, quoth *Smith*, you are very heartily welcome, pray how do all our Friends in the Country? Very well, *quoth the Rogue*, except your Uncle that is dead, who we hope is best of all. A little before his Death, he made his Will, and, Sir, hath made you his Heir, and left you all his personal Estate besides, save a few Legacies. To-Day he is to be bury'd by some of his Kindred, but before I came away, knowing my deceased Master your Uncle's Mind, I took an Inventory of all the Goods, and lock'd up all his Bonds and other Writings, and the Money and Plate, in one of the great Chests, and have brought the Key along with me, which I here present you with.

To have seen the perplexed Looks of this Ale-Draper, which he labour'd to frame to a Countenance of Grief, (but could not for his more prevalent Joys which visibly appear'd) would have made a Man split his Sides with laughing. At length, after a deep Sigh, and a few Ejaculations on the Certainty of Death, he unriddled his Face, and very heartily welcom'd the Fellow, brought him into his Kitchen, and cramm'd his Guts with good Victuals and Drink, commanding his Wife to make him what Cheer she could, since there was no recalling the Dead, though he was a dear Uncle, and the very best of Friends.

During this Preparation, the Fellow stands at some Distance, plucks off his Hat, and so keeps it, and much ado there was to persuade him to be cover'd, then he desired his new Master's Favour, that he might continue the Bailiff and Steward of his Lands, to which *Smith* readily assented, forepraising his Honesty and Faithfulness. After Supper, they resum'd the Discourse, with which *Smith* was much delighted. Then they began to consider of their Journey, the Expedition whereof this Fellow very much urged in Regard of those poor Kindred of his Uncle's, who, no doubt, would make

Havock of those Goods which where left about the House, and perchance might venture upon the Locks, and seize the rest, whereupon all Haste was used to begin the Journey, but *Smith* would not disgrace himself among his Kindred, and therefore would stay till he had provided himself and his Wife with new Mourning Cloaths, and Things suitable to his new Fortunes, with a black Suit and Cloak for the Man, who was to attend them into the Country, and bring them to this Inheritance.

When these were ready, they set forward, the Victualler having discharged his Man's Horse-Hire, and other Expences, besides Diet and Lodging, during his Stay in *London* Upon the Road he was very officiously waited upon by this new Servant the first four Days Journey, lodging the last Night, as this Impostor said, within ten Miles of the Place whither they were to go. But early in the Morning up gets the Spark, saddles his Horse with the Portmanteau and his Mourning in it, and away he gallops by another Road, leaving his Master to find out the *Utopia* of his great Windfall; who arising, and missing his Guide and Servant, that was lost beyond all Enquiry, began to suspect the Cheat; yet Covetousness prevailing against Reason, he resolv'd to pursue the Adventure, and having the Town in Mind, which he was inform'd was no farther than ten Miles off, he rode thither, where he could hear of no such Man, nor no such Matter

Vex'd, and yet asham'd to enquire any farther, or to make a Discovery of his own Folly, poor *Nick*

and *Froth* and his Doxy turn'd their Horses Heads, and sorowfully departed, cursing the Hour the/ ever saw this cheating Rogue, and to add to their Misfortunes, their Money was drawn very low, so that they were forced to make long Journies and short Meals in their Way homewards, and at last, to keep themselves, were fain to part with their Horses at St. *Alban*'s, whom their had Travel and harder Feeding had brought down to a Third of the Price they cost them in *London* After this on Foot, weary'd and wasted with Vexation, they at 1 arriv'd at *London*, and in the Evening crept into their House to avoid the Laughter of their Neighbours, among whom, before their setting out, they had nois'd their sudden Wealth, the Defeat whereof at length coming to their Knowledge, never was poor Man so flouted and jeer'd as he was for many Years after

But *Moll* did not very long outlive this Piece of Revenge, for still following the Art and Mystery of Shoplifting, she was apprehended for privately stealing a Piece of Sattin out of a Mercer's Shop on *Ludgate Hill*, whither she went in a very splendid Equipage, and personated the late Dutchess of *Norfolk*, to avoid Suspicion of her Dishonesty, but her greaceless Grace being sent to *Newgate*, and condemn'd for her Life at the *Old Bailey*, she was hang'd at *Tyburn* in the Twenty fifth Year of her Age, on *Friday* the Eighteenth Day of *December*, in the Year 1691.

The LIFE *of* TOM TAYLOR.

AT the same Time with *Moll Jones* was executed *Tom Taylor*, a Parson's Son, born at *Colechester* in *Essex*, who accustoming himself to Gaming from twelve Years of Age, was so addicted to Idleness, that he would not be brought up to any honest Employment Fathermore, rejecting the good Counsel of his Parents, and joining himself to bad Company, he soon got into a Gang of Pickpockets, with whom he often went out to learn their evil Profession, and find the ready Way to the Gallows Going once, with three or four of these Diving Sparks, to *Guildford*, a Market Town in *Surrey*, where there was next Day a Fair to be kept, fearing to be discover'd in that Concourse of so many People, they resolv'd to do their Business that very Evening, when the People were very busy in fitting up their Stalls, and some little Trading was stirring besides Their first Consultation was how to draw the Folks together to make one Jobb of it, which was agreed on in this Manner *Tom Taylor* pretended to be an ignorant Clown, got his Head into the Pillory, which was elevated near the Market House, as if he had only a Mind to be laugh-ed at. The Noise thereof causing the whole Town to run together to see this Spectacle, his Companions so ply'd their Work, while the People gaz'd, laugh'd, and star'd, that they left but few of them any Money in their Pockets Nay, the very Keeper of the Pillory, who was as well pleas'd at this

curious Sight as any Body, was serv'd in the same Manner with the rest

Tom seeing the Work was done, and having the Sign given him that his Comrades were departing, came down from his Wooden Machine, whereupon the Company dispers'd themselves A little while after, some of them clapping their Hands into their Pockets, they cry'd out with one Voice, that their Pockets were pick'd, while in the Confusion *Tom* slunk away to his Companions, who were out of the Reach of Apprehension

At last, *Taylor* being pretty expert at picking of Pockets, he set up for himself, and one Day going to the Playhouse in *Drury-Lane*, very well dress'd, he seated himself by a Gentleman in the Pit, whose Pocket he pick'd of about forty Guineas, and went clean off This good Success tempted *Tom* to go thither the next Day, in a different Suit of Cloaths, when perceiving the same Gentleman in the Pit, whose Pocket he had pick'd but the Day before, he takes his Seat by him again The Gentleman was so sharp, as to know his Face again, for all his Change of Apparel, though he seem'd to take no Notice of him, whereupon putting a great Quantity of Guineas into the Pocket next *Tom*, it was not long before he fell to diving for them The Gentleman had sew'd Fishing Hooks all round the Mouth of that Pocket, and our Gudgeon venturing too deep, by unconscionably plunging down to the very Bottom,

tom, his Hand was caught, and held so fast, that he could no manner of Way disentangle it.

Tom angled up and down in the Pocket for near a quarter of an Hour, the Gentleman all the While feeling his struggling to get his Hand out, took no Notice, till at last *Tom* very courteously pulling off his Hat, quoth he, *Sir, by a Mistake, I have somewhat put my Hand into your Pocket, instead of my own* The Gentleman, without making any Noise, arose and went to the *Rose Tavern*, at the Corner of *Bridges street*, and *Tom* along with him, with his Hand in his Pocket, where it remain'd till he had sent for some of his Cronies, who paid down Eighty Guineas to get the Gudgeon out of this dry Pond

However, the Gentleman being not altogether contented with this double Satisfaction for his Loss, he most unmercifully caned him, and then turning him over to the Mob, they as unmercifully pump'd him, and duck'd him in a Horse-Pond, and after that so cruelly us'd him, that they broke one of his Legs and an Arm

Tom meeting with such bad Usage in his first setting up for himself, he was so much out of Conceit with the Trade of picking Pockets, that he left it quite off, and follow'd House breaking, in which Kind of Villany he was so notorious, that he had committed above sixty Felonies and Burglaries only in the County of *Middlesex*, in less than fourteen Months. He reign'd eight Years in his Crimes, but at length setting a Barn on Fire betwixt *Brentford* and *Austirly*, a little Village lying about a Mile North from that Town, while the Servants came from the Dwelling House to quench it, he ran up into a Chamber, pretending to help to preserve the Goods, but ran away with a Trunk, in which was a great deal of Plate, and an Hundred and forty Pounds in Money He was apprehended before he got to *Hammersmith*, where being carry'd before a Magistrate,

he was committed to *Newgate*, and receiving Sentence of Death at the *Old Baily*; when about Twenty nine Years of Age. He was hang'd at *Tyburn* on *Friday* the eighteenth Day of *December*, in the Year 1691, as before mention'd Where he said he had been addicted to Swearing, Drunkenness, Whoredom, all all other Sins whatever, excepting Murder.

On the same Day, besides these Two, suffer'd, 1. One *William Horsey*, for the horrid Murder of two Men, one of which was his particular Friend; 2 *William Smith*, a Vintner, for Felony; 3. *Mary Motte*, for the barbarous Murder of her Male Bastard Child, by putting it up in a Basket, and exposing it in a Gutter, till'd it was starv'd; 4 *John Barret*, a Furrier's Son, who was put Apprentice to a Clothier, but serving only four Years of his Time, and getting into bad Company, he committed a Burglary, which brought him to this shameful Death 5 *William Good*, for robbing a Gentleman in *Hackney Fields* of a Silver-hilted Sword, a Gold Watch, and twenty eight Guineas, 6. *Richard Johnson*, for committing several most notorious Robberies in and about the Cities of *London* and *Westminster*, and other Places in the County of *Middlesex*, 7 *Anne Miller*, for Felony and Burglary, 8 and 9. *Edward Booth*, and *Humphrey Malice*, the last of whom was a Gardener at *Westminster*, for robbing a Gentleman in *Chelsea-Fields* of a Silver Snuff Box, a Gold Watch, a Periwig, a Beaver Hat, a Pair of Stone Buckles set in Silver, and Twenty four Shillings in Money. 10 A Glazier living in *Exeter-street*, for committing several notorious Robberies on the Highway, to the great Astonishment of all his Neighbours, among whom he seem'd to carry a very civil and honest Correspondence, and devoutly exclaim'd against all Manner of Vice, but as the old Proverb is, *The still Sow drinks all the Draught*

The LIFE of JACK WITHRINGTON.

THIS Fellow was the youngest of five Brothers, who were all born at *Blandford* in *Dorsetshire* The other four were all hang'd in the Country, for which Reason they must remain in Obscurity, but *Jack* had the good Fortune to be reserv'd for *Tyburn*, and by that Means to have his Name transmitted to Posterity He was bound to a Tanner in *Shaftsbury*, a Town in his native Country, with whom he served about three Years For being of an aspiring Mind, and thinking himself above any mechanical Drudgery, he scorn'd to be confined any longer, and like many Others, whom we have mentioned, chose rather to expose himself to the wide World, than receive a Maintenance for seven Years as the Reward of his Fidelity.

After his Elopement, he enter'd into the Earl of *Oxford's* Regiment of Horse, in which when *Monmouth's* Rebellion was suppress'd in the West of *England*, he came up to *London*, where he soon met

with Opportunities of discovering his Valour to the World These Occasions were two Quarrels in which he was engaged. The first with a Man famous for Fighting, against whom he behav'd with so much Bravery and Skill, that it won him a vast Reputation The second with a Person of great Estate, but a noted Coward, when he shew'd himself a Gentleman by his Adherence to the Point of Honour and good Breeding It must be confess'd, that to a Thinking Man, a Character founded upon such Excellencies as these must appear ridiculous; but as 'tis quite otherwise with Respect to the fashionable Part of Mankind, we need not wonder that *Withrington* by these Duels won abundance of Applause, so as thereby to contract a Familiarity with all the greatest Fighting Men of the Time, especially those in his own Regiment, and, what is the Consequence of the other, with all the noted Ladies of Pleasure, who, though in other Cases they are altogether mercenary,

cenary, think themselves obliged to be kind to Men of Bravery, there still subsisting a Sort of *Quixotism* among those People

Withrington however carry'd his Manhood so far, as to get himself turn'd out of the Regiment within a Year after, for challenging his Captain. He then became a perfect Bully and Gamester; and, being fortunate, in a little Time by these Means saw himself Master of a considerable Sum of Money Notwithstanding all this good Luck at first, he found himself afterwards subject to the Fate of Gamesters, *viz.* to be frequently without Money in Spite of his large Winnings.

This brought him at last to consider the Uncertainty of Fortune, and endeavour to make himself Master of her, by supplying with Fraud, what he might want in plain open Skill But this neither did not continue long, for every one began to be aware of him, as of a common Sharper, and none that knew him would venture to play with him

In the common Scale of Knavery, the next Step above a Sharper is a downright Thief *Witherington* made bold to ascend this Degree, and was resolv'd to take the most honourable Station thereon, that of a Highwayman. He had Money enough to buy him a good Horse, and Accoutrements, so that the Resolution and the real Attempt were not long asunder His first Adventure was with a Farmer, from whom he took Forty Pounds, giving him in Return only the following Harangue, occasion'd by the Countryman's reproaching him with the Robbery

And prithee Friend, says he, *who is there now adays that does not rob? The Taylor steals by cutting out the Cloth double for his Customer's Breeches, the Surgeon by prolonging a Cure, the Apothecary by his quid pro quo, without any Regard to the Constitution of his Patient; the Merchant by his Change-Alley Outcries, which enable him to raise and fall the Stocks at his Pleasure The Notary Publick gets a whole Lordship at once, once by an &c The —— robs us by imposing on our Credulity, the Lawyer by every thing he does In a Word, the Grocer uses false Weights; the Vintner adulterates his Wine, the Butcher blows up his Meat; the Victuallor draws in short Measures, the Cook roasts his Meat twice; and, to sum up all, the Bakers, and you Farmers, giving him a Stroke across the Shoulders with his Whip, you cheat us by mutually complaining against one another, and raising the Price of Bread in a Time of Plenty Now I profess Travelling, and why should not I have the Liberty to do in my Way of Trade as all others do in theirs, by stopping now and then a Man on the Road, and taking what he has*

We may suppose the Farmer was not much edify'd by this Discourse, because he gave the Orator no Thanks, and seem'd willing to get away as soon as he could

The next that fell in *Withrington*'s Way, whom we have an Account of, was Mr *Edward Clark*, Gentleman Usher to the Dutchess of *Mazarine* They met in *Devonshire*, in the Road between *Chudleigh* and *Ashburton* Mr *Clark* made some Resistance, so that in the Scuffle *Withrington*'s Masque fell off, and discover'd his Face, which Mr *Clark* knowing, he called him by his Name, and said he hoped he would not rob an old Acquaintance *Indeed I shall, Sir,* quoth *Withrington, for you get your Money much easier than I do, who am forced to venture my Life for a Maintenance; you have so much a Year for eating, drinking, and entertaining your Lady with Scandal and Nonsense What I shall take from you will do you little Harm, 'tis only putting a higher Price upon half a score Reputations, which you know*

how to do as well as any *Coxcomb* in England La dies never let such faithful Servants go unrewarded, nor will yours suffer your Loss to fall on yourself He got about eight Guineas out of this Gentleman's Pocket, and for old Acquaintance Sake bid him Good b'w' ye very heartily

Withrington's Robberies in less than a Year and a half were talk'd of almost all over the Kingdom But alas! he met with a Diversion, common to Mankind, that draws even the most stupid into the Rank of polite Persons The poor Man was in Love, and with whom but a rich Widow Innkeeper in *Bristol?* Farewel to the Highway, *Withrington* has another Scent to pursue No more Robberies to be thought of from a Man who was himself robb'd of his Heart' He employ'd an old Bawd in the Affair, who was intimately acquainted with our Hostess, and by this Flesh Broker's Mediation Things had like to have come to an Issue, and *Jack* to have been Master of the *Swan-Inn* In short, there was nothing prevented it but the accidental coming of a certain Gentleman, who knew our Highwayman, and inform'd his Mistress what he was The Effects of this Discovery were *Jack*'s being kick'd out of Doors by the Hostler and Chamberlain, and the Commitment of Madam the Negotiatress to *Bridewell*, in order to mill *Dolly*

Withrington carry'd it off as well as he could, though all his Acquaintance perceiv'd he was actually in Love He absolutely deny'd it *Why then did you not rob your Landlady according to Custom?* said they *Because,* said he, *I chose rather to rob her of Herself and of all she had at once, than to do Thing by Halves Curse on my Stars, that I have not succeeded* He would then pretend that when *Cupid* shot him,

—— He took his Stand
Upon the Widow's Jointure Land,

and that 'twas not the Woman but her Wealth that he was in Love with However for some Time there was as much Alteration in his Behaviour, as *Dryden* has described in that of *Cymon*, when he became enamour'd of *Iphigenia*, before which that excellent Poet gives us this Picture of him

A clownish Mien, a Voice with rustic Sound,
And stupid Eyes that ever lov'd the Ground
His Corn and Cattle were his only Care,
And his supreme Delight a Country Fair
His Quarter-Staff, which he could ne'er forsake,
Hung half before, and half behind his Back
He trudg'd along, unknowing what he sought,
And whistled as he went for want of Thought

But when he had beheld the fair One that captivated his Soul, then

Love, studious how to please, improv'd his Part,
With polish'd Manners, and adorn'd with Arts,
Awak'd the sleepy Vigor of his Soul,
And brushing o'er, gave Motion to the Pool,
To liberal Arts inclin'd the narrow soul'd,
Soften'd the fierce, and made the Coward bold

It was just the same Thing with *Withrington*, in Regard to his Morals, for he had even a Mind to turn honest, and never offend against the Laws of Hospitality and mutual Forbearance again while he liv'd But pinching Want, and a Prospect of nothing but Misery, ruin'd these good Beginnings, and turn'd the whole Stream of his Mind back into the former Chann

Channel, from whence it never afterwards was diverted

After his Return to the Highway, he, and one of his Companions, met with Mr *Thompson*, a noted Taylor, in a Part of *Hertfordshire* that was convenient for robbing. They took from him about 30 Pounds in Silver, and then dismounting him, they order'd him to stay where he was till they brought him more Company. As soon as they were gone from him, he remounted his Horse, and attempted to ride off as fast as he could But our Highwaymen perceiving what he was at, having the best Horses, they fetch'd him back, and mistrusting he had more Money, by his being in so much Haste, they search'd him afresh, he protesting all the while, that he had not so much as a Farthing left if it were to save his Soul In a literal Sense he might be right; but they made a shift to find Forty Guineas, which they thought better than Farthings *Withrington* upon this exclaim'd, *That 'twas a sad Thing that one Christian could not believe another!* They then shot his Horse, to put a Stop to his Speed, and so rode away and left him

In Conjunction with the same Accomplice, he stop'd a Gentleman and his Wife both on one Horse, betwixt St *Alban*'s and *Dunstable* They very submissively crav'd their Benevolence, which not being readily granted, they shot the Horse, and swore, *That if they could have no Money, they would have the Woman* This they perform'd by taking Madam aside into an adjacent Coppice, and each of them acting his Pleasure with her, while the other stood Centinel over the Husband When they had done, they rifled the Gentleman of eleven Guineas, telling him, *That was no more than their just Wages, for performing his Drudgery, and they would be paid for what they had done*

The last Robbery *Withrington* committed was alone He stopp'd a Nobleman on *Hounslow-Heath* attended by two Footmen There was a short Dispute, but *Withrington* having the best of it, he took a Portmanteau, in which was Two Hundred and Eighty Guineas, Sixty Pounds in Silver, and a Parcel of fine Linnen A Hue and Cry was soon issued out after him, and he was apprehended by Means of it at *Malmsbury* in *Wiltshire*, from whence he was remov'd to *London*, where he was condemn'd for this Fact

The Sentence of Death seem'd to have no Effect on his Temper, for he was as gay and humourous under that Circumstance as ever he had been before When he was riding up *Holborn Hill*, he order'd the Cart to stop, and calling up the Sheriff's Deputy, Sir, said he, *I owe a small Matter at the Three Cups, a little further, for which I am afraid of being arrested as I go by the Door, therefore I shall be much obliged to you, if you will be pleased to carry me down Shoe-Lane, and bring me up Drury-Lane again into the Road by which I am to travel this devilish long Journey.* The Deputy inform'd him, that if such a Mischance should happen, he should come to no Damage; for, says he, *I'll be Bail for you myself, rather than you shall go back to Prison again.* Thank you heartily, Sir, quoth *Jack*, *I protest, I could not have thought that I had a Friend in the World, who would have stood by me so in such a Time of Need* After this he rode very contentedly to the Place of Execution, where he was tuck'd up with as little Ceremony as usual. This fatal Day was *Wednesday* the first of *April*, in the Year 1691.

The Night before his Execution, he writ the following short Letter to a Friend in *Dorsetshire*

Dear Tom,

*A*S I very much question whether or no you may see any News-Papers in the Place where you live, I think it highly necessary to send you Word by Letter, that I am to be hang'd to-morrow; otherwise you may lose your old Correspondent, and never know the Reason of it I don't believe you'll be much surpriz'd at these Tidings, because you have often told me 'twas what I must come to, as to my own Part, I have a thousand times confessed, that I expected it.

But I send you this as a Secret, and as to my Friend and Confident, for though 'tis my Fate to be taken out of the World in good Health, there's no Need for all the Country to know it No, no, Tom, prithee take Care of my Reputation when I am gone, and don't let me be abus'd by Slanderers, for as big a Rogue as I have been, I believe there are some bigger, who have nevertheless left good Names behind them; and what need a Man wish for more?

I am apt to think they'll be so ill natur'd in the other World, as never to let me send to thee from thence, because we have never had a Line from any one of my Brothers But if a Body can't do a Thing, one can't I don't know what to say more, unless it be, that I should be very glad if I was along with you in Dorsetshire

Yours, &c

J Withrington

The LIFE of TOM COX.

THOMAS COX was born at *Blandford* in *Dorsetshire* He was the youngest Son of a Gentleman, so that having but a small Patrimony, he soon consumed it in riotous Living Upon the Decay of his Fortune he came up to *London*, where he fell in with a Gang of Highwaymen, and easily comply'd with their Measures, in order to support himself in his dissolute Course of Life. He was three Times try'd for his Life, before the last fatal Tryal, and had, after all these Imputations, a Prospect once more of making himself a Gentleman, so indulgent was Providence to him A young Lady fell in Love with him at *Worcester*, he being a very handsome Man, and she went so far as to communicate her Passion, and almost make him a direct Offer of herself and Fifteen Hundred Pounds *Cox* marry'd her, but, instead of settling himself in the World, and improving her Fortune, he spent it all in less than two Years, broke the poor Gentlewoman's Heart with his ill Usage, and then took to his old Courses again.

The Robberies he committed after this were almost innumerable We shall briefly mention a few, without dwelling on Particulars that are not material One Day he met with *Killigrew*, who had been Jester to King *Charles* the Second, and order'd him to deliver *Are you in Earnest, Friend?* said the Buffoon. *Tom* reply'd, *Yes, by G—d am I! for though you live by jesting, I can't* Killigrew found he spoke Truth ; for so well as he lov'd jesting, he could not conceive that to be a Jest which cost him Twenty five Guineas, for so much *Tom* took from him

Another Time he robb'd Mr *Hitchcock*, an Attorney of *New-Inn*, of Three Hundred and fifty Guineas, on the Road between *Midhurst* and *Tetworth* in the County of *Suffex*, giving him in Return a Lesson on the Corruption of his Practice, and throwing him a single Guinea to bear his Charges Mr *Hitchcock* was a little surprized at the Highwayman's Generosity, but more at his Morality, imagining the World must needs be near its End, when the Devil undertook to reform it

Mrs *Rox*, an infamous Bawd, living in *Fountain-Court*, in the *Strand*, was another that fell into his Hands She had been at *Litchfield* to receive Fifty Pounds, which was left her as a Legacy by a Sister *Cox* made bold to ease her of her Burden, and give her a great many hard Words into the Bargain He told her of the Vileness of her Profession, and that 'twas pure Envy made a Bawd For, *says he,* when you have lost all your own Teeth, and are grown as ugly as Imagination can figure, you decoy young Women, and make them subservient to your Pleasure, that you may hurry them by Diseases into your own Condition The old Haradan, being used to Scurrility, return'd his Compliments with others of the same Kind, which provoked *Cox* so far, that he made her come out of the Coach, where she was

alone, and pull off her Mourning-Clothes, telling her, That when she came home, she would have much more Reason to buy Mourning than at the Death of her Sister ; because by her Departure out of the World she had got something, but by this Adventure she had lost it all again

Tom Cox was as great a Libertine in his Sentiments as he was in his Practice, for he professed a Belief that the *Summum Bonum* of Man consisted in sensual Pleasures, as *Epicurus* is said to have thought formerly, whose Disciple he called himself 'Tis a common Thing to call Persons *Epicureans* that fall into these Notions, and I don't know whether in a Work of this Nature it may be worth while to prove that the Word is falsely apply'd ; since the Idea is all that we are to regard. However, 'tis Pity *Epicurus*, who was certainly a very good, as well as a very wise Man, should suffer in the Opinions of those who may not have Opportunity to inform themselves, Let *Epicurean* signify what it will, they are no Followers of *Epicurus* who are not Lovers of Virtue, and who do not place their supreme Happiness in the most exalted Pleasures of the Mind, as that great Philosopher certainly did

Our Offender was at last apprehended for a Robbery on the Highway, committed near *Chard* in *Somersetshire* But he had not been long confin'd in *Ilchester* Jail, before he found an Opportunity of escaping He broke out of his Ward into the Keeper's Apartment, who, as good Luck would have it, had been drunk over Night, and was now in a profound Sleep 'Twas a Moonlight Night, and *Cox* could see a Silver-Tankard on the Table in the Room which he secured, and then let himself out with Authority into the Street, by the Help of the Keys, leaving the Doors all unlock'd as he pass'd. The Tankard he had stole was worth Ten Pounds, and besides that he got into a Stable just by, and took a good Horse, with proper Furniture, to carry him off This he look'd upon as one of his fortunate Nights, to get his Liberty, and a good Booty into the Bargain

'Tis reported of *Tom Cox*, that he more than once robb'd Persons of his own Trade Indeed there is an old Proverb, that *two of a Trade can't agree*, but it must certainly be a very dangerous Thing for Highwaymen to make so bold one with another; because every one of them is so much exposed to the Revenge of the rest, and as *Cox* sometimes robb'd in Company, it discovers that he was not an unsociable Thief

One Time in particular he had Accomplices, when he formed a Project of robbing a Nobleman, well attended, who was travelling the Kingdom *Tom* associated himself with this Nobleman on the Road, and talk'd to him as they passed along of the Adventures he had met with, in such an agreeable Manner as gave a great deal of Pleasure They had not rid many Miles together, before two of *Tom's* Companions

...mpanions came up and bid them stand; but im-
...diately fled upon *Tom's* pulling out a Pistol, and
...king a little Bluster. The Nobleman attributed
...s Delivery to the Generosity and Bravery of this
...w Companion, putting still more Confidence in
...m, and desiring his Company as long as possible
...hey were to stay a whole Day at the next great
...own, in order to take a Ride round the Country,
...d see what was to be seen, according to the Custom
...nich this noble Friend of *Tom's* had practised all
...e Way. In the Morning the Saddle Horses were
...t ready, and our two Fellow-Travellers set out
...r the Tour of the Day, the Person of Quality re-
...g to take a Footman with him as usual, that he
...ing the more freely converse with his new Ac-
...aintance

We shall not trouble the Reader with what they
...w on the Way, and how much they were pleased,
...cause that is little to our Story. About Noon
...ey came to a convenient Place, when *Cox* suddenly
...rew off the Masque, and commanded his Com-
...nion to deliver his Money *Why ay, such a thing
ight be done here, for 'tis a devilish lonesome Coun-
y, but I can fear no Danger while you are with
e, you, whose Courage I have so lately experienced,*
...ys the Nobleman, not imagining but *Cox* had been
...l this Time mimicking the Adventure of the pre-
...ding Day, *Such a thing might be done? Why, in
le Name of Satan, I hope you don't think I have
pt you Company all this Time to play with you at
st, if you do, Sir, let me tell you, you are damna-
ly mistaken* With that he pull'd out a Pistol, and
...esented to his Breast, swearing and cursing like a
...adman, till he had given sufficient Proof that he
...as in Earnest. Fill'd with Astonishment and Con-
...sion, our Nobleman deliver'd a Diamond Ring, a
...old Watch, and near an Hundred Guineas in Mo-
...ey, staring all the while in *Tom's* Face with as much
...eadfastness as a Picture. To prevent a sudden Pur-
...it, *Tom* them dismounted his Companion, bound

him Hand and Foot, and kill'd his Horse, according
to the Custom of experienc'd Highwayman, taking
his Leave with a Sneer and *Good b' w' ye, Fellow-
Traveller, till I meet you again*

After this *Tom Cox* committed two other Robberies that were known One of them was on a Grasier, who had been at *Smithfield* and receiv'd about
Three Hundred Pounds for Cattle, a great Part of
which was in Silver, and consequently made it pretty
bulky. When he had got the Money he fell to caning the poor Sufferer in an unmerciful Manner, who
desired to know the Reason of such Usage after he
had taken all *Sirrah*, says *Tom*, *'tis for loading
my Horse at this Rate; that you may remember another Time to get your Money changed into Gold before you come out of Town, for who the Plague
must be your Porter?* We may reasonably suppose
the Grasier chose rather to pay for the Return of his
Money for the future, than carry so much about
him

Tom's last Robbery was on a Farmer, from whom
he took about Twenty Pounds. It was not above a
Week after the Fact before the said Farmer came to
London about Business, and saw *Tom* come out of his
Lodgings in *Essex* Street in the *Strand*, where upon
crying out *stop Thief*, he was immediately apprehended in St. *Clement's* Church-Yard, and committed by a neighbouring Magistrate to *Newgate*,
where he lived till the Sessions in an extravagant
Manner, being very full of Money Receiving Sentence of Death on the Farmer's Deposition at *Justice-
Hall*, on *Wednesday* the third Day of *June*, 1691,
he was hang'd at *Tyburn*, in the Twenty sixth Year
of his Age He was so resolute to the last, that when
Mr *Smith* the Ordinary ask'd him a few Moments
before he was turn'd off, whether he would join
with his Fellow Sufferers in Prayer? *D——n you,
No*, says he, and kick'd both Ordinary and Executioner out of the Cart

The LIFE of SIMON FLETCHER.

THIS Offender was a Son of a Baker in
Rosemary Lane, to which Trade he serv'd
about four Years with his Father; but hap-
ning several times to fall into bad Company, and
ing of a vicious Inclination, he was prevailed on,
thout much Difficulty, to run away from his Ser-
...de, and enter with a Gang of Thieves The
...ief Sort of Thieving at that Time was cutting off
...ople's Purses or Pockets, which was in Use long
...fore the modern and more dextrous Practice of
...king out the Money, and leaving the Case be-
...d The Latter, however, must be allow'd to be
...ly an Improvement of the former, and there-
...e the Performances of any of our Pick-Pockets
...not be said to derogate from the Merit of those
...ntlemen of the last Age, for the Inventors of
...Sciences have generally been look'd upon to

deserve a greater Share of Praise than they that
have brought those Sciences to Perfection, because
'tis much easier to refine upon the Thought of
another Person, than to start any new Thought of our
own.

Simon Fletcher was look'd upon to be the greatest
Artist of his Age by all his Contemporaries of the
same Trade, which is the Reason of our Introdu-
cing him into this Place There are some particular
Stories of his Performances in this Kind, which might
be here inserted, if they did not seem to be rather
Inventions than Realities, for which Reason we think
it proper to omit them He was not less knowing
in all the other Parts of Roguery that were then in
Practice, and 'tis affirmed, that he was constituted
Captain of all the Thieves in and about *London*, by
general Consent. All that we know more of him is,
that

that he was at laft taken, committed to _Newgate_, and hang'd at _Tyburn_. His Exit was in 1692, when he was about fifty three Years of Age.

Having mention'd his _cutting of Purfes_, and being made _Captain_ of the Thieves, no Place can be properer than this to give fome Account of thofe Words, we mean, to inform the Reader how _cutting of Purfes_ was perform'd, and what was the Office and Authority of a _Captain of the Thieves_.

The Women of thofe Times wore their Pockets more expos'd than they do at prefent, and 'twas very common for the Men to carry their Money in a Purfe or Bag ty'd about their Middle, almoft in the fame manner as the Women now tye their Pockets, or as fome publick Officers carry their Purfes to this Day on folemn Occafions; the Ufe of Fobs and Breeches Pockets not being then introduc'd, the Reafon of their Invention being perhaps only to prevent the Rogueries that were then committed. Now the Art of thefe Fellows confifted in cutting off thofe Purfes fo as not to be perceiv'd; for which Purpofe they haunted Fairs, Markets, Churches, and other publick Places, that fo they might take Advantage of the Throng. He who perform'd the Operation, had alway another ftanding near him, to whom he immediately gave the Purfe, and whofe Bufinefs it was to make off as faft as he could, while the other ftaid to brazen it out, if he were fufpected, clear himfelf, and prove his Accufer a Lyar.

A Captain of Thieves is a Sort of abfolute Lord over all thofe that put themfelves in Subjection to him. He has the Privilege to examine all Novices that are juft enter'd, put them to Tryals of their Skill, afk them Queftions relating to their Calling, and, finally, to affign them fuch Provinces in the Commonwealth of Thieves as he thinks moft fuitable to their Genius, to which they are obliged to keep

upon Forfeiture of their Honour. He has always a Referve of the moft experienc'd and active Fellows, whom he fends upon any fudden and difficult Enterprizes, and who are always to be near his Perfon. No Man in the Fraternity muft forget his Point of Duty, or exceed the Bounds of his Commiffion, by meddling with another Man's Charge, or attempting Things which he has been told are above his Capacity. The ufual Time of Probation is about three Months, during which the young Initiate is conftantly at his Exercife before the Captain, as a Trooper's Horfe that is not broke is at the Riding School. He muft fcale a Wall, fnatch off a Perriwig, fteal a Watch, and do a hundred Things of this Kind.

When his Abilities have been fufficiently prov'd and the Captain has pronounc'd what he is fit for, he is conftantly to wait upon his Honour once a Week, and give an Account of his Actions. At the fame Time he is to pay a Dividend out of what he has gotten towards the Captain's Maintenance, who reprehends, or praifes him, according as his Negligence or Vigilance have deferv'd, and appoints his Station for the enfuing Week. An Oath drawn up in the moft facred Terms is exacted of every Member for the Security of the Society.

There are Punifhments affign'd for thofe who fail in any of the abovemention'd Particulars. The firft Time, 'tis faid, they are abridg'd of Part of what they have taken; the fecond Time of a whole Week's Benefit, and fo on to a Deprivation fometimes of five or fix Months. But the moft difgraceful Penance is to be made a Spy or Follower to the reft for a certain Time. Thefe Punifhments have their defir'd Effect, and the whole Fraternity is kept in Order, becaufe if any Member were troublefome, the Captain would deliver him up to the common Law, and fee him fairly hang'd.

The LIFE _of_ PATRICK FLEMMING.

_P_ATRICK FLEMMING was a Native of _Ireland_, and born at _Athlone_, which is remarkably fituated in the Counties of _Eaft_ and _Weft Meath_, as well as in the Provinces of _Leinfter_ and _Connaught_. His Parents rented a Potato-Garden of about 15 s. _per Annum_, upon the Produce of which, and the Increafe of their Geefe, Hens, Pigs, &c. they wholly depended for the Subfiftence of themfelves and nine Children. They, and their whole Family of Swine, Poultry, and Progeny, all took up their Lodging at Night not only under the fame Roof, but in the fame Room, according to the Practice of Abundance of their Country-People, who build only for Neceffity, without any Idea of what we call Beauty and Order. One may guefs from the Circumftances of the Father, that the Son had fmall Share of liberal Education, tho' he had the moft Claim to it of any one of the Children, as he was the eldeft. But what he wanted in Acquirements was made up with Impudence, a Quality which in moft

ignorant People happily fills up their Void of Knowledge.

When he was about thirteen Years of Age the Countefs of _Kildare_ took him into her Service, in the Capacity of Footboy, and finding him fo utterly deftitute of Learning, fhe was fo indulgent as to put him to School. But inftead of being grateful to her Ladyfhip in improving his Time to the beft Advantage, he was entirely negligent, and difcover'd no Inclination to his Book. Her Lady admonifh'd him frequently, but to no Purpofe, for he grew not only carelefs but infolent, till at laft, being found incorrigible, he was difcharged from the Family.

It was not long, however, before he was fo fortunate as to get to be a Domeftick of the Earl of _Antrim_'s, but here his Behaviour was worfe than before. He was a Scandal to the whole Family, for the little Wit he had was altogether turned on Mifchief. His Lord bore it a pretty while, notwithftanding the repeated Complaints of his Fellow Servants,

vants, and took no Notice so long as he could avoid it; but at last this Nobleman also was obliged to turn him out of Doors, and this was the Occasion. The Earl of *Antrim* was a *Roman Catholick*, and kept a Priest in the House, as his Chaplain and Confessor, to whom every one of the Servants was requir'd to pay great Respect. *Patrick* on Account of his Disorderliness was often reprov'd by this Gentleman, and he receiv'd it very well till one Day he happen'd to find the holy Father asleep in some private Part of the House, in a very indecent Posture, whereupon he went and got all the Family to that Place, and shew'd them what he had discover'd as a Revenge upon the Parson, who at that Instant awak'd. With Respect to the Servants this had the desir'd Effect, and expos'd the Priest to Ridicule. But the Earl, when he heard it, took the Part of his Chaplain, believ'd the Story a Slander, and immediately gave *Flemming* a Discharge, as desir'd. *Patrick* found Means, however, before he entirely left the Neighbourhood, to rob his Lordship of Money and Plate to the Value of about Two hundred Pounds, with which he fled to *Athenrea* in the Province of *Connaught*.

He hid himself here in a little Hut that he found for ten or twelve Days, till he imagin'd the Hue and Cry after him might be over, and then made the best of his Way to *Dublin*, where he soon enter'd into a Gang of House-breakers, and during the Space of six Years was concern'd in more Robberies than had ever before been committed in that City in the Memory of Man.

While he continued in *Dublin*, he was twice in Danger of being hang'd for his Offences which were so great as to make him the publick Subject of Converfation all over the City. He now perceiv'd he began to be too well known to stay there any longer in Safety, and so he retir'd into the Country, and turn'd Highwayman. The chief Place of his Haunt was about the Bog of *Alan*, where he attack'd almost all that pass'd that Way, of whatever Quality, telling them, "That he was absolute Lord of that "Road, and had a Right to demand Contribution of "all that travell'd it, and to punish those with Death "who refus'd to comply; therefore, if they had "any Regard for their Lives, he advised them to de-"liver what they had peaceably, and not put him to "the Trouble of exerting his Prerogative." By these Means he became more dreaded in the Countries where he robb'd than any Thief of his Time. For he not only threaten'd those with Death who disputed with him, but actually murder'd several, and us'd many others with Abundance of Barbarity.

'Tis reported, that in a few Days he robb'd one hundred and twenty five Men and Women upon the Mountain of *Barnsmoor*, near which is a Wood which they call *Colorockedie*, where he had assembled a numerous Gang, out of which not a few at several Times were taken and executed. Persons of Quality he usually address'd in their own Style, and told them he was as well bred as they, and therefore they must subscribe towards maintaining him according to his Rank and Dignity.

Among the principal Persons whom he stopp'd and robb'd were the Archbishop of *Armagh*, and the Bishop of *Rapho*, both in one Coach, the Arch-bishop of *Tuam*, and the Lady *Baltimore*, with her young Son, a Child of four Years old, whom he took from her, and oblig'd her to send him a Ransom within twenty four Hours, or else he told her, he would cut the young Puppy's Throat and make a Pye of him. From the Archbishop of *Tuam* he got a Thousand Pounds. After this he fled into *Munster*, and continued the same Trade there, till he was apprehended for robbing a Nobleman of Two hundred and fifty Pound, for which Fact he was carry'd to *Cork*, and committed to Prison.

But even now they were far from having him so safe as they imagin'd; for the County-Jayl was not strong enough to hold him. He was no sooner confin'd than his Eyes were about him, and his Head plotting an Escape. At last he found Means to get up a Chimney, and by removing some few Obstacles, to get out at the Top, and so avoid Hanging for that Offence.

He follow'd his Villanies for some Years after his breaking out of Prison, during which Time he murder'd five Men, two Women, and a Boy of fourteen Years old. Besides which he mangled and wounded a great many others, in particular Sir *Donagh O Brian*, whose Nose, Lips, and Ears he cut off, for making some small Resistance while he robb'd him. At last he was apprehended by the Landlord of a House where he used to drink, near *Mancoth*. The Landlord sent Advice to the Sheriff of the County when he would be there with several of his Associates, and the Sheriff, according to the Instruction, came one Evening with a strong Guard, and beset the House. *Patrick* and his Company would have defended themselves, but the Landlord had taken Care to wet all their Fire-Arms, and prevent their going off, by which Means they became useless, and our Desperado with fourteen more were taken, carry'd to *Dublin*, and there executed on *Wednesday* the twenty-fourth of *April*, in the Year 1650. After which *Patrick Fleming* was hang'd in Chains on the high Road a little without the City.

The LIFE of SAWNY DOWGLAS.

NEXT after the Life of _Patrick Fleming_ it may not be amiss to give some Account of the Adventures of _Sawny Dowglas_, a _Scotchman_; who was the Son of a Tanner, and born at _Port Patrick_ in the Shire of _Galloway_, where he liv'd till the unnatural Civil War broke out in 1641 _Sawny_ at this Time being very zealous on the Side of the Kirk, and consequently against the King, enter'd himself into the Service of the Parliament, was at the Siege of _Dundee_, and boasted after that bloody Action was over, that he kill'd with his own Hands no less than twenty nine Persons. Those who have read the Histories of that Time will remember that _Dundee_ was taken by Storm, and that the Garrison was put to the Sword, which gave _Sawny_ an Opportunity to discover his Cruelty

After the Restoration of King _Charles_, the Second, when the _Scots_ were reduc'd to Obedience, _Sawny_ found himself oblig'd to seek some other Subsistance than the Army. He had now been a Soldier about twenty Years, and though he had never been advanc'd higher than to carry a Halbert, yet he was something loth to lay down his Commission However there was no opposing Necessity, and he was obliged to submit as well as many of his Betters, who were glad they could come off thus, after having been so deeply concern'd in the Rebellion

Coming into _England_, and being destitute of both Money and Bread, he was not long resolving what Course to take in order to supply himself The Highway, he thought, was as free for him as for any Body else, and he was both strong and desperate: But the Question was where should he get a Horse and Accoutrements _What_ (said he again) _should hinder my taking the first that comes in my Way, and seems fit for my Purpose?_ Pursuant to this last Resolution, he kept on the main Road with a good Crab-Tree Stick in his Hand, till he saw a Gentleman's Servant alone, well mounted, with Pistols before him. He had some Question ready to ask, and after that another, till the poor Footman was engaged in a Discourse with him, and rode along gently by his Side At last _Sawny_ observes an Opportunity, and takes him an effectual Knock on the Pate, which follow'd with four or five more left him insensible on the Ground, while our young Adventurer rode off with the Horse till he thought himself out of the Way of any Enquiry

The first Robbery he committed was in _Maidenhead-Thicket_, in _Berkshire_, in those Times a very noted Haunt for Highwaymen. The Person he stopp'd was one Mr _Thurston_, at that Time Mayor of _Thornbury_ in _Gloucestershire_; he got about 18 _l._ and was so uncivil as to refuse the poor Gentleman

Ten Shillings to bear his Charges home, which was all he requir'd, and for which he begg'd very hard.

Another Time he robb'd the Dutchess of _Albemarle_ of Diamond-Rings to the Value of 200 _l_ besides a Pearl Necklace, rich Bracelets, and Ear Rings After this he came and took Lodgings at the House of one Mr _Knowles_, an Apothecary in _Tuthil Street, Westminster_; where he set up for a Gentleman, appear'd very fine, and made Love to his Landlord's Daughter, who was reputed to be a 2000 _l_ Fortune For some Time he was very well receiv'd both by the young Lady and her Father; but when his Money was gone, and they found him full of Shifts, Arts, and Evasions, they not only discarded him as a Husband and Son in-law, but turn'd him fairly out of Doors

Sawny now took to the Road again, and committed more Robberies than before, ranging all over the North of _England_, and being often so fortunate as to escape Justice when it pursu'd him He moreover contracted a Familiarity with _Du Vall_, the most generous spirited Highwayman that ever liv'd, which Friendship continu'd till Death parted them by his Deputy _Jack Ketch_ _Sawny_'s last Attempt was on the Earl of _Sandwich_, who was afterwards Admiral in the _Dutch_ War, and unfortunately lost his Life together with his Ship This noble Commander bearing Arms in the Coach, resolv'd not to be insulted by a Highwayman, and discharged a Pistol into _Sawny_'s Horse, which immediately dropping down under him, the Servants came up and secur'd our bonny _North-Britain_, who was thereupon committed to _Newgate_, and in less than a Month after order'd for _Tyburn_

While he was under Sentence he behav'd in a very profane and indecent Manner; cursing the Bell man for his bad _English_, when he repeated the usual _Memento_ the Night before his Execution. At St _Sepulchre_'s the next Day, when the appointed Ceremony was perform'd, instead of composing his Countenance, and looking as a Man in his Condition ought to do, he only told the Spectators, _That 'twas hard a Man could not be suffer'd to go to the Gallows in Peace; and that he had rather be hang'd twice over without Ceremony, than once after this superstitious Manner._ He read no Prayer-Book, but carry'd the Ballad of _Chevy-Chace_ in his Hand all the Way to _Tyburn_: when he came thither he took no Notice of the Ordinary, but bid the Hangman be speedy, and not make a great deal of Work about nothing, or most about a meer Trifle He d_'_d _Sept_ 10, 1664, aged fifty three, and was bury'd in _Tyburn-Road_

The

The LIFE of WILLIAM BEW.

WE have little more to say of this Fellow, than that he was Brother of Captain *Bew*, the notorious Highwayman, who was kill'd some Years ago at *Knightsbridge*, by one *Figg*, and some Thief-Takers, and that he was himself as great an Offender in that Way as his said Brother for most of his Time, only his Reign was shorter than that of some Others, he being apprehended at *Branford* before he had pursued the Course many Years, brought from thence to *Newgate*, and at the next Execution tuck'd up at *Tyburn* This fatal Day to him was *Wednesday* the 17th of *April*, in the Year 1689

It cannot be expected that we should give a particular Detail of all the Actions of every one whom we introduce into this Collection; nor is it at all material, since the Reader cannot but think as well as we, that the most remarkable Particulars have been transmitted to us, and consequently, that those Things which are passed over in Silence, would, if they had been recorded, have afforded him but very little Pleasure. Captain *Smith* indeed, in his Lives, has generally found something to relate of every one he mentions, but then most of his Stories are such barefac'd Inventions, that we are confident those who have ever seen his Books will pardon us for omitting them It will not be long before we shall come down to more Certainty, and then a more particular Account of every Malefactor's Crimes may be procured, and we may be depended upon for taking Care on our Parts, that every Thing shall be related with the utmost Exactness. That this Life of *Bew* may not, however, appear more barren than any other, we shall insert in it two short Stories, which he used, as we are inform'd, to tell himself in his Life Time

The first of them is, that being at *Bristol*, he took a Lodging in the House of one Mr. *Stone*, who kept the *Dolphin-Inn* in *Dolphin-lane* This Landlord of his had never any Child, and was reputed to be a very covetous Fellow *Bew* lay in the next Room to him, and heard his Wife tell him one Night, that she believ'd she was with Child The old Gentleman upon this began to be terribly uneasy, and reckon'd up all the Charges that a Bantling would bring upon him, not forgetting the extraordinary Expences of a Lying in He then consider'd whether a Boy or a Girl would cost him most, and concluded, upon the whole, that a Son was likely to be soonest got off his Hands, and put into a Capacity to maintain himself Hereupon he told his Spouse very abruptly, *That he must have her bring him a Boy* Madam reply'd, *that it was not in the Power of her, or of any Woman living, to be deliver'd of which Sex she pleased* To this the old Man answer'd with a severe Snub, *that it was in vain for her to talk, for a Boy he must have, if he had any Child at all, and that if Na-*

ture sent a Girl into the World, he would metamorphose it into the Sex he liked, for he would put only *Boy's Clothes upon it, and oblige her never to let any Body into the Secret, at least till she was able to shift for herself* This Dialogue, doubtless, was pleasant enough to *Bew*, who did not stay to see the Event of his Landlady's great Belly But making himself merry was not the only Advantage he found in this Apartment, for he overheard the miserable old Wretch tell his Wife, every Night, whither he was to go the next Day, and upon what Business By this Means he got Intelligence of his being to go one Day a pretty Way out of Town, to receive One Hundred and thirty Pounds, and he took Care to lighten him of his Burden before he came home again, and rode off with it into another Part of the Kingdom, *it being worth while*, as he often merrily used to say, *to change his Quarters for such a Lump as this*.

The other Story is of an Adventure of *Bew's* with a young Lady, whom he overtook on the Road, with her Footman behind her He made bold to keep them Company a pretty Way, talking all along of the Lady's extraordinary Beauty, and carrying his Compliments to her to an unreasonable Height Madam was not at all displeased with what he said, for she look'd upon herself to be every bit as handsome as he made her However, she seem'd to contradict all he told her, and profess'd with a mighty formal Air, *That she had none of the Perfections he mentioned, and was therefore highly obliged to him for his good Opinion of a Woman who deserv'd it so little.* They went on in this Manner; *Bew* still protesting, that she was the most agreeable Lady he ever saw, and she declaring, that he was the most complaisant Gentleman she ever met with. This was the Discourse till they came to a convenient Place, when *Bew* took an Opportunity to knock the Footman off his Horse, and then addressing himself to the Lady, *Madam*, says he, *I have been a great while disputing with you about the Beauty of your Person, but you insist so strongly on my being mistaken, that I cannot in good Manners contradict you any longer However, I am not satisfy'd yet, that you have nothing handsome about you, and therefore I must beg Leave to examine your Pocket, and see what Charms are contain'd there* Having deliver'd his Speech, he made no more Ceremony, but thrust his Hand into her Pocket, and pull'd out a Purse with fifty Guineas in it *These are the Charms I mean*, says he, and away he rode, leaving her to meditate a little upon the Nature of Flattery, which commonly picks the Pocket of the Person 'tis most busy about

These two Relations, and what we have said at the Beginning concerning the Time of his Execution, are all the Particulars we know of *William Bew*.

The

The LIFE of JOHN COTTINGTON, alias MUL-SACK.

THE Father of *John Cottington*, or *Mul-Sack*, as he was oftener called, was a Haberdasher of Small Wares in *Cheapside*, and one Time reputed to be pretty wealthy, but having a large expensive Family, and being himself very fond of what is commonly called Good Company, he so far wasted his Substance, as to die very poor, even so poor as to be bury'd by the Parish. This was an unhappy Thing for his Children, who were no less than nineteen in Number, fifteen of which were Daughters, and *John* was the youngest of them all of either Sex, which exposed him perhaps to more Misfortunes than those who had some Reason to govern themselves by, at the Time when they became Orphans.

At about eight Years of Age he was put out Apprentice, to a Trade no less honourable than Chimney sweeping. He was bound for a great many Years, as he was so young at the Time of going to his Master, but he took Care not to make his Servitude longer than ordinary, for instead of adding six or seven Years, he cut off two from the usual Term, and ran away in the fifth Year of his Apprenticeship, apprehending that as he was got into his Teens he was as good a Man as his Master, and being confident that he had learn'd enough of his Trade for him to live upon.

He had not been long gone from his Master, before he perceived Business coming on him even as fast as he could wish, and he made all the Advantage possible of his good Fortune; not in the usual sneaking Manner, by hoarding up all he got, but by behaving himself like a Gentleman, swearing at every one that offended him, and assuming to himself almost as much State as the old Chimney-sweeper below, who we may be certain is haughty, because to say any One *is as proud as Lucifer* is become a Proverb. Nor was it only in *Cottington's* Carriage that you might observe the Effects of his good Fortune, for he lived in the best Manner possible, no Liquor but Sack, forsooth, would go down with him, and that too must always be mull'd, to make it the more pleasant. It was from this that he got his Name of *Mul-Sack*, by which he was commonly called, and by which we shall chuse to distinguish him in the following Account of his Exploits.

One Evening *Mul Sack* was drinking at the *Devil* Tavern in *Fleet-street*, when he observed what he thought was a beautiful Woman, and being naturally pretty amorous, and at that Time in particular warm with his Favourite Liquor, he made his Addresses to her. Madam appeared to be none of the coyest, for she received him very freely, only nothing but Matrimony would go down with her, which did not throughly please him: Yet why, (thought he at last) *should I be against it? I can*

keep myself and a Wife very well, and I never *saw* a Woman whom I could like better than this, *there-*fore, hang it, I'll e'en take her, for better *for* worse. Upon this, he immediately gave her his Hand, and there were no more Words to the Bargain, but away they tramp'd to the *Fleet* together, where Divinity link'd their Hands, pronounc'd 'em Man and Wife, and pray'd heartily for their Welfare, in particular, that they might be successful in their honest and lawful Endeavours for the Procreation of Children, which, as the holy Office of the Church informs us, is the principal End of Matrimony.

But how was our jolly Bridegroom deceived at Night, when he found himself espoused to an *Hermaphrodite*, and that the Lady he had marry'd was no other than a Person well known by the Name of *Aniseed Robin?* The Redundancy of Nature was soon discovered, and the Bride confess'd *her* Fault, or if you please *his* Fault, with abundance of seeming Contrition, while poor *Mul-Sack* had nothing more to do in Bed than to go to sleep as usual.

This Disappointment in Matrimony had a great Effect upon our Gentleman's Manners; for whereas he was never before known to be guilty of any worse Crime than spending his Money, sitting up late, and keeping jovial Company, he now run into all sorts of Extravagancies; in particular, he got acquainted with five noted *Amazons* in *Drury Lane*, who were called the *Women shavers*, and whose Actions were then much talk'd of about Town, till being apprehended for a Riot, and one or two of them severely punished, the rest fled to *Barbadoes*. *Mul Sack* was once present when these Furies got a poor Woman among them, whom one of them suspected of having been great with her Husband. As a Punishment for this they stripp'd her as naked as she was born, beat her with Rods in a terrible manner, and then shav'd off all the Hair about her whole Body: After that they sous'd her in a Tub of Soap suds over Head and Ears, and in fine almost kill'd her, in spite of all her Tears, Cries, and Protestations of Innocency.

After the Law, the greatest Enemy that People of this Character have in the World, had deprived *Mul Sack* of these worthy Companions, he resolv'd to pursue his Amours elsewhere, and to that purpose appeared when out of his Business in a very smart, and genteel manner; being withal a graceful Person, and having a very extraordinary Flow of Words for a Man of his Calling. With these Accomplishments, he found Means to insinuate himself into the good liking of a Merchant's Wife in *Mark lane*, who had before this none of the best of Characters. This Lady had originally been very handsome, but by a long Course of Amours, her Beauty was a little the worse for wearing when *Mul-Sack* became acquainted

quainted

John Cottington alias Mull Sack Robbing y Oxford Waggon Wherein he found Four Thousand Pounds in Money

ainted with her. However, what she wanted in
rson she made up in Purse; for our Smut made a
ft to squeeze out of her about 120 *l* before she
ll sick and dy'd, which happened not a great while
terwards.

Captain *Smith* has told a long Story of this Lady's
cknes, Death-bed Repentance, and Confession to
r Husband in her last Moments, the Substance of
hich is, that she desired her good Man to call up
ll her Children, to the Number of twelve, one of
hich she told him she believed might be his, be-
use she did not remember that any other Man had
nter'd upon the Premisses Time enough to have
ad any Share in it but for the rest, my Dear, (said
se with a deep Sigh) *I am afraid you are just as
uch their Father, as the Kings of England have
en Kings of France for some hundreds of Years
all, that is, you know very well, in Name only*
Iere she nam'd whom she believ'd to be the Father
of every one, tho' she could not be very positive in
ither, because always more than one Man had
een dabbling about the proper Time She con-
uded all with telling him, that as they were all
aken in his Net, she hoped he would not expose
imself and her after her Death, but put up his
Horns without Words, and contentedly act the Part
of a Father We have not heard how far the Hus-
and comply'd with his dying Wife's Request, but
there is good Reason to think it caused a grumbling in his Gizzard

Mul-Sack had lately been so plentifully supply'd
with Money, that, when his kind Benefactrets departed this Life, and changed this vain World, as
we ought in Christian Charity to believe, for a better, he could not think of applying himself to Business anew, and relapsing again to his Sooty Occupation. We may observe, that there is a sort of Vanity inherent in us all, that makes us try any Shift,
rather than go backwards in the World This Temper is doubtless the Original of Knavery in a great
measure. Citizens that have been reputed rich will
hold up their Heads to the last, and think it much
more honourable to pay Six-Pence in the Pound
after a Statute of Bankruptcy, provided they can be
trusted again, than honestly lay down their Trades
while they can pay Twenty Shillings, and seek a
meaner Way of Livelihood So a Courtier that
has attain'd to be first Minister of State, generally
prefers bringing his Neck to the Block, before at-
ending at the Levee of his Successor, after having
quitted his Post with universal Applause 'Tis just
the same in inferior Life, a Man that has once commenc'd Villain, seldom, as we said before, cares to
go backwards, till he is drawn backwards up *Holborn Hill*, or some other Place for the same Purpose.

After this short Digression then, we are to tell
ou, that *Mul-Sack* now turn'd Pickpocket, a Cal-
ing that generally serves for an Introduction to the
Gentlemen who make the Heroes of this History. As
a Tryal of his Dexterity, the first Thing he did was to
ake a very valuable Gold Watch, set with Diamonds, from a Lady of chief Quality in those Times
of Usurpation One Mr *Jacomb*, a Man very much
ollowed by the Precisians, preached at that Time a
Weekly Lecture at *Ludgate* Church, and the Gen-
ewoman we are speaking of was one of his Admirers
nd constant Attendants. *Mul-Sack* had taken No
ce for some Time how the pretty Bauble hung
angling at her Side by a Gold Chain One of the
Companions he had engaged on this Occasion found
Means to take out the Pin of one of the Coach-
Wheels, so that the Wheel fell, and the Coach caus-
d an Obstruction just under the Gate The End of
his was to make a Crowd, and oblige Madam to

alight before she came to the Church Door; all
which was effected, and *Mul-Sack* stood ready, dress'd
in what was then the Height of the Mode, to offer
the Lady his Arm into the Church He presented
himself very impudently, the favour was kindly accepted, and by the Way he found Means to cut the
Gold Chain in two, and secure the Watch as they
passed through the Crowd. The Loss was not perceived till Mr *Jacomb* concluded, when the devout
Gentlewomen was going to see how long the Spiritual
Meal had lasted But alas! all the Consolation she
had received vanish'd after her Darling Watch

It is reported that there never was in *England* a
more dexterous Gang of Pickpockets than in the
Time of this *Mul-Sack*. We might here introduce
by the Way of Episode, (as the Criticks phrase it)
abundance of their surprising Performances, but because we would avoid Prolixity, only remark in general, that they would lay Wagers of taking any Gentleman's Watch, tho' warned of it but a Minute before, and perform it by jostling them, asking a Question, pretending some urgent Business, giving them a
Letter, and a Thousand other Methods of diverting
their Attention, and leaving the Prize unguarded
long enough for them to accomplish their Pleasure :
Nor was there any one of these Fellows, who understood his Business better than our Hero, *Mul-Sack*,
so that it would be almost incredible to relate all the
Tricks of that Kind he play'd about the City, and
the numerous Stratagems he had Recourse to

We are inform'd, that, before *Mul-Sack* left off
this Trade, he was once so impudent as to attempt
the Pocket of *Cromwel* himself, and the Danger he
then run of being detected, was the Occasion of his
leaving this secret sort of Knavery, and taking to
Highway, in Company with one *Tom Cheney*

These two Fellows had the Courage and Confidence to set upon Colonel *Hewson*, a great Man in
those Times, and one who had been advanced from
a Cobler to the Dignity he then enjoy'd, merely because his Conscience was according to the Measure
of that Time , that is very large, or if you please
very small, which Expressions the witty Author of
Hudibras tells us, signify the same Thing The
Colonel's Regiment was then marching to *Hounslow*,
and he not so far before it, but some of the Troopers saw the Action of our Bravoes. No Body can
doubt but they were soon pursu'd , yet by the help
of a good Horse, *Mul-Sack* got clear off , but *Cheney's* Beast failing him, he was obliged to stand in
his own Defence, which he did very stoutly, till he
was overpower'd by Numbers, desperately wounded,
taken Prisoner, and carry'd to *Newgate* Sessions
began at the *Old Bailey* within a few Days after,
and *Cheney* being brought to the Bar, begg'd to have
his Tryal put off on Account of his Wounds But
the Favour could not be obtain'd , for they caused a
Chair to be brought for him to sit in, obliged him
to plead, and passed Sentence of *Death* upon him.
What he had urged as a Motive for putting off his
Tryal, was made the Means to hasten his Execution,
for tho' 'twas Two o'Clock in the Afternoon when
he was condemn'd, he was carry'd in a Cart that very
Day to *Tyburn*, and there executed, lest he should
have evaded the Sentence of the Law, by dying in
Newgate.

The next Companion *Mul-Sack* enter'd into Articles with was one Mr *Horne*, a very bold Man, and
a Pewterer by Trade, tho' he had been formerly a
Captain in Colonel *Downe*'s Regiment of Foot
Their Engagement was to act in Concert, offensively
and defensively, like generous *Highwaymen* But
neither did this Partnership subsist long , for the first
considerable Action they ventur'd on was fatal to the

poor

poor Captain, he being taken in the Pursuit, while *Mul-Sack* had still the good Fortune to escape. The Captain's Fate was the same as *Cheney's*, saving that he continued in good Health till the Hour of his Execution, when he behaved with so much Bravery and Gallantry, that his Death drew Tears from a great Part of the Spectators, particularly from that Sex, who know the Value of a brave Man so well, as always to be griev'd when such a One dies, especially at *Tyburn*.

His Companions having such ill Success *Mul-Sack* was resolv'd to try his Fortune alone, and he several times practis'd his calling upon Committee Men, Sequestrators, Members of Parliament, &c who were then almost the only Men in the Nation worth robbing, they having plunder'd every Body else, and gotten the Wealth of *England* into their own Hands In all these Adventures he was as fortunate as he could wish, which prompted him forwards to attempt still greater Things. Being inform'd that Four Thousand Pound was coming from *London*, to pay the Regiments quarter'd at *Oxford* and *Gloucester*, he resolv'd to venture his Life for so considerable a Sum, tho' two or three Men well arm'd were appointed for a Convoy. Just at the Close of Day, when the Waggon was past *Wheatley*, at the Foot of a Hill he started from an Ambuscade, presented his Pistol, and bid the Carrier *Stand*. He had certainly now gone to Pot, if the Guard had not thought it impossible he should attempt such an Action without Company, but the Apprehension of more behind the Hedge made these sturdy Fellows ride for their Lives, and leave our Adventurer to secure the Booty, which he spent with as much Mirth as he had obtain'd it with Danger.

There were also two or three Passengers in this Waggon, who were frighted terribly, but *Mul Sack* generously told them he had no Design upon what they had. *This* (says he) *that I have taken, is as much mine as theirs who own it, being all extorted from the Publick by the rapacious Members of our Commonwealth, to enrich themselves, maintain their Janizaries, and keep honest People in Subjection, the most effectual Way to do which, is to keep them very poor.*

It is said, that *Mul Sack* got more Money than any Highwayman of his Time, though no Man was less suspected than he by his Acquaintance in Town. When out of his Calling he appeared like a Merch-

ant, talk'd always about Business, and was seen on 'Change very often, being the Methods he us'd to conceal his Trade, for nothing betrays a Man so soon as endeavouring to hide himself

One Time having Notice that the Receiver-General at *Reading* was to send up Six Thousand Pound to *London* by an Ammunition Waggon, he immediately contrived to save that Trouble, and bring it up to Town himself on his own Horse. An Accomplice was necessary in this Undertaking, and he soon found one, by whose Assistance he set the Receiver's House the Night before the Money was to be carted. The Window they got in at, was next to the Garden, where they left the Ladder standing, and came off at the present very well, having bound all the Family to prevent any Alarm whereby they might be discover'd

But an Affair of this Kind, as might very well be expected, made a great Noise, and *Mul Sack* was apprehended in Town, by some who had seen him in *Reading* the Evening the Fact was committed. Upon this he was sent down to *Reading*, and try'd at the next Assizes for *Berkshire*, before Judge *Jamyn*, who did all he could to hang him. Nevertheless, by his Cunning, he found Means either to baffle the Evidence, or to corrupt the Jury by his Money, so far, that he was acquitted, the Proof against him being only circumstantial

Not long after this narrow Escape, our Offender growing in Wickedness, added Murder to his former Crimes. The Person on whom it was committed was one *John Bridges*, with whose Wife he had before contracted a Familiarity. On this Account he fled beyond Sea, and got himself introduc'd at the Court of King *Charles* the Second, who was then in Exile.

He got so much Intelligence here, that he returned home again, upon a Presumption of obtaining his Pardon from *Oliver Cromwell*, as a Reward for what he could discover of Affairs amongst the King's Friends. Accordingly he apply'd himself to the Usurper, confess'd his Crime, and made very large Promises, upon the Performance of which *Cromwell* assur'd him of his Life. But, whether could not be as good as his Word, or whether the Protector thought such an abandon'd Wretch utterly unfit to live, so it was, that he was apprehended, condemn'd, and executed in *Smithfield Rounds*, in *April*, 1658, being 45 Years of Age.

The LIFE of TOM AUSTIN.

NEVER was a more barbarous Villain than this of whom we are now to give some Account, nor is it possible there ever should be, nor, another may commit more Barbarities in ... than he did, but they cannot be more horrible in their Kind, and God knows to what a Number they would have increased, if he had not been so soon detected as he was But to proceed to the Narrative.

Thomas Austin was born at *Columpton* in *Devonshire*, of very honest Parents, who at their Death left him a Farm of their own, worth about Eighty Pounds *per Annum*, which is a pretty Estate in that Country, and as his Land was without Incumbrances, and he had a good Character at that Time, he soon got a Wife with a suitable Fortune, she having no less than Eight Hundred Pounds to her Portion But this Increase of his Riches, and the Thought of having so much Ready Money by him, made him neglect the Improvement of his Living, and take to an idle extravagant Course, by Means of which in less than four Years Time he had consumed all that his Wife brought him, and mortgaged his own Estate

Being now reduced to pinching Circumstances, and not knowing which Way to turn himself for a Livelihood, the Devil so far got the upper Hand of him, as to excite him to the Commission of all manner of unlawful Actions for the Support of himself and his Family Several Frauds he was detected in, which his Neighbours were so good as to forgive, out of Respect to his Family, and to what he had once been. At last he was so desperate as to venture on the Highway, where assaulting Sir *Zachary Wilmot*, on the Road between *Wellington* and *Taunton Dean*, that unfortunate Gentleman was murder'd by him, for making some Attempts to save his Money

The Booty he got from Sir *Zachary* was forty six Guineas, and a Silver-hilted Sword, with which he got home undiscover'd and unsuspected This did not however last him long, for he follow'd his old riotous Course. When 'twas all spent he pretended a Visit to an Uncle of his, who liv'd at about the Distance of a Mile from his own Habitation, and it was one of the bloodiest Visits that ever was made

When he came to the House he found no Body at home but his Aunt and five small Children, who informed him that his Uncle was gone out on Business, and would not be at home till Evening, desiring him to stay a little and keep them Company. He seemingly consented to stay ; but had not sate many Minutes before he snatch'd up a Hatchet that was at Hand, and cleaved the Scull of his Aunt in two, after which he cut the Throats of all the Children, and laid the dead Bodies in a Heap all weltring in their Gore Then he went up Stairs and robb'd the House of Sixty Pounds

He made all the Haste he could home to his Wife, who perceiving some Drops of Blood on his Clothes, ask'd him how they came there ? *You Bitch*, says he, *I'll soon shew you the Manner of it !* pulling at the same Time the bloody Razor which he had before used out of his Pocket, and cutting her Throat from Ear to Ear When he had gone thus far, to complete the Tragedy, he ripp'd out the Bowels of his own two Children, the eldest of whom was not three Years of Age

Scarcely had he finish'd all his Butcheries, before his Uncle, whom he had been to visit, came accidentally to pay him the same Compliment in his Way home, when entering the House, and beholding the horrid Spectacle, he was even Thunder-struck with the Sight, though as yet he little thought the same Tragedy had been acted on all his Family too, as he soon after fatally found What he saw however was enough to point out the Offender, whom he immediately laid hold off, and carry'd him before a Magistrate, who sent him to *Exeter* Jail.

In the Month of *August*, 1694, this inhuman Wretch suffer'd the Punishment provided by the Law, which appears much too mild for such a black unnatural Monster ! But the Laws of *England* aggravate nothing, and are content with barely taking away the Lives of the very worst of Criminals

Austin's Behaviour both in Prison and at the Gallows was very sullen and dogged, yet he would now and then say something that discover'd he was very far from having a just Sense of his Crimes An Instance of this was while the Halter was about his Neck, when he was ask'd by the Minister who attended him, what he had to say before he dy'd, *Only*, says he, *there's a Woman yonder with some Curds and Whey, and I wish I could have a Pennyworth of them before I am hang'd, because I don't know when I shall see any again* This extravagant Request was not granted, and so he was turned off without offering to give a Reason for his committing the Murder for which he suffer'd, nor indeed can it be thought he had any other Reason than his own inhuman Temper

The

The LIVES of EDWARD and JOAN BRACEY.

THESE two Criminals flourish'd from the Year 1680 to 1684, during which Time they committed a great Number of Robberies and Frauds. Their natural Inclinations to such a Manner of Living first brought them together, and kept up the Union between them till they were separated by Justice, though we cannot learn that they were ever marry'd, *Joan* only assuming the Name of her Companion, as is common in such Cases, the better to colour their living together, and impose on the World

Edward Bracey had been a Highwayman before he fell into Company with his pretended Wife, who was the Daughter of a wealthy Farmer in *Northamptonshire*, named *John Philips* The Beginning of their Acquaintance was *Bracey*'s making Love to her, in Hopes to get a large Sum of Money out of the Old Man for a Marriage-Portion, and then to have left both Wife and Father-in-law But he was very agreeably deceiv'd, for *Joan* was as good as he · She suffer'd herself to be first debauched by him, and then consented to rob her Father, and go along with him on the Pad; all which she accordingly accomplish'd They now passed for Husband and Wife wheresoever they went, frequently robb'd together on the Highway, and as often united in picking of Pockets and Shop-lifting at all the Country Fairs and Markets round about.

'Twas next to impossible that they should continue this Course of Life long together, without coming into Trouble One or t'other of them was often in Danger of the Gallows, but they had both the good Fortune to escape till they had got a large Quantity of Money. The Dread of Justice more than a Desire to live honestly now prevail'd upon them to quit their Vocation, and take to some creditable Business, in which they might spend the Remainder of their Days in Quiet, and live comfortably upon what they had acquir'd by their Industry. In order to this, they took an Inn in the Suburbs of *Bristol*, where they met with Success, having a large Trade in particular for Wine, which was occasion'd by the Beauty of our Landlady. 'Tis no uncommon Thing for a Husband to get Money by his having a handsome Wife, especially if they have both Art enough to manage an Intrigue, which was the present Case All the gay young Fellows of the Place came to drink with Madam *Bracey*, purely for the Sake of having an Opportunity to discover their Love. She gave them all Encouragement so long as they could spend a great deal of Money, and then took Care not only to turn them out of Doors, but to expose them sufficiently.

It may not be amiss to give an Instance of this her Manner of using her Suitors. One Mr *Day*, an eminent Citizen of *Bristol*, was among the Number

of her humble Servants He made her a great many fine Proposals, and she receiv'd 'em all with abundance of Complaisance, consenting at last that she should make use of the first Opportunity that offer'd to take a Night's Lodging with her. In a little Time Mr *Day* was inform'd that his Landlord *Bracey* was to be abroad such a Night, and that nothing could happen more favourably to his Wishes He went at the Time appointed with all the Ardor of a Lover, and was receiv'd by a Maid-Servant, who told him her Mistress was gone to Bed, and waited impatiently for him, but desiring him however to pull off his Clothes, and leave them in another Room, where he might be conceal'd, and have Time to dress himself again, in Case any Surprize should happen The innocent Mr *Day* thanked her for the Contrivance, and hugg'd himself in the Thought of the Mistress's sincere Affection, because the Maid was so careful for his Safety

Mrs *Abigal* led him to the Room appointed, put out the Candle on Account of mere Modesty, and staid at the Door while Mr *Day* undress'd himself, which he did in two Minutes Now the best of the Comedy was to be play'd; our tractable Maid conducted the Gallant to a Door, which she told him open'd into her Mistress's Chamber, bid him enter softly, and immediately turn'd the Key upon him. Here Mr *Day* wander'd about to find the Bed, and pronounc'd the Name of Mrs *Bracey* as loud as he dar'd, that she might give him Directions, but no Mrs *Bracey* answer'd. He was sufficiently amaz'd at the Oddness of the Scene, but was yet more surpriz'd when he tumbled down a Pair of Stairs against the Back Door of the House. The Contrivance was now plain, he saw that Mistress and Maid were agreed not only to baulk his Passion, but to strip him of his Clothes also 'Twas in vain to call, and make Protestations, he receiv'd no other Answer, than that the Back-Door was only bolted, and he might open it if he pleas'd, and go about his Business

This Door open'd into a narrow dirty Lane, down which the Common Sewer ran, and there was no going out at it, unless you got into a Coach, or upon a Horse, directly off the Steps, which was the only Use made of it, and that not often, especially in the Winter-Time, as it was at present Mr *Day* knew all these Inconveniences, but the terrible pinching Cold, and the Shame of being discover'd, if he stay'd till broad Day-light, made him go out, wade through the Mud, and make the best of his Way home, where he was heartily laugh'd at by those Friends to whom he told the Story, which were only such as he could not conceal it from, and even upon their he laid the severest Injunctions imaginable never to divulge a Word of it They kept the Secret from every Body se, but diverted themselves privately with poor Mr. Day all his Life afterwards

Every one whom our honeft Inn-keepers impos'd on were not however fo eafy as Mr. Day; fo that in lefs than a Twelvemonth's Time their Houfe became fo fcandalous that they were obliged to leave it, and then they had nothing to do but to take to their old Courfes again, being by this Time pretty well got over the Apprehenfions they were under of a Halter. At their firft fetting out again, they play'd fuch a Trick as was hardly ever match'd, which was the Woman's Contrivance as well as the former We fhall relate this alfo in as few Words as we can conveniently

A young Gentleman, who had fpent his Fortune, had us'd their Houfe all the Time they had been at *Briftol*, and got a pretty deal in their Debt They knew he was Heir to an Eftate of about an Hundred Pounds a Year, which was kept from him only by the Life of an old diftemper'd Uncle, and they had a mighty Itching to get this Reverfion into their Hands In order to this *Joan* threaten'd him grievoufly with Prifon for what he ow'd them, till fhe perceiv'd he was heartily frighten'd, and would do any Thing to keep his Liberty . She knew befides that he was vicioufly inclin'd, and only wanted a little Introduction to be made any Thing of that they could wifh Upon this fhe told him what fhe and her Hufband were going upon, and prevail'd with him to join them In a Day or two after, fhe inform'd him that a rich Tradefman was coming to *Briftol* with a large Quantity of Money, and that he muft accompany her Hufband To-morrow to take it from him. Accordingly *Bracey* and the young Man fet out, ftopp'd a Perfon on the Road, and took from him above an Hundred Pounds, with which they return'd home together. The Man that was robb'd had been fent out with the Money in his Pocket for that very Purpofe

As foon as the Fact was over, and they had got their Dupe fafe, Madam told him plainly, that he muft make over the Reverfion of his Eftate to them, or her Hufband fhould immediately fwear the Robbery upon him, and get him hang'd for it The Terror he was under, and the Promife of Liberty upon complying, made him do all they defir'd. After which they ftill kept him in their Houfe till they had fold it again, obliging him to affure the Purchafer, that he had receiv'd a valuable Confideration of Mr *Bracey*, which was readily enough believ'd, becaufe every Body knew the young Gentleman's Extravagancy They got Fourteen Hundred Pounds by this Bargain, with which they immediately made off, leaving the unfortunate Spark to lament his Folly. The Name of this young Man was *Rumbald*

Joan after this ufually drefs'd herfelf in Men's Apparel, and fhe and her Fellow Adventurer committed a great many Robberies together on the Highway,

At laft, however, *Fortune* put an End to their Progrefs in Iniquity , for as they were robbing a Perfon of Quality's Coach together in *Nottinghamfhire*, Madam was apprehended, and carry'd to *Nottingham*-Jayl. At the next Affizes fhe was condemn'd by the Name of *Joan Bracey*, and in *April*, 1685, fhe was executed, aged twenty nine Years.

Her pretended Hufband got off at the Time when fhe was taken, and conceal'd himfelf for fome Time after by fkulking about the Country. One Day being at a publick Inn he was feen by fome Body whom he had robb'd, who immediately got Affiftance, and came to take him, being at the Stair foot with armed Men before *Bracey* knew any thing of the Matter. It happen'd that in the Room where he was one of the Drawers had left his Cap and Apron, which *Bracey* in a Moment fnatch'd up, and put on, running down Stairs ready to break his Neck, and crying out as he run, *Coming, Gentlemen, coming* , as if he was waiting upon Company above This Stratagem preferv'd his Life a little longer, for the Gentleman, who came to fecure him, not apprehending any thing, let him pafs as a Drawer, though he had taken fo much Notice of his Face before; fo that he got his Horfe out of the Stable and rode off, while they were fearching the Houfe after him Two or three of his Companions, who were with him in the Inn, and knew nothing of the Occafion of his running down fo, were apprehended and brought to Juftice.

This Efcape however did him but little Service , for about three or four Days after, ftopping at a little Houfe to drink, and leaving his white Mare, on which he ufually robb'd, at the Door, another Gentleman who had fuffer'd by him came by, alarmed the Neighbourhood upon his Knowledge of the Beaft, and befet the Houfe, before he had the leaft Notice. As foon as he heard a Noife of Men at the Door, he ran out, and attempted to mount , but two or three Pieces were inftantly difcharged at him, one of them killing his Mare, and another taking off feveral of his Fingers He then endeavoured to leap over fome Pales, and get off by the Backfide off the Houfe, when another Difcharge was made at him from a Fowling-Piece, which lodg'd feveral great Goofe-Shot in his Guts, and wounded him fo that he dropp'd down on the Place, and dy'd in three Days afterwards

We fhould have mention'd before, that *Bracey*'s pretended Wife was handfomely bury'd by her Friends, and that a reputed Witch told him about the Time of her Execution, that he fhould not furvive her many Days, which happen'd to be verify'd This, at leaft, is what was reported in the Country, and thofe who give any Credit to the Stories of Witches, may believe as much of it as they pleafe. Thofe who laugh at thefe Things can't blame us for relating what we have been informed of

The LIFE of ANN HARRIS.

ANN HARRIS, alias *Sarah Davis*, alias *Thorn*, alias *Gothorn*, was born of honeft but poor Parents, in the Parifh of St *Giles's* without Cripplegate, but being debauch'd by one *James Wadfworth*, fhe foon abandoned all manner of Goodnefs This *Wadfworth* was otherwife call'd *Jemmy the Mouth* among his Companions He was hang'd for Felony and Burglary at *Tyburn*, in the twenty fourth Year of his Age, on *Friday* the twenty fourth of *September*, 1702 She lived next with one *William Pulman*, otherwife call'd *Norwich Will* from the Place of his Birth, who alfo made his *Exit* at *Hyde-Park Corner* on *Friday* the ninth of *March* 1704-5, aged twenty fix Years, for robbing one Mr *Jofeph Edwards* on the Highway, of a Pair of Leather Bags, a Shirt, two Neckcloths, two Pocket-Books, twenty five Guineas, a Half Broad Piece of Gold, and four Pounds in Silver

Now *Nan* being twice left a hempen Widow in lefs than three Years, fhe had learn'd in that Time to be as vicious as the very worft of her Sex, and was fo abfolutely enflav'd to all manner of Wickednefs thro' Cuftom and Opportunity, that good Admonitions could work no good Effects upon her. Her Inclination was entirely averfe to Honefty, as appears by the following Example

She went one Day to a Mercer's Shop on *Ludgate-Hill*, in a Hackney Coach, very finely drefs'd, with a pretended Footman waiting on her, where looking on feveral rich Pieces of Silk and Velvet, fhe bargained for as much as came to two hundred and odd Pounds, which being more Money than fhe had about her, fhe defired the Mercer to go along with her to her Houfe, and fhe would pay him all in ready Specie They putting the Goods into the Hackney Coach which brought her thither, the Mercer and fhe ftept in, and rid with all Speed to Dr. *Adams*, who kept a mad Houfe at *Fulham*, where being enter'd, and telling the Doctor this was the Gentleman of whom fhe had fpoken to him in the Morning, he, and three or four lufty Fellows, fet upon the Mercer like fo many mercilefs Bailiffs on a poor Prifoner, one taking him by the Arms, another by the Middle, another by the Legs, which ruftical Ufage made the poor Man afk the Meaning thereof, and bawl out for two hundred and odd Pounds *Ay, ay*, quoth the Doctor, *the poor Gentleman's very bad indeed, he's raving mad, tie him quickly down in that Chair, and prefently fhave his Head*

All the while they were lathering and fhaving him, his Cry was ftill either for Goods or Money, which made the Doctor fay, *Pray, Madam, See how his Lunacy makes him talk at Random !* She, fhaking her Head, replied, *True, Sir, but is there any Hopes of his Recovery ?* To which the Doctor anfwer'd, *You muft know, Madam, that there are three kinds of Frenzies, according to the three internal Senfes of Imagination, Cogitation, and Memory, which may*

be feverally hurt For fome are frantick, which can judge rightly of thofe Things that they fee, as touching common Senfe and Imagination, and yet in Cogitation and Fantafy they err from natural Judgment, Then fome others being frantick, err in Imagination, and there are fome frantick, who do err both in Senfe and Cogitation, that is, both in Imagination and Reafon, and do therewith alfo lofe their Memory, which is the worft of all Frenzies, and this it is which afflicts this unhappy Gentleman but I doubt not of making him Compos Mentis again in lefs than a Month

While the Doctor was fetting forth the Difference of Madnefs, the Mercer was ftruggling and raving like a Madman indeed, and when he faw *Nan* give the Doctor five Guineas, with all giving him a ftrict Charge to take great Care of her Hufband and he fhould want for no Encouragement, he cry'd out, 'She's a lying B——h, fhe's none of my Wife, 'my Wife's at home in *Ludgate-ftreet*, ftop her, 'ftop her, ftop her, fhe has cheated me of my Silk 'and Velvet I am not mad, I am not mad, but 'a Parcel of Rogues here will make me run out of 'my Senfes *Quoth Dr Adams then to his Men*, 'Poor Gentleman ! he's very bad indeed, we muft 'bleed him too, and give him a ftrong Glyfter at 'Night, confine him to a Room where there's no 'Light at all, and bind him faft down Hand and 'Feet in his Straw, and for one Week give him 'nothing but Water-gruel, with little or no Bread 'in it, but the Week after, if his Diftemper de- 'creafes, we may venture to give him a little Puf 'an broth boil'd with fome hufk'd Barley *The* '*Mercer hearing thefe Directions, cried out*, I'll have 'none of my Blood taken from me, I have had e 'nough taken from me already without paying for, 'I want no Glyfter, I tell you I am in my right 'Senfes, I'll have none of your Gruel and Devil's 'Broth, what cheat me and ftarve me too ! No, no, 'I am not lunatick *Quoth the Doctor*, You fhall 'not be ftarv'd, Sir ; what Diet I prefcribe now, is 'to reftore you to your Health again To Health, '*faid the Mercer again*, I think you are going to 'take it from me, as the Whore has my Goods '

But all the Mercer's talking was to no purpofe, for *Nan* being gone off with her Booty, he was hurried to his dark Room, where, being bound down to his Bed, a Glyfter was applied to him much againft his Will However, he obtain'd his Liberty in lefs than four Days, for *Nan Harris* fending a Penny-Poft Letter to his Wife, which inform'd her where her Hufband was, fhe and fome Friends, went with all Speed to Dr *Adams's*, in whofe Houfe they found the poor Mercer almoft mad indeed, for the Lofs of his Goods and Freedom too, fo they brought him home, but the Doctor never faw nor heard of *Nan Harris* any more

I think thofe who would arrive to as much Perfection as they are capable of enjoying here, muft as
well

well know bad, that they may avoid to shun it, as the good; which they ought rather to embrace; therefore to procure the Reformation of others, by the wicked Examples of such whom the Sword of Justice has cut off for their heinous Enormities, I shall relate another memorable Prank play'd by *Nan Harris*

She going once to Dr *Case*, Student in Physick and Astrology, when he liv'd in *Black Friers*, she was no sooner introdu'd into his Presence, with also one *Charles Moore*, but she thus declar'd the Cause of waiting on him Sir, the Report of your great Experience in your Practice hath brought me hither, humbly imploring your Assistance, and that instantly, if you have any Respect to the Preservation of Life The Trouble I shall put you to shall be gratefully recompenced to the utmost of my Ability The Doctor then inquiring of her, who it was, and what manner of Distemper the Person labour'd under, She told him, 'Twas her Husband, who being very drunk last Night, came to a sad Mischance in coming down a Pair of Stairs, but looking upon the Doctor to be a wise Man, she would give him leave to tell what his Ail might be, and for that Purpose had brought his Water Dr *Case* smelling by her former Words, what might afflict her Husband, he put the Water into an Urinal, and after well shaking it for about a Minute, quoth he, Good Woman, your Husband hath terribly bruised himself by falling down a Pair of Stairs, Ay (replied Nan) 'tis really true, Sir, what you say, I see, Sir, your Knowledge is infallible, but now, Sir, comes the Difficulty, can you tell me how many Stairs he fell down?

Here the Doctor was put to a *Ne plus ultra*; however, to save his Credit as well as he could, he takes the Urinal into his Hand again, and shaking it somewhat longer than before, quoth he, Your Husband fell down all the Stairs Nay (replied Nan) there you are out, Sir, for he fell down but half the Stairs The Doctor being now somewhat abashed at his false guessing, and shaking the Urinal again, quoth he to Nan, Is here all your Husband's Water? Said Nan, dropping a fine Courtesy at the same Time, No, Sir, here's but half his Water The Doctor then, who was a mighty cholerick Man, being in a great Passion, cry'd, A Pox on you, your bringing but half his Water, made me imagine your Husband fell down all the Stairs, when if you had brought all his Water, I could easily have told you, that he had fell down but half the Stairs

Nan upon this excusing her Ignorance, she desired Advice for the speedy Cure of her Husband's Bruises, and whilst the Doctor was writing a Receipt for her, pulling a Cord out of her Pocket, with a Noose, she and her Spark came behind him, and nimbly clapping it over his Head, they acted the

Part of a *Turkish* Mute on a Bashaw; for having almost strangled him with several sudden Jerks, they went away with a silver Tankard and Cup, leaving our old Friend in a sad *Case* indeed, till he came to himself again, which was not in half an Hour, in which Time the Booty was divided betwixt Nan and *Charles Moore*

This *Moore* was an infamous Rogue, who, for breaking open the House of Sir *John Buckworth*, Bart was executed on *Friday, Sept* 27. 1707 at *Tyburn*, where he told the Ordinary of *Newgate*, that if he had known when he was try'd, that he should have dy'd, he would have hang'd one or two with him for a Fancy; for then he would have made some Discovery of Persons concern'd with him in thieving, but now he was resolv'd to make none

Thus far have we proceeded on *Nan's* wicked Crimes, to deter others from the like Practices, because nothing renders Man or Woman more contemned and hated, than when their Actions only tend to Irregularity We have only to add, that biding adieu to every thing that looked like Virtue, she drove a great Trade among Goldsmiths, to whose Shops often going to buy gold Rings, she only cheapen'd till she had the Opportunity of stealing one or two, which she did by means of a little Ale held in a Spoon over the Fire, till it congeal'd thick like a Syrup, for by rubbing some of this on the Palm of her Hands, any light thing would stick to it, without the least Suspicion at all. She was as well known among the Mercers, Lacemen, and Linnen-Drapers, on *Ludgate* hill, *Cheapside*, or *Fleetstreet*, as that notorious Shoplift *Isabel Thomas*, who was condemned for the same Crimes

But at last she was apprehended for her Pranks, and being so often burnt in the Face, that there was no more room left for the Hangman to stigmatize her, the Court thought fit to condemn her for privately stealing a Piece of printed Callico out of the Shop of one Mr *John Andrews* Then, to evade their Sentence, she pleaded her Belly, and that she might succeed, used the old Stratagem of drinking new Ale very plentifully, to make her swell, cramming a Pillow under her Petticoats to make her look big Having Matrons of her own Profession ready at hand, who, right or wrong, bring in their wicked Companions quick with Child, to the great Impediment of Justice, her Sentence was respited But tho' she had the good luck to impose thus on the Bench after she was condemn'd, yet at the End of nine Months (all which time she was not wanting to procure a Pregnancy, if all the Men in the Goal could have done it for her, but they work'd in vain) she was call'd down to her former Judgment, and hang'd in the twentieth Year of her Age, at *Tyburn*, on *Friday July* the thirteenth

The LIFE *of* TOM SHARP.

THOMAS SHARP was born of very honest Parents at *Rygate* in *Surrey*, where he served his Time to a Glover But he had not been long out of his Apprenticeship, ere, by the Influence of bad Company, he was so harden'd in Villainy, as not to be reclaim'd either by wholsom Advice, Threats, or the Examples of his Companions, who where executed before him Nothing could put an End to his Roguery, but the Halter that put an End to his Life

To prove that this Fellow was not only *Sharp* by Name, but also sharp by Nature, we need only relate the following Adventures Dressing himself one Day in an old Sute of black Clothes, and an old tatter'd canonical Gown, he went to an eminent Tavern in the City, where at that Time was kept a great Feast of the Clergymen, and humbly begg'd one of the Drawers to acquaint some of the Ministers above Stairs, that a poor Scholar was waiting below, who crav'd their Charity. Accordingly the Drawer acquainted one of the Divines, that there was a poor Scholar below in a Parson's Habit The Gentleman going down, and commiserateing his seeming Poverty, introduc'd him into the Company of all the Clergymen, who made him eat and drink very plentifully, and gather'd him betwixt four and five Pounds, which he thankfully put into his Pocket. One of the Divines then, after asking Pardon for making so free, desired to know of him at what University he was bred Tom Sharp told them, he was never bred at any. *Can you speak Greek?* the Divine ask'd again *No*, replied *Tom Nor Latin?* the Divine ask'd. *No, Sir*, said *Tom. Can you write then*, quoth the Divine? *No, nor read neither*, replied *Tom*. At which they fell a laughing, and said, *He was a poor Scholar indeed. Then I have not deceived you Gentlemen*, quoth *Tom*, and so he brush'd off with their charitable Benevolence, as thinking himself not fit Company for such learned Sophisters.

This poor Scholar afterwards using the *Vine* Alehouse at *Charing Cross*, which was then kept by a rich old Man, who knew not that he was a Thief, he brought several of his Gang there once a Week, to keep a sort of a Club up one Pair of Stairs, with a Design to rob the Victualler Accordingly they had several Times struck all the Doors above Stairs with a *Dub*, that is, a Picklock, but could never light on his Mammon, whereupon, one Night, *Tom Sharp* puts the Candle to the old rotton Hangings that were in the Club-Room, and setting them in a Blaze, he and his Company cried out *Fire*. The Alarm brings up the old Man in a Trice, who in a great Fright ran up to secure his Money : *Tom*, runs softly after him at a Distance, to espy where his Hoard was, and in the mean Time, his Associates, with two or three Pails of Water, having quench'd the Flame, which had done no great Damage, the old Man, at the News, return'd down with a great

deal of Joy, leaving his Money where it was before. With this Information, the Night following, *Tom*, and two of his Companions having a great Supper there, with each his Lass, they took the Opportunity of taking away 500 Pounds in Money, which, when the old *Cove* miss'd, he was ready to hang himself in his own Garters

His chiefest Dexterity lay in robbing Waggons, which in their canting Language, they call *Tumblers* They who follow this sort of thieving, do generally wait in a dark Morning, in the Roads betwixt *London* and *Bow, Black heath, Newington, Islington, Highgate, Kensington Gravel Pits*, or *Knightsbridge*, and going in at the Tail of a Waggon, they take out Packs of Linnen or Woolen Cloth, Boxes, Trunks, or other Goods One Time above the rest, *Tom Sharp* and his Accomplices following a Waggon along *Tyburn* Road to St *Giles's* Pound, they had no Conveniency at all of entering it, by reason a Man drove the Team before, and the Master and his Son, a Lad of about thirteen Years of Age, rid behind on one Horse Still they follow'd the Waggon 'till it came just under *Newgate*, when *Tom Sharp*, who was a lusty hail Fellow, snatching the Boy off the Horse, he ran down the *Old Bailey* with him under his Arms, at which the Father cry'd out to his Man to stop the Waggon for a Rogue had stolen away his Son , so whilst the Master rid after *Tom. Sharp*, and the Man run after his Master, one of *Tom*'s Comrades slipt two Pieces of Woollen Cloth out of the Waggon The old Man got his Son again, for *Tom* dropp'd him at the Sessions-House Gate

Under this sort of thieving is also comprehended the robbing of Coaches in the Night Time in *London*, by cutting of Trunks and Boxes which are tied sometimes behind them , and also the *Chiving* Bags or Portmanteaus from behind Horses, that is cutting them of , for *Chive*, among Thieves, signifies a Knife. One Night *Tom. Sharp*, and another like himself, following a Man on Horse-back quite from *Charing-Cross* beyond the *Royal-Exchange*, they had no Opportunity of getting his Portmanteau, because he held one Hand on it all the Way , but coming just under *Aldgate*, acute Mr *Sharp*, took the Man a grievous Rap over the Knuckles, crying out at the same Time, *What a Pox, will you ride over People?* So whilst the Fellow clapt his Fingers to his Mouth, to suck them for Ease, *Tom*'s Comrade cut off the Portmanteau, in which was good Linnen, and other Things of value, which pretty well made amends for the long Fatigue they had after him and his *Prancer*, as they call a Horse.

For Offences of this Nature, *Tom Sharp* was in *Newgate* no less than eighteen Times before the last fatal Time Take the following Description of that Prison, as this Fellow deliver'd it to some of his Friends, in his half comic, half-tragic Strain

'Tis a Dwelling in more than *Cimmerian* Darkness,

ſs, an Habitation of Miſery, a confus'd *Chaos*, without any Diſtinction, a bottomleſs Pit of Violence, and a Tower of *Babel*, where are all Speakers, and no Hearers There is mingling the noble with the ignoble, the rich with the poor, the wiſe with the ignorant, and the Debtors with the worſt of Malefactors It is the Grave of Gentility, the Baniſhment of Courteſy, the Poiſon of Honour, the Center of Infamy, the Paradiſe of Couſenage, the Hell of Tribulation, the Treaſure of Deſpair, the Refuge of Vengeance, and Den of Foxes. There he that Yeſterday was great, To day is mean , he that was well fed abroad, there ſtarves , he that was richly clad, is ſtark naked ; he that commanded, obeys , and he that lay in a good Bed, is forc'd to reſt himſelf on the hard Boards, or cold Stones There Civility is metamorphos'd into Inſolence, Courage into Subtilty, Modeſty into Boldneſs, Knowledge into Ignorance, and Order into Confuſion There one weeps, whilſt another ſings, one prays, whilſt another ſwears , one goes out, another comes in , one is condemn'd, another abſolved , and in fine, one ſhall hardly find two Perſons of one Mind and Exerciſe There Hunger is their Appetite, their Times of Meals, always when they get any thing to eat, their Table, the Floor , their Sauce, the filthy Stinks of their Wards , and their Muſick, nothing but ſnoring, ſneezing, and belching The Hangings of their Chambers are ever in Mourning, adorn'd with large Borders of Cobwebs , their Seats the Ground , and they live Apoſtolically ; that is, without Script, without Staff, and without Shoes Many of their Collars are edg'd with a Piece of peeping Linnen, to repreſent a Neck cloth, but indeed it is only the forlorn Relicks of their Shirts crawling out at their Necks, and ſome of the Priſoners have their appointed Hours, wherein they fight their bodily Enemies, and evermore obtain the Victory, by continually bearing in Triumph the Blood of the Vermin they deſtroy on their Nails In a Word, Sighs are their chief Air, Coldneſs their Comfort, Deſpair their Food, rattling of Chains their Muſick, and Death and Damnation their ſole Inſpection , whilſt a Turnkey, with a grim Aſpect in his Countenance, makes them tremble with fear of a new Martyrdom , tho' the inſulting Raſcal, in the Height of his Pride, need not ſcrew his ill favour'd Face to a Frown, becauſe he knows not how to look otherwiſe, which ſo dejects the Spirits of thoſe poor impriſon'd Slaves, who fear him, that the Condition of their Looks ſeems to implore his Smiles, tho' his flinty Heart having renounc'd any Remorſe, caſts a Defiance in their ſad and piteous Faces

This may ſuffice for a Specimen of *Tom*'s Eloquence We ſhall now proceed to relate ſome more of his Adventures.

Going one Day into *Godlington*'s Coffee-Houſe, formerly at the Corner of *Parker's-Lane*, in *Drury-Lane*, and ſitting down at a common Table, as the Room is to all Comers, a little after came in one of his Comrades, and ſat himſelf down too *Tom Sharp* at the ſame Time was looking on a curious Gold Medal, which he had ſharp'd ſomewhere, and an Attorney of *New Inn*, ſitting oppoſite to him, he deſir'd the Favour of looking on't , which being granted him, and the Gentleman having view'd and commended it for a choice Piece, his Comrade, whom he ſeem'd not to know there, muſt needs have a Sight of it too from the Attorney, who thinking no harm, gave it into his Hands After he had fairly look'd on it a while, he has fairly march'd off with it *Tom Sharp* ſaw him, but would not in the leaſt take notice thereof, as knowing where to find him, and all this while the Gentleman imagin'd

nothing but that the right Owner had received it again. A little while after *Tom Sharp* demanded courteouſly his Medal, excuſing the Gentleman's Detention thereof upon the Account of Forgetfulneſs. The Gentleman ſtarting, replied, *Sir, I thought you had it long ſince* He told him, he had it not, and as he deliver'd it unto him, he ſhould require it from no other Perſon They came to high Words, the Gentleman piſh'd at it, and in the Concluſion, bade *Tom* take his Courſe , and ſo he did , for having firſt took Witneſs of the Standers by, he ſu'd him, and recover'd the Value of the Medal twice over

Another Time *Tom Sharp*, being very well dreſs'd, he went to one Counſellor *Manning*'s Chambers in *Gray's-Inn*, and demanded a hundred Pounds which he had lent him on a Bond The Barriſter was ſurpriz'd at his Demand, as not knowing him , but looking on the Bond, his Hand was ſo exactly counterfeited, that he could not in a manner deny it to be his own Writing However, as he knew his Circumſtances were ſuch, that he never was in any Neceſſity of borrowing ſo much Money of any Man, and that therefore he could not be indebted in any Sum, upon the Account of borrowing, he told *Tom* he would not pay a hundred Pounds in his own wrong Hereupon *Tom* taking his Leave, told him he muſt expect ſpeedy Trouble.

Mr *Manning* expecting to be arreſted, ſent for another Barriſter, to whom opening the Matter, they concluded it was a forg'd Bond, whereupon Mr *Manning*'s Counſel got a General Releaſe forg'd for the Payment of this hundred Pounds When Iſſue was join'd, and the Cauſe came to be try'd before the Lord Chief Juſtice *Holt*, the Witneſſes to *Tom Sharp*'s Bond ſwore ſo heartily to his lending of the Money to the Defendant, that he was in a very fair way of being caſt, 'till Mr *Manning*'s Counſel moving the Court in behalf of his Client acquainted his Lordſhip, that they did not deny the having borrow'd a hundred Pounds of the Plaintiff, but it had been paid above three Months *Three Months* (quoth his Lordſhip) *and why did not the Defendant take up his Bond, or ſee it cancell'd?* To this his Counſel reply'd, That when they paid the Money the Bond could not be found, whereupon the Defendant took a general Releaſe for Payment thereof, which being produc'd in Court, and two *Knights of the Poſt* ſwearing to it, the Plaintiff was caſt. This put *Tom Sharp* into a great Paſſion, ſo that he cry'd to his Companions, as he was coming through *Weſtminſter-Hall, Were ever ſuch Rogues ſeen in this World before, to ſwear they paid that which they never borrow'd?*

This Fellow's Inclination to Wickedneſs was ſo ſtrong, that it did not ſtop its Career in ſuch Crimes, which could only be puniſh'd with a Fine and Pillory , but being a Man of an undaunted Mind in acting any ſort of Villany, he was often wont to ſay, That that Man deſerv'd not the Fruition of the leaſt Happineſs here, that would not, rather than go without it, venture his Neck Thus Sin, if it be dreſs'd up in ſpacious Pretences, may be entertain'd as a Companion , but when it appears in its own Shape, it cannot but ſtrike Horror into the Soul of any, if not really ſtupefy'd, as *Tom, Sharp* was, who, to maintain himſelf in an idle Courſe of Life, would perpetrate any thing

Among many other Arts, peculiar to Perſons of his Profeſſion, *Tom* learn'd that of making *black Dogs*, which are Shillings, or other Pieces of Money, made only of Pewter, double waſh'd , by means of which he maintain'd himſelf for ſome time It may not be amiſs to obſerve here, that what the Profeſſors of this helliſh Art call *George Plaſteroon*, is all Copper within, with only a thin Plate about it; and they call what [*Compofitum*, is a mix'd Metal which will both touch and cut, but not endure the fiery Teft *Tom* had not been a great while at the Trade of Coining, before feveral of his Gang were apprehended, and fent Poft to the Gallows for their wicked Ingenuity, which oblig'd him to employ all the Powers of his Wit and Invention, in the Search of fomething elfe that might conduce to fupply him in his manifold Extravagancies

In the next place he went to picking of Pockets, at which being detected, he was committed to *New-Prifon*, where having a great many loofe Women coming after him, who fupply'd him with a great deal of Money, he had all the Priviledge imaginable in the Jail, and going to take his Trial at *Hicks's-Hall* for his Fact, one *John Lee*, a Turnkey, conducting him thither, gave him the Liberty of being fhav'd by the Way in a Barber's Shop. The Keeper having alfo a pretty long Beard, quoth *Tom Sharp*, *Come, we are Time enough yet, fit down, and I'll pay for taking your Beard off too*. Whilft he was trimming, *Tom* talk'd one Thing or other to hold him in Difcourfe, till at laft the Barber cry'd, *Shut, your Eyes, or elfe my Ball will offend 'em* The Man did as he was bid, and *Tom*. took this Occafion to flip out, the Barber not taking him for a Prifoner, and hid himfelf in an Alehoufe hard by. The Turnkey not hearing him talk, open'd his Eyes, and not feeing him in the Shop, rofe up fo haftily, that he overthrew *Cut-Beard*, Bafon, Water, and all upon him, and ran out into the Street with the Barber's Cloth about him, and Napkin on his Head The People feeing him thus, with the Froth about his Face, concluded him mad, and as he ran gave him the Way The Barber, with his Razor in his Hand, ran after the Turnkey, crying, *Stop Thief, ftop Thief*, but he never minding the Out-cry, ftill ran ftaring up and down, as if his Wits had lately ftolen away from him, and he was in purfuit of them, Some durft not ftop him, and other would not; till the Barber feiz'd him at laft, and getting his Cloth and Napkin from him, made him pay Six-pence befides for being but half fhav'd, while *Tom* in the time of this Hurly-burly, got clear off

Being afraid of being apprehended for this Efcape, he was obliged to lie *incognito* in a Garret in St *Andrew's ftreet*, by the *Seven-dials*, where alfo dwelling in the fame Houfe one *Baynham*, a poor illiterate Taylor, who was lately turn'd an Aftrologer, and had a mighty great Conceit of his own natural Parts, which were very extraordinary in ordinary Things, they became intimately acquainted one with another, and hearing this Star-gazer often wifh he could fpeak *Arabic*, for the Underftanding *Albumazar*, *Meffahalah*, *Abdilaxus*, *Ulugh Beigh*, and other Authors, who had written on the Art of Aftrology in that Language, *Tom Sharp* pretended he had that Tongue as perfect as his own, and would teach it him in three Months for forty Shillings, one half in Hand, and the other when he had perform'd his Bargain. *Baynham* was very glad of this Opportunity, and giving him twenty Shillings, he was to procure *Erpenius's Arabic* Grammer, which he underftood no more than a wild *Indian* did *Welfh* or *Irifh*. *Tom* proceeded with teaching his Pupil a great many cantuing Words, telling him *Autem* was *Arabic* for a Church, *Borde*, a Shilling; *Buffer*, a Dog. *Belly-cheat*, an Apron; *Cokir*, a Liar, *Cuffin*, a Man; *Canke*, dumb, *Cannakin*, the Plague, *Deufe-avil*, the Country, *Ferme*,

a Hole; *Flag*, a Groat, *Glymmer*, a Fire, *Gar, Lip*, *Gybe*, a Pafs; *Harmanback*, a Conftabl. *Jigger*, a Door; *Kinchin*, a Child, *Libege*, a Bed *Make*, a Half-penny, *Nab*, a Hat, *Prat*, a Thigh *Quarron*, a Body; *Ruffin*, the Devil; *Swag*, a Shop *Slat*, a Half-Crown; *Trin*, the Gallows, *Win*, Penny; *Yarum*, Milk, and abundance more to the fame Purpofe They went on in this Manner for two or three Days, when *Tom* abfconding from his Lodging, not one Digit of his Body was to be feen ever after Thus he trick'd the poor Aftrologer, as nicely as he had the Daughter of *James Gardner*, a Printer, out of above fifty Shillings, in telling her five or fix Years before, that fhe fhould have a Hufband in a fhort Time, and the poor Creature was not marr'ed at the Time of *Tom's* Adventure

Afterwards *Tom Sharp* equipping himfelf in a Cloak, he went to the *Portuguefe* Chapel in *Lincolns-Inn Fields*, and privately threw a Paper of Lamp black into the holy Water, plac'd by the Door, having firft changed the Silver Bafon for a Pewter one, which he had under his Cloak Soon after the Prieft came out and croffed himfelf, and having faid a fhort Fjaculation to himfelf, he look'd toward his bigotted Congregation, to blefs them with a *Pax vobifcum*, but when he faw them all have black Croffes on their Foreheads, and the People alfo faw one on his, there was fuch ftaring one upon the other, if they would have ftar'd thro' one another At length they found they were impos'd upon by fome Heretick, who was got far enough off before now, whereupon, highly refenting the Prophanation of that which they thought fufficent Proof againft the D——l, and all his Works, they prefently went to curfing of him with their greateft *Anathema* of Bell, Book, and Candle, but *Tom* being ready curs'd to their Hands, their Revenge did him no Injury at all

Tom's laft Fact was fhooting a Watchman, who oppos'd him in breaking open a Shoe-maker's Shop at the Corner of *Great Wild-ftreet*, facing up *Great Queen-ftreet* He was apprehended and condemn'd for this Murder, but fuch was his Impiety, whilft under Sentence of Death, that inftead of thanking fuch who had fo much Chriftianity in 'em as to bid him prepare for his latter End, he would bid them not to trouble his Head with the idle Whimfies of Heaven and Hell, for he was more a Man than to dread or believe any fuch Matter after this Life But when he came to the Place of Execution, which was at the End of *Long Acre* in *Drury-Lane*, and the Halter was put about his Neck, he then chang'd his Tone, and began to call out for Mercy, with fuch a forrowful Voice, which could not but awake the moft lethargick Confcience that ever the Devil lull'd afleep One there might plainly fee by the Deluge of Tears which fell from his Eyes, what Convulfion-Fits his poor Soul fuffer'd, whilft his own Mouth confefs'd how grievoufly his afflicted Spirit were ftretch'd on the Rack of black Defpair. Now was the Time that the voluminous Regifters of his ill Confcience, which formerly lay clafp'd in fome unfearch'd Corner of his Memory, were laid open before him; and the Devil, who hitherto gave him the leffening End of the Perfpective-Glafs to furvey his licentious Courfes, turn'd the magnifying End to his Eye, which made him implore Heaven for a gracious Pardon of his manifold Tranfgreffions In this manner he was turn'd off the Cart on *Friday* the twenty fecond Day of *September*, 1704, aged twenty nine Years

The

The LIFE of GEORGE SEAGER.

The following Account was sent in a LETTER from a Gentleman in London, to his Friend in the Country, in the Year 1697

SIR,

I Have no great Inclination to tell Stories, which perhaps is nothing, but the Effect of an ill-grounded Vanity, that makes me prefer the expressing of what I imagine, to the relating of what I have seen. The Profession of a Story Teller sits but aukwardly upon young People, and is downright Weakness in old Men. When our Wit is not arrived to its due Vigor, or when it begins to decline, we then take a Pleasure in telling what does no put us to any great Expence of Thought. However, in Compliance with your Request I will for once renounce the Pleasure which I generally take in my own Imagination, to relate the unaccountable Actions of *George Seager*, who was lately executed here.

This notorious Fellow, aged twenty six Years at the Time of his Death, was born at *Portsmouth* in *Hampshire*, where his Father and Mother dying, his Sister took Care of him for a while, but she not being able to support herself, left him to the Parish to keep him, the Overseers whereof placed him out to spin Pack Thread. After two Years he left that Employment, and went to a Silk-Throwster for a Year and half, when running away from his Master, he took bad Courses, as being addicted to Gaming, Swearing, Drunkenness, and Theft, but a Gang of the *Ruby* Man of War pressing him, he went on board that Ship to Sea, where robbing the Seamens Chests, he was often whipp'd at the Cap stern, put in the Bilboes and once Keel-haul'd. Keel-hauling a Man is tying a Rope round his Middle, to which two other Ropes are so fasten'd, that carrying him to the End of the Main-Yard-Arm on the Starboard-side of the Ship, he is flung from thence into the Water, and hauled under the Ship by a Man standing on the Main Yard-Arm on the Larboard side, where a Gun is fired over the Criminal's Head as he is drawing up. However, as no Punishment would deter him from pilfering, the Captain of the Ship, rather than be plagued with him, put him ashore at *Plymouth*, from whence he begg'd his Way to *Portsmouth*, where he listed himself into *Johnny Gibson*'s Regiment, to whom he was a continual Plague.

The first Time he mounted the Guard, being put Centry on the Ramparts, and ordered by the Corporal not to let the grand Rounds pass without challenging, he said, he would take Care of that, imagining that if he challenged them he must fight them too. So the grand Rounds going about at Twelve at Night, with *Johnny Gibson* at the Head of them, *Seager*, who had got a whole Hatful of Stones by him, because he chose to fight at a Distance cries out, *Who comes there?* Being told, they were the grand Rounds, Oh! d——mn ye, quoth *George*, the grand Rounds are ye! Have at you then, for I have waited for you this Hour and above. So pelting them with Stones as fast as he could fling, the grand Rounds could not pass any farther, till they called out to the Captain of *Lamport-Guard*, who sent the Corporal to relieve him, in order to his being examin'd, but *Johnny Gibson* finding him to be a raw Soldier, who had never been upon Duty before, he escaped any Punishment inflicted on Offenders by Martial Law.

Another Time, some arch Soldier putting a Whisp of Hay into the Mouth of the Wooden Horse, which stands at the End of the Parade by the Main Guard House, *Johnny Gibson* espying it, quoth he, *Ise warrant him an honest Fellow, who was so kind as to give my Horse some Hay, gin Ise ken who it was, Ise give him Saxpence to drink*. *George* standing by the Governor when he said so, quoth he, *It was I, Sir, who gave your Horse that Hay*. Said *Jonny* then, *Ise vow it was well done of thee, and there is Saxpence for thy Pains, but as you was so civil as to feed my Horse, you ought to ride him to Water too*. So commanding him presently to be mounted on it, with a fifty Pounds Weight at his Feet, he there sat for an Hour cursing *Jonny*'s Civility to him to the very Pit of Hell.

But not long after this Riding-Bout, *George* standing Centry one Night at *Jonny*'s Door, as he was coming homewards to his House, quoth he, *Who comes there?* *Jonny Gibson* the Governor reply'd, *A Friend, Lad.*——*What Friend? Stand, Sir.* Quoth *Jonny*, *Ise am the Governor*. *George* reply'd, *I don't know that, therefore stand off, till I call the Corporal, or else I'll shoot you*. *Jonny* would fain have press'd upon his Post, but when he saw himself frustrated in his Design, quoth he, *Ise see, honest Friend, that ye know yer Duty, therefore ye need no call the Corporal, there's a Shilling for ye, and if ye're hungry, ye may gang into my Kitchen and fill yer Belly, and in the mean Time Ise will stand for ye*. *George* refused his Favour several Times, but when *Jonny* as often promised him upon his Word and Honour, that not the least Harm should come to him for leaving his Post, he gave him his Musquet, and went into his Kitchen. When he had fill'd his Belly, he went out by a backward Door to the Guard-House, where being several Soldiers playing at Cards, he put in among them. While he was here the Corporal espying him, *Ha, ha,* quoth he, *how a Pox came you here from your Post already?* *George* reply'd, *Don't you trouble yourself about that, I have got one there to stand for me*.

The Corporal said no more to him then, but about an Hour and a half afterwards going to relieve the Centries, when he came to *George*'s Post, he was much surpriz'd to see *Johnny* walking there with a Musquet on his Shoulders, who cry'd out, *Come, make Haste Mon, and relieve me, for it is a very cold*

cold Night; but, by *my Sel*, *Ise will never stond for any Knave agen*, *till he gang to fill his Belly*; *however*, *Ise shall ken that ill faud Loan another Time from a black Sheep*. Some Time after, *George* being in *Johnny*'s own Company, and standing another Time Centry at his Door, wanting Shoes, he ask'd him for a Pair Quoth *Johnny*, *Haste thou ever a Piece of Chalk about thee?* *George* told him, *Yes*; and giving him a Piece, with which he drew out a Pair of Shoes on the Centry-Box; quoth he, *Thear's a Pair for thee* *George* could not well tell what to say to him, but as soon as *Jonny* went in a doors, he draws out a Man standing Centry on the Centry-Box, and went off from his Post Afterwards, the Governor coming out, and seeing what *George*, who was not there, had done, he presently went to the Guard-House to see for him, but finding none of Gentleman, he sent a Corporal with a File of Musqueteers to look for him. After long searching about the Town, they found him playing at *All-Fours* in an Ale-House, and brought him Prisoner to *Jonny*, who demanding how his Impudence could be so great as to quit his Post before he was reliev'd, he said, *He had left a Man to do his Duty* Yes, quoth *Johnny*, *a Man chalk'd out for me* Why, replies *George*, *I thought a Centry chalk'd out for you*, *would do as well as a Pair of Shoes for me*. But, to be short, *Johnny* committed him to the Hole, where living only upon the Allowance of Bread and Water for fourteen Days, he was then brought forth, and ran the Gauntloop six Times thro' the whole Regiment

After this *George* had also ran the Gauntloop several Times for robbing the Soldiers Barracks of Victuals, Linnen, or any thing else that he could find, but no Punishment deterring him from his pilfering Tricks, he was in a Draught sent over to *Flanders*, where going one Day into a great Church in *Brussels*, he espy'd a *Capuchin*-Fryar confessing a young Woman in a very private Place, and as soon as the good old Father had given Absolution to his Penitentiary, he made up to him under Pretence of confessing his Sins, for, as it happen'd, the Fryar was an *Englishman* But, instead of confessing his manifold Crimes, his Intention was to commit more; for, pulling a Pistol out of his Pocket, and clapping it to his Breast, quoth he, *Reverend Father*, *I perceived the young Gentlewoman*, *whom you just now confess'd*, *gave you something*; *but let it be more or less unless you surrender it to me*, *who have most Need of it*, *I will shoot you thro' the Heart*, *altho' I was sure to be hang'd this very Moment for it*

The Fryar being much surprized at these dangerous Words, and deeming Life sweet, he gave him what he had of his Female Penitentiary, which was two *Louis d'Ors*; then binding him Hand and Foot

in a Corner adjacent to his Confession-Box, he went away, and that same Day, deserting his Regiment, made the best of his Way for *England*, where he committed several most notorious Burglaries in the Cities of *London* and *Westminster*, and the Out Parts thereof; but at last being apprehended, and sent to *Newgate*, for breaking open the House of the Lord *Cutts*, and taking thence Plate and fine Linnen valued at Two Hundred and forty Pounds, he was hang'd at *Tyburn*, on *Wednesday*, the Twenty seventh Day of *January*, in the Year 1696-97

Thus have I given you all the Account I could collect, of a Man, who Life you were so desirous to be acquainted with, there is nothing very remarkable in his Actions, but his being your Countryman is a sufficient Excuse for your Curiosity,

I am, SIR, Yours, &c

We may add by way of *Postscript* to the foregoing Letter, that at the same Time and Place were executed the following Criminals, viz 1 *Joseph Potter*, aged Twenty seven Years, and born in *Southwark*, who running away from King *William*'s Service at Sea, broke open the Lady *Anverquerque's* House, and took from thence One Hundred and Thirty Pounds in Money, which he consumed in less than a Week, and when he came to the Tree, said was his Impudence as to say, *I must needs own that I have brought my Hogs to a fair Market*, *but what care I for hanging*, *since a short Life well spent is better than a long one!*

2 *Benjamin Ellison*, aged Twenty five Years, and born at *Wapping*, was condemn'd for breaking open the House of the Earl of *Albemarle*, and taking thence some Jewels, and a Gold Watch of great Value, but he was not much concerned at his untimely End, for, instead of repenting, he said, If *I now was to live my Life over again*, *I would be in other Trade but a Thief*, *because he has no sooner done his Work*, *but he is paid for his Labour*

3 *James Ayres*, aged Thirty Years, and born in *Scotland*, was condemn'd for committing several most notorious Robberies on the Highway, and being come to the Place of Execution, and espying a Country Fellow gazing earnestly upon him, quoth he, pointing at the same Time towards him, *I have got one Half Crown in my Breeches still*, *and believing you to be out of Business*, *I will give it you with all my Heart*, *to take but one Turn for me for half an Hour And let me tell you*, *a Crown an Hour is good Pay for any Working Man in England*

The LIFE *of* NED BONNET.

EDWARD *Bonnet* was born of very good and reputable Parents, in the Isle of *Ely*, in *Cambridgeshire*, who bestowing some small Education upon him, as Reading, Writing, and Casting Accompts, about the Fifteenth Year of his Age, he was put out an Apprentice to a Grocer, living at *Potten* in *Bedfordshire*, whom he served honestly. When he was out of his Time, he married a Neighbour's Daughter, by whom he had two small Children at the Time of his Death, and set up for himself in the Country, being at one Time worth above six hundred Pounds. He was ruined by a Fire, which burnt all his Goods and House to the Ground; and not being in a Condition to retrieve his Loss, he came up to *London*, to avoid the importunate Duns of Creditors, where lighting into a Gang of Highwaymen, he took to their Courses, to raise himself, if possible, once more. Having been upon several Exploits, wherein he was successful, the sweet Profit of his Enterprizes made him so in Love with robbing on the Highway, that he devoted himself wholly to it, and committed (as 'tis reported) above three hundred Robberies, particularly in *Cambridgeshire*, insomuch that he was as much dreaded by the People in that Country, as ever that great Tory, *Patrick Flemming*, was by the wild *Irish*.

After he was grown a good Proficient in the gainful Art and Mystery of robbing on the Highway, he ofentimes attempted to rob by himself, for he was an excellent Horse man, and kept the best of Horses which would leap a Hedge, Ditch, or Five-Bar Gate, with him on his Back, and knew the Road by Day or Night, in that Country, as perfectly as if was directed by a Compass.

Upon this Beast one Time he met a young *Cantabrigian*, who had more Money than Wit, recreating himself abroad in his Calash, with a brisk jolly Courtezan, belonging to bawdy *Barnwell*, a little Village, within a Mile of the University of *Cambridge*, well furnished with such sort of Cattle, as will sell the foul Disease to a Gentleman at a very moderate Price. He made up to these Gallants, and commanding them to stand, he very civilly demanded their Money, which they refusing, he took the Sum of six Pounds or thereabouts from 'em by Violence, and because they gave him some Trouble before they would part with what they had, he was resolved to put them to some Shame.

To accomplish this, he presented a Couple of Pistols towards them, and swore they should suffer no less than present Death, if they did not strip themselves stark naked, and they, to save their sweet Lives, obey'd his Commands. Then tying their Hands behind them, he bound their Legs one to the other, and flashing the Horse, away he ran upon a full Trot with these *Adamites*, home to his Inn in *Cambridge*. But as soon as they came into the Town, such a Multitude of Men, Women, and Children, were hallooing and hooting after them, that the like

to be sure was scarcely seen after the Lady *Godiva*, when she rid naked thro' the City of *Coventry* But their Shame did not end here, for the young Gentleman being call'd to an Account by the Vice-Chancellor, for this Scandal which he had brought on the Collegians, by his publickly keeping Company with lewd Women, he was expell'd by the University, and the Strumpet sent to the House of Correction, to do farther Pennance by Way of Mortification for the Flesh.

Having performed this Exploit, and removing his Quarters on t'other Side the Country, he met with his Taylor and Son, who had lately arrested him for a Sum of four or five Pounds, which he ow'd Mr *Stitch*. Resolving now to be revenged on him, he requested him to deliver his Purse, but the Taylor not approving of his Proposition, he us'd a great many Words and Ceremonies to divert *Ned Bonnet* from his Project. *Ned* not being to be Tongue padded, he, by force of Arms, took thirty six Pounds away from his former Creditor, and rid off; which made the Son say to his Father, *I wonder what these Fellows think of themselves? Surely they must go to Hell for committing these notorious Actions. G—d forbid,* reply'd the Taylor, *for to have Conversation of such Rogues there, would be worse than all the rest.*

After this, *Ned Bonnet* meeting on the Road betwixt *Cambridge* and *Ely*, Mr *Piggot* the Anabaptist Preacher in *Little-Wild street*, he commanded him to stand and deliver, whereupon, this pious and much Pains taking Propagator of the Gospel, being very loath to part with his *Mammon* to this D—l of a Robber, as thinking it false Heraulдry to put Metal to Metal, he dropp'd a great many devout Sayings to divert him from his intended Purpose. This putting *Ned Bonnet* into a great Passion, he said, *Pray, Sir, keep your Breath to cool your Porridge, and don't talk of religious Matters to me, for I'll have you to know, that, like all other true bred Gentlemen, I believe nothing at all of Religion; therefore deliver me your Money, and bestow your laborious Cant upon your Female Auditors, who'll never scold at their Maids without cudgelling them with broken Pieces of Scripture, which flow very fluently upon them on all Occasions.* So taking from him a good Watch, worth eight Pound, and as many Guineas, he ty'd his Leg, under his Horse's Belly, and left him to steer his Course as well as he could.

Another Time *Ned* and his Associates meeting with a Person of Quality, attended by four Servants, on the descending of a Hill into a hollow Way, the one Side whereof was inclos'd with a craggy shatter'd Rock, and the other with a large Wood, rising considerably higher than the Road, here they thought it very proper to assault the Nobleman and his Attendants, whom they commanded to stand and deliver what they had. At this the Person of

Quality fmil'd, (thinking, or at leaft diffembling that he thought fo) tnat they were only in Jeft, and told them, *He believed they were Gentleman only upon a Frolick, therefore, if they would accompany him to the next Town, they should be entertained with the beft the Place would afford* To this Ned and his Comrades reply'd furlily, *They muft convince him by ftronger Arguments if he perfifted not to deliver his Money,* which nolens volens *they were refolved to have* So having made ready, they bore up to feize his Horfe's Bridle Upon this, perceiving they were in Earneft, a fharp Difpute began betwixt them, but the Nobleman's Party being overpowered, they were forced to furrender themfelves Prifoners at Difcretion

The Robbers then taking from the Nobleman a Purfe full of Gold, a gold Snuff-Box, a gold Watch, and a rich diamond Ring, they carried him and his fervants into the adjacent Wood, where tying them Hands and Feet, they left them, but faying, *That they would bring them more Company prefently* Accordingly, they were as good as their Word, for in lefs than two Hours they made the Nobleman and his four Servants juft a dozen Perfons, whom alfo binding, quoth Ned Bonnet, ' There are now twelve ' of you, all good Men and true, fo bidding you ' farewel, you may give in your Verdict on us as you ' pleafe when we are gone, tho' it will be none of ' the beft, yet to give as little Trouble as may be, ' we fhall not ftay now to challenge any of you . So ' once more farewell

Ned Bonnet and his Comrades now going to their Place of Rendezvous, to make merry with what they had got, which was at a bye fort of an Inn ftanding fomewhat out of the high Road between *Stamford* and *Grantham,* it happened at Night to rain very hard, fo that one Mr. *Randal* a Pewterer, living near *Marygold-Alley* in the *Strand,* before it was burnt down, was oblig'd to put in there for Shelter. Calling for a Pot of Drink, whereon was the Innkeeper's Name, which was alfo *Randal,* the Pewterer afked him, as being his Name fake, to fit and bear him Company

They had not been long chattering before *Ned* and one of his Comrades, with a Trull, came down Stairs and placed themfelves at the fame Table, and underftanding, by the Means aforefaid, what this Stranger's Name was, one of the Rogues fixing his Eyes more intent than ordinary upon him, in a deal of feeming Joy, he leaped over the Table, and embracing the Pewterer, quoth he, ' Dear Mr. Ran- ' dol! who would have thought to have feen you ' here? 'Tis Ten Years, I think, fince I had the ' Happinefs to be acquainted with you

Whilft the Pewterer was recollecting whether he could call this Spark to mind or not, for it came not into his Memory, that he had ever feen him in his Life, the Highwayman again cry'd out, *Alas! Mr Randal, I fee now I am much altered, fince you have forgot me* So being here arrived to a *Ne plus ultra* how to go on, up ftarts *Ned,* and with as great feeming Admiration, faid to his Companion, *Is this, Harry, the honeft Gentleman in London, whom you fo often us'd to praife for his great Civility and Liberality to all People? Surely then we are very happy in meeting thus accidentally with him*

By this Difcourfe they would almoft have perfwaded Mr. *Randal* that they perfectly knew him, but being fenfible of the contrary, he very ferioufly affured them, that he could not remember them, he ever had feen any of them in his Life No! faid they, as ftruck with Admiration, *that's ftrange we fhould be altered fo much within thefe few Years* Then Mr *Randal* began to afk the Spark, who pretended to know him fo well, fome Queftions which

he was certain he could not pofitively anfwer, but fearing they fhould then be put to a Nonplus, they waved them, and ftrained Compliments with Mr *Randal* to fup with them, which all his Refufals could not avoid.

By that Time they had fupped, in came four more of *Ned*'s Comrades, who were invited alfo to fit down, and more Provifions were called for, which were as quickly brought, and as quickly devour'd When the Fury of confuming half a dozen good Fowls and other Victuals was over, befides feveral Flafks of Wine, there was not lefs than three Pound odd Money to pay At this they ftar'd on each other, and held a profound Silence, whilft Mr *Randal* was fumbling in his Pocket When they faw he only brought fourth a Moufe, which was only as much as came to his Share to pay, he that pretended to know him, ftarted up, and protefted he fhould be excus'd for old Acquaintance fake · But the Pewterer, not willing to be beholden, as indeed they never intended he fhould, to fuch Companions, left for the Civility they fhould expect greater Obligations from him, preffed them to accept his Dividend of the Reckoning, faying, *If they thought requifite he would pay more*

At laft their Trull taking the Wink, faid, *Come come, what needs all this ado? Let the Gentleman, if he fo pleafes, prefent us with this fmall Treat, and do you give him a larger at his taking his Farewell in the Morning* Mr *Randal* not liking this Propofal, it was ftarted that he and *Ned* fhould throw Dice to end the Controverfy, and fearing he was got into ill Company, to avoid Mifchief, *Randal* acquiefed to throw a Main for who fhould pay the whole Sho, which was fo managed that the Lot fell upon *Jinas* For putting the Change upon him, the Dice they threw with ran all Fives and Sixes on *Ned*'s Side, and but only Fours and Fives on the Pewterer's fide, which he perceiving, and going to detect them, the Strumpet fnatched them up, and by the Art of Hocus Pocus, converted them into regular ones By this Means *Randal,* having the Voice of the whole Board againft him, was deputed to pay the whole Reckoning, tho' the diffembling Villains vow'd and protefted they had rather it had fell to any of them to have had the Honour of treating him, with alfo making large Promifes what great Things they would do the next Morning, to make him amends

Mr. *Randal* diffembled his Difcontent at their fhirking Tricks as well as he could, and they perceiving he would not engage in Gaming, but counterfeited Drowfinefs, and defired to be a-bed, the Company broke up, and he was fhew'd to his Lodging, which he baricado'd as well as he could, by putting old Chairs, Stools, and Tables againft the Door Going to Bed and putting the Candle out, he fell afleep, but was foon awaked by a capering up and down the Room, and an Outcry of Murder and Thieves.

Upon this furprizing Noife he leaped out of Bed, and ran to the Door, to fee whether it was faft or not, and finding nothing removed (for the High waymen came into his Chamber by a Trap Door which was behind the Hangings) he wondered how the Noife fhould be there in his Apartment, unlefs it was enchanted But as he was about to remove the Barricade to run and raife the Houfe, he was furrounded with a Crew, who tying and gagging him, they took away all his Clooths, and left him to fhift for himfelf as well as he could

A little after, the Inn-keeper, the better to colour his Bufinefs, came thundering at tne Door, demanding what was the Caufe of this Clamour at that Time of Night? But hearing no Body anfwer, he jumbled

jumbled open the Door, and entered the Room with a Candle, bringing also his Hostler and Tapster along with him. Finding the Gentleman in that Condition, he soon unloos'd him, with a great deal of seeming Sorrow for this Disaster, for he had not only lost his Cloaths, but also forty Pounds which he had in Gold in his Breeches. In the mean while *Ned Bonnet* and one of his Comrades came into Mr. *Randal's* Chamber, to enquire the meaning of this Disturbance there, and when they were acquainted with his Loss, they swore, in a seeming great Rage, *they would find out the Rogues, if they went to a Conjuror.* But the poor Pewterer believed they need not consult the Devil to know who had robbed him, no more than they might have doubted going to him themselves when they died.

Mr *Randal* being thus cheated and robbed of all he had about him, he was obliged to borrow some old Cloaths of the Inn-keeper and then with a heavy Heart return early in the Morning home again, as being not able to prosecute his intended Journey, for want of Money to defray his Charges.

One Time *Ned Bonnet*, in a Rencounter on the Road, met with the Misfortune of having his Horse shot under him, whereupon, he was obliged to follow his Trade on Foot, till he could get another. But it was not long before he took a good Gelding out of the Grounds of a Man, who since kept the *Red Lyon Inn* in *Hounslow*, upon which, riding strait into *Cambridgeshire*, a Gentleman one Day overtook him on the Road, who had just like to have been robbed. Hearing *Ned Bonnet* to be tuning something of a Psalm, he, thereupon, took him to be a godly Man, and desired his Company to such a Place, to which he said he was also going, (for a Highwayman is never out of his Way, tho' he is going, against his Will, to the Gallows.) But at length, *Ned* coming to a Place convenient for his Purpose, he obliged the Gentleman to stand and deliver his Money, which being above eighty Guineas, he had the Conscience to give him half a Crown to bear his Charges, till he had Credit to recruit himself again. This Gentleman ever after could not endure the Tune of a Psalm, and had as great an Aversion against *Sterbold, Hopkins, Tate*, and *Brady*, as the Devil has to holy Water.

The Reader will observe by what precedes, that *Ned Bonnet* had always a sprightly Imagination, and this was yet more apparent before the Faculties of his Mind were debauched by evil Practices. We shall give one Instance, which was omitted at the Beginning, to prove the Liveliness of his Genius when he was but a Child. Being sent by his Father when he was no more than ten Years old, with a Present to the Parson of the Parish, he went and knocked manfully at the Door.

The Gift was a Spear-rib, the old Man having just killed a Hog, and it was wrapped up in a Cloth, and put into a Basket. A Servant comes to the Door, and demands of young *Bonnet* his Business. *I want to speak with your Master* says he. Immediately the Master was informed, and, he imagining what the Affair was, comes to receive the Dole of his pious Parishoner, a Thing that Gentlemen of the Cloth are as ready to do, as any Men in the World. *Well, my Dear,* quoth he, *What is your Business?* Why only my *Father has sent you this,* says *Ned,* and gives him the Basket, without moving his Hat. *O Fie, fie, Child,* says *Levi, have you no Manners? You should pull off your Hat, and say, Sir, my Father gives his Service to you, and desires you to accept this small Token. Come go out again with the Basket, and knock at the Door, and I'll let you in, and see how prettily you can perform it.*

The Parson waited within the Door till he was weary, expecting *Ned* to knock, till at last, imagining the Boy had mistook the Case, he opens the Door, and sees our Gentleman at a Distance, walking off with his Present. *So ho! So ho! Sirrah, where are you a going?* calls the Parson with a loud Voice. *Home, Sir,* answered the Boy as loudly. *Nay, but you must come back, and do as I bid you first,* says the Priest again. *Thank you for that, Sir,* quoth *Ned. I know better, and if you teach me Manners, I'll teach you Wit.* So away he fairly went with the Spear-rib, which his Father, upon hearing the Story, had Wit enough to keep, and laugh at the Parson into the Bargain.

At length one *Zachary Clare*, whose Father kept a Baker's Shop at *Hackney*, being apprehended for robbing on the Highway, and committed to *Cambridge* Goal, to save his own Bacon, he made himself an Evidence against *Ned Bonnet*, who being secured at his Lodging in *Old Street*, was sent to *Newgate*, where remaining till the Assizes held at *Cambridge*, before Mr Baron *Lovel*, he was carried down thither, and executed before the Castle, on *Saturday* the 28th of *March*, 1713, to the general Joy and Satisfaction of all the People in that Country, where a great Number on Horseback met him on the Road, when he was going down, to conduct him safe to Prison. Before he was turned off he shew'd himself very much troubled for the poor Condition in which he left his Wife and Children, and owned that his shameful Death was no more than what he deserved, in that he had been condemned for his Life not above three Years before, at *Chelmsford* in *Essex*, and was pardoned for the same, but not making good use of that Royal Mercy, which was extended towards him, the just Judgment of God had now overtook him for all his Wickedness.

The LIFE of JACK SHRIMPTON.

JOHN *Shrimpton* was born of good and reputable Parents, living at *Penns*, near *High-Wickham*, in *Buckinghamshire*, who bestowing so much Education upon him, as might qualify him for a Tradesman, he was put out an Apprentice when he was between 15 and 16 Years of Age, to a Soap-boiler in *Little-Briton*, in *London*, but not serving out his Apprenticeship there, he was turn'd over to another Soap-boiler in *Ratcliffe high-way*, where getting acquainted with a Parcel of unlucky Prentices, they went one Morning early to rob an Orchard a little out of Town. *Jack Shrimpton* getting into a Tree, whilst his Companions lay perdue, to prevent his Discovery, in the mean time a Sea Captain came out with another Brother Officer's Wife to re-create themselves, and just under this Tree wherein *Jack* was hid, our Gallant being dispos'd to give his Lady a Green gown, she denied his Civility, by Reason a great Dew being fell on the Grass, she was fearful of disobliging her fine Clothes. Hereupon the Gentleman spread his fine Cloak on the Ground, and giving his Mistress what pleas'd her, and praising his own Activity in the Sport of *Venus*, to a high Degree, *Jack Shrimpton* shaking the Tree, threw the Apples down in Shoals about their Ears. The two Lovers, in a great Fright and Consternation, ran into the House as fast as they could, without any Thoughts of the Cloak, which *Shrimpton*, when he came out of the Tree, with all Speed carried away, and sold it for Six Pounds.

When *Jack Shrimpton* was out of his Time, his Inclination not suiting with the Thoughts of getting a Livelihood by his honest Industry, he led a rakish Course of Life, and went into the Army, where he was some time in the Troop of Horse commanded by Major General *Wood*, but not finding such Preferment as he expected by being a Soldier, he came into *England*, and took to the High-way. He did always the most Damage betwixt *London* and *Oxford*, insomuch that scarce a Coach or Horseman could pass him without being robb'd.

One Time overtaking a certain Barrister at Law of the *Middle Temple*, in the Woods betwixt *Wickham* and *Stoken-Church*, the Gentleman lik'd *Shrimpton*'s Horse so extremely well, that he was pleas'd to proffer him 30 Guineas for it at first Word. But *Shrimpton* valuing his Horse at a higher Rate, would not take under 50 for him. The Gentleman told his new Companion, whom he had pick'd up upon the Road, that he had no more than 30 Guineas about him, and what would just bear his Charges to the Place whither he was going, however, because he had a great Fancy for the Horse, he would give him a Note, to be payable upon Sight in *London*, for 10 Pounds more. *Shrimpton* refus'd his Chapman's Offer, saying, Sir, mine is a Horse worth its Weight in Gold, and, if you was to know all, has procur'd me more Money than ever Bucephalus got for Alexander; therefore I shall not part with him on any Terms. But indeed, Sir, you must part with y'e 30 Guineas nevertheless, or otherwise we must dispute the Matter presently at Sword and Pistol. The Barrister was much startled at these Words, but *Jack Shrimpton* being very resolute in his Demand, he was oblig'd to part with his Money without having the Horse, which he so much admir'd to his Cost.

Some Time after the committing of this Robbery, Mr. *Shrimpton* (whose Practice in this unlawful Course of Life, plainly shew'd his main Industry was to ruin himself, in following a Profession which demonstrated an open Defiance to his Happiness) being in *London*, he accidentally lit into the Company of the Common Hangman, where he was taking a Glass of Wine; and coming to the Knowledge of his Occupation, he ask'd him this Question, What is the Reason, when you perform your Office, that you put the Knot just under the Ear; for in my Opinion, was you to fix it in the Nape of the Neck, it would be more easy to the Sufferer? The Hangman replied, If one Christian may believe another, I have hang'd a great many in my Time, but upon my Word, Sir, I never had any Complaint as yet. However, if it should be your good Luck to make use of me, I shall, to oblige you, be so civil as to hang you after your own Way. But *Shrimpton* not approving of the Hangman's Civility, he told him, that he desir'd none of his Favours, because they generally prov'd of a very dangerous Consequence.

One Mr *Littleton*, a Face Painter, living in Silver-street in *London*, was acquainted with several of *Shrimpton*'s Friends, by which means he had been often in his Company, and once having some Business which requir'd him into *Buckinghamshire*, he went and lodg'd at *Shrimpton*'s Brother's, who kept an Inn at *Wooburn*. Now whilst Mr *Littleton* was in the Country, *Jack Shrimpton* din'd with his Wife in *London*, on a Sunday, on the Tuesday following he din'd with Mr *Littleton* himself, in the County of *Bucks*, and the Day after, being Wednesday, overtaking Mr *Littleton* in a Coach, near *Gerrard's Cross*, where likewise were three or four other Coaches, *Shrimpton* spoke first to him, after the usual Words, stand and deliver. Pray, says he, what you do, do quickly, because I have a great deal of Work lies upon my Hands to finish betwixt this and Night. So Mr *Littleton* giving him 35 Shillings, he rid up to the Passengers in the other Coaches, from whom he took 150 Pounds. But three Days after the playing his Trick, *Shrimpton* sent to *Littleton* the following Letter by a Porter, with two Guineas inclos'd.

SIR,

THE last Time I had the Honour to see you was at Gerrard's Cross, which is all from your humble Servant to command

J Pu

Ano he

Another Time *Jack Shrimpton*, who also call'd himself *Parker*, meeting a Couple of Bailiffs beyond *Wickham*, carrying a poor Farmer to Goal, he desir'd to know what the Debt might be; and being told six Pounds odd Money, he requested them to go with him to the next Ale-house, and he would pay it They went along with him, where taking a Bond of the Farmer, whom he knew very well, he paid the Bailiffs their Prisoner's Debt and Fees, and then parted But *Jack Shrimpton* way-laying the Bailiffs, he had no more Mercy on them, than they had on the Farmer, for he took away what Money he paid 'em, and about 40 Shillings besides, after which he rid back again to the Farmer, and regaling him with a Treat of a Guinea, cancel'd his Bond, and then went in Pursuit of new Adventures

A little while after *Shrimpton* travelling the Road, he met with a poor Miller, who was going to turn Highwayman himself, for being very much indebted, so that he expected nothing but to be daily clapt up in a Jail, he was resolved to better his Fortune, or lose his Life Thus roving along, and meeting (as abovesaid) with *Shrimpton*, he held up an Oaken Plant, for he had no other Arms, and bad him stand, as thinking that Word was sufficient to scare any Man out of his Money.

Shrimpton perceiving the Simplicity of the Fellow, fir'd a Pistol at him, which (tho' he purposely miss'd him) put our new Robber into such an Agony, that he surrender'd himself to *Shrimpton's* Mercy; who presently said, *Surely, Friend, thou art but a young Highwayman, or else you would have knocked me down first, and have bid me stand afterwards.* The poor Miller told him his Misfortunes, on which *Shrimpton* taking some Compassion, quoth he, *I am a Highwayman myself, and am now waiting in this Road for a certain Neighbour of yours, who I expect will come this way by and by with six score Pounds, therefore if you will be assisting in the Robbery of him, you shall have half the Booty*

The Miller was very thankful for this kind Offer, and resolv'd to stand by him to the very utmost Then *Shrimpton* having told him again, that it was not long since he had robb'd one of his Neighbours of 150 Pounds, he farther said, "Honest Friend, "whilst I ride this Way, do you go that Way, and "if you should meet him whom I have told you of, "be sure knock him down, and take all he has from "him, without telling him why or wherefore, and "in case I should meet him, I'll serve him the same "Sauce"

They both separated, and went in Search for their Prey, till at last, upon the joining of two Roads, they met together again. *Shrimpton* wondering the Person he wanted should not yet come, order'd the Miller to follow him still, saying, *Without doubt we shall catch the old Cuff anon* But as he was thus encouraging his new Companion, who was just at his Horse's Heels, he takes up his Stick, and gave *Shrimpton* such a smart Blow betwixt Neck and Shoulders, that he fell'd him to the Ground, then being able to deal with him, he robb'd him of about fourscore Guineas, and bad him go quietly about his Business, or otherwise he would have him hang'd, according to his own Confession, for lately robbing his Neighbour Thus the Biter was bit but *Shrimpton* swore he would never more take upon him to learn Strangers how to rob on the Highway

This notorious Malefactor pursu'd his wicked Courses a long while, 'till at last being at *Bristol*, where he resided for some Months, he was drinking one Night very late at a Bawdy-house in St *James*'s Churchyard, when a Watchman going his Rounds, and hearing a great Noise of swearing and cursing in the House, he compell'd *Shrimpton* to go along with him to the Watch-house. As they were going together thro' *Wine-street*, he shot the Watch-man thro' the Body, and flung his Pistol away, that it might not be found, but some Men happening to go by at the same Time, they apprehended *Shrimpton*, and the Watchman dying on the Spot, they secur'd him till Morning, when carrying him before a Magistrate, he was committed to *Newgate* in *Bristol*, where he behaved himself very audaciously

At length being brought to a Trial, he was convicted not only for wilful Murder, but also for five Robberies on the Highway

After Sentence of Death was pass'd upon him, he was very careless of preparing himself for another World, whilst under Condemnation, for two Divines coming to him to admonish him, and give him good Advice about his latter End, he said, *Ye need not be so officious as ye are about my Soul, for 'tis Time enough to take Care of that when I come to the Gallows* So the Divines seeing him harden'd in his Sin, they left him to take his own Measures, and when he came to the Place of Execution at St *Michael's-Hill*, he was turn'd off without shewing any Signs of Repentance, on *Friday* the fourth of *September*, 1713 Thus died this incorrigible Offender, tho' he had several great Men to make Intercession to the Queen for a Pardon.

The LIVES of Christopher Dickson, John Gibson, *and* Charles Weymouth.

CHRISTOPHER DICKSON, the first of these Malefactors, aged 22 Years, was born at *White Chapel*, where he served five Years Apprenticeship with a Baker, and then by consent, parted with him. Afterwards he was Journeyman to another Baker, but staid not long there, before bad Company drew him away, and seduced him to follow wicked Courses The chief Persons who led him astray, were *John Gibson* and *Charles Weymouth*, the first of whom aged twenty Years, was born at *Newcastle under Line*, in *Staffordshire*, and was a Sea-faring Man, and the other aged twenty five Years, born at *Rediff*, had also been brought up to the Sea, and served the Queen on Board some of her Men of War, for several Years off and on

When these wicked Wretches first launched out into the Ocean of Iniquity, they met a poor old Man going to *Brentford* Market, whom they assaulted on the Highway, but finding nothing about him but an old Pair of Spectacles, *Kit Dickson* took them away for madness. The old Man begging hard for them, said, *Gentlemen, pray be so kind as to return me my Spectacles, for they are but little worth to you, and very serviceable to me, as fitting very well my Age, which is above threescore Years.* But *Dickson* swearing heartily at him, because he had no Money, told him, he would not part with them, till *Jack Gibson* said to his Comrade *Prithee, Dickson, give the poor old Fellow his Spectacles; for if we follow this Trade, we may assure our selves, we shall never reach his Years, to make any use of them.* whereupon *Dickson* returned the old Man his Spectacles again

One Morning before break of Day, these Sparks lying perdue for a Prey, where was a dead Horse flea'd in a Field, they threw the Carcass cross the Road, and a little after a Country Fellow riding before it was light, a full Gallop, and not perceiving the Obstacle laid in his Way, down fell his Horse, and flung him into a Ditch. In the mean Time, these acute Rogues coming to his Assistance, they very kindly helped him out of the Mire, but for Civility Money, they took three Pounds odd Money of him, and bound him both Hand and Foot, whilst his Horse was run quite away Some short Time after it being broad Day, some Passengers came by, to whom the Country Fellow crying out for Relief, they went and unbound him, and when he was on his Legs again, and saw the flea'd Horse lying in the Road, quoth he, *Gad's bleed, such Rogues ar these were never heard of before, for they have stolen the very Skin off of the Horse I rid on* Then going home on Foot, where he found his Horse was got before him, quoth he to his Wife and Servants, *Gad's bleed, how came Dobbin alive again? I'm sure it can't be him, it must be the Devil in his Shape, for my Horse was killed and flea'd not above three or four Hours ago, by a Parcel of Rogues that*

robbed me of all the Money I had about me And ever after, let his Wife and Servants say what they would to the contrary, they could never persuade him that it was the same Horse he rid out with

Another Time these accomplished Villains riding into the Country, they there killed an Ox, and cutting off three of its Feet, about the same Length that Neats Feet are usually sold at Market, they put them into their Portmanteau's, which were only stuff'd with Straw. Then going to an Inn in *Faringdon* in *Berkshire*, they called for a very plentiful Supper, and went up to their Chamber, in which was two Beds But before they turned into Bed, they cramm'd the Straw which they had in their Portmanteaus up the Chimney, and then filled them again with two good Pair of *Holland* Sheets, three Pillowbiers, two Pair of Callico Window Curtains, one fine Blanket, and a very good Quilt, and then went to their Repose.

In the Morning our Adventurers lying very late, the Chamberlain having the Curiosity of going softly up Stairs to see whether they were stirring, and peeping thro' the Keyhole of the Door, against which one of the Beds was placed, he perceived three cloven Feet, which they had tied to their Feet, danging out at the Bed's Foot At this sight running down Stairs again very much affrighted, (for his Hair stood on end, and the Sweat ran down his Face in Drops as big as Pease) quoth he to his Master and Mistress, *The three Strangers that came hither last Night, are three Devils, nay, I'm sure they must be Devils, for I saw their cloven Feet.*

The Master not believing this Relation without ocular Inspection himself, away he crept softly up Stairs, and peeping thro' the Keyhole too, he no sooner saw the black cloven Feet hanging out at the Bed's Foot, but he ran down Stairs faster than he went up, and told his Wife, That it was true what the Chamberlain said, furthermore adding, *I am ruined and undone, for if it should be known that my Devils haunt my House, I shall never have a Customer come to it again; and how to be rid of these Devils I can't tell.*

The Inn-keeper's Wife being much startled at what her Husband said, after some short Pause on the Matter, quoth she, *My Dear, I would have you go and fetch the Parson of the Parish hither presently, and see if he can rid the House of these infernal Guests by laying them.* Accordingly the Parson was fetched who positively assured them over a Pint of Sack, that he would soon send them all to Hell again, their proper Place of Rendezvous, in spite of their Teeth

The Parson now softly creeping up Stairs to behold them, he no sooner saw their cloven Feet too, but he ran down again in as great Precipitation as the Inn-keeper and Chamberlain had done before him, saying, ' Indeed, Neighbours, them Guests in
' that

that Room are certainly all Devils; therefore the only Advice I can give you is this, That when their Devilships are pleased to come down, you must give them very good Words, and take not one Farthing for what they have had for themselves or for their Horses

The Inn-keeper and his Wife promis'd to observe his Direction, altho' their Reckoning came to above Guinea, and at last the Devils coming down into the Kitchen, where they called for a good Breakfast, they demanded what was to pay? Quoth the Host, Not one Farthing, Gentlemen You are kindly welcome, without paying any Thing They still insisted upon paying their Reckoning, but when they found that their Landlord and Landlady would not take any Money, they took Horse and rid strait towards *London*. Afterwards the Chamberlain going to take the Linnen off the Bed and finding it ready took to his Hands, with divers other Things, as above specified, he acquainted his Master thereof, who said ' Why then I'm come off better still; for con- ' sidering they were thieving Devils, 'tis very well ' they did not take the House away with them, but ' I hope I shall never be troubled with such Guests ' again And indeed he had his Desire, for it was their Intention not to trouble him any more

At length the Devil indeed having left these sham Devils in the Lurch, they were met with at last, and sent to *Newgate*, and at Justice-Hall in the *Old-Bailey*, were indicted upon three special Indictments, for assaulting and robbing *John Edwards, Thomas Blake,* and *Samuel Slap,* on the Queen's Highway;

To all these Indictments *Weymouth* pleaded guilty, and the other two putting themselves upon their Trial, it was proved, That the several Persons robb'd, coming to Town to sell Cattle, staid to drink at the *Anchor* and *Hope* at *Stepney*, where the Prisoners were, with others of their Gang; and staying till near Ten o'Clock at Night, as they were coming over the Fields, were set upon; and they robbed *Edwards* of a Hat, value four Shillings, eleven Shillings, in Money, and a Pocket-Book, *Blake* of fourteen Shillings in Money, a Pocket-Book, a Pair of Scissars, and a Buckle, and *Slap* of twenty Shillings in Money, and a Hat *Edwards* having a Stick in his Hand, oppos'd them, and defended himself as long as he could, but they beat him so very barbarously, that he was in Danger of his Life, and could not appear against them.

William James one of their Accomplices, being sworn, depos'd, That he and the Prisoners, and *Charles Wade,* and *Henry Thompson,* not taken, being at the *Anchor* and *Hope* in *Stepney*, were told by a Woman, that there were three Men had Money; whereupon they went to the Sign of the *World's*

End, and stay'd till they came out, and then followed and robbed them The Evidence being so very plain, the Jury found them Guilty

When these Criminals were under Sentence of Death, they whistled and play'd at Cards, till the very Day before they were to die; when reflecting on the Past Follies of their ill spent Lives, they then began to bewail their Misfortunes; before this they were so little concerned for, for the dreadful Circumstances in which they lay, that instead of preparing themselves for their latter End, they only sung and damn'd. *Weymouth* particularly declared, That his coming to an untimely End, was occasion'd by his keeping Company with an old Bawd in *Grays-Inn-Lane,* of whom, and all others of that Profession, he gave the following Character

They are the Refuse and Sink of all human Society, who having pass'd thro' all the Degrees of Wickedness with their own Bodies, and finding they are incapable of acting any further Wickedness themselves, do (when they are grown old) become the Devil's Factors, and tempt others to do that which they are now unable to perform, and thereby do what in them lies to take the Devil's Work out of his Hands, their whole Business being to involve others in the same Damnation with themselves. These, wherever they are found, are the very Pests and Plagues of a Nation, and above all other Offenders, deserve to be made Examples of Publick Justice.

On *Wednesday* the 10th of *March,* 1713-14, they were convey'd up *Tyburn* Road At the same Time suffered Death with them, *Alexander Petre,* for privately stealing a great Quantity of Copper, of the value of twenty Pounds, out of the Warehouse of one Mr. *Thomas Chambers.* He readily confess'd that he was guilty of the Fact; but said, That one *Powel,* the Evidence against him, was the Person that enticed him to the Commission of that Crime. He was twenty two Years of Age, born at *Newcastle upon Tine,* in the County of *Northumberland,* his Calling a Sailor, having for twelve Years been employ'd on board several of her Majesty's Men of War, and the last of them on board which he serv'd was the *New Advice,* a fourth Rate. And also *Samuel Denny* alias *Appleby,* was hanged on the same Day, for stealing a Gelding from Mr *John Scagg,* and robbing him of twenty seven Shillings in Money, on the Queen's Highway, he was twenty three Years of Age, born at *Braintree* in *Essex,* and a Wheelwright by his Trade; but had served four Years as a private Centinel in the Army, which being a Soldier was the Occasion of his taking to ill Courses

The LIVES *of* Edward Burnworth, *alias* Frazier, William Blewit, Thomas Berry, Emanuel Dickenson, William Marjoram, John Higgs, &c.

Edward Burnworth, alias Frazier, was the extraordinary Person who framed a Project for bringing *Rapine* into Method, and bounding even the Practice of Licentiousness within some Kind of Order. It may seem reasonable therefore to begin with his Life, preferable to the rest, and in so doing, we must inform our Readers, that his Father was by Trade a Painter, though so low in his Circumstances, as to be able to afford his Son but a very mean Education. However, he gave him as much as would have been sufficient for him in that Trade to which he bound Apprentice; *viz* a Bucklemaker in *Grub-street*, where for some Time *Edward* lived honestly and much in the Favour of his Master; but his Father dying, and his unhappy Mother being reduced into very narrow Circumstances, Restraint grew uneasy to him, and the Weight of a Parent's Authority being lost, he began to associate himself with those incorrigible Vagrants, who frequent the Ring at *Moorfields*, and from Idleness and Debauchery, go on in a very swift Progression to Robbery and picking of Pockets. *Edward* was active in his Person, and enterprizing in his Genius; he soon distinguished himself in Cudgel-Playing, and such other *Moorfields* Exercises, as qualify a Man first for the Road, and then for the Gallows. The Mob who frequented this Place, where one *Frazier* kept the Ring, were so highly pleased with *Burnworth's* Performances, that they thought nothing could express their Applause so much as conferring on him the Title of young *Frazier*. This agreeing with the Ferocity of his Disposition, made him so vain thereof, that quitting his own Name, he chose to go by this, and accordingly was called so by all his Companions.

Burnworth's grand Associates were these, *William Blewit*, *Emanuel Dickenson*, *Thomas Berry*, *John Legee*, *William Marjoram*, *John Higgs*, *John Wilson*, *John Mason*, *Thomas Makins*, *William Gillingham*, *John Barton*, *William Swift*, and some others that is not material here to mention. At first they contented themselves with picking of Pockets, and other Exercises in the lowest Class of Thieving, in which, however, they did more Mischief than any Gang which had been before them for twenty Years. They rose afterwards to Exploits of a more hazardous Nature, *viz* snatching Womens Pockets, Swords, Hats, &c. The useful Places for their carrying on such infamous Practices, being about the *Royal-Exchange*, *Cheapside*, *St Paul's Church-Yard*, *Fleet-street*, the *Strand*, and *Charing-Cross*. Here they stuck a good while, nor is it probable they would ever have risen higher if *Burnworth* their Captain had not been detected in an Affair of this Kind, and

committed to *Bridewell*, from whence he was removed to *New-Prison*, where he projected an Escape, which he put in Execution. During this Imprisonment, instead of reflecting his evil Course of Life, he meditated only how to engage his Companions in Attempts of a higher Nature, and considering how large a Circle he had of wicked Associates, he began to entertain Notions of putting them in such a Posture as might prevent their falling easily into the Hands of Justice, which many of them within a Month or two last past had done.

Full of such Projects, and having once more regained his Freedom, he took much Pains to find out *Barton*, *Marjoram*, *Berry*, *Blewit*, and *Dickenson*, in whose Company he walked with strange Boldness, considering Warrants were out against the greatest Part of the Gang. In the Night-time *Burnworth* stroled about to such little Bawdy-Houses as he had formerly frequented, and where he yet fancied he might be safe. One Evening having wandered from the rest, he was so bold as to go into a House in the *Old-Bailey*, where he heard the Servants and Successors of *Jonathan Wild* were in close Pursuit of him, and that one of them was in the inner Room by himself. *Burnworth* loaded his Pistol under the Table, and having primed it, goes with it ready cocked into the Room where *Jonathan's* Foreman was, with a Quartern of Brandy and a Glass before him, Hark ye, *(says Edward)* You Fellow, who have served your Time to a *Thief-Taker*, what Business might you have with me or my Company? Do you think to gain a hundred or two by swearing our Lives away? If you do you are much mistaken, but that I may be some Judge of your Talent that Way, I must hear you swear a little on another Occasion. Upon which filling a large Glass of Brandy, and putting a little Gunpowder into it, he clapped it into the Fellows Hands, and then presenting his Pistol to his Breast, obliged him to wish most horrid Mischiefs upon himself, if ever he attempted to follow him or his Companions any more. No sooner had he done this, but *Frazier* knocking him down, quitted the Room, and went to acquaint his Companions with his notable Adventure, which, as it undoubtedly frightened the new Thief-Taker, so it highly exalted his Reputation for Bravery. A Thing not only agreeable to *Burnworth's* Vanity, but useful also to his Design, which was to advance himself to a Sort of absolute Authority. His Associates were not cunning enough to penetrate his Views, but without knowing it, suffered them to take Effect, so that instead of robbing as they used to do, as Accident directed them, or they received Intelligence of any Booty, they now submitted themselves to his Guidance,

...nce, and did nothing but as he commanded them. The Morning before the Murder of *Thomas Ball*, Burnworth and *Barton*, pitch'd upon the House of an old Justice of the Peace in *Clerkenwell*, to whom they had a particular Pique for having formerly committed *Burnworth*, and proposed it to their Companions to break it open that Night They put their Design in Execution successfully, carrying off some Things of real Value, and a considerable Parcel of what they took to be Silver Plate, with this they went into the Fields above *Islington*, and from thence to *Copenhagen-House*, where they spent the greatest Part of the Day On their parting the Booty, *Burnworth* perceived what they had taken for Silver was nothing more than a gilt Metal, at which he in a Rage would have thrown it away *Barton* opposed it, and said, *They should be able to sell it for something*, To which *Burnworth* replied, *That it was good for nothing but to discover them, and therefore it should not be preserved at any rate* Upon this they differed, and while they were debating, came *Blewit, Berry, Dickenson, Higgs, Wilson, Legee*, and *Marjoram*, who joined the Company *Burnworth* and *Barton* agreed to toss up at whose Disposal the Silver Ware should be, they did so, and it fell to *Burnworth* to dispose of it as he thought fit, upon which he carried it immediately to the *New-River-Side*, and threw it in there, adding, *He was sorry he had not the old Justice himself there, to share the same Fate*, being really as much out of Humour as if the Justice had imposed upon them in a fair Sale of the Commodity

They loiter'd up and down the Fields 'till towards Evening, when they thought they might venture into Town, and pass the Time in their usual Pleasures While they were thus murdering of Time, a Comrade of theirs came up puffing and blowing as if ready to break his Heart As soon as he reached them, *Lads*, (says he,) *beware of one thing, the Constables have been all about* Chick-Lane *in search of Folk of our Profession, and if ye venture to the House where we were to have met to-Night, 'tis Ten to one but we are all taken* This Intelligence occasioned a deep Consultation amongst them, what Method they had best take. *Burnworth* exhorted them to keep together, telling them, as they were armed with Pistols and Daggers, a small Force would not venture to attack them. This was approved by all the rest, and when they had made a solemn Oath to stand by one another in Case of Danger, they resolved, as Night grew on, to draw towards Town, *Barton* having quitted them and gone home As they came through *Turnmill Street*, they met the Keeper of *New Prison*, from whom *Burnworth* had escaped about six Weeks before He desired *Edward* to step cross the Way to him, adding, that he did not intend to do him any Prejudice *Burnworth* replied, *That he was no way in fear of any Injury he was able to do him* And so concealing a Pistol in his Hand, he stepped over to him, his Companions waiting for him in the Street, but the Neighbours having some Suspicion of the Methods they follow'd, began to gather about them, upon which they called to their Companion, to come away, which, after making a low Bow to the Captain of *New-Prison*, he did. Finding the People increase they thought it their most adviseable Method to retire back into the Fields, this they did, keeping close together, and in order to deter the People from making any Attempt, turn'd several times and presented their Pistols in their Faces, swearing they would murder the first Man who came near enough to them to touch him

As soon as they had dispersed their Pursuers, they entered into a fresh Consultation, in what Manner they should dispose of themselves. *Burnworth* heard what every one proposed, and said at last *That he thought the best Thing they could do, was to enter the other Quarter of the Town, and so go directly to the Water-Side.* They approved his Proposal, and accordingly getting down to *Black Fryers*, cross'd directly into *Southwark* They went afterwards to the Musick house, but did not stay there, retiring at last into St *George's-Fields*, where their last Counsel was held to settle the Operation of the Night There *Burnworth* exerted himself in his proper Colours, informing them that there was no less Danger of their being apprehended there than about *Chick-Lane*, for that one *Thomas Ball*, who kept a Gin-Shop in the *Mint*, and who was very well acquainted with most of their Persons, had taken it into his Head to venture upon *Jonathan Wild*'s Employment, and was indefatigable in searching out all their Haunts, that he might get a good Penny by apprehending them. He added, that but a few Nights ago, he himself narrowly missed being caught by him, being obliged to clap a Pistol to his Face, and threaten to shoot him dead Therefore, continued *Burnworth*, the surest Way is to go to this Rogue's House, and shoot him dead upon the Spot His Death will not only secure us from all Fears of his Treachery, but it will so terrify others, that no-body will take up the Trade of Thief catching in haste, and if it were not for such People, hardly one of our Profession in a Hundred would see the Inside of *Newgate*.

Burnworth had scarce made an End of his bloody Proposal, before they all testified their Assent to it, *Higgs* only excepted, who seeming to disapprove thereof, they upbraided him with being a Coward and a Scoundrel, unworthy of being any longer the Companion of such brave Fellows When *Frazier* had sworn them all to stick fast by one another, he put himself at their Head, and away they went directly to put their Design in Execution *Higgs* retreating under the Favour of the Night, being apprehensive that himself might share the Fate of *Ball*, upon the first Dislike of him, *Burnworth* and his Party, when they came to *Ball*'s House, and enquired of his Wife for him, were informed that he was gone to the next Door, a Publick-house, and that she would step and call him. *Burnworth* immediately followed her, and meeting *Ball* at the Door, took him fast by the Collar, dragged him into his own House, and began to expostulate with him why he had attempted to take him, and how ungenerous it was to seek to betray his old Friends and Acquaintance *Ball* apprehending their mischievous Intentions, addressed himself to *Blewit*, and beg'd of him to be an Intercessor for him, that they would not murder him But *Burnworth* with an Oath replied, *He would put it out of the Power of Ball ever to do him any farther Injury*, and thereupon immediately shot him Having thus done, they all went out of Doors again, and that the Neighbourhood might suppose the Firing the Pistol to have been without any ill Intention, *Blewit* fired another in the Street over the Tops of the Houses, saying aloud, *They were got safe into Town, and there was no Danger of meeting any Rogues there* *Ball* attempted to get as far as the Door, but in vain, for he dropped immediately, and died in a few Minutes afterwards.

Having thus executed their barbarous Design, they went down from *Ball*'s House directly towards the *Faulcon*, intending to cross the Water back

8 5   4 Q   again

again. By the Way they met with *Higgs*, who was making to the Water-side likewise; him they fell upon, and rated for a pusillanimous Dog: that would desert them in an Affair of such Consequence, and then *Burnworth* proposed to shoot him, which 'tis believed he would have done, had not *Marjoram* interposed, and pleaded for the sparing his Life. From the *Faulcon-Stairs* they crossed to *Pig-Stairs*; and there consulting how to spend the Evening, they resolved to go to the *Boar's-Head* Tavern in *Smithfield*, as not being there known, and being at a Distance from the Water-side, in Case any Pursuit should be made after them, on Account of the Murder. At this Place they continued till near Ten of the Clock, when they separated themselves into Parties for that Night. This Murder made them more cautious of appearing in publick, and *Blewit, Berry,* and *Dickenson* soon after set out for *Harwich*, and went over in a Packet-boat from thence for *Helvoet-Sluys*.

Higgs also being in Fear, shipped himself at *Spithead*, where he began to be a little at Ease, but Justice quickly overtook him, for his Brother who lived in Town, having wrote a Letter to him, and given it to a Ship-Mate of his, this Man accidentally fell into Company with one *Arthur* a Watchman, of St *Sepulchre's* Parish, and pulling the Letter by Chance out of his Pocket, the Watchman saw the Direction, and recollected that *Higgs* was a Companion of *Fraizer's*. Upon this he sends Word to Mr *Delafay*, Under Secretary of State, and proper Persons were immediately dispatched to *Spithead*, who seized and brought him up in Custody. *Wilson*, another of his Confederates, withdrew about the same Time, and preserved himself from being heard of for a considerable Time.

Burnworth with some Companions continued to carry on their rapacious Plunderings, and as they kept pretty well united, and were resolute, they were too strong to be apprehended. Amongst the rest of their Pranks, they stopped the Chair of the Earl of *Harborough* in *Piccadilly*, but the Chairmen drawing their Poles, and knocking one of the Robbers down, the Earl came out of the Chair, and after a smart Dispute, in which *Burnworth* shot one of the Chairmen in the Shoulder, they rais'd their wounded Companion, and withdrew. About this Time a Proclamation was published for the apprehending *Burnworth, Blewit,* &c it being justly suppos'd that none but Men guilty of these Out-rages, could be the Persons concerned in the Murder of *Ball*. A Gentleman who had bought one of these Papers, came into an Alehouse in *White-Cross-street*, and read it publickly. The Discourse of the Company turning upon the Impossibility of the Persons concerned making their Escape, *Marjoram* one of the Gang who was there, unknown, weighing the Thing with himself, retired immediately into the Fields, where loitering about till Evening, he then stole into *Smithfield*, and going to a Constable, surrendered himself as an Accomplice in the Murder of *Ball*, desiring to be carried before the Lord Mayor, that he might put himself in a Way of obtaining a Pardon, and the Reward promised by the Proclamation. That Night he was confined in *Woodstreet* Compter, his Lordship not being at Leisure to examine him.

The next Day the Noise of his Surrender being spread all over the Town, many of his Companions changed their Lodgings, and provided for their Safety, but *Barton* planting himself in the Way, as *Marjoram* was carrying to *Goldsmiths Hall*, he popped out upon him at once, though the Constable had him by the Arm, and presenting a Pistol to him,

said, D——— ye. I'll kill you. *Marjoram* at the Sound of his Voice duck'd his Head, and he immediately firing, the Ball graz'd only on his Back, without doing him any Hurt. The Surprize with which they were all struck who were assisting the Constable, gave an Opportunity to *Barton* to retire, after his committing such an Insult on publick Justice, as perhaps was never heard of. *Marjoram* proceeded, and made a full Discovery of all the Transactions in which he had been concerned, *Legee* being taken that Night by his Directions in *White-Cross Street*, and committed to *Newgate*.

Burnworth was now deprived of his old Associates, yet he went on at his old Rate by himself, for a few Nights after, he broke open the House of Mr. *Beezely* a great Distiller, in *Clare Market*, and took away from thence Notes to a very great Value, with a Quantity of Plate, which mistaking for white Metal he threw away. One *Benjamin Jones* picked it up, and was thereupon hanged, being one of the Number under Sentence, when the Condemned-Hold was shut up, and the Criminals refused to submit to the Keepers. *Burnworth* was particularly described in the Proclamation, and three hundred Pounds offered to any who would apprehend him, yet so audacious was he to come to a House in *Holburn*, and laying a Pistol down loaded on the Table, called for a Pint of Beer, which he drank and paid for, defying any Body to touch him, though they knew him to be the Person mentioned in the Proclamation.

It happened at this Time, that one *Christopher Leonard* was in Prison for some such Feats as *Burnworth* had been guilty of, who lodged at the same Time with *Leonard's* Wife and Sister, who supposing nothing could so effectually recommend to him the Mercy of the Government, as the procuring *Fraizer* to be apprehended, he, accordingly made the Proposal, by his Wife, to Persons in Authority, and the Project being approved, they appointed a sufficient Force to seize him, who were placed at an adjoining Alehouse, where the Wife of *Kit Leonard* was to give them the Signal. About Six of the Clock in the Evening, on *Shrove Tuesday*, *Kate Leonard* and her Sister and *Burnworth*, being all together, *Kate Leonard* proposed to fry some Pancakes for Supper, which the other two approved of; accordingly her Sister set about them. *Burnworth* had put off his Surtout Coat, in the Pocket whereof he had several Pistols. There was a little back Door which *Burnworth* usually kept upon the Latch, only in order to make his Escape, if he should be surprized. This Door *Kate* fastened unperceived by *Burnworth*, and whilst her Sister was frying the Pancakes, went to the Alehouse for a Pot of Drink; when having given the Men who were there waiting for him the Signal, she returned, and entring the House, pretended to lock the Door after her, but designedly missed the Staple: The Door being thus upon the jar only, as she gave the Drink to *Burnworth*, Six Persons rushed into the Room. *Burnworth* hearing the Noise, and fearing his Surprize, jump'd up, thinking to have made his Escape at the back Door, not knowing it to be bolted, but they were upon him before he could get it open, and holding his Hands behind him, one of them ty'd them, whilst another, to intimidate him, fired a Pistol over his Head. Having thus secured him, they immediately carried him before a Justice of the Peace, who after a long Examination committed him to *Newgate*. Notwithstanding his Confinement in that Place, he communicated to his Companions, the Suspicions he had of *Kate Leonard's* betraying him, and the Danger yer there was of her detecting some of the rest. They were easily induced to treat her as they had done *Ball*, and one of them fired a Pistol at her, just as she was entring her own House; but that missing, they made two or three other Attempts of the same Nature, untill the Justices of the Peace placed a Guard thereabouts in order to secure her from being killed, and if possible to seize those who should attempt it, after which they heard no more of these Attacks.

In *Newgate* they confined *Burnworth* to the Condemned-Hold, and took what other Precautions they thought proper, in order to secure so dangerous a Person, who they were aware, miditated nothing but how to escape. He was in this Condition when *Barton, Swift* &c. were under Sentence, and it was shrewdly suspected that he put them upon a new Attempt of breaking out, which failed of Success The Keepers upon Suspicion of his being the Projector of this Enterprize, removed him into the *Bilboa Room*, and there loaded him with Irons, yet nothing could break the Stubbornness of his Temper, which urged him continually to force his Way thro' all Opposition, and regain his Liberty, in order to practise more Villainies It is impossible to say how, but by some Method or other he had procured Saws, Files, and other Instruments for this Purpose With these he first released himself from his Irons, then broke thro' the Wall of the Room in which he was lodg'd, and got into the Woman's Apartment, the Window of which being fortified with three Tire of Iron Bars, he forced one of them in a little Time While he was filing the next, one of the Women gave the Keepers Notice, whereupon they came and dragged him back to the Condemned-Hold, and there stapled him down to the Ground.

WILLIAM BLEWIT, who next to *Frazier,* was the chief Person in the Gang, was one of *St Giles's* Breed, his Father a Porter, and his Mother at the Time of his Execution, selling Greens in the same Parish They were both of them unable to give their Son Education, or otherwise to provide for him, which occasioned his being put out by the Parish to a Perfumer of Gloves; but his Temper inclining him to wicked Practices, he soon got himself into a Gang of young Pick-pockets, with whom he practised several Years with Impunity, but being at last apprehended in the very Fact, he was committed to *Newgate,* convicted the next Sessions, and order'd for Transportation. Being shipped on Board the Vessel with other Wretches in the same Condition, he was quickly let into the Secret, of their having provided for an Escape. *Blewit* immediately foresaw Abundance of Difficulties in their designs and therefore resolved to make a sure use of it for his own Advantage, which he did, by communicating all to the Captain, who immediately seiz'd their Tools, and prevented the Loss of his Ship In return for this Service, *Blewit* obtained his Freedom, but before he had been two Months in Town, somebody seizing him, and committing him to *Newgate,* at the next Sessions he was tried for returning from Transportation, and convicted, but pleading the Service he had done, in preventing the Attempt of the other Malefactors, Execution was respited till the Return of the Captain, and on his Report the Sentence was changed into a new Transportation, to what foreign Port he would But he no sooner regain'd his Liberty, than he put into the same Use as before, till he got into Acquaintance with *Burnworth* and his Gang, who taught him other Methods of robbing He had, to his other Crimes, added the Marriage of several Wives, of which the first had

so great a Love for him, that upon her visiting him at *Newgate,* the Day before they sat out for *Kingston,* she fell down dead in the Lodge; another of his Wives married *Emanuel Dickenson,* and she survived them both.

His meeting *Burnworth* that Afternoon before *Ball's* Murder was accidental, but the Savageness of his Temper led him to quick Compliance with that wicked Proposition. After the Commission of that Fact, tho' he with his Companions went over to *Holland,* they were so uneasy there, that they were constantly perusing the *English* News Papers, at the Coffee-Houses in *Rotterdam,* that they might gain Intelligence of what Methods had been taken to apprehend the Persons concerned in *Ball's* Murther; resolving, on the first News of a Proclamation, or other Interposition of the State on that Occasion, to quit the Dominions of the Republick But as *Burnworth* had been betrayed by the only Persons from whom he could hope for Assistance, and *Higgs* seized on Board a Ship, where he fancied himself secure, so *Blewit* and his Associates, tho' they endeavoured to acquaint themselves with the Transactions at *London,* relating to them, fell also into the Hands of Justice, when they least expected it

The Proclamation for apprehending them came no sooner into the Hands of Mr *Finch* the *British* Resident at the *Hague,* but he caused an Enquiry to be made, whether any such Persons as were therein described, had been seen at *Rotterdam,* and being assured that there had, and that they were lodged at the *Hamburgh Arms* on the *Boom Keys* in that City, he sent away a special Messenger to enquire the Truth thereof; of which he was no sooner satisfied, than he procured an Order from the States-General for apprehending them any where within the Province By Virtue of this Order, the Messenger, with the Assistance of proper Officers, apprehended *Blewit* at the House whither they had been directed, but *Dickenson* and *Berry* had left him, and were gone on Board a Ship, not caring to remain any longer in *Holland* They conducted their Prisoner to the *Stadt-house* Prison in *Rotterdam,* and then went to the *Brill,* where the Ship, on Board which his Companions were, not being cleared out, they surprized them also, and sent them under a strong Guard to *Rotterdam,* where they were put in the same Place with their old Associate *Blewit.* We shall now take an Opportunity to speak of each of them.

EMANUEL DICKENSON was the Son of a very worthy Person The Lad was ever ungovernable in his Temper, and being left a Child at his Father's Death, himself, his Brother, and several Sisters, they unfortunately addicted themselves to evil Courses *Emanuel* having addicted him to picking of Pockets for a considerable Space, at last attempting to snatch a Gentleman's Hat off in the *Strand,* he was seized with it in his Hand, and committed to *Newgate,* and at the next Sessions convicted, and ordered for Transportation; but his Mother applying at Court for a Pardon, and setting forth the Merit of his Father, procured his Discharge; the only Use he made of which, was to associate himself with his old Companions, who, by Degrees, led him into greater Villainies, till he was with the rest drawn into the Murther of *Ball*

THOMAS BERRY was descended from Parents in the most wretched Circumstances, who suffered him to idle about the Streets, and get into such Gangs of Thieves, as taught him from his Infancy the Art of Diving. He did not always meet with Impunity, for besides getting into the little Prisons, and being whip'd feveral Times, he had been thrice in *Newgate*, and for the laft Faft ordered for Tranfportation · However, by fome Means or other, he got away from the Ship, and returned quickly to his old Employment ; in which he had not continued long, before falling into the Acquaintance of *Burnworth* it brought him to the Commiffion of Murder, and after that with great Juftice to an ignominious Death

After they were all Three fecured, the Refident difpatched an Account thereof to *England*, whereupon he received Directions for applying to the States General for Leave to fend them back This was readily granted, and fix Soldiers were ordered to attend them on Board, befides the Meffengers who were fend to fetch them Captain *Samuel Taylor*, in the *Delight* Sloop, brought them fafe to the *Nore*, where they were met by two other Meffengers, who affifted in taking Charge of them up the River In the Midft of all the Miferies they fuffered, and the Certainty they had of being doom'd to fuffer much more affoon as they came on Snore, yet they behaved themfelves with the greateft Gaity imaginable On their Arrival at the Tower, they were put into a Boat with the Meffengers, with three other Boats to guard them Each filled with a Corporal and a File of Mufqueteers , and in this Order they were brought to *Wefminfter* , where after being examined before Juftice *Cholk* and Juftice *Blackerby*, they were conducted by a Party of FootGuards to *Newgate*, through a continued Lane of Spectators, who proclaimed their Joy, at feeing thefe egregious Villains in the Hands of Juftice.

On their Arrival at *Newgate*, the Keepers having put them on each a Pair of the heavieft Irons in the Goal, they next did them the Honour of conducting them up Stairs, to their old Friend *Edward Burnworth*, who congratulated them on their fafe Arrival, and they condoled with him on his Confinement Being exhorted to apply the little Time they had to live in preparing themfelves for another World, *Burnworth* replied, *If they had any Inclination to think of a future State, yet fo many Perfons as were admitted to fee them, muft needs divert any good Thoughts* But their Minds were totally taken up with confulting the moft likely Means to make their Efcapes, and all their Actions fhewed their Thoughts were bent only on Enlargement, and that they were altogether unmindful of Death, or at leaft carelefs of the future Confequence thereof.

On *Wednefday* the 30th of *March*, 1726, *Burnworth, Blewit, Berry, Dickenfon, Legee* and *Higgs*, were all put into a Waggon, Hand cuff'd and chain'd and carried to *Kingfton*, under a Guard of the Duke of *Bolton*'s Horfe At their coming out of *Newgate* they were very merry, charging the Guard to take Care that no Misfortune happened to them, and calling upon the Spectators, as to fhew the Refpect they bore them, by Hallowing, and paying them the Compliments due to Gentlemen of their Profeffion As they paffed along the Road, they frequently threw Money among the People who followed them, diverting themfelves with feeing the others ftrive for it ; and particularly *Blewit* having thrown out fome Half-pence amongft the Mob, a little Boy picked up one of them, and calling out to *Blewit*, faid, *As fure as you will be condemned at* Kingfton, *fo fure will I have your Name engraved hereon.* Whereupon *Blewit* took a Shilling out of his Pocket, and gave it to the Boy, telling him, *There was fomething towards defraying the Charge of Engraving*

On the 31ft of **March**, the **Affizes** were opened,

before the *Right Hon. the Lord Chief Juftice* Raymond, and Mr. Juftice *Denton* , and the Grand Jury having found Indictments againft the Prifoners, they were feverally arraigned thereupon, when Five of them pleaded not guilty ; but *Burnworth* abfolutely refufed to plead at all , upon which, after being advifed by the Judge, not to force the Court upon that Rigour, his Thumbs were ty'd and ftrain'd with a Packthread ; which having no Effect upon him, the Sentence of the Prefs was read to him, and he ftill continuing contumacious, was carried down to the *Stock Houfe*, and the Prefs laid upon him He continued one Hour and three Minutes, under the Weight of three hundred, three Quarters, and two Pounds, endeavouring to beat out his Bruins againft the Floor ; during which Time, the High Sheriff himfelf was prefent, and frequently exhorted him to plead to the Indictment , which at laft he confented to do Being brought up to the Court, after a Trial which lafted from Eight in the Morning, till One in the Afternoon, on the firft Day of *April*, they were all Six found guilty of the Indictment, and being remanded back to the *Stock Houfe*, were all chained and ftapled down to the Floor While they were under Conviction, they diverted them felves with repeating Jefts and Stories of various Natures, particularly of the Manner of their Efcapes before out of the Hands of Juftice, and the Robberies and Offences they had committed , and it being propofed for the Satisfaction of the World, for them to leave the Particulars of the feveral Robberies by them committed, *Burnworth* replied, *That were he to write all the Robberies by him committed, an hundred Sheets of Paper, wrote as clofe as could be, would not contain them.*

On *Monday*, the 4th Day of *April*, they were brought up again from the *Stock-Houfe*, to receive Sentence of Death When Sentence was paffed, they entreated Leave for their Friends to vifit them in the Prifon, which was granted them by the Court, but with a ftrict Injunction to the Keeper to be careful over them After they returned to the Prifon, they bent their Thoughts wholly on making their Efcape, and for that Purpofe had procured proper Implements for the Execution of it *Burnworth*'s Mother being furprized with feveral Files, & about her, and the whole Plot difcovered by *Bifnett*'s Mother, who was heard to fay, *That fhe had forgot the Opium.* It feems the Scheme was to murder the two Perfons who attended them in the Goal, together with Mr *Elliot* the Turnkey After they had got out they intended to have fired a Stack of Hay, adjoining to the Prifon, and thereby amufed the Inhabitants while they got clear off *Burnworth*'s Mother was confined for this Attempt , in his Favour ; and fome leffer Implements that were fewed up in the Waiftbands of their Breeches being ripped out, all Hopes of Efcape whatfoever were now taken away , yet *Burnworth* affected to keep up the fame Spirit with which he hitherto behaved, and talked to one of his Guard, of coming in the Night in a dark Entry, and pulling him by the Nofe, if he did not fee him decently buried.

About Ten of the Clock on *Wednefday* Morning, (viz *April* the 6th, 1726) they, together with one *Blackburn*, who was condemned for robbing on the Highway, a Fellow groffly ignorant and ftupid, were carried out in a Cart to their Execution, being attended by a Company of Foot to the Gallows In their Paffage thither, that audacious Carriage in which they had fo long perfifted, totally forfook them, and they appeared with all that Serioufnefs and Devotion, which might be looked for, from Perfons in their

their Condition. *Blewit* perceiving one Mr *Warwick* among the Spectators, desired that he might stop to speak to him, which being granted, he threw himself upon his Knees, and earnestly entreated his Pardon, for having once attempted his Life, by presenting a Pistol at him, upon Suspicion that Mr *Warwick* had given an Information against him. When at the Place of Execution and tied up, *Blewit* and *Dickenson* especially, pray'd with great Fervour, and a becoming Earnestness exhorting all the young Persons they saw, to take Warning by them, and not follow such Courses as might in Time bring them to so terrible an End.

Blewit acknowledged, that for six Years he had lived by Stealing and Pilfering only. He had given all the Cloaths he had to his Mother, but being informed that he was to be hung in Chains, he desired his Mother might return them to prevent his being hung up in his Shirt. He then desired the Executioner to tye him up so, that he might be as soon out of his Pain as possible. Then he set the Penitential Psalm, and repeated the Words of it to the other Criminals, then they all kissed one another, and, after some private Devotions, the Cart drew away, and they were turned off. *Dickenson* died very hard, kicking off one of his Shoes, and loosing the other. Their Bodies were carried back under the same Guard which attended them to their Execution. *Burnworth* and *Blewit* were afterwards hung up in Chains, over-against the Sign of the *Fighting Cocks* in St *George's Fields*. *Dickenson* and *Berry* were hung up on *Kennington-Common*; but the Sheriff of *Surrey* had Orders to suffer his Relations to take down the Body of *Dickenson* after it's hanging up one Day, which Favour was granted on Account of his Father's Service in the Army, who was killed at his Post, when the Confederate Army besieged *Air*, in the late War. *Legee* and *Higgs* were hung up on *Putney Common*, beyond *Wandsworth*.

The LIFE of TOM KELSEY.

THOMAS KELSEY was born in *Leather-Lane*, in the Parish of St *Andrew's Holborn*, but his Mother being a Welch Woman, and she having an Estate of about 40 *l* per Annum, left her by an Uncle at *Wrexham* in *Denbighshire*, the whole Family went down thither to live upon it, which consisted only of the two old People, and this their Son.

Tom was from his Infancy a stubborn untoward Brat, and this Temper encreased as he grew up, so that at 14 Years of Age he was prevail'd on by one *Jones*, who has since been a Victualler in London, to leave his Father and come up to Town, in order to seek his Fortune. Having neither of them any Money, they were oblig'd to beg their Way along in the best English they were Masters of. Going one Day to a Gentleman's House with their Complaint, he took a liking to the Boys, and receiv'd them both into his House, *Kelsey* in the Quality of a Horse-keeper, and *Jones* as a Falconer. It may be supposed they were both awkard enough in their Callings, but *Tom's* Place was the least difficult, so that he kept it the longest, the Gentleman being soon weary of his Falconer, and glad to send him about his Business again.

Kelsey used to tell the following Story, as the Reason of *Jones's* Discharge, whether it were exactly true or no, there is something pleasant in it. One Day the Master and Man went out a Hawking together, and as soon as the Master discovered the Game, he gave the appointed Sign, and *Jones*, who had the Hawk on his Fist, let her fly. The poor Falcon, without pursuing the Game, mounted directly upwards, upon which the Gentleman began to be in a terrible Passion, not suspecting the Cause of her so doing. At last, when he saw no sign of her coming down again, I believe, says he, *the Hawk intends to lodge in the Sky To Night*. I believe so too, quoth *Jones*, for she took her *Night-Cap* along with her. The Gentleman was not long finding out what this *Night-Cap* was, for in a few Minutes the Bird dropp'd down dead by them with Hood on, having flown upwards till she was quite spent. This not only got *Jones* a Discharge, but procured him a handsome Caning into the Bargain, which he would have been very willing to have gone without.

Jones's being turned away, while *Kelsey* was retain'd, was the Occasion of breaking off their Acquaintance, which probably might save *Jones* from the Gallows; it being very likely that if they had continued together, they would both have shared the same Fate, whereas *Jones* now got a Tapster's Place in London, and continued ever after in the same Business either as a Servant or a Master. It was not a great while after, before Tom *Kelsey* was detected in some little pilfering Tricks, and turned out of Doors after his Companion, whom he could not find when he came to London. His being out of Place till he could subsist no longer, and his natural Inclination to Dishonesty, soon brought him forwards in the course of Life for which he was afterwards so infamous. He fell into Company with Thieves, and was as bold and as dextrous in a little Time as the best of them, if not even beyond them all.

Going one Day by the House of Mr *Norton*, a Silversmith in *Burleigh Street*, near *Exeter Change*, a couple of his Companions came by him like Strangers, and one of them snatch'd off his Hat, and flung it into the Goldsmiths Chamber Window, which stood open, running away as fast as they could. Tom, who had a Look innocent enough to deceive any Body, made a sad Complaint to Mr *Norton*, who stood at his Door, and saw all that past. It happened that at that Time there was no Body at Home but himself, of which Tom had got Intelligence before. Poor Lad! says Mr *Norton*, you shall not lose your Hat, go up Stairs and fetch it your self, for I cannot leave the Shop. This was just what Tom wanted, he went up and took his Hat, and with it a Dozen of Silver Spoons that lay in his Way, coming down in a Minute,

4 R   nute,

nute, and making a very submissive Bow to Mr *Norton* for his Civility, who let him go without Suspicion. This Prize was divided between him and his two Associates, as is common in such like Cases.

Tom was not, however, so successful in his Villainies, but that he was condemn'd to be hang'd before he was 16 Years of Age. The Fact was breaking open the House of one Mr. *Johnson*, a Grocer in the *Strand*, and stealing from thence two silver Tankards, a silver Cup, six silver Spoons, a silver Porringer, and 40 *l* in Money. But he got off this Time on account of his Youth, and the Interest his Father made at Court; for hearing of his Son's Condemnation, the old Gentleman came directly up to Town, and arrived before the Day appointed for his Execution, procuring a full Pardon by the Mediation of some powerful Friends.

To prevent his following the same Courses again, and exposing himself afresh to the Sentence of the Law, the old Gentleman put his Son Apprentice to a *Weaver*, but before he had served half a Year of his Time, he ran away from his Master, and took to his old Courses again. It was his Pride, to make all whom he conversed with as bad as himself, an Instance of which appeared in what he did by one *David Hudges*, a Cousin of his by the Mother's Side. This Youth going to *Kingston* Assizes along with *Tom*, a few Days after he came to Town, he was prevailed upon by him to pick a Pocket in the Court; in which Action being apprehended, he was immediately try'd, and condemned to be hang'd upon a Gibbet within Sight of the Bench, as a Terror to others. This Week was fatal enough to young *Hudges*; for he came to *London* on the *Monday*, on *Tuesday* and *Wednesday* spent and lost 10 *l*. which was all the Money he had, along with Whores and Sharpers, on *Thursday* in the Evening pick'd a Pocket, was condemned on *Friday* Morning, and hang'd on *Saturday*. This was the End of one of *Kelsey*'s hopeful Pupils, who had the Impudence to boast of it.

Another of the Actions of this Extravagant, was, his robbing the Earl of *Feversham*'s Lodgings. This Nobleman was General of the Forces in the Reign of King *James* the Second, and consequently had a Centinel always at his Door. *Tom* dress'd himself in a Foot Soldier's Habit one Evening, and went up to the Fellow who was then on Duty, asking him a great many Questions, and offering, at last, to make him drink, if he knew where to get a couple of Pots of good Beer. The Soldier told him there was very good a little beyond *Catherine-Street*, but he durst not leave his Post so long as to fetch it. Can't I

take your Place, brother Soldier? quoth *Tom*, I [...] sure if some Body be at the Post there can b[...] Danger. The Soldier thank'd him, took the Six[...] pence, and went his Way; mean while *Tom's* A[...] sociates got into the House, and were rifling it a[...] fast as they could. They had not quite done wh[...] the Soldier came back; whereupon *Tom* gave [...] Two-pence more, and desired him to get a little T[...] bacco also. While the poor Fellow was gone [...] this, the Villains came out, and *Tom* went w[...] them, carrying off not only above 200 *l* worth [...] Plate, but even the Soldier's Musquet. The ne[...] Day the Centinel was call'd to Account, and com[...] mitted to Prison. At the ensuing Court Martial [...] was ordered to run the Gantloop for losing his Pie[...] and then was sent to *Newgate*, and loaded with [...] rons, on Suspicion of being privy to the Robbery[...] where, after nine Months Confinement, he miserab[...] perished.

Kelsey, after this, broke open the House of th[...] Lady *Grace Pierpoint*, at *Thistleworth*, and to[...] from thence a great many valuable Things. B[...] soon after one of his Companions impeached hi[...] for this Fact; whereupon, being informed that th[...] Officers were in search after him, he fled to the Camp of King *William* in *Flanders*. Here he g[...] considerable Booty out of his Majesty's Tent, a[...] from other general Officers, with which he got t[...] *Amsterdam*, and sold it to a *Jew*; whom he als[...] robb'd afterwards, and sold what he had gotten to [...] nother *Jew* at *Rotterdam*, from whence he re-[...] bark'd for *England*.

He had not been long returned to his native Coun[...] try, before he was detected in breaking open the House of a *Linnen-Draper* in *Cheapside*, which pu[...] a final End to his Liberty, tho' not to his Villany. For being sent to *Newgate*, and having no Hope[...] of ever getting out any more, unless to go to *Ty-* *burn*, he grew desperate, and resolved to do all the Mischief he could there. Mr. *Goodman*, one of the Turnkeys of that Jayl, being one Day drinking in the Common Side Cellar, *Kelsey* privately stabb'd him into the Belly with a Knife, of which Wound he instantly died. For this Murder he received Sentence of Death at the next Sessions in the *Old-Baily*, and a Gibbet being erected in *Newgate-Street*, near the Prison, he was thereon executed on *Friday* the 13th of *June*, 1690, being then no more than twenty Years of Age. As a Terror to the other Prisoners who were then in Confinement, his Body was suffered to hang on the Gibbet the Space of three Hours.

The LIFE of RICHARD KEELE.

A More impudent Villain was never heard of than this of whom we are now to give some Account, who was born of very good and reputable Parents at *Rumsey* in *Hampshire*; and having no other Education bestowed upon him than meer Reading and Writing, he was put Apprentice to a Barber and Perriwigmaker living at *Winchester*, whose Daughter he married, but after seven or eight Years Cohabitation, left her, and married another Woman in *London*, who had fifty Pounds *per Annum*, during Life, quarterly paid her by a Justice of the Peace, living in St *Margaret*'s Church-Yard at *Westminster*.

His sole Delight and Pleasure was ever in keeping Company with the greatest Rogues, Whores, and Thieves, from whom he had learnt so much of their bad Manners, that he exceeded them all in Villany; specially when he came to be a Bailiff, the general Character of which Office is, that the Beginning is detestable, the Course desperate, and the End damnable. Soon after he was married to his last Wife, he kept an Ale-house in *Milk-Alley*, near St. *Ann*'s Church, but he had not been long in that Employment, ere he was arrested at the Suit of one *Thomas*, a Soldier in the First Regiment of Foot-Guards, in an Action of one hundred Pound, for keeping Company with his Wife *Isabella Thomas*, a most notorious Shoplift, whom he encouraged in her Thieving till she was condemned, but obtained Mercy.

Being now arrested, as aforesaid, and so little beloved that none would bail him, he was carried to the Gate-house Prison at *Westminster*, where he had not been a Week, before forty Robberies were laid to his Charge, for which he way heavy loaded with Irons, but no Prosecution commencing against him, he was admitted to Bail for them before Sir *Peter King*, then Recorder of *London*. But still being a Prisoner on *Thomas*'s Action, he removed himself by a Writ of *Habeas Corpus* to the *Fleet* Prison, from whence he was shortly after removed again to *Newgate*, upon an Information exhibited against him for speaking several blasphemous Expressions when in the Gatehouse; and being try'd for the same at the *Sessions House* in the *Old Bailey*, before the Lord Chief Justice *Parker*, the Sentence of the Court was, *That he should stand twice in the Pillory, once at Charing-Cross, and once without Temple Bar, and to suffer Imprisonment for a whole Year.*

When the Time of Confinement was expir'd, and his notorious Fellow had procured his Liberty, he then turned a Bailiff's Follower, but his Income thereby being being but very small, and supposing a ef the more profitable Employment, he stole a Coat and Perriwig, for which he was committed to Newgate. On his Trial being found guilty of Felony, he was burnt in the Hand, and ordered to hard Labour at the Workhouse for twelve Months. Accordingly being carried with one *William Low-*

ther, and *Charles Houghton*, two other Felons, to *Bridewell* in *Clerkenwell*, on the 19th of *September*, 1713, they made a Mutiny, upon Captain *Boreman*'s going to put Irons on them, to prevent their making an Escape out of his Goal. In this Fray *Charles Houghton* was shot dead on the Spot, *William Lowther* shot in several Parts of his Body, but not mortally wounded, and *Dick Keele* had one of his Eyes shot out. But these Villains having killed *Edward Perry*, one of the Turnkeys of *Bridewell*, *Keele* and *Lowther* were committed by Justice *Fuller* to *Newgate* again, where the former of them was kept in the Master side, at the Charge of *Isabel Thomas*, that notorious Shoplift; who being now at Liberty, by pleading to her Majesty's Pardon but in *August* last, and followed Shoplifting as much as ever, till at last she was apprehended and received Sentence of Death again, on *Monday* the 14th of *December*, 1713, for privately stealing 62 Yards of Silk, Value six Pounds, from the Shop of *Philip Bass*, a Mercer on *Ludgate-Hill*.

Now *Dick Keele* being afraid of coming to a Trial for the Murder of *Edward Perry* at the Sessions-House in the *Old-Bailey*, he put himself into a Salivation, and perhaps it might not be without a Cause, for he was such a common Fellow, that he would debauch himself with the very worst of Whores. But now having no other Device to delay his coming to Justice any longer, he was at the next Sessions brought to a Trial, on which the Evidence for the Queen being very full and clear to the Fact laid to his Charge, he and *William Lowther* were both found guilty of Wilful Murder. Notwithstanding this, such was the Assurance and Impudence of *Keele*, whilst in the Condemned Hold, that he was sure he should not die, and therefore made no Preparation for his approaching Death, as supposing his Sister, who lived with a Person of Quality, would procure his Pardon. However, mistaking his Aim, he and his Comrade *Will Lowther* were executed on *Clerkenwell Green*, on *Wednesday* the 23d of *December*, 1713, the first being 32 Years of Age, and the other but 23.

It was always the Custom of this unhappy Person to say, that he gloried in all manner of Wickedness; and if it ever was his Fate to come under the Circumstances of Death for the Breach of any Law, he should so far behave himself above the common Nature of Mankind, as not to shed Tears for his Offence, when launching into the very Gulph of Eternity, and therefore, like other warning Fools, he should not make any Confession of his Sins to any Person that presumed to ask him at the very Place of Execution, in case he was to come to such an untimely End.

But it is evidently seen, that a shameful Death commonly overtakes such Wretches for their Wickedness, and tho' this Fellow pretended to out-brave the very Terrors thereof, yet when he came under

the

tha unhappy Circumstance of being cut off by the Sword of Justice for his Crimes, no Man could bewail and bemoan himself more than he did, however, his Sorrow was not so much for the Thought of his Sins, as being sent out of the Land of the Living in his almost juvenile Years He stood to his Resolution of Silence, tho' not of Bravery, in not making a Confession of all his Sins, to those who desired it, for according to the Papers put out of him, he never discover'd in particular his robbing of a Shoemaker living once near Lincolns-Inn Fields, call'd Bond and Judgment. An Account whereof take as follows.

One Day Dick Keele being out of Money, by his paying twenty or thirty Pounds to an Adversary, whom that notorious Shoplift Isabel Thomas used to rob, he was resolved to make up those pull-backs by robbing himself. So meeting with Bond and Judgment, as aforesaid, (a very honest Man, so called upon his lending Money to People upon such an Assignment made over to him; and as soon as the Time was expired that the Money was to be paid, upon Non-payment, instantly, taking the Advantage thereof, and turned the Person and whole Family out of Doors, by seizing on all they had) I say, meeting with him not far from Paddington, and having been over-reached himself before upon an Occasion by the same Fellow, he commanded him to stand and deliver. Quoth Bond and Judgment, Don't you know me, Sir? Ay, reply'd Dick, you Son of a Whore, I know you to be a mercenary Rogue, that would send your Father and Mother to Gaol for the Fillip of a Farthing, therefore it is but a just Judgment befell you, to take all you have from you. So clapping a Pistol to his Breast, poor Bond and Judgment was obliged to stop the Fury of the Bullets, by giving him threescore Guineas, which was such a sinking of his Stock, that he went to Newgate quickly after, and was hard put to it to raise Money for an Habeus Corpus, to remove his corrupted Carcass to the Queen's Bench Prison in Southwark.

Another Time Dick Keele being very well mounted on a Horse, and accoutred with Sword and Pistols, who should he meet on Hounslow-Heath, but C———, lately a Tradesman, but then an Officer, as well mounted as himself. Nevertheless, he having as much Courage as the pretended Son of Mars, he gave him and ugly Word of Command, which was, stand and deliver.

Here our military Man was at a Stand indeed, what to say to him; but thinking the bloody Colour of his Cloaths might frighten him, quoth he, ' Don't ' you see whose Livery I wear? See whose Livery ' you wear, replied Dick, why, are you a Footman? ' No, said C——— again, I am an Officer in the ' Army, therefore to your Peril be it, if you pre- ' sume to stop me when I am about unlawful Occa-

sions. Nay, replied, Dick, if you are about law- ' ful Occasions, I am about unlawful Ones: ' Therefore deliver what you have, or else we must ' try who is the best Man, Said, C———I don't ' bear a Commission to fight with Highwaymen, ' I only wear Her Majesty's Cloth to fight for my ' Queen and Country Why then, replied Dick, ' that Cloth, nor any other, must not be Protection ' from my Arrest; therefore, as this Pistol is my ' Tip-staff, I demand your Money upon Pain of ' Death ' So taking (not finding any Money about him) his Coat, Waistcoat, and Breeches, he ordered him to take up another Sute on the regimental Account.

He utterly hated and abhorred his last Wife, for the sake of Arabella or Isabel Thomas, otherwise called Isabel Jones, alias Bolton, alias Wildman, alias King, besides several other Names, to shrow'd her from the Severity of Justice, of which Custom she had much Occasion, especially after her robbing a great Mercer in Cheapside, of about sixty Pounds worth of Silk, for which she had like to have been apprehended, but only she made her Escape thro' the back Alleys to her Lodgings in Jewin street

She was about thirty three Years of Age, born at Blackburn in Lancashire, and about eight Years before her Death came up to London, where she was a Servant in several worthy Families, in which she behaved herself very honestly, but falling at last into wicked Company, she soon learned to be wicked too, and committed divers Felonies in the Shops of Mercers, Linnen-Drapers, and Lace-men, living in and about the Cities of London and Westminster, some of which being clearly proved upon her, she was several Times burnt in the Hand.

She formerly received Sentence of Death for stealing several Yards of Muslin out of Mr Worman's Shop, a Linnen-Draper, living at the Corner of Barbican and Red-Cross street, but received Mercy, by pleading to the Queen's most gracious Pardon the August following Next she was apprehended for privately stealing fifty two Yards of Sarcenet, Value six Pounds, out of the Shop of Mr Phillip Bass, a Mercer on Ludgate-Hill, beforementioned, for which she received Sentence of Death again, and was executed at Tyburn, on Wednesday the 23d of December, 1713, with James Gosnel, Thomas Hudson, Tapster to Mr Richard Jewkes, a Victualler, at the Sign of the White Horse, in White Horse Yard, in Drury Lane, Giles Spencer, Samuel Hicks, James Gamblon, Anthony Martin, James Urwin, Richard Layton, Sarah Bugden, alias Small, alias Jones, alias Burgis, alias Evans, and Mary Baker, otherwise called Jane Cook, Lobby, and Hanun, or Harnale, from the four Men to whom she was marry'd, who were all alive together, for which she suffered Death.

The LIFE of PATRICK O-BRYAN.

THE Parents of *Patrick O-Bryan* were very poor, they liv'd at *Loughrea*, a Market Town in the County of *Galway* and Province of *Connaught* in *Ireland* *Patrick* came over into *England* in the Reign of King *Charles* the Second, and listed himself into his Majesty's *Coldstream* Regiment of Guards, so called from their being first raised at a Place in *Scotland* which bears that Name How good a Soldier he made is little to our Purpose, only we may observe, that 'twas not possible he should be more expert in the Use of his Arms than he was in the Practise of all manner of Vices, The Small Allowance of a private Centinel was far too little for him, and he was not like a great many poor Men, who make the same Complaint, yet sit down honestly to live on it, and only endeavour to make up the Scantiness of their Salary by their good Husbandry No, *Patrick*'s Maxims were widely different from those; he was resolv'd to have Money if there were any in the Land, and not to starve in the midst of Plenty, from a foolish Principle of Justice and Honour The first Thing he did was to run in Debt at all the Publick Houses and Shops that would trust him, and when his Credit would maintain him any longer, he had Recourse to borrowing of all he knew, being pretty well furnish'd with the common Defence of his Countrymen, a Front that would brazen out any Thing, and even laugh at the Persons whom he had imposed on, to their very Faces By such Means as these he subsisted for some Time

At last, when he found Fraud would no longer support him, he went out upon the Foot-pad Dr *Tewer* the Parson of *Croydon*, was one of those whom he stopp'd This Man had in his Youth been try'd at the *Old-Bailey*, and burnt in the Hand, for stealing a Silver Cup *Patrick* knew him very well, and greeted him upon their lucky Meeting; telling him, *That he could not refuse lending a little Assistance to one of his old Profession.* The Doctor assured him, *That he had not made a Word, if he had had any Money about him, but he had not so much as a single Farthing.* Then, says *Patrick*, I must have your Gown, Sir. *If you can win it,* quoth the Doctor, *so you shall, but let me have the Chance of a Game at Cards* To this O *Bryan* consented, and the Reverend Gentleman pull'd out a Pack of the Devil's Books; with which they fairly play'd at *All-fours*, to decide, who should have the black Robe. *Patrick* had the Fortune to win, and the other went home very contentedly, as he had lost his *Divinity* in such an equitable manner Indeed, according to the Idea which this Story seems to give of the Doctor, our Highwayman might become a Canonical Habit as well as he, and be no more a Scandal to the sacred Cloth

There was in *Patrick*'s Time a famous Posture-master in *Pall-Mall*, his Name was *Clark* Our Adventurer met him one Day on *Primrose-Hill*, and

saluted him with *Stand and deliver* But he was mightily disappointed, for the nimble *Harlequin* jump'd over his Head, and, instead of reviving his Heart with a few Guineas, made it sink into his Breeches for Fear, he imagining the Devil was come to be merry with him before his Time, for no human Creature, he thought could do the like This Belief was a little Mortification to him at first, but he soon saw the Truth of the Story in the publick Prints, where Mr *Clark*'s Friends took Care to put it, and then our *Teague*'s Qualm of Conscience was changed into a Vow of Revenge, if ever he met with his Tumblership again, which however he never did

Another Time *Patrick O-Bryan* was got behind a Hedge in the Way to *Hackney*, late in the Evening, in order to wait for a Booty He had not been here long before he heard a very merry Dialogue between one of the Sons of *Apollo*, and an old Bawd, whom he had employ'd to get him into the Company of a young Lady at a Boarding-School just by The Conversation ended so much to our Poet's Satisfaction, that pronounc'd the following Lines in a kind of Rapture

Oh! thou art wondrous in thy Art! thy Head
Was form'd for mighty Things, like those who rule
The Fates of Empires. But our kinder Stars
Have sent thee to direct the Realms of Love

Just as his Transport was over, out stepp'd O-*Bryan*, and presented a Pistol to the Head that conceiv'd those fine Imaginations It must be allow'd, that such a Surprize as this was enough to make the poor Bard a little cooler, but left it should not cool him enough, O *Bryan* order'd him to strip himself to the Skin, which he did with abundance of Reluctance, for the fine Embroider'd Sute of Clothes he had on was only hired as an additional Charm to his Verses, that he might the more effectually win the young Lady's Heart. Madam the Procuress was also dress'd in her richest Brocade, that her Visit might be perform'd with the better Grace. She suffer'd the same Fate, and was reduc'd to the Condition of our first Parents before the Fall; *Patrick* telling them both, *That as he perceived neither of them had any Religion before, 'twas proper they should begin to have some; and therefore out of Charity to their Souls he had converted them to Adamitism* We may suppose they did not very well like their new Religion But *Patrick* was a downright Pope, if they had not hearkened to his Arguments he would have made use of his Arms, and fairly have sent him out of the World, because they would not be implicitly obedient to their Superiors in it This they both consider'd, and so thought it their best Way to receive his *Ipse dixit*

O *Bryan* at last intirely deserted from his Regiment, and got a Horse, on which he robb'd on the Highway a long Time. One Day in particular he met *Nell Gwyn* in her Coach on the Road to *Winchester*, and addreſs himſelf to her in the following Manner *Madam, I am a Gentleman, and, as you may ſee, a very able one I have done a great many ſignal Services to the Fair Sex, and have in Return been all my Life long maintain'd by them Now, as I know you are a charitable W——e, and have a great Value for Men of my Abilities, I make bold to aſk you for a little Money, though I never have had the Honour of ſerving you in particular However, if an Opportunity ſhould ever fall in my Way, you may depend upon it I will exert myſelf to the uttermoſt, for I ſcorn to be ungrateful* Nell ſeem'd very well pleas'd with what he had ſaid, and made him a Preſent of ten Guineas ,However, whether ſhe wiſh'd for the Opportunity he ſpoke of, or no, cannot be determin'd, becauſe ſhe did not explain herſelf, but if a Perſon may gueſs from her general Character, ſhe never was afraid of a Man in her Life

While *Patrick* robb'd on the Highway, he perverted ſeveral young Men to the ſame bad Courſe of Life One *Claudius Wilt* in particular was hang'd at *Worceſter* for a Robbery committed in his Company, though 'twas the firſt he was ever concern'd in. Several others came to the ſame End through his Seducements, and he himſelf was at laſt executed at *Gloceſter*, for a Fact committed within two Miles of that City When he had hung the uſual Time, his Body was cut down and deliver'd to his Acquaintance, that they might bury him as they pleaſed, But being carry'd home to one of their Houſes, ſome Body imagin'd they perceiv'd Life in him, whereupon an able Surgeon was privately procured to bleed him, who by that and other Means which he uſed brought him again to his Senſes The Thing was kept an entire Secret from the World, and 'twas hoped by his Friends that he would ſpend the Remainder of his forfeited Life, which he had ſo ſurprizingly retriev'd, to a much better Purpoſe than he had employ'd the former Part of it

Theſe Friends offer'd to contribute in any manner he ſhould deſire towards his living privately and honeſtly. He promis'd them very fairly, and for ſome Time kept within due Bounds, while the Senſe of what he had eſcap'd remain'd freſh in his Mind, but the Time was not long before, in Spite of all the Admonitions and Aſiſtances he receiv'd, he return'd again to his Villainies like a Dog to his Vomit, leaving his kind Benefactors, ſtealing a freſh Horſe, and taking once more to the Highway, where he grew as audacious as ever

It was not above a Year after his former Execution, before he met with the Gentleman again who had convicted him before, and attack'd him in the ſame Manner The poor Gentleman was not ſo much ſurprized at being ſtopp'd on the Road as he was at ſeeing the Perſon who did it, being certain

'twas the very Man whom he had ſeen executed This Conſternation was ſo great, that he could not help diſcovering it, by ſaying, How comes this to paſs? I thought you had been hanged a Twelvemonth ago. So I was, ſays Patrick, and therefore you ought to imagine that what you ſee now is only my Ghoſt However, leſt you ſhould be ſo uncivil as to hang my Ghoſt too, I think it my beſt Way to ſecure you Up on this he diſcharg'd a Piſtol thro' the Gentleman's Head, and, not content with that, diſmounting his Horſe, he drew out a ſharp Hanger from his Side, and cut the dead Carcaſs into ſeveral Pieces

This piece of Barbarity was followed by another, which was rather more horrible yet *Patrick* with four more as bad as himſelf, having Intelligence that *Lancelot Wilmot*, Eſq; of *Wiltſhire*, had a great deal of Money and Plate in his Houſe, which ſtood in a lonely Place, at about a Mile and a half from *Trowbridge*, they beſet it one Night, and got in When they were entered, they ty'd and gagg'd the Servants, and then proceeded to the old Gentleman's Room, where he was in Bed with his Lady They ſerved both theſe in the ſame Manner, and then went in the Daughter's Chamber This young Lady they ſeverally forced after one another to their brutal Pleaſure, and when they had done, moſt inhuman, ſtabb'd her, becauſe ſhe endeavoured to get from their Arms. They next acted the ſame Tragedy on the Father and Mother, *which they told them, was becauſe they did not breed up their Daughter to better Manners* Then they rifled the Houſe of every Thing valuable which they could find in it, that was fit to be carried off, to the Value in all of 2500 *l*. After which they ſet the Building on fire, and left it to conſume with the unhappy Servants that was in it.

Patrick continued above two Years after this before he was apprehended, and poſſibly might never have been ſuſpected of this Fact, if one of his bloody Accomplices had not been hang'd for another Crime at *Bedford* This Wretch at the Gallows confeſſed all the Particulars, and diſcovered the Perſons concerned with him, a little while after which, *O Brian* was ſeized at his Lodging in *Little Suffolk Street*, near the *Hay-Market*, and committed to *Newgate*, from whence before the next Aſſizes he was convey'd to *Salſbury*, where he own'd the Fact himſelf, and all the other Particulars of his wicked Actions that have been here related He was now a ſecond Time executed, and great Care was taken to do it effectually There was not, indeed, much Danger of his recovering any more, becauſe his Body was immediately hung in Chains, near the Place where the barbarous Deed was perpetrated He was in the 31ſt Year of his Age at the Time of his Execution, which was on *Tueſday* the 30th of *April*, in the Year 1689.

The LIFE of ELEONER SYMPSON.

ELEONOR SYMPSON was born of very honeſt Parents, at *Henly* upon *Thames*, in *Oxfordſhire*. She laid a Baſtard, got on her by the Clerk of the Pariſh, to her own Father, who was a Farmer, for which Piece of Impudence being turned out of Doors, ſhe came up to *London*, and turned common Whore. Whilſt ſhe continued this wicked Courſe of Life, ſhe picked up late one Night a Linnen-Draper, to whom pretending ſo great Modeſty and Baſhfulneſs, that ſhe was aſham'd to go with a Man into a Tavern or an Alehouſe, they at laſt agreed to go into a dark Alley.

Here, whilſt the Cully was feeling what Gender he was of, ſhe in the mean Time was feeling for his Watch, which privately drawing half way out of his Fob, quoth ſhe, *The Watch is coming Sir* He being eager on the Game of High Gammer Cook, cry'd, *D——n the Watch, I don't value the Watch of a Farthing* At laſt, when ſhe had got the Watch out of his Fob indeed, and tranſported it into her own Pocket, ſhe ſaid again, *Pray, dear Sir, make Haſte, for I vow the Watch is juſt here.* He ſtill not apprehending her meaning, reply'd again, *D——n the Watch, I tell you I don't value the Watch of a Farthing*

The Sport being over, they parted, but he had not gone far, when beginning to have a Thought about him, he felt for his Watch, and finding it out of it's Precincts, he made all the Haſte he could after his Miſtreſs, and overtaking her in St *Martins-Lane*, charged her with a Conſtable, who committed her to the *Round Houſe* all Night.

Next Morning the Linnen Draper appeared againſt her at St *Martin's* Veſtry, where charging her upon Oath, before the Juſtices, of her robbing him of his Watch, Quoth one of the old *Mumpſimnſſes*, *Well, Mrs* Jelliver, *what have you to ſay for yourſelf now? you ſee the Fact is ſworn poſſitively againſt you* Mrs *Jelliver*, as he called her, dropping a very fine Courteſy, and looking as demure as a Whore at a Chriſtening, ſaid in her Defence, *That going home laſt Night to my Lodging, that Gentleman there, who is my Accuſer, did ſo far prevail with me as to be nought with him in a dark Alley, and whilſt he was jumbling me up againſt a Wall, Sirs, to paſs the Time away, I play'd with his Watch, which being half way out of his Fob, I told him, let him deny it if he can, that the Watch was coming, whereupon he reply'd, D——n the Watch, he did not value the Watch of a Farthing, nay, when I had the Watch quite out of his Fob, and had put it into my own Pocket, at the ſame Time pointing to it, and plainly telling him the Watch was here, ſtill he was ſo eager at his Work, that he ſaid again, D——n the Watch, I tell you I don't value it of a Farthing, ſo thinking it of more Conſequence than that comes to, I was carrying it home for my own Uſe, but ſince he requires it again, here it is Gentlemen, and I freely return it him again with all my Heart.* At this Confeſſion, the Juſtices were all ready to ſplit their Sides a Laughing; and making the Complainant give his Miſtreſs a Guinea for his Folly, he had his Watch again, and ſhe being diſcharged, went about her Buſineſs.

Another Time *Sympſon* being pick'd up by a Couple of Captains in the *Coldſtream*, or ſecond Regiment of *Foot Guards*, they carried her to *Rigby's* Ordinary, at the *Roe Buck* in *Suffolk Street*, where having a good Supper, and being alſo much elevated with Wine, they began to act ſeveral Beaſtialities upon her; but ſhe made them pay for their Frolick in the end, for having drank them to ſuch a Pitch, that they both fell into a ſound Sleep upon the Floor, honeſt *Sympſon* began to dive into their Fobs and Pockets, whence ſhe took a couple of gold Watches, two Purſes of Guineas, ſome Silver, two gold Snuff-Boxes, two diamond Rings off their Fingers, broke the ſilver Hilts off their Swords, then ſh——t——g in both their Perukes, which ſhe clapt on their Heads again, ſhe went off without ſaying ſo much as a Word to any Body. When they awoke, and found their Loſs, what Vollies of Oaths and Curſes flew about the Room, like Peals of great Ordnance! There was ſtriving betwixt them, who ſhould ſwear the faſteſt, but all to no Purpoſe, the Whore being gone they knew not whether, they were forced to be contented with their Calamity, and what was worſe too, to pay a Reckoning of four Pounds into the Bargain.

One Time *Nell* meeting a Butcher's Son of *Clare Market*, who was a J—— in the ſame County, he being diſpoſ'd to have a Game at *Tickle Tickle* with her, (for you muſt know, that by his Father's Trade, he was given to the Fleſh) ſhe takes him into *Piſſing-Alley*, in *Hollywell Street*, otherwiſe called the Backſide of St *Clements* in the *Strand*, ſo eminently noted for Taylors ſelling there their Cabbage. No ſooner were they arrived into that dark Hole, ſo fit for Fornication and Adultery, but as he was lugging out his Dagger, to whip her thro' the Beard, ſhe at the ſame Time lugged out his ſilver hilted Sword from his Side, which he never paid for to this Day, and cry'd, *Pray Sir, don't play the Spaniard upon me at once, I ſhall never be able to bear it* The J—— who was a Man of no great Metal at the beſt, reply'd, *My Dear, I'll uſe you gently,* and immediately, (being dead drunk) he fell down on his Arſe. Hereupon *Nell* takes up her Coats, ſtops his Mouth with her T——y M——y, and piſſes down his Throat His W—— now fancying himſelf in a Tavern, and taking *Nell's* warm Water for mull'd Wine, he ſaid, he was very well ſatisfied, and would pay the Reckoning next Day to a Farthing, and ſo fell aſleep, while *Nell* carried off his Sword, Wig, and Hat, and left him there wallowing in Sir Reverence, Urine, and other Naſtineſs, till ſomebody that came by carried him to the Place of his Habitation, laid him upon a Butcher's Block, and left him to ſhift for himſelf.

Now it happening to be about One of the Clock

on a

on a *Saturday* Morning, the Butcher who owned the Block was drinking at an adjacent Alehouse Whilst he was there, a Calf newly killed, but not drest, was stolen from before his Shop, which missing, he fell a swearing and staring like a Devil for his Loss, and called out to tne Man that was then putting out the Stands and Sheds against the Market-People came, and ask'd him if he knew any Thing of his Calf *D——n me,* reply'd the Fellow, *can't you see? why it lies upon your Block there By G——,* quoth he, *so it does; well,* Jack, *I beg your Pardon, for I did not see it till you told me* So taking out his Knife, and whetting it on his Steel, quoth he, *Prithee* Jack *come hither, and lend me a Hand to lift him on one of the Hooks, to flay him* The Butcher was briskly whetting his Knife still, and did not mind what his Calf was made of, till *Jack* coming to assist him, finding it was somewhat of a Man, said to him, *Master, this is* J——— *such a one, 'tis no Calf; but yet, Sir, as his Flesh may be a Novelty, I don't know but it may fetch a Penny in the Pound more than the best Mutton in the Market, considering he has fed himself a long Time upon laced Mutton, and will to his dying Day, if he can have it gratis, for he never loved to pay for any Thing in his Life, unless needs must when the Devil drives* The Butcher seeing his Mistake, kicks him off of the Block, but was bound over for it next Day, and had he not have made up his W——————p's Loss, by *Nel,* he had certainly been prosecuted for the Robbery

But a little after this Exploit, *Sympson* finding that her Tail brought her not the Comings in she expected, though she was a tolerable handsome Woman, and a good Tongue Pad, she was resolved to try what her Hands could do The first Experiment she made this Way, was at a certain Mercer's in *Bedford-street;* whither going in a Chair very well dress'd, with a Couple of sham Footmen attending her, in good Liveries, when she came into the Shop, she called for several Pieces of Silk to look on In the mean Time an Apple-Pasty coming in for the Family, she seemed on a sudden to be taken very ill and withdrew from the Place where she was, to the farther End of the Shop, and sat at the End of a Counter, under which was a great deal of rich Silks

Her Footman taking the Hint of her Illness, told the Journeyman, there happening then to be none but him, that they believed their Lady (who past for the Countess of *Colrain*) being newly married, longed for some of the Apple Pasty just then come in, for she was mighty apt to long of late for any Thing that was good The Journeyman pitying her Condition, presently ran up Stairs, and acquainted his Master and Mistress of the Matter They were mightily concerned at it, but before they came down, she gave her Footmen six whole Pieces of Silk, who put them into the Chair, the Chairmen not supposing any otherwise than that the suppos'd Lady had bought it

When the Mercer and his Wife came down, they invited her up Stairs, which Kindness, after some seeming Reluctancy, she accepted of, eat very heartily of the Pye, as she might have done of other Varieties which were there, but she refused them. When she had done, she returned them many Thanks

invited them to her Lodgings in St. *James's-Square,* and for their extraordinary Civility, promis'd to lay out five or six hundred Pounds with them, before she and her Lord went to *Ireland*

When she came down Stairs, she laid out four or five Guineas, and pitched upon other Silks, to the Value of one hundred and twenty Pounds, which ordering to be brought to her House as aforesaid in the Evening, (because she was going then to pay a Visit to the Dutchess of *Somerset* at *Northumberland House* at *Charing Cross,)* she then took Chair, and went off But within a few Hours afterwards, the Silks she had stol'n being miss'd, there was a great Outcry, the Mercer swearing that the longing Lady had long'd for more than she could eat, which proved as he said, for going to enquire after her in St. *James's-Square,* there was no finding the Lady *Colrain,* nor any Thing like it.

Another Time she went to a Dinnen-Draper's Shop in *Cornhill,* attended with a Couple of Foot men behind a hired Chariot, who knocking at the Door with an Authority, for it was then about eight or nine at Night in Winter Time, the Journeyman opened it, and gave Admission to this suppos'd Person of Quality, and her Attendants, whom she pretended to send to a Couple of Merchants by the *East-India-House* Being shew'd several Parcels of the finest Muslins, she pitched upon as much as came to eighty Pounds, when pulling out a Purse, in which she had not above twenty Guineas, and perhaps most of them Counters, quoth she, *Upon my Word, Sir, I have less Money about me than I thought for, so I cannot pay what I have agreed for, therefore I beg the Favour of you to let your young Lad, your Apprentice here, just step to Mr such a one, my Banker, in Lombard street, and telling him you are come from the Countess of Colrain, desire him to pay you one hundred Pounds upon Sight of this Note*

Away goes the Apprentice with the Note, and in came her two Footmen, who presently knocking down the Journeyman, stunn'd him to that Degree, that they carried off above two hundred Pounds worth of Muslin into the Chariot, and went off with it, before the other could recover himself After above a quarter of an Hour, calling down his Master he told him of the Disaster, and wondering the Apprentice did not come back in above an Hour's Time at last a Messenger was sent from the Banker, at whose House they found the Lad charged with a Constable, for bringing a forg'd Note But when the Master came in his Behalf, and told how the Matter was, to his Loss of above two hundred Pounds, he was discharged.

But not long after this notorious Robbery, *Sympson* was taken in the Act of Shoplifting at *Sturbridge* Fair, and was committed to *Cambridge* Gaol, and the Assizes following being try'd, she received Sentence of Death; whereupon she pleaded her Belly, and a Jury of Matrons being impannell'd, as is usual on such Occasions, she was brought in quick with Child, and was really so, for she was brought to Bed of a Girl before the Assizes following; when being called down to her former Judgment, she was hanged at *Cambridge,* upon *Saturday* the 10th of *July* 1714, aged twenty eight Years.

The LIFE *of* EDWARD HINTON.

EDWARD HINTON was born in *London* in the Year 1673 of very reputable Parents. In his younger Years he discover'd a strong Bent to Learning, which his Father cherish'd by putting him to St *Paul*'s School, that celebrated Seminary for Youth. This good Turn of Mind was however soon overcome by a vicious one, which seem'd also to be innate, and grew stronger as he grew older. Even at nine Years of Age, 'tis said, he robb'd one of his Sisters of Sixpences and other small Pieces to the Value of Thirty Shillings, and kept abroad in Company with Boys like himself till he had spent and lost it all. This was a very indifferent proof of what the old People were so proud of, his Integrity, and Inclination to Virtue.

Indulgent Parents are more forward to attribute the Faults of their Children to the want of knowing better, then to any Propensity which they have to be wicked. This was the Case here. After a little Correction, young *Hinton* was sent to School again, upon his promising to be a better Boy for the future. But in vain, alas! were his Promises. Thieving was grown into a Habit with him, and there was no Opportunity of getting Money or any Thing else conveniently that ever escap'd him. He went so far at last as to rob his Father's Counting-House of a considerable Sum of Money, which he carry'd to a lewd Woman, with whom he was soon after taken on *Cambridge Heath*.

Old Mr *Hinton* perceiv'd by this Time, that there was no Good to be expected from his Son if he let him stay any longer in *London*, so he thought it the best Way to send him where he might have no Room to practise his Villanies, and accordingly he procured the King's Letter to make him a Reformade on board a Man of War. In this Station he sail'd to the *Streights*, and behav'd himself handsomely in several Engagements. At *Cadiz* he fought with a *Spaniard*, who attack'd him one Day when he went ashore, left the Don dead on the Place, and made his Escape aboard the Ship again undiscover'd. But as soon as the Ship return'd to *England*, he quitted her, on a Pretence that a younger Reformade was preferr'd before him on the Death of a Lieutenant. Whether or know this was the real Cause is uncertain, but from this Time he became a profess'd Thief.

The first Action which he perform'd in Conjunction with others, was the robbing Admiral *Carter*'s Country-House. Soon after this he and his Comrades broke open the Lady *Dartmouth*'s House on *Black Heath*, and stole Plate to a great Value, which they sold to a Refiner near *Cripplegate*. We mention this last Circumstance, because the Refiner gave a signal Proof of his Exactness in Trade, and Caution of buying stollen Goods, for the Day after the Plate was sold, a Golden Cup and Cover were advertised among other Things, whereas the Thieves

had valued it all together as Silver, believing the Cup to be only gilt. When *Hinton* saw this Advertisement, he said smartly to his Companions, *What a Rogue was this to cheat us so! You see, there's no trusting any Body, nor any such Thing as a fair Dealer in the World.* This Reflection from him, without Doubt, was very entertaining.

Hinton was some Time after apprehended for this Robbery, and condemn'd at *Maidstone* Assizes, but his Youth, and the Intercession of his Friends procured him a Pardon. He was again taken up for breaking open and robbing the House of Sir *John Friend* at *Hackney*, for which he also receiv'd Sentence of *Death*, but was a second Time so far indulged as to have a Halter transmuted into *Transportation*, in order to which he was soon after put aboard with other Convicts. One would have thought he had now been safe enough, for he drew the rest of the Convicts into a Conspiracy, to get the Ship's Company under the Hatches, and make their Escape in the Long Boat, which they effected near the *Isle of Wight*, *Hinton* having first beat the Captain with a Rope's End, as a Return for being serv'd so himself.

He was no sooner ashore than he left his Company, and travell'd alone through the Woods and By-Ways, being in a very torn and rusty Habit. This Distress obliged him to sink from stealing to begging, which he practised all the Way to *Hounslow-Heath*, telling the People a lamentable Story of his having been shipwreck'd. But he soon alter'd his Tone when he saw a convenient Opportunity, for on *Hounslow-Heath* he unhors'd a Country Farmer and mounted in his Place. Nor was it long after before he changed this Horse for a better, and his own ragged Suit for a very genteel one, with a Gentleman he met.

Being now got among some of his old Gang, they continued some Months to rob on the Highway almost every Day that pass'd. The *Buckinghamshire* Lace-men, and Stage Coaches, in particular, were afraid to travel for them. *Hinton* by himself, at two several Times, robb'd a *Dutch* Colonel of his Money, Horse, Arms, and Cloak, and another Gentleman, who had Courage enough to exchange a Pistol with him. This Gentleman was wounded in the Leg by *Hinton*'s Fire, and our young Highwayman perceiving it, was so generous as to lend him his Assistance, and accompany him as far as within a little Way of *Epsom*, when he left him, in order to take Care of himself, for he very much question'd whether the Gentleman would act the same generous Part, if he once had his Enemy in his Power.

One Day, after robbing the Passengers in the *Southampton* Coach, they were so closely pursued, that some of the Gang were taken, and though *Hinton* had the good Fortune this Time to escape, yet the Society being broken, he did not care to venture any more on the Highway alone, whereupon he return'd to his old Vocation of House-breaking, picking of Pockets, &c till after the following Accident

An old *French* Gentlewoman had her House broke open one Night, and she was found the next Morning dead on the Floor, with her Mouth gagg'd, and her Chair upon her No Body could guess at the Villains, but they found on Examination that her Money was all gone, and they imagin'd her Death might be occasioned by her falling down in that Posture She was ty'd in the Chair, and therefore might easily be stifled A Night was appointed for the Funeral, and Providence was left to discover the Authors of this Tragedy When the Company were got together, who were to attend the Corpse, it was observ'd by some Body that one *Dewster*, a Grandson of the old Woman's, changed his Colour, and trembled, as they try'd his Gloves on This created such a Suspicion, that he was charged with the Fact, which he confess'd, and impeach'd his Accomplices, among whom his own Brother, and one *Butler*, were found guilty of the Murder and Robbery, and hang'd in Chains for the same

Hinton was nam'd as a Party concern'd, and talk'd of publickly as such, yet he remain'd unapprehended till after the Execution of those above mention'd At last he was taken and committed for some other Fact, of which being acquitted, a Bill was brought in against him for this *Dewster*, upon whose Evidence the two former were convicted, was not now to be found, nevertheless, the circumstantial Proofs against him were very strong, for it was sworn, that he was lurking about the old Woman's House, and that he was seen to go in, and come out, at her Door the Night before she was found dead But the Time that *Hinton* avoided being apprehended, had given him Opportunity to prepare against all this, for he had secured so many Evidences, and their Depositions were so positive, and so agreeable one to another, that the Court were induced to believe him innocent, and Discharged him accordingly As this was so extraordinary a Case, it may not be displeasing to our Readers, if we give some Account of the Witnesses, and the Substance of what they deposed

The first that appeared on his Behalf was a well dress'd young Man, who declared, That he and another Gentleman going through *Somerset-House-Yard*, on the Day set forth in the Indictment, they met Mr *Hinton*, who had been his School-Fellow, and whom he was surpriz'd to find there, having been inform'd that he was transported for Crimes, which he was very sorry for That Mr *Hinton* confess'd his having been order'd for *Transportation*, expressing at the same Time a great Concern for his Guilt, but that he had made his Escape, because he was put aboard as a common Felon, and was now waiting to see what his Friends would do for him, in order to his transporting himself, which he was resolv'd to do the first Opportunity That finding Mr *Hinton* so sensible of his Offences, he desired his Company to *Chelsea*, intending to make use of the Time they were together to exhort him to a more regular Course of Life for the future That Mr *Hinton* accepting the Offer, they took Water at *Somerset Stairs*, and went up to the *Star* at *Chelsea*, where they staid till Seven o'Clock at Night, and then came down to a Publick House on the *Bank-Side*, supp'd on a Dish of Fowls and Bacon, staid there till almost eleven, then cross'd the Water to *Somerset-Stairs*, went together into the *Strand*, and there parted

All this he deliver'd with a very good Grace,

and being ask'd how he came to remember the Day of the Month so exactly ? He reply'd, That a few Days after he heard a Paper of the Murder cry'd about the Street, and buying it, found Mr *Hinton's* Name among the Murderers, whereupon he made a *Memorandum* in his Pocket-Book. Here he shew'd his Pocket Book to the Court, and then went on telling them, That he made all the Speed he could to his Friend that was with them, and to the Waterman who carry'd them, shew'd them both the Paper, and desired them also to take Notice of the Day, because Mr *Hinton* being a Man of a bad Character if any Rogue should swear against him, he might be hang'd for what, as they were both sensible, he was entirely innocent of

The next of honest Mr *Hinton's* Evidences was the pretended Friend of the former, who said, That he saw the Prisoner and his Friend the last Deposer talk together in *Somerset-House Yard*, but knowing on what Subject That then they went to *Chelsea*, where the former Evidence was very earnest with the Prisoner to reform some ill Practices he had been guilty of, That a few Days after his Friend the former Evidence came to him, desired him to take Notice of the Day they went to *Chelsea*, and bear in Mind the Person that accompany'd them, which he did, and was certain the Prisoner at the Bar was the very Man This Evidence was also very positive on the other Circumstances, of their supping at the *Star Side*, coming over the Water together, and parting in the *Strand* at Eleven o'Clock at Night

Then the Waterman stood up, and affirmed, that he carry'd the two Gentlemen who spoke last to *Chelsea*, and a third Person with them Being ask'd, if the Prisoner at the Bar was that third Person, he said his Eyes were bad, but their going close to him, he turn'd again to the Court, and answer'd, Yes, my Lord, this is the Gentleman This Waterman then confirm'd all the Particulars concerning their Supper, and crossing the Water at eleven o'Clock, adding, that he had mark'd down the Day of the Month in Chalk, at the Desire of the first Witness

The pretended Landlord of the House where they supp'd, gave in his Deposition in the fourth Place, the Substance of it was a Repetition of what had been before said, concerning the Supper of Bacon and Fowls, and the staying at his House till almost Eleven o'Clock The Means of his remembering the Day of the Month, was his having started Beer that Day, and being very dirty when our three Gentlemen came *And look here, my Lord*, said he, and took his Book from under his Arm, *you may see all the Days of the Month when I started Beer for a while past.*

The last of all that appeared, was a Man, who told the Court, That he liv'd in *Burleigh Street* in the *Strand*, where Mr *Hinton* was his Lodger That Mr *Hinton* came home at Eleven o'Clock on the Night mention'd in the Indictment, and that he not only staid within all that Night, but all the next Day, complaining that he was not very well The Manner how this Witness remember'd the Day, was by his Landlord's Receipt, for he was very sure that he paid his Rent that Afternoon.

It must be acknowledg'd, that such a Sett of Witnesses as this was enough to dash Truth out of Countenance, nor is it at all to be wonder'd at that *Hinton* was easily discharged by the Court The Truth of the Story might have still been unknown, if he had not himself been so impudent as to boast in *Newgate* of this Master piece of Invention, as he frequently call'd it, and as every one must confess it to be, though 'tis enough at the same Time

Time to make any one weep, who confiders what a Pity 'tis that fo much Wit fhould be employ'd to fo bad a Purpofe

But the Storm was not yet over, for feveral Bills were prefented againft him, for Robberies committed in the Counties of *Surrey* and *Hertford*, to anfwer which he was detain'd a Prifoner One of his own Gang had made himfelf an Evidence againft him, which made the Cafe look very doubtful, yet even here he had again Hopes of efcaping, by ftopping the Mouth of this Fellow. Some of *Hinton's* Friends undertook to manage the Matter, and they threaten'd to bring in feveral Indictments againft their falfe Brother, if he did not retract in Court what he had before fworn, which for his own Safety he did, pretending that he had recollected himfelf, and that Mr *Hinton* was never concern'd with him in any Robbery whatfoever

This, and the other Affiftances he receiv'd from his old Friends, brought him off with Honour at the *Surrey* Affizes, and he did not at all doubt but he fhould efcape as well at *Hertford*, there being no Evidence againft him that he knew of, fo that he went thither with abundance of Confidence But when his Trial came on, in Spite of all that could be depos'd in his Favour, one of the Gentlemen whom he had robb'd, and whom he did not expect to appear, fwore fo pofitively, that he was the very Perfon who unhors'd him, and took away his Watch that the Court faw Reefon to believe him 'Tis true, they began before to imagine that he really muft be concern'd in fome of thofe Things that he got off of, becaufe 'tis unprecedented for a Man to be fo often accus'd, and not be at all guilty Befides, *Hinton* was known to be an old Offender, which gave Room both to fufpect the Evidences he brought, and to believe that he had not perfectly left off his Trade, though he had Art enough to make himfelf feem innocent In a Word, where *Hinton* fancy'd himfelf fafeft, he met with his deferved Fate, being convicted, condemn'd, and executed the fame Day A Thing feldom heard of, but at this Time occafion'd by the Judge's being inform'd what a dangerous Perfon he was,

on account of his Intereft among the Thieves, and how proper it would be to take him out of the Way as foon as poffibly they could, the Jailor protefting, that he was afraid he could not keep him a Week in Cuftody

At his Death he behav'd in an unconcerned, but not an impudent Manner He pray'd for Forgivenefs of all he had wrong'd, and complain'd mightily of his being executed fo fuddenly as not to have Time to prepare himfelf for Eternity He was but juft turn'd of twenty one Years of Age, which made it the more furprifing, that he could have run fuch a Length in Villainy, as to be the common Subject of Converfation at that Time but he had a very ready Wit, was full of fmart and lively Repartees, and arm'd with an undaunted Refolution, fo that there never was Man who feem'd more capable of being a diftinguifh'd Rogue than he *Mercury* among the Ancients was the God of Thieves as well as of Wit, and if we confider young *Hinton* in a phyfical Manner, it muft be allow'd that in every Refpect his Conftitution was perfectly mercurial 'Tis reported that he declared to a Perfon, who reprov'd him for his Practices, and put him in mind of an Eftate that was to come to him on the Death of a near and aged Relation, That if he had Five hundred Pounds a Year, his Propenfity to Thieving was fuch, that he believ'd he could never leave it off

If we may be allow'd upon fuch a Subject to give a little Scope to Fancy, it look'd as if *Mercury* had not only infpir'd him all his Days, but that the fame God even attended his dead Corpfe to the Grave, for the Perfons who brought his Body in a Coach from *Hertford* to *Mary-bone*, where he was bury'd, were robb'd a little before they came to the End of their Journey, one Woman lofing her Gold Chain, and another a pretty deal of Money Thus have we purfued from the Cradle to the Grave, a Man whofe Perfon and Fate were lamented by thofe who detefted his Crimes, a Man who, with a Stock of Virtue equal to his natural Endowments, might have been as remarkable for his Services to the Publick, as he was render'd notorious for his Villainies.

The LIFE of Captain WORLEY.

HIS Reign was but fhort, but his Beginning fomewhat particular, fetting out only in a fmall open Boat, with eight others, from *New York* This was as refolute a Crew as ever went upon this Account, They took with them a few Bifcuits, and a dry'd Tongue or two, a little Cag of Water, half a dozen old Mufkets, and Ammunition accordingly Thus provided, they left *New York* the latter End of *September* 1718, but it cannot be fuppofed, that fuch a Man of War as this could undertake any confiderable Voyage, or attempt any extraordinary Enterprize, fo they ftood down

the Coaft, till they came to *Delaware* River, which is about 150 Miles diftant, and not meeting with any Thing in their Way, they turned up the fame River as high as *Newcaftle*, near which Place they fell upon a Shallop belonging to *George Grant*, who was bringing Houfhold Goods, Plate, &c from *Oppoquenimt* to *Philadelphia*, they made Prize of the moft valuable Part of them, and let the Shallop go This Fact could not come under the Article of Pyracy, it not being committed *fuper altum Mare*, upon the High Sea, therefore was a fimple Robbery only, but they did not ftand for a Point of Law in the Cafe,

but

but eafing the Shallop Man of his Lading, the bold Adventurers went down the River again in queft of more Booty

The Shallop came ftraight to *Philadelphia*, and brought the ill News thither, which alarm'd the Government as much as if War had been declar'd againft them Expreffes were fent to *New York* and other Places, and feveral Veffels fitted out againft this powerful Rover, but to no manner of Purpofe, for after feveral Days Cruize, they all returned, without fo much as hearing what became of the Robbers

Worley and his Crew, in going down the River, met with a Sloop of *Philadelphia*, belonging to a Mulatto, whom they call'd *Black Robin*, they quitted their Boat for this Sloop, taking one of *Black Robin's* Men along with them, as they had alfo done from *George Grant*, befides two Negroes, which encreafed the Company one Third A Day or two after, they took another Sloop belonging to *Hull*, homeward bound, which was fomewhat fitter for their Purpofe they found aboard her Provifions and Neceffaries, which they ftood in need of, and which enabled them to profecute their Defign, in a Manner more fuitable to their Wifhes

Upon the Succefs of thefe Rovers, the Governor iffued out a Proclamation, for the apprehending and taking all Pyrates, who had refufed or neglected to furrender themfelves, by the Time limited in his Majefty's Proclamation of Pardon, and thereupon ordered his Majefty's Ship *Phœnix*, of 20 Guns, which lay at *Sandy Hook*, to Sea, to cruize upon this Pyrate, and fecure the Trade to that, and the adjoining Colonies

In all Probability, the taking this Sloop fav'd their Bacons for this Time, tho' they fell into the Trap prefently afterwards, for they finding themfelves in tolerable good Condition, having a Veffel newly clean'd, with Provifions, &c they ftood off to Sea, and fo miffed the *Phœnix*, who expected them to be ftill on the Coaft

About fix Weeks afterwards they returned, having taking both a Sloop and a Brigantine, among the *Bahama* Iflands, the former they funk, and the other they let go The Sloop belonged to *New York*, and they thought the finking of her good Policy, to prevent her returning to tell Tales at Home

Worley had by this Time encreafed his Company to about five and twenty Men, had fix Guns mounted, and fmall Arms as many as were neceffary for them, and feem'd to be in a good thriving fort of a Way He made a black Enfign, with a white Death's Head in the Middle of it, and other Colours fuitable to it They all figned Articles, and bound themfelves under a folemn Oath, to take no Quarters, but to ftand by one another to the laft Man, which was rafhly fulfilled a little afterwards

For going into an Inlet in *North Carolina* to clean, the Governor received Information of it, and fitted out two Sloops, one of eight Guns, and the other with fix, and about feventy Men between them *Worley* had clean'd his Sloop, and fail'd before the *Carolina* Sloops reach'd the Place, and fteered to the Northward, but the Sloops juft mentioned purfuing the fame Courfe, came in fight of *Worley* as he was cruifing off the Capes of *Virginia* Being in the Offing, he ftood in as foon as he faw the Sloops, in-

tending thereby to have cut them off from *James* River, for he verily believed they had been bound thither, not imagining, in the leaft, they were in Purfuit of him

The two Sloops ftanding towards the Capes at the fame Time, and *Worley* hoifting his black Flag, the Inhabitants of *James* Town were in the utmoft Confternation, thinking that all three had been Pyrates, and that their Defign had been upon them, fo that all the Ships and Veffels that were in the Road, or in the Rivers up the Bay, had Orders immediately to hale into the Shore, for their Security, or elfe to prepare for their Defence, if they thought themfelves in a Condition to fight Soon after two Boats, which were fent out to get Intelligence, came crowding in and brought an Account, that one of the Pyrates was in the Bay, being a fmall Sloop of fix Guns The Governor (expecting the reft would have followed, and all together have made fome Attempt to land, for the fake of Plunder) beat to Arms, and collected all the Force that could be got together, to one of them, he ordered all the Guns out of the Ships to make a Platform, and, in fhort, put the whole Colony in a warlike Pofture, but was very much furprifed at laft, to fee all the fuppofed Pyrates fight with one another

The Truth of the Matter is, *Worley* gained the Bay, thinking to make fure of his two Prizes by keeping them from coming in, but by the hoifting of the King's Colours, and firing a Gun, he quickly was fenfible of his Miftake, and too foon perceived that the Tables were turned upon him, and that inftead of keeping them out, he found himfelf by a fuperior Force kept in When the Pyrates faw how Things went, they refolutely prepared themfelves for a defperate Defence, and tho' three to one and great Odds, yet *Worley* and his Crew determined to ftand to the laft Gafp, and receive no Quarters, agreeable to what they had before fworn, fo that they muft either die or conquer upon the Spot

The *Carolina* Men give the Pyrate a Broadfide, and then Boarded him, one Sloop getting upon his Quarter, and the other on his Bow, *Worley* and his Crew drew up upon the Deck, and fought very obftinately, Hand to Hand, fo that in a few Minutes, abundance of Men lay weltering in their Gore The Pyrates proved as good as their Words, not a Man of them cry'd out for Quarter, nor would accept of fuch when offered, but were all kill'd except the Captain and another Man, whom they referved for the Gallows, and thofe very much wounded They were brought afhore in Irons, and the next Day, which was the 17th Day of *February* 1718-19, they were both hanged up, for fear they fhould die, and efcape the Punifhment which was thought due to their Crimes

The Reader will fee a very good Reafon for this great Difproportion in the Length of thefe Lines fome of the Pyrates having continued their Depredations but a fhort Time, and that too in a Capacity much inferior to others Nor is it poffible to give long Accounts of all that may deferve it, with any degree of Certainty, and we chufe rather to make the Narrative fhort, than lengthen it with Stories that have no other Foundation than our own Fancy or, what is as little to be built upon, the many lying Reports which thefe Fellows always occafion

Cap.ᵗ GEORGE LOWTHER and his Company at Port Mayo, in the Gulph of Matique.

The LIFE of Capt GEORGE LOWTHER.

GEORGE LOWTHER sail'd out of the River of Thames, in one of the Royal *African* Company's Ships, called the *Gambia Castle*, of 16 Guns and 30 Men, *Charles Russel* Commander, of which Ship the said *Lowther* was second Mate Aboard of the same Vessel was a certain Number of Soldiers, commanded by one *John Massey*, who were to be carry'd to one of the Company's Settlements, on the River of *Gambia*, to garrison a Fort, which was sometime ago taken and destroy'd by Captain *Davis* the Pyrate

In *May* 1721, the *Gambia Castle* came safe to her Port in *Africa*, and landed Captain *Massey* and his Men on *James*'s Island, where he was to command under the Governor, Colonel *Whitney*, who arrived there at the same Time in another Ship: And here, by a fatal Misunderstanding between the military Folks and the trading People, the Fort and Garrison not only came to be lost again to the Company, but a fine Galley well provided, and worth 10,000 *l* turn'd against her Masters

The Names of *Governor* and *Captain* sounded great, but when the Gentlemen found that the Power that generally goes along with those Titles was oversway'd and born down by the Merchants and Factors (mechanick Fellows as they thought them) they grew very impatient and disatisfy'd, especially *Massey*, who was very loud in his Complaints against them, particularly at the small Allowance of Provision to him and his Men, for the Garrison and Governor too were victualled by the Merchants, which was no small Grievance and Mortification to them And the want of Eating was the only Thing that made the great *Sancho* quit his Government, so did it here rend and tare theirs to Pieces *Massey* told them, that he did not come there to be a *Guiney* Slave, and that he had promised his Men good Treatment, and Provisions fitting for Soldiers That as he had the Care of so many of his Majesty's Subjects, if they would not provide for them in a handsome Manner, he should take suitable Measures for the Preservation of so many of his Countrymen and Companions

The Governor at this Time was very ill of a Fever, and, for the better Accommodation in his Sickness, he was carry'd aboard the Ship *Gambia Castle*, where he continued for about three Weeks, and therefore could have little to say in this Dispute, tho' he resolv'd not to stay in a Place where there was so little Occasion for him, and where his Power was so confin'd The Merchants had certainly Orders from the Company, to issue the Provisions out to the Garrisons, but whether they had cut them short of the Allowance that was appointed them, we can't say, if they did, then was the Loss of the Ship and Garrison owing principally to their ill Conduct

However, an Accident that happen'd on board the Ship, did not a little contribute to this Misfortune, which was a Pique that the Captain of her

took against his second Mate, *George Lowther*, the Man who is the Subject of this short History, and who, losing his Favour, found Means to ingratiate himself into the good liking of the common Sailors, insomuch that when Captain *Russel* order'd him to be punish'd, the Men took up Handspikes, and threatned to knock that Man down who offered to lay hold of the Mate This served but to widen the Differences between him and the Captain, and more firmly attach'd *Lowther* to the Ship's Company, the greatest Part of which he found ripe for any Mischief in the World

Captain *Massey* was not a Whit the better reconcil'd to the Place by a longer Continuance, nor to the Usage he met with there, and having often Opportunities of conversing with *Lowther*, with whom he had contracted an Intimacy in the Voyage, they aggravated one another's Grievances to such a Height, that they resolved upon Measures to curb the Power that controul'd them, and to provide for themselves after another Manner

When the Governor recovered of his Fever, he went ashore to the Island, but took no Notice of *Massey*'s Behaviour, tho' it was such as might give Suspicion of what he design'd, and *Lowther* and the common Sailors, who were in the Secret of Affairs, grew insolent and bold, even refusing to obey when commanded to their Duty by Captain *Russel* and the chief Mate. The Captain seeing how Things were carried, goes ashore early one Morning to the Governor and Factory in order to hold a Council; which *Lowther* apprehending was in order to prevent his Design, he sent a Letter in the same Boat to *Massey*, intimating it to him, and *that he should repair on board, for it was high Time to put their Project in Execution*

As soon as *Massey* received this Letter, he went to the Soldiers at the Barracks, and said to them, and others, *You that have a Mind to go to England, now is your Time* They generally consenting, *Massey* went to the Store-room, burst open the Door, set two Centinels upon it, and order'd that no Body should come near it, then he went to the Governor's Apartment, and took his Bed, Baggage, Plate, and Furniture, in Expectation, that the Governor himself, as he had promised *Massey*, would have gone on board, which he afterwards refused, by Reason, as he said, he believed they were going a pyrating, tho' at first, whatever *Lowther* design'd, *Massey* certainly proposed only the going to *England* When this was done, he sent the Boat off to the chief Mate with this Message, *That he should get the Guns ready, for that the King of* Barro [a Negroe Kingdom near the Royal *African* Settlement] *would come aboard to Dinner* But *Lowther* understanding best the Meaning of those Orders, he confined the chief Mate, shotted the Guns, and put the Ship in a Condition for sailing. In the Afternoon *Massey* came on board with the Governor's Son, having sent off all the Provisions vifions of the Ifland, and eleven Pipes of Wine, leaving only two half Pipes in the Store-houfe, and difmounting all the Guns of the Fort

In the Afternoon they weigh'd one Anchor, but fearing to be too late to get out of the River, they flipped the other, and fo fell down, in doing of which, they run the Ship a-ground Maffey fhew'd himfelf a Soldier upon this Accident; for as foon is the Misfortune happen'd, he left the Ship with about fixteen Hands, and row'd directly to the Fort, remounted the Guns, and kept Garrifon there all the Night, while the Ship was afhore; and obliged fome of the Factory to affift in getting her clear In the mean while Ruffel came off, but not being fuffered to come on board, he called to Lowther, and offer'd him and the Company whatever Terms they would accept of, upon Condition of furrendering up the Ship, but this had no Effect upon any of them In the Morning they got her afloat, and Maffey and his Men came aboard, having nailed up and difmounted all the Cannon of the Fort They put the Governor's Son, and two or three others afhore, who were not willing to go without the Governor, and fail'd out of the River, having exchang'd feveral Shot with the Martha, Otter, &c that lay there, without doing Execution on either Side.

When the the Ship came out to Sea, Lowther call'd up all the Company, and told them, *That it was the greateft Folly imaginable to think of returning to England, for what they had already done, could not be juftify'd upon any Pretence whatfoever, but would be look'd upon, in the Eye of the Law, as a capital Offence, and none of them were in a Condition to withftand the Attacks of fuch powerful Adverfaries, as they would meet with at Home For his Part,* he told them, *he was determined not to run fuch a Hazard, and therefore if his Propofal was not agreed to, he defired to be fet afhore in fome Place of Safety· That they had a good Ship under them, a Parcel of brave Fellows in her, that it was not their Bufinefs to ftrave, or be made Slaves, and therefore, if they were all of his Mind, they should feek their Fortunes upon the Seas, as other Adventurers had done before them* They one and all came into the Meafures, knocked down the Cabins, made the Ship flufh fore and aft, prepared black Colours, new nam'd her The Delivery, having about 50 Hands and 16 Guns, and then the following fhort Articles were drawn up, figned, and fworn to, upon the Bible.

The Articles of Captain *George Lowther*, and his Company.

1. T*HE Captain is to have two full Shares, the Mafter is to have one Share and a half, the Doctor, Mate, Gunner, and Boatfwain, one Share and a quarter*

2. *He that fhall be found guilty of taking up any unlawful Weapon on board the Privateer, or any Prize by us taken, fo as to ftrike or abufe one another, in any regard, fhall fuffer what Punifhment the Captain and majority of the Company fhall think fit*

3 *He that fhall be found guilty of Cowardice in the Time of Engagement, fhall fuffer what Punifhment the Captain and majority fhall think fit*

4 *If any Gold, Jewels, Silver, &c be found on board of any Prize or Prizes, to the Value of a Piece of Eight, and the Finder do not deliver it to the Quarter mafter, in the Space of 24 Hours, he fhall fuffer what Punifhment the Captain and majority fhall think fit*

5. *He that is found guilty of Gaming, or Defraud-*

ing another to the Value of a Shilling, fhall fuffer what Punifhment the Captain and majority of the Company fhall think fit

6. *He that fhall have the Misfortune to lofe a Limb, in Time of Engagement, fhall have the Sum of One hundred and fifty Pounds Sterling, and remain with the Company as long as he fhall think fit*

7 *Good Quarters fhall always be given when call'd for*

8 *He that fees a Sail firft fhall have the beft Piftol, or fmall Arms on board her*

It was on the 13th of *June* that Lowther left this Settlement, and on the 20th, being then within 10 Leagues of Barbadoes, he came up with a Brigantine, belonging to Bofton, called the Charles, James Douglas Mafter, which they plunder'd in a pyratical Manner, and let the Veffel go, but leaft fhe fhould meet with any of the Station Ships, and fo give Information of the Robbery, in Terrorem, to prevent a Purfuit, Lowther contrived a fort of a Certificate, which he directed the Mafter to fhew to their Confort, if they fhould meet with her, and upon Sight of it the Brigantine would pafs unmolefted This Confort, he pretended, was a 40 Gun Ship, and cruifing thereabouts

After this the Delivery proceeded to Hispaniola, near the Weft End of the Ifland fhe met with a French Sloop loaden with Wine and Brandy Aboard of this Veffel went Captain Maffey, as a Merchant, and ask'd the Price of one Thing, and then another, bidding Money for the greateft Part of her Cargo, but after he had trifled a while, he whifper'd a fecret in the Frenchman's Ear, viz That they muft have it all without Money Monfieur prefently underftood their Meaning, and unwillingly agreed to the Bargain They took out of her thirty Casks of Brandy, five Hogfheads of Wine, feveral Pieces of Chintzes, and other valuable Goods, and about 70 l. Englifh, in Money, of which Lowther generoufly returned five Pounds back to the French Mafter for his Civilities

But as all Conftitutions grow old, and thereby fhake and totter, fo did their Commonwealth, in about a Month of its Age, feel Commotions, and inteftine Difturbances, by the Divifions of its Members, which had near hand terminated in its Deftruction Thefe civil Difcords were owing to the following Occafion Captain Maffey had been a Soldier almoft from his Infancy, but was very indifferently acquainted with maritime Affairs, and having an enterprifing Soul, nothing could fatisfy him, but he muft be doing Bufinefs in his own Way, therefore he required Lowther to let him have thirty Hands to land with, and he would attack the French Settlements, and bring aboard the Devil and all of Plunder

Lowther did all that he could do, and faid all that he could fay, to diffuade Maffey from fo rafh and dangerous an Attempt, pointing out to him the Hazard the Company would run, and the Confequences to them all, if he fhould not fucceed, and the little Likelihood there was to expect Succefs from the Undertaking: But 'twas all one for that, Maffey would go and attack the French Settlements, for any thing Lowther could fay againft it, fo that he was obliged to propofe the Matter to the Company, among whom Maffey found a few Fellows as refolute as himfelf, however, a great Majority being againft it, the Affair was over ruled in Oppofition to the Captain Upon this Maffey grew fractious, quarrel'd with Lowther, and the Men divided into Parties, fome fiding with the Land Pyrate, and fome with

with the Sea Rover, and were all ready to fall together by the Ears

In the Midst of this Squabble the Man at the Mast-head cry'd out, a Sail! a Sail! then they gave over the Dispute, set all their Sails, and steer'd after the Chace In a few Hours they came up with her, she being a small Ship from *Jamaica*, bound to *England*, they took what they thought fit out of her, and a Hand or two, and then *Lowther* was for sinking the Ship, with several Passengers that were in her, for what Reason no body knows; but *Massy* interposed in this Affair, prevented their cruel Fate, and the Ship safely arrived afterwards in *England*

The next Day they took a small Sloop, an interloping Trader, which they detain'd with her Cargo All this while *Massey* was uneasy, and declared his Resolution to leave them, and *Lowther* finding him a very troublesome Man to deal with, consented that he should take the Sloop last made Prize of, with what Hands had a Mind to go with him, and shift for himself Whereupon *Massey*, with about ten more Malecontents, goes aboard the Sloop, and comes away in her directly for *Jamaica*

Notwithstanding what had passed, Captain *Massey* puts a bold Face upon the Matter, and goes to Sir *Nicholas Laws*, the Governor, informs him of his leaving *Lowther* the Pirate, owns, *That he assisted in going off with the Ship, at the River* Gambia, but said, 'twas to save so many of his Majesty's Subjects from perishing, and that his Design was to return to *England*, till Lowther, conspiring with the greater Part of the Company, went a pyrating with the Ship, upon which, he had taken this Opportunity to leave him, and surrender himself and Vessel to his Excellency

Massey was very well received by the Governor, and had his Liberty given him, with a Promise of his Favour, and so forth, and, at his own Request, he was sent on board the happy Sloop, Captain *Laws*, to cruise off *Hispaniola* for *Lowther*, but not being so fortunate as to meet with him, Captain *Massey* returned back to *Jamaica* in the Sloop, and getting a Certificate, and a Supply of Money, from the Governor, he came home Passenger to *England*

When *Massey* came to Town, he writes a long Letter to the Deputy Governor and Directors of the *African* Company, wherein he imprudently relates the whole Transactions of his Voyage, the going off with the Ship, and the Acts of Pyracy he had committed with *Lowther*, but excuses it as Rashness and Inadvertency in himself, occasioned by his being ill used, contrary to the Promises that had been made him, and the Expectations he had entertained He own'd however, that he deserved to die for what he had done; yet, if they had Generosity enough to forgive him, as he was still capable to do them Service, as a Soldier, so he would be very ready to do it, but if they resolved to prosecute him, he begg'd only this Favour, that he might not be hang'd like a Dog, but suffer'd to die like a Soldier, as he had been bred from his Childhood, that is, that he might be shot

This was the Substance of the Letter, which, however, did not produce so favourable an Answer as he hoped for, Word being brought back to him, *That he should be fairly hang'd* Upon this, *Massey* resolved not to go out of the Way, when he found what important Occasion there was likely to be for him, but takes a Lodging in *Aldersgate street*, and the next Day goes to the Lord Chief Justice's Chambers, and enquires, if my Lord had granted a Warrant against Captain *John Massey* for Pyracy Being told by the Clerks, that they knew of no such Thing, he

inform'd them, he was the Man, that my Lord would soon be applied to for that Purpose, and the Officer might come to him at such a Place, where he lodg'd. They took the Direction from him in Writing, and in a few Days, a Warrant being issued, the Tipstaff went directly, by his own Information, and apprehended him, without any other Trouble than walking to his Lodging

There was then no Person in Town to charge him with any Fact, upon which he could be committed; nor could the Letter be proved to be his Hand-writing, so that they had been obliged to let him go again, if he had not helped his Accusers out at a Pinch: The Magistrate was reduced to the putting of this Question to him, *Did you write this Letter?* He answer'd, *I did* And not only that, but confessed all the Contents of it, upon which, he was committed to *Newgate*, but was afterwards admitted to a hundred Pounds Bail, or thereabouts

On the 5th of *July* 1723, he was brought to his Tryal, at a Court of Admiralty held at the *Old Bailey*, when Captain *Russel*, Governor *Whitney*'s Son, and others, appeared as Evidences, by whom the Indictment was plainly proved against him, tho' if this had not been done, the Captain was of such an heroick Spirit, that, in all probability, he would have denied nothing, for instead of making a Defence, he only entertain'd the Court with a long Narrative of his Expedition, from the first setting out, to his Return to *England*, mentioning two Acts of Piracy committed by him, which he was not charged with, often challenging the Evidences to contradict him, if in any Thing he related the least Untruth; and instead of denying the Crimes set forth in the Indictment, he charged himself with various Circumstances, which fixed the Facts more home upon him Upon the whole, the Captain was found Guilty, received Sentence of Death, and was executed three Weeks after, at *Execution Dock*

We return now to *Lowther*, whom we left cruising off *Hispaniola*, from whence he ply'd to Windward, and near *Porto Rico*, chased two Sail, and spoke with them, they proved to be a small *Bristol* Ship, commanded by Captain *Smith*, and a *Spanish* Pyrate, who had made Prize of the said Ship *Lowther* examined the *Spaniard*'s Authority, for taking an *English* Vessel, and threatened to put every Man of them to death, for so doing, so that the *Spaniards* fancied themselves in a very pitiful Condition, till Matters clear'd up, and then they found their Masters as great Rogues as themselves, from whom some Mercy might be expected, in regard to the near Relation they stood with them, as to their Profession In short, *Lowther* first rifled, and then burnt both the Ships, sending the *Spaniards* away in their Launch, and turning all the *English* Sailors into Pyrates

After a few Days Cruise, *Lowther* took a small Sloop belonging to St *Christophers*, which they mann'd and carried along with them to a small Island, where they cleaned, and staid some Time to take their Diversions, which consisted in unheard of Debaucheries, with drinking, swearing, and rioting, in which there seem'd to be a kind of Emulation among them, they resembling rather Devils than Men, and striving who should out do the rest in new invented Oaths and Execrations

They all got aboard about *Christmas*, observing neither Times nor Seasons for perpetrating their villainous Actions, and sailed towards the Bay of *Honduras*, but stopping at the *Grand Caimanes*, for Water, they met with a small Vessel with 13 Hands, in the same honourable Employment with themselves, the Captain of this Gang was one *Edward Low*, whose

Whose Life will be inserted in this Collection *Lowther* received them as Friends, and treated them with all imaginable Reefpect, inviting them, as they were few in Number, and in no Condition to pursue the Account (as they called it) to join their Strength together, which on the Confideration aforesaid, was accepted of, *Lowther* still continuing Commander, and *Low* being made Lieutenant The Veffel the new Pirates came out of, they funk, and the Confederates proceeded on the Voyage that *Lowther* before intended

On the 10th of *January*, the Pyrates came into the Bay, and fell upon a Ship of 200 Tun, called the *Greyhound, Benjamin Edwards* Commander, belonging to *Boston Lowther* hoifted his pyratical Colours, and fired a Gun for the *Greyhound* to bring to, which fhe refufing, the *Happy Delivery* (the Name of the Pyrate) edg'd down, and gave her a Broadfide, which was returned by Captain *Edwards* very bravely, and the Engagement held for an Hour, but Captain *Edwards* finding the Pyrate too ftrong for him, and fearing the Confequence of too obftinate a Refiftance againft thofe lawlefs Fellows, ordered his Enfign to be ftruck The Pyrates Boat came aboard, and not only rifled the Ship, but whipp'd, beat, and cut the Men in a cruel Manner, turned them aboard their own Ship, and then fet Fire to theirs

In cruifing about the Bay, they met and took feveral other Veffels without any Refiftance, *viz* two Brigantines of *Boston* in *New England*, one of which they burnt, and funk the other, a Sloop belonging to *Connecticut*, Captain *Airs*, which they alfo burnt, a Sloop of *Jamaica*, Captain *Hamilton*, which they took for their own Ufe, a Sloop of *Virginia* they unladed, and were fo generous as to give her back to the Mafter that own'd her They took a Sloop of 100 Tun, belonging to *Rhode Ifland*, which they were pleas'd to keep, and mount with eight Carriage, and ten Swivel Guns.

With this little Fleet, *viz* Admiral *Lowther*, in the *Happy Delivery*, Captain *Low*, in the *Rhode Ifland* Sloop, Captain *Harris* (who was fecond Mate in the *Greyhound* when taken) in *Hamilton*'s Sloop, and the little Sloop formerly mentioned, ferving as a Tender, I fay, with this Fleet the Pyrates left the Bay, and came to *Port Mayo* in the Gulph of *Matique*, and there made Preparations to careen, they carried afhore all their Sails, and made Tents by the Water fide, wherein they laid their Plunder, Stores &c and fell to work, and at the Time that the Ships were upon the Heel, and the good Folks employ'd in heaving down, fcrubbing, tallowing, and fo forth, of a fudden came down a confiderable Body of the Natives and attack'd the Pyrates unprepared As they were in no Condition to defend themfelves, they fled to their Sloops, leaving them Mafters of the Field and the Spoil thereof, which was of great Value, and fet Fire to the *Happy Delivery*, their capital Ship

Lowther made the beft Provifion he could in the largeft Sloop, which he called the *Ranger*, having ten Guns and eight Swivels, and fhe failing beft, the Company went all aboard of her, and left the other at Sea Provifion was now very fhort, which, with the late Lofs, put them in a confounded ill Humour, infomuch that they were now and then going together by the Ears, laying the Blame of their ill Conduct fometimes upon one, then upon another

The Beginning of *May* 1722, they got to the *Weft-Indies*, and near the Ifland of *Defeada* they took a Brigantine, one *Payne* Mafter, that afforded them what they ftood in need of, which put them in better Temper, and Bufinefs feemed to go on well again After they had pretty well plundered the Brigantine, they fent her to the Bottom They went into the Ifland and watered, and then ftood to the Northward, intending to vifit the Main Coaft of *America*

In the Latitude of 38 they took a Brigantine, called the *Rebecca* of *Boston*, Captain *Smith*, bound thither from St *Chriftophers*. At the taking of this Veffel, the Crews divided, for *Low*, whom *Lowther* joined at the *Grand Caimanes*, proving always a very unruly Member of the Commonwealth, continually afpiring, and never fatisfy'd with the Proceedings of the Commander, he thought it the fafeft Way to get rid of him, upon any Terms; and, according to the Vote of the Company, they parted the Bear Skin between them *Low* with 44 Hands went aboard the Brigantine, and *Lowther* with the fame Number ftaid in the Sloop, and fo they feparated that very Night, being the 28th of *May* 1722

Lowther proceeded on his Way to the Main Coaft, took three or four fifhing Veffels off *New York*, which was no great Booty to the Captors On the 3d of *June*, they met with a fmall *New England* Ship, bound home from *Barbadoes*, which ftood an Attack a fmall Time, but finding it to no Purpofe, yielded herfelf a Prey to the Booters The Pyrates took out of her fourteen Hogfheads of Rum, fix Barrels of Sugar, a large Box of *English* Goods, feveral Cafks of Loaf Sugar, a confiderable Quantity of Pepper, fix Negroes, befides a Sum of Money and Plate, and then let her go on her Voyage

The next Adventure was not fo fortunate for them, for coming pretty near the Coaft of *South Carolina*, they met with a Ship juft come out, on her Voyage to *England*, *Lowther* gave her a Gun, and hoifted his pyratical Colours, but this Ship, which was called the *Amy*, happening to have a brave gallant Man to command her, who was not any ways daunted with that terrible Enfign, the black Flag he, inftead of ftriking immediately, as it was expected, let fly a Broadfide at the Pyrate *Lowther* (not at all pleafed with the Compliment, though he put up with it for the prefent) was for taking Leave, but the *Amy* getting the Pyrate between her and the Shore, ftood after him to clap him aboard, to prevent which, *Lowther* run the Sloop a-ground, and landed all the Men with their Arms Captain *Gwatkins*, the Captain of the *Amy*, was obliged to ftand off, for fear of running his own Ship afhore, but at the fame Time thought fit, for the publick Good, to deftroy the Enemy, and thereupon went into the Boat, and rowed towards the Sloop, in order to fet her on Fire, but before he reached the Veffel, a fatal Shot from *Lowther*'s Company afhore, put an End to their Defign and Captain *Gwatkins*'s Life. After this unfortunate Blow, the Mate returned aboard with the Boat, and, not being inclined to purfue them any farther, took Charge of the Ship

Lowther got off the Sloop after the Departure of the *Amy*, and brought all his Men aboard again, but was in a poor fhattered Condition, having fuffered much in the Engagement, and had a great many Men kill'd and wounded He made Shift to get into an Inlet fomewhere in *North Carolina*, where he ftaid a long while before he was able to put to Sea again

He and his Crew laid up all the Winter, and fhifted as well as they could among the Woods, divided themfelves into fmall Parties, and hunted generally in the Day time, killing black Cattle, Hogs &c for

for their Subſiſtence, and in the Night retired to their Tents and Huts, which they made for Lodging, and ſometimes, when the Weather grew very cold, they would ſtay aboard of their Sloop

In the Spring of the Year 1723, they made Shift to get to Sea, and ſteered their Courſe for *Newfoundland,* and upon the Banks took a Scooner, call'd the *Swift,* *John Hood* Maſter, they found a good Quantity of Proviſions aboard her, which they very much wanted at that Time, and after taking three of their Hands, and plundering her of what they thought fit, they let her depart They took ſeveral other Veſſels upon the Banks, and in the Harbour, but none of any great Account, and then ſteering for a warmer Climate, in *Auguſt* they arrived at the *Weſt-Indies* In their Paſſage thither they met with a Brigantine, called the *John* and *Elizabeth, Richard Stanny* Maſter, bound for *Boſton,* which they plundered, took two of her Men, and diſcharged her

Lowther cruiſed a pretty while among the Iſlands without any extraordinary Succeſs, and was reduc'd to a very ſmall Allowance of Proviſions, till they had the Luck to fall in with a *Martinico* Man, which proved a ſeaſonable Relief to them, and after that a *Guiny* Man had the ill Fortune to become a Prey to the Rovers, ſhe was called the *Princeſs,* Captain *Wickſted* Commander

It was now thought neceſſary to look out for a Place to clean their Sloop in, and prepare for new Adventures Accordingly the Iſland of *Blanco* was pitched upon for that Purpoſe, which lies in the Latitude of 11° 50 m N about 30 Leagues from the Main of the *Spaniſh America,* between the Iſlands of *Margarita* and *Rocas,* and not far from *Tortuga* It is a low even Iſland, but healthy and dry, uninhabited, and about two Leagues in Circumference, with plenty of *Lignum Vitæ* Trees thereon growing in Spots, with ſhrubby Buſhes of other Wood about them There are, beſides Turtle, great Numbers of *Guanoes,* which is an amphibious Creature like a Lizard, but much larger, the Body of it being as big as a Man's Leg They are very good to eat, and are much uſed by the Pyrates that come here They are of divers Colours, but ſuch as live upon dry Ground, as here at *Blanco,* are commonly yellow On the North weſt End of this Iſland, there is a ſmall Cove of ſandy Bay; all round the reſt of the Iſland is deep Water, and ſteep cloſe to the Iſland Hither *Lowther* reſorted to, about the Beginning of *October,* unrigged his Sloop, ſent his Guns, Sails, Rigging, &c aſhore, and put his Veſſel upon the Careen The *Eagle* Sloop of *Barbadoes,* belonging to the *South Sea* Company, with 35 Hands, commanded by *Walter Moore,* coming near this Iſland, in her Voyage to *Comena,* on the *Spaniſh* Continent, ſaw the ſaid Sloop juſt careen'd, with her Guns out, and Sails unbent, which ſhe ſuppoſed to be a Pyrate, becauſe it was a Place where Traders did not commonly uſe, and ſo took the Advantage of attacking of her, as ſhe was then unprepared The *Eagle* having fired a Gun to oblige her to ſhew her Colours, the Pyrates hoiſted the St *George's* Flag at their Topmaſt-Head, as it were to bid Defiance to her, but when they found *Moore* and his Crew reſolved to board them in good Earneſt, the Pyrates cut their Cable, and hawled their Stern on Shore, which obliged the *Eagle* to come to an Anchor athwart her Hawſire, where ſhe engaged them till they called for Quarter and ſtruck, at which Time *Lowther* and twelve of the Crew made their Eſcape out of the Cabin Window The Maſter of the *Eagle* got the Pyrate Sloop off, ſecured her, and went aſhore with 25 Hands, in Purſuit of *Lowther* and his Gang, but after five Days Search, they could find but five of them, which they brought aboard, and then proceeded with the Sloop and Pyrates to *Comena* aforeſaid, where they ſoon arrived

The *Spaniſh* Governor, being informed of this brave Action, condemned the Sloop to the Captors, and ſent a ſmall Sloop with 25 Hands to ſcour the Buſhes, and other Places of the Iſland of *Blanco,* for the Pyrates that remained there, and took four more, with ſeven ſmall Arms, leaving behind them Captain *Lowther,* three Men, and a little Boy, which they could not take, the above four the *Spaniards* try'd, and condemned to Slavery for Life, three to the Gallies, and the other to the Caſtle of *Arrana*

The *Eagle* Sloop brought all their Priſoners afterwards to St *Chriſtophers,* where the following were try'd by a Court of Vice Admiralty, there held *March* the 11th, 1722, viz *John Churchill, Edward Mackdonald, Nicholas Lewis, Richard Weſt, Samuel Levercott, Robert White, John Shaw, Andrew Hunter, Jonathan Delve, Matthew Freebarn, Henry Watſon, Roger Grange, Ralph Candor,* and *Robert Wills* The three laſt were acquitted, the other eleven were found Guilty, two of which were recommended to Mercy by the Court, and accordingly pardoned, and the reſt executed at that Iſland, on the 20th of the ſame Month

As for Captain *Lowther,* it is ſaid, that he afterwards ſhot himſelf upon that fatal Iſland, where his Pyracies ended, being found, by ſome Sloop's Men, dead, and a Piſtol burſt by his Side.

The LIFE of Captain SPRIGGS.

SPRIGGS fail'd with *Low* for a pretty while, and came away from *Lowther* along with him, he was Quarter-Master to the Company, and consequently, had a great Share in all the Barbarities committed by that execrable Gang, till the Time they parted; which was about *Christmas* 1723, when *Low* took a Ship of twelve Guns on the Coast of *Guiney*, call'd the *Delight*, (formerly the *Squirrel* Man of War,) commanded by Captain *Hunt*. *Spriggs* took possession of this Ship with eighteen Men, left *Low* in the Night, and came to the *West Indies* This Separation was occasion'd by a Quarrel with *Low*, concerning a Piece of Justice to be executed upon one of the Crew, for killing a Man in cold Blood; *Spriggs* insisting that he should be hang'd, and the other that he should not

A Day or two after they parted, *Spriggs* was chosen Captain by the rest, and a black Ensign was made, which they call'd *Jolly Roger*, with the same Device that Captain *Low* carry'd, *viz* a white Skeleton in the Middle of it, with a Dart in one Hand, striking a bleeding Heart, and in the other an Hour-Glass; when this was finish'd and hoisted, they fired all their Guns to salute their Captain and themselves, and then look'd out for Prey

In their Voyage to the *West-Indies*, these Pyrates took a *Portuguese* Bark, wherein they got valuable Plunder; but not contented with that alone, they said they would have a little Game with the Men, and so order'd them a Sweat, more for Diversion of these brutal Wretches than the poor Man's Health What they mean by a Sweat is performed after this Manner They stick up lighted Candles circularly round the Mizon-Mast, between Decks, within which the Patients one at a Time enter: Without the Candles the Pirates post themselves, as many as can stand, forming another Circle, and armed with Pen-Knives, Tucks, Forks, Compasses, &c and as he runs round and round, the Musick playing at the same Time, they prick him with those Instruments This usually lasts for ten or twelve Minutes, which is as long as the miserable Man can support himself. When the Sweating was over, they gave the *Portuguese* their Boat, with a small Quantity of Provisions, and set their Vessel on Fire

Near the Island of St *Lucia*, they took a Sloop belonging to *Barbadoes*, which they plundered, and then burnt, forcing some of the Men to sign their Articles, the others they beat and cut in a barbarous Manner, because they refuse to take on with the Crew, and then sent them away in the Boat, in which they all got safe afterwards to *Barbadoes*

The next was a *Martinico* Man, the Crew of which they served as bad as they had done the others, but did not burn the Ship Some Days afterwards, in running down to Leeward, they took one Captain *Hawkins*, coming from *Jamaica*, laden chiefly with Logwood, they took out of this Vessel,

Stores, Arms, Ammunition, and several other Things, as they thought fit, and what they did not want they threw over-board or destroy'd They cut the Cables to Pieces, knock'd down the Cabins, broke all the Windows, and in short took all the Pains in the World to be mischievous They took by Force, out of her, Mr *Burridge* and Mr *Stephens*, the two Mates, and some other Hands, and after containing the Ship from the twenty second of *March*, to the twenty ninth, they let her go On the twenty seventh they took a *Rhode-Island* Sloop, Captain *Pike*, and all his Men were oblig'd to go aboard the Pyrate, but the Mate, being a grave sober Man, and not inclinable to stay, they told him, he should have his Discharge, and that it should be immediately writ on his Back, whereupon, he was sentenced to receive ten Lashes from every Man in the Ship, which was rigorously put in Execution

The next Day Mr *Burridge*, Captain *Hawkin's* Mate, sign'd their Articles, which was so agreeable to them (he being a good Artist and Sailor) that they gave three Huzza's, fir'd all the Guns in the Ship, and appointed him Master The Day was spent in boisterous Mirth, roaring and drinking of Healths, among which was that of King *George* the II For now and then these Gentry are provok'd to sudden Fits of Loyalty, by the Expectation of an Act of Grace, which they thought would be past at the Accession of his present Majesty to the Throne, who was then Prince of *Wales* It seems Captain *Pike* had heard at *Jamaica* by mistake, that the late King was dead, so the Pyrates immediately hoisted their Ensign Half-Mast (the Death Signal) and proclaimed his Royal Highness, saying, *They doubted not but there would be a general Pardon in a twelve Month, which they would embrace and come in upon, but if they should be excepted out of it, they would murder every* Englishman *that should fall into their Hands*

The second of *April*, they spy'd a Sail, and gave her Chace till twelve o'Clock at Night The Pyrates believed her to be a *Spaniard*, and so when they came close up to her, they discharg'd a Broadside, with small and great Shot, which was follow'd by another but the Ship making a lamentable Cry for Quarters, they ceas'd firing, and ordered the Captain to come aboard, which he did, but how disappointed the Rogues were when they found 'twas their old Friend Captain *Hawkins*, whom they had sent away three Days before, worth not one Penny? This was such a Baulk to them, that they resolved he should suffer for falling in their Way, tho' it was so contrary to his own Inclinations About fifteen of them surrounded the poor Man with sharp Cutlasses, and fell upon him, where by he was soon laid flat on the Deck At that Instant *Burridge* flew amongst the thickest of the Villains, and begg'd earnestly for his Life, upon whose Request

Request it was granted They were now moft of 'em drunk, as is ufual at this time of Night, fo they unanimoufly agreed to make a Bonfire of *Hawkins*'s Ship, which was immediately done, and in half an Hour fhe was all of a Blaze

After this, they wanted a little more Diverfion, and fo Captain *Hawkins* was fent for down to the Cabin to Supper What fhould the Provifion be, but a Difh of Candles, which he was forced to eat; having a naked Sword and a Piftol held to his Breaft all the while, when this was over, they buffeted him about for fome Time, and fent him forward amongft the other Prifoners, who had been treated with the fame Delicacies.

Two Days afterwards, they anchor'd at a little uninhabited Ifland, call'd *Rattan*, near the Bay of *Honduras*, and put afhore Captain *Hawkins*, and feveral other Men; one of which was his Paffenger, woo dy'd there of the Hardfhips he underwent They gave them Powder and Ball, and a Mufquet, with which they were to fhift as they could, failing away the next Day for other Adventures

Captain *Hawkins*, and his unfortunate Companions, ftaid nineteen Days upon this Ifland, fupplying themfelves with both Fifh and Fowl, fuch as they were. At the End of that Time came two Men in a Canoe, that had been left upon another Maroon Ifland near *Benacca*, who carry'd the Company at feveral Times thither, it being more convenient in having a good Well of frefh Water, and Plenty of Fifh, &c Twelve Days afterwards they fpy'd a Sloop off at Sea, which, upon their making a great Smoke, ftood in, and took them off, fhe was the *Merriam*, Captain *Jones*, lately efcap'd out of the Bay of *Honduras*, from being taken by the *Spaniards*

At an Ifland to the Weftward, the Pyrates clean'd their Ship, and fail'd towards the Ifland of St *Chriftopher*, to wait for one Captain *Moor*, who commanded the *Eagle*-Sloop, when fhe took *Lowther*'s upon the Careen, at *Blanco* *Spriggs* refolved to put him to Death, wherever he took him, for falling upon his Friend and Brother, but, inftead of *Moor*, he found a *French* Man of War from *Martinico* upon the Coaft; which *Spriggs* not thinking fit to contend with, run away with all the Sail he could make. The *French* Man crowded after *Spriggs*, and was very likely to fpeak with him, when unfortunately his Main-Top-Maft came by the Board, which obliged him to give the Chafe

Spriggs then ftood to the Northward, towards *Bermudas*, or the *Summer Ifles*, and took a Scooner belonging to *Bofton* He took out all the Men, and funk the Veffel, and had the Impudence to tell the Mafter, that he defign'd to increafe his Company on the Banks of *Newfoundland*, and then he would fail for the Coaft of *New England*, in queft of Captain *Solgard*, who attack'd and took their Confort *Charles Harris* *Spriggs* was at that Time in Company with *Low*, who very fairly ran for it The Pyrate afk'd the Mafter if he knew Captain *Solgard*? who anfwering *No*, he afk'd another the fame Queftion, who denying alfo, he put the fame Queftion to a Third, who faid he knew him very well, upon which *Spriggs* ordered him to be fweated, which was done in the manner before defcrib'd

Inftead of going to *Newfoundland*, as the Pyrates threatened, they came back to the Iflands, and to the Windward of St *Chriftopher*'s, on the fourth of *June*, they took a Sloop, *Nicholas Trot* Mafter, belonging to St *Euftatia* Wanting at this Time a little Diverfion, they hoifted the Men as high as the Main and Fore-Tops, and let them down fuddenly, enough to break all the Bones in their Skins; and after they had pretty well crippled 'em by this cruel Ufage, and whipp'd them about the Deck, they gave *Trot* his Sloop, and let him go, keeping back only two of his Men, befides the Plunder of the Veffel.

Within two or three Days after they took a Ship, coming from *Rhode-Ifland* to St *Chriftopher*'s laden with Provifions and fome Horfes; the Pyrates mounted the Horfes, and rid them about the Deck backwards and forwards a full Gallop, like Madmen at *New-Market*, curfing, fwearing, and hallooing, at fuch a Rate, as made the poor Creatures wild Two or three of them at length throwing their Riders, they fell upon the Ship's Crew, and whipped, and cut, and beat 'em in a barbarous manner, tilling 'em, it was for bringing Horfes without Boots and Spurs, for want of which they were not able to ride 'em

In this Manner thefe Wretches went on as long as they could maintain their Community, taking from all they met, every Thing they pleafed Nor is it any Wonder that Men who have taken Pains to diveft themfelves of Humanity fhould act thus, fince when we once lofe the Notions of Right and Property, which keep up the mutual Dependance among mankind, we have nothing within us, that can lay any Reftraint upon our Actions

The LIFE *of Captain* PHILIP ROCHE, &c.

PHILIP *Roche* was born in Ireland, of mean Parents, and from his Youth had been bred up to the Sea, where he apply'd the little Leisure he had, to the improving the small Share of Learning he had received at School He was a brisk genteel Fellow, about thirty Years of Age at the Time of his Death, one whose black and savage Nature did no Ways answer the Comliness of his Person, his Life being almost one continued Scene of Villainy, before he was discovered to have committed the horrid Murders we are now speaking of

This inhuman Monster had been concerned with others, in insuring Ships to a great Value, and then destroying them, by which Means and other Rogueries, he had got a little Money By these Means becoming Mate of a Ship, he was diligent enough in trading for himself between *Ireland* and *France*, so that he was in a Way of getting himself a comfortable Livelihood But, as he resolved to be Rich, and finding fair Dealing brought in Wealth but slowly, he confessed he had put other Methods in Execution. What these Methods were, he would never own, but 'tis thought he had murthered several innocent Persons in the Prosecution of his abominable Schemes However, as we cannot have the particular Circumstances of these Facts, we shall confine ourselves to the horrid Deed for which he suffered

Roche getting acquainted with one *Neal*, a Fisherman at *Cork*, whom he found ignorantly bold and ready for any villainous Attempt, he imparted the Design to him, which they afterwards executed *Neal* being pleas'd with the Project, brings one *Pierce Cullen* and his Brother into the Confederacy, together with one *Wise*, who, at first, was very unwilling to come into their Measures, and, indeed, had the least Hand of them all in the Perpetration of what follows

They pitch'd upon a Vessel in the Harbour, belonging to *Peter Tartoue*, a *French* Man, to execute their cruel Intentions upon, because it was a small one, and had not a great Number of Hands on board, and 'twas easy afterwards to exchange it for one more fit for Pyracy, and therefore they apply'd themselves to the Master of her for a Passage to *Nantz*, whereto the Ship was bound

Accordingly, in the Beginning of *November*, 1721, they went on board, and when at Sea, *Philip Roche* being an experienced Sailor, the Master of the Vessel readily trusted him with the Care of her, at Times, while he and the Mate went to rest

This was the unhappy Case on the fifteenth of *November*, at Night, the Time design'd for the Tragedy Before the Action, *Francis Wise* relented, and appeared desirous to divert them from their bloody Purposes; whereupon *Roche* told him, *That as* Cullen *and he had sustained great Losses at Sea, unless every* Irishman *present would assist in repairing their Losses, by murthering all the* French *Rogues, and running away with the Ship, he should suffer the same*

Fate with the French *Men; but if all would assist, all should have a Share in the Booty* Upon this, they all resolved alike, and *Roche* ordered three *French* Men and a Boy up to hand the Topsails, the Master and Mate being then asleep in their Cabins. The two first that came down, they beat out their Brains and threw them overboard The other, two seeing what was done, ran up to the Topmast Head, but *Cullen* followed them, and taking the Boy by the Arm, threw him into the Sea, then driving down the Man, those below knocked him on the Head, and threw him over-board

Those who were asleep, being awakened by the dismal Shrieks and Groans of dying Men, ran upon Deck in Confusion, to enquire into the Cause of such unusual Noises, but the same Cruelty was immediately acted towards them, e'er they could be sensible of the Danger that threatened them

They were now (as *Roche* himself afterwards confess'd) all over as wet with the Blood that had been spilt, as if they had been dipp'd in Water, or stood in a Shower of Rain, nor did they regard it any, yet *Roche* said, Captain *Tartoue* used many Words to Mercy, and ask'd them, if he had not used them with Civility and Kindness? If they were not of the same Christian Religion, and owned the same blessed Jesus, and the like? But they, not regarding what he said, took Cords, and bound the poor Master and his Mate Back to Back While that was doing, both of them begged with the utmost Earnestness, and used the most solemn Intreaties, that they would at least allow them a few Minutes to say their Prayers, and crave Mercy of God for the various Sins and Offences of their Lives But it did not move them, (although all the rest were dead, and no Danger could be apprehended from these two alone) but the bound Persons were hurry'd up, and thrown into the Sea after the rest

The Massacre being finish'd, they wished themselves a little from the Blood, and searched the Chests, Coffers, and all Places about the Ship, and then sate down in the Captain's Cabin, and refresh'd them selves with some Rum they found there, being (as *Roche* confess'd) never merrier in their Lives They invested *Roche* with the Command of the Ship, and calling him Captain, talked over their Liquor, what rare Actions they would perform about Cape *Britas*, *Sable Isle*, and the Banks of *Newfoundland*, whither they design'd to go as soon as they had recruited their Company, and got a better Ship, which they proposed speedily to do

Roche taking upon himself the Command of the Vessel, *Andrew Cullen* was to pass for a Merchant, or Super-Cargo, but when they bethought themselves, they were in Danger of being discovered by the Papers of the Ship, relating to the Cargo, as Bills of Lading, &c they erased and took out the Name of the *French* Master, and instead thereof inserted the Name of *Roche*, so that it stood in the Ship'

Ship's Papers, *Peter Roche* Master Having so few Hands on board, they contrived if they met any Ships, to give out, that they had lost some Hands by their being wash'd overboard in a Storm, by which Means they thought to screen themselves from being suspected of having committed any such wicked Act For, the small Number of their Men might otherwise have given ground for such a Suspicion They also supposed, that by this Means they might prevail with the first Ship they met to spare them some, on Consideration of their pretended Disaster

In going to *Cales* they were in Distress by the Weather, and being near *Lisbon,* they made Complaint to a Ship, but obtain'd no Assistance They were then oblig'd to fall back for *England,* and put into the Port of *Dartmouth,* but then they were in fear lest they might be discover'd To prevent that, they resolv'd to alter the Ship, and getting Workmen, they took down the Mizzen-Mast, built a Spar-Deck, and made Rails (on pretence that the Sailors had been wash'd overboard) to secure the Men Then they took down the Image of St *Peter* at the Head of the Ship, and put a Lion in its place, painted over the Stern of the Ship with Red, and new-nam'd her the *Mary Snow* The Ship being thus alter'd, that they thought it could not be known, they fancy'd themselves pretty secure, but wanting Money to defray the Charge of these Alterations, *Roche,* as Master of the Vessel, and *Andrew Cullen,* as Merchant, apply'd themselves to the Officers of the Customs for Liberty to dispose of some of the Cargo, in order to pay the Workmen Having obtain'd Leave, they sold fifty-eight Barrels of Beef, and then hiring three more Hands, they set Sail for *Ostend,* and there sold more Barrels of Beef, thence they steer'd their Course to *Rotterdam,* dispos'd of the rest of the Cargo, and took in one Mr *Annesly,* who freighted the Ship for *England*; but in their Passage, in a stormy Night, it being very dark, they took up Mr *Annesly* their Passenger, and threw him into the Sea; who swam about the Ship a pretty while, calling out for Life, and telling 'em they should have all his Goods, if they would receive him again into the Vessel but in vain were his Cries!

After this, they were obliged to put into several Ports, and, by contrary Winds, came to the Coast of *France,* where, hearing there was an Enquiry made after the Ship, *Roche* quits her at *Havre de Grace,* and leaves the Management to *Cullen* and the rest; who, having shipp'd other Men, sail'd away to *Scotland,* and there left the Vessel, which was afterwards seiz'd and brought into the River of *Thames*

Some Time after this, *Philip Roche* came to *London,* and making some Claim for Money he had made Insurance of, in the Name of *John Euslace,* the Officer was apprized of the Fraud, and he arrested, and flung into the Compter, from whence directing a Letter to his Wife, she shew'd it to a Friend, who discover'd by it, that he was the principal Villain concern'd in the Destruction of *Peter Tartoue,* and the Crew Upon this, an Information was given to my Lord *Carteret,* that the Person who went by the Name of *John Euslace,* was *Philip Roche,* as aforesaid, and being brought down by his Lordship's Warrant, he stisly deny'd it for some Time, notwithstanding a Letter was found in his Pocket, directed to him by the Name of *Roche* At last, being confronted by a Captain of a Ship, who knew him well, he confessed his Name, but prevaricated in several Particulars, whereupon he was committed to *Newgate* upon violent Suspicion, and the next Day was brought down again at his own Request, confessed the whole, desir'd to be made an Evidence, and promis'd to convict three Men worse than himself *Neal* and *Cullen* were discover'd by him, who dy'd miserably in the *Marshalsea,* and *Roche* himself was afterwards try'd, found guilty of the Pyracy, and executed at *Tyburn,* no more of his Crew than the two just mention'd being apprehended

He appear'd not very sollicitous at his Tryal; knowing it was impossible to get clear of the Pyracy But when the Order for his Execution came from *Hanover,* he complain'd of being hardly us'd, for, he depended upon having his Life given him, when he made himself an Evidence against his Companions

The LIFE *of Captain* JOHN GOW, *alias* SMITH.

JOHN *Gow*, fail'd from *Amfterdam* in *July* 1724, on board the *George* Galley of that Place, *Oliver Ferneau* Mafter They went firft to *Santa Cruz*, in South *Barbary*, where they took in Bee's-W*ax*, and ftaid till the Beginning of *November*. On the fecond or third Day of that Month, they weigh'd Anc^or, and failed out of the Bay, about three Hours after which was acted the following horrible Tragedy, they being at that Time bound for the Streights

A Combination having been formed between *Gow* and feveral others, that will be occafionally nam'd in this Relation, *Melvin*, one of the Confpirators, was heard to cry out, *There is a Man over-board* The Captain thereupon, came inftantly to the Side of the Ship, and look'd over; when *Melvin* and *Rolfon*, another Confpirator, feiz'd him, and endeavoured to throw him into the Sea, but by ftruggling hard he got from them At that Inftant, one *John Winter* came up with a Knife in his Hand, and cut the Captain acrofs the Throat, but not fo as to kill him, for, in all Probability he miffed his Wind pipe The former two laid hold of him again, and try'd to throw him over-board, yet he ftill ftruggled fo as to prevent them, till *Gow*, who was then fecond Mate and Gunner, ftept up to him with a Piftol in his Hand, and fhot him thro' the Body, after which they threw him over as they at firft intended

After they had difpatch'd the Captain, they were to proceed with all the reft, whom they look'd upon as dangerous Perfons One *Daniel Maccawly* cut the Clerk's Throat, whofe Name was *Stephen Algiers*, as he lay afleep in his Hammock, but not thoroughly, (as *Maccawly* afterwards ufed frequently to fwear) for he awak'd and got out in the Struggle, whereupon *James Williams* meeting him, took Care to finifh the bloody Action *Williams* firft afk'd him for his Watch, but *Algiers* faid he had it not about him, gave him the Key of h s Cheft, and begg'd very hard for a little Time to fay his Prayers, but the barbarous Villain was deaf to all his Cries, fhot him directly thro' the Head with a Piftol loaded fo high, that it burft in firing, and had like to have deftroyed the Murderer too *John Peterfon* cut the Throat of *Bonaventure Jelphs* the chief Mate, and then *Melvin* ty'd a Rope about his Neck, dragg'd him to the Side, and threw him over board, *Michael Moore*, who ftood Centry over the Arms, fhooting him as he was drawn along

All thefe Murders took up about Half an Hour's Time, and as foon as they were over, *James Williams* came upon the Quarter Deck, ftruck upon a Gun with his Cutlafs, and faluted *Gow* (alias *Smith*) in the following Manner *Captain* Smith

you are welcome! welcome to your new Command! Then *Williams* himfelf was declared Lieuten.nt *Peter Rolfon* was made Gunner, and *James Belvin* Boatfwain The Officers being thus fettled, the new Captain made a fhort and pithy Speech to his Men, to this Effect *If hereafter I fee any of you whifpering together, or if any of you refufe to obey my Orders, let every fuch Man depend upon it, that he fhall certainly go the fame Way as thofe that are juft gone before* This laconick Harangue was very well received by the Confpirators, and all who had not engaged in the Confederacy, was immediately confined to the great Cabin the remaining Part of the Night

William Booth, who was afterwards a Witnefs againft this Crew at their Trial, was afleep in his Hammock, all the Time whil'e thefe Barbarities were perpetrated, when he awaked and heard a Noife, he afked one of the Company what was the Matter, but was inftantly anfwered with, *You Dog, if I had a Piftol I wou'd tell you!* But *James Belvin*, tho' not at firft in the Secret, declared impudently the next Day, *That he was very forry he was not told of the Defign the Night before, for he would have lent them a Hand with all his Heart* This was afterwards fwore againft him at the Seffions-Houfe in the *Old-Bailey*, where he was condemned with the reft of his inhuman Companions

The Day after the Perpetration of thefe Cruelties, *Phinnes*, who was an Evidence at the *Old-Bailey*, afked *Gow*, whether or no he was fure he hit the Captain when he fhot at him, fhowing at the fame Time the Mark of a Piftol-Ball in the Side of the Ship· To which *Gow* replied with an Oath, that the Piftol was loaded with two Balls, and he was certain one of them went thro' the Body of the *French* Son of a B——h Thus did they delight to glory in their Villainies

They had not been long Mafters of the Veffel before they took the *Sarah Snow*, of *Briftol*, when Captain *Gow* made a Declaration to the Crew, *That if any of them chofe to go, they might, but if they were willing to ftay with him, they fhould find good Ufage* There was but one of all the Ship's Company, who wou'd condefcend to turn Pyrate, his Name was *Alexander Rob* The reft were difcharged, after they had rifled their Prize of every Thing they thought proper

The next Ship that was fo unhappy as to fall into their Hands, was the *Delight* of *Pool*, *Thomas Wife* Mafter Out of her they took only one thoufand pound weight of Fifh About a Mo th after wards *(viz.)* on the eighteenth of *December* they took the *Batchelor*, *Benjamin Crofs* Mafter, with in twenty Leagues of the Rock of *Lifbon* Here they

they found two thousand pound Weight of Bread, two Barrels of Beef, and one of Pork, all which they seized They had besides two Hands out of this Ship, whose Names were *Harvey* and *Teague*: These Men were both taken against their Consent, and begged hard to be discharged, but the Captain would not grant it, for he had picked them out of the whole Ship's Company. *Harvey* afterwards had projected an Escape along with some others, who went off without him, while he went back to fetch something he had left behind These Particulars being sworn at the *Old-Bailey*, the two Men were thereupon discharged

A *French* Ship, call'd the *Lewis* and *Joseph*, was so unlucky as to be in the Way of these Rovers, on the 27th of *December* The Master's Name was *Henry Mens*. *English* and *French* were all the same to them, provided there was any Thing to be got They had before taken Meat and Bread, here they found twelve Pipes of Wine, forty Barrels of Oil, one hundred and twenty Barrels of Figs, and one hundred and thirty Chests of Lemons and Oranges in all to the Value of about 500*l Sterl* This they look'd upon as an indifferent good Prize, considering they were young Traders

On the sixth of *January* following, within thirty Leagues of *Vigo*, they took the *Triumvirate, Joel Davis* Master; they pillaged her of two Caggs of Butter, ten Anchors of Brandy, thirty Gallons of Rum, a Silver Cup, six Silver Spoons, a Silver Watch, and several other Things This Vessel made no Resistance, and so they let her go as soon as they had plunder'd her This was their last Expedition, and these five were all the Ships they ever took, at least all that have come to our Knowledge

Soon after this Adventure with the *Triumvirate*, they made away for the Isles of *Orkney*, in order to clean their Ship; But an End was soon put to their Depredations; for, being stranded upon the Coast, they were apprehended by Mr *Fea*, a Gentleman of that Country, and brought up to *London*,

where a High Court of Admiralty was held for their Tryal, before Sir *Henry Penrice*, Judge of that Court, assisted by Mr Justice *Tracy* and Mr Justice *Reynolds*, on *Wednesday* and *Thursday*, the 26th and 27th of *May*, 1725

When the first Indictment was read, *Gow* obstinately refus'd to plead, for which the Court ordered his Thumbs to be ty'd together with Whip-cord. The Punishment was several times repeated by the Executioner and another Officer, they drawing the Cord every time till it broke But he still being stubborn, refusing to submit to the Court the Sentence was pronounc'd against him, which the Law appoints in such Cases, that is, That he should be taken back to Prison, and there press'd to Death The Jaylor was then order'd to conduct him back, and see that the Sentence was executed the next Morning, mean while the Tryals of the Prisoners, his Companions, went forwards.

But the next Morning, when the Press was prepar'd, pursuant to the Order of the Court the Day before, he was so terrify'd with the Apprehension of dying in that manner, that he sent his humble Petition to the Court, praying that he might be admitted to plead This Request being granted, he was brought again to the Bar, and arraign'd upon the first Indictment, to which he pleaded, *Not guilty*. Then the Depositions that had been given against the other Prisoners were repeated, upon which he was convicted, and receiv'd Sentence of Death accordingly

The Names of the rest of his Crew that were condemn'd with him, were *James Williams, Daniel Maccawly, Peter Rolson*, alias *Rollinson, John Peterson, John Winter, William Melvin, William Moore, James Belvin*, and *Alexander Rob*, who were afterwards executed, along with *Brigstock Weaver* and *William Ingram*, condemn'd at the same Time.

The LIFE of Captain BRIGSTOCK WEAVER, and WILLIAM INGRAM.

BRIGSTOCK WEAVER and *William Ingram* were both on board the *Good Fortune* Brigantine, *Thomas Anstis* Commander, when that Pyrate took the *Morning Star* in the Manner related in his Life Ingram was made Gunner of the *Morning Star*, after she was converted to *Anstis*'s Use, and *Weaver* succeeded *Anstis* in the Command of the *Good Fortune* These Particulars were depos'd at the Tryal of our Two Offenders by *Ezekiel Davis*, who was on board the *Morning-Star* when she was taken, and was detain'd by the Pyrates above ten Months after this Action It was further prov'd, that *Weaver* had been Master under *Anstis* before this, and that *Ingram* came voluntarily on board, and sign'd the Articles, while *Anstis* lay at Anchor.

Weaver seem'd at first unwilling to accept the Command of the *Good Fortune*, but was afterwards present at the taking between fifty and sixty Sail of Ships in the *West Indies* and on the Banks of *Newfoundland*, all which Time he seem'd pretty active, and discover'd but little sign of Remorse Tho' *Davis* confess'd that in private he had sometimes talk'd pretty freely about leaving the Ship, and had always behav'd himself in a very civil manner But as for *Ingram*'s Part, he was so far from being unwilling to leave his Companions, that he did all he could to prevent any Body else from getting away In particular, while they were at *Cuba*, one *Mayork*, a *Portuguese*, desir'd Leave to go ashore, which was granted him, and he took his
Gun

Gun and went But *Ingram* miftrufted he had a Defign to efcape, and therefore immediately follow'd him The poor *Portuguefe*, as foon as he was loofe, took to his Heels, and dropp'd his Gun for Expedition fake, whereupon *Ingram* drew his Cutlafs, and purfu'd, took up the Gun, and fir'd it at him, and, at laft, when he faw he could not overtake him, he return'd in a great Rage, and fwore, if he could have catch'd him, he would have cut him in two

The Stories of thefe Two Men are fo interwoven with Others, that 'twill be impoffible to diftinguifh many of their particular Actions They were, however prov'd to have been concern'd, if not the principal Actors, in the following Pyracies. 1ft, The feizing a *Dutch* Ship in *Auguft*, 1722, and taking from thence an hundred Pieces of Holland, Value 800 *l* a Thoufand Pieces of Eight, Value 250 *l* 2 ly, the entering and pillaging the *Dolphin* of *London*, *William Haddock*, out of which they got three hundred Pieces of Eight, Value 75 *l*, forty Gallons of Rum, and other Things, on the twentieth of *November* in the fame Year 3dly, The ftealing out of a Ship call'd the *Don Carlos*, *Lot Neekins* Mafter, four hundred Ounces of Silver, Value 100 *l* fifty Gallons of Rum, Value 30 *s* a Thoufand Pieces of Eight, an hundred Piftoles, and other valuable Goods, and 4thly, The taking from a Ship call'd the *Portland* ten Pipes of Wine, Value 250 *l* The two latter Facts both in the Year 1721

Weaver came in *May*, 1723, to the Houfe of Mr *Thomas Smith* in *Briftol*, with whom he had been acquainted nine or ten Years before, in a very ragged Condition, and told him that he had been taken by Pyrates, and made his Efcape from 'em Mr *Smith* pity'd his Condition, and immediately lent him fome Money, and one Captain *Edwards* fupply'd him with 10 *l* more, to buy him Clothes, and other Neceffaries They moreover provided a Lodging for him at the *Griffin*, a publick Inn, and he walk'd openly about the Town From thence he went to *Hereford* to fee his Relations, being born in that City, where he ftaid fome Weeks, and then came back to *Briftol*, ftill continuing to walk up and down unmolefted, till about *Michaelmas* he was taken up by Captain *Jofeph Smith*, who was Commander of the *Hamilton*, when fhe was taken by *Anftis*, at which Time *Weaver* was Mafter of the *Good Fortune* Brigantine His Apprehenfion was in the following manner

Weaver was walking along one of the Streets of *Briftol* when he met the Captain, and was known

by him The Captain afk'd him how he did, and defir'd to drink a Bottle with him, which being agreed to, when they came to the Tavern, he told *Weaver*, that he had been a great Sufferer by his boarding the Ship, and had in particular loft a confiderable Quantity of Liquor, *therefore, Mr* Weaver (fays he) *as I underftand you are in good Circumftances, I expect you will make me fome Reftitution, which if you do, I will never hurt a Hair of your Head, becaufe you was very civil to me when I was in your Hands* The Equivalent demanded was four Hogfheads of Cyder; which whether *Weaver* was able to procure or not, or whether he imagin'd himfelf fafe enough without it, we can't determine However fo it was, that the Cyder was not produc'd, and *Weaver* was apprehended, brought to *London*, try'd along with *Ingram*, and received Sentence of Death at the fame Time with *Gow* and his Crew

Ingram appear'd, according to all the Evidence, to have been a very refolute hardened Fellow, always one of the forwardeft in any Action It was depofed againft him in particular, That one *Benjamin Sates* defired to leave the Pyrate Service, and all the Crew confented to it but *Ingram*, fo he was detained only upon his Oppofition. every Man, it feems, among the Pyrates having Liberty to hinder another from going away. This was the Fact before related concerning the *Portuguefe*, made his Cafe look very darkly.

But every Body, on the contrary, gave *Weaver* a good Character, with refpect to his Behaviour, tho' his having acted as a Pyrate was as clear as the Sun at Noon day. One Mr *Parker*, a Surgeon declar'd in particular, That when he was taken by the *Good Fortune*'s Company, they put burning Matches between his Fingers, and twice threw him overboard But *Weaver* took his Part, though he gain'd the ill Will of a great Part of the Ship's Crew by fo doing

When Mr. *Weaver* and Others, continued he, came on board our Veffel, he faid to me, Well, Doctor, *what do you think of it? how fhall you like to be a Prifoner ———— I can't fay I have any great Liking to it, faid I, but what muft be, muft be, You fay right,* (quoth *Weaver*) *I am a Prifoner as well as you, but as your Ship fell in our Way, was oblig'd to fpeak with you Now we have got our Hands in the Lyon's Mouth, we muft draw them out again as gently as we can* This and a great deal more was faid on his Behalf; but nothing was fufficient to invalidate the plain Matter of Fact that was produc'd

The LIFE of Captain JOHN UPTON.

HE was about fifty Years of Age at the
Time of his Execution in *May*, 1729 He
was born at *Deptford*, of honeft Parents,
who gave him an Education fuitable to their Station,
teaching him to read and write, and making him fit
for Bufinefs   He ferv'd his Time to a Waterman on
the River with Approbation, having always a good
Character, 'till his laft unhappy Voyage   From his
leaving his Mafter 'till his Death, he had fpent the
greateft Part of his Time at Sea, chiefly to Men of
War, aboard of which he had commonly ferv'd as
Boatfwain, Quarter-Mafter, or fome other inferior
Officer   When he was at home, he liv'd in Reputation among his Neighbours, having a Wife and Family   And this had been his Manner of Living for
twenty eight Years

The Reafon of his going abroad the laft Time,
and leaving behind him four Orphans, he declared to
have been his receiving Information that five Actions
were taken out againft him, for Debts contracted by
his Wife in his Abfence, of which he knew nothing
till after her Death, when Creditors came to him
hourly for Sums of Money on his faid deceafed Wife's
Account   The Surprize of thefe Difcoveries, and
the Fear of an Imprifonment, made him precipitately
leave his Habitation, and fly to *Pool* in *Dorfetfhire*,
whence he fet fail as Boatfwain, on board the *John
and Elizabeth* Merchant-man, Captain *Hooper* Commander, being bound for *Bonavifta* in *Newfoundland*,
and never returned to *England* again till he was
brought Prifoner by the *Nottingham* Man of War, in
Order to his fubfequent Trial   It was on the 12th
of *July*, 1723 that he departed from the *English*
Coaft.

The Fact for which he fuffered was fworn on him
by *Charles Dimmock*, chief Mate, and *Henry Eaton*,
fecond Mate, of the *Perry* Galley, and *Peter Pur-
nell*, a Paffenger in the fame Veffel   We will firft relate their Depofitions, and then the Malefactor's own
Account of his Voyage, as it was extracted from his
Pocket Journal, which is the only Thing we could
have any Information of, as he had never attained to
the fupreme Command among the Pirates, and confequently his Story could never make any Figure in the
general Account

The Subftance of what they depofed was, That
Upton was Boatfwain of their Galley in a Voyage
from *Barbadoes* to *Briftol*, when, on the 14th of
November, 1725, in the Latitude of forty Deg. N
fhe was taken by a Pyrate Sloop, called the *Night
Rambler*, of which one *Cooper* was Commander
That the Prifoner expreffed great Satisfaction at
meeting of the Pirates, voluntarily lifted with them,
and fign'd their Articles   That foon after they took
a *French* Sloop, which with the *Perry-Galley* they
carry'd to *Aruba*, an Ifland near *Curafao*, where
the Prizes were both plunder'd, and a Divifion of

the Booty made, when *Upton* had his Share along
with the reft, there being out of the *Perry-Galley*
alone three hundred and fifty Pounds in Money, befides her Provifions, Stores, Rigging, &c: That
they (the Evidences) were kept on that Ifland feventeen Days, during which Time they muft have
ftarv'd had not the Doctor of the Pirates relieved
them, which Tendernefs of the Doctor *Upton* obferving, he fwore at him, and faid, *Damn 'em let
'em ftarve*   That the Prifoner advis'd the Pirates to
burn the *Perry Galley*, with her Captain and chief
Mate in her, and appear'd to be more cruel in his
Behaviour, than any of the older Pirates   That, in
particular, he made a Cat of nine Tails, and faw the
firft Mate receive two hundred Lafhes with it, and
that he endeavour'd, by the moft inhuman Treatment, to oblige the fecond Mate to join with them.

Upton could not fay a great deal in his own Defence, the Evidence againft him having been fo full
and clear, what he urged moft was, his having been
forced to join the Pirates   He called fome Perfons
to vindicate his Character; but they could fay no
thing with refpect to the Facts that were charged
upon him, nor did he pretend himfelf abfolutely to
deny them, only endeavoured to palliate all the moft
criminal Circumftances.   He faid, he never fign'd
their Articles, that his Name on the Lift was written
by fomebody elfe, and that whatever Service he did,
'twas for Fear of being murder'd   He confeffed his
making the Cat of nine Tails, but faid it was upon
exprefs Orders, which he durft not difobey   In a
Word, the Jury brought him in Guilty, and Sentence of Death was pronounced againft him accordingly

We fhall now proceed with the Account extracted
from his Journal   It has been already mentioned,
that he was bound for *Bonavifta* from *England*   He
arrived there, and was difcharge by mutual confent,
when, being at Liberty, he contracted with one
William Knight, a Planter there, to ferve him a
Twelvemonth in Furring and Fifhing for 18 l Wages,
which Agreement he punctually fulfill'd, and then left
his Service to feek fomething further

On the 31ft of *Auguft*, 1724 he went Paffenger in
a Sloop to *Bofton* in *New-England*, whence he fhipp'd
himfelf on board the *Mary* Merchant-man, *John
Kent* Mafter, made a Voyage in her to the Bay of
Honduras, and fo returned to *New-England*   It
was after this that he went on board the *Perry Galley*,
Captain *King* Commander, bound to *Barbadoes* and
Briftol   At *Barbadoes* the Ship was del vered and
laden again, and then they prepared for *England*
Before their Departure, *Upton* defired the Captain to
difcharge him, and fuffer him to go on board his
Majefty's Ship the *Lynn*, Captain *Cooper* Com-
mander, but Captain *King* abfolutely deny'd his Requeft

November the 9th, 1725 the *Perry Galley* set sail, and on the 12th of the same Month they were taken by the Pirates, who commanding them to hoist their Boat out, they ordered the Captain and Mate to come there n aboard their Vessel, which was done accordingly The Pirates then returned with the Boat to the Galley, and made themselves absolute Masters of her immediately One of them according to this Journal, swore at *Upton* in a terrrible Manner, and said, D——n you, you old Son of a B——h, *I know you, and you shall go along with us, or else I'll cut your Liver out* After this he beat him violently with his Cutlash, and the same Evening, when *Upton* was carried on board the Pirate Ship, three of the Gang attacked him, one with a Pistol cock'd and levelled at his Forehead, another with a Pistol at his right Ear, and a third with a Fork in each Hand pointing at his Breast, swearing, *That they would blow out his Brains, if he did not sign their Articles that Instant* The Journal added, that *Upton* refused, and desired them to defer till next Morning, urging his four Children, and the Dislike he had to their Way of Life and that when they insisted on his Compliance, he called the Captain as a Witness of his being forced, while one of the Company subscrib'd his Name

This is his own Account concerning his Entering, but it is very probable this Journal might be a Contrivance to confront the Evidence against him, if ever it should be taken; for the Deponents swore positively and circumstantially; and they were all three Men of an undoubted Character

The Journal goes on with saying, that the Pirates carried the *Perry Galley* and her Men to the Island of *Ruby*, where they were kept till the 10th of *December*, about which Time one informed the Pirate that he saw her a Sail to Offing, upon which they made after her and took her, then she proved to be a small *Dutch* Sloop *Upton* and some others were sent on board this Vessel, where watching an Opportunity, they made their Escape, carry'd away the Sloop, and got her down to the Point of *Gourda*, joining to the *Moskitta* Shore What their Design was in this Action, we cannot determine, having only his Word for it, which to be sure gives us the best Side of Things. But to proceed, according to the best Light we have,

In the Month of *January*, 1725 he got his Passage along with the Traders to *Carpenter's* River, otherwise called the *Matine*, belonging to the *Spaniards*, to which Place they traffick for Cocoa He arriv'd there on the 12th of *February*, when the Governor gave him Leave to go to *Porto Bello*, by the Way of *Panama*, there being no other safe Passage thither on Account of the wild *Indians* In twenty-eight Days he set out with the Mules for the City of *Carritago*, lying fifty-six Leagues on the burning Mountains, and esteemed to be about Midway between the North and South Seas When he came thither, he was taken up by the Governor for a Spy, and kept Prisoner three three Month and four Days, after which he was sent to *Kildare*, on the South Sea, being still confin'd, where he staid a Month longer, waiting for the Barks which came out of the Lake of *Granada*, and were bound for *Panama* At last he was sent on board the Admiral of *New Spain*, who commanded the *Lima* Fleet in the *South Sea*, where he was again very strictly examined

The *Spaniards* desired him to enter into their Service, which he absolutely refused to comply with, and desired to go on Shore for *Porto Bello*, but as he would not agree to their Proposals, they would not grant him his Request, and so, instead of setting him ashore where he desired, they sent him to *Panama*, where he was imprisoned four Months and five Days longer After this, with thirty two *Dutchman*, who were also detained Prisoners, he was sent to *Porto bello*, and there put on board the Galleons bound for *Old Spain* From them he found some Means of escaping, but does not say in what Manner, and then he entered on board a *New York* Sloop, Captain *Phœnix* Commander, bound for *Jamaica*, where they arrived on the 28th of *December*, 1726 He had not been here long, before he was press'd on board his Majesty's Ship the *Nottingham*, commanded by Captain *Charles Cotterel*, where he remained more than two Years in the Quality of Quarter-Master, behaving himself all the Time very obediently to his Officers Commands, till he was accused of Piracy, and brought home in order to his Trial For the Truth of this latter Part of the Story, he said, he appealed to Captain *Cotterel*

At the Place of Execution he made some Reflections that are not proper to be rehears'd, and said, he forgave all his Enemies Being ask'd at the Desire of a Gentleman, whether or no he persuaded the Pirates to burn the *Perry* Galley, with Captain *King*, and Mr *Dimmock* the chief Mate, on board of her, he stedfastly denied the Fact, protesting that he never either proposed such a Thing himself, or gave his Vote for the doing it One would think the Words of a dying Man should have some Weight, yet how can we believe the Truth of what was now asserted, after three such creditable Witnesses had sworn the direct contrary, and declared to his Face, that he actually did persuade this Piece of Villany There was no Need for them to have added such a Circumstance, if it had not been true, because there was enough without it to have procured the Sentence that was passed on him, and have given him all the Satisfaction they could now expect I mean, that of seeing him suffer what was the just Punishment due for his Crimes

The LIFE *of* Captain EDWARD LOW.

EDWARD *Low* was born in *Westminster*, and had his Education there, such as it was, for he could neither write or read Nature seem to have design'd him for a Pyrate from his Childhood, for he very early began the Trade of Plundering, and was wont to raise Contributions among all the Boys of *Westminster*, and if any were bold enough to refuse it, a Battle was the Consequence, but *Low* was so hardy, as well as bold, that there was no getting the better of him, so that he robbed the Youths of their Farthings, with Impunity, when he grew bigger, he took to Gaming in a low Way, for it was commonly among the Footmen in the Lobby of the House of Commons, where he used to play the whole Game (as they term it) that is, cheat all he could, and those who pretended to dispute it with him, must fight him

The Virtues of some of his Family were equal to his, one of his Brothers was a Youth of Genius, when he was but seven Years old, he used to be carried in a Basket upon a Porter's Back, into a Crowd and snatch Hats and Wigs According to the exact Chronology of *Newgate*, he was the first who practised this ingenious Trick After this, he applied himself to picking of Pockets When he increased in Strength, he attempted greater Things, such as House breaking, &c But after he had run a short Race, he had the Misfortune of ending his Days at *Tyburn*, in Company with *Stephen Bunce*, and the celebrated *Jack Hall* the Chimney Sweeper

But to return to *Ned*, when he came to Man's Estate, at his eldest Brother's Desire, he went to Sea with him, and so continued for three or four Years, and then they parted *Ned* work'd in a Rigging-House in *Boston*, in *New-England*, for a while About the Year 1717, he took a Trip home to *England*, to see his Mother, who was then living His Stay was not long here, but taking Leave of his Friends and Acquaintance, for the last Time he should see them (for so he was pleased to say) he returned to *Boston*, and work'd a Year or two longer at the Rigging Business But being too apt to disagree with his Masters, he left them, and shipp'd himself in a Sloop that was bound to the Bay of *Honduras*

When the Sloop arrived in the Bay, *Ned Low* was appointed Patron of the Boat, which was employ'd in cutting of Logwood, and bringing it aboard to lace the Ship, for that is the Commodity they make the Voyage for In the Boat were twelve Men besides *Low* who all went arm'd, because of the *Spaniards*, from whom this Logwood is but little better than Stole It happen'd that the Boat one Day came aboard just before Dinner was ready, and *Low* desir'd that they might stay and dine, but the Captain, being in a hurry for his Lading, order'd them a Bottle of Rum, and to take t'other Trip, because no Time should be lost This provok'd the Boat's Crew, but particularly *Low*, who took up a loaded

Musquet and fired at the Captain, but missing him, he shot another poor Fellow thro' the Head, then put off the Boat, and with his twelve Companions got to Sea The next Day they took a small Vessel, and went into her, made a black Flag, and declared War against all the World

They then proceeded to the Island of the *Grand Caimanes*, intending to have fitted up their small Vessel, and prepare themselves, as well as their Circumstances would permit, for their honourable Employment, but falling in Company with *George Lowther*, another Pyrate there, and he paying his Compliments to *Low*, as great Folks do to one another when they meet, and offering himself is an Ally, *Low* accepted the Terms, and so the Treaty was sign'd without Plenipo's, or any other Formalities

We have already given an Account of their joint Pyracies, under *Lowther* as chief Commander, till the 28th of *May* 1722, when they took a Brigantine of *Boston*, bound thither from St *Christophers*, at which they parted, and *Edward Low* went into the Brigantine, with forty four others, who chose him their Captain They took with them two Guns, four Swivels, six Quarter casks of Powder, some Provisions and so left *Lowther* to prosecute his Adventures, with the Men he had left

Their first Adventure in the Brigantine was on *Sunday*, the 3d Day of *June*, when they took a Vessel belonging to *Amboy*, *John Hance* Master, whom he rifled of his Provisions, and let go, the same Day he met with a Sloop, *James Colquhoon* Master, off *Rhode Island*, bound into that Port This Ship he first Plundered, and then cut away his Boltsprit, and all his Rigging, as also his Sails from his Yards, and wounded the Master, to prevent his getting in to give Intelligence, and then stood away to the South Eastward, with all the Sail he could make, there being but little Wind

Low judged right in making Sail from the Coast, for a longer stay had proved fatal to him, for notwithstanding the disabled Condition he had brought the Sloop into, she made shift to get into *Block-Island*, at 12 o'Clock that Night, and immediately dispatch'd a Whale Boat to *Rhode Island*, which got thither by seven the next Morning, with an Account of the Pyrate, his Force, and what had happened to him As soon as the Governor had received this Information, he ordered a Drum to beat up for Voluntiers, and two of the best Sloops then in the Harbour to be fitted out He gave Commissions to one Captain *John Headland*, and Captain *John Brown*, and in ten Days, the former had eight Guns and two Swivels, and the latter six Guns, well fitted with small Arms, and in both Sloops 140 stout Fellows All this was performed with so much Expedition, that before Sun set they were under Sail, turning out of the Harbour, at the same Time the Pyrate was seen from *Block Island*, which gave great Hope, that the Sloops would be Masters of her the

next

next Day This however did not happen, for the Sloops returned into the Harbour some Days afterwards, without so much as seeing their Enemy.

After this Escape, Captain *Low* went into Port upon the Coast, for he had not fresh Water enough to run to the Islands, where he staid a few Days, getting Provisions and what Necessaries the Crew wanted, and then sail'd for Purchase (as they call it) steering their Course for *Marblehead*.

About the 12th of *July*, the Brigantine sailed into the Harbour of Port *Rosemary*, and there found thirteen Ships and Vessels, but none of Force, at Anchor, they spread their black Flag, and ran in among them, *Low* telling them from the Brigantine, that they should have no Quarters if they resisted. In the mean Time they mann'd and arm'd their Boat, and took Possession of every one of them, plunder'd them of what they thought fit, and converted one to their own Use, *viz* a Scooner of 80 Tuns. Aboard of this they put 10 Carriage Guns, and 50 Men, and *Low* himself went Captain, and named her the *Fancy*, making one *Charles Harris* (who was at first forced into their Service out of the *Greyhound* of *Boston*, by *Lowther*, of which Ship *Harris* was second Mate) Captain of the Brigantine. Out of the Vessels they took several Hands, and encreased the Company to 80 Men, who all signed the Articles, some willingly, and a few perhaps by force, and so they sailed away from *Marblehead*.

Some Time after this, they met with two Sloops bound for *Boston*, with Provisions for the Garrison, the Scooner coming up first, she attacked them; but there happening to be an Officer and some Soldiers on board, who gave them a warm Reception, *Low* chose to stay till he could be joined by the Brigantine, in the mean while the Sloops made the best of their Way, and the Pyrates gave them Chace two Days, and at last lost Sight of them in a Fog.

They now steer'd for the Leeward Islands, but in their Voyage met with such a Hurricane of Wind, that the like had not been known, the Sea ran Mountain high, and seemed to threaten them every Moment with Destruction. It was no Time now to look out for Plunder, but to save themselves, if possible, All Hands were continually employed Night and Day, on board the Brigantine, and all little enough, for the Waves went over her, so that they were forced to keep the Pump constantly going, besides their Buckets. Notwithstanding which, finding themselves not able to keep her free, and seeing the utmost Danger before their Eyes, they turn'd to the Tackle, and hoisted out their Provisions, and other heavy Goods, and threw them over board, with six of their Guns, so that by lightening the Vessel, she might rise to the Top of the Sea with the Waves. They were also going to cut away their Mast; but considering how dangerous it would be to be left in such a Condition, they resolv'd to delay it to the last, which was a great deal of Prudence in them, for a Ship without Masts or Sails lies like a Log upon the Water, and, if attack'd must fight with Disadvantage, the working of her being the most artful Part of the Engagement, because she may sometimes bring all her great Guns on one Side, to bear upon her Enemy, when the disabled Ship can do little or nothing.

But to proceed, by their throwing over-board the heavy Goods, the Vessel made considerable less Water, and they could keep it under with the Pump only, which gave them Hopes and new Life, so that instead of cutting all away, they took necessary Measures to secure the Mast, by making Preventor-

Shrowds, &c and then they wore and lay too on the other Tack, till the Storm was over. The Scooner made some somewhat better Weather of it of the two, but was pretty roughly handled notwithstanding, having split her Main sail, sprung her Bowsprit, and cut her Anchors from her Bows. The Brigantine by running away to Leeward, when she wore upon the Larboard Tack, had lost Sight of the Scooner, but not knowing whether she might be safe or not, as soon as the Wind abated, she set her Main Sail and Top-Sail, and made short Trips to Windward; and the next Day had the good Fortune to come in Sight of her Consort, who, upon a Signal, which the other knew, bore down to her, and the Crew were overjoy'd to meet again, after such ill Treatment from the Winds and Seas.

After the Storm, *Low* got safe to a small Island, one of the Weathermost of the *Caribbees*, and there fitted their Vessels, as well as the Place could afford. They got Provisions of the Natives in exchange for Goods of their own, and as soon as the Brigantine was ready, 'twas judg'd necessary to take a short Cruise, and leave the Scooner in the Harbour till her Return. The Brigantine sail'd out accordingly, and had not been out many Days before they met a Ship at Sea, that had lost all her Masts. On board of her they went, and took from her in Money and Goods, to the Value of 1000*l* and so left her in the Condition they found her. This Ship was bound home from *Barbadoes*, but losing her Masts in the late Storm, was making for *Antegoa*, to refit, where she afterwards arriv'd.

The Storm just spoken of, was found to have done incredible Damage in those Parts of the World, but however, it appear'd to have been more violent at *Jamaica*, both to the Island and Shipping. There was such a prodigious Swell of the Sea, that several hundred Tuns of Stones and Rocks, were thrown over the Wall of the Town of *Port-Royal* and the Town it self was overflowed, and above half destroy'd, there being the next Morning five Foot Water from one End to the other, the Cannon of Fort *Charles* were dismounted, and some washed into the Sea, and four hundred People lost their Lives, a more melancholly Sight was scarce ever seen when the Water ebb'd away all the Streets being covered with Ruins of Houses, Wrecks of Vessels, and a great Number of dead Bodies, for forty Sail of Ships in the Harbour, were cast away.

The Brigantine returned to the Island, where she had left the Scooner, who being ready to sail, it put to the Vote of the Company, what Voyage to take next, and herein they follow'd the Advice of the Captain, who thought it not advisable to go any farther to Leeward, because of the Men of War who were cruising in their several Stations, which they were not at all fond of meeting, and therefore it was agreed to go to the *Azores*, or Western Islands.

The latter End of *July*, *Low* took a *French* Ship of 34 Guns, and carried her along with him to the *Azores*. He came into St *Michael's* Road the 3d of *August*, and took seven Sail that were lying there, *viz* the *Nostre Dame Mere de Dieu*, Captain *Roche* Commander, the *Dove*, Captain *Cox*, the *Rose* Pink, formerly a Man of War, Captain *Thompson*, another *English* Ship, Captain *Chandler*, and three other Vessels. He threatned all with present Death who resisted, which struck such a Terror to them, that they yielded themselves up a Prey to the Villains, without firing a Gun.

The Pyrates being in great Want of Water and fresh Provisions, *Low* sent to the Governor of St *Michael's* for a Supply, and promised upon that

Conditio.

Condition to releafe the Ships he had taken, but otherwife to burn them all This Demand the Governor thought it not prudent to refufe, but fent the Provifion he required, upon which, he releafed fix of the Ships (after he had plundered them of what he thought fit) and the other, viz. the Rofe Pink, was made a Pyrate Ship, which Low himfelf took the Command of.

The Pyrates took feveral of the Guns out of the French Ship, which proved not very fit for their Turn, fo that they mounted them aboard the Rofe, and condemned the former to the Flames. They took all the Crew out of her, but the Cook, who, they faid, being a greafy Fellow would fry well in the Fire, fo the poor Man was bound to the Mainmaft, and burnt in the Ship, to the no fmall Diverfion of Low and his Mirmidons.

Low ordered the Scooner to lie in the Rare between St Michael's and St Mary's, where, about the 20th of Auguft, Captain Carter in the Wright Galley had the ill Fortune to come in her Way, and becaufe at firft they fhewed Inclinations to defend themfelves and what they had, the Pyrates cut and mangled them in a barbarous Manner; particularly fome Portuguefe Paffengers, two of which being Friers, they tied them up at each Arm of the Fore-Yard, but let them down again before they were quite dead, and this they repeated feveral Times out of Sport.

Another Portuguefe, who was alfo Captain Carter's Paffenger, putting on a forrowful Countenance at what he faw acted, one of this vile Crew attacked him upon the Deck, faying, he did not like his Looks, and thereupon gave him one Blow a-crofs his Belly with his Cutlafh, that cut out his Bowels, and he fell down dead without fpeaking a Word At the fame Time, another of thefe Rogues cutting at a Prifoner, miffed his Mark, and Low ftanding in his Way, very opportunely received the Stroke upon his under Jaw, which laid the Teeth bare, upon this the Surgeon was called, who immediately ftitched up the Wound, but Low finding Fault with the Operation, the Surgeon being tollerably drunk, as it was cuftomary for every Body to be, ftruck Low fuch a Blow with his Fift, that broke out all the Stitches, and then bid him few up his Chops himfelf and be damned, fo that Low made a very pitiful Figure for fome Time after.

When they had plundered Captain Carter's Ship, feveral of them were for burning her, as they had done the Frenchman, but it was otherwife refolved at laft, for, after they had cut her Cables, Rigging, and Sails to Pieces, they left her to the Mercy of the Sea.

After thefe Depredations, they fteered for the Ifland of Madera, where miffing other Booty, they took up with a Fifhing Boat, with two old Men and Boy in her, one of which they detained on board, and fent the other afhore with a Flag of Truce, demanding a Boat of Water of the Governor, on Pain of taking away the old Man's Life, whom they threatned to hang at the Yard Arm, upon their Refufal, but the Thing being comply'd with, the old Man was honourably (as the Pyrates fay) difcharged, and all the three much handfomer cloathed than when they took them From this Ifland they failed to the Canaries, where meeting no Prey, they continued their Courfe for the Cape de Verd Iflands, and at Bonvifta took a Ship called the Liverpool Merchant, Captain Goulding, from whom they ftole a great quantity of Provifions and dry Goods, 300 Gallons Brandy, two Guns and Carriages, a Maft, Yard, and Hawfers, befides fix of his Men, and then

would not let them trade there, nor at St Nicholas, but obliged Captain Goulding to go with his Snip to the Ifle of May.

The Pyrate alfo took among thefe Iflands a Ship belonging to Leverpool, one Scot Commander, two Portuguefe Sloops bound for Brafil; a fmall Englifh Sloop trading there, James Peafe Mafter, bound to Santa Cruz, and three Sloops from St Thomas bound to Curafo, the Mafters Names were Lilly, Staples, and Simpkins, all which they plundered, and then let them go about their Bufinefs, except one Sloop, which they fitted up for the following Purpofe.

Low had heard by one of the above-mentioned Ships, that two fmall Gallies were expected every Day at the Weftern Iflands, viz. the Greyhound, Captain Glafs, and the Joliff, Captain Aram, the former of which was defigned to be fitted for the pyratical Trade to Brafil, if Things had happened to their Minds They mann'd the Sloop, and fent her in queft of one or both of thefe Ships to the Weftern Iflands aforefaid, whilft they careen'd their Ship Rofe, at one of the Cape de Verd's But now Fortune, that had hitherto been fo propitious to them, left her Minions, and baffled for the prefent all their Hopes, for the Sloop miffing of their Prey, was reduc'd to great Neceffities for want of Provifions and Water, fo that they ventured to go afhore at St Michael's for a Supply, and to pafs for a Trader, but they play'd their Parts fo aukwardly, that they were fufpected by the Governor to be what they really were, and he was foon put out of Doubt by a Vifit fome Portuguefe made them, who happened unluckily to be Paffengers in Captain Carter's Ship, when Low took her, and knew the Gentlemen's Faces very well, upon which the whole Crew was conducted into the Caftle, where they were provided for as long as they liv'd.

Low, in the mean Time, did not fire quite fo ill, but had his intended Voyage to Brafil fpoil'd, by the overfetting of his Ship, when fhe was upon the Careen, whereby fhe was loft, fo that he was reduc'd to his old Scooner, which he called the Fancy, aboard of which they all went, to the Number of 100, as vile Rogues as ever ended their Lives at Tyburn They proceeded now to the Weft Indies, but before they had gotten far on their Voyage, they attacked a rich Portuguefe Snip, called the Noftra Signiora de Victoria, bound home from Bahia, and after fome Refiftance took her Low tortured feveral of the Men, to make them declare where the Money (which he fuppofed they had on board) lay, and extorted by that Means, a Confeffion that the Captain had, during the Chace, hung out of the Cabin Window, a Bag with 11,000 Moidores, and that, as foon as he was taken, he cut the Rope off, and let it drop into the Sea.

Low, upon hearing what a Prize had efcaped him, raved like a Fury, fwore a thoufand Oaths, and ordered the Captains Lips to be cut off, which he broil'd before his Face, and afterward murthered him and all his Crew, being thirty two Perfons.

After this bloody Action, they continued their Courfe, till they came to the Northward of all the Iflands, where they cruifed for about a Month, in which Time they made Prizes of the following Veffels, viz. a Sloop from New York to Curacoa, Robert Leonard Mafter, a Sloop from the Bay, bound to New York, Craig Mafter, a Snow from London and Jamaica, bound to New York, and the Stanhope Pink, Andrew Delbridge Mafter, from Jamaica to Bofton, which laft they burnt, becaufe of Low's irreconcileable Averfion to New England Men

After

After this Cruise, they went into one of the Islands and clean'd, and then steer'd by the Bay of *Honduras*, where they arrived about the Middle of *March* 1722 3, and met a Sloop turning out of the said Bay The Pyrates had hoisted up *Spanish* Colours, and continued them till they drew near the Sloop : then they hall'd them down, hoisted their black Flag, fired a broadside, and boarded her This Sloop was a *Spaniard* of six Guns, and 70 Men, that came into the Bay that Morning, and meeting there with five *English* Sloops and a Pink, had made Prizes of them all, plundered them, and brought the Masters of the Vessels away Prisoners, for the Ransom of the Logwood , their Names were *Tutbell*, *Norton*, *Newbury*, *Spratfort*, *Clark*, and *Parrot* The *Spaniards* made no Resistance, so that the *English* Pyrates soon became their Masters, and fell to rifling , but finding the above mentioned People in the Hold, and several English Goods, they consulted *Low* their Captain thereupon, and without examining any further, the Resolution pass'd to kill all the Company ; and the Pyrates, without any Ceremony, fell Pell-Mell to Execution, with their Swords, Cutlashes, Pole-Axes, and Pistols, cutting, slashing, and shooting the poor *Spaniards*, at a sad Rate Some of the miserable Creatures jump'd down into the Hold, but could not avoid the Massacre , they met Death every where, for if they escap'd it from one Hand, they were sure to perish by another , the only Prospect they had of Life, was to fly from the Rage of those merciless Men, and to trust to the more merciful Sea , and accordingly a great many leap'd overboard, and swam for the Shore

Low perceiving this, ordered the Canoe to be mann'd, and sent in Pursuit of them , by which Means several of the poor unhappy Men were knocked on the Head in the Water, as they endeavouring to get to Land , however, about twelve of them reached to the Shore, but in a miserable Condition, being very much wounded, and what became of them afterwards was not known , except that one, who, while the Pyrates were at their Sports and Pastimes ashore, finding himself very weak, and fainting with his Wounds, and not knowing where to go for Help and Relief, in this Extremity, he came back to them, and begg'd for God sake, in the most earnest Manner possible, that they would give him Quarters , upon which, one of the Villains took hold of him, and said, G— d——n him, he *would give him good Quarters presently*, and made the poor *Spaniard* down on his Knees ; then taking his Fusee, put the Muzzle of it into his Mouth, and fired down his Throat. 'Twas thought the rest did not long survive their miserable Condition, and could not prolong their Lives, to add to the Misery of them

When the murdering Work was over, they rumaged the *Spanish* Pyrate, and brought all the Booty aboard their own Vessels The six Masters aforementioned, found in the Hold, they restored to their respective Vessels · They forced away the Carpenter from the Pink, and then set Fire to the Spanish Sloop, and burnt her , which last Scene concluded the Destruction of their Enemy, Ship, and Crew

Low set the Masters of the Vessels free, but would not suffer them to steer for *Jamaica*, where they were bound, for fear the Men of War should get Intelligence of them , but forced them all to go to *New York*, threatning them with Death, when they met them again, if they refused to comply with his Demands

In the next Cruise, which was between the Leeward Islands and the Main, they took two Snows, bound from *Jamaica* to *Liverpool*, and a Snow from *Jamaica* to *London*, *Bridds* Master ; as also a Ship from *Biddiford* to *Jamaica*, *John Pinkham* Commander ; and two Sloops from *Jamaica* to *Virginia*.

On the 27th of *May*, *Low* and his Consort *Harris*, came off *South Carolina*, and met with three good Ships, viz the *Crown* Captain *Loveriegn*, the *King William*, the *Carteret*, and a Brigantine, who all came out of *Carolina* together two Days before, The Pyrates were at the Trouble of chasing them, and Captain *Lovereign* being the sternmost, she fell first a Prey into their Hands , and they spent all the Day in coming up with the rest

Within a few Days they took a Ship called the *Amsterdam Merchant*, Captain *Willard*, from *Jamaica*, but belonging to *New-England*, as *Low* let none of that Country depart without some Marks of his Rage, he cut off this Gentleman's Ears, slit up his Nose, and cut him in several Places of his Body, and after plundering his Ship, let him pursue his Voyage

After this he took a Sloop bound to *Amboy*, *William Frazier* Master, with whom Mr *Low* happening to be displeased, he order'd lighted Matches to be ty'd between the Mens Fingers which burnt all the Flesh off the Bones, they then cut them in several Parts of their Bodies with Knives and Cutlashes, afterwards they took all their Provisions away, and set some of them ashore in an uninhabited Part of the Country

The *Kingston*, Captain *Estwick* , another Ship, one *Burrington* Master , two Brigantines from *Carolina* to *London* , a Sloop from *Virginia* to *Bermudas*, a Ship from *Glascow* to *Virginia* , a Scooner from *New York* to *South Carolina* ; a Pink from *Virginia* to *Dartmouth* , and a Sloop from *Philadelphia* to *Surinam*, all fell a Prey to these Villains upon this Cruise, besides the above mentioned

It happened that at this Time one of his Majesty's Ships was upon the Cruise, on this Station, and got Intelligence of some of the mischievous Actions of this Miscreant, by one of the Vessels that had been plundered by him , upon which, steering as directed, she came in Sight of the Pyrates by break of Day, on the 10th of *June* The Rovers looking out for Prey, soon saw, and gave Chace to the Man of War, which was called the *Greyhound*, a Ship of 20 Guns, and 120 Men, rather inferior in Force than otherwise, to the two Pyrate Vessels The *Greyhound*, finding them so eager, was in no Doubt what they should be, and therefore tack'd and stood from them, giving the Pyrates an Opportunity to chace her for two Hours, till all Things were in Readiness for an Engagement, and the Pyrates about Gun shot off, then the *Greyhound* tack'd again, and stood towards the two Sloops One of these Sloops was called the *Fancy*, and commanded by *Low* himself, and the other the *Ranger*, commanded by *Harris*, who which hoisted their pyratical Colours, and fired each a Gun. When the *Greyhound* came within Musquet shot, she halled up her Main sail, and clapp'd close upon a Wind, to keep the Pyrates from running to Leeward, and then engag'd But when the Rogues found who they had to deal with, they edg'd away under the Man of War's Stern, and the *Greyhound* standing after them, they made a running Fight, for about two Hours, but little Wind happening, the Sloops gained from her, by the Help of their Oars, upon which the *Greyhound* left off firing, and turned all Hands to their own Oars, and at three in the Afternoon came up with them The Pyrates haul'd upon a Wind to receive the Man of War, and the Fight was immediately renew'd, with a brisk Fire on both Sides, till the *Ranger*'s Main Yard was shot down,

down, and the *Greyhound* pressing close upon the disabled Sloop, *Low*, in the other, thought fit to bear away and leave his Consort a Sacrifice to his Enemy, who (seeing the Cowardice and Treachery of his Commodore and Leader, having ten or twelve Men killed and wounded, and finding there was no Possibility of escaping) called out for Quarters, and surrender'd themselves to Justice, which proved severe enough to them a while afterwards

The Conduct of *Low* was surprizing in this Adventure, because his reputed Courage and Boldness had, hitherto, so possessed the Minds of all People, that he became a Terror, even to his own Men; but his Behaviour throughout this whole Action, shewed him to be a base cowardly Villain, for had *Low*'s Sloop fought half so briskly as *Harris*'s had done (as they were under a solemn Oath to do) the Man of War, in the Opinion of some present, could never have escur'd them

The *Greyhound* carried in their Prize to *Rhode Island*, to the great Joy of the whole Province, tho' the Satisfaction had been more compleat, if the great *Low* himself had grac'd the Triumph The Prisoners were strongly secured in a Goal, till a Court of Vice Admiralty could be held for their Tryals, which began on the 10th Day of *July*, at *Newport*, and continued three Days

This narrow Escape of *Low* and his Companions, one would have thought, might have brought them to a little Consideration of their black and horrid Crimes, and to look upon this Interval as an Opportunity put into their Hands by Providence, to reconcile themselves to God, by a hearty and sincere Repentance But alas! they were dead to all Goodness, and had not so much as one Spark of Virtue to stir them up to be thankful for such an eminent Deliverance But instead thereof, vented a Million of Oaths and Curses upon the Captain of the *Greyhound*, vowing to execute Vengeance upon all they should meet with afterwards, for the Indignity he put upon them

The first Prey that they met with, after their Fight, was a small Sloop belonging to *Nantucket*, a Whale Fishing, about 80 Miles from Land, the Master of which, one *Nathan Skiff*, a brisk young Fellow, the Pyrates cruelly whipp'd naked about the Deck, making his Torture their Sport, after which they cut off his Ears, and last of all shot him through the Head, and then sunk his Vessel, putting the rest of the Hands into their Whale Boat, with a Compass, a little Water, and a few Biskets Nevertheless, it being good Weather, they providentially got safe to *Nantucket*, beyond all Expectation

There was another Whale Boat, belonging to this Sloop last mentioned, which happened to be at some Distance from her, and, perceiving what was doing, rowed with all Speed to another Sloop not far off, to acquaint her with the Misfortune, that the Men might take care of themselves, by which Means she happily got away in Time Some Days after, *Low* took a Fishing Boat off of *Block Island*, but did not perpetrate so much Cruelty on her, contenting himself with only cutting off the Master's Head But after taking two Whale-Boats near *Rhode Island*, he caused one of the Master's Bodies to be ripp'd up, and his Intrails to be taken out, and cut off the Ears of the other, and made him eat them himself with Pepper and Salt, which hard Injunction he comply'd with, without making a Word Several other Persons he would have murthered, but Humanity prevailing in the Hearts of his Companions, they refused to put his Orders in Execution

From the Coast of *New-England*, *Low* sailed directly for *Newfoundland*, and, near Cape *Britton*,

took two or three and twenty *French* Vessels; one of which, of 22 Guns, he mann'd with Pyrates, making a sort of a Man of War of her. With this Ship he scower'd the Harbours and Banks of *Newfoundland*, and took sixteen or eighteen other Ships and Vessels, all which they plunder'd, and some they destroy'd

Thus these inhumane Wretches went on, not contented to satisfy their Avarice only, and travel in the common Road of Wickedness, but, like their Patron, the Devil, they made Mischief their Sport, Cruelty their Delight, and damning of Souls their constant Employment Of all the pyratical Crews that were ever heard of, none of the *English* Name came up to this in Barbarity, their Mirth and their Anger had much the same Effect, for both were usually gratify'd with the Cries and Groans of their Prisoners, so that they almost as often murthered a Man from the Excess of good Humour, as out of Passion and Resentment, and the Unfortunate could never be assured of Safety from them, for Danger lurked in their very Smiles An Instance of this had like to have happened to one Captain *Graves*, Master of a *Virginia* Ship which they had taken, for as soon as he came aboard of the Pyrate, *Low* took a Bowl of Punch in his Hand, and drank to him, saying, Captain *Graves*, here's half this to you But the poor Gentleman, being too sensibly touched at the Misfortune of falling into his Hands, modestly desired to be excused, for that he could not drink; whereupon *Low* draws out a Pistol, cocks it, and with the Bowl in t'other Hand, told him, he should either take one or the other. So *Graves*, without Hesitation, made Choice of the Vehicle that contained the Punch, and gutled down about a Quart, when he had the least Inclination that ever he had in his Life to be merry

About the latter End of *July* 1723, *Low* took a large Ship called the *Merry Christmas*, and fitted her for a Pyrate, cut several Ports in her, and mounted her with 34 Guns He goes aboard of this Ship himself, assumes the Title of Admiral, and hoists a black Flag, with the Figure of Death in red, at the Maintopmast Head, and takes another Voyage to the *Western Islands*, where he arrived at the Beginning of *September* The first Vessel he met with there was a Brigantine, formerly an *English* Sloop, commanded by *Elias Wild*, but lately bought by a *Portuguese* Nobleman, and altered She was manned partly with *English*, and partly with *Portuguese*, the latter *Low* caused to be hang'd, by Way of Reprisal, for some of his own Men sent thither in a Sloop from the *Cape de Verd Islands*, as has been mentioned The *English* Men he thrust into their own Boat, to shift for themselves, and set Fire to the Vessel

At St *Michael*'s, they sent in their Boats, and cut out of the Road a new *London* built Ship of 14 Guns, commanded by Captain *Tompson*, who was taken there the Year before, by *Low*, in the *Rose Pink* The Boats had fewer Men than the Ship, and Captain *Thompson* would have defended himself, but his Men through Cowardice, or too great an Inclination of becoming Pyrates themselves, refused to stand by him, and he was obliged to surrender When he came aboard the Pyrate, he and his Ears cut off close to his Head, for only proposing to resist Admiral *Low*'s black Flag, they then gave him one of his own Boats, and burnt his Ship

The next was a *Portuguese* Bark that fell into their Hands, whose Men came off somewhat better than usual, for they only cut them with their Cutlashes, out of Wantonness, turned them all into their Boat, and set their Vessel on Fire When the Boat was

going

going from the Side of the Ship, one of *Low's* Men, who, we may suppose, was forced into the Gang, was drinking with a Silver Tankard at one of the Ports, and took his Opportunity to drop into the Boat among the *Portuguese*, and lie down in the Bottom, in order to escape along with them After he had stowed himself in the Boat, so as not to be seen, it came into his Head, that the Tankard might prove of some Use to him where he was going, so he got up again, laid hold of the Utensil, and went off, without being discovered In which Attempt had he failed, no doubt his Life, if not the Lives of all the People in the Boat, would have paid for it The Name of this Man was *Richard Hains*.

Low took his old Tour to he *Canaries, Cape de Verd* Islands, and so to the Coast of *Guiney*, but nothing extraordinary happened till he arrived near *Sierraleon* in *Africa*, where he met with a Ship called the *Delight*, Captain *Hunt* Commander, the Ship the Pyrates thought fit for their own Purpose, for she had been a small Man of War, and carried 12 Guns, however, they mounted 16 on board her, mann'd her with 60 Men, and appointed one *Spriggs*, who was then their Quarter maiter, to be Captain of her, who, two Days after, separated from the Admiral, and went to the *West Indies* a pyrating, upon his own and particu'ar Company's Account, where for the present we shall leave them

---

The LIFE of Captain JOHN JAEN.

IT cannot be amiss to conclude the Lives of the Pyrates with an Account of Captain *Jaen*, who was condemn'd by an High Court of Admiralty for the Murder of his Cabin Boy, and executed at *Execution Dock* · For, tho' this Malefactor was no Pyrate, yet the said Circumstances, and his suffering for a Crime committed on the High Seas, makes this a properer Place for what we have to say concerning him, than any other in the Book We shall be as brief in our Relation as the Nature of the Case will admit, because of proceeding with the Highwaymen, &c

The Parents of *John Jaen* liv'd in very good Circumstances at *Bristol*, they bred this their Son up in the Knowledge of every Thing that was requisite for a Youth whom they designed to put to a Trade; nor did he at all balk their Expectation in the Progress he made, for he became not only a Proficient in Writing and Accompts, but attained also a considerable Insight into the *Latin* Tongue When he had finish'd the Course of his Learning, under the best Masters his Friends could provide for him, he was removed from his Pursuit of the Muses, and bound Apprentice to a Cooper in his native City, with whom he serv'd out his Time with Industry and Fidelity, tho' there was always a remarkable Severity in his Temper, which Disposition, we may suppose, at last prompted him to the barbarous Act for which he suffer'd, as soon as it found Scope to exert itself, of which it had too much at Sea, where the Master's Command is too absolute to be put into the Hands of any Man who wants Compassion

After he had compleated the Time of his Servitude, he apply'd himself to his Trade with the same Diligence he had discover'd while he was an Apprentice, going sometimes to Sea for the Advancement of his Fortune, which desir'd Effect happen'd in the Year 1724, when he became Master of a Ship called the *Burnett*, fitted out by some Merchants of *Bristol* for *South Carolina* This was the first and last Voyage in which he was Commander, for it was in his Return home in *March*, 1725, that he committed the Murder of which we shall now give such Account as was deposed against him in Court.

Being apprehended as soon as he came on Shore, and sent up to *London*, he was indicted at the same Sessions of Admiralty, where *Gow*, *Weaver*, and their Companions, received Sentence of *Death*, for the Murder of *Richard Pye* on the high Seas, within thirty Leagues of *Carolina*, and within the Jurisdiction of the Admiralty of *England*, by beating and striking the said *Richard Pye* with a Rope, on the Head, Shoulders, Arms, Back, Breast, and Sides, on the 15th of *March* last, of which beating and striking the said *Richard Pye* did languish till the 21st of the same Month, and then dy'd But the Prisoner making Affidavit in Court, that two of his material Witnesses, Captain *Samuel Jennings* and *John Morpeth*, were absent at Sea, having been gone about a Fortnight before, the Court deferr'd his Trial till another Time This Sessions of Admiralty, at which he was first indicted, was held on the 26th and 27th of *May*, in the same Year the Fact was committed, and not above nine Weeks after the Death of the Boy

On the 27th of *April*, 1726, another Sessions of Admiralty was held it the *Old Bailey*, before the Honourable Sir *Henry Penrice*, Judge, assisted by the Honourable Mr *Baron Fiole*, at which Captain *Creagh* was indicted for felo io sly sinking the good Ship the *Friendship*, of which he was Commander, but there appearing no Evidence sufficient to convict him of such a Charge, he was acquitted Captain *John Jaen* was then set to the Bar again, and a second Time arraign d on an Indictment for the Murder of his Cabin Boy *Richard Pye*, which Fact was set forth in the Words before related

It appeared by the Evidence produced against him, that he either whipp'd the Boy himself, or caused him to be whipp d, every Day during the Voyage, that he caused him to be ty'd to the Main Mast with Ropes for nine Days together, extending his Arms and Legs to the uttermost, whipping him with a *Cat*, as it is commonly called, made of five small Cords, till he was bloody, and then causing his Wounds to be several times wash'd with Brine and Pickle, that under this terrible Usage the Boy grew speechless very soon, that the Captain, notwithstanding

withstanding, continued his barbarous Usage, stamping on him, beating him, and abusing him, nay even obliging him to eat his own Excrements, though it immediately forced its Way up again; that when the Boy, in his Agony and Pain, made Signs for a Dram, the said Captain in Derision took a Glass, carried it into the Cabin and made Water therein, and then brought it to the Boy to drink, who refused the same; that the lamentable Condition the Boy was in made no Impression on the Captain, who continued to treat him with the same Barbarity, by whipping, pickling, kicking, beating and bruising him, all the while he was lingering out his miserable Life, that on the very last Day of his said Life, he gave him eighteen Lashes with the aforesaid Cat of five Tails, in a little Time after which the unhappy Wretch dy'd

The Evidences farther deposed, That when they were sewing up the Boy's Body in a Hammock, in order to its being thrown overboard, it had in it as many Colours as the Rainbow, that his Flesh was in many Places as soft as a Jelly, and his Head swell'd as big as two. Upon the whole it appeared, that a more bloody, premeditated, and wilful Murder was never committed, and Sir *Henry Penrice* declar'd, when he pronounced Sentence of *Death*, that in all the Time he had had the Honour of sitting on the Bench, he never heard any thing like it, and he added, that he hoped no Person who might sit there after him, would ever have a Parallel Case brought before him In a Word, every Body was shock'd at the very Rehearsal of this Action

Under Sentence of *Death* he behav'd with a great deal of seeming Piety and Resignation, tho' he did not frequent the publick Chapel, for which he gave the Ordinary two Reasons, which were just enough First, That the Number of Strangers, who were admitted thither, to stare at Persons under his unhappy Circumstances, was generally very great, and their Behaviour sometime very indiscreet Secondly, That the Fact for which he was to suffer had procured him many Enemies, who would take a Pleasure in coming thither to insult him under his Misfortunes. As he was sure, (he said) these Things must of Necessity wholly interrupt his Devotion, he thought it more eligible only to receive the Assistance of a Minister privately in his Chamber, which he had daily till his Execution

He was very open in confessing the general Offences of his Life, but took abundance of Pains to palliate the particular Fact for which he was to die particularly he often professed, that he never intended to murder the Boy, but only to correct him as he deserved, he being exceeding wicked and ungovernable When they first went out (he said) the Boy was very much given to thieving, and grew

worse continually, one Evening, for Instance, when they were upon their Return home, and he was asleep in the Cabin, the Boy broke open his Lockers, and took out a Bottle of Rum, of which he drank near a Pint, making himself therewith so drunk, that his Excrements fell involuntarily from him, and stunk so abominably that it awaken'd him Upon this, he called in several Men, who found the Boy in a sad nasty Condition, and were obliged to sit down and smoke Tobacco, in order to overcome the Stench he had raised This Action of the Boy's produced the terrible Punishment of tying him to the Mast for several Days, and offering him his Excrements, as had been deposed

Notwithstanding the Captain owned all this, yet he could not forbear reflecting very hardly on those who had given in their Evidence against him, charging them with Perjury and a Conspiracy to ruin him; tho' it appear'd from the Manner in which they deliver'd their Testimony.

As the Time appointed for his Execution drew nearer, the Fear of Death, and that Remorse of Conscience which naturally attends Persons in his Condition, brought him into such a low and bad State of Health, that he could scarce speak to any Body, or attend to the Discourse of others, but he lay in a languishing Condition, frequently fainting away, and appearing in fine not unlike a Person who had taken something to procure a sudden Death, in order to prevent a publick and ignominious one However, when these Suspicions were mentioned to him, he declared that they were utterly without any Foundation, and that he had never suffer'd such a Thought to come into his Head His Wife also, who attended him constantly whilst he was in Prison, declared, she loved him too well to become his Executioner, being positive nothing unwholsome had been administer'd to him, since his Confinement

He appeared to be so very much spent when he was carry'd to the Place of Execution, that it was thought he would hardly have lived to reach thither There was present a Minister of Distinction, who assisted him, and pray'd by him till he was thrown off His Execution was on the 13th Day of *May*, 1726, when he was about twenty nine Years of Age As soon as his Body was cut down, it was put into Chains, in order to be hung up over against the King's Powder-House, as a Warning to Others who serve in the same Station, how they abuse the great Power, with which 'tis necessary they should be invested while they are abroad, for the Sake of Order and Decorum, but of which 'tis the Privilege of those that serve under them to require an Account when they come home, that so no Subject of *Great Britain* may be oppressed, much less murder'd, by another entrusted with a greater Share of Authority

The LIFE *of* NED WICKS.

THIS wretched Person, *Edward Wicks*, was born of very good Parents, who kept an Inn at *Coventry*, and bestowed on him so much Education in Reading, Writing, and Casting Accompts, as qualify'd him to be a Clerk for extraordinary Business. He was an Exciseman about fourteen Month, but not thinking that a Post sufficient enough to cheat Her Majesty's Subjects, he was resolved to impose upon them more, by taking all they had on the Highway. Being well Equipp'd for such Enterprizes, he travelled the Roads to seek his Fortune, and had the good Luck to commit two Robberies without any Discovery. But a third Time being apprehended for a Robbery committed not far from *Croydon* in *Surrey*, he was sent to the *Marshalsea* in *Southwark*.

However, *Wicks* was not long under Confinement, before he obtained his Liberty, by his Friends making up the Business with his Adversary, to whom sixty Guineas were given, for taking from him but thirty Shillings. Then running *Jehu* like to his Destruction as fast as he could, he kept Company with one *Joe Johnson*, alias *Sanders*, with whom going once on the Road, they met, between *Hounslow* and *Colebrook*, with a Stage Coach, having four Gentlemen in it, who seeing them come pretty near the Coach, and perceiving they had Masks on, were apprehensive of their Intention of robbing them, and upon that, to be beforehand with them, one of them shot *Joe Johnson* with a Brass Piece or Blunderbuss, and lodged seven or eight large Shot in his Body. *Wicks* now rode clear off, without any Hurt, whilst his Comrade was apprehended, and, on Suspicion, sent to *Newgate*, where he was charged by one Mr *Woolly*, with robbing him of a silver Watch, and some Money, on the Highway; for which he was hanged at *Tyburn*, on *Wednesday* the 17th of *February*, 1704-5, aged twenty two Years.

But the untimely End of this Fellow making no Impression on *Wick's* bad Manners, he still pursues his wicked Courses with a great deal of Pleasure and Satisfaction, and one Day the Duke of *Marlborough* being at St *Albans*, after he was in Disgrace, *Ned* being then in the Town, and ruminating on the old Proverb, *Fallere fallentem non est fraus*, he thought it no Injustice to finger a little of his Grace's Money, but having too great a Retinue with him when he left that Place, our Highwayman durst not venture to make an Attack, whereupon, riding towards *Cheshunt*, in the same County, he put into a bye sort of a House a little out of the Road, in which, finding only a poor old Woman, bitterly weeping, and asking her the Reason of shedding those Tears, she told him, That she was a poor Widow, and being somewhat indebted for Rent to her Landlord, she expected him every Minute to come and seize what few Goods she had, which would be her utter Ruin.

Wicks bid the old Woman rest contented, and he would make Things easy, so pulling off his rich lac'd Cloaths, and putting on an old Coat which his Land lady lent him, and having also secur'd his Horse in an old Barn, presently after, the old Miser of a Land lord came and demanded his Rent. Hereupon, *Ned* rising out of the Chimney Corner, with a short Pipe in his Mouth, quoth he, *I understand, Sir, that my Sister here, poor Woman! is behind hand for Rent, and that you design to seize her Goods, but as she is a desolate Widow, and hath not wherewithal to pay you at present, I hope you will take so much Pity and Compassion on her mean Circumstances, as not to be too severe. Pray let me persuade you to have a little Forbearance.* The Landlord reply'd, *Don't tell me of Forbearance, I'll not pity People to ruin myself, I'll have my Money, I want my Rent, and if I am not paid now, I'll seize her Goods forthwith, and turn her out of my House.*

When *Ned* found that no Intreaties nor Persuasions would prevail with the old Cuff to have Patience with the poor Woman a little longer, he said, *Come, come, let's see a Receipt in full, and I'll pay it.* Accordingly a Receipt was given, and the Rent paid. Then the Landlord being upon going away, quoth *Wicks, 'Tis drawing towards Night, Sir, and there is great robbing abroad, therefore I would advise you to stay here till To-morrow, and take the Day before you. No, no,* reply'd the Country fellow, *I'll go home now, I shall reach seven Miles yet, by that Time it is dark. Ah! Sir, said Ned again, but let me persuade you to tarry here, for indeed there is great robbing abroad. I don't care, cry'd the Landlord what robbing there is abroad, I'll go home now, besides, I don't fear being robbed by any one Man, let him be who he will.*

So taking his Horse, away the old Fellow rid, and *Wicks* after, arested then in his fine Cloaths, and meeting him at a Pond where he knew he must pass by, he did not only bid him stand and de'iver, but presenting him also with a whole Volley of h[.] rate Oaths, he so frightened him out of his Wits, that he delivered all the Money he had lately received, and as much more to it.

Then *Wicks* riding back to the old Woman again, and disguising himself as before, it was no long[...] ter, ere the Landlord came to the House again, and knocking at the Door, quoth *Wicks, Who's there*, The Landlord said, *'Tis I,* reply'd *Wicks,* What I? *Why, it is I,* quoth the Country Fellow again. At these Words, the old Woman cried, *O! 'tis my Landlord.* So letting him in, he told his Grievance with a great deal of Sorrow, as how he was robbed by a R[...] in a lac'd Coat, who swore a thousand Oaths at him, and had certainly killed him, if he had not given him all his Money. *Ay (quoth Wicks) I told you there was great robbing abroad, but you would not take my Advice, now I hope you will stay here, Sir, till Morning.* However, he did not, for having given an Account of his Misfortune, he made the best of his Way homewards, having nothing more to lose.							A

A little after the Performance of this Exploit, Wicks being in *London*, and going one Night along *Drury-Lane*, dressed much like a Gentleman, who should make a sham stumble by him, but one Madam *Toby*, a noted Jilt, whereupon, catching hold on her Arm to save her from falling, she returned him many Thanks, and for his Civility, invited him to her Lodging just by, in *Princes street*, where she would also make him a suitable Return for his Courtesy. Now *Wicks*, by his Behaviour in not speaking, seemed to be dumb, but nevertheless, by the Signs he made, he intimated that he accepted of Madam *Toby*'s Proffer, who thinking him to be really speechless, she said as they went along, *Oh! dear, Sir, 'tis a thousand Pities that such a handsome likely Man as you are, should be dumb.*

As soon as he came to her Lodgings, he made a Sign for Pen, Ink, and Paper, to be brought him, whereby signifying his Desire of having a Couple of Bottles of Clarret and a Fowl for Supper, he gave the Maid a Guinea to provide it. Whilst she was gone to get what was ordered, he, by writing his Mind, desired to know of Madam *Toby*, who was every now and then crying, *What a Pity it is such a well-bred Gentleman should be dumb*, the Price of a Nights Lodging, which was two Guineas, as she signified by holding up two Fingers — So the Bargain being made, after Supper they went very lovingly to Bed, but in the middle of the Night, *Ned Wicks* arising, and taking a Couple of Pistols out of his Pockets, which he presented to Madam *Toby*'s Breast, quoth he, *You jilting B——h, I must have my two Guineas again, and more to boot, therefore if you offer to make the least Noise, these fatal Instruments of Death shall send your Soul to the Devil.*

Our Lady of Iniquity was in a great Surprize to hear her suppos'd Cully use his Tongue, but not daring to speak for her Life, he did not only tie her Hand and Foot, but also took from her a very good Watch, a gold Locket, a gold Bracelet, a silver Cup, half a dozen silver Spoons, a velvet Hood, and velvet Scarf, and then left her in a a deep Study how to get more. When *Wicks* was gone, she cry'd out, *Murder and Thieves*, with such an audible Voice, that alarming all the House, the Landlord, Landlady, and Maid, came running naked into Madam *Toby*'s Chamber, where finding her bound fast to her good Behaviour, after they had set her loose, she told them of her irretrievable Loss, and swore that she would never pick up dumb Men again.

Another Time *Wicks* meeting with the late Lord M—— on the Road betwixt *Windsor* and *Colebrook*, attended only with a Groom and one Footman, he commanded his Lordship to stand and deliver, for he was in great Want of Money, and Money he would have before they parted. His Honour pretending to have a great deal of Courage, swore he should fight for it then. *Wicks* very readily accepted the Proposal, and preparing his Pistols for an Engagement, his Lordship seeing his Resolution, he began to hang an Arse, which his Antagonist perceiving, he began to swagger, saying, *All the World knows me to be a Man, and tho' your Lordship was concerned in the cowardly murdering of M——d the Player, and Captain C——t, yet I'm not to be frightened at that, therefore down with your Gold, or else expect no Quarter.*

His Lordship now meeting with his Match, it put him into such a passionate Fit of swearing, that *Wicks*, not willing to be outdone in any Wickedness, said, *My Lord, I perceive you swear perfectly well extempore. Come, I'll give your Honour a fair Chance for your Money, and that is, he that swears best of us two, shall keep his own, and his that loseth.* His Lordship agreed to that Bargain, and throws down a Purse of fifty Guineas, which *Wicks* matched with a like Sum. After a quarter of an Hour's swearing most prodigiously on both Sides, it was left to my Lord's Groom to decide the Matter, who said, *Why, indeed your Honour swears as well as ever, I heard a Person of Quality in my Life, but to give the strange Gentleman his due, he has won the Wager, if it was for a thousand Pounds.* Whereupon, *Wicks* taking up the Gold, he gave the Groom a Guinea, and rode about his Business.

But not long after this, *Wicks* being apprehended in *London*, for a Robbery done in *Warwickshire*, he was committed to *Newgate*; from whence attempting to break out, he was quickly removed to *Warwick* Gaol, where being try'd the next *July*, he was condemned to be hang'd. His Parents made great Intercession for this their only Child, but in vain, for he was executed on *Saturday* the 29th of *August*, 1713, aged twenty nine Years.

The LIFE *of* NAN HEREFORD.

WHETHER it be that we entertain a greater Regard for the Female Sex than for the other, or whether Instances of their falling into those Sorts of Vices that expose them to the Cognizance of the Law are less frequent, or whatever else may be the Cause of it, 'tis certain, that a Female Offender excites our Curiosity more than a Male, if she has any Way distinguish'd her self in the Course of her Actions. Some indeed will say, that we need not be at a loss to find the Reason of this, because a Woman always discovers more Art and Cunning than a Man, when she applies her self to the Practice of Fraud. We will not dispute any Point of Honour with the subtil soft fair Sex, since 'tis our Duty to yield to them, as we are taught by the Example of our common Father *Adam*. Let it be their finer Genius, or whatever else they, or their greatest Admirers will call it, that gives 'em this Advantage, we must still acknowledge it, and confess that an *Anne Bonny*, or a *Mary Read*, are greater Names than a *Blackbeard*, an *Avery*, or a *Roberts*, and that the Tricks of a *German Princess* leave stronger Impressions than the open Robberies of *Hind* and *Du Vall*, &c.

But not to amuse the Reader with a long Preface to a short Life, we would only observe, that *Anne Hereford*, the Person of whom we are now to write, was one of those Women who, in her Time, was more famous than almost any one of the Male Robbers, whose Actions have adorn'd, as well as fill'd, this Work, which extraordinary Reputation (if we may use a Word here that is commonly taken in a good Sense) was, we believe, chiefly owing to her Sex, and the Manner in which she imposed on Mankind. One Instance, out of many, shall suffice to give an Idea of her Cunning, and one Instance of this Kind is as good as one thousand, since, however they may be diversify'd by Circumstances, all these Sort of Stratagems tend to one Thing, and 'tis easy at the Beginning of a Story to know where it will end. But first take this short Account of her Original. She was born at *Ipswich* in *Suffolk*, of very honest Parents, who both died when she was about seventeen Years of Age. No sooner was she an Orphan than she came up to *London*, where she got a Service, and lived in it above half a Year. It was then her Misfortune to fall into bad Company, who seduced her from her Place, and brought her to be a Partner with them in their evil Courses, which she pursu'd afterwards all the Days of her Life, taking Care still to keep herself genteely, and not to be seen among her Associates, by which Means she long escap'd unsuspected, and during which Time she executed the following Piece of Invention.

She took very good Lodgings in *King-street, Westminster*, where she entertain'd an experienced old Beldam as her Assistant, knowing very well, that she could not pursue her Enterprizes without Help. It was the Business of this old Woman to enquire about for a rich young Novice in that Neighbourhood, who might be a proper Subject to work on. Upon a diligent Search, she found there was a young Shopkeeper, by Trade an Apothecary, who was both rich and covetous. These two Qualities were look'd upon as a sufficient Excuse for their taking him in, for first, as he was so very wealthy, he might spare a few Hundred Pounds without hurting himself; and then, secondly, his being covetous made it a Sort of Duty, in their Opinion, to take from him what they could use, though he had not the Heart to do it. There is a Sort of natural Antipathy between those Free-baters and an avaritious Person, whereas, in Reality, a Robber should at least speak well of a Miser, because 'tis through his Means that the other often gets so much Money at a Time. But *Nan* did not reason in this Manner, she used to say, 'twas a just Judgment upon them for their grievous Sins, when any such Person was stripp'd of his Gold, or, in other Words, of his God.

Nan kept herself up close at home, and the old Woman was sent of many an idle Errand to the Apothecary's Shop, one Time for *Pomatum*, another Time for *Mithridate*, another for *Diascordium*, and so continually for such Things as the Use of was well known. This frequent coming induced the Apothecary to take Notice of her, and talk to her in a more free and pleasant Manner than at first. She took [Care to improve those Opportunities, which were all she came for, and to run from indifferent Things to his domestick Affairs, asking him, in particular, *Why he did not marry?* His Answer was such as might be expected from a Miser, *That the Times were hard, Trading dead, and Housekeeping expensive*. *That's true*, said she, *but a rich Wife, Man, would make amends for all this*. *A good one, and a rich one too*, quoth he, *would be a brave Thing indeed I must confess, I should be glad to embrace such an Opportunity of altering my Condition*. The old Woman had now nothing to do, but to insinuate, that she was certain such Fortunes might be had, and raise a Curiosity in him of knowing farther what she meant. This Part she acted to Admiration, till she made the young Fellow stark mad to draw the Secret from her, and he was almost ready to throw himself at her Feet when she told him, *That there was a young Gentlewoman of her Acquaintance, who was Niece to a very eminent Citizen of London, and had Two Thousand Pounds to her Portion, lodg'd in her Uncle's Hands, which must be paid her upon the Day of Marriage, if demanded*. The next Question was, *How he should get into the young Lady's Company*. To this 'twas as readily reply'd, *That her Uncle kept a strict Hand over her, and permitted her to go abroad but very seldom, but that she had now and then the Liberty of making our old Lady a Visit, she having been formerly a Nurse in her Father's Family. And every Time the poor Thing is at my House*, says the crafty old Baggage, *she complains of her Uncle's*

Uncle's Severity, and wishes she could meet with a good Opportunity of altering her Condition with a Man who would use her well, and take her entirely out of the old Man's Tutelage The Apothecary was charm'd, and engaged the old Dame to do all she could for him

Having taken down the Names both of the Uncle and the Damsel, he goes the next Day into the City, and makes Inquiry concerning them, with as much Care as an old Usurer would examine his Security before he put out his Money. He soon found that there was such a Man as had been describ'd, and that he had a Niece with Two Thousand Pounds The old Woman had been very exact in these Particulars, for Fear he should give himself this Trouble, which she afterwards wish'd he might, the better to confirm his good Opinion of her Sincerity He had no Business to enquire any further, than whether or no there were such Persons, and such a Sum of Money; because he had been before caution'd against letting the Uncle see him, or know any thing of his Design To be sure he was now very earnest to see his good Angel again, as he afterwards call'd her, that they might concert further Measures, and that they might engage her more strongly to his Interest by a Promissory Note, to be paid as soon as ever he got the young Lady Our Go-between was not long absent from his Shop, but when he made his Proposal to her, she seem'd more cold than before, and told him, that she would not for the World be concern'd in the Match, if he had nothing in View but getting the Money *However,* said she, *since I have promised you, I'll bring you together, and if you like her Person, and she likes yours, then we will talk further of Conditions, for as I am but a poor Woman my self, a small Gratuity would not be unacceptable, if I do you any Service*

In a few Days our Apothecary was introduced to the Company of *Nan Hereford*; who receiv'd him like a Girl that had never seen a Man in her Life before, such Modesty, such Silence, so many Blushes, were enough to deceive almost the Devil himself The Interview was but very short, for the Lady was afraid of staying long abroad, lest her Uncle should be angry Her Coldness made *Galen* the warmer, till the old Woman whisper'd him not to say too much at first, for Fear he should spoil all. In a Word, Miss went home, without so much as promising him positively that she would endeavour to come again; however, she gave him Room to hope a little The next Time the old Woman saw our Gallant, he renew'd his Proposal to her, protested, he liked her Choice beyond any Woman he had ever seen in is Life, and begg'd of her to proceed as vigorously for him as she was able After a few Compliments, a Bond was drawn up for an Hundred Pounds, payable to the old Woman on the Day of Marriage, in Case she effected what she had undertaken He seemed to give this Bond more willingly than she receiv'd it, and would almost have doubled it, when, a few Days after his Angel told him, *That she had seen Miss, and perceiv'd she entertain'd a good Opinion of him, for she had promis'd to come to her House again*

The next Meeting was something longer, and even long enough to finish the whole Affair. He told her plainly that he lov'd her, could maintain her handsomly, and would make her his Wife, if she pleased, without any further Ceremony The Counterfeit Fortune seem'd to consent, but withal intimated, that she left her Uncle only because he did not use her well, and allow her any Money;

and that therefore she hoped he would not serve her in the same Manner. *I have been hitherto,* says she, *kept so short, as not to be allow'd Apparel suitable to my Condition, and I shall think it hard to be used so by you too My Uncle will suspect some Design of leaving him, if I should now press him more than ordinary for a Suppl, and as I am, I am unfit to appear as your Wife My Fortune may be demanded when we are marry'd, and 'tis best not to trouble the old Man till all be secure* Thus she ran on, talking at a Distance, but plain enough for him to see what she meant, and it was now proper to try his Mettle If she found him bleed well, as the Phrase among these People is, 'twould be worth while to tickle him a little longer, and even marry him, if it were necessary; but otherwise Madam had nothing else to do, but to give him the Bag, and look out for fresh Sport The Stratagem succeeded beyond her most extravagant Expectations; for he fetch'd Two Hundred and fifty Guineas, to give the more signal Proofs of his Sincerity, and leave her no Room to suspect his loving her All this he threw into her Lap, told her he had three times as much more at home, and she should enjoy whatever was in his Power to procure

In a Word, they were soon after marry'd, and bedded the same Day, because Madam durst not be absent from her Uncle's House all Night When he had enjoy'd the Darling of his Soul, as she now began to be in Earnest, he sent her home with a thousand Sighs and Expressions of Fondness, promising to come in a few Days, and demand both her and her Fortune of her Uncle In the mean while he continued very impatient, till Time would allow him in good Manners to make his Claim; and Madam and her old Procuress made off the Ground to fresh Lodgings, far enough from him, and where he was never like to see, or hear of her any more

When three Days were over, our Apothecary dress'd himself up in his best Clothes (which were entirely new on the Wedding-Day, to answer what his Spouse had bought with his Money) took a Coach, and drove into the City, up to the Door of the supposed Uncle. He expected a warm Reception, and had fortify'd his Mind to bear it, so that, when he had knock'd, and was admitted to the old Gentleman's Presence, he peremptorily said, *He was come to demand his Wife I know nothing of your Wife, nor you neither,* quoth the old Man, *and desire therefore that you'd explain your Meaning.* *Galen* smartly reply'd, *I mean your Niece, Sir, who is my lawful Wife Your Wife, Man?* said t'other; *since how long, pray?* The Apothecary here named the Day and the Circumstances, to convince him of the Truth of what he said, but the old Man told him his Niece was not out on the Day specify'd, and that he could not comprehend his Drift. In short, they came at last to high Words, and the Apothecary seemed so positive and sincere all the while, that the Uncle began to think he had been imposed on, whereupon he ask'd him, *If he knew his Wife when he saw her? I should be glad,* reply'd Mr *Gallipot, if you would try me.* The old Man agreed to send for his Niece, and she came accordingly. *This is none of my Wife,* said the disappointed young Man But this is my Niece though, quoth the other, *and all the Nieces I have in the World too* They both stood aghast, and the young Lady is as much surprized as they, to hear her self talk'd of by the Name of *Wife*, when she was certain she had never had the Pleasure of being one

The

The old Man having fully weigh'd the Cafe, *Friend*, fays he, *be convinc'd that fome Trick has been play-ed you, and be fo kind as to relate the Particulars of your Courtſhip, and every Thing that has paſs'd between you* This was no fooner demanded than confented to, and one particular clear'd up another through the whole Courfe of the Affair, till the A-pothecary was as fully convinc'd as any Body that he had met with a Couple of Sharpers All he had now to do, was to think of *Job*, go peaceably home, tell over the Money he had left, and advance one Penny *per* Shilling on his Medicines

This Relation has been fomewhat long, but as 'tis the only Story in this Life 'twill be the more excufable We fhall now conclude what we have to fay of this Criminal in as few Words as poſſible After this Adventure *Nan* grew enamour'd with one *Kirkham* a Player, who confented to live with her To maintain their juſt Extravagancies, ſhe went a Shop lifting, and he on the Highway He had the Fortune to be taken on his firſt Progreſs, and hang'd

for what he had done in good Time, but *Nan* continued her Occupation for fix Years longer, ſtealing from Mercers, Linen Drapers, and Lace men, as much Goods as were fuppoſ'd to be worth above Four Thoufand Pounds However, at laſt, ſhe alſo was detected, at a Linen Draper's Shop in *Cornhill*, as ſhe was endeavouring to fecure a Piece of Muſlin, after ſhe had come to the Shop in a Chair, with two or three Footmen at her Heels Before the Seſſions, 'tis faid, ſhe offer'd an Hundred Guineas to prevent her Adverfary's appearing againſt her, but in vain, for he was refolv'd to profecute her to the utmoſt She alfo attempted to fet *Newgate* on Fire, for which ſhe was very heavily fetter'd and Hand cuff'd Being condemn'd at the *Old Baily*, ſhe was executed before the Prifon ſhe had endeavour'd to deſtroy, on *Monday*, the twenty fecond Day of *December*, in the 1690, aged twenty eight Years Her Body was given to the Surgeons for a Skeleton.

The LIFE *of* TOM MARSH.

THIS Fellow being one who, (like all other Rogues) employ'd his Wits in all manner of Villany, to fupport himfelf in the Purfuit of his unlawful Appetites, he one while uſed an Ale houfe in *Leiceſter Fields*, the Man whereof having a very handfome Wife to fit in the Bar, ſhe brought a great many Cuſtomers, who were in Hopes of qualifying her Husband for Horn Fur But the Hoſteſs being as cunning as her Guefts, ſhe would not be like a Glove, for every one's drawing on, for if ſhe had any Gallants, it was her Refolution that they ſhould be of the beſt, and thofe ſhe counted fo, who had the moſt Money in their Pockets Her Carriage in all Company feemed to be varnifhed with a very great Modeſty; but it was only counterfeited, for feveral having laid Siege to the Fortreſs of her Chaſtity, ſhe had furrendered it for the Prefents of fine Hoods, Scarves, Gloves, Rings, or other fuch womanifh Toys

Among the Crowd of this Woman's Admirers, was *Thomas Marſh*, who difcovering his flaming Paſſion to her, ſhe as foon made him fenfible by what means he muſt cool it, which was, by giving her a filk Night-Gown, fo, after promifing her one, they parted, and he went Home, to contrive how to be as good as his Word, whilſt the other found ont a Way to procure her Husband's Abfence for a Night or two This ſhe accomplifhed by fending him fifteen Miles off, to *Watford* in *Hertfordſhire*, to fee her Mother, who then lay a dying

In the mean Time *Tom* finding the Strength of his Pocket was not fufficient to accomplifh his Promife, he fupply'd that Defect by this Stratagem Vifiting a Woman of his particular Acquaintance, who had then lately ſtolen a very rich Gown (namely *Eleanor Jackſon*, alias *Scotch Nell*, who was fince hang'd at *Tyburn*, for ſtealing a calicoe Petti-

coat from one Mrs *Margaret Stephens*) and acquainting her with his Defign, which was more than mere Love, as you will find by the Sequel of the Story, he beg'd the Favour of her to lend it him, to facilitate his Intention Accordingly ſhe did as he defired, upon Affurance that he would fee it forth coming, then fending it by a Porter to the Victualler's Wife, ſhe accepted it and the following Letter, with a fmiling Countenance

My Dear,

'HAving fent you a Gown by the Bearer, this is alfo to acquaint you, that I muſt die to ' fee you To-day Never Man lov'd to fuch a De-' gree as I do, but it is true, never Man lov'd ' fo amiable a Creature You may be fure of my ' Company at the Time appointed If I had a ' thoufand Lives, I would expofe them all for fo ' dear a Bleſſing How long will this Day feem to ' me! How many tirefome Minutes am I to paſs, ' before that I arrive at that which is the Perfection ' of my Happineſs! Thus dearly Love will make ' us pay for his Joy! But I ſhall owe him the ' more, if in this Time of my Pennance I can pre ' vail upon you to believe that never Man deferved ' more to poſſeſs you! I ſhall give a Proof of it, ' and if you give all your Heart, I'll venture for ' mine

Your humble Servant,

THO MARSH

Towards the Evening this paſſionate Lover paid her

her a Visit, being very merry at her House till late at Night, when preparing for Bed, they took up some good Liquors, as Cyder, Stout, and Brandy, to enjoy themselves in private, but *Tom* had put a small Dose of *Laudanum* into his Beloved's Cup, which made her, after but one Enjoyment, fall so fast asleep, that you might as well awake the Dead as her Ladyship. Now *Tom*, thinking it was good to make Hay while the Sun shin'd, took three gold Rings off her Fingers, then taking the Keys of a Chest of Drawers out of her Pocket, he rifled them of the best of her Cloaths, and forty Pounds in Money, which bundling up in his Friend's Gown, he left Madam *Nick and Froth* to retrieve her Loss by the old Way of scoring two for one.

After this he cheated the Country up and down, by pretending to be a disbanded Soldier, or shipwreck'd Seaman, for which Purpose he made false Passes, and counterfeited their Seals, after this Manner. Going to three or four Magistrates, and procuring their Warrants, signed and sealed, by swearing the Peace against *Tom a Nokes*, or *Jack a Stiles*, he would take a Piece of Clay, which being rubb'd with a bit of Butter, that it might not stick to the Wax, the Impression thereon would come off very clean, then dry it very hard, and it gives the same Impression on Wax. But *Tom* being once detected in this sort of Forgery, he was whipt at *Turtle-Fields Bridewell*, a Place where all the Senses of a Man may enjoy a peculiar Pleasure, by seeing nothing but the Marks of Poverty, smelling the fragrant Odour of that Commodity, which they often beat for their own Destruction, hearing the harmonious Noise made with Beetle and Punny, tasting Water without Adulteration, and feeling a good Bull's Pizzle in Case they won't work.

Once *Tom Marsh* lodging at one Mr *Bennet's* House near *Mutton Lane*, who and his Wife were strong Presbyterians, he seemed to be a Precisian too, which made his Landlord and Landlady have a great Respect for their seemingly serious Lodger. *Tom* made Use of their good Opinion, and one Sunday in the Evening, coming Home from a Meeting-House, he sat down by the Fire, in a very devout Sort of a Posture, as having his Glove on his Head, and Arms a cross, then desiring the old People to fetch him a Bible, they, glad to see him in this goodly Frame of Mind, brought him one presently. Taking it in his Hand, he pitch'd on that Chapter of the Gospel, which tells the Evangelical Story

of our Saviour's bidding the lame Man take up his Bed and walk, which he read with a great Emphasis, and afterwards going to his Repose, he, very early in the Morning, bundled up his Bed, which flung out of the Window, he carried clean away.

About Noon the Landlord's Daughter going to make *Tom*'s Bed, she came down in a great Agony to her Mother, to whom telling what had happen'd, she made as terrible an Outcry of her Loss, in the Neighbourhood, as the People did of the wild *Irish* coming hither, a little before the Prince of *Orange* arriv'd at *London*, but her Husband being a moderate Man, and, for his Profession, a merry one too, he bid her be quiet, because *Tom* had been so civil as to prove over Night by Scripture, that he ought to walk away with it.

This wicked Person was born near *Ludlow* in *Shropshire*, a Mason by Trade, and coming up to *London*, married a very honest Woman, by whom he left a Girl behind him, but being of an idle lazy Disposition, he took to ill Courses, and had not only been whipt at the Cart's Tail, for stealing Lead off St *Paul's* Cathedral, but for a Trespass, in entring a Man's Yard, with a Design to rob him, he was also fin'd twenty Pounds, and committed to *Newgate* till he paid the Sum, where he remained 4 Years, except some little Time when he broke out, which he did twice, but was both Times soon retaken, and punish'd with Hand-Cuffs, the Neck-Collar, and double Irons.

Whilst he was under Confinement, he had a Child by one *Elizabeth Key*, a notorious Whore, a Prisoner in the same Goal for Debt, whom, as being of a fickle or rather lustful Temper, he slighted, for the sake of *Jane Hays*, another Prisoner there for Debt. It was not long after his Correspondence with the last, that he got his Fine remitted, and obtain'd his Liberty. But he did not enjoy it long, for committing a Burglary at *Hampstead*, he was committed to *Newgate* again, and on the 20th of *December*, 1710, hang'd at *Tyburn*, where he confessed 'twas he that murdered the Farmer at *Shipperton*, in the County of *Middlesex*, and not Mr *Charles Dean* the Attorney, who, a little before was wrongfully executed for it, at that same Time that one Mr *Crouch* was try'd on the same Account at *Justice-Hall* in the *Old-Bailey*, but was honourably acquitted.

The LIFE *of* JACK ADDISON.

THIS Fellow was born of very honest Parents, in the Parish of *Lambeth*, and for some Time had been in the Sea and Land Service, but for the moſt Part of his Life followed the Trade of a Butcher, to which he was brought up He kept Company much with ill Women, eſpecially one *Kate Speed*, a Perſon both Whore and Thief, and, for the Maintenance of her, he went upon the Footpad, committing ſeveral moſt notorious Robberies of that Nature, with one *William Jewel*, and *Peter Cartwright*, the latter of which was hang'd at *Tyburn* on *Wedneſday* the 18th of *July*, 1711

One Time meeting with a Parſon between *Weſtbourne-Green* and *Paddington*, he took from him five Guineas ; which putting in to his own Pocket, quoth *Jack*, 'Tis as ſafe there as in yours That I believe, reply'd the Parſon, but I hope, Sir, yo 'll be ſo civil as to give me ſome of it back again Said *Jack* then, Alas ! Sir, I wonder how a Man in your Coat can be ſo unconſcionable as to deſire any Thing out of this ſmall Matter ; but I tell you what ; Sir, if you can tell me what Part of Speech your Gold is, I'll return it all again. The Parſon, thinking the Money was his own again, told him it was a Noun Subſtantive, as an, Thing was to which he could put A, or The No, no, reply'd *Jack* you are out now, I perceive you are no good Grammarian, for where your Gold is at preſent, it is a Noun Adjective, becauſe it can be neither ſeen, felt, heard, nor underſtood So leaving the Parſon to ruminate on his Miſtake, away *Jack* went about his unlawful Buſineſs again.

A little while after this, meeting on the Road betwixt *Hammerſmith* and *Kenſington*, with one *Palmer*, a Victualler, who formerly kept the *King's-Head* Alehouſe, in *King's-Head-Court*, in *Drury-Lane*, he took from him a ſilver Watch, and eighteen Shillings ; and Mr *Palmer* deſiring *Jack* to give him ſome ſmall Matter to bear his Charges up to *London*, quoth he, Had you been an honeſt Tradeſman, perhaps I might have conſidered you ; but as I know you wear a blue Flag, I will not give you a Farthing, becauſe all of your Profeſſion neither eat, drink, or think, but at other Mens Charges

Another Time meeting with a Captain of the Foot Guards, betwixt *Marybone* and *Tottenham Court*, knocking him down, quoth *Jack*, Thou great Defender of Women, whoſe Sword is your Plough, which Honour and Geneva, two fiery mettled Jades, are ever drawing, I muſt make bold now to bid you Stand, and doubt not but you'll forgive my Rudeneſs, becauſe your Charity goes beyond the Clergy's, in loving your greateſt Enemies beſt, that is to ſay, much drinking So ſtunning the Officer with a ſecond Blow, he took three Guineas from him and a gold Watch

One Evening meeting a Town Miſs whom he knew well, coming from *Chelſea*, after he ſtopp'd her, he ſaid, Oh ! you B——h of H——ll, where have you been all this while, that I muſt wait two or three Hours for your Strumpetſhip ? I ſuppoſe you have been dreſſing all Day, to be taſted with the better Appetite at Night Come, come, let's ſee what Money you have in your Pockets So taking about three or four Shillings from her, he gave her a green Gown, by tying her Neck and Heels on the Graſs, where ſhe remained till next Morning before ſhe was releas'd by ſome Hay makers.

Afterwards meeting betwixt *Hampſtead* and *Kentiſh-Town*, with a Barriſter of *Lincolns-Inn*, and taking from him a gold Watch, a ſilver Snuff Box, and two Guineas, quoth he to *Jack*, I'd have you take Care what you do, for I am a Lawyer, and if you ſhould come into my Hands, I ſhould be very ſevere upon you, *Addiſon* reply'd, I value not the Severity of all the Lawyers in *England*, who only learn to frame their Caſes from publick Riddles, and imitating *Merlin*'s Prophecies, and ſo ſet all the Croſs Row together by the Ears, yet your whole Law is not able to decide *Lucian*'s old Controverſy, 'twixt *Tau* and *Sigma* So binding the Lawyer Hand and Foot, he left him to plead his Cauſe by himſelf.

Another Time *Jack* meeting with a Chamber-Maid, whom he knew belong'd to the Dutcheſs of M————, betwixt *Kenſington* and *Knightsbridge*, he civilly deſired her to Stand and Deliver, but ſquawling out, and making a great Clutter, rather than part with what ſhe had, he laid violent Hands on her, ſaying at the ſame Time, ' You covetous B——h, how loth you are to lend an honeſt Man a ' little Money, to do him a Kindneſs ; when I warrant you, if you had a good ſwinging Clap now, ' you would divide it equally betwixt your M—— ' and his Footmen, as if you had cut out the getting of it by a Thread ' So taking about twenty three Shillings from her, he made the beſt of his Way to *London*

Not long after this Exploit, *Jack* meeting a Serjeant of the *Poultry* Compter, coming from *Iſlington*, he commanded him to Stand and Deliver, or elſe he would ſhoot him through the Head Th Fellow being ſurpriz'd, gave him forty Shillings, deſiring, at the ſame Time, that he would be ſo civil as to return him what he pleaſed back again. But *Jack* knowing his raſcally Function, quoth he, ' Sirrah, was the tenth Part of a Farthing to ſave ' your Life, nay, your Soul, I would not give ' it, becauſe thou art the Spawn of a broken Shop ' keeper, who takes Delight in the Ruin of thy ' Fellow-Creatures ! The Miſery of a poor Man, is ' the Offals on which you feed, and Money is the ' Cruſt you leap at ; your Walks in Term Time, ' are up *Fleet-ſtreet*, but at the End of the Term, ' up *Holborn*, and ſo to *Tyburn*, for the Gallows ' is your Purlieu, in which you and the Hangman ' are Quarter-Rangers, the one turns off, and the ' other

'other cuts down ' At these Words, quoth the Serjeant, ' And I hope I shall have the Happiness of cutting you down too, one of these Days. Perhaps ' so, reply'd *Jack*, but you shall devour a great many ' more of the Sheriffs Custards first ' So tying him Neck and Heels, he bound the Serjeant to his good Behaviour, till some Passengers came by to release him

He had committed 56 Robberies thus on Foot, and at last being apprehended, upon the Information of one *Will Jewel*, a Prisoner in the *Marshalsea* Prison, in *Southwark*, for robbing His Excellency the Duke *D'Aumont*, the *French* Ambassador here of late, he was committed to *Newgate*, and try'd at *Justice Hall* in the *Old Bailey*, for assaulting and robbing on the Queen's Highway, Mr *Matthew Beazly*, Mr. *William Winflow*, Mr *Disury Stanniford*, Mr

Robert Sherwood, and Mr *Joseph Ashton*, on the 30th of *November*, and 20th of *December*, 1710, and the 6th of *February*, 1710-11; and for which being cast and condemned, he was hang'd at *Tyburn* on *Friday* the 2d of *March* following, aged 23 Years

But before I conclude this Fellow's Life, I must not forget his once robbing mad *Wigmore*, whom meeting betwixt *Kentish Town* and *London*, raving along with a Quarter-Staff in his Hand, and a great Pair on Boots on his Legs, he oblig'd him to Stand and Deliver, without much Opposition, for presenting a couple of Pistols at him, *Wigmore* was not so mad as to lose his Life for the Value of ten or twelve Shillings, which *Jack* took from him, besides cutting the Madman's Boots to Pieces, so that he was obliged to go through Thick and Thin, it being then very dirty Weather, barefoot Home

---

The LIFE *of* ANDREW BAYNES.

THIS *Andrew Baynes* was from his Infancy of a vicious Inclination, and tho' he had the natural Sense to know he was in an Error, yet was he resolved his Heart should be still the same When he first display'd his Vanity, he began with defrauding and cheating all he had to deal with, especially by taking great Houses, and then getting Upholsters to furnish 'em, which when he had done, he would run away with their Goods by Night Thus would he also trick Brasiers, Pewterers, Limners, Cabinet-Makers, and other Tradesmen, as particularly once by taking a House in *Red-Lyon-Square*, from whence he carried above four hundred Pounds worth of Goods into the *Mint*, but was took out from thence by Virtue of a *Posse Comitatus*, and sent to Gaol.

Another Time being in great Want of Money, (for what such Rogues get by Villany, is always spent in Luxury and Excess, he went to a Justice of the Peace at *Norwich*, before whom he swore (tho' he had not lost a Farthing) that he was robb'd of one hundred and fifty Pounds, within five Miles of that City, betwixt Sun and Sun; and brought three or four as great Knaves as himself, to depose he had, to their Knowledge, so much Money when he left such a Place, then suing the County, he recovered his pretended Loss

Afterwards his profligate course of Life tempting him to greater Villanies, he turned House breaker with one *Tom Betts*, who was a notorious Offender in this kind This *Betts* being cast once for a Felony at the Sessions-House in the *Old Bailey*, he was, by an Order of the Court, sent into the Foot Service in *Flanders*; after which he suffered a great deal of Hardship For, being first commanded into *Germany*, he was there taken Prisoner by the *French*, and carried to *Lewk* After a long starving Confinement, he made his Escape, and went to *Fern* in *Sweden*, where being listed into that King's Service to go into *Poland*, he ran away Then coming into *Holland*, he entered himself on board a *Dutch* Man of War, that was

to convoy a Fleet from *Moscovy*, where going ashore, he stole one of the Czar's Bears in the Night, and returning to *Holland* again, shew'd it, after his Discharge from five Months Service, about *Amsterdam*, and getting Money thereby, he came over to *England*; where he was hanged at *Tyburn*, on *Wednesday* the 15th of *May*, 1706, for robbing the House of the Lord *Georges* in *Covent-Garden*

But his untimely End working no good Effects in his Comrade *Andrew Baynes*, he still followed the Faculty of House-breaking, till he was condemned for it in 1709, and had the good Fortune to be repriev'd, yet not making good Use of that Mercy, a little after his Liberty was obtain'd, he robb'd the Earl of *Westmorland*'s House, taking from thence several good Medals, his Lordship's Parliament Robes, damask Curtains, Cloaths, Linnen, and other Goods, to the Value of five hundred Pounds, for which being apprehended upon the Information of one *Daniel Waters*, (a Shoemaker concerned with him in the same Fact, and hanged in *August*, 1713, at *Maidstone* in *Kent*) he was committed to the *Marshalsea* Prison, in *Southwark*, from whence being removed by a Writ of *Habeas Corpus* to *Newgate*, he was condemned again, but saved his Life once more, by a Restitution of most part of the Goods which he had stolen from that Peer.

Having obtain'd his Enlargement a second Time, and being so unsuccessful in House breaking, he resolved to try his Fortune in turning Foot Pad, so he and his Comrades (who likewise followed this Exercise, which is the high Road to Hell) meeting with one Mr *Archer*, a Taylor, living in *Blackmore street* by *Clare Market*, coming one Evening from *Highgate*, they set upon him, but he having some Knowledge of *Andrew Baynes*, who was indebted to him for making a Coat, when once in *Newgate*, quoth he, Mr *Baynes*, *don't you know me? Yes*, reply'd *Baynes*, *I know you well enough, and therefore am resolved to send you home like a Gentleman, for you shall have no Money in your Pockets.*

Searching him, they found about eight Shillings in his Breeches, and a silver Watch; which taking from him, quoth *Baynes,* who had a good Bull-Dog with him, *By G——d I fancy it is pretty Sport to see a live Taylor batted, therefore I'll bait this Fellow to try the Experiment* So stripping him stark naked, they bound him to a Tree, then setting the Dog at him, he flew like a Dragon on the Taylor, who cry'd and roar'd like a Bull indeed, and had had a Mischief done him, if *Baynes*'s Companions had not been more merciful, in timely taking off the Dog, which had grievously bit him in several Parts of the Body: But for this Civility, they kept his Cloaths, as looking upon him to be a sort of an *Alchymist,* who could soon extract another Sute out of Customers Apparel.

Another Time *Andrew Baynes,* and his Associates, meeting, betwixt *Hampstead* and *London,* with one Mr *Blachard* a Shoe-maker, formerly living in the *Strand,* they commanded him, with out much Ceremony, to Stand and Deliver; but not obeying the Word of Command, he begg'd 'em to use Conscience, and not to ruin him and his Family at once. Quoth *Baynes, You Son of a Whore, don't talk of Conscience to us, for we shall now stretch it at large as you do your Leather.* So rifling his Pockets, they found about sixty Pounds, most in Gold, received that Evening of a Customer, then, as they were tying his Hands and Feet, quoth *Baynes* again, *Is this all the Money you have?* The poor Shoe-maker answer'd, *Yes,* indeed Mr *Baynes* cry'd, *You Son of a B——h, you ought to have every Bone in your Skin broke for bringing no more with you, for this small Matter is no more in our Pockets than a Man in Paul's* In the mean Time the Shoe-maker begg'd and pray'd, that if they would not give him all his Money, they would give him but some, but *Baynes* said, *How can you be so unconscionable,* Crispen, *as to ask for our Charity out of this little Sum? Pray hold your chattering, for was you to stand as hard with us, as for a Piece of Carrot, we would not give you a Dott, so stay here till we come to unloose you, which may be about the Day of Judgment*

Not long after this Robbery, *Andrew Baynes* and his Comrades meeting three Women, who were *Quakers,* coming from a little Way out of Town, they set upon these holy Sisters, and having first searched all their Pockets, in which was not above two Guineas, and twelve Shillings in Silver, they thought this a very small Prey, without taking their Cloaths too So stripping them stark naked, quoth one of the Lambs, as they were tying her to a Tree, *Ye Men of* Belial*! what is the Meaning of all this Violence, in taking away our Garments?* Andrew Baynes reply'd, *Nothing at all, beloved ones, but only to make your Bodies as light as your Souls, and on my Word, if ye always keep in this manner, as ye came into the World, ye will never offend the Statute made against the Excess of Apparel.*

Now *Andrew*'s Comrades, because they were tolerably handsome, were for untying them, saying,

' 'Twas easy to get away, without any Danger of
' their having us secured But Andrew Baynes, in
' a great Passion, reply'd, They shall not be unty'd,
' for tho' I'm of no Religion myself, yet I mortally
' hate a *Quaker,* or any other *Precisian,* because he
' is a demure Creature, only full of oral Sanctity,
' and mental Impiety Though he will not swear,
' he'll lye confoundedly, nevertheless, his Presump-
' tion is so sure of his Salvation, that he will not
' change Places in Heaven with the *Virgin Mary* He
' will not stick out from committing Fornication or
' Adultery, so it be done for the Propagation of the
' Godly, and can find in his Heart to lye with any
' Whore, but the Whore of *Babylon* He thinks
' every Organist is in the State of Damnation, and
' had rather hear a Ditty of his own making, than
' the best Hymn a *Cherubim* can sing. In fine, he
' had rather See *Antichrist* himself, than Pictures
' in a Church Window; and prophanely thinks his
' Discourse is so good, that he durst challenge the
' Almighty to talk with him *extempore.* Truly
' this Character I have heard discreet Men give of
' this sort of Cattle, and for this Reason the Spirit
' moves me to shew no Favour here to these female
' Hypocrites, who we'll leave in the Dark, till their
' own Light conducts them to a better Place ' So
his Companions being satisfy'd with what he said,
they left the three *Yeas and Nays* to hold forth by
themselves.

Andrew Baynes being once impress'd by *Dent,* the informing Constable, (who was kill'd in *Covent Garden,* by one *Tooly,* a Soldier) and sent to *Flanders,* he ran away from his Colours into *England,* and being one Day at a House in *Chelsea,* where *Dent* was also drinking, and knowing him again, he and another way-laid him at *Bloody-Bridge,* where setting on him, quoth *Baynes, Thou insolent Rascal! who hast sold many a Man's Blood at twenty Shillings per Head, I am sensible you can use your long Staff well enough, I'll see how you can exercise your short one* So pulling out his Generation Tool, they applied a Blister Plaister to it, bought for that Purpose at an Apothecary's in the abovesaid Town, and tying his Hands and Feet, left him in that Condition till Morning, before any Passengers came by to release him

This Malefactor, executed at *Tyburn,* in 1711, aged 26 Years, was born in *Essex,* and served as a Drawer last at the *Blue Posts* Tavern, at the Corner of *Portugal street,* by *Lincolns-Inn* Back-Gate He was very undutiful to his ancient Mother, who went a begging; and the Woman he kept Company with, was called *Flum,* from her formerly selling Flummery, being the Leavings of one *George Purchas,* a Bailiff, condemned (but repriev'd) for high Treason, with one *Dammary,* a Waterman, for the Insurrection made by the Rabble in *London,* when Dr *Henry Sacheverell was try'd by the Peers, upon several Articles exhibited against him by the House of Commons.*

The

The LIFE *of* JAMES FILEWOOD.

THIS Fellow was often called *Vilet,* tho' *Filewood* was his right Name He was born of honest Parents in the Parish of St *Pe- ters Cornhill* His Father was a Poulterer; which Occupation he, and two or three other Brothers, pretended originally to follow, but finding the fid- dling Work of scalding, picking, and gutting Cocks and Hens, and other Poultry, was not so beneficial as picking of Pockets, they took up that Employ- ment, as knowing there was their ready Money as soon as they had done their Work.

When this Fellow suffered Death, 'twas thought there were some of his Brothers who deserved it more, one of them having been formerly condemn'd, gave Proof that the Mercy was ill bestowed, for he lived to do a great deal of Mischief, and another of them had been at *Old Bridewell* by *Fleet-Ditch,* where he was two Years at hard Labour, which going hard against the Grain, he and some others mutiny'd, with a Design to break out, but the Keepers and Blue- coat Boys soon quelled them. And in this rash At- tempt, one *Isaac Rag,* a Prisoner then with him, and who was afterwards an Evidence against *White,* and another Person hanged with him, for the hor- rid Murder of Mrs. *Knap* in *Jockey-Fields,* had one of his Eyes shot out,

But to return to *James Filewood* As soon as he had listed himself under the Banners of Wicked- ne's, he first went a *Clouting,* that is, picking Hand- kerchiefs out of Pockets. in which having pretty well improved himself, after often being duck'd in a Horse-pond, or pumped, he next ventured to pick Pockets and Fobs and Money and Watches To which Purpose, he always gave his constant Atten- dance at the King's going to the Parliament-House, the Lord-Mayor's Show, the Artillery Men making a Mock Fight, Entries of Ambassadors, *Bartholo- mew* and *Southwark* Fairs, *Drury-Lane* and *Lincolns. Inn* Play-Houses, or any other Place where a great Concourse of People is drawn together upon any Oc- casions; and to be sure he never miss'd going on *Sun- days* to Church, tho' it was more to serve the Devil, than that omnipotent Majesty, to whose Honour and Glory the House of Prayer is erected, and here he would, as well as pick Pockets, change an old Hat or two for a new one.

In the late Queen's Reign, *Vilet* being try'd at the Assizes at *Oxford,* for a Matter in which he was allowed the Benefit of Clergy, being put to read his Neck Verse, a Student standing at the Bar, took so much Compassion as to instruct him The Words were *Lord have Mercy upon us.* So he held the Book, and the Scholar bid him say after him *O Lord,* says the Scholar, *O Lord,* says *Vilet,* and and his Thumb being upon the other Part of it, the Scholar said, *Take away thy Thumb,* says *Vilet* then, *O Lord, take away thy Thumb* Quoth the Judge, *Legit, aut non legit, ut Clericus!* And he that was appointed to answer, being pleas'd to favour the

Criminal, reply'd, *Legit ut Clericus,* by which Means he saved his Neck this Time

One Day this *Vilet* meeting with another of his own Profession, named *Clark, Come Clark,* quoth he, *since we have so happily stumbled upon one ano- ther, let us take a Pint together* A Match, says the other, so they went into a Tavern in *Holborn.* But drinking about for a While, when they came to examine their Pockets, they found themselves de- ceived, one thinking the one had, and the other thin- king the other had, Money enough to defray the Reckoning, when indeed both of them could make not above a Groat *Hang it then,* (said the Inviter) *we had as good be in for a great deal as a little.* So they called lustily till it came to five or six Shil- lings, then looking out at the Window, as if they had been viewing the Descent, says one to the other, I have it now Upon that, knocking and desiring to speak with the Master, up he came, *Sir, says Vi- let, we came hither about a mathematical Business, to measure from your Window to the Ground I have laid upon 13 Foot my Friend on 13 Foot 9 Inches, and you are to be Judge that I slip not this Line* (which was Packthread upon a Piece of Brass, which Joyners and Carpenters use in Mensuration) *till he goes down, to see whether from this Knot,* (shew- ing it him) *which is just so much, it reaches to the Ground* The Vintner was content The other Sharper being below in the Street, cry'd, *It did not reach by eleven Inches.* Pray, Sir, said *Vilet* to the Vintner, *Hold it here till I step down and see, for I won't believe him* So down he went, telling the Drawer he'd paid his Master, and away they both scoured, leaving the String for the Reckoning

Once *Jemmy Vilet* having stolen an Alarum Watch, stifly denied it before the Justice, so that upon the slender Evidence he was discharged, but before he got out of his Worship's Presence, the Alarum went, and he was ordered to be brought back again, and searched, at which he cry'd out, *What devilish Luck have I, that I should so easily baffle both Justice and Constable, and yet am trapanned by the Watch!* But for all his Jesting, the Justice was in such good earn- est now, that he committed him to *Newgate,* and had he not so far made it up with the Prosecutor to throw in a Bill of *Ignoramus* at Sessions, he might perhaps been hanged then

Once *Vilet* having been at some Country Fairs, he got a pretty deal of Money, but falling into Play with a Shoemaker at *Lincoln,* it was his Misfortune to lose it, Cloaths and all *Crispin* give him his old Cloaths, and his leather Apron, and when he depart- ed from *Lincoln,* was so civil, as to put twenty Shil- lings into his Pockets to bear his Charges With this he sets out to travel, and coming to a lone Inn betwixt *Grantham* and *Stamford,* he puts in there, and spending four or five Shillings, the People pro- vided him a good Lodging, and *Jemmy* went to Bed betimes It so fell out, that they had several Guests

came

came to the Inn, which took up their Lodgings, so that a Parson coming in very late, they had no room for him The Parson rather than go farther, chose to accept of a Bedfellow , but there was none cared to be disturbed at that Time of Night but *Vilet* whom they took for a Shoemaker, and who was well enough pleased with the Honour of having such such a Bedfellow.

Matters being thus accommodated, and the Parson a bed, he soon fell asleep, and slept very heartily, being tired with the Fatigue of his Days Journey, but *Vilet* having slept well before, had no mind to sleep any more that Night, but lay awake meditating Mischief; and seeing the Parson had a great deal of Money in his Pockets, which he pulled out to pay for a Pot of Beer which he called for to make his Bedfellow drink, he was contriving how to change Breeches with him, well knowing his own Pockets were but thin lin'd with that precious Metal. After having resolved what he would do, he gets up at the dawning of the Day, and puts on not only the Parson's Breeches, but also all his sacerdotal Garments, finding they fitted him very well , and being rigg'd in those sacred Habiliments, down Stairs he goes very softly, and calls the Hostler, bidding him bring his Boots, and make ready his Horse

Now the Hostler, not in the least mistrusting, but that *Vilet* being in that Dress, was really the Parson, brought him his Boots, and ask'd him what Corn he must have ? He told him half a Peck of Oats, which was accordingly given him , and *Vilet* was very uneasy till the Horse had eat them , but in the mean Time, that he might be the sooner ready to go, he called to pay , and was answered he had paid all last Night but for his Horse The Horse having eat up his Corn he was very much in Haste to be gone , but the Hostler asking what it was a Clock by his Watch, which he saw the Parson pull out the Night before, it put *Vilet* to a little Stand, not having so far examin'd his Pockets as to know whether he had or no, and therefore being loath to make a vain Essay, he answered that his Watch was down, and so got upon his Horse, and giving the Hostler a Shilling, rid away as fast as he could , and it being Summer Weather, he had a long Day before him After he had rid a considerable Way, he examines his Pockets, and finds in them six Guineas, four Pounds odd Money in Silver, and a very good Watch, and having found himself so well provided, he rid away the merrily, resolving to live well as long as that lasted.

But let us return to the true Parson, whom he left fast asleep in his Bed, About Seven in the Morning, it being in *June*, the Parson awakes, and going to bid his Bedfellow good Morrow, he soon found not only that the Bird was flown, but also that he had flown away with his Feathers, for he saw nothing

there but some old Cloath's which he suppos'd belonged to his Bedfellow; whereupon he calls for somebody to come up , but the Servants, who supposed it to be only the Shoemaker, ask'd him, what a Pox ail'd him to make such a Noise, and bid him quiet, or else they'd make him quiet This vex'd the Parson, and made him knock the harder, till the Chamberlain came up, and threatened to thrash his Sides, if so he would not be quiet.

The Minister wondring at this rude Treatment, ask'd, *Where was his Cloaths?* The Chamberlain still taking him for St *Hugh*, reply'd, *Where the Plague should they be but upon the Chair, where you left them? Who the Devil do ye think would meddle with your Cloaths? They an't so much worth I'm sure, you need not fear any Body's stealing them* The Man's mad, I think, replies the Parson , *Do you know who ye speak to? Speak to*, says the Fellow , *Yes, sure, I think I do If you did, you'd use better Words*, says the Parson *Better Words*, says the Man ; *my Words are good enough for a drunken Shoemaker Shoemaker!* says the Parson , *I am no Shoemaker, I am the Minister that came in here last Night* The *Devil you are*, replies the Chamberlain, *I am sure the Minister went away soon after three a Clock this Morning.* With that the Minister gets out of Bed in his Shirt, and taking hold of the Chamberland, *Sirrah*, says he, *bring me my Cloaths, my Mony, and my Watch, or I'll break your Neck down Stairs* With this Noise and Scuffle comes up the Master of the Inn, and some other of the Servants , who presently knew that was none of him whom they took for a Shoemaker , and upon a little Enquiry into the Matter, found that St *Hugh* had made an Exchange with the Parson Whereupon the Master of the Inn furnished him with a Suit of his own, and Money to bear his Charges, till they could hear what became of the Thief

He was at length taken in picking a Pocket, and tho' the Value he took from the Person did not come to ten Shillings, yet he was convicted thereof, and likewise upon another Indictment preferr'd against him by Mrs. *Frances Baldock*, for snatching from her a Pocket valued at one Shilling, and in which were twelve Guineas and two Pistoles For these Facts he received Sentence of Death at Justice Hall in the *Old Bailey* , but no Report being immediately given in to the King of the Malefactors condemned the Sessions he was try'd, he remained in the *condemned Hold* till another Sessions, when the dead Warrant being signed for eight Criminals, he was one among them appointed for Death, and accordingly on the 31st of *October*, 1718, he took shipping at *Newgate*, sailed with a fair Wind up *Holborn* River, and striking against the Rock of St. *Giles's*, was cast away at *Tyburn*, in the 27th Year of his Age

The

The LIVES of WILLIAM WARD, SAMUEL LYNN, RALPH EMMERY, ROBERT VICKERS, JOHN PRIOR, *and* FRANCIS PARQUET.

AS all these Malefactors were executed at the same Time, and as we have not many Particulars to relate of any one of them, we thought it best to put them all into one Chapter

William Ward was born at *Drydocking* in the County of *Norfolk* When he was but three Years old, his Parents removed from thence to the City of *Norwich* His Father who was a Mill Wright by Trade, made him, when capable, to work with him in that Occupation Afterwards he came up to *London*, where he married a very honest Woman, and at *Bow*, and other Places thereabouts, followed the Business he was brought up to; but unhappily falling into ill Company, he was too easily seduced to follow their bad Examples The first Fact he committed, was the taking off from a Hackney-Coach standing at the four *Swans-Inn* Door within *Bishops-Gate*, a Portmanteau corded under the Coachman's Seat, in which there was a gold Watch and Chain, Cloaths, and several other Things of Value, which were sold together for fourteen Guineas, and shared between him and two others concerned with him in that Fact However, the right Owner had them again for twenty one Guineas

Another Time *Will Ward* riding thro' *Holborn* in a Hackney-Coach, and espying a Porter with a great Trunk on his Back, bids the Coachman stop, and call the Porter to him, accordingly the Man of Carriage comes, to whom giving a Shilling to step just by of an Errand, he bade him lay his Load into the Coach, of which he would take Care No sooner was the Porter gone, but *Ward* calls to the Coachman again, who was feeding his Horses, and bids him drive to such a Place, where the Porter (he said) was to meet him. He is driven to an Alehouse in *Lutener's Lane*, which harbours all Sorts of Villains, where opening the Trunk to find what Prize he had got, he found therein about eighty Pounds in Money, besides a great Quantity of rich Cloaths, both Woollen and Linnen, in the mean Time the Porter was making a great Outcry all thro' *Holborn* for his Loss, but all to no Purpose, for the Owner of the Trunk sued his Sureties, which are Ticket-Porters give, and they again su'd the Porter, who was put in Gaol for his Folly

Not long after, *Ward* committed another Robbery at the four *Swans Inn* in *Bishopsgate-street*, taking from another Hackney Coach a Portmanteau Trunk, but being presently stopped and seized with it, was carried to the Poultry Compter, from whence he was committed to *Newgate* so that he had no Opportunity to know what was in it At the Sessions held at the *Old Bailey* in *October* 1718, he was try'd for it, and found guilty of his Last Fact, which proving

but a single Felony, he was thereupon only ordered for Transportation, but whilst he lay under Confinement he was convicted upon two other Indictments First for breaking open the House of *Thomas Lane*, and stealing ten Pounds Weight of Tea, on the 12th of *April* 1717, and Secondly, for a Burglary committed by him and *Samuel Lynn* hereafter mentioned in the House of Mr *Julian Bailey*, in the Parish of St *Giles's Cripplegate*, from whence they took divers Pieces of Plate to the Value of forty Pounds, on the 24th of *July*, 1717, and on *Monday* the 16th of *February* 1718-19, he was executed, being twenty two Years of Age, at *Tyburn*, where he confess'd that about a Twelvemonth before then, he and *Sam Lynn* took from off a Coach standing at the *Spread Eagle* in *Gracechurch street* a Portmanteau with Goods in it, belonging to Dr *Treburg*, and had also been concerned together in several other Facts, but could not particularly recollect themselves about them

SAMUEL LYNN was born at *Brampton* in *Norfolk*, and for some Time lived at a neighbouring Town called *Shesington* When he was Young, his Father (a Grocer and Tallow Chandler) removed to the City of *Norwich*, where he was bound Apprentice to him, and afterwards wrought Journey-work there, and then came up to *London*, where falling into ill Company, he soon took to picking of Pockets, for which he was brought to Justice, particularly for picking the Pocket of the Lady *Dorcas Roberts*, from whom he took a green silk Purse with three Guineas, and sixteen Shillings in it, on the 16th of *March*, 1713-14, and a little after was try'd and received Sentence of Death for the same, but afterwards received the King's gracious Pardon, and pleaded it at the *Old Bailey* on the 16th of *August* 1715, the Conditions of that Pardon (which he did not observe) being, that he should transport himself within six Months out of His Majesty's Dominions in *Europe*, but wanting Grace to improve this Mercy, he not only fell in again among his wicked Acquaintance, but returned to his former Trade of Thieving, till he was condemned for the same Fact as *Ward* abovementioned, and at the same Time hanged at *Tyburn*, aged 19 Years

RALPH EMMERY, was executed at the same Time, for a Murder and Robbery committed by him on the Body of *Nathaniel Asser*, on the 28th of *June*, 1718 He was born in *Old street*, in the Parish of St *Giles's Cripplegate* He was a Parish-Boy, and bound for nine Years to a *Cane-Chair maker*, whom he served faithfully all that Time,

Time, which when expired he followed that Business for himself, going about the Streets to get mending Work of that Sort, whereby he got a Livelyhood The Murder he stood condemned for, was committed in *Stepney-Fields*, in Company with *William Audley*, and *Sarah Brown*, executed some Time before *Emmery* took out of the Deceased's Pocket a Pocket Book, and some Coffee, however, he deny'd the bloody Fact, saying, that he never was guilty of any Murder, but could not justify himself in other Matters, for he had lived a long Time in Fornication and Adultery, had been a prophane Swearer, a vile Drunkard, and all along neglected the Service of God, that he had abandoned himself to a sinful Course of Life, and for Six Years past made it his common Practice to pick Pockets, That for these and the like Wicked Facts he was committed once to the Gaol in *White-Chapel*, and six times to *Newgate*. that he had took several Trials, been thrice whipt, and sent twice to *Bridewell*, but none of those Corrections working any Reformation in him, he still pursued his wicked Course of Life

The aforesaid *Ralph Emmery* had likewise been upon the Foot-pad, and with two others meeting just upon the Close of the Evening with a Nonjuring Parson just beyond the Halfway House to *Hampstead*, one of them justled the honest Doctor, which the other two perceiving, they seem'd to take the Doctor's Part, saying, go along with us, Sir, for that's some Rogue without doubt So these two Rogues went scolding along with the single Rogue, getting the Doctor betwixt 'em to protect him from robbing, till coming to a Ditch *Emmery* pushes the Doctor into it Look you there now, said the other two, did we not tell you before that he was a Rogue; we hope you'll be pleased to bestow something on us for conducting you hither The Doctor did not at all like his Guardians, and indeed he had no Reason, for taking his Peruke, Coat, and Sword, from him, they search'd his Breeches, in which finding about Eight Shillings, they then left him to get out of the Ditch

JOHN PRIOR was born at *Carsoo* in *Bedfordshire*, of such poor Parents, that they could not bestow any Education upon him, insomuch that he could neither write nor read, for a Livelihood he follow'd Husbandry in the Country, but leaving both Husbandry and Country, he came up to *London* about the Beginning of the Year 1716. and listed himself in the second Regiment of Foot-Guards, soon after which giving way to a lewd Life, he committed several most notorious Robberies on the Foot-pad, at many Country Places about the Cities of *London* and *Westminster*.

He was at last condemn'd for the following Robberies on the Highway, with *Robert Vickers* and *Francis Parquot* First, for assaulting and robbing *William Spinnage*, Gent. and taking from him a Purse with Fourteen Guineas, and a Half Guinea, a Watch, value Eight Pounds, and other Things, as he was riding in a Hackney Coach in *Farringdon-Lane*, near *Hornsey*, on the eighteenth of *August* 1718. Next

for a like Assault and Robbery by them jointed committed on the Person of *George Floyer* Esq; on Horseback, near *Tottenham-Court*, in the Parish of St *Pancras*, from whom they took a Pair of Pistols, value Forty Shilling, and a Gelding value Thirty Pounds, on the eighteenth of *September* following And lastly, for such another Assault and Robbery, which the said *Prior* and *Vickers* committed on Mr *William Squire*, who was by them roughly handled, and threaten'd to be kill'd (besides their taking from him Five Guineas, a Watch with a Chain and Seal, and Ten Shillings in Silver, near the Turnpike at *Tottenham*) without any Reward to the said Mr *Squire*'s Character, being one of his Majesty's Messengers After his Condemnation he was very impudent in the Condemn'd Hold, and was in great Hopes of a Reprieve, but he was nevertheless hang'd at *Tyburn* on *Monday* the Sixteenth of *February* beforemention'd, aged 34 Years

ROBERT VICKERS, hang'd also at the same Time, aged twenty three Years, was born at *Nethercot* in *Warwickshire*, and when but very young going from thence to *Westbury* in *Buckinghamshire*, he was there bound Apprentice to a Baker. When his Time was expired, he came up to *London*, and was Journeyman to a Baker in *Cow Cross*, and afterwards to another in *Golden Lane*, in the Parish of St *Giles's Cripplegate* But he growing weary of his Employment, listed himself in the second Regiment of Foot Guards, where he had not been very long before he began to be loose, and follow ill Courses, especially going on the Foot pad

The first Person whom he attack'd in this Manner was a certain *Irish* Barrister of the *King's Bench Walk* in the *Temple*, who was very well known for his not taking the Oaths to the then present Government This Lawyer *Vickers* meeting one Night walking from *Mary-le bone*, cross the Fields towards *Southampton-House*, he did not only take what Money he had, but also stript him to his Shirt, which dawbing all over with Dirt in a Pond, he put it on the Lawyer, saying, *that now he looked something like a Limb of the Law, since he was in black* Then tying him Neck and Heels, he left him there to ponder till next Morning, on *Wingate*'s Statutes, *Coke* upon *Littleton*, *Magna Charta*, old *Plowden*, *Levinz*'s Reports, and other musty Authors of the Law

FRANCIS PARQUOT, hang'd also with the above mentioned Malefactors, aged thirty Years, was born in *France*, at a Seaport Town call'd *Marrines*, near *Rochel* When he was about fifteen Years old he came into *England*, where he lived three Years with a *French* Jeweller Then leaving his Master he went to the City of *Bath*, and there kept a Shop for some time, but being in debt, was forced to leave that Place, and come up to *London*, where he privately follow'd his Occupation, till falling into ill Company, he betook himself to House breaking, which he follow'd till his Acquaintance with *Prior* and *Vickers* brought him to share their Fates

The LIVES *of* John Trippuck *the* Golden-Tinman, Robert Cane, Thomas Charnock, *and* Richard Shepherd.

THE firft of thefe Offenders had been an old Sinner, and had acquir'd the nick Name of the *Golden Tinman*, in the fame Manner as a former Practitioner in his wretched Calling, did that of the *Golden Farmer* Trippuck had robbed alone and in Company for a confiderable Space, till his Character was grown very notorious Some fhort Time before his being taking up for his laft Offence, he had by dint of Money and Intereft procured a Pardon However, venturing on the Fact which brought him to Death, the Perfon injured foon feized him, and being inexorable in his Profecution, *Trippuck* was caft and received Sentence But having ftill fome Money, he did not lofe all Hope of a Reprieve, but kept up his Spirits, by flattering himfelf with his Life being preferved, till within a very few Days of Execution If the Ordinary fpoke to him of the Affairs of his Soul, *Trippuck* immediately cut him fhort with, *D'ye believe I can obtain a Pardon? I don't know that indeed,* fays the Doctor, *But you know one Counfellor fuch a one,* fays Trippuck, *prithee make Ufe of your Intereft with him, and fee whether you can get him to ferve me, I'll not be ungrateful Doctor*

The Ordinary was almoft at his Wits End with this fort of crofs Purpofes ; however, he went on to exhort him to think of the great Work he had to do, and entreated him to confider the Nature of that Repentance, which muft attone for all his numerous Offences *Trippuck* upon this, opened his Breaft, and fhewed him a great Number of Scars, amongft which were two very large ones, out of which he faid two Mufquet Bullets had been extracted *And will not thefe good Doctor,* quoth he, *and the vaft Pains I have endured in their Cure, in fome fort leffen the Heinoufnefs of the Facts I may have committed No,* faid the Ordinary, *what Evils have fallen upon you in fuch Expeditions you have drawn upon yourfelf, and are not to imagine that thefe will in any Degree, make amends for the multitude of your Offences You had much better clear your Confcience, by a full and ingenuous Confeffion of your Crimes, and prepare in earneft for another World, fince I dare affure you, you need no Hopes of ftaying in this*

Trippuck as foon as he found the Ordinary was in the right, and that all Expectation of a Reprieve or Pardon were totally in vain, began, as moft of thofe fort of People do, to lofe much of that ftubbornnefs, they miftake for Courage ; He now felt all the Terrors of an awakened Confcience, and therefore perfifted no longer in denying the Crime for which he [...], but at firft ac...ed it altogether at [...]hood, and Convicted his Companion had devil't even to De...

It [...] ...rippuck was the

Man who killed Mr *Hull* towards the end of the Summer before on *Black Heath*, but when this Story reached his Ears, he declar'd it was an utter Falfity, repeating this Affertion to the Ordinary a few Moments before his being turned off, pointing to the Rope about him, faid, *As you fee this Inftrument of Death about me, what I fay is the real Truth* He died at laft with all outward Signs of Penitence

ROBERT CANE was a young Man, of about twenty two Years of Age, at the Time he fuffered Having a tollerable Genius when a Youth, his Friends put him Apprentice twice, but to no Purpofe, for having got rambling Notions in his Head, he would needs go to Sea There too but for his own unhappy Temper he might have done well, for the Ship of War in which he failed, was fo fortunate as to take, after eight Hours fharp Engagement, a *Spanifh* Veffel, of an immenfe Value, but the large Share he got here did him little Service. *Robert* as foon as he came home made a quick Hand of it, and when the ufual Train of fenfual Delights, which pafs for Pleafures in low Life, had exhaufted him to the laft Farthing, Neceffity, and the Defire of ftill indulging his Vices, made him fall into the worft, and moft unlawful Methods, to obtain the Means by which he might purfue them.

Sometime after this, the unhappy Man of whom we are fpeaking, fell in Love with a virtuous young Woman, who lived with her Mother, a poor well-meaning Creature, utterly ignorant of *Cane's* Behaviour, or that he had ever committed any Crimes punifhable by Law. The Girl, as fuch filly People are wont, yielded quickly to Marriage, which was to be confummated privately, becaufe *Cane's* Relations were not to be difobliged, who it feems did not think him totally ruined, while he efcaped Matrimony But the unhappy Youth not having Money enough to procure a Licenfe, and being afhamed to put the Expence on the Woman and her Mother, in a Fit of amorous Diftraction, he went out from them one Evening, and meeting a Man fomewhat fuddled in the Street, he threw him down, and took away his Hat and Coat The Fellow was not fo drunk, but that he cried out, and People coming to his Affiftance, *Cane* was immediately apprehended, and to this Fact, inftead of raifing him Money enough to be married, brought him to Death in the moft ignominious Way

While he lay in *Newgate*, the miferable young Creature who was to have been his Wife, came conftantly after him to cry with him, and deplore their mutual Misfortunes, which were encreafed by the Girl's Mother falling fick, and being confined to her

her Bed through Grief for her defign'd Son-in-Law's fad Fate   When the Day of his fuffering drew on, this unhappy Man compofed himfelf to fubmit to it with great Serenity   He profeffed abundance of Contrition for the Wickednefs of his former Life, and lamented with much Tendernefs thofe Evils he had brought upon the Girl and her Mother   The foftnefs of his Temper, and the fteady Affection he had for the Maid, contributed to make his Exit much pity'd, which happened at *Tyburn* in the 22d Year of his Age   He left a Paper behind him, which he alfo read at the Tree, containing a Confeffion of his Crime, a Vindication of his Sweetheart's Character, and a Profeffion of his Faith, and univerfal Charity

RICHARD SHEPHERD was born of very honeft and reputable Parents in the City of *Oxford*, who were careful in giving him a fuitable Education, which he through the Wickednefs of his future Life utterly forgot, infomuch, that he knew fcarce the *Creed* and *Lord's Prayer*, at the Time he had moft need of them   When he grew a tollerable big Lad, his Friends put him out Apprentice to a Butcher, where having ferved a great Part of his Time, he fell in Love with a young Country Lafs hard by, and his Paffion growing outragious, he attacked her with all the amorous Strains of Gallantry he was able   The Hearts of young uneducated Wenches, like unfortify'd Towns, make little Refiftance when once befieged, and thereof *Shepherd* had no great Difficulty in making a Conqueft   However the Girl infifted on honourable Terms, and unfortunately for the poor Fellow they were married before his Time was out   *An error in Conduct, which in low Life is feldom retrieved*

It happened fo here, *Shepherd's* Mafter was not long before he difcovered this Wedding, he thereupon gave the poor Fellow fo much Trouble, that he was at laft forced to give him forty Shillings down, and a Bond for twenty eight Pounds more, which having totally ruined him, *Dick* fell unhappily into the Way of difhoneft Company, who foon drew him into their manner of gaining Money, and fupplying his Neceffities at the Hazard both of his Confcience, and his Neck   He became an expert Proficient, yet could never acquire any Thing confiderable thereby, but was continually embroiled and in Debt, his Wife bringing in every Year a Child, contributing not a little thereto

When he firft began his Robberies, he went on Houfe breaking, and committed feveral Facts in the City of *Oxford* itfelf, but thofe Things not being fo eafily concealed there, as at *London*, report quickly began to grow very loud about him, and *Dick* was forced to make fhift with pilfering in other Places, in which he was fo unlucky, that the fecond or third

Fact he committed in *Hertfordfhire*, he was detected and feized, and at the next Affizes capitally convicted, yet his Friends out of Compaffion to his Youth, and in Hopes he might be fufficiently check'd by fo narrow Efcape from the Gallows, procured him firft a Reprieve and then a Pardon

But this proximity to Death made little Impreffion on his Heart, which is too often the Fault of Perfons, who receive Mercy, and have too little Grace to make ufe of it.   *Dick*, partly driven by Neceffity (for few People cared after his Releafe, to employ him) partly through the inftigations of his own wicked Heart, went again upon the old Trade, for when he was fo lately like to have fuffered; but thieving was ftill an unfortunate Profeffion to him   He foon after fell again into the Hands of Juftice, from whence he efcaped by impeaching *Allen* and *Chambers*, two of his Accomplice, and fo evaded *Tyburn* a fecond Time, yet all this fignified nothing to him, for as foon as at home, he was at work in his old Way, till apprehended and executed for his Wickednefs

No unhappy Criminal had ever more Warning than *Shepherd*, of his approaching miferable Fate, if he would have fuffered any Thing to have detered him, but alas! what are Advices, what are Terrors, what even the Sight of Death itfelf, to Souls hardened in Sin, and Confciences fo feared as his   He was taken up, carried before Col   *Ellis* and committed to *Newprifon* for a capital Offence   He had not remained there long, before he wrote the Colonel a Letter, in which (provided he were admitted an Evidence) he offered to make large Difcoveries   His Offers were accepted, and both convicted capitally at the *Old-Bailey*, by him, were executed at *Tyburn*, whither *Shepherd* quickly followed them

Shepherd had picked up while in *Newgate*, a thoughtlefs Refolution as to dying, not uncommon to old Malefactors, who having been often condemned, grow at laft hardened to the Gallows   When he was exhorted to think ferioufly of making his Peace with God, he replied, It was done, and he was fure of going to Heaven

THOMAS CHARNOCK, executed with thefe, was a young Man well and religioufly Educated   He had by his Friends been placed in the Houfe of a very eminent Trader, and being feduced by ill Company, yielded to a Defire of making a Shew in the World, and in order to it, robbed his Mafter's Accompting-Houfe, which Fact made him indeed confpicuous, but in a very indifferent Manner from what he had flattered himfelf with   They died tolerably Submiffive and Penitent, this laft Malefactor efpecially, who had rational Ideas of Religion   The Day of their Execution was *January* the 29th, 1719-20.

The LIVES of JOHN HAWKINS and GEORGE SYMPSON.

JOHN *HAWKINS* at the Time of his Death was about thirty Years old. His Father was a Farmer at *Stains* in *Middlesex*, very honest, but poor; and therefore could not give his Son but a slender Education. At fourteen *John* waited on a Gentleman, but soon left him to be a Tapster's Boy at the *Red Lyon* in *Brentford*, where he continued till he got into another Gentleman's Service. But being of an unsettled Temper, he seldom tarried long in a Place. The last Family he was in was Sir *Dennis Dutry*'s, where he was Butler, and might have have lived happily, for being a handsome creditable Servant, he was approved of by his Master and Lady. But the Opinion he had of his own Person made him too assuming, and he thought it a small Fault to be out two or three Nights a Week at the Gaming Tables. By his repeated Neglect of his Master's Business, the Family was incensed against him, he was turned away, not without a Suspicion of having first been a Confederate in robbing the House of a considerable Value in Plate. Having been instructed in the Nature of trading to France and Flanders, in Wares, Brandies, &c. He joined with his Brother, a Captain of a Vessel or Sloop, in fetching those Commodities from those Places, and commonly paid the King's Custom for them. This Way of Life was very agreeable to him, but having a strong and violent Inclination to arrive at great Riches and Splendour, on a sudden, he left the uncertain Way of dealing at Sea, to deal in the *South Sea*, and the Bubbles, from which he had recourse to Bubbling in another Way, as some others besides have done, in which vicious Courses he had Success for a considerable Time.

He was now twenty four. His first Expedition was to *Hounslow Heath*, where he stopp'd a Coach, and eas'd the Passengers of about eleven Pounds. With this Booty he returned safe to *London*, and repairing immediately to the *King's Head* at *Temple-Bar*, he threw it all off. It was he went on a pretty while by himself, losing all Prey what he had got upon the Road. But finding some Difficulties in robbing alone, he chose for his Companions *Ryley*, *Commerford*, *Reeves*, and *Leonard*, an *Irish* Captain. With these he committed several Robberies on *Hounslow* and *Bagshot* Heaths. But tho' he sometimes acquired considerable Prizes by such Means, they did him but little Service, for he still had such an Itching to Gaming, that he could never forbear 'till he had lost the last Penny, so that he was often put to the pitiful shift of bilking an Ordinary for a Dinner.

Having follow'd this Course about two Years he was made a State Prisoner, for being concerned in the *Preston* Rebellion, and *Hawkins* and one *Wortley*, for attempting to rescue him, were apprehend-

ed by the King's Messengers, but in a short Time they were both discharged. A few Days after this, *Commerford*, *Reeves*, and *Ryley*, were seized at *Guilford*. *Hawkins* had been with them, but could not get a Horse. The two former were executed, and *Ryley* transported, and the Government took Care of *Leonard*.

Hawkins now engaged with a new Gang, among which was one *Pocock*, who being apprehended, impeach'd all the rest. This quickly dispers'd them, and one *Ralphson*, to whom they had entrusted most of their Stock, went off with it to *Holland*. By which Means *Hawkins* was left without Money or Companions, for they had all forsaken the Town, except his Brother *Will* and *James Wright*. *Will* was taken on *Pocock*'s Information, and *Wright* was in a Salivation. *Hawkins* himself skulk'd about Town, not daring to appear but in such Houses as he could confide in, one of which *Wilson*, who was Evidence against him at his Trial, frequented. They soon became as familiar as ever, and believing *Wilson* wou'd not betray him for the sake of the Reward, *Hawkins* told him every Thing that we have related concerning him and his Companions, and other Passages that are omitted. As that he was present when Colonel *Floyer* shot *Woldridge*, and that he himself shot General *Evans*'s Footman, which he said happened thus: He stopp'd the General and another Gentleman in a Coach, the General and the Gentleman both fired at him, upon which he shot directly into the Coach, but miss'd them and killed the Servant who was behind it.

Hawkins often lamented this Misfortune, and when he fell into Company with a Clergyman, would always be asking some casuistical Questions on Cases parallel to his own, but tho' he fancied this was no Murder because he had no Design against the Deceas'd, yet he was always told, that the Design against the Master made the Person as Guilty, as if it had been intended against the Man who was killed.

Wilson took so much Pleasure in hearing *Hawkins* relate his Pranks and Robberies, that he grew very fond of his Company. *Wright* being now recover'd, he and *Hawkins* fell to their old Sport, and when they came home at Night, *Wilson* used to drink with them. Their first Robbery after this Reunion was in *Richmond* Lane, upon the Earl of *Pomfret*? and the Lord *Bruce*, from whom they took twenty Pounds, two gold Watches, and a fine Ring, for which his Lordship offered 100*l.* to *Justice* — *Will* Brown pretended he sold it for five Pounds, and poor *Wright* thought that a good Price, and gladly accepted of three Pounds for his Share, tho' *Hawkins* then had the Ring in his own Possession, and afterwards sold it in *Holland* for forty Pounds.

James Wright was born of honest Parents, and bred a Barber. He was one of the best Temper, and greatest Fidelity to his Companions, that ever was known of a Highwayman. How his Acquaintance begun with *Hawkins* is uncertain, but they two for about a Month after *Wright*'s Salvation, went on very prosperously together, before *Wilson* engaged with them.

About this Time a good natur'd Countryman lent *Wilson* ten Pounds who had been starving for some Weeks, notwithstanding which, he made all the Haste he could to the Tables and lost it every Farthing. From the Table he went to *Hawkins* and *Wright*, and having drank freely, *Hawkins* begun to talk about robbing, but said a third Man was necessary, and ask'd *Wilson* if he durst take a Pistol. *Wilson* answered, *Yes, as well as any Man, for the want of Money has made me ready for any Thing.* He, who was always glad of new Companions, proffered very kindly to get a Horse against next Night. They agreed, and so went to Bed.

Hawkins was as good as his Word, and in the Evening they sat to drinking again. At a proper Hour *Hawkins* told us all was ready, and so they mounted about Ten a Clock, and soon after robbed Sir *David Dalrymple* near *Winstanley*'s Water-Works. They put on upon stopping the Coach, to try how capable he was of becoming a Man of Business. And he perform'd so well, that *Hawkins* never after cared to part with him.

They took from Sir *David* about three Pounds in Money, a Snuff Box, and a Pocket Book, for which last, Sir *David* offer'd sixty Pounds to *Wild*, but they return'd it by a Porter, *gratis*, for they had no dealings with *Wild*, nor did he know either of them.

The next Coach they robbed was Mr *Hide*'s of *Hackney*, they took from him ten Pounds and a Watch, but miss'd three hundred Pounds in Bank Notes. They seldom fail'd of committing two or three Robberies in a Week, for a Month together. They scarce ever went above five Miles out of Town, and when they returned to it again, they attack'd the Coaches in *Chancery-Lane*, another in *Lincolns Inn Fields*, and in going off stumbled upon my Lord *Westmoreland*, who had three Footmen behind his Coach. They had some Difficulty in robbing his Lordship, for the Watch pour'd in upon them, but at hearing a Pistol fir'd over their Heads, they retired as fast, and gave them an Opportunity of escaping.

Will Hawkins, the Brother of *John*, and *Wright*, were soon after both Prisoners, *Hawkins* could not impeach any Body, because he was impeached himself. *Wright* indeed might have taken that Advantage to have saved his own Life, but he told *Jack Hawkins*'s Wife that he would hurt no Body, and much less her Husband, because of his Children. How well this Generosity was returned will appear hereafter. *Hawkins* and *Wilson*, to conceal themselves, went to *Oxford*, and staid there a Month, in which Time *Hawkins* defac'd some Pictures in the Gallery over the *Bodleian* Library. The University offered a hundred Pounds to any that would discover the Person who did it, and a poor Taylor, who had distinguished himself for a Whig, was taken up and imprison'd on Suspicion, and narrowly escaped a Whipping.

The Sessions at the *Old Bailey* being ended, *Hawkins* was discharged, and *Wright* reserved for *Kingston* Assizes. The two Brothers then went to *Holland* with all *Wright*'s Goods to the Value of fifty Pounds, and left him starving in Jail.

About the end of *October* they both returned to *London*, where *Wilson* joined with them, and they went on together till *Christmas*, when *Wilson* became of age, and was in Possession of a small Estate his Father left him, which he sold for three hundred and fifty Pounds. But he soon lost it all at play, except what he lent to *Jack* and *Will* to buy Horses.

One Night *Hawkins* and *Wilson* took a Ride to *Hampstead*, and being elevated with Wine, resolved as they returned, to rob the first Coach they met. It happened that about a hundred Yards on this side of *Lane*, they met a Chariot with two Gentlemen in it. As soon as they pass'd them they muffled up with Cape and Handkerchief, and overtook 'em at the Lower end of *Fig-Lane*. The Coachman stopt at the first Word, and down went the Sashes, *Wilson* on one side, and *Hawkins* on the other. The Gentlemen fired both at once. One of them lodg'd three Slugs in *Hawkins*'s Shoulder, but the other miss'd *Wilson*, had they fetch'd them to come nearer they might have shattered them to pieces. However our Highwaymen thought it best to move off, to prevent Murder on both sides.

This Action was follow'd with such bad Weather, that they could do nothing; and when fair Weather came, their Horses Heads were so swell'd that they could not get 'em out of the Stable, and so they agreed to rob on Foot in Hide Park. The first Coach they attempted there was Mr *Green* the Brewer's but the Coachman whipt his Horses and left them. However *Wilson* shot one of his Horses, and endeavouring to fire again shot himself thro' the Hand, which made his retreat very difficult having the Wall to get over.

Being thus disabled *Wilson* had Leisure to reflect on his deplorable Condition, and was convinced that Vengeance would one Day overtake him, and such a Course of Life be finish'd with Scandal at *Tyburn*. These Reflections brought him to a Resolution of leaving the Town, pursuant to which he borrow'd Money of a Friend, took a Horse out of the Stable and set forward for *Yorkshire*, *Feb* 1 1721.

Thus prepared for an honest Life arrived at *Whitby*, where in a few Days he fell into his Mother's Business, and followed it diligently till the succeeding *August*, when one day being sent for to a Publick House, to his great Surprize, he found his old friend *John Hawkins*, and a new Companion *George Simpson*. After the usual Salutations, *Hawkins* told *Wilson* that as he had been like other Men, he was now as liable to suffer as any Body, for his Brother *Will* had impeached him and all the rest of his Companions, and he should be fetch'd away in a few Days. This startled *Wilson*, that he agreed to go with them. So they also bought Horses, and came to *London*. Then *Wilson* found that *Hawkins* had deceived, me, for I was not impeach'd nor was his Brother in Custody.

George Simpson was about twenty eight Years of Age when he died. He was born at *Putney*, in *Surrey*, and brought up at *Coure* in *Lincolnshire*. He had no Education, and but poor natural Parts. He was never capable of designing, but when any thing was contrived for him, no one was more speedy or bold in the Execution, for he was equally brisk and stout. He had been Bailiff of a Hundred in *Lincolnshire*, but for some Misdemeanor, flying the Country, he came to *London*, and served the Lord *Castlemain* and other Gentlemen in quality of a Footman. But discontented with that condition of Life, and becoming acquainted with *Jack Hawkins* he commenced Collector of the Highway.

However it was not long before *Hawkins* was in a and taken by the Servants of Sir *Edward Lawrence* whom he and *Butler Fox* had robbed in the *Hunnington* Coach. *Will* impeached every Body that had been concerned with him, tho' none but *Fox* and *Wright* were apprehended. *Wright* was acquitted at *Kingston* the *Summer* Affizes before, and having obtain'd his Liberty, fell into an honest Imployment, which he follow'd till *Hawkins* impeached him. He was convicted of a Street-Robbery, done about two Years before, and hanged. And thus was poor *Wright* s Generosity repaid. He faves *Hawkins* to be hang'd himself.

Butler Fox was a Porter in *Milk-street*. He had a Wife and three Children. His Acquaintance with *Will Hawkins* began at *Carter's* House by *London Wall*, a Nest for Highwaymen. *Hawkins* impeach'd him of robbing Colonel *Hamilton*, and at the Trial swore, that himself and *Fox* committed that Robbery, tho' neither of them was concerned in it, for it was done by *Jack Hawkins* and *George Simpson*, and no other Person, and they, the same Night, informed *Will* of all the Particulars. This I had from *Jack* himself, who own'd he had often exclaim'd against *Will* for swearing *Fox* into this Robbery.

All this Time the rest of the Gang play'd least in Sight, their most convenient House was by *London Wall*. The Landlord knew all their Circumstances, and found his Account in that Knowledge, for they seldom committed a Robbery, but he had his Snack by way of Reckoning. As he kept a Livery Stable, there had an Opportunity of riding out at all Hours, so that they harrass'd most of the Morning Stage-Coaches in *England*. One Morning they robb'd the *Worcester*, the *Glocester*, the *Cirencester*, the *Bristol*, and the *Oxford* Coaches all together. Next Morning the *Chichester* and *Ipswich*, and the third Morning the *Portsmouth* Coach. They were constant Customers to the *Bury* Coach, and touch'd it no less than ten Times. And for any of these they seldom rode farther than the *Stones End*. When they met with any Portmanteaus, they carried them to *Carter*, and ransack'd 'em.

Their Evening Enterprizes were commonly between *Richmond*, *Hackney*, *Hampstead*, or *Bow*, and *London*, and often behind *Buckingham Wall*. They committed innumerable Robberies with great Success, and might perhaps, have continued much longer if they had not meddled with the Mails.

One Time as they were making up to the *Portsmouth* Coach, a Gentleman upon it fired at them, before they spoke to the Coachman, for their passing the Coach and immediately returning, was a plain Indication of what they aimed at. They were treated in the like Manner in attempting a mourning Coach, but with worse Luck, for *Wilson*'s Horse received a Wound, of which he died. One Thing was remarkable enough, and that was their meeting Mr *Green* and his Lady behind *Buckingham Wall*, and robbing them, because when they once before attacked the same Coach, and being on Foot the Coachman drove away, upon which *Wilson* told him they should have the Luck to meet him again, when they were mounted.

Thus they went on till the Beginning of *April*, 1722, when they began to talk of robbing the Mails. This Design was first concerted with their Landlord *Carter*. He propos'd to begin with the *Harwich* Mail, but that being as uncertain as the Wind, they could not agree to wait for it. At last, they pitched upon the *Bristol* Mail, and prepared every Thing for that Purpose.

On *Sunday*, *April* the 15th, they set out, and next Morning they took the Mail, and again on *Wednesday* Morning. They robbed it the second Time, to get the Halves of some Bank Notes, the other Halves of which, they had taken the first Time.

On *Monday*, *April* the 23d, *Wilson* went after Dinner to see his Horse in *Fenchurch-street*; and from thence to *Carter's*, where he found two or three Men, whose Looks made him withdraw abruptly to *Moregate* Coffee House ——— There he fell into a Sett of Company, among whom was one who appeared to be a *Quaker*, and told him there was great Enquiry made after the Robbers of the *Bristol* Mail, and that some were even then searching for them in the Neighbourhood. This confirming *Wilson*'s Suspicion, he paid for his Gill, left the Coffee House, and took a turn in *Bedlam*, where he determined in his Mind to take a Passage that Night for *Newcastle*.

With this Resolution he went towards *Moregate* Coffee House again, and in his Way, met the Persons he had seen at *Carter's*. As soon as he past 'em, they turned about and followed him, tho' not so closely but he got into the Coffee House unperceived by them, for they went thro' *Moregate* Arch. He then went out at the Fore Door, where they stood watching in the Street, and as soon as they saw him, they seized him. They carried him to the Post-Office, where he was examined by the Post-Master General, who could make nothing of him that Night. Next Morning he was carried before him again, four or five Times to as little Purpose, tho' Mr *Carteret* used the most prevailing Arguments to procure a Discovery. All the Post Officers, in short, were very pressing to no Purpose, till one of them called *Wilson* aside, and shewed him the following Letter.

SIR,

I AM one of those Persons who robbed the Mails, which I am sorry for, and to make amends, I will secure my two Companions, as soon as may be. He whose Hand this shall appear to be, will, I hope, be entitled to the Reward and his Pardon.

Wilson knew this to be *Simpson*'s Letter, and so presently made a Discovery, whereupon *Hawkins* and *Simpson* were apprehended on the *Thursday* following.

At their Trial *Hawkins* pray'd the Court that all the King's Witnesses might be examin'd a-part, which the Court granted.

Thomas Green, the Postboy, depos'd thus. On *Monday* the 16th of *April*, about one in the Morning, as I was riding by the *Pyde Horse* at *Slough*, and blowing my Horn, I was overtaken by *James Ladbrook*, who was travelling the same Way. We rode in Company to *Langley-Broom*, where a Man on a Chesnut Horse made up to us, and went off again. We rode thro' *Colebrook*, and then perceived that two Men follow'd us at a Distance, and on this side *Longford* they came up to us, with Handkerchiefs in their Mouths, and their Wigs and Hats pulled forward over their Faces. The foremost of them was on a Chesnut Horse. He held a Pistol to my Head, and said, *You must go along with me*, and then taking hold of my Horse's Bridle he led me down a narrow Lane, and the other Man brought *Ladbrook* after me in the same manner. Then they making us both dismount, he on the Chesnut Horse said to me, *Are you the Lad that swore against Child?* No, I said, *I have been Post-Boy but a very little while. Have you ever been rob'd yet* says he, No, says I. *Why then,* says he, *you must pay Beverage now, for God damn my Blood and Ouns I'll be revenged upon somebody for poor Child's sake.* Then

he

le cut *Ladbrook*'s Horfe a Bride, and turned him adrift, and that being done, he went off with the Black Gelding I rode upon As foon as he was gone, the other Man tied our Hands behind us, bound us Back to Back, and fo faftened us to a Tree in a Ditch Then he afke Ladbrook what Money he had about him *Ladbrook* told him he had about 3 s 6 d He fearched *Ladbrook*'s Pocket, and finding no more, he did not take that nor any Thing elfe from him, but left us bound, and went after his Companions Ladbrook and I, with a great deal of ftruggling, got from the Tree, but could not get from one another And fo ty'd Back to Back, we went to an Inn in *Longford*, from whence the Hoftler came with us, and we went down the Lane together, and there we found the Gelding loofe, and the Bags cut open It was pretty dark, fo that I cannot fwear to their Perfons or their Horfes, only I could perceive that one was a Chefnut Horfe

James Ladbrook confirmed all the Poft boy's Evidence

Ralph Wilfon I have known *John Hawkins* thefe two Years, but was not acquainted with *Simpfon* till *Auguft* laft. We had often confulted together about robbing fome Mail, but did not agree upon what Mail, till five Days before the Fact was committed, and then we refolved it fhould be the *Briftol* Mail Purfuant to this Refolution, about 11 o'Clock on *Sunday* Morning, the 15th of *April*, we all three took Horfe at the *Blue Boar-Inn* in *Southwark*, Hawkins on a tall Bay, or Brown Gelding, Simpfon on a Chefnut or Sorrel Mare, and I on a dapple Grey We croffed the Water at *Kew* Ferry, dined at the *Three Pidgeons* in *Brentford*, ftaid there till fix in the Evening, called at the Poft-noufe at *Hounflow*, and loitered on the Road till we came to the Poft office at *Colebrook*, where we fupped on Horfeback, we enquired of the Hoftler what Time the *Briftol* Mail would come by, and he told us between one and two o'Clock in the Morning We went thence and came to *Langly* Broom about Midnight, where we agreed to difpatch *Simpfon* alone to meet the Mail He went, and we loitered about, waiting for his Return And about one o'Clock we faw the Poft boy and a Traveller with him, and *Simpfon* following them Then we met *Simpfon*, and held a frefh Confultation, in which at laft it was agreed, that the and I fhould follow the Mail, and that *Hawkins* fhould watch at a Diftance, becaufe he being pretty bulky, would be more remarkable Then *Hawkins* and I changed Horfes, and I and *Simpfon* followed the Boy and Traveller through *Colebrook*, and on this Side of *Longford* we rode up to them, and taking hold of their Horfes Bridles, led them down *Harmerfworth*-Lane, where we made them difmount I left *Simpfon* to bind them, and took the Boy's Gelding and Mail to the End of the Lane, where I found *Hawkins* waiting, and in a little Time *Simpfon* came to us We rifled the Bags, and carried feveral of them to *Hounflow* Heath, where we felected thofe of *Bath* and *Briftol*, and left the reft. Thence we rode thro' *Kingfton* and *Wandfworth*, and going down a bye Road, we fe rched the Bags, took out what we thought fit, moft of which we put in two riding Bags, and the reft into our Pocket, and what we thought would be of no Service to us, we put into the *Briftol* and *Bath* Bags again, and fo threw them over a Hedge Then taking our Way thro' *Camberwell*, we came along *Greenwich* Road, to the *Hand Inn* in *Barnaby* ftreet, between five and fix on *Monday* Morning There we put up our Horfes, and drank a Pint of burnt Wine, and after fome Time took Coach, and drove to the *Minories*, where to avoid Sufpicion, we parted, and went by different Ways to

Frank Green's at the *Cock and George* in the M We went in to a Room by our felves, and to take all Miftruft, we called for a Candle, Wax, Pper, Pen and Ink, and then locking the Door we examined our Prize We referved only the Bank Note and burnt all the other Notes and the Letters with the Candel which we fet in the Chimney, we found three 20 l Bank Notes, one of 25 l half of a 5 l and two halves of 25 l each, which we equally divided I was apprehended on the Monday following, and made this fame Confeffion before Mr *Carteret*, the Poft Mifter-General, and by my Directions the Prifoners were taken at Mrs *Bowen*'s (a Midwife) in *Green Arbour Court*, in the *Little Old-Bailey*

The Hoftlers at the feveral Inns where they had been, confirmed almoft all the Circumftances of *Wilfon*'s Depofition

Richard Room, Conftable I went with *Richard Mills* and others, to apprehend the Prifoners at a Midwife's Houfe in *Green Arbour-Court*, in the Little *Old-Bailey*, between Eight and Nine at Night A Woman came to the Door, and afked what we wanted? We bid her not be frighted, but bring a Candle, for we were come to fearch for ftolen Goods The Prifoners, who were above, overheard us, called out and faid, we are the Men you want, but G——d d——n ye, the firft that comes up is a dead Man We told them we were provided for them, let them fire as foon as they would Then *Hawkins*'s Brother came down foremoft, and perfuaded them to furrender quietly I told them we were come upon *Wilfon*'s Information. Are you fo, fays the Prifoner *Hawkins*, why then we are dead Men, but we had rather lofe our Lives, than fave them in fuch a bafe and infamous a Manner as that Villain *Wilfon* faved his

Richard Mills depofed the fame in Subftance The Prifoners then brought feveral Evidences to vindicate their Characters, one of which gave the Court fome Trouble, on Account of a Receipt which he produced, the whole Affair is too long to be related In fine, at the fecond going out, the Jury brought them in Guilty

The Verdict being recorded, *Hawkins* expreffed himfelf to this Purpofe I am altogether innocent of this Robbery, though I don't blame my Countrymen for their Verdict, for their Intentions were honourable, but they were over ruled by a partial Judge I have been ill dealt by My Friend has been Brow beat, and hardly fuffered to fpeak Ie jeft to die, but yet I would not change Conditions with the Villain that has faved his own Life, by fwearing away mine. For I prefer Death to a Life faved in fuch an infamous Manner My Blood lies upon his Head, and upon fome others —— I hope your Lordfhip is not concerned in it

When they were conveyed to Execution, not being allowed the Privilege of a Coach, they appeared in the Carts with uncommon Tokens of Repentance, fcarce ever raifing their Eyes from their Books or regard the Crowds about them, nor tarrying to drink Quantities of Liquor, as is ufually done

Being come to the Place of Execution, *Hawkins* in fome Confufion, was turned off, and died with prodigous Difficulty and Struggling, contrary to his Friend, who was more compofed before he died, and more eafily loft his Breath

The fame Day their Bodies were carried to *Hounflow-Heath*, and there hanged in Irons on a Gibbet erected for that Purpofe, not far from the on which *Benjamin Child* was hanged in the fame Manner

He was convicted at *Ailefbury* Affizes, on the F
dence

dence of his Man *William Wade* and the Post Boy) for robbing the *Bristol Mail.* On *Monday* the Eighth of *March*, 1722, he was carried out on Horseback from *Aylesbury* Goal, to the *Bear* at *Slough*, where he lay that Night, and about Ten next Day was carried in a Coach to the Place of Execution.

The LIVES of WILL OGDEN and TOM REYNOLDS.

THE first of these Villains was born in *Wall-Nut Tree Alley*, in *Tooley-street*, in *Southwark*, being a Waterman by his Calling, and the other was born in *Cross-Key Alley*, in *Barnaby street*, being Apprentice to a Dung Barge Man, living between *Vaux Hall* and the *Nine Elms*, but running away from his Master before he had served his Time, and taking ill Courses with *Ogden*, they first robbed several Ships, Hoys, and other Vessels below Bridge, for above two Years, when being very like to have been once apprehended for this fort of Theft, they left it off, and took to Housebreaking.

Several Houses they had broke open and robb'd in and about the Borough of *Southwark.* But at last being apprehended for breaking open a Watchmaker's Shop in the City of *London*, and stealing thence twenty six Watches, in Company of another Rogue, who made himself an Evidence against them, they were committed to *Newgate*, and condemned, however, they both had the good Fortune to be repriev'd, and in *August* 1713, pleaded her Majesty's most gracious Pardon, after which they obtained their Liberty.

Nevertheless, these hardened Rogues not making good Use of that Mercy which they had received, they turned Foot-pads, and one of them, namely *Ogden*, meeting one Night, when the Moon was up, with a Parson who lived at *Peckham*, pretending to be a Seaman, out of all Business, and in great Distress, he humbly begg'd an Alms of him, whereupon the Parson taking Compassion on the dismal Story which he told him of his extream Poverty, he gave him Six-pence, and so they parted. The Parson had not gone above the length of a Field before *Ogden* met him again, going over a Stile, and begging his Charity again, quoth the Gentleman, *You are the most impudent Beggar that ever I met with.* *Ogden* then telling him that he was in very great Want, and that the Six-pence which he gave him would not relieve his pressing Necessities, he gave him half a Crown, whereupon *Ogden* saying, *These are very sad Times, for there's horrid robbing abroad, therefore if you have any Money about you, you may as well let me have it as another, who perhaps may abuse you, and binding you Hand and Foot, make you lie in the Cold all Night, but if you'd give me your Money, I'll take Care of you, and conduct you very safe Home.*

The Parson then gave him all his Money, which was about forty Shillings. Quoth *Ogden*, *I see you have a Watch, Sir, you may as well let me have that too.* The Parson gave him that also, and as

they were trudging along, out came two or three Fellows upon them, to whom *Ogden* crying, *The Moon shines bright*, they let them pass quietly, and shortly after two or three other Fellows came suddenly on to whom *Ogden* crying again *The Moon shines bright*, they also permitted them to pass by. At last *Ogden* brought the Parson to his Door, where the Parson invited him to walk in, with a Promise that he would not hurt a Hair of his Head on any Account, but *Ogden* refusing the Parson's Proffer, he called for a Bottle of Wine, and drinking to *Ogden* to whom he gave the Bottle and Glass to help himself, he ran away with them, saying, he would drink the Wine to them that should certainly drink his Health.

Not long after this Civility shewed the Parson *Ogden* and *Reynolds* one Evening meeting with Beau *Medlicote*, walking near *Marybone*, they commanded him to stand and deliver. He made some Refusal at first, pretending as if he would defend himself by his Sword, but presenting their Pistols at him, and knowing how a Gentleman had once caned him for making Love to his Wife, quoth they, if you do not presently deliver your Money we shall serve you worse than Sir *Robert Atkins* did, whereupon searching his Pockets, and finding therein two half Crowns, one of which was Brass, they most grievously thrashed the Spark for carrying bad Money about him.

Another Time *Ogden* and *Reynolds* in Company with one *John Bradshaw*, who was Grandson of that infamous Villain, Serjeant *Bradshaw*, who passed Sentence on King *Charles* the First to be beheaded watching for a Prey in a Wood near *Shooter's Hill*, in *Kent*, one *Cecilia Fowler*, a Servant Wench, just come out of Service, happening then to be passing by with a Box on her Head, *Jack Bradshaw* went up to her by himself, being, as he thought, sufficient enough to deal with her, and taking her Box from her, in which was her Clothes and fifteen Shillings in Money, which she had received for a Quarter's Wages, whilst he was rifling of it, after he had broke it open, a Hammer being therein, she takes it up, and striking him on the left Temple with it, the Blow felled him to the Ground on his Back. She then seconded it with the Claw of the Hammer, by striking it into his Windpipe, of which Wound the Rogue instantly died.

In a very short time a Gentleman riding by, to whom she cried out *Stop*, he made up to the deceased, in whose Pockets he found eighty Guineas, and a Whistle with which whistling, *Ogden* and *Reynolds* came presently, running out of the Wood, but perceiving it to be a wrong Person that whistled, they assembly ran into the Wood again. Then the Gentlemen carried the Maid before a Magistrate, where he was bound for her Appearance at the Assizes held at *Rochester*, in *March* 1714, when she came there to take her Trial, and was acquitted.

Once *Ogden* and *Reynolds*, meeting a Tallyman near *Camberwell*, very well noted for his dealing with most of the poor People in the Parish of St *Giles's in the Fields*, especially Hawkers, whom he lay with first, and sent next to the *Marshalsea*, they commanded him to stand and deliver, he us'd many Expostulations with them, hoping they would have Pity on a poor Man, who took a great deal of Pains for his Bread. Quoth *Ogden*, thou *Spawn of Hell! have Pity on thee? No Sirrah, I know thee too well, and would almost as soon be kind to a Bailiff, or an informing Constable, A Tallyman and a Rogue are Synonimous, or at least convertible Terms. Every* Friday *you set up a Tenter in the* Marshalsea *Court, upon which you rack and stretch poor Prisoners like English Broad Cloth, beyond the Staple of the Wool, till the Threads crack, and that causes them with the least Wet to shrink, and presently wear bear. Money is so much thy Darling that for this you would fall down and worship the Image of a Nero, nay of a Devil, rather than want the single Penny that bears it, yet you pretend to Honesty, but again, I say, that you, and all your Calling, are worse Rogues then ever were hanged at* Tyburn. So taking from him a silver Watch, two gold Rings, and twenty eight Shillings, they then stripped him, and binding him Hand and Foot, left him under a Hedge to shift for himself.

These Criminals were great Cronies of one *Thomas Jones*, a Victualler's Son at *Deptford*, and *John Richardson*; the former of whom was Butler, and the other Footman, to an Esquire living at *Eltham*. These Fellows one Day robbing a Gentleman on *Black-Heath*, and leaving him there bound Hand and Foot, their Master, within some few Hours after, riding by the same Place, where he saw the Gentleman bound, he ordered him to be loos'd, and taking him into his Coach, brought him to his House, where refreshing him with a Glass of Wine, the Butler had no sooner filled it out, whom he knew again, but he charged him with the Robbery. This surprising the Esquire, he could scarce believe it, till he described what Horse he rode on, and the other Horse and Person on him, which proved to be one of his Footmen, and they not denying the Fact, they were carried before a Magistrate committed to *Maidstone* Gaol, and hanged at *Rochester* on *Friday* the 2d of *April*, 1714.

As for *Ogden* and *Reynolds*, pursuing these wicked Courses, without any Fear of the Laws, either of God or Man, they were at last apprehended for robbing one *Simon Hasey*, and one *John Boyont*, committed to the *Marshalsea* Prison in *Southwark* and hanged, the first aged twenty five Years, the other twenty two, at *Kingston upon Thames*, on *Saturday* the 23d of *April*, 1714.

Whilst they were under Sentence of Death, they attempted to break out of the *Stock House*, in which they were confin'd at *Kingston*, and as they were riding to the Place of Execution, *Ogden* flung a Handful of Money out of the Cart to the People, saying, *Gentlemen here is poor Will's Farewel*. And when he was turning off, he gave two such extraordinary Jirks with his Legs, as was much admired by all the Spectators.

The LIFE *of* ZACHARY CLARE.

ZACHARY CLARE was a Baker's Son, born at *Hackney,* and by his Father bred up to his Trade , but becoming acquainted with *Ned Bonnet,* who learned him the Trade of robbing on the Highway, they practifed it together with good Succefs for three or four Years, in the Counties of *Hartford* and *Cambridge* , and became fuch a Terror to the People of the Ifle of *Ely,* that they durft hardly ftir out far from home, unlefs they were half a Dozen, or half a Score in a Body together, but at length *Clare* being apprehended as robbing one Day by himfelf, to fave his own Neck he made himfelf an Evidence againft *Ned Bonnet,* who being apprehended, was committed to *Newgate,* from whence was convey'd to *Cambridge,* and there hanged as before related

One would think that untimely End of his Companion, would have reclaimed him, but inftead of being reformed, he withdrew himfelf again from under his Father's Tuition, and took to his old Courfes, with a Refolution of never leaving them off till he was hanged too However, dreading a Halter, he was refolved to rob by Stratagem , and accordingly one Afternoon riding over *Bagfhot Heath,* he falls to blowing of a Horn, juft as if he had been a Poft, whereupon three or four Gentlemen then on the Road gave him the Way, as is ufual in fuch Cafes, and being not rightly acquainted with the Place where they were, they made what Hafte they could after him for a Guide, promifing to give him fomewhat for conducting them to fuch a Town *Clare* accepts of their Civility, and being come upon the Middle of the aforefaid Heath, where was a lone Houfe upon the Side of the Road, pretending to be Thirfty, he crav'd the Favour of the Gentlemen to beftow a little Drink upon him, withal faying there was a Cup of very good Liquor They acquiefced to his Requeft, and rid up to the Houfe, where a Couple of his Companions being planted, ready mounted, they attacked the Gentlemen at Sword and Piftol, with fuch Fury, that after a fhort Refiftance, they obliged them to pay their Poftman about two hundred and thirty Pound, for fafely conducting them into their Clutches

Shortly after this Adventure, being thro' his Extravagance deftitute of a Horfe, Piftols, and Accoutrements, fitting for a *Gentleman-Thief,* he puts himfelf into the Difguife of a Porter, with an old Frock on his Back, Leather Breeches, a broad Belt about his Middle, a having Hat on his Head, a Knot on his Shoulders, a fmall Cord (an Emblem of what would be his Fate) at his Side, and a fham Ticket hanging at his Girdle ; fo going up and down the Streets to fee how Fortune might favour his Defigns, it was his good Luck one Evening to go thro' *Lombard ftreet,* when a Gentleman was fealing up a couple of hundred Pound Bags He takes the Advantage to walk by juft as the aforefaid Gentleman came to the Door, where calling for a Porter, he p'ies him, and the Money was delivered to him, to carry along with the Gentleman to one Efq. *Macklethwait*'s living near *Red Lyon-Square* But *Zachary Clare,* being tired of his Burden, turns up St *Martin's le Grand,* and made the beft of his Way to lighten himfelf as foon as he could of his Load

The Gentleman turning about and miffing his fuppos'd Porter, ran up and down like a diftracted Lunatick broke out of *Bedlam,* out of one Street into another, in this Lane, and that Alley, this Court and that Houfe, crying out, *Did you fee the Man that's run away with my two hunared Pounds!* But all his Scrutiny was to no Purpofe, for *Zachary* having a light Pair of Heels, made, no doubt, what Hafte he could to fuch Quarters where he might have a fafe Retreat from Juftice

Clare being thus recruited, he foon metamorphofed his Porter's Habit into that of a Gentleman's , and from a Man of Carriage, transform'd himfelf into an abfolute Highwayman again One of his Conforts buys him a good Horfe in *Weft-Smithfield,* whilft another buys Piftols, and other Materials, requifite for a Perfon that lives by the Words *Stand and Deliver* Being thus equipped, he bids *London* adieu for ever , for it was the laft Time he ever faw it His Progrefs now was towards the Weft of *Engrland* , where he and his Affociates robbed the Welch Drovers, and feveral Waggons, befides Coaches, infomuch that they were a Dread and Terror to all thofe Parts which border upon *Wales*

But ftaying there till the Country was too hot for them, they fteered their Courfe into *Warwickfhire ;* where they committed feveral Robberies, with very good Succefs , till one Day *Zachary Clare,* and only one more in Company with him, going to give their Horfes a Breathing upon *Dunmore-Heath,* they attacked Sir *Humphry Jennifon* and his Lady in their Coach, who had then above one thoufand one hundred Pounds in the Seat of it, and the Knight being unwilling to lofe it, he came out to give them Battle An Engagement began betwixt the Highwaymen and Sir *Humphrey,* one of whofe two Footmen was wounded in the Arm, and the other had his Horfe fhot in the Buttock But ftill Sir *Humphrey*'s Courage was not quell'd, he maintained the Fight more vigoroufly with what Piftols he had , till the Coachman difcharging a Blunderbufs, fhot *Zachary*'s Horfe dead on the Spot, and himfelf in the Foot His Comrade feeing him difmounted and wounded into the Bargain, he fled as faft as he could *Clare* was now taken, and Sir *Humphrey* mounting his Footman's Horfe, that was not wounded, purfued *James Lawrence,* the Highwyman that had left *Clare* in the Lurch, and took him

Tha

Then tying them behind one another, with the Legs of them under the Horse's Belly, they were brought into *Warwick*, and being examined before a Magistrate he committed them to Gaol

Now being in close Confinement, they made several Attempts to break open the Prison, and in order thereto, they had Files, Chisels, Ropes, and *Aqua Fortis*, to facilitate their Escape But being detected by one of their Fellow Prisoners, they were loaded with the heaviest Irons the Gaol afforded, and were stapled down to the Floor, under which strict Restraint they continued for above four Months, when the Assizes coming on, they were both brought to a Trial, having a great Number of Indictments exhibited against them, to the great Surprize of the whole Court, who try'd them upon no less than ten, of every one of which the Jury found them Guilty

Being ask'd what they had to say for themselves, before Sentence of Death was past upon them according to Law, *James Lawrence* said, *He had always been an unfortunate Son of a Whore, however, if his Lordship would be pleas'd but to be hanged for him, for one half Hour or so, it should be the last Favour that ever he should ask of him any more* Being told he was a hardened impudent Rogue, *Zachary Clare* was ask'd what he had to say for himself, who answered, *My Lord, I have hanged one Man already by swearing to save myself, and to save it once more, if your Lordship pleases, I'll*

swear right or wrong, against the whole J[..], hang them too, for I vow they have done [..] th[e] great Diskindness that ever any Men did [..] [..]fe

Being condemned, they where remanded back to Gaol again, and secur'd in a dark Dungeon under Ground, where instead of preparing for their la[..]ter End, they did nothing but sing, swear, play at Cards, and get drunk from Morning till Night So audacious were they, that a grave Minister coming to give them good Counsel, they had the Impudence to throw a Pot of Drink in his Face, crying out at the same Time, *Begone you old formal Son of a Whore! Have we nothing else to do do you think, than stand to be surfeited with your damned Cant?* They were no less impudent when they were conveyed to the Place of Execution, and when they were there, they would neither pr[..] nor make Confession When the Sheriff ask'd them if they had any Thing to say before they were turn'd off, *Lawrence* reply'd, *I wish I was safe in Bed with your Wife now!* and *Clare* cry'd, *I wish I might have the getting of that young [..] man's Maidenhead there!* The Ladder upon th[..] was immediately drawn from under them, and [..] they miserably ended their Lives, in *August*, 171[..] the first of them aged thirty two, and the other twenty six Years

An Account of SARAH MALCOLM.

OF the following Paper its needs only be said, that it was written by this unfortunate Person with her own Hand in the *Press Yard* of *Newgate*, on *Tuesday* the 6th of *March*, 1732 3 the Day before her Suffering She spent the greatest Part of the Day in writing it, and when it was finished she read it over several Times, being often admonished to be careful to write nothing but what was Truth She then folded it up with her own Hands before the Rev Dr *Middleton*, Lecturer of St *Bride's*, and *Rowland Ingram*, Esq, Keeper of his Majesty's Goal of *Newgate*, who both sealed it with their own Seals; in which manner she delivered it to the Rev Mr *Piddington*, with a desire that it might be published

After the Execution was over, the Paper was opened before the worshipful the *Sheriffs* of *London* and *Middlesex*, Dr *Middleton*, Mr *Peters*, Mr *Broancker*, and Mr *Ingram*, and being read, was again sealed up, and produced two Nights after, before the Honourable the Masters of the Bench of the *Inner* and *Middle Temples*, who read and returned it to one said Reverend Person in the manner where in it afterwards appear'd to the World, signed with his Name

March, the 6th, 1732 3

SIR,

YOU cannot be, nor are not unsensible that there is a just God, before whom we must give an exact Account of all our Actions, at the End of our Lives

So as my Life is at an End, and I must appear before the All-seeing Judge of Heaven and Earth, to give an Account of mine, so I take that great Judge to witness, that what I here declare is true

January the 28th, which was *Sunday*, after my Master was gone to Commons, *Mary Tracy* came to me, and drank Tea, and then it was I did give my Consent to that unhappy Act of Robbing Mrs *Duncomb*, but I do declare before the Almighty, before whom I shortly shall appear, I did not know of the Murder.

And on *Saturday* the 3d of *February* was the Time appointed, and accordingly they came about ten a Clock at Night, and *Mary Tracey* came to Mr. *Kerrsl's* Chambers, and I went to Mrs *Duncomb's*, and on the Stairs I met the Maid, and she did ask me whether I was going to the old Maid, and I answered I was, and as soon as I thought she had got down Stairs, I would have gone in myself, but I thought that I should give some Suspicion, and so I asked which would go in, and *James Alexander* replied he would, and the Door being

left open for the Maid, against her Return, or otherways I was to have knocked at the Door, and after to have let them in, but it being open hindred it, and I gave *James Alexander* Directions to lie under the Maid's Bed, and desired *Mary Tracy* and *Thomas Alexander* to go and stay for me at my Master's Door until my Return, and accordingly they did, and when I came, I desired they would go and stay for me at Mrs *Duncomb's* Stairs, until my Return, and I went and lighted a Candle, and stirred the Fire in my Master's Chamber, and went again to *Mary Tracey* and *Thomas Alexander*, who were on Mrs *Duncomb's* Stairs, and there we waited until after two a Clock on the *Sunday* which was the 4th of *February*, and then I would have gone in, but when *Thomas Alexander* and *Mary Tracey* interrupted me, and said if you go in, and they awake, they will know you, and if you stay on the Stairs, it may be that some one will come up and see you, but I made Answer, that no one lives up so high but Madam *Duncomb*.

And at length it was concluded that *Mary Tracey* and the other *Alexander* should go in, and shut the Door, and accordingly they did, and there I remained until between 4 and 5 a Clock, and then they came out, and said, *Hip*, and I came higher up, and they did ask, which way they should shut the Door and I told them to run the Bolt back, and it would spring into its Place, and accordingly they did, and came down, and having come down, they asked, where they should divide what they had got, I asked how much that was, they said, about three hundred Pounds in Goods and Money, but said they were forced to gag them all

I desired to know, where they had found it, they said, that fifty Guineas of it was in the old Maid's Pocket in a leathern Purse, besides Silver, that they said was loose, and above an hundred and fifty Pounds in a Drawer, besides the Money that they had out of a Box, and the Tankard and one silver Spoon, and a Ring which was looped with Thread, and one square piece of Plate, one pair of Sheets, and two Pillowbiers and five Shifts, and we did divide all this, near *Fig Tree Court*, as also near *Pump Court*; and they did say unto me, before that you bury the Cole and Plate under Ground, until the Robbery is all over I or if you be seen flush with Cole, you will be suspected, and on *Monday*, before, about 3 or 4 a Clock, you come to the *Pewter Platter* on *Holborn Bridge*

I being apprehended on the *Sunday* Night, on the *Monday* Morning, when I was in the *Compter*, I happened to see one *Bridgewater* he said, he was sorry to see me there, I also was sorry to see him a Brother in Affliction, he desired me to give him a Dram, for he was a great while in Prison, and I

99

5 H   threw

threw him a Shilling and a Farthing And I walking about the Room, I was furprifed to hear me called by my Name, and looking about, I obferved at the Head of the Bed fomething move, and I pulled back the Curtain, and there I faw this *Bridgewater*, and he afked, whether I had fent for any Friends. I told him I had, and not long after he called me again, and faid, there was a Friend come to me, and I looked thorough the Hole in the Wall, and afked, whether that was *Will Gibbs*, and he anfwered me yes; and I afked him, how the *Alexanders* were, he faid, they were well, he afked me how I came to be taken, and I told him, my Mafter having found the Tankard, and fome Linnen, and he having feen ninety Pounds and fixteen Shillings on the *Sunday* the 4th of *February*, but it might through Surprize be forgot, but I had it all He faid, if I would give him fome Money, he would get People that would fwear that the Tankard was my Mother's according as I would direct, but faid I, you muft get fome one to fwear, that I was at their Houfe, he faid, it muft be a Woman, and he faid, fhe would not go without four Guineas, and the four Men muft have two Guineas a-piece So I gave him twelve Guineas, and he faid, he and his Friends would be at the *Bull's Head* in *Breadftreet*, but when I afked for them, I could not hear of them, and when I came before the Worfhipful Alderman *Brocas*, I was committed to *Newgate*

And when I was brought up to the Common Side, I was bid to pull off my Riding-hood, and one *Peter Buck* a Prifoner obferved a Bulk in my Hair to hang down behind, and told one *Roger Johnfon*, that I certainly had Money in my Hair, and Mr *Johnfon* brought me down in a Cellar, and told me that *Peter Buck* faid, I had Money in my Hair, and bid me take it out, and fo I did, and he counted the Moidores and eighteen Guineas, and 6 broad Pieces, and two of them were 25 Shillings, and four were 23 Shilling Pieces, and half a 23 Shillings, and five Crowns, and two half Crowns, and one Shilling, and ne faid in the Condemned Hole, he would be cleared and get out of Gaol on that Account

In the feal'd Cover, wherein the foregoing Paper was enclos'd, were thefe Words written alfo with her own Hand.

THE enclos'd contains fix Sides of Paper, which I take Almighty God and my own Confcience to witnefs, is nothing but the very Truth, as witnefs my Hand,

Sarah Malcolm.

When this unhappy Malefactor was brought into Fleet-ftreet, over-againft Fetter-Lane End, the Place of her Execution, on Wednefday the 7th of March, fhe declared fhe died in Peace with all the Wolld, and earneftly defired to fee her Mifter *Kerrol*, but as fhe could not, protefted that all Accufations and Afperfions concerning him, were entirely falfe, and that all Confeffions, except thofe delivered as above, were entirely groundlefs, and likewife fo lemnly declared that the Contents of the foregoing Paper were true

The LIFE of TOM DORBEL.

THE Person of whom we are now going to speak, was born of very good Parents at *Shaftsbury* in *Dorsetshire*, and put out by them an Apprentice to a Glover at *Blandford*, in the same County ; but being very early of a vicious Inclination, he ran away from his Master before he had serv'd half his Time, and coming up to *London*, he soon became acquainted with ill Company, and as soon learnt their Vices. To support himself in an extravagant way of Living, he ventur'd to go on the Highway when he was but seventeen Years of Age, but in his first Attempt of that Nature, he had like to have been cropt in the Bud The Story was as follows

Meeting a sturdy *Cambro Briton* on the Road, and demanding his Money, otherwise he would shoot him, quoth the *Welshman*, *Hur has no Money of bur own, but has Threescore Pounds of bur Master's, but Cots plood bur must not give away bur Master's Money, wh* *would bur Master then say for bur doing so?* Tom Dorbel reply'd, *You must not put m off thus with your Cant, for Money I want, and Money I will have, let it be whose it will, or expect to be shot presently thro' the Head* Hereupon the *Welshman* gave *Tom* his Money, withal saying, *What bur gives you is none of ber own, and that bur Master may not think bur has spent bur Money, bur desires you to be so kind as to shoot some Holes thro' bur Coat Lappets, that bur Master may see bur was robb'd* So the *Welshman* pulling off his Coat, and hanging it on a Tree, *Tom* was so civil as to fire his Pistol thro' it, which made *Taffy* say, *Cots splutter-a-nails, this is a pretty Pounce, pray give bur another Pounce for bur Money* *Tom* fires another Pistol thro' *Taffy's* Coat, which made him cry out by St *Davy, This is a better Pounce than t'other, pray give her one Pounce more* Quoth *Tom, I have never another Pounce left.* Why then, reply'd *Taffy, Hur has one Pounce left for bur, and if bur will not give bur bur Money again, bur will pounce this o' bur Pody* *Tom* finding himself thus outwitted, he quietly return'd the *Welshman* his Money, who rid away without troubling himself about taking our young Highway man

But after this ill Success, *Tom* was pretty successful in his Villainy for about five Years During this Time a certain Gentleman's Son being in *Winchester* Goal for robbing on the Highway, and fearing he should be hang'd, because he had receiv'd Mercy once before for the like Crime, *Tom* undertook for five Hundred Pounds to bring him off The Gentleman's Father paid 250 Pounds in Hand, and the other half he was to have when he had perform'd his Bargain At last the Assizes was held at *Winchester*, when the young Gentleman coming on his Trial, the Witnesses proved the Matter of Fact so plainly against him, that the Jury brought the Prisoner in guilty of robbing on the Highway Then the Judge going to pass Sentence on him, quoth *Tom, Oh! what a sad*

Thing it is to shed innocent Blood! Oh! what a sad Thing it is to shed innocent Blood! And repeating it over and over, with an audible Voice, insomuch that the Court took Notice thereof, he was took into Custody, and the Judge asking him what he meant by his crying out *What a sad Thing it is to shed innocent Blood!* quoth *Tom, May it please your Lordship, it is a very hard Thing for a Man to die wrongfully, but one may see how hard mouth'd some People are, by the Witnesses swearing that this Gentleman here at the Bar now robbed them on the Highway at such a Time, when indeed, my Lord, I was the Man that committed that Robbery*

Hereupon the Gentleman was acquitted, and *Tom* took into Custody, and sent to *Winchester* Gaol, where he remained till the Assizes following, when being brought to his Trial, and ask'd, whether he was Guilty or not Guilty, he pleaded not Guilty. 'Not Guilty!' *replied the Judge,* Why did not you 'last Assizes, when I was here, own yourself Guilty 'of such a Robbery? *quoth* Tom, I don't know how 'far I was Guilty then, but upon my Word I am not 'Guilty now, therefore, if any Person can accuse 'me of committing such a Robbery, I desire they 'may appear to prove the same But no Witnesses appearing against him, because they must have proved themselves perjured in swearing against him, when they had sworn so positively before against another Person, he was acquitted

Tom having lived at an extravagant Rate the six Months that he was in *Winchester* Gaol, he had not much of his five hundred Pounds left when he was at Liberty again, whereupon, endeavouring to recruit his Pockets, by following his old Trade, he attacked the Duke of *Norfolk's* Coach, as passing over *Salisbury* Plain But his Grace refusing to gratify his Desire, an Engagement soon became betwixt them, in which *Tom* having his Horse shot under him, his Grace's Servants soon secured him, and carrying him, with his Arms pinion'd close down, into the City of *Salisbury*, he was there committed to Gaol, and when the Assizes came to be held there, he was condemned for his Life

Whilst he was under Condemnation, finding a Lawyer in that Place who engaged to procure him a Pardon for fifty Guineas, he gave him a Bond to pay him so much Money as soon as he had obtained it Accordingly the Lawyer rid to *London*, and by an Interest that he had with some Nobleman at Court, procured what he had promised, then making what Haste he could back again, he came with the Reprieve just as *Dorbel* was going to be cast off the Gallows. The Lawyer had rid so fast, that he had no sooner delivered the Reprieve to the Sheriff, but his Horse dropp'd down dead; nevertheless, when *Tom* was at Liberty, he was so ungrateful as not to pay the Lawyer a Farthing, who had thus saved his Life, whereupon they went to Law; but *Dorbel* cast him, by reason no Writing stands good in our Laws of Eng-

k 2,

land, which is given by a Man under Sentence of Death

Now *Dorbel* was so much affrighted by this narrow Escape of hanging, that he was resolved to live honest, and accordingly lived in several Places in the Quality of a Footman, but last of all he served for six or seven Years a Gentlewoman in *Ormond-Street*, near *Lambs Conduit-Fields*, who prevailing upon her Brother *Nevil Thompson*, a Linnen-Draper in the City of *Bristol*, to send his only Daughter, who was entring the 16th Year of her Age, to *London*, to be bettered in her Education, he took a Place for her in the Coach, on *Monday* the 22d of *February*, 1714, and also for the Messenger *Tom Dorbel*, to whose Care, as being sent purposely to fetch her up, she was committed, for great Confidence was reposed in him, because he had been an old Servant of his Sister's, who had sent him very frequently upon important Messages to this her Brother at *Bristol*

Now the Villain being very sensible of the great Charge which this young Gentlewoman had about her, as a gold Watch, diamond Ring, and Jewels, to the Value of one hundred and ten Pounds, his wicked Inclination was to rob her, and in order thereto, being alone with her in the Coach, he very impudently pretended Courtship to her This piece of Freedom the young Gentlewoman most sharply reprimanded, but little valuing her Anger, he took out a Penknife, and swore, that if she did not consent to lie with him, he would immediately cut her Throat These mighty Threats frightning the young Gentlewoman into a Swoon, the Rogue took the Advantage thereof, by tying her Hands to each Knee, and in that Manner most inhumanly debauched her, and stole away all she had, excepting one Crown and her Cloaths Then this barbarous Villain cutting his Way thro' the back of the Coach, he slipt out unknown to the Coachman

Still the young Gentlewoman continued in her Swoon, from four of the Clock till six in the Evening, being the Time the Coach put up in its Inn The Coachman opening the Coach Door, and finding the Gentlewoman in the aforesaid Posture, with the Villain's Neckcloth also tied round her Mouth, and her Face all bruised and bloody with the jogging of the Coach, he was frightned, and cried out to the People of the House for Assistance, who sending immediately for an able Surgeon, upon his coming to her, she seemed to be just expiring, but by the Skill he used, he brought her so much to herself by nine of the Clock, that she was able to speak, and declare the Abuse which had been done her

Her surprizing Relation alarm'd the whole Town with the Horror of the Villain's inhuman Lust, and several good People pursuing the Villain in several Ways on Horseback, they took him on the *Wednesday* following at *Hammersmith*, near which Place he had but just robbed a Gentleman of three Pounds five Shillings Being carried before a Magistrate, he was committed to *Newgate* in *London*, from whence he was removed within a Week after, by Virtue of a Writ of *Habeas Corpus*, to *Newgate* in *Bristol*

In the mean Time, the young Gentlewoman, seeing the Reflections which the World might cast upon her, and thinking her Reputation was utterly lost, altho' the Loss of her Virginity was forced, she laid it so deeply to Heart, that at the Arrival of her Mother to her Bed side the next Day, she only changed a few Words with her, and then she died, to the great Grief of the old Gentlewoman, who ran distracted, and her sorrowful Father soon lost his Senses too

At length, the Villain being brought to Trial, he received Sentence of Death for the perpetrating this most inhuman Crime All the while he was under Condemnation, he shewed not the least Remorse, and when he was hanged on *Saturday* the 23d of *March*, 1714, in the 45th Year of his Age, he died with a great deal of Impenitency, and was very obstinate in not hearkening to any wholsome Advice which was given him, in order to prepare himself as he ought, before he launched out into the unfathomable Gulph of Eternity After he was executed on St *Michael's-Hill*, he was cut down, and hanged up in Chains in the Road without *Lafford's* Gate

The LIVES of JACK COLLINGS, KIT MOOR, and DANIEL HUGHES.

JACK COLLINGS, alias *John Collinson*, was born of mean Parents at *Fauſtone*, near *Hull* in *Yorkſhire*, and being brought up to no Trade, he had been a Footman to ſeveral Gentlemen, both in the Country, and here in *London*, where he was ſome time a Coachman to one Colonel *Kendal* This Gentlemen ſending *Jack* to ſell a Pair of Coach-Horſes, becauſe they were not well match'd, *Jack* obey'd his Maſter's Order, and ran away with the Money Afterwards his Maſter taking him, he committed him to the *Marſhal's* in the *Savoy*, from whence he ſent him for a Soldier into *Flanders*, but quickly deſerting his Colours, he came into *England* again, where being much addicted to keep Company with lewd Women, he got ſadly pox'd

Getting himſelf cur'd, when the Apothecary brought in his Bill, which came to Forty eight ſhillings and four pence, *Jack* ſwore it was a very unconſcion ble Bill, and if he wou'd not be contented with a Groat, he would never pay him a Farthing The Apothecary ſwore and curs'd like a Madman, ſaying, he would never take that, and away he flounce'd out of the Room in a great Paſſion But on the Stairs pauſing to himſelf, and conſidering it was better to take that Groat than to loſe all, he went up again, ſaying, Come, ſir, ſince you'll pay me no more, let's ſee that Groat So having given *Jack* a Receipt in full of all Accounts, when he was going out of the Room again, quoth he, Let me be ſ———n'd, Sir, if I have got any more than one poor Two pence halfpenny by you *Jack* thinking the Profit large, and it being towards Evening, he follow'd the Apothecary towards the Halfway Houſe betwixt *London* and *Hampſtead*, where a good Opportunity favouring his Deſign, he commanded *Galen* to ſtand and deliver, or elſe he would ſhoot him a thro' the Head *Jack's* Order being obey'd, he did not only take his Groat from him again, but alſo robb'd him of a good ſilver Watch, and Twenty four ſhillings

In this Exploit he had like to have been taken, and more his Eſcape ſo narrowly, that being afraid to go on the Foot pad again, he follow'd Houſe-breaking altogether, in which he was ſucceſsful for many Years, but betwixt while he was a Soldier for ſix Years, and attain'd to the Office of a Serjeant in Colonel *W——ng's* Regiment However, being not ſatisfied with his Station, he ſtill purſued unlawful Courſes then too, even to the Time that he was diſbanded, and then keeping Company with an ill Woman, he cou'd not whom he wrong'd to ſupport her, and yet that ſame Strumpet whom he maintain'd or harbouring his Neſt, was a Witneſs againſt him in his Life, as it appears in his Trial, which is partly thus

He was indicted for breaking the Houſe of *John Halloway*, and ſtealing from thence two *Exchequer* Notes, value a Hundred Pounds each, One hundred thirty ſeven Pounds ten Shillings in Money, and One hundred ninety foar Pounds in Gold It appear'd by the Evidence, that Mr *Halloway* being at *London*, the Priſoner was at his Houſe at *Chelſea*, to intreat his Favour for a Ticket of Re-entrance into the Royal Hoſpital there, and Mrs *Halloway* permitted him to go up Stairs, and the Money and Bills being in a Cloſet in the Room, he found an Opportunity to break it open, and carry them off

The Woman he kept Company with ſwore, That going to look for him, ſhe met in a Coach, and upbraiding him for riding ſo, while ſhe wanted, he gave her Money to pay off her Lodging, and bid her do it and come to him again, which ſhe did, and ſhe ſaw a great Bag of Money in the Coach, which he told her was worth Six hundred pounds, and that he had it, out of the Proſecutor's Cloſet They then went to a Lodging at *Wapping*, and he bought her Clothes, and himſelf a Coat and Wig to diſguiſe him

Mrs *Griffin*, their Landlady at *Wapping*, depos'd, That the Priſoner and the Witneſs having taken a Lodging at her Houſe, ſhe ſuſpected them to be looſe People, and that the Priſoner having ſent her Man to borrow the *Gazette*, he look'd upon it, and laid it down, ſaying, There was nothing in it, and ſo went up Stairs, and that cauſing her Man to look over the *Gazette*, ſhe found the Priſoner deſcrib'd, and ſo got a Conſtable and ſecur'd him

He had Seventy pounds ſeventeen ſhillings found upon him when taken, and Twenty two Guineas and a half, and a Broad piece He ow'd to the Conſtable who took him, he had robb'd Mr *Halloway*, but did not ſay of ſo much as was mention'd in the Indictment The Fact being plainly prov'd upon him, he was found guilty

He was alſo a ſecond Time indicted for robbing Mr *James Boyce* on the Queen's Highway, of a ſilver Watch, value Three pounds, and Ten ſhillings in Money

Mr *Boyce* depos'd, That coming out of *Bedſhire* in a Coach the Priſoner ſet upon him on this ſide *Kentiſh town*, about three of the Clock in the Afternoon, and after he had got his Watch and Money, aſk'd him for his green Purſe, and he telling him he had none, he made him turn his Pockets out and pull off his Gloves, to ſhew he had no Rings

The Priſoner call'd ſome Witneſſes to prove he was at another Place when that was done, but none appearing, he was found guilty too of that Indictment and hang'd at *Tyburn*, on *Wedneſday* the 15th of ——— 1714, aged 42 Years

On the same Day were also executed two other House-breakers, namely, *Kit Moor*, and *Daniel Hughes*

Chriſtopher Moor, the firſt of theſe, aged 20 Years, born in the Pariſh of St *Giles*'s in the Fields, for the moſt part of his Life had been a Tapſter in ſome Victualling Houſes in and about *London*, he confeſs'd that a little before that, he one Night robb'd a Houſe in *Grey Friers*, near *Chriſt's Hoſpital*, by lifting up a Saſh Window, and entring the Parlour, that he took from thence ſix Silver Tea-Spoons, and a Strainer, with a Silk Handkerchief Ell-wide, which he ſold for Three Shillings, and as for the Plate, that he ſold it with a larger Parcel, (amounting to a hundred Ounces) for four Shillings an Ounce Furthermore he ſaid, that he had wrong'd one Mr *Johnſon*, a working Silverſmith, by ſwearing falſly heretofore that he had bought of him, and one *Roderick Audery*, another moſt notorious Rogue, ſome Plate that he had ſtolen out of the Lady *Edwin*'s Houſe But the Fact for which he was condemn'd to die, was for a Burglary committed in breaking open the Houſe of one Mr *Thomas Wright*, in the Night, and taking thence a Pair of Silver Branches, and eight Tea ſpoons, two Tea-pots, a Lamp, and a large Quantity other Plate He would not diſcover where it might be found, that the right Owner might have it again, for when he was preſs'd by the Ordinary of *Newgate* to make a Diſcovery thereof if he could, he did not ſo much alledge his Incapacity, as he plainly ſhew'd his Unwilling-neſs of doing it, ſaying, *That tho' he could do it, yet he would make no ſuch Diſcovery, if he was ſure to be d——n'd for it*

Daniel Hughes, the other Perſon, aged but Sixteen Years, born at *Graveſend* in the County of *Kent*, was brought up to the Sea, and condemn'd for the ſame Fact with *Kit Moor*, and ſuch was their Impudence to the very laſt, that when they went into the Cart, which was to carry them to the Place of Execution, they were no ſooner ty'd to the Copſe, but they pull'd off their Snoes, and flinging them among the Spectators, repeated this common Speech of ſuch Wretches *Our Parents often ſaid we ſhould die on a Fiſh Day, and with our Shoes on, but tho' the former part of their Prediction is true, yet we will make them all Liars in the latter part of it*

It is to be obſerv'd, that tho' the Ages of theſe two unfortunate Lads together made but 36 Years, yet they were as vicious as more noted Rogues, taking pride in all manner of Laſciviouſneſs, Sabbath-breaking, Drunkenneſs, Swearing, Curſing, Gaming, and all ſorts of Vices whatever They had committed between them above fifty Burglaries in *London*, *Weſtminſter*, and *Southwark* In fine, the Obſtinacy of the two young Malefactors in their Iniquity, and their impudent Behaviour towards all who came to ſee them, was ſcarce ever parallel'd, ſo that it was very requiſite Juſtice ſhould lay hold of them, and prevent their doing further Miſchief

---

The LIFE of JOHN PRICE.

IT would be but little Benefit and Satisfaction to the Reader to have an Account of this Criminal's Extraction, becauſe it is ſo extraordinary mean, 'tis enough to ſay, that he firſt drew his Breath in the Fag-end of the Suburbs of *London*, and, like *Mercury*, became a Thief as ſoon as ever he peeped out of the Shell

Fortune having reduced his miſerable Parents to ſuch Extremity, that they could not beſtow on this their Son, any Education, it was his Misfortune to improve himſelf in all manner of Wickedneſs, before he was turn'd of Seven So prone was he to Vice, that as ſoon as he could ſpeak, he would curſe and ſwear with as great a Paſſion and Vileneſs, as is frequently heard round any Gaming-Table Moreover, to this unprofitable Talent of Prophaneneſs, he added that of Lying, at which he was ſo dextrous, that it was once a Means of his ſaving his Life

For when *John Price* was about eighteen Years of Age, living with a Gentleman in the Country, he turned him out of his Service, purely upon the Account of his exceſſive Lying, when going towards *London*, and robbing a Market Woman of about eighteen Shillings near *Brentwood* in *Eſſex* he was taken by ſome Travellers coming ſuddenly on him in the Fact, and committed by a Magiſtrate to *Chelmsford* Gaol, where at the Aſſizes pleading Guilty, he received Sentence of Death, but his late Maſter being then High Sheriff of the County of *Eſſex*, and taking Compaſſion on his Servant's Misfortunes did not permit his Sentence to be put in Force againſt him, of which the Judges being informed the next Aſſizes, they ſeverely blamed for his Neglect, eſpecially ſince the Criminal had pleaded guilty to the Crime laid to his Charge The Sheriff ſaid, *He acknowleaged that ſuch a Man had been condemned the laſt Aſſizes, but then he knew the Fellow to be ſuch an unaccountable Lyar, that there was no believing one Word he ſaid, ſo his pleading guilty to what was laid to his Charge, was, in his Opinion, an eminent Sign he ought to be believed innocent of the Fact, and he would not be guilty of hanging an innocent Man for the World* This facetious Story of Mr Sheriff making the Judges ſmile, they repriev'd the Criminal, but with a ſevere reprimand, and ſtrict Charge of never coming before them any more

Soon after this Eſcape *John Price* made the beſt of his Way for *London*, where he aſſociated himſelf with a Tribe of Pick-pockets and Gypſies, with whom he kept up and down the Country, frequenting quitting all Fairs and Concourses of People, till he was catch'd diving in a Pocket that was none of his own, and committed to *Newgate* in *Bristol* Being there severely whipt for his Fault, he went on board a Merchant Ship, and afterwards served in two Men of War, but not forbearing to pilfer from the Seamen, after having been whipt at a Gun, pickled with Brine, and Keel-hawl'd, he was discharged Coming ashore at *Portsmouth*, he got to beloved *London* again, where he would never hearken to any wholsome Counsel, but was resolved to break thro all virtuous Sentiments, and wholly to betake himself to all manner of Wickedness Entring himself into a Gang of Foot pads, they one Night divided themselves into three Bands, and an Attorney then falling into their Hands near *Hampstead*, his Money being demanded, with a Thousand Oaths and Curses According to their Demand he gave them what Money he had about him, which was eight Guineas, rejoicing howsoever that he had now past, as he thought, all Danger When lo, suddenly as he came up to the Halfway House, betwixt that Place and *London*, he was again surrounded with a second Band of these Rogues, who viewing him nearly, demanded whence he came, and where he was going He related his piteous Adventure, and into what cruel Hands he had fallen, *Crack!* answered one of the Gang, *How durst you use these Terms? And who made you so bold as to talk to us with your Hat on? Pray, Sir, be pleased, henceforwards to learn more Manners* Which saying, they snatched his Hat and Wig off his Head, and took a diamond Ring off his Finger, in all to the value of fifteen Pounds What could our poor Lawyer now do? To return back again, was to leap out of the Frying-Pan into the Fire, wherefore he faintly puts on When scarce he had got past *Kentish Town*, but the third Band, who lay as Centinels in this Place, made up to him, bringing along with them a Man who had not a rag of Cloaths on his Back no not so much as a Shirt, a dreadful Thing, considering the Time of the Year, it being then in the Depth of Winter Sir, (said *Price*, who was in this Party,) *You'll do a charitable Deed, to let this poor Wretch, whom we have just now stript, have your upper Coat, or rather both upper and under for you see he is almost dead with Cold* The Lawyer would willingly have pleaded that Charity begins at home, and that every Man is bound by the Laws of Nature to conserve his own Being rather then anothers But Alas! his Judges were other kind of Men than to be moved by the Laws of the Land or Nature either, wherefore they took from him both his Coats and his Wastecoat, telling him it was a Favour that they took not from him his Life also, seeing that he made so much bad Use of it

Not long after this, *Price* and one of his wicked Associates privately conveying themselves one Evening into a House in *Fleet street*, crept up into a Garret fill'd with nothing but Lumber, with an Intent to rob the People, but in the Night bustling about in the Dark, as *Price* was going to a Table for a Pistol he had laid there, he no sooner laid his Hand on it, but it presently discharges, and awakened them of the House, who immediately began to rise to secure the Thieves, *Price's* Comrade flies presently to the Window, where they had fastened a Rope ready for their Escape, and offers to slide down, when scarcely had he got above a Story and half but the Rope broke, and he fell down Here he, as naught is never in Danger, he received no so much Hurt, but that he made a shift to scramble away

In the mean Time *Price* being left behind, and

seeing himself alone three or four Stories high, without any Possibility of following his Companion, he resolved to venture Neck or nothing, so quickly removes the remaining Part of the Rope to another Window, whereby he might let himself down into the Balcony, whither he was no sooner got to, but all the People of the House were in an Alarm, upon which he jumps out full into a great Basket of Eggs, which a Man coming from *Newgate* Market had on his Head The Eggs running all about his Ears, nay, all his whole Body, as he lay upon the Ground, there was then as great an Outcry of Murder, as there was of Thieves, but all to no Purpose, for *Price* having broke his Fall by his Jump into that brittle Commodity, he made his Escape likewise, to reign longer in his Villany

Jack Price having go clear this Time, and beginning to be very much noted about Town, he takes a Journey into the Country, stripping all the Hedges he met with that had any Linnen on them, till he had reached *Cumberland*, where putting into a little Inn, the People whereof being none of the honestest, and finding by his Discourse that he was a Servant fit for their turn, he was entertained as their Tapster, and let into the Secret of their murdering Travellers that sometimes lay there, but long he had not been in this Imployment, before a Gentleman happened to put into this Inn for Lodging, who being in his Chamber, was secretly informed by a Maid of the Danger he was in Amongst other Things she told him, 'twas the Inn-keeper's Custom to ring a Bell, at the Sound of which several Rogues came running; when presently one of them feigning to be Servant to the Inn, comes to the Chamber where the Guests are, and making as he would snuff the Candle, puts it out, upon which the other Villians enter, and most cruelly murder them This Gentleman considering with himself what to do, caused the Maid to bring him a Larthorn, puts a Candle lighted into it, and hiding it under a Stool, lays ready his Arms, and stands upon his Guard When scarcely had he sat himself down, but a great boorish Fellow enters, who very officiously so to suit the Candle, that he snuffs it out But the Gentleman presently bid his Man bring out the Lanthorn, repelled the Villains, killed two of them, and put the others to flight Then he seized on the Inn keeper and his Wife, delivered them into the Hands of Justice, and at the Assizes being proved by the Maid they had murdered at several Times fourteen of their Guests, whose Bodies were found in an arched Vault in the Garden, to which they had a secret Passage out of a Cellar, they were both condemned and executed, the Inn keeper himself being afterwards hanged in Chains

Being at last committed to *Newgate* for Petit Larceny, he was only whipt at the Cart's Arse, and upon paying his Fees, obtained his Liberty again Afterwards endeavouring to mend his Fortune by Marriage, he entered into the State of Matrimony, with a young Woman called *Betty*, whose Employment was daily to attend the Gaol of *Newgate*, and to run on Prisoners Errands By this Means and his own good Behaviour, he quickly raised himself to Preferment, for he was made Hangman for the County of *Middlesex* But the first Day he officiated at the Sessions in the *Old Bailey*, going to the Blue Boar Alehouse, situated not far from Justice Hall, it was his misfortune to have his burning Iron slip out of his Pocket, for which he was forced to pawn his Wastcoat to have them back again However, he soon retrieved this Loss, for what with gladly putting a T, which was all the Letters he knew of the whole Alphabet, on a Thief's Hand,

Hand, and correcting others with a gentle Lash, he redeemed his Waistcoat, and bought a Shirt into the Bargain Moreover, at the first Call of his Office he performed at *Tyburn*, he made as much of the executed Persons Cloaths among the Brokers in *Monmouth Street* and *Chick Lane*, as procured him several drunken Bouts Though he was bad enough in many Things, yet he had one good Principle in him while he was hangman, for let him have owed Money to any Body, if he could not pay them, he was very willing to work it out whenever they pleased, a Principle indeed which every Rogue is not endued with

Whilst he was in this Post, he took upon him a great deal of State, making every *Geneva* Shop his Office, and every Bawdy-house his *Seraglio* Instead of one Wife he had two, and on every Execution Day he had a great Levee as some Persons of Quality, being attended on by Broom Men for old Hats, Perriwig Makers for old Wigs, Brokers for old Coats, Suits and Cloaks, and Coblers for old Shoes Indeed, he was a Man every Way qualified for this Station, for he had Impudence in Abundance, Cruelty at his Fingers-end, Drunkenness to Perfection, and could swear as well without Book as within However, these natural Parts could not protect him, for several envying his Felicity, they endeavoured to lower his Top fail, and at last blew him out of the Haven of his reputable Business by his manifold Failings

Some were glad he was to catch no body any more at *Hyde-Park-Corner*, and others as sorry, especially those whom he often obliged with an old Shirt or an Handkerchief, and indeed, that which most troubled him for the Loss of his Place, was only that he could not any more send Men out of the World, without being called to an Account for it Now he was left to shift for himself again, and indeed, so long as he had any Fingers he could make as good a shift as any Body, for there was nothing, excepting it lay out of his Reach, but what he made his own.

What brought him to his End, was his going one Night over *Bunhill-Fields*, in his drunken Airs, when he met an old Woman, named *Elizabeth White*, a Watchman's Wife, who sold Pastry-Ware

about the Streets This poor Creature he would have ravished, and, because she resisted the Heat of his Lust, be violently assaulted her in a barbarous Manner, almost knocking one of her Eyes out of her Head giving her several Bruises about her Body, breaking one of her Legs, and wounding her in the Belly Whilst he was acting this Inhumanity, two Men coming along at the same Time, and hearing dreadful Groans, supposed somebody was in Distress, and having the Courage to pursue the Sound as well as they could, at last came up to the distressed Woman, which made *Price* damn them for their Impudence However, they secured him, and brought him to the Watchouse in *Old street*, from whence Couple of Watchmen were sent to fetch the old Woman out of *Bunhill Fields*, who within a Day or two dy'd under the Surgeons Hands

Price was sent to *Newgate*, where he seemed to be under a great Surprize and Concern for the Death of the Woman, till being try'd and condemned for her, he was no sooner confin'd in the *Condemned Hole*, but laying aside all Thoughts of preparing himself for his latter End, he appeared quite void of all Grace, and instead of repenting for his manifold Sins and Transgressions, he would daily go up to Chapel intoxicated with cursed Geneva, comforting himself even to the very last that he should fare as well in a future State, as those who had gone the same Way before him Thus his Conscience was eas'd with the Pleasure of thinking he should have Company under the State of Damnation At length the fatal Day came, wherein he was to bid Adieu to the World, which was on *Saturday* the 31st of *May* 1718 As he was riding in the Cart, he several Times pulled a Bottle of Geneva out of his Pocket, to drink before he came to the Place of Execution, which was in *Bunhill-Fields*, where he committed the Murder Being arrived at the fatal Tree, he was upon Mr *Ordinary*'s Examination, found so ignorant in the Grounds of Religion, that he troubled himself not much about it, but valuing himself upon his former Profession of being Hangman, stil'd himself *Finisher of the Law*, and so was turn'd off the Gibbet aged upwards of forty Years, and the same Day was hanged at *Stone Bridge* at *Kingsland* in Chains

The LIVES of Tom Garret, Kit Bani-ster, *and* John Wheeler.

WE are induced to put thefe Lives together, for the fame Reafon as the foregoing, for tho' thefe three Malefactors were not exe-cuted at the fame Place, nor precifely the fame Time, yet all their Exits happened within the Compafs of a Month.

THOMAS GARRET was born at *Ipfwich,* in *Suf-folk,* his Parents living in good Credit and Reputa-tion, and having no other Son but this, they put him Apprentice to an Ironmonger, in the City of *Nor-wich,* and when he had ferved his Time out, he was put up with a Thoufand Pound Stock, and fhortly after married a Wife with whom he had a Portion of eight hundred Pounds

But ill Company enticing him to Gaming, making nothing to lofe forty or fifty Pounds, and fometimes more, in a Night, he foon wafted his Stock; and in lefs than two Years breaking, to avoid the Profecu-tion of his Creditors, who plagu'd him with conti-nual Duns, he fent his Wife, and one Child he had by her, to her own Friends, and came up to *London,* where he foon became acquainted with the feveral Vices of the Town, addicting himfelf to all manner of Lewdnefs and Whoredom to fupport himfelf, in which he took to the Highway

He had committed feveral Robberies, which came to his Father's Ears, who thereupon came up to *Lon-don,* and finding him out, would have took him Home, which Kindnefs he refufed, alledging he was fo far crackt in the Country, that he was refolv'd not to fee it for one While His Father then, upon the Son's Promife of Amendment of Life, bought a Free-dom for him in the City of *London,* and fet him up with a Thoufand Pounds more in *Leadenhall ftreet;* but being corrupted with a vicious Inclination, he would ftill fhake his Elbow, and now and then go out privately on the Road, with a certain Mercer in *Cheapfide,* and take a Purfe

Garret and his Companion being at an Inn at St. *Albans* in *Hertfordfhire,* a certain Gentleman put up there too for a Night, and gave his Portmanteau to the Inn keeper to lay fafe up for him till Morning The Inn keeper locking it up, came to *Garret* and his friend, for he knew their Employment, and told them, *That he had a Portmanteau now in keeping, that he believed would be worth their While to take, for it was very heavy,* I'll go, fays he, *and perfuade the Gentleman to come in to you; and fifting him which Way he goes To morrow, you know how to order Mat-ters, I need not inftruct you* Accordingly going to the Gentleman, he faid to him, *Sir, I fee you are all alone, there are a Couple of honeft Gentlemen, in the Parlour, whom I know very well, would be glad of your Company, if you pleafe to accept it, follow me, Sir, and I'll introduce you* Upon thefe Words, and the Recommendation of the Gentlemen by the Land-

lord, he was willing to participate of their Converfa-tion till Bed time He was brought into the Parlour, where they refpectfully faluted him, and had a great deal of Difcourfe without fo much as an Oath, or any prophane Word in it Supper was brought to the Table, after which they drank their Bottle of Wine a-piece, and the Reckoning coming to be paid, they would not let the ftrange Gentleman pay one Farthing towards it, which extraordinary Piece of Civility made the Gentleman return them many Thanks, ad-ding, *That if they went his Way next Day, which was towards* London, *he fhould be glad of their good Company, and endeavour to retaliate their Kind-nefs*

They then went to their refpective Beds In the Morning took a hearty Breakfaft, towards which *Garret* and his Comrade would not then let the Gen-tleman pay any thing, and then they proceeded on their Journey When they came to *Coney-Hatch,* or thereabouts, feeing the Coaft clear, they fet upon the Gentleman, opened the Portmanteau, out of which they took one hundred Pounds, and rode off

The Gentleman finding he had paid too dear for his Supper and Breakfaft, alights off his Horfe, and fills the Vacancy they had made in his Portmanteau with Stones, and then with a Penknife pricking the Horfe fo under the Hoof, as to make him go lame, he rid back again to the fame Inn, and telling the Landlord he had a Mifchance befell his Horfe, or-dered a Farrier to be prefently fent for, and gave him his Portmanteau to lay up for him The Landlord feeling it to be as heavy as before, fuppos'd *Garret* and his Comrade had not took the Prize, out of which he was to have a fnack for his Intelligence, and curs'd them heartily to himfelf Whilft the Far-rier was dreffing the Gentleman's Horfe, he defir'd the Landlords Company to drink with him, calling in very brifkly for one Bottle after another All his Difcourfe was on the two Gentlemen's great Favour fhew'd him over Night and that Morning, drinking their Healths over and over, and faying alfo that if he knew their Names, and where they lived, he would make them amends for their Generofity; nay, he would bring them down fhortly thither and give them a Treat of Ten Guineas with his Landlord and Land-lady Thefe Words confirming the Inn keeper's Suf-picion that they had not robbed him, and being a little elevated with Liquor, and having Hopes too of the ten Guineas to be fpent at his Houfe, made him then tell their Names and Places of Abode, for which the Gentleman feemed to be extreme glad, for he faid, *He was refolved to fee them as foon as he cou'd* His Horfe being dreff'd by the Farrier who told him he might ride him fafe enough to *London,* he mounts with his Portmanteau, and arrived in Town by Night

about Five the next Morning, he went to *Garret*'s Houfe

House first, and knocks at the Door, which being opened by a Servant, he told him, *He must speak with his Master* The Servant told him, *He was not stirring and believed would not till Ten or Eleven of the Clock, as being much weary and fatigued in coming off a Journey late last Night* Quoth the Gentleman, *It is upon such extraordinary Business I want to see him, that I must and will speak with him just now.* Upon this Urgency the Servant went up to his Master and told him, *There was a Gentleman below Stairs, who says, he must and will speak with you presently* Garret being conscious of somewhat ill approaching him, slips on his Night-Gown, and comes down, and seeing 'twas the Gentleman he had robbed the Day before, takes him into a back Room, where the Gentleman told him, *That he had lately borrowed a hundred Pounds of him, which if he did not then pay, he must expect to feel the utmost Severity of Justice* Garret pays him the Money, upon Sight, and then he went to his Comrade's House in *Cheapside*, where making the same Uproar as he did at the same Place from whence ne came last, he got there another hundred Pounds, by which he was so much gainer

Tho' the Gentleman told the Story among all his Acquaintance, yet he would not discover the Persons Names who robbed him Nevertheless, the Matter being nois'd about so much, that it came to the Ears of Garret and his Comrade, and they having a Guilty Conscience and Dread that it would at last be disclos'd, they went off by Night, and pursu'd their old Courses more openly, till Garret began to be so publickly noted over most Countries in *England*, that he left off robbing on the Highway, and turn'd Housebreaker, as supposing he should thus longer screen himself from Justice, but long he had not practis'd the Art of Felony and Burglary, before he was apprehended for breaking open the House of one *Thomas King*, in the County of *Kent*, and taking thence Money, Rings and Plate, to the Value of three hundred Pounds and upwards, for which he was condemned at the Assizes held at *Rochester*, on *Monday the* 9th *of March*, 1718-19, before the Right Honourable the Lord Chief Justice *Pratt*, and receiving Sentence of Death, was hang'd on the *Saturday* Seven Night following, aged twenty nine Years

CHRISTOPHER BANISTER was born at *Colanprow* in *Devonshire*, and put Apprentice to a Gun-Smith, and coming up to *London*, wrought for the Master of the Ordnance He had lived near forty Years in *East Smithfield*, and other Places contiguous to the Metropolis of this Nation, in which Time he had also followed the Employment of a Bailiff, and of late Years that of lending Money upon Pawns

He had been a most notorious Villain in all his Occupations, for when he belonged to the Tower, he was turn'd out by the Master of the Ordnance, for pilfering the royal Stores, when he turned Bailiff, he would set poor People together by the Ears, and encourage them to arrest one another for the Value of a Groat, take Bribes of them he were to arrest, to cheat their Plaintiff, and when he transformed himself into that most detestable and damnable Profession of a Pawn broker, he would make the poor pay fifty *per Cent* for what they borrowed, and very often cheat them of their Pledges if any Thing valuable, especially silver Plate, Watches, or gold Rings

Among the many Sins he was addicted to, Whoredom was very predominate in him, keeping a common Jilt under his Wife's Nose, even in his own House, against whom, one *Powel Reval* having a Writ, and serving it on her in *Banister's* House, he

ran up Stairs for a Dagger then lying in his Bed Chamber, and coming down again, most barbarously murdered the aforesaid Officer, whose Brother some short Time afterwards was one of the Turnkeys to the Master Side of *Neugate*, and next a Tip-staff to one of the Courts of *Westminster-Hall* This Murder was committed on the Eighth of *January*, 1712-13, and he received Sentence of Death for it the Sessions next ensuing in the same Month, but thro' the Expence of a great deal of Money, which he then had by him, he obtained her late Majesty's Pardon for it, and pleaded it there on *Wednesday* the 12th of *August*, 1713

He was no sooner discharged, but he returned to the wicked Course of Life he had been before addicted to, insomuch, that in Process of Time, by his Progress in Iniquity, he brought himself under the Lash of the Law again, as being burnt in the Hand, on *Saturday* the 4th of *June* 1715, for a Felony He was a little after try'd at *Maidstone* in *Kent*, for robbing on the Highway, and tho' guilty of the Crime, was yet acquitted for Want of sufficient Evidence But at last Justice pursuing this notorious Fellow, he was committed to *Neugate*, and at the Sessions held at the *Old Bailey* in *February* 1718-19, took his Trial for robbing on the Highway, which take as follows

Christopher Banister, of St *Botolph Aldgate*, was indicted for assaulting *Dorothy Thompson* on the Highway, putting her in bodily Fear, and taking from her a Muslin Hood, value four Shillings and ten Pence, the 21st of *January* last, about 10 o'Clock at Night The Prosecutor depos'd, that as she was coming out of *Minories*, the Prisoner catch'd her by the Throat and said he'd Throttle her, but she crying out, a young Man came to her Assistance, where upon the Prisoner snatched her Hood off her Head, and run away with it She was positive the Prisoner was the Person, and had on a laced Hat and white Cloak, that she saw him plainly by the Light of two Lamps, (one on each Side the Door) and knew him, he having lived some Time in the same Street

The Prisoner deny'd the Fact, and pleaded in his Defence, that about fourteen Months ago he lent the Prosecutor one Pound one Shilling and Six pence, for which he had a Note under her Hand, and produced a Note in a Court, and that he arrested her a Month ago for the Money, which was the Occasion of this Prosecution He called one Mrs *Boon* to prove it, who swore, that the Prosecutor told her the Prisoner had arrested her, but there was a Hoop Petticoat stole, and she would swear it against him She farther depos'd, that the Prosecutor was a Woman of the Town, and that the House she lived in had been reputed a Bawdy House above half a Year He likewise called one Mr *Dawnes* to discredit the Prosecutor, who did not, but gave him a very ill Character, and said that they had some Trouble to rout him out of the Neighbourhood, being afraid of being robbed by him every Night

The Prosecutor deny'd the Note, or that she ever gave him one, or ever had any Dealings with him She also called one Mrs *Meal* to her Reputation, who said she was a very civil industrious Woman, and made Perriwig Cauls for her Livelihood, which she sold to the Barbers and Perriwig makers, and that she lived in a private House of good Repute The Constable likewise depos'd, that he enquired after her in the Neighbourhood, and found a good Character of her, and that the Prisoner would have agreed it up both before and after they went before the Justice The Jury found him Guilty

Whilst he was under Sentence of Death, he was no

no Changeling, for he would swear, curse, damn and sink in the *Condemned Hold*, as if he had not been to have died at all, and being convey'd in a Coach to *Tyburn*, on *Monday* the 23d of *March*, 1718-19, he most blasphemously said, *He was as innocent as our Saviour* And afterwards was turned off the Cart, aged sixty Years

JOHN WHEELER was born in the Parish of St *Bridget* in *London*, and at about sixteen Years of Age was put Apprentice to a Joyner in *Bartholomew-Close*, which is the Parish of St *Bartholomew* the Great, and having served out his Apprenticeship, he became an Inmate in St *Sepulchre's* Parish, for the last nine Years of his Life, in all which While he wrought Journey work at his Trade, whereby he maintained himself and his Family pretty well, for being a very good Workman he was commonly in Business, but only this was his Misfortune, that he never worked in any House, but what he would be sure to rob, as soon as Opportunity served

He was induced to follow a vicious Course of Life by the Perfuasion of a near Relation of his, who was an Accomplice with him in most of the Robberies which he committed He was altogether for House breaking, excepting once when he stole a Horse out of a Field at *Hackney*, from a Gentleman who set such a Value upon his Beast, which cost him forty Pounds, that he was daily cursing the Thief, whom he could not discover, for above a Twelvemonth

But when the aforesaid *John Wheeler* was wont to go upon any Burglary, or breaking open a House in the Night Time, he commonly carried a young Kitten in his Coat-Pocket, so that if he should happen to make any Noise that should occasion the People to go and hearken at the Chamber-Door in which he was, he would severely pinch the Kitten's Tail, which making it to Mew very loud, the Listners would return from hearkening, saying, *Is it you Mrs Pufs, c'es Mew and be poxt, what a cluter you make! the Devil is in you for catterwauling* So by this Means the Thief proceeded in his Robbery, without any farther Interruption

One Time *Wheeler* breaking into the House of one *Hodder* a Shoemaker, keeping a Bawdy-House in *Denmark Court* in the *Strand*, and there being at that Time a Covey of no less than half a dozen

Whores sleeping and snoring in their Beds, he pack'd up all their Mantetus, Petticoats, Linnen, and every Thing that was worth taking, as silk Stockings and laced Shoes, which throwing out to his Comrade, he jump'd after, and went off But in the Morning when the Strumpets came to rise, and found all their Cloaths gone, what a Holobo loo was there! worse than what the wild *Irish* make at the Funeral of a *Bogtrotter* There was swearing and cursing, by Wholesale, till quite weary with venting Imprecations, they were obliged to lie in Bed till they could agree with any man to new rig them

Another Time he broke into the House of one Mrs *Clark* an eminent Midwife, living in *Exeter-street*, out of which he stole a large silver Cup, a dozen of silver Spoons, a dozen of silver Forks, a dozen of silver hafted Knives, besides Money and rich Apparel He also robbed one *Snead* a Taylor, in the *Strand*, of two rich Suits of Cloaths, which were made for a Person of Quality, worth above eighty Pounds Likewise he robbed one Mr *Coon* an Upholderer near the Star Inn in the *Strand*, of a set of rich Tapestry Hangings, worth two hundred and fifty Pounds And he robbed one Mr *Atkinson* a Taylor in Fountain Court in the *Strand*, of forty Pounds in Money, and a silver Tankard and Punch-Bowl

Whilst he followed Thieving, with his Relation aforementioned, he broke open above a hundred Houses in the Night-time, and robbed them, but at last being apprehended, and committed to *Newgate* for his most notorious Villanies, he was try'd, convicted, and condemn'd, at the Sessions House in the *Old Bailey*, upon two Indictments, first, for breaking open the House of one *Samuel Mead*, and stealing thence ten pewter Dishes, thirty six Plates, a brass Porridge Pot, two Stew Pans, and other Goods, on the 20th of *January*, 1718-19, and secondly, for another Burglary committed in the House of one *Joshua Winefinose*, out of which he took three silver Spoons, a silver Cup, and a silver quartern Pot, *March* the 4th, 1718 19 Whilst he was under Sentence, he gave Satisfaction to some whom he had injur'd, particularly to a Gentlewoman whom he had robb'd of her wearing Apparel He was executed alone at *Tyburn*, on *Monday* *May* the 25th, 1719, aged 32 Years.

The

The LIFE of CATHERINE HAYES.

Catherine Hall, afterwards Catherine Hayes, was born in the Year 1690, at a Village on the Borders of Warwickshire, within four Miles of Birmingham. Her Parents were so poor as to receive the Assistance of the Parish, and so careless of the Daughter, that they never gave her the least Education. While a Girl she discovered Marks of so violent and turbulent a Temper, that she totally threw off all Respect and Obedience to her Parents, giving a loose to her Passions, and gratifying herself in all her vicious Inclinations.

About the Year 1705, some Officers coming into the Neighbourhood to recruit, Kate was so much taken with the Fellows in Red, that she stroled away with them, till they came to a Village called Great Ombersley in Warwickshire, where they very ungenerously left her behind them. This Elopement of her Sparks drove her almost mad, so that she went like a distracted Creature about the Country, till coming to Mr Hayes's Door, his Wife in Compassion took her in out of Charity. The eldest Child in the Family was John Hayes the Deceased, who being then about 21 Years of Age, found so many Charms in this Catherine Hall, that he quickly made Proposals to her of Marriage. There is no Doubt of their being readily enough received, and as they both were sensible how disagreeable a Thing it would be to his Parents, agreed to keep it secret. They quickly adjusted the Measures that were to be taken, in order to their being married at Worcester. Mrs John Hayes pretended that she wanted some Tools in the Way of his Trade, viz that of a Carpenter, for which it was necessary he should go to Worcester, and under this Colour he procured also as much Money as was sufficient to defray the Expence of the intended Wedding.

Catherine having privately quitted the House, and meeting at the appointed Place, they accompanied each other to Worcester, where the Wedding was soon celebrated. The same Day Mrs Catherine Hayes had the Fortune to meet with some of her Acquaintance, who had dropped her at Ombersley, who understanding where the Nuptials were to be solemnized, consulted among themselves how to make a Penny of the Bridegroom. Accordingly, at Evening, just as Mr Hayes was got into Bed to his Wife, they coming to the House where he lodged, forcibly entered the Room, and dragged the Bridegroom away, pretending to impress him for her Majesty's Service. This Proceeding broke the Measures Mr John Hayes had concerted with his Wife, to keep their Wedding secret, for finding no Redemption without a larger Sum of Money than he was Master of, he was necessitated to let his Father know of his Misfortune. Mr Hayes hearing of his Son's Adventure, his Resentment did not extinguish his Affection for him as a Father, but he resolved to deliver him from his Troubles, and accordingly taking a Gentleman in the Neighbourhood along with him, he went for

Worcester. At their Arrival there, they found Mr John Hayes in the Hands of the Officers, who insisted upon the detaining him for her Majesty's Service, but his Father, and the Gentleman he brought with him, soon made them sensible of their Error, and they were glad to discharge him immediately. But Mrs Catherine, who better approved of a travelling than a settled Life, persuaded her Husband to enter himself a Voluntier, in a Regiment then at Worcester which he did, and went abroad with them, where he continued for some Time.

Mr John Hayes being in Garrison in the Isle of Wight, and not content with such a lazy, indolent Life, sollicited his Father to procure his Discharge, which at length he was prevailed upon to consent to, but the several Journeys he was necessitated to take, and the Expences of procuring such Discharge, amounted to about sixty Pounds. The Father then, the better to induce him to settle himself in the Country, put him into an Estate of ten Pounds per annum, but Mr John Hayes representing to his Father, that it was not possible for him and his Wife to live on that, persuaded him to let him have also a Leasehold of sixteen Pounds per annum, upon which he lived during the Continuance of the Lease.

The Characters of Mr John Hayes and his Wife were vastly different. He had the Repute of a sober honest peaceable Man, and a very good Husband, the only Objection against him was, that he was of too frugal a Temper, and rather too indulgent of his Wife. She was on all Hands allowed to be a very turbulent Person, never free from Quarrels in the Neighbourhood, and fomenting Disputes to the Disturbance of all her Friends. They lived in the Country for the Space of about six Years, until the Lease of the last mentioned Farm expired, about which Time, Mrs Hayes persuaded her Husband to leave the Country, and come to London.

In the Year 1719, upon their Arrival in Town, they took a House, Part of which they let out in Lodgings, and sold Sea Coal, Chandlery Ware &c, whereby they lived in a handsome creditable Manner. In this Business they picked up Money, and Mr Hayes received the yearly Rent of the first mentioned Estate, tho' in Town, and by lending out Money in small Sums amongst his Country People improved the same considerably. She would frequently, in speaking of Mr Hayes, give him the best of Characters, tho' to some of her particular Cronies, who knew not Mr Hayes's Temper, she would complain against him, and say, that it was no Sin to beat him, and that one Time or other she might give him a Pot. Afterwards they removed into Tottenham Court Road, where they lived ten Pounds, following the same Business as formerly, from whence about two Years afterwards they removed into Tyburn Road a few Doors above where the Murder was committed. There they lived about twelve Months,

Months, Mr *Hayes* still supporting himself in lending out Money upon Pledges, and sometimes working at his Profession, and in Husbandry, till it was computed he had picked up a pretty handsome Sum of Money. About ten Months before the Murder, they removed to the House of Mr *Whinyard,* where the Murther was committed, taking Lodgings up two Pair of Stairs There it was, that *Thomas Billings* a Taylor, who wrought Journeywork about *Monmouth-street,* under Pretence of being Mrs *Hayes's* Countryman, came to see them They invited him to lodge with them , he did so, and continued in the House till about six Weeks before the Death of Mr *Hayes* About the same Time *Thomas Wood,* who was a Neighbours Son in the Country, and an intimate Acquaintance both of Mr *Hayes* and his Wife, came to Town, and pressing being at that Time very hot, he was obliged to quit his Lodgings, whereupon Mr *Hayes* very kindly invited him to accept of the Conveniences of theirs *Wood* accepted the Offer, and lay with *Billings* In three or four Days Time Mrs. *Hayes* having taken an Opportunity, opened to him a Desire of being rid of her Husband, at which *Wood* as he very well might, was exceedingly surprized, and demonstrated the Baseness as well as Cruelty there would be in such an Action, if committed by him, who besides the general Ties of Humanity, stood particularly oblig'd to him as his Neighbour and his Friend Mrs *Hayes* in order to hush these Scruples, persuaded him that her Husband was void of all Religion and Goodness, an Enemy to God, and therefore unworthy of his Protection , that he had killed a Man in the Country, and destroyed two of his and her Children, one of which was buried under an Apple-Tree, the other under a Pear-Tree, in the Country To these fictitious Tales, she added another, which perhaps had the greatest Weight, viz That if he were dead she should be Mistress of fifteen hundred Pounds, *And then,* says she, *you may be Master thereof if you will help to get him out of the Way,* Billings *has agreed to it if you'll make a Third, and so all may be finished without Danger,*

A few Days after this, *Wood*'s Occasions called him out of Town On his Return, which was on the 1st Day of *March,* he found Mr *Hayes* and his Wife, and *Billings,* very merry together. Amongst other Things which passed in Conversation, Mr *Hayes* happened to say, *That he and another Person once drank as much Wine between them, as came to a Guinea, without either of them being fuddled* Billings upon this proposed a Wager on these Terms, That half a dozen Bottles of the best Mountain should be fetched, which if Mr *Hayes* could drink without being disordered, then *Billings* should pay for it, but if not, then it should be at the Cost of Mr *Hayes,* who accepting of this Proposal, Mrs *Hayes* and the two Men went to the *Brawns Head* in *New Bond-street* to fetch the Wine. As they were going thither, she put them in Mind of the Proposition she made them to Murder Mr *Hayes,* and said they could not have a better Opportunity then when he should be intoxicated with Liquors, whereupon *Wood* made Answer, that it would be a most inhuman Act to Murder a Man in cool Blood, and that too when he was in Liquor Mrs *Hayes* had recourse to her old Arguments, and *Billings* joining with her, *Wood* suffer'd himself to be over-power'd When they came to the Tavern they called for a Pint of the best Mountain, and after they had drank it order'd a Gallon and a Half to be sent home to their Lodgings , which was done accordingly, and Mrs *Hayes* paid Ten Shillings and six Pence for it, which was what

it came to Then they came all back and sat down together to see Mr *Hayes* drink the Wager, and while he swallowed the Wine, they called for two three full Pots of Beer, in order to entertain themselves

Mr *Hayes* when he had almost finished his Wine, began to grow very merry, Singing and Dancing about the Room, with all the Gaity which is natural But Mrs *Hayes* fearful of his not having his Dose, sent away privately for another Bottle, of which having drank some also, it quite finished the Work, by depriving him totally of his Understanding ; however, reeling into the other Room, he there threw himself a-cross the Bed, and fell fast asleep No sooner did his Wife perceive it, than she came to the two Men to go in and do the Work , then *Billings* taking a Coal Hatchet in his Hand going into the other Room, struck Mr *Hayes* therewith on the Back of his Head, which Blow fractur'd his Skull, and made him, thro' the Agony of the Pain, stamp violently upon the Ground , insomuch that it alarmed the People who lay in the Garret ; and *Wood* fearing the Consequence, went in and repeated the Blows, tho' that was needless, since the first was mortal of itself, and he already lay quiet By this Time Mrs *Springate,* whose Husband lodged over Mr *Hayes's* Head, on hearing the Noise, came down to enquire the Reason of it, complaining at the same Time, that it so disturbed her Family, that they could not rest Mrs *Hayes* thereupon told her, *That her Husband had had some Company with him, who growing merry with their Liquor were a little noisy, but that they were going immediately, and desired she would be easy* Upon this she went up again for the present, and the three Murderers began immediately to consult how to get rid of the Body

The Men were in so much Terrour and Confusion, that they knew not what to do , but the Wife of the Deceased quickly thought of an Expedient in which they all agreed she said, *That if the Head was cut off, there would not be near so much Difficulty in carrying off the Body, which could not be known.*

In order to put this Design in Execution, they got a Pail, and she herself carrying the Candle, they all entered the Room where the deceased lay, Then the Woman holding the Pail, *Billings* drew the Body by the Head over the Bed side, that the Blood might run the more freely into it, and *Wood* with his Pocket Penknife cut it off Assoon as it was severed from the Body, and the Bleeding was over, they poured the Blood down a Wooden Sink at the Window, and after it several Pails of Water in order to wash it quite away, that it might not be perceiv'd in the Morning , however, their Precautions were not altogether effectual, for *Springate* the next Morning found several Clods of Blood, but not suspecting any thing of the Matter, threw them away , neither had they escaped letting some Tokens of their Cruelty fall upon the Floor, stained the Wall of the Room, and even the Ceiling, which it may be supposed happened at the giving the first Blow. When they had finished this Decollation, they again consulted what was next to be done Mrs. *Hayes* was for boiling it in a Pot, till nothing but the Skull remained, which would effectually prevent any body's knowing to whom it belonged, but the two Men thinking this too dilatory a Method, they resolved to put it in a Pail, and go together and throw it in the *Thames* *Springate* hearing a bustling in Mr *Hayes's* Room for some Time, and then somebody going down Stairs, called again to know who it was and what was the Occasion of it, (it being then about Eleven a Clock) to which Mrs *Hayes*

answered

anſwered, *It was her Husband, who was going a Journey into the Country*

Billings and *Wood* being thus gone to diſpoſe of the Head, went towards *Whitehall* intending to have thrown it into the River there ; but the Gates being ſhut up, they were obliged to go forward as far as Mr *Macreth's* Wharf, near the *Horſe-Ferry* at *Weſtmuſter* where *Billings* ſetting down the Pail from under his Great Coat, *Wood* took up the ſame with the Head therein, and threw it into the Dock before the Wharf It was expected the ſame would have been carried away by the Tide, but the Water being then ebbing, it was left behind There were alſo ſome Lighters lying over-againſt the Dock and one of the Lightermen walking then on board, ſaw them throw the Pail into the Dock, but by the Obſcurity of the Night, the Diſtance, and having no Suſpicion, did not apprehend any thing of the Matter Having thus done, they returned home again to Mrs *Hayes's*, where they arrived about Twelve a Clock, and being let in, found the Wife of the Deceaſed had been very buſily employed in waſhing the Floor, and ſcraping the Blood off from it, and from the Wall, &c, After which they all three went into the Fore Room , *Billings* and *Wood* went to Bed there, and Mrs *Hayes* ſat by them till Morning

In the Morning of the Second of *March*, about the dawning of the Day, one *Robinſon* a Watchman ſaw a Man's Head lying in the Dock, and a Pail near it His Surprize occaſioned his calling ſome Perſons to aſſiſt in taking up the Head, and finding the Pail bloody, they conjectured the Head had been brought thither in it Their Suſpicions were fully confirmed therein by the Lighterman, who ſaw *Billings* and *Wood* throw the ſame into the Dock, as beforementioned It was now Time for Mrs *Hayes*, *Billings* and *Wood*, to conſider how they ſhould diſpoſe of the Body Mrs *Hayes* and *Wood* propoſed to put it in a Box, where it might lay conceiled till a convenient Opportunity offered for removing it , this being approved of, Mrs *Hayes* brought a Box, but upon their endeavouring to put it in, the Box was not big enough to hold it They had before wrapped it up in a Blanket, out of which they took it Mrs *Hayes* propoſed to cut off the Arms and Legs, and they again attempted to put it in, but the Box would not hold it , then they cut off the Thighs, and laying them Piece meal in the Box, concealed them till Night In the mean Time Mr *Hayes's* Head, which had been found as before, had ſufficiently alarmed the Town, and Information was given to the neighbouring Juſtices of the Peace The Pariſh Officers did all that was poſſible towards the Diſcovery of the Perſons guilty of ſo horrid an Action , they cauſed the Head to be cleaned, the Face to be waſhed from the Dirt and Blood, and the Hair to be combed, and then the Head to be ſet upon a Poſt in publick View in St *Margaret's* Church-Yard, *Weſtminſter*, that every Body might have free Acceſs to ſee the ſame, with ſome of the Pariſh Officers to attend, hoping by that Means a Diſcovery of the ſame might be attained The High Conſtable of *Weſtminſter* Liberty, alſo iſſued private Orders to all the petty Conſtables, Watchmen, and other Officers of that Diſtrict, to keep a ſtrict Eye on all Coaches, Carts &c paſſing in the Night through their Liberty, imagining that the Perpetrators of ſuch a horrid Fact would endeavour to free themſelves of the Body, in the ſame Manner as they had done of the Head Theſe Orders were executed for ſome Time, with all the Secrecy imaginable, under various Pretences, but inſucceſsfully , the Head alſo continued to be expoſed for ſome Days in the Manner before deſcribed which

drew a prodigious Number of People to ſee it, but without attaining any Diſcovery of the Murderers

On the Second of *March* in the Evening, *Catherine Hayes*, *Thomas Wood*, and *Thomas Billings* took the Body and diſjointed Members out of the Box, and wrapped them up in two Blankets, *viz* the Body in one, and the Limbs in the other Then *Billings* and *Wood* firſt took up the Body, and about Nine a Clock in the Evening carried it by Turns into *Mary le bone Fields*, and threw the ſame into a Pond, (which *Wood* in the Day time had been hunting for) and returning back again about Eleven, took up the Limbs in the other old Blanket, and carried them by Turns to the ſame Place, throwing them in alſo About Twelve o'Clock the ſame Night, they returned back again, and knocking at the Door, were let in by *Mary Springate* They went up to Bed in Mrs *Hayes's* Fore room, and Mrs *Hayes* ſtaid with them all Night, ſometimes ſitting up, and ſometimes laying down upon the Bed by them The ſame Day one *Bennet*, the King's Organ maker's Apprentice, going to *Weſtminſter* to ſee the Head, believed it to be Mr *Hayes's*, he being intimately acquainted with him, and thereupon went and informed Mrs *Hayes*, that the Head expoſed to View in St *Margaret's* Church-Yard, was ſo very like Mr *Hayes*, that he believed it to be his , upon which Mrs *Hayes* aſſerted him to be Mr *Hayes* was very well, and reproved him very ſharply for forming ſuch an Opinion, telling him he muſt be very cautious how he rais'd ſuch falſe and ſcandalous Reports, for that he might thereby bring himſelf into a great deal of Trouble This Reprimand put a Stop to the Youth's ſaying any thing more about it The ſame Day alſo Mr *Samuel Patrick* having been at *Weſtminſter* to ſee the Head, went from thence to Mr *Granger's* at the *Dog* and *D* in *Monmouth ſtreet*, where Mr *Hayes* and his Wife were intimately acquainted, and told that the Head in his Opinion was the moſt like to their Countryman *Hayes*, of any he ever ſaw

Billings being there then at Work , ſome of the Servants replied it could not be his, becauſe there being one of Mrs *Hayes's* Lodgers there they ſhould have heard of it by him if Mr *Hayes* had been miſſing, or any Accident had happen'd to him , to which *Billings* made Anſwer that Mr *Hayes* was alive and well, and that he left him in Bed when he came to work in the Morning The third Day of *March*, Mrs *Hayes* gave *Wood* a white Coat and a pair of Leathern Breeches of Mr *Hayes's*, which he carried with him to *Greenford*, near *Harrow* on the ſaid Mrs *Springate* obſerving *Wood* carrying theſe Things down Stairs bundled up in a white Cloath told Mrs *Hayes*, who replied it was a Suit of Cloaths he had borrowed of a Neighbour, and was going to carry them home again On the Fourth of *March*, one Mrs *Longmore* coming to Viſit Mrs *Hayes*, enquired how Mr *Hayes* did and where he was Mrs *Hayes* anſwered, that he was gone to take a walk, and then enquired what News there was about Town Her Viſiter told her that moſt People's Diſcourſe run upon the Man's Head that had been found at *Weſtminſter* Mrs *Hayes* ſeemed to wonder very much at the wickedneſs of the Age, and exclaimed vehemently againſt ſuch barbarous Murderers, adding, here is a Diſcourſe too in our Neighbourhood, of a Woman who has been found in the fields mangled and cut to pieces It may be ſo reply'd, Mr , *Longmore*, but I have heard nothing of it On the Sixth of *March*, the Pariſh Officers conſidering that it might putrify if it continued longer in the Air, agreed with one Mr *Weſtbrook*, a Surgeon, to have it preſerved in Spirits He having accordingly provided a proper Glass put it therein, and shewed it to all Persons who were desirous of seeing, yet the Murther remained still undiscover'd, and notwithstanding the Multitude which had seen it, yet none pretended to be directly positive to the Face, tho' many agreed in their having seen it before

In the mean Time Mrs *Hayes* quitted her Lodgings, and removed from where the Murther was committed to Mr *Jones*'s a Distiller in the Neighbourhood, with *Billings*, *Wood*, and *Springate*, for whom she paid one Quarters Rent at her old Lodgings She now employed herself in getting as much of her Husbands Effects as possible she could, and amongst other Papers and Securities, finding a Bond due to Mr *Hayes* from *John Davis*, who had married Mr *Hayes*'s Sister, she consulted how to get in that Money To which purpose she sent for one Mr *Leonard Myring* a Barber, and told him, that she knowing him to be her Husband's particular Friend, and he then being under some Misfortune, thro' which she feared he would not presently return, she knew not how to recover several Sums of Money that were due to him, unless by sending fictitious Letters in his Name, to the several Persons from whom the same was due, Mr *Myring* considering the Consequences of such a Proceeding, declining it But she prevailed upon some other Person to write Letters in Mr *Hayes*'s Name, particularly one to his Mother, on the 14th of *March*, to demand Ten Pounds of the abovementioned Mr *Davis*, threatning if he refused, to sue him for it This Letter Mr *Hayes*'s Mother received, and acquainting her Son in Law *Davis* with the Contents thereof, he offered to pay the Money, on sending down the Bond, of which she by a Letter acquainted Mrs *Hayes* on the Twenty-second of the same Month

During these Transactions, several Persons came daily to Mr *Westbrook*'s to see the Head A poor Woman at *Kingsland*, whose Husband had been missing the Day before it was found, was one amongst them She at first sight fancied it bore some Resemblance to that of her Husband, but was not positive enough to swear it, yet her Suspicion as first was sufficient to ground a Report, which flew about the Town in the Evening, and some Enquires were made after the Body of the Person to whom it was suppos'd to belong, but to no Purpose. Mrs *Hayes* in the mean While took all the Pains imaginable to propagate a Story of Mr *Hayes*'s withdrawing on Account of an unlucky Blow he had given a Person in a Quarrel, and which made him apprehensive of a Prosecution, though he was then in Treaty with the Widow in order to make it up This Story she at first told with many Injunctions of Secresy, to Persons who she had good Reasons to believe, would tell it again It happened in the Interim, that one *Joseph Ashby*, who had been an intimate Acquaintance of Mr *Hayes*'s, came to see her She with a great deal of pretended Concern, communicated the Tale she had framed to him Mr *Ashby* asked whether the Person he had killed was him to whom the Head belonged She said, No, the Man who died by Mr *Hayes*'s Blow, was buried entire, and Mr *Hayes* had given, or was about to give, a Security to pay the Widow fifteen Pounds per annum, to hush it up Mr *Ashby* enquired next, Where Mr *Hayes* was gone She said, to Portugal, with three or four foreign Gentlemen, and he thereupon took his Leave But going from thence to Mr *Henry Longmore*, Cousin to Mr *Hayes*, he related to him the Story Mrs *Hayes* had told him, and expressed a great deal of Dissatisfaction therein,

desiring Mr *Longmore* to go to her and make the same Enquiry as he had done, but without taking Notice they had seen one another Mr *Longmore* went thereupon directly to Mrs *Hayes*'s and enquired in a peremptory Tone for her Husband She in Answer said, She suppos'd Mr *Ashby* had acquainted him with the Misfortune which had befallen him Mr *Longmore* replied, He had not seen Mr *Ashby* for a considerable Time, and knew nothing of his Cousin's Misfortune He then asked if he was in Prison for Debt? She answered him, No, 'twas worse than that Mr *Longmore* again importuning her to know what he had done, to occasion his absconding so, saying, I suppose he has no murdered any Body? she replied, He had, and beckoning him to come on the Stairs, related to him the Story as before mentioned Mr *Longmore* being inquisitive which Way he was gone, she told him in to *Herefordshire*, and that he had taken four Pistols with him for his Security, one under each Arm, and two in his Pockets Mr *Longmore* answered, 'twould be dangerous for him to travel in that Manner, because any Person seeing him so armed, might cause him to be apprehended on Suspicion of being an Highwayman She offered him, that once he was apprehended on Suspicion of being an Highwayman, but that a Gentleman who knew him, accidentally came in, and seeing him in Custody, passed his Word for his Appearance, by which he was discharged Mr *Longmore* made Answer, that it was very improbable he was ever stopped on Suspicion of being an Highwayman, and discharged upon a Man's only passing his Word for his Appearance He then demanded which Way he was supplied with Money for his Journey? She told him, she had sewed twenty six Guineas into his Cloaths, and that he had about seventeen Shillings in new Silver She added, that *Springate* who lodged there was privy to the whole Transaction, for which Reason she paid a Quarters Rent for her at her old Lodging, and the better to maintain what she had averred, called *Springate* to justify the Truth of it In concluding the Discourse, she reflected on the unkind Usage of Mr *Hayes* towards her, which surprized Mr *Longmore*, more than any Thing else she had said, because he had often been a Witness to her giving Mr *Hayes* the Character of a most indulgent tender Husband

Mr *Longmore* then took his Leave of her, and returned back to his Friend Mr *Ashby*, when after comparing their several Notes together, they judged that Mr *Hayes* must have had very ill Play shewn him upon which they agreed to go to Mr *Eaton* a Lifeguardman, who was also an Acquaintance of Mr *Hayes*'s, which accordingly they did, intending him to have gone to Mrs *Hayes* also, to have heard what Relation she would give him concerning her Husband They went and enquired at several Places for him, but he was not then to be found, upon which they went down to *Westminster* to see the Head at Mr *Westbrook*'s Mr *Ashby* first went up Stairs to look on it, and coming down, told Mr *Longmore* he really thought it to be Mr *Hayes*'s Head, upon which Mr *Longmore* went up to see it, and after examining it more particularly, confirmed their Suspicion Then they returned to seek out Mr *Eaton*, and finding him at Home, informed him of their Proceedings, with the Reasons on which their Suspicions were grounded, and compelled him to go with them to enquire into the Affair Mr *Eaton* dispatched them to try Dinner with him, which at first they agreed to, but after with him, which at first they agreed to, but after testing their Minds went down to Mr *Longmore*

Ho

Houfe, and there renewed their Sufpicions, not only of Mr. *Hayes*'s being murdered, but alfo that his Wife was privy to the fame, but in order to be more fully fatisfied, they agreed that Mr *Eaton* fhould in a Day or two's Time go and enquire for Mr *Hayes*, taking no Notice of his having feen them. In the mean Time *Longmore*'s Brother interfered, faying, *That it feemed apparent to him, that his Coufin* Hayes *had been murderer, and that Mrs* Hayes *appeared Guilty, with* Wood *and* Billings, *who, fhe told him, had drank with him the Night before his Journey* He added, moreover, *that he thought Time was not to be delayed, becaufe they might remove from their Lodgings upon the leaft Apprehenfions of a Difcovery*

His Opinion prevailed as the moft reafonable, and Mr *Longmore* faid, *they would go about it immediately* Accordingly to Mr Juftice *Lambert* he immediately applied, and acquainted him with the Grounds of their Sufpicions, and their Defire of his granting a Warrant for the Apprehending of the Parties The Juftice, on hearing the Story, not only readily complied with their Demand, but faid alfo, he would get proper Officers to execute it in the Evening, about Nine o'Clock, putting Mrs *Hayes*, *Thomas Wood*, *Thomas Billings*, and *Mary Springate*, into a fpecial Warrant for that Purpofe At the Hour appointed they met, and Mr *Eaton* bringing two Officers of the Guards along with him, they went altogether to the Houfe where Mrs. *Hayes* lodged They went directly in, and up Stairs, at which Mr. *Jones* who kept the Houfe, immediately demanded who and what they were? He was anfwered, that they were fufficiently authorized in all that they did, defiring at the fame Time to bring Candles, and he fhould fee on what Occafion they came Light being brought, they went all up Stairs together Juftice *Lambert* wrapped at Mrs *Hayes*'s Door with his Cane She demanded who was there, for fhe was in Bed, on which fhe was bid to get up and open the Door, or they would break it open. After fome little Time taken to put on her Cloaths, fhe came and opened it, and as foon they were in the Room, they faw *Billings*, who was fitting upon her Bed-fide, without either Shoes or Stockings on. The Juftice afk'd whether he had been in Bed with her? She faid no, but that he fat there to mend his Stockings Why then, replied Mr *Lambert*, he had very good Eyes to fee to do it without Fire or Candle Hereupon they feized him too, and leaving Perfons below to guard them, went up and apprehended *Springate*, and after an Examination, in which they would confefs nothing, committed *Billings* to New-Prifon, *Springate* to the Gate-houfe, and Mrs *Hayes* to Tothill Fields Bridewell

Mrs *Hayes* was very Affiduous in contriving fuch a Method of Behaviour as might carry the greateft Appearance of Innocence. She entreated Mr *Longmore* that fhe might be admitted to fee the Head, and Mr *Lambert* ordered her to have a Sight of it as fhe came from *Tothill Fields Bridewell* to her Examination Accordingly Mr *Longmore* attending the Officers ordered the Coach to ftep at Mr *Weftbrook*'s Door, and as foon as we was admitted into the Room fhe threw her felf down upon her Knees, crying out in great Agonies, Oh it is my dear Hufband's Head! it is my dear Hufbands Head! and embracing the Glafs in her Arms, kiffed the outfide of it feveral Times Mr *Weftbrook* coming in, told her, that if it was his Head fhe fhould have a plainer View of it, fo taking it out of the Glafs by the Hair he brought it to her She taking it in her Arms, kiffed it, and feemed in great Confufion, withall begging to have a Lock of his Hair, but Mr.

Weftbrook replied, that he was afraid fhe had had too much of his Blood already, At which fhe fainted away, and after recovering, was carried to Mr *Lambert*, to be examined before him and fome other Juftices of the Peace While thefe Things were in Agitation, one Mr *Huddle* and his Servant walking in *Mary le bone Fields* in the Evening, efpied fomething lying in one of the Ponds, which after they had examined, found to be the *Legs*, *Thighs*, and *Arms* of a Man They being very much furprized at this, determined to fearch farther; and the next Morning getting Affiftance ordained the Pond, where to their further Aftonifhment they pulled out the Body of a Man wrapped up in a Blanket, with the News of which, while Mrs *Hayes* was under Examination, Mr *Crofby* a Conftable came down to the Juftices, not doubting but this was the Body of Mr *Hayes*. Yet tho' fhe was fomewhat confounded at the new Difcovery made hereby, fhe could not be prevailed on to make any Acknowledgment of her knowing any thing of the Fact, whereupon the Juftices who examined her, committed her that Afternoon to *Newgate*, the Mob attending her thither with as loud Acclamations of Joy, at her Commitment, as if they were already convinc'd of her Guilt

Sunday Morning following, *Thomas Wood* came to Town from *Greenford* near *Harrow*, having heard nothing of the taking up of Mrs *Hayes*, *Billings*, or *Springate* The firft Place he went to, was Mrs *Hayes*'s old Lodging, where he was anfwer'd that fhe was removed to Mr. *Jones*'s a Diftiller, a little farther in the Street, thither he went, where the People, knowing him to be fufpected of the Murther, faid Mrs *Hayes* was gone to the *Green Dragon* in *King's ftreet*, which is Mr *Longmore*'s Houfe, and a Man who was there told him moreover that he was going thither and would fhew him the way *Wood*, being on Horfeback followed him, and he led him the way to Mr *Longmore*'s Houfe, when Mr *Longmore*'s Brother coming to the Door, and feeing *Wood*, immediately feized him, and unhorfing him dragged him in Doors, fent for Officers and charged them with him on fufpicion of the Murder. From thence he was carried before Mr *Juftice Lambert*, who afked him many Queftions in Relation to the Murder, but he would confefs nothing, whereupon he was committed to *Tothill Fields Bridewell* While he was there he heard the various Reports of Perfons concerning the Murder, and Judging it impoffible to prevent a Difcovery or evade the Proofs that were againft him, he refolved to make an ample Confeffion of the whole Affair, of which Mr *Lambert* being acquainted, he, with *John Mohun* and *Thomas Salt*, Efqrs two other Juftices of the Peace, went to *Tothill Fields Bridewell*, to take his Examination, in which he feem'd very ingenuous and ample, declaring all the particulars before mentioned, with this Addition, that he had been drawn into the Commiffion thereof partly thro' Poverty, and partly thro' her crafty Infinuations, who by feeding him with Liquors, had fpirited him up to the Commiffion of fuch a Piece of Barbarity He farther acknowledged, that ever fince the Commiffion of the Fact, he had had no Peace, but that every Day, before he came from *Greenford*, he was fully perfuaded within himfelf, that he fhould be feized for the Murther when he came to Town, notwithftanding which, he could not refrain coming, tho' under a kind of Certainty of being taken, and dying for the Fact

Having thus made a full and ample Confeffion, and figned the fame, on the 27th of *March*, his Mittimus was made by Juftice *la ...*, and he was committed to *Newgate,* whether he was carried under a guard of a Serjeant and eight Soldiers, with Musquets and Bayonets, to keep off the Mob, who were so exasperated against the Actors of such a piece of Barbarity, that without that Caution it would have been very difficult to have carried him thither alive.

On *Monday* the 28th of *March,* after Mrs *Hayes* was committed to *Newgate,* being the Day after *Wood*'s Apprehension, *Joseph Mercer* going to see Mrs. *Hayes,* she told him as he was *Thomas Billings*'s Friend as well as he s, she desired he would go to him and tell him, 'twas in vain to deny any longer the Murder of her Husband, for they were equally guilty, and both must die for it *Billings* hearing this, and that *Wood* was apprehended, and had fully confess'd the whole Affair, thought it needless to persist any longer in a Denial, and therefore the next Day, being the 29th of *March,* he made a full and plain Discovery of the whole Fact, agreeing with *Wood* in all the Particulars, which Confession was made and signed in the Presence of *Gideon Harvey* and *Oliver Lambert,* Esqrs, two of His Majesty's Justices of the Peace, whereupon he was removed to *Newgate* the same Day that *Wood* was Wood and Billings acquitting *Springate* of the aforesaid Murder, she was soon discharged from her Confinement, but this Discovery making a great Noise in the Town, divers of Mrs *Hayes*'s Acquaintance, went to visit her in *Newgate,* and examin'd into the Reasons that induced her to commit the said Fact, Her Acknowledgment in general was that Mr *Hayes* had proved but an indifferent Husband to her, that one Night he came home drunk and struck her, that upon complaining to *Billings* and *Wood,* they, or one of them, said, such a Fellow ought not to live, and that they would murder him for a Halfpenny She took that Opportunity to propose her bloody Intentions to them, and her Willingness that they should do so, that she was acquainted with their Design, heard the Blow given to Mr *Hayes* by *Billings,* and then went with *Wood* to them into the Room, that she held the Candle while his Head was cut off, and in Excuse for this bloody Fact, said, the Devil was got into them all that made them do it. When she was made sensible that her Crime in Law was not only Murder but petty Treason, she began to shew great Concern indeed, making Enquiries into the Nature of the Proof which was necessary to convict, having possessed herself with a Notion, that unless it appeared she murthered him with her own Hands, it would not touch her Life, and therefore she was very angry that either *Billings* or *Wood* should acknowledge her guilty of the Murther, and subject her to that Punishment which of all others she most feared, often repeating it, that it was hard they would not suffer her to be hanged with them

There are a Set of People about *Newgate,* who get their Living by imposing on unhappy Criminals, and persuading them that Guilt may be covered, and Justice avaded, by certain artful Contrivances in which they profess themselves Masters Some of these had got access to this unhappy Woman, and had instilled into her a Notion, that the Confession of *Wood* and *Billings* could no Ways affect her Life This made her vainly imagine, that there was no positive Proof against her, and that Circumstantials only, would not convict her For this Reason she resolved to put herself upon a Trial contrary to her first Intentions Accordingly being arraigned, she pleaded not Guilty, and put herself upon her

Trial *Wood* and *Billings,* both pleaded Guilty to the same Indictment, at the same Time acknowledging their Guilt, and desiring to make Attonement for the same by the Loss of their Blood, only praying the Court would be graciously pleased to favour them so much as to dispense with their being hanged in Chains,

Mrs *Hayes* having thus put herself upon her Trial, the King's Council opened the Indictment, setting forth the Heinousness of the Fact, the premeditated Intentions, and inhuman Method of acting it Then *Richard Bromage, Robert Wilkins, Leonard Myring, Joseph Mercer, John Blakesly, Mary Springate* and *Richard Bows* were called into Court, the Substance of whose Evidence was, that the Prisoner being interrogated about the Murther, when in *Newgate,* said, The Devil put it into her Head; but however, John Hayes *was none of the best of Husbands, for she had been half starved ever since she was married to him, that she did not in the least repent of any Thing she had done, but only disowning those two poor Men into this Misfortune, that she was six Weeks importuning them to do it, that they denied it two or three Times, but at last agreed, that she was in the Fore Room on the same Floor when he was killed, that when he was quite dead, she went in and held the Candle whilst Wood cut his Head off, that it would signify nothing to make a long Preamble, she could hold up her Hand, and say she was guilty, for nothing could save her, no body could forgive her; that the first Occasion of this Design to murther him was, because he came home one Night and beat her, upon which Billings said, this Fellow deserves to be killed, and Wood, said he'd be his Butcher for a Penny* Many other Circumstances equally with these appeared, and a Cloud of Witnesses, many of whom, the Thing appearing so plain, were sent away unexamined She herself confessed at the Bar, her previous Knowledge of their Intent, yet foolishly insisted on her Innocence, because the Fact was not committed by her own Hands The Jury without staying long to consider on it, found her Guilty, and she was taken from the Bar in a very weak and faint Condition On her Return to *Newgate,* she was visited by several Persons of her Acquaintance, who where so far from doing her any Good, that they in the interrupted her in those Preparations which became her One old Gentleman indeed, who seemed to have no other Motive in coming to see her, took an Opportunity of discoursing to her in a suitable and very rational Manner. This Discourse was taken down, but is too long to insert

When they were brought up to receive Sentence, *Wood* and *Billings* renewed their former Request to the Court, that they might not be hung in Chains Mrs *Hayes* also made Use of her former Assertion, that she was not guilty of actually committing the Fact, and therefore begged of the Court, that she might at least have so much Mercy shewn her, as not to be burnt alive The Judges then sentenced the two men, with the other Malefactors to be hanged, and Mrs *Hayes,* as in all Cases of Petit Treason, to die by Fire at a Stake, at which the screamed, and being carried back to *Newgate,* fell into violent Agonies Perhaps no Body ever kept their Thoughts so long and so closely united in the World, as appeared by the frequent Messages she sent to *Wood* and *Billings,* and that Tenderness which she expressed for both of them, lamenting in the softest Terms, her having involved those two poor Men to the Commission of a Fact, for which they were

now

no v to lose their Lives. In which indeed, they deserved Pity, since they were Persons of unblemished Characters until misled by her

As to the Sense she had of her own Circumstances, there has been scarce any in her State known to behave with so much indifference. She said often, that Death was neither grievous nor terrible to her in itself, but was in some Degrees shocking from the Manner in which she was to die. Her fondness for *Billings* hurried her into Indecencies of a very extraordinary Nature, such as sitting with her Hand in his at Chapel, leaning upon his Shoulder, and refusing upon being reprimanded, to make any Amendment in Respect of those shocking Passages, between her and the Murderers of her Husband. One of her last Expressions was to enquire of the *Executioner*, whether he had hang'd her dear Child, and this, as she was going from the Sledge to the Stake, so strong and lasting were the Passions of this Woman

The *Friday* Night before her Execution, being assured she should die on the *Monday* following) she had procured a Bottle of strong Poison, designing to have taken the same; but a Woman who was in the Place with her touching it with her Lipes found it burnt them to an extraordinary Degree, and spilling a little on her Handkerchief, perceived it burnt that also, upon which suspecting her Intention, she broke the Viol. On the Day of her Execution she was at Prayers, and received the Sacrament in the Chapel, where she still shewed her Tenderness for *Billings*. About Twelve the Prisoners were severally carried to Execution. *Billings* with eight others for various Crimes were put into three Carts, and *Catherine Hayes* was drawn upon a Sledge. *Billings* with eight others, after having had some Time for their private Devotions, were turned off. After which, *Catherine Hayes* being brought to the Stake, was chained thereto with an iron Chain, running round her Waist, and under her Arms, and a Rope about her Neck, which was drawn thro' a Hole in the Post, then the Faggots, intermixed with light Brush, Wood, and Straw, being piled all round her, the Executioner put Fire thereto in several Places, which immediately blazing out, as soon as it reached her, with her Arms she pushed down those that were before her, when she appeared in the Middle of the Flames as low as her Waist.

The Executioner got hold of the End of the Cord which was round her Neck, and pulled it tight, in order to strangle her, but the Fire soon reach his Hand and burnt it, so that he was obliged to let go again. More Faggots were immediately thrown up on her, and in about three or four Hours she was reduced to Ashes. In the mean time *Billings*'s Irons were put upon him as he was hanging on the Gallows, after which being cut down, he was carried to the *Gibbet*, about one hundred Yards Distance, and there hung up in Chains.

Mrs *Hayes* some time before her Execution, confidently averred, that *Billings* was the Son both of Mr *Hayes* and herself, that his Father not liking him, he was put out to Relations of hers, and took the Name of *Billings* from his God father. But Mr. *Hayes*'s Relations confidently deny'd all this, and he himself said he knew nothing more, than that he called a Shoemaker, Father, in the Country, himself being put Apprentice to a Taylor, with whom he served his Time, and then came up to *London* to Work Journey-work.

Th

The LIFE of Mr. ROBERT FOULKES.

THIS 'unhappy Gentleman was a Divine of the Church of *England*, and had been very much efteem'd for his Learning, and Abilities Few Men were more capable of fhining in a Church, or had a greater Share of that facred Eloquence, fo requifite in a Preacher He was Minifter of *Stanton-Lacy* in the County of *Salop*, where he was exceedingly follow'd and admir'd till his Crimes came to be known, and where he might have been belov'd till Death in a natural Way had taken him hence, and then univerfally lamented, if his Heart had been as well furnifh'd with Grace, as his Head was with Knowledge, and his Tongue with Expreffions

A young Gentlewoman of a confiderable Fortune, who had been left an Infant by her Parents, was committed to his Care by her Executors, as to a Man who they trufted, would not only deal juftly by her, but alfo inftruct her betimes in the Principles of Religion, and her feveral Duties as a Chriftian But, alas! how weak is human Nature, and how foon are we temp'ed afide from the Ways of Piety! Mr *Foulkes*, inftead of anfwering the Purpofe of the young Woman's Friends, was foon fmitten with her Charms, and took an Opportunity of difcovering a criminal Paffion for her, tho' he had at that Time a virtuous Wife and two Children living The young Lady too eafily confented to gratify his Luft, and they continued their Converfation together till fhe became pregnant

All the Means he could think of to procure Abortion were now try'd, and they all prov'd ineffectual, fo that they muft be both expos'd to Scandal, unlefs fhe could be remov'd to fome convenient Place, remote from the Eyes of the World, and from the Jealoufies of Mrs *Foulkes*, where fhe might be deliver'd of her Burden, which was not yet perceiv'd. A plaufible Excufe for his going up to *London* was foon form'd, and for his taking Mifs along with him, who at that Time was under twenty Years of Age When they were arriv'd in Town, they took a Lodging in *York-Buildings* in the *Strand*, where fhe lay in, and where (fhocking to think of!) the Child was privately murder'd, to prevent the Infamy that might follow.

But divine Vengeance would not fuffer this horrible Deed to remain long conceal'd, for before Mr *Foulkes* went out of Town, the Girl was examin'd upon the Sufpicion of fome Women, when fhe confefs'd the whole, and charged Mr *Foulkes* with the Murder, who was thereupon apprehended and committed to *Newgate*, in a fhort Time after which he was condemn'd at the Seffions Houfe in the *Old-Bailey*, upon the Evidence of the young Woman On the thirty firft of *January*, 1678-79, he was executed at *Tyburn*, when he made the following Speech to the Spectators

Good Chriftian People,

' I Intend not to make any long Difcourfe at
' this Time, and I hope no Body will expect
' it of me! What I have to fay more particular-
' ly is exprefs'd in a Paper which I have fent to the
' Reverend Dr *Lloyd*, Dean of *Bangor*, and which
' I have defir'd him to publifh As I fhall by and
' by anfwer to the God of Truth, there is no-
' thing but the Truth therein contain'd, and my
' Cafe is fet in a better Light than I could poffibly
' have fhewn it in here

' In a few Words therefore,

' You may fee in me what Sin is, and what it
' will end in You may fee in me the lamenta-
' ble and irreparable Mifchiefs of Uncleannefs and
' Hypocrify, and in particular, what it is for one
' who was a Member of Chrift, to make himfelf
' the Member of an Harlot It is a Sin that fel-
' dom goes fingly and alone It is the Mother-
' Sin to a great many more, and they more ugly
' and deformed than itfelf I have found fo by fa-
' tal Experience It led me to Lying, Oaths, and
' Execrations, to conceal and defend it Nay, I
' went further, to advife, contrive, and affift in,
' what might procure Abortion, which certainly,
' in the Sight of God, was Murder in Intention.
' Nor ftopp'd I there, but went forward to Murder
' in Act and Execution, for which crying Sin I am
' come hither to fatisfy the Laws of the King-
' dom, and I acknowledge the Juftice of my Sen-
' tence And Oh! that you may fear and tremble
' at God's holy and righteous Judgments, which
' have now overtaken me, and that, from my Ex-
' ample, you may be warned to avoid the Snares
' of a whorifh Woman, and keep the Marriage-
' Bed undefil'd

' Beware of hypocrital Pretences to Religion, and
' of coming to the holy Sacrament while you live
' in any filthy Practices Do not grieve nor quench
' the good Spirit of God, nor ftifle the Convic-
' tions of your own Confciences, left God fhould
' leave you, as he did me, to work all Uncleannefs
' with Greedinefs, and left at laft ye be brought
' to this moft miferable Condition into which he has
' fuffer'd me to fall His Judgment is righteous,
' and I humbly fubmit to it! I forgive all the World
' as I defire to find Mercy at the Hands of God
' through Jefus Chrift Be intreated to take Warn-
' ing by me not to continue in Sin, for (let me
' repeat it) Juftice will find you out

' With refpect to my Crimes, I have but two
' Things to fay, with which I fhall conclude

' Firft, That I have Caufe to lament exceeding-
' ly for the great Scandal I have thereby brought
' upon Religion, and the facred Function of the
' Miniftry This I look upon to be the moft hei nous
' and aggravating Circumftance of my wicked and
' licentious Life, which by this laft Sin will be ill
' laid open to the World Let me beg of you there-
                                                     ' fore,

‘ fore, not to entertain any Prejudices against the
‘ Ambaſſadors of the Goſpel upon my Account,
‘ they are generally holy and good Men, and they
‘ grant no Licence at all to ſuch ungodly Practices
‘ as I have been guilty of This I am obliged to
‘ ſay in Juſtice to their Order

‘ In the ſecond Place I muſt expreſs my Joy that
‘ I hope my Sins, however great and numerous, are
‘ all pardon’d by God, and atton’d for by the Me-
‘ rits of Jeſus Chriſt ’Tis true, the Crime I die
‘ for has expos’d the whole Nation to judgment,
‘ for thro’ *Blood the Land is defil’d* But as I ſuf-
‘ fer the Sentence of God and Man, the Judgment
‘ falls upon my own Head, and I hope, through
‘ divine Mercy, it will proceed no farther than my
‘ Body All I have to add, is, Be admoniſh’d by
‘ me, *to ceaſe to do Evil, and learn to do well*

*Now the Lord have Mercy upon my poor depart-
ing Soul ! In this Petition I deſire you to join with
me, and pray for me to the laſt Moment of my
Life.*

*A genuine Copy of the Paper ſent by Mr Foulkes
to the Reverend Dr* Lloyd, *and mention’d by him
in the foregoing Speech.*

SIR,

I Send the following Account to you, as to my
once very good Friend, though now, alas ! no
good Man can be fond of that Appellation from
me I deſire you would publiſh it, that thoſe who
are Spectators of my End might not be diſappointed
in what they expected to hear from me, and that
my Example may be tranſmitted to Poſterity, as a
Terror to the Workers of Iniquity

Such have my Irregularities always been, that I
have long ago deſerv’d to ſmart under the Severity of God’s Reproof, but theſe Things were hitherto conceal’d Now the Hand of Juſtice has
found me out, and I am to become a publick Spectacle of Shame and Reproach I have no Intereſt
therefore any longer in hiding my Iniquities from
the World. No, I will confeſs them to Mankind,
that they may be warn’d and inſtructed, and that
God may be vindicated in my Puniſhment

My Birth and Education was not amongſt them
that are Aliens from the Commonwealth of *Iſrael,*
and Strangers to the Covenant of Promiſe ; but within the Pale of the Church of *England,* a Church
not ſupported by Error and Superſtition, a Church
ſo refin’d and reform’d, that it is become the pu-
reſt upon Earth Nor was this all neither, for
God, by the outward Miniſtration of his Word, and
the inward Operation of his holy Spirit, ſo wrought
upon my Heart, that for ſome Time his Fear was
before my Eyes I ſerv’d him in ſecret, and ſtudy’d
to glorify him in my whole Life and Converſation

In this Path I walk’d when I was dedicated more
immediately to the Service of my Creator, by the
Impoſition of Epiſcopal Hands. God had alſo bleſſed with competent Abilities for the Diſcharge of
that Office, ſo that had I proſecuted my Studies
with the ſame Diligence and Induſtry as I did my
Follies, I might not only have been a learned and
judicious Man myſelf, but an uſeful Inſtrument in
the Hand of God for enlightening the Underſtand-
ings of others Providence alſo ſupply’d me with
the Favour of a noble and honourable Patron, thro’
whoſe Means I was ſettled very comfortably as to
the Concerns of human Life My Portion was ſo
far from being ſcanty, that I had enough and to
ſpare I was belev’d by my Pariſhioners, and re-

ſpected by my Neighbours The ſame bountiful
Providence bleſs’d me with as worthy Relations,
a very faithful and affectionate Wife, tender of my
Perſon, careful and induſtrious about my Affairs
One, in ſhort, that had as good a Right as any Wo-
man to *Solomon’s* Character in the laſt Chapter of
Proverbs ; one that bleſſed me with four ſweet Chil-
dren, and was to me *as a fruitful Vine*

In a Word, to God’s Glory and my own Shame
I confeſs, that the Hand of Heaven had been exceeding liberal to me upon all Accounts, and that I
had no Reaſon to murmur, as if my Heritage had
been ſparing, either in ſpiritual or temporal Things

And now I come to the laſt and worſt Part of my
melancholly Story That Tenderneſs that was on
my Conſcience was not long liv’d My Corruptions,
with the Devil’s Temptations, ſoon overcame it
Then I forfeited my Baptiſmal Vows, and my Ordination Engagements, then I renounc’d the Faith
of Wedlock, and *had my Eyes full of Adultery that
could not ceaſe from Sin* The Devil had prepar’d
for me a fatal Companion and Partner in my Debaucheries, one who was eaſily tempted by me, and
was afterwards a conſtant Temptation to me, till ſhe
prov’d the great Occaſion of this diſmal Concluſion
of my wretched Courſe of Life Open your Eyes,
therefore, O Adulterers and Adultereſſes ! contem-
plate this woful and tragick Inſtance, be not en-
ſnared with a Whore’s Charms, truſt not to her
Kindneſs, tho’ confirm’d with Oaths, Execrations,
and Tears They lead on to all manner of
Sin, they will waſte your Eſtate, divide your Family, ruin your Health, deſtroy your Soul, and, if
ever you need her Friendſhip, ſhe will moſt perfidi-
ouſly betray you

I thought my Sin well ſecured under the Protection of ſeeming Religion, and vainly fancy’d it was
done in ſecret, and that it ſhould never be brought
to Light but I was deceiv’d a Suſpicion of my
Guilt was whiſper’d about, and came to the Ears of
my Right Reverend Diocefan, the Lord Biſhop of
Hereford, who reprov’d and admoniſh’d me for it
This made me more conſtant and poſitive in my De-
nials, which I confirmed in the moſt ſolemn Manner I could, uſing ſuch Expreſſions for my Purga-
tion as I trembled to think of, when I conſider how
juſtly I was accus’d As for my Neighbours, I
threaten’d ſuch of them with Proſecutions as ſhould
defame my Character, and was mighty exact with
them upon Points of Law, which I thought would
have borne me out But all this while I was a very
Slave to my Luſt, though I briſkly receiv’d the Af-
ſaults of all my Accuſers, and promiſ’d my ſelf as
compleat a Victory over them as I had obtain’d over
my own Conſcience, whoſe Warnings I had almoſt
perfectly ſtifled

“ I was now arriv’d at the very Height of Impiety,
to which I had aſcended by a long Courſe of A-
dulteries, Falſhoods, and Hypocriſy When there
was no other Way of hiding my Shame, from my
injur’d dear Wife, and from all the World, I found
my Conſcience ſo ſear’d, and ſo paſt feeling, that
I was not afraid to commit the horrid Murder for
which the Law has ſo juſtly adjudg’d me to die
A Crime that not only bids Defiance to God and all
Religion, but to the very Dictates and Principles of
Nature and Humanity ! To deſtroy an innocent
Babe had Cruelty enough in the Act itſelf, but to
offer Violence to the Fruit of one’s own Body was a
great Aggravation of the Crime, and makes it, in
Truth, a monſtrous Piece of Barbarity God grant
my Repentance may bear ſome Proportion to my
Sin, and be acceptable to him whom I have offend-
ed !

Now

Now I have made this full Confeſſion, be pleas'd, Sir, to hear my ſhort Apology againſt the ſeveral Calumnies, which my Partner in Guilt, though not in Condemnation, has been pleas'd to load me with

Firſt, It was alledg'd, that ſhe was committed to my Charge and Government by her Father, in her Minority, which has been thought a great heightening of my Sin To this I declare, that her Father was a Gentleman I never ſaw, or had the leſt intercourſe with, ſhe being put into my Hands only as a Boarder by her Guardians

Secondly, It was ſaid, that I attempted to vitiate her at nine Years of Age, and bad for that Purpoſe corrupted her Judgment, by informing her that Polygamy was lawful This I alſo declare to be a Falſhood, and proteſt that I never proſtitut ed the ſacred Word of God to ſerve the Turn of any Luſt, nor ever had ſuch a Thought in my Soul

Again, ſhe has ſaid, ſhe knew nothing of the Fact for which we were jointly queſtion'd, and I con demn'd In Anſwer to this I call God to witneſs, that ſhe both ſaw, and acted in, all that was done

I have now done with the World, and have no more Part to act therein; I pray God therefore, who

has ſuffer'd me to be taken out of it in this ignominious Way, that if he has not already open'd my Eyes by this ſevere Courſe of Providence, and alarmed me ſufficiently to repent, he would now be pleaſed to do it, e'ie all will be too late! I thank God for giving me Time conſiderable, and great Aſſiſtances, to turn to him withal! I might have been ſurpriz'd with ſome ſudden Death, and infallibly ſent into Hell headlong, from which I have now ſome Hope to be preſerv'd, thro' the Mercy of God, and the Merits of my Bleſſed Saviour and Redeemer, to whom be Glory for ever

The preceding Speech and Paper, though ſomewhat long, were thought proper to be inſerted, as they give more Light into the Caſe than any other Help we could obtain 'Tis difficult to account for the ſevere Reflections he has thrown on the young Lady, who could hardly be more than Second in the Crime at worſt, and doubtleſs the Influence of ſuch a Man wrought much on her in all their criminal Acquaintance We can ſay no more at this Diſtance of Time than that we hope he obtain'd the Mercy he ſeem d ſo confident of

---

The LIFE of Colonel JAMES TURNER.

THIS Gentleman was born in the City of *Worceſter*, in the Year 1609, of very wealthy Parents, who plac'd him with a Goldſmith of Reputation in *London*, as ſoon as of Years for a Trade With this Man he ſerv'd his Apprenticeſhip very faithfully, and had the Character of being a young Man well qualify'd for Buſineſs When his Father thought proper to put him into Trade for himſelf, he gave him a Stock of no leſs than Three Thouſand Pounds, to which he ſoon added Two Thouſand Pounds more by Marriage He had great Succeſs in Buſineſs for ſome Years, and was eſteem'd the wealthieſt Man in his Neighbourhood, ſo that his Word would have paſs'd for almoſt any Sum

Mr *Turner* had always a conſiderable Inclination for Pleaſure and Company, taking peculiar Delight in aſſociating himſelf with the Gentlemen who were Officers of the City Militia Among theſe he was complimented with a Captain's Commiſſion, then a Major's, then a Lieutenant Colonel's, and at laſt with the Command of one of the Regiments, in which he continu'd till the unhappy Action that brought him to his End was diſcover'd, to the Surprize of all the World

The Colonel's Temper was very generous and noble, which, 'tis thought, in ſome meaſure, brought on him that Decay of his Fortune which he afterwards labour'd under In his Poſt, particularly, whenever he march'd out with his Regiment, he was very liberal in his Entertainments, and com monly run himſelf to four times the Expence that was neceſſary 'Twas the ſame on every other Occaſion, no Man was more free with his Money, or more ambitious of living in Splendor and Repu tation, than Colonel *Turner*

This Diſpoſition had with him the ſame Effect as it commonly has with others who ruin themſelves by their Generoſity He had no Notion of retrenching his Expences when he perceiv'd his Subſtance waſte, but was reſolv'd to ſupport himſelf with the ſame Pomp as uſual, however he came by the Money 'Twas eaſy for ſuch a Man to commit a great many little ſecret Actions, that were in themſelves diſhonourable, before he loſt his Character, on Account of his great Buſineſs Several of theſe Things diſcover'd themſelves after he was convicted, which even the Perſons that were wrong'd did not ſuſpect before One Inſtance in particular will be well worth relating, and was as follows

He apply'd himſelf one Day to a Merchant, and bought of him as much Train Oil and Rice, as came to Three hundred and ſixty Pounds, which he promis'd to pay for as ſoon as the Goods were deliver'd Accordingly the Day after he went to the Merchant's Houſe, and give him the full Sum in Money and Notes, for which the Merchant wrote a Receipt, while it all lay on the Deſk Two of *Turner's* Accomplices (for he made uſe of Aſſiſtants) came juſt at this Time, and pretended ſome urgent Buſineſs with the Merchant, and, in ſhort, play'd their Part ſo well, that one of them got off with the greateſt Part of *Turner's* Payment, while the other kept the innocent Man in Diſcourſe Neither of them took any more Notice of the Colonel than if they had not known him, nor did the Merchant imagine he had any Concern in the Matter till he was found guilty of another Crime, of which take this ſhort Account

There was one Mr *Francis Tryon*, a great Merchant, who liv'd in *Lime ſtreet*, whom Colonel *Turner* knew to be very rich In order to rob this Man, one of the abovemention'd Fellows convey'd himself into his Cellar in the Dusk of the Evening, and as soon as Mr *Tryon* was abed, and as he thought asleep, he let the Colonel in at the Door They went up together to his Bed-Chamber, bound him, gagg'd him, and us'd him in a very barbarous manner, and then going into his Warehouse, they took from thence, a large Quantity of Diamonds, Saphires, Rubies, *&c* which *Turner* knew where to find Then they took all the Money in the House, which amounted to a vast large Sum, so that the whole Booty was reputed to be the Value of Five Thousand nine hundred and forty six Pounds, four Shillings, and three Pence They made off with all this quietly Mr *Tryon* had a Man and a Maid-Servant, but they both lay abroad this Night by Permission, of which the Colonel had before receiv'd Information

Strict Enquiry was made after the Thieves, and all such Jewels as were remarkable were particularly describ'd, while *Turner* thought himself secure in his Character, which had so long screen'd him But some of the Things describ'd were seen in his House, and the Discoverers were resolv'd to examine further Whereupon the Colonel, his Wife, and his three Sons, *John, William,* and *Ely,* were apprehended, and upon Search almost all the Jewels were found There was now no Room for Evasion, the whole Family was carry'd before Sir *Thomas Allen,* Knight and Alderman, and all committed to *Newgate*

At the next Sessions they were all indicted for the said Robbery, but after a full Examination of what Evidence they had, and considering what the Colonel himself said in his Defence, 'twas thought proper by the Court to acquit the Wife and Sons, and to bring the Colonel in *guilty*, whereupon the usual Sentence of *Death* was pass'd on him, and executed on the Twenty first of *January*, 1662 63, when he was drawn in a Cart from *Newgate* to the End of *Lime street* in *Leadenhall street*, and there hang'd on a Gibbet erected for that Purpose, being 53 Years old

The Colonel left a Paper behind him full of Expressions of Piety and Contrition, too long to be inserted here We would only observe, that tho' all who knew him, wonder'd at the Fact, yet every one believ'd him *guilty*, because the Proof, were so clear

There was a Robbery in his Life-time, which no Body could then find out, but after his Death 'twas generally thought he was the Manager A Letter was sent to a wealthy Dealer at *Chichester,* sign'd with the Name of a Merchant his Acquaintance in *London,* informing him of a profitable Purchase in his Way, and inviting him to Town The *Chichester* Man had before receiv'd Advices of this Kind from the same Friend, and found them of Service, therefore scrupled not, but set out the next Day with what Money and Notes he had in the House; but before he got half Way to *London,* he was robb'd of all by two Men in Disguise. He soon found his Correspondent had not sent to him, and was astonish'd However, Colonel *Turner*'s Death clear'd all, he knowing both their Circumstances.

The

The LIFE *of* HARMAN STRODTMAN.

THE *following Account was taken in Writing from the Criminal's own Mouth, the Day before he was executed at Tyburn, which was on Wednesday the 18th Day of June, 1701 The Relation seems to be made with so much Sincerity, that we thought it best to use his own Words, in which he has express'd his Case, and given us a Sketch of his Life, as briefly, and yet as fully as can be expected*

In the Year 1683, or a little before, I was born at *Revel* in *Liefland*, and had the Happiness to come of a good Family; my Parents being Persons of some Account in the World, and also godly and religious People, who took great Care of my Education

About the Year 1694, my Father sent me to School to *Lubeck*, where I continued till *Michaelmas*, 1698 From thence I went to *Hamburgh*, and stay'd there till I set out for *England* I arriv'd at *London* the 18th Day of *March* following, together with one *Peter Wolter*, who came with me from my native Place We were both bound Apprentice to Mr *Stein* and Mr *Dorten*, Merchants and Partners in *London*

Peter Wolter and myself having been Fellow-Travellers, and being now Fellow-Prentices, we liv'd for some time very friendly and lovingly together, till about *August* last, when his Sister was married to Mr *Dorten*, one of our Masters Then he began to be so proud, and so very domineering over me, and abusive to me, that I could not bear it We had several Fallings-out, and he did twice beat me, once before the Maids of the House in the Kitchen, and at another Time in the Compting House, and did, besides that, often complain and tell Tales of me to my Masters, thereby raising their Displeasure against me, and creating me their Ill-will, so that they kept me close at home, and would not give me the same Liberty which my Fellow-Apprentice, and myself before, had, of going abroad sometimes for Recreation Upon this Account I conceiv'd an implacable Hatred against him, and the Devil put it into my Heart to be reveng'd on him at any rate

First I design'd to do it by Poison, having to that purpose mixt some *Mercury* with a certain white Powder, which he had always in a Glass in the Chamber, and of which he us'd to take a Dose very often, for the Scurvy But it being then Winter time (I think the latter End of *December*, or Beginning of *January*) I found he had left off taking his Powder, and so I might wait long enough before I could see the Effects of my Poison, if I stay'd till the Time he was to take that Powder again Therefore I thought of another Way to dispatch him, and that was by stabbing him

On *Good-Friday* Morning, my Masters sending me on an Errand, I took from thence Opportunity to go to *Greenwich*, from whence not returning till the *Thursday* following, my Masters were so very angry with me, that they bid me be gone Upon this I went away, and took Lodgings in *Moor-fields* And

two Days after I took other Lodgings at the Sign of the *Sun*, in Ale-house in *Queen-street*, in *London*

Now I had a Key of the Fore Door of my Master's House, which I got made for me a long time before *Christmas*, by that which was my Master's, and this was for my private Use, that I might, unknown to my Masters, go in and out at any time when I had a Mind to it, but at last the Devil taught me another Use of this Key, for by the Help of it I came to my Master's House on *Saturday*, about half an Hour past eight at Night, and being got in, I went up two Pair of Stairs, and having got into an empty Room, adjoining to *Peter Wolter*'s Chamber, I shut myself in there, and some time after fell asleep

About twelve o'Clock being awake, after I had been some time hearkening, perceiving all was very quiet in the House, I went down to a Room one Pair of Stairs, where a Tinder Box lay, and having lighted a Candle, enter'd the Compting House, and there took out several Notes and Bills, and some Money too Then I went up again two Pair of stairs carrying with me a certain Piece of Wood, wherewith they us'd to beat Tobacco, which I found in my Chamber When I was got up Stairs, I sprang into *Peter Wolter*'s Room, and coming to his Bed-side, open'd the Curtains, and with my Tobacco beater knock'd him on the Head, giving him four or five Blows on the left Side of it, and another on the right Thus it was that I most barbarously murder'd this poor Creature, whom I intended, had this fail'd, to have shot to Death, having brought with me two Pistols, ready charged, for that wicked Purpose

When I perceiv'd *Peter Wolter* was quite dead, I proceeded to search his Breeches, and Chest of Drawers, and took a Note of Twenty Pounds, with some Money, out of his Pocket, which Money, with that I had taken in the Compting House, amounted to eight or nine Pounds Then I pick'd up some of his Linnen and Woollen Cloaths, and having made a Bundle of them, went down with it one Pair of Stairs, and out of a Window there threw it into the next House, where no body dwelt Then I went up Stairs again, and having cut my Candle in two, both Pieces being lighted, I set one in the Chest of Drawers, and the other on a Chair, close by the Bed Curtains, intending to have burnt the House, in order to conceal by this heinous Fact, the other two of Theft and Murder, which, thro' the Instigation of the Devil, I had now most barbarously committed Then I went thro' a Window, out of the House, into that where I had flung the Bundle, and staying there till about five in the Morning, went away with the Bundle, and what else I had taken, to my Lodgings in *Queen-street*, where I put on clean Cloaths, and then went to the *Swedes* Church in *Trinity Lane*

The next Day, being the second *Monday* after *Easter*, I went to a Goldsmith, one that I knew, in *Lombard-street*, where I found Mr *Stein*, with another

another Gentleman My Master ask'd me, whether I would go willingly to his House, or be carried thither by two Porters I said I would go So, after some Questions about the horrid Facts I had committed at his House, and my denying of them, I was search'd, and the Bill of twenty Pounds, which was in the Deceased's Pocket, was found upon me

Then my Master asking me where I lay, I told him in *Moor Fields*, so we went thither, and came to my former Lodging, but the People of the House took him, I did not lie there now By this my Master finding that I was unwilling to let him know where I had lain, or how I had dispos'd of the Things which I had stoll'n out of his House, he promis'd me, that if I would confess, no harm should come to me, for he would take care to send me presently beyond Seas Upon this I freely told him the Truth, where I lay, and where those Goods of his were, as we were walking together So he presently took Coach, and carried me first to my Lodgings in *Queen-street*, where he received the Bills, Clothes, Money and all that I had thus stolen, and then he carried me to Sir *Humphry Edwin*; who upon his Examination of me, and my own Confession of all these

Facts, did most justly commit me to *Newgate*, where I must leave it to others to relate how I behaved myself during my Confinement.

I have freely given this true and impartial Account of myself, and my sinful Actions, to the World, that all Men, both young and old, might take warning by me, who once little thought I should ever be capable of committing such foul and enormous Crimes And now I am going to leave this World for ever, before I have lived long enough in it (as being but about eighteen Years of Age) to know either it or myself But I thank the divine Grace, that has open'd my Eyes, and set me in a clearer Light, by which I am come within Sight and Apprehension of better Things Let me therefore, for once and ever, advise all Men to be warn'd by my Fall, and take great care to their Ways, that they do not stumble upon the Snares of *Satan*, as I have done, for perhaps all may not have the same divine Mercy and Help given them for their Recovery, as I have had, for which I love and praise my great Maker and Redeemer, and will adore him to all Eternity

---

The LIFE *of* JACK COLLET,
alias COLE

THIS unfortunate Person was the Son of a Grocer in the Borough of *Southwark*, where he was born, and from whence at fifteen Years of Age he was put out Apprentice to an Upholsterer in *Cheapside* He did not serve above four Years of his Time before he ran away from his Master, and took to the Highway We have not an Account of abundance of his Robberies, tho' 'tis said he committed a great many, but there is this remarkable Particular recorded of him, That he frequently robb'd in the Habit of a Bishop, with fore or five of his Companions at his Heels in the Quality of Servants, who were ready to assist him on Occasion Some, who love to make themselves merry with the Reverend and the Right Reverend the Clergy, would be apt to insinuate, that 'tis no very uncommon Thing to see a Thief in the Habit of a Clergyman. For our Parts, we are so far from making any such prophane Observation, that we think the sacred Order give daily Proofs, that *England* has but very few Wolves in Sheep's Cloathing Give us Leave to add however, concerning our Adventurer, that he generally got much larger Booties on the Road than most of our Lay Highwaymen

Collet had once the ill Fortune to lose his Canonical Habit at Dice, so that he was forced to take a Turn or two on the Road to supply his present Necessities, in unsanctify'd Garments But it was not long before he met with a good Opportunity of taking Orders again, and becoming as holy as ever Riding from *London* down into *Surrey*, a little on this

Side *Farnham*, he met with Dr *Mew*, Bishop of *Winchester*, and commanded his Coachman to stop The Bishop was not at all surpriz'd at being ask'd for his Money, because when he saw his Coach stopp'd he expected that would follow But when *Collet* told him he must have his Robes too, his Lordship thought him a Madman. There was no resisting however, the old Doctor was obliged to strip into his Waistcoat, besides giving him about fifty Guineas; which *Collet* told him he had now a Right to demand, by having the Sacerdotal Habit in his Possession For that, you know, Doctor, quoth he, *is a Proof of my indelible Character, and the Property I have in the Revenues of the Church, and as good a Proof, I believe, as many Others can shew, who have just as much Learning and Honesty as I have, and yet are acknowledg'd to be good Clergymen, and some of the Receivers General of Heaven*

Collet follow'd this Trade till he was about thirty two Years of Age, and, as if he had been determin'd to live by the Church, he was at last apprehended for Sacrilege and Burglary, in breaking open the Vestry of *Great St. Bartholomew's* in *London*, in Company with one *Christopher Assley, alias Brown*, and stealing from thence the Pulpit Cloth, and all the Communion-Plate For this Fact he receiv'd Sentence of *Death*, and was executed at *Tyburn*, on *Friday* the fifth of *July*, in the Year 1691 This *Brown* and *Collet* had before robb'd *St. Saviour's* Church in *Southwark* in Conjunction

The

The LIFE of JOCELIN HARWOOD.

EVERY Day's Experience may serve to confirm the old English Proverb, *That a good Father may have a bad Son.* Virtue is not convey'd .... ls of Nature, and two Men may be of ...... me Blood, yet ve different in respect of their Actions. It must be allow'd indeed, that the Son ..... virtuous Father if he falls into Exceffes, com..... much greater Crime then one who has never ..... the Advantage of good Instruction, and, what is ..... more powerful, good Example But this is only ..... Reflexion, and doe not at all involve te ..... we have said, the truth of which is proved ..... observation

Jocelin Harwood was a degenerated Plant from a ...... His Father was once moderately rich ...... undoubted Reputation And the greatest Misfortune of his Life was the having a Child so unworthy of him. Jocelin was born in the Year 16.. at Wateringbury in Kent, where he was edu-ced with all the Caution neceffary in such Cases ...... that he not set him to neglect the Care that was taken of him but rendered himself deferving of it by his Improvement, promising a much better Method then afterwards afforded But no body ..... account for their Changes

When he grew toward feventeen Years of Age, he ran away from his Father, carrying off with him .... Pound Children often begin the Pri-..... Thieving upon their Parents, becaus the ...... there learn Life to them, or at least, becaue they hope, if they are detected, to meet with more Mercy than from other Hands But this is only an Artifice of the great Deceiver of Mankind, who knows the Temper of our Souls too well, and in what Manner to lead us on from Step to Step till we arrive at the very Height of Iniquity

Thus Harwood, when he had wasted what he took from his Father in Luxury and Wantonnefs, made no Scruple of getting more in the fame difhonest Way Being now in London alfo, he had every Diffair.... get that a young Man can have, who has given Way a little to the Allurements of Vice His Money brought him into bad Company, and then the bad Company perfuaded him to feek for more Money He fubmitted at first only to pilfering and picking of Pockets, which he followed for about the Years, and then he refolved to move in a nigher Sphere, make a greater Bize in the World for a Time and receive his Fate, when it came, with more Honour

The ill Success of his first Adventure on the High-way was enough to have reform'd him had he had any ..... from ever attempting the like again He had .... Bridle, Saddle, Holfters, and Piftol ..... when he fet out on Black Heath, and was fo .... two Men at once to stand and ...... the Gentleman engaged him, for his new .... the Encounter had not difabled them

from exciting themfelves Harwood was terribly frightened at the Bravery of his Antagonifts, and was glad he could get off without a Horfe

The next Night he broke open a Stable at Dartford in Kent, and remounted himfelf, though but indifferently He had not been many Hours upon the Road before he overtook one Mr Payne, a Lifeguard man, with whom he fell into Difcourfe upon the Goodnefs of their two Horfes Mr Payne laugh'd at Harwood for mentioning fuch a defpicable Beaft as the other Pray, fays Harwood, what may be the extraordinary Qualities of your Horfe, that you boaft of him fo? I confefs he has a better Appearance then mine, but I will undertake to leap with you for what you dare, or travel a Day's Journey

The Lifeguard man could not help admiring what Harwood faid, though he did not believe but 'twas all Lies He would not however tell him fo, but thought to convince him genteely of his Miftake the first Opportunity that offer'd They came at laft to a Gate, that led into a Bye Road, but was always faft except on particular Occafions Harwood knew whither 'twould carry him, though the other did not When Mr Payne faw this Gate, he immediately gave his Horfe a Kick, and over he went, coming back again with the like Air of Surprife me, Sir faid Harwood I could never have believed fuch a Thing if I had not feen it but pray would you Horfe do the fame with another Perfon on his Back? Certainly, fays the other, you pull try him if you pleafe Harwood feemed tired of being thrown off, however he accepted the Offer for the Sake of faying he had rid fuch a Horfe

In a Word, Harwood got upon the Lifeguard-man's Horfe, and leap'd the Gate, with as much Eafe as it had been done juft before And now pray Sir, fays he, at what do you value this fine Beaft? At forty Guineas, faid Payne Well, I confefs you are very reafonable, faid Jocelin, but I have not fo much about me However the fift time I fee you after your Horfe has earned fo much, you fhall have the Money And fo away he rode, the Soldier being able to purfue him only with his Eyes and his Oaths

Jocelin continued to rob on the Highway for about two or three Years, during which Time he lived in all manner of Excefs, pafhng from County to County as it fuited either with his Pleafure or his Safety If he had been any thing frugal, he might in this Time have amaffed a prodigious Sum of Money, but he was too much of a Gentleman not to fpend all as faft as he could after he had got it booty

The laft and worft Action of his Life was commit-ted at the Houfe of Sir Henrich Borroughs in Shrop-fhire, where he was informed of an imminent Trea-fure, in Plate and Money In Company with two more, he went one Night, and broke open this Houfe, gagging and binding all the Servants as faft as they could get into their Chambers When the reft of the Family was fecure, he went to the Knight, and bound him and his Lady, and then going into his Daughters Room, one of the young Ladies faid to *Harwood, Pray Sir, ufe us cruelly; which if you do, we will ufe you in the fame Manner, in Cafe you and your Companions fhould be taken, for I am fure we fhall know you again. Shall youfo?* faid the inhuman Wretch, *I'll take Care then to prevent your doing any Mifchief* Upon this he cut them both in Pieces with his Hanger, and then running into the old People's Room again, *What,* fays he, *and do you know me too?* They told him *No* *D——n you,* faid he, *you are only a little more artful than the B——s your Daughters, but I fhan't truft you* Then he run them both thorough, and left them wallowing in their Blood, feeming as well fatisfy'd as if he had done a meritorious Deed

His Companions were fo aftonifhed at the Barbarity of this Fellow, that they ftood like Stocks, unable either to prevent him in his bloody Attempts, or to apprehend him for them on the Place, which latter they had moft Mind to But the Horror continued fo ftrong on their Minds, that, tho' they were both old Offenders themfelves, they could not help expofing him to Juftice as foon as they had left the Houfe of this unhappy Family Being on the Road, one of them by Agreement fhot his Horfe, and then they joined to bind him Hand and Foot, and leave him on the Ground, with a Piece of the Knight's Plate by his Side, telling him 'twas but a juft Requital for his Inhumanity

The next Day, an Enquiry being made all over the Country, he was found in the Condition he had been left by his Companions The Excufe he made to thofe who difcover'd him, was, that he had been robb'd himfelf by fome Rogues, who dropp'd that Piece of Plate by him in their Hurry But this Pretence did him little Service; for upon fearching his Pockets they found a great deal of Money there, befides Cords, a dark Lanthorn, Watches, and a Tinder-Box, all which made his Cafe very fufpicious. When he came into the Prefence of the Servants of the Family, they all fwore he was one of the Men who had bound and gagg'd them What made the Proofs yet ftronger was a Letter, which his Companions fent with an exact State of the Affair, and the Manner of their leaving him

Upon all this Evidence he was fent under a ftrong Guard to *Shrewfbury* Jail, where he behaved very audacioufly At his Trial he was even fo impudent as to fpit in the Faces of the Judge and Jury, and talk to them without any Regard to Decency The Matter of Fact being plainly proved againft him, he was condemn'd to be firft hang'd on the Gallows till he was dead, and then to have his Body hang'd in Chains on a Gibbet, for a publick Spectable This Sentence made no Impreffion on him; fo that he continued the fame horrid Courfe of Oaths, Profanenefs, and Blafphemies, till his Death By thefe Methods, and his getting drunk the very Morning he was to die, he fo exafperated every Body againft him, that the common People of the Place would have executed Juftice on him, if the Law had not, the firft Time they could have laid Hold of him When he was at the Gallows, with a fteddy Countenance, he faid, *That he fhould act the fame Murder again, in the fame Cafe* This was all he would fay to any Body 'Tis fhocking to think that fuch a Wretch fhould be but twenty three Years of Age at the Time of his Death, which was in the Year 1692

The LIFE *of* RICHARD WALTON, commonly call'd the CONJUROR.

THIS Criminal was several Years confined to his Bed, notwithstanding which, he was drawn from the same by a Rope, and executed at *Warwick*, on *Friday* the 10th of *August*, 1733 For promoting and encouraging *Humphry Mousall*, *Morris Walker*, and *William Coley*, to commit several Robberies, &c Of which he gives the following Account of himself when under Sentence of Death, and delivered to the Sub-Sheriff at the Place of Execution

I WAS born in the City of *Litchfield* in the County of *Stafford*, the 15th of *November*, 1691, when the Sun was in the Meridian, *i e* Noon I had the Happiness to be born of honest and reputable Parents, by whose Care I was early instructed in the Principles of the Episcopal Religion My Learning was Mean, but I sufficiently instructed in all moral Duties, and in the flower of my Youth was shew'd the unavoidable Punishment that would certainly be inflicted upon those that practised Iniquity, and the blessed Reward for such that did well

When I came to Man's Estate I was Servant three Years to one of those People call'd Quakers, and about one Year of that Time, I usually frequented their Meetings, being hugely betaken with a Book call'd *Barclay's Apology*, but when my Service dropt, my appearing at their Meetings dropt also Yet I cannot say, that I went amongst them to please my Master, or from any hope of Favour from him, for I was much affected with some of their Writings, particularly the Book above mentioned, which without doubt is an excellent Performance, and does certainly point the very Root and Substance of the Gospel Ordinances, and only dissuades from empty Shadows, which in themselves have no Life, being but little (nay none at all) better than the Prodigal's Husks But alas! notwithstanding these Things with their talk of Illumination, to their very great Shine be it spoken, I have seen as much Covetousness, Self endedness, Deceit, desirousness of Vainglory amongst them as any People whatsoever And even in the place where I last cohabited, many of them full well know how they lusted after Chambering and Wantonness, desiring to shelter themselves (in committing their Nastiness) under my Roof, tho' thanks be to God, none of them all had their wicked Ends I say no more of them, only with with all my Spirit, notwithstanding the Illumination they boast themselves of, that they could see a little further into their own Hearts, and not pretend to so much Outwardness in their being Followers of Christ and his Apostles, even pretending to the very Substance thereof whilst secretly they practice the reverse

In the 19th Year of my Age I married a Wife,

very much against the Consent of my aged Parents, for which I am heartily sorry, and beg that my heavenly Father will graciously forgive me the Sin of Undutifulness, which I was too much guilty of

'Tis about twenty Years since my Country was some small sufferer by my imitating the King's Stamp, and tho' it was not alleag'd against me, yet who knows but this may be one Thing that may be a Means of bringing me to this shameful Death; from whence we may see that capital Crimes seldom go unpunished

In 1733, I was indicted as a Promoter and Encourager of *Humphry Mousall* and *Morris Walker*, to steal two black Mares the Property of *William Guest* in *Worcestershire* The Witness to prove me a Promoter or Encourager was *Morris Walker*, who said he asked me to look in the *Almanack*, to see whether he shou'd come to any Damage, by going with *Humphry Mousall* that Night This Deponent further said, that he heard me tell *Mousall*, that he need not want Money

The next Evidence was a Piece of Parchment produced by *Mousall*, who said that I give him that it to protect him in Horse stealing, and that would keep him from all Harm By the aforesaid Evidence of *Walker*, and the producing of the Parchment I was by the Jury found Guilty, and by the Judge sentenc'd to Die

Now as near as I can remember the Mares of *William Guest* were rode away by *Mousall* and *Walker* on the 12th of *January* last, and on the 13th of the same Month were brought back by the same Men, and turn'd up near the same Place they were taken from, and on the third Day the Owner had his Mares again Nor was it ever known who rode them away till about three Months after when *Mousall* being in custody on Suspicion of other Matters, of his own accord acknowledged that he and *Walker* rode away with the Mares

And as to the Parchment that was produc'd against me, there was wrote in it, the first six Verses of the first Chapter of St *John's* Gospel, and several other Sentences out of the Scriptures All which, if the unthinking Gentlemen of the Jury would have seriously consider'd, would not in the least have supposed that to have any Appearance in it of a *Protection for Horse stealing*, especially if they had consider'd the Words that it was concluded with, viz. *That the Angel of God would preserve from Witchcraft or evil Tongues, all that did belong to Humphry Mousall* And as I am a dying Man, I will declare the true intent for which this Parchment was given, which is as follows

Towards the latter end of the Year 1731, *Humphry Mousall* came to my House, and told me that he had a Heiffer that was ill, being handled or afflicted

flicted after a strange and surprizing Manner, and that he and his Neighbours which saw her, did imagine that she had Damage done her by Witchcraft, or the unlawful Tricks of a neighbouring Woman, whereupon I gave him that Parchment, written, as before mention'd, bidding him bury it in the Corner of the Garden, towards Sun rising, about a Foot deep in the Ground, laying a green Turf upon it, and then fill up the Hole again This is the whole Truth and nothing but the Truth, as I hope for Mercy in and thro' the Merits of Jesus Christ my Redeemer '

This Day seventh Day is my last and solemn Farewell to this World, therefore I will leave behind me a frank Acknowledgment of what I was really privy to, and in relation to what I did certainly know touching the Facts which were committed by *Humphry Mousall* and *Morris Walker*

About *November* 1732, *Humphry Mousall* came to my House, and told me the great necessity he was in for some Money to discharge a Debt of about 12 Pounds, desiring me it possibly to consider of some proper Person that was likely to supply his present Occasion, till he could raise some Money out of his own Stock of Cattle Now I had made fruitless Application to Mr *F——*, and Mr *C——l*, Attornies at Law on the like occasion for him not long before, there are I tried several other People, but the like Success, at last a Writ came out against him, and through a mistake of the Bailiffs his Brother *Andrew Mousall* was arrested in his stead, which gave *Humphry* Notice to avoid the Danger, which accordingly did, by sheltering himself at my House, (it being in another County) two or three Days a Week, for the space of two Months, sometimes Cursing and Swearing, other times he would Weep and seem sorrowful on the account of his Children, and then again cursing his Relations for not making it to Matters up, often protesting Revenge on them, saying, he would ride away with a Horse of his Cousins, and sell him, tho' by me often persuaded to the contrary, at last he and *Morris Walker* takes a turn in the Closes adjoining to my House, and in the Evening returning back, *Walker* softly asked me if he might safely go with *Mousall* that night? the Almanack lying before me, I carelesly cast my Eye thereon (not having respect to the Question he asked me) and answer'd Yes So away they both went from me, it being on *Thursday* Night the 11th of *January*, 1732 3 And about 7 o'Clock on *Saturday* Night following, *Mousall* came again to my House, and finding me engaged in Company, he took an Opportunity of whispering to me, that *Walker* and he rode away with two Mares down to *Stafford*, but there being no Fair that Day, they brought them back and turn'd them up again, and so *Mousall* went home to his own House, and being Glad in my Heart that they had been so disappointed

On the next Day came a Stranger to me (which proved to be Mr *Guest*,) who own'd the two Mares, and asked me if I could give any Intelligence which way he shou'd seek his Mares, whereupon I gave him Directions, and he accordingly had them again The Day following being *Monday*, he came and gave me two Guinea, which Reward he had promised in a printed Advertisement, published before he came to me This is the Truth, and altho' I knew no more of it than what is here express'd, yet I was most notoriously to blame for taking the Money of him

About a Month after this, *Mousall* brings one *William Coley* to my House, and when my Servant was gone to Bed, as we were drinking share of a

Mug or two of Ale, they told me their Intentions, *viz* that they designed to steal Mr *Hill* Mare at Night, which was in a Stable adjoining to my House, I said but little against it I own, verily thinking to put it by another way And betwixt ten and eleven of the Clock they both went out together to put Matters in order for their Design, leaving me a Candle before me, which immediately I put out, thrusting the Candlestick and other things which were before me, on my board, upon the Ground, whereupon I early told them that *Sarah* (which was my Servant's Name) had been down Stairs, and finding them not with me, said she was sure they were gone to do some Mischief, and that she would certainly be the first that should discover it, directly charging that the Mischief before mentioned, assuring them that she should never on *Coley* look'd up — — —— down, saying, he would not — — — had not the time fixed — — — bent, now threatening *Coley* unwillingly that I could fly, so that I was well — — — Morning came round to my will and since the Mare was gone

Some few Days after this, *Mousall* came again, and told me he had sold the Mare for six pounds, and give me Ten Shillings, to which I replied, *Humph*, Do not think I will have any share of it Money you sold the Mare for, for I will be under no Obligations, nor will I have any share of stoln Goods, further adding, *Humphry*, My Nativity look a little Dangerous, that I should suffer by the Sentence of a Judge, was I ever to come before one, tho' for ever so small a Matter, I should certainly die And as sure as the Sun is in the Firmament at Noon-Day, I uttered these Words to him more than ten Times To which he replied, He did not desire me to take it on that Account, he freely gave it me in part of the Money he ow'd me This is the real Truth as I am now Alive, and yet lo I must Die !

An Elegy on the Death of Richard Walton.

DEATH is the common Lot impos'd on all, The Brave and Virtuous with the Vulgar fall, Insatiate Power ! the scientific Head, Stript of its Honours sinks among the Dead, D *Escartes* and *Newton* whom the World regret, And *Walton* late has paid the mighty Debt, Sages who shew'd us Nature as she was, And from effects could latent cause trace See in the *Womb* of fate a future Birth, And paint the Time when it shou'd issue forth

Much suffering *Walton* ! much lamented Name ! Immortal as thy Knowledge be thy Fame, For Arts and Arms, eternal Honours grow, And wreaths of fading Grace thee blest Brow Else might thy Presence with thy Carcase die And thy Arts buried in Oblivion lie

Oh ! if the learn'd Associate, as below, And kindred shades releas'd, each other know, Methinks I see thee in Assembly met, With *Gadb'ry*, *Partridge*, and wise *Lilly* set, Despising *Death*, informing every Age, Thy *Genius*, *Conduct*, *Morals* in thy Age, How when you last arriv'd at those cross Skies, (On agonizing Sight !) proud *Leo* rise, His Tail the truest emblem of a *Rope*, Hung gaping like a hempen Noose slope, 'Twas fate and who contemns that great Decree ? It summon'd you, and late has summon'd me

To

'To some near Cloud, if thou haft Power, repair,
(Variety may pleafe above, as here)
See every Moth is bufy with thy Name,
And Songsters publickly rehearfe thy Fame
Walton is Dead! In vain the Virgin Dreams,
In vain, with Joys her pregnant Fancy Teems,
In vain, at morn diviner flumbers fpread,
A train of Vifions round *Corinna's* Head,
Walton is Dead! and who fhall dare t'explain,
The crude Concept ons of her fleeping Brain,
Who, but a cunning Wizard cou'd forefee
That Peace and Plenty were decreed for thee?
In ta' Field the Soldier leaves his fleeting Breath,
And finks, and bravely Triumphs over Death,
The Vulgar die in Beds to thee 'twas given,
To fving in open Air the nearest Heaven

EPITATH.

HERE on his Back old Walton lies,
Who yet to's Power looks to'ai as the Skies,
Weep not for him, tho' he cou'd tell,
Your Fortunes when on Earth fo well,
I dare engage if's Grave, ou'll feek,
(Who'd know your Fortune) once a Week,
This Earth which bears his Body's print,
You'll find bis fo much Vertue in't,
That it will all your Dubs remove
Concerning ftolen Goods, or Love,
As well as he cou'd when above.

The LIFE of JOHN STEVENS, alias HENRY COOK.

THE following Account this Criminal gave of himfelf, and of the feveral Robberies he had committed, which he deliver'd to his Friend, and defired im got be publifh'd, after his Execution which was at *Tyburn* on *Wednesday* the 16th of *September* 1741

I HENRY COOK, aged 27 Years, was born in *Houndfditch*, of honest, reputable Parent, who fill live there, my Father having a great Number of Children, at leaft 19 or 20, now but Eight living, all which he has handfomely brought up

When I was of proper Age, I was put to School to a Gentleman in *Sandy Court*, near *Houndfditch*, with whom I continued, and was inftructed, till I could write tollerable well, and had learnt Arithmetick, as far as the Rule of Three and Practice My Father being in the Leather-Cutting Bufinefs, he inftructed me in that Art, fo far that I thought I was fufficiently qualified to act for myfelf There being a Shoemaker's Shop to be Let at *Stratford* in *Effex*, my Father hearing thereof, at my Requeft inftantly took it for me, ftock'd it with Leather, and other Neceffaries, for me to begin Trade, and at the fame Time furnifhed me two Rooms with Goods.

Here I lived very well, and had good Bufinefs for about two Years, then I got acquainted with the eldeft Daughter of one *Joseph Alexander*, Beadle of *Stratford*, to whom I have been married about five Years, which, with the additional Expence of three Children, by that Time, had reduced me to fo low a Ebb, and involv'd me fo much in Debt, that I could no longer ftand my Ground, for fear of being Arrefted Where to go for Refuge I could not tell, my Father's in *Houndfditch* being an improper Place, on Account I had taken up Goods in his Name, of as many of his Dealers in *London*, as I could get to Credit me, at which my Father was very much difpleafed, as I did it without his Confent and Knowledge

By this Time I had contracted an Intimacy with moft of the loofe and diforderly Sparks in and about *Stratford*, but particularly with one Y——g, an Apothecary, who then kept a Shop in *Stratford*, (now in *London*, near *Monmuth ftreet*) With him, &c of Nights, (after I had been fecreted all Day for Fear of a Knap) I ufed to go robbing of Gentlemens Fifh Ponds, ftealing Fowls, &c till Mr *Monk*, a Gentleman in the Neighbourhood, advertifed two Guineas Reward for fome Ducks he had loft, as alfo a Farrier in the Town half a Guinea, for fome he had loft, &c Being fufpected by every Body to be guilty, and knowing myfelf fo, I made up what Money I could, and retired to a Relation of mine, who keeps the Sign of the *Rofe* and *Crown*, at *Grays*, down the River, where I was concealed about two Months I diverted myfelf a days in fhooting of Rabits, &c, which was a good Prefence for my carrying a Gun, to fecure myfelf from the Bailiffs, if they had fcente! where I was, not that I had any particular Malice againft them, more than one who lives at the Foot of *Bow-Bridge*, he having Actions againft me, protefting he would catch me, if I was above Ground, of which I was informed, whereupon I fent him Word to take Care of himfelf, for that I was provided with Piftols, &c and that if he did not defift his Refolution in taking me, I would certainly make it my Bufinefs to lay wait for him, and blow his Brains out, of him I heard no more

Two Months being gone, and my Money all fpent, I was at a Lofs what Courfe to fteer, however I refolved to venture Home to my Wife again, which I did about Eleven o'Clock at Night, when to my expreffible Surprize and Grief I found a certain Perfon in the Houfe, which at that Time gave me great Uneafinefs, tho' I have fince reflected I had no great Occafion to be fo, however the World muft imagine it did not a little furprize and confound me, but is a y Circumftance,

were then so bad, I was obliged to be silent, but determined never to live with her more, for a Constancy

The next Morning about five, I went into the Shop, strip't it of what I could conveniently carry off, and came directly to *London*, where I pawn'd them for two Pound ten Shillings

Not daring to go to my Fathers, I went to one R——— S———, a *Gardener* in *Shoreditch*, who married one of my Sisters. He very kindly received me, telling me he had heard before of my bad Circumstances, and would do all in his Power to serve me, with whom I staid about six Weeks, in which Time I had pretty well made even with my two Pounds ten Shillings, how, or which Way to get more, I was in a Consternation to know, resolving not to go to my Wife again

As I was walking over *Moorfields* one Day, I espied a Brace of second hand Pistols at a Broker's Shop, which I cheapen'd, and bought for seven Shillings and six Pence After I had provided myself with Powder, Balls and Flints, I return'd to my Sister's, where I dined, and soon after took my Leave, and went towards *Newington*; and a little on this Side the Town, I stopped a Man in the Dusk of the Evening, in the Foot Path, from whom I took fifteen Shillings, this being the first Robbery of that Kind I ever committed, the World must needs think it a little startled me

From thence I turned off for *Finchley Common*, intending there to stop the first Man I met, rob and take his Horse from him, which, luckily for me, fell out just as I would have it I had not been on the Common ten Minutes, before I met a Man well mounted, who was agoing towards *Coney-Hatch*, it being dark, I sat down on the Road Side till he came up with me, I then rushed up, and seized his Horse's Bridle, demanded him to dismount and deliver his Money He at first spur'd his Horse and would have forced him over me, but upon my threatning to blow his Brains out, he surrendered both Horse and Money, desiring I would send his Horse to an Inn at St *Alban's*, where three Guineas should be left for the Person who brought it I promised him I would, but after I had rode him a little Way, I thought him of more Worth to keep for my Business, than return to the Owner

I accordingly went forward that Night with my Horse and Booty, which was about two Pounds fifteen Shillings to my Brother in-Law, S———'s Mother, who kept an Alehouse the Side of *Enfield-Chase* Here I was kindly received, telling them I was obliged to fly for Debt, and must keep close that nobody must see me.

Here I tarried two Days, and as they kept a Publick House, I lived after a very extravagant Manner From hence I went down the Chace to *Fortyhill*, from thence towards *Tottenham*, between which Place, I stopped a Gentleman, from whom I took about six Pounds, went on to *London*, set up my Horse at an Inn in *Bishopsgate-street*, and went and staid all Night at my Brother S———'s, who was surprized to see me have so much Money, and strictly examined me how I came by it I desired him to be silent, which he was The next Morning I took my Leave, and went and bought a Pair of Boots, &c After which I set out for St *Alban's*, and just on this Side the Turnpike, I stopp'd the St *Alban's* Stage Coach, from whence I took about eight Pounds

At Night I returned to S———'s Mother at *Enfield Chase*, where I got the News-Papers, upon Perusal of which, I found my Horse was advertised

with a full Description, and three Guineas Reward, to have it paid by the Master of the *White Hart Inn* at St *Alban's*

A few Days after I turned out again with an intent to take the first sightly Horse I could meet on the Road, which happened that Night upon *Hadly Common*, where I overtook a Gentleman, as I then thought him to be, whom I robbed of about four Pound, and then exchanged Horses with him He told me what he was and where he liv'd, which was at a Publick House near *Moorgate*, as well as I can remember

A short Time after this, crossing the Country from *Mims* to St *Alban's* and being at the *Bull* at Mr *French's*, one of the Passengers, an elderly Woman, who I had robbed in the Stage-Coach, was in the Kitchen, where I at my alighting went I recollected her Face the Minute I saw her, as I perceived she did mine, whereupon I directly ran to the Stable, and having saddled my Horse I set out for *Barnet*

On the Road I struck in with some Company who were coming the same Way, with whom I joined myself We had not rode together a Mile, before one challenged by Horse to be advertised, and that it was taken at such a Time and Place by a Highwayman, and he knowing the Horse and Owner very well, demanded of me to give an Account of myself, and how *I* came by the Horse, which *I* soon would have done, but there being in Company seven or eight, all well mounted, and who, if *I* had either shot him or his Horse, would inevitably have taken me, *I* therefore told him *I* lived in *London*, but had bought the Horse a few Days before, of a Man at the *Bell-Inn* at *Edmonton*, where, if he would go with me, he might be satisfied of the Truth of what *I* said, *I* thinking thereby to get him to go over *Enfield* Chase, by which Means, as it was out of the strait Road to *London*, *I* thought the rest of his Company would have kept on, which if they had, *I* intended to have given him his Friend's Horse to carry Home, and have taken his in the stead, with what Cash he had about him But in this *I* was disappointed, by all the Company going with us.

When we came near the *Bell*, I was in a flutter to guess which was the best Method to disengage myself from my new Companions, when just as we all came to the Gateway of the said *Inn*, I clapt Spurs to my Horse, and turned down a Line the Corner of the *Inn*, which came from *Finchley* Common Their Horses being fresher than mine, very closely pursued · *I* took to the Fields, and made for a Wood, when *I* wanted to have got therein, but could not get my Horse to leap, in which Time four Men came within twenty Yards of me, whereupon *I* turned about, and fired a Pistol at them, (which did no Damage) and demanded them to keep off; at which they stopped *I* called out and told them, there was their Friend's Horse, so *I* quitted him, and ran into the Wood, by which Means, with the Darkness of the Evening, *I* then escaped.

After this miraculous Deliverance I went home as I then called it, to my Brother-in-law S———'s, in *Shoreditch*, who judged something to be the matter with me, by the Confusion I appeared to be in He taxed me hard with going on the Highway, but to no Purpose, I desired his Silence, or otherwise I must seek a new Lodging, after which Time go or come when I would, he said nothing.

Here I continued a Week, or 9 Days, without doing any one Thing to get a Shilling, in which

Time my Mony was near exausted, the major part of which, I spent in Bawdy-houses, in and about *Shoreditch*, when I determin'd upon *Finchley Common*, being the Place of Action, when I came there, I saunter'd some Time upon the Common without doing any Business, being a little fearful from the narrow Escape I had the last Time I was out, I suffer'd several to pass by unmolested, 'till it was almost dark, when I espied an old Man poorly mounted with a Basket on his Arm coming towards me, he I thought might have been at *London* at Market, and able to replenish my empty Purse I therfore prepared for an Attack, when he came up with me after the Word of Command, to stop and deliver, I dismounted him, he protesting for some time to have no more Money than 5 s. wherupon I search'd him, and found above four Guineas, I took both his Horse and Money tho' a poor one, mounted and was going to my old Lodging near the Chace, intending to do no more that Night, but before I got off the common, just at the End of the Road which leads to *Finchley Town*, I met a Man going but easily along, I stop'd and rob'd him of some Silver, and his Silver Buckles, exchanged Horses, as his seemed much better then mine, and so I soon found and left him mine to carry him home, he had not got half way over the Common, before he met the old Market-Men, I had just before rob'd of both Horse and Money, the old Man thinking it was me, said I wish you a good Night, and good Success the other answer'd, I hope better then I have just now met with, the old Man perceiving it not to be me tho' his Horse, desired the Man to dismount telling him, that was his Horse, and if he did not immediately deliver it, he should charge him with the Robbery, the other begin to D——m and swear there was nothing but Thieves and Highwaymen upon the Road; however, he gave the old Man his Horse and walked home on foot, to the *Axe Inn*, in *Aldermanbury*, he being *Chamberlain*, his Name was *Thomason*, who in a short Time after had my Life in his Power, as I shall soon relate, I directly proceeded from hence to my Lodging on the Chace, where I spent that Night and the next two Days in Boozing and Carousing with my Acquaintance, a pretty many by that Time I had there, the third Day in the Morning, I sent for the News-Papers, wherein I found my Mare advertised with a full Description of her I put the News-Papers in my Pocket, saddled my Mare and came for *Finchley Common*, in order to rob, and exchange my Nagg with the first Man I Met, and should like his, when I came within 500 Yards as near as I can guess of the Place I took the Mare and rob'd the Man, I to my Astonishment! was seiz'd by him and three more before I saw them, the first Salutation I met with was a Knock on the Head, which brought me to the Ground, when being surrounded by a Mob before I could recover, I was forced to submit; they immediately upon searching me, found a Brace of loaded Pistols, Powder and Bullets, a Silver Watch and some Money, I was directly carried before a Magistrate, who committed me to *Newgate*, but upon my requesting him, to return me my Money, he readily did, leaving my Watch (which was never own'd) and Pistols in the Custody of the Constable, a Person who liv'd about *Finchley*, and in *October* Sessions, 1710 I was Tryed at the *old Baile*, for the said Offence, when by the Favourableness, of my then Prosecutor, in not Swearing I was the Man who rob'd him, altho' I was taken upon the Mare he lost, and I am well assured he could, had he been inclinable to it, I had

nothing to say in my own Defence, but that I found the Mare turn'd up in the Road, and seeing the Advertisement which I then had about me, was bringing her Home, and as that was the first Time of my being call'd before a Court of Justice, my Father and Neighbours at *Stratford*, appeared in my Behalf, tho' I had my Landlady and four more from *Enfield Chace*, to have swore if there had been a Necessity that I was at her House the Time the Robbery was committed, but as I was not positively swore to be the Man, I was discharged without their Assistance

Being thus happily deliver'd, to the great Joy of my Father, and seemingly of all my Acquaintance and Neighbours at *Stratford*, I was by them prevailed upon to return Home to my Wife and Family at *Stratford*, which I thought was the least Return of Gratitude I could make them, after shewing their Friendship in serving me

The very Day I was discharged I accompanied my Neighbours to *Stratford*, where for that Night we were very merry, they all hoping my narrow Escape would be a Warning to me for the future I on my Part, promised to return to my Wife, and by my more than ordinary Diligence for the Time to come, to repair not only my Reputation, but my Circumstances, when we parted they went to their separate Homes, I to mine to my Wife, who was that Day Churched The next Day I examin'd how Matters stood in the Shop and Book, which I found if possible, in a worse Condition than when I left them, by her lying in, and *William Taylor* the Man who managed Business, neglecting it in coming after me to *Newgate*, this I thought a poor Prospect, to perform my Promise in retrieving my Reputation and Circumstances I examin'd the said *Taylor*, if there were were any good Debts, which might be immediately collected, he reply'd not one as he knew of, how to act in this Case I knew not, whether to stand my Ground, or *turn out* again on the Road, when I resolved with myself to come to *London*, and purchase a Brace of second Hand Pistols, which when I had done, I thought I could have gone an Evening and robb'd betwixt my House and the Forest, and return Home unsuspected, which I did for about a Fortnight, in which Time I had got and saved about 30 l. this I had a Thought of laying out in a Stock of Leather, &c. when consulting with the said *William Taylor* what was most wanting, and telling him what Sum I had to lay out, he freely told me how I came by it, and instead of advising me for the best as an honest Man, he reply'd, what signifies that Sum, lets go with you and make it ten Times as much, and then think of buying Leather

This was no sooner by him proposed, than by me accepted, I well knowing from his former Scene of Life in Smuggling, that I could have no properer Person for a Companion, he and I come directly to *London*, where we equipt ourselves with what was wanting and necessary for Gentlemen of our Profession, as we then stiled ourselves, that Night we return'd Home to *Stratford* without doing any Thing, the next Day I and my Man, as he insisted I should call him, not only from being the Manager of my Business in the Shoemaking Way, but from my Experience and Seniority in our new Profession Going as far as *Rumford*, &c. with an Intent, as it was my fixed Maxim, to stop the first Man we met on Horseback, rob and dismount him, till we were both on our Horses, then stop and rob both Coaches and Horsemen, till we came near Home, and then turn up our Horses

The Sweets and Benefits arising from this new Profession, my Man I'll soon found, for he would of ten fay when he had taken any Thing of a Booty, is 16 this better than Shoemaking Matters In this auda-cious Manner did we continue both Night and Morn-ing, to ftop moft or all the Stage Coaches, &c on that Road, of which one Capt *Mawley*, who had been before robb'd was appriz'd, he coming that Road in the *Colchefter* Stage Coach, had provided himfelf with Fire Arms, and conceal'd himfelf in the Bafket behind the faid Coach, in Expectation of our meeting 'em as ufual My Man *Will* and I had been out about two Hours before the *Colchefter* Coach came by, in which Time we had ftop'd and robb'd feveral that paffed and repaffed, of whom we could get no Horfes, and knowing the faid Coach was a coming, we agreed to take the two Horfes which were at Grafs in a Field joining to the Road, having two Bridles, and one Saddle concealed in a Hedge near the Field, but before we could catch the faid Horfes, or either of them, we heard the Coach coming, when we left the Horfes and ran to meet it, and juft at *Gal-lows Green* we ftop'd it, I giving the Word of Com-mand to ftop, *Will* on the other Side demanding their Money, which he had no fooner done, than Capt *Mawley* in the Bafket behind fhot him thro' the Head, upon which he dropp'd, which I feeing ran directly towards the Captain in the Bafket, who faluted me with a Brace of Balls from a Piftol, which took me directly upon the right Shoulder, in which Hand my Piftol was, I being at fome Diftance, the Balls did not penetrate the Skin, only knocked me backwards, and numm'd it for the prefent, notwithftanding which I took up my Piftol in my left Hand, ran to the Captain, and would have fhot him, but my Piftol miffed fire, by the Dirt getting in the Pan by the Fall, however I robb'd him of about 19s all in Sil-ver, though I underftand he denies loofing any Thing, however I declare it to be true, and as foon as I had done, I bid the Coachman drive on, which he did as faft as poffible

I looked at my Man *Will*, and faw he was juft ex-piring, he had then about 7l in his Pocket, which we had taken that Morning and the over Night, and when I wanted to have taken from him, but the Mob coming, I jump'd over a Gate, and croffed the Fields towards *Upton*, but before I got there, it came in my Head to return Home, and as it was very early in the Morning, to go to Bed to prevent a Sufpi-cion of my being concern'd with my Man *Will Tay-lor*

I had not croffed two Fields before I heard a Thou-fand People were alarmed with *Will's* being fhot, and that I muft certainly be the Man who was with him, and was efcaped, however I ventured fo near the Place as the other Side of the Hedge, where the Mob was gather'd, and carrying *Will* out of the Road I had it ftill in my Head to go Home and to Bed, but fome of the Mob called out, let's go and fearch *Cook's* Lodging, at which faying, I thought it the moft prudent Way to make of, which I did to the Sign of the *L——* and *C——* at *N—— G——*

Here I fecreted myfelf about three Days, in which Time I lived in fo extravagant a manner, as to fpend 5l by which I was well efteem'd there, and might have been fecreted to this Day had I Money fuffici-ent to have maintain'd me in the fame Manner Here I fent for my Brother in law *S———*, and defired he would go to *Stratford*, and enquire how Mat-ters ftood there, he readily comply'd, and at his Return told me, the Juftice had been fo good as to let my Man *Will* be buried, in as decent a manner as the Money he had in his Pocket when fhot would ad-mit off, and that there was Warrants againft me,

and I would certainly be taken if I went near *Strat-ford*

I promifed him I would not, but on the contrary go to Sea, at which he was feemingly well pleafed, and faid, he would go to Doctor *Y——* in *London*, and try to get me fome Money as he ow'd me, about 25l which I had lent him when living at *Stratford*, my Brother ufed his Endeavours but to no Pur-pofe

Whilft I was here it came in my Head to go in Purfuit of the Conftable who had got my Watch and Piftols, fince the Time of my being taken, who I had fuch a Spite and Hatred againft, that I was determi-ned if ever I met him to take his Life, but Provi-dence directed to the contrary, for I never could hear what was become of him

Going to Sea I thought a Hardfhip, efpecially for a Gentleman as I then thought I was entituled to by my Profeffion, and therefore refolved to continue is fuch, and revenge the Death of my poor Man *Will*, for whom I had a very great Regard and Efteem, not only from his Valour and Courage in the Profeffion of a Gentleman Collector, but for his civil Behaviour and good Nature, and had he not depended fo much upon his Strength, his Reign might have been longer

When upon the Road, he inftead of clapping a Pif-tol to a Man's Breaft, would often take a Man by the Collar, and once as he ftopt a Gentleman's Ser-vant near *Burntwood* upon his Refiftance tie ing no Pif-tol, they both tumbled from their Horfes into a great Ditch, I ftood looking on fome Time, till the Gen-tleman's Servant was too many for *Will*, I came up and prefented a Piftol, which foon ended the Difpute, from whom we took a Bafket, wherein was a Pound or thereabouts of Hyfon Tea, Sugar and Plumb, &c and feveral Pounds of Starch, this was a Prefent for a Lady, as feveral other Things had been before, that I had robb'd people of, all which fhe was thankful for, and willing to take, had there been a thoufand Times as much, notwithftanding fhe well knew how I came by them

Thus to revenge the Death of my poor Man *Will*, I provided myfelf with a good Nag, &c went down to *Rumford*, in hopes of hearing there who was the Perfon that was in the Bafket and fhot *Will*, but could hear no further, than it was one Capt *Mawley* of *Colchefter* I was at the Inn all Night when the whole Talk was about me, nothing but *Cook* was the r Subject throughout the whole Houfe

The next Morning feveral fetting out from that Inn for *London*, who had lain there, and at private Houfes in the Town, among whom was a Gentleman I had a great Sufpicion was my bitter Enemy, *Mawley* I let the Coach go on about half an Hour, I then call'd for my Horfe, after paying my Reckoning, the Land-lord bidding me a good Morning, and a fafe arrival in Town, hoping I fhould efcape the noted *Cook* and his Gang, I thanked him and fet out after my prey, the Stage-Coach, wherein was gone the very Anti-dote of my Soul, I purfued with a Refolution, not only to fhoot the Man I fufpected, but for a certainty all in the Coach, when I came up with them, my Soul was fo full of Envy, Hatred and Malice againft him, that I fcarce could bid the Coachman ftop with-out blowing his Brains out, when I came to the Door of the Coach, I demanded which was Capt *Maw-ley*, who had fhot my Companion, and endeavour'd the fame to me, I told them, they who were not He, had better difcover which He was, otherwife I would deftroy them all; when a beautiful young Lady who was in the Coach, fell upon her knees, imploring my Mercy, and protesting he was not there, as did all the rest the same, this instantly excited my Compassion, and moved me to Pity As I always had, and professed a great Veneration for the Fair Sex, I put up my Pistol, defiring the Gentlemen to be speedy in giving me their Money, &c which they did to the amount of above 30 *l* all I demanded of the Fair one, was a kind Salute, which she readily complied with, with which I took my Leave, telling the Gentlemen if Capt *Mawley* was amongst them, for him never to venture out without Arms, for that I was resolved tho' at the Loss of my own Life, to have his, —— and for that end, as well as to be revenged on some others, I went to *London*, sent for two old Companions in Vice, and Iniquity from *Stratford*, who h'd before wanted me to admit them into my Company, they no sooner received my Message, than they complied therewith, they having each an Acquaintance in *London*, who were hearty, stout Fellows, and would be glad to be admitted of the Society, which I readily consented to, they being short of Money, proposed going a Street robbing, till they had raised a Bank sufficient to equip them for the Road, this I rejected, as being Generalissimo, and having the Command over them, by Seniority, and Election, after a short Debate, it was my Resolution to take the Road, which we all did, I having no Horse no more than they, *Epping Forrest* being the Place appointed, as I knew little or nothing of any other Road, except *Finchley*, about *London*, and beg that all the injured Part of the World who have been robb'd on any other round *London*, will believe the same, when I declare upon the Words of a dying Man, it's Truth

From hence I went to *Wooburn* in *Bedfordshire*, between which Place and *Bedford* Town in the Road I was overtaken by a Countryman well mounted, the Bridle of whose Horse I laid hold of, presented a Pistol to him, demanded him to dismount and deliver his Money, he with a great Stick he had in his Hand struck at me, which Blow I received with my Arm, at which I gave the Bridle a Snatch, which brought my Countryman down, notwithstanding which he resisted and had once like to have snatch'd my Pistol out of my Hand, but finding I was resolute and swearing I wou'd shoot him, he surrender'd both Money and Horse, which was to the amount of about 50 *l* but beg'd hard to have his Horse again, which was the principal Thing I wanted, so I mounted and rode off telling the Countryman to sue the County, which I heard and saw in the News-Papers he did

From hence, I went to *Birmingham*, where I put up at the *Swan* Inn, having about 40 *l* and liking the Town I was determin'd to stay there some Time, in a few Days I sold my Horse for 10 Guineas tho' he was worth more, and never should have defired a better for my Business

Here I took a Lodging, at a Publick House, having a Liking to my Landlord, who was a merry Companion, he and I talking about Trade and Business, thereby understanding I was a *Shoemaker*, he said, Mr *Stevens*, (I then going by that Name) there is a Shop to be let over the Way, which will do for your Purpose; the next Day I took it and laid out most of my Money in Stocking it, and my Room, which when I had done, I was at a Loss for a House-keeper, but that Piece of Furniture as well as any other I was soon provided with, whose Name was soon changed by all that knew her, from that of *Molly Barrett*, to that of Mrs *Stevens* Here I had a fair Prospect of doing well, and was encouraged and esteemed by all who knew me in the Town, but I and my new Wife

108

as I then called her, minded the Gaiety and Pleasures of Life, in going from Place to Place to see Horse-racing and other Diversions, more than Business, 'till I had run and raced away not only my ready Money, but my Stock in Trade, which put me in Mind of the old Saying, *What is got over the Devil's Back, is spent under his Belly*, and now to deceive the World in repairing my Circumstances to prevent any Suspicion of my being a Highwayman? I told my Spouse Mrs *Barrett*, and the rest of my Acquaintance, that I had an old rich Aunt who liv'd in *Herefordshire*, and allow'd me sometimes a Hundred Pounds a Year, and sometimes more, which I received Quarterly, this every Body believ'd, I told of it I thereupon prepared for my Journey, as they thought, to *Herefordshire*, to my pretended Aunt, leaving Mrs *Molly* my House keeper in Care of the Shop, telling her, I should return in a Fort night or 3 Weeks, from hence to *Northampton*, I went in the Stage Coach, intending to visit my Lucky County of *Bedford* again, I stay'd here 2 Days in Hopes of meeting with an Opportunity to replenish my empty Pockets, when I was informed most of the *London* Dealers went the other Way, that is through *Dun Church*, with that, I set out for the same Place, where both Roads come into the main *Chester* Road, here I stop'd a Man, robb'd him of 16 *l* and took his Horse, which was a very good one, with which Booty I thought to return to *Birmingham*, but being overtaken that Night, by a *Manchester* Dealer, at the *Horseshoe Inn*, at *Daintry*, who was going in the Country to buy Goods, we go ing both to the same Inn, supp'd together of a boil'd Rabbit smother'd with Onions and a roasted Fowl after Supper, we drank two or three Bowls of Punch, a Bottle of Wine and smoak'd several Pipes of Tobacco, I knowing who must smoke for it the next Day, I used all the Arts and Means I possibly could to found the Depth of his Pockets, which he was too close to let me that Night; the next Morning we breakfasted together, (as I had told him the over Night I would accompany him to *Liverpool* in *Lancashire*) set forward for *Coventry*, where at the *White Bear* we din'd, it being the Post House, as that was a fixed Rule with me to do, for the Benefit of the News-Papers Here after Dinner we refreshed ourselves with a Bottle of Wine, and smoaked a Pipe 'til it was near 3 o'Clock in the afternoon, whilst we was a drinking our Bottle after Dinner, I told my Fellow Traveller, it was a dangerous Road we had to pass that Evening, and therefore thought it very adviseable to conceal our Money in our Boots or some other secure Place; he at first refused, but upon seeing me put my Purse down my Boot, he drew out his Bag, which revived my drooping Spirits, my wish was granted to a few Miles riding for Opportunity He answer'd and I will put mine down my Side-pocket, which he did, about 3 as I said before, we set forward intending to go that Night to *Litchfield*, we rode very lovingly 'till we came to a Place called *Cookbows Corner*, which parts the Roads, here I told my Companion it was at my Journey's End, telling him he must draw to his Side pocket directly for there was no Time to dispute, his Answer was I really thought as much, and suspected it from the first Hour I came into your Company, I took his Bag wherein was contain'd (besides some Silver in his Pocket, which I left him to carry him to his Journey's End,) the Sum of 35 Guineas, besides his Watch, which I took, dismounted him and turn'd up his Horse, I should have taken him but thought my own better, from hence I had not above 7 Miles to *Birmingham*, where I went that Night, my House keeper was surprised to see me returned so soon, as was most of my Acquaintance

quaintance, believing every Thing I had related a-
bout my Aunt was true, with this Cash, I restock'd
my Shop, which by that Time look'd naked, and
paid what Debts I had contracted in the Town,
which put me in the good Esteem of all who knew
me there, soon after I sold my Horse for 6 *l* after
this, I contracted a Friendship with one Mr *Insal*,
who was very Friendly, and told me when ever I
wanted a Horse to ride out, he had one at my Service, accordingly, I made bold with a Mare of his
the next Time I wanted to make a Visit to my pretended Aunt, leaving mine to ride when Occasion
offer'd, for which I must now pay no less a Ransome
than my Life

This my so speedy leaving of *Birmingham* the second Time, was in some Measure owing to a *London*
Dealer, who was there, enquiring who I was, and
how long I had been there, which I did not greatly
like From whence I crossed the Country for *Lon-*
don, just as Fancy led me, picking up what I could
towards defraying travelling Charges, till I met Mr
Zachary, as he related on my Trial, (for the Particulars whereof I refer to the same) whose Testimony,
as I am a dying Man, I declare to be true and just in
every Particular

Being thus near *Stratford*, and finding myself well
mounted, I was determined to ride through the Town,
which I did, seeing several that I knew, and who
knew me, to many of whom I spoke, as they did to
me At Night I returned to my Lodging, the *C—*
and L—, where I sent for my Brother *S—*, who
was not then at Home

The next Morning I went to his his House, but
not soon enough to catch him at Home I saw my
Sister, his Wife, with whom I talked, and desired her
to send her Husband to me at the *C— and L—*,
when he came in. She thereupon gave me to understand, that somebody had given Information of my
resorting to that House when about *London*, and advised me to leave it, which I accordingly did, and
by her Directions went to one *S—*, a Relation of
her Husband's, who keeps the Sign of the *Badger* at
Mims Wash, where I was kindly received, upon letting them know who I was, and making use of their
Names Here I continued from *Thursday* to *Sunday*
for my Brother-in-law *S—*'s coming, which he
then did; after some Talk, I told him that I had
five Watches, which I begged he would take and secure for me He then refused them, but told me if
I would come on *Tuesday*, and send for him in the
Neighbourhood, he would take them When he
was for going Home, I ordered my Horse to be got
ready to accompany him, which I did as far as *Finch-*
ley-Common, where we parted, and whilst we were a
talking, a single Horse Chaise passed us for *London*,
with two Men in it, which as soon as we had parted
I pursu'd, and about the *Red Lyon* on *Highgate* Hill
I overtook them, which being near the Houses, I
desisted from stopping them there, but followed them
thro' the Town and Turnpike, till they came within
a Hundred Yards of *Whittington*'s-Stone

I rode by them, and gave them the Meeting and
Word of Command, which they were so far from
complying with, that they whipt my Horse, and
would have forced me into the Ditch, they kept
whipping their own Horse, and went at a great Rate,
notwithstanding which I got up with them a second
Time, when I told them I certainly would blow
the Brains of both of them out, if they made any
further Resistance, which they not regarding, I fired
and shot one through the Arm with a Brace of Balls,
and would have served the other the same, had they
not drove up to an Alehouse in the Road, the Sign

of *Old Mother Red Cap* and alarmed the People of
the House by making a great Noise

Thus disappointed of my Booty, (which I was inform'd after was about 50 *l*) I return'd to my Lodgings at *Mims*, and staid there till ten a Clock on
Monday, then went for St *Alban's* and came to
London that Night by the Carravan, leaving my
Pistols as well as my Horse at *Mims* Wash, which
was never before done by me to leave my Pistols

On *Monday* Night the 17th of *July*, I lay at the
Bell Inn in *West Smithfield*, and on *Tuesday* Morning
the 28th, according to my Promise, I went to meet
my Brother in Law *S—*, about my five Watches,
and the Reason of my going down *Cheapside* from
Smithfield to *Norton Folgate*, was, that I repented
leaving my Pistols at *Mims*, and thought to have
bought a Brace behind the *Royal Exchange*, which I
should have done, had the People of the Shop been
up

When I came to Mr *Taylor's*, the Sign of the
Wise Man of Gotham, I called for a Pint of Ale, and
wrote a Letter to my Brother in Law *S—*, that
I was there according to Appointment, and called
a Porter and sent it to him, when *Martha Underwood*
who formerly knew me at *Stratford*, saw me pass
by *Bow* Church in *Cheapside*, who lodg'd and fixed me at the abovesaid Mr *Taylor's*, she immediately acquainted *Haines* the Constable therewith, who
with Assistance came and seiz'd me, and upon searching me took my five Watches and 9 *l* odd Money
from me, and carried me before Justice *Chandler*,
who upon my being proved to be *Cook* the *Strat-*
ford Shoemaker, by some out of that Town, and
Mr *Zachary* swearing to his Watch, I was committed to *Newgate*, which had been my old Lodging, about eleven Months ago, for five Weeks

This I declare upon the Words of a dying Man,
to be the Truth and Substance of my Life, as near
as I can, through my Infirmity of Body, since my
Conviction, recollect.

The following Letter was sent by Mary Barret, *at*
Birmingham, to Cook, *viz*

' T H I S is to let you know that I receiv'd your
' Letter with some Satisfaction, and am glad to
' hear that you are in good Health, and had Pleasure
' in your Journey, for that is more than I have had
' at Home ever since you went, till now as I receiv'd
' your Letter, for I thought that Pens, Ink and Paper
' was very hard to find, and your Hands and your
' Thought was very much confin'd, that you could
' not write before, tho' I did excuse the first Post
' day with a great deal of Uneasiness, for I was very
' sorry to think that I was forc'd to write to you,
' first upon such an Account as I did, the very Day
' after you set out. I wrote to you to let you know
' the Report and Scandal that was raised on you
' when you was gone, for some said you had stole
' a Horse, and rode away with him, and got a Han-
' ger and a Brace of Pistols, and was turn'd High
' wayman, and durst not come no more to *Birming*
' *ham*, it was best known to yourself, how that
' was, but I think you have got a very fine Chara-
' cter, by your going in such a silly Manner, by your
' Writing, you have not receiv'd the Letter, and if
' you have not, I desire you will go to Mr *Wilson*,
' at Mr *Ward's*, in *Salisbu y Court*, at the *Black*
' *Lyon*, where you was to take that Letter for my
' Mother, and they will give it you, I could tell no
' other Way to write to you then, and not hearing
' from you so long after promis'd, I was afraid that
' you was under Confinement, for you was promised
' very

' very fair for it by Mr *Infal* I am very glad to
' hear that your four leg'd Horse carried you easy to
' your Journey's End ; you bid me be a good Girl
' and mind Shop, till you come Home, I told you
' when you went, that I would as well as I could,
' and what I promise if I can, I will perform till you
' return, which I hope will not be long before you
' do, for you must think it is very lonesome, for to
' have the Shop open from Morning till Night, and
' nobody in it but myself, accept my Mother, and
' that you may think is but little concerning you,
' and you said your Thoughts was always on me, but
' I believe I have thought as much on you as you
' could on me, for my Uneasiness has been so great
' that I could not avoid it, but I hope you will think
' of me and these Letters, and return as soon as pos-
' sible you can, for I am sure that it will be more to
' your Profit and my Satisfaction, to have you here,
' and I hope that your next Letter will let me know
' how long it will be before you return I have ne-

' ver been at Mrs *Cotton*'s but twice since you went,
' for who could think of its being nothing else but a
' parcel of false Reports from the first beginning of
' it. My Father and Mother both join in Love to
' you, and long to have you at Home, that you
' may convince the World All Friends desire to be
' remembered to you , let me know if you will have
' the Room kept till you come again, for Nurse wont
' let it to nobody while you are away, unless she hears
' from you or me

*So no more at present from your loving and
sincere Friend till Death,*

Mary Barrat.

Pray let me hear from you the next Post after you
receive this, and I will make myself as easy as I can
till I see you again, pray excuse so much to any one before.

July 18 1741

N B I hope this will be a Companion for the
Handkerchief

(*The* E N D.)

A COMPLETE

INDEX

OF

Malefactor's Names.

F I N I S.

Lightning Source UK Ltd.
Milton Keynes UK
UKHW031856071220
374783UK00016B/314